Mike Holt's Illustrated Guide to

Understanding the
NATIONAL
ELECTRICAL CODE®

Volume 1 • Articles 90 - 480

Based on the 2011 NEC®

Since 1974
www.MikeHolt.com

Mike Holt Enterprises, Inc.
888.NEC.CODE (632.2633) • www.MikeHolt.com • Info@MikeHolt.com

NOTICE TO THE READER

The publisher does not warrant or guarantee any of the products described herein or perform any independent analysis in connection with any of the product information contained herein. The publisher does not assume, and expressly disclaims, any obligation to obtain and include information other than that provided to it by the manufacturer.

The reader is expressly warned to consider and adopt all safety precautions that might be indicated by the activities herein and to avoid all potential hazards. By following the instructions contained herein, the reader willingly assumes all risks in connection with such instructions.

The publisher makes no representation or warranties of any kind, including but not limited to, the warranties of fitness for particular purpose or merchantability, nor are any such representations implied with respect to the material set forth herein, and the publisher takes no responsibility with respect to such material. The publisher shall not be liable for any special, consequential, or exemplary damages resulting, in whole or part, from the reader's use of, or reliance upon, this material.

Mike Holt's Illustrated Guide to Understanding the 2011 National Electrical Code, Volume 1

First Printing: February 2011

Technical Illustrator: Mike Culbreath
Cover Design: Madalina Iordache-Levay
Layout Design and Typesetting: Cathleen Kwas

COPYRIGHT © 2011 Charles Michael Holt
ISBN 978-1-932685-51-0

For more information, call 888.NEC.CODE (632.2633), or E-mail Info@MikeHolt.com.

NEC, NFPA, and *National Electrical Code* are registered trademarks of the National Fire Protection Association.

This logo is a registered trademark of Mike Holt Enterprises, Inc.

If you are an instructor and would like to request an examination copy of this or other Mike Holt Publications:

Call: 888.NEC.CODE (632.2633) • Fax: 352.360.0983

E-mail: Info@MikeHolt.com • Visit: www.MikeHolt.com

You can download a sample PDF of all our publications by visiting www.MikeHolt.com

I dedicate this book to the
Lord Jesus Christ,
my mentor and teacher.
Proverbs 16:3

One Team

To Our Instructors and Students:

We're committed to providing you the finest product with the fewest errors, but we're realistic and know that there'll be errors found and reported after the printing of this book. The last thing we want is for you to have problems finding, communicating, or accessing this information. It's unacceptable to us for there to be even one error in our textbooks or answer keys. For this reason, we're asking you to work together with us as One Team.

Students: Please report any errors you may find to your instructor.

Instructors: Please communicate these errors to us by sending an email to corrections@mikeholt.com.

Our Commitment:

We'll continue to list all of the corrections that come through for all of our textbooks and answer keys on our Website. The most up-to-date answer keys will always be available to instructors to download from our instructor Website. We don't want you to have problems finding this updated information, so we're outlining where to go for all of this below:

To view textbook and answer key corrections: Students and instructors go to our Website, www.MikeHolt.com, click on "Books" in the sidebar of links, and then click on "Corrections."

To download the most up-to-date answer keys: Instructors go to our Website, www.MikeHolt.com, click on "Instructors" in the sidebar of links and then click on "Answer Keys." On this page you'll find instructions for accessing and downloading these answer keys.

If you're not registered as an instructor you'll need to register. Your registration will be sent to our educational director who in turn will review and approve your registration. In your approval E-mail will be the login and password so you can have access to all of the answer keys. If you have a situation that needs immediate attention, please contact the office directly at 888.NEC.CODE (632.2633).

Call 888.NEC.CODE (632.2633) or visit us online at www.MikeHolt.com

Table of Contents

Table of Contents

Table of Contents

Introduction

Mike Holt's Illustrated Guide to Understanding the National Electrical Code, Volume 1

This edition of *Mike Holt's Illustrated Guide to Understanding the National Electrical Code, Volume 1* textbook is intended to provide you with the tools necessary to understand the technical requirements of the *National Electrical Code (NEC)*®. The writing style of this textbook, and in all of Mike Holt's products, is meant to be informative, practical, useful, informal, easy to read, and applicable for today's electrical professional. Just like all of Mike Holt's textbooks, this textbook contains hundreds of full-color illustrations to help you see the safety requirements of the *NEC* in practical use, helping you visualize the Code in today's electrical installations.

This illustrated textbook contains cautions regarding possible conflicts or confusing *Code* requirements, tips on proper electrical installations, and warnings of dangers related to improper electrical installations. In spite of this effort, some rules may seem to be unclear or need additional editorial improvement.

This textbook can't eliminate confusing, conflicting, or controversial *Code* requirements, but we do try to put these requirements into sharper focus to help you understand their intended purpose. Sometimes a requirement is so confusing nobody really understands its actual application. When this occurs, we'll point the situation out in an up-front and straightforward manner. We apologize in advance if that ever seems disrespectful, but our intention is to help the industry understand the current *NEC* as best as possible, point out areas that need refinement, and empower *Code* users to be a part of the process of change to create a better *NEC* for the future.

The *NEC* is updated every three years to accommodate new electrical products and materials, changing technologies, improved installation techniques, and make editorial improvements to improve readability. While the uniform adoption of each new edition of the *Code* is the best approach for all involved in the electrical industry, many inspection jurisdictions modify the *NEC* when it's adopted. To further complicate this situation, the *Code* allows the authority having jurisdiction (AHJ) the authority to waive *NEC* requirements or permit alternative wiring methods contrary to *Code* requirements. This is only allowed when the completed electrical installation is assured to provide an equivalent level of safety [90.4].

Keeping up with requirements of the *NEC* should be the goal of everyone involved in the safety of electrical installations. This includes electrical installers, contractors, owners, inspectors, engineers, instructors, and others concerned with electrical installations.

About the 2011 *NEC*

The actual process of changing the *Code* takes about two years, and it involves thousands of individuals making an effort to have the *NEC* as current and accurate as possible. Let's review how this process works:

Step 1. Proposals—November, 2008. Anybody can submit a proposal to change the *Code* before the proposal closing date. Over 5,000 proposals were submitted to modify the 2011 *NEC*. Of these proposals, over 300 rules were revised that significantly effect the electrical industry. Some changes were editorial revisions, while others were more significant, such as new articles, sections, exceptions, and Informational Notes.

Step 2. *Code*-Making Panel(s) Review Proposals—January, 2009. All *Code* proposals were reviewed by *Code*-Making Panels. There were 19 panels in the 2011 *Code* process who voted to accept, reject, or modify them.

Step 3. Report on Proposals (ROP)—July, 2009. The voting of the *Code*-Making Panels on the proposals was published for public review in a document called the "Report on Proposals," frequently referred to as the "ROP."

Step 4. Public Comments—October, 2009. Once the ROP was available, public comments were submitted asking the *Code*-Making Panel members to revise their earlier actions on change proposals, based on new information. The closing date for "Comments" was October, 2009.

Step 5. Comments Reviewed by *Code* Panels—December, 2009. The *Code*-Making Panels met again to review, discuss, and vote on public comments.

Step 6. Report on Comments (ROC)—April, 2010. The voting on the "Comments" was published for public review in a document called the "Report on Comments," frequently referred to as the "ROC."

Step 7. Electrical Section—June, 2010. The NFPA Electrical Section discussed and reviewed the work of the *Code*-Making Panels. The

Electrical Section developed recommendations on last-minute motions to revise the proposed *NEC* draft that would be presented at the NFPA annual meeting.

Step 8. NFPA Annual Meeting—June, 2010. The 2011 *NEC* was voted by the NFPA members to approve the action of the *Code*-Making Panels at the annual meeting, after a number of motions (often called "floor actions") were voted on.

Step 9. Standards Council Review Appeals and Approves the 2011 *NEC*—July, 2010. The NFPA Standards Council reviewed the record of the *Code*-making process and approved publication of the 2011 *NEC*.

Step 10. 2011 *NEC* Published—September, 2010. The 2011 *National Electrical Code* was published, following the NFPA Board of Directors review of appeals.

> **Author's Comment:** Proposals and comments can be submitted online at the NFPA Website (www.nfpa.org). From the homepage, click on "Codes and Standards" at the top of the page, then from the Codes and Standards page click on "Proposals and Comments" in the box on the right-hand side of the page. The deadline for proposals to create the 2014 *National Electrical Code* is November 5, 2011. If you would like to see something changed in the *Code*, you're encouraged to participate in the process.

The Scope of this Textbook

This textbook, *Understanding the National Electrical Code, Volume 1*, covers the general installation requirements that Mike considers to be of critical importance in Articles 90 through 480 (*NEC* Chapters 1 through 4). This textbook is written with these stipulations:

- **Power Systems and Voltage.** All power-supply systems are assumed to be solidly grounded ac such as: 120V single-phase, 120/240V single-phase, 120/208V three-phase, 120/240V three-phase, or 277/480V three-phase, unless identified otherwise.

- **Electrical Calculations.** Unless the question or example specifies three-phase, the questions and examples are based on a single-phase power supply.

- **Rounding.** All calculations are rounded to the nearest ampere in accordance with 220.5(B).

- **Conductor Material.** All conductors are considered copper, unless aluminum is identified or specified.

- **Conductor Sizing.** All conductors are sized based on a THHN copper conductor terminating on a 75°C terminal in accordance with 110.14(C)(1), unless the question or example identifies otherwise.

- **Overcurrent Device.** The term "overcurrent device" in this textbook refers to a molded case circuit breaker, unless identified otherwise. If a fuse is identified in the text, it's to be of the single-element type, also known as a "one-time fuse," unless identified otherwise.

Mike Holt's Detailed *NEC* Library

If you want to really understand the 2011 *National Electrical Code,* then Mike Holt's Detailed *Code* Library is ideal for you. This program covers general installation requirements, branch circuits, feeders, services and overcurrent protection, grounding and bonding, conductors, cables and raceways, boxes, panels, motors, transformers, and much more. Summary questions are included in all books to help you test your knowledge.

This program includes 3 textbooks and 10 DVDs:

- *Understanding the National Electrical Code Volume 1* textbook
- *Understanding the National Electrical Code Volume 2* textbook
- *NEC Exam Practice Questions* book
- General Requirements Part 1 DVD and Part 2 DVD
- Grounding vs. Bonding Part 1 DVD and Part 2 DVD
- Wiring Methods Part 1 DVD and Part 2 DVD
- Equipment for General Use DVD
- Special Occupancies DVD
- Special Equipment DVD
- Limited Energy and Communication Systems DVD

Order Mike Holt's Detailed *Code* Library by calling 888.NEC.CODE (632.2633) or visiting www.MikeHolt.com

What is the QR code above? See page xviii.

About This Textbook

This textbook is to be used along with the *NEC*, not as a replacement for it, so be sure to have a copy of the 2011 *National Electrical Code* handy. Compare what Mike is explaining in this book to what the *Code* book says, and discuss any topics that you find difficult to understand with others.

You'll notice that in this book, a great deal of the *NEC* wording has been paraphrased, and some of the article and section titles appear different from the wording in the actual *Code*. Mike believes doing so makes it easier to understand the content of the rule, so keep this in mind when comparing this textbook against the actual *NEC*.

We hope that as you read through this textbook, you'll allow sufficient time to review the text along with the outstanding graphics and examples, which are invaluable to your understanding.

Textbook Format

This textbook follows the *NEC* format, but it doesn't cover every *Code* requirement. For example, it doesn't include every article, section, subsection, exception, or Informational Note. So don't be concerned if you see the textbook contains Exception 1 and Exception 3, but not Exception 2.

Important Features for the 2011 Edition of This Textbook

In order to better meet the needs of our customers, we have improved the layout of this textbook with some new feaures, in addition to the features from the 2008 edition which were so successful. These features include:

- Special Sections which contain additional information to better help you understand a concept are identified with a light gray background and colored frame.

- Graphics that contain a 2011 *Code* change will have a green border with a green 2011 CC icon next to the heading.

- Any *NEC* changes will be in green underlined text in all graphics. If you see a green bordered graphic with no green underlined text, it most likely indicates that the *Code* change is the removal of some text. Graphics without a color border support the concept being discussed, but nothing in the graphic was affected by a change for 2011.

- Any 2011 *Code* is denoted by <u>underlined text and in the corresponding chapter color</u>. For example, in Chapter 1 the change text will be red and underlined; Chapter 2 the change text will be cyan and underlined, and so on.

- Examples or practical application questions with their answer and solution have a light yellow background.

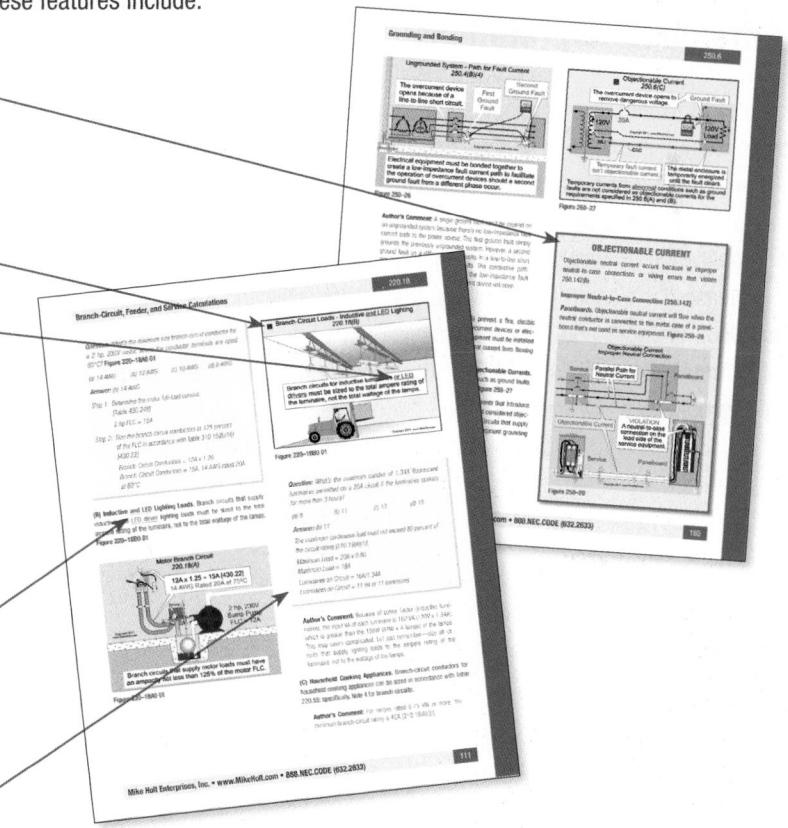

Cross-References and Author's Comments

Cross References. This textbook contains several *NEC* cross-references to other related *Code* requirements to help you develop a better understanding of how the *NEC* rules relate to one another. These cross-references are indicated by *Code* section numbers in brackets, an example of which is "[90.4]."

Author's Comments. "Author's Comments," written by Mike, are intended to help you understand the *NEC* material, and to bring to your attention things of which you should be aware.

Difficult Concepts

As you progress through this textbook, you might find that you don't understand every explanation, example, calculation, or comment. Don't become frustrated, and don't get down on yourself. Remember, this is the *National Electrical Code* and sometimes the best attempt to explain a concept isn't enough to make it perfectly clear. If you're still confused, visit www.MikeHolt.com, and post your question on the *Code* Forum for help.

Different Interpretations

Some electricians, contractors, instructors, inspectors, engineers, and others enjoy the challenge of discussing the *NEC* requirements, hopefully in a positive and productive manner. This give-and-take is important to the process of better understanding the *Code* requirements and application. However, if you're going to get into an *NEC* discussion, please don't spout out what you think without having the actual *Code* book in your hand. The professional way of discussing an *NEC* requirement is by referring to a specific section, rather than talking in vague generalities.

QR Codes

QR Code

What is this? It is a QR Code and gives you the ability to use your smartphone to take a photo (using a barcode reader app) and be directed to a website. For example, the QR Code to the left when captured will direct your smartphone to the Mike Holt Enterprises website. We have included these in various places in our book to make it easier for you to go directly to the website page referenced. In order to use a QR code, you will need an app for your phone that allows your phone to read this barcode. Your phone may already have the ability to scan this barcode, but if not visit the website www.mobile-barcodes.com/qr-code-software for more information.

Textbook Errors and Corrections

Humans develop the text, graphics, and layout of this textbook, and since currently none of us are perfect, there may be a few errors. This can occur because the *NEC* is dramatically changed each *Code* cycle; new articles are added, some are deleted, some are relocated, and many are renumbered. We take great care in researching the *NEC* requirements to ensure this textbook is correct. If you believe there's an error of any kind in this textbook (typographical, grammatical, technical, or anything else), no matter how insignificant, please let us know.

Any errors found after printing are listed on our Website, so if you find an error, first check to see if it's already been corrected. Go to www.MikeHolt.com, click on the "Books" link, and then the "Corrections" link (www.MikeHolt.com/bookcorrections.htm).

If you don't find the error listed on the Website, contact us by sending an E-mail to Corrections@MikeHolt.com. Be sure to include the book title, page number, and any other pertinent information.

You Tube

Visit the Mike Holt channel on YouTube to see video clips that accompany this and our other 2011 books (www.youtube.com/user/MikeHoltNEC).

How to Use the
National Electrical Code

The *National Electrical Code* is written for persons who understand electrical terms, theory, safety procedures, and electrical trade practices. These individuals include electricians, electrical contractors, electrical inspectors, electrical engineers, designers, and other qualified persons. The *Code* isn't written to serve as an instructive or teaching manual for untrained individuals [90.1(C)].

Learning to use the *NEC* is like learning to play the game of chess; it's a great game if you enjoy mental warfare. When learning to play chess, you must first learn the names of the game pieces, how the pieces are placed on the board, and how each piece moves.

Once you understand the fundamentals, you're ready to start playing the game. Unfortunately, at this point all you can do is make crude moves, because you really don't understand how all the information works together. To play chess well, you'll need to learn how to use your knowledge by working on sub-tle strategies before you can work your way up to the more intriguing and complicated moves.

Not a Game

Electrical work isn't a game, and it must be taken very seriously. Learning the basics of electricity, important terms and concepts, as well as the basic layout of the *NEC* gives you just enough knowledge to be dangerous. There are thousands of specific and unique applications of electrical installations, and the *Code* doesn't cover every one of them. To safely apply the *NEC*, you must understand the purpose of a rule and how it affects the safety aspects of the installation.

NEC Terms and Concepts

The *NEC* contains many technical terms, so it's crucial for *Code* users to understand their meanings and their applications. If you don't understand a term used in a *Code* rule, it will be impossible to properly apply the *NEC* requirement. Be sure you understand that Article 100 defines the terms that apply to two or more *Code* articles. For example, the term "Dwelling Unit" is found in many articles; if you don't know what a dwelling unit is, how can you apply the requirements for it?

In addition, many articles have terms unique for that specific article and definitions of those terms are only applicable for that given

article. For example, Section 250.2 contains the definitions of terms that only apply to Article 250—Grounding and Bonding.

Small Words, Grammar, and Punctuation

It's not only the technical words that require close attention, because even the simplest of words can make a big difference to the application of a rule. The word "or" can imply alternate choices for equipment wiring methods, while "and" can mean an additional requirement. Let's not forget about grammar and punctuation. The location of a comma can dramatically change the requirement of a rule.

Slang Terms or Technical Jargon

Electricians, engineers, and other trade-related professionals use slang terms or technical jargon that isn't shared by all. This makes it very difficult to communicate because not everybody understands the intent or application of those slang terms. So where possible, be sure you use the proper word, and don't use a word if you don't understand its definition and application. For example, lots of electricians use the term "pigtail" when describing the short conductor for the connection of a receptacle, switch, luminaire, or equipment. Although they may understand it, not everyone does.

NEC Style and Layout

Before we get into the details of the *NEC*, we need to take a few moments to understand its style and layout. Understanding the structure and writing style of the *Code* is very important before it can be used and applied effectively. The *National Electrical Code* is organized into ten major components.

1. Table of Contents
2. Article 90 (Introduction to the *Code*)
3. Chapters 1 through 9 (major categories)
4. Articles 90 through 840 (individual subjects)
5. Parts (divisions of an article)
6. Sections and Tables (*Code* requirements)

7. Exceptions (*Code* permissions)

8. Informational Notes (explanatory material)

9. Annexes (information)

10. Index

1. Table of Contents. The Table of Contents displays the layout of the chapters, articles, and parts as well as the page numbers. It's an excellent resource and should be referred to periodically to observe the interrelationship of the various *NEC* components. When attempting to locate the rules for a particular situation, knowledgeable *Code* users often go first to the Table of Contents to quickly find the specific *NEC* Part that applies.

2. Introduction. The *NEC* begins with Article 90, the introduction to the *Code*. It contains the purpose of the *NEC*, what's covered and what isn't covered along with how the *Code* is arranged. It also gives information on enforcement and how mandatory and permissive rules are written as well as how explanatory material is included. Article 90 also includes information on formal interpretations, examination of equipment for safety, wiring planning, and information about formatting units of measurement.

3. Chapters. There are nine chapters, each of which is divided into articles. The articles fall into one of four groupings: General Requirements (Chapters 1 through 4), Specific Requirements (Chapters 5 through 7), Communications Systems (Chapter 8), and Tables (Chapter 9).

Chapter 1 General

Chapter 2 Wiring and Protection

Chapter 3 Wiring Methods and Materials

Chapter 4 Equipment for General Use

Chapter 5 Special Occupancies

Chapter 6 Special Equipment

Chapter 7 Special Conditions

Chapter 8 Communications Systems (Telephone, Data, Satellite, Cable TV and Broadband)

Chapter 9 Tables–Conductor and Raceway Specifications

4. Articles. The *NEC* contains approximately 140 articles, each of which covers a specific subject. For example:

Article 110 General Requirements

Article 250 Grounding and Bonding

Article 300 Wiring Methods

Article 430 Motors and Motor Controllers

Article 500 Hazardous (Classified) Locations

Article 680 Swimming Pools, Fountains, and Similar Installations

Article 725 Remote-Control, Signaling, and Power-Limited Circuits

Article 800 Communications Circuits

5. Parts. Larger articles are subdivided into parts.

Because the parts of a *Code* article aren't included in the section numbers, we have a tendency to forget what "part" the *NEC* rule is relating to. For example, Table 110.34(A) contains working space clearances for electrical equipment. If we aren't careful, we might think this table applies to all electrical installations, but Table 110.34(A) is located in Part III, which only contains requirements for "Over 600 Volts, Nominal installations." The rules for working clearances for electrical equipment for systems 600V, nominal, or less are contained in Table 110.26(A)(1), which is located in Part II—600 Volts, Nominal, or Less.

6. Sections and Tables.

Sections. Each *NEC* rule is called a "*Code* Section." A *Code* section may be broken down into subsections by letters in parentheses (A), (B), and so on. Numbers in parentheses (1), (2), and so forth, may further break down a subsection, and lowercase letters (a), (b), and so on, further break the rule down to the third level. For example, the rule requiring all receptacles in a dwelling unit bathroom to be GFCI protected is contained in Section 210.8(A)(1). Section 210.8(A)(1) is located in Chapter 2, Article 210, Section 8, Subsection (A), Sub-subsection (1).

Many in the industry incorrectly use the term "Article" when referring to a *Code* section. For example, they say "Article 210.8," when they should say "Section 210.8." Section numbers in this book are shown without the word "Section," unless they begin a sentence. For example, Section 210.8(A) is shown as simply 210.8(A).

Tables. Many *Code* requirements are contained within tables, which are lists of *NEC* requirements placed in a systematic arrangement. The titles of the tables are extremely important; you must read them carefully in order to understand the contents, applications, limitations, and so forth, of each table in the *Code*. Many times notes are provided in or below a table; be sure to read them as well since they're also part of the requirement. For example, Note 1 for Table 300.5 explains how to measure the cover when burying cables and raceways, and Note 5 explains what to do if solid rock is encountered.

7. Exceptions. Exceptions are *Code* requirements or permissions that provide an alternative method to a specific requirement. There are two types of exceptions—mandatory and permissive. When a rule has several exceptions, those exceptions with mandatory requirements are listed before the permissive exceptions.

Mandatory Exceptions. A mandatory exception uses the words "shall" or "shall not." The word "shall" in an exception means that if you're using the exception, you're required to do it in a particular way. The phrase "shall not" means it isn't permitted.

Permissive Exceptions. A permissive exception uses words such as "shall be permitted," which means it's acceptable (but not mandatory) to do it in this way.

8. Informational Notes. An Informational Note contains explanatory material intended to clarify a rule or give assistance, but it isn't a *Code* requirement.

9. Annexes. Annexes aren't a part of the *NEC* requirements, and are included in the *Code* for informational purposes only.

Annex A. Product Safety Standards
Annex B. Application Information for Ampacity Calculation
Annex C. Raceway Fill Tables for Conductors and Fixture Wires of the Same Size
Annex D. Examples
Annex E. Types of Construction
Annex F. Critical Operations Power Systems (COPS)
Annex G. Supervisory Control and Data Acquisition (SCADA)
Annex H. Administration and Enforcement
Annex I. Recommended Tightening Torques

10. Index. The Index at the back of the *NEC* is helpful in locating a specific rule.

Changes to the *NEC* since the previous edition(s), are identified by shading, but rules that have been relocated aren't identified as a change. A bullet symbol "•" is located on the margin to indicate the location of a rule that was deleted from a previous edition. New articles contain a vertical line in the margin of the page.

How to Locate a Specific Requirement

How to go about finding what you're looking for in the *Code* depends, to some degree, on your experience with the *NEC*. *Code* experts typically know the requirements so well they just go to the correct rule without any outside assistance. The Table of Contents might be the only thing very experienced *NEC* users need to locate the requirement they're looking for. On the other hand, average *Code* users should use all of the tools at their disposal, including the Table of Contents and the Index.

Table of Contents. Let's work out a simple example: What *NEC* rule specifies the maximum number of disconnects permitted for a service? If you're an experienced *Code* user, you'll know Article 230 applies to "Services," and because this article is so large, it's divided up into multiple parts (actually eight parts). With this knowledge, you can quickly go to the Table of Contents and see it lists the Service Equipment Disconnecting Means requirements in Part VI.

> **Author's Comment:** The number 70 precedes all page numbers because the *NEC* is NFPA Standard Number 70.

Index. If you use the Index, which lists subjects in alphabetical order, to look up the term "service disconnect," you'll see there's no listing. If you try "disconnecting means," then "services," you'll find that the Index specifies that the rule is located in Article 230, Part VI. Because the *NEC* doesn't give a page number in the Index, you'll need to use the Table of Contents to find the page number, or flip through the *Code* to Article 230, then continue to flip through pages until you find Part VI.

Many people complain that the *NEC* only confuses them by taking them in circles. As you gain experience in using the *Code* and deepen your understanding of words, terms, principles, and practices, you'll find the *NEC* much easier to understand and use than you originally thought.

Customizing Your *Code* Book

One way to increase your comfort level with the *Code* is to customize it to meet your needs. You can do this by highlighting and underlining important *NEC* requirements, and by attaching tabs to important pages. Be aware that if you're using your *Code* book to take an exam, some exam centers don't allow markings of any type.

Highlighting. As you read through this textbook, be sure you highlight those requirements in the *Code* that are the most important or relevant to you. Use yellow for general interest and orange for important requirements you want to find quickly. Be sure to highlight terms in the Index and the Table of Contents as you use them.

Underlining. Underline or circle key words and phrases in the *NEC* with a red pen (not a lead pencil) and use a 6-inch ruler to keep lines straight and neat. This is a very handy way to make important requirements stand out. A small 6-inch ruler also comes in handy for locating specific information in the many *Code* tables.

Tabbing the *NEC*. By placing tabs on *Code* articles, sections, and tables, it will make it easier for you to use the *NEC*. However, too many tabs will defeat the purpose. You can order a set of *Code* tabs designed by Mike Holt online at www.MikeHolt.com, or by calling 1.888.NEC.CODE (632.2633).

About the Author

Mike Holt

Mike Holt worked his way up through the electrical trade from an apprentice electrician to become one of the most recognized experts in the world as it relates to electrical power installations. He has worked as a journeyman electrician, master electrician, and electrical contractor. Mike's experience in the real world gives him a unique understanding of how the *NEC* relates to electrical installations from a practical standpoint. You'll find his writing style to be direct, nontechnical, and practical.

Did you know that he didn't finish high school? So if you struggled in high school or if you didn't finish it at all, don't let this get you down, you're in good company. As a matter of fact, Mike Culbreath, Master Electrician, who produces the finest electrical graphics in the history of the electrical industry, didn't finish high school either. So two high school dropouts produced the text and graphics in this textbook! However, realizing success depends on one's continuing pursuit of education. Mike immediately attained his GED (as did Mike Culbreath) and ultimately attended the University of Miami's Graduate School for a Master's degree in Business Administration (MBA).

Mike Holt resides in Central Florida, is the father of seven children, and has many outside interests and activities. He's a six-time National Barefoot Water-Ski Champion (1988, 1999, 2005, 2006, 2007, and 2008), has set many national records, has competed in three World Championships (2006, 2008, and 2010) and continues to train and work out year-round so that he can qualify to ski in the 2012 World Barefoot Championships at the age of 61!

What sets him apart from some, is his commitment to living a balanced lifestyle; placing God first, family, career, then self.

Mike Holt—Special Acknowledgments

First, I want to thank God for my godly wife who's always by my side and my children, Belynda, Melissa, Autumn, Steven, Michael, Meghan, and Brittney.

A special thank you must be sent to the staff at the National Fire Protection Association (NFPA), publishers of the *NEC*—in particular Jeff Sargent for his assistance in answering my many *Code* questions over the years. Jeff, you're a "first class" guy, and I admire your dedication and commitment to helping others understand the *NEC*. Other former NFPA staff members I would like to thank include John Caloggero, Joe Ross, and Dick Murray for their help in the past.

A personal thank you goes to Sarina, my long-time friend and office manager. It's been wonderful working side-by-side with you for over 25 years nurturing this company's growth from its small beginnings.

About the Graphic Illustrator

Mike Culbreath

Mike Culbreath devoted his career to the electrical industry and worked his way up from an apprentice electrician to master electrician. While working as a journeyman electrician, he suffered a serious on-the-job knee injury. With a keen interest in continuing education for electricians, he completed courses at Mike Holt Enterprises, Inc. and then passed the exam to receive his Master Electrician's license. In 1986, after attending classes at Mike Holt Enterprises, Inc., he joined the staff to update material and later studied computer graphics and began illustrating Mike Holt's textbooks and magazine articles. He's worked with the company for almost 25 years and, as Mike Holt has proudly acknowledged, has helped to transform his words and visions into lifelike graphics.

Special Acknowledgments

I want to thank my wonderful children, Dawn and Mac, who have had to put up with me during the *Code* revision seasons.

I would like to thank Steve Arne, our amazing technical editorial director, Eric Stromberg, an electrical engineer and super geek (and I mean that in the most complimentary manner, this guy is brilliant), and Ryan Jackson, an outstanding and very knowledgeable code guy, for helping me keep our graphics as technically correct as possible.

I also want to give a special thank you to Cathleen Kwas for making me look good with her outstanding layout design and typesetting skills. I would also like to acknowledge Belynda Holt Pinto, our Chief Operations Officer and the rest of the outstanding staff at Mike Holt Enterprises, for all the hard work they do to help produce and distribute these outstanding products.

And last but not least, I need to give a special thank you to Mike Holt for not firing me about 25 years ago when I "borrowed" one of his computers and took it home to begin the process of learning how to do computer illustrations. He gave me the opportunity and time needed to develop my computer graphic skills. He's been an amazing friend and mentor since I met him as a student many years ago. Thanks for believing in me and allowing me to be part of the Mike Holt Enterprises family.

Mike Holt Enterprises Team

Editorial Team

I want to thank **Toni Culbreath** and **Barbara Parks** who worked tirelessly to proofread and edit the final stages of this publication. Their attention to detail and dedication to this project is greatly appreciated.

Production Team

I want to thank **Cathleen Kwas** who did the layout and production of this book. Her desire to create the best possible product for our customers is greatly appreciated.

Video Team Members

The following special persons provided assistance in the development of this textbook; particularly in ensuring that the technical content is accurate. In addition, they all provided outstanding technical advice as they served on the video team along with author Mike Holt and a guest appearance by graphic illustrator Mike Culbreath.

Steve Arne
Technical Training Consultant
Arne Electro Tech
Rapid City, S.Dak.
ElectricalMaster.com

Steve Arne has worked in various positions in the electrical industry since 1974 including electrician, electrical contractor, full-time instructor, and department chair in technical postsecondary education. Steve has developed and taught curriculum for many electrical training courses as well as university business and leadership courses. He's completed a Bachelor's degree in Technical Education and a Master's degree in Administrative Studies. Currently, he provides electrician exam prep and continuing education *Code* classes in South Dakota, Wyoming, and surrounding states using Mike Holt's textbooks and material. He enjoys seeing a student's "lights come on" as they come to a point of understanding and have the "ah-ha" experience of learning something new.

Steve has worked for Mike Holt as a technical editor and video team participant since 2002, and used Mike Holt's books in his classes for a number of years before that. Steve is very thankful to have been associated with an industry leader like Mike who provides excellent training products to help students progress in the electrical industry. Steve has been active in the South Dakota Electrical Council, serving on the Board of the Black Hills Chapter in various capacities and is the current Chapter President.

Steve and his wife Deb live in Rapid City, S.Dak. where they're both active in their church and community, and love to spend time with their children and grandchildren. Most of all, Steve and Deb both endeavor to put God first in their lives and in their home.

Victor M. Ammons
Electrical Department Manager
TMG Engineers, Inc.
Edison, New Jersey
tmg-engr.com

Victor Ammons was born in North Carolina, but has lived primarily in New Jersey since the age of five. He spent his high school and college vacation times working in a small, family-owned electrical contracting firm. Vic married Anne, his high school sweetheart, after his sophomore year at North Carolina State University, from which both graduated with honors two years later. After four years in the Army, during which time their first child was born in Germany, Vic and Anne alternated getting MBA degrees. They now have three married children and three grandchildren.

Vic is a licensed electrical contractor and has spent several years running the family contracting business while his father's health declined. He later trained and turned the business over to his brother-in-law and then returned to the engineering field. Vic is a registered Professional Engineer in New Jersey, is LEED accredited, and has served in several officer positions for the local branch of the National Professional Engineers Society. He is now the Electrical Department Manager for TMG Engineers in Edison, New Jersey.

Vic now resides in west central New Jersey in an area with a few dozen families among nearly a thousand acres of woodlands. Yes, there are still woodlands in New Jersey; they haven't gotten around to paving them all yet. Vic and Anne celebrated their 41ᵗʰ anniversary in 2010, are avid square and round dancers, and are active in several clubs. He's also an amateur beekeeper. Both are active in several capacities in their church.

Ryan Jackson
Electrical Inspector
Draper City, Ut
West Valley City, UT

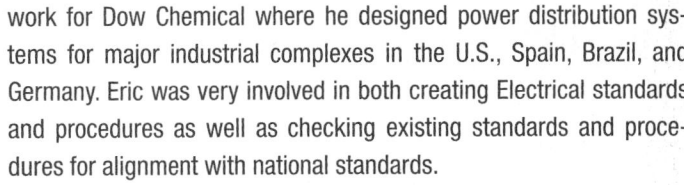

Ryan Jackson is a combination inspector in the Salt Lake City, Utah, area. He began doing electrical work at the age of 18. At the age of 23 Ryan landed his first job as an electrical inspector, and subsequently became certified in building, plumbing, and mechanical inspection (commercial and residential), as well as building and electrical plan review. Two years after becoming an inspector, he was approached by a friend in the area asking him to fill in at an electrical seminar for him. After his first class he was hooked, and is now a highly sought-after seminar instructor. Ryan has taught in several states, and loves helping people increase their understanding of the *Code*.

In 2005, Ryan met Mike Holt in Salt Lake City, and they became friends immediately. He helped Mike with his *Understanding the NEC, Volume 2* videos and began editing his books as well. Ryan believes that there are only a small handful of opportunities that change a person's life and career, and meeting Mike was one of them.

Ryan can often be found in his garage turning wood on his lathe, and in the autumn you'll find him at as many University of Utah football games as he can attend, which is typically all of them. Ryan married his high school sweetheart, Sharie, and they have two beautiful children together: Kaitlynn and Aaron.

Eric Stromberg
Electrical Engineer/Instructor
Stromberg Engineering, Inc.
Lake Jackson, TX
www.strombergengineering.com

Eric Stromberg started in the Electrical field by working as a journeyman electrician for a small contractor in the Houston area while going to college pursuing a degree in Electrical Engineering. After graduation, in 1982, Eric worked as an electronic technician where he installed and maintained life safety control systems in high rise buildings. In 1989, Eric went to work for Dow Chemical where he designed power distribution systems for major industrial complexes in the U.S., Spain, Brazil, and Germany. Eric was very involved in both creating Electrical standards and procedures as well as checking existing standards and procedures for alignment with national standards.

He also worked as a Construction Manager where he ensured *Code* compliancy of installations as well as provided field engineering support. Eric currently has his own business and spends a good deal of time teaching classes in both the *National Electrical Code* and electrical circuits. He is also a member of the Electrical Safety and Licensing Advisory Board for the State of Texas.

Eric lives in Lake Jackson, Texas, with his wife Jane. They have three children: Ainsley, Austin, and Brieanna. Ainsley is a teacher in Boston who will be getting married in the summer of 2011. Austin will be enlisting in the Air Force, and Brieanna started college in the Fall of 2010.

J. Kevin Vogel
Professional Engineer/Instructor
Crescent Electric Supply
Coeur d'Alene, ID
www.cesco.com and www.trindera.com.

Kevin Vogel graduated from Santa Clara University in 1964 with a Bachelor of Science degree in Mechanical Engineering. A licensed Professional Engineer since 1969, he worked as Chief Engineer for a division of Square D Company that manufactured electric heaters and thermoplastic outlet boxes. He also was employed as an electrician and holds a Master Electrician's license.

In 1978, Kevin co-founded an electrical wholesale distribution business that was acquired in 1991 by Crescent Electric Supply Company. Kevin continues to work in that part of the industry, and is a certified instructor for *National Electrical Code* classes in the states of Idaho and Washington. He also serves as a consultant to Trindera Engineering, an electrical engineering firm located in Coeur d'Alene.

Kevin and his beloved wife Linda have been married since 1966, and have been blessed with 13 wonderful children and 20 (so far) grandchildren. Kevin is extremely grateful to God for all of the gifts He has bestowed on him and his loved ones.

Notes

ARTICLE 90

Introduction to the *National Electrical Code*

INTRODUCTION TO ARTICLE 90—INTRODUCTION TO THE *NATIONAL ELECTRICAL CODE*

Many *NEC* violations and misunderstandings wouldn't occur if people doing the work simply understood Article 90. For example, many people see *Code* requirements as performance standards. In fact, the *NEC* requirements are bare minimums for safety. This is exactly the stance electrical inspectors, insurance companies, and courts take when making a decision regarding electrical design or installation.

Article 90 opens by saying the *NEC* isn't intended as a design specification or instruction manual. The *National Electrical Code* has one purpose only, and that's the "practical safeguarding of persons and property from hazards arising from the use of electricity." It goes on to indicate that the *Code* isn't intended as a design specification or instruction manual. The necessity to carefully study the *NEC* rules can't be overemphasized, and the role of textbooks such as this one is to help in that undertaking. Understanding where to find the rules in the *Code* that apply to the installation is invaluable. Rules in several different articles often apply to even a simple installation.

Article 90 then describes the scope and arrangement of the *NEC*. The balance of Article 90 provides the reader with information essential to understanding those items you do find in the *NEC*.

Typically, electrical work requires you to understand the first four chapters of the *Code* which apply generally, plus have a working knowledge of the Chapter 9 tables. That knowledge begins with Article 90. Chapters 5, 6, and 7 make up a large portion of the *NEC*, but they apply to special occupancies, special equipment, or other special conditions. They build on, modify, or amend the rules in the first four chapters. Chapter 8 contains the requirements for communications systems, such as telephone systems, antenna wiring, CATV, and network-powered broadband systems. Communications systems aren't subject to the general requirements of Chapters 1 through 4, or the special requirements of Chapters 5 through 7, unless there's a specific reference in Chapter 8 to a rule in Chapters 1 through 7.

90.1 Purpose of the *NEC*.

(A) Practical Safeguarding. The purpose of the *NEC* is to ensure that electrical systems are installed in a manner that protects people and property by minimizing the risks associated with the use of electricity.

(B) Adequacy. The *Code* contains requirements considered necessary for a safe electrical installation. If an electrical installation is installed in compliance with the *NEC*, it will be essentially free from electrical hazards. The *Code* is a safety standard, not a design guide.

NEC requirements aren't intended to ensure the electrical installation will be efficient, convenient, adequate for good service, or suitable for future expansion. Specific items of concern, such as electrical energy management, maintenance, and power quality issues aren't within the scope of the *Code*. **Figure 90–1**

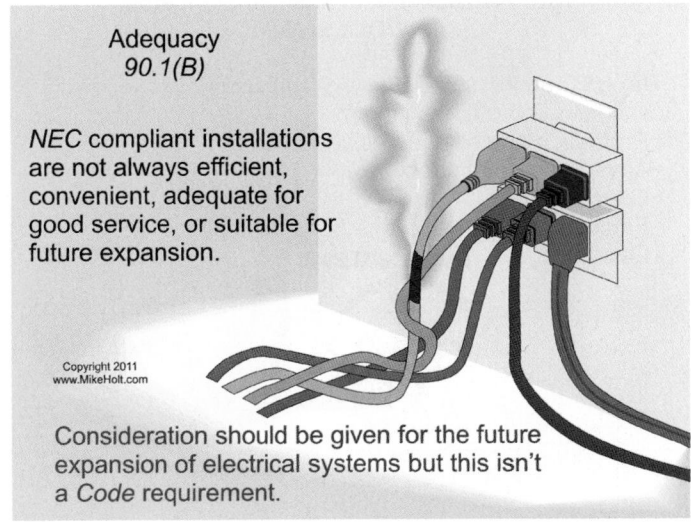

Adequacy
90.1(B)

NEC compliant installations are not always efficient, convenient, adequate for good service, or suitable for future expansion.

Copyright 2011
www.MikeHolt.com

Consideration should be given for the future expansion of electrical systems but this isn't a *Code* requirement.

Figure 90–1

Note: Hazards in electrical systems often occur because circuits are overloaded or not properly installed in accordance with the *NEC*. These often occur if the initial wiring didn't provide reasonable provisions for system changes or for the increase in the use of electricity.

Author's Comments:

- See the definition of "Overload" in Article 100.

- The *NEC* doesn't require electrical systems to be designed or installed to accommodate future loads. However, the electrical designer, typically an electrical engineer, is concerned with not only ensuring electrical safety (*Code* compliance), but also with ensuring the system meets the customers' needs, both of today and in the near future. To satisfy customers' needs, electrical systems are often designed and installed above the minimum requirements contained in the *NEC*. But just remember, if you're taking an exam, licensing exams are based on your understanding of the minimum Code requirements.

(C) Intention. The *Code* is intended to be used by those skilled and knowledgeable in electrical theory, electrical systems, construction, and the installation and operation of electrical equipment. It isn't a design specification standard or instruction manual for the untrained and unqualified.

(D) Relation to International Standards. The requirements of the *NEC* address the fundamental safety principles contained in the International Electrotechnical Commission (IEC) standards, including protection against electric shock, adverse thermal effects, overcurrent, fault currents, and overvoltage. **Figure 90–2**

NEC Relation to International Standards
90.1(D) and Note

The *NEC* addresses the safety principles contained in the IEC such as:
- Protection against electric shock
- Adverse thermal effects
- Overcurrent
- Fault currents
- Overvoltage

NFPA 70

nec 2011

Copyright 2011
www.MikeHolt.com

Figure 90–2

Author's Comments:

- See the definition of "Overcurrent" in Article 100.

- The *NEC* is used in Chile, Ecuador, Peru, and the Philippines. It's also the electrical code for Colombia, Costa Rica, Mexico, Panama, Puerto Rico, and Venezuela. Because of these adoptions, the *NEC* is available in Spanish from the National Fire Protection Association, 617.770.3000, or www.NFPA.Org.

90.2 Scope of the *NEC*.

(A) What is Covered. The *NEC* contains requirements necessary for the proper installation of electrical conductors, equipment, and raceways; signaling and communications conductors, equipment, and raceways; as well as optical fiber cables and raceways for the following locations: **Figure 90–3**

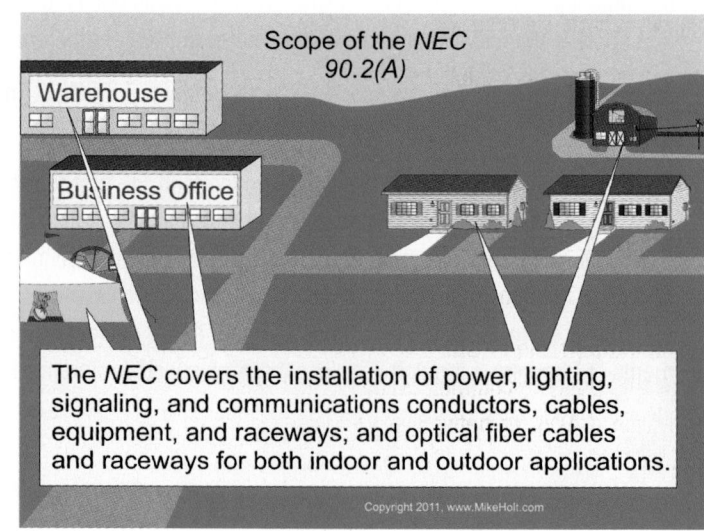

Scope of the *NEC*
90.2(A)

Warehouse

Business Office

The *NEC* covers the installation of power, lighting, signaling, and communications conductors, cables, equipment, and raceways; and optical fiber cables and raceways for both indoor and outdoor applications.

Copyright 2011, www.MikeHolt.com

Figure 90–3

(1) Public and private premises, including buildings or structures, mobile homes, recreational vehicles, and floating buildings.

(2) Yards, lots, parking lots, carnivals, and industrial substations.

(3) Conductors and equipment connected to the utility supply.

(4) Installations used by an electric utility, such as office buildings, warehouses, garages, machine shops, recreational buildings, and other electric utility buildings that aren't an integral part of a utility's generating plant, substation, or control center. **Figure 90–4**

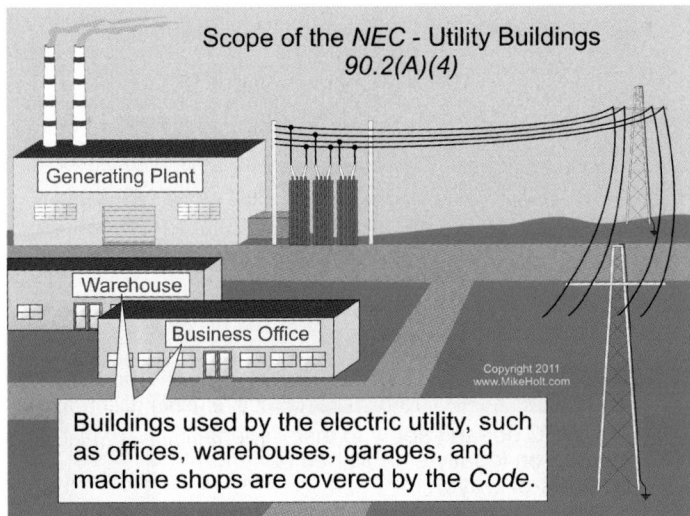

Scope of the *NEC* - Utility Buildings
90.2(A)(4)

Generating Plant

Warehouse

Business Office

Buildings used by the electric utility, such as offices, warehouses, garages, and machine shops are covered by the *Code*.

Figure 90–4

(B) What Isn't Covered. The *NEC* doesn't apply to:

(1) Transportation Vehicles. Installations in cars, trucks, boats, ships and watercraft, planes, electric trains, or underground mines.

(2) Mining Equipment. Installations underground in mines and self-propelled mobile surface mining machinery and its attendant electrical trailing cables.

(3) Railways. Railway power, signaling, and communications wiring.

(4) Communications Utilities. The installation requirements of the *NEC* don't apply to communications (telephone), Community Antenna Television (CATV), or network-powered broadband utility equipment located in building spaces used exclusively for these purposes, or outdoors if the installation is under the exclusive control of the communications utility. **Figures 90–5 and 90–6**

> **Author's Comment:** Interior wiring for communications systems, not in building spaces used exclusively for these purposes, must be installed in accordance with the following Chapter 8 Articles:
>
> • Telephone and Data, Article 800
> • CATV, Article 820
> • Network-Powered Broadband, Article 830

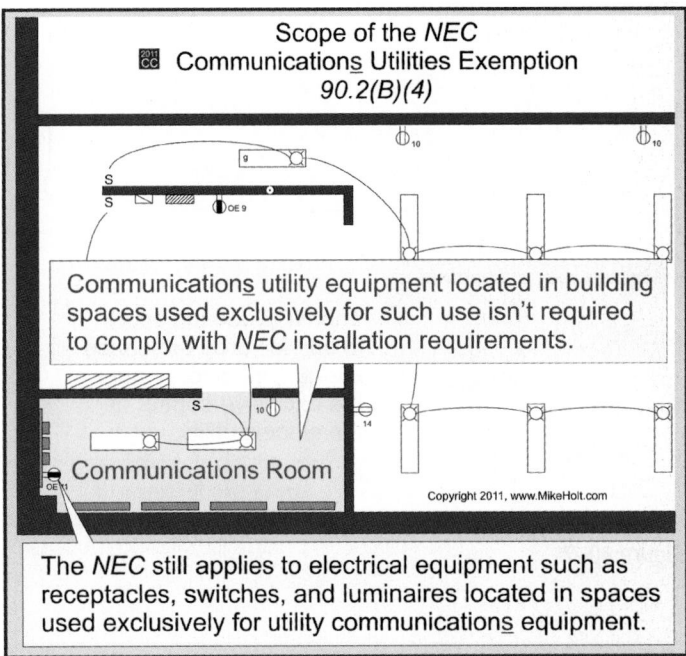

Scope of the *NEC*
Communications Utilities Exemption
90.2(B)(4)

Communications utility equipment located in building spaces used exclusively for such use isn't required to comply with *NEC* installation requirements.

Communications Room

The *NEC* still applies to electrical equipment such as receptacles, switches, and luminaires located in spaces used exclusively for utility communications equipment.

Figure 90–5

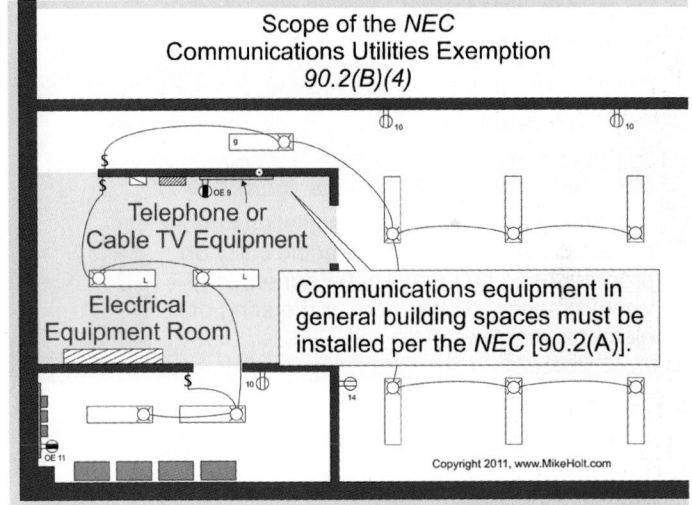

Scope of the *NEC*
Communications Utilities Exemption
90.2(B)(4)

Telephone or Cable TV Equipment

Electrical Equipment Room

Communications equipment in general building spaces must be installed per the *NEC* [90.2(A)].

Figure 90–6

(5) Electric Utilities. The *NEC* doesn't apply to installations under the exclusive control of an electric utility where such installations:

   a. Consist of service drops or service laterals and associated metering. **Figure 90–7**

   b. Are on property owned or leased by the electric utility for the purpose of generation, transformation, transmission, distribution, or metering of electric energy. **Figure 90–8**

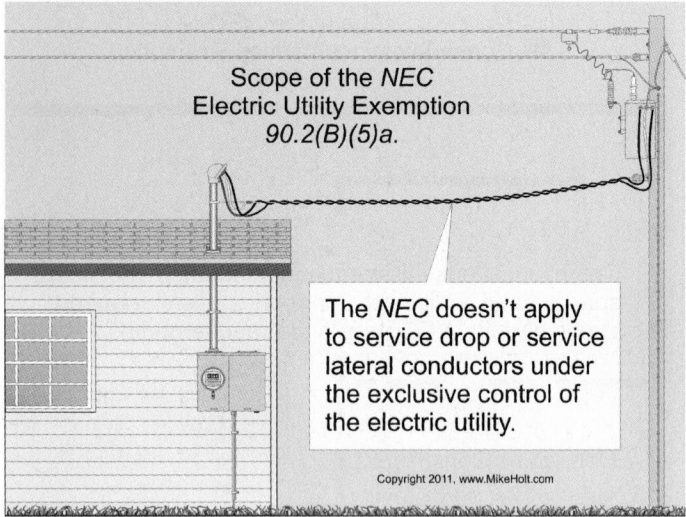

Figure 90–7

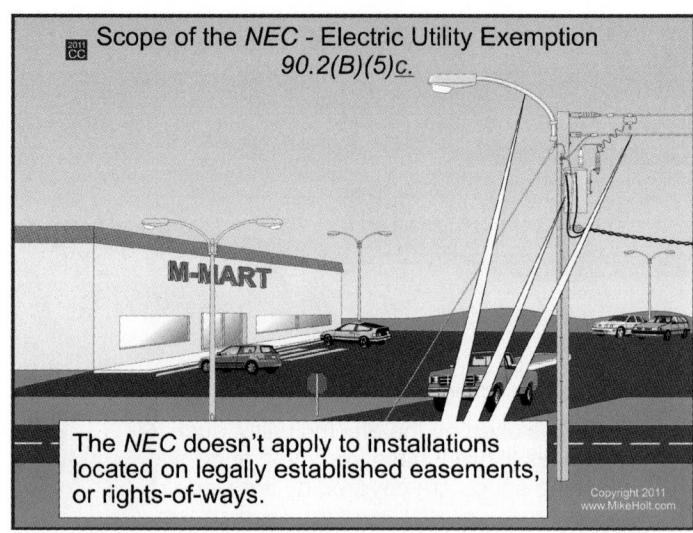

Figure 90–9

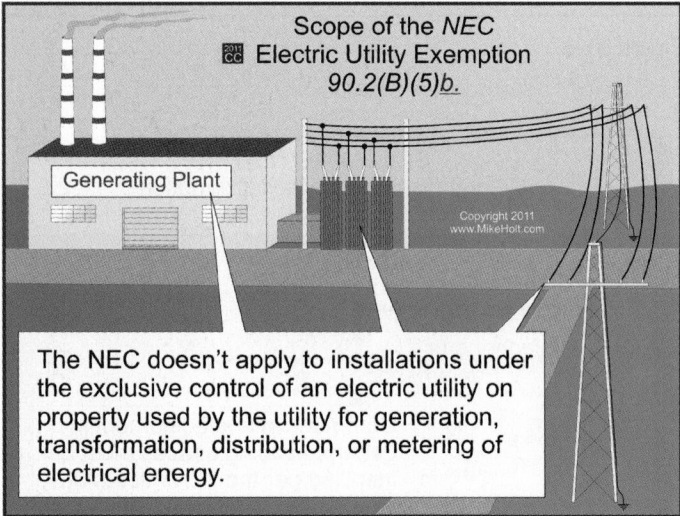

Figure 90–8

Author's Comment: Luminaires located in legally established easements, or rights-of-way, such as at poles supporting transmission or distribution lines, are exempt from the *NEC*. However, if the electric utility provides site and public lighting on private property, then the installation must comply with the *Code* [90.2(A)(4)].

c. Are located on legally established easements, or rights-of-way. **Figure 90–9**

d. Are located by other written agreements either designated by or recognized by public service commissions, utility commissions, or other regulatory agencies having jurisdiction for such installations; limited to installations for the purpose of communications, metering, generation, control, transformation, transmission, or distribution of electric energy where legally established easements or rights-of-way can't be obtained. These installations are limited to federal lands, Native American reservations through the U.S. Department of the Interior Bureau of Indian Affairs, military bases, lands controlled by port authorities and state agencies and departments, and lands owned by railroads.

Note to 90.2(B)(4) and (5): Utilities include entities that install, operate, and maintain communications systems (telephone, CATV, Internet, satellite, or data services) or electric supply (generation, transmission, or distribution systems) and are designated or recognized by governmental law or regulation by public service/utility commissions. Utilities may be subject to compliance with codes and standards covering their regulated activities as adopted under governmental law or regulation.

90.3 *Code* Arrangement. The *Code* is divided into an introduction and nine chapters. **Figure 90–10**

General Requirements. The requirements contained in Chapters 1, 2, 3, and 4 apply to all installations.

Author's Comment: These first four chapters may be thought of as the foundation for the rest of the *Code*, and are the main focus of this textbook.

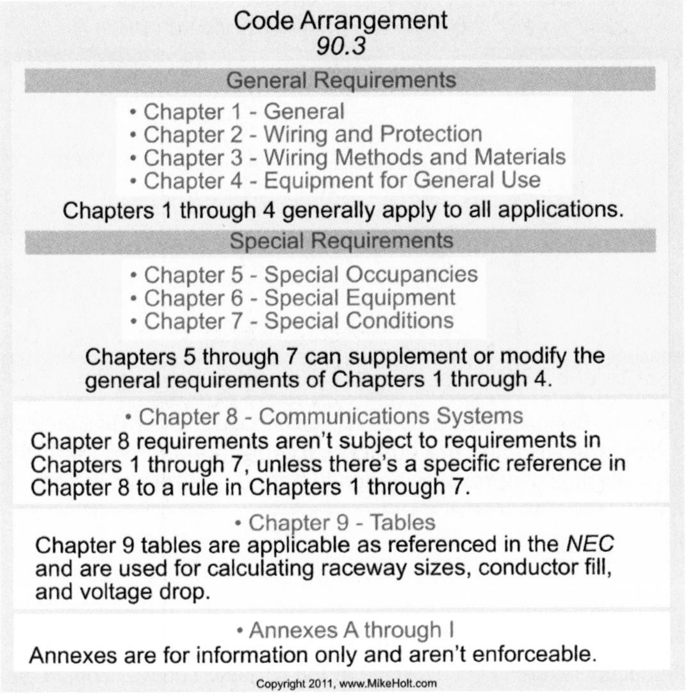

Code Arrangement
90.3

General Requirements

- Chapter 1 - General
- Chapter 2 - Wiring and Protection
- Chapter 3 - Wiring Methods and Materials
- Chapter 4 - Equipment for General Use

Chapters 1 through 4 generally apply to all applications.

Special Requirements

- Chapter 5 - Special Occupancies
- Chapter 6 - Special Equipment
- Chapter 7 - Special Conditions

Chapters 5 through 7 can supplement or modify the general requirements of Chapters 1 through 4.

- Chapter 8 - Communications Systems

Chapter 8 requirements aren't subject to requirements in Chapters 1 through 7, unless there's a specific reference in Chapter 8 to a rule in Chapters 1 through 7.

- Chapter 9 - Tables

Chapter 9 tables are applicable as referenced in the *NEC* and are used for calculating raceway sizes, conductor fill, and voltage drop.

- Annexes A through I

Annexes are for information only and aren't enforceable.

Copyright 2011, www.MikeHolt.com

Figure 90–10

Special Requirements. The requirements contained in Chapters 5, 6, and 7 apply to special occupancies, special equipment, or other special conditions. These chapters can supplement or modify the requirements in Chapters 1 through 4.

Communications Systems. Chapter 8 contains the requirements for communications systems, such as telephone systems, antenna wiring, CATV, and network-powered broadband systems. Communications systems aren't subject to the general requirements of Chapters 1 through 4, or the special requirements of Chapters 5 through 7, unless there's a specific reference in Chapter 8 to a rule in Chapters 1 through 7.

> **Author's Comment:** An example of how Chapter 8 works is in the rules for working space about equipment. The typical 3 ft working space isn't required in front of communications equipment, because Table 110.26(A)(1) isn't referenced in Chapter 8.

Tables. Chapter 9 consists of tables applicable as referenced in the *NEC*. The tables are used to calculate raceway sizing, conductor fill, the radius of raceway bends, and conductor voltage drop.

Annexes. Annexes aren't part of the *Code*, but are included for informational purposes. There are eight Annexes:

- Annex A. Product Safety Standards
- Annex B. Application Information for Ampacity Calculation

- Annex C. Raceway Fill Tables for Conductors and Fixture Wires of the Same Size
- Annex D. Examples
- Annex E. Types of Construction
- Annex F. Critical Operations Power Systems (COPS)
- Annex G. Supervisory Control and Data Acquisition (SCADA)
- Annex H. Administration and Enforcement

90.4 Enforcement. The *Code* is intended to be suitable for enforcement by governmental bodies that exercise legal jurisdiction over electrical installations for power, lighting, signaling circuits, and communications systems, such as: **Figure 90–11**

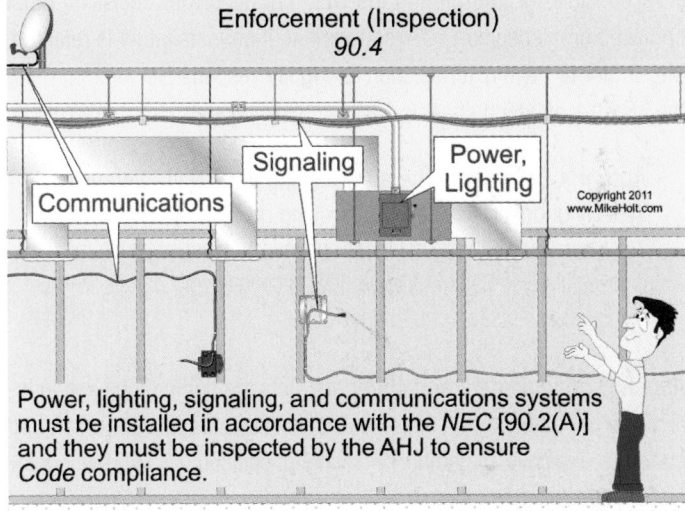

Power, lighting, signaling, and communications systems must be installed in accordance with the *NEC* [90.2(A)] and they must be inspected by the AHJ to ensure *Code* compliance.

Figure 90–11

Signaling circuits which include:

- Article 725 Class 1, Class 2, and Class 3 Remote-Control, Signaling, and Power-Limited Circuits
- Article 760 Fire Alarm Systems
- Article 770 Optical Fiber Cables and Raceways

Communications systems which include:

- Article 800 Communications Circuits (twisted-pair conductors)
- Article 810 Radio and Television Equipment (satellite dish and antenna)
- Article 820 Community Antenna Television and Radio Distribution Systems (coaxial cable)
- Article 830 Network-Powered Broadband Communications Systems

Author's Comment: The installation requirements for signaling circuits and communications circuits are covered in Mike Holt's *Understanding the National Electrical Code, Volume 2* textbook.

The enforcement of the *NEC* is the responsibility of the authority having jurisdiction (AHJ), who is responsible for interpreting requirements, approving equipment and materials, waiving *Code* requirements, and ensuring equipment is installed in accordance with listing instructions.

Author's Comment: See the definition of "Authority Having Jurisdiction" in Article 100.

Interpretation of the Requirements. The authority having jurisdiction is responsible for interpreting the *NEC*, but his or her decisions must be based on a specific *Code* requirement. If an installation is rejected, the authority having jurisdiction is legally responsible for informing the installer of which specific *NEC* rule was violated.

Author's Comment: The art of getting along with the authority having jurisdiction consists of doing good work and knowing what the *Code* actually says (as opposed to what you only think it says). It's also useful to know how to choose your battles when the inevitable disagreement does occur.

Approval of Equipment and Materials. Only the authority having jurisdiction has authority to approve the installation of equipment and materials. Typically, the authority having jurisdiction will approve equipment listed by a product testing organization, such as Underwriters Laboratories Inc. (UL). The *NEC* doesn't require all equipment to be listed, but many state and local AHJs do. See 90.7, 110.2, 110.3, and the definitions for "Approved," "Identified," "Labeled," and "Listed" in Article 100. **Figure 90–12**

Author's Comment: According to the *NEC*, the authority having jurisdiction determines the approval of equipment. This means he or she can reject an installation of listed equipment and can approve the use of unlisted equipment. Given our highly litigious society, approval of unlisted equipment is becoming increasingly difficult to obtain.

Waiver of Requirements. By special permission, the authority having jurisdiction can waive specific requirements in the *Code* or permit alternative methods where it's assured equivalent safety can be achieved and maintained.

Author's Comment: Special permission is defined in Article 100 as the written consent of the authority having jurisdiction.

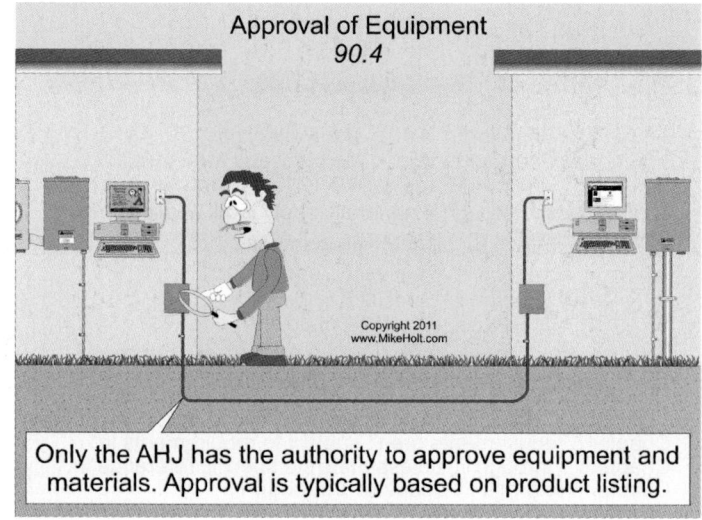

Only the AHJ has the authority to approve equipment and materials. Approval is typically based on product listing.

Figure 90–12

Waiver of New Product Requirements. If the 2011 *NEC* requires products that aren't yet available at the time the *Code* is adopted, the authority having jurisdiction can allow products that were acceptable in the previous *Code* to continue to be used.

Author's Comment: Sometimes it takes years before testing laboratories establish product standards for new *NEC* requirements, and then it takes time before manufacturers can design, manufacture, and distribute these products to the marketplace.

90.5 Mandatory Requirements and Explanatory Material.

(A) Mandatory Requirements. In the *NEC* the words "shall" or "shall not," indicate a mandatory requirement.

Author's Comment: For the ease of reading this textbook, the word "shall" has been replaced with the word "must," and the words "shall not" have been replaced with "must not." Remember that in many places, we will paraphrase the *Code* instead of providing exact quotes, to make it easier to read and understand.

(B) Permissive Requirements. When the *Code* uses "shall be permitted" it means the identified actions are permitted but not required, and the authority having jurisdiction isn't permitted to restrict an installation from being done in that manner. A permissive rule is often an exception to the general requirement.

Author's Comment: For ease of reading, the phrase "shall be permitted," as used in the *Code*, has been replaced in this textbook with the phrase "is permitted" or "are permitted."

(C) Explanatory Material. References to other standards or sections of the *NEC*, or information related to a *Code* rule, are included in the form of <u>Informational Notes</u>. Such notes are for information only and aren't enforceable as a requirement of the *NEC*.

For example, Informational Note 4 in 210.19(A)(1) recommends that the voltage drop of a circuit not exceed 3 percent. This isn't a requirement; it's just a recommendation.

Author's Comment: For convenience and ease of reading in this textbook, I will identify Informational Notes simply as "Note."

(D) <u>Informative</u> Annexes. Nonmandatory information annexes contained in the back of the *Code* book are for information only and aren't enforceable as a requirement of the *NEC*.

90.6 Formal Interpretations.
To promote uniformity of interpretation and application of the provisions of the *NEC*, formal interpretation procedures have been established and are found in the NFPA Regulations Governing Committee Projects.

Author's Comment: This is rarely done because it's a very time-consuming process, and formal interpretations from the NFPA aren't binding on the authority having jurisdiction.

90.7 Examination of Equipment for Product Safety.
Product evaluation for safety is typically performed by a testing laboratory, which publishes a list of equipment that meets a nationally recognized test standard. Products and materials that are listed, labeled, or identified by a testing laboratory are generally approved by the authority having jurisdiction.

Author's Comment: See Article 100 for the definition of "Approved."

Listed, factory-installed, internal wiring and construction of equipment need not be inspected at the time of installation, except to detect alterations or damage [300.1(B)]. **Figure 90–13**

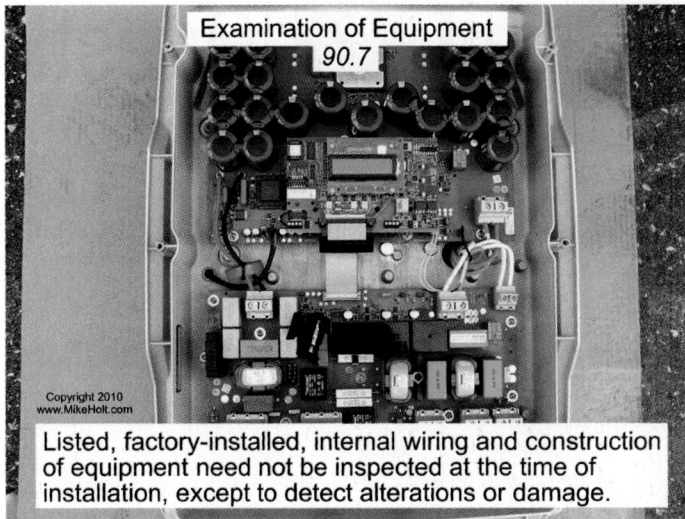

Figure 90–13

90.9 Units of Measurement.

(B) Dual Systems of Units. Both the metric and inch-pound measurement systems are shown in the *NEC*, with the metric units appearing first and the inch-pound system immediately following in parentheses.

Author's Comment: This is the standard practice in all NFPA standards, even though the U.S. construction industry uses inch-pound units of measurement. You will need to be cautious when using the tables in the *Code* because the additional units can make the tables more complex and more difficult to read.

(D) Compliance. Installing electrical systems in accordance with the metric system or the inch-pound system is considered to comply with the *Code*.

Author's Comment: Since compliance with either the metric or the inch-pound system of measurement constitutes compliance with the *NEC*, this textbook uses only inch-pound units.

These questions are based on the 2011 *National Electrical Code*. Please use the 2011 *NEC Code* book to answer the following questions.

Article 90. Introduction—Practice Questions

1. The *NEC* is _____.

    (a) intended to be a design manual
    (b) meant to be used as an instruction guide for untrained persons
    (c) for the practical safeguarding of persons and property
    (d) published by the Bureau of Standards

2. Hazards often occur because of _____.

    (a) overloading of wiring systems by methods or usage not in conformity with the *NEC*
    (b) initial wiring not providing for increases in the use of electricity
    (c) a and b
    (d) none of these

3. This *Code* covers the installation of _____ for public and private premises, including buildings, structures, mobile homes, recreational vehicles, and floating buildings.

    (a) optical fiber cables
    (b) electrical equipment
    (c) raceways
    (d) all of these

4. Installations of communications equipment that are under the exclusive control of communications utilities, and located outdoors or in building spaces used exclusively for such installations _____ covered by the *NEC*.

    (a) are
    (b) are sometimes
    (c) are not
    (d) may be

5. Utilities may be subject to compliance with codes and standards covering their regulated activities as adopted under governmental law or regulation.

    (a) True
    (b) False

6. Communications wiring such as telephone, antenna, and CATV wiring within a building shall not be required to comply with the installation requirements of Chapters 1 through 7, except where specifically referenced in Chapter 8.

    (a) True
    (b) False

7. The _____ has the responsibility for deciding on the approval of equipment and materials.

    (a) manufacturer
    (b) authority having jurisdiction
    (c) testing agency
    (d) none of these

8. The authority having jurisdiction has the responsibility for _____.

    (a) making interpretations of rules
    (b) deciding upon the approval of equipment and materials
    (c) waiving specific requirements in the *Code* and permitting alternate methods and material if safety is maintained
    (d) all of these

9. When the *Code* uses "_____," it means the identified actions are allowed but not required, and they may be options or alternative methods.

    (a) shall
    (b) shall not
    (c) shall be permitted
    (d) a or b

10. Explanatory material, such as references to other standards, references to related sections of the *NEC*, or information related to a *Code* rule, are included in the form of Informational Notes.

    (a) True
    (b) False

Notes

GENERAL

INTRODUCTION TO CHAPTER 1—GENERAL

A young child doesn't begin reading and writing until they have an understanding of some of the basic words of the language. Similarly, you must be familiar with a few basic rules, concepts, definitions, and requirements that apply to the rest of the *NEC* and you must maintain that familiarity as you continue to apply the *Code*.

Chapter 1 consists of two topics. Article 100 provides definitions so people can understand one another when trying to communicate about *Code*-related matters and Article 110 provides the general requirements needed to correctly apply the rest of the *NEC*.

Time spent learning this general material is a great investment. After understanding Chapter 1, some of the *Code* requirements that seem confusing to other people—those who don't understand Chapter 1—will become increasingly clear to you. The requirements will strike you as being "common sense," because you'll have the foundation from which to understand and apply them. When you read the *NEC* requirements in later chapters, you'll understand the principles upon which many of them are based, and not be surprised at all. You'll read them and feel like you already know them.

- **Article 100—Definitions.** Part I of Article 100 contains the definitions of terms used throughout the *Code* for systems that operate at 600V, nominal, or less. The definitions of terms in Part II apply to systems that operate at over 600V, nominal.

  Author's Comment: This textbook covers the requirements for systems that operate at 600V, nominal, or less.

Definitions of standard terms, such as volt, voltage drop, ampere, impedance, and resistance, aren't listed in Article 100. If the *NEC* doesn't define a term, then a dictionary suitable to the authority having jurisdiction should be consulted. A building code glossary might provide better definitions than a dictionary found at your home or school.

Definitions located at the beginning of an article apply only to that specific article. For example, the definition of a "Swimming Pool" is contained in 680.2, because this term applies only to the requirements contained in Article 680—Swimming Pools, Fountains, and Similar Installations. As soon as a defined term is used in two or more articles, its definition is included in Article 100.

- **Article 110—Requirements for Electrical Installations.** This article contains general requirements for electrical installations for the following:
  - Part I. General
  - Part II. 600V, Nominal, Or Less

Notes

ARTICLE 100

Definitions

INTRODUCTION TO ARTICLE 100—DEFINITIONS

Have you ever had a conversation with someone, only to discover that what you said and what he or she heard were completely different? This often happens when people in a conversation don't understand the definitions of the words being used, and that's why the definitions of key terms are located right at the beginning of the *NEC* (Article 100), or at the beginning of each article.

If we can all agree on important definitions, then we speak the same language and avoid misunderstandings. Because the *Code* exists to protect people and property, it's very important to know the definitions presented in Article 100.

Now, here are a couple of things you may not know about Article 100:

Article 100 contains many, but not all, of the terms defined by the *NEC*. In general, only those terms used in two or more articles are defined in Article 100. Those terms used only within one article are located within that article, often near the beginning of the article.

- Part I of Article 100 contains the definitions of terms used throughout the *Code* for systems that operate at 600V, nominal, or less.
- Part II of Article 100 contains only terms that apply to systems that operate at over 600V, nominal.

How can you possibly learn all of these definitions? There seem to be so many. Here are a few tips:

- Break the task down. Study a few words at a time, rather than trying to learn them all at one sitting.
- Review the graphics in the textbook. These will help you see how a term is applied.
- Relate them to your work. As you read a word, think about how it applies to the work you're doing. This will provide a natural reinforcement to the learning process.

DEFINITIONS

Accessible (as it applies to equipment). Admitting close approach and not guarded by locked doors, elevation, or other effective means.

Accessible (as it applies to wiring methods). Not permanently closed in by the building structure or finish and capable of being removed or exposed without damaging the building structure or finish. **Figure 100–1**

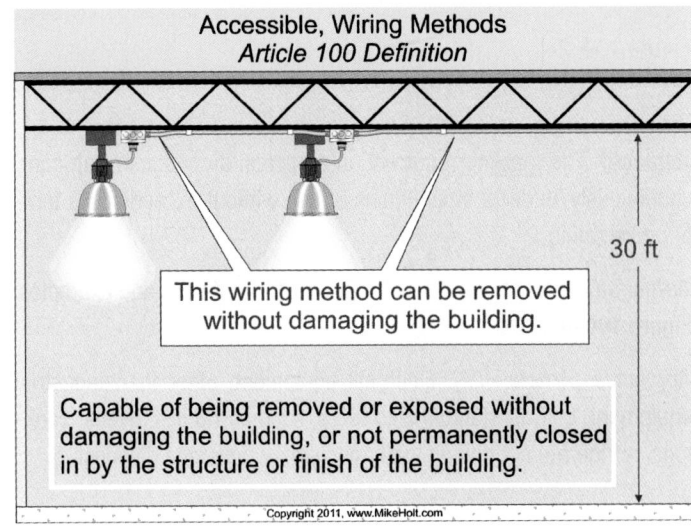

Figure 100–1

Author's Comments:

- Conductors in a concealed raceway are considered concealed, even though they may become accessible by withdrawing them from the raceway. See the definition of "Concealed" in this article.

- Raceways, cables, and enclosures installed above a suspended ceiling or within a raised floor are considered accessible, because the wiring methods can be accessed without damaging the building structure. See the definitions of "Concealed" and "Exposed" in this article.

Accessible, Readily (Readily Accessible). Capable of being reached quickly without having to climb over or remove obstacles, or resort to portable ladders. **Figures 100–2 and 100–3**

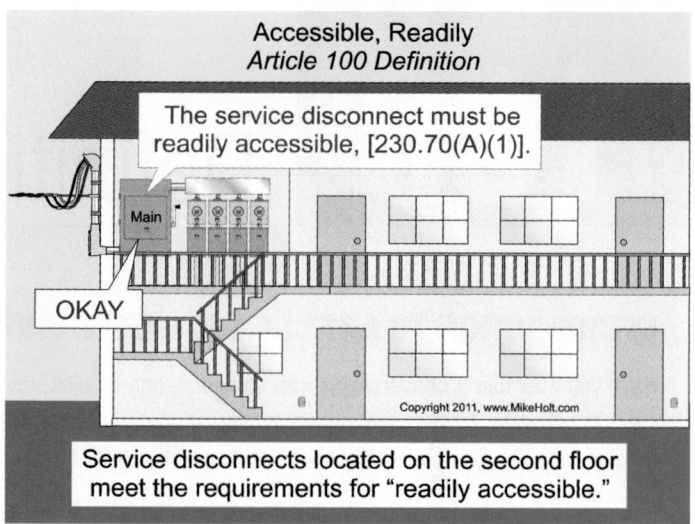

Figure 100–3

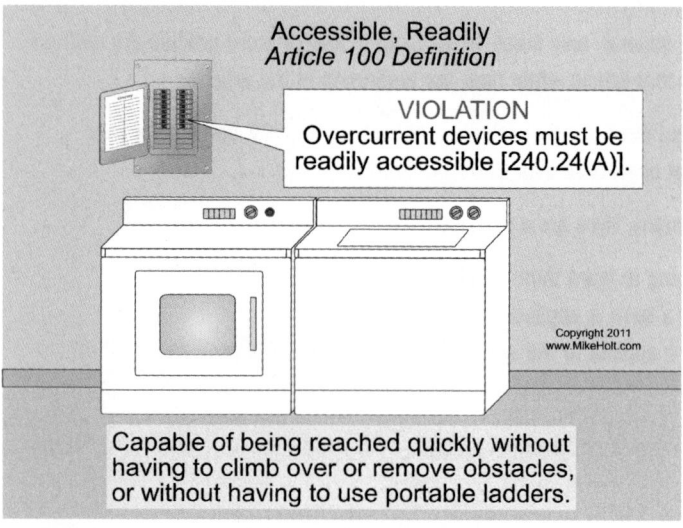

Figure 100–2

Ampacity. The <u>maximum</u> current, in amperes, a conductor can carry continuously, under the conditions of use without exceeding its temperature rating.

Author's Comment: See 310.10 and 310.15 for details and examples. **Figure 100–4**

Appliance [Article 422]. Electrical equipment, other than industrial equipment, built in standardized sizes, such as ranges, ovens, cooktops, refrigerators, drinking water coolers, or beverage dispensers.

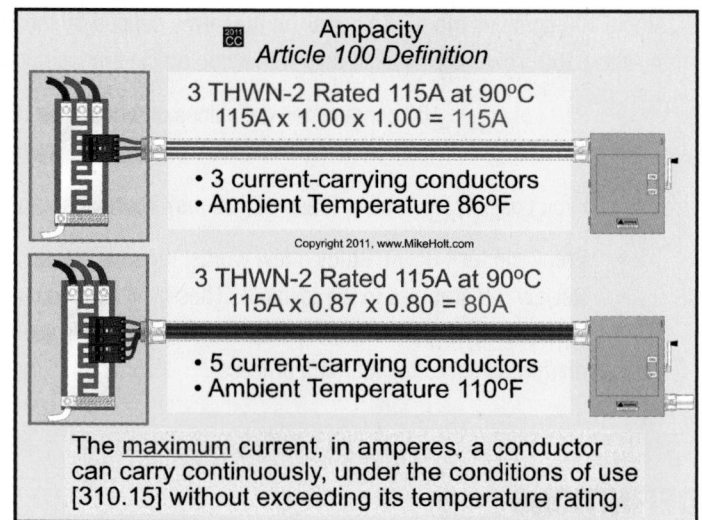

Figure 100–4

Approved. Acceptable to the authority having jurisdiction, usually the electrical inspector.

> **Author's Comment:** Product listing doesn't mean the product is approved, but it's a basis for approval. See 90.4, 90.7, 110.2, and the definitions in this article for "Authority Having Jurisdiction," "Identified," "Labeled," and "Listed."

Arc-Fault Circuit Interrupter (AFCI). <u>An arc-fault circuit interrupter is a device intended to de-energize the circuit when it detects the current waveform characteristics unique to an arcing fault.</u> **Figures 100–5 and 100–6**

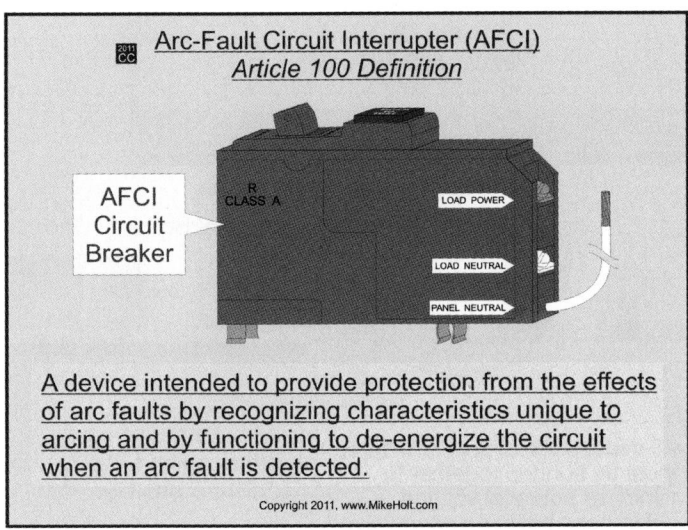

Figure 100–5

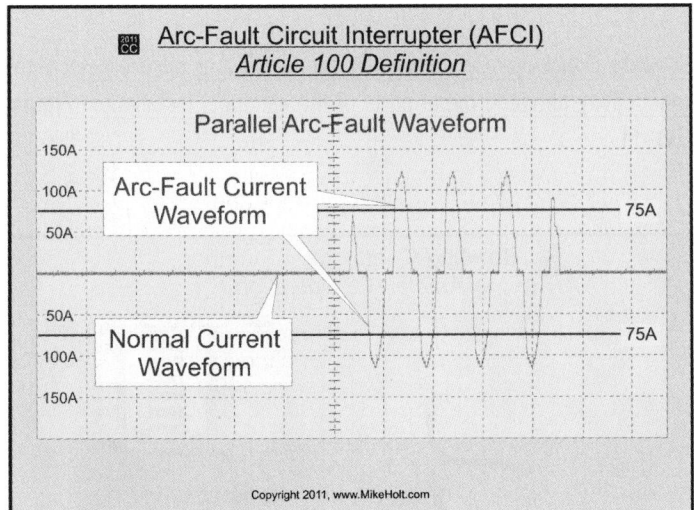

Figure 100–6

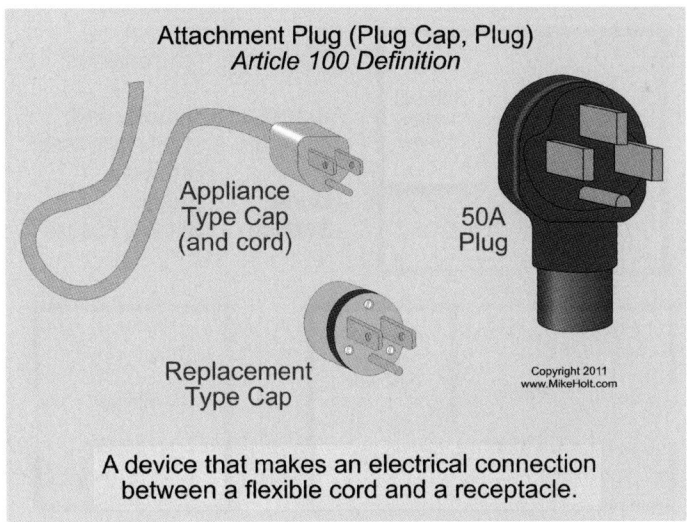

Figure 100–7

Attachment Plug (Plug Cap), (Plug) [Article 406]. A wiring device at the end of a flexible cord intended to be inserted into a receptacle in order to make an electrical connection. **Figure 100–7**

> **Author's Comment:** The use of cords with attachment plugs is limited by 210.50(A), 400.7, 410.24, 410.62, 422.16, 422.33, 590.4, 645.5 and other sections.

Authority Having Jurisdiction (AHJ). The organization, office, or individual responsible for approving equipment, materials, an installation, or a procedure. See 90.4 and 90.7 for more information.

Note: The authority having jurisdiction may be a federal, state, or local government department or an individual, such as a fire chief, fire marshal, chief of a fire prevention bureau or labor department or health department, a building official or electrical inspector, or others having statutory authority. In some circumstances, the property owner or his/her agent assumes the role, and at government installations, the commanding officer, or departmental official may be the authority having jurisdiction.

Author's Comments:

- Typically, the authority having jurisdiction is the electrical inspector who has legal statutory authority. In the absence of federal, state, or local regulations, the operator of the facility or his or her agent, such as an architect or engineer of the facility, can assume the role.

- Some believe the authority having jurisdiction should have a strong background in the electrical field, such as having studied electrical engineering or having obtained an electrical contractor's license, and in a few states this is a legal requirement. Memberships, certifications, and active participation in electrical organizations, such as the International Association of Electrical Inspectors (IAEI), speak to an individual's qualifications. Visit www.IAEI.org for more information about that organization.

Automatic. Functioning without the necessity of human intervention.

Bathroom. A bathroom is an area that includes a basin as well as one or more of the following: a toilet, urinal, tub, shower, bidet, or similar plumbing fixture. **Figure 100–8**

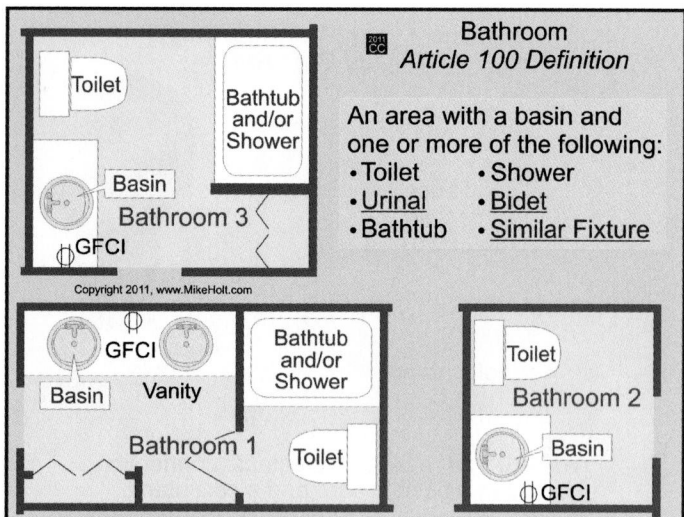

Figure 100-8

Author's Comment: All 15A and 20A, 125V receptacles located in bathrooms must be GFCI protected [210.8(A)(1) and 210.8(B)(1)].

Bonded (Bonding). Connected to establish electrical continuity and conductivity. **Figure 100-9**

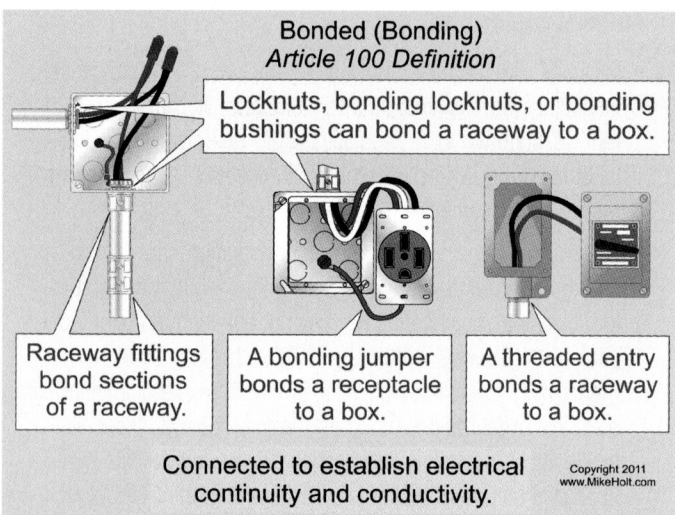

Figure 100-9

Author's Comment: The purpose of bonding is to connect two or more conductive objects together to ensure the electrical continuity of the fault current path, provide the capacity and ability to conduct safely any fault current likely to be imposed, and to minimize potential differences (voltage) between conductive components. **Figure 100-10**

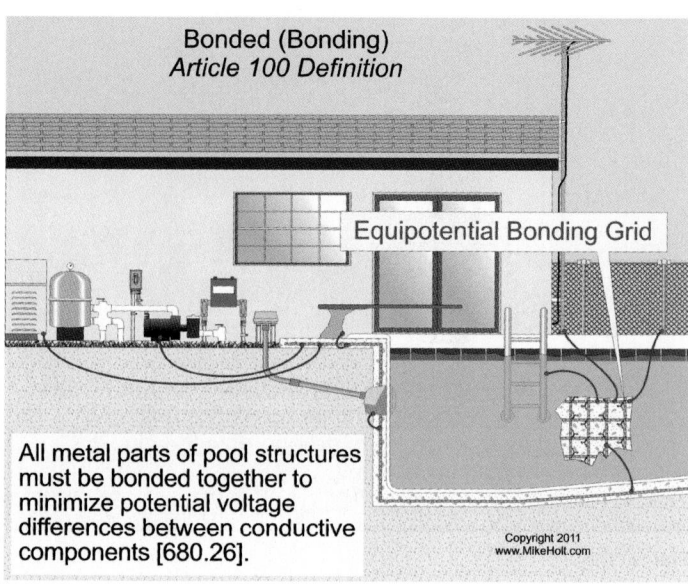

Figure 100-10

Bonding Conductor or Jumper. A conductor that ensures electrical conductivity between metal parts of the electrical installation. **Figure 100-11**

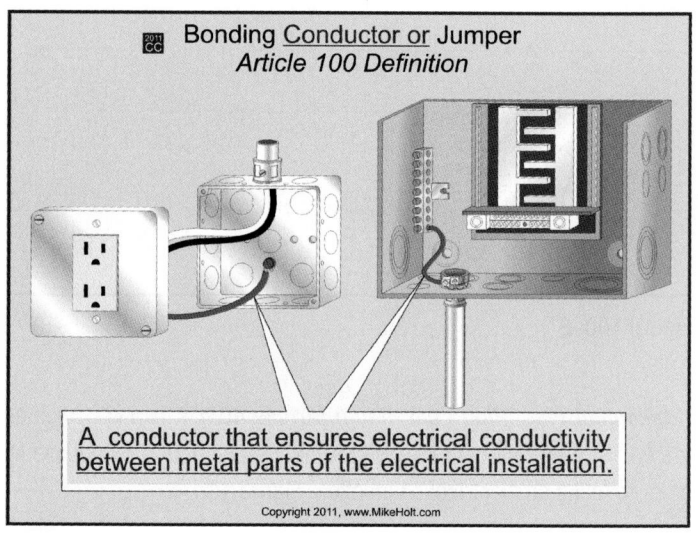

Figure 100-11

Bonding Jumper, Main. A conductor, screw, or strap that connects the circuit equipment grounding conductor to the neutral conductor at service equipment in accordance with 250.24(B) [250.24(A)(4), 250.28, and 408.3(C)]. **Figure 100-12**

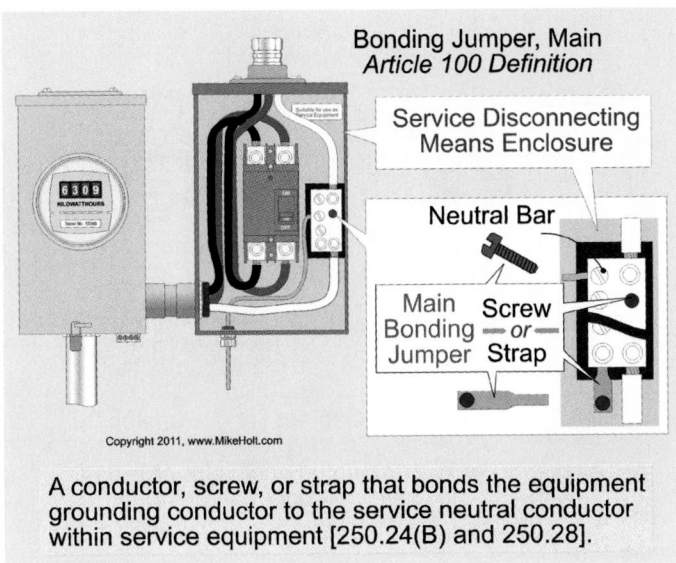

A conductor, screw, or strap that bonds the equipment grounding conductor to the service neutral conductor within service equipment [250.24(B) and 250.28].

Figure 100–12

Bonding Jumper, System. The connection between the neutral conductor and the supply-side bonding jumper or equipment grounding conductor, or both, at a separately derived system. **Figure 100–13**

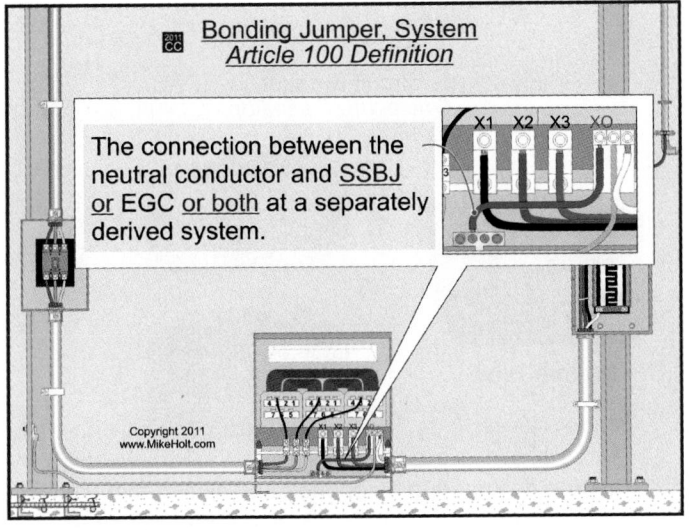

Figure 100–13

Branch Circuit [Article 210]. The conductors between the final overcurrent device and the receptacle outlets, lighting outlets, or other outlets as defined in this article. **Figure 100–14**

Branch Circuit, Individual. A branch circuit that only supplies one load.

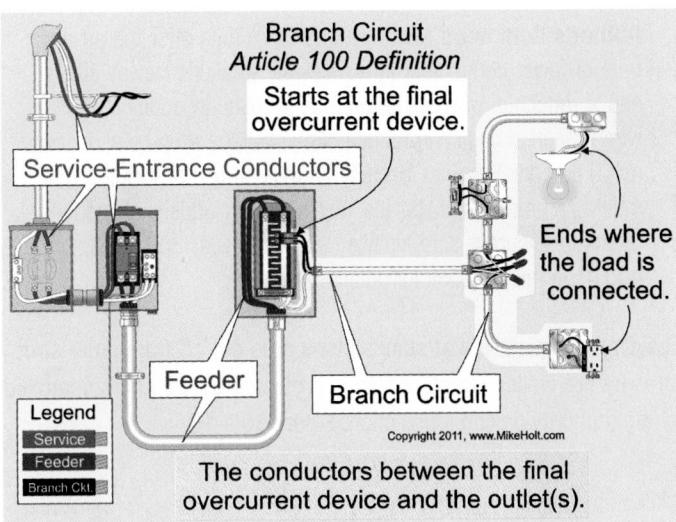

Figure 100–14

Branch Circuit, Multiwire. A branch circuit that consists of two or more ungrounded circuit conductors with a common neutral conductor. There must be a voltage between the ungrounded conductors and an equal difference of voltage from each ungrounded conductor to the common neutral conductor. **Figure 100–15**

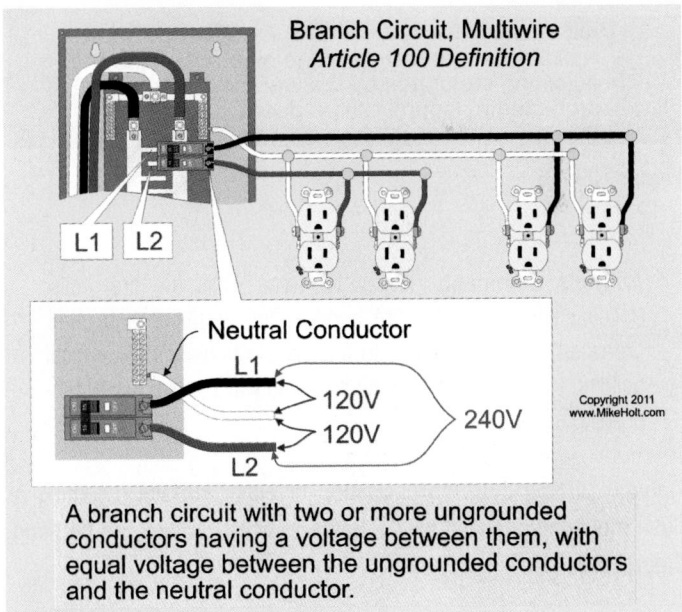

Figure 100–15

Author's Comment: Multiwire branch circuits offer the advantage of fewer conductors in a raceway, smaller raceway sizing, and a reduction of material and labor costs. In addition, multiwire branch circuits can reduce circuit voltage drop by as much as 50 percent. However, because of the dangers associated with multiwire branch circuits, the *NEC* contains additional requirements to ensure a safe installation. See 210.4, 300.13(B), and 408.41 in this textbook for details.

Building. A structure that stands alone or is cut off from other structures by fire walls with all openings protected by fire doors approved by the authority having jurisdiction. **Figure 100–16**

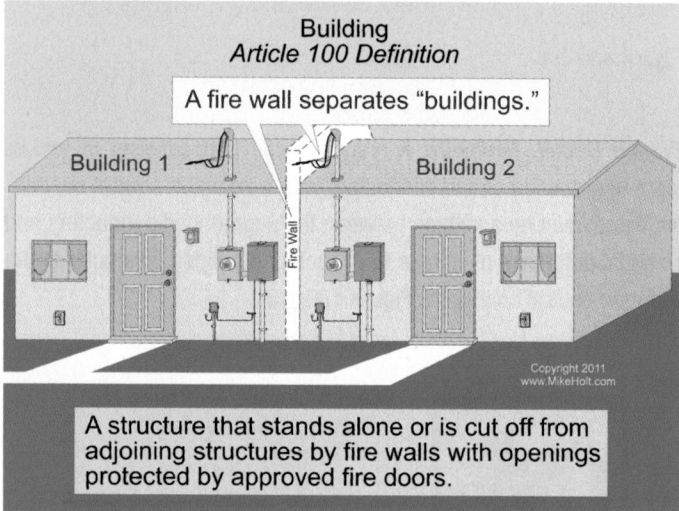

A structure that stands alone or is cut off from adjoining structures by fire walls with openings protected by approved fire doors.

Figure 100–16

Author's Comment: Not all fire-rated walls are fire walls. Building codes describe fire barriers, fire partitions and other fire-rated walls, in addition to fire walls. Check with your local building inspector to determine if a rated wall creates a separate building (fire wall).

Cabinet [Article 312]. An enclosure for either surface mounting or flush mounting provided with a frame in which a door can be hung. **Figure 100–17**

Author's Comment: Cabinets are used to enclose panelboards. See the definition of "Panelboard" in this article.

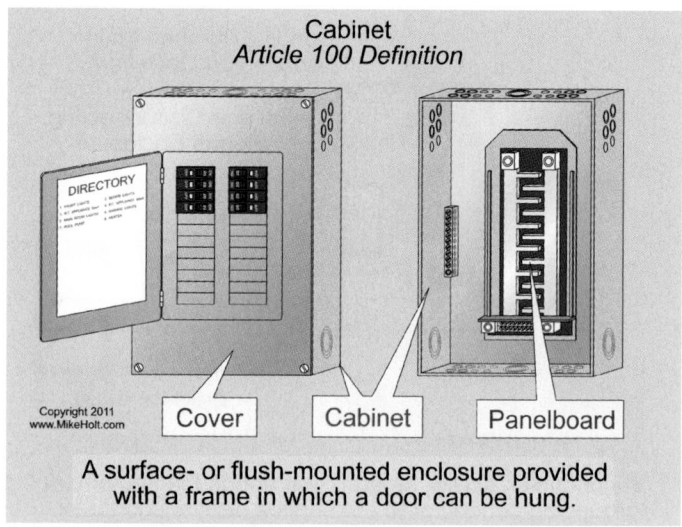

A surface- or flush-mounted enclosure provided with a frame in which a door can be hung.

Figure 100–17

Circuit Breaker. A device designed to be opened and closed manually, and which opens automatically on a predetermined overcurrent without damage to itself. Circuit breakers are available in different configurations, such as inverse time, adjustable trip (electronically controlled), and instantaneous trip/motor-circuit protectors. **Figure 100–18**

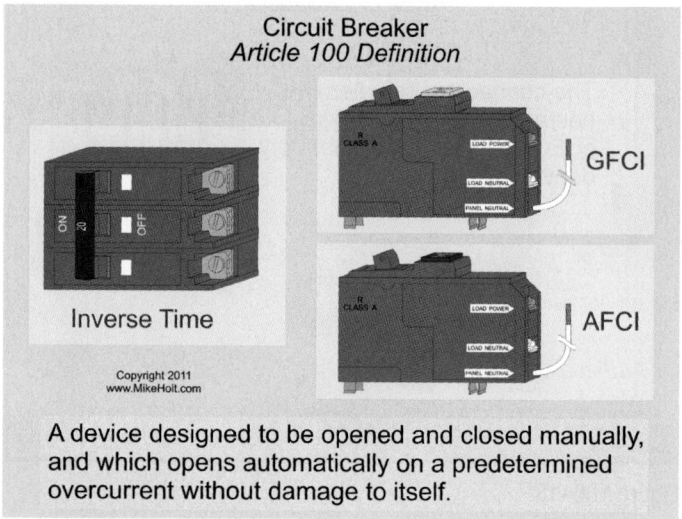

A device designed to be opened and closed manually, and which opens automatically on a predetermined overcurrent without damage to itself.

Figure 100–18

- *Inverse Time:* Inverse time breakers operate on the principle that as the current increases, the time it takes for the devices to open decreases. This type of breaker provides overcurrent protection (overload, short circuit, and ground fault). This is the most common type of circuit breaker that you'll buy over-the-counter.

- *Adjustable Trip:* Adjustable trip breakers permit the thermal trip setting to be adjusted. The adjustment is often necessary to coordinate the operation of the circuit breakers with other overcurrent devices.

Author's Comment: Coordination means that the devices with the lowest ratings, closest to the fault, operate and isolate the fault and minimize disruption so the rest of the system can remain energized and functional. This sounds simple, but large systems (especially emergency systems) may require an expensive engineering study; so if you're responsible for bidding a project, be aware of this requirement.

- *Instantaneous Trip:* Instantaneous trip breakers operate on the principle of electromagnetism only and are used for motors. Sometimes these devices are called motor-circuit protectors. This type of overcurrent device doesn't provide overload protection. It only provides short-circuit and ground-fault protection; overload protection must be provided separately.

Author's Comment: Instantaneous trip circuit breakers have no intentional time delay and are sensitive to current inrush, and to vibration and shock. Consequently, they shouldn't be used where these factors are known to exist.

Clothes Closet. A non-habitable room or space intended primarily for the storage of garments and apparel. **Figure 100–19**

Author's Comment: The definition of "Clothes Closet" provides clarification in the application of overcurrent devices [240.24(D)] and luminaires [410.16] in clothes closets.

Communications Equipment. Electronic telecommunications equipment used for the transmission of audio, video, and data, including support equipment such as computers. **Figure 100–20**

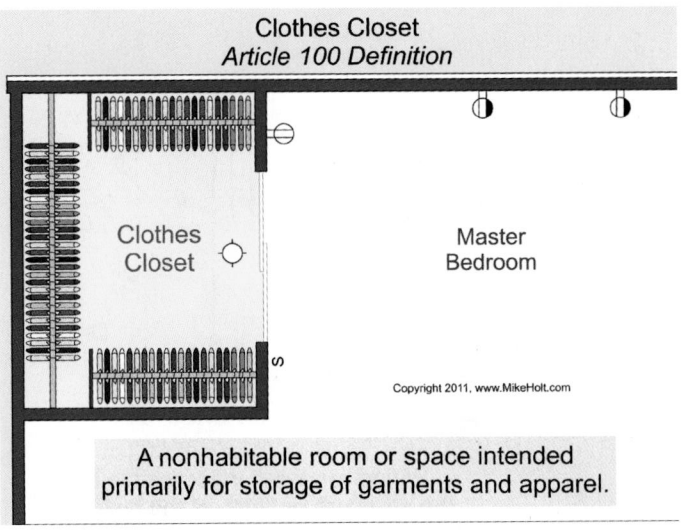

Figure 100–19

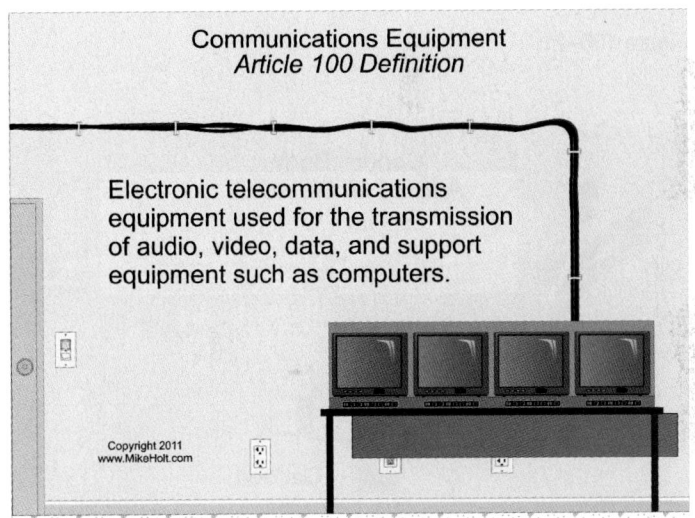

Figure 100–20

Concealed. Rendered inaccessible by the structure or finish of the building. Conductors in a concealed raceway are considered concealed, even though they may be made accessible by withdrawing them from the raceway. **Figure 100–21**

Author's Comment: Wiring behind panels designed to allow access, such as removable ceiling tile, is considered exposed.

Conduit Body. A fitting that's installed in a conduit or tubing system and provides access to conductors through a removable cover. **Figure 100–22**

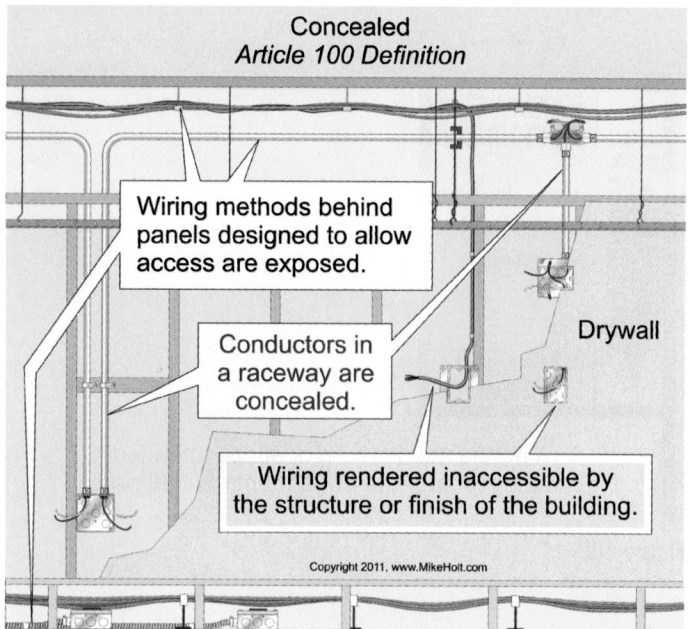

Figure 100–21

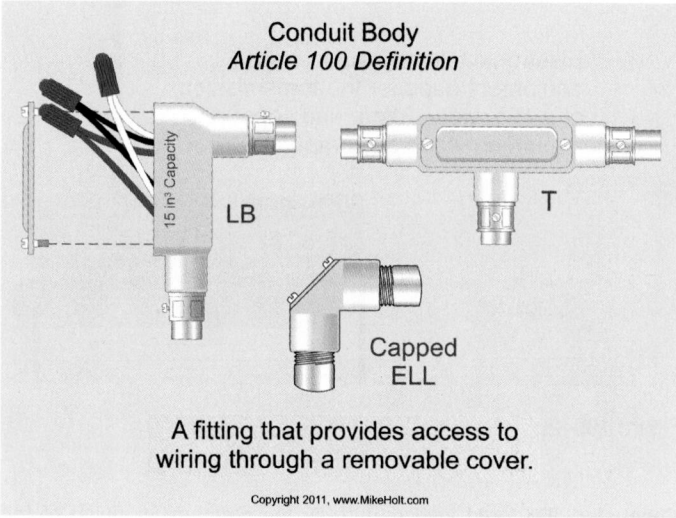

Figure 100–22

Connector, Pressure (Solderless). A device that establishes a conductive connection between conductors or between a conductor and a terminal by the means of mechanical pressure.

Continuous Load. A load where the maximum current is expected to exist for 3 hours or more continuously, such as store or parking lot lighting.

Controller. A device that controls the electric power delivered to electrical equipment in some predetermined manner. This includes time clocks, lighting contactors, photocells, and equipment with similar functions. **Figure 100–23**

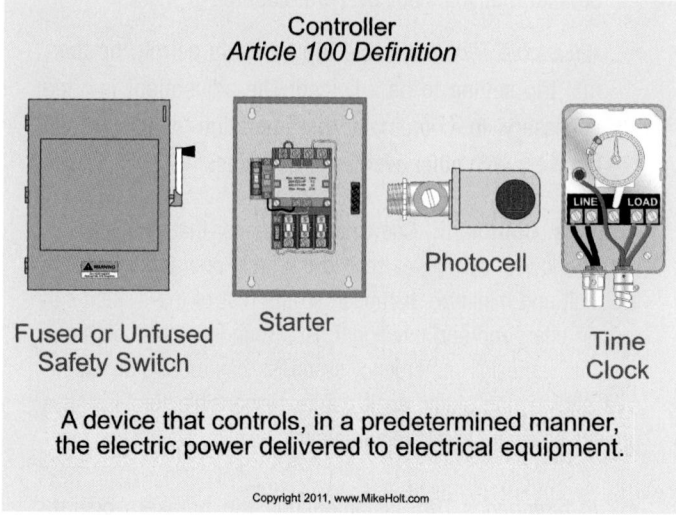

Figure 100–23

Author's Comment: For the definition of "Motor Controller," see 430.2.

Coordination (Selective). Localization of an overcurrent condition to restrict outages to the circuit or equipment affected, accomplished by the choice of overcurrent devices. **Figure 100–24**

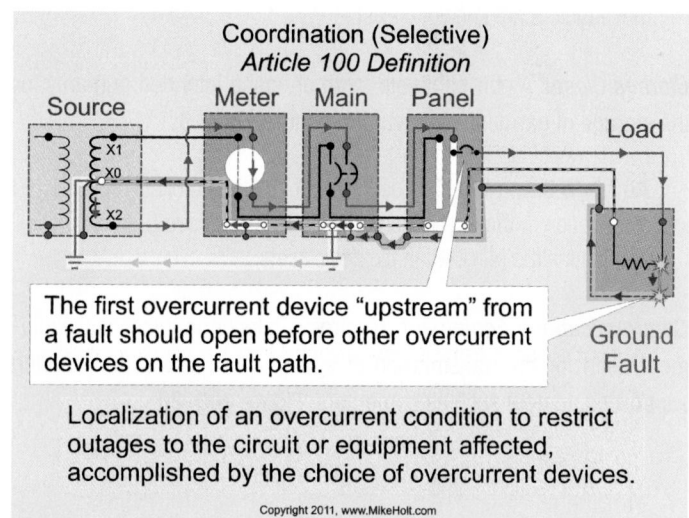

Figure 100–24

Author's Comment: Selective coordination means the overcurrent protection scheme confines the interruption to a particular area rather than to the whole system. For example, if someone plugs in a space heater and raises the total demand on a 20A circuit to 25A, or if a short circuit or ground fault occurs with selective coordination, the only breaker or fuse that will open is the one protecting just that branch circuit. Without selective coordination, an entire building can go dark!

Cutout Box [Article 312]. Cutout boxes are designed for surface mounting with a swinging door or covers secured directly to the box.

Demand Factor. The ratio of the maximum demand to the total connected load.

Author's Comment: This definition is primarily used in the application of the requirements of Article 220—Branch-Circuit, Feeder, and Service Calculations.

Device. A component of an electrical installation intended to carry or control electric energy as its principal function. Figure 100–25

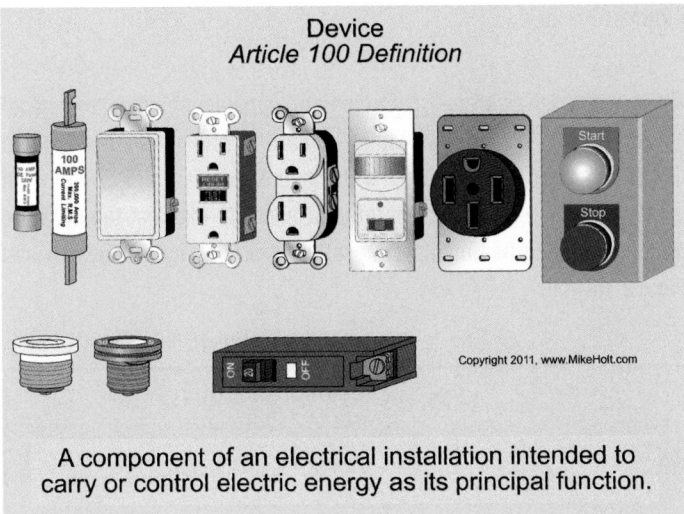

Device
Article 100 Definition

A component of an electrical installation intended to carry or control electric energy as its principal function.

Figure 100–25

Author's Comment: Devices include wires and busbars, receptacles, switches, illuminated switches, circuit breakers, fuses, time clocks, controllers, and so forth, but not locknuts or other mechanical fittings. A device may consume very small amounts of energy, such as an illuminated switch, but still be classified as a device based on its principal function.

Disconnecting Means. A device that opens all of the ungrounded circuit conductors from their power source. This includes devices such as switches, attachment plugs and receptacles, and circuit breakers. Figure 100–26

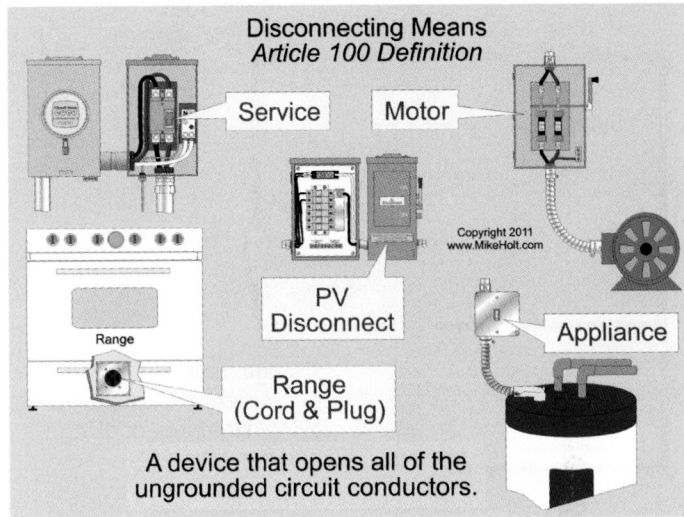

Disconnecting Means
Article 100 Definition

Service   Motor

PV Disconnect

Range

Appliance

Range (Cord & Plug)

A device that opens all of the ungrounded circuit conductors.

Figure 100–26

Author's Comment: Review the following for the specific requirements for equipment disconnecting means:

- Air-conditioning and refrigeration equipment, 440.14
- Appliances, Article 422, Part III
- Buildings supplied by a feeder, Article 225, Part II
- Electric space-heating equipment, 424.19
- Electric duct heaters, 424.65
- Luminaires, 410.130(G)
- Motor control conductors, 430.75
- Motor controllers, 430.102(A)
- Motors, 430.102(B)(1)
- Refrigeration equipment, 440.14
- Services, Article 230, Part VI
- Swimming pool, spa, hot tub, and fountain equipment, 680.12

Dusttight. Constructed so that dust will not enter the enclosure or case under specified test conditions.

Duty, Continuous. Operation at a substantially constant load for an indefinitely long time.

Duty, Varying. Operation at loads, and for intervals of time, which may both be subject to wide variation.

Dwelling Unit. A space that provides independent living facilities, with space for eating, living, and sleeping; as well as permanent facilities for cooking and sanitation. **Figure 100–27**

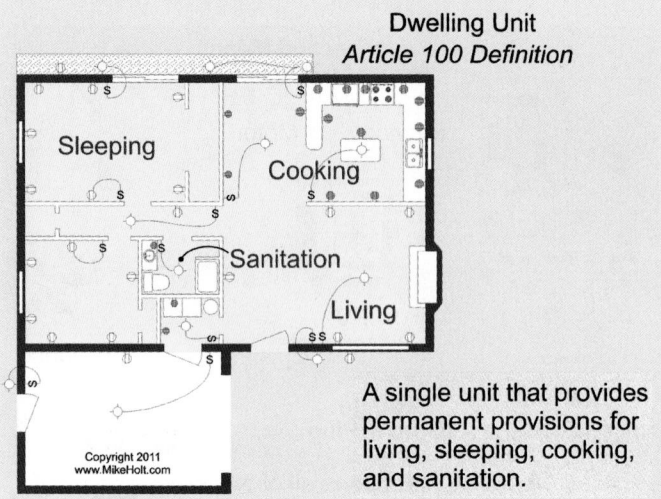

Figure 100–27

Dwelling, Multifamily. A building that contains three or more dwelling units. **Figure 100–28**

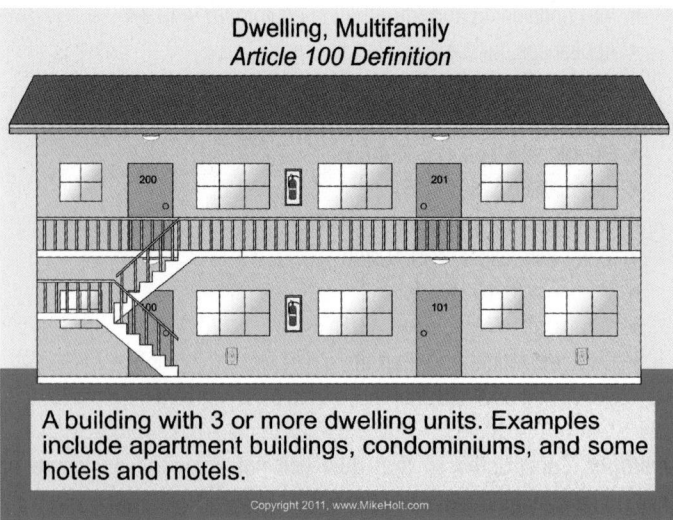

Figure 100–28

Electric Sign [Article 600]. A fixed, stationary, or portable self-contained, electrically illuminated piece of equipment with words or symbols designed to convey information or attract attention.

Enclosed. Surrounded by a case, housing, fence, or wall(s) that prevents accidental contact with energized parts.

Energized. Electrically connected to a source of voltage.

Equipment. A general term including fittings, devices, appliances, luminaires, machinery, and the like. **Figure 100–29**

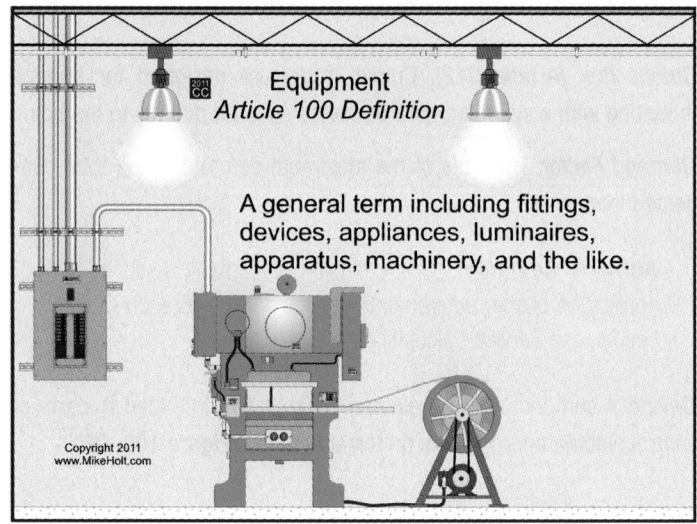

Figure 100–29

Explosionproof Equipment. Equipment capable of withstanding an explosion that may occur within it, and of preventing the ignition of gas or vapor surrounding the enclosure by sparks, flashes, or an explosion within, and that operates at such an external temperature that surrounding flammable atmosphere won't be ignited by its heat. **Figure 100–30**

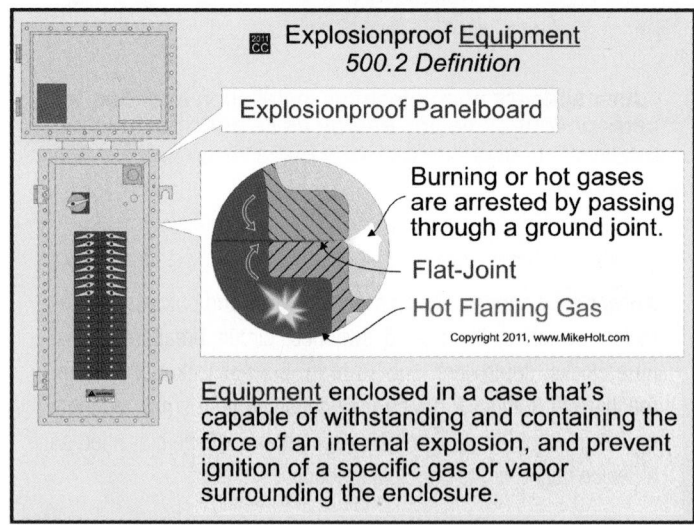

Figure 100–30

Exposed (as applied to live parts). Capable of being touched if not suitably guarded, isolated, or insulated.

Exposed (as applied to wiring methods). On or attached to the surface of a building, or behind panels designed to allow access.

Author's Comment: An example is wiring located in the space above a suspended ceiling or below a raised floor. **Figure 100–31**

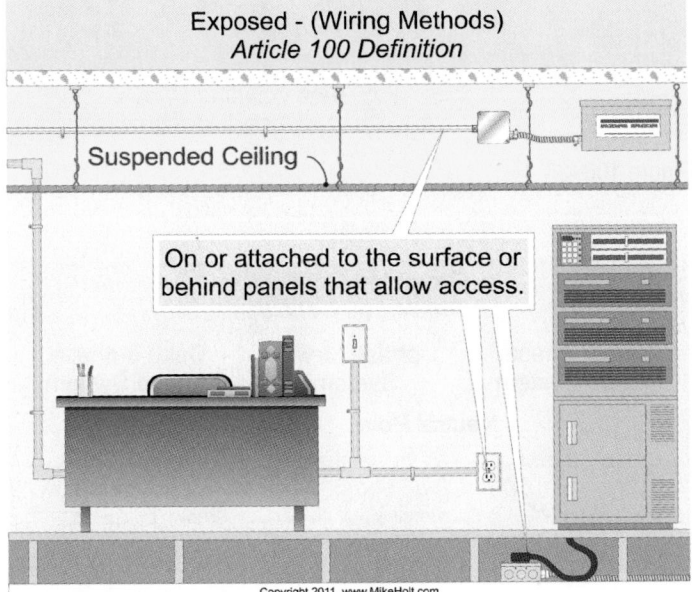

Figure 100–31

Feeder [Article 215]. The conductors between the service equipment, a separately derived system, or other power supply and the final branch-circuit overcurrent device. **Figure 100–32**

Author's Comments:

- An "other power source" includes a solar energy (photovoltaic) system.
- To have a better understanding of what a feeder is, be sure to review the definitions of "Service Equipment" and "Separately Derived System."

Fitting. An accessory, such as a locknut, intended to perform a mechanical function.

Garage. A building or portion of a building where self-propelled vehicles can be kept.

Ground. The earth. **Figure 100–33**

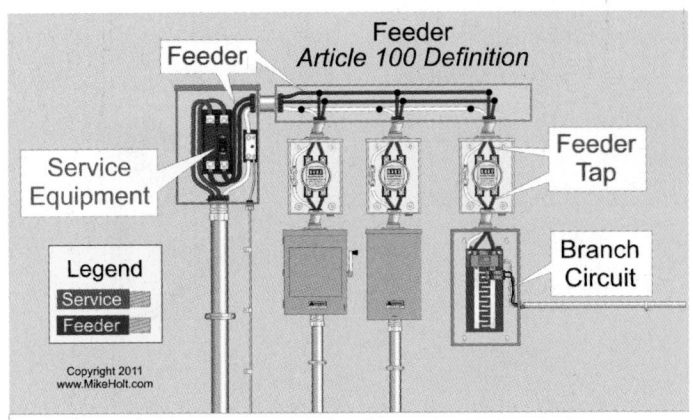

Conductors between service equipment, a separately derived system, or other power supply, and the final branch-circuit overcurrent device.

Figure 100–32

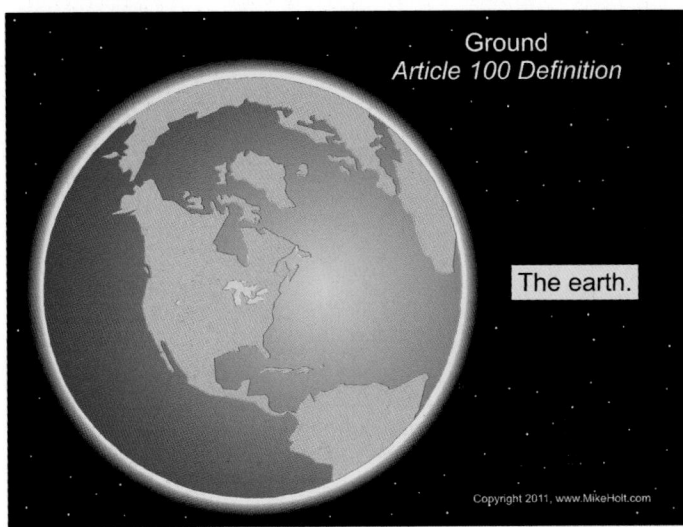

Figure 100–33

Ground Fault. An unintentional electrical connection between an ungrounded conductor and the metal parts of enclosures, raceways, or equipment. **Figure 100–34**

Grounded (Grounding). Connected to ground or to a conductive body that extends the ground connection.

Author's Comment: An example of a "body that extends the ground (earth) connection" is the termination to structural steel that's connected to the earth either directly or by the termination to another grounding electrode in accordance with 250.52. **Figure 100–35**

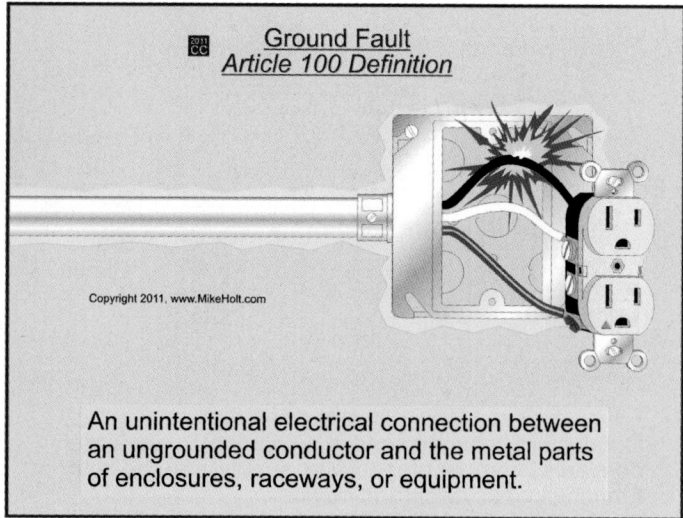

An unintentional electrical connection between an ungrounded conductor and the metal parts of enclosures, raceways, or equipment.

Figure 100–34

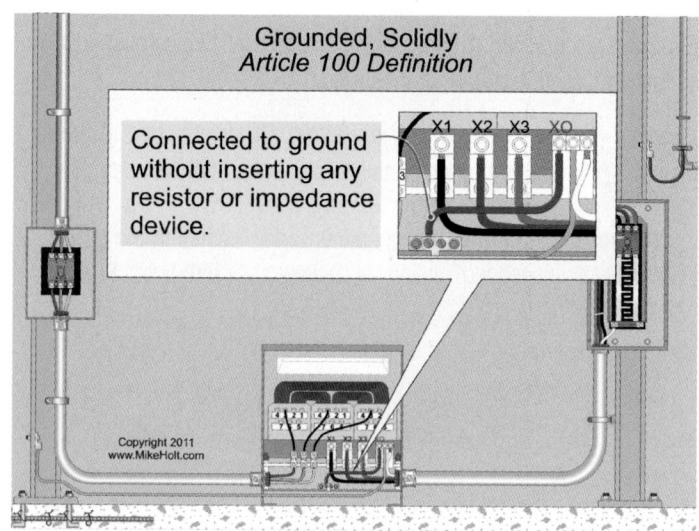

Figure 100–36

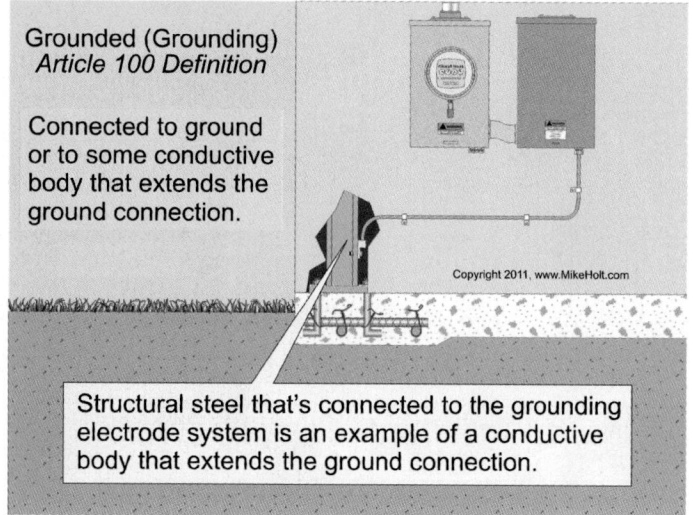

Figure 100–35

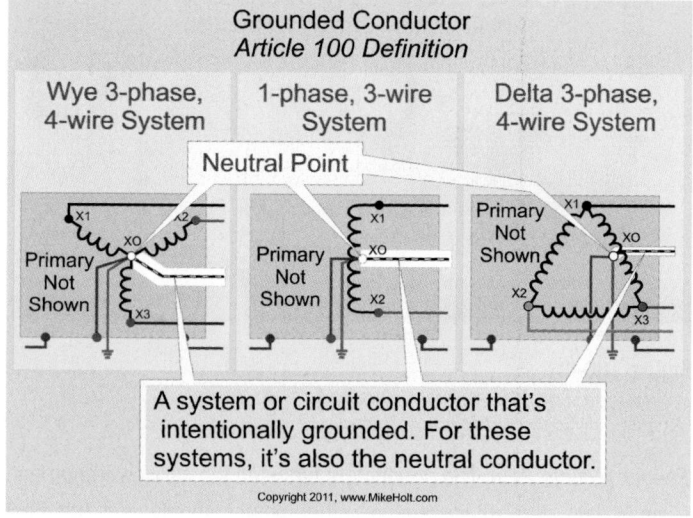

Figure 100–37

Grounded, Solidly. Connected to ground without inserting any resistor or impedance device. **Figure 100–36**

Grounded Conductor [Article 200]. The system or circuit conductor that's intentionally grounded (connected to the earth). **Figure 100–37**

> **Author's Comment:** Because the neutral conductor of a solidly grounded system is always grounded (connected to the earth), it's both a "grounded conductor" and a "neutral" conductor. To make it easier for the reader of this textbook, we'll refer to the "grounded" conductor of a solidly grounded system as the "neutral" conductor, except for the applications contained in Article 690—Solar Photovoltaic Systems.

Ground-Fault Circuit Interrupter (GFCI). A device intended to protect people by de-energizing a circuit when the current to ground exceeds the value established for a "Class A" device.

> **Note:** A "Class A" ground-fault circuit interrupter opens the circuit when the current to ground has a value of 6 mA or higher and doesn't trip when the current to ground is less than 4 mA. **Figure 100–38**

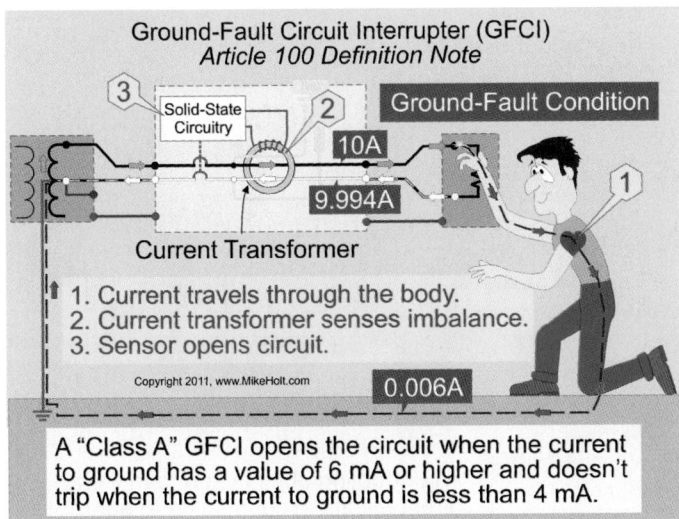

Ground-Fault Circuit Interrupter (GFCI)
Article 100 Definition Note

Solid-State Circuitry

Ground-Fault Condition

10A

9.994A

Current Transformer

1. Current travels through the body.
2. Current transformer senses imbalance.
3. Sensor opens circuit.

Copyright 2011, www.MikeHolt.com

0.006A

A "Class A" GFCI opens the circuit when the current to ground has a value of 6 mA or higher and doesn't trip when the current to ground is less than 4 mA.

Figure 100–38

Author's Comment: A GFCI operates on the principle of monitoring the unbalanced current between the current-carrying circuit conductors. On a 120V circuit, the GFCI will monitor the unbalanced current between the ungrounded and neutral conductors; on 240V GFCIs, this monitoring is between ungrounded conductors. GFCI-protective devices are commercially available in receptacles, circuit breakers, cord sets, and other types of devices. **Figure 100–39**

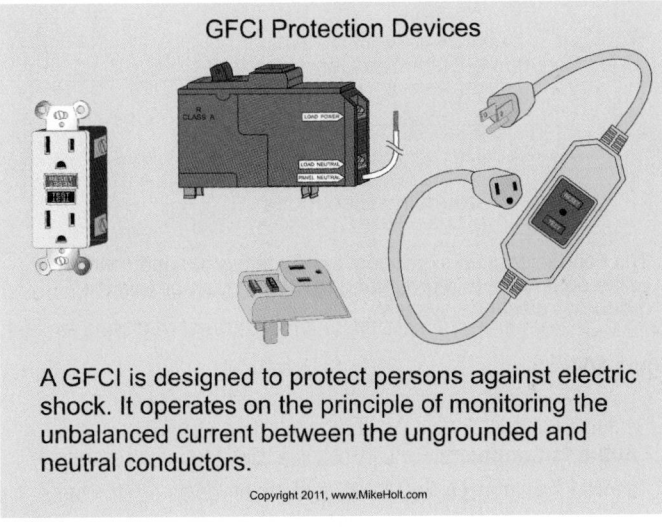

GFCI Protection Devices

A GFCI is designed to protect persons against electric shock. It operates on the principle of monitoring the unbalanced current between the ungrounded and neutral conductors.

Copyright 2011, www.MikeHolt.com

Figure 100–39

Ground-Fault Protection of Equipment. A system intended to provide protection of equipment from damaging ground-fault currents by opening all ungrounded conductors of the faulted circuit. This protection is provided at current levels less than those required to protect conductors from damage through the operation of a supply circuit overcurrent device [215.10, 230.95, and 240.13].

> **Author's Comment:** This type of protective device isn't intended to protect people and trips at a higher level than required for "Class A" GFCIs. This type of device is typically referred to as ground-fault protection for equipment, or GFPE, but should never be called a GFCI.

Grounding Conductor, Equipment (EGC). The conductive path(s) that connect metal parts of equipment to the system neutral conductor, to the grounding electrode conductor, or both [250.110 through 250.126]. **Figure 100–40**

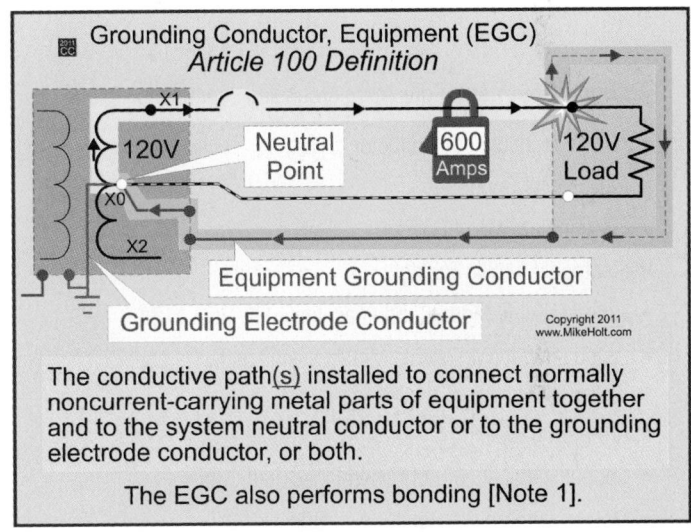

Grounding Conductor, Equipment (EGC)
Article 100 Definition

X1

Neutral Point

600 Amps

120V

120V Load

X0

X2

Equipment Grounding Conductor

Grounding Electrode Conductor

Copyright 2011 www.MikeHolt.com

The conductive path(s) installed to connect normally noncurrent-carrying metal parts of equipment together and to the system neutral conductor or to the grounding electrode conductor, or both.

The EGC also performs bonding [Note 1].

Figure 100–40

Note 1: The circuit equipment grounding conductor also performs bonding.

> **Author's Comment:** To quickly remove dangerous touch voltage on metal parts from a ground fault, the equipment grounding conductor must be connected to the system neutral conductor at the source, and have low enough impedance so that fault current will quickly rise to a level that will open the branch-circuit overcurrent device [250.2 and 250.4(A)(3)].

Note 2: An equipment grounding conductor can be any one or a combination of the types listed in 250.118. **Figure 100–41**

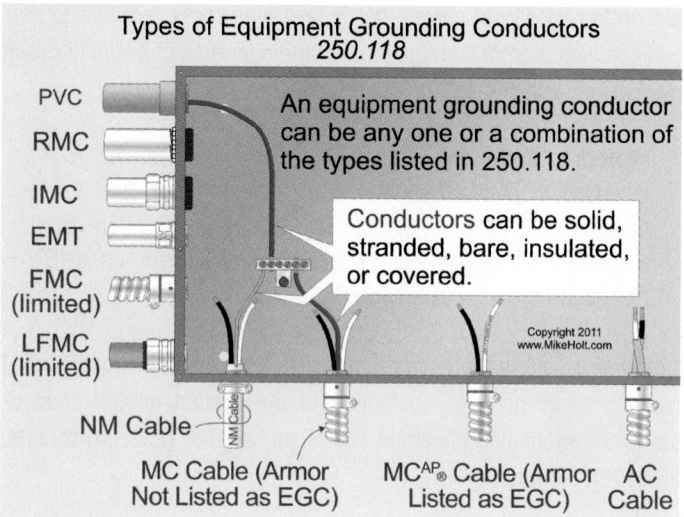

Figure 100–41

Author's Comment: Equipment grounding conductors include:

- A bare or insulated conductor

- Rigid Metal Conduit

- Intermediate Metal Conduit

- Electrical Metallic Tubing

- Listed Flexible Metal Conduit as limited by 250.118(5)

- Listed Liquidtight Flexible Metal Conduit as limited by 250.118(6)

- Armored Cable

- Copper metal sheath of Mineral Insulated Cable

- Metal-Clad Cable as limited by 250.118(10)

- Metallic cable trays as limited by 250.118(11) and 392.60

- Electrically continuous metal raceways listed for grounding

- Surface Metal Raceways listed for grounding

Grounding Electrode. A conducting object used to make a direct electrical connection to the earth [250.50 through 250.70]. **Figure 100–42**

Grounding Electrode Conductor (GEC). The conductor used to connect the system grounded conductor (neutral) to a grounding electrode or to a point on the grounding electrode system. **Figure 100–43**

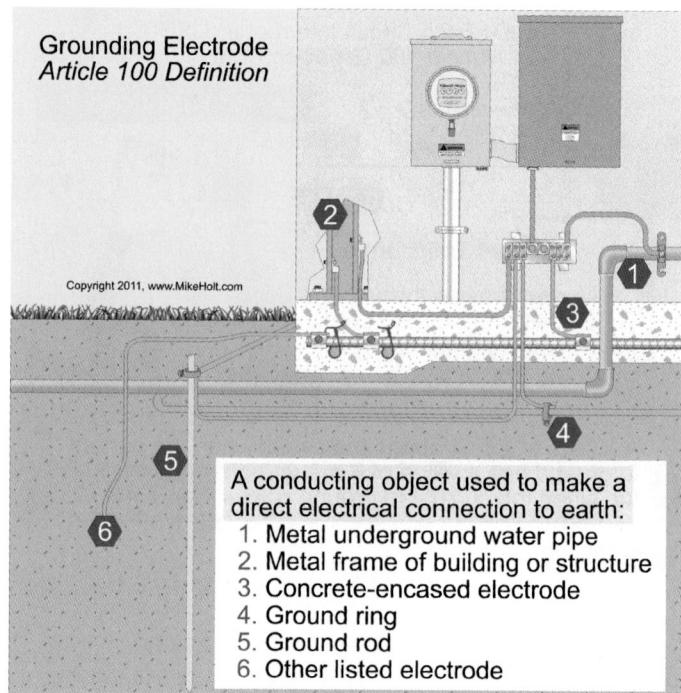

Figure 100–42

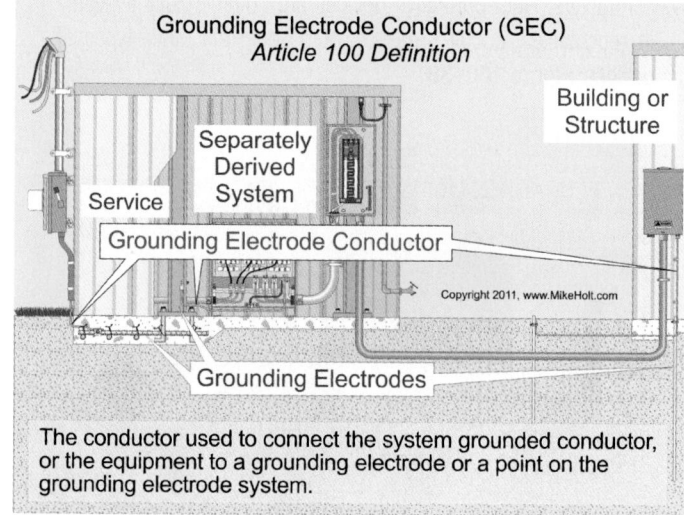

Figure 100–43

Author's Comment: For services see 250.24(A), for separately derived systems see 250.30(A), and for buildings or structures supplied by a feeder see 250.32(A).

Guest Room. An accommodation that combines living, sleeping, sanitary, and storage facilities. **Figure 100–44**

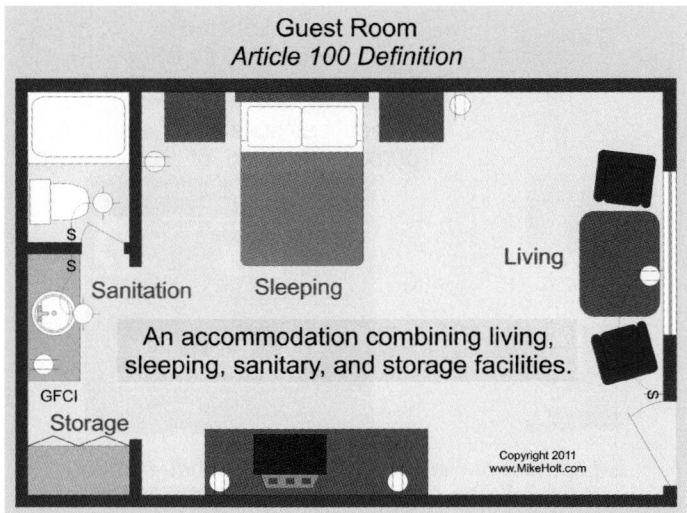

Figure 100–44

Guest Suite. An accommodation with two or more contiguous rooms comprising a compartment, with or without doors between such rooms, that provides living, sleeping, sanitary, and storage facilities.

Handhole Enclosure. An enclosure for underground system use sized to allow personnel to reach into it for the purpose of installing or maintaining equipment or wiring. It may have an open or closed bottom. **Figure 100–45**

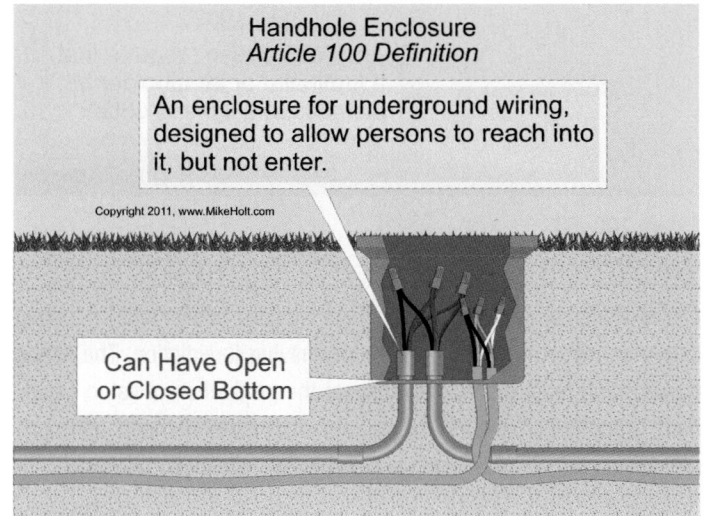

Figure 100–45

> **Author's Comment:** See 314.30 for the installation requirements for handhole enclosures.

Hoistway. A vertical opening or space in which an elevator is designed to operate.

Identified Equipment. Recognized as suitable for a specific purpose, function, or environment by listing, labeling, or other means approved by the authority having jurisdiction.

> **Author's** Comment: See 90.4, 90.7, 110.3(A)(1), and the definitions for "Approved," "Labeled," and "Listed" in this article.

In Sight From (Within Sight). Visible and not more than 50 ft away from the equipment. **Figure 100–46**

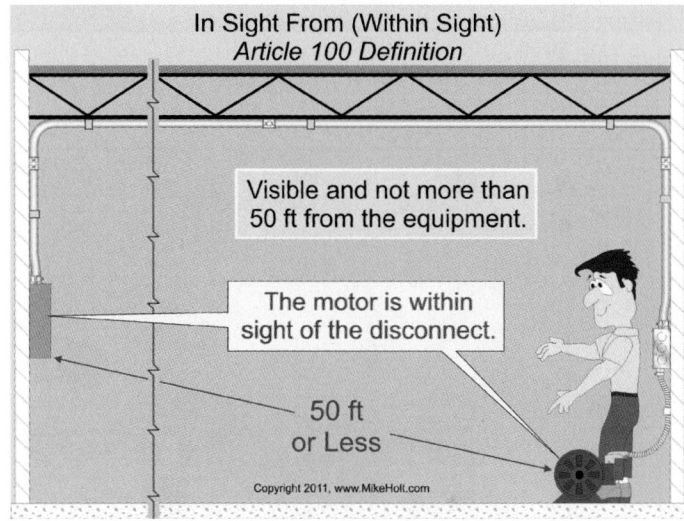

Figure 100–46

Interrupting Rating. The highest short-circuit current at rated voltage the device is identified to interrupt under standard test conditions.

> **Author's Comment:** For more information, see 110.9 in this textbook.

Intersystem Bonding Termination. A device that provides a means to connect bonding conductors for communications systems to the grounding electrode system, in accordance with 250.94. **Figure 100–47**

Isolated. Not readily accessible to persons unless special means for access are used.

Kitchen. An area with a sink and permanent provisions for food preparation and cooking. **Figure 100–48**

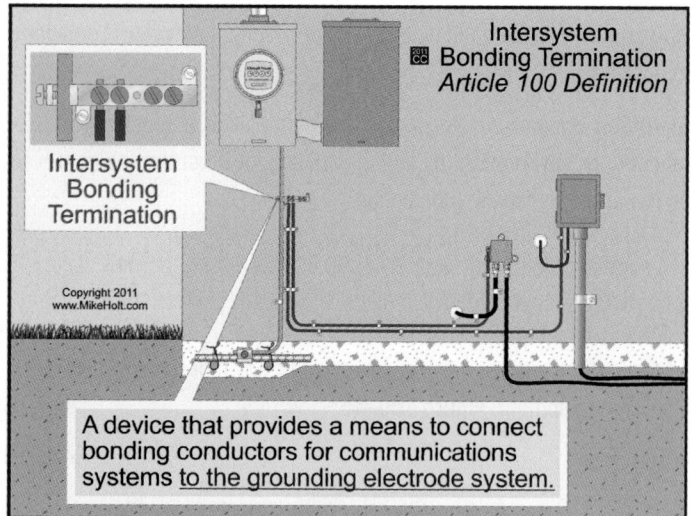

Figure 100–47

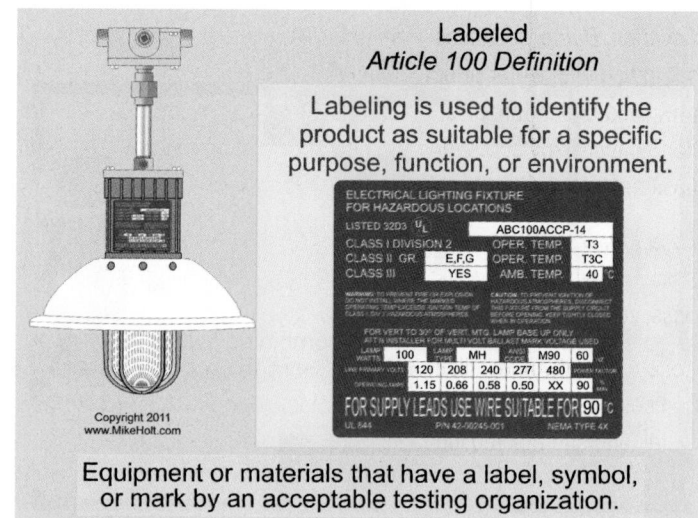

Figure 100–49

Figure 100–48

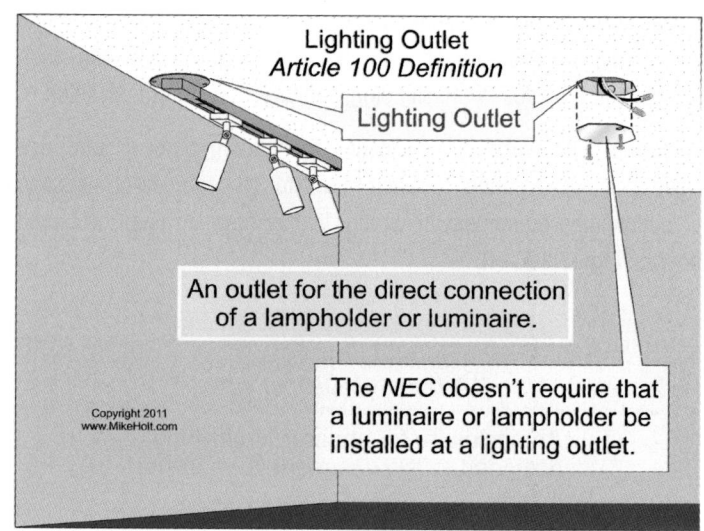

Figure 100–50

Labeled. Equipment or materials that have a label, symbol, or other identifying mark in the form of a sticker, decal, printed label, or molded or stamped into the product by a testing laboratory acceptable to the authority having jurisdiction. **Figure 100–49**

> **Author's Comment:** Labeling and listing of equipment typically provides the basis for equipment approval by the authority having jurisdiction [90.4, 90.7, 110.2, and 110.3].

Lighting Outlet. An outlet for the connection of a lampholder or luminaire. **Figure 100–50**

Listed. Equipment or materials included in a list published by a testing laboratory acceptable to the authority having jurisdiction. The listing organization must periodically inspect the production of listed equipment or material to ensure the equipment or material meets appropriate designated standards and is suitable for a specified purpose.

> **Author's Comment:** The *NEC* doesn't require all electrical equipment to be listed, but some *Code* requirements do specifically require product listing. Organizations such as OSHA increasingly require that listed equipment be used when such equipment is available [90.7, 110.2, and 110.3].

Location, Damp. Locations protected from weather and not subject to saturation with water or other liquids. This includes locations partially protected under canopies, marquees, roofed open porches, and interior locations subject to moderate degrees of moisture, such as some basements, barns, and cold-storage warehouses.

Location, Dry. An area not normally subjected to dampness or wetness, but which may temporarily be subjected to dampness or wetness, such as a building under construction.

Location, Wet. An installation underground, in concrete slabs in direct contact with the earth, as well as locations subject to saturation with water, and unprotected locations exposed to weather. **Figure 100–51**

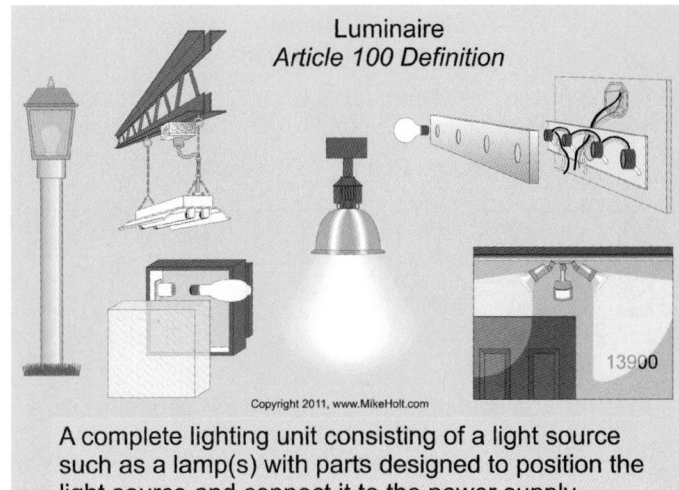

A complete lighting unit consisting of a light source such as a lamp(s) with parts designed to position the light source and connect it to the power supply.

Figure 100–52

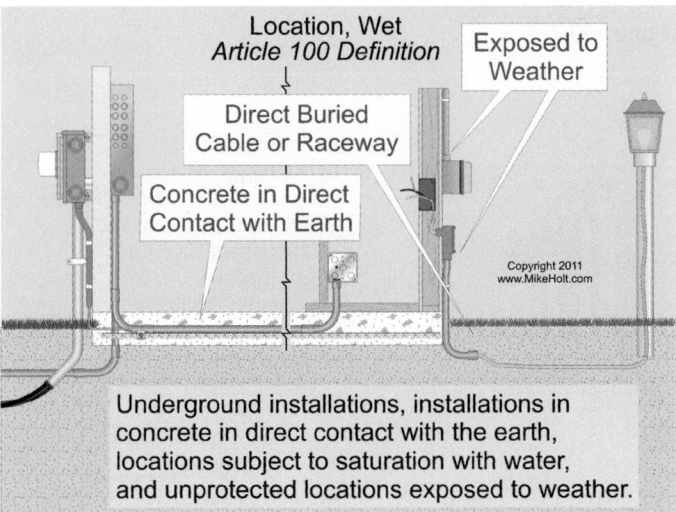

Figure 100–51

Author's Comment: The interior of a raceway installed in wet locations is considered to be a wet location, and the conductors used must be suitable for wet locations [300.5(B) and 300.9].

Luminaire [Article 410]. A complete lighting unit consisting of a light source with the parts designed to position the light source and connect it to the power supply and distribute the light. A lampholder by itself isn't a luminaire. **Figure 100–52**

Multioutlet Assembly [Article 380]. A surface, flush, or freestanding raceway designed to hold conductors and receptacles. **Figure 100–53**

Neutral Conductor. The conductor connected to the neutral point of a system that's intended to carry current under normal conditions. **Figure 100–54**

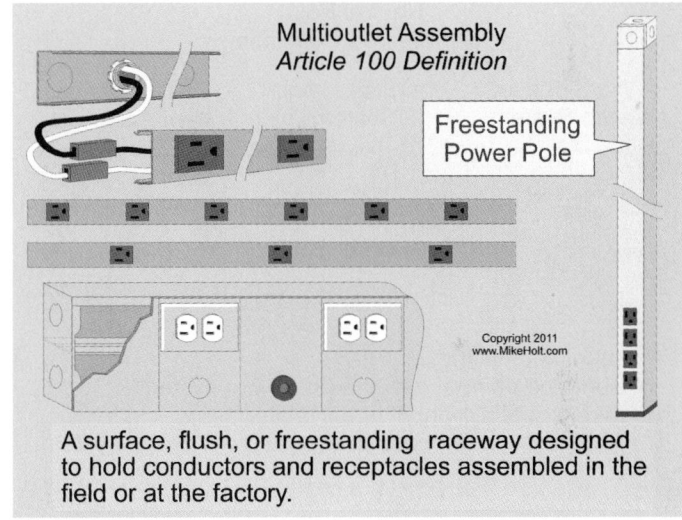

A surface, flush, or freestanding raceway designed to hold conductors and receptacles assembled in the field or at the factory.

Figure 100–53

Author's Comment: The neutral conductor of a solidly grounded system is required to be grounded (connected to the earth), therefore this conductor is also called a "grounded conductor."

Neutral Point. The common point of a 4-wire, three-phase, wye-connected system; the midpoint of a 3-wire, single-phase system; or the midpoint of the single-phase portion of a three-phase, delta-connected system. **Figure 100–55**

Nonautomatic. Requiring human intervention to perform a function.

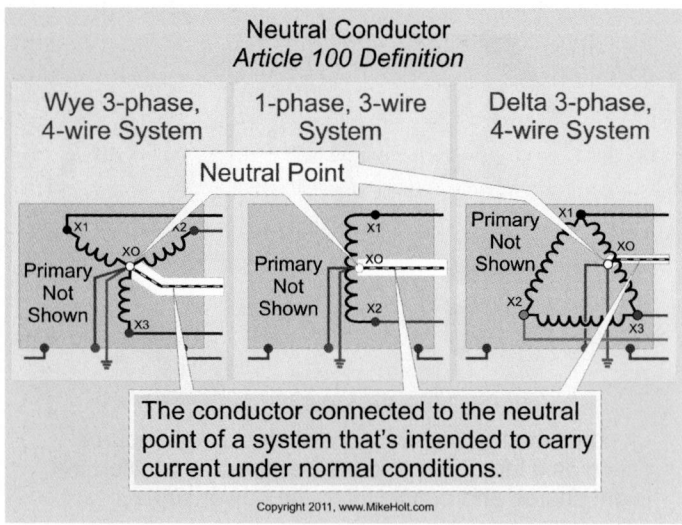

Figure 100–54

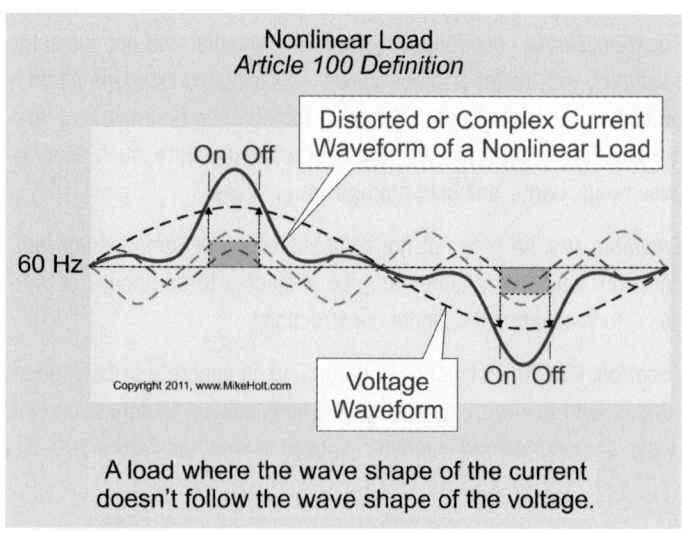

Figure 100–56

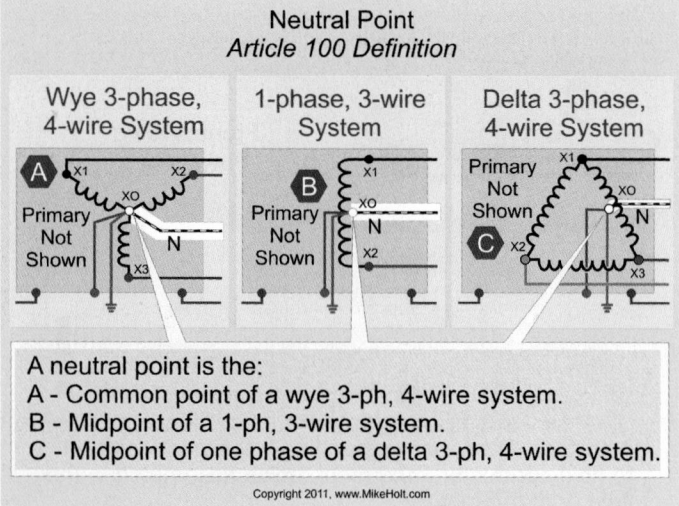

Figure 100–55

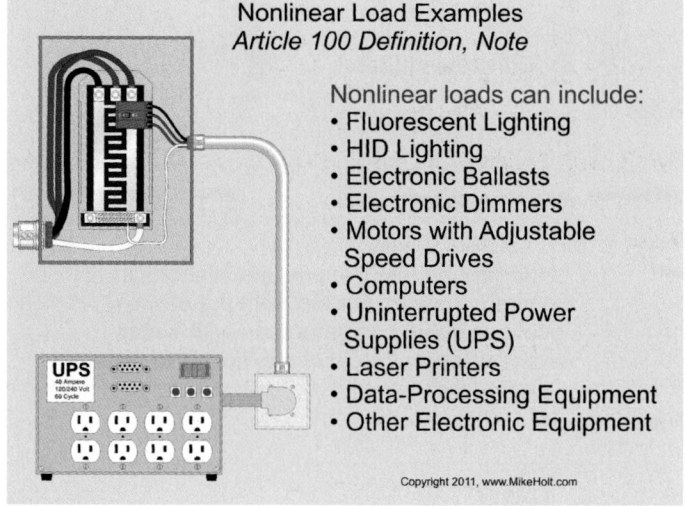

Figure 100–57

Nonlinear Load. A load where the current waveform doesn't follow the applied sinusoidal voltage waveform. **Figure 100–56**

Note: Single-phase nonlinear loads include electronic equipment, such as copy machines, laser printers, and electric-discharge lighting. Three-phase nonlinear loads include uninterruptible power supplies, induction motors, and electronic switching devices, such as adjustable speed drives (variable frequency drives). **Figure 100–57**

Author's Comment: The subject of nonlinear loads is beyond the scope of this textbook. For more information on this topic, visit www.MikeHolt.com, click on the "Technical" link, then on the "Power Quality" link.

Outlet. A point in the wiring system where electric current is taken to supply a load (utilization equipment). This includes receptacle outlets and lighting outlets, as well as outlets for ceiling paddle fans and smoke alarms. **Figure 100–58**

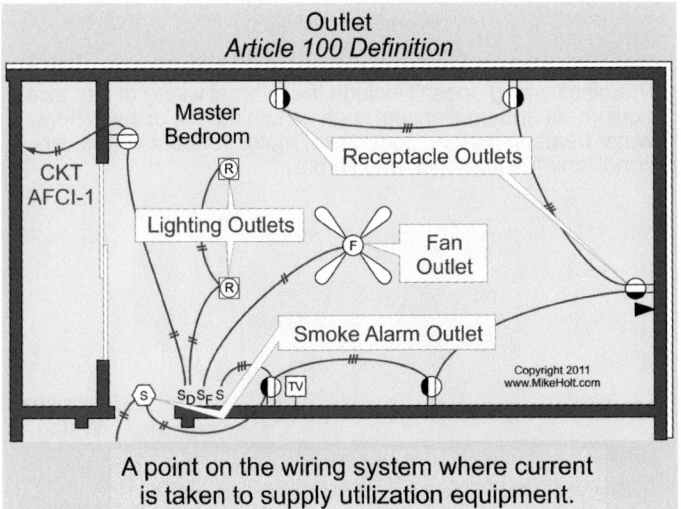

Figure 100–58

Outline Lighting [Article 600]. An arrangement of incandescent lamps, electric-discharge lighting, or other electrically powered light sources to outline or call attention to certain features such as the shape of a building or the decoration of a window.

Overcurrent. Current, in amperes, greater than the rated current of the equipment or conductors resulting from an overload, short circuit, or ground fault. **Figure 100–59**

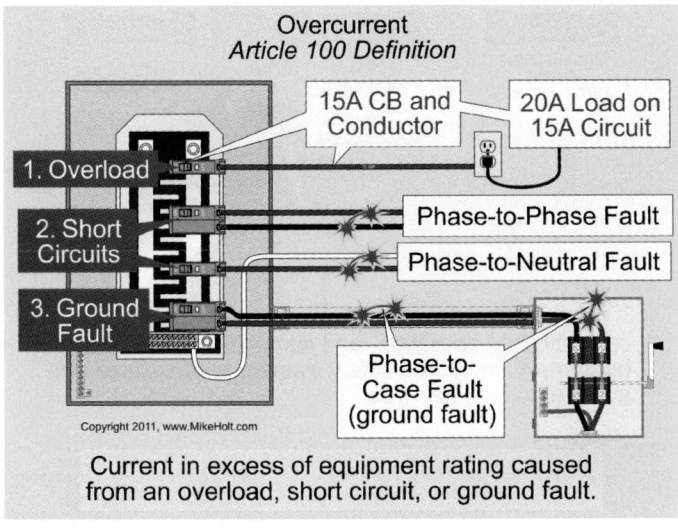

Figure 100–59

Author's Comment: See the definitions of "Ground Fault" in 250.2 and "Overload" in this article.

Overcurrent Protective Device, Supplementary. A device intended to provide limited overcurrent protection for specific applications and utilization equipment, such as luminaires and appliances. This limited protection is in addition to the required protection provided in the branch circuit by the branch-circuit overcurrent device. **Figure 100–60**

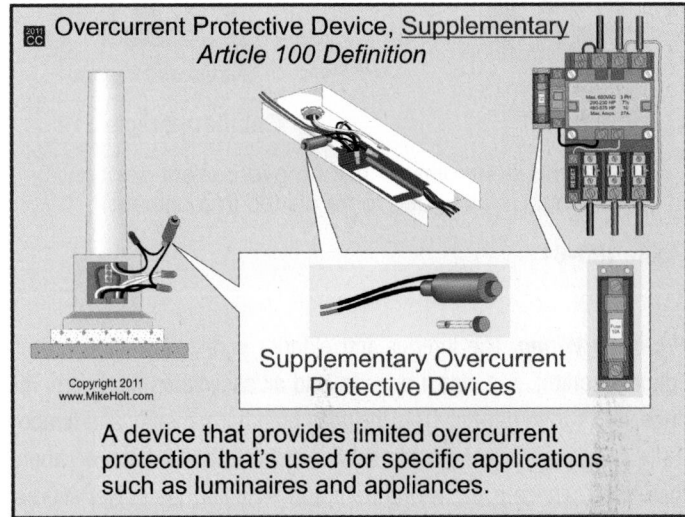

Figure 100–60

Overload. The operation of equipment above its current rating, or current in excess of conductor ampacity. When an overload condition persists for a sufficient length of time, it can result in equipment failure or in a fire from damaging or dangerous overheating. A fault, such as a short circuit or ground fault, isn't an overload.

Panelboard [Article 408]. A distribution point containing overcurrent devices and designed to be installed in a cabinet. **Figure 100–61**

Author's Comments:

- See the definition of "Cabinet" in this article.
- The slang term in the electrical field for a panelboard is "the guts." This is the interior of the panelboard assembly and is covered by Article 408, while the cabinet is covered by Article 314.

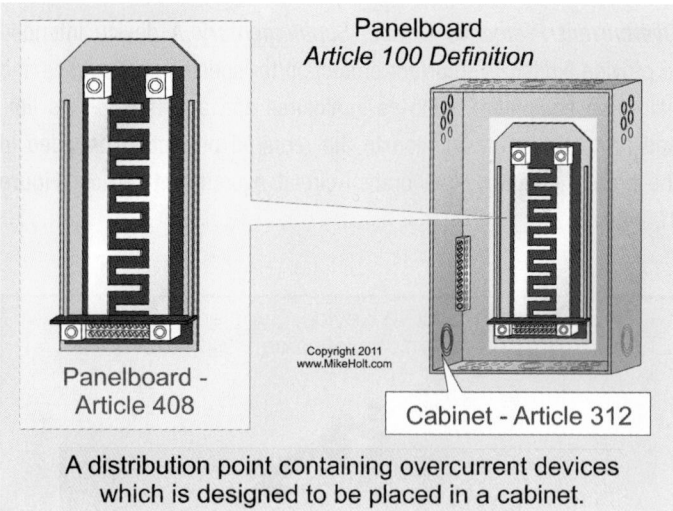

A distribution point containing overcurrent devices which is designed to be placed in a cabinet.

Figure 100–61

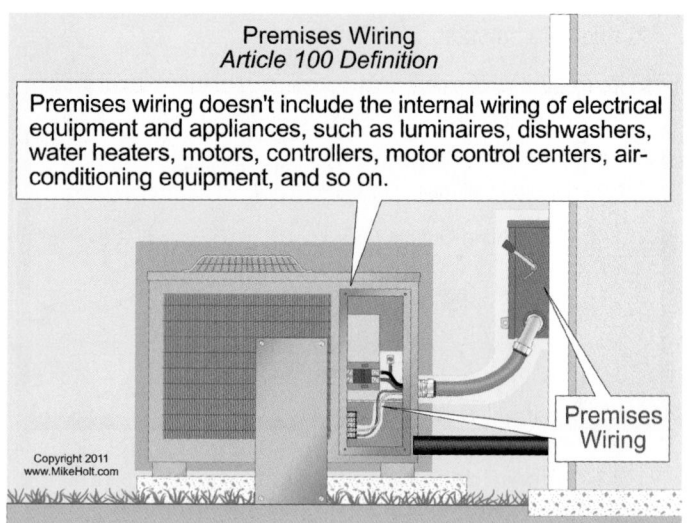

Figure 100–63

Premises Wiring. The interior and exterior wiring, including power, lighting, control, and signal circuits, and all associated hardware, fittings, and wiring devices. This includes both permanently and temporarily installed wiring from the service point to the outlets, or where there's no service point, wiring from and including the power source, such as a generator, transformer, or photovoltaic system to the outlets. **Figure 100–62**

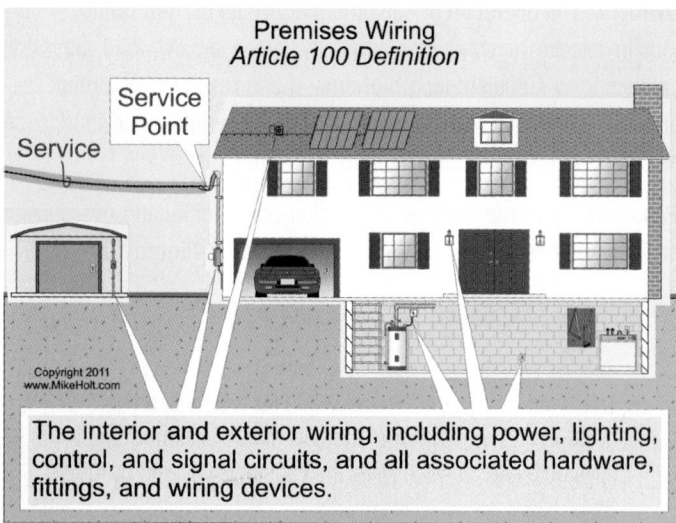

The interior and exterior wiring, including power, lighting, control, and signal circuits, and all associated hardware, fittings, and wiring devices.

Figure 100–62

Premises wiring doesn't include the internal wiring of electrical equipment and appliances, such as luminaires, dishwashers, water heaters, motors, controllers, motor control centers, air-conditioning equipment, and so on [90.7 and 300.1(B)]. **Figure 100–63**

Qualified Person. A person who has the skill and knowledge related to the construction and operation of electrical equipment and its installation. This person must have received safety training to recognize and avoid the hazards involved with electrical systems. **Figure 100–64**

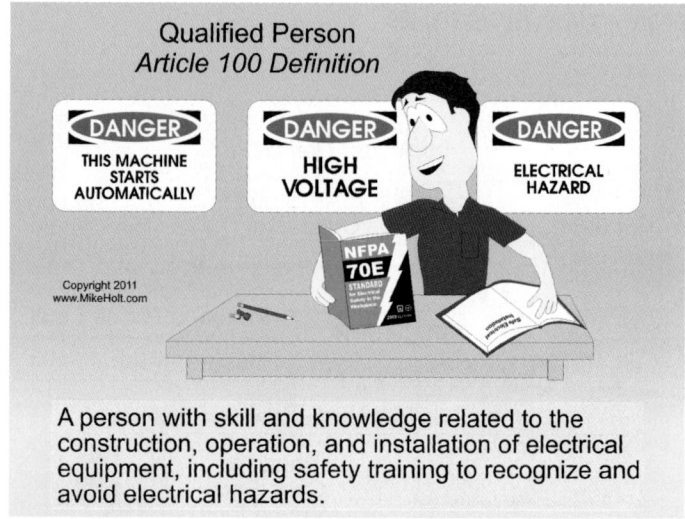

A person with skill and knowledge related to the construction, operation, and installation of electrical equipment, including safety training to recognize and avoid electrical hazards.

Figure 100–64

Note: NFPA 70E, *Standard for Electrical Safety in the Workplace*, provides information on safety training requirements expected of a "qualified person."

Author's Comments:

- Examples of this safety training include, but aren't limited to, training in the use of special precautionary techniques, of personal protective equipment (PPE), of insulating and shielding materials, and of using insulated tools and test equipment when working on or near exposed conductors or circuit parts that can become energized.

- In many parts of the United States, electricians, electrical contractors, electrical inspectors, and electrical engineers must complete from 6 to 24 hours of *NEC* review each year as a requirement to maintain licensing. This in itself doesn't make one qualified to deal with the specific hazards involved with electrical systems.

Raceway. An enclosure designed for the installation of conductors, cables, or busbars. Raceways in the *NEC* include:

Raceway Type	Article
Busways	368
Electrical Metallic Tubing	358
Electrical Nonmetallic Tubing	362
Flexible Metal Conduit	348
Intermediate Metal Conduit	342
Liquidtight Flexible Metal Conduit	350
Liquidtight Flexible Nonmetallic Conduit	356
Metal Wireways	376
Multioutlet Assembly	380
Rigid Metal Conduit	344
PVC Conduit	352
Surface Metal Raceways	386
Surface Nonmetallic Raceways	388

Author's Comments: A cable tray system isn't a raceway; it's a support system for cables and raceways [392.2].

Rainproof. Constructed, protected, or treated so as to prevent rain from interfering with the successful operation of the apparatus under specified test conditions.

Raintight. A raintight enclosure is constructed or protected so that exposure to a beating rain will not result in the entrance of water under specified test conditions.

Receptacle [Article 406]. A contact device installed at an outlet for the connection of an attachment plug. A single receptacle contains one device on a strap (mounting yoke), and a multiple receptacle contains more than one device on a common yoke. **Figure 100–65**

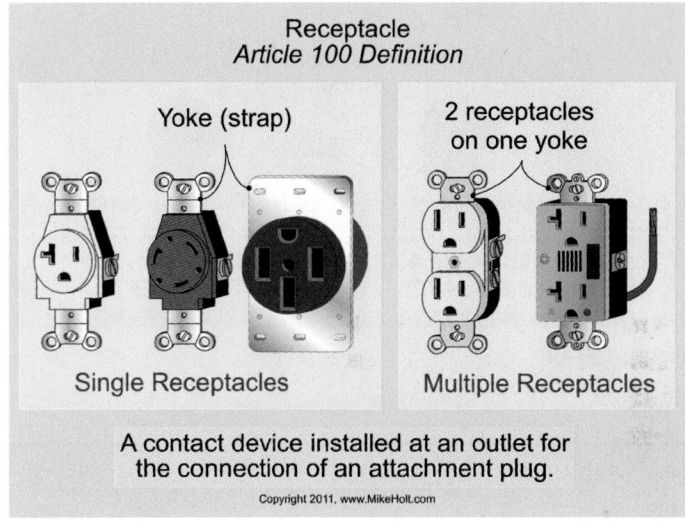

Figure 100–65

Receptacle Outlet. An opening in an outlet box where receptacles have been installed.

Remote-Control Circuit [Article 725]. An electric circuit that controls another circuit by a relay or equivalent device installed in accordance with Article 725. **Figure 100–66**

Sealable Equipment. Equipment enclosed with a means of sealing or locking so that live parts cannot be made accessible without opening the enclosure.

Separately Derived System. A wiring system whose power is derived from a source of electric energy or equipment other than the electric utility service. This includes a generator, a battery, a solar photovoltaic system, a transformer, or a converter winding, where there's no direct electrical connection from circuit conductors of one system to circuit conductors of another system, other than connections through the earth, metal raceways, or equipment grounding conductors. **Figure 100–67 and 100–68**

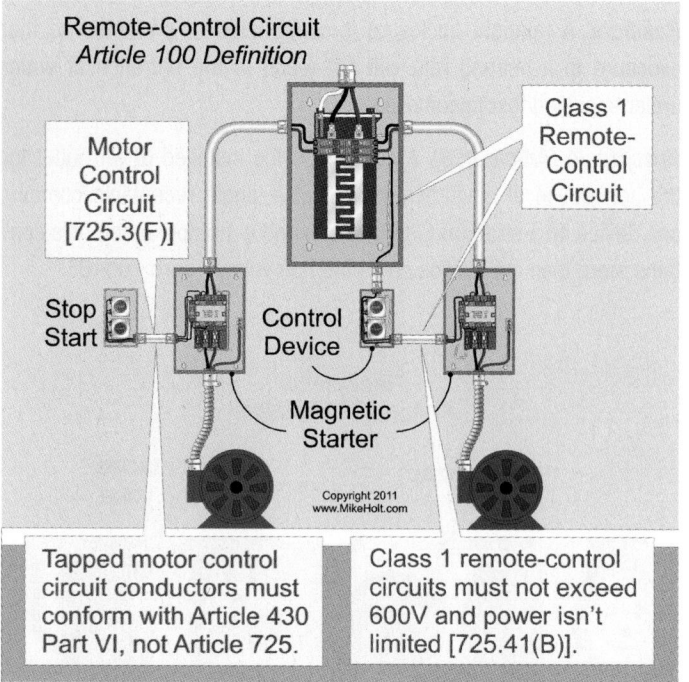

Figure 100–66

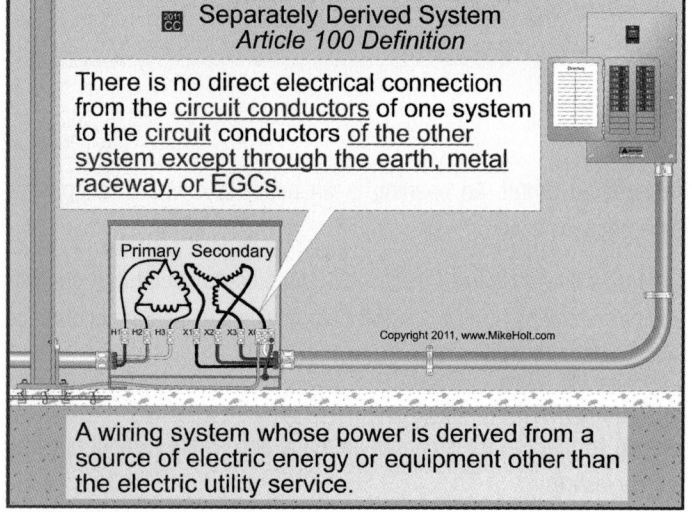

Figure 100–67

Author's Comments:

- This definition clarifies that separately derived systems also include equipment such as transformers, converters, and inverters, which might not be considered sources of energy.

- Separately derived systems are actually a lot more complicated than the above definition suggests, and understanding them requires additional study. For more information, see 250.30.

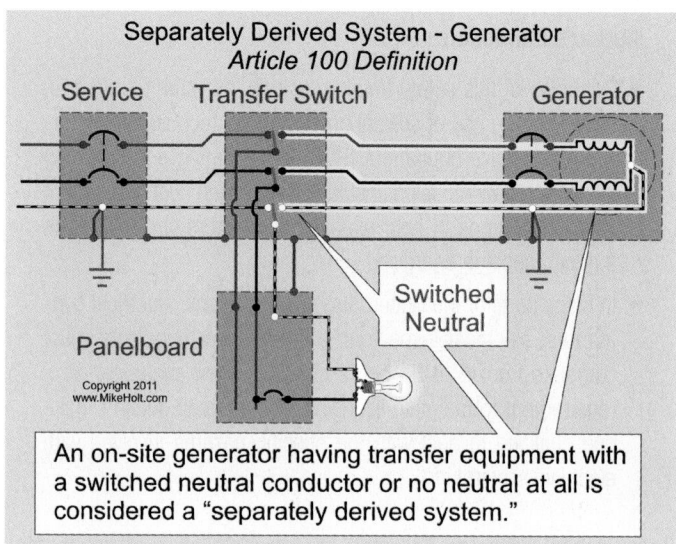

Figure 100–68

Service [Article 230]. The conductors from the electric utility that deliver electric energy to the wiring system of the premises. **Figure 100–69**

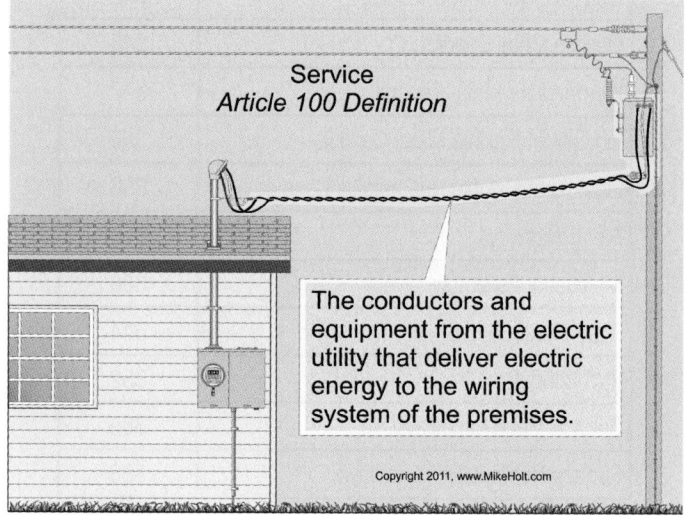

Figure 100–69

Author's Comment: Conductors from a UPS system, solar photovoltaic system, generator, or transformer aren't service conductors. See the definitions of "Feeder" and "Service Conductors" in this article.

Service Conductors. The conductors from the service point to the service disconnecting means. **Figure 100–70**

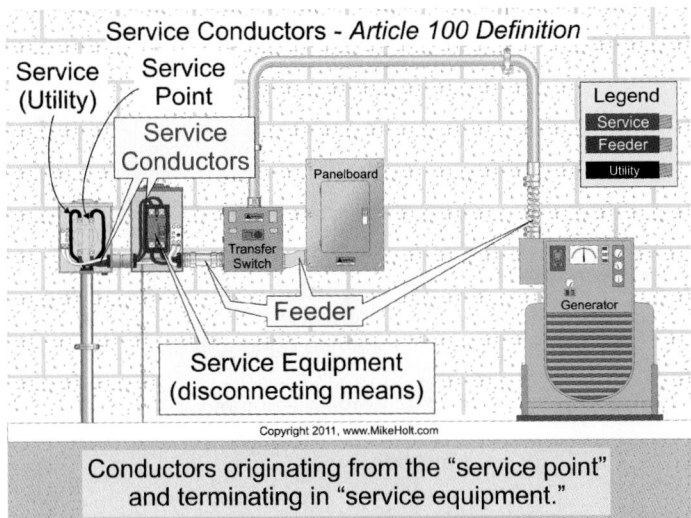

Figure 100–70

Author's Comments:

- These conductors fall within the requirements of Article 230, since they are not under the exclusive control of the electric utility.

- "Service Conductors" is a term that that can include service drop, service lateral, and service-entrance conductors.

Service Conductors, Overhead. Overhead conductors between the service point and the first point of connection to the service-entrance conductors at the building/structure. **Figure 100–71**

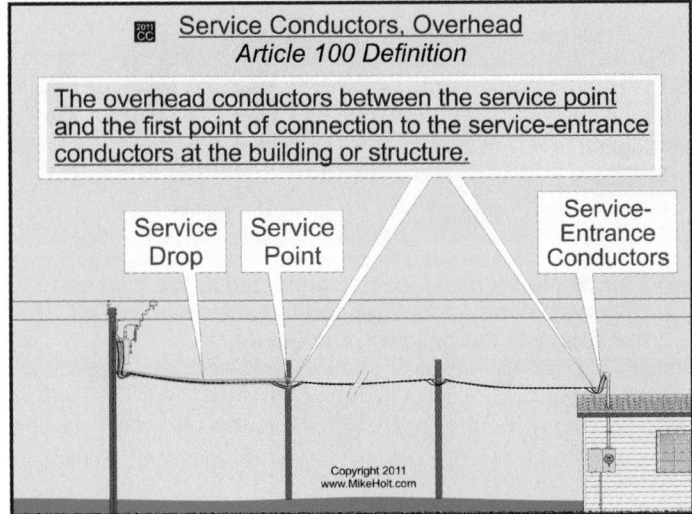

Figure 100–71

Author's Comment: These conductors fall within the requirements of Article 230, since they aren't under the exclusive control of the electric utility.

Service Conductors, Underground. Underground conductors between the service point and the first point of connection to the service-entrance conductors in a terminal box, meter, or other enclosure, inside or outside the building wall. **Figure 100–72**

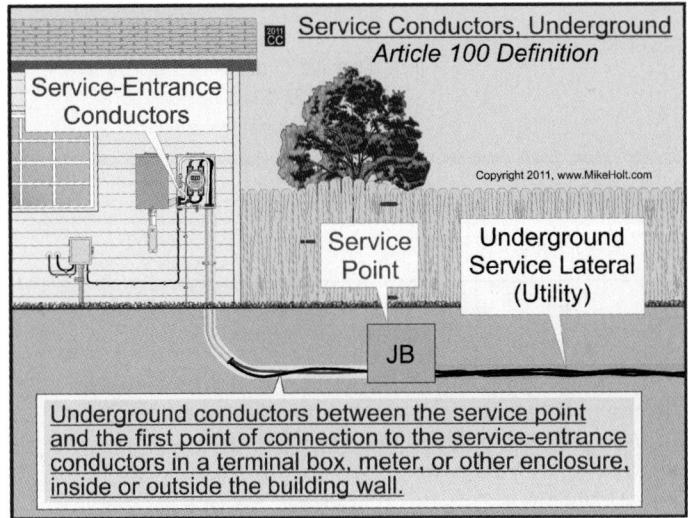

Figure 100–72

Author's Comment: These conductors fall within the requirements of Article 230, since they aren't under the exclusive control of the electric utility.

Note: Where there's no terminal box, meter, or other enclosure, the point of connection is the point of entrance of the service conductors into the building.

Service Drop. Overhead conductors between the utility electric supply and the service point. **Figures 100–73 and 100–74**

Author's Comment: These conductors don't fall within the requirements of Article 230, since they're under the exclusive control of the electric utility.

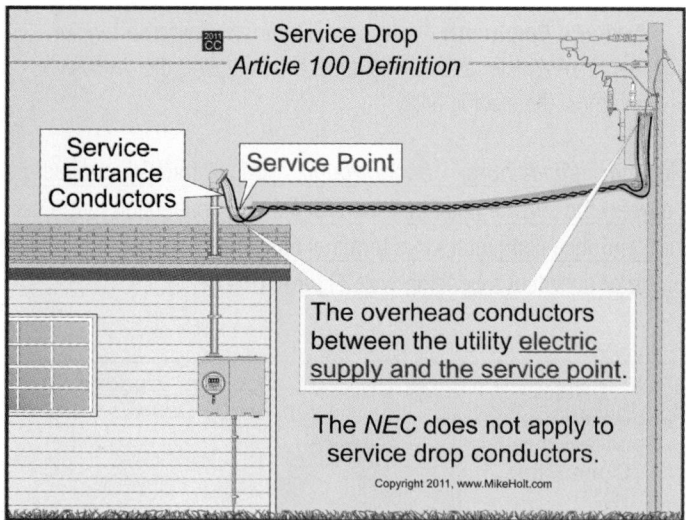

Figure 100-73

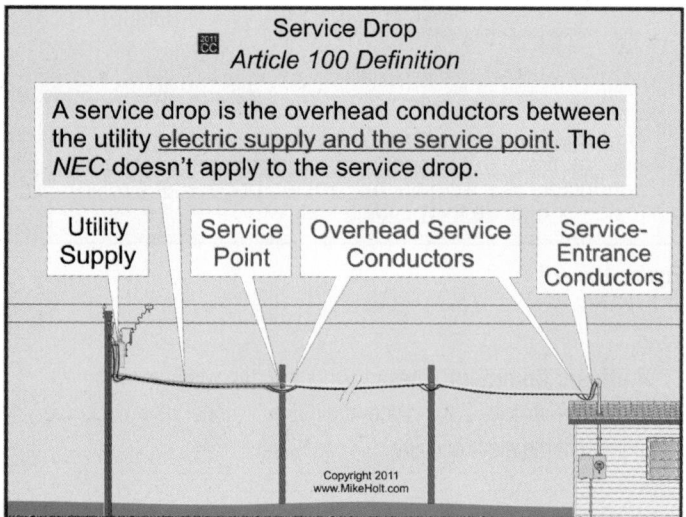

Figure 100-74

Service-Entrance Conductors, Overhead System. The conductors between the terminals of service equipment and service drop or overhead service conductors. **Figure 100-75**

> **Author's Comment:** These conductors fall within the requirements of Article 230, since they aren't under the exclusive control of the electric utility.

Service-Entrance Conductors, Underground System. The conductors between the terminals of service equipment and service lateral or underground service conductors.

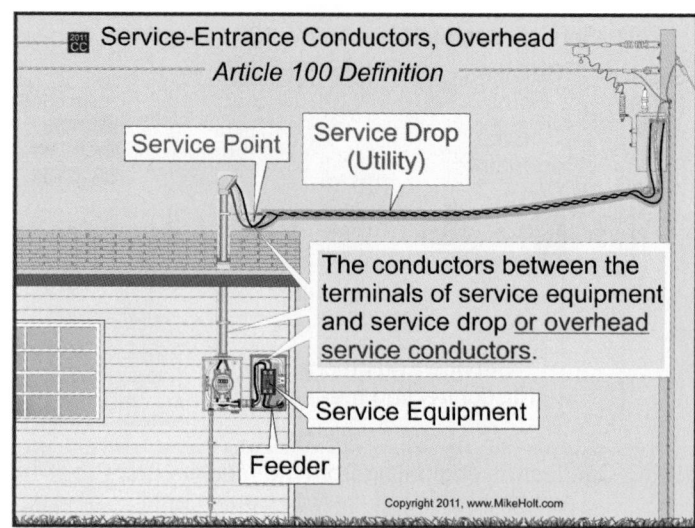

Figure 100-75

> **Author's Comment:** These conductors fall within the requirements of Article 230, since they aren't under the exclusive control of the electric utility.

Service Equipment [Article 230]. Circuit breaker(s) or switch(es) connected to the load end of service conductors, intended to control and cut off the service supply to the building/structure. **Figure 100-76**

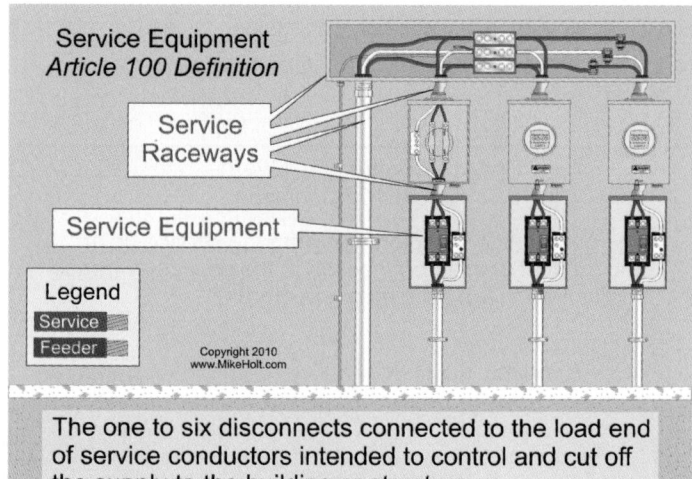

Figure 100-76

Author's Comments:

- It's important to know where a service begins and where it ends in order to properly apply the *NEC* requirements. Sometimes the service ends before the metering equipment. **Figure 100–77**

- Service equipment is often referred to as the "service disconnect" or "service disconnecting means."

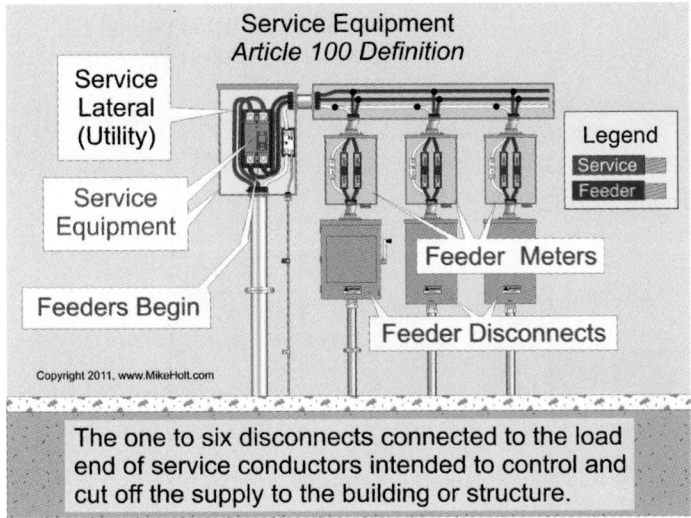

The one to six disconnects connected to the load end of service conductors intended to control and cut off the supply to the building or structure.

Figure 100–77

Service Lateral. Underground conductors between the utility electric supply and the service point. **Figure 100–78**

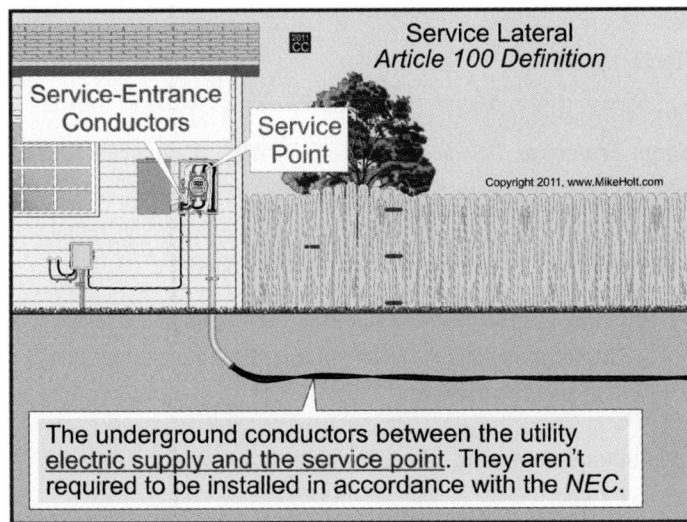

The underground conductors between the utility electric supply and the service point. They aren't required to be installed in accordance with the *NEC*.

Figure 100–78

Author's Comment: These conductors don't fall within the requirements of Article 230, since they're under the exclusive control of the electric utility.

Service Point [Article 230]. The point where the electrical utility conductors make contact with premises wiring. **Figure 100–79**

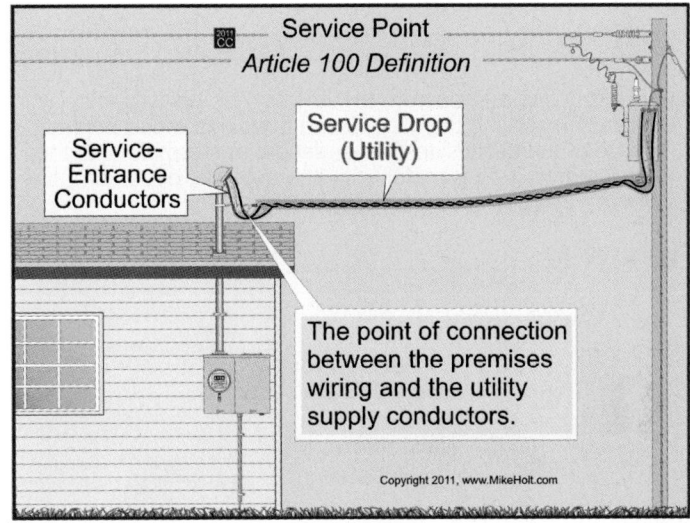

Figure 100–79

Note: The service point is the point where the serving utility ends and the premises wiring begins.

Author's Comments:

- For utility-owned transformers, the service point will be at the utility transformer secondary terminals, at the service drop, or the meter socket enclosure, depending on where the utility conductors terminate. **Figure 100–80**

- For customer-owned transformers, the service point will be at the termination of the utility conductors, often at the utility pole. **Figure 100–81**

Short-Circuit Current Rating. The prospective symmetrical fault current at a nominal voltage that electrical equipment is able to be connected to without sustaining damage exceeding defined acceptance criteria.

Signaling Circuit [Article 725]. A circuit that energizes signaling equipment. **Figure 100–82**

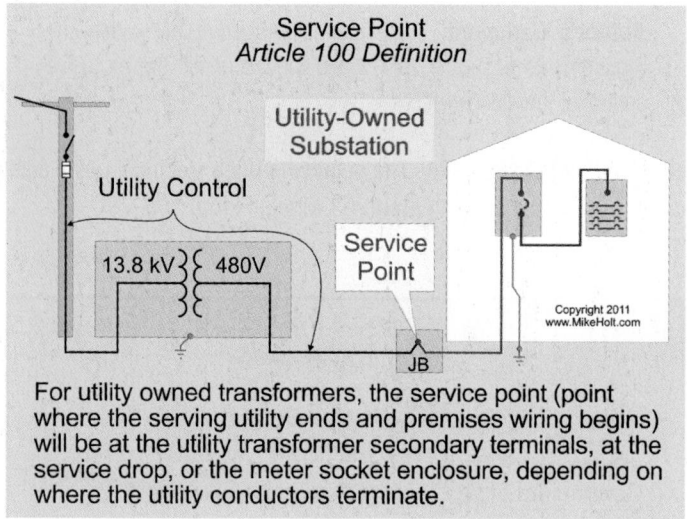

Service Point
Article 100 Definition

For utility owned transformers, the service point (point where the serving utility ends and premises wiring begins) will be at the utility transformer secondary terminals, at the service drop, or the meter socket enclosure, depending on where the utility conductors terminate.

Figure 100–80

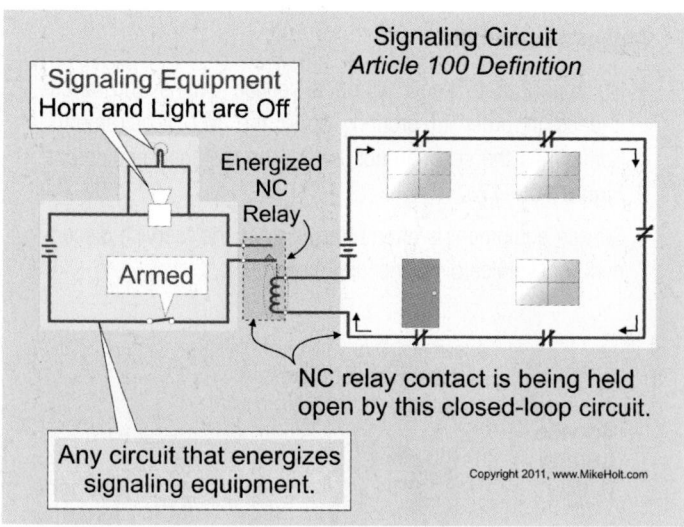

Signaling Circuit
Article 100 Definition

NC relay contact is being held open by this closed-loop circuit.

Any circuit that energizes signaling equipment.

Figure 100–82

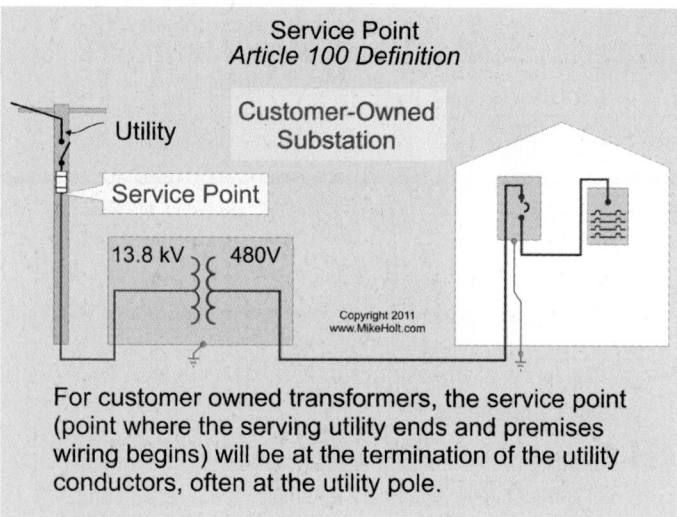

Service Point
Article 100 Definition

For customer owned transformers, the service point (point where the serving utility ends and premises wiring begins) will be at the termination of the utility conductors, often at the utility pole.

Figure 100–81

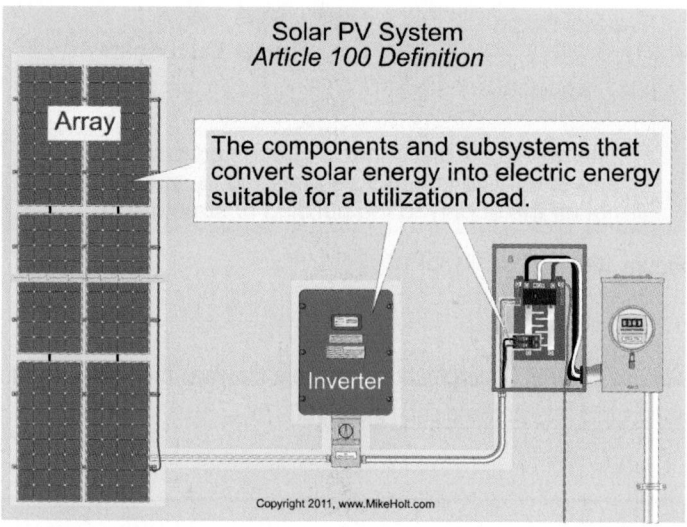

Solar PV System
Article 100 Definition

The components and subsystems that convert solar energy into electric energy suitable for a utilization load.

Figure 100–83

Solar Photovoltaic System. The combination of all components and subsystems that convert solar energy into electrical energy suitable for connection to a utilization load. **Figure 100–83**

Special Permission. Written consent from the authority having jurisdiction.

> **Author's Comment:** See the definition of "Authority Having Jurisdiction" in this article.

Structure. That which is built or constructed.

Surge Protective Device (SPD) [Article 285]. A protective device intended to limit transient voltages by diverting or limiting surge current and preventing the continued flow of current while remaining capable of repeating these functions. **Figure 100–84**

- *Type 1:* A permanently connected surge protective device listed for installation between the utility transformer and the service equipment.

> **Author's Comment:** The 2005 *NEC* referred to a Type 1 device as a surge arrester.

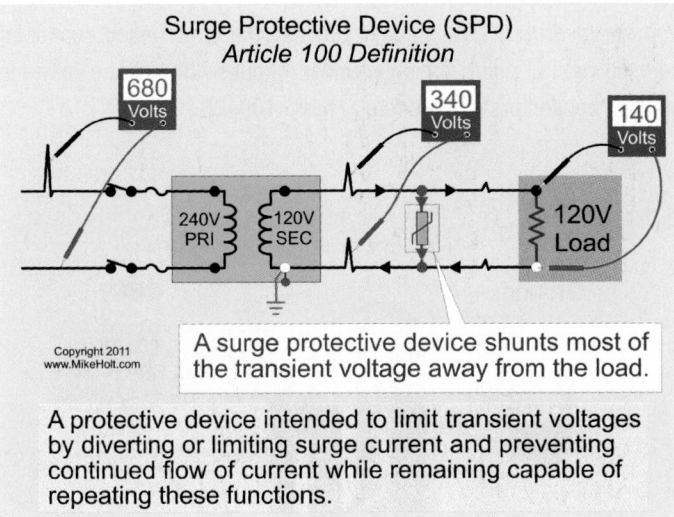

Surge Protective Device (SPD)
Article 100 Definition

A surge protective device shunts most of the transient voltage away from the load.

A protective device intended to limit transient voltages by diverting or limiting surge current and preventing continued flow of current while remaining capable of repeating these functions.

Figure 100–84

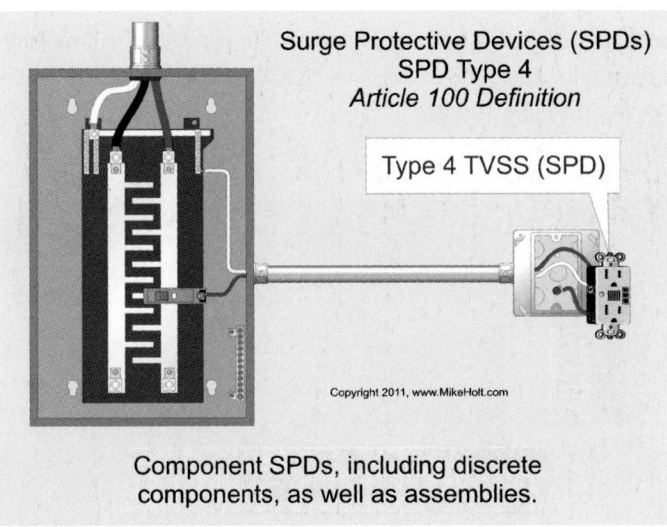

Surge Protective Devices (SPDs)
SPD Type 4
Article 100 Definition

Type 4 TVSS (SPD)

Component SPDs, including discrete components, as well as assemblies.

Figure 100–85

- *Type 2:* A permanently connected surge protective device listed for installation on the load side of the service disconnecting means.

Author's Comment: The 2005 *NEC* referred to a Type 2 device as a transient voltage surge suppressor (TVSS).

- *Type 3:* A surge protective device listed for installation on branch circuits.

Author's Comment: Type 3 surge protective devices can be installed anywhere on the load side of branch-circuit overcurrent protection up to the equipment served, provided there's a minimum of 30 ft of conductor length between the connection and the service or separately derived system [285.25].

- *Type 4:* A component surge protective device; this includes those installed in receptacles and relocatable power taps (plug strips). **Figure 100–85**

Note: For further information see UL 1449, *Standard for Surge Protective Devices.*

Switch, General-Use Snap. A switch constructed to be installed in a device box or a box cover.

Ungrounded. Not connected to the ground (earth) or a conductive body that extends the ground (earth) connection. **Figure 100–86**

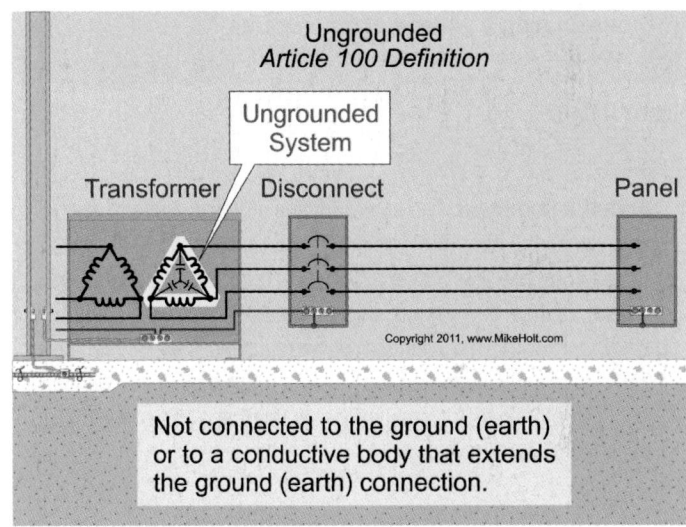

Ungrounded
Article 100 Definition

Ungrounded System

Transformer   Disconnect   Panel

Not connected to the ground (earth) or to a conductive body that extends the ground (earth) connection.

Figure 100–86

Author's Comment: The use of this term relates to an ungrounded system, where one of the system's current-carrying conductors isn't grounded (connected to the earth) [250.4(B) and 250.30(B)].

Utilization Equipment. Equipment that utilizes electricity for electronic, electromechanical, chemical, heating, lighting, or similar purposes.

Voltage of a Circuit. The greatest effective root-mean-square difference of potential between any two conductors of the circuit.

Voltage, Nominal. A value assigned for the purpose of conveniently designating voltage class, such as 120/240V, 120/208V, or 277/480V [220.5(A)]. **Figure 100–87**

Voltage-to-Ground. The voltage between the ungrounded conductor and the neutral point; for ungrounded circuits, the voltage between any two conductors of the circuit. **Figure 100–88**

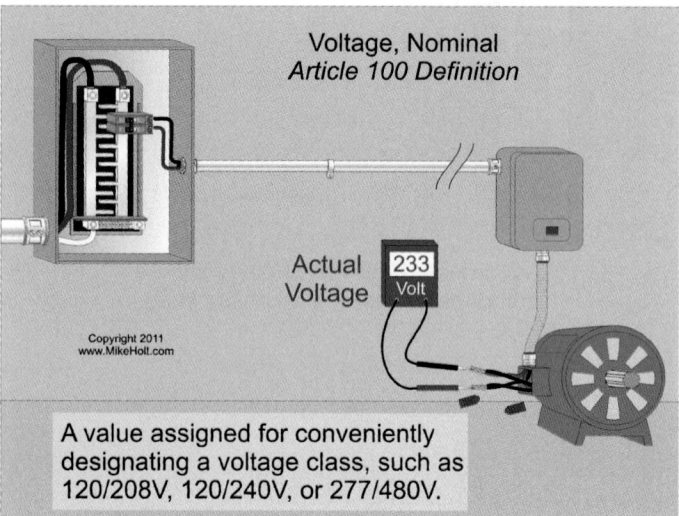

Figure 100–87

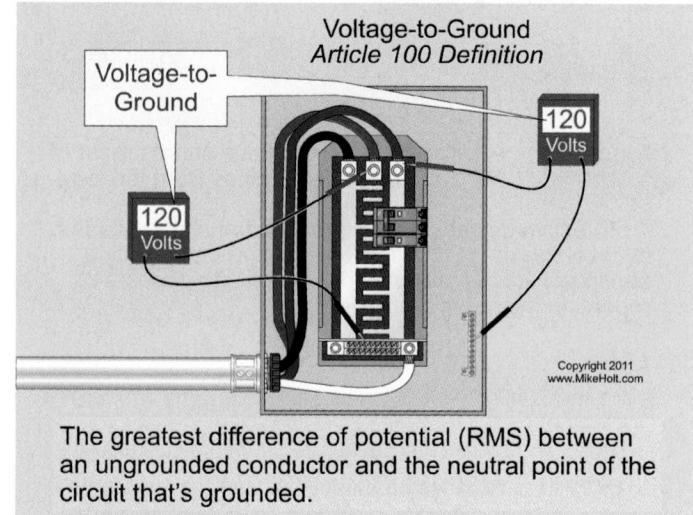

Figure 100–88

Author's Comment: The actual voltage at which a circuit operates can vary from the nominal within a range that permits satisfactory operation of equipment. In addition, the common voltage ratings of electrical equipment are 115V, 200V, 208V, 230V, and 460V. The electrical power supplied might be at the 240V, nominal voltage, but the voltage at the equipment will be less. Therefore, electrical equipment is rated at a value less than the nominal system voltage.

Watertight. Constructed so that moisture won't enter the enclosure under specific test conditions.

Weatherproof. Constructed or protected so that exposure to the weather won't interfere with successful operation.

Requirements for Electrical Installations

INTRODUCTION TO ARTICLE 110—REQUIREMENTS FOR ELECTRICAL INSTALLATIONS

Article 110 sets the stage for how you'll implement the rest of the *NEC*. This article contains a few of the most important and yet neglected parts of the *Code*. For example:

- How should conductors be terminated?
- What kinds of warnings, markings, and identification does a given installation require?
- What's the right working clearance for a given installation?
- What do the temperature limitations at terminals mean?
- What are the *NEC* requirements for dealing with flash protection?

It's critical that you master Article 110, and that's exactly what this *Illustrated Guide to Understanding the National Electrical Code* is designed for. As you read this article, you're building your foundation for correctly applying the *NEC*. In fact, this article itself is a foundation for much of the *Code*. The purpose for the National Electrical Code is to provide a safe installation, but Article 110 is perhaps focused a little more on providing an installation that is safe for the installer and maintenance electrician, so time spent in this article is time well spent.

PART I. GENERAL REQUIREMENTS

110.1 Scope. Article 110 covers the general requirements for the examination and approval, installation and use, access to and spaces about electrical equipment; as well as general requirements for enclosures intended for personnel entry (manholes, vaults, and tunnels).

110.2 Approval of Conductors and Equipment. The authority having jurisdiction must approve all electrical conductors and equipment. **Figure 110–1**

> **Author's Comment:** For a better understanding of product approval, review 90.4, 90.7, 110.3 and the definitions for "Approved," "Identified," "Labeled," and "Listed" in Article 100.

110.3 Examination, Identification, Installation, and Use of Equipment.

(A) Guidelines for Approval. The authority having jurisdiction must approve equipment. In doing so, consideration must be given to the following:

(1) Suitability for installation and use in accordance with the *NEC*

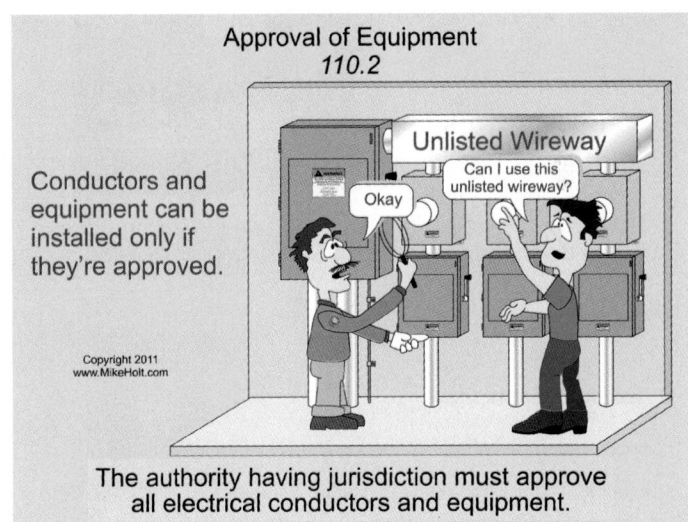

Approval of Equipment
110.2

Conductors and equipment can be installed only if they're approved.

Okay

Unlisted Wireway

Can I use this unlisted wireway?

Copyright 2011
www.MikeHolt.com

The authority having jurisdiction must approve all electrical conductors and equipment.

Figure 110–1

> **Note:** Suitability of equipment use may be identified by a description marked on or provided with a product to identify the suitability of the product for a specific purpose, environment, or application. Special conditions of use or other limitations may be marked on the equipment, in the product instructions, or appropriate listing and labeling information. Suitability of equipment may be evidenced by listing or labeling.

(2) Mechanical strength and durability

(3) Wire-bending and connection space

(4) Electrical insulation

(5) Heating effects under all conditions of use

(6) Arcing effects

(7) Classification by type, size, voltage, current capacity, and specific use

(8) Other factors contributing to the practical safeguarding of persons using or in contact with the equipment

(B) Installation and Use. Equipment must be installed and used in accordance with any instructions included in the listing or labeling requirements. **Figure 110–2**

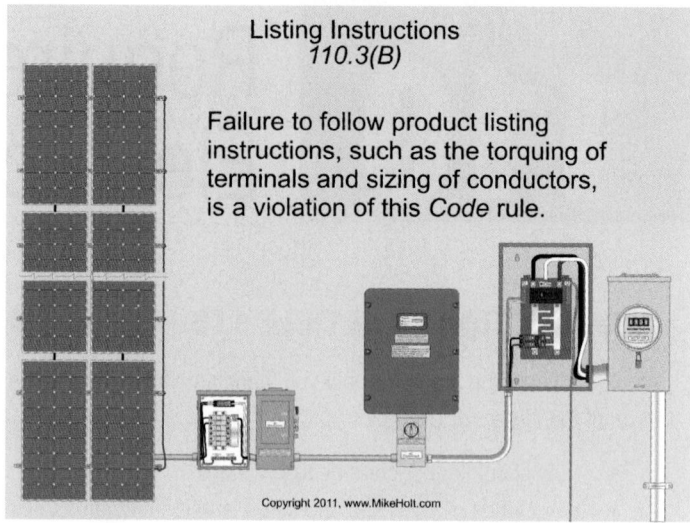

Figure 110–3

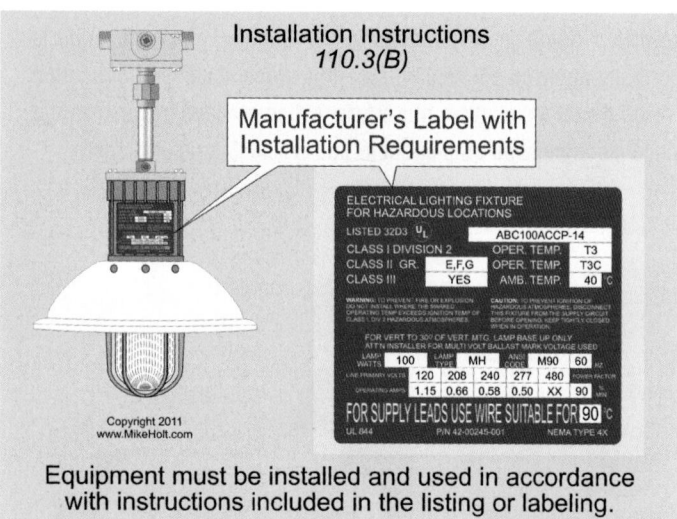

Figure 110–2

Author's Comments:

• See the definitions of "Labeling" and "Listing" in Article 100.

• Failure to follow product listing instructions, such as the torquing of terminals and the sizing of conductors, is a violation of this *Code* rule. **Figure 110–3**

• When an air conditioner nameplate specifies "Maximum Fuse Size," one-time or dual-element fuses must be used to protect the equipment. **Figure 110–4**

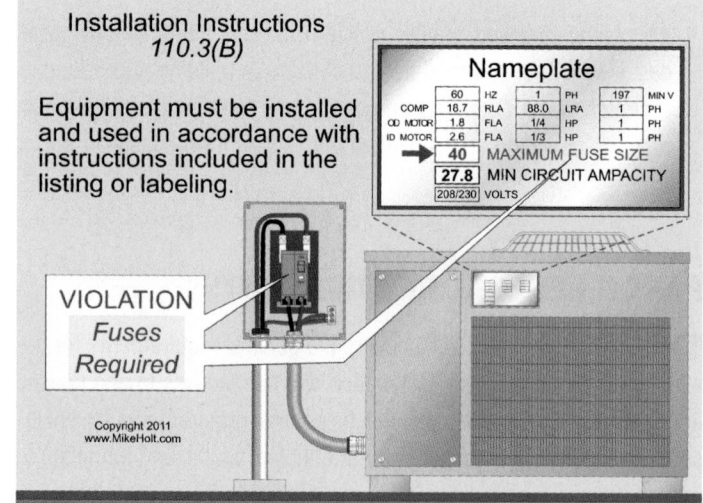

Figure 110–4

110.4 Voltages. The voltage rating of electrical equipment is not permitted to be less than the nominal voltage of a circuit to which it is connected. **Figure 110–5**

110.5 Copper Conductors. When the conductor material (copper/aluminum) isn't specified in a rule, the material and sizes is based on a copper conductor.

110.6 Conductor Sizes. Conductor sizes are expressed in American Wire Gage (AWG), typically from 18 AWG up to 4/0 AWG. Conductor sizes larger than 4/0 AWG are expressed in kcmil (thousand circular mils). **Figure 110–6**

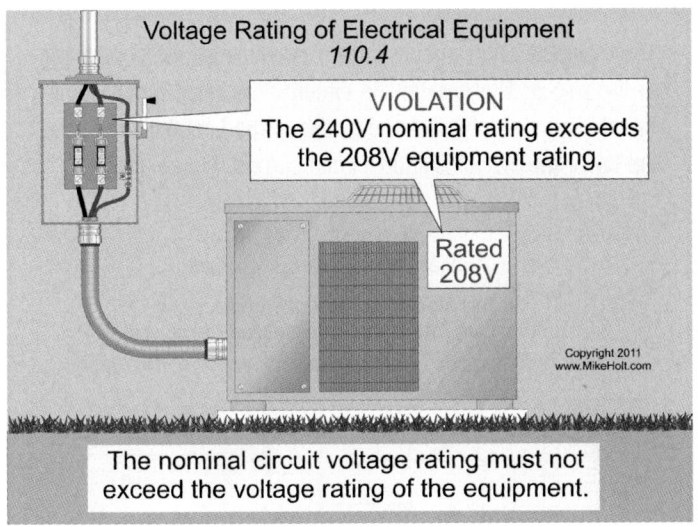

Figure 110–5

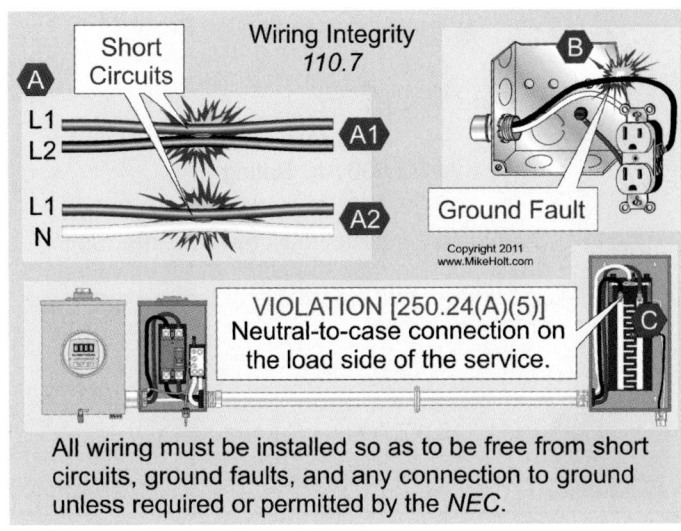

Figure 110–7

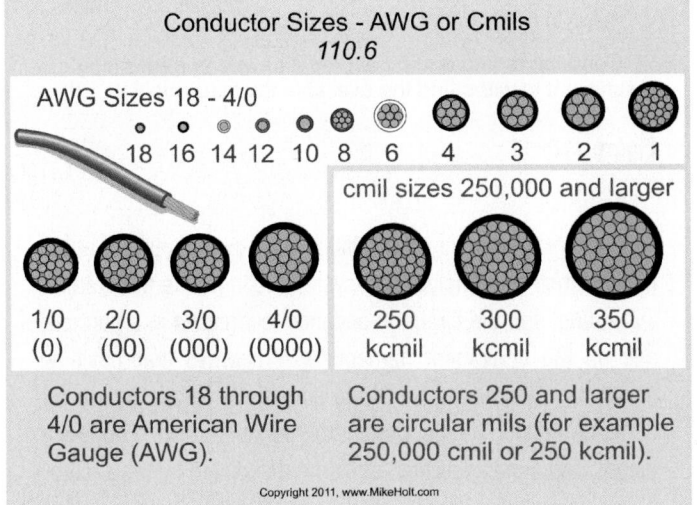

Figure 110–6

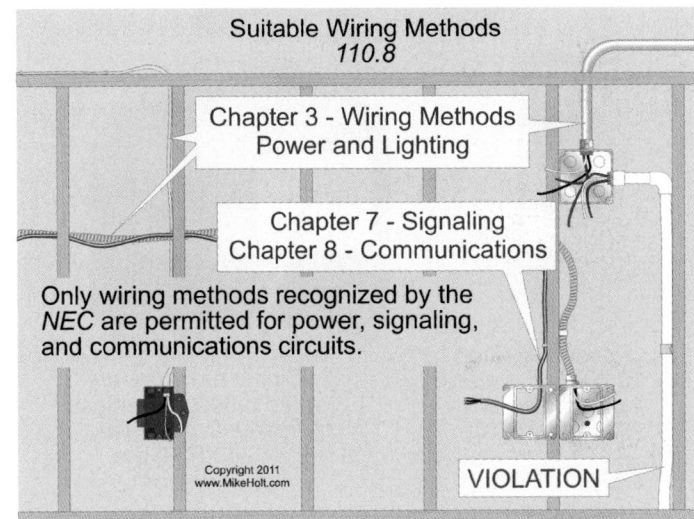

Figure 110–8

110.7 Wiring Integrity. Completed installations must be free from short circuits, ground faults, or any connections to ground unless required or permitted by the *Code*. **Figure 110–7**

110.8 Suitable Wiring Methods. Only wiring methods recognized as suitable are included in the *NEC*, and they must be installed in accordance with the *Code*. **Figure 110–8**

> **Author's Comment:** See Chapter 3 for power and lighting wiring methods, Chapter 7 for signaling, remote-control, and power-limited circuits, and Chapter 8 for communications circuits.

110.9 Interrupting Protection Rating. Overcurrent devices such as circuit breakers and fuses are intended to interrupt the circuit, and they must have an interrupting rating <u>not less than</u> the nominal circuit voltage and the current that's available at the line terminals of the equipment. **Figure 110–9**

> **Author's Comments:**
>
> • See the definition of "Interrupting Rating" in Article 100.
>
> • Unless marked otherwise, the ampere interrupting rating for circuit breakers is 5,000A [240.83(C)], and for fuses it's 10,000A [240.60(C)(3)]. **Figure 110–10**

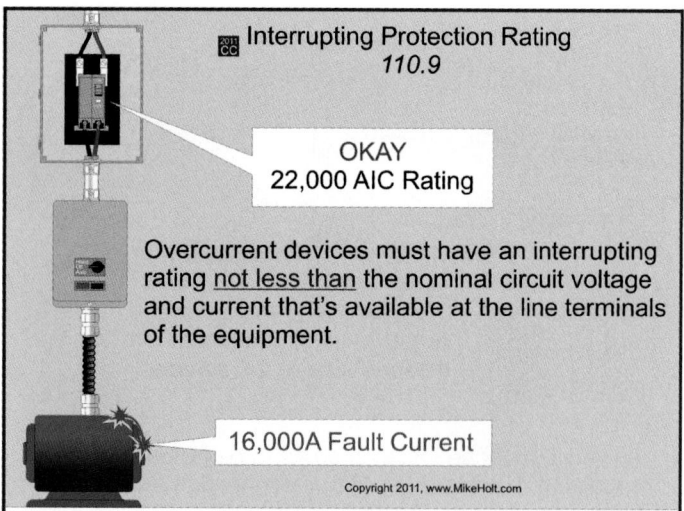

Figure 110-9

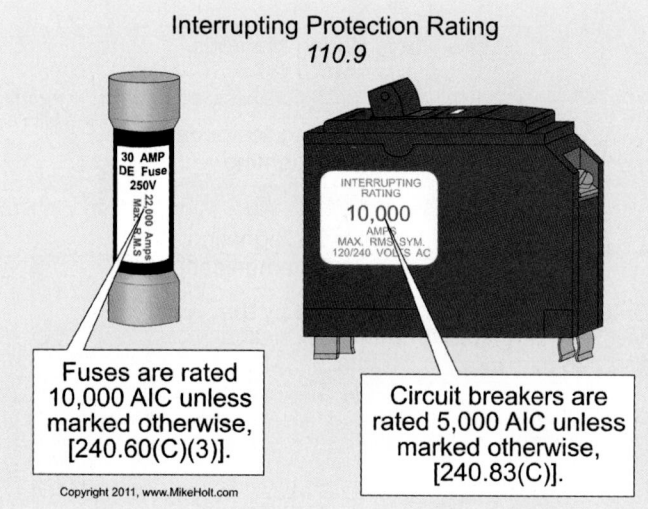

Figure 110-10

AVAILABLE SHORT-CIRCUIT CURRENT

Available short-circuit current is the current, in amperes, available at a given point in the electrical system. This available short-circuit current is first determined at the secondary terminals of the utility transformer. Thereafter, the available short-circuit current is calculated at the terminals of service equipment, then at branch-circuit panelboards and other equipment. The available short-circuit current is different at each point of the electrical system. It's highest at the utility transformer and lowest at the branch-circuit load.

The available short-circuit current depends on the impedance of the circuit. The greater the circuit impedance (utility transformer and the additive impedances of the circuit conductors), the lower the available short-circuit current. **Figure 110-11**

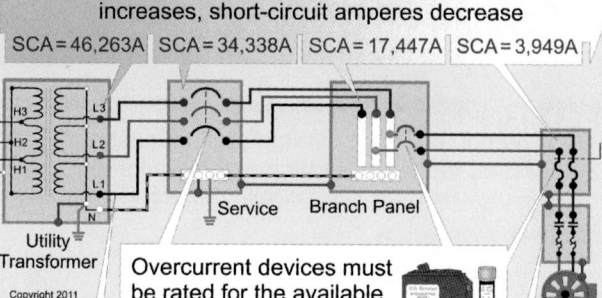

Figure 110-11

The factors that affect the available short-circuit current at the utility transformer include the system voltage, the transformer kVA rating, and the circuit impedance (expressed in a percentage on the equipment nameplate). Properties that have an impact on the impedance of the circuit include the conductor material (copper versus aluminum), conductor size, conductor length, and motor-operated equipment supplied by the circuit.

Author's Comment: Many people in the industry describe Amperes Interrupting Rating (AIR) as "Amperes Interrupting Capacity" (AIC).

 DANGER: *Extremely high values of current flow (caused by short circuits or ground faults) produce tremendously destructive thermal and magnetic forces. Overcurrent protection devices not rated to interrupt the current at the available fault values at its listed voltage rating can explode while attempting to open the circuit overcurrent device from a short circuit or ground fault, which can cause serious injury or death, as well as property damage.* **Figure 110-12**

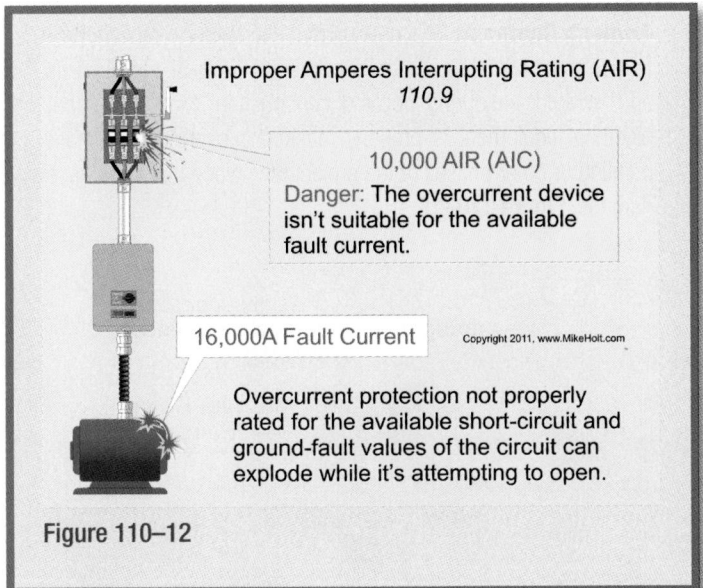

Figure 110–12

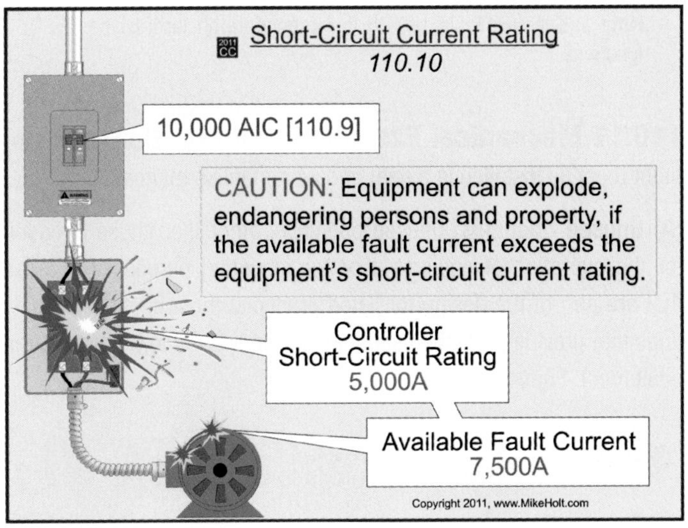

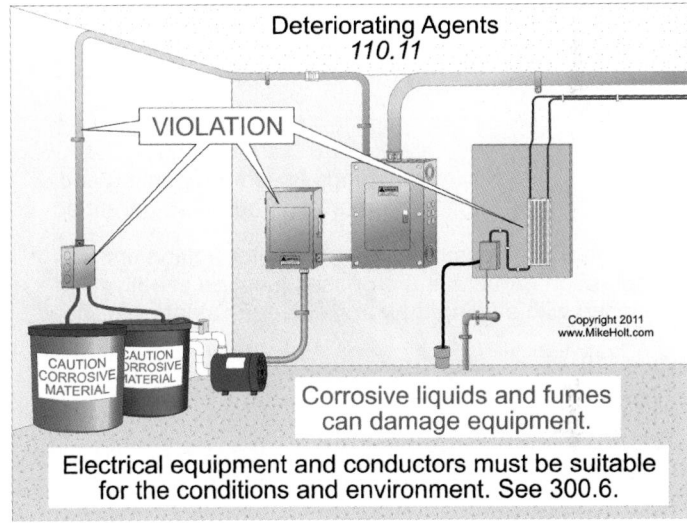

Figure 110–13

110.10 Circuit Impedance, Short-Circuit Current Rating, and Other Characteristics. Electrical equipment must have a short-circuit current rating that permits the circuit protective device to open from a short circuit or ground fault without extensive damage to the electrical equipment of the circuit. This fault is assumed to be either between two or more of the circuit conductors or between any circuit conductor and the equipment grounding conductor(s) permitted in 250.118. Listed equipment applied in accordance with their listing is considered to have met the requirements of this section.

> **Author's Comment:** For example, a motor controller must have a sufficient short-circuit rating for the available fault current. If the fault current exceeds the controller's short-circuit current rating, the controller can explode, endangering persons and property. **Figure 110–13**

110.11 Deteriorating Agents. Electrical equipment and conductors must be suitable for the environment and conditions of use. Consideration must also be given to the presence of corrosive gases, fumes, vapors, liquids, or other substances that can have a deteriorating effect on the conductors or equipment. **Figure 110–14**

> **Author's Comment:** Conductors must not be exposed to ultraviolet rays from the sun unless identified for the purpose [310.10(D)].

Figure 110–14

Note 1: Raceways, cable trays, cablebus, cable armor, boxes, cable sheathing, cabinets, elbows, couplings, fittings, supports, and support hardware must be of materials that are suitable for the environment in which they're to be installed, in accordance with 300.6.

Note 2: Some cleaning and lubricating compounds contain chemicals that can cause deterioration of the plastic used for insulating and structural applications in equipment.

Equipment not identified for outdoor use and equipment identified only for indoor use must be protected against damage from the weather during construction.

Note 3: See *NEC* Table 110.28 for appropriate enclosure-type designations.

110.12 Mechanical Execution of Work. Electrical equipment must be installed in a neat and workmanlike manner.

(A) Unused Openings. Unused openings, other than those intended for the operation of equipment or for mounting purposes, or those that are part of the design for listed products, must be closed by fittings that provide protection substantially equivalent to the wall of the equipment. **Figure 110–15**

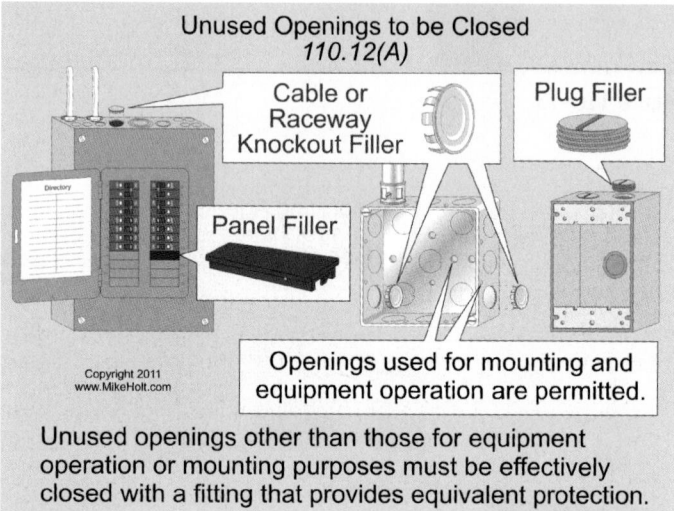

Figure 110–15

Note: Accepted industry practices are described in ANSI/NECA 1, *Standard Practices for Good Workmanship in Electrical Contracting.*

Author's Comment: The National Electrical Contractors Association (*NECA*) created a series of National Electrical Installation Standards (NEIS)® that established the industry's first quality guidelines for electrical installations. These standards define a benchmark or baseline of quality and workmanship for installing electrical products and systems. They explain what installing electrical products and systems in a "neat and workmanlike manner" means. For more information about these standards, visit www.neca-neis.org/.

(B) Integrity of Electrical Equipment. Internal parts of electrical equipment must not be damaged or contaminated by foreign material, such as paint, plaster, cleaners, and so forth.

Author's Comment: Precautions must be taken to provide protection from contamination of the internal parts of panelboards and receptacles during building construction. Make sure that electrical equipment is properly masked and protected before painting or other phases of the project take place that can cause damage. **Figure 110–16**

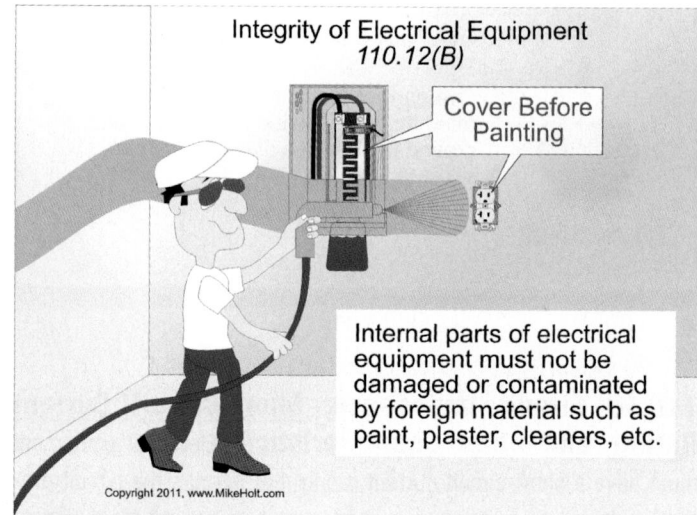

Figure 110–16

Electrical equipment that contains damaged parts may adversely affect safe operation or mechanical strength of the equipment and must not be installed. This includes parts that are broken, bent, cut, or deteriorated by corrosion, chemical action, or overheating.

Author's Comment: Damaged parts include cracked insulators, arc shields not in place, overheated fuse clips, and damaged or missing switch handles or circuit-breaker handles. **Figure 110–17**

110.13 Mounting and Cooling of Equipment.

(A) Mounting. Electrical equipment must be firmly secured to the surface on which it's mounted.

Author's Comment: See 314.23 for similar requirements for boxes.

110.14 Conductor Termination and Splicing. Conductor terminal and splicing devices must be identified for the conductor material and they must be properly installed and used. **Figure 110–18**

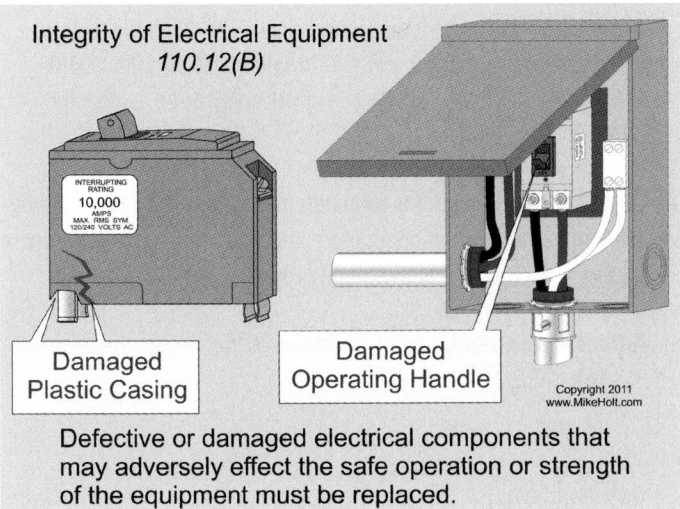

Defective or damaged electrical components that may adversely effect the safe operation or strength of the equipment must be replaced.

Figure 110–17

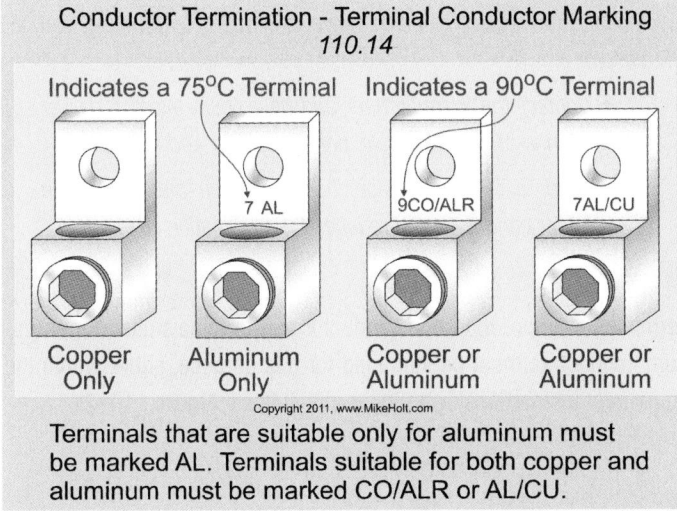

Terminals that are suitable only for aluminum must be marked AL. Terminals suitable for both copper and aluminum must be marked CO/ALR or AL/CU.

Figure 110–18

Connectors and terminals for conductors more finely stranded than Class B and Class C, as shown in Table 10 of Chapter 9, must be identified for the conductor class. **Figure 110–19**

Author's Comments:

- According to UL Standard 486 A-B, a terminal/lug/connector must be listed and marked for use with conductors stranded in other than Class B. With no marking or factory literature/instructions to the contrary, terminals may only be used with Class B stranded conductors.

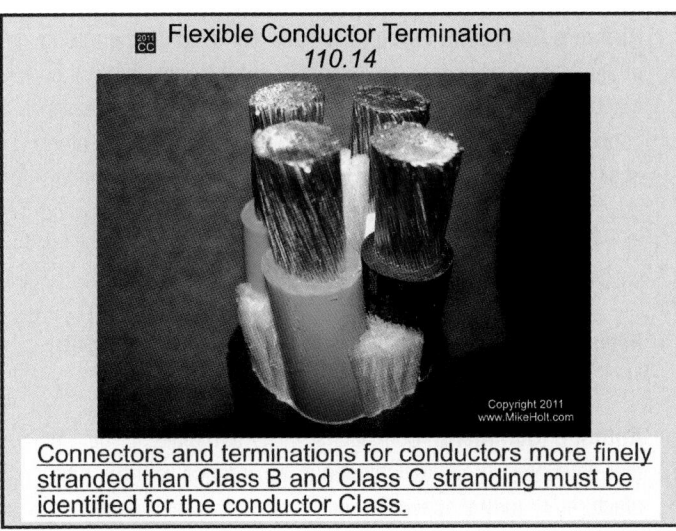

Connectors and terminations for conductors more finely stranded than Class B and Class C stranding must be identified for the conductor Class.

Figure 110–19

- Class D stranding has 37 strands of wire per conductor in sizes 18-2 AWG, 61 strands in sizes 1-4/0 AWG, and 91 strands in sizes 250-500 kcmil.

Switches and receptacles marked CO/ALR are designed to ensure a good connection through the use of the larger contact area and compatible materials. The terminal screws are plated with the element called "Indium." Indium is an extremely soft metal that forms a gas-sealed connection with the aluminum conductor.

Author's Comments:

- See the definition of "Identified" in Article 100.
- Conductor terminations must comply with the manufacturer's instructions as required by 110.3(B). For example, if the instructions for the device state "Suitable for 18-12 AWG Stranded," then only stranded conductors can be used with the terminating device. If the instructions state "Suitable for 18-12 AWG Solid," then only solid conductors are permitted, and if the instructions state "Suitable for 18-12 AWG," then either solid or stranded conductors can be used with the terminating device.

Copper and Aluminum Mixed. Copper and aluminum conductors must not make contact with each other in a device unless the device is listed and identified for this purpose.

Author's Comment: Few terminations are listed for the mixing of aluminum and copper conductors, but if they are, that will be marked on the product package or terminal device. The reason copper and aluminum shouldn't be in contact with each other is because corrosion develops between the two different metals due to galvanic action, resulting in increased contact resistance at the splicing device. This increased resistance can cause the splice to overheat and cause a fire.

Note: Many terminations and equipment are marked with a tightening torque, see Table I.1 in Informative Annex I.

Author's Comment: Conductors must terminate in devices that have been properly tightened in accordance with the manufacturer's torque specifications included with equipment instructions. Failure to torque terminals can result in excessive heating of terminals or splicing devices due to a loose connection. A loose connection can also lead to arcing which increases the heating effect and also may lead to a short circuit or ground fault. Any of these can result in a fire or other failure, including an arc-flash event. In addition, this is a violation of 110.3(B), which requires all equipment to be installed in accordance with listing or labeling instructions. **Figure 110–20**

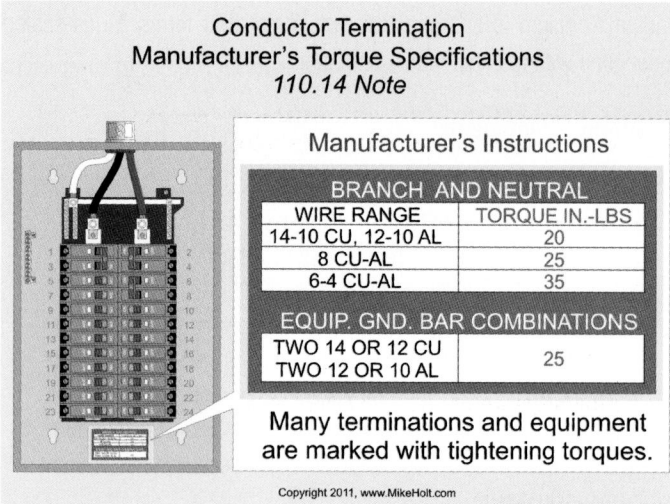

Conductor Termination
Manufacturer's Torque Specifications
110.14 Note

Manufacturer's Instructions

BRANCH AND NEUTRAL	
WIRE RANGE	TORQUE IN.-LBS
14-10 CU, 12-10 AL	20
8 CU-AL	25
6-4 CU-AL	35

EQUIP. GND. BAR COMBINATIONS	
TWO 14 OR 12 CU TWO 12 OR 10 AL	25

Many terminations and equipment are marked with tightening torques.

Copyright 2011, www.MikeHolt.com

Figure 110–20

Question: What do you do if the torque value isn't provided with the device?

Answer: Call the manufacturer, visit the manufacturer's Website, or have the supplier make a copy of the installation instructions.

Author's Comment: Terminating conductors without a torque tool can result in an improper and unsafe installation. If a torque screwdriver isn't used, there's a good chance the conductors aren't properly terminated.

(A) Terminations. Conductor terminals must ensure a good connection without damaging the conductors and must be made by pressure connectors (including set screw type) or splices to flexible leads.

Author's Comment: See the definition of "Connector, Pressure" in Article 100.

Question: What if the conductor is larger than the terminal device?

Answer: This condition needs to be anticipated in advance, and the equipment should be ordered with terminals that will accommodate the larger conductor. However, if you're in the field, you should:

• Contact the manufacturer and have them express deliver you the proper terminals, bolts, washers, and nuts, or

• Order a terminal device that crimps on the end of the larger conductor and reduces the termination size.

Terminals for more than one conductor and terminals used for aluminum conductors must be identified for this purpose, either within the equipment instructions or on the terminal itself. **Figure 110–21**

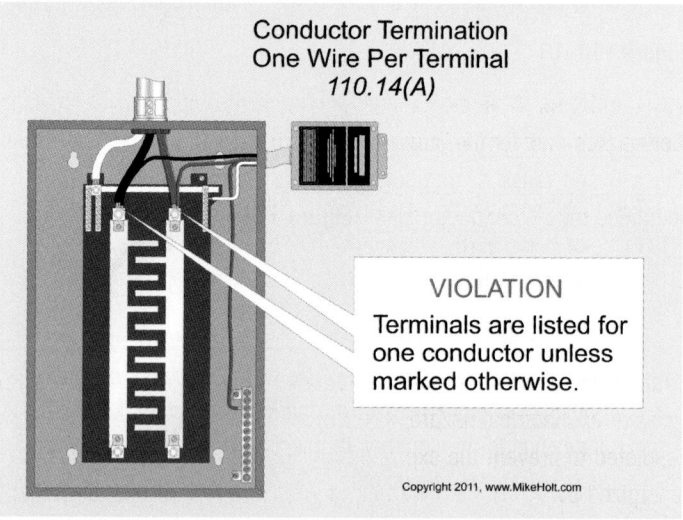

Conductor Termination
One Wire Per Terminal
110.14(A)

VIOLATION
Terminals are listed for one conductor unless marked otherwise.

Copyright 2011, www.MikeHolt.com

Figure 110–21

Author's Comments:

- Split-bolt connectors are commonly listed for only two conductors, although some are listed for three conductors. However, it's a common industry practice to terminate as many conductors as possible within a split-bolt connector, even though this violates the *NEC*. **Figure 110–22**

- Many devices are listed for more than one conductor per terminal. For example, some circuit breakers rated 30A or less can have two conductors under each lug. Grounding and bonding terminals are also often listed for more than one conductor under the terminal.

- Each neutral conductor within a panelboard must terminate to an individual terminal [408.41].

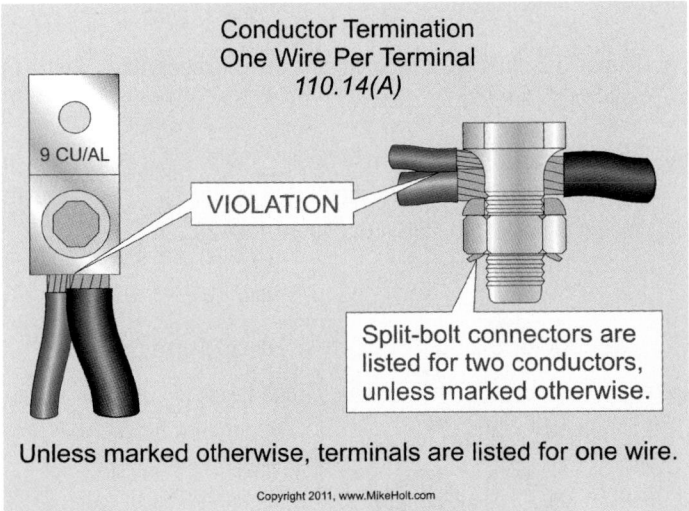

Figure 110–22

(B) Conductor Splices. Conductors must be spliced by a splicing device identified for the purpose or by exothermic welding.

Author's Comment: Conductors aren't required to be twisted together prior to the installation of a twist-on wire connector, unless specifically required in the installation instructions. **Figure 110–23**

Unused circuit conductors aren't required to be removed. However, to prevent an electrical hazard, the free ends of the conductors must be insulated to prevent the exposed end of the conductor from touching energized parts. This requirement can be met by the use of an insulated twist-on or push-on wire connector. **Figure 110–24**

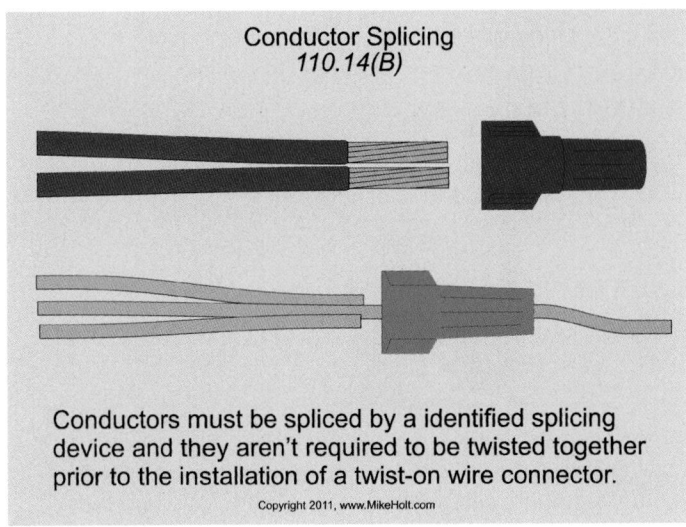

Figure 110–23

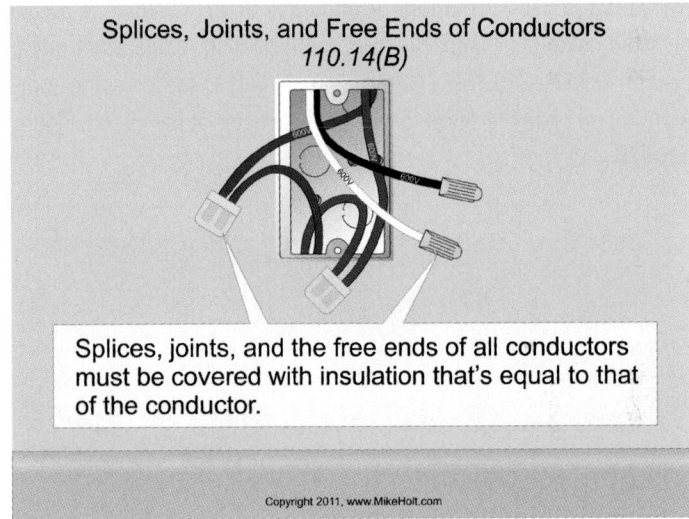

Figure 110–24

Author's Comment: See the definition of "Energized" in Article 100.

Underground Splices:

Single Conductors. Single direct burial conductors of types UF or USE can be spliced underground without a junction box, but the conductors must be spliced with a device listed for direct burial [300.5(E) and 300.15(G)]. **Figure 110–25**

Multiconductor Cable. Multiconductor UF or USE cable can have the individual conductors spliced underground without a junction box as long as a listed splice kit that encapsulates the conductors as well as the cable jacket is used.

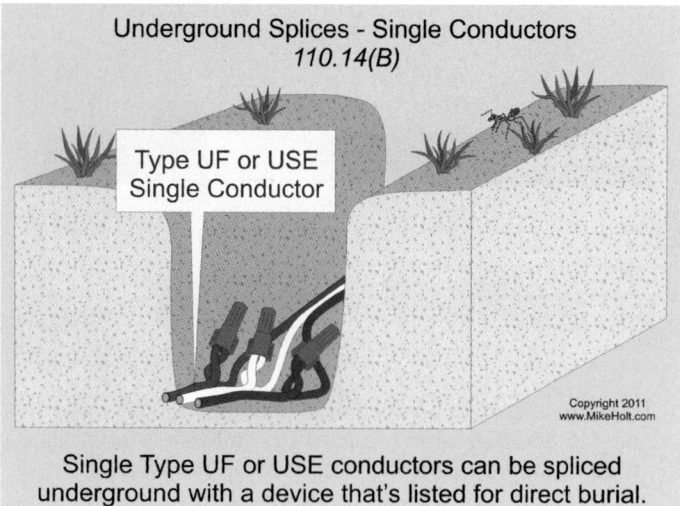

Figure 110–25

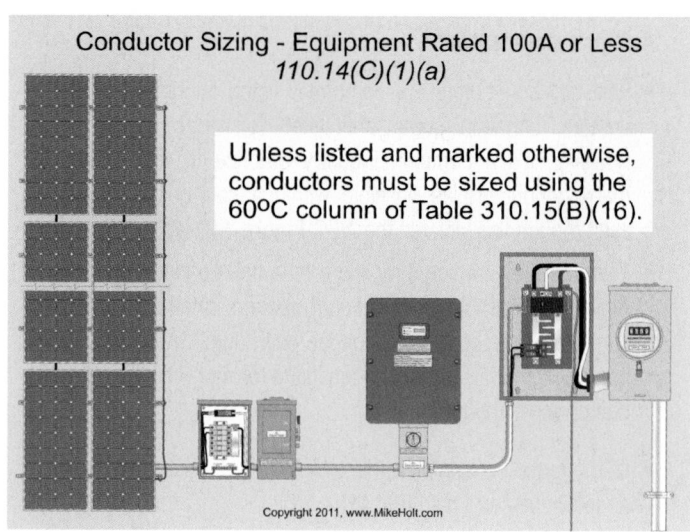

Figure 110–27

(C) Temperature Limitations (Conductor Size). Conductors are to be sized using their ampacity from the insulation temperature rating column of Table 310.15(B)(16) that corresponds to the lowest temperature rating of any terminal, device, or conductor of the circuit. **Figure 110–26**

(1) Conductors must be sized using the 60°C temperature column of Table 310.15(B)(16).

(3) Conductors terminating on terminals rated 75°C are sized in accordance with the ampacities listed in the 75°C temperature column of Table 310.15(B)(16). **Figure 110–28**

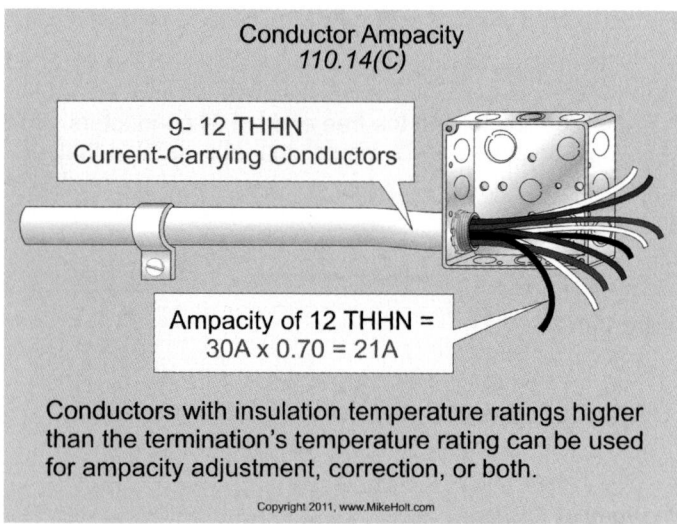

Figure 110–26

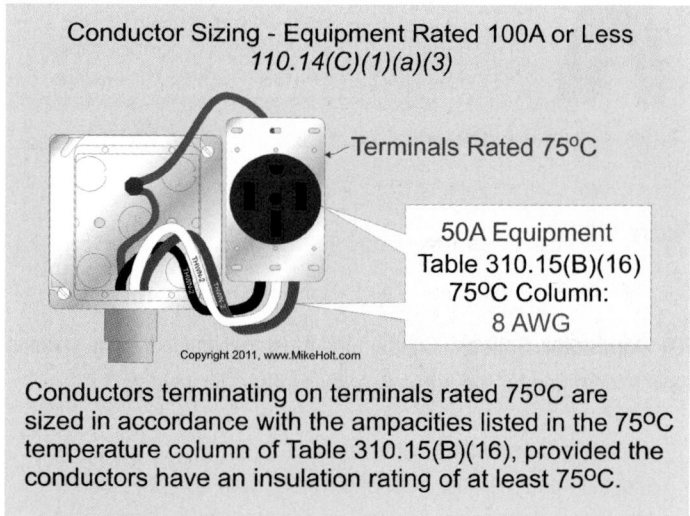

Figure 110–28

(1) Equipment Temperature Rating Provisions. Unless the equipment is listed and marked otherwise, conductor sizing for equipment terminations must be based on Table 310.15(B)(16) in accordance with (a) or (b):

(a) Equipment Rated 100A or Less. Figure 110–27

(b) Equipment Rated Over 100A.

(1) Conductors must be sized using the 75°C temperature column of Table 310.15(B)(16). **Figure 110–29**

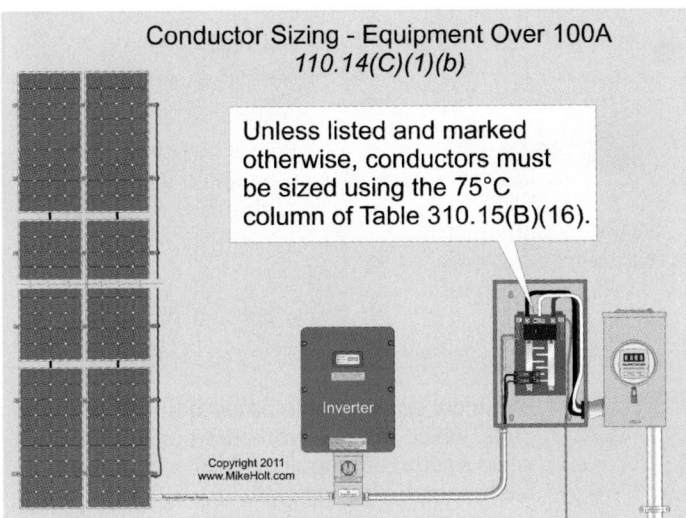

Figure 110–29

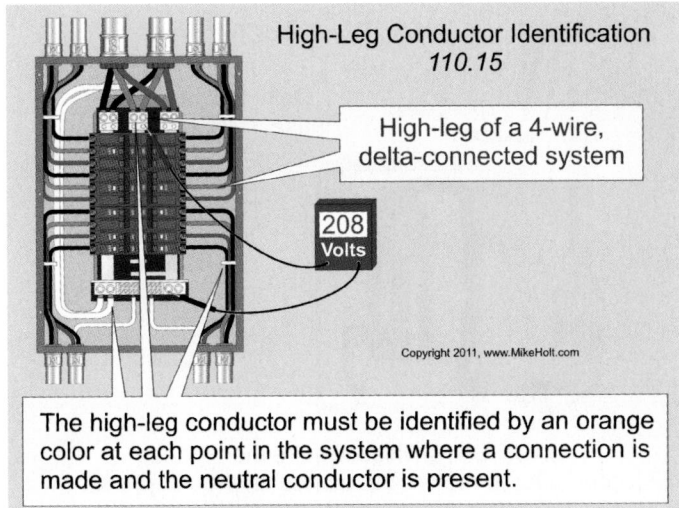

Figure 110–31

(2) Separate Connector Provisions. Conductors can be sized to the 90°C column of Table 310.15(B)(16) if the conductors and pressure connectors are rated at least 90°C. **Figure 110–30**

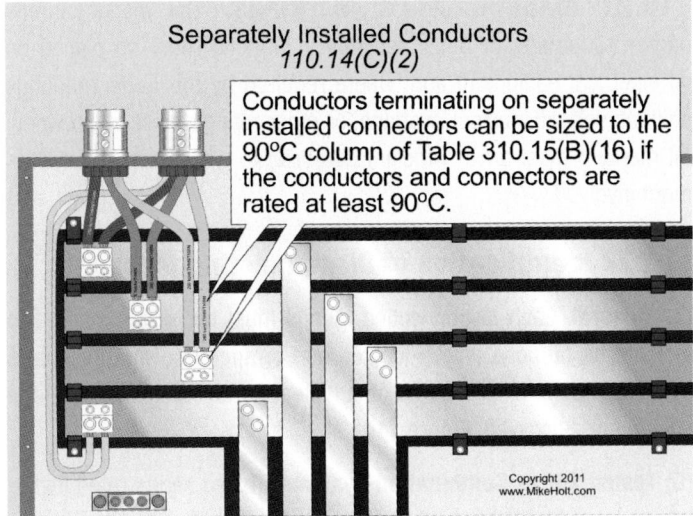

Figure 110–30

110.15 High-Leg Conductor Identification. On a 4-wire, delta-connected, three-phase system, where the midpoint of one phase winding of the secondary is grounded (a high-leg system), the conductor with 208V to ground must be durably and permanently marked by an outer finish orange in color, or other effective means. Such identification must be placed at each point on the system where a connection is made if the neutral conductor is present [230.56]. **Figure 110–31**

Author's Comments:

- The high-leg conductor is also called the "wild leg," "stinger leg," or "bastard leg."

- Other important *NEC* rules relating to the high leg are as follows:

  - **Panelboards.** Since 1975, panelboards supplied by a 4-wire, delta-connected, three-phase system must have the high-leg conductor terminate to the "B" phase of a panelboard [408.3(E)]. Section 408.3(F)(1) requires panelboards to be field-marked with "Caution Phase B Has 208V to Ground."

  - **Disconnects.** The *NEC* doesn't specify the termination location for the high-leg conductor in switch equipment (Switches—Article 404), but the generally accepted practice is to terminate this conductor to the "B" phase.

  - **Utility Equipment.** The ANSI standard for meter equipment requires the high-leg conductor (208V to neutral) to terminate on the "C" (right) phase of the meter socket enclosure. This is because the demand meter needs 120V, and it obtains that voltage from the "B" phase. **Figure 110–32**

- Also hope the utility lineman isn't color blind and doesn't inadvertently cross the "orange" high-leg conductor (208V) with the red (120V) service conductor at the weatherhead. It's happened before...

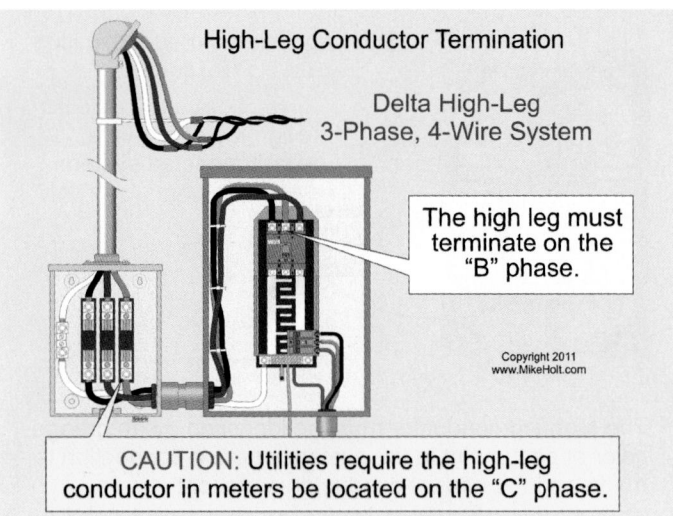

High-Leg Conductor Termination

Delta High-Leg
3-Phase, 4-Wire System

The high leg must terminate on the "B" phase.

Copyright 2011
www.MikeHolt.com

CAUTION: Utilities require the high-leg conductor in meters be located on the "C" phase.

Figure 110–32

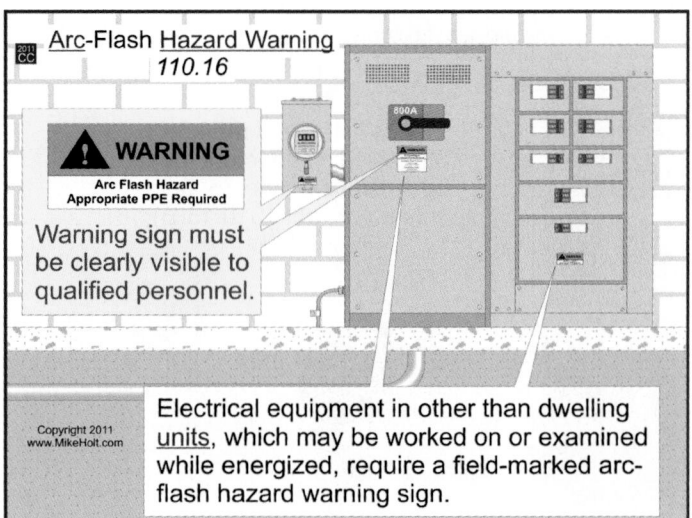

Arc-Flash Hazard Warning
110.16

⚠ **WARNING**
Arc Flash Hazard
Appropriate PPE Required

Warning sign must be clearly visible to qualified personnel.

Copyright 2011
www.MikeHolt.com

Electrical equipment in other than dwelling units, which may be worked on or examined while energized, require a field-marked arc-flash hazard warning sign.

Figure 110–33

WARNING: *When replacing equipment in existing facilities that contain a high-leg conductor, care must be taken to ensure the high-leg conductor is replaced in its original location. Prior to 1975, the high-leg conductor was required to terminate on the "C" phase of panelboards and switchboards. Failure to re-terminate the high leg in accordance with the existing installation can result in 120V circuits being inadvertently connected to the 208V high leg, with disastrous results.*

110.16 Arc-Flash Hazard Warning.

Electrical equipment such as switchboards, panelboards, industrial control panels, meter socket enclosures, and motor control centers in other than dwelling units that are likely to require examination, adjustment, servicing, or maintenance while energized must be field-marked to warn qualified persons of the danger associated with an arc flash from short circuits or ground faults. The field-marking must be clearly visible to qualified persons before they examine, adjust, service, or perform maintenance on the equipment. **Figure 110–33**

Author's Comments:

- See the definition of "Qualified Person" in Article 100.

- This rule is meant to warn qualified persons who work on energized electrical systems that an arc flash hazard exists so they'll select proper personal protective equipment (PPE) in accordance with industry accepted safe work practice standards.

Note 1: NFPA 70E, *Standard for Electrical Safety in the Workplace*, provides assistance in determining the severity of potential exposure, planning safe work practices, and selecting personal protective equipment.

110.21 Manufacturer's Markings.

The manufacturer's name, trademark, or other descriptive marking must be placed on all electrical equipment and, where required by the *Code*, markings such as voltage, current, wattage, or other ratings must be provided. All marking must have sufficient durability to withstand the environment involved.

110.22 Identification of Disconnecting Means.

(A) General. Each disconnecting means must be legibly marked to indicate its purpose unless located and arranged so the purpose is evident. The marking must be of sufficient durability to withstand the environment involved. **Figure 110–34**

(C) Tested Series Combination Systems. Tested series-rated installations must be legibly field-marked in accordance with 240.86(B) to indicate the equipment has been applied with a series combination rating.

110.24 Available Fault Current.

(A) Field Marking. Service equipment in other than dwelling units must be legibly field-marked with the maximum available fault current, including the date the fault current calculation was performed and be of sufficient durability to withstand the environment involved. **Figure 110–35**

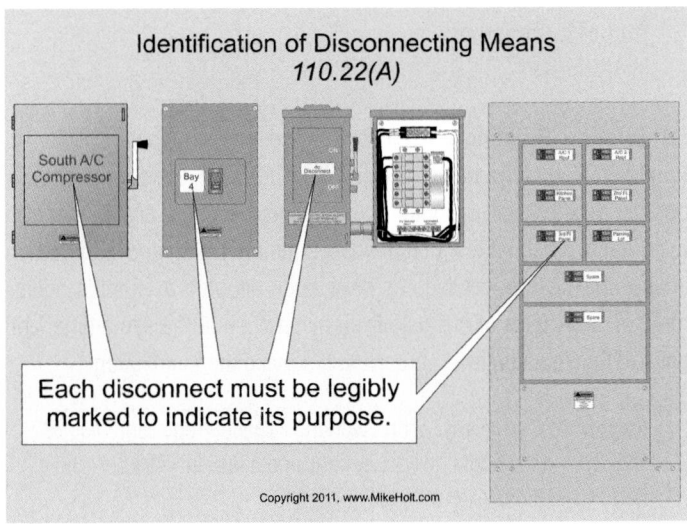

Figure 110–34

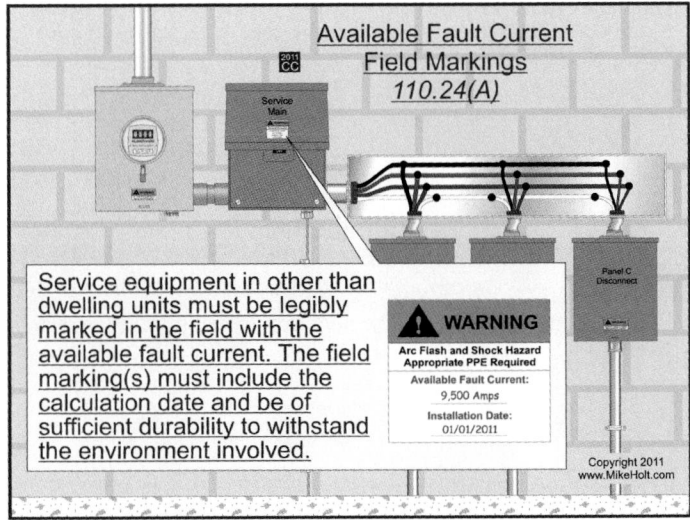

Figure 110–35

(B) Modifications. When modifications to the electrical installation affect the maximum available fault current at the service, the maximum available fault current must be recalculated to ensure the service equipment ratings are sufficient for the maximum available fault current at the line terminals of the equipment. The required field marking(s) in 110.24(A) must be adjusted to reflect the new level of maximum available fault current.

Ex: Field markings aren't required for industrial installations where conditions of maintenance and supervision ensure that only qualified persons service the equipment.

PART II. 600V, NOMINAL, OR LESS

110.26 Spaces About Electrical Equipment. For the purpose of safe operation and maintenance of equipment, access and working space must be provided about all electrical equipment.

(A) Working Space. Equipment that may need examination, adjustment, servicing, or maintenance while energized must have working space provided in accordance with (1), (2), and (3):

> **Author's Comment:** The phrase "while energized" is the root of many debates. As always, check with the AHJ to see what equipment he or she believes needs a clear working space.

(1) Depth of Working Space. The working space, which is measured from the enclosure front, must not be less than the distances contained in Table 110.26(A)(1). **Figure 110–36**

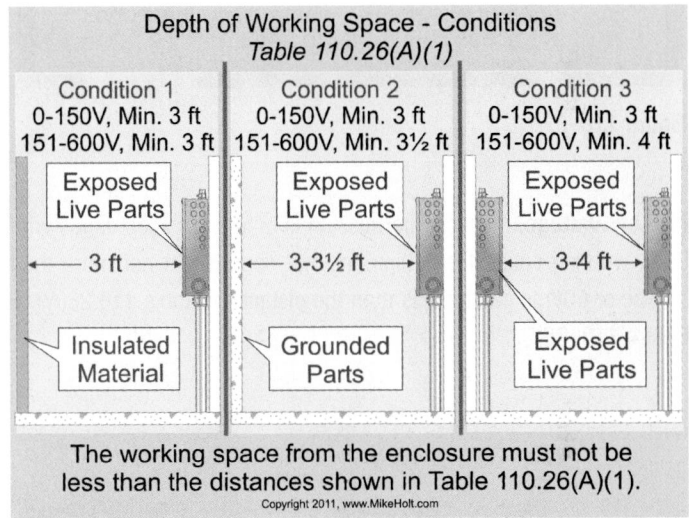

Figure 110–36

Table 110.26(A)(1) Working Space			
Voltage-to-Ground	Condition 1	Condition 2	Condition 3
0–150V	3 ft	3 ft	3 ft
151–600V	3 ft	3½ft	4 ft

• *Condition 1—Exposed live parts on one side of the working space and no live or grounded parts, including concrete, brick, or tile walls are on the other side of the working space.*
• *Condition 2—Exposed live parts on one side of the working space and grounded parts, including concrete, brick, or tile walls are on the other side of the working space.*
• *Condition 3—Exposed live parts on both sides of the working space.*

(a) Rear and Sides. Working space isn't required for the back or sides of assemblies where all connections and all renewable or adjustable parts are accessible from the front. **Figure 110–37**

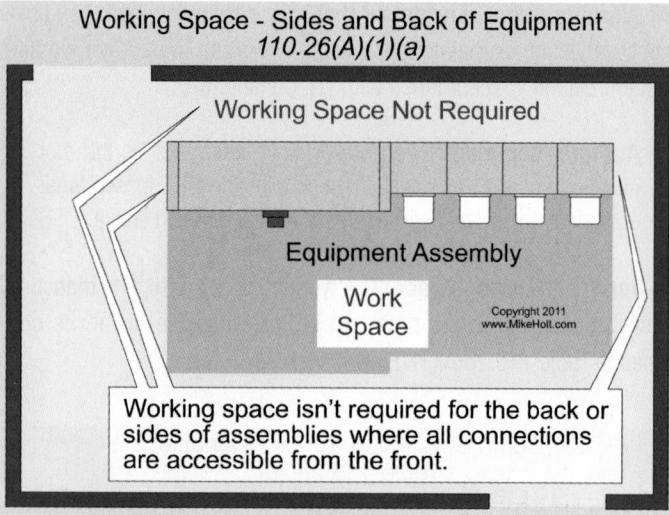

Figure 110–37

(b) Low Voltage. If special permission is granted in accordance with 90.4, working space for equipment that operates at not more than 30V ac or 60V dc can be less than the distance in Table 110.26(A)(1). **Figure 110–38**

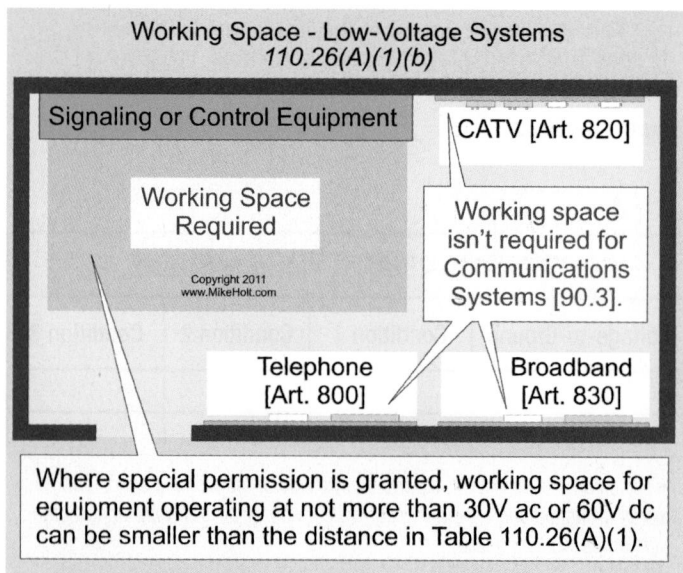

Figure 110–38

Author's Comment: See the definition of "Special Permission" in Article 100.

(c) Existing Buildings. If electrical equipment is being replaced, Condition 2 working space is permitted between dead-front switchboards, panelboards, or motor control centers located across the aisle from each other where conditions of maintenance and supervision ensure that written procedures have been adopted to prohibit equipment on both sides of the aisle from being open at the same time, and only authorized, qualified persons will service the installation.

Author's Comment: The working space requirements of 110.26 don't apply to equipment included in Chapter 8—Communications Circuits [90.3].

(2) Width of Working Space. The width of the working space must be a minimum of 30 in., but in no case less than the width of the equipment. **Figure 110–39**

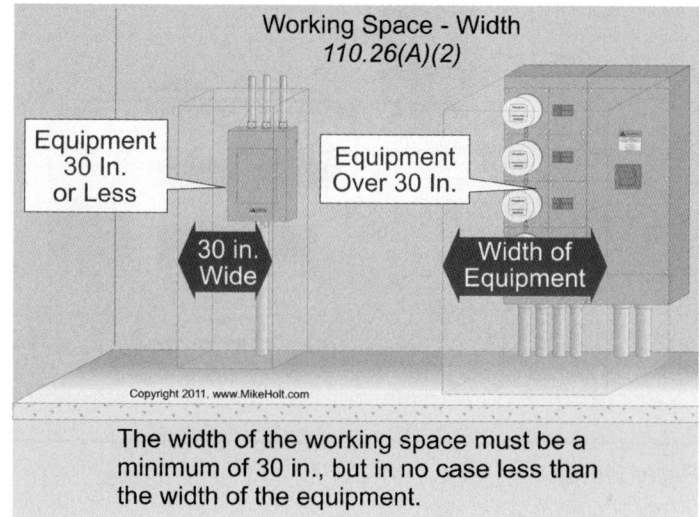

Figure 110–39

Author's Comment: The width of the working space can be measured from left-to-right, from right-to-left, or simply centered on the equipment, and the working space can overlap the working space for other electrical equipment. **Figure 110–40**

In all cases, the working space must be of sufficient width, depth, and height to permit all equipment doors to open 90 degrees. **Figure 110–41**

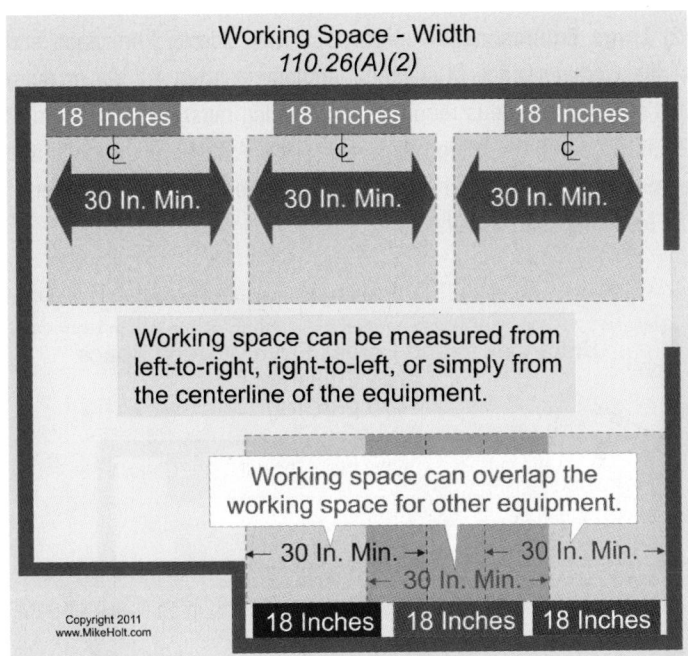

Figure 110–40

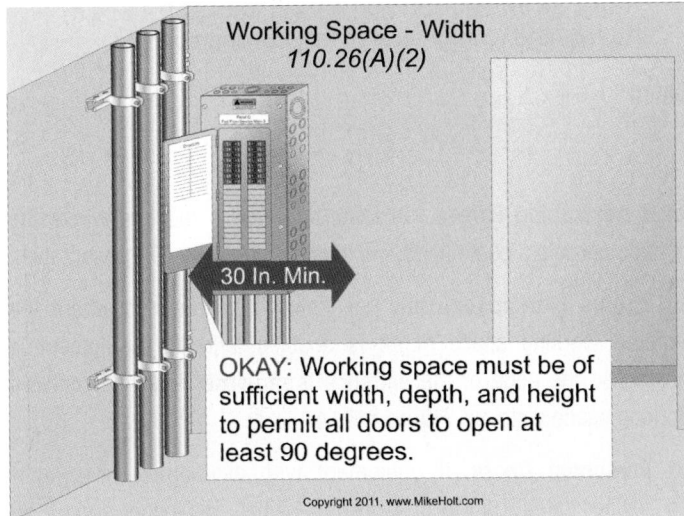

Figure 110–41

(3) Height of Working Space (Headroom). The height of the working space in front of equipment must not be less than 6½ ft, measured from the grade, floor, platform, or the equipment height, whichever is greater. Figure 110–42

Equipment such as raceways, cables, wireways, cabinets, panels, and so on, can be located above or below electrical equipment, but must not extend more than 6 in. into the equipment's working space. Figure 110–43

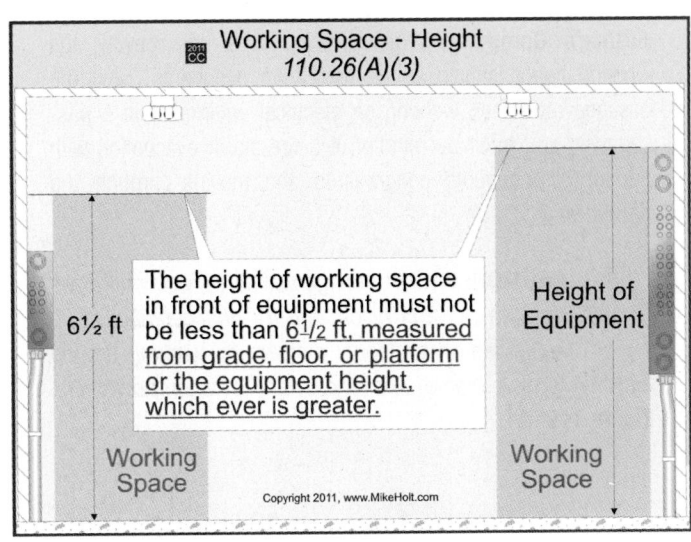

Figure 110–42

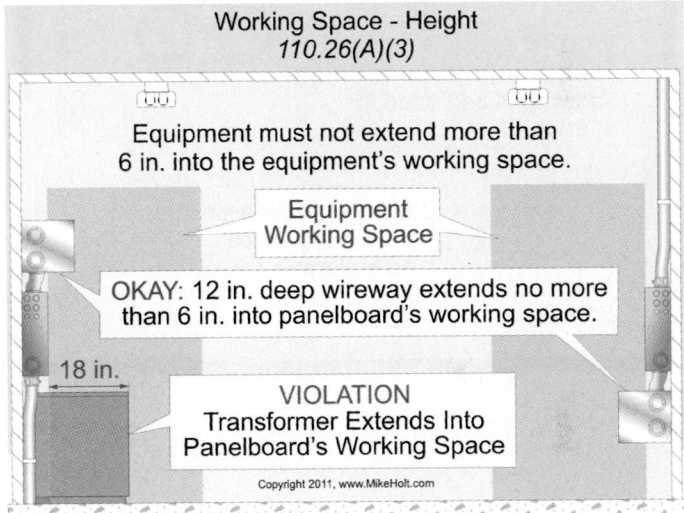

Figure 110–43

Ex 1: The minimum headroom requirement doesn't apply to service equipment or panelboards rated 200A or less located in an existing dwelling unit.

Author's Comment: See the definition of "Dwelling Unit" in Article 100.

Ex 2: Meters are permitted to extend beyond the other equipment.

(B) Clear Working Space. The working space required by this section must be clear at all times. Therefore, this space isn't permitted for storage. When normally enclosed live parts are exposed for inspection or servicing, the working space, if in a passageway or general open space, must be suitably guarded.

Author's Comment: When working in a passageway, the working space should be guarded from occupants using the passageway. When working on electrical equipment in a passageway one must be mindful of a fire alarm evacuation with numerous occupants congregated and moving through the passageway.

⚠ **CAUTION:** *It's very dangerous to service energized parts in the first place, and it's unacceptable to be subjected to additional dangers by working around bicycles, boxes, crates, appliances, and other impediments.* **Figure 110–44**

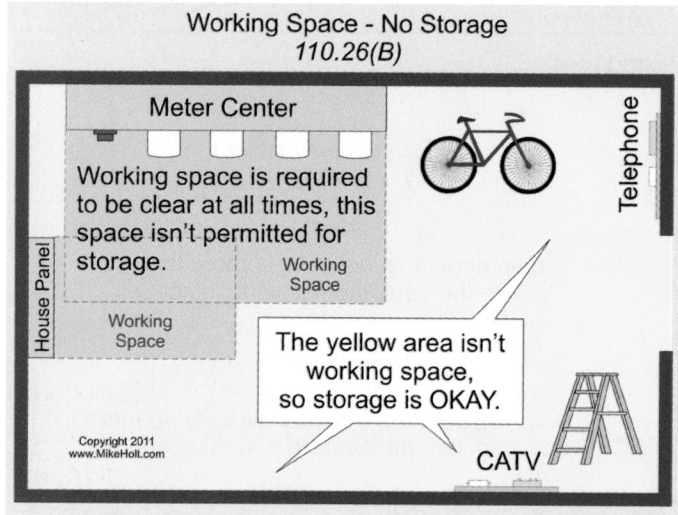

Figure 110–44

Author's Comment: Signaling and communications equipment must not be installed in a manner that encroaches on the working space of the electrical equipment.

(C) Entrance to and Egress from Working Space.

(1) Minimum Required. At least one entrance of sufficient area must provide access to and egress from the working space.

Author's Comment: Check to see what the authority having jurisdiction considers "Sufficient Area." Building codes contain minimum dimensions for doors and openings for personnel travel.

(2) Large Equipment. An entrance to and egress from each end of the working space of electrical equipment rated 1,200A or more that's over 6 ft wide is required. The opening must be a minimum of 24 in. wide and 6½ ft high. **Figure 110–45.** A single entrance to and egress from the required working space is permitted where either of the following conditions is met:

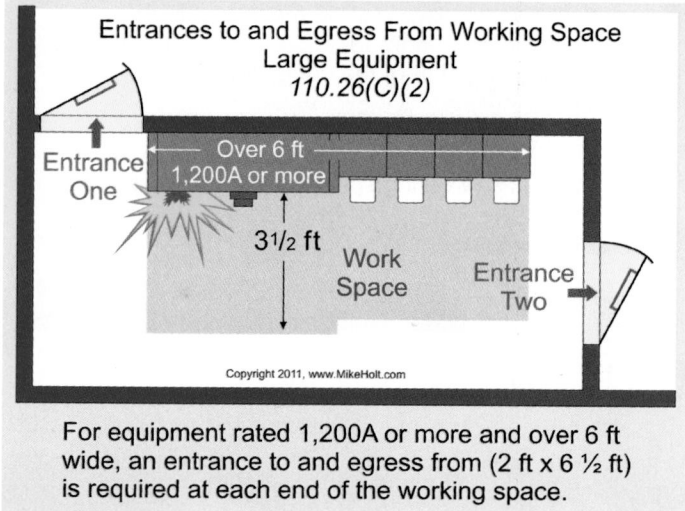

For equipment rated 1,200A or more and over 6 ft wide, an entrance to and egress from (2 ft x 6 ½ ft) is required at each end of the working space.

Figure 110–45

(a) Unobstructed Egress. Only one entrance is required where the location permits a continuous and unobstructed way of egress travel.

(b) Double Workspace. Only one entrance is required where the required working space depth is doubled, and the equipment is located so the edge of the entrance is no closer than the required working space distance. **Figure 110–46**

(3) Personnel Doors. If equipment with overcurrent or switching devices rated 1,200A or more is installed, personnel door(s) for entrance to and egress from the working space located less than 25 ft from the nearest edge of the working space must have the door(s) open in the direction of egress and be equipped with panic hardware or other devices that open under simple pressure. **Figure 110–47**

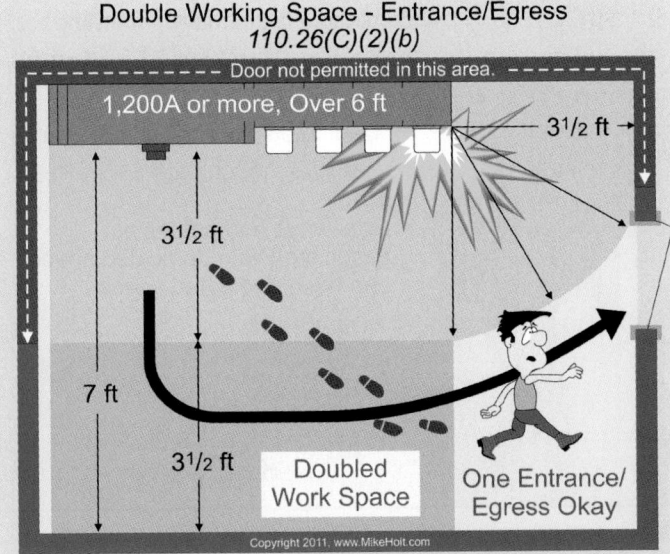

Double Working Space - Entrance/Egress
110.26(C)(2)(b)

One entrance/egress is permitted where the required working space is doubled, and equipment is located so the edge of the entrance is no closer than the required working space distance.

Figure 110–46

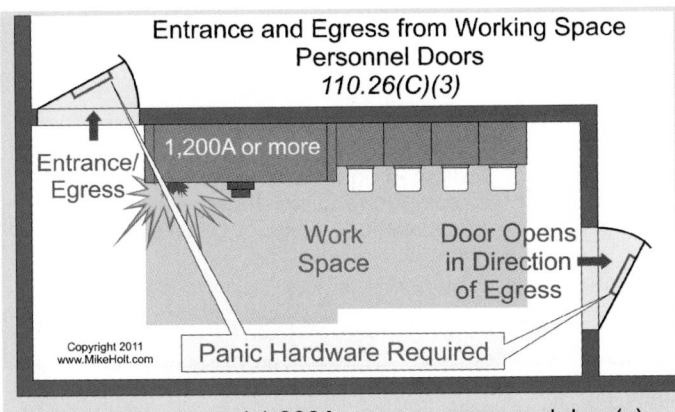

Entrance and Egress from Working Space Personnel Doors
110.26(C)(3)

For equipment rated 1,200A or more, personnel door(s) located less than 25 ft from the nearest edge of working space must open in the direction of egress and have panic hardware or devices that open under simple pressure.

Figure 110–47

Author's Comments:

- History has shown that electricians who suffer burns on their hands in electrical arc flash or arc blast events often can't open doors equipped with knobs that must be turned.

- Since this requirement is in the *NEC*, the electrical contractor is responsible for ensuring that panic hardware is installed where required. Some electrical contractors are offended at being held liable for nonelectrical responsibilities, but this rule is designed to save the lives of electricians. For this and other reasons, many construction professionals routinely hold "pre-construction" or "pre-con" meetings to review potential opportunities for miscommunication—before the work begins.

(D) Illumination. Service equipment, switchboards, panelboards, as well as motor control centers located indoors must have illumination located indoors and must not be controlled by automatic means only. Figure 110–48

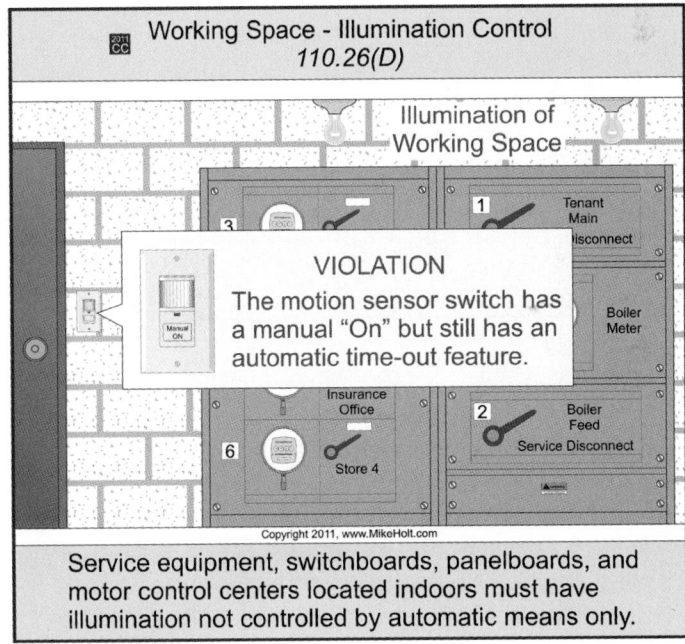

Working Space - Illumination Control
110.26(D)

Service equipment, switchboards, panelboards, and motor control centers located indoors must have illumination not controlled by automatic means only.

Figure 110–48

Author's Comment: The *Code* doesn't provide the minimum foot-candles required to provide proper illumination. Proper illumination of electrical equipment rooms is essential for the safety of those qualified to work on such equipment.

(E) Dedicated Equipment Space. Switchboards, panelboards, and motor control centers must have dedicated equipment space as follows:

(1) Indoors.

(a) Dedicated Electrical Space. The footprint space (width and depth of the equipment) extending from the floor to a height of 6 ft above the equipment or to the structural ceiling, whichever is lower, must be dedicated for the electrical installation. No piping, ducts, or other equipment foreign to the electrical installation can be installed in this dedicated footprint space. **Figure 110–49**

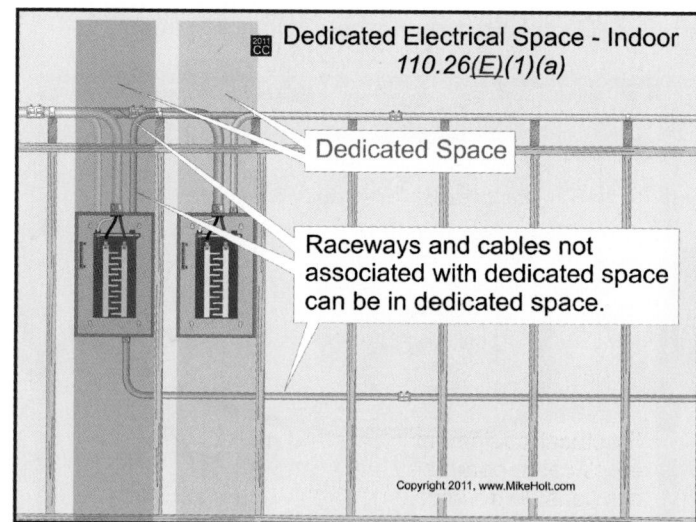

Figure 110–50

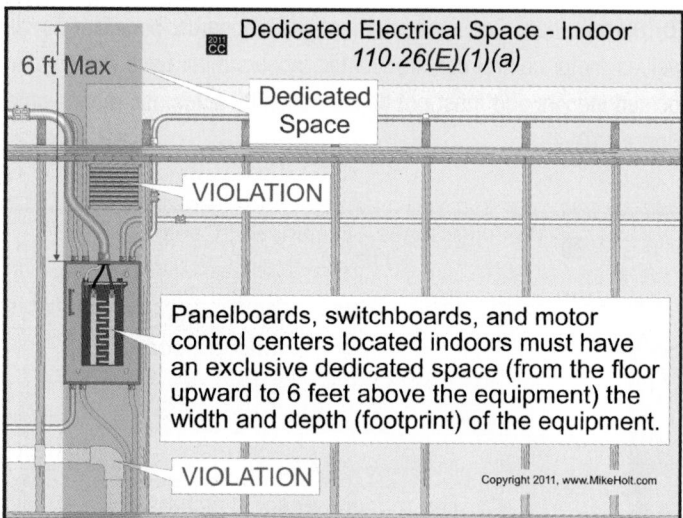

Figure 110–49

Ex: Suspended ceilings with removable panels can be within the dedicated footprint space [110.26(E)(1)(d)].

> **Author's Comment:** Electrical raceways and cables not associated with the dedicated space can be within the dedicated space. These aren't considered "equipment foreign to the electrical installation." **Figure 110–50**

(b) Foreign Systems. Foreign systems can be located above the dedicated space if protection is installed to prevent damage to the electrical equipment from condensation, leaks, or breaks in the foreign systems, which can be as simple as a drip-pan. **Figure 110–51**

(c) Sprinkler Protection. Sprinkler protection piping isn't permitted in the dedicated space, but the *NEC* doesn't prohibit sprinklers from spraying water on electrical equipment.

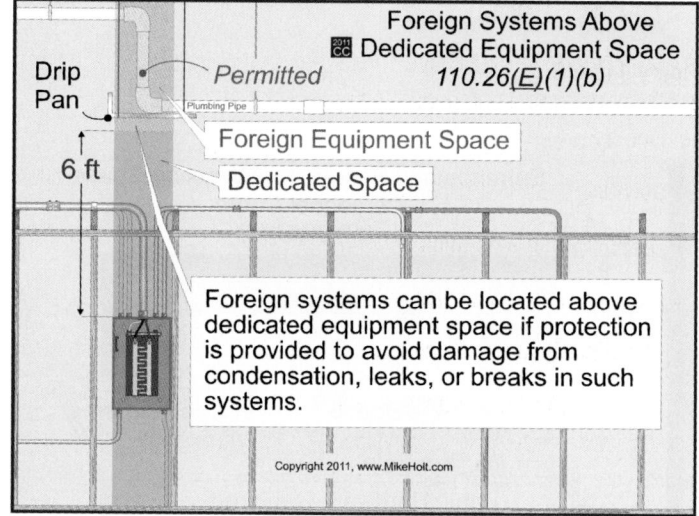

Figure 110–51

(d) Suspended Ceilings. A dropped, suspended, or similar ceiling isn't considered a structural ceiling.

(F) Locked Electrical Equipment Rooms or Enclosures. Electrical equipment rooms and enclosures housing electrical equipment can be controlled by locks because they are still considered to be accessible to qualified persons who require access. **Figure 110–52**

> **Author's Comment:** See the definition of "Accessible as it applies to equipment" in Article 100.

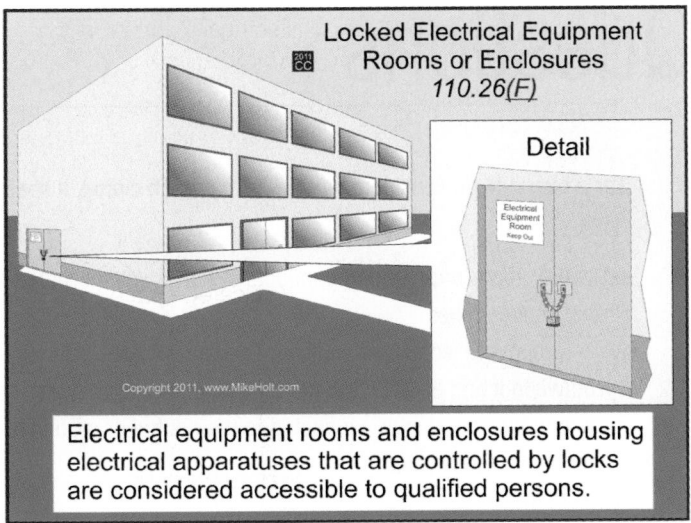

Figure 110–52

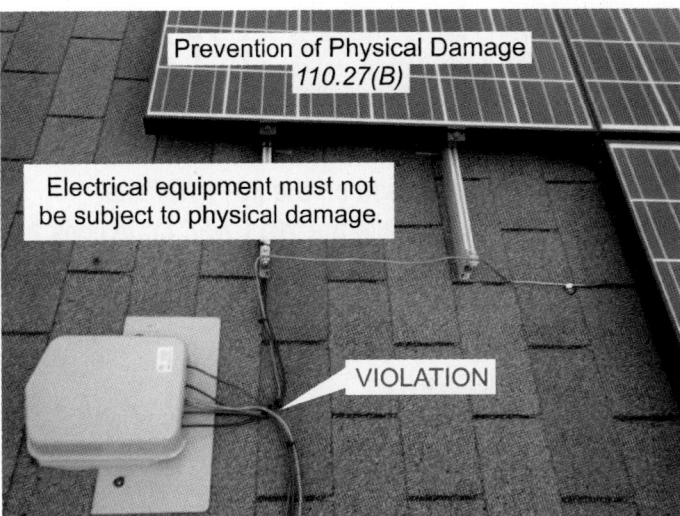

Figure 110–53

110.27 Guarding.

(A) Guarding Live Parts. Live parts of electrical equipment operating at 50V or more must be guarded against accidental contact. This can be done by:

(1) Locating them in a separate room, vault, or enclosure.

(2) Guarding with a partition or screen.

(3) Locating them on a balcony or platform.

(4) Elevating them 8 ft or more above the floor or working surface.

(B) Prevent Physical Damage. Electrical equipment must not be installed where subject to physical damage, unless enclosures or guards are arranged and they are of sufficient strength to prevent damage. **Figure 110–53**

(C) Warning Signs. Entrances to rooms and other guarded locations containing exposed live parts must be marked with conspicuous signs forbidding unqualified persons from entering.

110.28 Enclosure Types. Enclosures must be marked with an enclosure-type number and be suitable for the location in accordance with Table 110.28.

The enclosures aren't intended to protect against condensation, icing, corrosion, or contamination that might occur within the enclosure or that enters via the raceway or unsealed openings.

> **Note:** Raintight enclosures include Types 3, 3S, 3SX, 3X, 4, 4X, 6, and 6P; rainproof enclosures are Types 3R, and 3RX; watertight enclosures are Types 4, 4X, 6, and 6P; driptight enclosures are Types 2, 5, 12, 12K, and 13; and dusttight enclosures are Types 3, 3S, 3SX, 3X, 5, 12, 12K, and 13.

These questions are based on the 2011 *National Electrical Code*. Please use the 2011 *NEC Code* book to answer the following questions.

CHAPTER 1. GENERAL

Article 100. Definitions

1. Capable of being reached quickly for operation, renewal, or inspections without resorting to portable ladders and such is known as _____.

    (a) accessible (as applied to equipment)
    (b) accessible (as applied to wiring methods)
    (c) accessible, readily
    (d) all of these

2. "_____" means acceptable to the authority having jurisdiction.

    (a) Identified
    (b) Listed
    (c) Approved
    (d) Labeled

3. Where no statutory requirement exists, the authority having jurisdiction can be a property owner or his/her agent, such as an architect or engineer.

    (a) True
    (b) False

4. The conductors between the final overcurrent device protecting the circuit and the outlet(s) are known as "_____ conductors."

    (a) feeder
    (b) branch-circuit
    (c) home run
    (d) none of these

5. For a circuit to be considered a multiwire branch circuit, it shall have _____.

    (a) two or more ungrounded conductors with a voltage potential between them
    (b) a grounded conductor having equal voltage potential between it and each ungrounded conductor of the circuit
    (c) a grounded conductor connected to the neutral or grounded terminal of the system
    (d) all of these

6. A load is considered to be continuous if the maximum current is expected to continue for _____ or more.

    (a) one-half hour
    (b) 1 hour
    (c) 2 hours
    (d) 3 hours

7. A _____ is a single unit that provides independent living facilities for persons, including permanent provisions for living, sleeping, cooking, and sanitation.

    (a) one-family dwelling
    (b) two-family dwelling
    (c) dwelling unit
    (d) multifamily dwelling

8. The *NEC* defines a "_____" as all circuit conductors between the service equipment, the source of a separately derived system, or other power-supply source and the final branch-circuit overcurrent device.

    (a) service
    (b) feeder
    (c) branch circuit
    (d) all of these

9. A device intended for the protection of personnel that functions to de-energize a circuit or portion thereof within an established period of time when the current to ground exceeds the values established for a Class A device, is a(n) "_____."

   (a) dual-element fuse
   (b) inverse time breaker
   (c) ground-fault circuit interrupter
   (d) safety switch

10. A Class A GFCI protection device is designed to trip when the ground-fault current to ground is _____ or higher.

    (a) 4 mA
    (b) 5 mA
    (c) 6 mA
    (d) none of these

11. Recognized as suitable for the specific purpose, function, use, environment, and application is the definition of "_____."

    (a) labeled
    (b) identified (as applied to equipment)
    (c) listed
    (d) approved

12. Within sight means visible and not more than _____ ft distant from the equipment.

    (a) 10
    (b) 20
    (c) 25
    (d) 50

13. Equipment or materials to which a symbol or other identifying mark of a product evaluation organization that is acceptable to the authority having jurisdiction has been attached is known as "_____."

    (a) listed
    (b) labeled
    (c) approved
    (d) identified

14. Equipment or materials included in a list published by a testing laboratory acceptable to the authority having jurisdiction is said to be "_____."

    (a) book
    (b) digest
    (c) manifest
    (d) listed

15. Conduit installed underground or encased in concrete slabs that are in direct contact with the earth is considered a _____ location.

    (a) dry
    (b) damp
    (c) wet
    (d) moist

16. A single receptacle is a single contact device with no other contact device on the same _____.

    (a) circuit
    (b) yoke
    (c) run
    (d) equipment

17. An opening in an outlet box where one or more receptacles have been installed is called "_____."

    (a) a device
    (b) equipment
    (c) a receptacle
    (d) a receptacle outlet

18. The _____ is the necessary equipment, usually consisting of a circuit breaker(s) or switch(es) and fuse(s) and their accessories, connected to the load end of service conductors, and intended to constitute the main control and cutoff of the supply.

    (a) service equipment
    (b) service
    (c) service disconnect
    (d) service overcurrent device

19. Special permission is the written consent from the _____.

    (a) testing laboratory
    (b) manufacturer
    (c) owner
    (d) authority having jurisdiction

Article 110. Requirements for Electrical Installations

1. In judging equipment for approval, considerations such as the following shall be evaluated:

    (a) mechanical strength
    (b) wire-bending space
    (c) arcing effects
    (d) all of these

2. Conductors shall be _____ unless otherwise provided.

    (a) bare
    (b) stranded
    (c) of copper
    (d) of aluminum

3. Unless identified for use in the operating environment, no conductors or equipment shall be _____ having a deteriorating effect on the conductors or equipment.

    (a) located in damp or wet locations
    (b) exposed to fumes, vapors, liquids or gases
    (c) exposed to excessive temperatures
    (d) all of these

4. Unused openings other than those intended for the operation of equipment, intended for mounting purposes, or permitted as part of the design for listed equipment shall be _____.

    (a) filled with cable clamps or connectors only
    (b) taped over with electrical tape
    (c) repaired only by welding or brazing in a metal slug
    (d) effectively closed to afford protection substantially equivalent to the wall of the equipment

5. Connection by means of wire-binding screws, studs, or nuts having upturned lugs or the equivalent shall be permitted for _____ or smaller conductors.

    (a) 12 AWG
    (b) 10 AWG
    (c) 8 AWG
    (d) 6 AWG

6. Separately installed pressure connectors shall be used with conductors at the _____ not exceeding the ampacity at the listed and identified temperature rating of the connector.

    (a) voltages
    (b) temperatures
    (c) listings
    (d) ampacities

7. Concrete, brick, or tile walls are considered _____, as applied to working space requirements.

    (a) inconsequential
    (b) in the way
    (c) grounded
    (d) none of these

8. The minimum height of working spaces about electrical equipment, switchboards, panelboards, or motor control centers operating at 600V, nominal, or less and likely to require examination, adjustment, servicing, or maintenance while energized shall be 6½ ft or the height of the equipment, whichever is greater, except for service equipment or panelboards in existing dwelling units that do not exceed 200A.

    (a) True
    (b) False

9. All switchboards, panelboards, and motor control centers shall be _____.

    (a) located in dedicated spaces
    (b) protected from damage
    (c) in weatherproof enclosures
    (d) a and b

10. In locations where electrical equipment is likely to be exposed to _____, enclosures or guards shall be so arranged and of such strength as to prevent such damage.

(a) corrosion
(b) physical damage
(c) magnetic fields
(d) weather

Notes

CHAPTER 2

WIRING AND PROTECTION

INTRODUCTION TO CHAPTER 2—WIRING AND PROTECTION

Chapter 2 provides general rules for wiring and the protection of conductors. The rules in this chapter apply to all electrical installations covered by the *NEC*—except as modified in Chapters 5, 6, and 7 [90.3].

Communications Systems (Chapter 8 systems) aren't subject to the general requirements of Chapters 1 through 4, or the special requirements of Chapters 5 through 7, unless there's a specific reference in Chapter 8 to a rule in Chapters 1 through 7 [90.3].

As you go through Chapter 2, remember its purpose. Chapter 2 is primarily concerned with correctly sizing and protecting circuits. Every article in Chapter 2 deals with a different aspect of this purpose. This differs from the purpose of Chapter 3, which is to correctly install the conductors that make up those circuits.

Chapter 1 introduced you to the *NEC* and provided a solid foundation for understanding the *Code*. Chapters 2 (Wiring and Protection) and 3 (Wiring Methods and Materials) continue building the foundation for applying the *NEC*. Chapter 4 applies the preceding chapters to general equipment. It's beneficial to learn the first four chapters of the *Code* in a sequential manner because each of the first four chapters builds on the preceding chapter. Once you've mastered the first four chapters, you can learn the next four in any order you wish.

- **Article 200—Use and Identification of Grounded Conductors.** This article contains the requirements for the use and identification of the neutral conductor and its terminals.

  Author's Comment: Because the neutral conductor of a solidly grounded system is connected to the earth, it's both a "grounded conductor" and a "neutral conductor." To make it easier for the reader of this textbook, we'll refer to the "grounded conductor" as the "neutral conductor."

- **Article 210—Branch Circuits.** Article 210 contains the requirements for branch circuits, such as conductor sizing, identification, GFCI protection, as well as receptacle and lighting outlet requirements.

- **Article 215—Feeders.** This article covers the requirements for the installation, minimum size, and ampacity of feeders.

- **Article 220—Branch-Circuit, Feeder, and Service Calculations.** Article 220 provides the requirements for calculating the minimum size for branch circuits, feeders, and services. This article also aids in determining related factors such as the number of receptacles on a circuit in nondwelling installations, and the minimum number of branch circuits required.

- **Article 225—Outside Branch Circuits and Feeders.** This article covers the installation requirements for equipment, including conductors located outside that run on or between buildings, poles, and other structures on the premises.

- **Article 230—Services.** Article 230 covers the installation requirements for service conductors and equipment. It's very important to know where the service begins and ends when applying Article 230.

Author's Comment: Conductors from a battery, uninterruptible power supply, solar photovoltaic system, generator, or transformer aren't considered service conductors; they're feeder conductors.

- **Article 240—Overcurrent Protection.** This article provides the requirements for overcurrent protection and overcurrent devices. Overcurrent protection for conductors and equipment is provided to open the circuit if the current reaches a value that will cause an excessive or dangerous temperature on the conductors or conductor insulation.

- **Article 250—Grounding and Bonding.** Article 250 covers the grounding requirements for providing a low-impedance path to the earth to reduce overvoltage from lightning, and the bonding requirements for a low-impedance fault current path necessary to facilitate the operation of overcurrent devices in the event of a ground fault.

- **Article 285—Surge Protective Devices (SPDs).** This article covers the general requirements, installation requirements, and connection requirements for surge protective devices (SPDs) permanently installed on both the line side and load side of service equipment.

Use and Identification of Grounded Conductors

INTRODUCTION TO ARTICLE 200—USE AND IDENTIFICATION OF GROUNDED CONDUCTORS

This article contains the requirements for the identification of the grounded conductor and its terminals. Article 100 contains definitions for both "Grounded Conductor" and "Neutral Conductor." In some cases, both of these terms apply to the same conductor. **Figures 200–1 and 200–2**

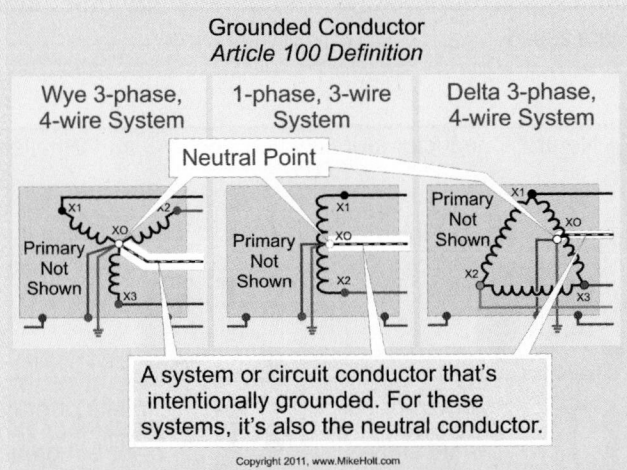

Grounded Conductor
Article 100 Definition

Wye 3-phase, 4-wire System | 1-phase, 3-wire System | Delta 3-phase, 4-wire System

Neutral Point

A system or circuit conductor that's intentionally grounded. For these systems, it's also the neutral conductor.

Copyright 2011, www.MikeHolt.com

Figure 200–1

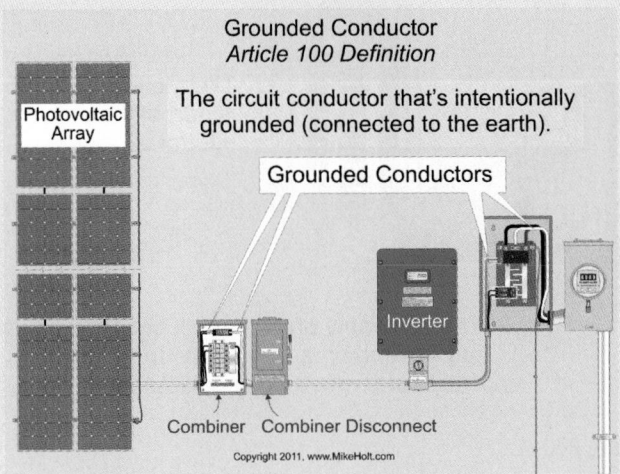

Grounded Conductor
Article 100 Definition

The circuit conductor that's intentionally grounded (connected to the earth).

Grounded Conductors

Photovoltaic Array

Inverter

Combiner   Combiner Disconnect

Copyright 2011, www.MikeHolt.com

Figure 200–2

In a system that produces direct-current, such as a photovoltaic system, the "grounded conductor" is not a neutral conductor. **Figure 200–3**

Author's Comment: Throughout this book, we will use the term "neutral" when referring to the grounded conductor when the application is not related to PV systems or corner-grounded delta-connected systems.

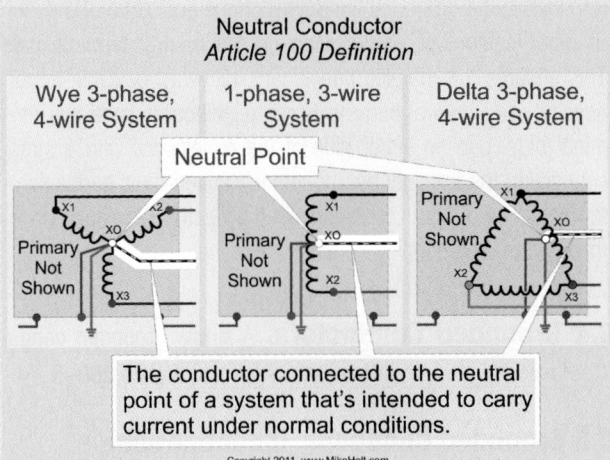

Neutral Conductor
Article 100 Definition

Wye 3-phase, 4-wire System | 1-phase, 3-wire System | Delta 3-phase, 4-wire System

Neutral Point

The conductor connected to the neutral point of a system that's intended to carry current under normal conditions.

Copyright 2011, www.MikeHolt.com

Figure 200–3

PART I. GENERAL

200.1 Scope. Article 200 contains requirements for the use and identification of grounded conductors and terminals.

200.2 General.

(B) Continuity. The continuity of the grounded conductor isn't permitted to be dependent on metal enclosures, raceways, or cable armor. **Figure 200–4**

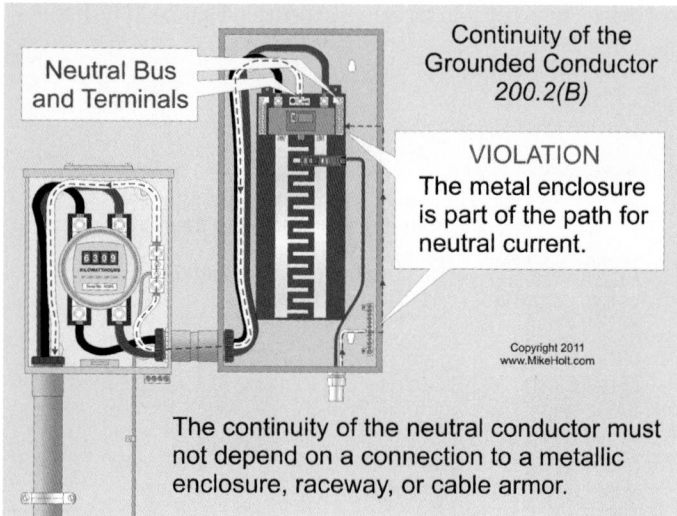

Continuity of the Grounded Conductor
200.2(B)

VIOLATION
The metal enclosure is part of the path for neutral current.

Neutral Bus and Terminals

Copyright 2011
www.MikeHolt.com

The continuity of the neutral conductor must not depend on a connection to a metallic enclosure, raceway, or cable armor.

Figure 200–4

Author's Comment: This requirement prohibits the practice of terminating the grounded conductor on the enclosure of a panel or other equipment, rather than on the neutral terminal bar. This ensures the metallic panelboard, raceway, or cable armor doesn't carry neutral current. Some panelboards have two terminal bars, one on either side of the panelboard with a strap connecting the terminal bars together. Caution must be taken to terminate the neutral conductor to the neutral terminal, not to the equipment grounding conductor terminal.

200.4 Grounded Conductors. A single grounded conductor can't be used for more than one branch circuit. **Figure 200–5**

200.6 Grounded Conductor Identification.

(A) Size 6 AWG or Smaller. Grounded conductors 6 AWG and smaller must be identified by one of the following means: **Figure 200–6**

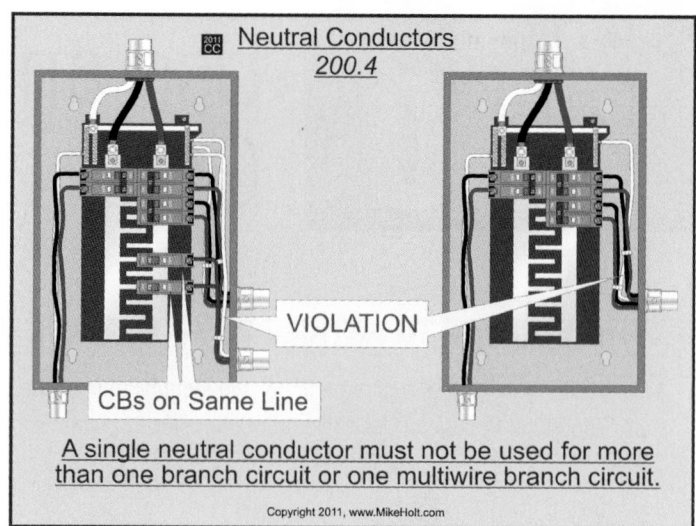

Neutral Conductors
200.4

VIOLATION

CBs on Same Line

A single neutral conductor must not be used for more than one branch circuit or one multiwire branch circuit.

Copyright 2011, www.MikeHolt.com

Figure 200–5

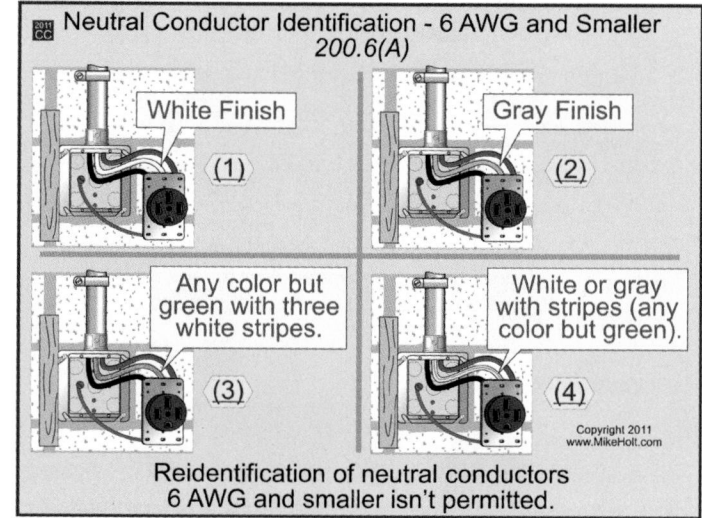

Neutral Conductor Identification - 6 AWG and Smaller
200.6(A)

White Finish (1)

Gray Finish (2)

Any color but green with three white stripes. (3)

White or gray with stripes (any color but green). (4)

Copyright 2011
www.MikeHolt.com

Reidentification of neutral conductors 6 AWG and smaller isn't permitted.

Figure 200–6

(1) By a continuous white outer finish.

(2) By a continuous gray outer finish.

(3) By three continuous white stripes along its entire length on other than green insulation.

(4) Wires that have their outer covering finished to show a white or gray color but have colored tracer threads in the braid identifying the source of manufacture are considered to meet the provisions of this section.

Author's Comment: The use of white tape, paint, or other methods of identification isn't permitted for grounded conductors 6 AWG or smaller. **Figure 200–7**

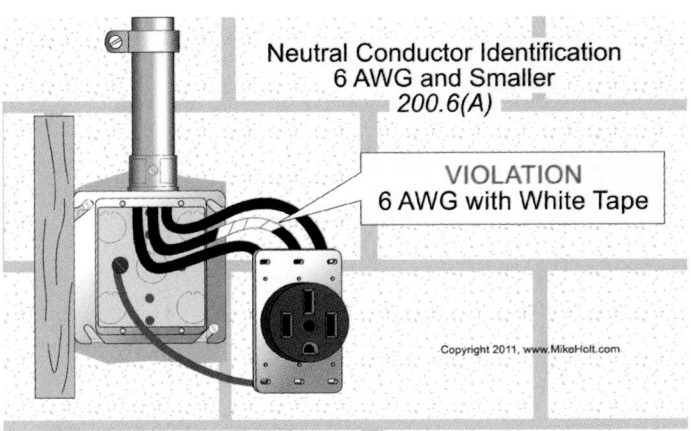

Figure 200–7 caption (in figure):
Neutral Conductor Identification
6 AWG and Smaller
200.6(A)

VIOLATION
6 AWG with White Tape

Copyright 2011, www.MikeHolt.com

White tape, paint, or other methods of identification aren't permitted for neutral conductors 6 AWG or smaller.

Figure 200–7

(6) A single-conductor, sunlight-resistant, outdoor-rated cable used as the grounded conductor in photovoltaic power systems as permitted by 690.31(B) can be identified by distinctive white marking at all terminations. **Figure 200–8**

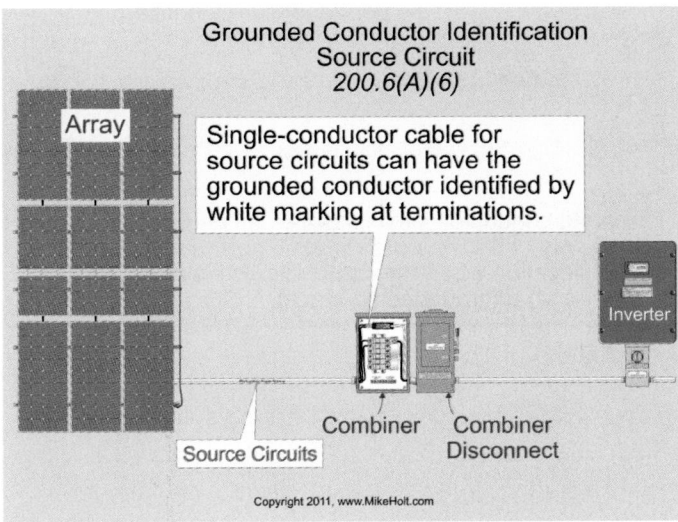

Figure 200–8 (in figure):
Grounded Conductor Identification
Source Circuit
200.6(A)(6)

Array

Single-conductor cable for source circuits can have the grounded conductor identified by white marking at terminations.

Inverter

Combiner   Combiner
Disconnect

Source Circuits

Copyright 2011, www.MikeHolt.com

Figure 200–8

(B) Size 4 AWG or Larger. Grounded conductors 4 AWG or larger must be identified by one of the following means: **Figure 200–9**

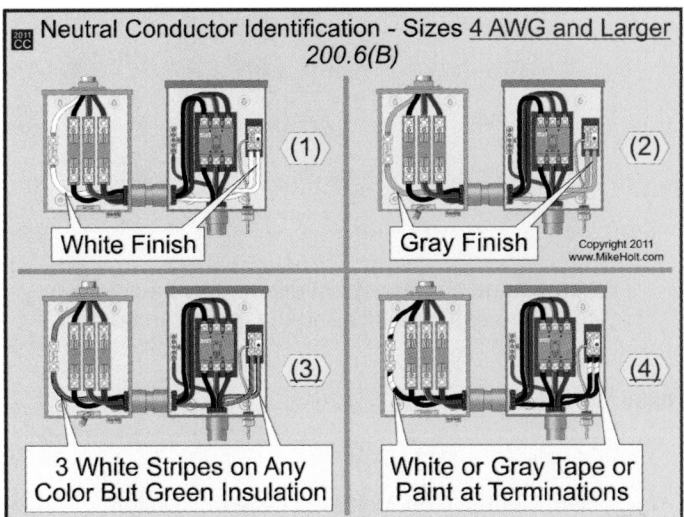

Figure 200–9 (in figure):
Neutral Conductor Identification - Sizes 4 AWG and Larger
200.6(B)

(1) White Finish
(2) Gray Finish
(3) 3 White Stripes on Any Color But Green Insulation
(4) White or Gray Tape or Paint at Terminations

Copyright 2011
www.MikeHolt.com

Figure 200–9

(1) A continuous white outer finish along its entire length.

(2) A continuous gray outer finish along its entire length.

(3) Three continuous white stripes along its length.

(4) White or gray tape or markings at the terminations.

(D) Grounded Conductors of Different Systems. If grounded conductors of different voltage systems are installed in the same raceway, cable, or enclosure, each system grounded conductor must be identified by:

(1) A continuous white or gray outer finish along its entire length. **Figure 200–10**

(2) The grounded conductor of the other system must have a different outer covering of continuous white or gray outer finish along its entire length or by an outer covering of white or gray with a readily distinguishable color stripe (other than green) along its entire length. **Figure 200–11**

(3) Other identification allowed by 200.6(A) or (B) that distinguishes the grounded conductor from other systems.

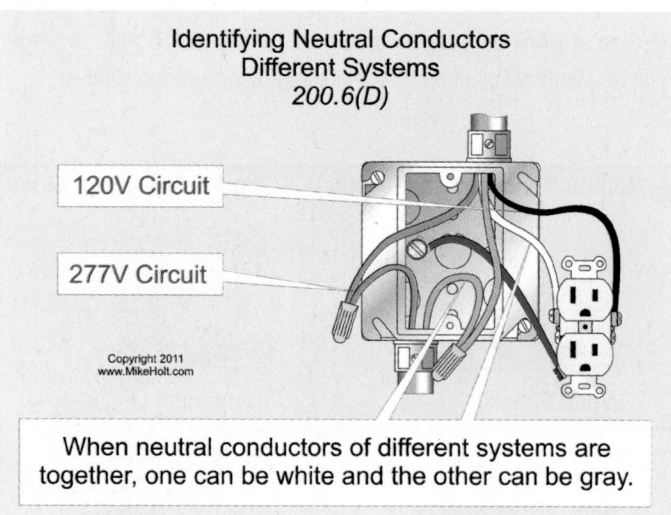

Identifying Neutral Conductors
Different Systems
200.6(D)

120V Circuit

277V Circuit

Copyright 2011
www.MikeHolt.com

When neutral conductors of different systems are together, one can be white and the other can be gray.

Figure 200–10

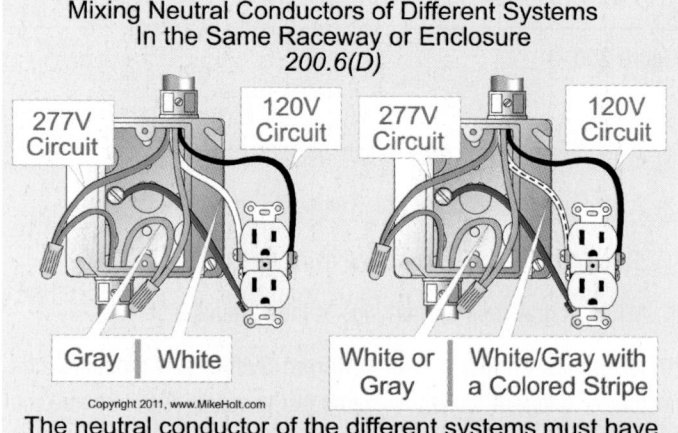

Mixing Neutral Conductors of Different Systems
In the Same Raceway or Enclosure
200.6(D)

277V Circuit | 120V Circuit | 277V Circuit | 120V Circuit

Gray | White | White or Gray | White/Gray with a Colored Stripe

Copyright 2011, www.MikeHolt.com

The neutral conductor of the different systems must have an outer covering of continuous white or gray finish along its entire length or by an outer covering of white or gray with a readily distinguishable colored stripe (other than green) along its entire length.

Figure 200–11

200.7 Use of White or Gray Color.

(C) Circuits of 50V or More. A conductor with white insulation can only be used for the ungrounded conductor as follows:

(1) Cable Assembly. The white conductor within a cable can be used for the ungrounded conductor, if permanently reidentified by marking tape, painting, or other effective means at each location where the conductor is visible to indicate its use as an ungrounded conductor. Identification must encircle the insulation and must be a color other than white, gray, or green. **Figure 200–12**

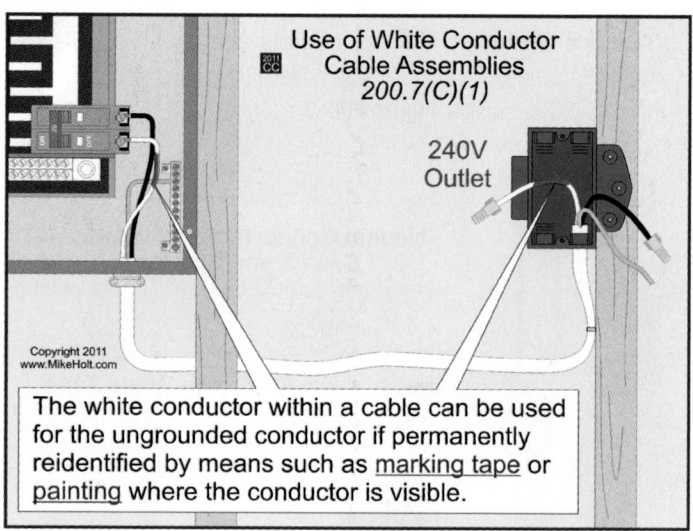

Use of White Conductor
Cable Assemblies
200.7(C)(1)

240V
Outlet

Copyright 2011
www.MikeHolt.com

The white conductor within a cable can be used for the ungrounded conductor if permanently reidentified by means such as marking tape or painting where the conductor is visible.

Figure 200–12

The white conductor within a cable can be used to supply power to single-pole, 3-way, and 4-way switch loops, as well as travelers for 3-way and 4-way switching if permanently reidentified at each location where the conductor is visible to indicate its use as an ungrounded conductor. **Figures 200–13 and 200–14**

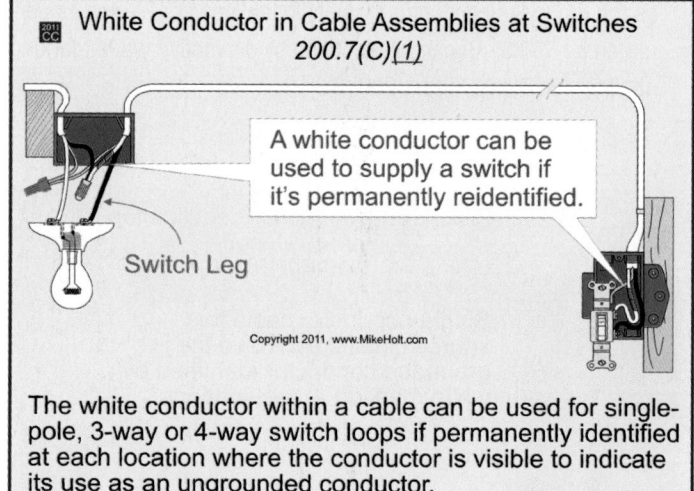

White Conductor in Cable Assemblies at Switches
200.7(C)(1)

A white conductor can be used to supply a switch if it's permanently reidentified.

Switch Leg

Copyright 2011, www.MikeHolt.com

The white conductor within a cable can be used for single-pole, 3-way or 4-way switch loops if permanently identified at each location where the conductor is visible to indicate its use as an ungrounded conductor.

Figure 200–13

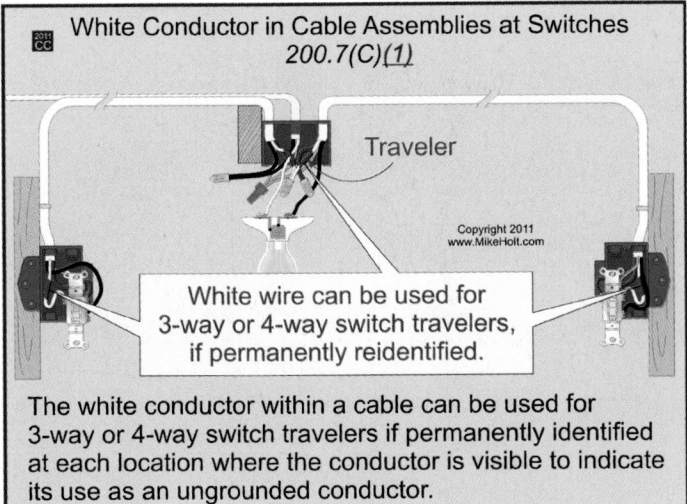

White Conductor in Cable Assemblies at Switches
200.7(C)(1)

Traveler

Copyright 2011
www.MikeHolt.com

White wire can be used for
3-way or 4-way switch travelers,
if permanently reidentified.

The white conductor within a cable can be used for
3-way or 4-way switch travelers if permanently identified
at each location where the conductor is visible to indicate
its use as an ungrounded conductor.

Figure 200–14

(2) Flexible Cord. The white conductor within a flexible cord can be used for the ungrounded conductor for connecting an appliance or equipment as permitted by 400.7.

Note: Care should be taken when working on existing systems because a gray insulated conductor may have been used in the past as an ungrounded conductor.

Author's Comment: The *NEC* doesn't permit the use of white or gray conductor insulation for ungrounded conductors in a raceway, even if the conductors are permanently reidentified. Figure 200–15

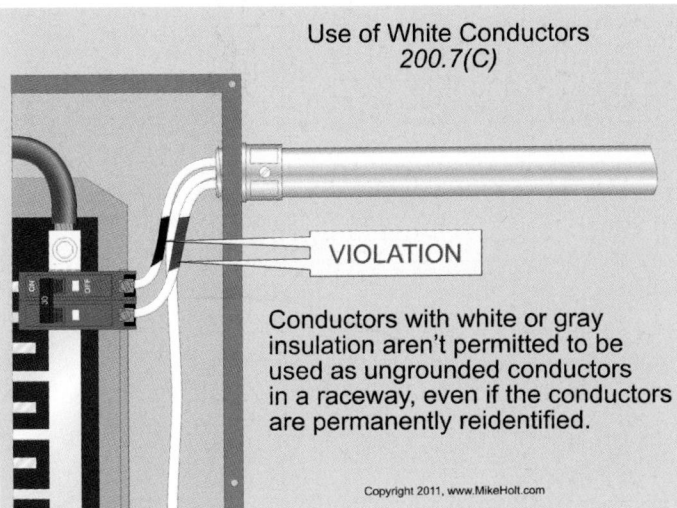

Use of White Conductors
200.7(C)

VIOLATION

Conductors with white or gray
insulation aren't permitted to be
used as ungrounded conductors
in a raceway, even if the conductors
are permanently reidentified.

Copyright 2011, www.MikeHolt.com

Figure 200–15

200.9 Terminal Identification. The terminal for the grounded conductor must be colored white (actually silver). The terminal for the ungrounded conductor must be a color readily distinguishable from white (brass or copper).

Author's Comment: Terminals for the circuit equipment grounding conductor must be green [250.126 and 406.10(B)].

200.10 Identification of Terminals.

(B) Receptacles, Plugs, and Connectors. Receptacles must have the terminal intended for connection to the grounded conductor identified by:

(1) A metal or metal coating that's substantially white in color or marked by the word white or the letter W.

(2) If the terminal isn't visible, the conductor entrance hole must be marked with the word white or the letter W.

(C) Screw Shell. To prevent electric shock, the screw shell of a luminaire or lampholder must be connected to the grounded conductor [410.90]. Figure 200–16

Screw-Shell Terminal Identification
200.10(C)

The neutral conductor must
be connected to the screw shell.

VIOLATION
Reverse Polarity

Correct polarity of a screw shell
keeps the screw shell threads
from being energized. This
reduces the chance of getting a
shock when replacing a lamp.
See 200.11.

Copyright 2011, www.MikeHolt.com

Figure 200–16

Author's Comment: See the definition of "Luminaire" in Article 100.

200.11 Polarity. A grounded conductor must not be connected to terminals or leads that will cause reversed polarity [410.50]. See Figure 200–16.

Notes

ARTICLE 210

Branch Circuits

INTRODUCTION TO ARTICLE 210—BRANCH CIRCUITS

This article contains the requirements for branch circuits, such as conductor sizing and identification, GFCI protection, and receptacle and lighting outlet requirements. It consists of three parts:

- Part I. General Provisions
- Part II. Branch-Circuit Ratings
- Part III. Required Outlets

Table 210.2 of this article identifies specific-purpose branch circuits. The provisions for branch circuits that supply equipment listed in Table 210.2 amend or supplement the provisions given in Article 210 for branch circuits, so it's important to be aware of the contents of this table.

The following sections contain a few key items on which to spend extra time as you study Article 210:

- **210.4—Multiwire Branch Circuits.** The conductors of these circuits must originate from the same panel.

- **210.8—GFCI Protection.** Crawl spaces, unfinished basements, and boathouses are just some of the many locations that require GFCI protection.

- **210.11—Branch Circuits Required.** With three subheadings, 210.11 gives summarized requirements for the number of branch circuits in certain situations, states that a load calculated on a VA per area basis must be evenly proportioned, and covers some minimum branch circuit rules for dwelling units.

- **210.12—Arc-Fault Circuit-Interrupter Protection.** An arc-fault circuit interrupter is a device intended to de-energize a circuit when it detects the current waveform characteristics unique to an arcing fault. The purpose of an AFCI is to protect against a fire hazard, whereas the purpose of a GFCI is to protect people against electrocution.

- **210.19—Conductors—Minimum Ampacity and Size.** This section covers the basic rules for sizing branch-circuit conductors, including continuous and noncontinuous loads.

- **210.21—Outlet Devices.** Outlet devices must have an ampere rating at least as large as the load to be served, as well as following the other rules of this section.

- **210.23—Permissible Loads.** This is intended to prevent a circuit overload from occurring because of improper design and planning of circuitry.

- **210.52—Dwelling Unit Receptacle Outlets.** There are some specific receptacle spacing rules and branch-circuit requirements for dwelling units that don't apply to other occupancies.

Mastering the branch-circuit requirements in Article 210 will give you a jump-start toward completing installations that are free of *Code* violations.

PART I. GENERAL PROVISIONS

210.1 Scope. Article 210 contains the requirements for conductor sizing, overcurrent protection, identification, and GFCI protection of branch circuits, as well as receptacle outlets and lighting outlet requirements.

> **Author's Comment:** Article 100 defines a "branch circuit" as the conductors between the final overcurrent device and the receptacle outlets, lighting outlets, or other outlets. **Figure 210–1**

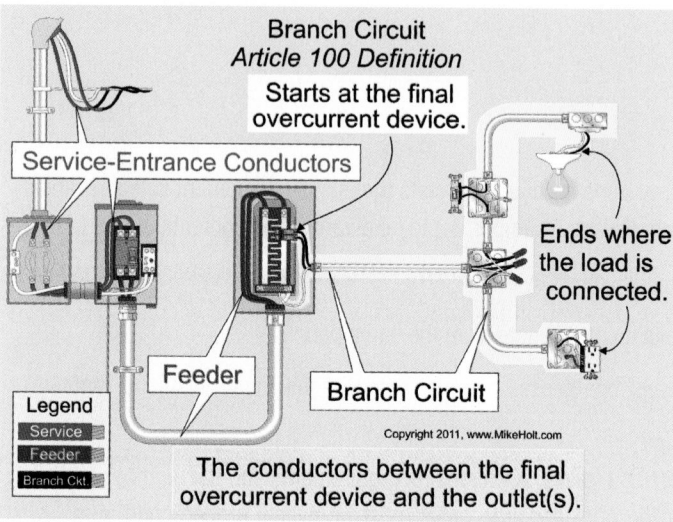

Figure 210–1

210.2 Other Articles. Other *NEC* sections that have specific requirements for branch circuits include:

- Air-Conditioning and Refrigeration, 440.6, 440.31, and 440.32
- Appliances, 422.10
- Data Processing (Information Technology) Equipment, 645.5
- Electric Space-Heating Equipment, 424.3(B)
- Generators, 445.20
- Motors, 430.22
- Signs, 600.5

210.3 Branch-Circuit Rating. The rating of a branch circuit is determined by the rating of the branch-circuit overcurrent device, not the conductor size.

> **Author's Comment:** For example, the branch-circuit ampere rating of a 10 THHN conductor on a 20A circuit breaker is 20A. **Figure 210–2**

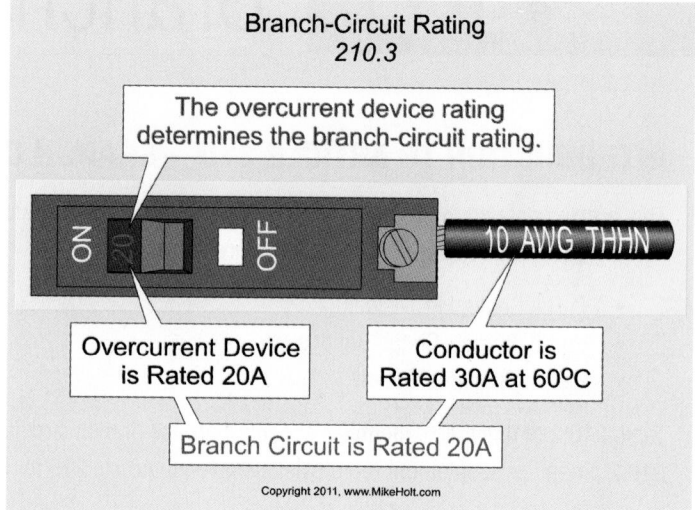

Figure 210–2

210.4 Multiwire Branch Circuits.

> **Author's Comment:** A multiwire branch circuit that consists of two or more ungrounded circuit conductors with a common neutral conductor. There must be a difference of potential (voltage) between the ungrounded conductors and an equal difference of potential (voltage) from each ungrounded conductor to the common neutral conductor. **Figure 210–3**

(A) General. A multiwire branch circuit can be considered a single circuit or a multiple circuit.

To prevent inductive heating and to reduce conductor impedance for fault currents, all conductors of a multiwire branch circuit must originate from the same panelboard.

> **Author's Comment:** For more information on the inductive heating of metal parts, see 300.3(B), 300.5(I), and 300.20.

> **Note:** Unwanted and potentially hazardous harmonic neutral currents can cause additional heating of the neutral conductor of a 4-wire, three-phase, 120/208V or 277/480V wye-connected system, which supplies nonlinear loads. To prevent fire or equipment damage from excessive harmonic neutral currents, the designer should consider: (1) increasing the size of the neutral conductor, or (2) installing a separate neutral for each phase. See 220.61(C)(2) and 310.15(B)(5)(c) in this textbook for additional information. **Figures 210–4 and 210–5**

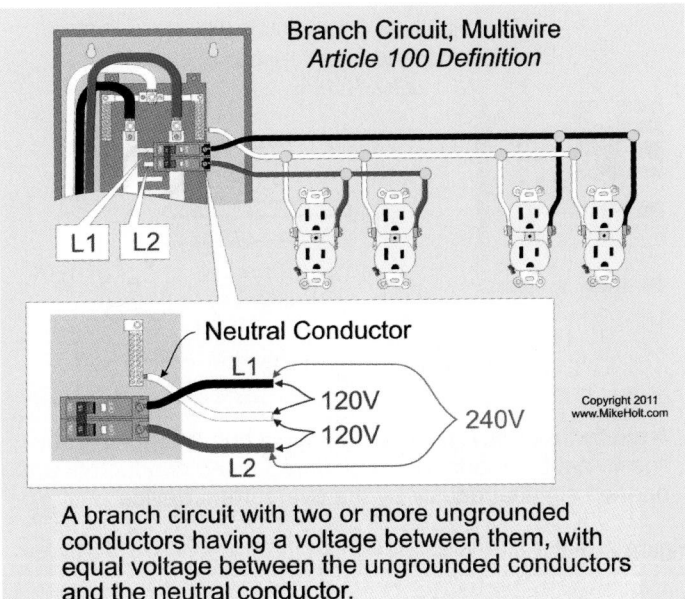

Branch Circuit, Multiwire
Article 100 Definition

Neutral Conductor

L1

120V
120V 240V

L2

Copyright 2011
www.MikeHolt.com

A branch circuit with two or more ungrounded conductors having a voltage between them, with equal voltage between the ungrounded conductors and the neutral conductor.

Figure 210–3

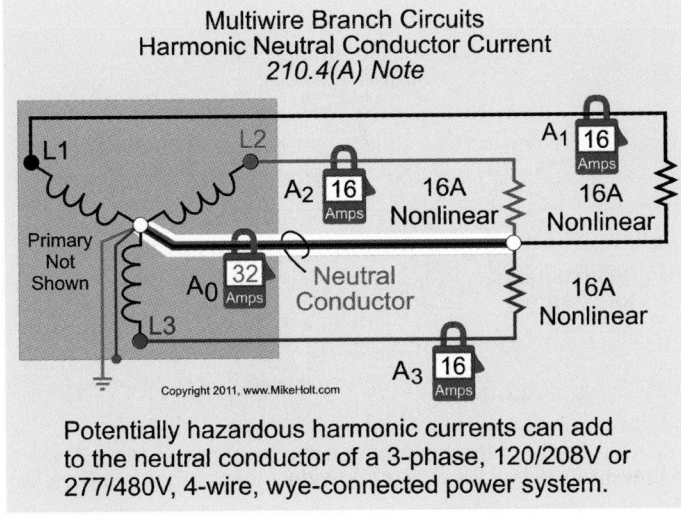

Multiwire Branch Circuits
Harmonic Neutral Conductor Current
210.4(A) Note

L1 L2 A₁ 16 Amps

A₂ 16 Amps 16A Nonlinear 16A Nonlinear

Primary Not Shown A₀ 32 Amps Neutral Conductor 16A Nonlinear

L3

A₃ 16 Amps

Copyright 2011, www.MikeHolt.com

Potentially hazardous harmonic currents can add to the neutral conductor of a 3-phase, 120/208V or 277/480V, 4-wire, wye-connected power system.

Figure 210–4

Author's Comments:

- See the definition of "Nonlinear Load" in Article 100.

- For more information, please visit www.MikeHolt.com. Click on "Technical Information" on the left side of the page, and then select "Power Quality."

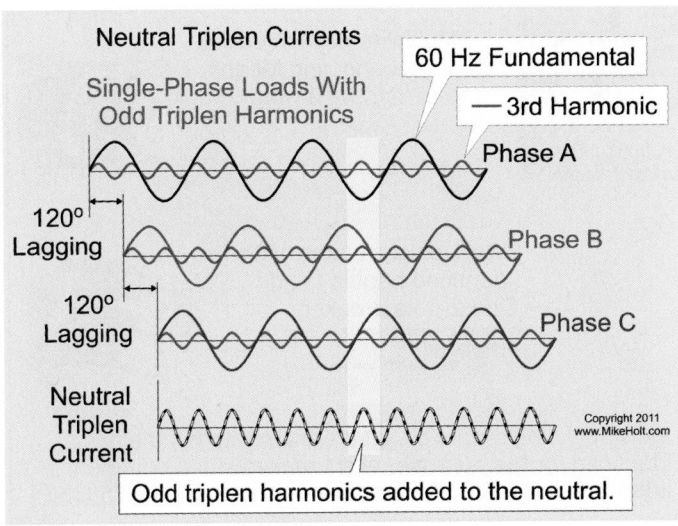

Neutral Triplen Currents

60 Hz Fundamental
3rd Harmonic

Single-Phase Loads With Odd Triplen Harmonics

Phase A

120° Lagging Phase B

120° Lagging Phase C

Neutral Triplen Current

Copyright 2011
www.MikeHolt.com

Odd triplen harmonics added to the neutral.

Figure 210–5

(B) Disconnecting Means. Each multiwire branch circuit must have a means to simultaneously disconnect all ungrounded conductors at the point where the branch circuit originates. **Figure 210–6**

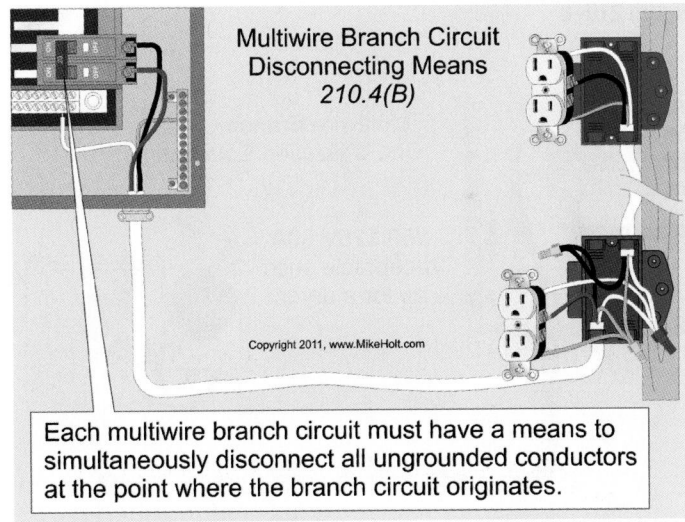

Multiwire Branch Circuit
Disconnecting Means
210.4(B)

Copyright 2011, www.MikeHolt.com

Each multiwire branch circuit must have a means to simultaneously disconnect all ungrounded conductors at the point where the branch circuit originates.

Figure 210–6

Note: Individual single-pole circuit breakers with handle ties identified for the purpose can be used for this application [240.15(B)(1)].
Figure 210–7

 CAUTION: *This rule is intended to prevent people from working on energized circuits they thought were disconnected.*

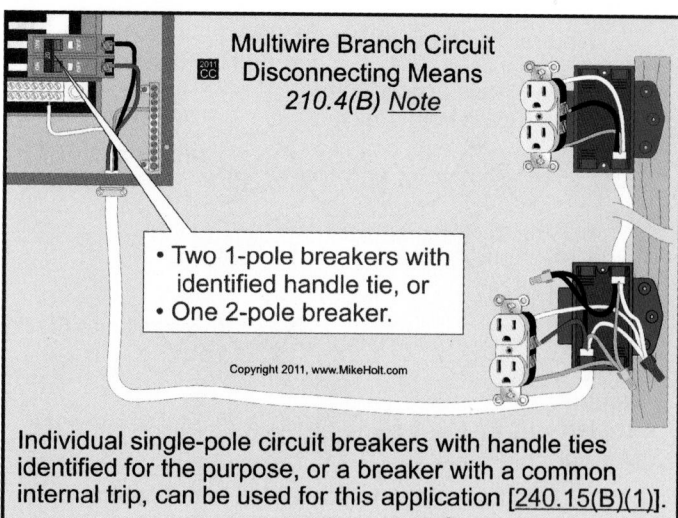

Multiwire Branch Circuit Disconnecting Means 210.4(B) Note

- Two 1-pole breakers with identified handle tie, or
- One 2-pole breaker.

Copyright 2011, www.MikeHolt.com

Individual single-pole circuit breakers with handle ties identified for the purpose, or a breaker with a common internal trip, can be used for this application [240.15(B)(1)].

Figure 210–7

(C) Line-to-Neutral Loads. Multiwire branch circuits must supply only line-to-neutral loads.

Ex 1: A multiwire branch circuit is permitted to supply an individual piece of line-to-line utilization equipment, such as a range or dryer. Figure 210–8

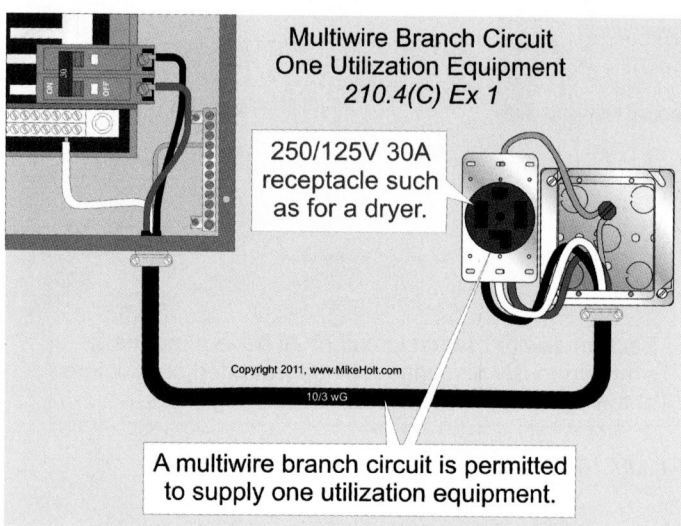

Multiwire Branch Circuit One Utilization Equipment 210.4(C) Ex 1

250/125V 30A receptacle such as for a dryer.

Copyright 2011, www.MikeHolt.com

10/3 wG

A multiwire branch circuit is permitted to supply one utilization equipment.

Figure 210–8

Ex 2: A multiwire branch circuit is permitted to supply both line-to-line and line-to-neutral loads if the circuit is protected by a device such as a multipole circuit breaker with a common internal trip that opens all ungrounded conductors of the multiwire branch circuit simultaneously under a fault condition. Figure 210–9

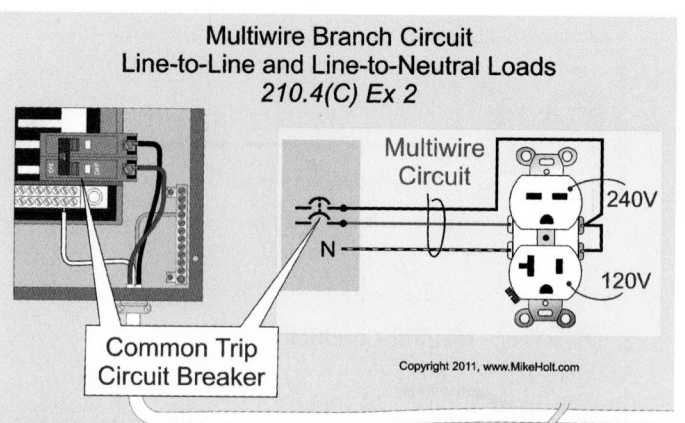

Multiwire Branch Circuit Line-to-Line and Line-to-Neutral Loads 210.4(C) Ex 2

Multiwire Circuit

240V

N

120V

Common Trip Circuit Breaker

Copyright 2011, www.MikeHolt.com

A multiwire branch circuit can supply both line-to-line and line-to-neutral loads where all ungrounded conductors are opened simultaneously by the overcurrent device.

Figure 210–9

Note: See 300.13(B) for the requirements relating to the continuity of the neutral conductor on multiwire branch circuits. **Figure 210–10**

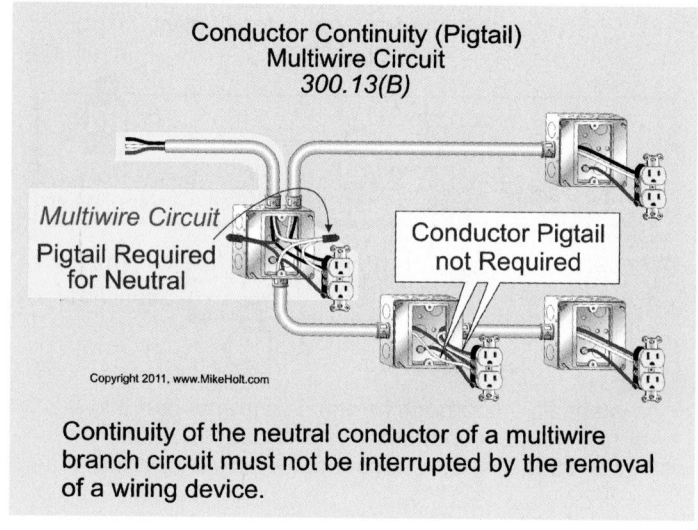

Conductor Continuity (Pigtail) Multiwire Circuit 300.13(B)

Multiwire Circuit

Pigtail Required for Neutral

Conductor Pigtail not Required

Copyright 2011, www.MikeHolt.com

Continuity of the neutral conductor of a multiwire branch circuit must not be interrupted by the removal of a wiring device.

Figure 210–10

⚠ **CAUTION:** *If the continuity of the neutral conductor of a multiwire circuit is interrupted (opened), the resultant over- or undervoltage can cause a fire and/ or destruction of electrical equipment. For details on how this occurs, see 300.13(B) in this textbook.* **Figures 210–11 and 210–12**

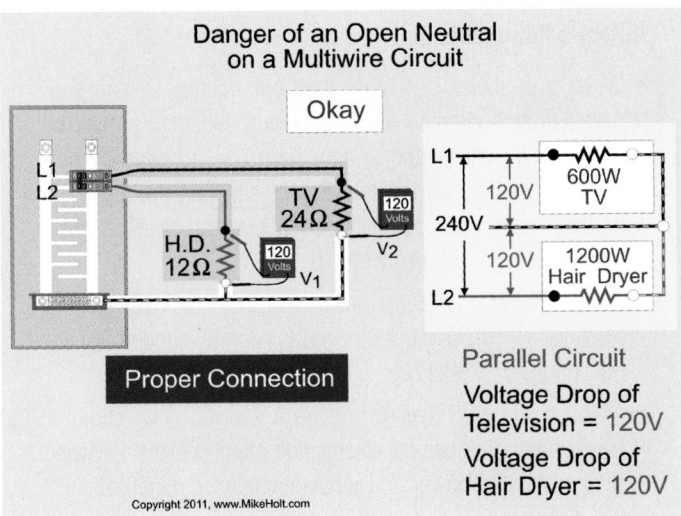

Figure 210–11

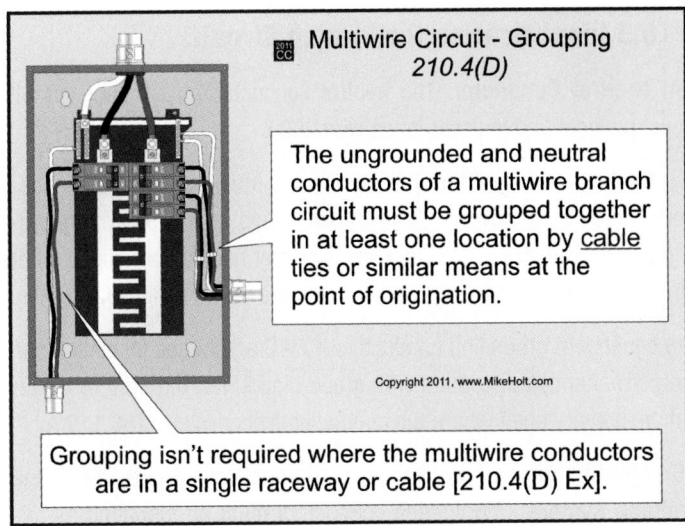

Figure 210–13

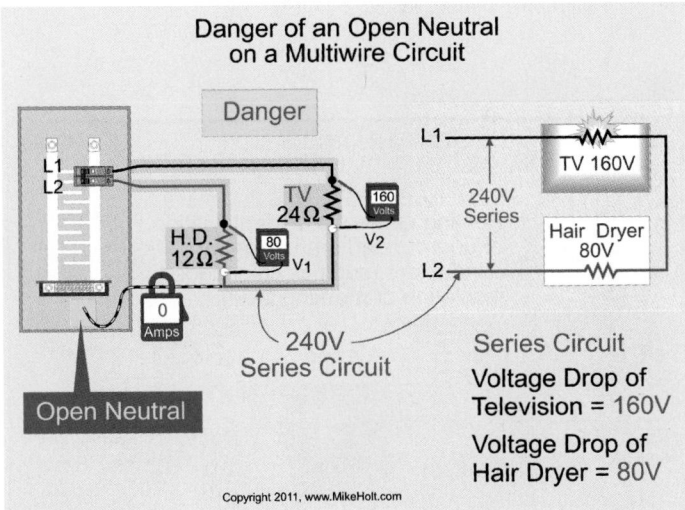

Figure 210–12

(D) Grouping. The ungrounded and neutral conductors of a multi-wire branch circuit must be grouped together by cable ties or similar means at the point of origination. Figure 210–13

Ex: Grouping isn't required where the circuit conductors are contained in a single raceway or cable unique to that circuit that makes the grouping obvious.

Author's Comment: Grouping all associated conductors of a multiwire branch circuit together by cable ties or other means within the point of origination makes it easier to visually identify the conductors of the multiwire branch circuit. The grouping will assist in making sure that the correct neutral is used at junction

points and in connecting multiwire branch-circuit conductors to circuit breakers correctly, particularly where twin breakers are used. If proper diligence isn't exercised when making these connections, two circuit conductors can be accidentally connected to the same phase.

⚠️ **CAUTION:** *If the ungrounded conductors of a multi-wire circuit aren't terminated to different phases or lines, the currents on the neutral conductor won't cancel, but will add, which can cause an overload on the neutral conductor.* Figure 210–14

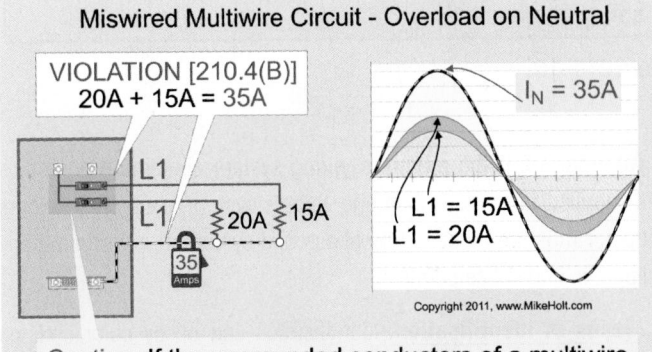

Caution: If the ungrounded conductors of a multiwire circuit aren't terminated to different phases or lines, the currents on the neutral conductor won't cancel, but will add, which can cause a dangerous overload on the neutral conductor.

Figure 210–14

210.5 Identification for Branch Circuits.

(A) Neutral Conductor. The neutral conductor of a branch circuit must be identified in accordance with 200.6.

(B) Equipment Grounding Conductor. Equipment grounding conductors can be bare, covered, or insulated. Insulated equipment grounding conductors size 6 AWG and smaller must have a continuous outer finish either green or green with one or more yellow stripes [250.119].

On equipment grounding conductors 4 AWG and larger, insulation can be permanently reidentified with green marking at the time of installation at every point where the conductor is accessible [250.119(A)].

(C) Identification of Ungrounded Conductors—More Than One Voltage System. Ungrounded conductors must be identified as follows: Figure 210–15

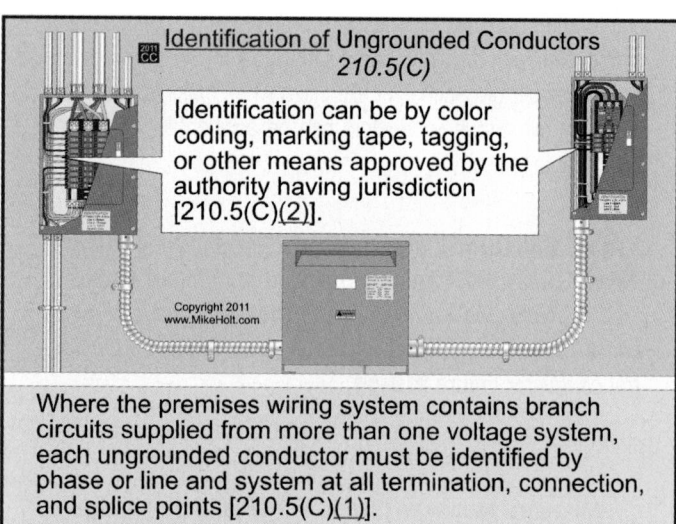

Where the premises wiring system contains branch circuits supplied from more than one voltage system, each ungrounded conductor must be identified by phase or line and system at all termination, connection, and splice points [210.5(C)(1)].

Figure 210–15

(1) Application. If the premises wiring system contains branch circuits supplied from more than one voltage system, each ungrounded conductor must be identified by phase and system at all termination, connection, and splice points.

(2) Means of Identification. Identification can be by color coding, marking tape, tagging, or other means approved by the authority having jurisdiction.

(3) Posting. The method of identification must be documented in a manner that's readily available or permanently posted at each branch-circuit panelboard.

Author's Comments:

- When a premises has more than one voltage system supplying branch circuits, the ungrounded conductors must be identified by phase and system. This can be done by permanently posting an identification legend that describes the method used, such as color-coded marking tape or color-coded insulation. **Figure 210–16**

- Conductors with insulation that's green or green with one or more yellow stripes can't be used for an ungrounded or neutral conductor [250.119].

- Although the *NEC* doesn't require a specific color code for ungrounded conductors, electricians often use the following color system for power and lighting conductor identification:

  - 120/240V, single-phase—black, red, and white
  - 120/208V, three-phase—black, red, blue, and white
  - 120/240V, three-phase—black, orange, blue, and white
  - 277/480V, three-phase—brown, orange, yellow, and gray; or, brown, purple, yellow, and gray

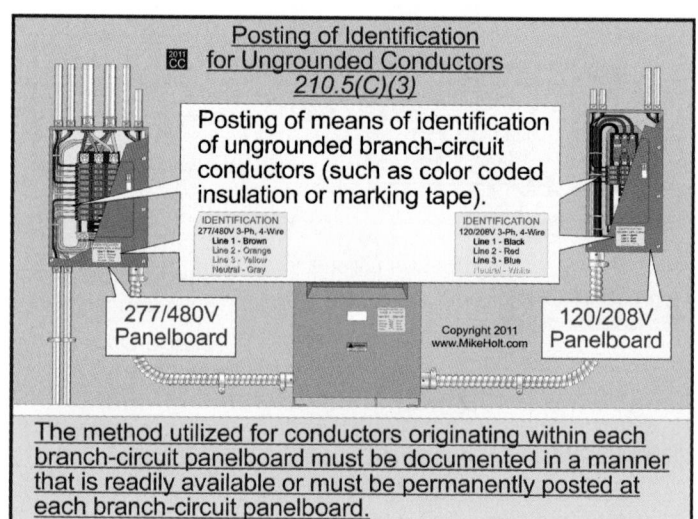

The method utilized for conductors originating within each branch-circuit panelboard must be documented in a manner that is readily available or must be permanently posted at each branch-circuit panelboard.

Figure 210–16

210.6 Branch-Circuit Voltage Limitations.

(A) Occupancy Limitation. In dwelling units, the voltage between conductors must not exceed 120V, nominal, when they supply the terminals of:

(1) Luminaires.

(2) Cord-and-plug-connected loads of 1,440 VA or less or less than ¼ hp.

210.7 Multiple Branch Circuits. If two or more branch circuits supply devices or equipment on the same yoke, a means to disconnect simultaneously all ungrounded conductors that supply those devices or equipment is required at the point where the branch circuit originates. **Figure 210–17**

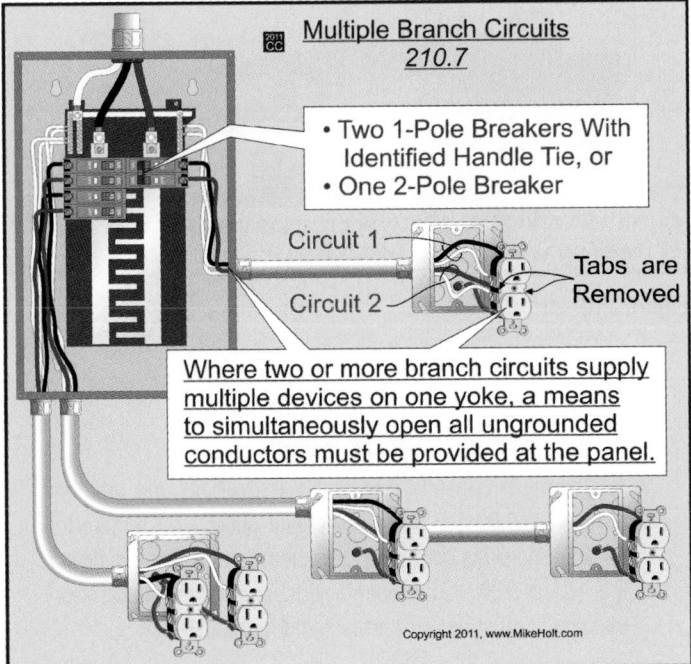

Figure 210–17

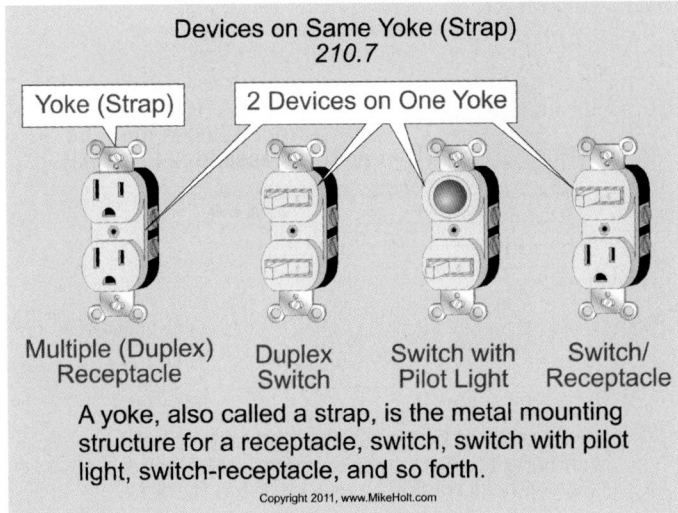

Figure 210–18

Author's Comments:

• A yoke, also called a strap, is the metal mounting structure for a receptacle, switch, switch with pilot light, switch-receptacle, and so forth. **Figure 210–18**

• Individual single-pole circuit breakers with handle ties identified for the purpose, or a circuit breaker with a common internal trip, can be used for this application [240.15(B)(1)].

210.8 GFCI Protection. Ground-fault circuit interruption for personnel must be provided as required in 210.8(A) through (C). The ground-fault circuit-interrupter device must be installed at a readily accessible location. **Figure 210–19**

Author's Comment: According to Article 100, readily accessible means capable of being reached quickly without having to climb over or remove obstacles, or resort to portable ladders. **Figure 210–20**

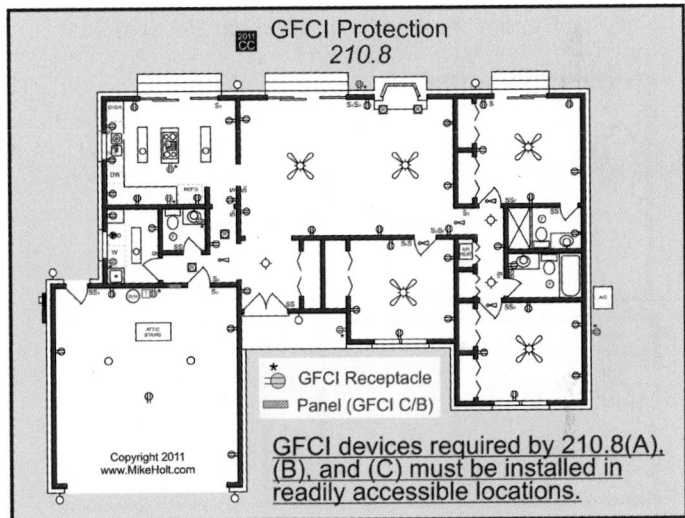

Figure 210–19

(A) Dwelling Units. GFCI protection is required for all 15A and 20A, 125V receptacles located in the following locations:

Author's Comment: See the definitions of "GFCI" and "Dwelling Unit" in Article 100.

(1) Bathroom Area. GFCI protection is required for all 15A and 20A, 125V receptacles in the bathroom area of a dwelling unit. **Figure 210–21**

Accessible, Readily
Article 100 Definition

VIOLATION
Overcurrent devices must be readily accessible [240.24(A)].

Copyright 2011
www.MikeHolt.com

Capable of being reached quickly without having to climb over or remove obstacles, or without having to use portable ladders.

Figure 210–20

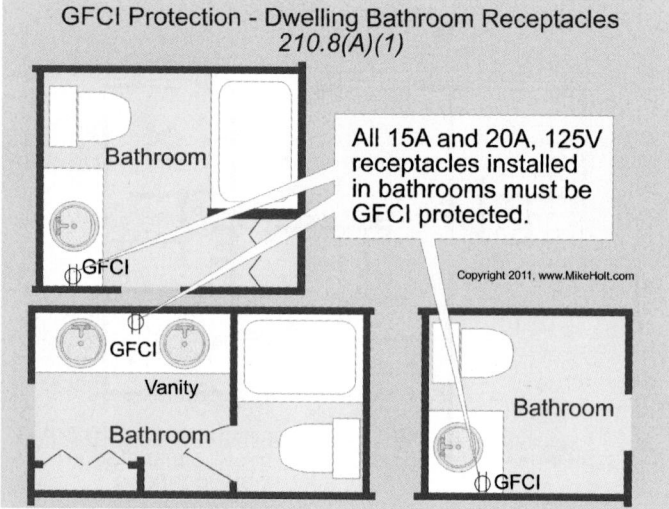

GFCI Protection - Dwelling Bathroom Receptacles
210.8(A)(1)

Bathroom

All 15A and 20A, 125V receptacles installed in bathrooms must be GFCI protected.

GFCI

GFCI

Vanity

Copyright 2011, www.MikeHolt.com

Bathroom

Bathroom

GFCI

Figure 210–21

Author's Comments:

- See the definition of "Bathroom" in Article 100.

- In the continued interests of safety, proposals to allow receptacles for dedicated equipment in the bathroom area to be exempted from the GFCI protection requirements have been rejected.

(2) Garages and Accessory Buildings. GFCI protection is required for all 15A and 20A, 125V receptacles in garages, and in grade-level portions of accessory buildings used for storage or work areas of a dwelling unit. **Figure 210–22**

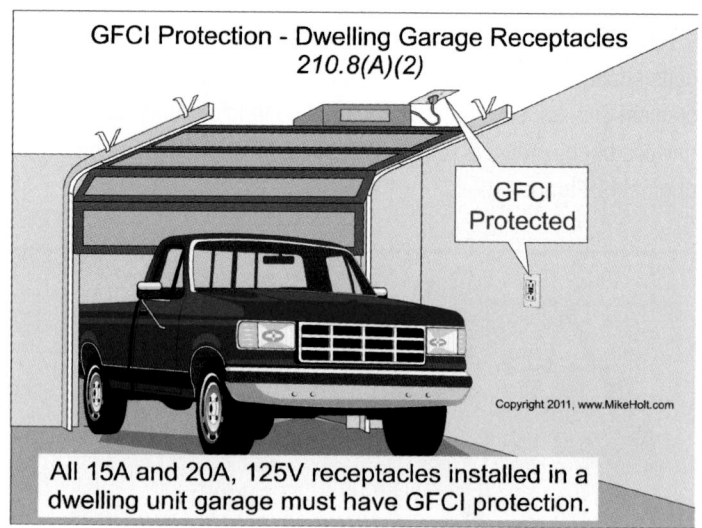

GFCI Protection - Dwelling Garage Receptacles
210.8(A)(2)

GFCI
Protected

Copyright 2011, www.MikeHolt.com

All 15A and 20A, 125V receptacles installed in a dwelling unit garage must have GFCI protection.

Figure 210–22

Author's Comments:

- See the definition of "Garage" in Article 100.

- A receptacle outlet is required in a dwelling unit attached garage [210.52(G)], but a receptacle outlet isn't required in an accessory building or a detached garage without power. If a 15A or 20A, 125V receptacle is installed in an accessory building, it must be GFCI protected. **Figure 210–23**

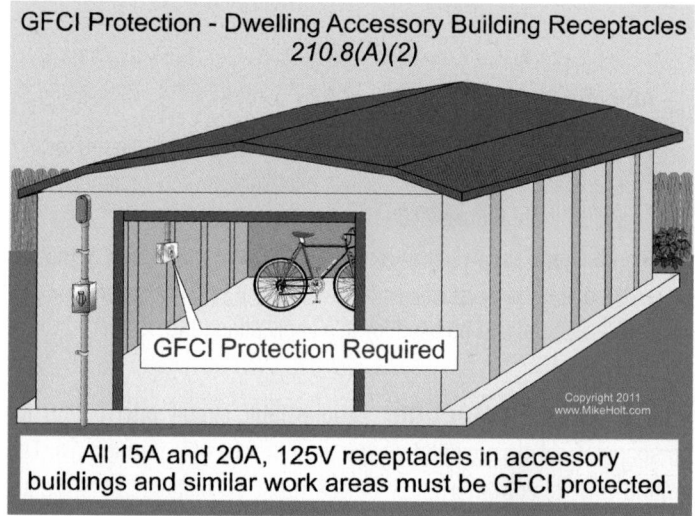

GFCI Protection - Dwelling Accessory Building Receptacles
210.8(A)(2)

GFCI Protection Required

Copyright 2011
www.MikeHolt.com

All 15A and 20A, 125V receptacles in accessory buildings and similar work areas must be GFCI protected.

Figure 210–23

(3) Outdoors. All 15A and 20A, 125V receptacles located outdoors of dwelling units, including receptacles installed under the eaves of roofs, must be GFCI protected. **Figure 210–24**

Figure 210-24

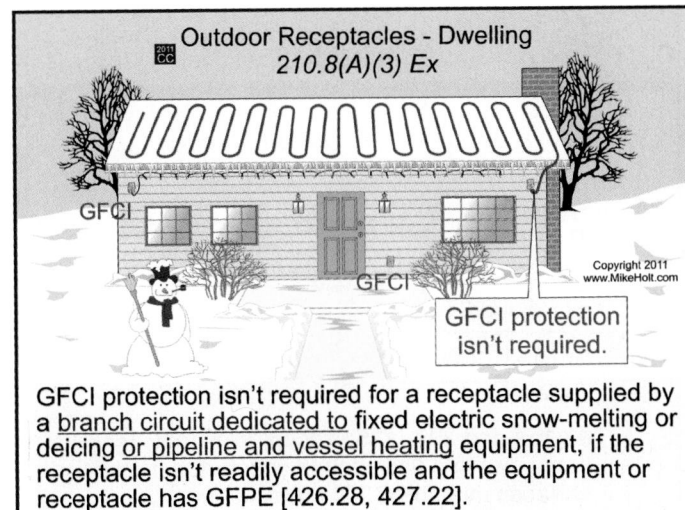

Figure 210-25

Author's Comments:

- Each dwelling unit of a multifamily dwelling that has an individual entrance at grade level must have at least one GFCI-protected receptacle outlet accessible from grade level located not more than 6½ ft above grade [210.52(E)(2)].

- Balconies, decks, and porches that are attached to the dwelling unit and are accessible from inside the dwelling must have at least one GFCI-protected receptacle outlet accessible from the balcony, deck, or porch [210.52(E)(3)].

Ex: GFCI protection isn't required for a receptacle that's supplied by a branch circuit dedicated to fixed electric snow-melting or deicing or pipeline and vessel heating equipment, if the receptacle isn't readily accessible and the equipment or receptacle has ground-fault protection of equipment (GFPE) [426.28 and 427.22]. **Figure 210-25**

(4) Crawl Spaces. All 15A and 20A, 125V receptacles installed in crawl spaces at or below grade of a dwelling unit must be GFCI protected.

> **Author's Comment:** The *Code* doesn't require a receptacle to be installed in a crawl space, except when heating, air-conditioning, and refrigeration equipment is installed there [210.63].

(5) Unfinished Basements. GFCI protection is required for all 15A and 20A, 125V receptacles located in the unfinished portion of a basement not intended as a habitable room and limited to storage and work areas. **Figure 210-26**

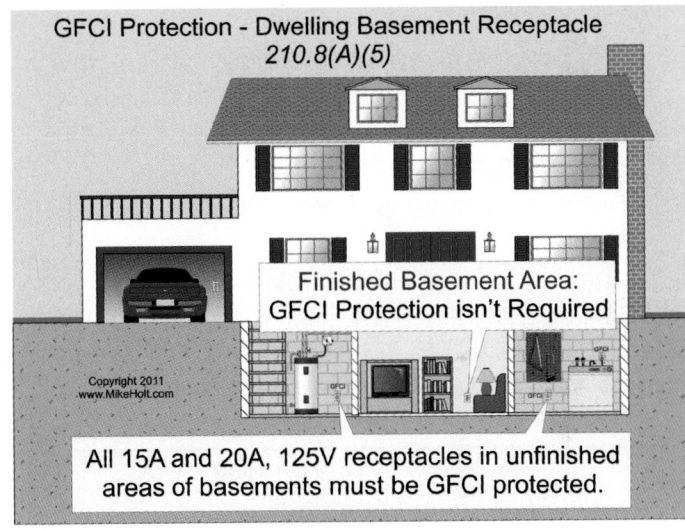

Figure 210-26

Ex: A receptacle supplying only a permanently installed fire alarm or burglar alarm system isn't required to be GFCI protected [760.41(B) and 760.121(B)].

> **Author's Comment:** A receptacle outlet is required in each unfinished portion of a dwelling unit basement [210.52(G)].

(6) Kitchen Countertop Surfaces. GFCI protection is required for all 15A and 20A, 125V receptacles that serve countertop surfaces in a dwelling unit. **Figure 210-27**

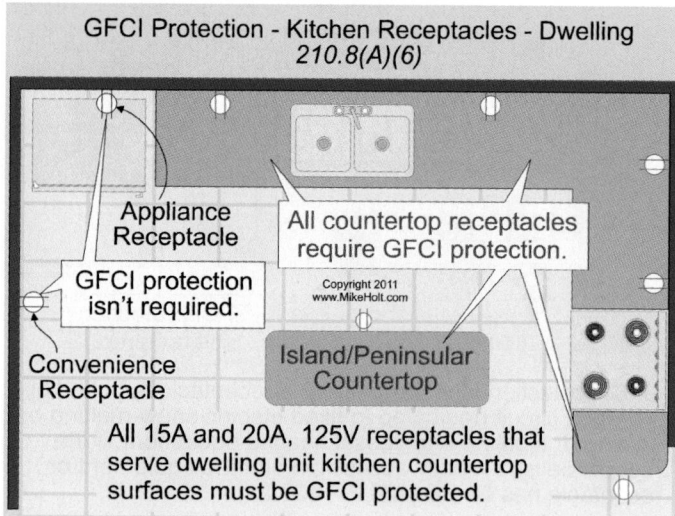

Figure 210–27

Author's Comments:

- GFCI protection is required for all receptacles that serve countertop surfaces, but GFCI protection isn't required for receptacles that serve built-in appliances, such as dishwashers or kitchen waste disposals.

- See 210.52(C) for the location requirements of countertop receptacles.

(7) Sinks. For other than kitchen sinks, GFCI protection is required for all 15A and 20A, 125V receptacles located within an arc measurement of 6 ft from the outside edge of the sink. **Figure 210–28**

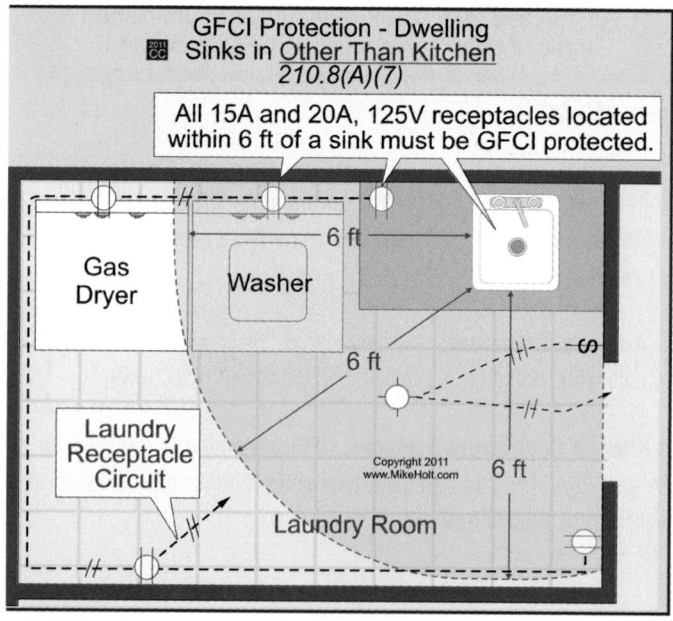

Figure 210–28

(8) Boathouses. GFCI protection is required for all 15A and 20A, 125V receptacles located in a dwelling unit boathouse. **Figure 210–29**

Figure 210–29

Author's Comment: The *Code* doesn't require a 15A or 20A, 125V receptacle to be installed in a boathouse, but if one is installed, it must be GFCI protected.

(B) Other than Dwelling Units. GFCI protection is required for all 15A and 20A, 125V receptacles installed in the following commercial/industrial locations:

(1) Bathrooms. All 15A and 20A, 125V receptacles installed in commercial or industrial bathrooms must be GFCI protected. **Figure 210–30**

Author's Comments:

- See the definition of "Bathroom" in Article 100.

- A 15A or 20A, 125V receptacle isn't required in a commercial or industrial bathroom, but if one is installed, it must be GFCI protected.

(2) Kitchens. All 15A and 20A, 125V receptacles installed in a kitchen, even those that don't supply the countertop surface, must be GFCI protected. **Figure 210–31**

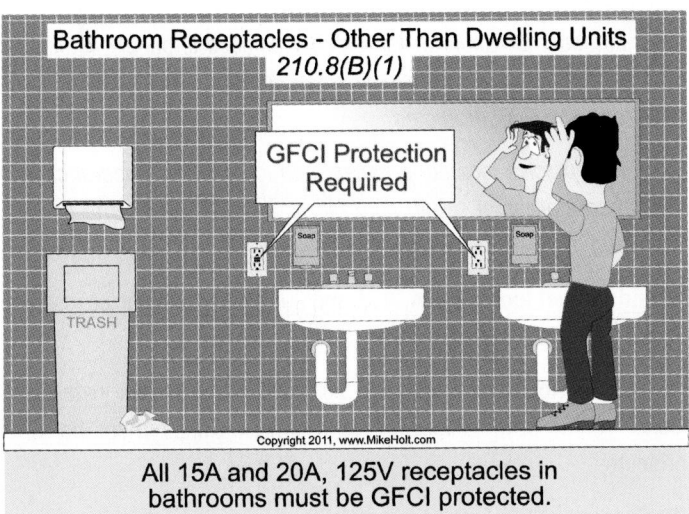

Figure 210–30

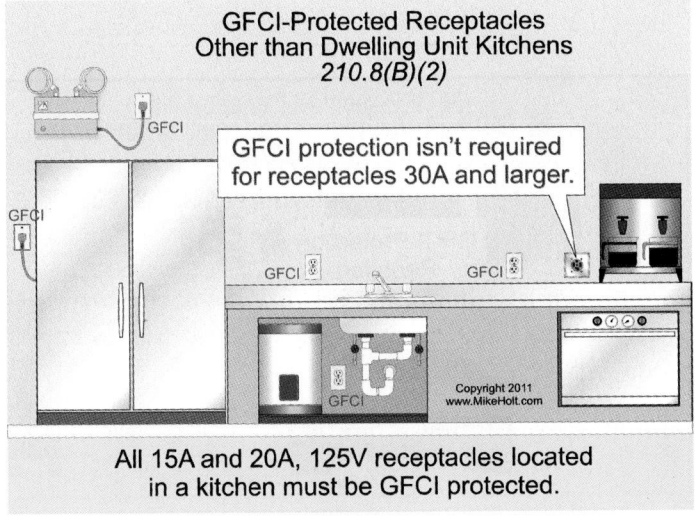

Figure 210–31

Author's Comments:

- A kitchen is an area with a sink and permanent provisions for food preparation and cooking [Article 100]

- GFCI protection isn't required for receptacles rated other than 15A and 20A, 125V in these locations.

- GFCI protection isn't required for hard-wired equipment in these locations.

- An area such an employee break room with a sink and cord-and-plug-connected cooking appliance such as a microwave oven isn't considered a kitchen. **Figure 210–32**

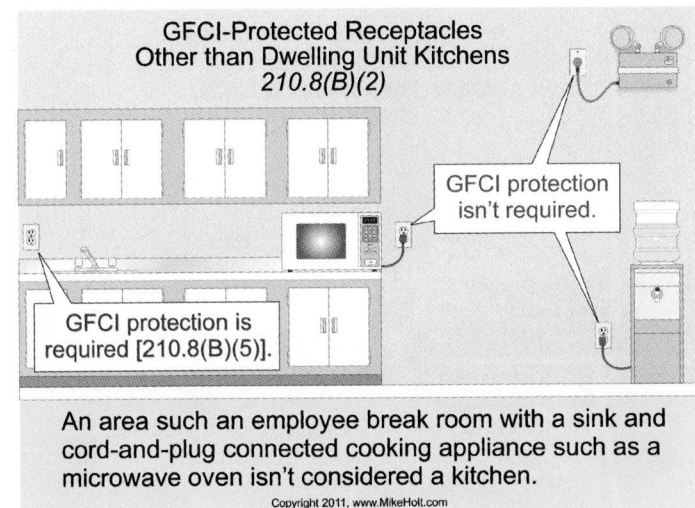

Figure 210–32

(3) Rooftops. All 15A and 20A, 125V receptacles installed on rooftops must be GFCI protected. **Figure 210–33**

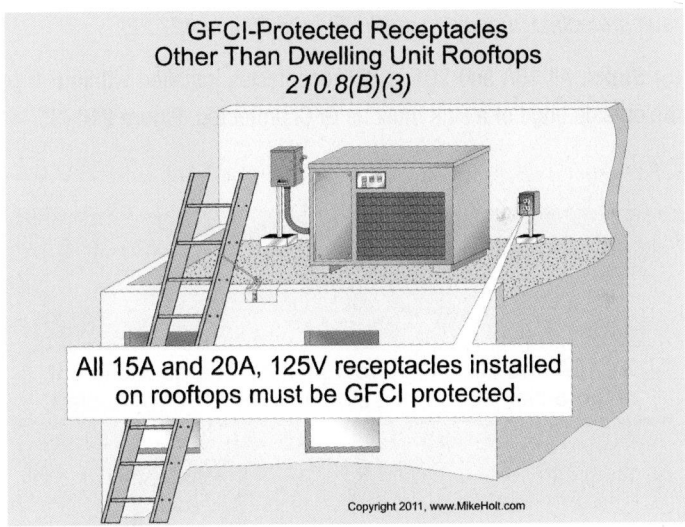

Figure 210–33

Author's Comment: A 15A or 20A, 125V receptacle outlet must be installed within 25 ft of heating, air-conditioning, and refrigeration equipment [210.63].

(4) Outdoors. All 15A and 20A, 125V receptacles installed outdoors must be GFCI protected. **Figure 210–34**

Figure 210–34

Ex 1 to (3) and (4): GFCI protection isn't required for a receptacle that's supplied by a branch circuit dedicated to fixed electric snow-melting or deicing or pipeline and vessel heating equipment, if the receptacle isn't readily accessible and the equipment or receptacle has ground-fault protection of equipment (GFPE) [426.28 and 427.22].

(5) Sinks. All 15A and 20A, 125V receptacles installed within 6 ft of the outside edge of a sink must be GFCI protected. **Figure 210–35**

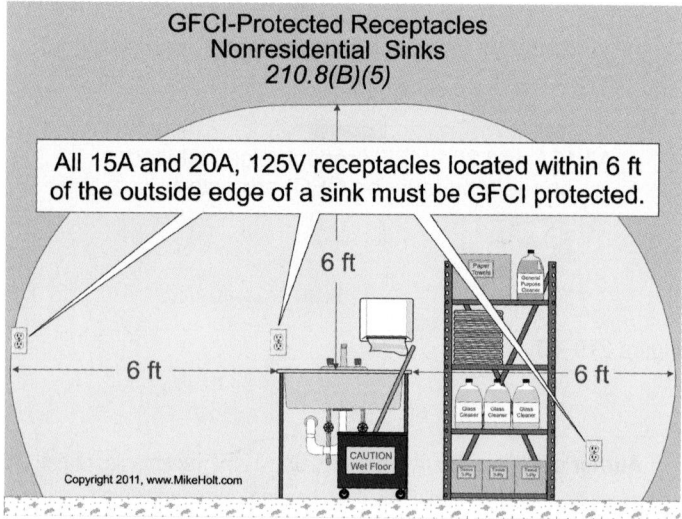

Figure 210–35

Ex 1: In industrial laboratories, receptacles used to supply equipment where removal of power would introduce a greater hazard aren't required to be GFCI protected.

Ex 2: Receptacles located in patient bed locations of general care or critical care areas of health care facilities aren't required to be GFCI protected.

(6) Indoor wet locations. All 15A and 20A, 125V receptacles installed indoors in wet locations must be GFCI protected.

(7) Locker Rooms. All 15A and 20A, 125V receptacles installed in locker rooms with associated showering facilities must be GFCI protected.

(8) Garages. All 15A and 20A, 125V receptacles installed in garages, service bays, and similar areas where electrical diagnostic equipment, electrical hand tools, or portable lighting equipment are to be used must be GFCI protected. **Figure 210–36**

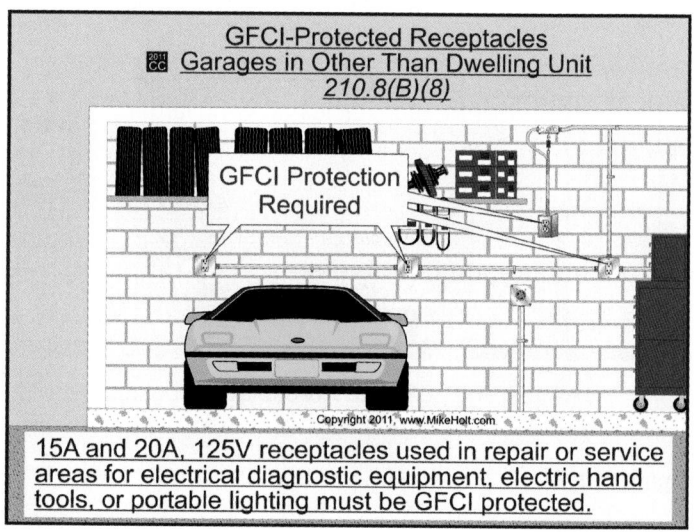

Figure 210–36

(C) Boat Hoists. GFCI protection is required for outlets supplying boat hoists in dwelling unit locations. **Figure 210–37**

Author's Comments:

- See the definition of "Outlet" in Article 100.
- This ensures GFCI protection regardless of whether the boat hoist is cord-and-plug-connected or hard-wired.

GFCI protection is required for outlets not exceeding 240V that supply boat hoists in dwelling unit locations.

Figure 210–37

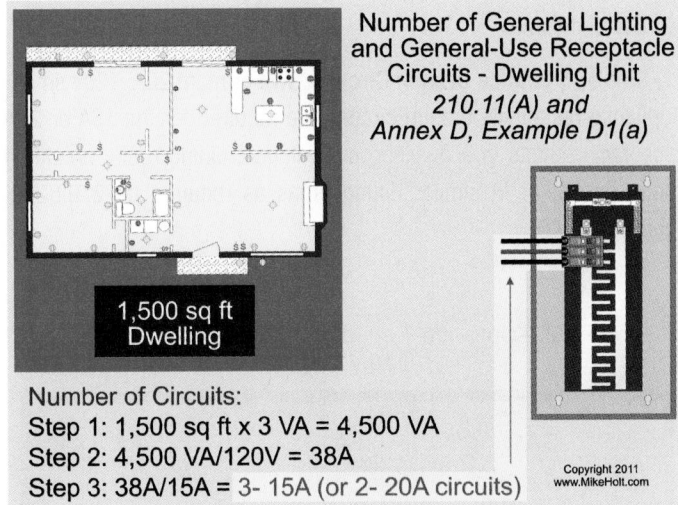

Number of Circuits:
Step 1: 1,500 sq ft x 3 VA = 4,500 VA
Step 2: 4,500 VA/120V = 38A
Step 3: 38A/15A = 3- 15A (or 2- 20A circuits)

Figure 210–38

210.11 Branch Circuits Required.

(A) Number of Branch Circuits. The minimum number of general lighting and general-use receptacle branch circuits must be determined by dividing the total calculated load in amperes by the ampere rating of the circuits used.

Question: How many 15A, 120V circuits are required for the general lighting and general-use receptacles for a dwelling having floor area of 1500 ft2, exclusive of an unfinished cellar not adaptable for future use [Example D1(a) in Annex D]. **Figure 210–38**

(a) 1   (b) 2   (c) 3   (d) 4

Answer: (d) 4

Step 1: Determine the total VA load:

$VA = 1,500$ sq ft x 3 VA per sq ft [Table 220.12]
$VA = 4,500$ VA

Step 2: Determine the amperes:

$I = VA/E$
$I = 4,500VA/120V$
$I = 38A$

Step 3: Determine the number of circuits:

Number of Circuits = 38A/15A
Number of Circuits = Three 15A, or two 20A, 120V

Author's Comment: There's no limit to the number of receptacles on a circuit in a dwelling unit.

(B) Load Evenly Proportioned Among Branch Circuits. If the load is calculated on the volt-amperes/square foot, the wiring system must be provided to serve the calculated load, with the loads evenly proportioned among multioutlet branch circuits within the panelboard. **Figure 210–39**

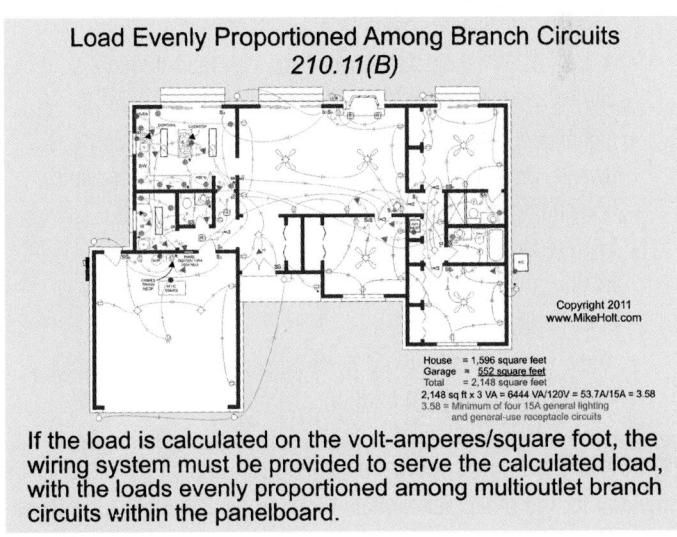

If the load is calculated on the volt-amperes/square foot, the wiring system must be provided to serve the calculated load, with the loads evenly proportioned among multioutlet branch circuits within the panelboard.

Figure 210–39

(C) Dwelling Unit.

(1) Small-Appliance Branch Circuits. Two or more 20A, 120V small-appliance receptacle branch circuits are required for the 15A or 20A receptacle outlets in a dwelling unit kitchen, dining room, breakfast room, pantry, or in similar dining areas as required by 210.52(B). **Figure 210–40**

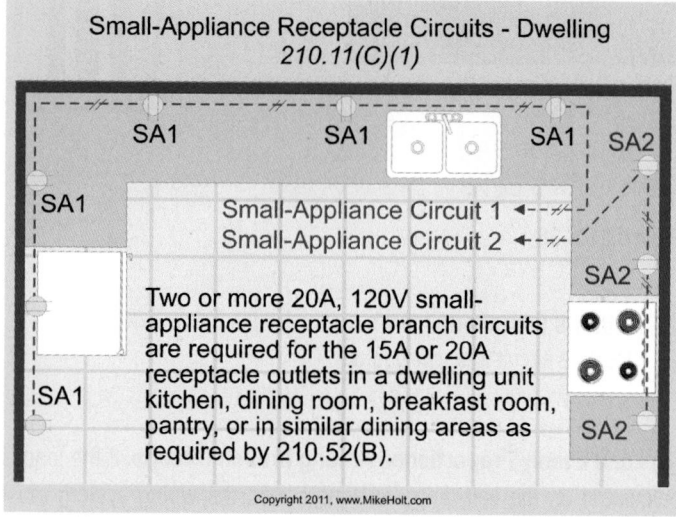

Figure 210–40

Author's Comments:

- See the definition of "Receptacle Outlet" in Article 100.

- A 15A, 125V receptacle is rated for 20A feed-through, so it can be used for this purpose [210.21(B)(3)].

- Lighting outlets or receptacles located in other areas of a dwelling unit must not be connected to the small-appliance branch circuit [210.52(B)(2)].

- The two 20A small-appliance branch circuits can be supplied by one 3-wire multiwire circuit or by two separate 120V circuits [210.4(A)].

- Each separate countertop must be supplied with two small-appliance circuits [210.52(B)(3)].

(2) Laundry Branch Circuit. One 20A, 120V branch circuit must be provided for the receptacle outlets required by 210.52(F) for a dwelling unit laundry room. The 20A laundry room receptacle circuit is permitted to supply more than one receptacle in the laundry room. The 20A laundry receptacle must not serve any other outlets, such as the laundry room lighting or receptacles in other rooms. **Figure 210–41**

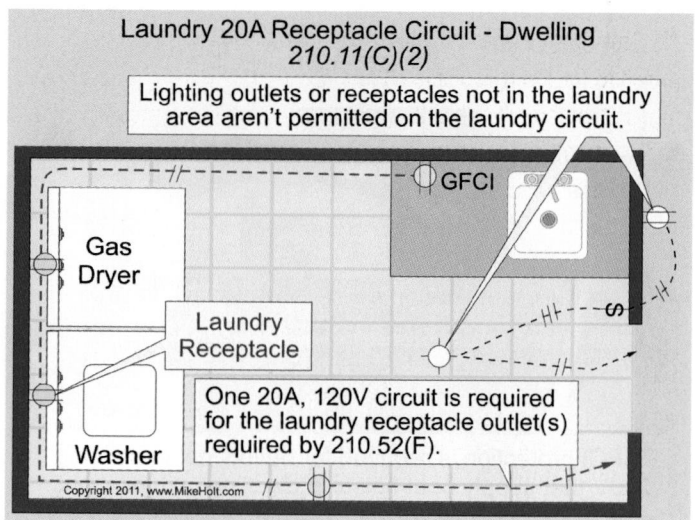

Figure 210–41

Author's Comments:

- The 20A, 120V laundry branch circuit is required, even if the laundry appliance installed is a 30A, 230V combination washer/dryer. **Figure 210–42**

- A 15A receptacle is rated for 20A feed-through, so it can be used for this purpose [210.21(B)(3)].

- GFCI protection isn't required for 15A and 20A, 125V receptacles located in a laundry room, unless they're within 6 ft of a sink [210.8(A)(7)].

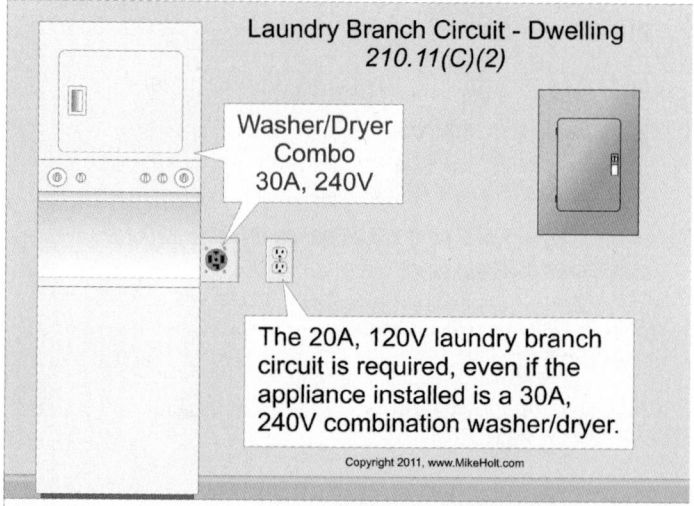

Figure 210–42

(3) Bathroom Branch Circuit. One 20A, 120V branch circuit must be provided for the receptacle outlets required by 210.52(D) for a dwelling unit bathroom. This 20A bathroom receptacle circuit must not serve any other outlet, such as bathroom lighting outlets or receptacles in other rooms. **Figure 210–43**

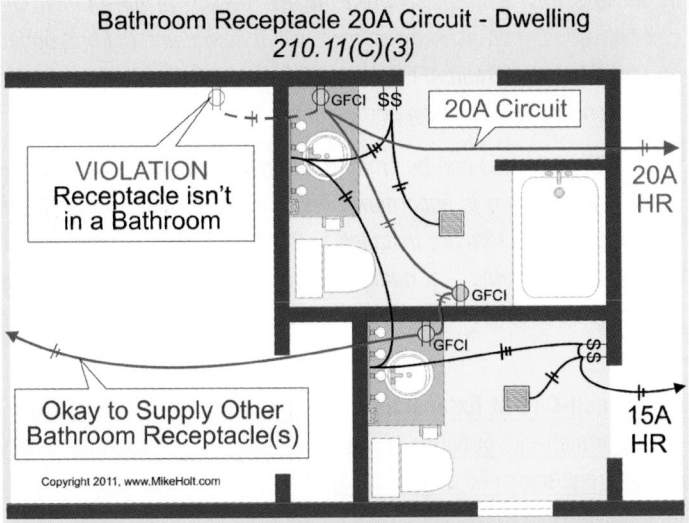

A minimum of one 20A circuit is required to supply the required bathroom receptacles. Other outlets aren't permitted on the bathroom receptacle circuit.

Figure 210–43

Author's Comment: A 15A, 125V receptacle is rated for 20A feed-through, so it can be used for this purpose [210.21(B)(3)].

Ex: A single 20A, 120V branch circuit is permitted to supply all of the outlets in a single bathroom, as long as no single load fastened in place is rated more than 10A [210.23(A)]. **Figure 210–44**

Question: Can a luminaire, ceiling fan, or bath fan be connected to the 20A, 120V branch circuit that supplies one bathroom?

Answer: Yes.

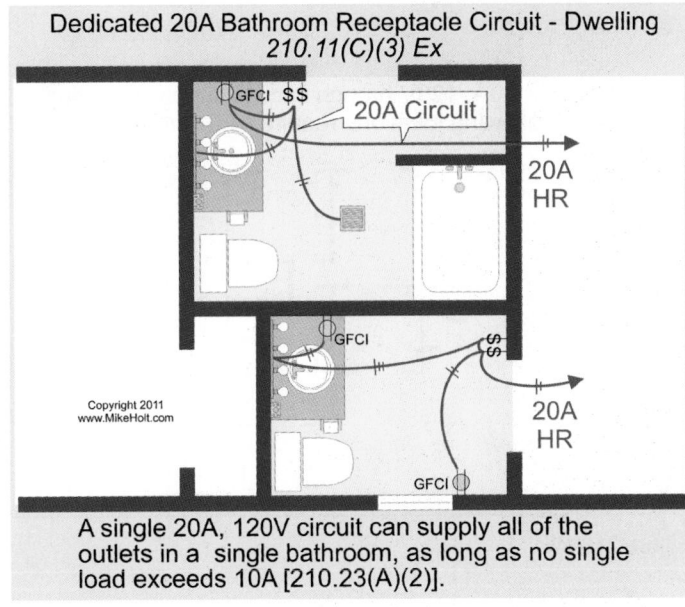

A single 20A, 120V circuit can supply all of the outlets in a single bathroom, as long as no single load exceeds 10A [210.23(A)(2)].

Figure 210–44

210.12 Arc-Fault Circuit-Interrupter Protection for Dwelling Units

Author's Comment: The combination AFCI is a circuit breaker that protects downstream branch-circuit wiring as well as cord sets and power-supply cords; an outlet branch circuit AFCI (receptacle) is installed as the first outlet in a branch circuit to protect downstream branch-circuit wiring, cord sets, and power-supply cords.

(A) Where Required. All 15A or 20A, 120V branch circuits in dwelling units supplying outlets in family rooms, dining rooms, living rooms, parlors, libraries, dens, bedrooms, sunrooms, recreation rooms, closets, hallways, or similar rooms or areas must be protected by a listed AFCI device of the combination type. **Figure 210–45**

Author's Comment: The 120V circuit limitation means AFCI protection isn't required for equipment rated 230V, such as a baseboard heater or room air conditioner. For more information, visit www.MikeHolt.com, click on the "Search" link, and search for "AFCI."

Note 3: See 760.41(B) and 760.121(B) for power-supply requirements for fire alarm systems.

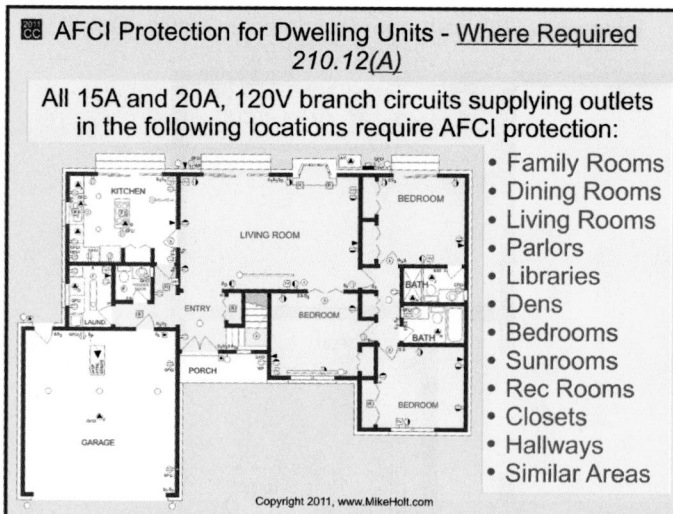

Figure 210–45

Author's Comment: Smoke alarms connected to a 15A or 20A circuit of a dwelling unit must be AFCI protected if the smoke alarm is located in one of the areas specified in 210.12(A). The exemption from AFCI protection for the "fire alarm circuit" contained in 760.41(B) and 760.121(B) doesn't apply to the single- or multiple-station smoke alarm circuit typically installed in dwelling unit bedroom areas. This is because a smoke alarm circuit isn't a fire alarm circuit as defined in NFPA 72, *National Fire Alarm Code*. Unlike single- or multiple-station smoke alarms, fire alarm systems are managed by a fire alarm control panel. **Figure 210–46**

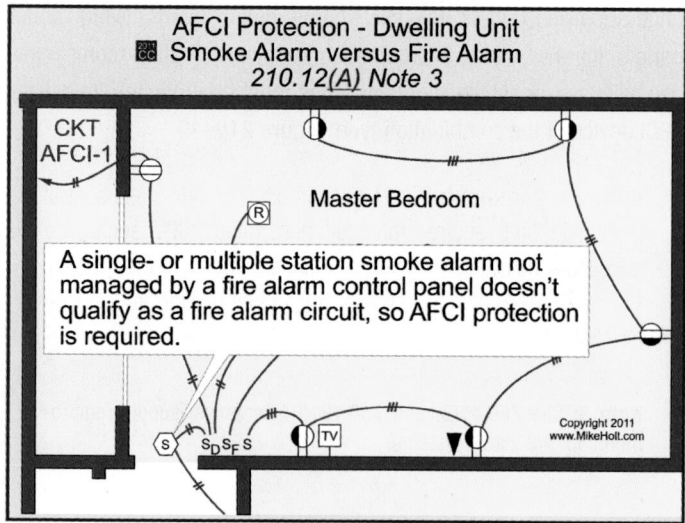

Figure 210–46

Ex 1: AFCI protection can be of the branch-circuit type located at the first outlet if the circuit conductors are installed in RMC, IMC, EMT, or Type MC or steel armored Type AC cable meeting the requirements of 250.118, and the AFCI device is contained in a metal outlet or junction box.

Ex 2: Where a listed metal or nonmetallic conduit or tubing is encased in not less than 2 in. of concrete for the portion of the branch circuit between the branch-circuit overcurrent device and the first outlet, an outlet branch-circuit AFCI at the first outlet is permitted to provide protection for the remaining portion of the branch circuit.

Ex 3: AFCI protection can be omitted for an individual branch circuit to a fire alarm system in accordance with 760.41(B) and 760.121(B), if the circuit conductors are installed in RMC, IMC, EMT, or steel sheath Type AC or MC cable that qualifies as an equipment grounding conductor in accordance with 250.118, with metal outlet and junction boxes.

(B) Branch-Circuit Extensions or Modifications—Dwelling Units. Where branch-circuit wiring is modified, replaced, or extended in any of the areas specified in 210.12(A), the branch circuit must be protected by:

(1) A listed combination AFCI located at the origin of the branch circuit; or

(2) A listed outlet branch circuit AFCI located at the first receptacle outlet of the existing branch circuit.

210.18 Guest Rooms and Guest Suites. Guest rooms and guest suites provided with permanent provisions for cooking must have branch circuits installed in accordance with the dwelling unit requirements of 210.11.

> **Author's Comment:** See the definitions of "Guest Room" and "Guest Suite" in Article 100.

PART II. BRANCH-CIRCUIT RATINGS

210.19 Conductor Sizing.

(A) Branch Circuits.

(1) Continuous and Noncontinuous Loads. Conductors must be sized no less than 125 percent of the continuous loads, plus 100 percent of the noncontinuous loads, based on the terminal temperature rating ampacities as listed in Table 310.15(B)(16), before any ampacity adjustment [110.14(C)(1)].

Ex 1: If the assembly and the overcurrent device are both listed for operation at 100 percent of its rating, the conductors can be sized at 100 percent of the continuous load.

Author's Comments:

- Equipment suitable for 100 percent continuous loading is rarely available in ratings under 400A.

- See the definition of "Continuous Load" in Article 100.

- See 210.20 for the sizing requirements for the branch-circuit overcurrent device for continuous and noncontinuous loads.

Question: What size branch-circuit conductors are required for the ungrounded conductors of a 44A continuous load, if the equipment terminals are rated 75°C? **Figure 210–47**

(a) 10 AWG   (b) 8 AWG   (c) 6 AWG   (d) 4 AWG

Answer: (c) 6 AWG

Since the load is 44A continuous, the ungrounded conductors must be sized to have an ampacity of not less than 55A (44A x 1.25). According to the 75°C column of Table 310.15(B)(16), a 6 AWG conductor is suitable, because it has an ampere rating of 65A at 75°C before any conductor ampacity adjustment for ambient temperature [310.15(B)(2)(a)], conductor bundling [310.15(B)(3)(a)], or both.

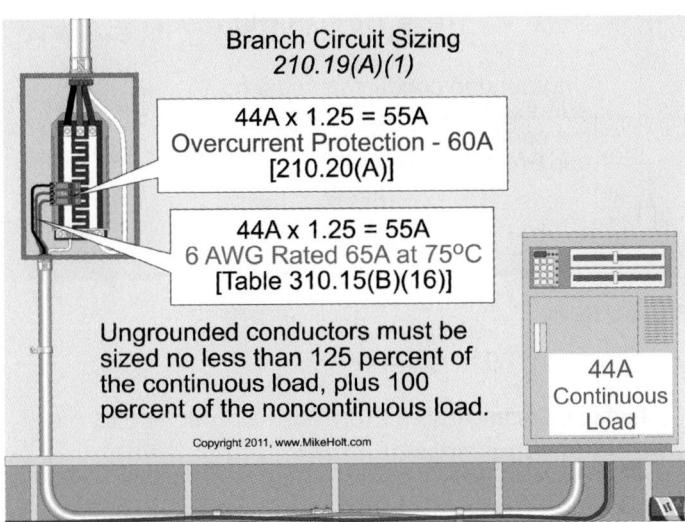

Branch Circuit Sizing
210.19(A)(1)

44A x 1.25 = 55A
Overcurrent Protection - 60A
[210.20(A)]

44A x 1.25 = 55A
6 AWG Rated 65A at 75°C
[Table 310.15(B)(16)]

Ungrounded conductors must be sized no less than 125 percent of the continuous load, plus 100 percent of the noncontinuous load.

44A Continuous Load

Copyright 2011, www.MikeHolt.com

Figure 210–47

Note 4: To provide reasonable efficiency of operation of electrical equipment, branch-circuit conductors should be sized to prevent a voltage drop not to exceed 3 percent. In addition, the maximum total voltage drop on both feeders and branch circuits shouldn't exceed 5 percent. **Figures 210–48 and 210–49**

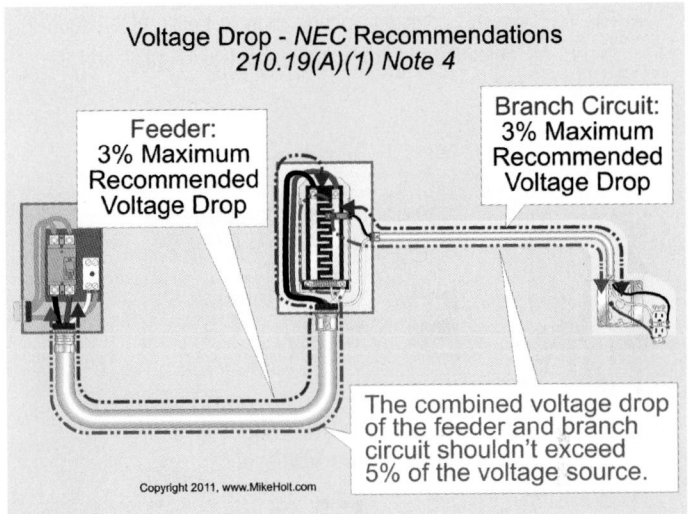

Voltage Drop - *NEC* Recommendations
210.19(A)(1) Note 4

Feeder:
3% Maximum
Recommended
Voltage Drop

Branch Circuit:
3% Maximum
Recommended
Voltage Drop

The combined voltage drop of the feeder and branch circuit shouldn't exceed 5% of the voltage source.

Copyright 2011, www.MikeHolt.com

Figure 210–48

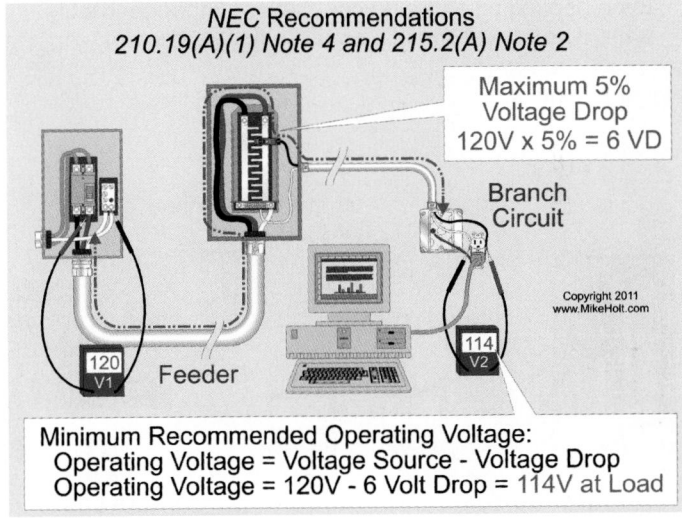

***NEC* Recommendations**
210.19(A)(1) Note 4 and 215.2(A) Note 2

Maximum 5%
Voltage Drop
120V x 5% = 6 VD

Branch Circuit

Feeder

Copyright 2011
www.MikeHolt.com

Minimum Recommended Operating Voltage:
Operating Voltage = Voltage Source - Voltage Drop
Operating Voltage = 120V - 6 Volt Drop = 114V at Load

Figure 210–49

Author's Comments:

- Many believe the *NEC* requires conductor voltage drop, as per Note 4 to be applied when sizing conductors. Although this is often a good practice, it's not a *Code* requirement because Notes are only advisory statements [90.5(C)]. **Figures 210–50 and 210–51**

- The *NEC* doesn't consider voltage drop to be a safety issue, except for sensitive electronic equipment [647.4(D)] and fire pumps [695.7].

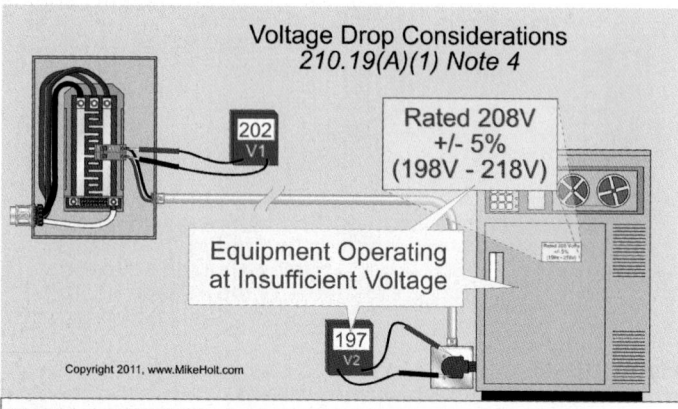

Figure 210–50

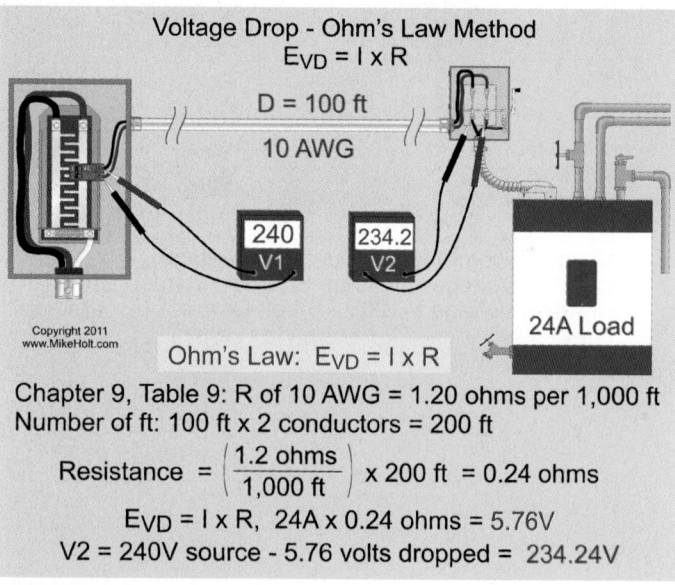

Figure 210–51

(2) Branch Circuits Supplying More than One Receptacle. Branch circuits that supply more than one receptacle must have an ampacity not less than the rating of the circuit overcurrent device [210.3].

(3) Household Ranges and Cooking Appliances. Branch-circuit conductors that supply household ranges, wall-mounted ovens or counter-mounted cooking units must have an ampacity not less than the rating of the branch circuit, and not less than the maximum load to be served. For ranges of 8¾ kW or more rating, the minimum branch-circuit ampere rating is 40A.

Ex 1: Conductors tapped from a 50A branch circuit for electric ranges, wall-mounted electric ovens and counter-mounted electric cooking units must have an ampacity not less than 20A, and must have sufficient ampacity for the load to be served. The taps must not be longer than necessary for servicing the appliances.

210.20 Overcurrent Protection.

(A) Continuous and Noncontinuous Loads. Branch-circuit overcurrent devices must have a rating of not less than 125 percent of the continuous loads, plus 100 percent of the noncontinuous loads. **Figure 210–52**

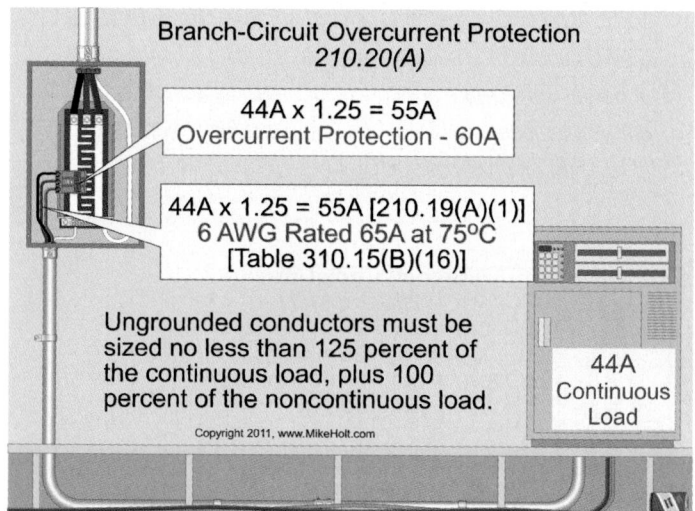

Figure 210–52

Author's Comment: See 210.19(A)(1) for branch-circuit conductor sizing requirements.

Ex: If the assembly and the overcurrent devices are both listed for operation at 100 percent of their rating, the branch-circuit overcurrent device can be sized at 100 percent of the continuous load.

Author's Comment: Equipment suitable for 100 percent continuous loading is rarely available in ratings under 400A.

(B) Conductor Protection. Branch-circuit conductors must be protected against overcurrent in accordance with 240.4.

(C) Equipment Protection. Branch-circuit equipment must be protected in accordance with 240.3.

210.21 Outlet Device Rating.

(A) Lampholder Ratings. Lampholders connected to a branch circuit rated over 20A must be of the heavy-duty type.

Author's Comment: Fluorescent lampholders aren't rated heavy duty, so fluorescent luminaires must not be installed on circuits rated over 20A.

(B) Receptacle Ratings and Loadings.

(1) Single Receptacles. A single receptacle on an individual branch circuit must have an ampacity not less than the rating of the overcurrent device. **Figure 210–53**

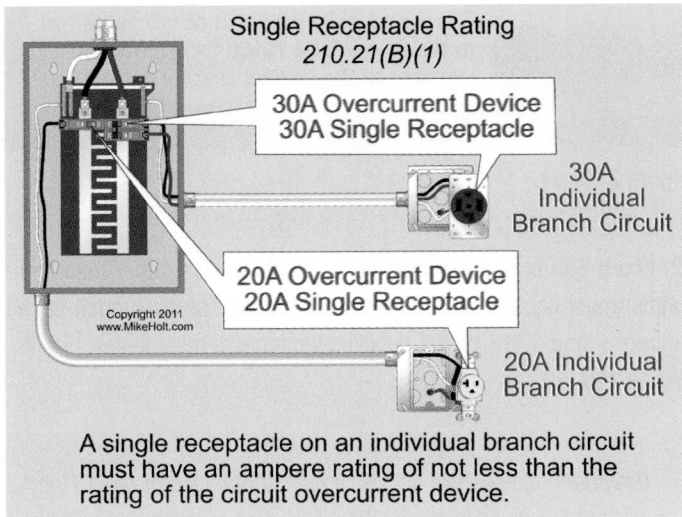

Single Receptacle Rating
210.21(B)(1)

30A Overcurrent Device
30A Single Receptacle

30A Individual Branch Circuit

20A Overcurrent Device
20A Single Receptacle

20A Individual Branch Circuit

Copyright 2011
www.MikeHolt.com

A single receptacle on an individual branch circuit must have an ampere rating of not less than the rating of the circuit overcurrent device.

Figure 210–53

Note: A single receptacle has only one contact device on its yoke [Article 100]; this means a duplex receptacle is considered as two receptacles.

(2) Multiple Receptacle Loading. If connected to a branch circuit that supplies two or more receptacles, the total cord-and-plug-connected load must not exceed 80 percent of the receptacle rating.

Author's Comment: A duplex receptacle has two contact devices on the same yoke [Article 100]. This means even one duplex receptacle on a circuit makes that circuit a multioutlet branch circuit.

(3) Multiple Receptacle Rating. If connected to a branch circuit that supplies two or more receptacles, receptacles must have an ampere rating in accordance with the values listed in Table 210.21(B)(3). **Figure 210–54**

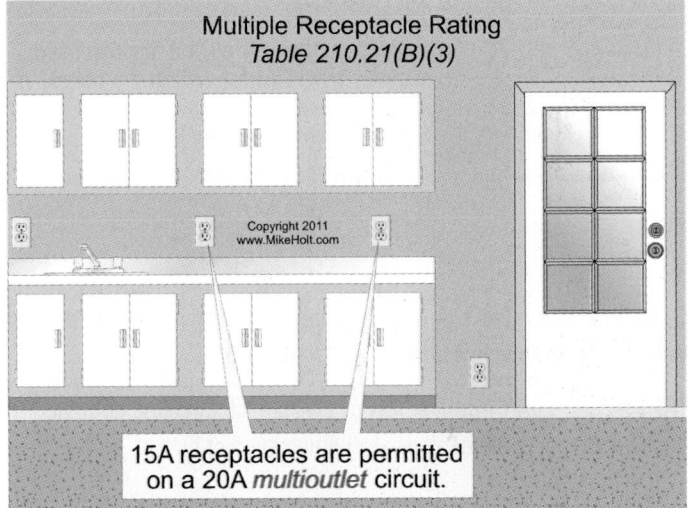

Multiple Receptacle Rating
Table 210.21(B)(3)

Copyright 2011
www.MikeHolt.com

15A receptacles are permitted on a 20A *multioutlet* circuit.

Figure 210–54

Table 210.21(B)(3) Receptacle Ratings	
Circuit Rating	Receptacle Rating
15A	15A
20A	15A or 20A
30A	30A
40A	40A or 50A
50A	50A

210.23 Permissible Loads. An individual branch circuit is permitted to supply any load for which it's rated, but in no case is the load permitted to exceed the branch-circuit ampere rating. **Figure 210–55**

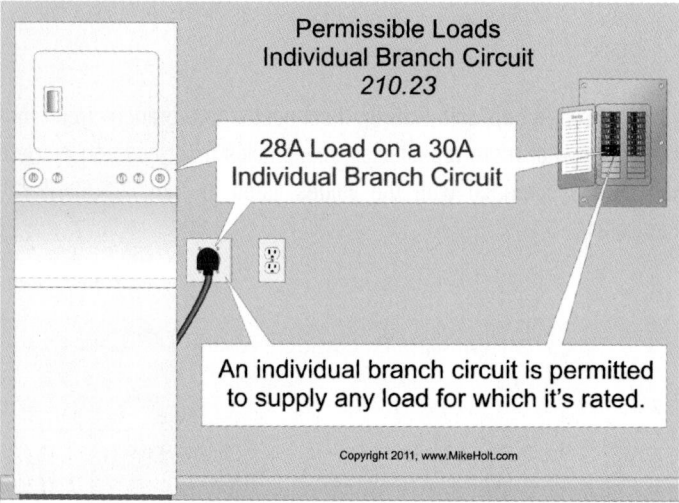

Figure 210–55

Branch circuits rated 15A or 20A supplying two or more outlets must only supply loads in accordance with 210.23(A).

(A) 15A and 20A Circuit. A 15A or 20A branch circuit is permitted to supply lighting, equipment, or any combination of both.

> **Author's Comment:** Except for temporary installations [590.4(D)], 15A or 20A circuits can be used to supply both lighting and receptacles on the same circuit. **Figure 210–56**

(1) Cord-and-Plug-Connected Equipment Not Fastened in Place. Cord-and-plug-connected equipment not fastened in place, such as a drill press or table saw, must not have an ampere rating more than 80 percent of the branch-circuit rating. **Figure 210–57**

> **Author's Comment:** UL and other testing laboratories list portable equipment (such as hair dryers) up to 100 percent of the circuit rating. The *NEC* is an installation standard, not a product standard, so it can't prohibit this practice. There really is no way to limit the load to 80 percent of the branch-circuit rating if testing laboratories permit equipment to be listed for 100 percent of the circuit rating.

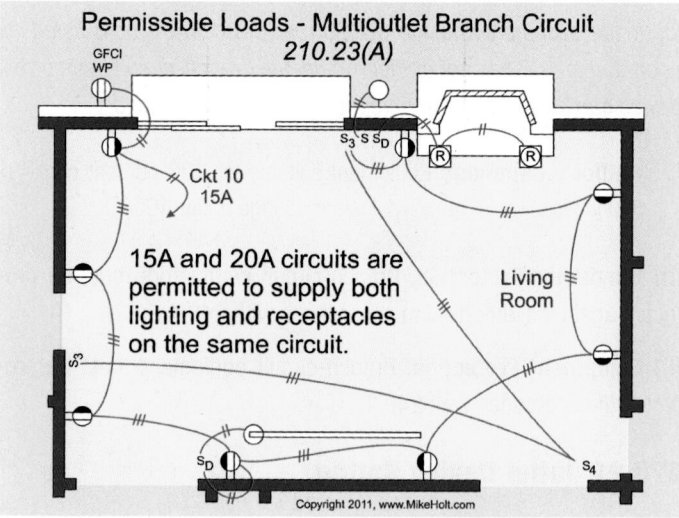

Figure 210–56

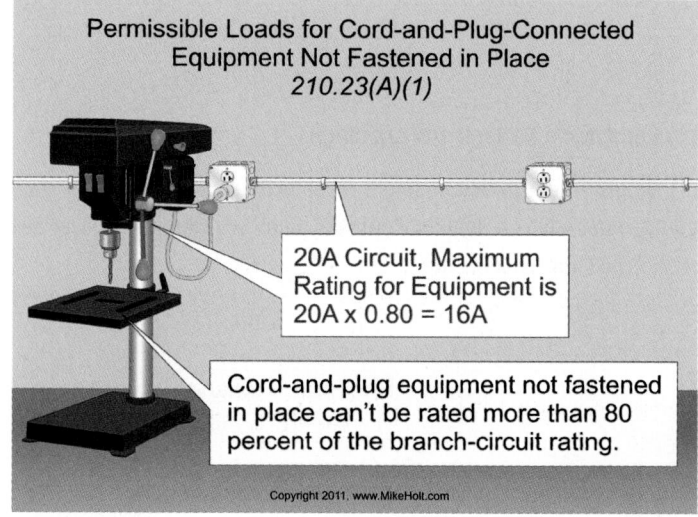

Figure 210–57

(2) Fixed Equipment. Equipment fastened in place (other than luminaires) must not be rated more than 50 percent of the branch-circuit ampere rating if this circuit supplies luminaires, receptacles, or both. **Figure 210–58**

> **Question:** *Can a whole house (central) vacuum motor rated 13A be installed on an existing 20A circuit that supplies more than one receptacle outlet?*
>
> **Answer:** *No, an individual 15A or 20A branch circuit will be required.*

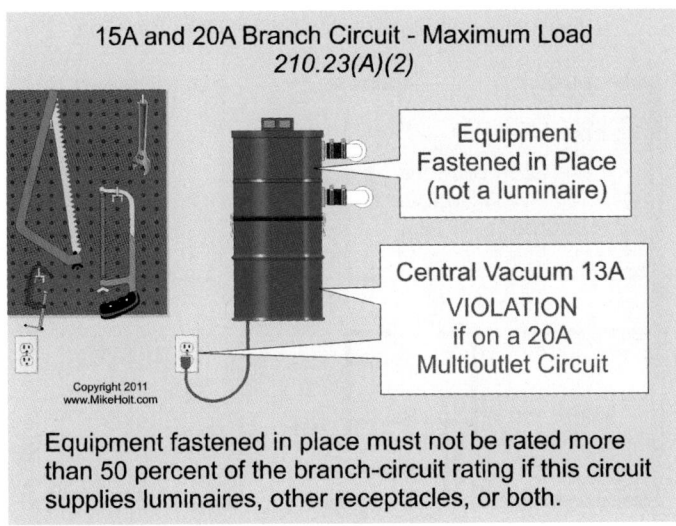

15A and 20A Branch Circuit - Maximum Load
210.23(A)(2)

Equipment Fastened in Place (not a luminaire)

Central Vacuum 13A
VIOLATION
if on a 20A
Multioutlet Circuit

Copyright 2011
www.MikeHolt.com

Equipment fastened in place must not be rated more than 50 percent of the branch-circuit rating if this circuit supplies luminaires, other receptacles, or both.

Figure 210–58

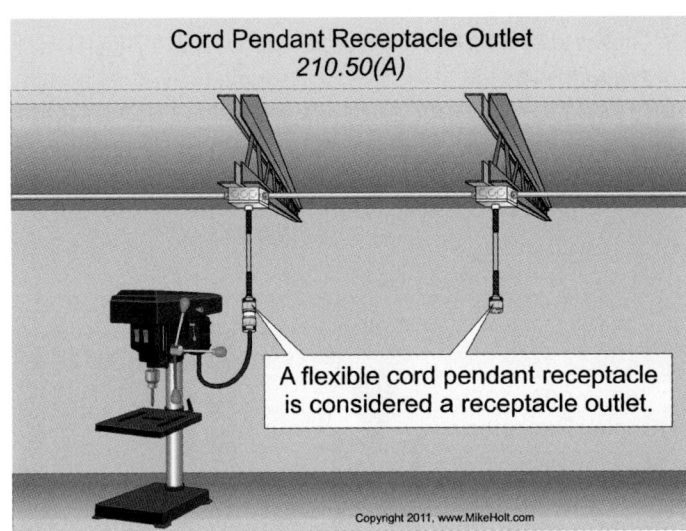

Cord Pendant Receptacle Outlet
210.50(A)

A flexible cord pendant receptacle is considered a receptacle outlet.

Copyright 2011, www.MikeHolt.com

Figure 210–59

210.25 Branch Circuits in Buildings with Multiple Occupancies.

(A) Dwelling Unit Branch Circuits. Dwelling unit branch circuits are only permitted to supply loads within or associated with the dwelling unit.

(B) Common Area Branch Circuits. Branch circuits installed for public or common areas of a multi-occupancy building aren't permitted to originate from equipment that supplies an individual dwelling unit or tenant space.

> **Author's Comment:** This rule prohibits common area branch circuits from being supplied from an individual dwelling unit or tenant space to prevent common area circuits from being turned off by tenants or by the utility due to nonpayment of electric bills.

PART III. REQUIRED OUTLETS

210.50 General. Receptacle outlets must be installed in accordance with 210.52 through 210.63.

(A) Cord Pendant Receptacle Outlet. A permanently installed flexible cord pendant receptacle is considered a receptacle outlet. **Figure 210–59**

> **Author's Comment:** Only cords identified for use as pendants in Table 400.4 may be used for pendants,, also see 314.23(H) for the requirements for boxes at pendant outlets.

(C) Appliance Receptacle Outlets. Receptacle outlets installed in a dwelling unit for a specific appliance, such as a clothes washer, dryer, range, garage door opener or refrigerator, must be within 6 ft of the intended location of the appliance. **Figure 210–60**

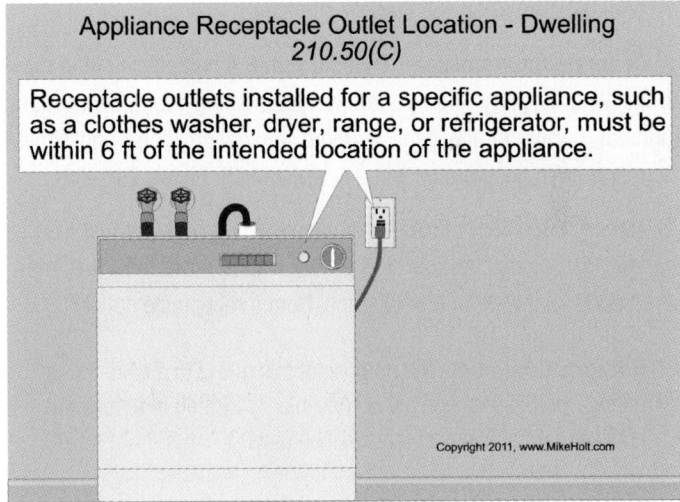

Appliance Receptacle Outlet Location - Dwelling
210.50(C)

Receptacle outlets installed for a specific appliance, such as a clothes washer, dryer, range, or refrigerator, must be within 6 ft of the intended location of the appliance.

Copyright 2011, www.MikeHolt.com

Figure 210–60

210.52 Dwelling Unit Receptacle Outlet Requirements. This section provides requirements for 15A and 20A, 125V receptacle outlets. The receptacles required by this section are in addition to any receptacle that is:

(1) Part of a luminaire or appliance,

(2) Controlled by a wall switch in accordance with 210.70(A)(1), Ex 1. **Figure 210–61**

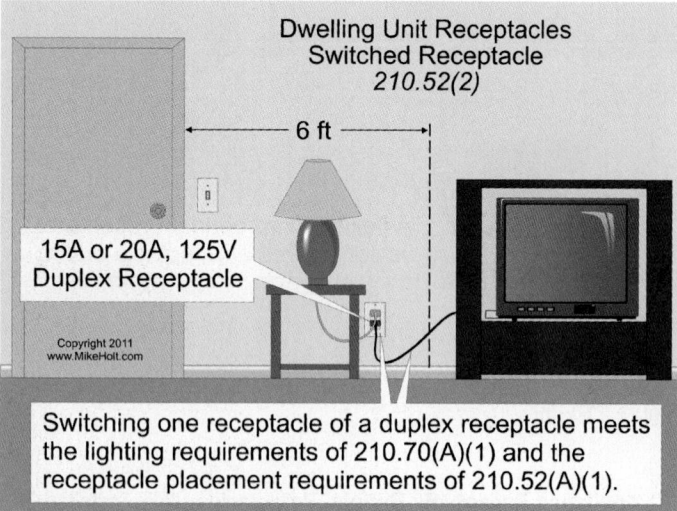

Figure 210–61

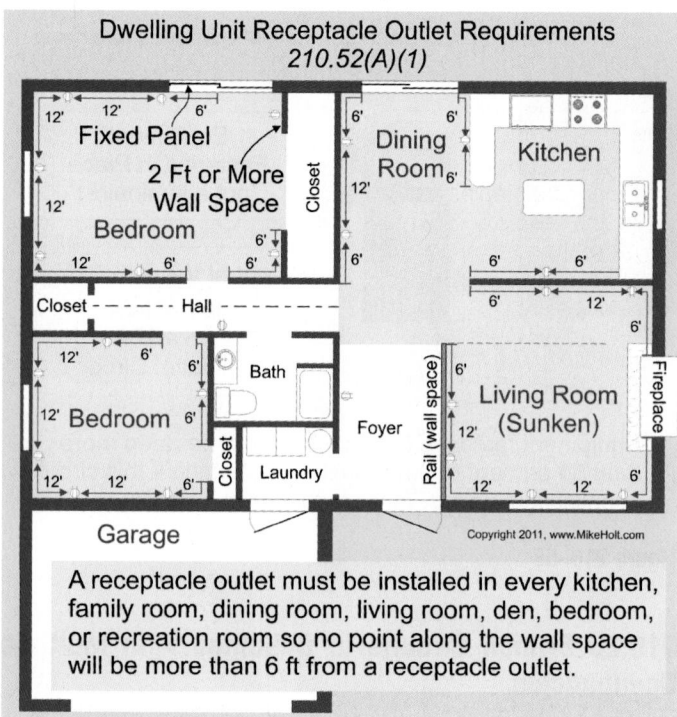

Figure 210–62

(3) Located within cabinets or cupboards, or

(4) Located more than 5½ ft above the floor.

(A) General Requirements—Dwelling Unit. A receptacle outlet must be installed in every kitchen, family room, dining room, living room, sunroom, parlor, library, den, bedroom, recreation room, and similar room or area in accordance with (1), (2), and (3): **Figure 210–62**

(1) Receptacle Placement. A receptacle outlet must be installed so that no point along the floor line of any wall is more than 6 ft, measured horizontally along the floor line, from a receptacle outlet.

> **Author's Comment:** The purpose of this rule is to ensure that a general-purpose receptacle is conveniently located to reduce the chance that an extension cord will be used.

(2) Definition of Wall Space.

(1) Any space 2 ft or more in width, unbroken along the floor line by doorways <u>and similar openings</u>, fireplaces, <u>and fixed cabinets</u>. **Figure 210–63**

(2) The space occupied by fixed panels in exterior walls.

(3) The space occupied by fixed room dividers, such as freestanding bar-type counters or guard rails.

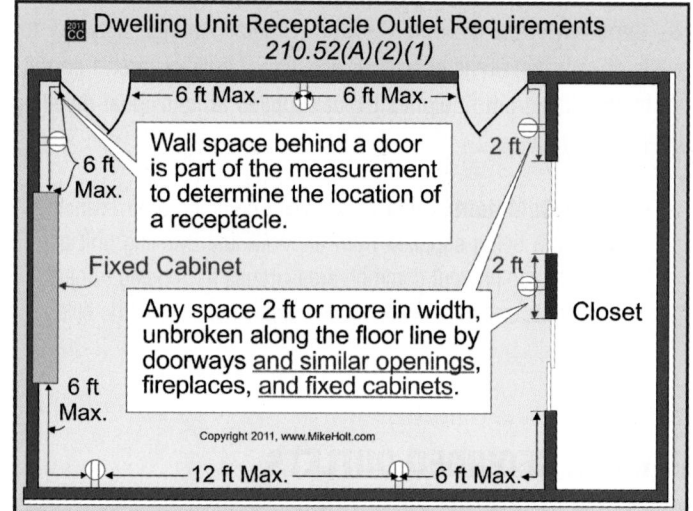

Figure 210–63

(3) Floor Receptacle Outlets. Floor receptacle outlets aren't counted as the required receptacle wall outlet if they're located more than 18 in. from the wall. **Figure 210–64**

(4) Countertop Receptacles. Receptacles installed for countertop surfaces as required by 210.52(C), can't be used to meet the receptacle requirements for wall space as required by 210.52(A). **Figure 210–65**

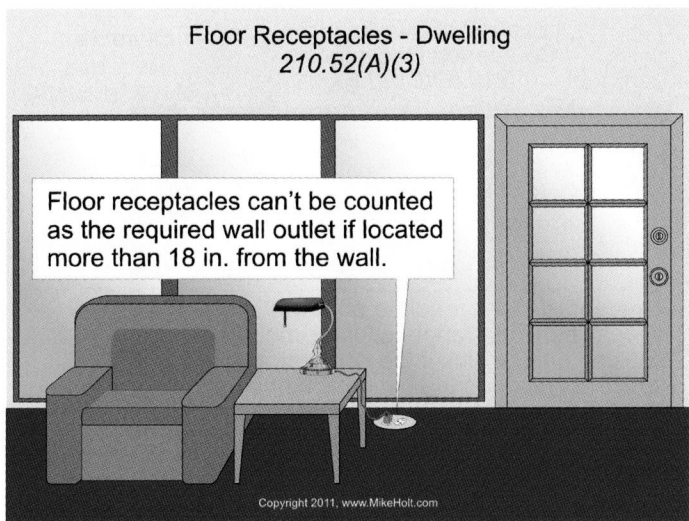

Figure 210–64

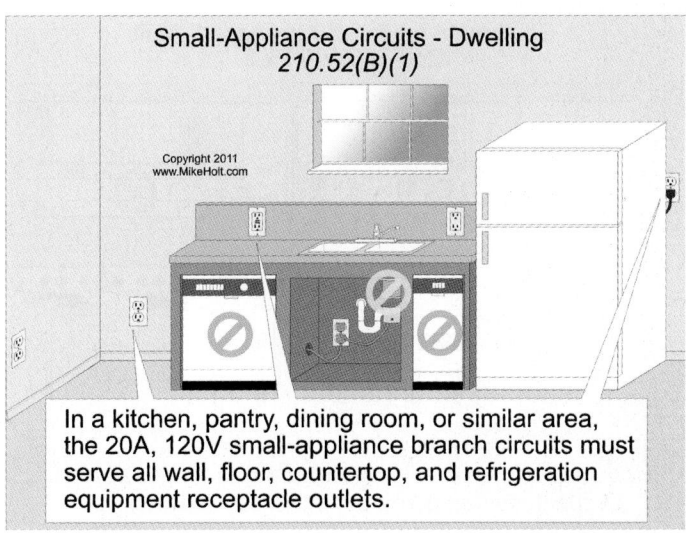

Figure 210–66

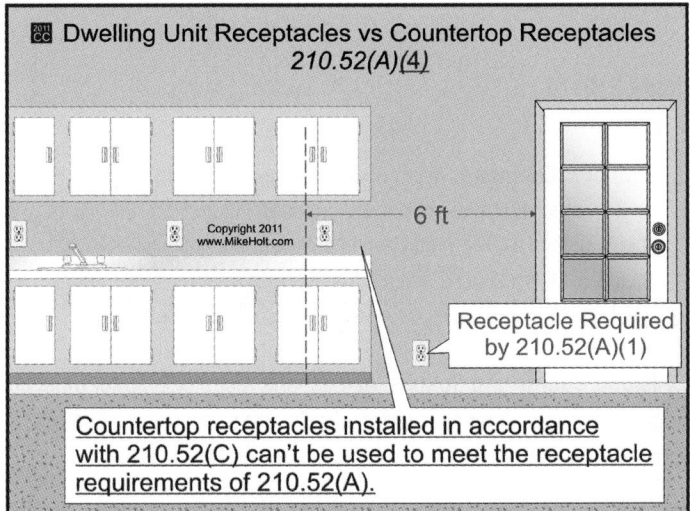

Figure 210–65

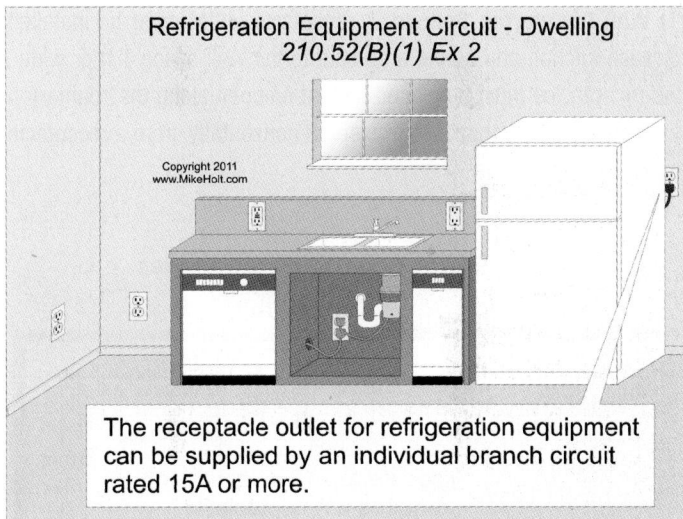

Figure 210–67

(B) Small-Appliance Circuits.

(1) Receptacle Outlets. The two or more 20A, 120V small-appliance branch circuits serving the kitchen, pantry, breakfast room, and dining room area of a dwelling unit [210.11(C)(1)] must serve all wall, floor and countertop receptacle outlets [210.52(C)], and the receptacle outlet for refrigeration equipment. **Figure 210–66**

Ex 2: The receptacle outlet for refrigeration equipment can be supplied from an individual branch circuit rated 15A or greater. **Figure 210–67**

(2) Not Supply Other Outlets. The 20A, 120V small-appliance circuits required by 210.11(C)(1) must not supply outlets for luminaires or appliances.

Ex 1: The 20A, 120V small-appliance branch circuit can be used to supply a receptacle for an electric clock.

Ex 2: A receptacle can be connected to the small-appliance branch circuit to supply a gas-fired range, oven, or counter-mounted cooking unit. **Figure 210–68**

> **Author's Comment:** A range hood or above the range microwave listed as a range hood must be supplied by an individual branch circuit [422.16(B)(4)(5)].

(C) Countertop Receptacles. In kitchens, pantries, breakfast rooms, dining rooms, and similar areas of dwelling units, receptacle outlets for countertop spaces must be installed according to (1) through (5) below.

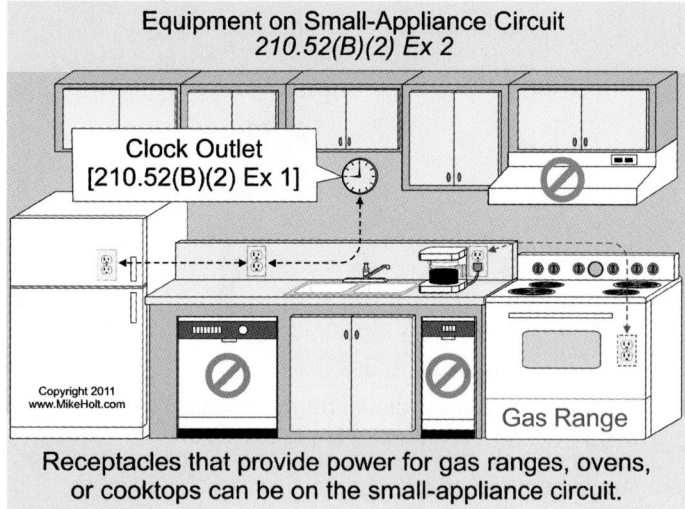

Figure 210-68

(1) Wall Countertop Spaces. A receptacle outlet must be installed for each kitchen and dining area countertop wall space 1 ft or wider, and receptacles must be placed so that no point along the countertop wall space is more than 2 ft, measured horizontally, from a receptacle outlet. Figure 210-69

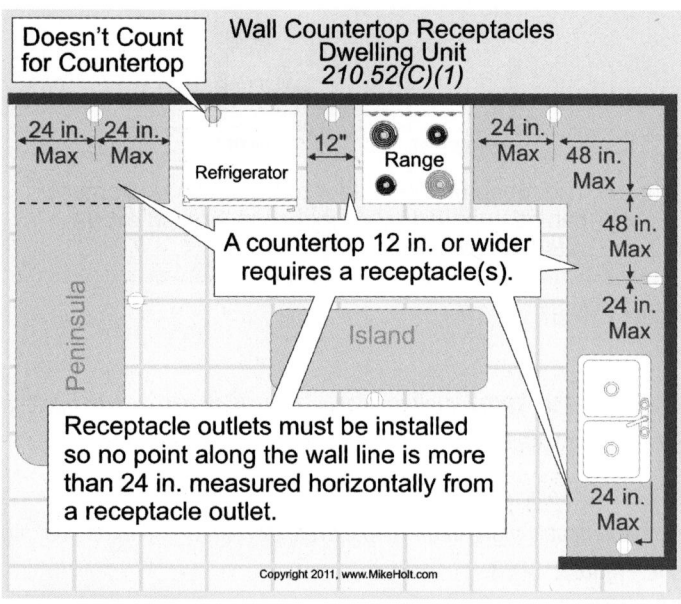

Figure 210-69

Ex: A receptacle outlet isn't required on a wall directly behind a range, counter-mounted cooking unit, or sink, in accordance with Figure 210.52(C)(1) in the NEC. Figure 210-70

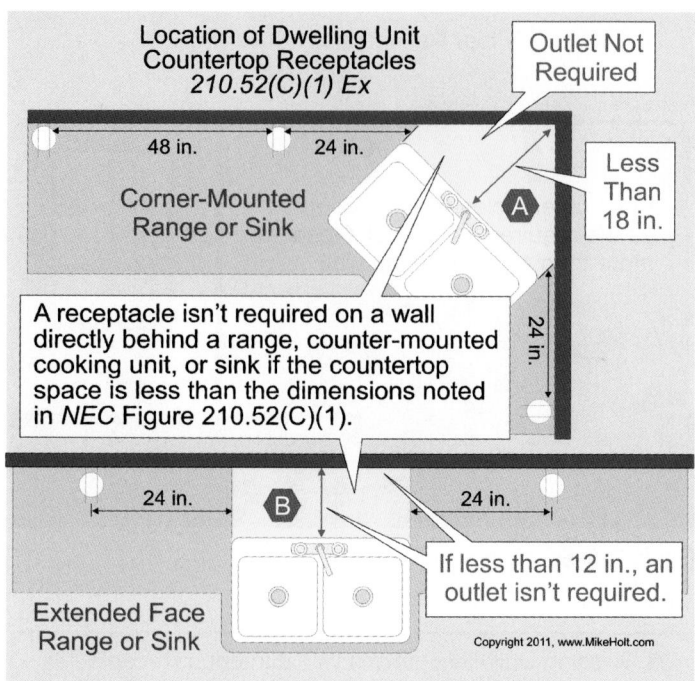

Figure 210-70

Author's Comment: If the countertop space behind a range or sink is larger than the dimensions noted in Figure 210.52(C)(1) of the *NEC*, then a GFCI-protected receptacle must be installed in that space. This is because, for all practical purposes, if there's sufficient space for an appliance, an appliance will be placed there.

(2) Island Countertop Spaces. At least one receptacle outlet must be installed at each island countertop space with a long dimension of 2 ft or more, and a short dimension of 1 ft or more. Figure 210-71

(3) Peninsular Countertop Spaces. At least one receptacle outlet must be installed at each peninsular countertop with a long dimension of 2 ft or more, and a short dimension of 1 ft or more, measured from the connecting edge. Figure 210-72

Author's Comment: The *Code* doesn't require more than one receptacle outlet in an island or peninsular countertop space, regardless of the length of the countertop, unless the countertop is broken as described in 210.52(C)(4).

(4) Separate Countertop Spaces. When breaks occur in countertop spaces for rangetops, refrigerators, or sinks, each countertop space is considered as a separate countertop for determining receptacle placement. Figure 210-73

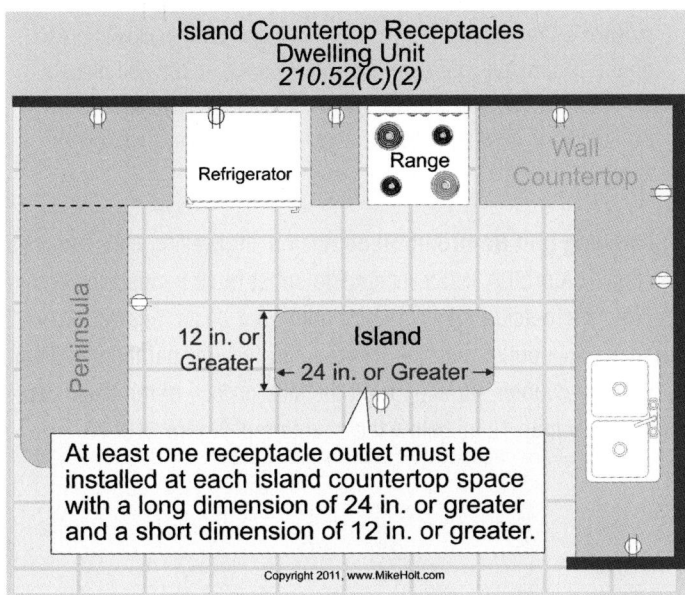

Figure 210–71

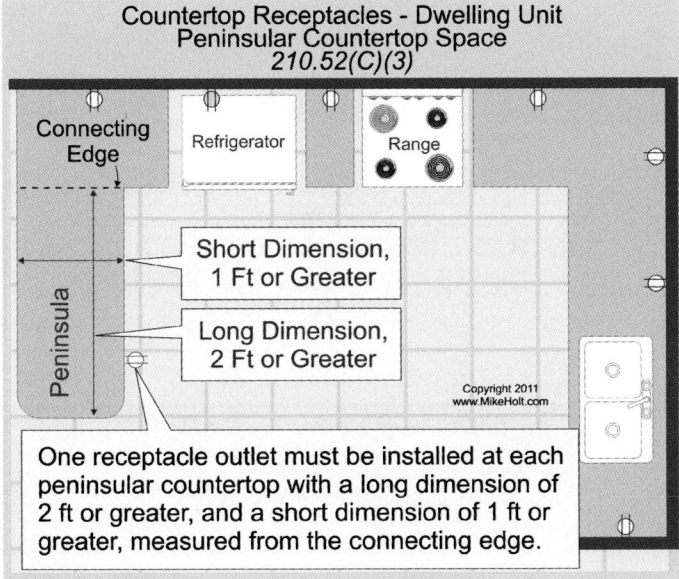

Figure 210–72

If a range, counter-mounted cooking unit, or sink is installed in an island or peninsular countertop, and the depth of the counter behind the range, counter-mounted cooking unit, or sink is less than 12 in., the countertop space is considered to be two separate countertop spaces. **Figure 210–74**

Author's Comment: GFCI protection is required for all 15A and 20A, 125V receptacles that supply kitchen countertop surfaces [210.8(A)(6)].

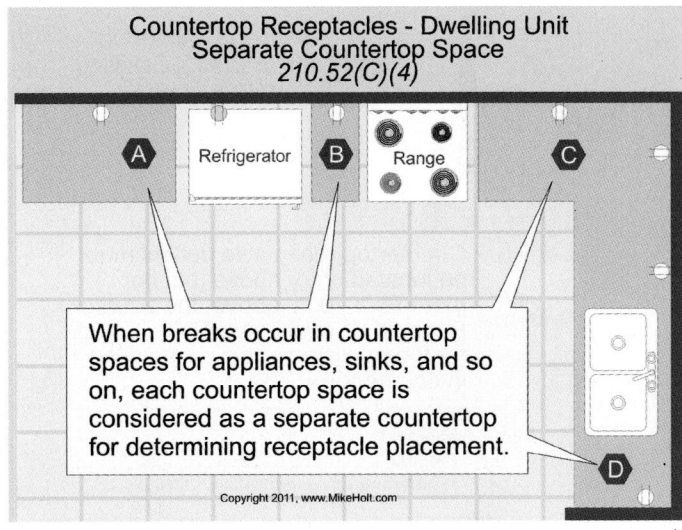

Figure 210–73

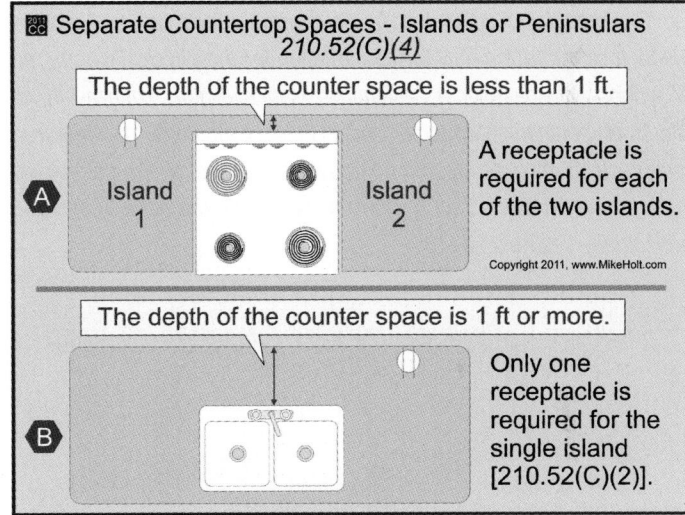

Figure 210–74

(5) Receptacle Location. Receptacle outlets required by 210.52(C)(1) for the countertop space must be located on or above, but not more than 20 in. above, the countertop surface. Receptacle outlet assemblies listed for the application can be installed in countertops. **Figure 210–75**

Note: Receptacles must not be installed in a face-up position in countertops or similar work surface areas in a dwelling unit [406.5(E)].

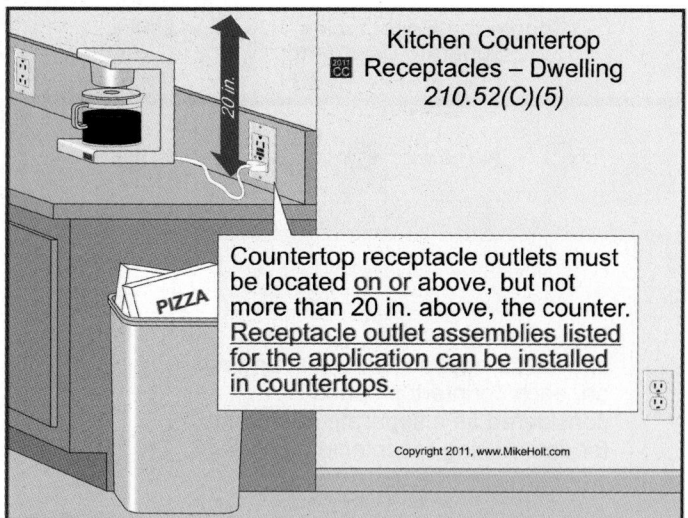

Figure 210–75

Ex: The receptacle outlet for the countertop space can be installed below the countertop only for construction for the physically impaired or when wall space or a backsplash isn't available, such as in an island or peninsular counter. Under these conditions, the required receptacle(s) must be located no more than 1 ft below the countertop surface and no more than 6 in. from the countertop edge, measured horizontally. **Figure 210–76**

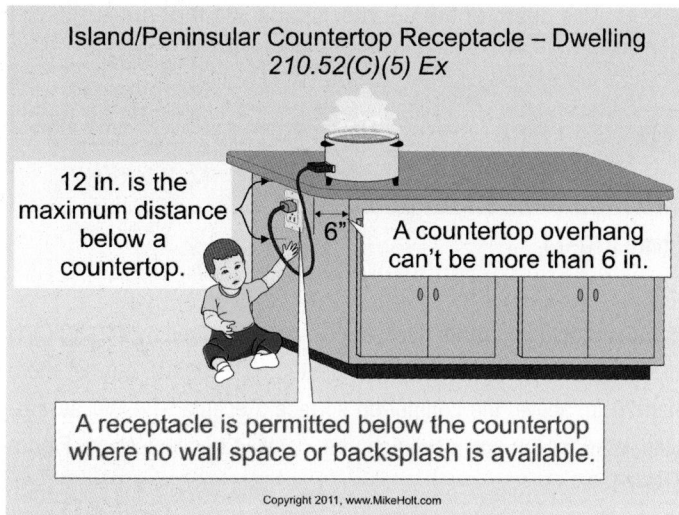

Figure 210–76

Receptacle outlets rendered not readily accessible by appliances fastened in place, located in an appliance garage, behind sinks, or rangetops [210.52(C)(1) Ex], or supplying appliances that occupy dedicated space don't count as the required countertop receptacles.

Author's Comment: An "appliance garage" is an enclosed area on the countertop where an appliance can be stored and hidden from view when not in use. If a receptacle is installed inside an appliance garage, it doesn't count as a required countertop receptacle outlet.

(D) Dwelling Unit Bathroom Receptacles. In dwelling units, not less than one 15A or 20A, 125V receptacle outlet must be installed within 3 ft from the outside edge of each bathroom basin. **Figure 210–77**. The receptacle outlet must be located on a wall or partition adjacent to the basin counter surface, or on the side or face of the basin cabinet not more than 12 in. below the countertop. **Figure 210–78**

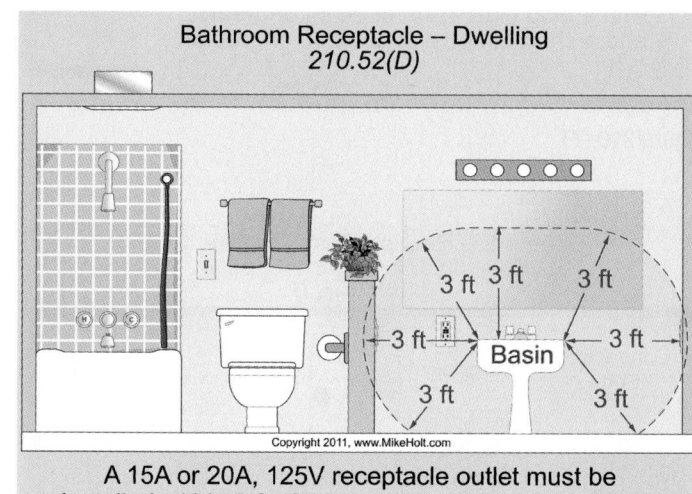

Figure 210–77

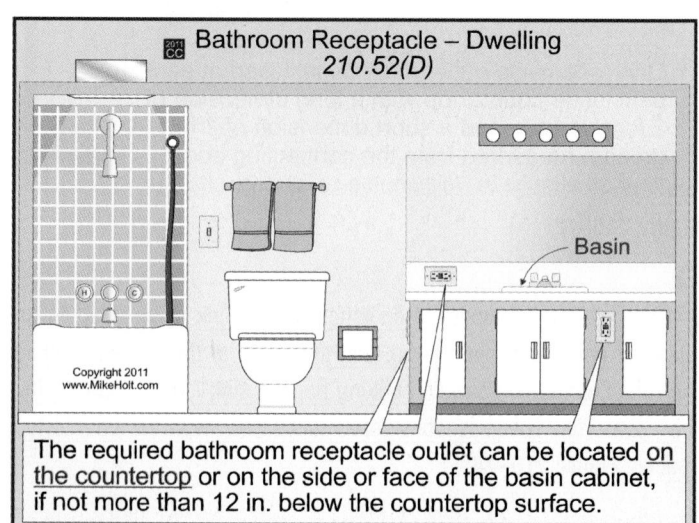

Figure 210–78

<u>Receptacle outlet assemblies listed for the application can be installed in countertops.</u>

Note: Receptacles must not be installed in a face-up position in countertops or similar work surface areas in a dwelling unit [406.5(E)].

Author's Comments:

- One receptacle outlet can be located between two basins to meet this requirement, but only if it's located within 3 ft of the outside edge of each basin. **Figure 210–79**
- The bathroom receptacles must be GFCI protected [210.8(A)(1)].

Figure 210–79

One 15A or 20A, 125V receptacle outlet must be installed within 3 ft from the outside edge of each bathroom basin.

(E) Dwelling Unit Outdoor Receptacles.

(1) One- and Two-Family Dwellings. Two GFCI-protected 15A or 20A, 125V receptacle outlets that are accessible while standing at grade level must be installed outdoors for each dwelling unit, one at the front and one at the back, no more than 6½ ft above grade. **Figure 210–80**

(2) Multifamily Dwelling. Each dwelling unit of a multifamily dwelling that has an individual entrance at grade level must have at least one GFCI-protected 15A or 20A, 125V receptacle outlet accessible from grade level located not more than 6½ ft above grade. **Figure 210–81**

(3) Balconies, Decks, and Porches. At least one 15A or 20A, 125V receptacle must be installed within the perimeter and not more than

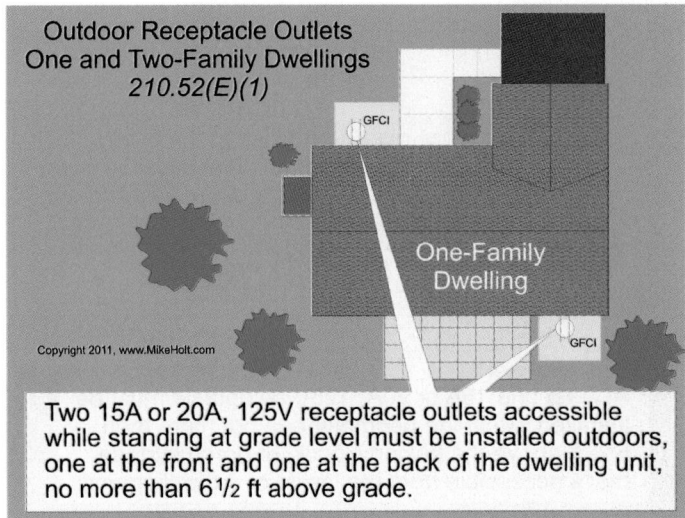

Figure 210–80

Two 15A or 20A, 125V receptacle outlets accessible while standing at grade level must be installed outdoors, one at the front and one at the back of the dwelling unit, no more than 6½ ft above grade.

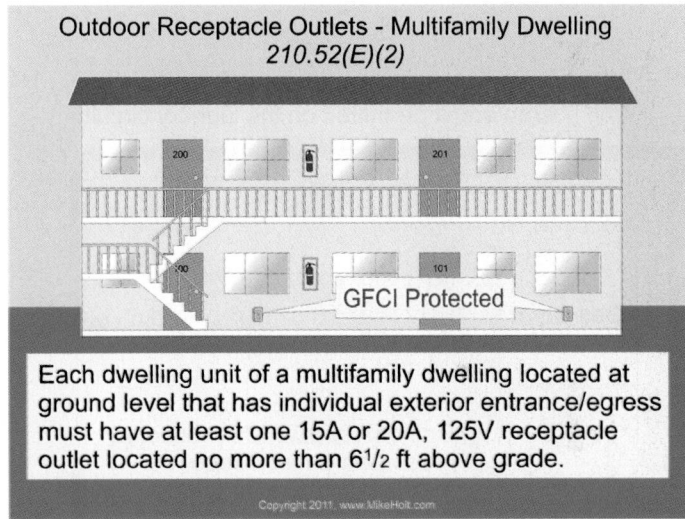

Figure 210–81

Each dwelling unit of a multifamily dwelling located at ground level that has individual exterior entrance/egress must have at least one 15A or 20A, 125V receptacle outlet located no more than 6½ ft above grade.

6½ ft above the balcony, deck, or porch surface that's accessible from the inside of a dwelling unit. **Figure 210–82**

> **Author's Comment:** These receptacles must be GFCI protected [210.8(A)(3)].

(F) Dwelling Unit Laundry Area Receptacles. Each dwelling unit must have not less than one 15A or 20A, 125V receptacle installed in the laundry area. The receptacle(s) must be supplied by the 20A, 120V laundry branch circuit, which must not supply any other outlets [210.11(C)(2)]. **Figure 210–83**

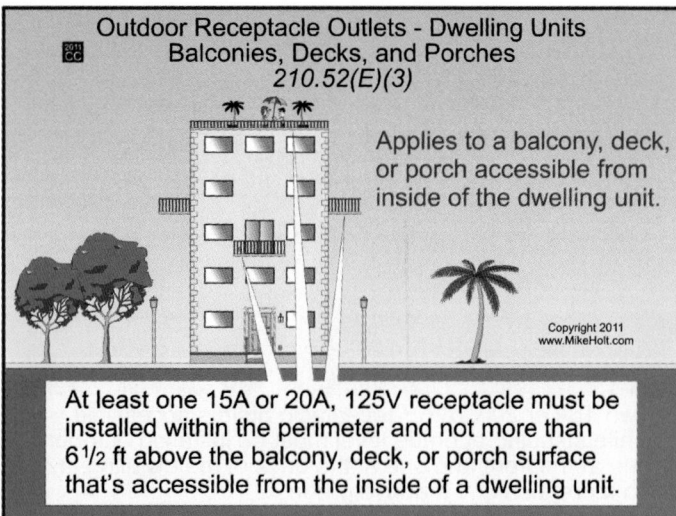

Figure 210–82

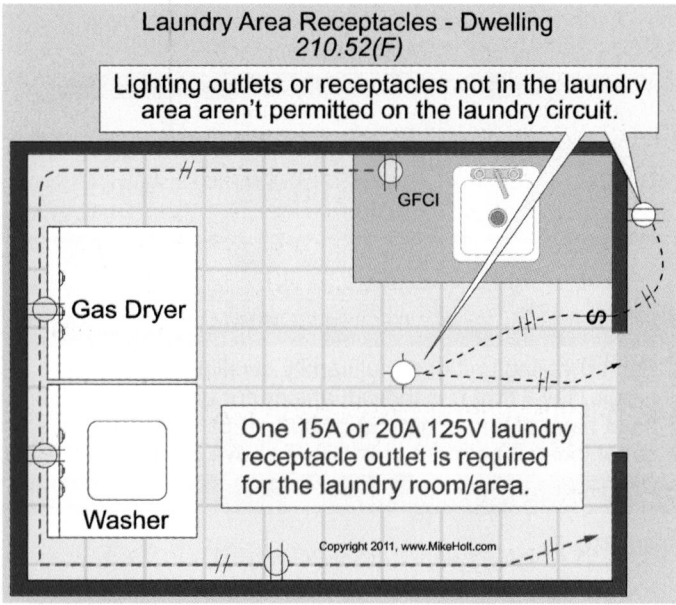

Figure 210–83

Author's Comment: Receptacles located within 6 ft of a laundry room sink require GFCI protection [210.8(A)(7)].

Ex 1: A laundry receptacle outlet isn't required in a dwelling unit located in a multifamily building with laundry facilities available to all occupants.

(G) Dwelling Unit Garage, Basement, and Accessory Building Receptacles.

(1) Not less than one 15A or 20A, 125V receptacle outlet, in addition to any provided for a specific piece of equipment, must be installed in each basement, in each attached garage, and each detached garage or accessory building with electric power. **Figure 210–84**

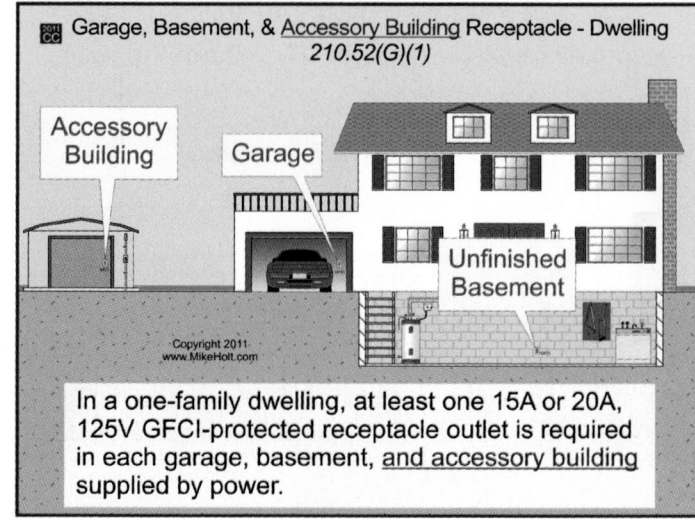

Figure 210–84

Author's Comment: GFCI protection is required for all 15 or 20A, 125V receptacles installed in unfinished basements [210.8(A)(5)], garages and accessory buildings [210.8(A)(2)] of dwelling units.

(2) If a portion of the basement is finished into habitable rooms, each separate unfinished portion must have a 15A or 20A, 125V receptacle outlet installed. **Figure 210–85**

Author's Comment: The purpose of this requirement is to prevent an extension cord from a non-GFCI-protected receptacle from being used to supply power to loads in the unfinished portion of the basement.

(H) Dwelling Unit Hallway Receptacles. One 15A or 20A, 125V receptacle outlet must be installed in each hallway that's at least 10 ft long, measured along the centerline of the hallway without passing through a doorway. **Figure 210–86**

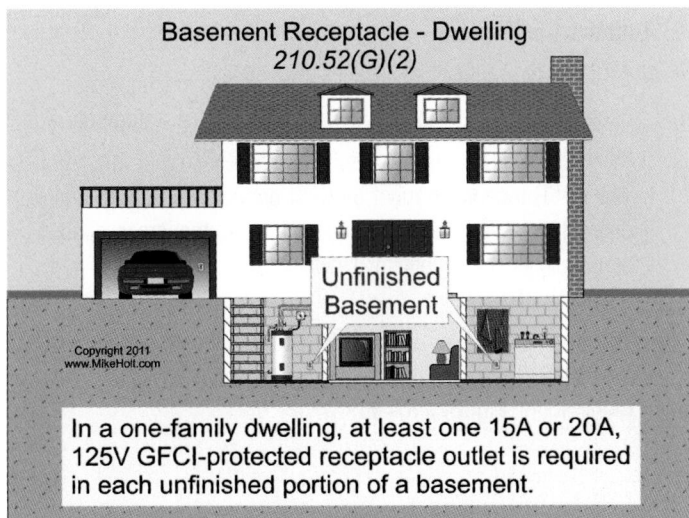

Figure 210–85

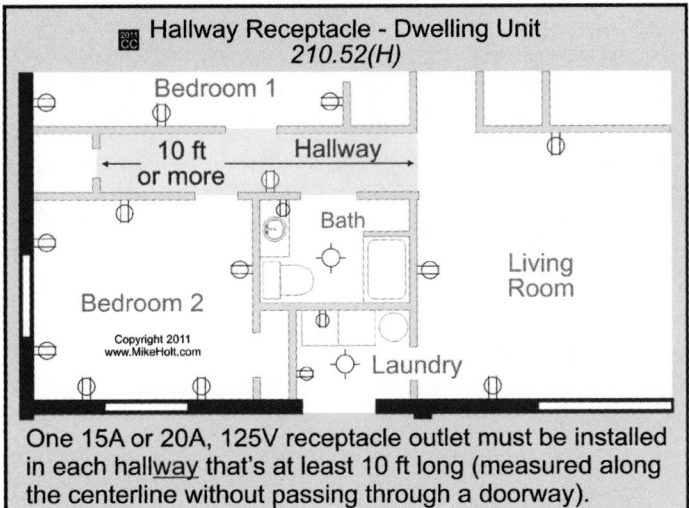

Figure 210–86

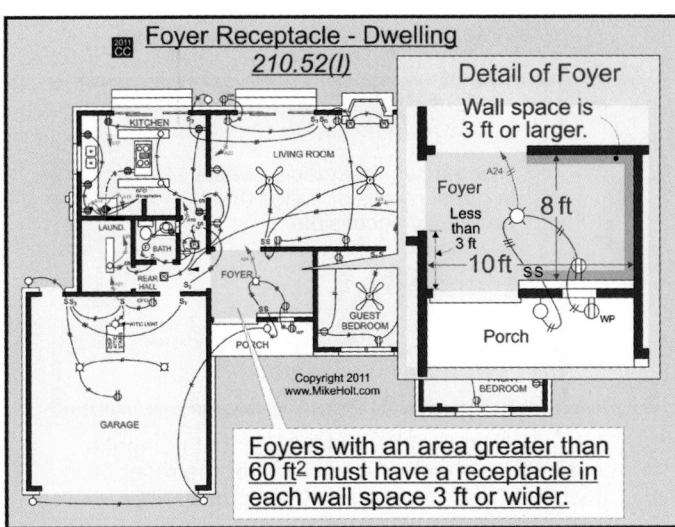

Figure 210–87

(I) Foyer Receptacles. Foyers that aren't part of a hallway [210.52(H)] having an area greater than 60 sq ft must have a receptacle located on any wall space 3 ft or more in width and unbroken by doorways, floor to ceiling windows, and similar openings. **Figure 210–87**

210.60 Receptacles in Guest Rooms, Guest Suites, Dormitories, and Similar Occupancies.

(A) General Requirements. Guest rooms or guest suites in hotels, motels, and sleeping rooms in dormitories and similar occupancies, must have receptacle outlets installed in accordance with all the requirements for a dwelling unit as described in 210.52(A) and 210.52(D).

Guest rooms with permanent provisions for living, sleeping, cooking, and sanitation must have receptacles installed in accordance with the dwelling unit requirements of 210.52.

(B) Receptacle Placement. The number of receptacle outlets required for guest rooms must not be less than that required for a dwelling unit, in accordance with 210.52(A). To eliminate the need for extension cords by guests for ironing, computers, refrigerators, and so forth, receptacles can be located to be convenient for permanent furniture layout, but not less than two receptacle outlets must be readily accessible.

Receptacle outlets behind a bed must be located so the bed won't make contact with the attachment plug, or the receptacle must be provided with a suitable guard. **Figure 210–88**

> **Author's Comment:** See the definition of "Attachment Plug" in Article 100.

210.62 Show Windows. At least one receptacle outlet must be installed within 18 in. of the top of a show window for each 12 linear feet or major fraction thereof measured horizontally at its maximum width.

> **Author's Comment:** See the definition of "Show Window" in Article 100.

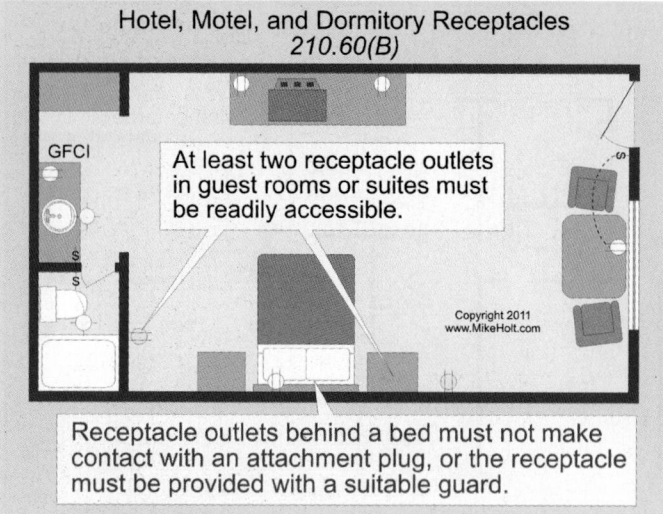

Figure 210–88

210.63 Heating, Air-Conditioning, and Refrigeration (HACR) Equipment.

A 15A or 20A, 125V receptacle outlet must be installed at an accessible location for the servicing of heating, air-conditioning, and refrigeration equipment. The receptacle must be located within 25 ft of, and on the same level as, the heating, air-conditioning, and refrigeration equipment. **Figure 210–89**

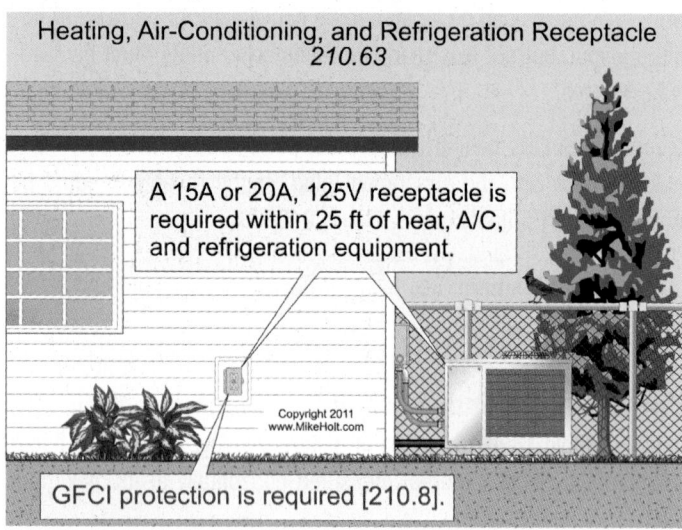

Figure 210–89

Author's Comments:

- A receptacle outlet isn't required for ventilation equipment, because it's not heating, air-conditioning, or refrigeration equipment.

- The HACR receptacle must be GFCI protected if located outdoors [210.8(A)(3) and 210.8(B)(5)] or in the crawl space or unfinished basement of a dwelling unit [210.8(A)(4) and 210.8(A)(5)].

- The outdoor 15A or 20A, 125V receptacle outlet required for dwelling units [210.52(E)(1)] can be used to satisfy this requirement. **Figure 210–90**

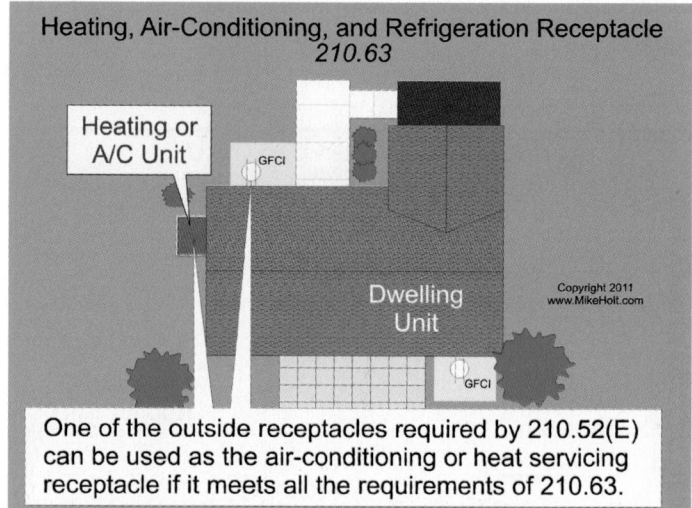

Figure 210–90

Ex: A receptacle outlet isn't required at one- and two-family dwellings for the service of evaporative coolers.

210.70 Lighting Outlet Requirements.

(A) Dwelling Unit Lighting Outlets. Lighting outlets must be installed in:

(1) Habitable Rooms. At least one wall switch-controlled lighting outlet must be installed in every habitable room and bathroom of a dwelling unit. Figure 210–91

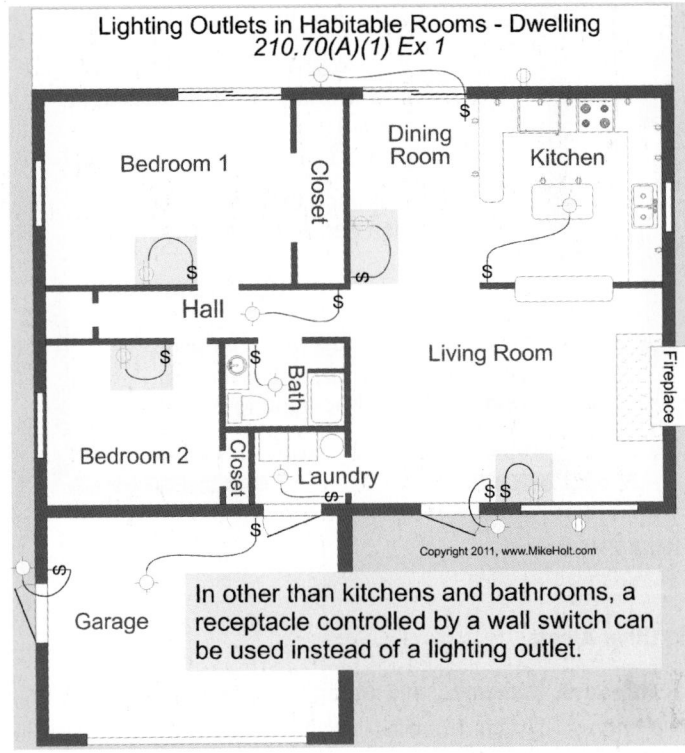

Figure 210–92

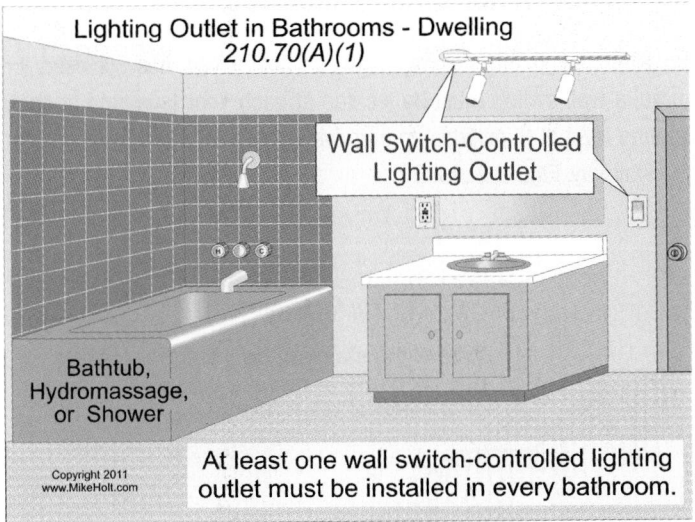

Figure 210–91

Author's Comment: See the definition of "Lighting Outlet" in Article 100.

Ex 1: In other than kitchens and bathrooms, a receptacle controlled by a wall switch can be used instead of a lighting outlet. Figure 210–92

Ex 2: Lighting outlets can be controlled by occupancy sensors equipped with a manual override that permits the sensor to function as a wall switch. Figure 210–93

Author's Comment: The *Code* specifies the location of the wall switch-controlled lighting outlet, but it doesn't specify the switch location. Naturally, you wouldn't want to install a switch behind a door or other inconvenient location, but the *NEC* doesn't require you to relocate the switch to suit the swing of the door. When in doubt as to the best location to place a light switch, consult the job plans or ask the customer. **Figure 210–94**

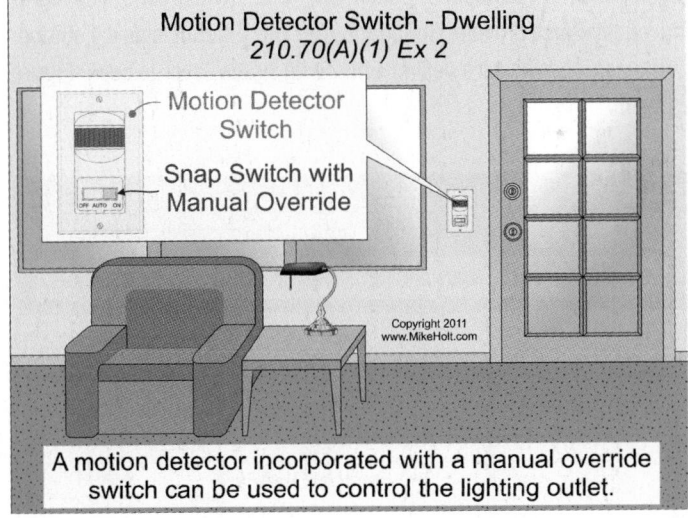

Figure 210–93

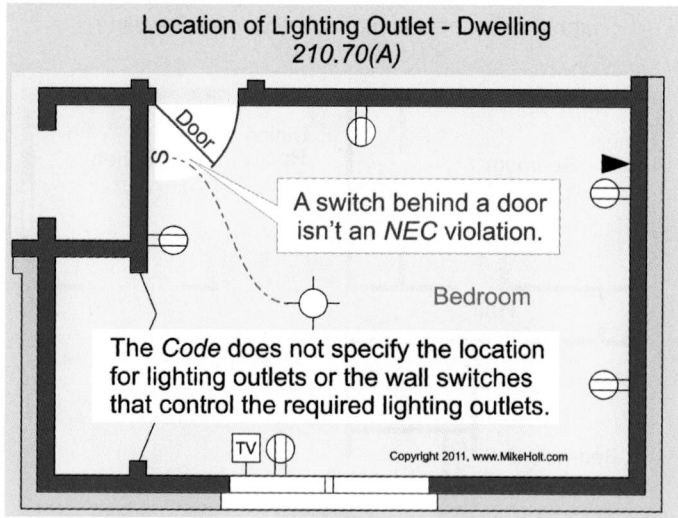

Figure 210–94

(2) Other Areas.

(a) Hallways, Stairways, and Garages. In dwelling units, not less than one wall switch-controlled lighting outlet must be installed in hallways, stairways, attached garages, and detached garages with electric power.

(b) Exterior Entrances. At least one wall switch-controlled lighting outlet must provide illumination on the exterior side of outdoor entrances or exits of dwelling units with grade-level access. **Figure 210–95**

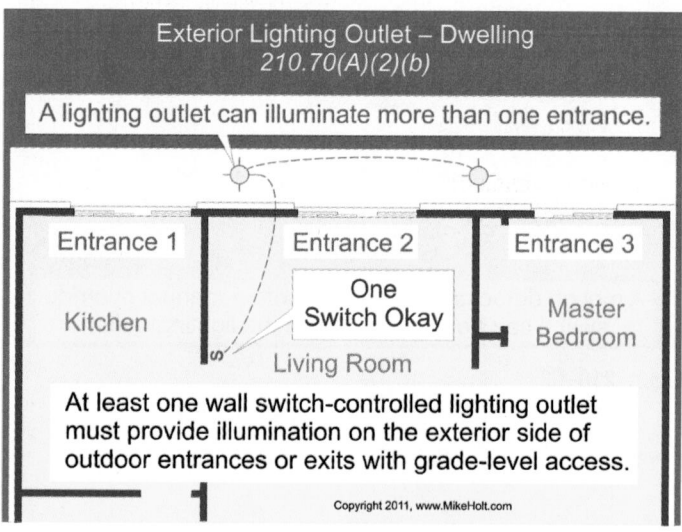

Figure 210–95

Author's Comments:

- The *NEC* doesn't require a switch adjacent to each outdoor entrance or exit. The *Code* considers switch location a "design issue" which is beyond the purpose of the *NEC* [90.1(C)]. For this reason, proposals to mandate switch locations have been rejected.

- A lighting outlet isn't required to provide illumination on the exterior side of outdoor entrances or exits for a commercial or industrial occupancy.

(c) Stairway. If the stairway between floor levels has six risers or more, a wall switch must be located at each floor level and at each landing level that includes an entryway to control the illumination for the stairway. **Figure 210–96**

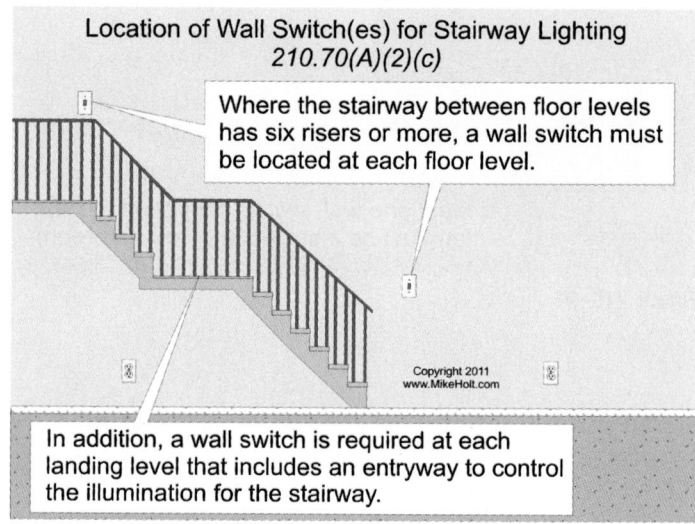

Figure 210–96

Ex to (a), (b), and (c): Lighting outlets for hallways, stairways, and outdoor entrances can be switched by a remote, central, or automatic control device. **Figure 210–97**

(3) Storage and Equipment Rooms. At least one lighting outlet that contains a switch or is controlled by a wall switch must be installed in attics, underfloor spaces, utility rooms, and basements used for storage or containing equipment that requires servicing. The switch must be located at the usual point of entry to these spaces, and the lighting outlet must be located at or near the equipment that requires servicing. **Figure 210–98**

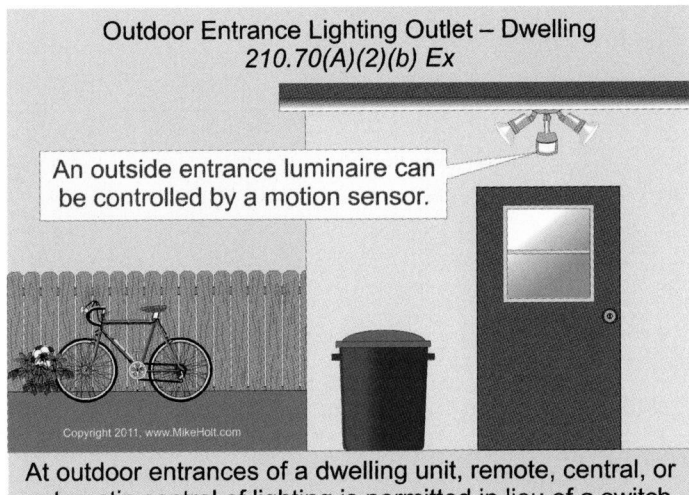

Outdoor Entrance Lighting Outlet – Dwelling
210.70(A)(2)(b) Ex

An outside entrance luminaire can be controlled by a motion sensor.

At outdoor entrances of a dwelling unit, remote, central, or automatic control of lighting is permitted in lieu of a switch.

Figure 210–97

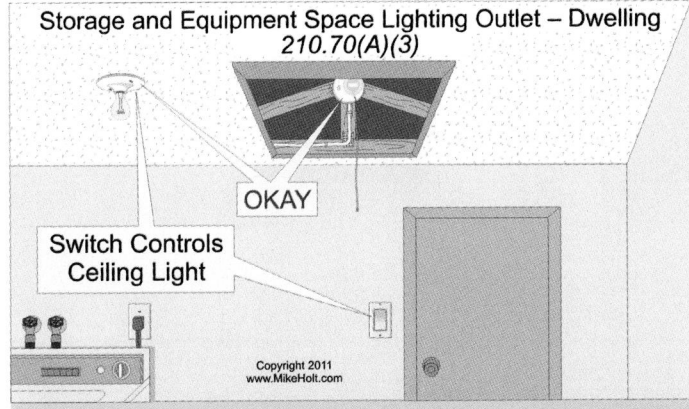

Storage and Equipment Space Lighting Outlet – Dwelling
210.70(A)(3)

OKAY

Switch Controls Ceiling Light

For attics, underfloor spaces, utility rooms, and basements, at least one lighting outlet containing a switch, or controlled by a wall switch, must be installed where these spaces are used for storage or contain equipment needing servicing.

Figure 210–98

(B) Guest Rooms or Guest Suites. At least one wall switch-controlled lighting outlet must be installed in every habitable room and bathroom of a guest room or guest suite of hotels, motels, and similar occupancies.

Ex 1: In other than bathrooms and kitchens, a receptacle controlled by a wall switch is permitted in lieu of lighting outlets. **Figure 210–99**

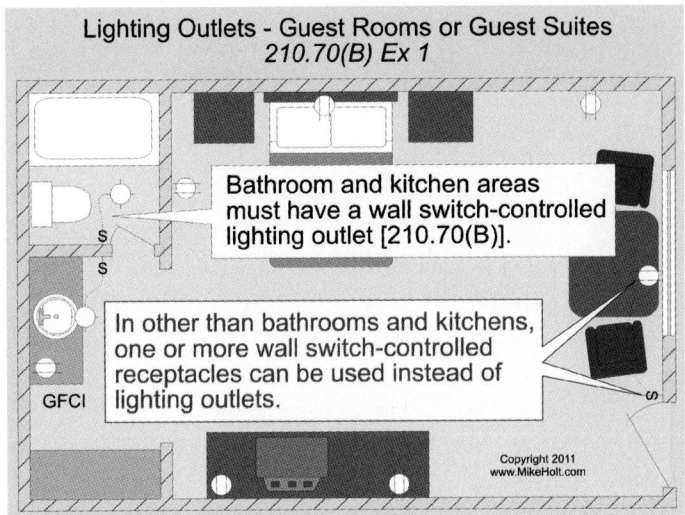

Lighting Outlets - Guest Rooms or Guest Suites
210.70(B) Ex 1

Bathroom and kitchen areas must have a wall switch-controlled lighting outlet [210.70(B)].

In other than bathrooms and kitchens, one or more wall switch-controlled receptacles can be used instead of lighting outlets.

GFCI

Figure 210–99

Ex 2: Lighting outlets can be controlled by occupancy sensors equipped with a manual override that permits the sensor to function as a wall switch.

(C) Other Than Dwelling Units. At least one lighting outlet that contains a switch or is controlled by a wall switch must be installed in attics and underfloor spaces containing equipment that requires servicing. The switch must be located at the usual point of entry to these spaces, and the lighting outlet must be located at or near the equipment requiring servicing.

> **Author's Comment:** A 15A or 20A, 125V receptacle must be installed within 25 ft of HACR equipment [210.63].

Notes

ARTICLE
215

Feeders

INTRODUCTION TO ARTICLE 215—FEEDERS

Article 215 covers the rules for the installation, minimum size, and ampacity of feeders. The requirements for feeders have some similarities to those for branch circuits, but in some ways, feeders bear a resemblance to service conductors. It's important to understand the distinct differences between these three types of circuits in order to correctly apply the *Code* requirements.

Feeders are the conductors between the service equipment, the separately derived system, or other supply source and the final branch-circuit overcurrent device. Conductors past the final overcurrent device protecting the circuit and the outlet are branch-circuit conductors and fall within the scope of Article 210 [Article 100 Definitions].

Service conductors are the conductors from the service point of the electric utility to the service disconnecting means [Article 100 Definition]. If there's no serving utility, and the electrical power is derived from a generator or other on-site power source, then the conductors from the supply source are defined as feeders and there are no service conductors.

It's easy to be confused between feeder, branch circuit, and service conductors, so it's important to evaluate each installation carefully using the Article 100 Definitions to be sure the correct *Code* rules are followed.

215.1 Scope. Article 215 covers the installation, conductor sizing, and protection requirements for feeders.

> **Author's Comment:** Article 100 defines feeders as the conductors between service equipment, a separately derived system, or other power supply, and the final branch-circuit overcurrent device. **Figure 215–1**

215.2 Minimum Rating.

(A) Feeder Conductor Size.

(1) Continuous and Noncontinuous Loads. The minimum feeder conductor ampacity, before the application of ambient temperature correction [310.15(B)(2)(a)], conductor bundling adjustment [310.15(B)(3)(a)], or both, must be no less than 125 percent of the continuous load, plus 100 percent of the noncontinuous load, based on the terminal temperature rating ampacities as listed in Table 310.15(B)(16) [110.14(C)(1)]. **Figure 215–2**

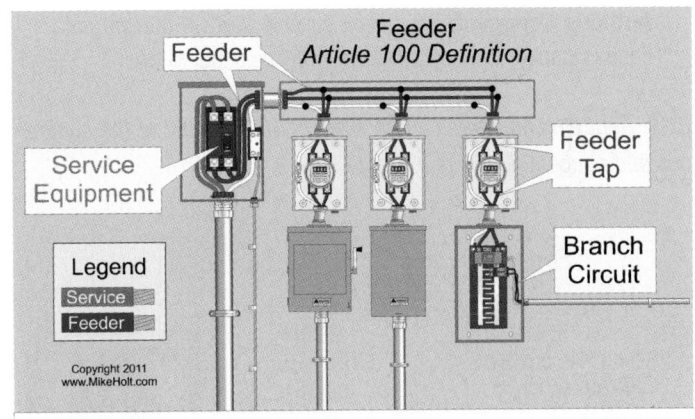

Conductors between service equipment, a separately derived system, or other power supply, and the final branch-circuit overcurrent device.

Figure 215–1

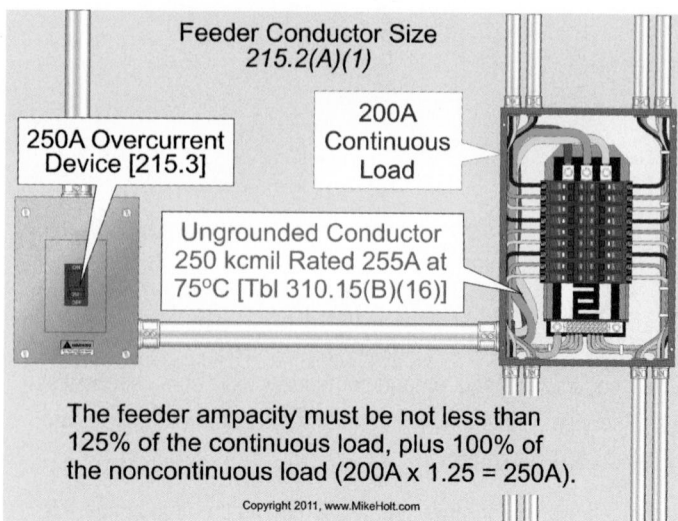

Figure 215–2

Author's Comment: See 215.3 for the feeder overcurrent device sizing requirements for continuous and noncontinuous loads.

Ex 1: If the assembly and the overcurrent device are both listed for operation at 100 percent of its rating, the conductors can be sized at 100 percent of the continuous load.

Author's Comment: Equipment suitable for 100 percent continuous loading is rarely available in ratings under 400A.

Ex 2: Neutral conductors can be sized at 100 percent of the continuous and noncontinuous load. Figure 215–3

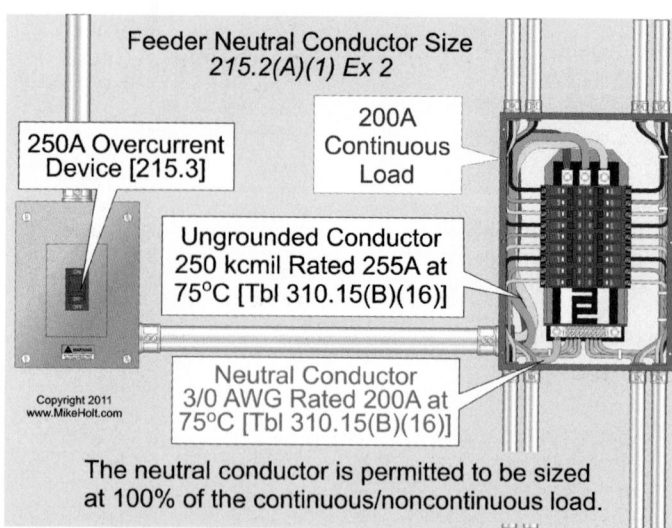

Figure 215–3

Question: *What size feeder conductors are required for a 200A continuous load if the terminals are rated 75ºC?*

(a) 2/0 AWG ungrounded conductors and a 1/0 AWG neutral conductor

(b) 3/0 AWG ungrounded conductors and a 1/0 AWG neutral conductor

(c) 4/0 AWG ungrounded conductors and a 1/0 AWG neutral conductor

(d) 250 kcmil ungrounded conductors and a 3/0 AWG neutral conductor

Answer: *(d) 250 kcmil AWG ungrounded conductors and a 3/0 AWG neutral conductor*

Since the load is 200A continuous, the feeder conductors must have an ampacity of not less than 250A (200A x 1.25). The neutral conductor is sized to the 200A continuous load according to the 75ºC column of Table 310.15(B)(16). According to the 75ºC column of Table 310.15(B)(16), 250 kcmil has an ampacity of 255A, and 3/0 has an ampacity of 200A.

(2) Neutral Conductor Size. The feeder neutral conductor must be sized to carry the maximum unbalanced load, in accordance with 220.61, and must not be smaller than the size listed in 250.122, based on the rating of the feeder overcurrent device. The sizing requirements of 250.122(F) for parallel conductors don't apply.

Question: *What size neutral conductor is required for a feeder consisting of 250 kcmil ungrounded conductors and one neutral conductor protected by a 250A overcurrent device, where the unbalanced load is only 50A, with 75ºC terminals?* **Figure 215–4**

(a) 6 AWG   (b) 4 AWG   (c) 1/0 AWG   (d) 3/0 AWG

Answer: *(b) 4 AWG [based on Table 250.122]*

Table 310.15(B)(16) and 220.61 permit an 8 AWG neutral conductor, rated 50A at 75ºC to carry the 50A unbalanced load, but the neutral conductor isn't permitted to be smaller than 4 AWG, as listed in Table 250.122, based on the 250A overcurrent device.

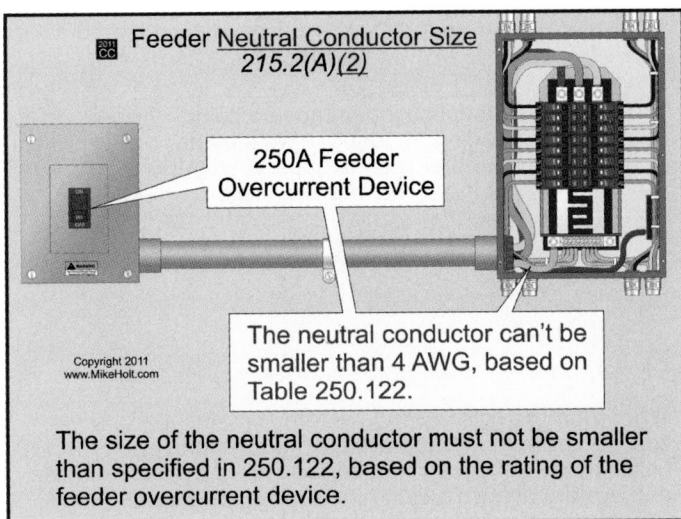

Figure 215–4

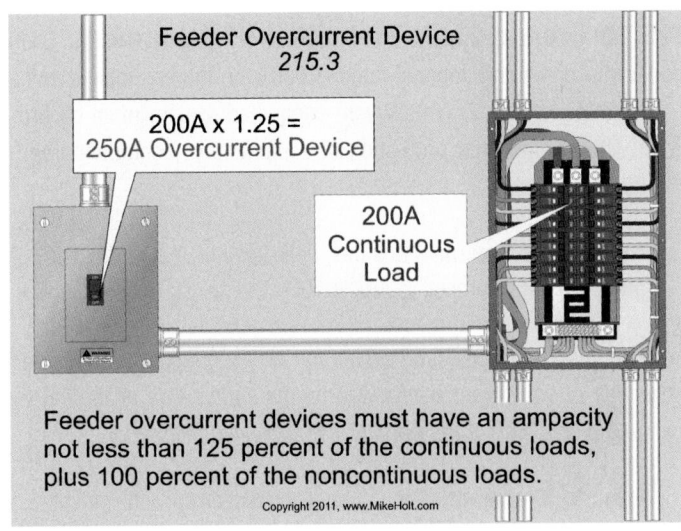

Figure 215–5

(3) Ampacity Relative to Service Conductors. The feeder conductor ampacity must not be less than that of the service conductors where the feeder conductors carry the total load supplied by service conductors with an ampacity of 55A or less.

(4) Dwelling Unit and Mobile Home Feeder Sizing. Feeder conductors for individual dwelling units or mobile homes need not be larger than service conductors sized to 310.15(B)(7).

Note 2: To provide reasonable efficiency of operation of electrical equipment, feeder conductors should be sized to prevent a voltage drop not to exceed 3 percent. In addition, the maximum total voltage drop on both feeders and branch circuits shouldn't exceed 5 percent.

Note 3: See 210.19(A), Note 4, for voltage drop for branch circuits.

215.3 Overcurrent Protection Sizing. Feeder overcurrent devices must have a rating of not less than 125 percent of the continuous loads, plus 100 percent of the noncontinuous loads. Figure 215–5

Author's Comment: See 215.2(A)(1) for feeder conductor sizing requirements.

Ex: If the assembly and the overcurrent device are both listed for operation at 100 percent of its rating, the overcurrent device can be sized at 100 percent of the continuous load.

Author's Comment: Equipment suitable for 100 percent continuous loading is rarely available in ratings under 400A.

215.4 Feeders with Common Neutral Conductor.

(A) Feeders with Common Neutral. Up to three sets of 3-wire feeders or two sets of 4-wire feeders can use the same neutral conductor.

Author's Comment: The neutral conductor must be sized to carry the total unbalanced load for all feeders as determined in Article 220, see 220.61.

215.6 Equipment Grounding Conductor. Feeder circuits must include or provide an equipment grounding conductor of a type listed in 250.118, and it must terminate in a manner so that branch-circuit equipment grounding conductors can be connected to it, and installed in accordance with 250.134. Figure 215–6

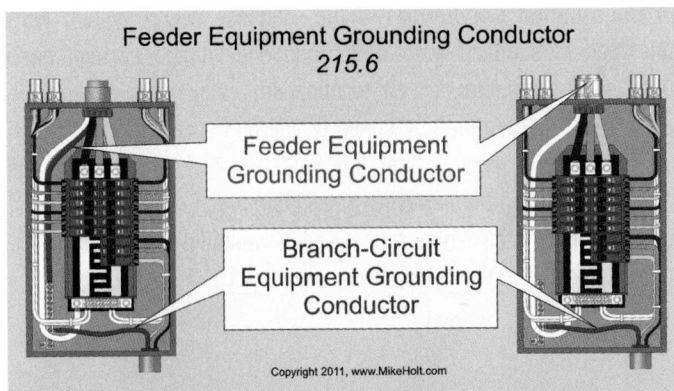

Figure 215–6

215.10 Ground-Fault Protection of Equipment.

Each feeder disconnecting means rated 1,000A or more supplied by a 4-wire, three-phase, 277/480V wye-connected system must be provided with ground-fault protection of equipment in accordance with 230.95 and 240.13.

Author's Comment: See the definition of "Ground-Fault Protection of Equipment" in Article 100.

Ex 2. Equipment ground-fault protection isn't required if ground-fault protection of equipment is provided on the supply side of the feeder and on the load side of the transformer supplying the feeder.

Author's Comment: Ground-fault protection of equipment isn't permitted for fire pumps [695.6(H)], and it's not required for emergency systems [700.26] or legally required standby systems [701.17].

215.12 Conductor Identification.

(A) Neutral Conductor. The neutral conductor of a feeder must be identified in accordance with 200.6.

(B) Equipment Grounding Conductor. Equipment grounding conductors can be bare, and individually covered or insulated equipment grounding conductors sized 6 AWG and smaller must have a continuous outer finish either green or green with one or more yellow stripes [250.119].

Insulated equipment grounding conductors 4 AWG and larger can be permanently reidentified with green marking at the time of installation at every point where the conductor is accessible [250.119(A)].

(C) Ungrounded Conductors. If the premises wiring system contains feeders supplied from more than one voltage system, each ungrounded conductor, at all termination, connection, and splice points, must be identified by phase or line and system. Identification can be by color coding, marking tape, tagging, or other means approved by the authority having jurisdiction. Such identification must be documented in a manner that's readily available, or it must be permanently posted at each panelboard. Figure 215–7

Ungrounded Conductor Identification 215.12(C)

Identification can be by color coding, marking tape, tagging, or other means approved by the authority having jurisdiction.

Copyright 2011
www.MikeHolt.com

Where the premises wiring system contains feeders supplied from more than one voltage system, each ungrounded conductor must be identified by phase or line and system at termination, connection, and splice points.

Figure 215–7

Author's Comment: Although the *NEC* doesn't require a specific color code for ungrounded conductors, electricians often use the following color system for power and lighting conductor identification:

- 120/240V, single-phase—black, red, and white
- 120/208V, three-phase—black, red, blue, and white
- 120/240V, three-phase—black, orange, blue, and white
- 277/480V, three-phase—brown, orange, yellow, and gray; or, brown, purple, yellow, and gray

ARTICLE 220

Branch-Circuit, Feeder, and Service Calculations

INTRODUCTION TO ARTICLE 220—BRANCH-CIRCUIT, FEEDER, AND SERVICE CALCULATIONS

This five-part article focuses on the requirements for calculating the minimum size of branch circuit, feeder, and service conductors.

Part I describes the layout of Article 220 and provides a table of where other types of load calculations can be found in the *NEC*. Part II provides requirements for branch-circuit calculations and for specific types of branch circuits. Part III covers the requirements for feeder and service calculations, using what's commonly called the standard method of calculation. Part IV provides optional calculations that can be used in place of the standard calculations provided in Parts II and III—if your installation meets certain requirements. Farm Load Calculations are discussed in Part V of the article.

In many cases, either the standard method (Part III) or the optional method (Part IV) can be used; however, these two methods don't yield identical results. In fact, sometimes these two answers may be diverse enough to call for different service sizes. There's nothing to say that either answer is right or wrong. If taking an exam, read the instructions carefully to be sure which method the test wants you to use. As you work through Article 220, be sure to study the illustrations to help you fully understand it. Also be sure to review the examples in Annex D of the *NEC* to provide more practice with these calculations.

PART I. GENERAL

220.1 Scope. This article contains the requirements necessary for calculating branch circuits, feeders, and services. In addition, this article can be used to determine the number of receptacles on a circuit and the number of general-purpose branch circuits required.

220.3 Application of Other Articles. Other articles contain calculations that are in addition to, or modify, those contained within Article 220. Take a moment to review the following additional calculation requirements found in these sections:

- Air-Conditioning and Refrigeration Equipment, 440.6, 440.21, 440.22, 440.31, 440.32, and 440.62
- Appliances, 422.10 and 422.11
- Branch Circuits, 210.19 and 210.20(A)
- Computers (Data Processing Equipment), 645.4 and 645.5(A)
- Conductors, 310.15
- Feeders, 215.2(B) and 215.3
- Fire Pumps, 695.7
- Fixed Electric Space-Heating Equipment, 424.3(B)
- Marinas, 555.12, 555.19(A)(4), and 555.19(B)

- Mobile Homes and Manufactured Homes, 550.12 and 550.18
- Motors, 430.6(A), 430.22, 430.24, 430.52, and 430.62
- Overcurrent Protection, 240.4 and 240.15
- Refrigeration (Hermetic), 440.6 and Part IV
- Recreational Vehicle Parks, 551.73(A)
- Electronic Equipment, 647.4(D)
- Services, 230.42(A) and 230.79
- Signs, 600.5
- Transformers, 450.3

220.5 Calculations.

(A) Voltage Used for Calculations. Unless other voltages are specified, branch-circuit, feeder, and service loads must be calculated on nominal system voltages, such as 120V, 120/240V, 120/208V, 240V, 277/480V, or 480V. Figure 220–1

> **Author's Comment:** A nominal value is assigned to a circuit for the purpose of convenient circuit identification. The actual voltage at which a circuit operates can vary from the nominal within a range that permits satisfactory operation of equipment [Article 100].

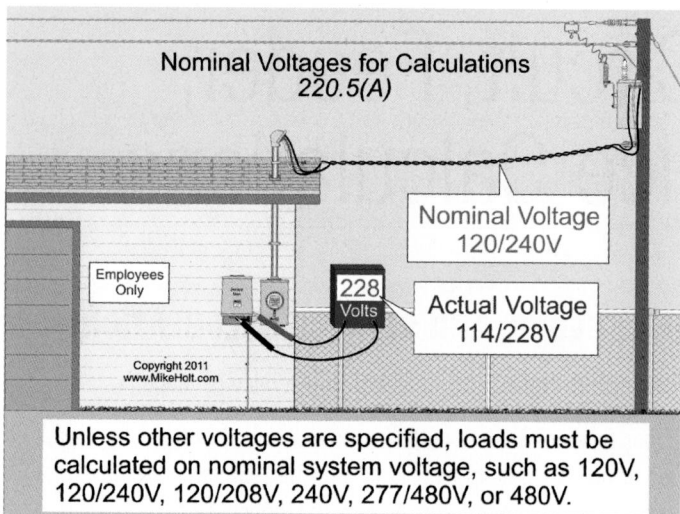

Figure 220–1

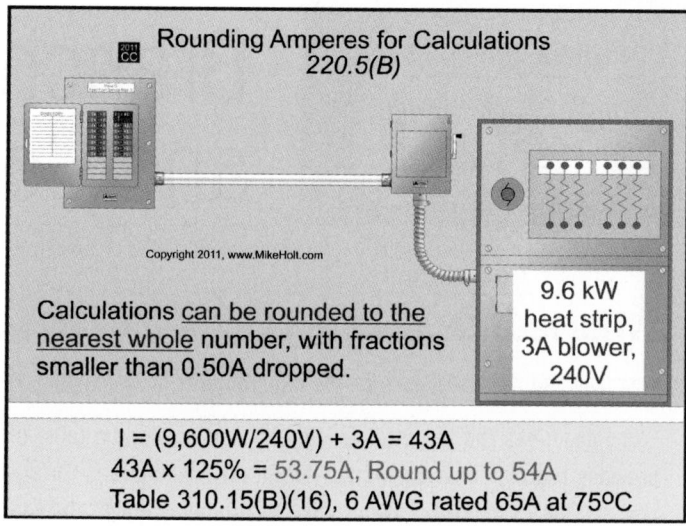

$$I = (9,600W/240V) + 3A = 43A$$
$$43A \times 125\% = 53.75A, \text{ Round up to } 54A$$
Table 310.15(B)(16), 6 AWG rated 65A at 75°C

Figure 220–2

(B) Fractions of an Ampere (Rounding Amperes). Calculations can be rounded to the nearest whole number and fractions less than 0.50A can be dropped.

Author's Comment: When do you round—after each calculation, or at the final calculation? The *NEC* isn't specific on this issue, but rounding at each calculation can lead to accumulated errors that can be an issue with the authority having jurisdiction.

Question: According to 424.3(B), the branch-circuit conductors and overcurrent device for electric space-heating equipment must be sized at no less than 125 percent of the total load. What size conductor is required to supply a 9.60 kW (40A), 240V, single-phase fixed space heater with a 3A blower motor, if the equipment terminals are rated 75°C? **Figure 220–2**

(a) 10 AWG   (b) 8 AWG   (c) 6 AWG   (d) 4 AWG

Answer: (c) 6 AWG

Step 1: Determine the load for the heater:

$$I = VA/E$$
$$I = 9,600 \, VA/240V$$
$$I = 40A$$

Step 2: Conductor size at 125% of the load:

$$\text{Conductor Size} = (40A + 3A) \times 1.25$$
$$\text{Conductor Size} = 53.75A, \text{ round up to } 54A$$

PART II. BRANCH-CIRCUIT LOAD CALCULATIONS

220.12 General Lighting. The general lighting load specified in Table 220.12 must be calculated from the outside dimensions of the building or area involved. **Figure 220–3**

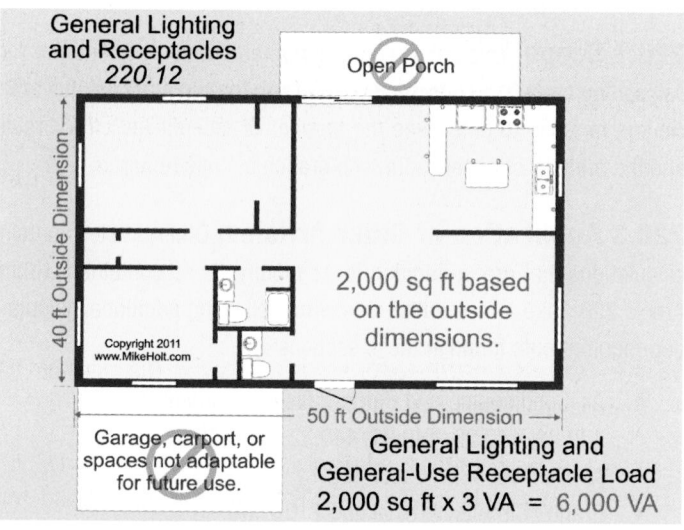

Figure 220–3

Table 220.12 General Lighting VA per Square Foot

Occupancy	VA/Sq. Ft
Armories and auditoriums	1
Assembly halls and auditoriums	1
Banks	3½[b]
Barber shops and beauty parlors	3
Churches	1
Clubs	2
Courtrooms	2
Dwelling units	3[a]
Garages—commercial (storage)	½
Halls, corridors, closets, stairways	½
Hospitals	2
Hotels and motels without cooking facilities	2
Industrial commercial (loft buildings)	2
Lodge rooms	1½
Office buildings	3½[b]
Restaurants	2
Schools	3
Storage spaces	¼
Stores	3
Warehouses (storage)	¼

Note a: The VA load for general-use receptacles, bathroom receptacles [220.14(J)(1) and 210.11(C)(3)], outside receptacles, as well as garage, basement receptacles [220.14(J)(2), 210.52(E) and (G)], and lighting outlets [220.14(J)(3), 210.70(A) and (B)] in a dwelling unit are included in the 3 VA per-square-foot general lighting [220.14(J)].

Note b: The receptacle calculated load for banks and office buildings is the largest calculation of either (1) or (2) [220.14(K)].

220.14 Other Loads—All Occupancies.
The minimum VA load for each outlet must comply with (A) through (L).

(A) Specific Equipment. The branch-circuit VA load for equipment and appliance outlets must be calculated on the VA rating of the equipment or appliance.

(B) Electric Dryers and Electric Cooking Appliances in Dwelling Units. The branch-circuit VA load for household electric dryers must comply with 220.54, and household electric ranges and other cooking appliances must comply with 220.55.

(C) Motor Loads. The motor branch-circuit VA load must be determined by multiplying the motor full-load current (FLC) listed in Table 430.248 or 430.250 by the motor table voltage, in accordance with 430.22 [430.6(A)(1)].

(D) Luminaires. The branch-circuit VA load for recessed luminaires must be calculated based on the maximum VA rating for which the luminaires are rated.

(E) Heavy-Duty Lampholders. The branch-circuit VA load for heavy-duty lampholders must be calculated at a minimum of 600 VA.

(F) Sign Outlet. Each commercial occupancy that's accessible to pedestrians must have at least one 20A sign outlet [600.5(A)], which must have a minimum branch-circuit load of 1,200 VA. **Figure 220–4**

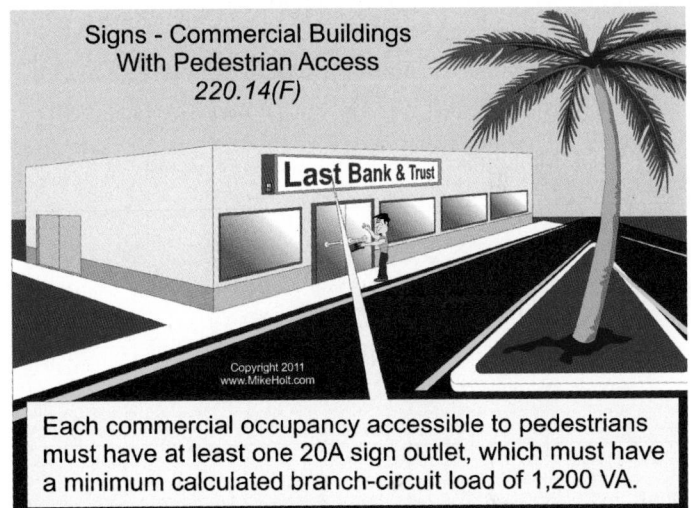

Each commercial occupancy accessible to pedestrians must have at least one 20A sign outlet, which must have a minimum calculated branch-circuit load of 1,200 VA.

Figure 220–4

(G) Show Windows. The branch-circuit VA load for show-window lighting must be calculated in accordance with (1) or (2):

(1) 180 VA <u>for each</u> outlet in accordance with 220.14(L), or

(2) 200 VA <u>for each</u> linear foot of show-window lighting [220.43]. **Figure 220–5**

(H) Fixed Multioutlet Assemblies. Fixed multioutlet assemblies in commercial occupancies used in other than dwelling units, or in the guest rooms of hotels or motels, must be calculated in accordance with (1) or (2). **Figure 220–6**

(1) If appliances are unlikely to be used simultaneously, each 5 ft or fraction of 5 ft of multioutlet assembly is considered as one outlet of 180 VA.

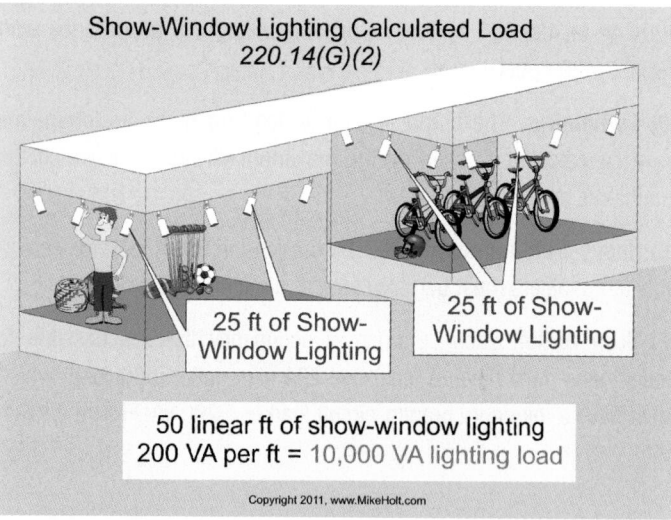

Figure 220–5

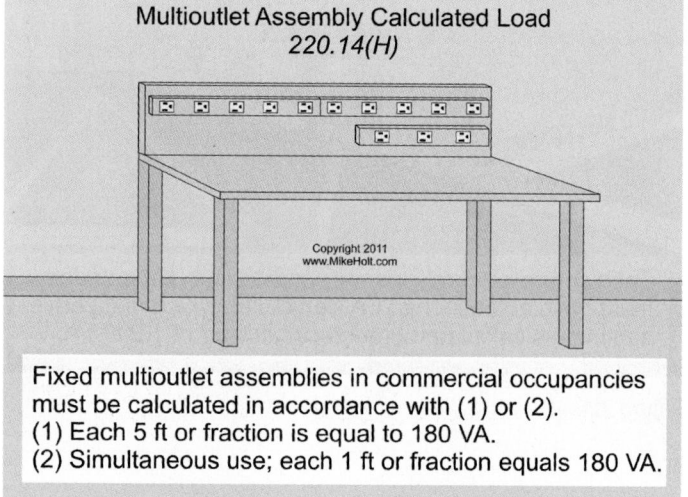

Multioutlet Assembly Calculated Load
220.14(H)

Fixed multioutlet assemblies in commercial occupancies must be calculated in accordance with (1) or (2).
(1) Each 5 ft or fraction is equal to 180 VA.
(2) Simultaneous use; each 1 ft or fraction equals 180 VA.

Figure 220–6

(2) If appliances are likely to be used simultaneously, each 1 ft or fraction of a foot of multioutlet assembly is considered as one outlet of 180 VA.

Author's Comments:

- See the definition of "Multioutlet Assembly" in Article 100.

- The feeder or service calculated load for fixed multioutlet assemblies can be calculated in accordance with the demand factors contained in 220.44.

(I) Receptacle Outlets. 180 VA per mounting strap for each 15A or 20A, 125V general-use receptacle outlet, except as covered in 200.14(J) and (K). Figure 220–7

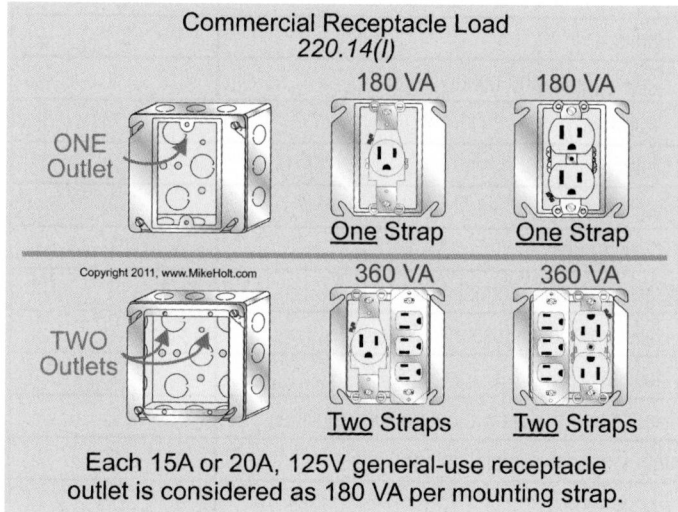

Commercial Receptacle Load
220.14(I)

Each 15A or 20A, 125V general-use receptacle outlet is considered as 180 VA per mounting strap.

Figure 220–7

A single device consisting of four or more receptacles is considered as 90 VA <u>for each</u> receptacle (360 VA for a quad receptacle). Figure 220–8

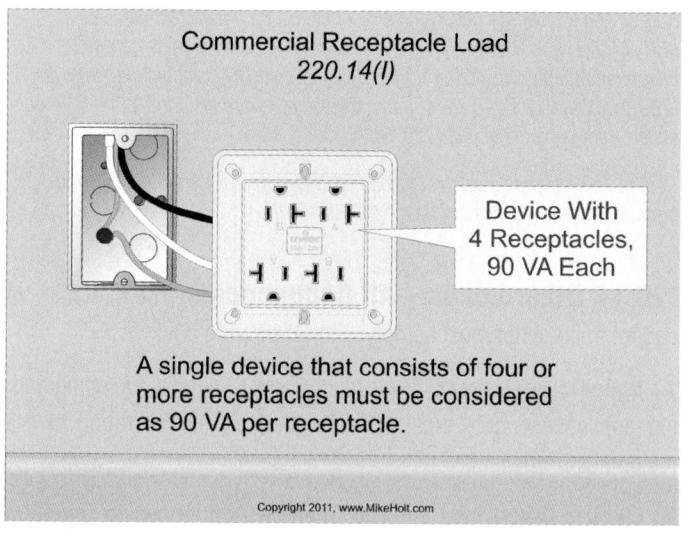

Commercial Receptacle Load
220.14(I)

Device With 4 Receptacles, 90 VA Each

A single device that consists of four or more receptacles must be considered as 90 VA per receptacle.

Figure 220–8

Question: What's the maximum number of 15A or 20A, 125V receptacle outlets permitted on a 20A, 120V general-purpose branch circuit in a commercial occupancy? **Figure 220–9**

(a) 4   (b) 6   (c) 10   (d) 13

Answer: (d) 13

Circuit VA = Volts x Amperes

Circuit VA = 120V x 20A

Circuit VA = 2,400 VA

Number of Receptacles = 2,400 VA/180 VA

Number of Receptacles = 13

Author's Comment: There's no VA load for 15A and 20A, 125V general-use receptacle outlets, because the loads for these devices are part of the 3 VA per-square-foot for general lighting as listed in Table 220.12 for dwelling units.

Question: What's the maximum number of 15A or 20A, 125V receptacle outlets permitted on a 15A or 20A, 120V general-purpose branch circuit in a dwelling unit? **Figure 220–10**

(a) 4   (b) 6   (c) 8   (d) No limit

Answer: (d) No limit

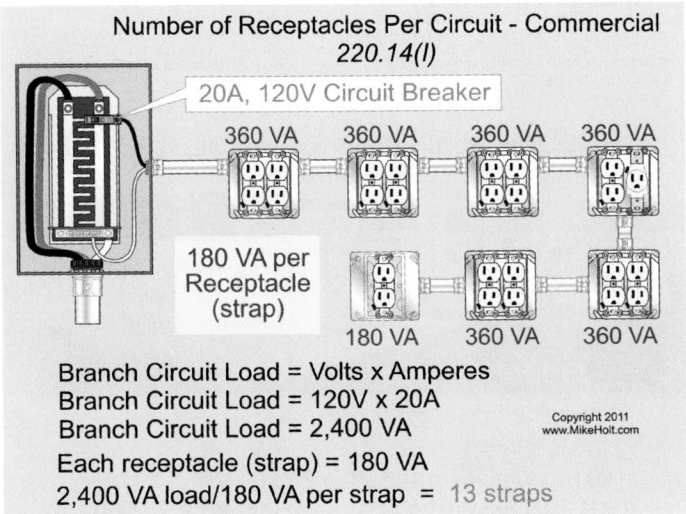

Number of Receptacles Per Circuit - Commercial 220.14(I)

20A, 120V Circuit Breaker

360 VA   360 VA   360 VA   360 VA

180 VA per Receptacle (strap)

180 VA   360 VA   360 VA

Branch Circuit Load = Volts x Amperes
Branch Circuit Load = 120V x 20A
Branch Circuit Load = 2,400 VA
Each receptacle (strap) = 180 VA
2,400 VA load/180 VA per strap = 13 straps

Copyright 2011
www.MikeHolt.com

Figure 220–9

Number of Outlets Per Circuit - Dwelling Unit 220.14(J)

Bedroom 1

Hall

Bath

Bedroom 2

Laundry

Living Room

The *NEC* doesn't limit the number of receptacle and lighting outlets on a general-purpose circuit in a dwelling unit.

Copyright 2011, www.MikeHolt.com

Figure 220–10

Author's Comment: According to the *NEC* Handbook, published by the NFPA, general-purpose receptacles aren't considered a continuous load.

(J) Residential Receptacle Load. In one-family, two-family, and multifamily dwellings, and in guest rooms of hotels and motels, the outlets specified in (1), (2), and (3) are included in the general lighting load calculations of 220.12.

(1) General-use receptacle outlets, including the receptacles connected to the 20A bathroom circuit [210.11(C)(3)].

(2) Outdoor, garage, and basement receptacle outlets [210.52(E) and (G)].

(3) Lighting outlets [210.70(A) and (B)].

Author's Comment: The *NEC* doesn't limit the number of receptacle outlets on a general-purpose branch circuit in a dwelling unit. See the *NEC Handbook* for more information.

 CAUTION: *There might be a local Code requirement that limits the number of receptacle outlets on a general-purpose branch circuit.*

Author's Comment: Although there's no limit on the number of receptacle outlets on dwelling general-purpose branch circuits, the *NEC* does require a minimum number of circuits to be installed for general-purpose receptacles and lighting outlets [210.11(A)]. In addition, the receptacle and lighting loads must be evenly distributed among the required circuits [210.11(B)].

(K) Banks and Office Buildings. The receptacle calculated load for banks and office buildings is the largest calculation of either (1) or (2).

(1) Determine the receptacle calculated load at 180 VA per receptacle yoke [220.14(I)], then apply the demand factor from Table 220.44, or

(2) Determine the receptacle load at 1 VA per sq ft.

Bank or Office General Lighting and Receptacle—Example 1

Question: What's the calculated receptacle load for an 18,000 sq ft bank with 160 15A, 125V receptacles? **Figure 220–11**

(a) 15,400 VA   (b) 19,400 VA   (c) 28,800 VA   (d) 142 kVA

Answer: (b) 19,400 VA

[220.14(K)(1) and 220.14(I)]
160 Receptacles x 180 VA = 28,800 VA
First 10,000 at 100% = –   **10,000 VA** x 1.00 =   10,000 VA
Remainder at 50% =   18,800 VA x 0.50 = + 9,400 VA
Receptacle Calculated Load =   19,400 VA

[220.14(K)(2)]
18,000 x 1 VA per sq ft   18,000 VA
                                               (smaller, omit)

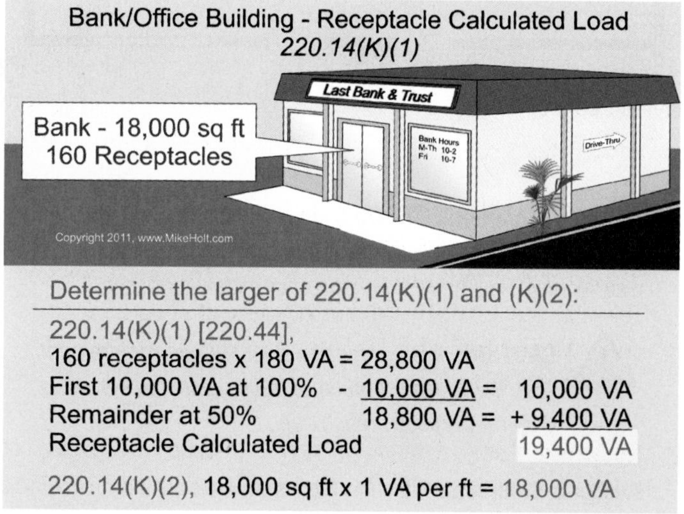

Bank or Office General Lighting and Receptacle—Example 2

Question: What's the receptacle calculated load for an 18,000 sq ft bank with 140 15A, 125V receptacles? **Figure 220–12**

(a) 15,000 VA   (b) 18,000 VA   (c) 23,000 VA   (d) 31,000 VA

Answer: (b) 18,000 VA

[220.14(K)(1) and 220.14(I)]
140 Receptacles x 180 VA = 25,200 VA
First 10,000 at 100% =   –10,000 VA x 1.00 = 10,000 VA
Remainder at 50% =   15,200 VA x 0.50 = + 7,600 VA
Receptacle Calculated Load =   17,600 VA
                                               (smaller, omit)

[220.14(K)(2)]
18,000 x 1 VA per sq ft =   18,000 VA

Bank/Office Building - Receptacle Calculated Load
220.14(K)(1)

Bank - 18,000 sq ft
160 Receptacles

Copyright 2011, www.MikeHolt.com

Determine the larger of 220.14(K)(1) and (K)(2):
220.14(K)(1) [220.44],
160 receptacles x 180 VA = 28,800 VA
First 10,000 VA at 100%   - 10,000 VA = 10,000 VA
Remainder at 50%   18,800 VA = + 9,400 VA
Receptacle Calculated Load   19,400 VA
220.14(K)(2), 18,000 sq ft x 1 VA per ft = 18,000 VA

Figure 220–11

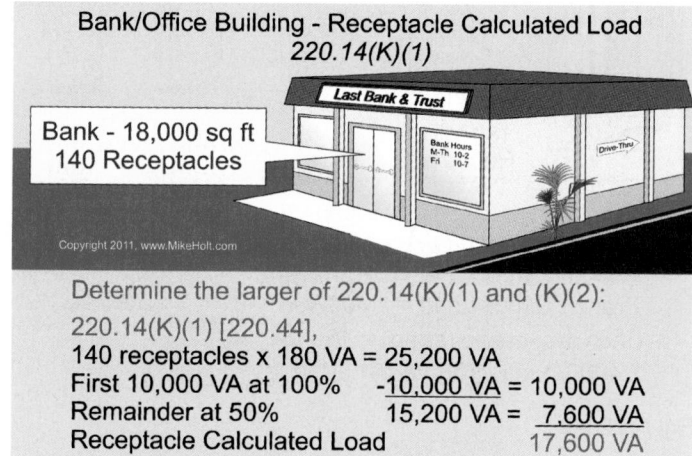

Bank/Office Building - Receptacle Calculated Load
220.14(K)(1)

Bank - 18,000 sq ft
140 Receptacles

Copyright 2011, www.MikeHolt.com

Determine the larger of 220.14(K)(1) and (K)(2):
220.14(K)(1) [220.44],
140 receptacles x 180 VA = 25,200 VA
First 10,000 VA at 100%   -10,000 VA = 10,000 VA
Remainder at 50%   15,200 VA = 7,600 VA
Receptacle Calculated Load   17,600 VA
220.14(K)(2), 18,000 sq ft x 1 VA per ft = 18,000 VA

Figure 220–12

(L) Other Outlets. 180 VA for <u>each</u> receptacle and lighting outlet not covered in (A) through (K).

220.18 Maximum Load on a Branch Circuit.

(A) Motor Operated Loads. Branch circuits that supply motor loads must be sized not less than 125 percent of the motor FLC, in accordance with 430.6(A) and 430.22.

Question: What's the minimum size branch-circuit conductor for a 2 hp, 230V motor, where the conductor terminals are rated 75°C? **Figure 220–13**

(a) 14 AWG   (b) 12 AWG   (c) 10 AWG   (d) 8 AWG

Answer: (a) 14 AWG

Step 1: Determine the motor full-load current:
[Table 430.248]
2 hp FLC = 12A

Step 2: Size the branch-circuit conductors at 125 percent of the FLC in accordance with Table 310.15(B)(16) [430.22]:
Branch-Circuit Conductors = 12A x 1.25
Branch-Circuit Conductors = 15A, 14 AWG rated 20A at 75°C.

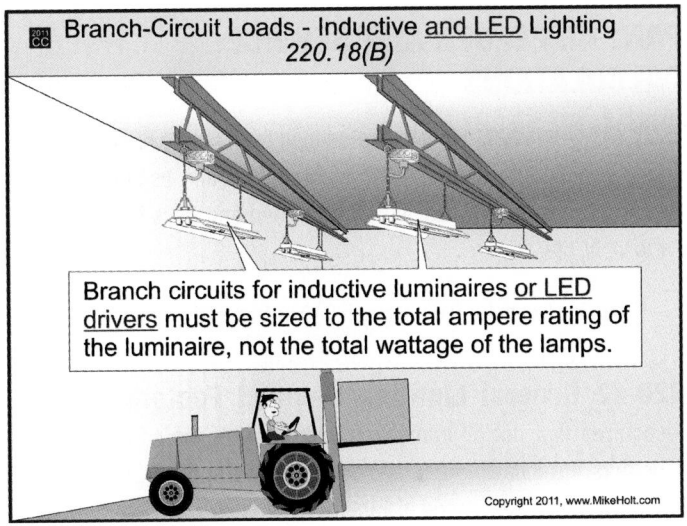

Branch circuits for inductive luminaires or LED drivers must be sized to the total ampere rating of the luminaire, not the total wattage of the lamps.

Copyright 2011, www.MikeHolt.com

Figure 220–14

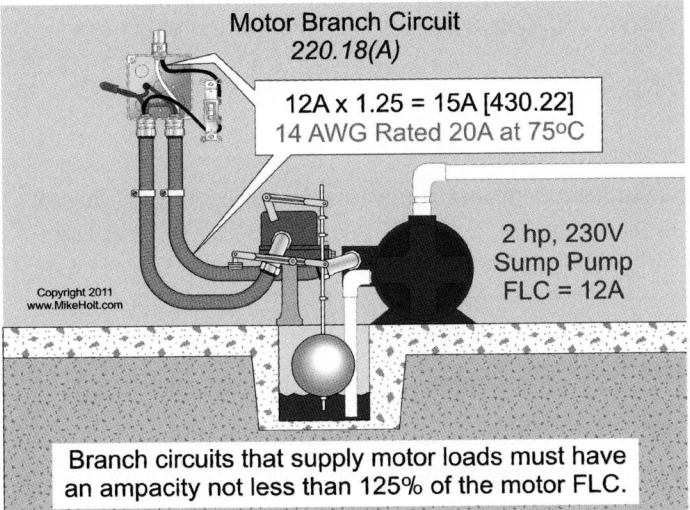

Motor Branch Circuit
220.18(A)

12A x 1.25 = 15A [430.22]
14 AWG Rated 20A at 75°C

2 hp, 230V
Sump Pump
FLC = 12A

Copyright 2011
www.MikeHolt.com

Branch circuits that supply motor loads must have an ampacity not less than 125% of the motor FLC.

Figure 220–13

Question: What's the maximum number of 1.34A fluorescent luminaires permitted on a 20A circuit if the luminaires operate for more than 3 hours?

(a) 8   (b) 11   (c) 13   (d) 15

Answer: (b) 11

The maximum continuous load must not exceed 80 percent of the circuit rating [210.19(A)(1)].

Maximum Load = 20A x 0.80
Maximum Load = 16A
Luminaires on Circuit = 16A/1.34A
Luminaires on Circuit = 11.94 or 11 luminaires

(B) Inductive and LED Lighting Loads. Branch circuits that supply inductive and LED driver lighting loads must be sized to the total ampere rating of the luminaire, not to the total wattage of the lamps. Figure 220–14

Author's Comment: Because of power factor (inductive luminaires), the input VA of each luminaire is 162 VA (120V x 1.34A), which is greater than the 136W (34W x 4 lamps) of the lamps. This may seem complicated, but just remember—size all circuits that supply lighting loads to the ampere rating of the luminaire, not to the wattage of the lamps.

(C) Household Cooking Appliances. Branch-circuit conductors for household cooking appliances can be sized in accordance with Table 220.55; specifically, Note 4 for branch circuits.

Author's Comment: For ranges rated 8.75 kW or more, the minimum branch-circuit rating is 40A [210.19(A)(3)].

PART III. FEEDER AND SERVICE CALCULATIONS

220.40 General. The calculated load for a feeder or service must not be less than the sum of the branch-circuit loads, as determined by Part II of this article, as adjusted for the demand factors contained in Parts III, IV, or V.

Note: See Examples D1(a) through D10 in Annex D.

220.42 General Lighting Demand Factors. The *Code* recognizes that not all luminaires will be on at the same time, and it permits the following demand factors to be applied to the general lighting load as determined in Table 220.42.

Table 220.42 General Lighting Demand Factors		
Type of Occupancy	Lighting VA Load	Demand Factor
Dwelling Units	First 3,000 VA Next 117,000 VA Remainder at	100% 35% 25%
Hotels/motels without provision for cooking	First 20,000 VA Next 80,000 VA Remainder at	50% 40% 30%
Warehouses (storage)	First 12,500 VA Remainder at	100% 50%
All others	Total VA	100%

Question: What's the general lighting and receptacle calculated load, after demand factors, for a 40 x 50 ft (2,000 sq ft) dwelling unit? **Figure 220–15**

(a) 2,050 VA   (b) 3,050 VA   (c) 4,050 VA   (d) 5,050 VA

Answer: (c) 4,050 VA

General Lighting = 40 x 50 ft
General Lighting = 2,000 sq ft x 3 VA per sq ft
General Lighting = 6,000 VA

First 3,000 VA at 100% 3,000 VA x 1.00 =	3,000 VA
Next 117,000 VA at 35% 3,000 VA x 0.35 =	+ 1,050 VA
General Lighting and General-Use Receptacles Calculated Load =	4,050 VA

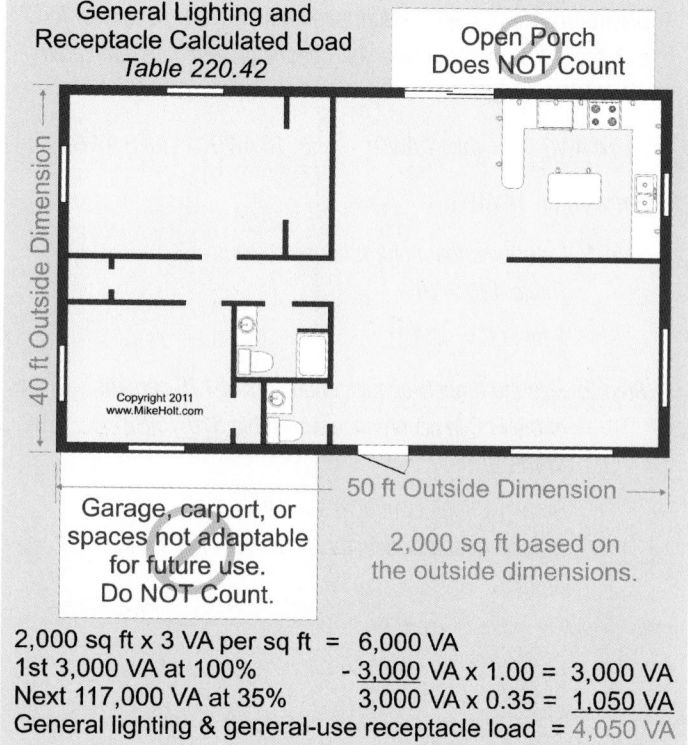

General Lighting and Receptacle Calculated Load Table 220.42

Open Porch Does NOT Count

40 ft Outside Dimension

Copyright 2011 www.MikeHolt.com

Garage, carport, or spaces not adaptable for future use. Do NOT Count.

50 ft Outside Dimension

2,000 sq ft based on the outside dimensions.

2,000 sq ft x 3 VA per sq ft = 6,000 VA
1st 3,000 VA at 100%   - 3,000 VA x 1.00 = 3,000 VA
Next 117,000 VA at 35%   3,000 VA x 0.35 = 1,050 VA
General lighting & general-use receptacle load = 4,050 VA

Figure 220–15

Author's Comment: For commercial occupancies, the VA load for receptacles [220.14(I)] and fixed multioutlet assemblies [220.14(H)] can be added to the general lighting load and subjected to the demand factors of Table 220.42 [220.44].

220.43 Commercial—Show Window and Track Lighting Load.

(A) Show Windows. The feeder/service VA load must not be less than 200 VA per linear foot.

(B) Track Lighting. The feeder/service VA load must not be less than 150 VA for every 2 ft of track lighting or fraction of that length. **Figure 220–16**

Ex: Track lighting supplied through a device that limits the current to the track can have the load calculated based on the current rating of the limiting device.

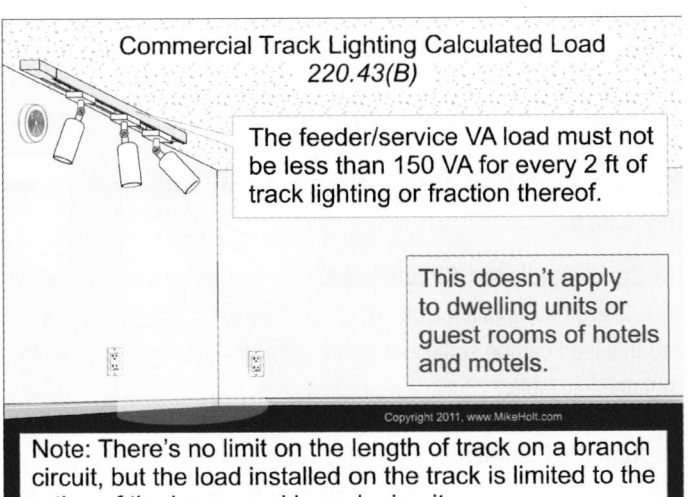

Commercial Track Lighting Calculated Load
220.43(B)

The feeder/service VA load must not be less than 150 VA for every 2 ft of track lighting or fraction thereof.

This doesn't apply to dwelling units or guest rooms of hotels and motels.

Copyright 2011, www.MikeHolt.com

Note: There's no limit on the length of track on a branch circuit, but the load installed on the track is limited to the rating of the lamps and branch circuit.

Figure 220–16

Author's Comments:

- There's no limit on the length of track that can be supplied by a single branch circuit.

- If a feeder or service supplies continuous loads, the minimum feeder or service conductor ampacity, before the application of ambient temperature correction [310.15(B)(2)(a)], conductor bundling adjustment [310.15(B)(3)(a)], or both, must have an allowable ampacity of at least 125 percent of the continuous load [215.2(A)(1) for feeders and 230.42(A) for services].

Question: What's the approximate feeder/service calculated load for conductor sizing for 150 ft of track lighting in a commercial occupancy?

(a) 10,000 VA (b) 12,000 VA (c) 14,000 VA (d) 16,000 VA

Answer: (c) 14,000 VA

Feeder Calculated Load = 150 ft/2 ft
Feeder Calculated Load = 5 units x 150 VA
                          x 1.25 (continuous load)
Feeder Calculated Load = 14,063 VA

Author's Comment: This rule doesn't apply to branch circuits. Therefore, the maximum number of lampholders permitted on a track lighting system is based on the wattage rating of the lamps and the voltage and ampere rating of the circuit [410.151(B)]. Because lighting is a continuous load, the maximum load on a branch circuit must not exceed 80 percent of the circuit rating [210.19(A)(1)].

Question: How many 75W lampholders can be installed on a 20A, 120V track lighting circuit in a commercial occupancy if the track is 32 ft long?

(a) 10   (b) 15   (c) 20   (d) 25

Answer: (d) 25

Maximum Load Permitted on Circuit = 20A x 0.80
Maximum Load Permitted on Circuit = 16A

Maximum Load in VA = 120V x 16A
Maximum Load in VA = 1,920 VA

Number of Lampholders = 1,920 VA/75 VA
Number of Lampholders = 25.60

Author's Comments:

- There's no limit on the length of track lighting that can be supplied by a branch circuit.

- The total wattage of the lamps on the track isn't permitted to exceed the rating of the track [410.151(B)].

220.44 Other than Dwelling Unit—Receptacle Load.

The feeder/service VA load for general-purpose receptacles [220.14(I)] and fixed multioutlet assemblies [220.14(H)] is determined by:

- Adding the receptacle and fixed multioutlet assembly VA load with the general lighting load [Table 220.12] and adjusting this VA value by the demand factors contained in Table 220.42, or

- Applying a 50 percent demand factor to that portion of the receptacle and fixed multioutlet receptacle load that exceeds 10 kVA.

Question: *What's the calculated feeder/service VA load, after demand factors, for 150 general-purpose receptacles and 100 ft of fixed multioutlet assembly in a commercial occupancy? The appliances powered by the multioutlet assembly aren't used simultaneously.* **Figure 220–17**

(a) 8,500 VA   (b) 10,000 VA   (c) 20,300 VA   (d) 27,000 VA

Answer: *(c) 20,300 VA*

Step 1:   Determine the total connected load:

Receptacle Load = 150 receptacles x 180 VA
Receptacle Load = 27,000 VA [220.14(I)]

Multioutlet Load = 100 ft/5 ft
Multioutlet Load = 20 sections x 180 VA
Multioutlet Load = 3,600 VA [220.14(H)]

Step 2:   Apply Table 220.44 demand factor:

Total Connected Load = 30,600 VA
First 10,000 VA at 100% = 10,000 VA x 1.00 =   10,000 VA
Remainder at 50% = 20,600 VA x 0.50 =   +10,300 VA
Receptacle Calculated Load =   20,300 VA

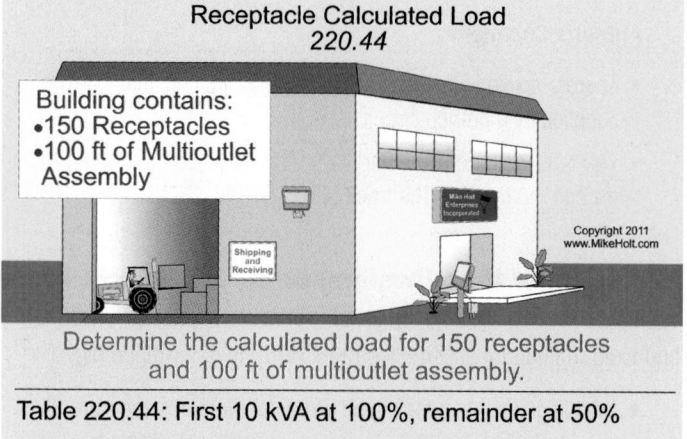

Receptacle Calculated Load
220.44

Building contains:
• 150 Receptacles
• 100 ft of Multioutlet Assembly

Copyright 2011
www.MikeHolt.com

Determine the calculated load for 150 receptacles
and 100 ft of multioutlet assembly.

Table 220.44: First 10 kVA at 100%, remainder at 50%

150 receptacles x 180 VA = 27,000 VA [220.14(I)]
100 ft/5 ft = 20 sections x 180 VA = 3,600 VA [220.14(H)]
Total Connected Load = 30,600 VA
1st 10,000 VA at 100% = -10,000 VA x 1.00 = 10,000 VA
Remainder at 50% =   20,600 VA x 0.50 = +10,300 VA
Receptacle Calculated Load =   20,300 VA

Figure 220–17

220.50 Motor Load. The feeder/service load for motors must be sized not less than 125 percent of the largest motor load, plus the sum of the other motor loads. See 430.24 for example.

220.51 Fixed Electric Space-Heating Load. The feeder/service load for fixed electric space-heating equipment must be calculated at 100 percent of the total connected load.

220.52 Dwelling Unit—Small-Appliance and Laundry Load.

(A) Small-Appliance Circuit Load. The feeder/service VA load for each 20A small-appliance circuit covered by 210.11(C)(1) is 1,500 VA, and this load can be subjected to the general lighting demand factors contained in Table 220.42.

Author's Comments:

• Each dwelling unit must have a minimum of two 20A, 120V small-appliance branch circuits for the kitchen and dining room receptacles [210.11(C)(1)].

• The bathroom circuit covered by 210.11(C)(3) isn't included in the service/feeder calculations.

(B) Laundry Circuit Load. The feeder/service VA load for each 20A laundry circuit covered by 210.11(C)(2) is 1,500 VA, and this load can be subjected to the general lighting demand factors contained in Table 220.42.

Author's Comment: A laundry circuit isn't required in each dwelling unit of a multifamily building if laundry facilities are provided on the premises for all building occupants [210.52(F) Ex 1].

220.53 Dwelling Unit—Appliance Load. A demand factor of 75 percent can be applied to the total connected load of four or more appliances on the same feeder/service. This demand factor doesn't apply to electric space-heating equipment [220.51], electric clothes dryers [220.54], electric ranges [220.55], electric air-conditioning equipment [Article 440, Part IV], or motors [220.50].

Question: *What's the feeder/service appliance calculated load for a dwelling unit that contains a 1,000 VA disposal, a 1,500 VA dishwasher, and a 4,500 VA water heater?* **Figure 220–18**

(a) 3,000 VA   (b) 4,500 VA   (c) 6,000 VA   (d) 7,000 VA

Answer: *(d) 7,000 VA*

No demand factor applies for three appliances.

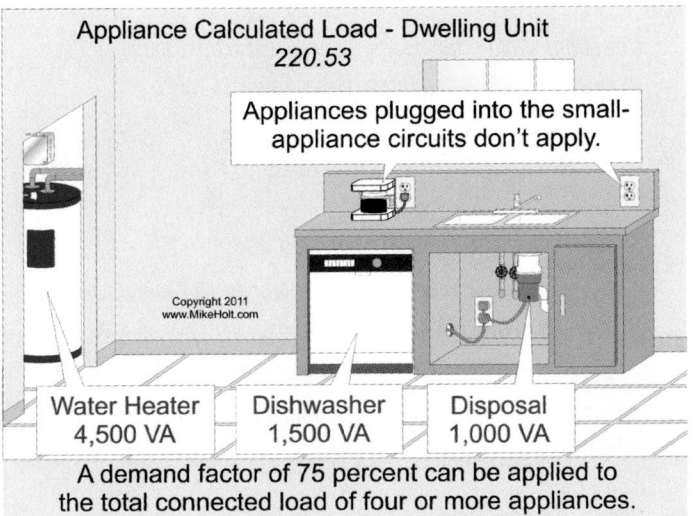

Appliance Calculated Load - Dwelling Unit
220.53

Appliances plugged into the small-appliance circuits don't apply.

Copyright 2011
www.MikeHolt.com

| Water Heater 4,500 VA | Dishwasher 1,500 VA | Disposal 1,000 VA |

A demand factor of 75 percent can be applied to the total connected load of four or more appliances.

Figure 220–18

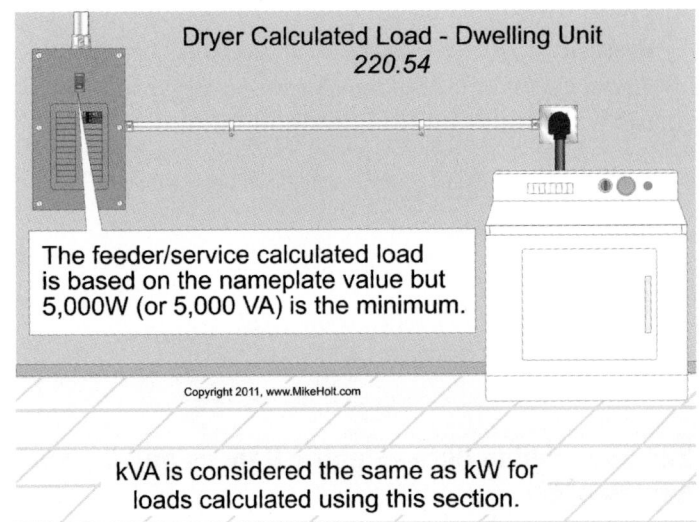

Dryer Calculated Load - Dwelling Unit
220.54

The feeder/service calculated load is based on the nameplate value but 5,000W (or 5,000 VA) is the minimum.

Copyright 2011, www.MikeHolt.com

kVA is considered the same as kW for loads calculated using this section.

Figure 220–19

Question: What's the feeder/service appliance calculated load, after demand factors, for a 12-unit multifamily dwelling if each unit contains a 1,000 VA disposal, a 1,500 VA dishwasher, and a 4,500 VA water heater?

(a) 23,000 VA   (b) 43,500 VA   (c) 63,000 VA   (d) 71,000 VA

Answer: (c) 63,000 VA

Calculated Load = 7,000 VA x 12 units x 0.75*
Calculated Load = 63,000 VA

*Each dwelling unit has only three appliances, but the feeder supplies a total of 36 appliances (12 units x 3 appliances).

220.54 Dwelling Unit—Electric Clothes Dryer Load.

The feeder/service load for electric clothes dryers located in a dwelling unit must not be less than 5,000W (5,000 VA), or the nameplate rating of the equipment if more than 5,000W (5,000 VA). Kilovolt-amperes (kVA) is considered equivalent to kilowatts (kW) for loads calculated in this section. Figure 220–19

When a building contains five or more dryers, it's permissible to apply the demand factors listed in Table 220.54 to the total connected dryer load.

Author's Comment: A clothes dryer load isn't required if the dwelling unit doesn't have an electric clothes dryer circuit receptacle outlet.

Table 220.54 Dwelling Unit Dryer Demand Factors

Number of Dryers	Demand Factor(Percent)
1–4	100%
5	85%
6	75%
7	65%
8	60%
9	55%
10	50%
11	47%
12–23	47% minus 1% for each dryer exceeding 11
24–42	35% minus 0.50% for each dryer exceeding 23
43 and over	25%

Question: What's the feeder/service calculated load for a 10-unit multifamily building that contains a 5 kW dryer in each unit?

(a) 25,000W   (b) 43,500W   (c) 63,000W   (d) 71,000W

Answer: (a) 25,000W

Table 220.54 demand factor for 10 units is 50%

Calculated Load = 10 units x 5,000W x 0.50
Calculated Load = 25,000W

220.55 Dwelling Unit—Electric Ranges and Cooking Appliances

Household cooking appliances rated over 1.75 kW can have the feeder/service load calculated according to the demand factors of Table 220.55. See the *NEC* for the actual Table.

Note 1: For identically sized ranges individually rated more than 12 kW, the maximum demand in Column C must be increased 5 percent for each additional kilowatt of rating, or major fraction thereof, by which the rating of individual ranges exceeds 12 kW.

Question: What's the feeder/service calculated load for three 15.60 kVA ranges?

(a) 14 kVA   (b) 15 kVA   (c) 17 kVA   (d) 21 kVA

Answer: (c) 17 kVA (closest answer)

Step 1: Determine the Column C demand load for 3 units: 14 kVA.

Step 2: Because each 15.60 kVA range exceeds 12 kVA by 3.60 kVA, increase the Column C demand load by 5% for each kVA or major fraction of kVA in excess of 12 kVA.

Step 3: Because 3.60 kVA is 3 kVA plus a major fraction of a kVA, increase the Column C value by 4 x 5% = 20%

Increase the Column C load (14 kVA) by 20%:
14 kVA x 1.20 = 16.80 kVA.

Note 2: For ranges individually rated more than 8.75 kW, but none exceeding 27 kW, and of different ratings, an average rating must be calculated by adding together the ratings of all ranges to obtain the total connected load (using 12 kW for any range rated less than 12 kW) and dividing this total by the number of ranges. Then the maximum demand in Column C must be increased 5 percent for each kilowatt, or major fraction thereof, by which this average value exceeds 12 kW.

Question: What's the feeder/service calculated load for three ranges rated 9 kVA and three ranges rated 14 kVA?

(a) 22 kVA   (b) 36 kVA   c) 42 kVA   (d) 78 kVA

Answer: (a) 22 kVA

Step 1: Determine the total connected load:

9 kVA (minimum 12 kVA); 3 Ranges x 12 kVA = 36 kVA
14 kVA; 3 Ranges x 14 kVA =   + 42 kVA
Total Connected Load =   78 kVA

Step 2   Determine the average of range ratings:

78 kVA/6 units = 13 kVA average rating

Step 3: Demand load from Table 220.55 Column C:

6 ranges = 21 kVA

Step 4: Because the average of the ranges (13 kVA) exceeds 12 kVA by 1 kVA, increase the Column C demand load (21 kVA) by 5%:

Calculated Load = 21 kVA x 1.05
Calculated Load = 22.05 kVA

Note 4: It's permissible to compute the branch-circuit load for one range in accordance with Table 220.55.

Question: What's the branch-circuit calculated load in amperes for a single 12 kW range connected on a 120/240V circuit? **Figure 220–20**

(a) 20A   (b) 33A   (c) 41A   (d) 50A

Answer: (b) 33A

Column C Calculated Load = 8 kW
Branch-Circuit Load in Amperes, I = P/E

P = 8,000W

E = 240V

I = 8,000W/240V
I = 33.33A

Note 4: The branch-circuit load for one wall-mounted oven or one counter-mounted cooking unit must be the nameplate rating of the appliance.

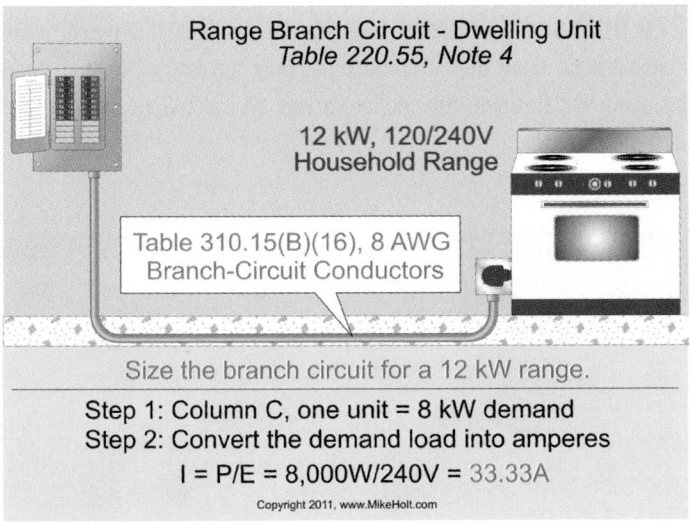

Figure 220–20

Question: What size branch-circuit conductors are required for a 6 kW wall-mounted oven connected on a 120/240V circuit? **Figure 220–21**

(a) 14 AWG   (b) 12 AWG   (c) 10 AWG   (d) 8 AWG

Answer: (c) 10 AWG

Branch-circuit load in amperes, I = P/E

P = 6,000W
E = 240V

I = 6,000W/240V

I = 25A, 10 AWG rated 35A at 75°C, [Table 310.15(B)(16) and 110.14(C)(1)]

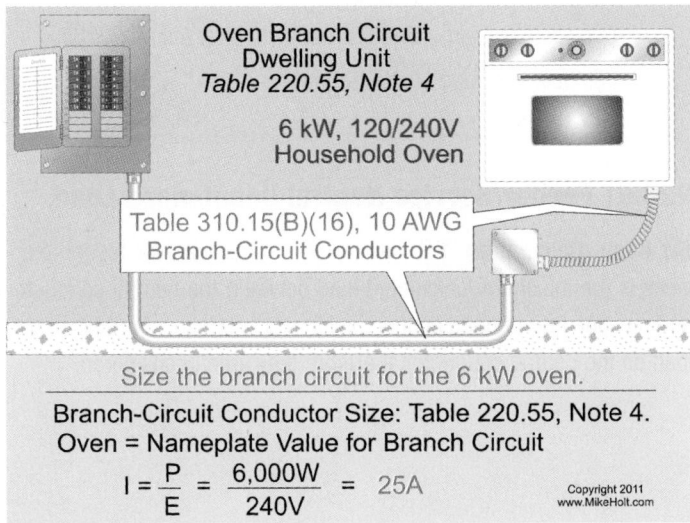

Figure 220–21

Note 4: The branch-circuit load for one counter-mounted cooking unit and up to two wall-mounted ovens is determined by adding the nameplate ratings together and treating that value as a single range.

Question: What size branch circuit is required for one 6 kW counter-mounted cooking unit and two 3 kW wall-mounted ovens connected on a 120/240V circuit? **Figure 220–22**

(a) 14 AWG   (b) 12 AWG   (c) 10 AWG   (d) 8 AWG

Answer: (d) 8 AWG

Step 1: Determine the total connected load:

Total Connected Load = (6 kW + 3 kW + 3 kW).
Total Connected Load = 12 kW

Step 2: Determine the calculated VA load as a single 12 kW range:

Table 220.55 Column C = 8 kW

Step 3: Determine the branch-circuit load in amperes, I = P/E:

P = 8,000W
E = 240V
I = 8,000W/240V
I = 33.33A, 8 AWG rated 40A at 60°C [Table 310.15(B)(16) and 110.14(C)(1)]

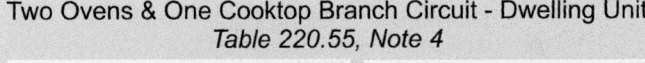
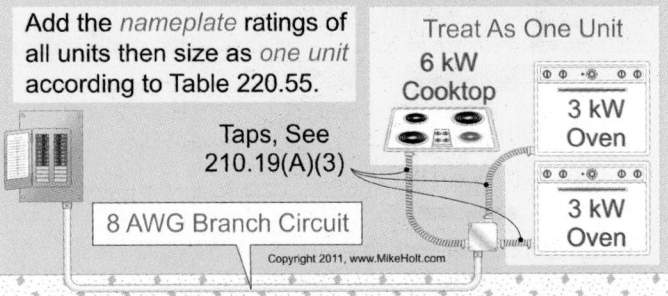

Figure 220–22

Author's Comment: For ranges rated 8.75 kW or more, the minimum branch-circuit rating is 40A [210.19(A)(3)].

220.56 Commercial—Kitchen Equipment Load. Table 220.56 can be used to calculate the feeder/service load for thermostat-controlled or intermittently used commercial electric cooking equipment, such as dishwasher booster heaters, water heaters, and other kitchen loads. The kitchen equipment feeder/service calculated load must not be less than the sum of the two largest kitchen equipment loads. Table 220.56 demand factors don't apply to space-heating, ventilating, or air-conditioning equipment.

> *Question:* What's the feeder/service calculated load for one 15 kW booster water heater, one 15 kW water heater, one 3 kW oven, and one 2 kW deep fryer in a commercial kitchen? **Figure 220–23**
>
> (a) 15 kW   (b) 20 kW   (c) 26 kW   (d) 30 kW
>
> *Answer:* (d) 30 kW
>
> Step 1: Determine the total connected load:
>
> > Total Connected Load = 15 kW + 15 kW + 3 kW + 2 kW
> > Total Connected Load = 35 kW
>
> Step 2: Determine the feeder/service calculated load:
>
> > 35 kW x 0.80 = 28 kW, but it must not be less than the sum of the two largest appliances, or 30 kW.

Commercial Cooking Equipment
Service/Feeder Calculated Load
220.56

| Booster Heater 15 kW* | Water Heater 15 kW* | Oven 3 kW | Deep Fryer 2 kW |

Copyright 2011
www.MikeHolt.com

Determine the kitchen equipment calculated load.

Table 220.56, 4 units, 80% of connected load.

Water Heater	15.00 kW*	*The calculated load can't
Booster Heater	15.00 kW*	be less than the sum of the
Oven	3.00 kW	two largest appliances.
Deep fryer	2.00 kW	
Total Connected	35.00 kW x 0.80 DF = *28 kW Demand

*Two Largest Appliances:

Water Heater	15.00 kW
Booster Heater	15.00 kW
	30.00 kW which exceeds 28 kW

Feeder/Service Calculated Load = 30 kW

Figure 220–23

220.60 Noncoincident Loads. If it's unlikely that two or more loads will be used at the same time, only the largest load(s) must be used to determine the feeder/service VA calculated load. **Figure 220–24**

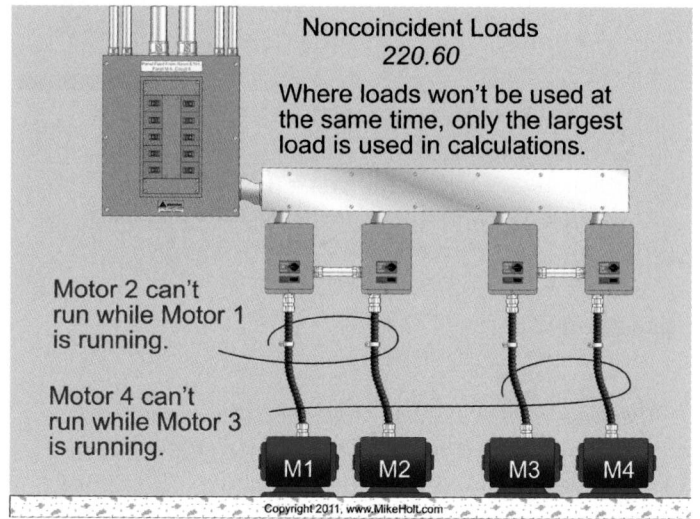

Noncoincident Loads
220.60

Where loads won't be used at the same time, only the largest load is used in calculations.

Motor 2 can't run while Motor 1 is running.

Motor 4 can't run while Motor 3 is running.

M1 M2 M3 M4

Copyright 2011, www.MikeHolt.com

Figure 220–24

> *Question:* What's the feeder/service calculated load for a 5 hp, 230V air conditioner having a rated load current of 28A versus three electric space heaters, each rated 3 kW? **Figure 220–25**
>
> (a) 5,000W   (b) 6,000W   (c) 7,500W   (d) 9,000W
>
> *Answer:* (d) 9,000W
>
> Air-Conditioning Load = 230V x 28A
> Air-Conditioning Load = 6,440 VA (omit, smaller than 9,000W)
> Electric Space Heating Load = 9,000W

220.61 Feeder/Service Neutral Unbalanced Load.

(A) Basic Calculation. The calculated neutral load for feeders/services is the maximum calculated load between the neutral conductor and any one ungrounded conductor. Line-to-line loads don't place any load on the neutral conductor, therefore they aren't considered.

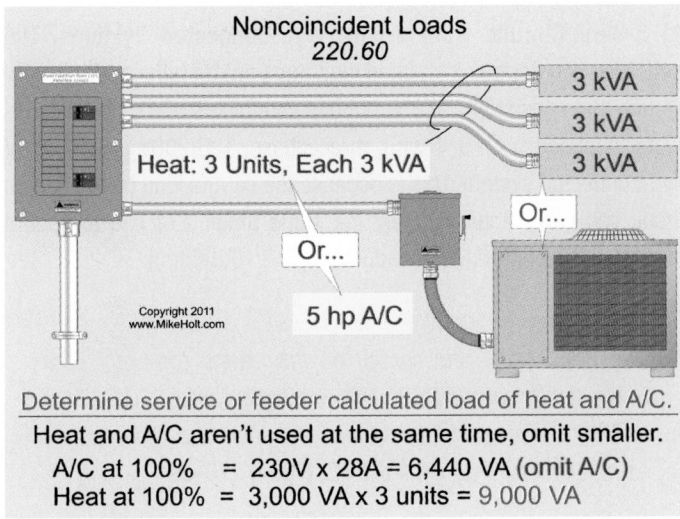

Determine service or feeder calculated load of heat and A/C.

Heat and A/C aren't used at the same time, omit smaller.
A/C at 100%   = 230V x 28A = 6,440 VA (omit A/C)
Heat at 100% = 3,000 VA x 3 units = 9,000 VA

Figure 220–25

Question: What's the minimum neutral conductor size for a 200A feeder, of which 100A is line-to-line loads with a maximum unbalanced neutral load of 100A? **Figure 220–26**

(a) 3/0 AWG   (b) 1/0 AWG   (c) 1 AWG   (d) 3 AWG

Answer: (d) 3 AWG

200A total load less 100A line-to-line loads = 100A neutral load

Table 310.15(B)(16), 75°C column, 3 AWG rated 100A

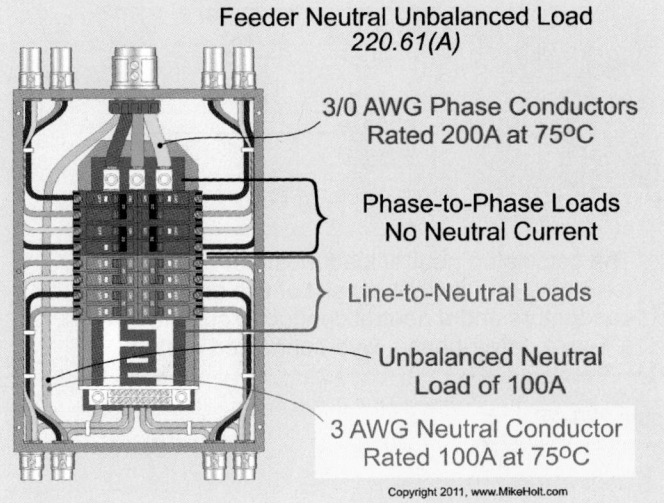

Figure 220–26

(B) Permitted Reductions.

(1) Dwelling Unit Cooking and Dryer Load.

Cooking Load. The feeder/service neutral calculated load for household electric ranges, wall-mounted ovens, or counter-mounted cooking units can be calculated at 70 percent of the cooking equipment calculated load in accordance with Table 220.55.

Question: What's the feeder/service calculated neutral load for nine 12 kW household ranges?

(a) 13 kW   (b) 14.70 kW   (c) 16.80 kW   (d) 24 kW

Answer: (c) 16.80 kW

Step 1: Table 220.55 Column C = 24 kW

Step 2: Neutral Load = 24 kW x 0.70
         Neutral Load = 16.80 kW

Dryer Load. The feeder/service neutral calculated load for household electric dryers can be calculated at 70 percent of the dryer calculated load in accordance with Table 220.54.

Question: A 10-unit multifamily building has a 5 kW electric clothes dryer in each unit. What's the feeder/service neutral load for these dryers?

(a) 17.50 kW   (b) 23.50 kW   (c) 33 kW   (d) 41 kW

Answer: (a) 17.50 kW

Step 1: Table 220.54 = 10 units x 5 kW x 0.50
         Table 220.54 = 25 kW

Step 2: Neutral Load = 25 kW x 0.70
         Neutral Load = 17.50 kW

(2) Over 200A Neutral Reduction. The feeder/service calculated neutral load for a 3-wire, single-phase, or 4-wire, three-phase system, can be reduced for that portion of the unbalanced load over 200A by a multiplier of 70 percent.

Question: *What's the feeder/service neutral calculated load for the following? The voltage system is 120/240V, single phase.* **Figure 220–27**

- *100A of line-to-line loads*
- *100A of household ranges*
- *50A of household dryers*
- *350A of line-to-neutral loads*

(a) 200A   (b) 379A   (c) 455A   (d) 600A

Answer: *(b) 379A*

Step 1: Determine the total feeder/service neutral load:

Line-to-line	100A	0A
Ranges	100A	70A (100A x 0.70)
Dryers	50A	35A (50A x 0.70)
Line-to-neutral	**+ 350A**	**+ 350A**
Total Load =	600A	455A

Step 2: Determine the demand feeder/service neutral load:

Total Neutral Load	455A		
First 200A at 100%	**– 200A** x 1.00 =	200A	
Remainder at 70%	255A x 0.70 =	**179A**	
Total Demand Neutral Load =		379A	

(1) 3-Wire Circuits from 4-Wire Wye-Connected Systems. The feeder/service neutral calculated load must not be reduced for 3-wire circuits that consist of two ungrounded conductors and a neutral conductor supplied from a 4-wire, three-phase, 120/208V or 277/480V wye-connected system. This is because the neutral load on the 3-wire circuit will carry approximately the same amount of line-to-neutral current as the ungrounded conductors [310.15(B)(5)(c)].

Question: *What's the current on the neutral conductor of a 3-wire feeder supplied from a 4-wire, three-phase, 120/208V or 277/480V wye-connected system? The ungrounded conductors carry 200A of line-to-neutral loads.* **Figure 220–28**

(a) 200A   (b) 379A   (c) 455A   (d) 600A

Answer: *(a) 200A*

$$I_N = \sqrt{(I_{Line1}^2 + I_{Line2}^2) - (I_{Line1} \times I_{Line2})}$$
$$I_N = \sqrt{200A^2 + 200A^2 - (200A \times 200A)}$$
$$I_N = \sqrt{80,000 - 40,000}$$
$$I_N = \sqrt{40,000}$$
$$I_N = 200A$$

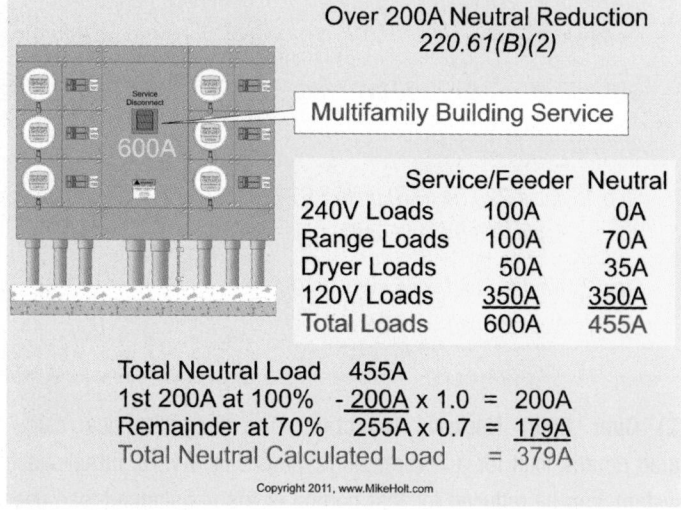

Over 200A Neutral Reduction
220.61(B)(2)

Multifamily Building Service

600A

	Service/Feeder	Neutral
240V Loads	100A	0A
Range Loads	100A	70A
Dryer Loads	50A	35A
120V Loads	350A	350A
Total Loads	600A	455A

Total Neutral Load   455A
1st 200A at 100%   -200A x 1.0   =   200A
Remainder at 70%   255A x 0.7   =   179A
Total Neutral Calculated Load   =   379A

Copyright 2011, www.MikeHolt.com

Figure 220–27

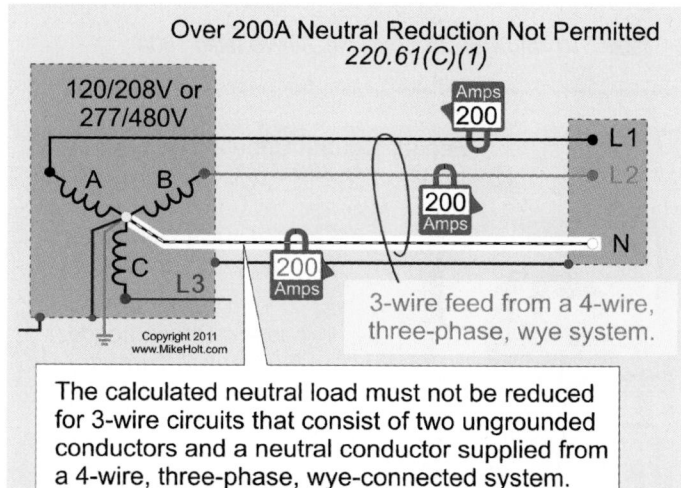

Over 200A Neutral Reduction Not Permitted
220.61(C)(1)

120/208V or
277/480V

Amps
200

Amps
200

L1

L2

200
Amps

N

200
Amps

3-wire feed from a 4-wire,
three-phase, wye system.

Copyright 2011
www.MikeHolt.com

The calculated neutral load must not be reduced for 3-wire circuits that consist of two ungrounded conductors and a neutral conductor supplied from a 4-wire, three-phase, wye-connected system.

Figure 220–28

(C) Prohibited Reductions. No reduction of the neutral conductor calculated feeder/service load is permitted for the following:

(2) Nonlinear Loads. The feeder/service neutral calculated load must not be reduced for nonlinear loads supplied from a 4-wire, three-phase, 120/208V or 277/480V wye-connected system.

Question: What's the feeder/service neutral calculated load for the following?

- *200A of line-to-line loads*
- *200A of line-to-neutral nonlinear loads*
- *200A of line-to-neutral linear loads*

(a) 200A   (b) 400A   (c) 500A   (d) 600A

Answer: *(d) 400A*

 CAUTION: *The current on the neutral conductor for nonlinear loads can be as much as twice the maximum neutral load.*

	Feeder/Service	Neutral Load
Line-to-Line Loads	200A	0A
Nonlinear Line-to-Neutral Loads	200A	200A
Linear Line-to-Neutral Loads	200A	200A
Total Calculated Load	600A	400A

PART IV. OPTIONAL CALCULATIONS FOR COMPUTING FEEDER AND SERVICE LOADS

220.82 Dwelling Unit—Optional Load Calculation.

(A) Feeder/Service Load. The 3-wire feeder/service load for a dwelling unit can be calculated by adding the calculated loads from 220.82(B) and (C). The feeder/service neutral calculated load must be determined in accordance with 220.61.

(B) General Loads. The feeder/service calculated load must not be less than 100 percent of the first 10 kVA, plus 40 percent of the remainder of the following:

(1) General Lighting. The general lighting load is based on 3 VA per sq ft for general lighting and general-use receptacles. The floor area is calculated from the outside dimensions of the dwelling unit, not including open porches, garages, or unused or unfinished spaces not adaptable for future use.

(2) Small-Appliance and Laundry Circuits. A load of 1,500 VA for each 20A small-appliance and laundry branch circuit [220.11(C)(1) and (2)]. Since a minimum of two small-appliance circuits and a laundry circuit are required, the minimum load for calculation purposes is 4,500 VA.

(3) Appliances. The nameplate rating of the following:

- a. Appliances fastened in place, permanently connected or located to be on a specific circuit

- b. Ranges, wall-mounted ovens, counter-mounted cooking units

- c. Clothes dryers

- d. Water heaters

(4) Motor VA. The VA nameplate rating of all motors not part of an appliance.

(C) Air-Conditioning and Heating Equipment. The larger of (1) through (6):

(1) Air-Conditioning Equipment. 100 percent of the nameplate rating(s).

(2) Heat-Pump Compressor without Supplemental Heating. 100 percent of the heat-pump nameplate rating.

(3) Heat-Pump Compressor and Supplemental Heating. 100 percent of the nameplate rating of the heat pump and 65 percent of the supplemental electric heating. If the heat-pump compressor is prevented from operating at the same time as the supplementary heat, it can be omitted in the calculation.

(4) Space-Heating Units (three or fewer units). 65 percent of the space-heating nameplate rating.

(5) Space-Heating Units (four or more units). 40 percent of the space-heating nameplate rating.

(6) Thermal Storage Heating. 100 percent of the thermal storage heating nameplate rating.

> **Author's Comment:** One form of thermal storage heating involves heating bricks or water at night when the electric rates are lower. Then during the day, the building uses the thermally stored heat.

Question: Using the optional calculation method, what size 3-wire, single-phase, 120/240V feeder/service ungrounded conductors are required for a 1,500 sq ft dwelling unit that contains the following loads?

- Dishwasher   1,200 VA
- Disposal   900 VA
- Cooktop   6,000 VA
- Oven   3,000 VA
- Dryer   4,000 VA
- Water heater   4,500 VA
- Heat-pump compressor having a rating of 5 hp, with supplemental electric heat having a rating of 7 kW.

(a) 100A   (b) 110A   (c) 125A   (d) 150A

Answer: (c) 125A

Step 1: Determine the total feeder/service calculated load:

Lighting, receptacles, and appliance calculated load [220.82(B)]

Small appliance	1,500 VA x 2 =	3,000 VA
Laundry	1,500 VA x 1 =	1,500 VA
General lighting	1,500 sq ft x 3 VA/sq ft =	4,500 VA
Dishwasher	1,200 VA x 1 =	1,200 VA
Disposal	900 VA x 1 =	900 VA
Cooktop	6,000 VA x 1 =	6,000 VA
Oven	3,000 VA x 1 =	3,000 VA
Dryer	4,000 VA x 1 =	4,000 VA
Water heater	4,500 VA x 1 =	+ 4,500 VA
		28,600 VA

First 10,000 VA at 100%
10,000 VA x 1.00 =   10,000 VA
Remainder at 40% 18,600 VA x 0.40 =   + 7,440 VA
220.82(B) Calculated Load =   17,440 VA

Largest of Air-Conditioning or Heat [220.82(C)]
Heat pump 5 hp compressor at 100%
230V x 28A =   6,440 VA

Supplemental heat at 65% =
7,000 VA x 0.65 =   **+ 4,550 VA**

Total Calculated Load 220.82(B) and (C)
17,440 VA + 6,440 VA + 4,550 VA =   28,430 VA

Step 2: Determine the feeder/service calculated load in amperes:

$I = VA/E$
$I = 28,430 \text{ VA}/240\text{V}$
$I = 119\text{A}$, 2 AWG [215.2(A)(4) and 310.15(B)(7)]

220.83 Existing Dwelling Unit Calculations.

It's permissible to calculate the total load in accordance with 220.83(A) or (B).

(B) If Additional Air-Conditioning Equipment or Electric Space-Heating Equipment Is to Be Installed. The larger of the air-conditioning or space-heating load, plus the first 8 kVA of the following loads (1 through 3) at 100 percent, and the remainder of the loads at 40 percent:

(1) General lighting and general-use receptacles 3 volt-amperes/ft^2 as per 220.12

(2) 1,500 VA for 20A small-appliance and laundry branch circuits as per 210.11(C)(1) and (C)(2)

(3) The nameplate rating of:

     a. All appliances that are fastened in place, permanently connected, or located to be on a specific circuit

     b. Ranges, wall-mounted ovens, counter-mounted cooking units

     c. Clothes dryers

     d. Water heaters

Question: For an existing dwelling, what size 3-wire, single-phase, 120/240V feeder/service ungrounded conductors are required for a 1,500 sq ft dwelling unit that contains the following loads?

- Dishwasher   1,200 VA
- Disposal   900 VA
- Cooktop   6,000 VA
- Oven   3,000 VA
- Dryer   4,000 VA
- Water heater   4,500 VA
- Air-Conditioning compressor having a rating of 5 hp, with electric heat having a rating of 7 kW.

(a) 100A   (b) 110A   (c) 125A   (d) 150A

Answer: (c) 125A

Step 1: Determine the total feeder/service calculated load:

(1) General Lighting at 3 VA/sq ft
1,500 sq ft x 3 VA/sq ft =   4,500 VA

(2) Small and Laundry Appliance Circuits

Small appliance	1,500 VA x 2 =	3,000 VA
Laundry	1,500 VA x 1 =	1,500 VA

(3) Nameplate of all appliances

Dishwasher	*1,200 VA x 1 =*	*1,200 VA*
Disposal	*900 VA x 1 =*	*900 VA*
Cooktop	*6,000 VA x 1 =*	*6,000 VA*
Oven	*3,000 VA x 1 =*	*3,000 VA*
Dryer	*4,000 VA x 1 =*	*4,000 VA*
Water heater	*4,500 VA x 1 =*	*+ 4,500 VA*
		28,600 VA

First 8,000 VA at 100%
8,000 VA x 1.00 =   *8,000 VA*
Remainder at 40%   20,600 VA x 0.40 =   *+ 8,240 VA*
220.82(B) Calculated Load =   *16,240 VA*

Largest of Air-Conditioning or Heat [220.82(C)]
Air-Conditioner, 5 hp compressor
at 100%   230V x 28A =   *6,440 VA*
Heat at100% =   **7,000 VA**

Total Calculated Load
16,240 VA + 7,000 VA =   *23,2400 VA*

Step 2: Determine the feeder/service calculated load in amperes:

$I = VA/E$
$I = 23,240 VA/240V$
$I = 97A, 4 AWG [215.2(A)(4) and 310.15(B)(7)]$

220.84 Multifamily—Optional Load Calculation.

(A) Feeder or Service Load. The feeder/service calculated load for a building with three or more dwelling units equipped with electric cooking equipment, and either electric space heating or air-conditioning, can be in accordance with the demand factors of Table 220.84, based on the number of dwelling units. The feeder/service neutral calculated load must be determined in accordance with 220.61.

(B) House Loads. House loads are calculated in accordance with Part III of Article 220, and then added to the Table 220.84 calculated load.

Author's Comment: House loads are those not directly associated with the individual dwelling units of a multifamily dwelling. Some examples of house loads are landscape and parking lot lighting, common area lighting, common laundry facilities, common pool and recreation areas, and so on.

(C) Connected Loads. The connected loads from all of the dwelling units are added together, and then the Table 220.84 demand factors are applied to determine the calculated load.

(1) 3 VA per sq ft for general lighting and general-use receptacles.

(2) 1,500 VA for each 20A small-appliance circuit as required by 210.11(C)(1) (a minimum of two circuits per dwelling unit), and 1,500 VA for each 20A laundry circuit as required by 210.11(C)(2).

Author's Comment: A laundry circuit isn't required in an individual unit of a multifamily dwelling if common laundry facilities are provided [210.52(F) Ex 1].

(3) **Appliances.** The nameplate rating of the following:

a. Appliances fastened in place, permanently connected or located to be on a specific circuit

b. Ranges, wall-mounted ovens, counter-mounted cooking units

c. Clothes dryers not connected to the required laundry circuit specified in 210.11(C)(2)

d. Water heaters

(4) The nameplate rating of all motors not part of an appliance.

(5) The larger of the air-conditioning load or fixed electric space-heating load.

Question: What size 4-wire, three-phase, 120/208V service is required for a multifamily building with twenty 1,500 sq ft dwelling units, where each unit contains the following loads?

• *Dishwasher*	*1,200 VA*
• *Water heater*	*4,500 VA*
• *Disposal*	*900 VA*
• *Dryer*	*4,000 VA*
• *Cooktop*	*6,000 VA*
• *Oven*	*3,000 VA*
• *Heat*	*7,000 VA*
• *Air-Conditioning, 5 hp compressor*	*6,440 VA*

(a) 400A   (b) 600A   (c) 800A   (d) 1,200A

Answer: *(c) 800A [240.4 and 240.6(A)]*

(Steps to solution continued on next page)

Step 1: Determine the dwelling unit connected load:

General lighting	1,500 sq ft x 3 VA/sq ft =	4,500 VA
Small appliance	1500VA x 2 =	3,000 VA
Laundry	1,500 VA x 1 =	1,500 VA
Dishwasher	1,200 VA x 1 =	1,200 VA
Water heater	4,500 VA x 1 =	4,500 VA
Disposal	900 VA x 1 =	900 VA
Dryer	4,000 VA x 1 =	4,000 VA
Cooktop	6,000 VA x 1 =	6,000 VA
Oven	3,000 VA x 1 =	3,000 VA
Air-Conditioning		
5 hp (omit)	0 VA x 1 =	0 VA
Heat =		+ 7,000 VA
Total Dwelling Unit Load =		35,600 VA

Step 2: Determine the calculated load for the multifamily building:

Demand Factor for 20 units = 0.38
   [Table 220.84]

35,600 VA x 20 x 0.38 =   270,560 VA

Step 3: Determine feeder/service conductor size:

$I = VA/(E \times \sqrt{3})$

$I = 270,560 \ VA/(208V \times 1.732)$

$I = 751A$

I of Each Conductor Parallel Set = 751A/2 conductors

I of Each Conductor Parallel Set = 376A

Conductor = 500 kcmil, rated 380A at 75°C x 2

Conductor = 760A, Table 310.15(B)(16)

220.85 Optional Calculation—Two Dwelling Units.
If two dwelling units are supplied by a single feeder, and where the standard calculated load in accordance with Part II of this article exceeds that for three identical units calculated in accordance with 220.84, the lesser of the two calculated loads may be used.

220.87 Determining Existing Loads. The calculation of a feeder or service load for existing installations can be based on:

(1) The maximum demand data for one year.

Ex: If the maximum demand data for one year isn't available, the maximum power demand over a 15-minute period continuously recorded over a minimum 30-day period using a recording ammeter or power meter connected to the highest loaded phase, based on the initial loading at the start of the recording is permitted. The recording must be taken when the building or space is occupied based on the larger of the heating or cooling equipment load.

225 Outside Branch Circuits and Feeders

INTRODUCTION TO ARTICLE 225—OUTSIDE BRANCH CIRCUITS AND FEEDERS

This article covers the installation requirements for equipment, including conductors, located outdoors on or between buildings, poles, and other structures on the premises. Conductors installed outdoors can serve many purposes such as area lighting, power for outdoor equipment, or providing power to a separate building or structure. It's important to remember that the power supply for buildings or structures aren't always service conductors, but in many cases may be feeders or branch-circuit conductors originating in another building. Be careful not to assume that the conductors supplying power to a building are service conductors until you've identified where the utility service point is and reviewed the Article 100 Definitions for feeders, branch circuits, and service conductors. If they're service conductors, use Article 230. For outside branch circuit and feeder conductors, whatever they feed, use this article.

Section 225.2 provides a listing of other articles that may furnish additional requirements, then Part I of Article 225 goes on to address installation methods intended to provide a secure installation of outside conductors while providing sufficient conductor size, support, attachment means, and maintaining safe clearances.

Part II of the article limits the number of supplies (branch circuits or feeders) permitted to a building or structure and provides rules regarding disconnects for them. These rules include the disconnect rating, construction characteristics, labeling, and where to locate the disconnecting means and the grouping of multiple disconnects.

Outside branch circuits and feeders over 600V are the focus of Part III of Article 225.

PART I. GENERAL

225.1 Scope. Article 225 contains the installation requirements for outside branch circuits and feeders installed on or between buildings, structures, or poles. **Figures 225–1 and 225–2**

> **Author's Comment:** Review the following definitions in Article 100:
>
> - "Branch Circuit"
> - "Building"
> - "Feeder"
> - "Structure"

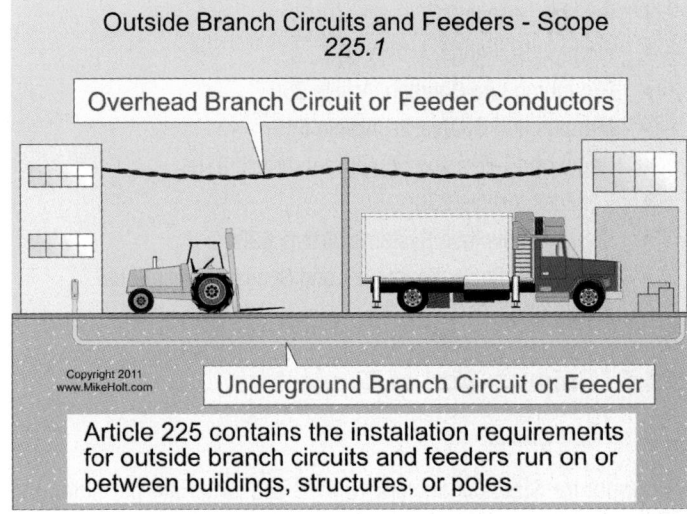

Figure 225–1

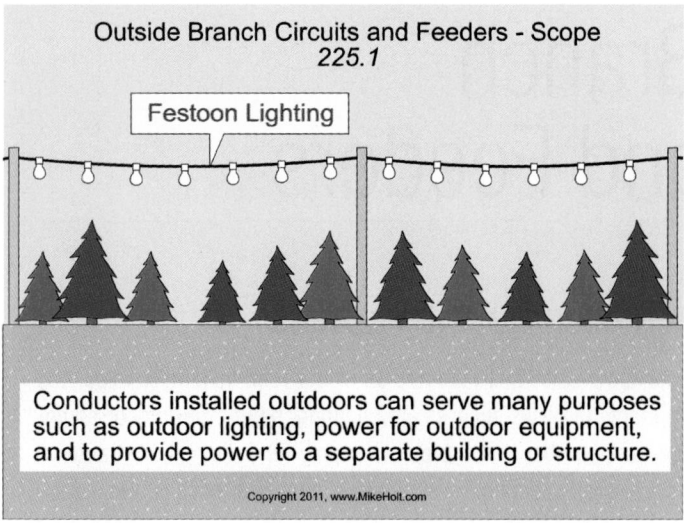

Figure 225–2

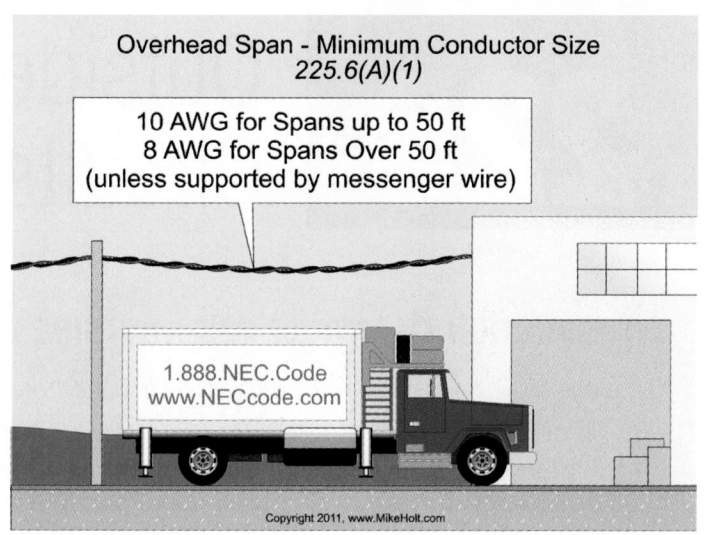

Figure 225–3

225.2 Other Articles. Other articles containing important requirements include:

- Branch Circuits, Article 210
- Class 1, Class 2, and Class 3 Remote-Control, Signaling, and Power-Limited Circuits, Article 725
- Communications Circuits, Article 800
- Community Antenna Television and Radio Distribution Systems, Article 820
- Conductors for General Wiring, Article 310
- Electric Signs and Outline Lighting, Article 600
- Feeders, Article 215
- Floating Buildings, Article 553
- Grounding and Bonding, Article 250
- Marinas and Boatyards, Article 555
- Radio and Television Equipment, Article 810
- Services, Article 230
- Solar Photovoltaic Systems, Article 690
- Swimming Pools, Fountains, and Similar Installations, Article 680

225.6 Minimum Size of Conductors.

(A) Overhead Spans.

(1) Conductor Size. Conductors 10 AWG and larger are permitted for overhead spans up to 50 ft long. For spans over 50 ft in length, the minimum size conductor is 8 AWG, unless supported by a messenger wire. **Figure 225–3**

(B) Festoon Lighting. Overhead conductors for festoon lighting must not be smaller than 12 AWG, unless messenger wires support the conductors. The overhead conductors must be supported by messenger wire, with strain insulators, whenever the spans exceed 40 ft in length. **Figure 225–4**

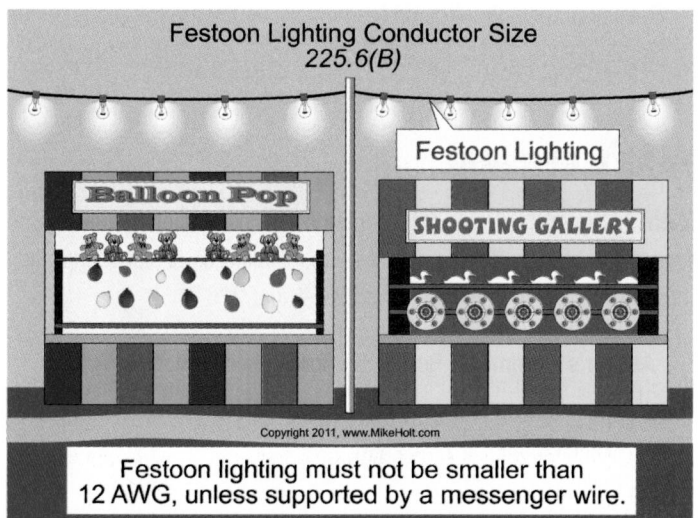

Figure 225–4

Author's Comment: Festoon lighting is a string of outdoor lights suspended between two points [Article 100]. It's commonly used at carnivals, circuses, fairs, and Christmas tree lots [525.20(C)].

225.7 Luminaires Installed Outdoors.

(C) 277V to Ground Circuits. 277V and 480V branch circuits are permitted to supply luminaires for lighting outdoor areas of industrial establishments, office buildings, schools, stores, and other commercial or public buildings. **Figure 225–5**

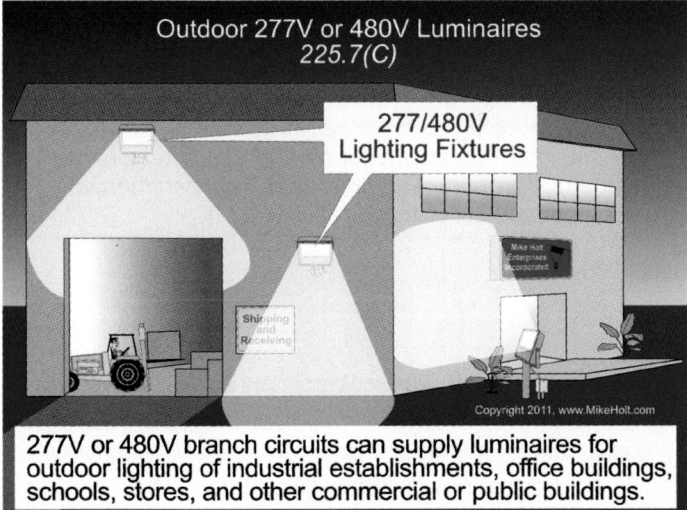

Figure 225–5

Author's Comment: See 210.6(C) for the types of luminaires permitted on 277V or 480V branch circuits.

225.15 Supports Over Buildings.
Conductor spans over a building must be securely supported by substantial structures. If practicable, such supports must be independent of the building [230.29].

225.16 Attachment.

(A) Point of Attachment. The point of attachment for overhead conductors must not be less than 10 ft above the finished grade, and it must be located so the minimum conductor clearance required by 225.18 can be maintained.

⚠️ **CAUTION:** *Conductors might need to have the point of attachment raised so the overhead conductors will comply with the clearances from building openings and other building areas required by 225.19.* **Figure 225–6**

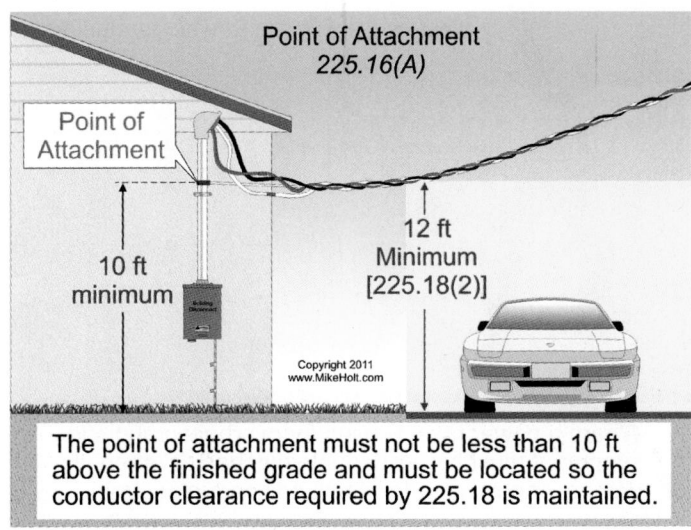

Figure 225–6

(B) Means of Attachment to Buildings. Open conductors must be attached to fittings identified for use with conductors, or to noncombustible, nonabsorbent insulators securely attached to the building or other structure.

Author's Comment: The point of attachment of the overhead conductor spans to a building or other structure must provide the minimum clearances as specified in 225.18 and 225.19. In no case can this point of attachment be less than 10 ft above the finished grade.

225.17 Masts as Support.
If a mast is used for overhead conductor support, it must have adequate mechanical strength, braces, or guy wires to withstand the strain caused by the conductors. Only branch-circuit or feeder conductors can be attached to the mast. **Figure 225–7**

Author's Comment: Aerial cables and antennas for radio and TV equipment must not be attached to the feeder or branch-circuit mast [810.12]. In addition, 800.133(B) prohibits communications cables from being attached to raceways, including a mast for power conductors. **Figure 225–8**

225.18 Clearance for Overhead Conductors.
Overhead conductor spans must maintain vertical clearances as follows:

(1) 10 ft above finished grade, sidewalks, platforms, or projections from which they might be accessible to pedestrians for 120V, 120/208V, 120/240V, or 240V circuits.

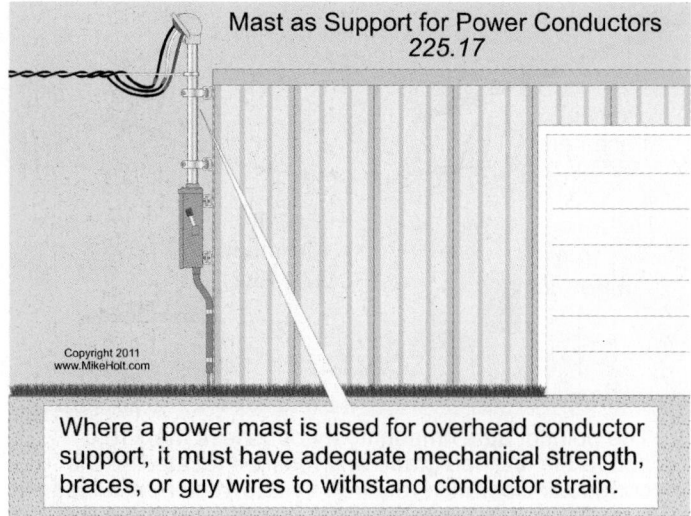

Mast as Support for Power Conductors
225.17

Where a power mast is used for overhead conductor support, it must have adequate mechanical strength, braces, or guy wires to withstand conductor strain.

Figure 225–7

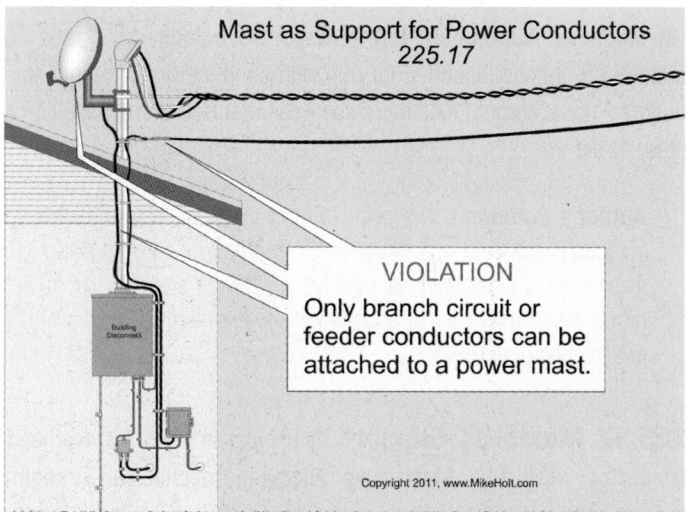

Mast as Support for Power Conductors
225.17

VIOLATION

Only branch circuit or feeder conductors can be attached to a power mast.

Figure 225–8

(2) 12 ft above residential property and driveways, and those commercial areas not subject to truck traffic for 120V, 120/208V, 120/240V, 240V, 277V, 277/480V, or 480V circuits. Figure 225–9

(4) 18 ft over public streets, alleys, roads, parking areas subject to truck traffic, driveways on other than residential property, and other areas traversed by vehicles (such as those used for cultivation, grazing, forestry, and orchards).

(5) 24½ ft over track rails of railroads.

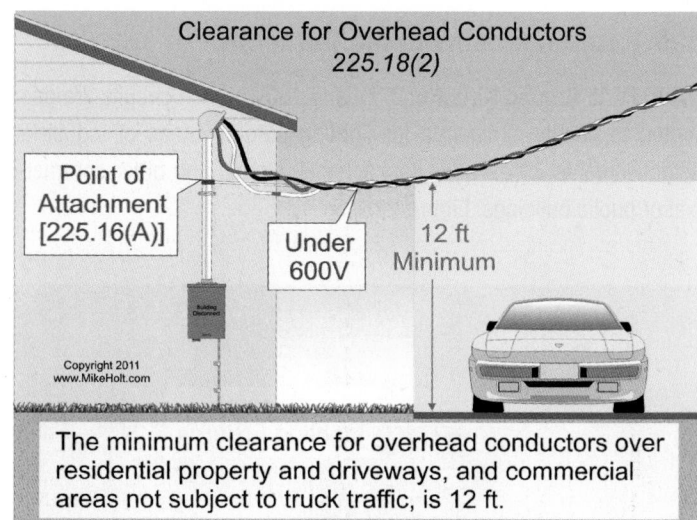

Clearance for Overhead Conductors
225.18(2)

Point of Attachment [225.16(A)]

Under 600V

12 ft Minimum

The minimum clearance for overhead conductors over residential property and driveways, and commercial areas not subject to truck traffic, is 12 ft.

Figure 225–9

Author's Comment: Overhead conductors located above pools, outdoor spas, outdoor hot tubs, diving structures, observation stands, towers, or platforms must be installed in accordance with the clearance requirements in 680.8.

225.19 Clearances from Buildings

(A) Above Roofs. Overhead conductors must maintain a vertical clearance of 8 ft above the surface of a roof and must be maintained for a distance of at least 3 ft from the edge of the roof. Figure 225–10

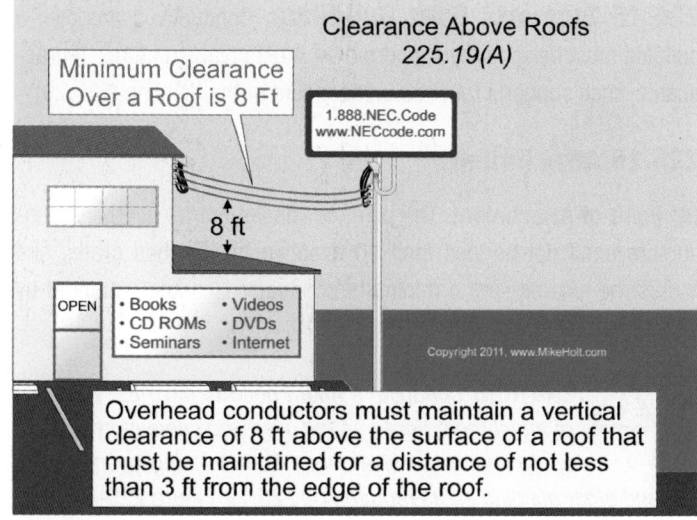

Clearance Above Roofs
225.19(A)

Minimum Clearance Over a Roof is 8 Ft

1.888.NEC.Code
www.NECcode.com

8 ft

OPEN
• Books   • Videos
• CD ROMs   • DVDs
• Seminars   • Internet

Overhead conductors must maintain a vertical clearance of 8 ft above the surface of a roof that must be maintained for a distance of not less than 3 ft from the edge of the roof.

Figure 225–10

Ex 2: The overhead conductor clearances from the roof can be reduced from 8 ft to 3 ft if the slope of the roof meets or exceeds 4 in. of vertical rise for every 12 in. of horizontal run.

Ex 3: For 120/208V or 120/240V circuits, the conductor clearance over the roof overhang can be reduced from 8 ft to 18 in., if no more than 6 ft of conductor passes over no more than 4 ft of roof. **Figure 225-11**

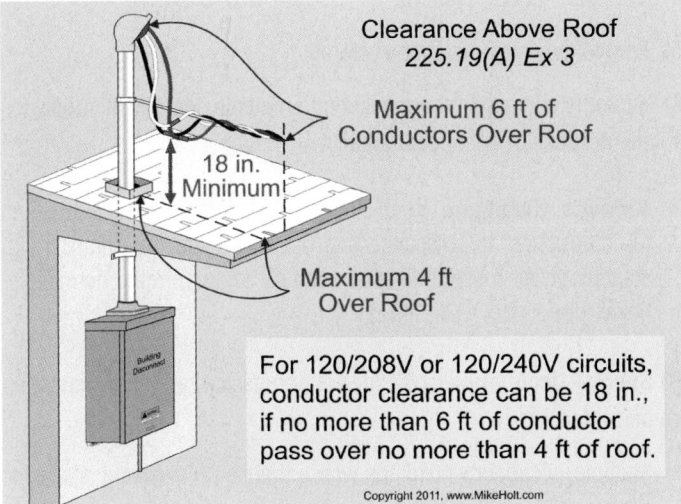

Figure 225–11

Ex 4: The 3 ft clearance from the roof edge doesn't apply when the point of attachment is on the side of the building below the roof.

(B) From Other Structures. Overhead conductors must maintain a clearance of at least 3 ft from signs, chimneys, radio and television antennas, tanks, and other nonbuilding or nonbridge structures.

(D) Final Span Clearance.

(1) Clearance from Windows. Overhead conductors must maintain a clearance of 3 ft from windows that open, doors, porches, balconies, ladders, stairs, fire escapes, or similar locations. **Figure 225–12**

Ex: Overhead conductors installed above a window aren't required to maintain the 3 ft distance from the window.

(2) Vertical Clearance. Overhead conductors must maintain a vertical clearance of at least 10 ft above platforms, projections, or surfaces from which they might be reached. This vertical clearance must be maintained for 3 ft, measured horizontally from the platforms, projections, or surfaces from which they might be reached.

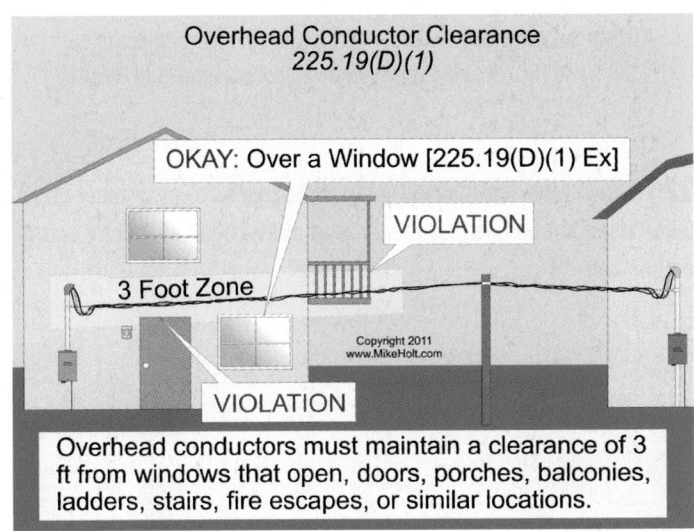

Figure 225–12

(3) Below Openings. Overhead conductors must not be installed under an opening through which materials might pass, and they must not be installed where they will obstruct an entrance to building openings. **Figure 225–13**

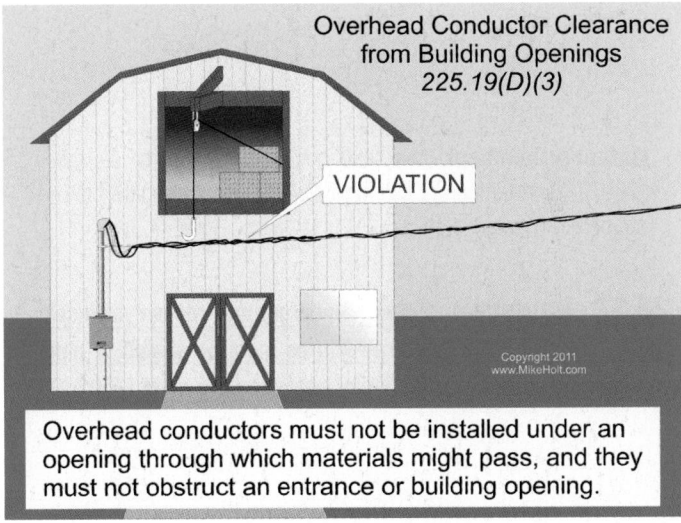

Figure 225–13

225.22 Raceways on Exterior Surfaces of Buildings or Other Structures.
Raceways on exterior surfaces of buildings or other structures must be arranged to drain, and be suitable for use in wet locations.

Author's Comment: A "Wet Location" is an area subject to saturation with water and unprotected locations exposed to weather [Article 100].

225.26 Trees for Conductor Support. Trees or other vegetation must not be used for the support of overhead conductor spans. Figure 225–14

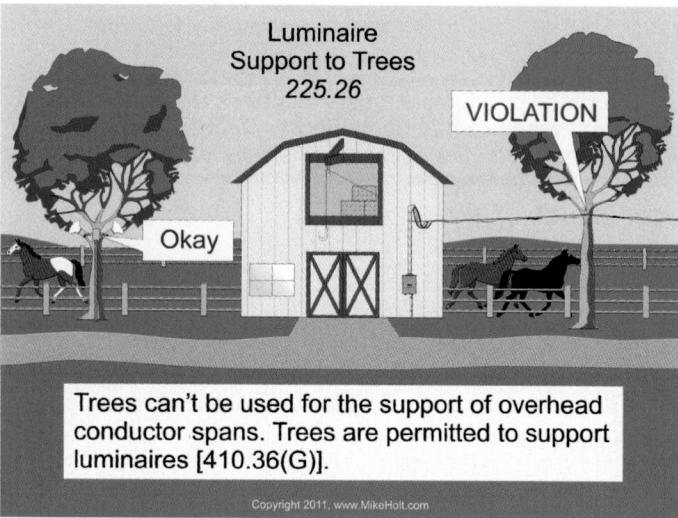

Figure 225–14

Author's Comment: Overhead conductor spans for services [230.10] and temporary wiring [590.4(J)] aren't permitted to be supported by vegetation.

225.27 Raceway Seal. Underground raceways (used or unused) entering buildings or structures must be sealed or plugged to prevent moisture from contacting energized live parts [300.5(G)].

PART II. BUILDINGS OR OTHER STRUCTURES SUPPLIED BY A FEEDER(S) OR BRANCH CIRCUIT(S)

225.30 Number of Supplies. If more than one building or other structure is on the same property, each building/structure must be served by no more than one feeder or single or multiwire branch circuit, except as permitted in (A) through (E).

Author's Comment: Article 100 defines a "Structure" as, "That which is built or constructed."

(A) Special Conditions. Additional supplies are permitted for:

(1) Fire pumps

(2) Emergency systems

(3) Legally required standby systems

(4) Optional standby systems

(5) Parallel power production systems

(6) Systems designed for connection to multiple sources of supply for the purpose of enhanced reliability.

Author's Comment: To minimize the possibility of accidental interruption, the disconnecting means for the fire pump or standby power must be located remotely away from the normal power disconnect [225.34(B)].

(B) Special Occupancies. By special permission, additional supplies are permitted for:

(1) Multiple-occupancy buildings where there's no available space for supply equipment accessible to all occupants, or

(2) A building/structure so large that two or more supplies are necessary.

(C) Capacity Requirements. Additional supplies are permitted for a building/structure where the capacity requirements exceed 2,000A.

(D) Different Characteristics. Additional supplies are permitted for different voltages, frequencies, or uses, such as control of outside lighting from multiple locations.

(E) Documented Switching Procedures. Additional supplies are permitted where documented safe switching procedures are established and maintained for disconnection.

225.31 Disconnecting Means. A disconnect is required for all conductors that enter or pass through a building/structure.

225.32 Disconnect Location. The disconnecting means for a building/structure must be installed at a readily accessible location either outside or inside nearest the point of entrance of the conductors. Figure 225–15

Supply conductors are considered outside of a building or other structure where they're encased or installed under not less than 2 in. of concrete or brick [230.6]. Figure 225–16

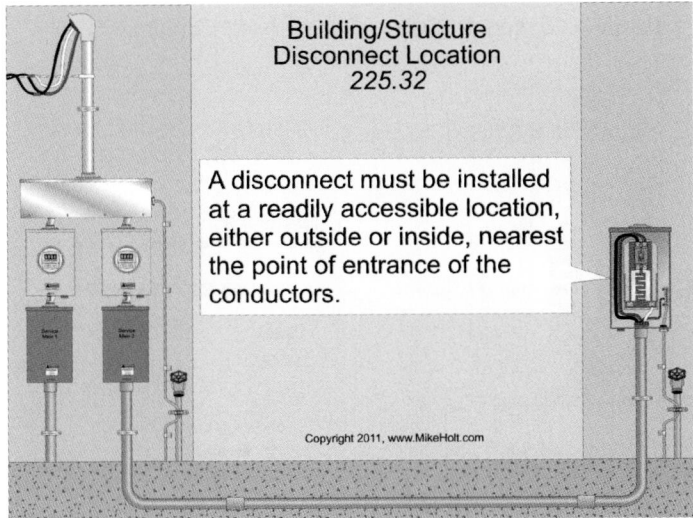

Building/Structure
Disconnect Location
225.32

A disconnect must be installed at a readily accessible location, either outside or inside, nearest the point of entrance of the conductors.

Copyright 2011, www.MikeHolt.com

Figure 225–15

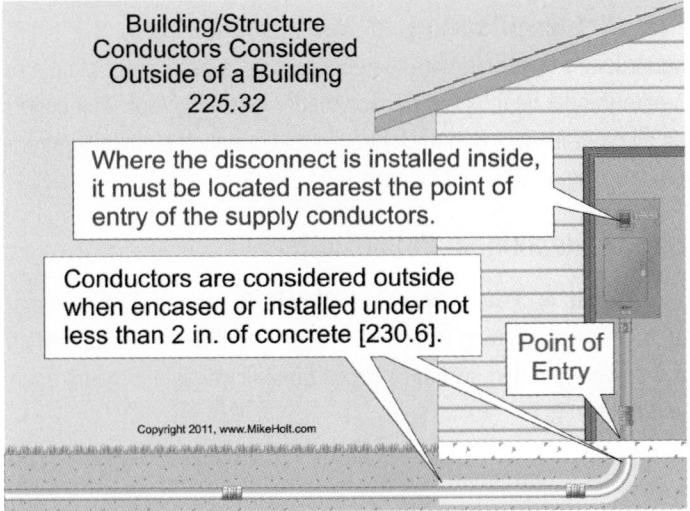

Building/Structure
Conductors Considered
Outside of a Building
225.32

Where the disconnect is installed inside, it must be located nearest the point of entry of the supply conductors.

Conductors are considered outside when encased or installed under not less than 2 in. of concrete [230.6].

Point of Entry

Copyright 2011, www.MikeHolt.com

Figure 225–16

Ex 1: If documented safe switching procedures are established and maintained, the building/structure disconnecting means can be located elsewhere on the premises, if monitored by qualified persons.

> **Author's Comment:** A "Qualified Person" is one who has skills and knowledge related to the construction and operation of the electrical equipment and installation, and has received safety training to recognize and avoid the hazards involved with electrical systems [Article 100].

Ex 3: A disconnecting means isn't required within sight of poles that support luminaires. **Figure 225–17**

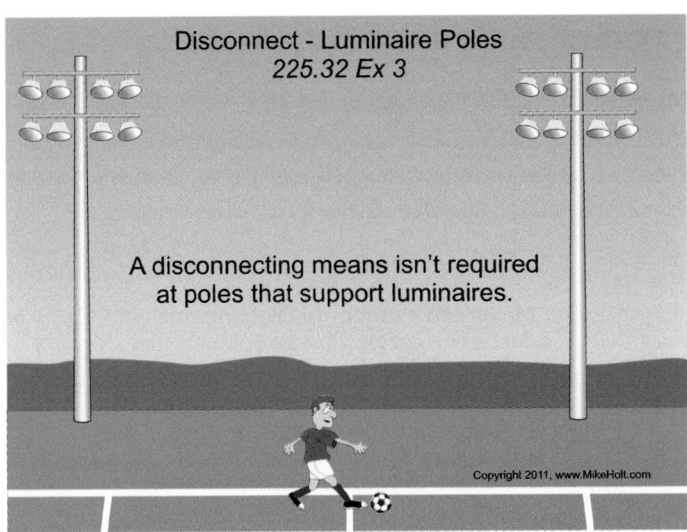

Disconnect - Luminaire Poles
225.32 Ex 3

A disconnecting means isn't required at poles that support luminaires.

Copyright 2011, www.MikeHolt.com

Figure 225–17

> **Author's Comment:** According to Article 100, within sight means that it's visible and not more than 50 ft from one to the other.

Ex 4: The disconnecting means for a sign must be controlled by an externally operable switch or circuit breaker that opens all ungrounded conductors to the sign. The sign disconnecting means must be within sight of the sign, or the disconnecting means must be capable of being locked in the open position [600.6(A)]. **Figure 225–18**

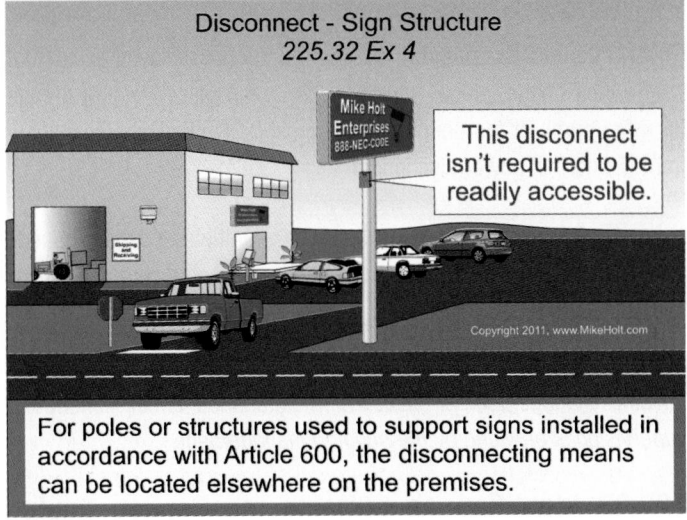

Disconnect - Sign Structure
225.32 Ex 4

Mike Holt
Enterprises
888-NEC-CODE

This disconnect isn't required to be readily accessible.

Copyright 2011, www.MikeHolt.com

For poles or structures used to support signs installed in accordance with Article 600, the disconnecting means can be located elsewhere on the premises.

Figure 225–18

225.33 Maximum Number of Disconnects.

(A) General. The building/structure disconnecting means can consist of no more than six switches or six circuit breakers in a single enclosure, or separate enclosures for each supply grouped in one location as permitted by 225.30. **Figure 225–19**

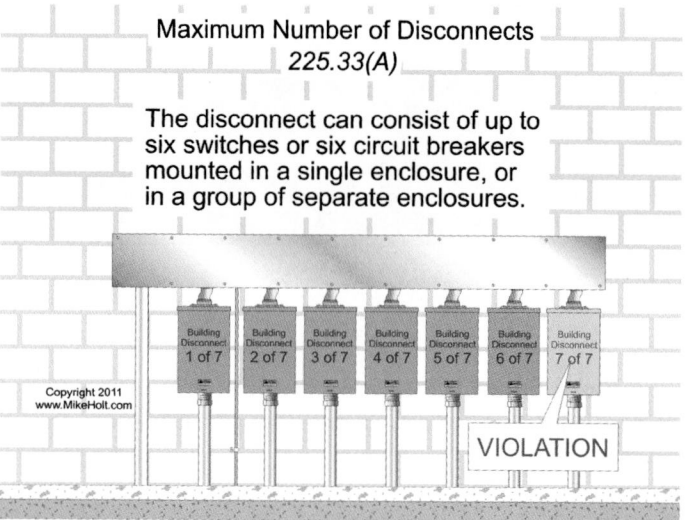

Figure 225–19

225.34 Grouping of Disconnects.

(A) General. The building/structure disconnecting means must be grouped in one location, and they must be marked to indicate the loads they serve [110.22].

(B) Additional Disconnects. To minimize the possibility of accidental interruption of the critical power systems, the disconnecting means for a fire pump or for standby power must be located remotely away from the normal power disconnect.

225.35 Access to Occupants. In a multiple-occupancy building, each occupant must have access to the disconnecting means for their occupancy.

Ex: The occupant's disconnecting means can be accessible to only building management, if electrical maintenance under continuous supervision is provided by the building management.

225.36 Identified as Suitable for Service Equipment. The building/structure disconnecting means must be comprised of a circuit breaker, molded case switch, general-use switch, or snap switch "suitable for use as service equipment". **Figure 225–20**

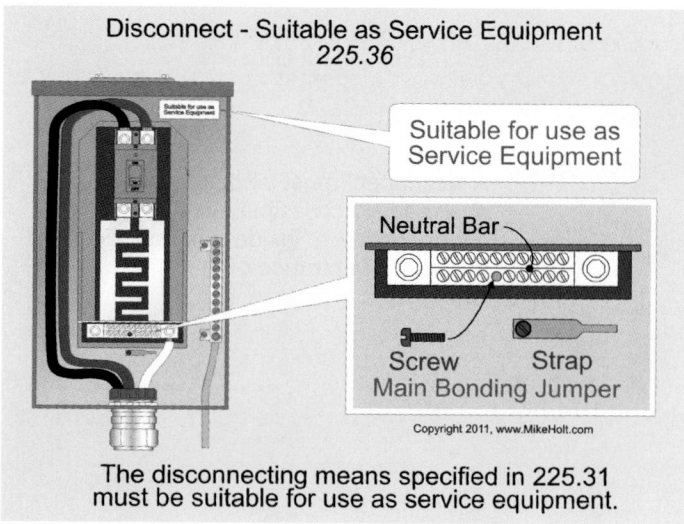

Figure 225–20

225.37 Identification of Multiple Feeders. If a building/structure is fed by more than one supply, a permanent plaque or directory must be installed at each feeder disconnect location denoting all other feeders or branch circuits that supply that building/structure, and the area served by each.

225.38 Disconnect Construction.

(A) Manual or Power-Operated Circuit Breakers. The building/structure disconnecting means can consist of either a manual switch or a power-operated switch or circuit breaker capable of being operated manually.

> **Author's Comment:** A shunt-trip pushbutton can be used to open a power-operated circuit breaker. The circuit breaker is the disconnecting means, not the pushbutton.

(D) Indicating. The disconnecting means for a building supplied by a feeder must plainly indicate whether it's in the open or closed position.

225.39 Rating of Disconnecting Means. A single disconnecting means for a building/structure must have an ampere rating not less than the calculated load as determined by Article 220. If the disconnecting means consists of more than one switch or circuit breaker, the combined ratings of the circuit breakers must not be less than the calculated load as determined by Article 220. In addition, the disconnecting means must not be rated lower than:

(A) One-Circuit Installation. For installations consisting of a single branch circuit, the disconnecting means must have a rating of not less than 15A.

(B) Two-Circuit Installation. For installations consisting of two 2-wire branch circuits, the feeder disconnecting means must have a rating of not less than 30A.

(C) One-Family Dwelling. For a one-family dwelling, the feeder disconnecting means must have a rating of not less than 100A, 3-wire.

(D) All Others. For all other installations, the feeder or branch-circuit disconnecting means must have a rating of not less than 60A.

230 Services

INTRODUCTION TO ARTICLE 230—SERVICES

This article covers the installation requirements for service conductors and service equipment. The requirements for service conductors differ from those for other conductors. For one thing, service conductors for one building/structure can't pass through the interior of another building or structure [230.3], and you apply different rules depending on whether a service conductor is inside or outside a building/structure. When are they "outside" as opposed to "inside?" The answer may seem obvious, but Section 230.6 should be consulted before making this decision.

Let's review the following definitions in Article 100 to understand when the requirements of Article 230 apply:

- Service Point—The point of connection between the serving utility and the premises wiring.
- Service Conductors—The conductors from the service point to the service disconnecting means. Service-entrance conductors can either be overhead or underground.
- Service Equipment—The necessary equipment, usually consisting of circuit breakers or switches and fuses and their accessories, connected to the load end of service conductors at a building or other structure, and intended to constitute the main control and cutoff of the electrical supply. Service equipment doesn't include individual meter socket enclosures [230.66].

After reviewing these definitions, you should understand that service conductors originate at the serving utility (service point) and terminate on the line side of the service disconnecting means. Conductors and equipment on the load side of service equipment are considered feeder conductors or branch circuits, and must be installed in accordance with Articles 210 and 215. They must also comply with Article 225 if they're outside branch circuits and feeders, such as the supply to a building/structure. Feeder conductors include: **Figures 230–1 and 230–2**

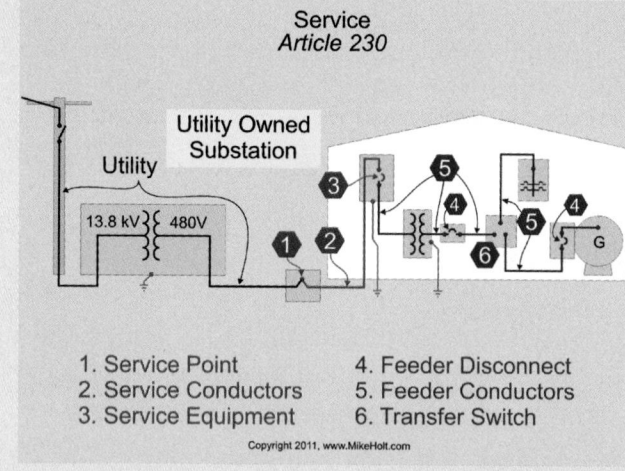

Figure 230–1

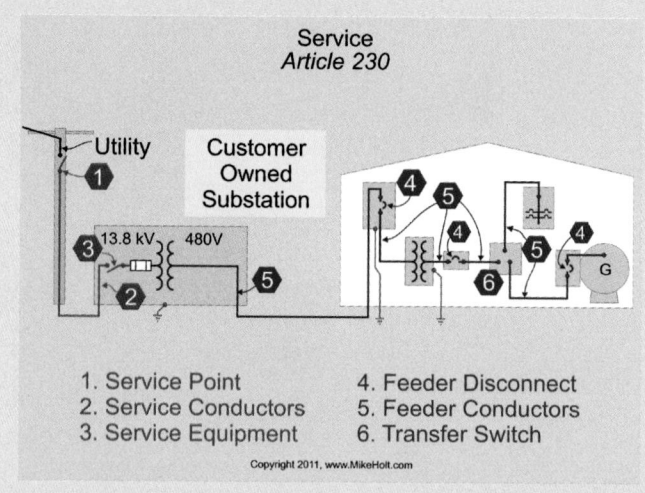

Figure 230–2

- Secondary conductors from customer-owned transformers,
- Conductors from generators, UPS systems, or photovoltaic systems, and
- Conductors to remote buildings or structures

Article 230 consists of seven parts:

- Part I. General
- Part II. Overhead Service Conductors
- Part III. Underground Service Conductors
- Part IV. Service-Entrance Conductors
- Part V. Service Equipment
- Part VI. Disconnecting Means
- Part VIII. Overcurrent Protection

PART I. GENERAL

230.1 Scope. Article 230 covers the installation requirements for service conductors and service equipment.

230.2 Number of Services. A building/structure can only be served by one service drop or service lateral, except as permitted by (A) through (D). **Figure 230–3**

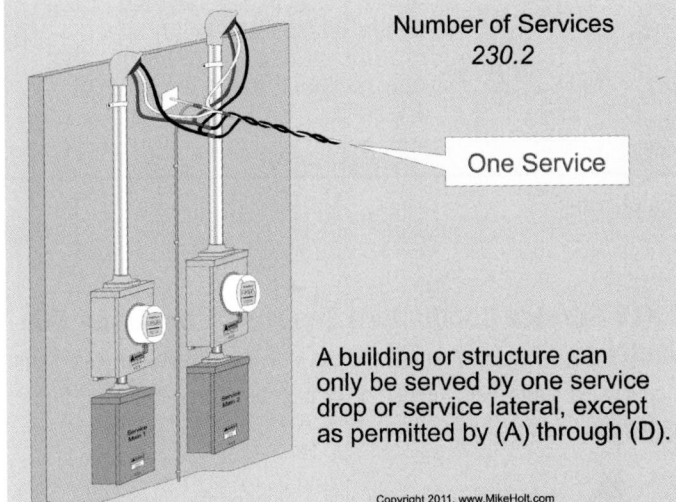

Number of Services
230.2

One Service

A building or structure can only be served by one service drop or service lateral, except as permitted by (A) through (D).

Copyright 2011, www.MikeHolt.com

Figure 230–3

Service laterals 1/0 AWG and larger run to the same location and connected together at their supply end, but not connected together at their load end, are considered to be a single service.

(A) Special Conditions. Additional services are permitted for the following:

(1) Fire pumps

(2) Emergency systems

(3) Legally required standby systems

> **Author's Comment:** A separate service for emergency and legally required systems is permitted only when approved by the authority having jurisdiction [700.12(D) and 701.11(D)].

(4) Optional standby power

(5) Parallel power production systems

(6) Systems designed for connection to multiple sources of supply for the purpose of enhanced reliability.

> **Author's Comment:** To minimize the possibility of accidental interruption, the disconnecting means for the fire pump, emergency system, or standby power system must be located remotely away from the normal power disconnect [230.72(B)].

(B) Special Occupancies. By special permission, additional services are permitted for:

(1) Multiple-occupancy buildings where there's no available space for supply equipment accessible to all occupants, or

(2) A building or other structure so large that two or more supplies are necessary.

(C) Capacity Requirements. Additional services are permitted:

(1) If the capacity requirements exceed 2,000A, or

(2) If the load requirements of a single-phase installation exceed the utility's capacity, or

(3) By special permission.

> **Author's Comment:** Special permission is defined in Article 100 as "the written consent of the authority having jurisdiction."

(D) Different Characteristics. Additional services are permitted for different voltages, frequencies, or phases, or for different uses, such as for different electricity rate schedules.

(E) Identification of Multiple Services. If a building/structure is supplied by more than one service, or a combination of feeders and services, a permanent plaque or directory must be installed at each service and feeder disconnect location to denote all other services and feeders supplying that building/structure, and the area served by each. **Figure 230–4**

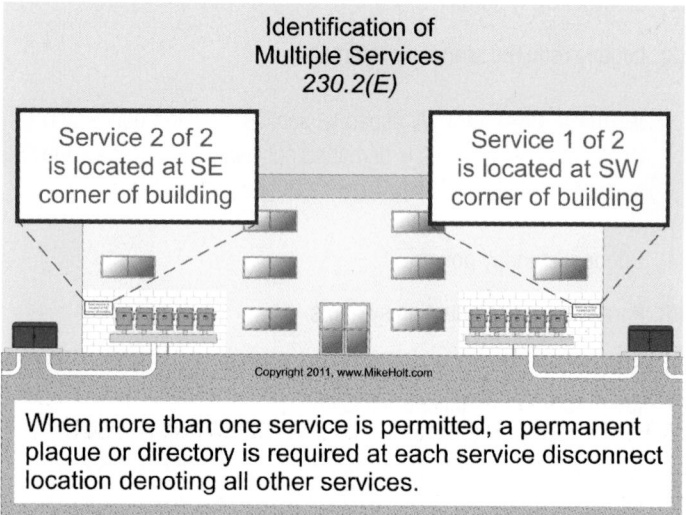

Figure 230–4

230.3 Not to Pass Through a Building/Structure. Ser-
vice conductors must not pass through the interior of another building or other structure.

230.6 Conductors Considered Outside a Build-
ing. Conductors are considered outside of a building when they're installed:

(1) Under not less than 2 in. of concrete beneath a building/structure. **Figure 230–5**

(2) Within a building/structure in a raceway encased in not less than 2 in. of concrete or brick.

(3) In a vault that meets the construction requirements of Article 450, Part III.

(4) In a raceway under not less than 18 in. of the earth beneath a building/structure.

(5) In an overhead service mast on the outside surface of the building that only passes through the eave of the building. **Figure 230–6**

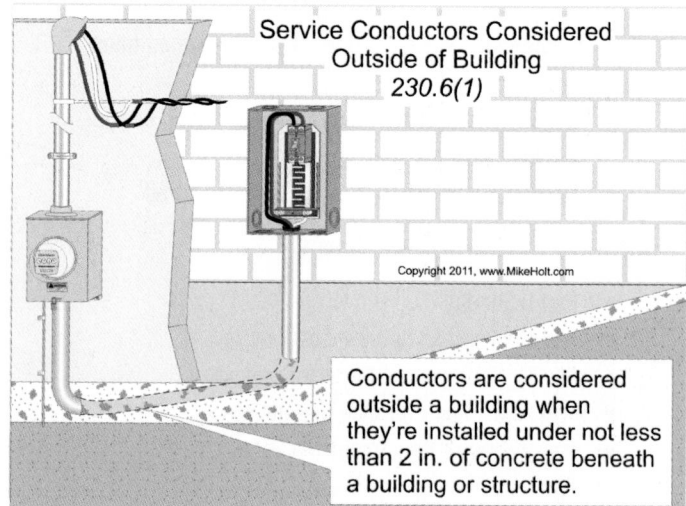

Figure 230–5

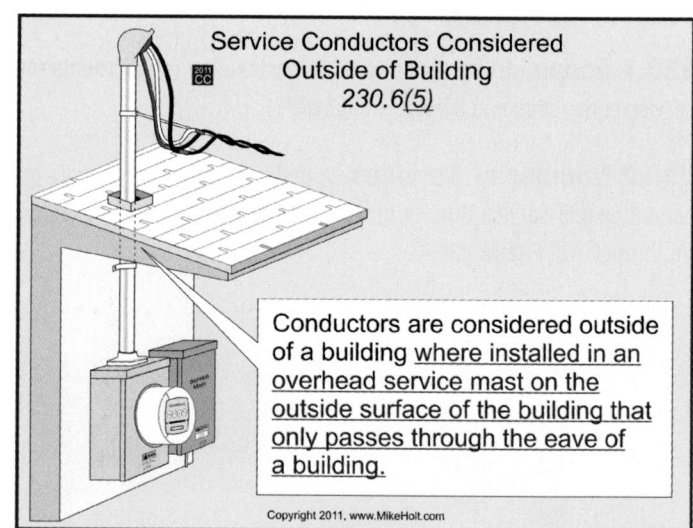

Figure 230–6

230.7 Service Conductors Separate from Other Con-
ductors. Service conductors must not be installed in the same raceway or cable with feeder or branch-circuit conductors. **Figure 230–7**

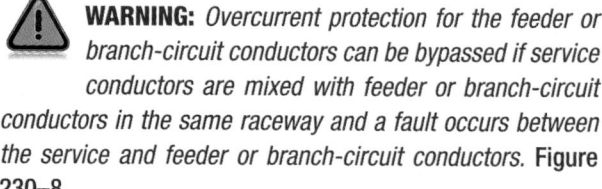 **WARNING:** *Overcurrent protection for the feeder or branch-circuit conductors can be bypassed if service conductors are mixed with feeder or branch-circuit conductors in the same raceway and a fault occurs between the service and feeder or branch-circuit conductors.* **Figure 230–8**

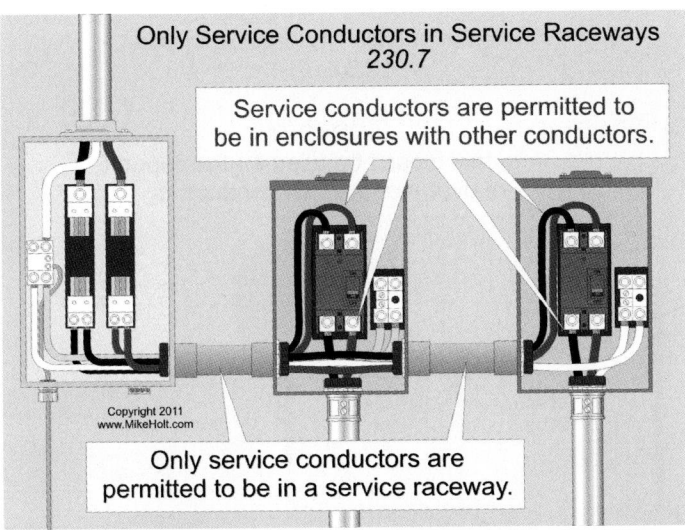

Only Service Conductors in Service Raceways
230.7

Service conductors are permitted to be in enclosures with other conductors.

Only service conductors are permitted to be in a service raceway.

Figure 230–7

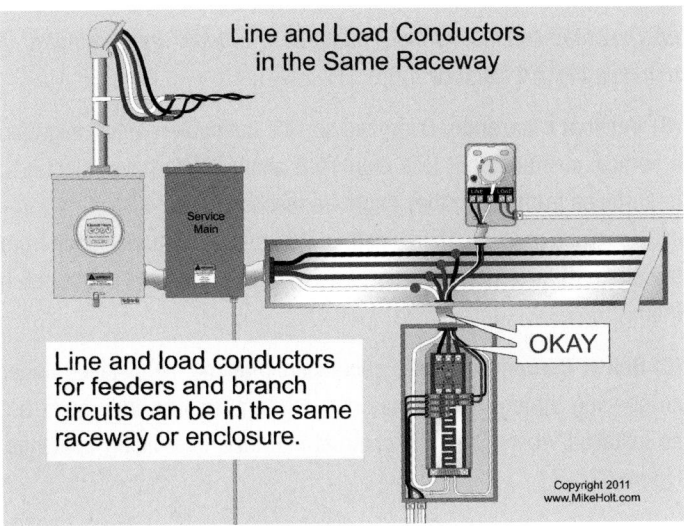

Line and Load Conductors in the Same Raceway

Line and load conductors for feeders and branch circuits can be in the same raceway or enclosure.

OKAY

Figure 230–9

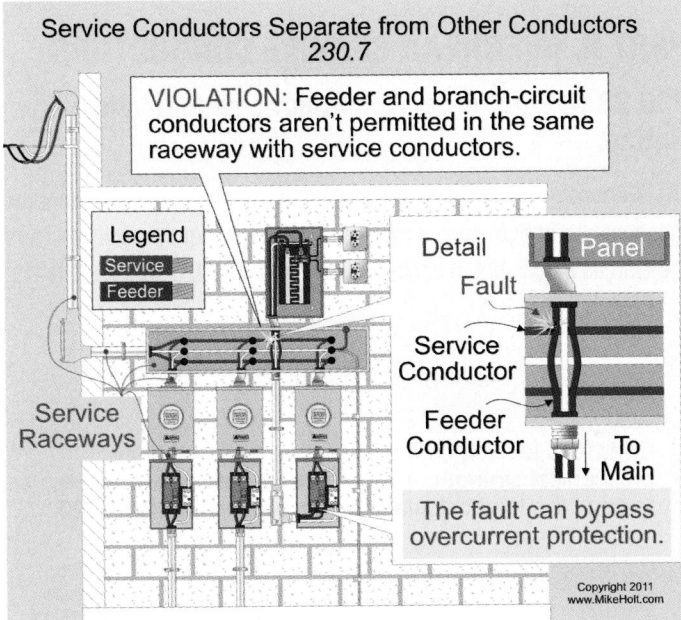

Service Conductors Separate from Other Conductors
230.7

VIOLATION: Feeder and branch-circuit conductors aren't permitted in the same raceway with service conductors.

Legend
Service
Feeder

Service Raceways

Detail
Fault
Panel
Service Conductor
Feeder Conductor
To Main

The fault can bypass overcurrent protection.

Figure 230–8

Author's Comments:

- This rule doesn't prohibit the mixing of service, feeder, and branch-circuit conductors in the same service equipment enclosure.

- This requirement may be the root of the misconception that "line" and "load" conductors must not be installed in the same raceway. It's true that service conductors must not be installed in the same raceway with feeder or branch-circuit conductors, but line and load conductors for feeders and branch circuits can be in the same raceway or enclosure. **Figure 230–9**

230.8 Raceway Seals. Underground raceways (used or unused) entering buildings or structures must be sealed or plugged to prevent moisture from contacting energized live parts [300.5(G)].

230.9 Clearance from Building Openings.

(A) Clearance. Overhead service conductors must maintain a clearance of 3 ft from windows that open, doors, porches, balconies, ladders, stairs, fire escapes, or similar locations. **Figure 230–10**

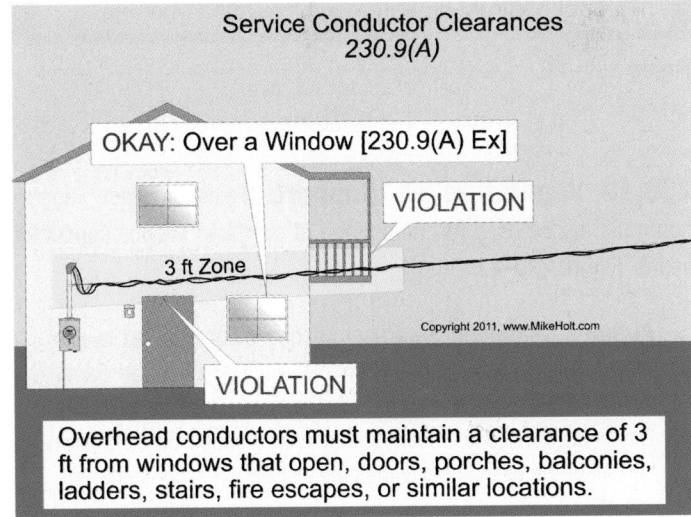

Service Conductor Clearances
230.9(A)

OKAY: Over a Window [230.9(A) Ex]

VIOLATION

3 ft Zone

VIOLATION

Overhead conductors must maintain a clearance of 3 ft from windows that open, doors, porches, balconies, ladders, stairs, fire escapes, or similar locations.

Figure 230–10

Ex: Overhead conductors installed above a window aren't required to maintain the 3 ft distance.

(B) Vertical Clearance. Overhead service conductors must maintain a vertical clearance not less than 10 ft above platforms, projections, or surfaces from which they might be reached [230.24(B)]. This vertical clearance must be maintained for 3 ft, measured horizontally from the platform, projections, or surfaces from which people might reach them.

(C) Below Openings. Service conductors must not be installed under an opening through which materials might pass, and they must not be installed where they will obstruct entrance to building openings. Figure 230–11

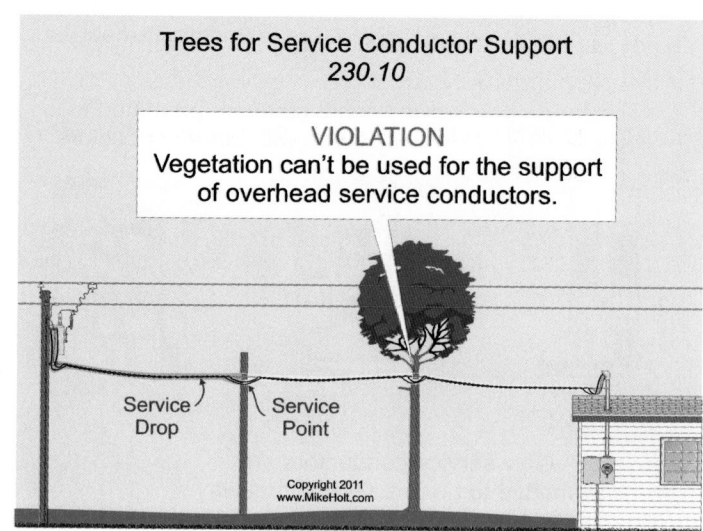

Figure 230–12

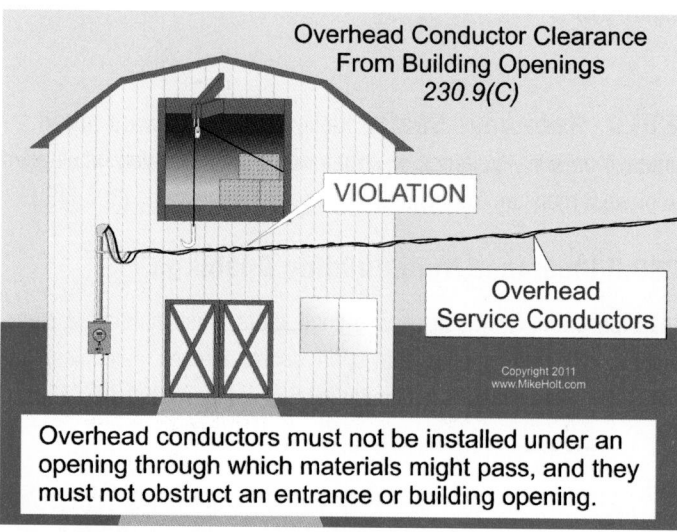

Figure 230–11

230.10 Vegetation as Support. Trees or other vegetation must not be used for the support of overhead service conductor spans. Figure 230–12

> **Author's Comment:** Service-drop conductors installed by the electric utility must comply with the *National Electrical Safety Code* (NESC), not the *National Electrical Code* [90.2(B)(5)]. Overhead service conductors that aren't under the exclusive control of the electric utility must be installed in accordance with the *NEC*.

PART II. OVERHEAD SERVICE CONDUCTORS

230.23 Overhead Service Conductor Size and Rating.

(A) General. Overhead service conductors must have adequate mechanical strength, and they must have sufficient ampacity to carry the load as calculated in accordance with Article 220. Figure 230–13

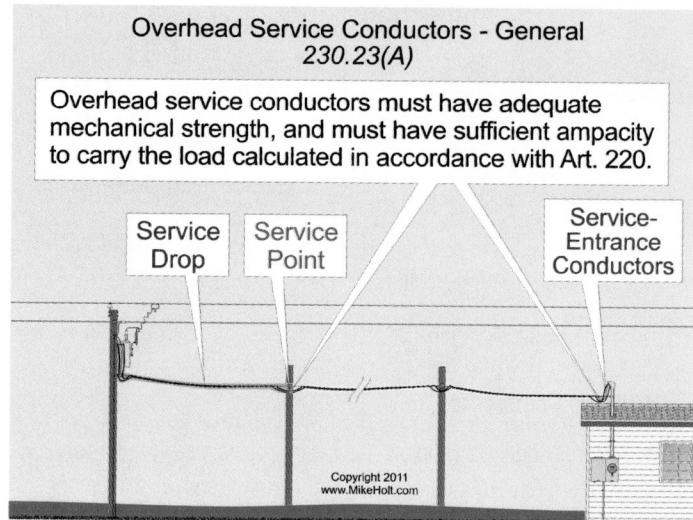

Figure 230–13

(B) Ungrounded Conductor Size. Overhead service conductors must not be smaller than 8 AWG copper or 6 AWG aluminum.

Ex: Overhead service conductors can be as small as 12 AWG for limited-load installations.

(C) Neutral Conductor Size. The neutral overhead service conductor must be sized to carry the maximum unbalanced load, in accordance with 220.61, and it must not be sized smaller than required by 250.24(C).

⚠️ **WARNING:** *In all cases, the service neutral conductor size must not be smaller than required by 250.24(C) to ensure that it has sufficiently low impedance and current-carrying capacity to safely carry fault current in order to facilitate the operation of the overcurrent device.*

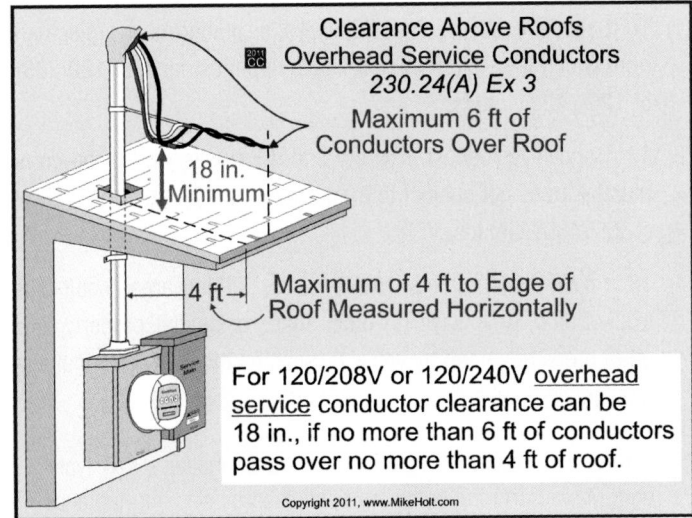

Figure 230–14

Question: *What size neutral conductor is required for a structure with a 400A service supplied with 500 kcmil conductors if the maximum line-to-neutral load is no more than 100A?*

(a) 3 AWG   *(b) 2 AWG*   *(c) 1 AWG*   *(d) 1/0 AWG*

Answer: *(d) 1/0 AWG*

According to Table 310.15(B)(16), 3 AWG rated 100A at 75°C [110.14(C)(1)] is sufficient to carry 100A of neutral current. However, the service neutral conductor must be sized not smaller than 1/0 AWG, in accordance with Table 250.66, based on the area of the service conductor [250.24(C)].

230.24 Vertical Clearance for Overhead Service Conductors. Overhead service conductor spans must maintain the vertical clearances as follows:

(A) Above Roofs. A minimum of 8 ft above the surface of a roof for a minimum distance of 3 ft in all directions from the edge of the roof.

Ex 2: If the slope of the roof exceeds 4 in. of vertical rise for every 12 in. of horizontal run, 120/208V or 120/240V overhead service conductor clearances can be reduced to 3 ft over the roof.

Ex 3: If no more than 6 ft of conductors pass over no more than 4 ft of roof, 120/208V or 120/240V overhead service conductor clearances over the roof overhang can be reduced to 18 in. **Figure 230–14**

Ex 4: The 3 ft vertical clearance for overhead service conductors that extends from the roof doesn't apply when the point of attachment is on the side of the building below the roof.

Ex 5: If the voltage between conductors doesn't exceed 300V and the roof area is guarded or isolated, a reduction in clearance to 3 ft is permitted.

(B) Vertical Clearance for Overhead Service Conductors. Overhead service conductor spans must maintain the following vertical clearances: **Figure 230–15**

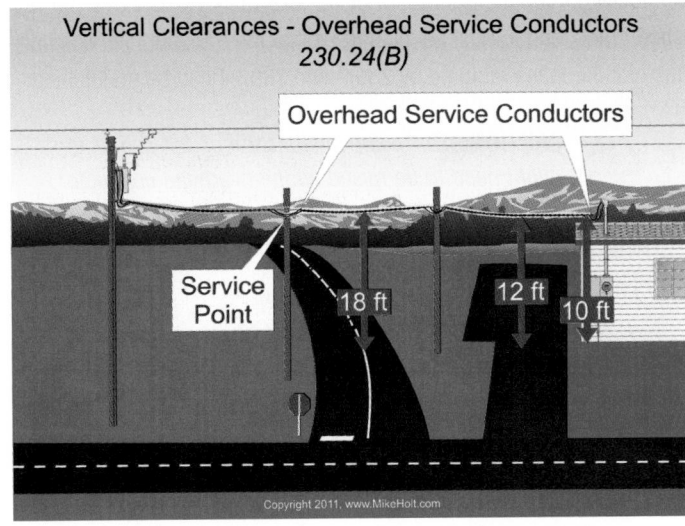

Figure 230–15

(1) 10 ft above finished grade, sidewalks, or platforms or projections from which they might be accessible to pedestrians for 120/208V or 120/240V circuits.

(2) 12 ft above residential property and driveways, and those commercial areas not subject to truck traffic for 120/208V, 120/240V, or 277/480V circuits.

(4) 18 ft over public streets, alleys, roads, parking areas subject to truck traffic, driveways on other than residential property, and other areas traversed by vehicles, such as those used for cultivation, grazing, forestry, and orchards.

Author's Comment: Department of Transportation (DOT) type right-of-ways in rural areas are often used by slow-moving and tall farming machinery to avoid impeding road traffic.

(D) Swimming Pools. Overhead service conductors that aren't under the exclusive control of the electric utility located above pools, outdoor spas, outdoor hot tubs, diving structures, observation stands, towers, or platforms must be installed in accordance with the clearance requirements contained in 680.8.

(E) Clearance from Communications Cables. Where communications cables and electric light or power conductors are supported by the same pole, communications cables must have a minimum separation of 12 in. at any point in the span, including the point of attachment to the building [800.44(A)(4)].

230.26 Point of Attachment. The point of attachment for service-drop conductors must not be less than 10 ft above the finished grade, and it must be located so that the minimum service conductor clearances required by 230.9 and 230.24 can be maintained.

CAUTION: *The point of attachment for conductors might need to be raised so the overhead conductors will comply with the clearances from building openings required by 230.9 and from other areas by 230.24.* Figure 230–16

230.27 Means of Attachment. Multiconductor cables used for overhead service conductors must be attached to buildings or other structures by fittings identified for use with service conductors.

Open conductors must be attached to fittings identified for use with service conductors or to noncombustible, nonabsorbent insulators securely attached to the building or other structure.

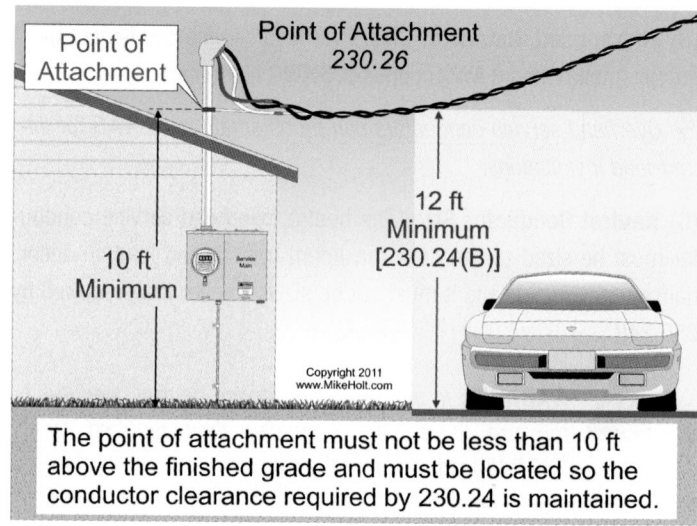

The point of attachment must not be less than 10 ft above the finished grade and must be located so the conductor clearance required by 230.24 is maintained.

Figure 230–16

230.28 Service Masts Used as Supports. The service mast used as the overhead conductor support must have adequate mechanical strength, or braces or guy wires to support it, to withstand the strain caused by the service-drop conductors.

Author's Comment: Some local codes require a minimum 2 in. rigid metal conduit for the service mast. In addition, many electric utilities contain specific requirements for the installation of the service mast.

Only electric utility service-drop conductors can be attached to a service mast.

Author's Comment: 810.12 and 820.44(C) specify that aerial cables for radio, TV, or CATV must not be attached to the service mast, and 810.12 prohibits antennas from being attached to the service mast. In addition, 800.133(B) and 830.133(B) prohibit broadband communications cables from being attached to raceways, including a service mast. **Figure 230–17**

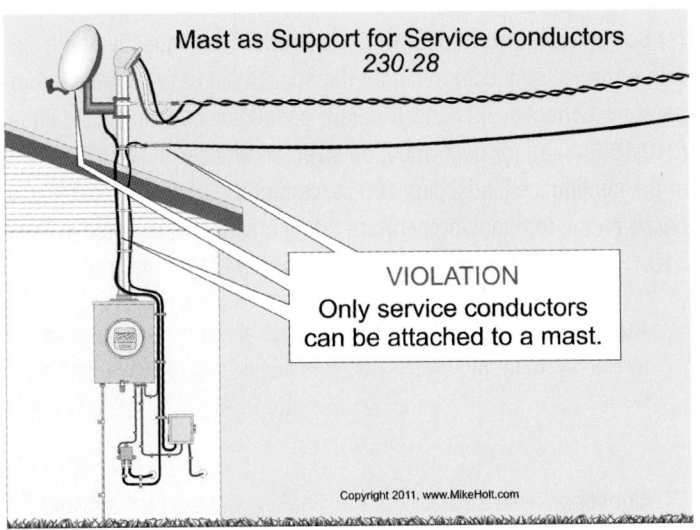

VIOLATION
Only service conductors
can be attached to a mast.

Figure 230–17

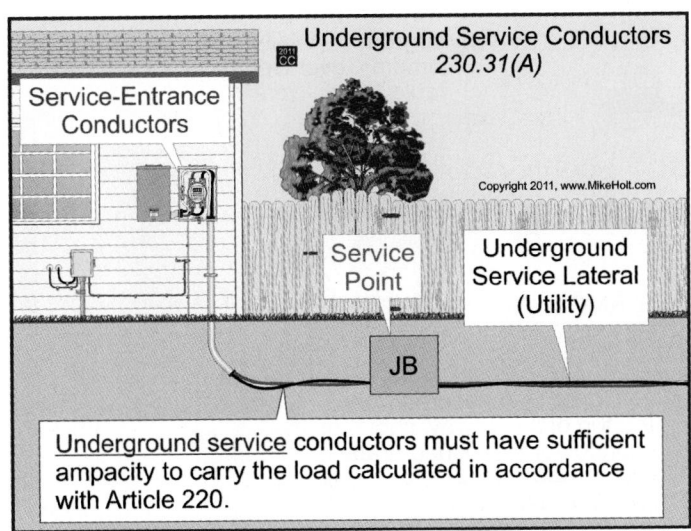

Underground service conductors must have sufficient
ampacity to carry the load calculated in accordance
with Article 220.

Figure 230–18

PART III. UNDERGROUND SERVICE CONDUCTORS

Author's Comment: Underground service conductors installed by the electric utility must comply with the *National Electrical Safety Code* (NESC), not the *National Electrical Code* [90.2(B)(5)]. Underground conductors that aren't under the exclusive control of the electric utility must be installed in accordance with the *NEC*.

230.31 Underground Service Conductor Size and Rating.

(A) General. Underground service conductors must have sufficient ampacity to carry the load as calculated in accordance with Article 220. **Figure 230–18**

(B) Ungrounded Conductor Size. Underground service conductors must not be smaller than 8 AWG copper or 6 AWG aluminum.

Ex: Underground service conductors can be as small as 12 AWG for limited-load installations.

(C) Neutral Conductor Size. The neutral conductor must be sized to carry the maximum unbalanced load in accordance with 220.61, and it must not be sized smaller than required by 250.24(C).

Author's Comment: 250.24(C) requires the service neutral conductor to be sized no smaller than Table 250.66.

230.32 Protection Against Damage. Underground service conductors must be installed in accordance with 300.5, and have minimum cover in accordance with Table 300.5. **Figures 230–19 and 230–20**

Underground Installations - Minimum Cover Depths Table 300.5				
	UF or USE Cables or Conductors	RMC or IMC	PVC not Encased in Concrete	Residential 15A & 20A GFCI 120V Branch Ckts
Street Driveway Parking Lot	24 in.	24 in.	24 in.	24 in.
Driveways One - Two Family	18 in.	18 in.	18 in.	12 in.
Solid Rock With not Less than 2 in. of Concrete	Raceway Only			Raceway Only
All Other Applications	24 in.	6 in.	18 in.	12 in.

Copyright 2011, www.MikeHolt.com

Figure 230–19

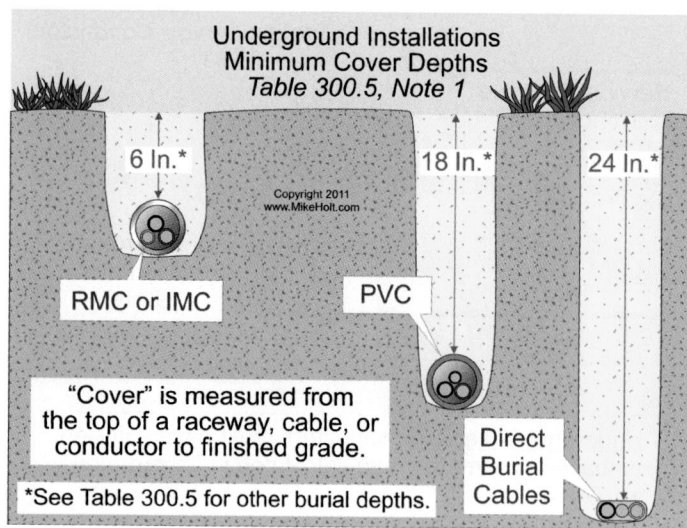

Figure 230–20

PART IV. SERVICE-ENTRANCE CONDUCTORS

230.40 Number of Service-Entrance Conductor Sets.
Only one set of service conductors (drop, overhead, or underground) is permitted to supply a building/structure.

Ex 2: Service conductors can supply two to six service disconnecting means as permitted in 230.71(A).

Ex 3: A single-family dwelling unit and its accessory structure(s) can have one set of service conductors run to each structure.

Ex 4: Two-family dwellings, multifamily dwellings, and multiple occupancy buildings are permitted to have one set of service conductors to supply branch circuits for public or common areas.

Ex 5: One set of service-entrance conductors connected to the supply side of the normal service disconnecting means can supply standby power systems, fire pump equipment, and fire and sprinkler alarms [230.82(5)].

230.42 Size and Rating.

(A) Load Calculations. Service-entrance conductors must have sufficient ampacity for the loads to be served in accordance with Parts III, IV, or V of Article 220.

(1) Continuous and Noncontinuous Loads. The ampacity of the service-entrance conductors, before the application of any ambient temperature correction [310.15(B)(2)(a)], conductor bundling adjustment [310.15(B)(3)(a)], or both, must be sized no smaller than 125 percent of the continuous loads, plus 100 percent of the noncontinuous loads, based on the terminal temperature rating ampacities as listed in Table 310.15(B)(16), before any ampacity adjustment [110.14(C)(1)].

> **Author's Comment:** See 215.3 for the sizing requirements of feeder overcurrent devices for continuous and noncontinuous loads.

Question: What size service-entrance conductors are required for a 200A continuous load, if the terminals are rated 75°C?
Figure 230–21

(a) 2/0 AWG (b) 3/0 AWG (c) 4/0 AWG (d) 250 kcmil

Answer: (d) 250 kcmil

Since the load is 200A continuous, the service-entrance conductors must have an ampacity not less than 250A (200A x 1.25). According to the 75°C column of Table 310.15(B)(16), 250 kcmil conductors are suitable because they have an ampere rating of 255A at 75°C, before the application of ambient temperature correction [310.15(B)(2)(a)], conductor bundling adjustment [310.15(B)(3)(a)], or both.

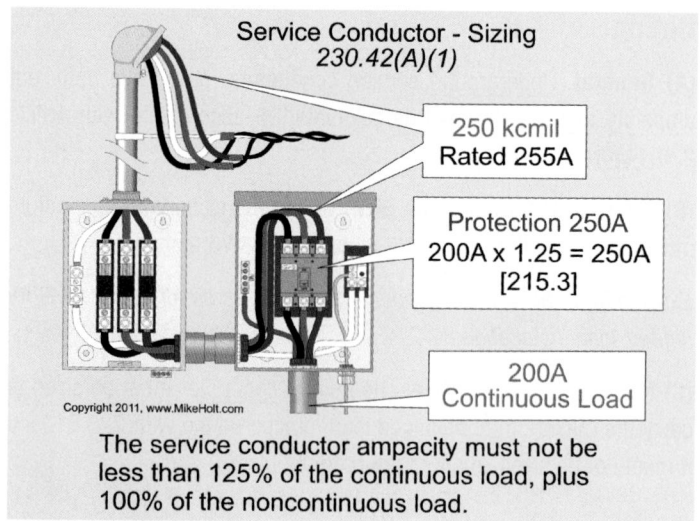

Figure 230–21

(C) Neutral Conductor Size. The service neutral conductor must be sized to carry the maximum unbalanced load in accordance with 220.61, and must not be sized smaller than required by 250.24(C).

⚠️ **WARNING:** *In all cases the service neutral conductor size must not be smaller than required by 250.24(C) to ensure that it has sufficiently low impedance and current-carrying capacity to safely carry fault current in order to facilitate the operation of the overcurrent device.*

230.43 Wiring Methods. Service-entrance conductors must be installed with one of the following wiring methods:

(1) Open wiring on insulators

(3) Rigid metal conduit

(4) Intermediate metal conduit

(5) Electrical metallic tubing

(6) Electrical nonmetallic tubing

(7) Service-entrance cables

(8) Wireways

(9) Busways

(11) PVC Conduit

(13) Type MC Cable

(15) Flexible metal conduit or liquidtight flexible metal conduit not longer than 6 ft

(16) Liquidtight flexible nonmetallic conduit

(17) High-Density Polyethylene Conduit (HDPE)

(18) Nonmetallic Underground Conduit with Conductors (NUCC)

(19) Reinforced Thermosetting Resin Conduit (RTRC)

230.46 Spliced Conductors. Service-entrance conductors can be spliced or tapped in accordance with 110.14, 300.5(E), 300.13, and 300.15. Figure 230–22

230.50 Protection Against Physical Damage.

(A) Underground Service-Entrance Conductors. Underground service-entrance conductors must be protected against physical damage in accordance with 300.5.

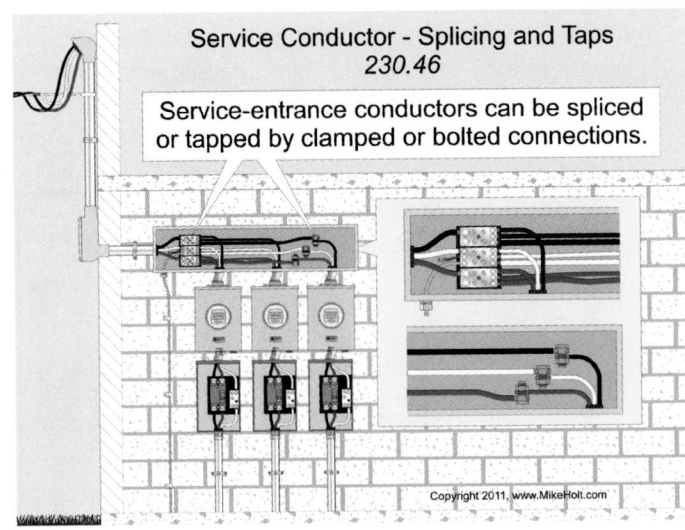

Figure 230–22

(B) All Other Service-Entrance Conductors.

(1) Service-Entrance Cables. Service-entrance cables that are subject to physical damage must be protected by one of the following: Figure 230–23

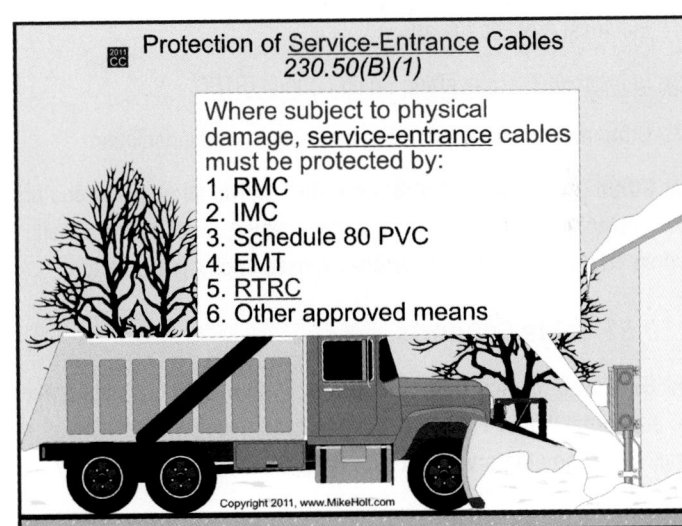

Figure 230–23

(1) Rigid metal conduit

(2) Intermediate metal conduit

(3) Schedule 80 PVC conduit

Author's Comment: If the authority having jurisdiction determines the raceway isn't subject to physical damage, Schedule 40 PVC conduit can be used. **Figure 230–24**

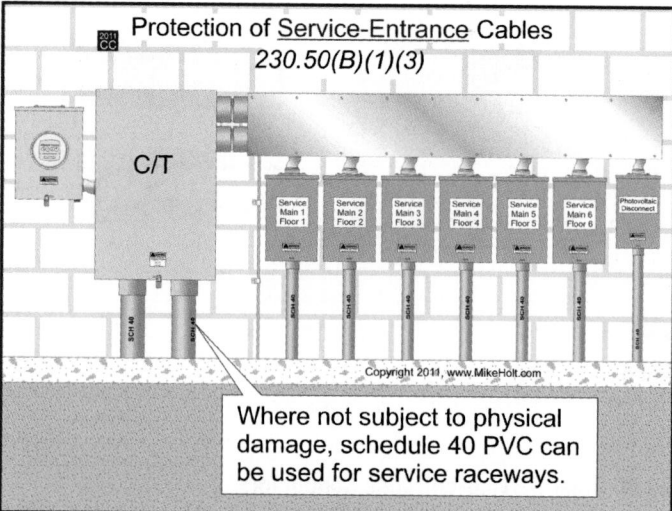

Figure 230–24

(4) Electrical metallic tubing

(5) Reinforced Thermosetting Resin Conduit (RTRC)

(6) Other means approved by the authority having jurisdiction

(2) Other Than Service-Entrance Cable. Individual open conductors and cables, other than service-entrance cables, must not be installed within 10 ft of grade level or where exposed to physical damage.

230.51 Cable Supports.

(A) Service-Entrance Cable Supports. Service-entrance cable must be supported within 1 ft of the weatherhead, raceway connections or enclosure, and at intervals not exceeding 30 in.

230.54 Overhead Service Locations.

(A) Service Head. Raceways for overhead service drops or overhead service conductors must have a weatherhead listed for wet locations.

(B) Service-Entrance Cable. Service-entrance cables must be equipped with a weatherhead listed for wet locations.

Ex: SE cable can be formed into a gooseneck and taped with self-sealing weather-resistant thermoplastic.

(C) Above the Point of Attachment. Service heads and goosenecks must be located above the point of attachment for service-drop or overhead service conductors. See 230.26.

Ex: If it's impractical to locate the service head above the point of attachment, it must be located within 2 ft of the point of attachment.

(D) Secured. Service-entrance cables must be held securely in place.

(E) Opposite Polarity Through Separately Bushed Holes. Service heads must provide a bushed opening, and ungrounded conductors must be in separate openings.

(F) Drip Loops. Drip loop conductors must be connected to the service-drop or overhead service conductors below the service head or termination of the service-entrance cable sheath.

(G) Arranged so Water Won't Enter. Service entrance and overhead service conductors must be arranged to prevent water from entering service equipment.

230.56 High-Leg Identification. On a 4-wire, delta-connected, three-phase system, where the midpoint of one phase winding is grounded (high-leg system), the conductor with the higher phase voltage-to-ground (208V) must be durably and permanently marked by an outer finish that's orange in color, or by other effective means. Such identification must be placed at each point on the system where a connection is made if the neutral conductor is present [110.15]. **Figure 230–25**

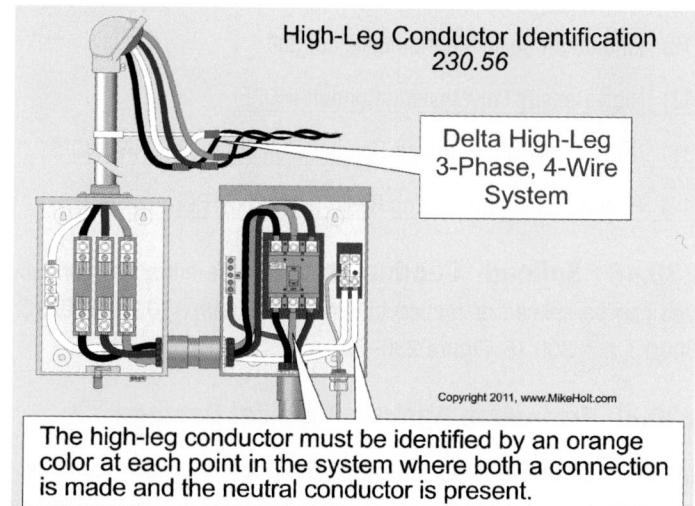

Figure 230–25

Author's Comments:

- The high-leg conductor is also called the "wild leg," "stinger leg," or "bastard leg."

- Since 1975, panelboards supplied by a 4-wire, delta-connected, three-phase system must have the high-leg conductor (208V) terminate to the "B" (center) phase of a panelboard [408.3(E)].

- The ANSI standard for meter equipment requires the high-leg conductor (208V to neutral) to terminate on the "C" (right) phase of the meter socket enclosure. This is because the demand meter needs 120V and it gets this from the "B" phase. Hopefully, the utility lineman isn't colorblind and doesn't inadvertently cross the "orange" high-leg conductor (208V) with the red (120V) service conductor at the weatherhead. It's happened before… **Figure 230–26**

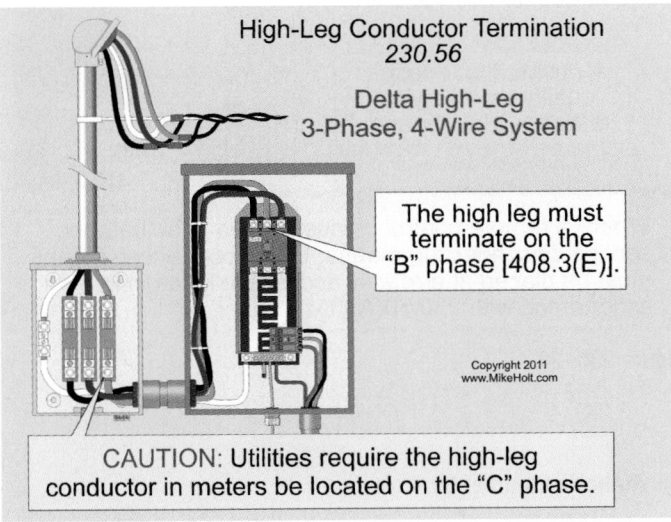

Figure 230–26

PART V. SERVICE EQUIPMENT—GENERAL

230.66 Listed as Suitable for Service Equipment. The service disconnecting means must be listed as suitable for use as service equipment.

> **Author's Comment:** "Suitable for use as service equipment" means, among other things, that the service disconnecting means is supplied with a main bonding jumper so a neutral-to-case connection can be made, as required in 250.24(C) and 250.142(A). **Figure 230–27**

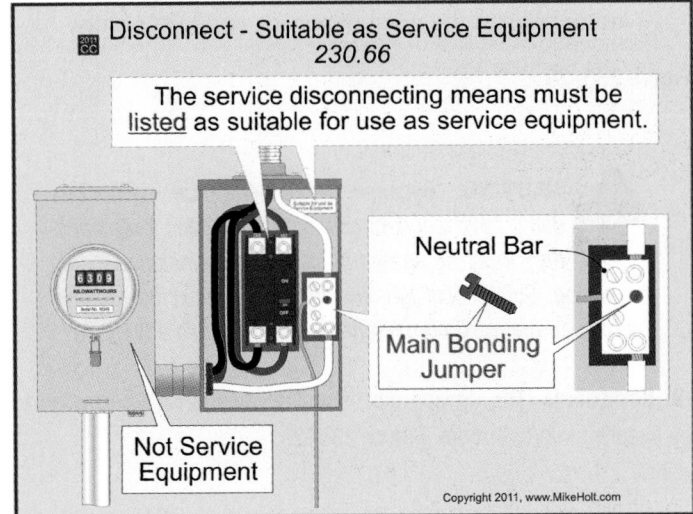

Figure 230–27

PART VI. SERVICE EQUIPMENT— DISCONNECTING MEANS

230.70 Disconnect Requirements. The service disconnecting means must open all service-entrance conductors from the building/structure premises wiring.

(A) Location.

(1) Readily Accessible. The service disconnecting means must be placed at a readily accessible location either outside the building/structure, or inside nearest the point of service conductor entry. **Figure 230–28**

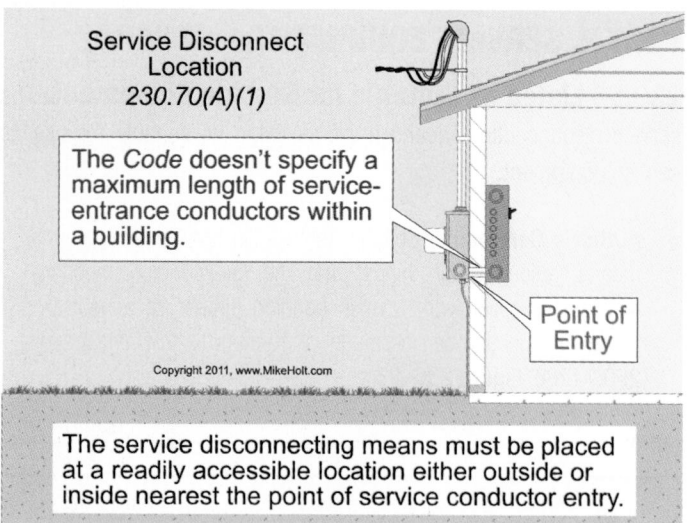

Service Disconnect
Location
230.70(A)(1)

The *Code* doesn't specify a maximum length of service-entrance conductors within a building.

Point of Entry

Copyright 2011, www.MikeHolt.com

The service disconnecting means must be placed at a readily accessible location either outside or inside nearest the point of service conductor entry.

Figure 230–28

WARNING: *Because service-entrance conductors don't have short-circuit or ground-fault protection, they must be limited in length when installed inside a building. Some local jurisdictions have a specific requirement as to the maximum length permitted within a building.*

(2) Bathrooms. The service disconnecting means isn't permitted to be installed in a bathroom. **Figure 230–29**

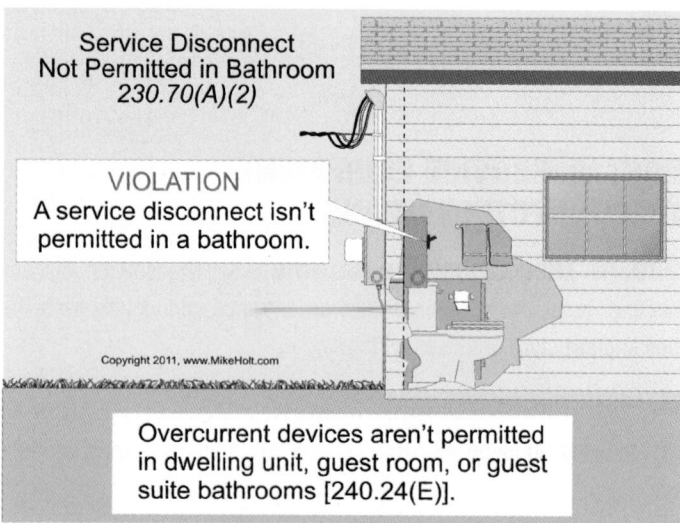

Service Disconnect
Not Permitted in Bathroom
230.70(A)(2)

VIOLATION
A service disconnect isn't permitted in a bathroom.

Copyright 2011, www.MikeHolt.com

Overcurrent devices aren't permitted in dwelling unit, guest room, or guest suite bathrooms [240.24(E)].

Figure 230–29

Author's Comment: Overcurrent devices must not be located in the bathrooms of dwelling units, or guest rooms or guest suites of hotels or motels [240.24(E)].

(3) Remote Control. If a remote-control device (such as a pushbutton for a shunt-trip breaker) is used to actuate the service disconnecting means, the service disconnecting means must still be at a readily accessible location either outside the building/structure, or nearest the point of entry of the service conductors as required by 230.70(A)(1). **Figure 230–30**

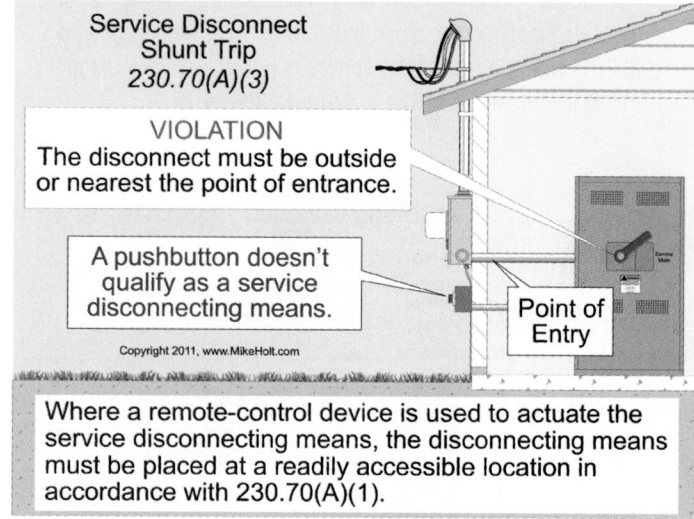

Service Disconnect
Shunt Trip
230.70(A)(3)

VIOLATION
The disconnect must be outside or nearest the point of entrance.

A pushbutton doesn't qualify as a service disconnecting means.

Point of Entry

Copyright 2011, www.MikeHolt.com

Where a remote-control device is used to actuate the service disconnecting means, the disconnecting means must be placed at a readily accessible location in accordance with 230.70(A)(1).

Figure 230–30

Author's Comments:

- See the definition of "Remote Control" in Article 100.
- The service disconnecting means must consist of a manually operated switch, a power-operated switch, or a circuit breaker that's also capable of being operated manually [230.76].

(B) Disconnect Identification. Each service disconnecting means must be permanently marked to identify it as part of the service disconnecting means. **Figure 230–31**

Author's Comment: When a building/structure has multiple services and/or feeders, a plaque is required at each service or feeder disconnect location to show the location of the other service or feeder disconnect locations. See 230.2(E).

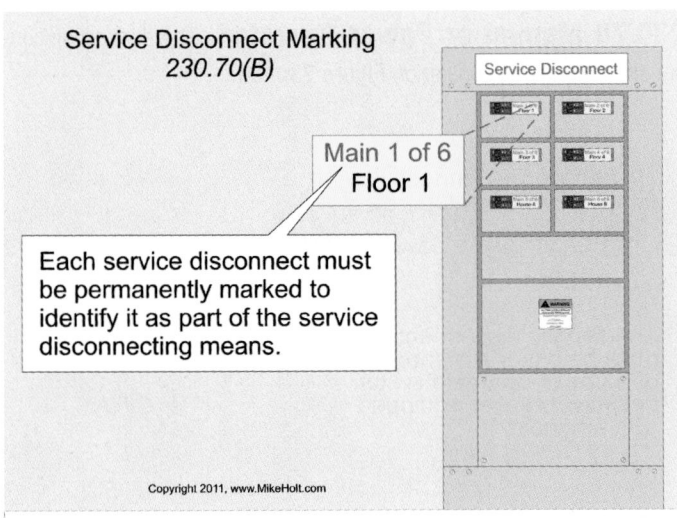

Service Disconnect Marking
230.70(B)

Main 1 of 6
Floor 1

Each service disconnect must be permanently marked to identify it as part of the service disconnecting means.

Copyright 2011, www.MikeHolt.com

Figure 230–31

(C) Suitable for Use. Each service disconnecting means must be suitable for the prevailing conditions.

230.71 Number of Disconnects.

(A) Maximum. There must be no more than six service disconnects for each service permitted by 230.2, or each set of service-entrance conductors permitted by 230.40 Ex 1, 3, 4, or 5. 230-71A0 02

The service disconnecting means for each service grouped in one location [230.72(A)] can consist of up to six switches or six circuit breakers mounted in a single enclosure, in a group of separate enclosures, or in or on a switchboard. **Figure 230–32**

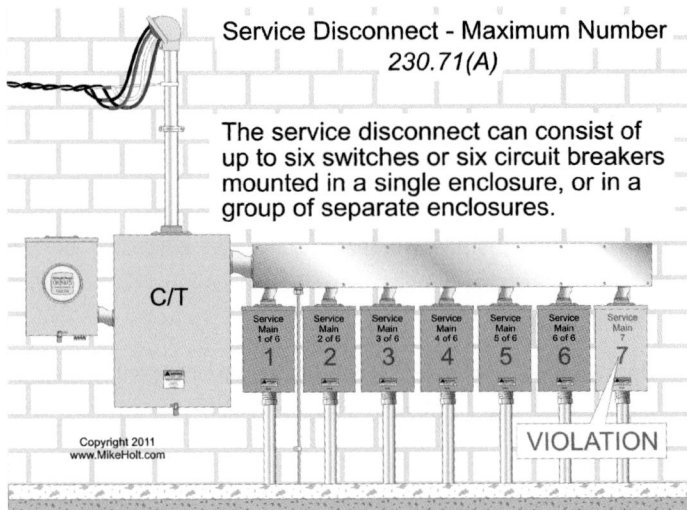

Service Disconnect - Maximum Number
230.71(A)

The service disconnect can consist of up to six switches or six circuit breakers mounted in a single enclosure, or in a group of separate enclosures.

C/T

Service Main 1 of 6 — 1
Service Main 2 of 6 — 2
Service Main 3 of 6 — 3
Service Main 4 of 6 — 4
Service Main 5 of 6 — 5
Service Main 6 of 6 — 6
Service Main 7 — 7

VIOLATION

Copyright 2011
www.MikeHolt.com

Figure 230–32

CAUTION: *The rule is six disconnecting means for each service, not for each building. If the building has two services, then there can be a total of 12 service disconnects (six disconnects per service).* **Figure 230–33**

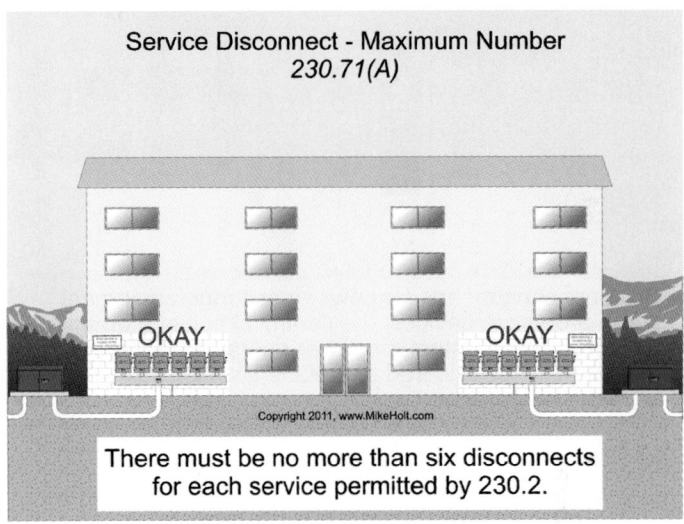

Service Disconnect - Maximum Number
230.71(A)

OKAY   OKAY

Copyright 2011, www.MikeHolt.com

There must be no more than six disconnects for each service permitted by 230.2.

Figure 230–33

Disconnecting means used for the following are not considered a service disconnecting means:

(1) Power monitoring equipment

(2) Surge-protective device(s). **Figure 230–34**

(3) Control circuit of the ground-fault protection system

(4) Power-operable service disconnecting means

> **Author's Comment:** A photovoltaic system disconnect connected to the supply-side of service equipment as permitted by 230.82(6) and 705.12(A) is not considered a service disconnecting means. **Figure 230–35**

230.72 Grouping of Disconnects.

(A) Two to Six Disconnects. The service disconnecting means for each service must be grouped.

(B) Additional Service Disconnecting Means. To minimize the possibility of accidental interruption of power, the disconnecting means for fire pumps [Article 695], emergency [Article 700], legally required standby [Article 701], or optional standby [Article 702] systems must be located remote from the one to six service disconnects for normal service.

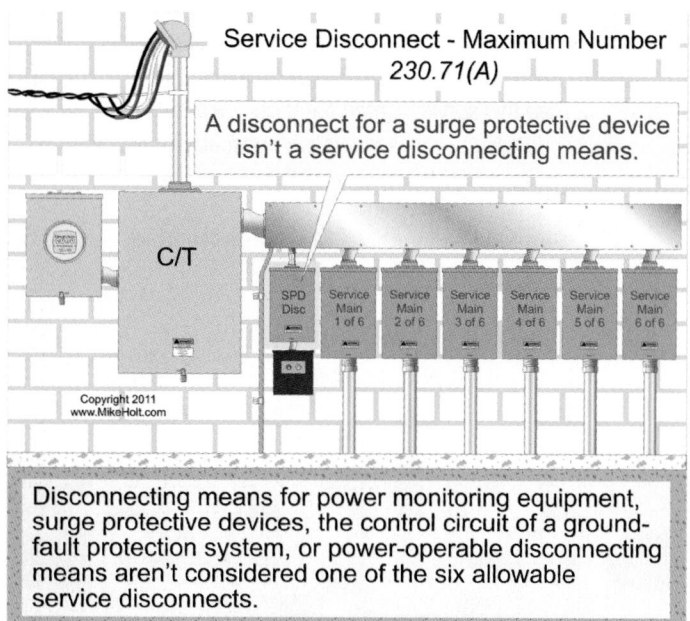

Figure 230–34

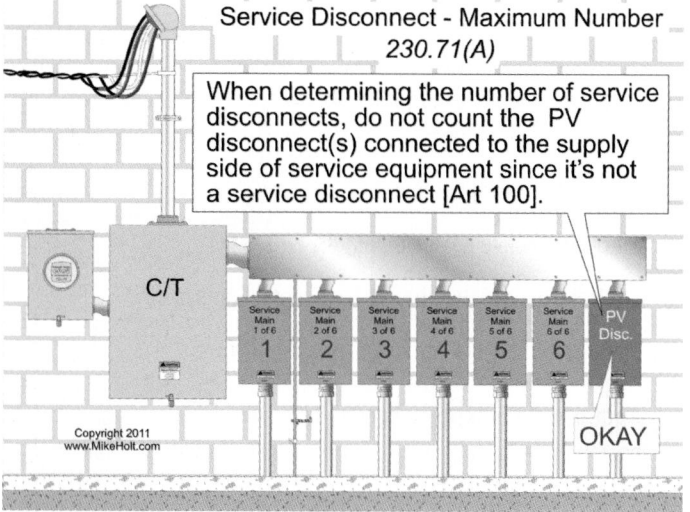

Figure 230–35

Author's Comment: Because emergency systems are just as important as fire pumps and standby systems, they need to have the same safety precautions to prevent unintended interruption of the supply of electricity.

(C) Access to Occupants. In a multiple-occupancy building, each occupant must have access to their service disconnecting means.

Ex: In multiple-occupancy buildings where electrical maintenance is provided by continuous building management, the service disconnecting means can be accessible only to building management personnel.

230.76 Manual or Power Operated. The service disconnecting means can consist of: **Figure 230–36**

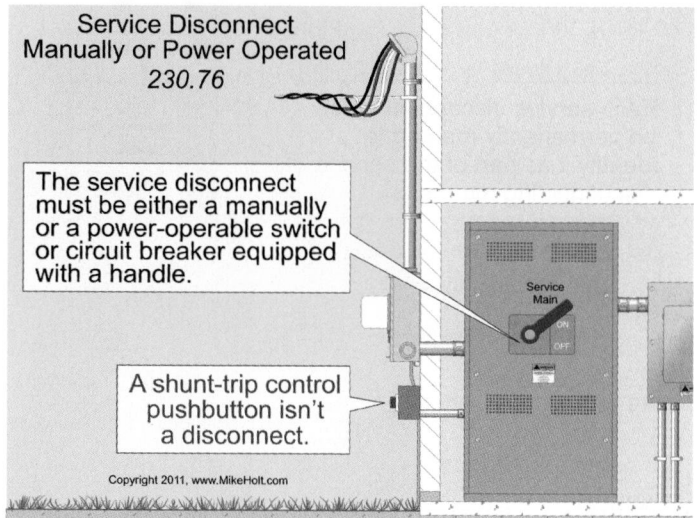

Figure 230–36

(1) A manually operable switch or circuit breaker equipped with a handle or other suitable operating means.

(2) A power-operated switch or circuit breaker, provided it can be opened by hand in the event of a power supply failure.

230.77 Indicating. The service disconnecting means must indicate whether it is in the off (open) or (closed) position.

230.79 Rating of Disconnect. The service disconnecting means for a building/structure must have an ampere rating of not less than the calculated load according to Article 220, and in no case less than:

(A) One-Circuit Installation. For installations consisting of a single branch circuit, the disconnecting means must have a rating not less than 15A.

(B) Two-Circuit Installation. For installations consisting of two 2-wire branch circuits, the disconnecting means must have a rating not less than 30A.

(C) One-Family Dwelling. For a one-family dwelling, the disconnecting means must have a rating not less than 100A, 3-wire.

(D) All Others. For all other installations, the disconnecting means must have a rating not less than 60A.

Author's Comment: A shunt-trip button doesn't qualify as a service disconnect because it doesn't meet any of the above requirements.

230.81 Connection to Terminals.
The service conductors must be connected to the service disconnecting means by pressure connectors, clamps, or other means approved by the authority having jurisdiction. Connections must not be made using solder.

230.82 Connected on Supply Side of the Service Disconnect.
Electrical equipment must not be connected to the supply side of the service disconnect enclosure, except for the following:

(2) Meters and meter sockets.

(3) Meter disconnect switches. **Figure 230–37**

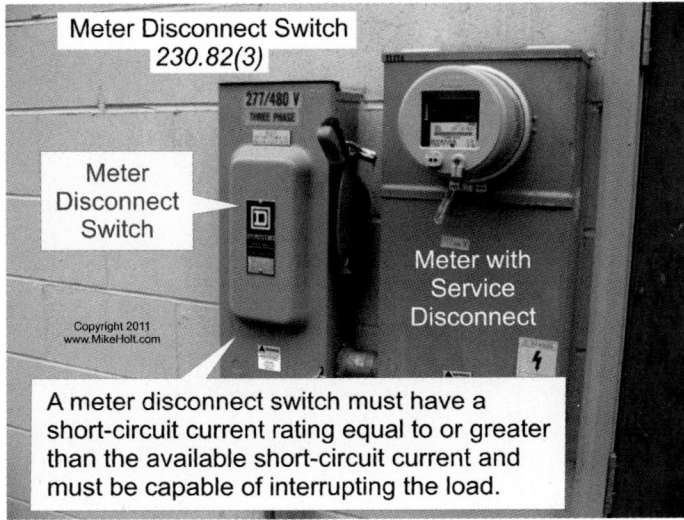

Figure 230–37

Author's Comment: Electric utilities often require a meter disconnect switch for 277/480V services to enhance safety for utility personnel when they install or remove a meter.

(4) Type 1 surge protective devices.

Author's Comment: A Type 1 surge protective device is listed to be permanently connected on the line side of service equipment [285.23].

(5) Taps used to supply legally required and optional standby power systems, fire pump equipment, fire and sprinkler alarms, and load (energy) management devices.

Author's Comment: Emergency standby power must not be supplied by a connection ahead of service equipment [700.12]. **Figure 230–38**

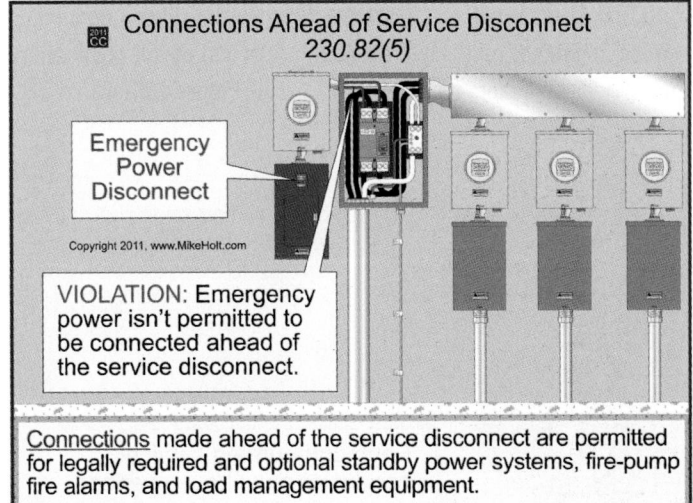

Figure 230–38

(6) Solar photovoltaic systems. **Figure 230–39**

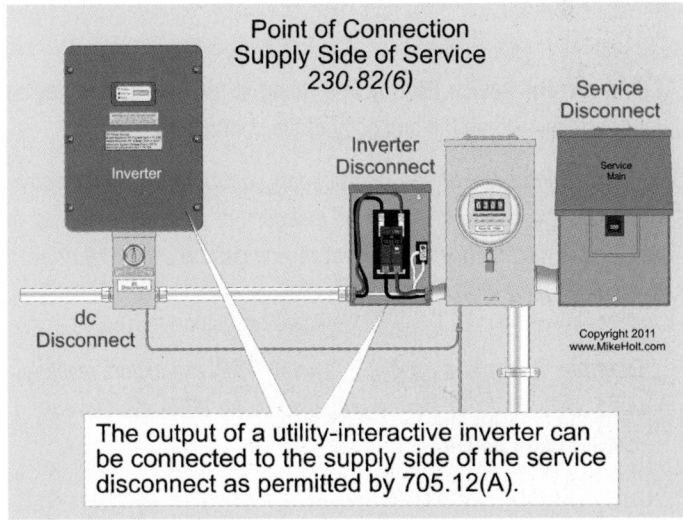

Figure 230–39

PART VII. SERVICE EQUIPMENT OVERCURRENT PROTECTION

Author's Comment: The *NEC* doesn't require service conductors to be provided with short-circuit or ground-fault protection, but the feeder overcurrent device provides overload protection for the service conductors.

230.90 Overload Protection Required. Each ungrounded service conductor must have overload protection at the point where the service conductors terminate [240.21(D)]. **Figure 230–40**

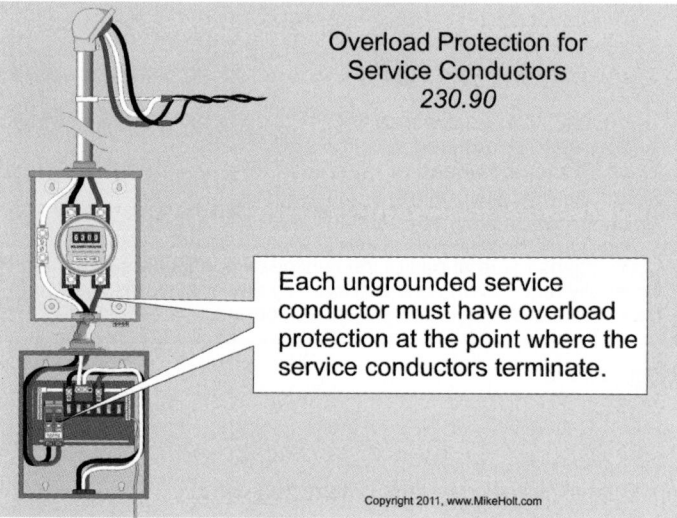

Overload Protection for Service Conductors 230.90

Each ungrounded service conductor must have overload protection at the point where the service conductors terminate.

Copyright 2011, www.MikeHolt.com

Figure 230–40

(A) Overcurrent Device Rating. The rating of the overcurrent device must not be more than the ampacity of the conductors.

Ex 2: If the ampacity of the ungrounded conductors doesn't correspond with the standard rating of overcurrent devices as listed in 240.6(A), the next higher overcurrent device can be used, if it doesn't exceed 800A [240.4(B)].

> **Example:** *Two sets of parallel 500 kcmil THHN conductors (each rated 380A at 75°C) can be protected by an 800A overcurrent device.* **Figure 230–41**

Ex 3: The combined ratings of two to six service disconnecting means can exceed the ampacity of the service conductors provided the calculated load, in accordance with Article 220, doesn't exceed the ampacity of the service conductors. **Figure 230–42**

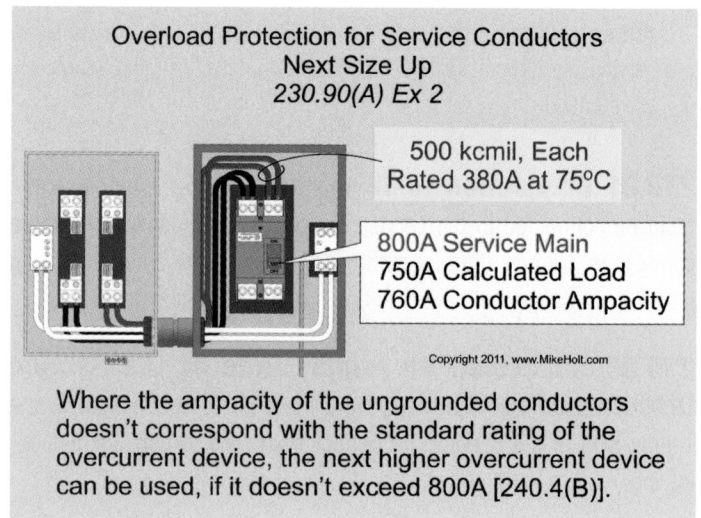

Overload Protection for Service Conductors Next Size Up 230.90(A) Ex 2

500 kcmil, Each Rated 380A at 75°C

800A Service Main
750A Calculated Load
760A Conductor Ampacity

Copyright 2011, www.MikeHolt.com

Where the ampacity of the ungrounded conductors doesn't correspond with the standard rating of the overcurrent device, the next higher overcurrent device can be used, if it doesn't exceed 800A [240.4(B)].

Figure 230–41

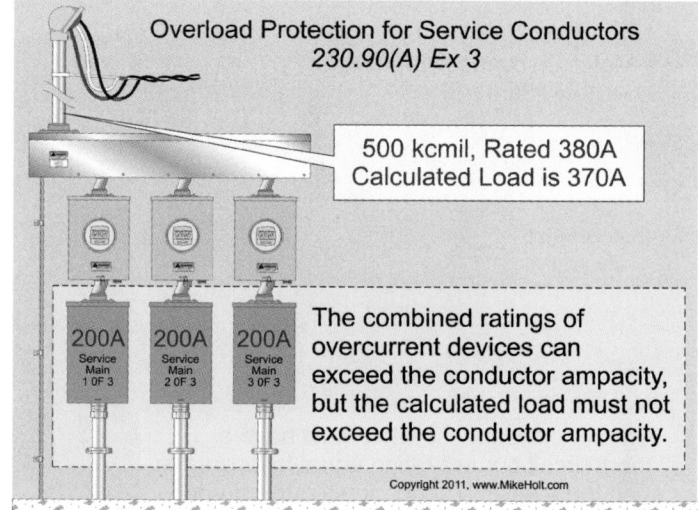

Overload Protection for Service Conductors 230.90(A) Ex 3

500 kcmil, Rated 380A Calculated Load is 370A

| 200A Service Main 1 OF 3 | 200A Service Main 2 OF 3 | 200A Service Main 3 OF 3 |

The combined ratings of overcurrent devices can exceed the conductor ampacity, but the calculated load must not exceed the conductor ampacity.

Copyright 2011, www.MikeHolt.com

Figure 230–42

Ex 5: Overload protection for 3-wire, single-phase, 120/240V dwelling unit service conductors can be in accordance with 310.15(B)(7). **Figure 230–43**

230.95 Ground-Fault Protection of Equipment. Ground-fault protection of equipment is required for each service disconnecting means rated 1,000A or more that's supplied by a 4-wire, three-phase, 277/480V wye-connected system.

The rating of the service disconnecting means is considered to be the rating of the largest fuse that can be installed or the highest continuous current trip setting of a circuit breaker.

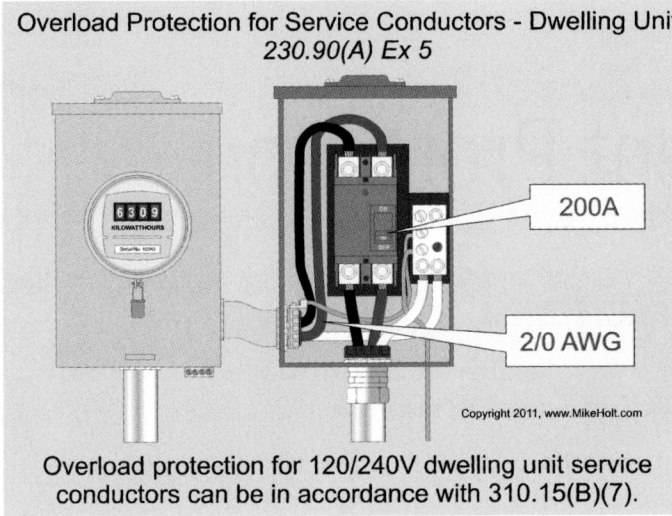

Overload Protection for Service Conductors - Dwelling Unit
230.90(A) Ex 5

200A

2/0 AWG

Copyright 2011, www.MikeHolt.com

Overload protection for 120/240V dwelling unit service conductors can be in accordance with 310.15(B)(7).

Figure 230–43

Author's Comments:

- Ground-fault protection of equipment isn't permitted for fire pumps [695.6(H)] and it's not required for emergency systems [700.26] or legally required standby systems [701.17].

- Article 100 defines "Ground-Fault Protection of Equipment" as a system intended to provide protection of equipment from ground faults by opening the overcurrent device at current levels less than those required to protect conductors from damage. This type of protective system isn't intended to protect people, only connected equipment. See 215.10 for similar requirements for feeders.

(A) Setting. The maximum setting for ground-fault protection in a service disconnecting means is 1,200A.

(C) Performance Testing. The ground-fault protection system for service equipment must be performance tested when first installed on-site.

> **Note 1:** Ground-fault protection that functions to open the service disconnect won't protect service conductors or the service equipment from faults on the line side of the protective element.

> **Note 2:** When service equipment has ground-fault protection installed, it may be necessary to review the overall wiring system for proper selective overcurrent protection coordination.

ARTICLE 240

Overcurrent Protection

INTRODUCTION TO ARTICLE 240—OVERCURRENT PROTECTION

This article provides the requirements for selecting and installing overcurrent devices. Overcurrent exists when current exceeds the rating of equipment or the ampacity of a conductor. This can be due to an overload, short circuit, or ground fault [Article 100].

Overload. An overload is a condition where equipment or conductors carry current exceeding their current rating [Article 100]. A fault, such as a short circuit or ground fault, isn't an overload. An example of an overload is plugging two 12.50A (1,500W) hair dryers into a 20A branch circuit.

Ground Fault. A ground fault is an unintentional, electrically conducting connection between an ungrounded conductor of an electrical circuit and the normally noncurrent-carrying conductors, metallic enclosures, metallic raceways, metallic equipment, or the earth [Article 100]. During the period of a ground fault, dangerous voltages will be present on metal parts until the circuit overcurrent device opens.

Short Circuit. A short circuit is the unintentional electrical connection between any two normally current-carrying conductors of an electrical circuit, either line-to-line or line-to-neutral.

Overcurrent devices protect conductors and equipment. Selecting the proper overcurrent protection for a specific circuit can become more complicated than it sounds. The general rule for overcurrent protection is that conductors must be protected in accordance with their ampacities at the point where they receive their supply [240.4and 240.21]. There are many special cases that deviate from this basic rule, such as the overcurrent protection limitations for small conductors [240.4(D)] and the rules for specific conductor applications found in other articles, as listed in Table 240.4(G). There are also a number of rules allowing tap conductors in specific situations [240.21(B)]. Article 240 even has limits on where overcurrent devices are allowed to be located [240.24].

An overcurrent protection device must be capable of opening a circuit when an overcurrent situation occurs, and must also have an interrupting rating sufficient to avoid damage in fault conditions [110.9]. Carefully study the provisions of this article to be sure you provide sufficient overcurrent protection in the correct location.

PART I. GENERAL

240.1 Scope. Article 240 covers the general requirements for overcurrent protection and the installation requirements of overcurrent devices. **Figure 240–1**

> **Author's Comment:** Overcurrent is a condition where the current exceeds the rating of equipment or ampacity of a conductor due to overload, short circuit, or ground fault [Article 100]. **Figure 240–2**

Note: An overcurrent device protects the circuit by opening the device when the current reaches a value that will cause excessive or dangerous temperature rise (overheating) in conductors. Overcurrent devices must have an interrupting rating sufficient for the maximum possible fault current available on the line-side terminals of the equipment [110.9]. Electrical equipment must have a short-circuit current rating that permits the circuit's overcurrent device to clear short circuits or ground faults without extensive damage to the circuit's electrical components [110.10].

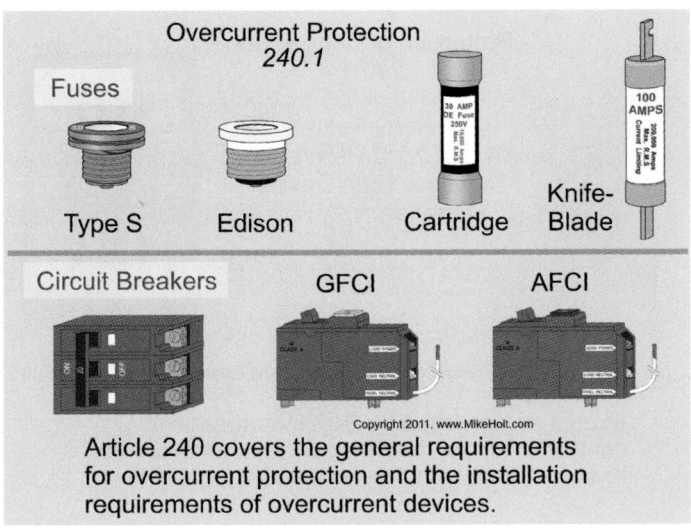

Figure 240–1

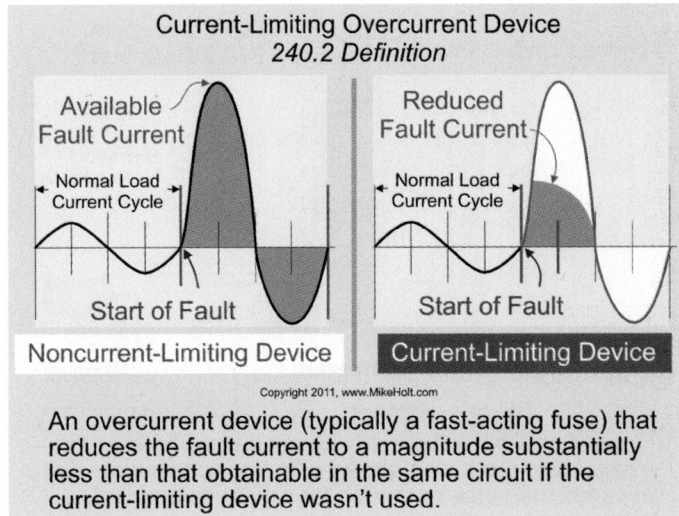

Figure 240–3

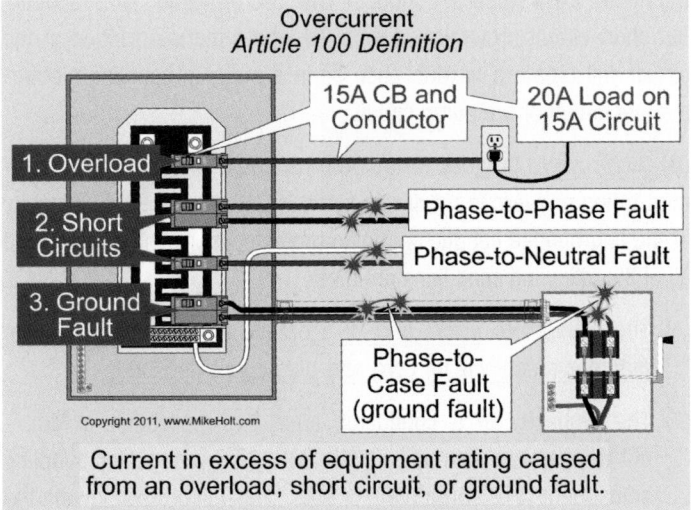

Figure 240–2

240.2 Definitions.

Current-Limiting Overcurrent Device. An overcurrent device (typically a fast-acting fuse) that reduces the fault current to a magnitude substantially less than that obtainable in the same circuit if the current-limiting device wasn't used. See 240.40 and 240.60(B). **Figure 240–3**

Author's Comment: A current-limiting fuse is a type of fuse designed for operations related to short circuits only. When a fuse operates in its current-limiting range, it will begin to melt in less than a quarter of a cycle, and it will open a bolted short circuit in less than half a cycle. This type of fuse limits the instantaneous peak let-through current to a value substantially less than what will occur in the same circuit if the fuse is replaced with a solid conductor of equal impedance. If the available short-circuit current exceeds the equipment/conductor short-circuit current rating, then the thermal and magnetic forces can cause the equipment circuit conductors, as well as the circuit equipment grounding conductors, to vaporize. The only solutions to the problem of excessive available fault current are to:

- Install equipment with a higher short-circuit rating, or

- Protect the components of the circuit by a current-limiting overcurrent device such as a fast-clearing fuse, which can reduce the let-through energy.

A breaker or a fuse does limit current, but it may not be listed as a current-limiting device. A thermal-magnetic circuit breaker typically clears fault current in less than three to five cycles when subjected to a short circuit or ground fault of 20 times its rating. A standard fuse will clear the same fault in less than one cycle and a current-limiting fuse in less than half of a cycle.

Tap Conductors. A conductor, other than a service conductor, that has overcurrent protection rated more than the ampacity of a conductor. See 240.21(A) and 240.21(B) for details. **Figure 240–4**

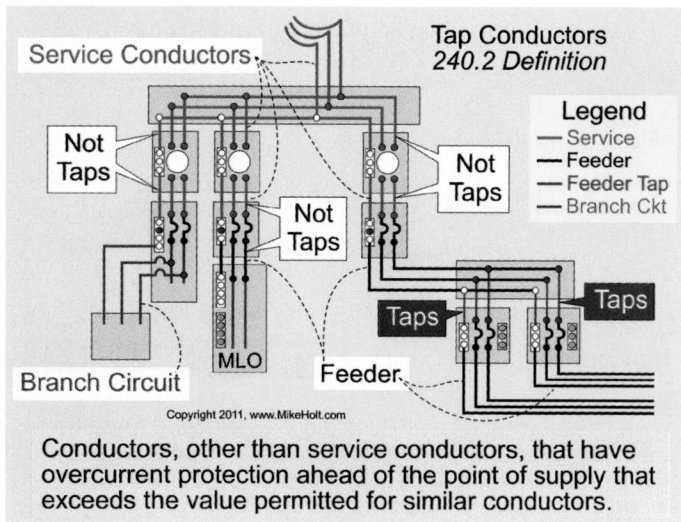

Conductors, other than service conductors, that have overcurrent protection ahead of the point of supply that exceeds the value permitted for similar conductors.

Figure 240–4

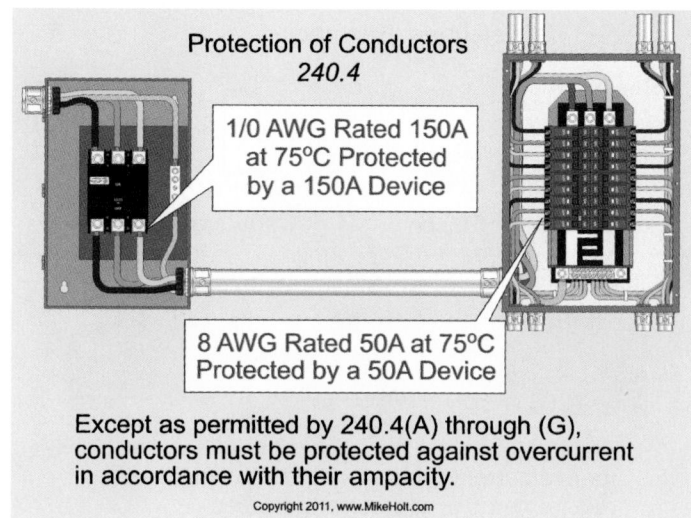

Except as permitted by 240.4(A) through (G), conductors must be protected against overcurrent in accordance with their ampacity.

Copyright 2011, www.MikeHolt.com

Figure 240–5

240.3 Protection of Equipment. The following equipment and their conductors are protected against overcurrent in accordance with the article that covers the type of equipment:

Table 240.3—Other Articles

Equipment	Article	Section
Air-Conditioning and Refrigeration Equipment	440	440.22
Appliances	422	All
Audio Circuits	640	640.9
Branch Circuits	210	210.20
Class 1, 2, and 3 Circuits	725	All
Feeder Conductors	215	215.3
Flexible Cords	240	240.5(B)(1)
Fire Alarms	760	All
Fire Pumps	695	All
Fixed Electric Space-Heating Equipment	424	424.3(B)
Fixture Wire	240	240.5(B)(2)
Panelboards	408	408.36
Service Conductors	230	230.90(A)
Transformers	450	450.3

240.4 Protection of Conductors. Except as permitted by (A) through (G), conductors must be protected against overcurrent in accordance with their ampacity after ampacity correction and adjustment as specified in 310.15. **Figure 240–5**

(A) Power Loss Hazard. Conductor overload protection isn't required, but short-circuit protection is required where the interruption of the circuit will create a hazard; such as in a material-handling electromagnet circuit or fire pump circuit.

(B) Overcurrent Devices Rated 800A or Less. The next higher standard rating of overcurrent device listed in 240.6 (above the ampacity of the ungrounded conductors being protected) is permitted, provided all of the following conditions are met:

(1) The conductors aren't part of a branch circuit supplying more than one receptacle for cord-and-plug-connected loads.

(2) The ampacity of a conductor, after the application of ambient temperature correction [310.15(B)(2)(a)], conductor bundling adjustment [310.15(B)(3)(a)], or both, doesn't correspond with the standard rating of a fuse or circuit breaker in 240.6(A).

(3) The overcurrent device rating doesn't exceed 800A.

Example: A 400A overcurrent device can protect 500 kcmil conductors, where each conductor has an ampacity of 380A at 75°C, in accordance with Table 310.15(B)(16). **Figure 240–6**

Author's Comment: This "next size up" rule doesn't apply to feeder tap conductors [240.21(B)] or transformer secondary conductors [240.21(C)].

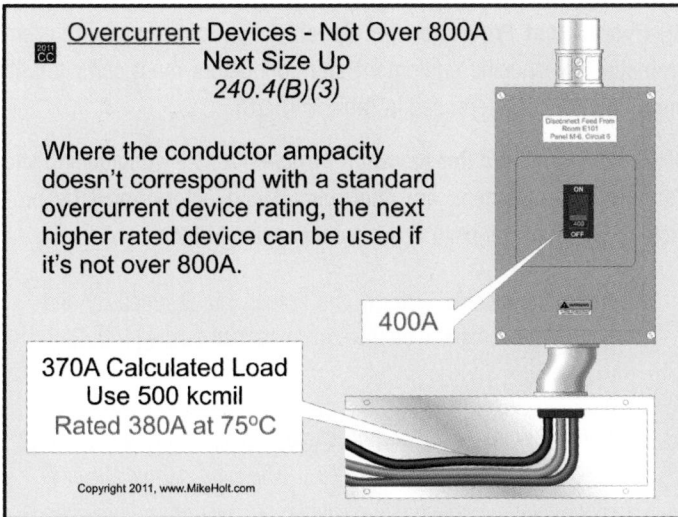

Figure 240–6

(C) <u>Overcurrent</u> **Devices Rated Over 800A.** If the circuit's overcurrent device exceeds 800A, the conductor ampacity (after the application of ambient temperature correction [310.15(B)(2)(a)], conductor bundling adjustment [310.15(B)(3)(a)], or both, must have a rating of not less than the rating of the overcurrent device defined in 240.6.

> **Example:** *A 1,200A overcurrent device can protect three sets of 600 kcmil conductors per phase, where each conductor has an ampacity of 420A at 75°C, in accordance with Table 310.15(B)(16).* **Figure 240–7**

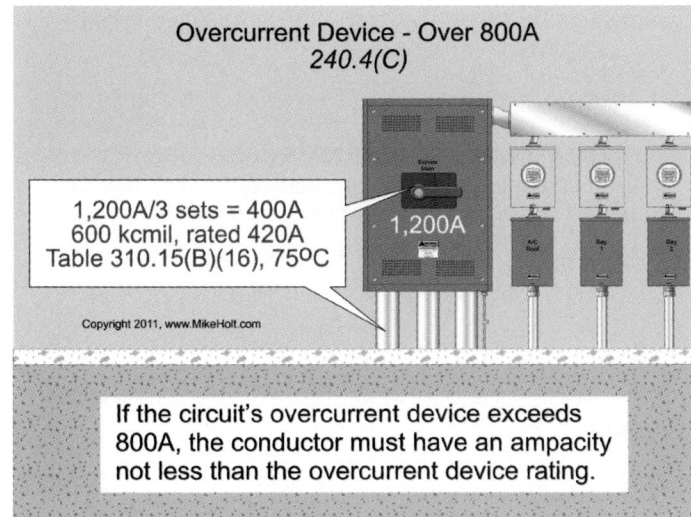

Figure 240–7

(D) Small Conductors. Unless specifically permitted in 240.4(E) or (G), overcurrent protection must not exceed the following: **Figure 240–8**

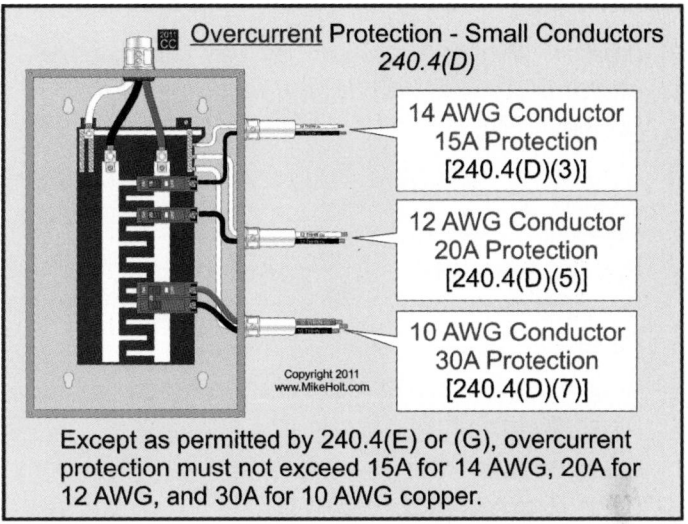

Figure 240–8

(1) 18 AWG Copper—7A

(2) 16 AWG Copper—10A

(3) 14 AWG Copper—15A

(4) 12 AWG Aluminum/Copper-Clad Aluminum—15A

(5) 12 AWG Copper—20A

(6) 10 AWG Aluminum/Copper-Clad Aluminum—25A

(7) 10 AWG Copper—30A

(E) Tap Conductors. Tap conductors must be protected against overcurrent as follows:

(1) Household Ranges and Cooking Appliances and Other Loads, 210.19(A)(3) and (4)

(2) Fixture Wire, 240.5(B)(2)

(3) Location in Circuit, 240.21

(4) Reduction in Ampacity Size of Busway, 368.17(B)

(5) Feeder or Branch Circuits (busway taps), 368.17(C)

(6) Single Motor Taps, 430.53(D)

(F) Transformer Secondary Conductors. The primary overcurrent device sized in accordance with 450.3(B) is considered suitable to protect the secondary conductors of a 2-wire (single voltage) system, provided the primary overcurrent device doesn't exceed the value determined by multiplying the secondary conductor ampacity by the secondary-to-primary transformer voltage ratio.

> **Question:** What's the minimum secondary conductor size required for a 2-wire, 480V to 120V transformer rated 1.50 kVA? **Figure 240–9**
>
> (a) 16 AWG   (b) 14 AWG   (c) 12 AWG   (d) 10 AWG
>
> **Answer:** (b) 14 AWG
>
> **Primary Current = VA/E**
>
> VA = 1,500 VA
>
> E = 480V
>
> Primary Current = 1,500 VA/480V
>
> Primary Current = 3.13A
>
> Primary Protection [450.3(B)] = 3.13A x 1.67
>
> Primary Protection = 5.22A or 5A Fuse
>
> Secondary Current = 1,500 VA/120V
>
> Secondary Current = 12.50A
>
> Secondary Conductor = 14 AWG, rated 20A at 75°C, [Table 310.15(B)(16)]
>
> The 5A primary overcurrent device can be used to protect 14 AWG secondary conductors because it doesn't exceed the value determined by multiplying the secondary conductor ampacity by the secondary-to-primary transformer voltage ratio (5A = 20A x 120V/480V).

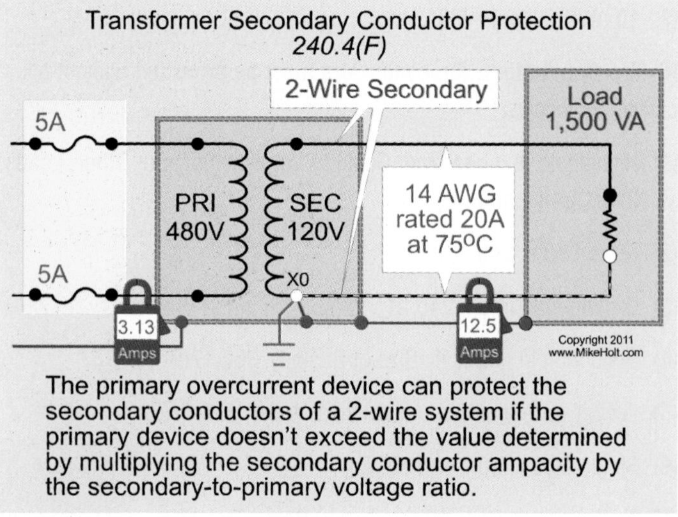

(G) Overcurrent Protection for Specific Applications. Overcurrent protection for specific equipment and conductors must comply with the requirements referenced in Table 240.4(G).

Air-Conditioning and Refrigeration [Article 440]. Air-conditioning and refrigeration equipment, and their circuit conductors, must be protected against overcurrent in accordance with 440.22.

> **Author's Comment:** Typically, the branch-circuit ampacity and protection size is marked on the equipment nameplate [440.4(A)].

> **Question:** What size branch-circuit overcurrent device is required for an air conditioner (18A) when the nameplate indicates the minimum circuit ampacity is 23A, with maximum overcurrent protection of 40A? **Figure 240–10**
>
> (a) 12 AWG, 40A protection   (b) 12 AWG, 50A protection
> (c) 12 AWG, 60A protection   (d) 12 AWG, 70A protection
>
> **Answer:** (a) 12 AWG, 40A protection

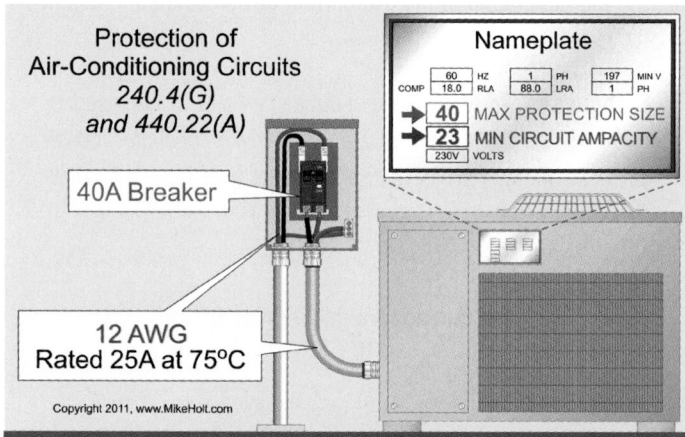

Air-conditioning and refrigeration equipment must be protected against overcurrent in accordance with 440.22.

Figure 240–10

> **Author's Comment:** Air-conditioning and refrigeration nameplate values are calculated by the manufacturer according to the following:
>
> • Branch-Circuit Conductor Size [440.32]
>   18A x 1.25 = 22.50A, 12 AWG rated 25A at 75°C
>
> • Branch-Circuit Protection Size [440.22(A)]
>   18A x 2.25 = 40.50A, 40A maximum overcurrent protection size [240.6(A)]

Transformer Secondary Conductor Protection 240.4(F)

The primary overcurrent device can protect the secondary conductors of a 2-wire system if the primary device doesn't exceed the value determined by multiplying the secondary conductor ampacity by the secondary-to-primary voltage ratio.

Figure 240–9

- Motors [Article 430]. Motor circuit conductors must be protected against short circuits and ground faults in accordance with 430.52 and 430.62 [430.51].

If the nameplate calls for fuses, fuses must be used to comply with the manufacturer's instructions [110.3(B)].

Question: What size branch-circuit conductor and overcurrent device (circuit breaker) is required for a 7½ hp, 230V, three-phase motor? **Figure 240–11**

(a) 10 AWG, 50A breaker   (b) 10 AWG, 60A breaker
(c) a or b   (d) none of these

Answer: (c) a or b

Step 1: Determine the branch-circuit conductor size [Table 310.15(B)(16), 430.22, and Table 430.250]:

FLC = 28A [Table 430-250]

22A x 1.25 = 28A, 10 AWG, rated 35A at 75°C

Step 2: Determine the branch-circuit protection size [240.6(A), 430.52(C)(1) Ex 1, and Table 430.250].

Inverse Time Breaker: 22A x 2.50 = 55A

Next size up = 60A

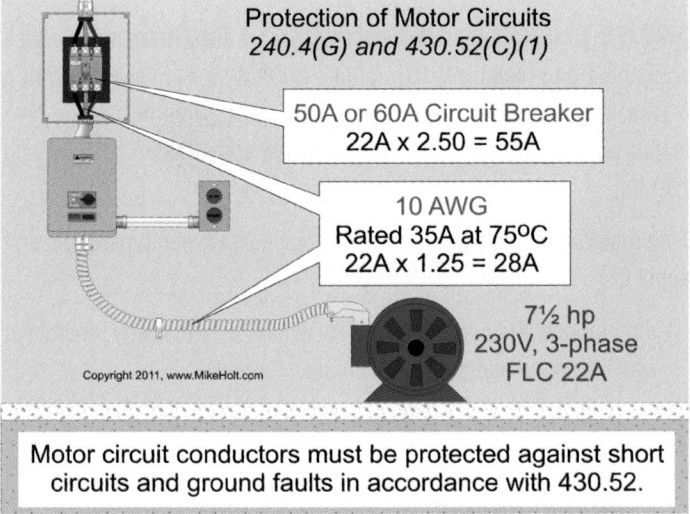

Protection of Motor Circuits
240.4(G) and 430.52(C)(1)

50A or 60A Circuit Breaker
22A x 2.50 = 55A

10 AWG
Rated 35A at 75°C
22A x 1.25 = 28A

7½ hp
230V, 3-phase
FLC 22A

Copyright 2011, www.MikeHolt.com

Motor circuit conductors must be protected against short circuits and ground faults in accordance with 430.52.

Figure 240–11

Motor Control [Article 430]. Motor control circuit conductors must be sized and protected in accordance with 430.72.

Remote-Control, Signaling, and Power-Limited Circuits [Article 725]. Remote-control, signaling, and power-limited circuit conductors must be protected against overcurrent in accordance with 725.43.

240.5 Protection of Flexible Cords and Fixture Wires.

(A) Ampacities. Flexible cord must be protected by an overcurrent device in accordance with its ampacity as specified in Table 400.5(A)(1) or Table 400.5(A)(2). Fixture wires must be protected against overcurrent in accordance with their ampacity as specified in Table 402.5. Supplementary overcurrent protection, as discussed in 240.10, is permitted to provide this protection.

(B) Branch-Circuit Overcurrent Protection.

(1) Cords for Listed Appliances or Luminaires. If flexible cord is used with a specific listed appliance or luminaire, the conductors are considered protected against overcurrent when used within the appliance or luminaire listing requirements.

> **Author's Comment:** The *NEC* only applies to premises wiring, not to the supply cords of listed appliances and luminaires.

(2) Fixture Wire. Fixture wires can be tapped to the following circuits:

(1) 20A–18 AWG, up to 50 ft of run length

(2) 20A–16 AWG, up to 100 ft of run length

(3) 20A–14 AWG and larger

(3) Extension Cord Sets. If flexible cord is used in listed extension cord sets, the conductors are considered protected against overcurrent when used within the extension cord's listing requirements. **Figure 240–12**

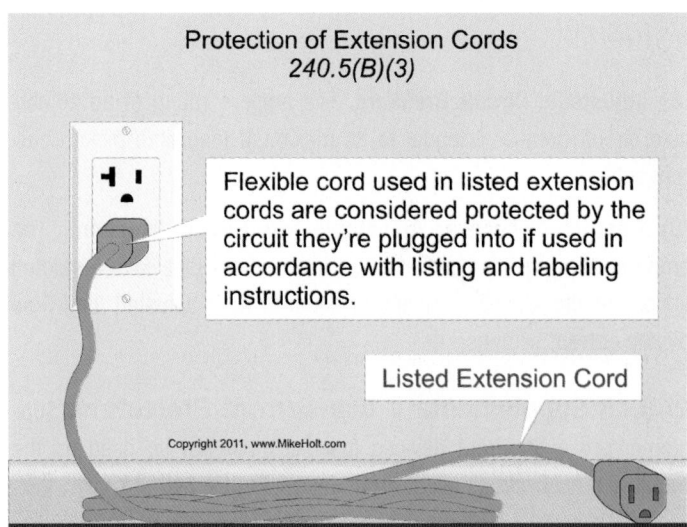

Protection of Extension Cords
240.5(B)(3)

Flexible cord used in listed extension cords are considered protected by the circuit they're plugged into if used in accordance with listing and labeling instructions.

Listed Extension Cord

Copyright 2011, www.MikeHolt.com

Figure 240–12

240.6 Standard Ampere Ratings.

(A) Fuses and Fixed-Trip Circuit Breakers. The standard ratings in amperes for fuses and inverse time breakers are: 15, 20, 25, 30, 35, 40, 45, 50, 60, 70, 80, 90, 100, 110, 125, 150, 175, 200, 225, 250, 300, 350, 400, 450, 500, 600, 700, 800, 1,000, 1,200, 1,600, 2,000, 2,500, 3,000, 4,000, 5,000 and 6,000. **Figure 240–13**

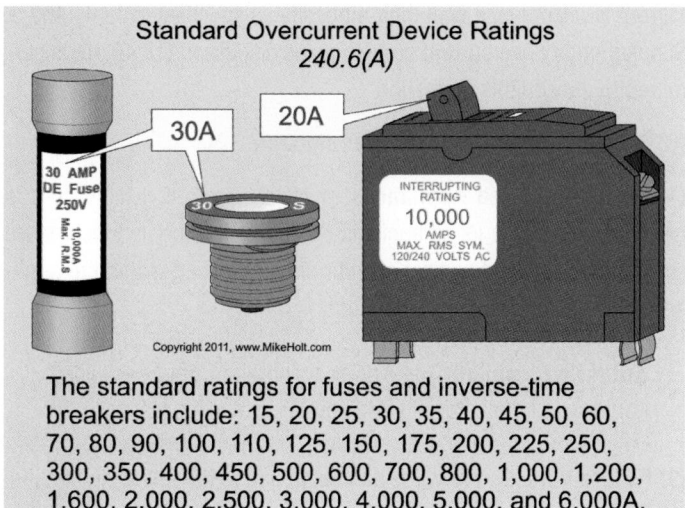

The standard ratings for fuses and inverse-time breakers include: 15, 20, 25, 30, 35, 40, 45, 50, 60, 70, 80, 90, 100, 110, 125, 150, 175, 200, 225, 250, 300, 350, 400, 450, 500, 600, 700, 800, 1,000, 1,200, 1,600, 2,000, 2,500, 3,000, 4,000, 5,000, and 6,000A.

Figure 240–13

Additional standard ampere ratings for fuses include 1, 3, 6, 10, and 601.

> **Author's Comment:** Fuses rated less than 15A are sometimes required for the protection of fractional horsepower motor circuits [430.52], motor control circuits [430.72], small transformers [450.3(B)], and remote-control circuit conductors [725.43].

(B) Adjustable Circuit Breakers. The ampere rating of an adjustable circuit breaker is equal to its maximum long-time pickup current setting.

(C) Restricted Access, Adjustable-Trip Circuit Breakers. The ampere rating of adjustable-trip circuit breakers that have restricted access to the adjusting means is equal to their adjusted long-time pickup current settings.

240.10 Supplementary Overcurrent Protection. Supplementary overcurrent devices (usually must not be used as the required branch-circuit overcurrent device. **Figure 240–14**

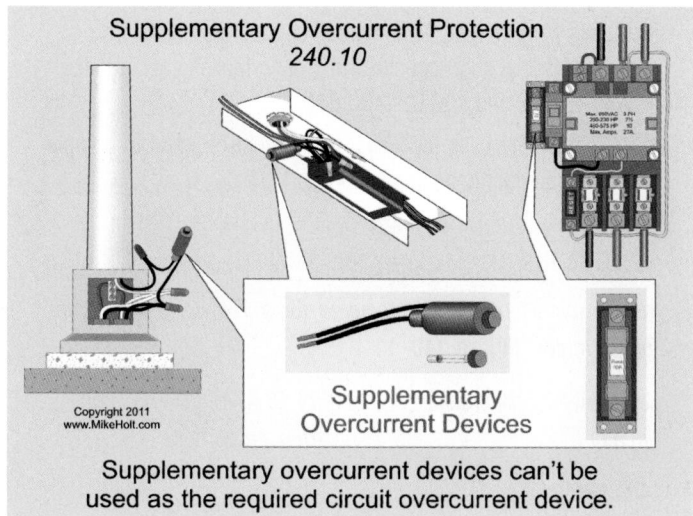

Supplementary overcurrent devices can't be used as the required circuit overcurrent device.

Figure 240–14

A supplementary overcurrent device isn't required to be readily accessible [240.24(A)(2)].

> **Author's Comment:** Article 100 defines a "Supplementary Overcurrent Device" as a device intended to provide limited overcurrent protection for specific applications and utilization equipment. This limited protection is in addition to the protection provided in the required branch circuit by the branch-circuit overcurrent device.

240.13 Ground-Fault Protection of Equipment. Service equipment and feeder circuits rated 1,000A or more, supplied from a 4-wire, three-phase, 277/480V wye-connected system must be protected against ground faults in accordance with 230.95 [215.10 and 230.95].

The requirement for ground-fault protection of equipment doesn't apply to:

(1) Continuous industrial processes where a nonorderly shutdown will introduce additional or increased hazards.

(2) Installations where ground-fault protection of equipment is already provided.

(3) Fire pumps [695.6(H)].

Author's Comments:

- Article 100 defines "Ground-Fault Protection of Equipment" as a system intended to provide protection of equipment from ground faults by opening the overcurrent device at current levels less than those required to protect conductors from damage. This type of protective system isn't intended to protect people, only connected equipment. See 215.10 and 230.95 for similar requirements for feeders and services.

- Ground-fault protection of equipment isn't required for emergency power systems [700.26] or legally required standby power systems [701.17].

240.15 Ungrounded Conductors.

(A) Overcurrent Device Required. A fuse or circuit breaker must be connected in series with each ungrounded conductor.

(B) Circuit Breaker as an Overcurrent Device. Circuit breakers must automatically (and manually) open all ungrounded conductors of the circuit, except as follows:

(1) Multiwire Branch Circuits. Individual single-pole breakers with identified handle ties are permitted for a multiwire branch circuit that only supplies line-to-neutral loads. **Figure 240–15**

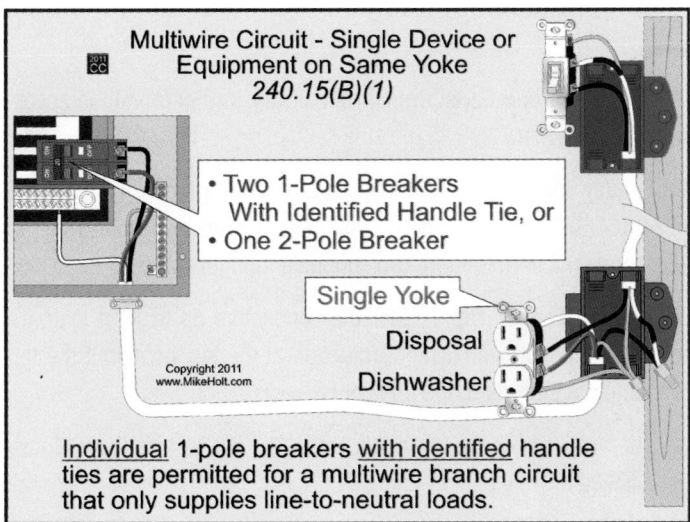

Figure 240–15

Author's Comments:

- According to Article 100, "Identified" means recognized as suitable for a specific purpose, function, or environment by listing, labeling, or other means approved by the authority having jurisdiction. This means handle ties made from nails, screws, wires, or other nonconforming materials aren't suitable. **Figure 240–16**

- Single-pole AFCI or GFCI circuit breakers aren't suitable for protecting multiwire branch circuits. AFCI or GFCI circuit breakers for multiwire branch circuits must be of the 2-pole type. **Figure 240–17**

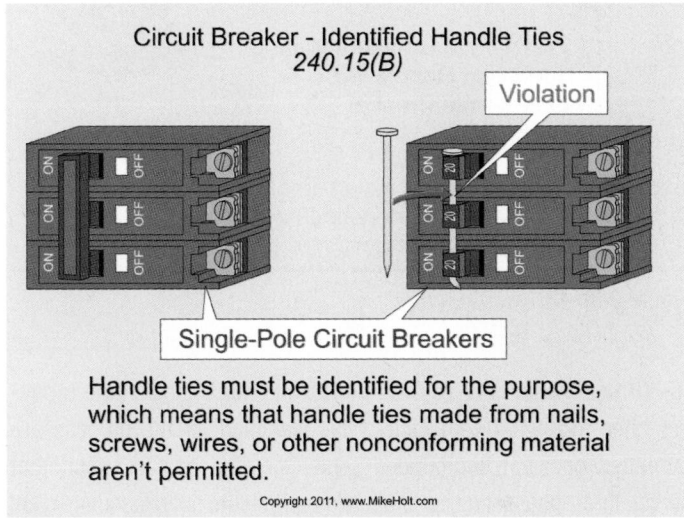

Figure 240–16

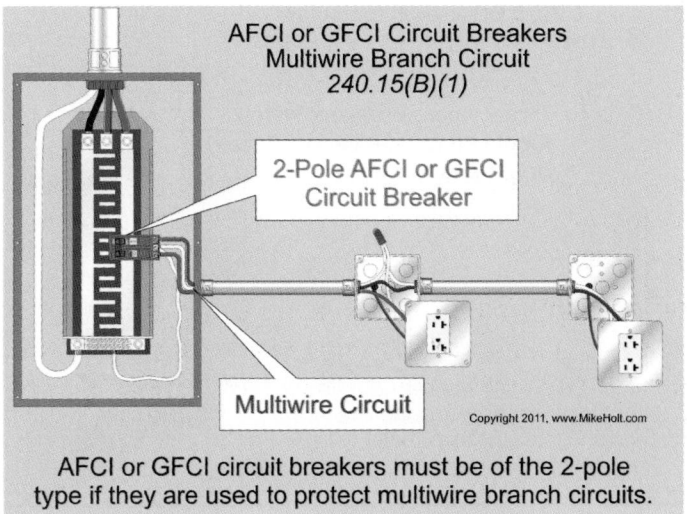

Figure 240–17

(2) Single-Phase, Line-to-Line Loads. Individual single-pole circuit breakers rated 120/240V with handle ties identified for the purpose are permitted on each ungrounded conductor of a branch circuit that supplies single-phase, line-to-line loads. **Figure 240–18**

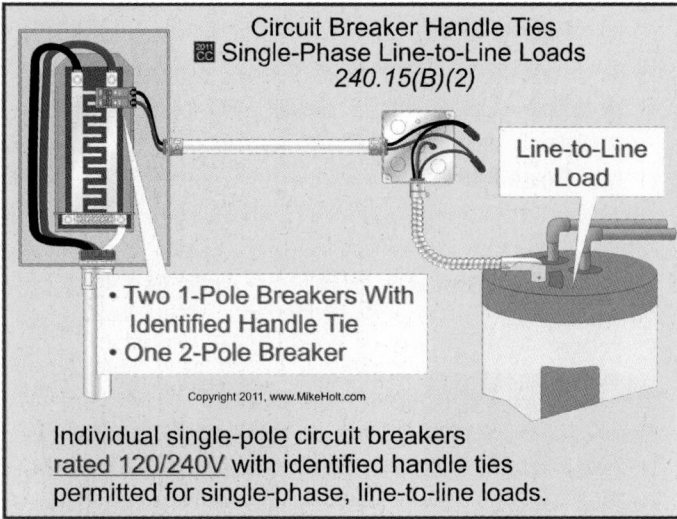

Figure 240–18

(3) Three-Phase, Line-to-Line Loads. Individual single-pole breakers rated 120/240V with handle ties identified for the purpose are permitted on each ungrounded conductor of a branch circuit that serves three-phase, line-to-line loads on systems not exceeding 120V to ground. **Figure 240–19**

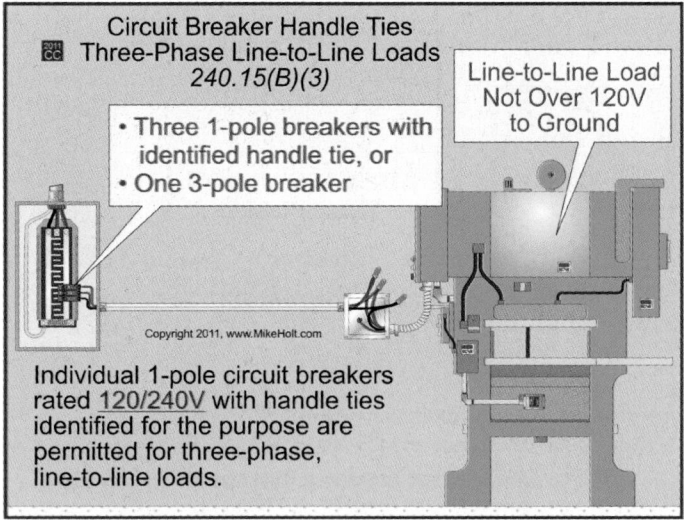

Figure 240–19

PART II. LOCATION

240.21 Overcurrent Protection Location in Circuit.
Except as permitted by (A) through (H), overcurrent devices must be placed at the point where the branch circuit or feeder conductors receive their power. Taps and transformer secondary conductors aren't permitted to supply another conductor (tapping a tap isn't permitted). **Figure 240–20**

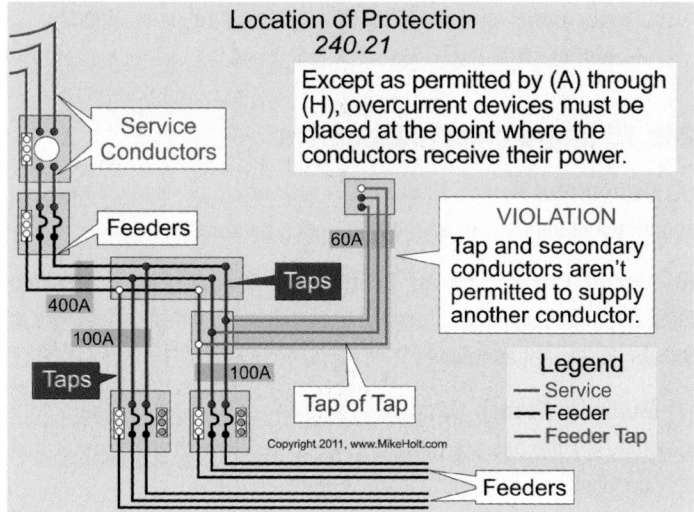

Figure 240–20

(A) Branch-Circuit Taps. Branch-circuit taps are permitted in accordance with 210.19.

(B) Feeder Taps. Conductors can be tapped to a feeder as specified in 240.21(B)(1) through (B)(5). The "next size up protection rule" of 240.4(B) is not permitted for tap conductors. **Figure 240-21**

(1) 10-Foot Feeder Tap. Feeder tap conductors up to 10 ft long are permitted without overcurrent protection at the tap location if the tap conductors comply with the following:

(1) The ampacity of the tap conductor must not be less than: **Figure 240–22**

    a. The calculated load in accordance with Article 220, and

    b. The rating of the device or overcurrent device supplied by the tap conductors.

(2) The tap conductors must not extend beyond the equipment they supply.

(3) The tap conductors are installed in a raceway if they leave the enclosure.

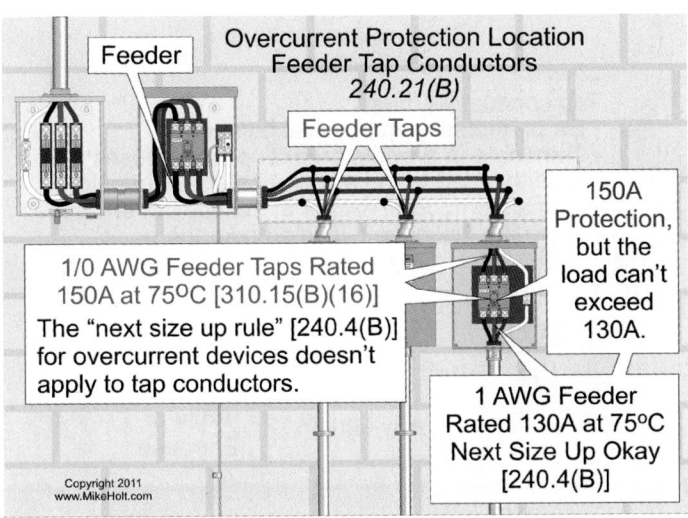

1/0 AWG Feeder Taps Rated 150A at 75°C [310.15(B)(16)]

The "next size up rule" [240.4(B)] for overcurrent devices doesn't apply to tap conductors.

150A Protection, but the load can't exceed 130A.

1 AWG Feeder Rated 130A at 75°C Next Size Up Okay [240.4(B)]

Copyright 2011 www.MikeHolt.com

Figure 240-21

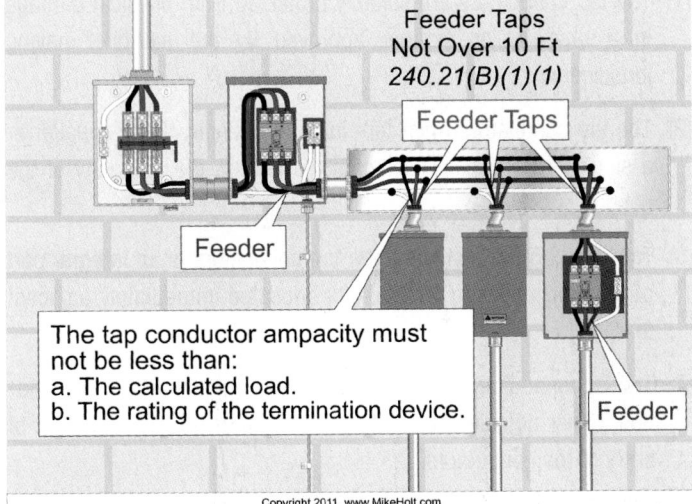

The tap conductor ampacity must not be less than:
a. The calculated load.
b. The rating of the termination device.

Copyright 2011, www.MikeHolt.com

Figure 240–22

(4) If the tap conductors leave the enclosure or vault in which the tap is made, the tap conductors must have an ampacity not less than 1/10th of the rating of the overcurrent device that protects the feeder.

Note: See 408.36 for the overcurrent protection requirements for panelboards.

Example: A 400A breaker protects a set of 500 kcmil feeder conductors. There are three taps fed from the 500 kcmil feeders that supply disconnects with 200A, 150A, and 30A overcurrent devices. What are the minimum size conductors for these taps? **Figure 240–23**

- 200A: 3/0 AWG is rated 200A at 75°, and is greater than 10 percent of the ampacity of 500 kcmil, which is rated 380A at 75°.

- 150A: 1/0 AWG is rated 150A at 75°, and is greater than 10 percent of the ampacity of 500 kcmil, which is rated 380A at 75°.

- 30A: 8 AWG is rated 50A at 75°, and is greater than 10 percent of the ampacity of 500 kcmil, which is rated 380A at 75°. Anything smaller than 8 AWG can't be used, as it will have an ampacity of less than 10 percent of 380A (38A) in the 75° column of 310.15(B)(16).

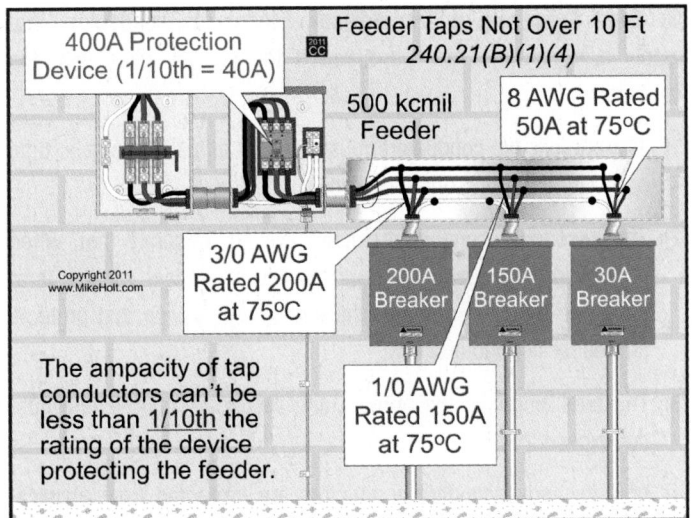

Figure 240–23

(2) 25-Foot Feeder Tap. Feeder tap conductors up to 25 ft long are permitted without overcurrent protection at the tap location if the tap conductors comply with the following: **Figure 240–24**

(1) The ampacity of the tap conductors must not be less than one-third the rating of the overcurrent device that protects the feeder.

(2) The tap conductors terminate in a single circuit breaker, or set of fuses rated no more than the tap conductor ampacity in accordance with 310.15 [Table 310.15(B)(16)].

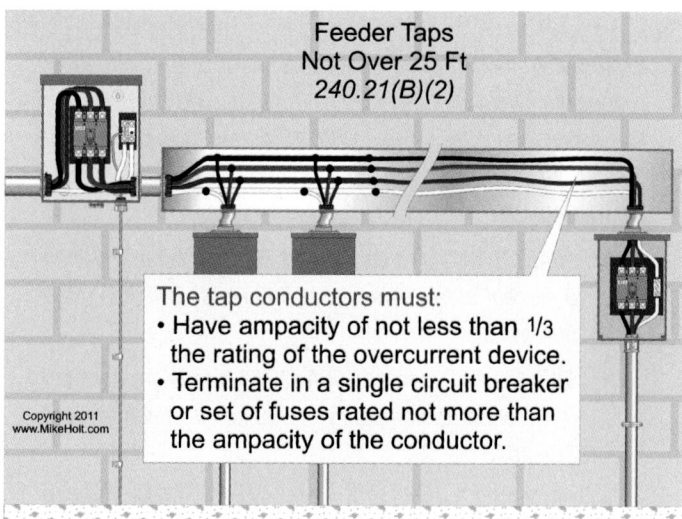

Figure 240–24

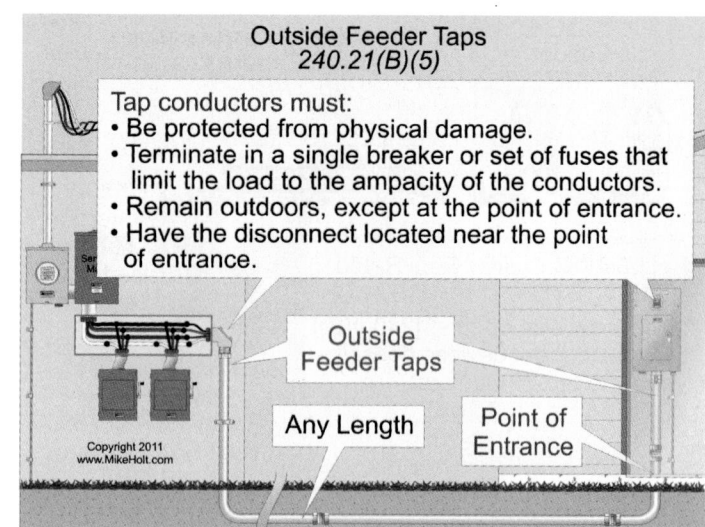

Figure 240–25

(3) The tap conductors are protected from physical damage by being enclosed in a manner approved by the authority having jurisdiction, such as within a raceway.

(3) Taps Supplying a Transformer. Feeder tap conductors that supply a transformer are permitted if the tap complies with the following:

(1) The primary tap conductors must have an ampacity not less than one-third the rating of the overcurrent device.

(2) The secondary conductors must have an ampacity that, when multiplied by the ratio of the primary-to-secondary voltage, is at least one-third the rating of the overcurrent device that protects the feeder conductors.

(3) The total length of the primary and secondary conductors must not exceed 25 ft.

(4) Primary and secondary conductors are protected from physical damage by being enclosed in a manner approved by the authority having jurisdiction, such as within a raceway.

(5) Secondary conductors terminate in a single circuit breaker or set of fuses rated no more than the tap conductor ampacity in accordance with 310.15 [Table 310.15(B)(16)].

(5) Outside Feeder Taps of Unlimited Length. Outside feeder tap conductors can be of unlimited length, without overcurrent protection at the point they receive their supply, if they comply with the following: **Figure 240–25**

(1) The tap conductors are suitably protected from physical damage in a raceway or manner approved by the authority having jurisdiction.

(2) The tap conductors must terminate at a single circuit breaker or a single set of fuses that limits the load to the ampacity of the conductors.

(3) The overcurrent device for the tap conductors is an integral part of the disconnecting means, or it's located immediately adjacent to it.

(4) The disconnecting means is located at a readily accessible location, either outside the building/structure, or nearest the point of entry of the conductors.

(C) Transformer Secondary Conductors. A set of conductors supplying single or separate loads is permitted to be connected to a transformer secondary without overcurrent protection in accordance with (1) through (6).

> **Author's Comment:** The permission of the 'next size up' protection rule when the conductor ampacity does not correspond with the standard size overcurrent protection device of 240.4(B) shall does not apply to transformer secondary conductors. **Figure 240–26**

(1) Protection by Primary Overcurrent Device. The primary overcurrent device sized in accordance with 450.3(B) is considered suitable to protect the secondary conductors of a 2-wire (single-voltage) system, provided the primary overcurrent device doesn't exceed the value determined by multiplying the secondary conductor ampacity by the secondary-to-primary transformer voltage ratio.

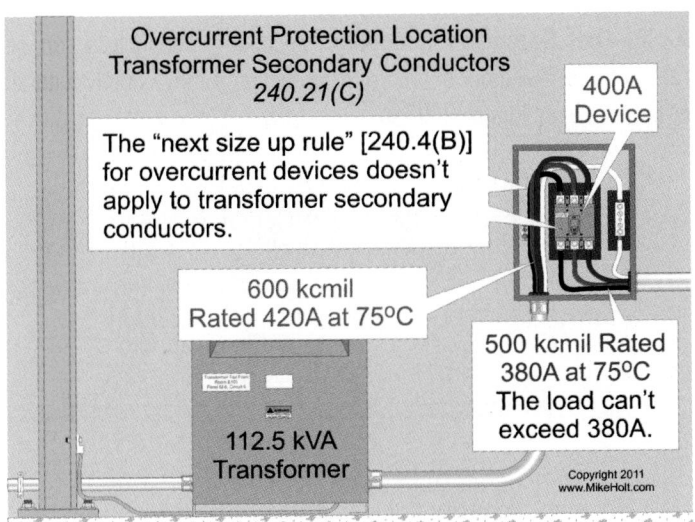

Overcurrent Protection Location
Transformer Secondary Conductors
240.21(C)

400A
Device

The "next size up rule" [240.4(B)] for overcurrent devices doesn't apply to transformer secondary conductors.

600 kcmil
Rated 420A at 75ºC

500 kcmil Rated 380A at 75ºC
The load can't exceed 380A.

112.5 kVA
Transformer

Copyright 2011
www.MikeHolt.com

Figure 240–26

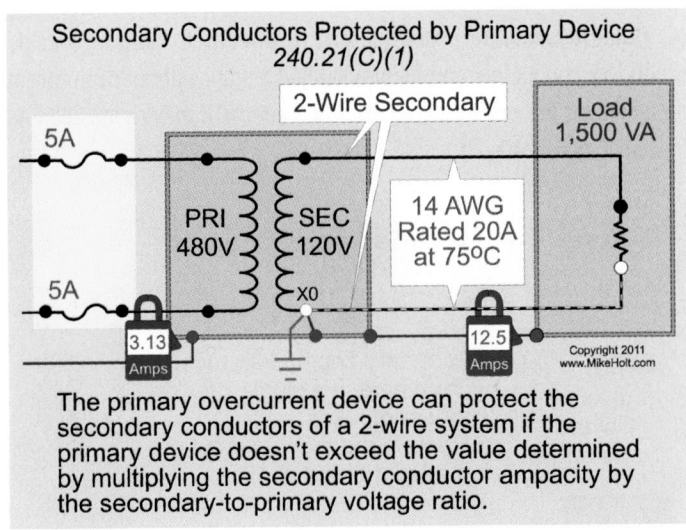

Secondary Conductors Protected by Primary Device
240.21(C)(1)

2-Wire Secondary

5A

Load
1,500 VA

PRI
480V

SEC
120V

14 AWG
Rated 20A
at 75ºC

5A

X0

3.13
Amps

12.5
Amps

Copyright 2011
www.MikeHolt.com

The primary overcurrent device can protect the secondary conductors of a 2-wire system if the primary device doesn't exceed the value determined by multiplying the secondary conductor ampacity by the secondary-to-primary voltage ratio.

Figure 240–27

Question: *What's the minimum size secondary conductor required for a 2-wire, 480V to 120V transformer rated 1.50 kVA?* **Figure 240–27**

(a) 16 AWG   (b) 14 AWG   (c) 12 AWG   (d) 10 AWG

Answer: *(b) 14 AWG*

Primary Current = VA/E

VA = 1,500 VA

E = 480V

Primary Current = 1,500 VA/480V

Primary Current = 3.13A

Primary Protection [450.3(B)] = 3.13A x 1.67

Primary Protection [450.3(B)] = 5.22A or 5A Fuse

Secondary Current = 1,500 VA/120V

Secondary Current = 12.50A

Secondary Conductor = 14 AWG, rated 20A at 60ºC, [Table 310.15(B)(16)]

The 5A primary overcurrent device can be used to protect 14 AWG secondary conductors because it doesn't exceed the value determined by multiplying the secondary conductor ampacity by the secondary-to-primary transformer voltage ratio (5A = 20A x 120V/480V).

(2) 10 Ft Secondary Conductors. Secondary conductors can be run up to 10 ft without overcurrent protection if installed as follows:

(1) The ampacity of the secondary conductor must not be less than: **Figure 240–28**

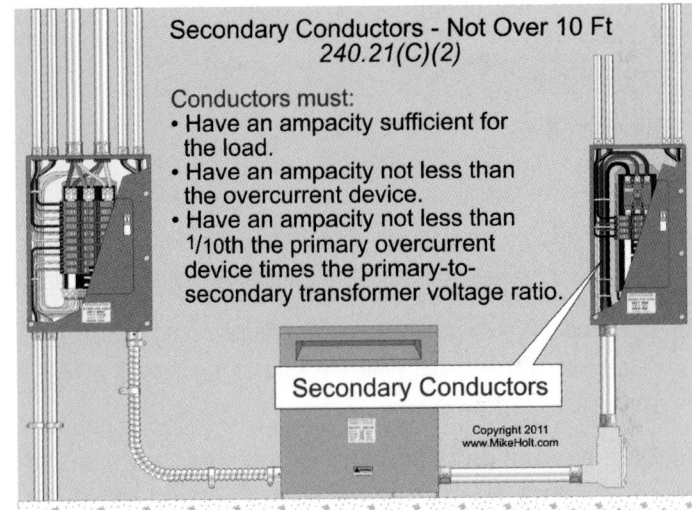

Secondary Conductors - Not Over 10 Ft
240.21(C)(2)

Conductors must:
• Have an ampacity sufficient for the load.
• Have an ampacity not less than the overcurrent device.
• Have an ampacity not less than 1/10th the primary overcurrent device times the primary-to-secondary transformer voltage ratio.

Secondary Conductors

Copyright 2011
www.MikeHolt.com

Figure 240–28

a. The calculated load in accordance with Article 220,

b. The rating of the device supplied by the secondary conductors or the overcurrent device at the termination of the secondary conductors, and

(2) The secondary conductors must not extend beyond the switchboard, panelboard, disconnecting means, or control devices they supply.

(3) The secondary conductors are enclosed in a raceway.

(4) Not less than one-tenth the rating of the overcurrent device protecting the primary of the transformer, multiplied by the primary-to-secondary transformer voltage ratio.

(4) Outside Secondary Conductors of Unlimited Length. Outside secondary conductors can be of unlimited length, without overcurrent protection at the point they receive their supply, if they're installed as follows: **Figure 240–29**

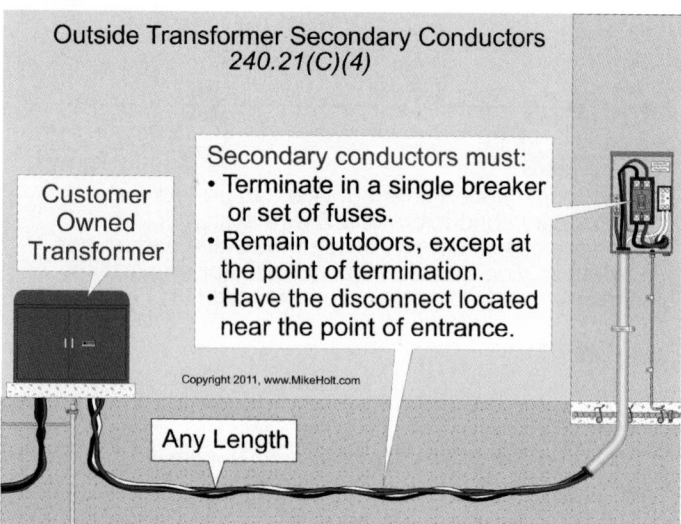

Figure 240–29

(1) The conductors are suitably protected from physical damage in a raceway or manner approved by the authority having jurisdiction.

(2) The conductors must terminate at a single circuit breaker or a single set of fuses that limit the load to the ampacity of the conductors.

(3) The overcurrent device for the ungrounded conductors is an integral part of a disconnecting means or it's located immediately adjacent thereto.

(4) The disconnecting means is located at a readily accessible location that complies with one of the following:

   a. Outside of a building/structure.

   b. Inside, nearest the point of entrance of the conductors.

   c. If installed in accordance with 230.6, nearest the point of entrance of the conductors.

(5) Secondary Conductors from a Feeder Tapped Transformer. Transformer secondary conductors must be installed in accordance with 240.21(B)(3).

(6) 25-Foot Secondary Conductor. Secondary conductors can be run up to 25 ft without overcurrent protection if they comply with all of the following: **Figure 240–30**

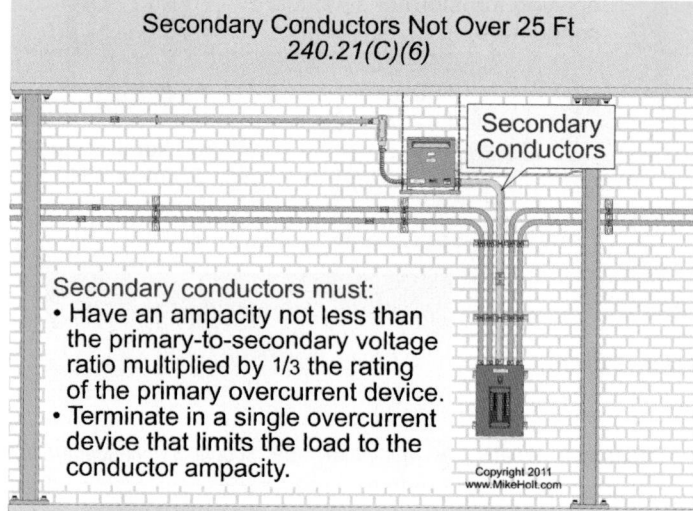

Figure 240–30

(1) The secondary conductors have an ampacity not less than the value of the primary-to-secondary voltage ratio multiplied by one-third of the rating of the overcurrent device that protects the primary of the transformer.

(2) Secondary conductors terminate in a single circuit breaker or set of fuses rated no more than the tap conductor ampacity in accordance with 310.15 [Table 310.15(B)(16)].

(3) The secondary conductors are protected from physical damage by being enclosed in a manner approved by the authority having jurisdiction, such as within a raceway.

(D) Service Conductors. Service conductors are protected against overload by the service disconnect overcurrent device in accordance with 230.91.

(H) Battery Conductors. Overcurrent protection is installed as close as practicable to the storage battery terminals.

240.24 Location of Overcurrent Devices.

(A) Readily Accessible. Circuit breakers and fuses must be readily accessible, and they must be installed so the center of the grip of the operating handle of the fuse switch or circuit breaker, when in its highest position, isn't more than 6 ft 7 in. above the floor or working platform, unless the installation is for: **Figure 240–31**

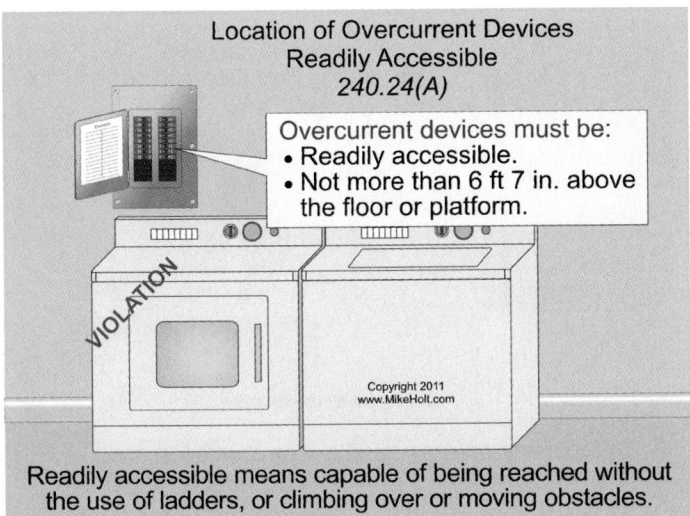

Figure 240–31

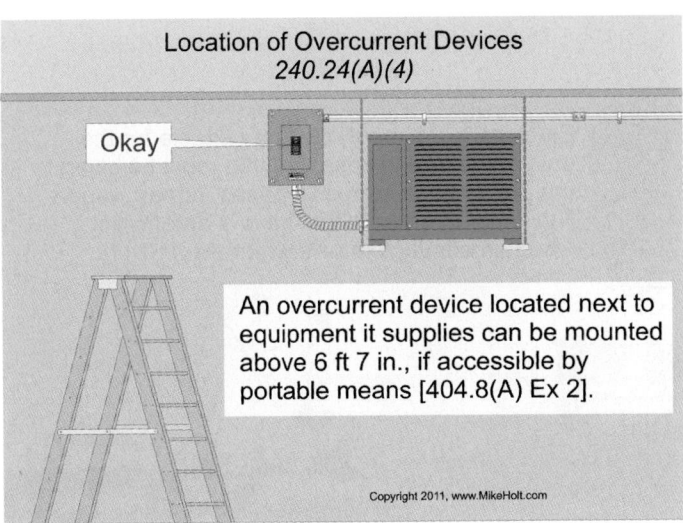

Figure 240–33

(1) Busways, as provided in 368.17(C).

(2) Supplementary overcurrent devices are not required to be readily accessible [240.10]. **Figure 240–32**

(C) Not Exposed to Physical Damage. Overcurrent devices must not be exposed to physical damage. **Figure 240–34**

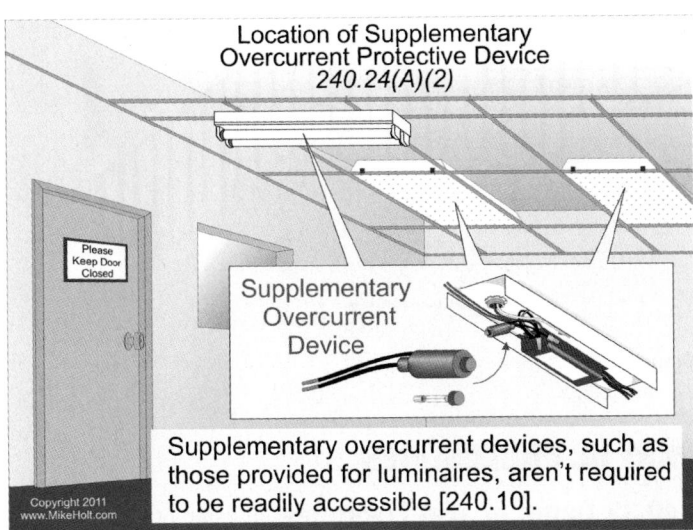

Figure 240–32

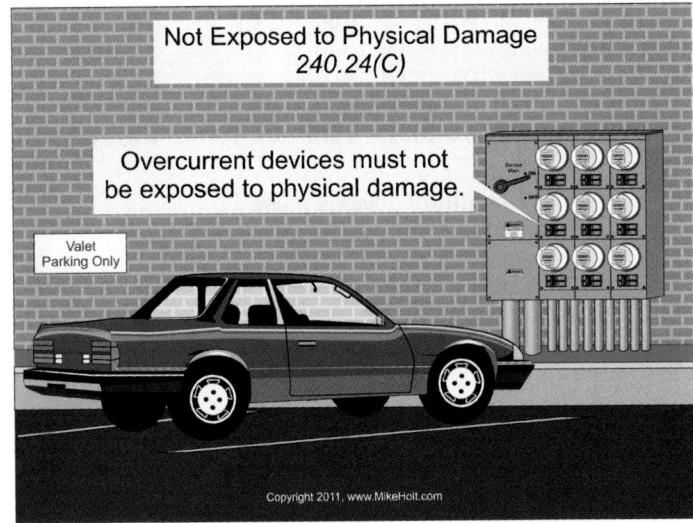

Figure 240–34

(3) For overcurrent devices, as described in 225.40 and 230.92.

(4) Overcurrent devices located next to equipment can be mounted above 6 ft 7 in., if accessible by portable means [404.8(A) Ex 2]. Figure 240–33

Note: Electrical equipment must be suitable for the environment, and consideration must be given to the presence of corrosive gases, fumes, vapors, liquids, or chemicals that have a deteriorating effect on conductors or equipment [110.11]. **Figure 240–35**

(D) Not in Vicinity of Easily Ignitible Material. Overcurrent devices must not be located near easily ignitible material, such as in clothes closets. **Figure 240–36**

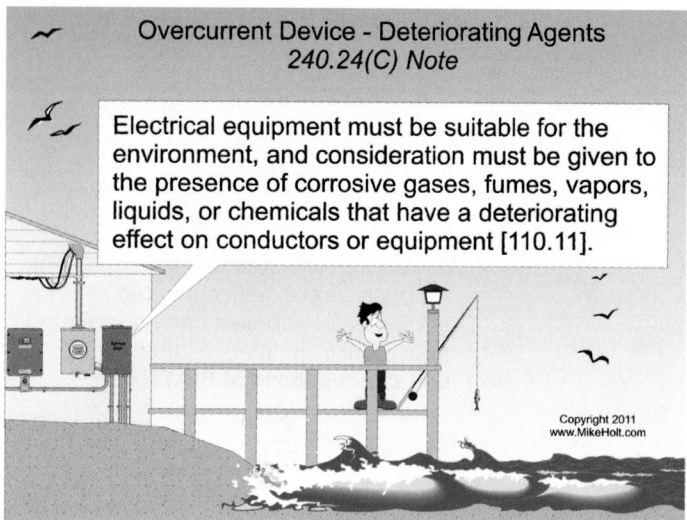

Figure 240–35

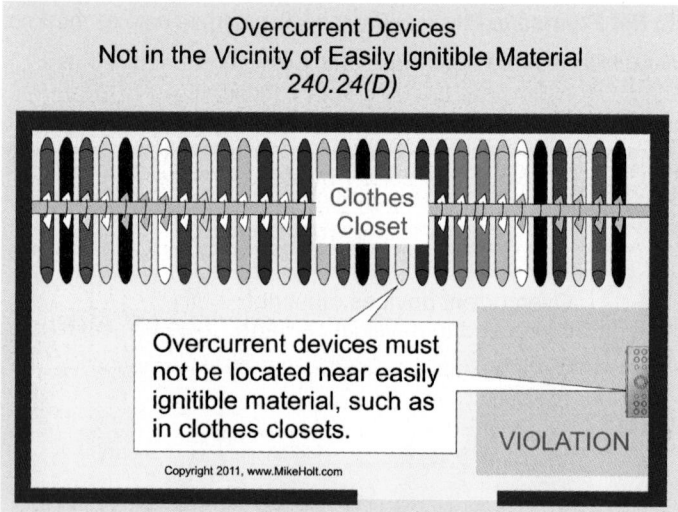

Figure 240–36

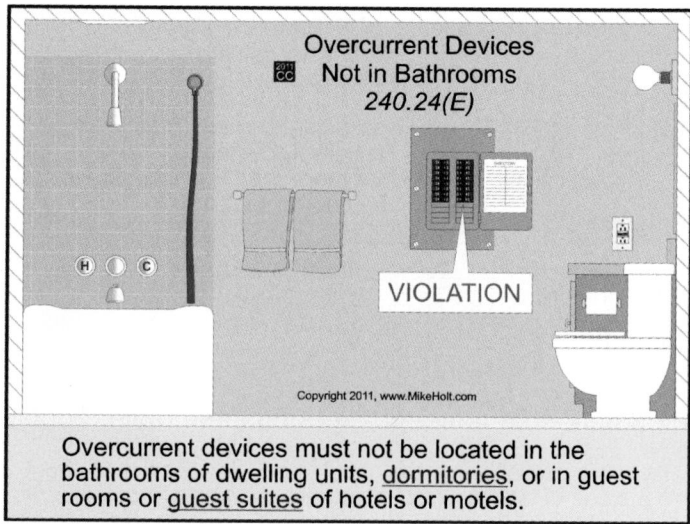

Figure 240–37

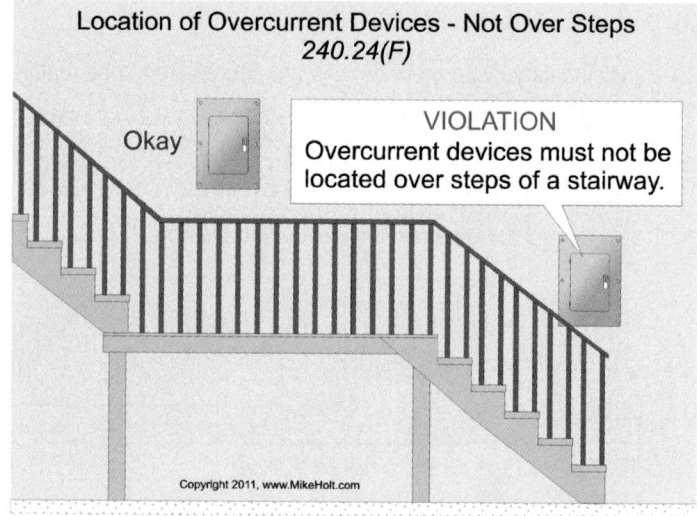

Figure 240–38

(E) Not in Bathrooms. Overcurrent devices aren't permitted to be located in the bathrooms of dwelling units, dormitories, or guest rooms or guest suites of hotels or motels. **Figure 240–37**

> **Author's Comment:** The service disconnecting means must not be located in a bathroom, even in commercial or industrial facilities [230.70(A)(2)].

(F) Over Steps. Overcurrent devices must not be located over the steps of a stairway. **Figure 240–38**

> **Author's Comment:** Clearly, it's difficult for electricians to safely work on electrical equipment that's located on uneven surfaces such as over stairways.

PART III. ENCLOSURES

240.32 Damp or Wet Locations. In damp or wet locations, enclosures containing overcurrent devices must prevent moisture or water from entering or accumulating within the enclosure. When the enclosure is surface mounted in a wet location, it must be mounted with not less than ¼ in. of air space between it and the mounting surface. See 312.2.

240.33 Vertical Position. Enclosures containing overcurrent devices must be mounted in a vertical position unless this isn't practical. Circuit-breaker enclosures can be mounted horizontally if the circuit breaker is installed in accordance with 240.81. **Figure 240–39**

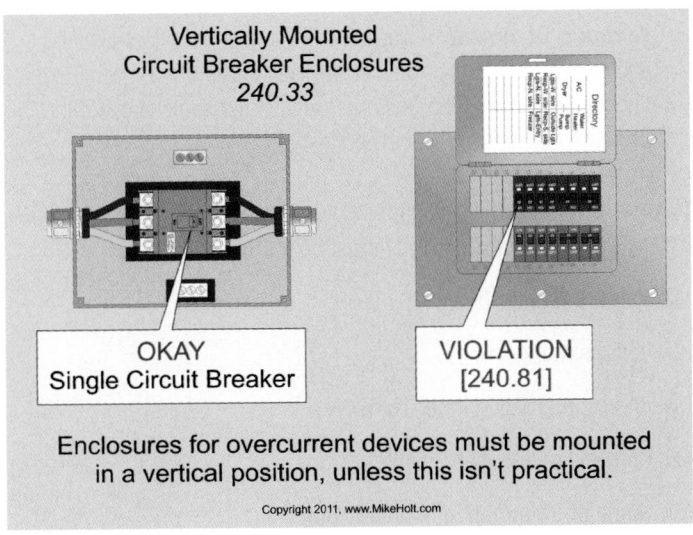

Vertically Mounted
Circuit Breaker Enclosures
240.33

OKAY
Single Circuit Breaker

VIOLATION
[240.81]

Enclosures for overcurrent devices must be mounted
in a vertical position, unless this isn't practical.

Figure 240–39

Author's Comment: Section 240.81 specifies that where circuit-breaker handles are operated vertically, the "up" position of the handle must be in the "on" position. So, in effect, an enclosure that contains one row of circuit breakers can be mounted horizontally, but an enclosure that contains a panelboard with multiple circuit breakers on opposite sides of each other will have to be mounted vertically.

PART V. PLUG FUSES, FUSEHOLDERS, AND ADAPTERS

240.50 General.

(A) Maximum Voltage. Plug fuses are permitted to be used only when:

(1) The circuit voltage doesn't exceed 125 volts between conductors.

(2) The circuits are supplied by a system with a line-to-neutral voltage not exceeding 150V.

(C) Hexagon Configuration. Plug fuses of 15A or lower rating must be identified by a hexagonal configuration of the window, cap or other prominent part.

240.51 Edison-Base Fuses.

(A) Classification. Edison-base fuses are classified to operate at not more than 125V and have an ampere rating of not more than 30A.

(B) Replacement Only. Edison-base fuses are permitted only for replacement in an existing installation where there's no evidence of tampering or overfusing.

240.52 Edison-Base Fuseholders. Edison-base fuseholders must be used only if they're made to accept Type S fuses by the use of adapters.

240.53 Type S Fuses.

(A) Classification. Type S fuses operate at not more than 125V and have ampere ratings of 15A, 20A, and 30A. **Figure 240–40**

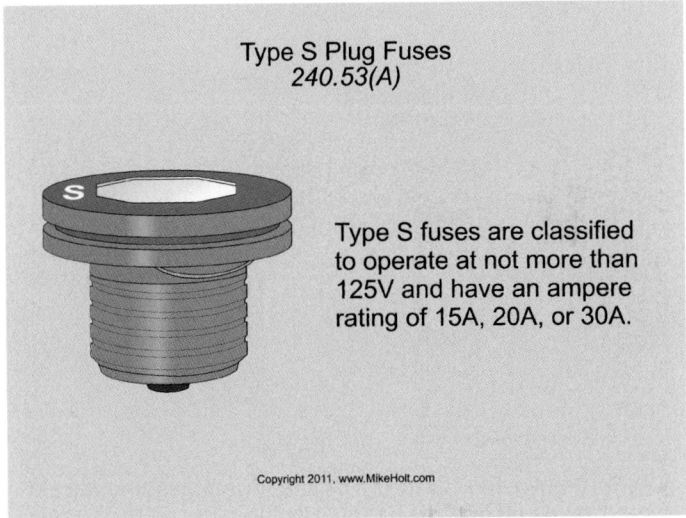

Type S Plug Fuses
240.53(A)

Type S fuses are classified
to operate at not more than
125V and have an ampere
rating of 15A, 20A, or 30A.

Figure 240–40

(B) Not Interchangeable. Type S fuses are made so different ampere ratings aren't interchangeable.

240.54 Type S Fuses, Adapters, and Fuseholders.

(A) Type S Adapters. Type S adapters are designed to fit Edison-base fuseholders.

(B) Prevent Edison-Base Fuses. Type S fuseholders and adapters are designed for Type S fuses only.

(C) Nonremovable Adapters. Type S adapters are designed so they can't be removed once installed.

(D) Nontamperable. Type S fuses, fuseholders and adapters must be designed so that tampering or shunting would be difficult.

(E) Interchangeability. Dimensions of Type S fuses, fuseholders, and adapters shall be standardized to permit interchangeability regardless of the manufacturer.

PART VI. CARTRIDGE FUSES AND FUSEHOLDERS

Author's Comment: There are two basic designs of cartridge fuses, the ferrule type with a maximum rating of 60A and the knife-blade type rated over 60A. The fuse length and diameter varies with the voltage and current rating. **Figure 240–41**

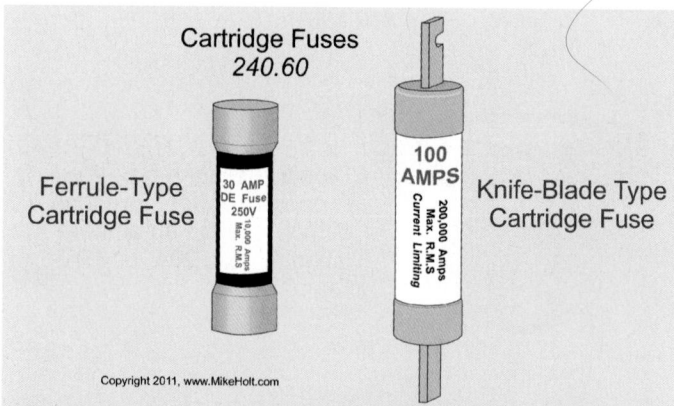

There are two basic designs of cartridge fuses, the ferrule type (maximum 60A) and the knife-blade type. The size of the fuse varies with the fuse voltage and current rating.

Figure 240–41

240.60 General.

(A) Maximum Voltage—300V Type. Cartridge fuses and fuseholders of the 300V type can only be used for:

- Circuits not exceeding 300V between conductors.
- Circuits not exceeding 300V from any ungrounded conductor to the neutral point.

(B) Noninterchangeable Fuseholders. Fuseholders must be designed to make it difficult to interchange fuses of any given class for different voltages and current ratings.

Fuseholders for current-limiting fuses must be designed so only current-limiting fuses can be inserted.

Author's Comment: A current-limiting fuse is a fast-clearing overcurrent device that reduces the fault current to a magnitude substantially lower than that obtainable in the same circuit if the current-limiting device isn't used [240.2].

(C) Marking. Cartridge fuses have an interrupting rating of 10,000A, unless marked otherwise. They must be marked with:

(1) Ampere rating

(2) Voltage rating

(3) Interrupting rating if not 10,000A

(4) Current limiting if applicable

(5) Name or trademark of manufacturer

WARNING: *Fuses must have an interrupting rating sufficient for the short-circuit current available at the line terminals of the equipment. Using a fuse with an inadequate interrupting current rating can cause equipment to be destroyed from a line-to-line or ground fault, and result in death or serious injury. See 110.9 for more details.* **Figure 240–42**

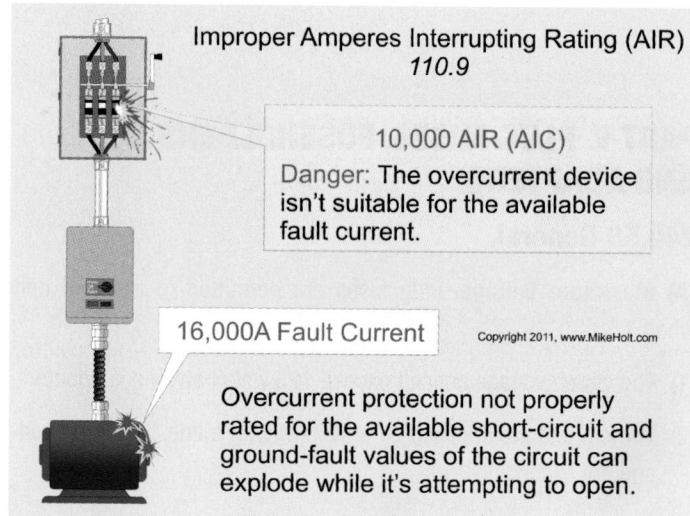

Figure 240–42

240.61 Classification.
Cartridge fuses and fuseholders are classified according to voltage and amperage ranges. Fuses rated 600V, nominal, or less are permitted for voltages at or below their ratings.

PART VII. CIRCUIT BREAKERS

240.80 Method of Operation.
Circuit breakers must be capable of being opened and closed by hand. Nonmanual means of operating a circuit breaker, such as electrical shunt trip or pneumatic operation, are permitted as long as the circuit breaker can also be manually operated.

240.81 Indicating.
Circuit breakers must clearly indicate whether they're in the open "off" or closed "on" position. When the handle of a circuit breaker is operated vertically, the "up" position of the handle must be the "on" position. See 240.33 and 404.6(C). Figure 240–43

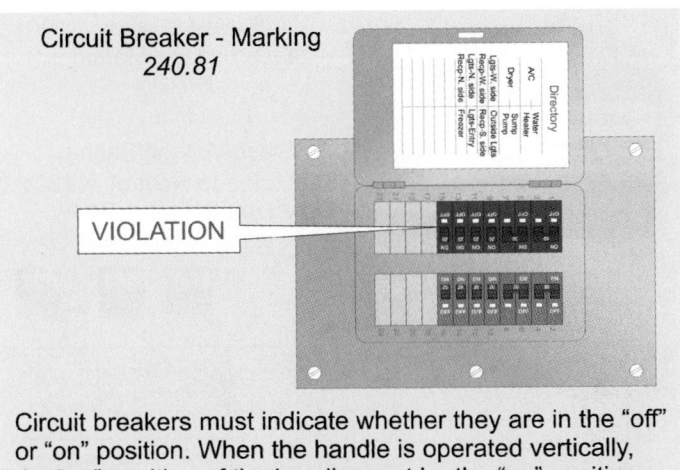

Figure 240–43

240.82 Nontamperable.
A circuit breaker must be designed so that any alteration of its trip point (calibration) or the time required for its operation requires dismantling of the device or breaking of a seal for other than intended adjustments.

240.83 Markings.

(A) Durable and Visible. Circuit breakers must be marked with their ampere rating in a manner that's durable and visible after installation. Such marking is permitted to be made visible by removal of a trim or cover.

(C) Interrupting Rating. Circuit breakers have an interrupting rating of 5,000A unless marked otherwise.

WARNING: *Take care to ensure the circuit breaker has an interrupting rating sufficient for the short-circuit current available at the line terminals of the equipment. Using a circuit breaker with an inadequate interrupting current rating can cause equipment to be destroyed from a line-to-line or ground fault, and result in death or serious injury. See 110.9 for more details.* **Figure 240–44**

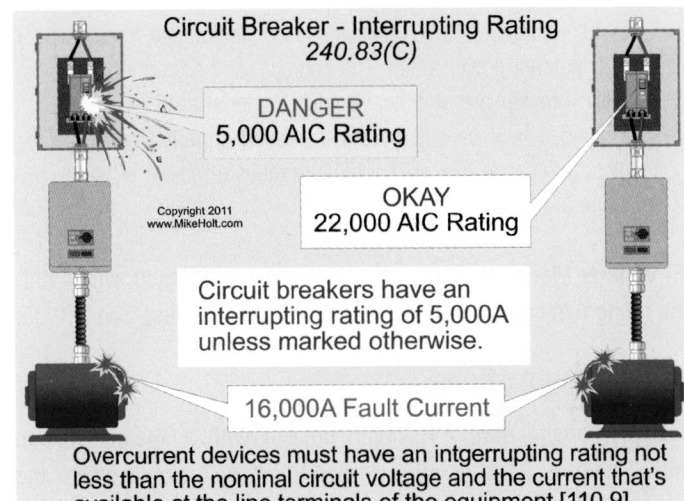

Figure 240–44

(D) Used as Switches. Circuit breakers used to switch 120V or 277V fluorescent lighting circuits must be listed and marked SWD or HID. Circuit breakers used to switch high-intensity discharge lighting circuits must be listed and marked HID. **Figure 240–45**

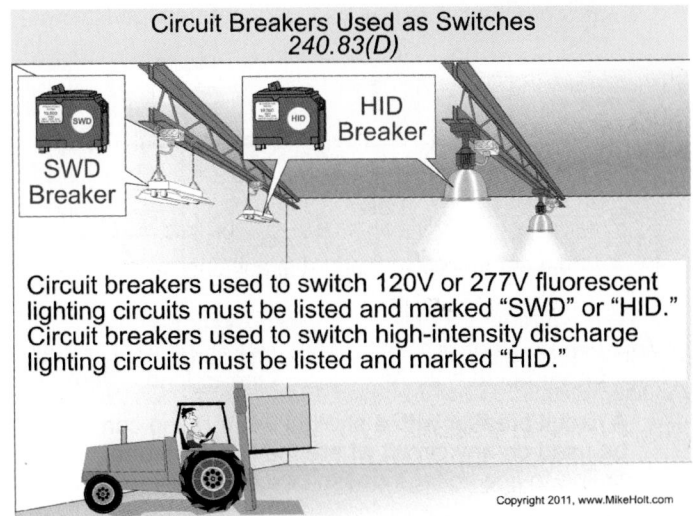

Figure 240–45

Author's Comments:

- This rule applies only when the circuit breaker is used as the switch. If a general-use snap switch or contactor is used to control the lighting, this rule doesn't apply.

- UL 489, *Standard for Molded Case Circuit Breakers*, permits "HID" breakers to be rated up to 50A, whereas an "SWD" breaker can only be rated up to 20A. The tests for "HID" breakers include an endurance test at 75 percent power factor, whereas "SWD" breakers are endurance-tested at 100 percent power factor. The contacts and the spring of an "HID" breaker are of a heavier-duty material to dissipate the increased heat caused by the increased current flow in the circuit, because the "HID" luminaire takes a minute or two to ignite the lamp.

(E) Voltage Markings. Circuit breakers must be marked with a voltage rating that corresponds with their interrupting rating. See 240.85.

240.85 Applications

Straight Voltage Rating. A circuit breaker with a straight voltage rating, such as 240V or 480V, is permitted on a circuit where the nominal voltage between any two conductors (line-to-neutral or line-to-line) doesn't exceed the circuit breaker's voltage rating. **Figure 240–46**

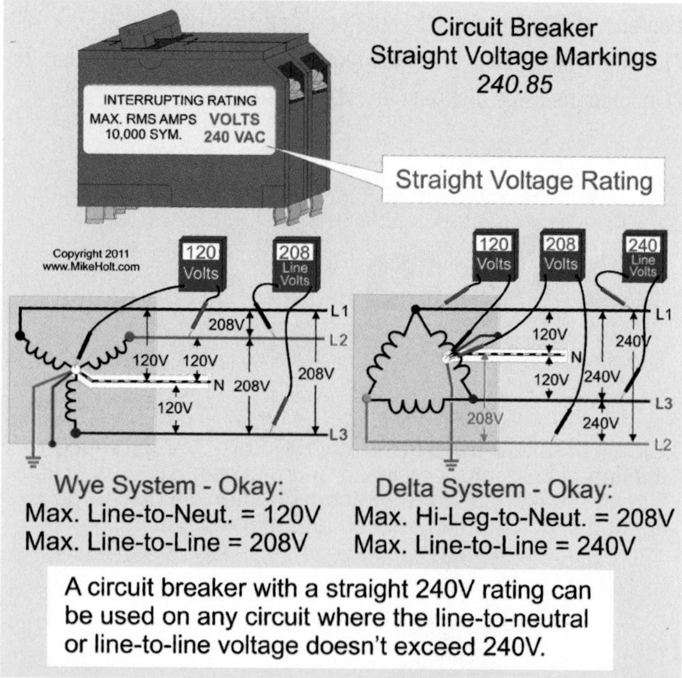

![Circuit Breaker Straight Voltage Markings 240.85. INTERRUPTING RATING, MAX. RMS AMPS 10,000 SYM. VOLTS 240 VAC. Straight Voltage Rating. Copyright 2011 www.MikeHolt.com. Wye System - Okay: Max. Line-to-Neut. = 120V, Max. Line-to-Line = 208V. Delta System - Okay: Max. Hi-Leg-to-Neut. = 208V, Max. Line-to-Line = 240V. A circuit breaker with a straight 240V rating can be used on any circuit where the line-to-neutral or line-to-line voltage doesn't exceed 240V.]

Figure 240–46

Slash Voltage Rating. A circuit breaker with a slash rating, such as 120/240V or 277/480V, is permitted on a solidly grounded system where the nominal voltage of any one conductor to ground doesn't exceed the lower of the two values, and the nominal voltage between any two conductors doesn't exceed the higher value.

⚠ **CAUTION:** *A 120/240V slash circuit breaker must not be used on the high leg of a solidly grounded 4-wire, three-phase, 120/240V delta-connected system, because the line-to-ground voltage of the high leg is 208V, which exceeds the 120V line-to-ground voltage rating of the breaker.* **Figure 240–47**

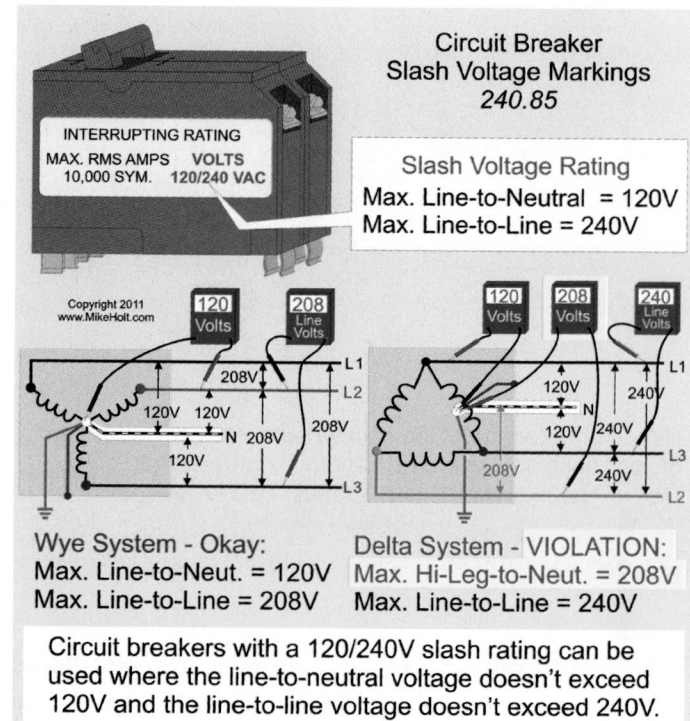

Circuit breakers with a 120/240V slash rating can be used where the line-to-neutral voltage doesn't exceed 120V and the line-to-line voltage doesn't exceed 240V.

Figure 240–47

Note: When installing circuit breakers on corner-grounded delta systems, consideration needs to be given to the circuit breakers' individual pole-interrupting capability.

Grounding and Bonding

INTRODUCTION TO ARTICLE 250—GROUNDING AND BONDING

No other article can match Article 250 for misapplication, violation, and misinterpretation. Terminology used in this article has been a source for much confusion, but that has improved during the last few *NEC* revisions. It's very important to understand the difference between grounding and bonding in order to correctly apply the provisions of Article 250. Pay careful attention to the definitions that apply to grounding and bonding both here and in Article 100 as you begin the study of this important article. Article 250 covers the grounding requirements for providing a path to the earth to reduce overvoltage from lightning, and the bonding requirements for a low-impedance fault current path back to the source of the electrical supply to facilitate the operation of overcurrent devices in the event of a ground fault.

Over the past five Code cycles, this article was extensively revised to organize it better and make it easier to understand and implement. It's arranged in a logical manner, so it's a good idea to just read through Article 250 to get a big picture view—after you review the definitions. Next, study the article closely so you understand the details. The illustrations will help you understand the key points.

PART I. GENERAL

250.1 Scope. Article 250 contains the following grounding and bonding requirements:

(1) What systems and equipment are required to be grounded.

(3) Location of grounding connections.

(4) Types of electrodes and sizes of grounding and bonding conductors.

(5) Methods of grounding and bonding.

250.2 Definitions.

Bonding Jumper, Supply-Side. A conductor on the supply side or within a service or separately derived system to ensure the electrical conductivity between metal parts required to be electrically connected. **Figures 250–1 and 250–2**

Effective Ground-Fault Current Path. An intentionally constructed low-impedance conductive path designed to carry fault current from the point of a ground fault on a wiring system to the electrical supply source. **Figure 250–3**

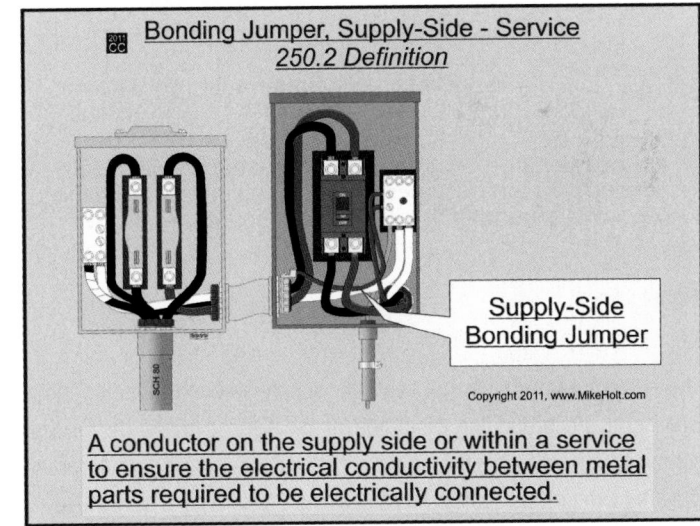

A conductor on the supply side or within a service to ensure the electrical conductivity between metal parts required to be electrically connected.

Figure 250–1

Author's Comment: In **Figure 250–3**, EGC represents the equipment grounding conductor [259.118], MBJ represents the main bonding jumper, SNC represents the service neutral conductor (grounded service conductor), GEC represents the grounding electrode conductor.

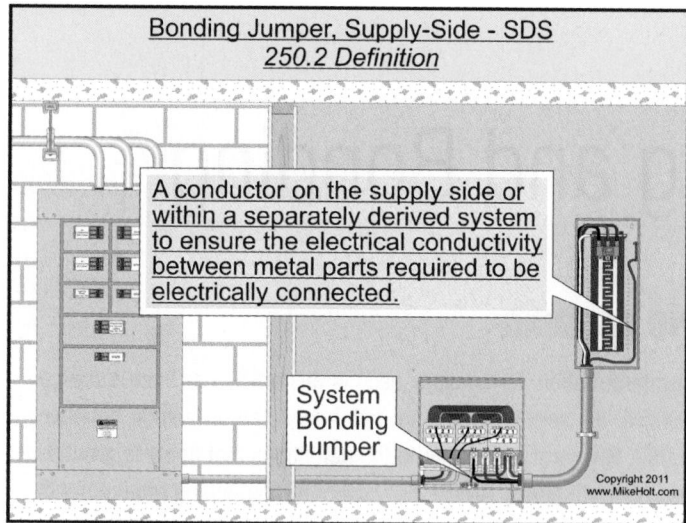

Figure 250–2

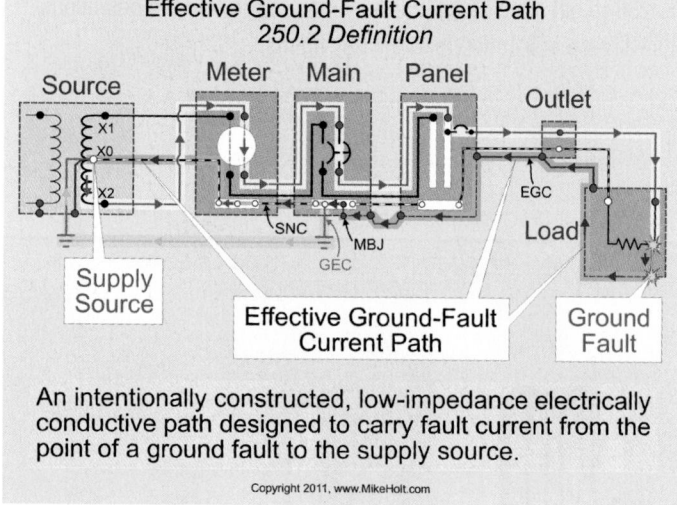

Figure 250–3

The current path shown between the supply source grounding electrode and the grounding electrode at the service main shows that some current will flow through the earth but the earth is not part of the effective ground-fault current path.

The effective ground-fault current path is intended to help remove dangerous voltage from a ground fault by opening the circuit overcurrent device. **Figure 250–4**

Ground-Fault Current Path. An electrically conductive path from a ground fault to the electrical supply source.

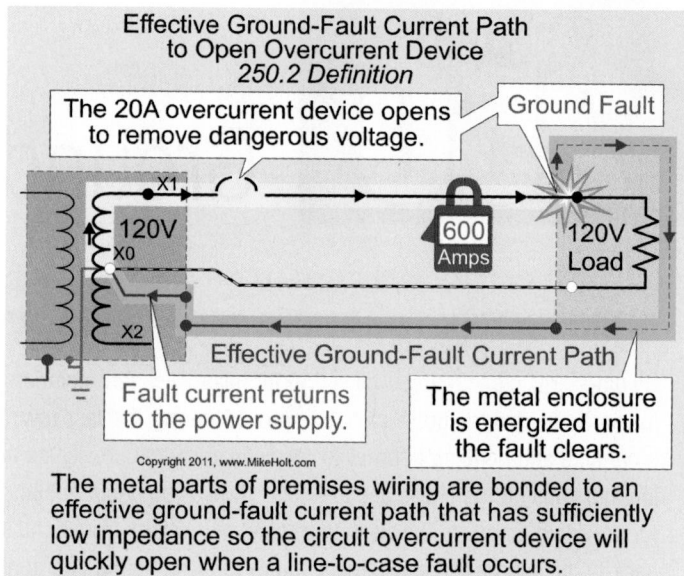

Figure 250–4

Note: The ground-fault current path could be metal raceways, cable sheaths, electrical equipment, or other electrically conductive materials, such as metallic water or gas piping, steel-framing members, metal ducting, reinforcing steel, or the shields of communications cables. **Figure 250–5**

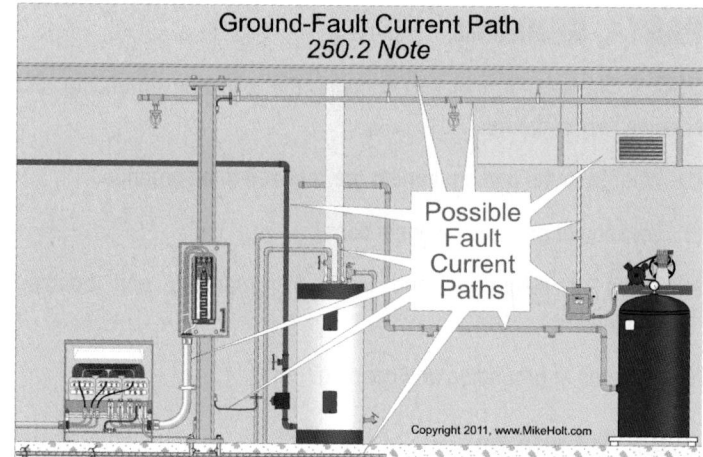

Figure 250–5

Author's Comment: The difference between an "effective ground-fault current path" and a "ground-fault current path" is the effective ground-fault current path is "intentionally" constructed to provide a low-impedance fault current path to the electrical supply source for the purpose of clearing a ground fault. A ground-fault current path is all of the available conductive paths over which fault current flows on its return to the electrical supply source during a ground fault.

250.4 General Requirements for Grounding and Bonding.

(A) Solidly Grounded Systems.

(1) Electrical System Grounding. Electrical power systems, such as the secondary winding of a transformer are grounded (connected to the earth) to limit the voltage induced by lightning, line surges, or unintentional contact by higher-voltage lines. **Figure 250–6**

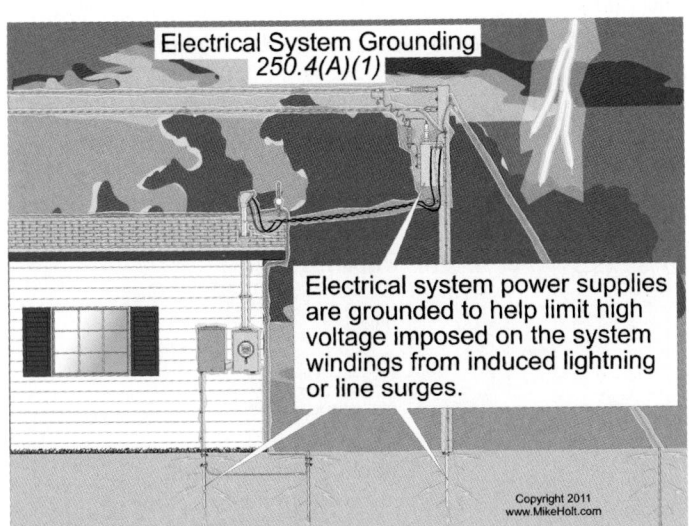

Figure 250–6

Author's Comment: System grounding helps reduce fires in buildings as well as voltage stress on electrical insulation, thereby ensuring longer insulation life for motors, transformers, and other system components. **Figure 250–7**

Note: An important consideration for limiting imposed voltage is to remember that grounding electrode conductors shouldn't be any longer than necessary and unnecessary bends and loops should be avoided. **Figure 250–8**

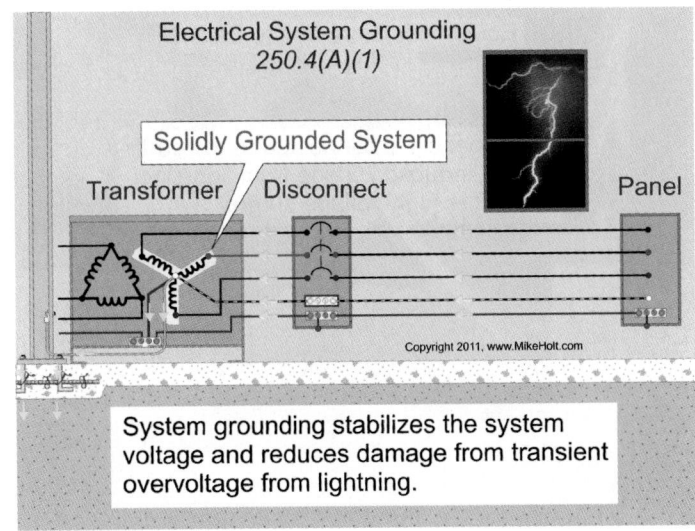

Figure 250–7

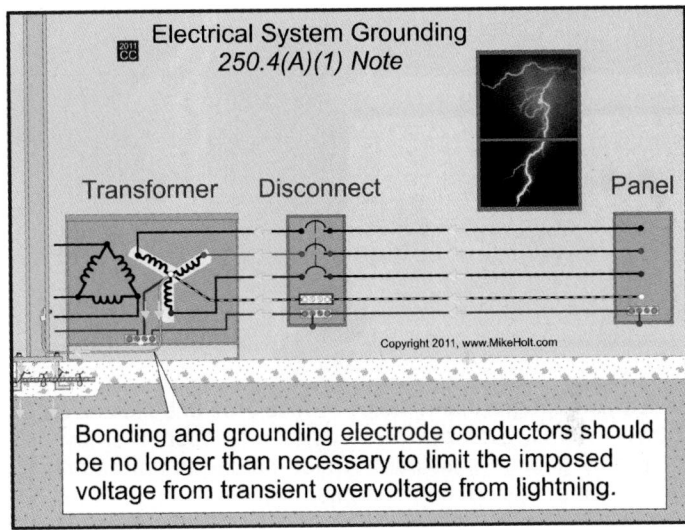

Figure 250–8

(2) Equipment Grounding. Metal parts of electrical equipment are grounded (connected to the earth) to reduce induced voltage on metal parts from exterior lightning so as to prevent fires from an arc within the building/structure. **Figure 250–9**

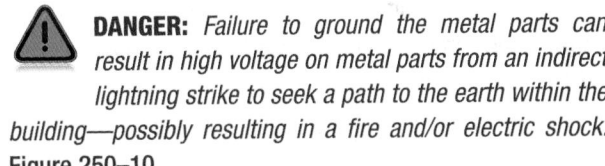 **DANGER:** *Failure to ground the metal parts can result in high voltage on metal parts from an indirect lightning strike to seek a path to the earth within the building—possibly resulting in a fire and/or electric shock.* **Figure 250–10**

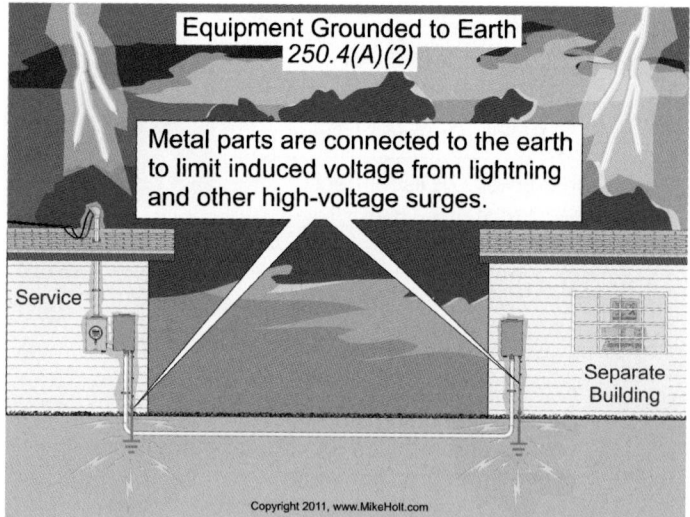

Figure 250–9

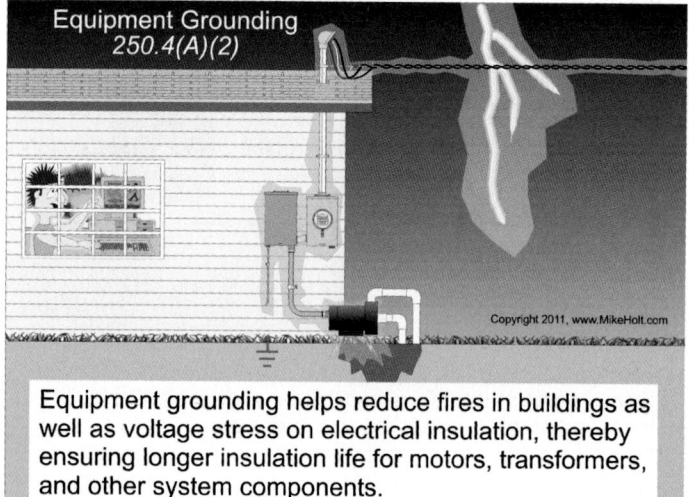

Figure 250–10

Author's Comment: Grounding metal parts helps drain off static electricity charges before flashover potential is reached. Static grounding is often used in areas where the discharge (arcing) of the voltage buildup (static) can cause dangerous or undesirable conditions [500.4 Note 3].

⚠ **DANGER:** *Because the contact resistance of an electrode to the earth is so high, very little fault current returns to the power supply if the earth is the only fault current return path. Result—the circuit overcurrent device won't open and clear the ground fault, and all metal parts associated with the electrical installation, metal piping, and structural building steel will become and remain energized.* Figure 250–11

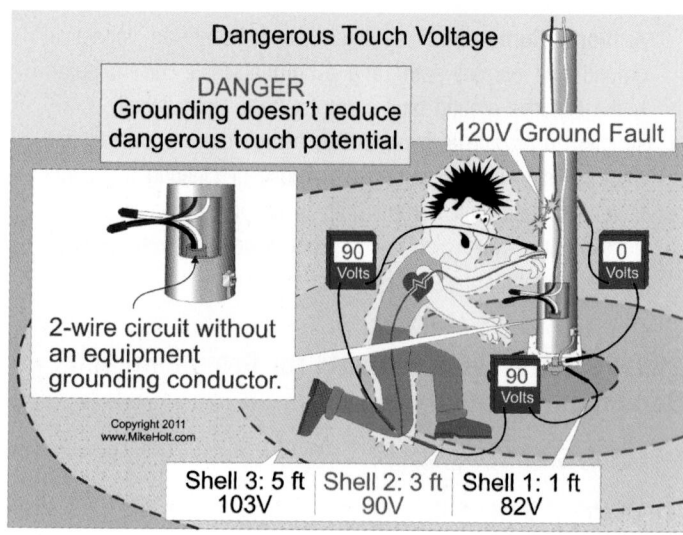

Figure 250–11

(3) Equipment Bonding. Metal parts of electrical raceways, cables, enclosures, and equipment must be connected to the supply source via the effective ground-fault current path. **Figures 250–12 and 250–13**

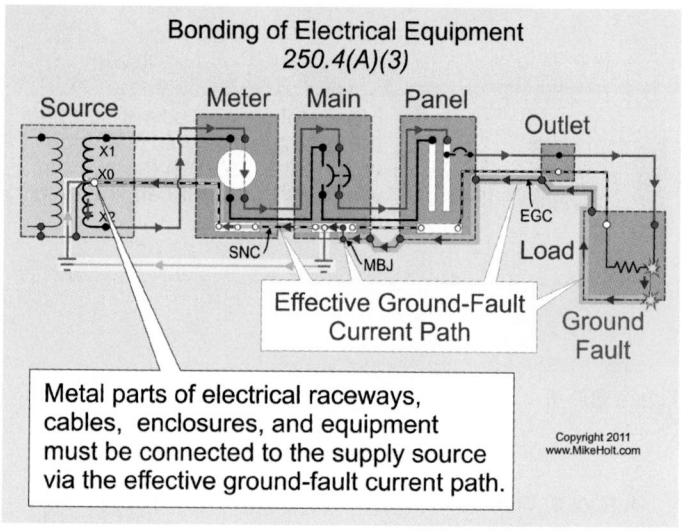

Figure 250–12

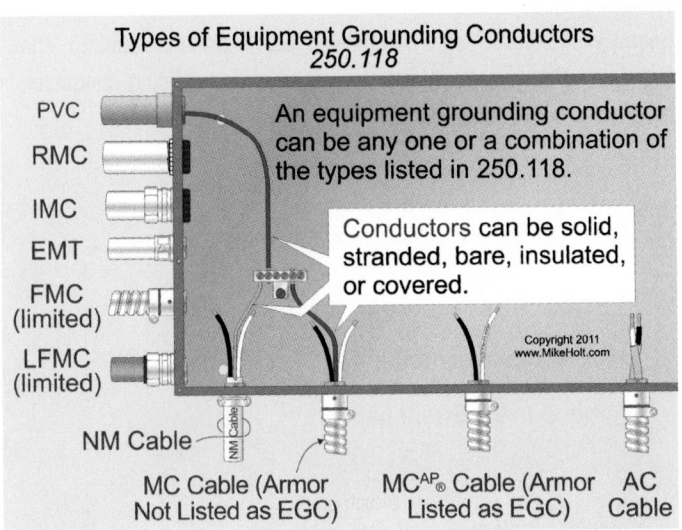

Figure 250–13

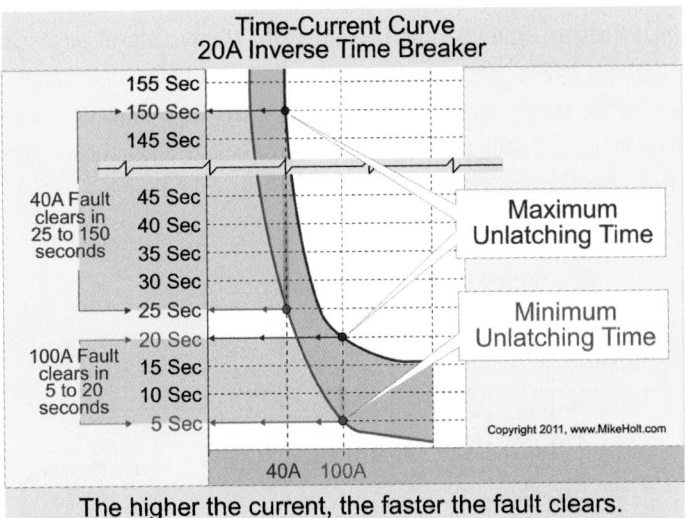

The higher the current, the faster the fault clears.

Figure 250–15

Author's Comments:

- To quickly remove dangerous touch voltage on metal parts from a ground fault, the fault current path must have sufficiently low impedance to the source so that fault current will quickly rise to a level that will open the branch-circuit overcurrent device. **Figure 250–14**

- The time it takes for an overcurrent device to open is inversely proportional to the magnitude of the fault current. This means the higher the ground-fault current value, the less time it will take for the overcurrent device to open and clear the fault. For example, a 20A circuit with an overload of 40A (two times the 20A rating) takes 25 to 150 seconds to open the overcurrent device. At 100A (five times the 20A rating) the 20A breaker trips in 5 to 20 seconds. **Figure 250–15**

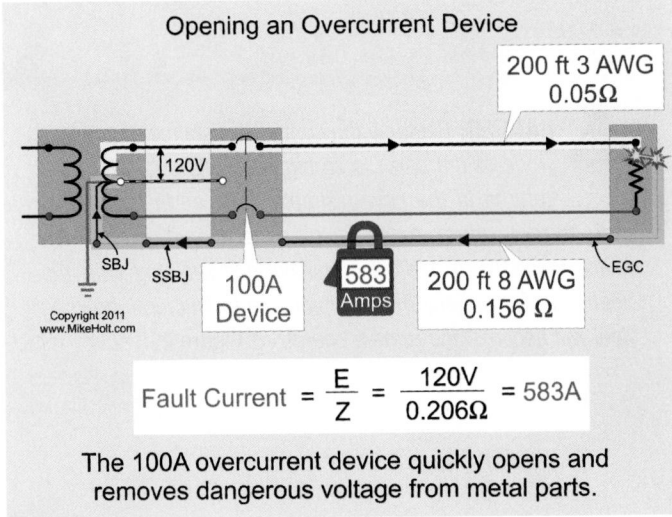

The 100A overcurrent device quickly opens and removes dangerous voltage from metal parts.

Figure 250–14

(4) Bonding Conductive Materials. Electrically conductive materials such as metal water piping systems, metal sprinkler piping, metal gas piping, and other metal-piping systems, as well as exposed structural steel members likely to become energized, must be connected to the supply source via an equipment grounding conductor of a type recognized in 250.118. **Figure 250–16**

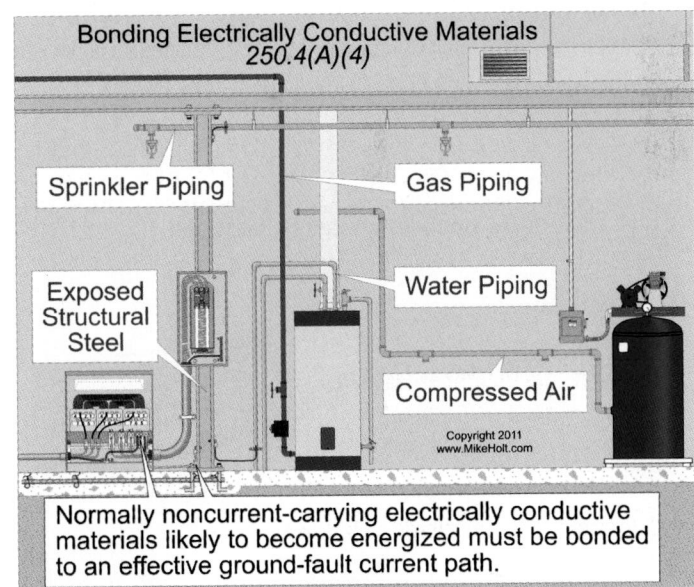

Figure 250–16

Author's Comment: The phrase "likely to become energized" is subject to interpretation by the authority having jurisdiction.

(5) Effective Ground-Fault Current Path. Metal parts of electrical raceways, cables, enclosures, or equipment must be bonded together and to the supply system in a manner that creates a low-impedance path for ground-fault current that facilitates the operation of the circuit overcurrent device. **Figure 250–17**

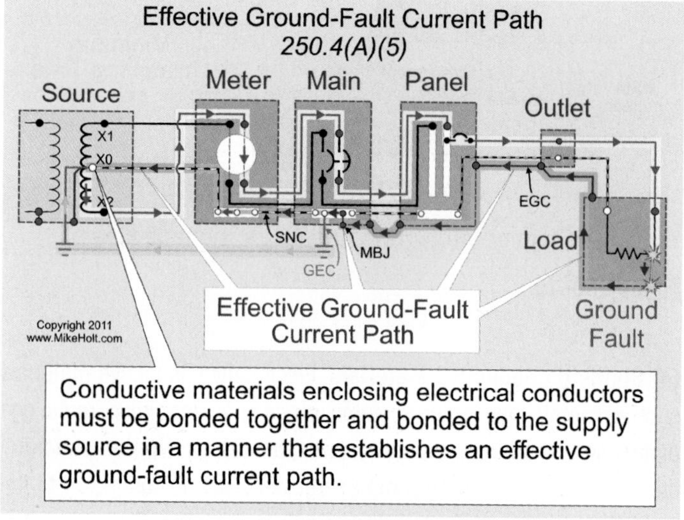

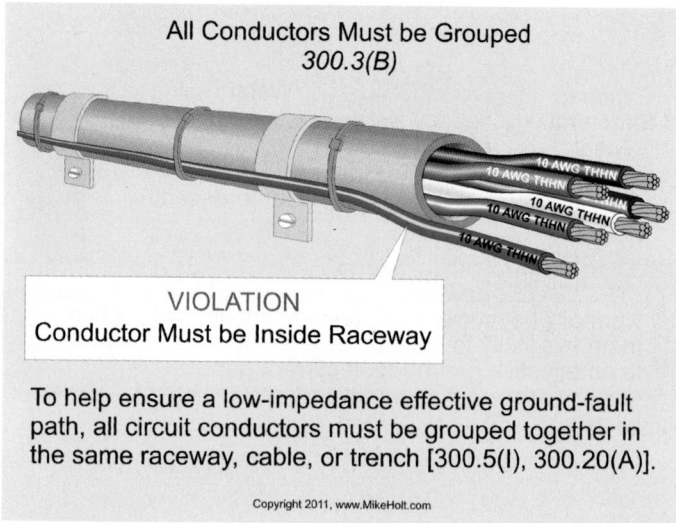

Figure 250–17

Author's Comment: To ensure a low-impedance ground-fault current path, all circuit conductors must be grouped together in the same raceway, cable, or trench [300.3(B), 300.5(I), and 300.20(A)]. **Figure 250–18**

All Conductors Must be Grouped
300.3(B)

VIOLATION
Conductor Must be Inside Raceway

To help ensure a low-impedance effective ground-fault path, all circuit conductors must be grouped together in the same raceway, cable, or trench [300.5(I), 300.20(A)].

Copyright 2011, www.MikeHolt.com

Figure 250–18

Because the earth isn't suitable to serve as the required effective ground-fault current path, an equipment grounding conductor is required to be installed with all circuits. **Figure 250–19**

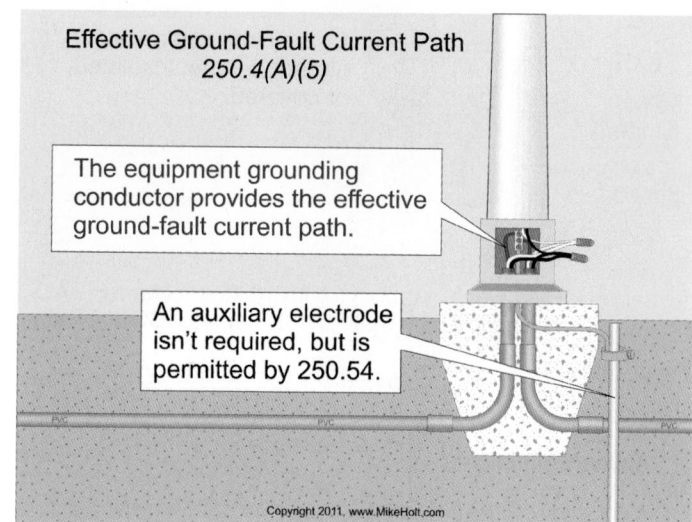

Figure 250–19

> **Question:** What's the maximum fault current that can flow through the earth to the power supply from a 120V ground fault to metal parts of a light pole that's grounded (connected to the earth) via a ground rod having a contact resistance to the earth of 25 ohms? **Figure 250–20**
>
> (a) 4.80A   (b) 20A   (c) 40A   (d) 100A
>
> **Answer:** (a) 4.80A
>
> I = E/R
>
> I = 120V/25 ohms
>
> I = 4.80A

⚠ **DANGER:** Because the contact resistance of an electrode to the earth is so high, very little fault current returns to the power supply if the earth is the only fault current return path. Result—the circuit overcurrent device won't open and all metal parts associated with the electrical installation, metal piping, and structural building steel will become and remain energized. **Figure 250–21**

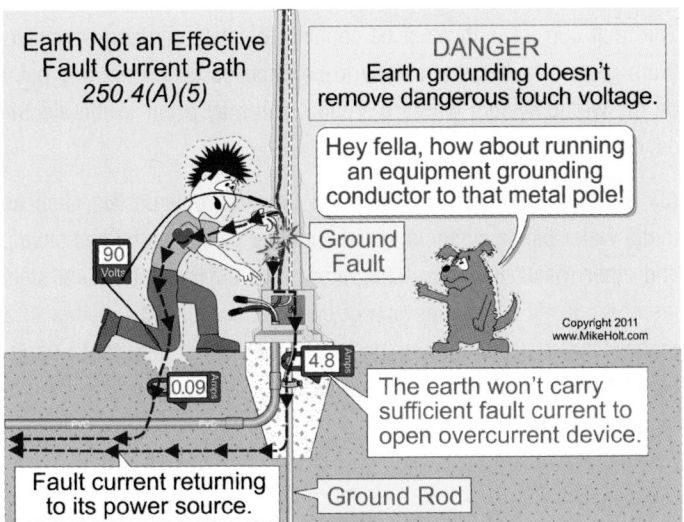

Figure 250–20

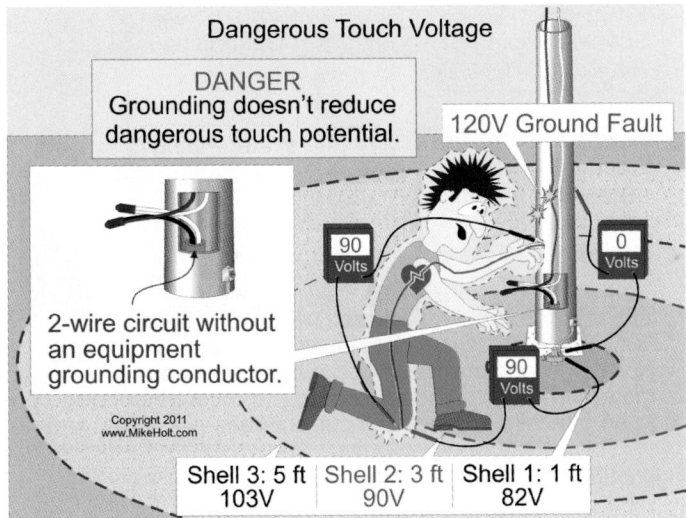

Figure 250–21

EARTH SHELLS

According to ANSI/IEEE 142, *Recommended Practice for Grounding of Industrial and Commercial Power Systems* (Green Book) [4.1.1], the resistance of the soil outward from a ground rod is equal to the sum of the series resistances of the earth shells. The shell nearest the rod has the highest resistance and each successive shell has progressively larger areas and progressively lower resistances. Don't be concerned if you don't understand this statement; just review the table below. **Figure 250–22**

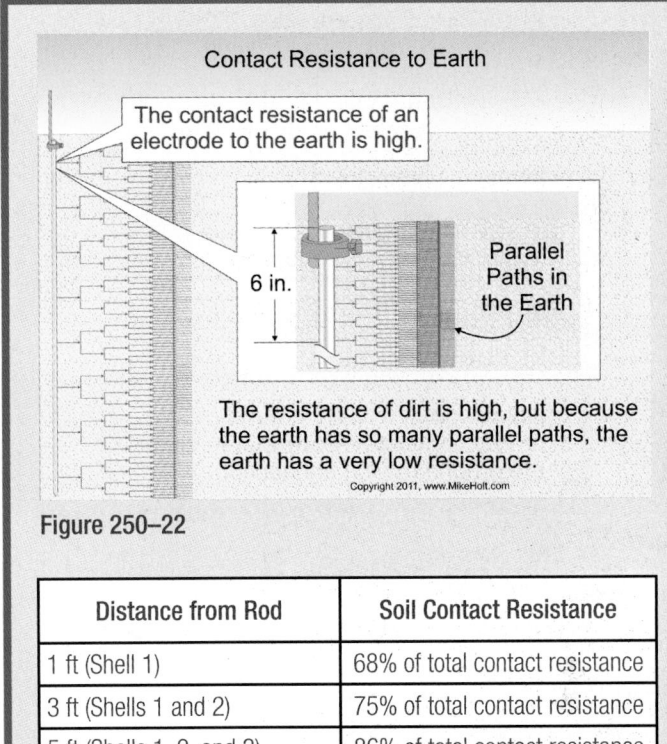

Figure 250–22

Distance from Rod	Soil Contact Resistance
1 ft (Shell 1)	68% of total contact resistance
3 ft (Shells 1 and 2)	75% of total contact resistance
5 ft (Shells 1, 2, and 3)	86% of total contact resistance

Since voltage is directly proportional to resistance, the voltage gradient of the earth around an energized ground rod will be as follows, assuming a 120V ground fault:

Distance from Rod	Soil Contact Resistance	Voltage Gradient
1 ft (Shell 1)	68%	82V
3 ft (Shells 1 and 2)	75%	90V
5 ft (Shells 1, 2, and 3)	86%	103V

(B) Ungrounded Systems.

Author's Comment: Ungrounded systems are those systems with no connection to the ground or to a conductive body that extends the ground connection [Article 100]. **Figure 250–23**

(1) Equipment Grounding. Metal parts of electrical equipment are grounded (connected to the earth) to reduce induced voltage on metal parts from exterior lightning so as to prevent fires from an arc within the building/structure. **Figure 250–24**

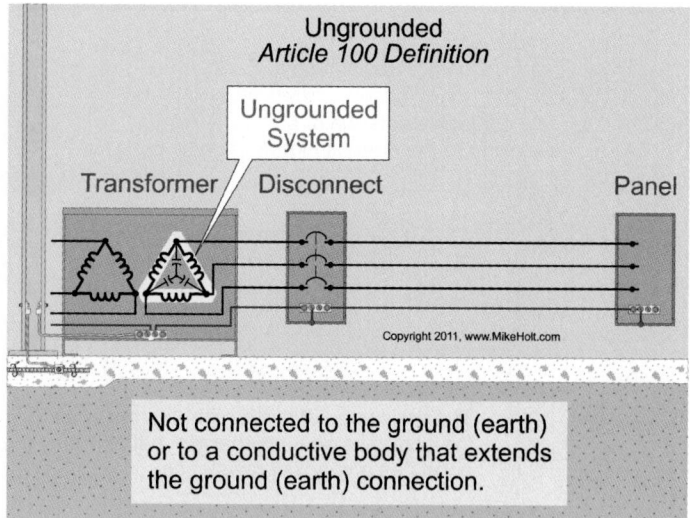

Figure 250–23

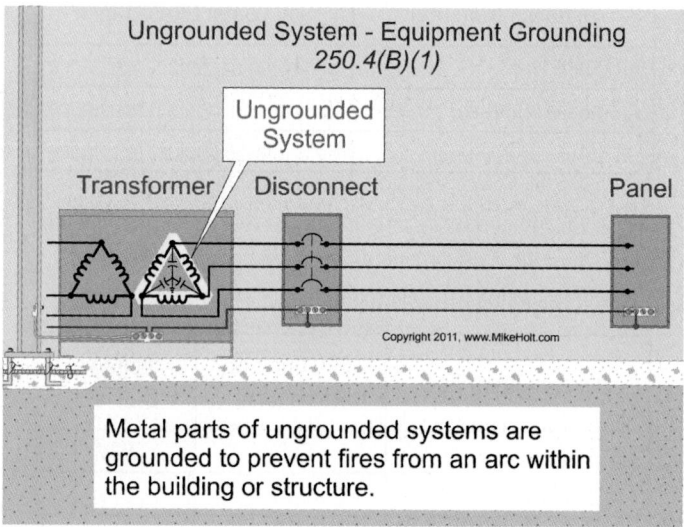

Figure 250–24

Author's Comment: Grounding metal parts helps drain off static electricity charges before an electric arc takes place (flashover potential). Static grounding is often used in areas where the discharge (arcing) of the voltage buildup (static) can cause dangerous or undesirable conditions [500.4 Note 3].

 CAUTION: *Connecting metal parts to the earth (grounding) serves no purpose in electrical shock protection.*

(2) Equipment Bonding. Metal parts of electrical raceways, cables, enclosures, or equipment must be bonded together in a manner that creates a low-impedance path for ground-fault current to facilitate the operation of the circuit overcurrent device.

The fault current path must be capable of safely carrying the maximum ground-fault current likely to be imposed on it from any point on the wiring system where a ground fault may occur to the electrical supply source.

(3) Bonding Conductive Materials. Conductive materials such as metal water piping systems, metal sprinkler piping, metal gas piping, and other metal-piping systems, as well as exposed structural steel members likely to become energized must be bonded together in a manner that creates a low-impedance fault current path that's capable of carrying the maximum fault current likely to be imposed on it. Figure 250–25

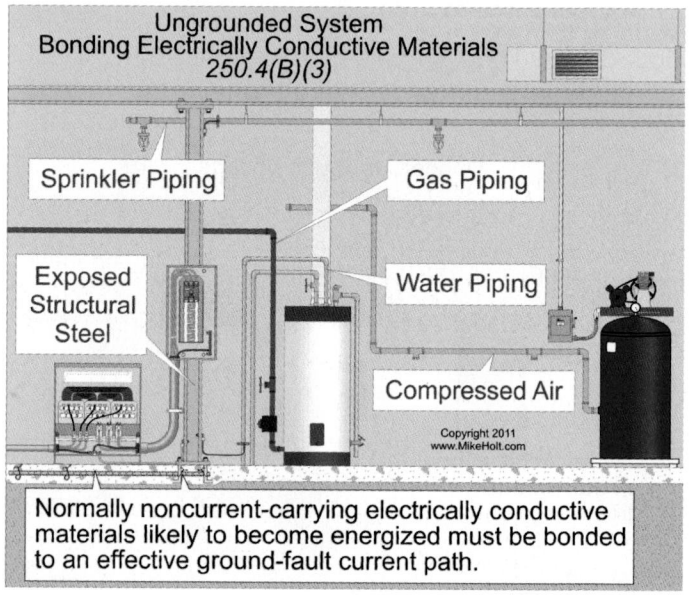

Figure 250–25

Author's Comment: The phrase "likely to become energized" is subject to interpretation by the authority having jurisdiction.

(4) Fault Current Path. Electrical equipment, wiring, and other electrically conductive material likely to become energized must be installed in a manner that creates a low-impedance fault current path to facilitate the operation of overcurrent devices should a second ground fault from a different phase occur. Figure 250–26

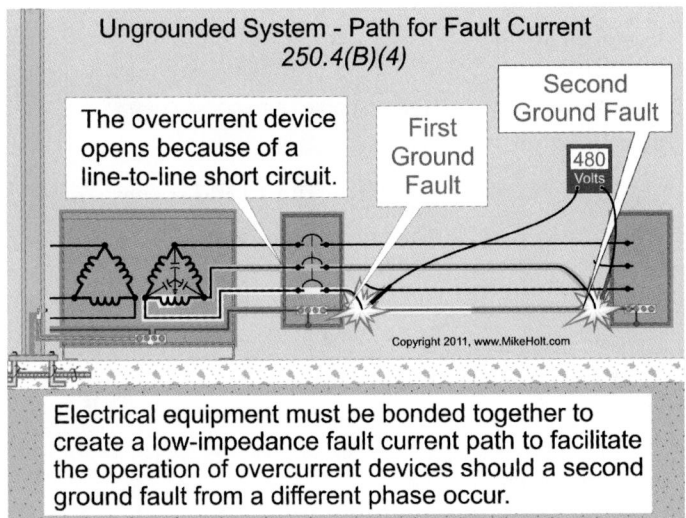

Figure 250–26

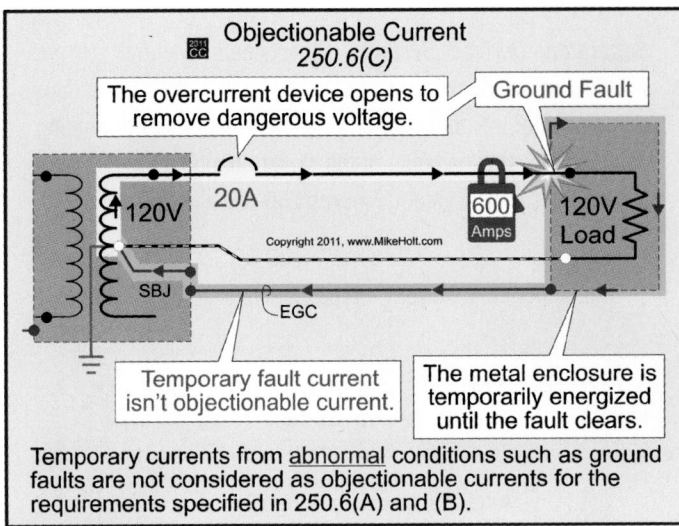

Figure 250–27

Author's Comment: A single ground fault can't be cleared on an ungrounded system because there's no low-impedance fault current path to the power source. The first ground fault simply grounds the previously ungrounded system. However, a second ground fault on a different phase results in a line-to-line short circuit between the two ground faults. The conductive path, between the ground faults, provides the low-impedance fault current path necessary so the overcurrent device will open.

250.6 Objectionable Current.

(A) Preventing Objectionable Current. To prevent a fire, electric shock, or improper operation of circuit overcurrent devices or electronic equipment, electrical systems and equipment must be installed in a manner that prevents objectionable neutral current from flowing on metal parts.

(C) Temporary Currents Not Classified as Objectionable Currents. Temporary currents from <u>abnormal</u> conditions, such as ground faults, aren't to be classified as objectionable current. **Figure 250–27**

(D) Limitations to Permissible Alterations. Currents that introduce noise or data errors in electronic equipment are not considered objectionable currents for the purposes of this section. Circuits that supply electronic equipment must be connected to an equipment grounding conductor.

OBJECTIONABLE CURRENT

Objectionable neutral current occurs because of improper neutral-to-case connections or wiring errors that violate 250.142(B).

Improper Neutral-to-Case Connection [250.142]

Panelboards. Objectionable neutral current will flow when the neutral conductor is connected to the metal case of a panelboard that's not used as service equipment. **Figure 250–28**

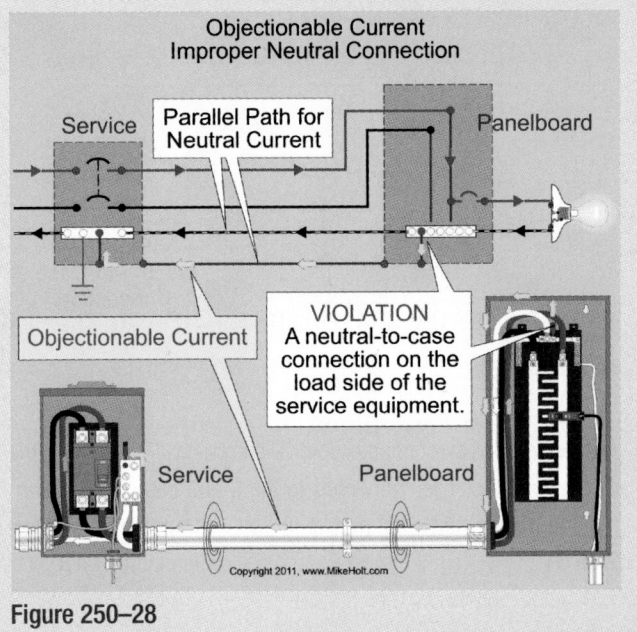

Figure 250–28

Separately Derived Systems. Objectionable neutral current will flow on conductive metal parts and conductors if the neutral conductor is connected to the circuit equipment grounding conductor on the load side of the system bonding jumper for a separately derived system. **Figures 250–29 and 250–30**

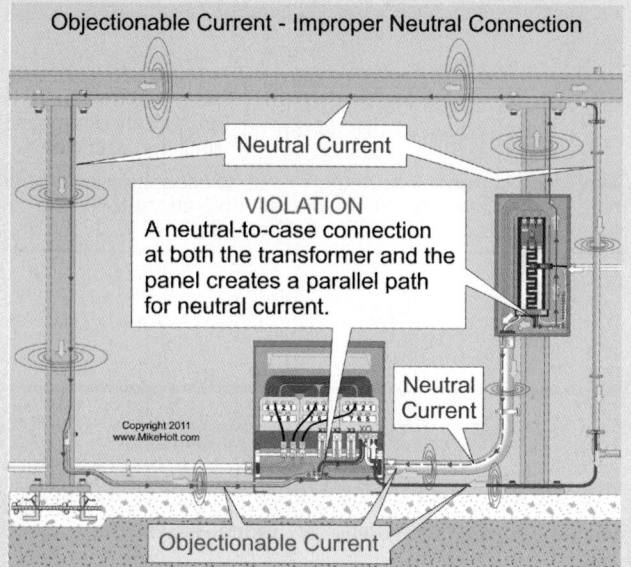

Figure 250–29

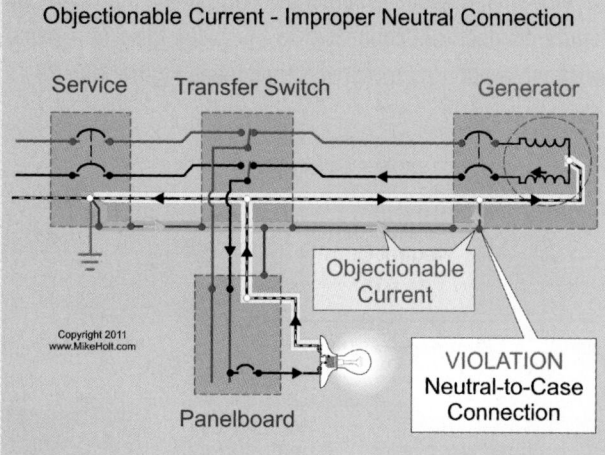

Figure 250-30

Disconnects. Objectionable neutral current will flow when the neutral conductor is connected to the metal case of a disconnecting means that's not part of the service equipment. **Figure 250–31**

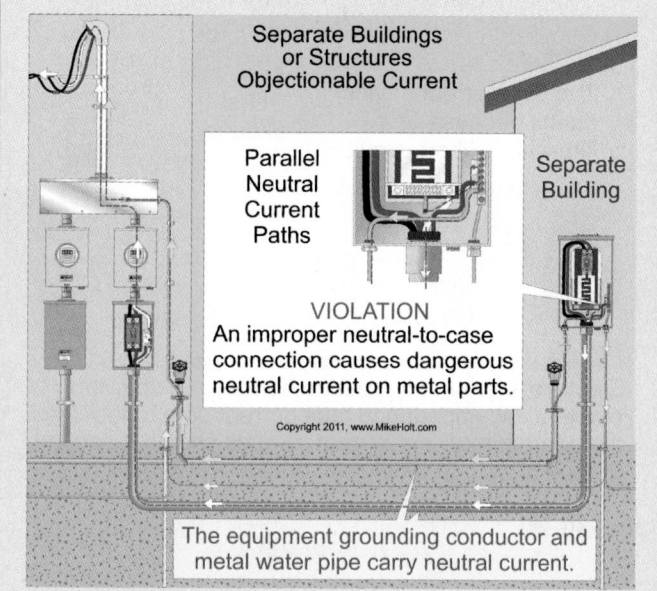

Figure 250–31

Wiring Errors. Objectionable neutral current will flow when the neutral conductor from one system is connected to a circuit of a different system. **Figure 250–32**

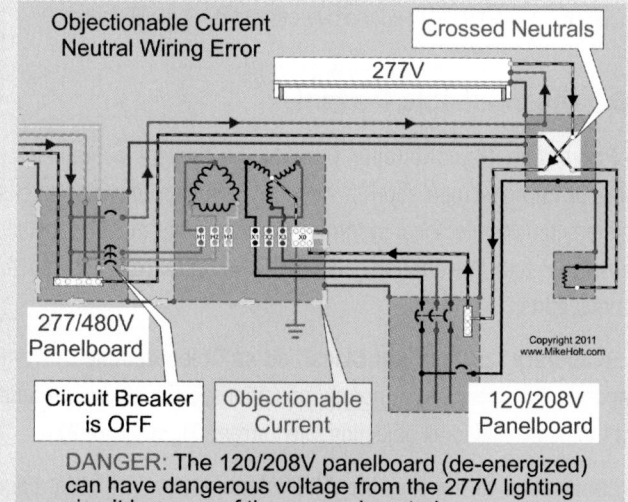

Figure 250–32

Objectionable neutral current will flow on metal parts when the circuit equipment grounding conductor is used as a neutral conductor such as where:

- A 230V time-clock motor is replaced with a 115V time-clock motor, and the circuit equipment grounding conductor is used for neutral return current.

- A 115V water filter is wired to a 240V well-pump motor circuit, and the circuit equipment grounding conductor is used for neutral return current. **Figure 250–33**

- The circuit equipment grounding conductor is used for neutral return current. **Figure 250–34**

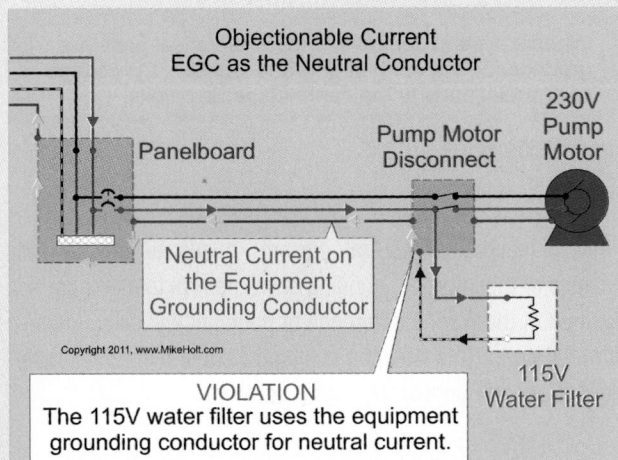

Figure 250–33

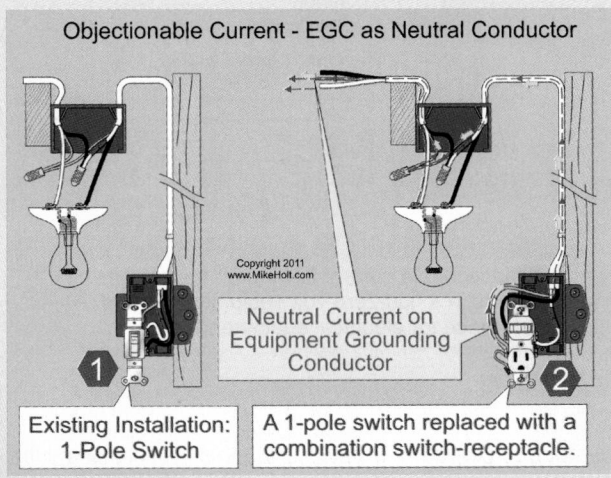

Figure 250–34

DANGERS OF OBJECTIONABLE CURRENT

Objectionable neutral current on metal parts can cause electric shock, fires, and improper operation of electronic equipment and overcurrent devices such as GFPs, GFCIs, and AFCIs.

Shock Hazard. When objectionable neutral current flows on metal parts, electric shock and even death can occur from the elevated voltage on those metal parts. **Figures 250–35 and 250–36**

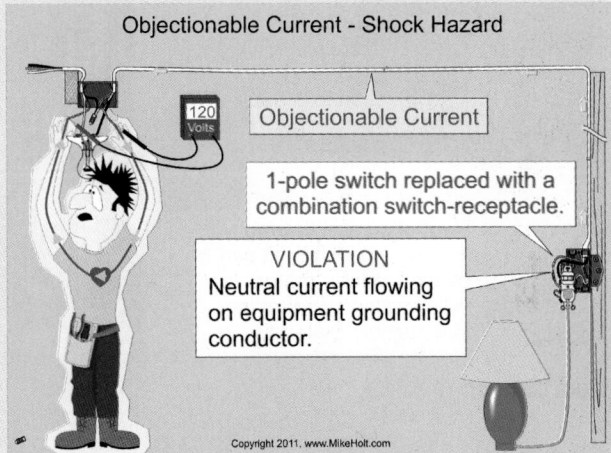

Figure 250–35

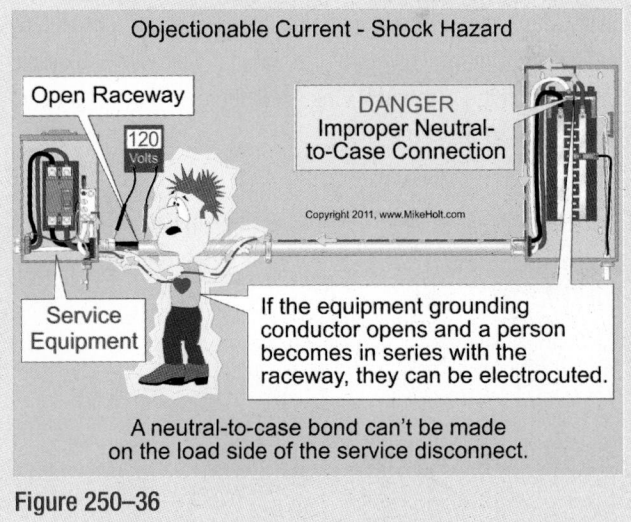

Figure 250–36

Fire Hazard. When objectionable neutral current flows on metal parts, a fire can ignite adjacent combustible material. Heat is generated whenever current flows, particularly over high-resistance parts. In addition, arcing at loose connections is especially dangerous in areas containing easily ignitible and explosive gases, vapors, or dust. **Figure 250–37**

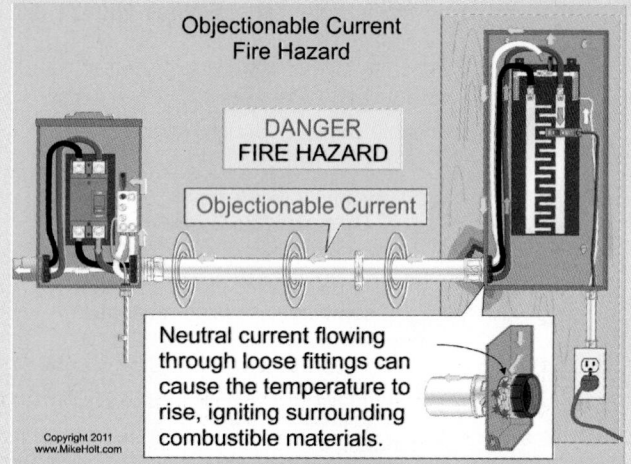

Figure 250–37

Improper Operation of Electronic Equipment. Objectionable neutral current flowing on metal parts of electrical equipment and building parts can cause electromagnetic fields which negatively affect the performance of electronic devices, particularly medical equipment. For more information, visit www.MikeHolt.com, click on the "Technical Link," and then on "Power Quality." **Figure 250–38**

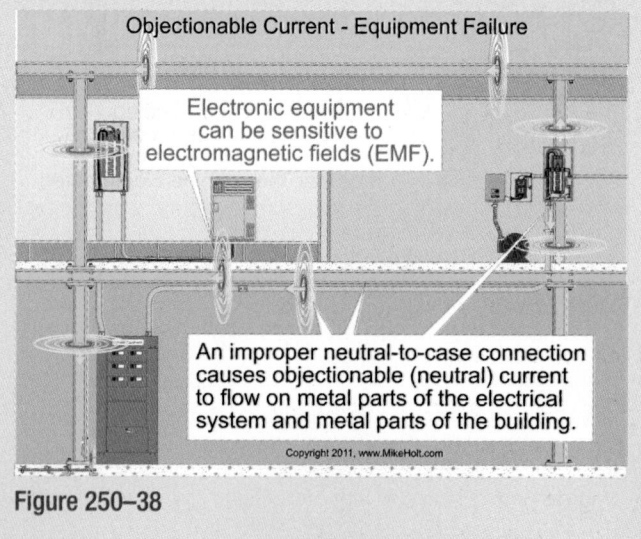

Figure 250–38

When a system is properly grounded and bonded, the voltage of all metal parts to the earth and to each other will be zero. **Figure 250–39**

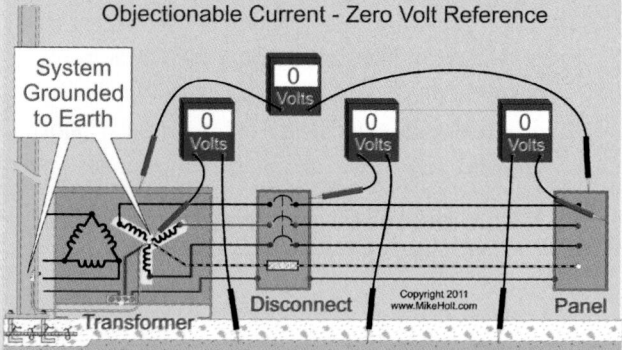

Figure 250–39

When objectionable neutral current travels on metal parts because of the improper bonding of the neutral to metal parts in violation of the *NEC*, a difference of potential will exist between all metal parts. This situation can cause some electronic equipment to operate improperly. **Figure 250–40**

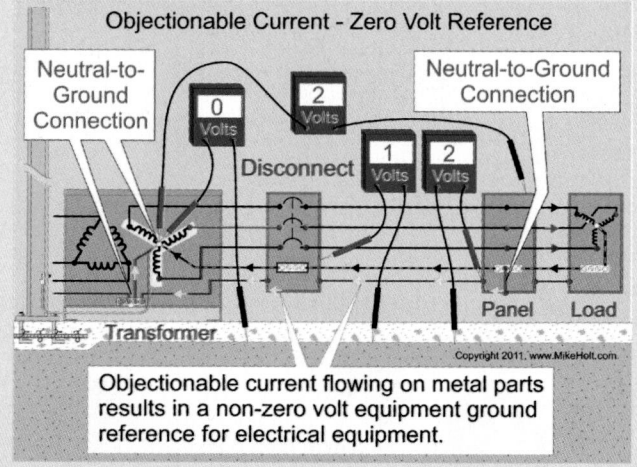

Figure 250–40

Operation of Overcurrent Devices. When objectionable neutral current travels on metal parts, tripping of electronic overcurrent devices equipped with ground-fault protection can occur because some neutral current flows on the circuit equipment grounding conductor instead of the neutral conductor.

250.8 Termination of Grounding and Bonding Conductors.

(A) Permitted Methods. <u>Equipment</u> grounding conductors, <u>grounding electrode conductors,</u> and bonding jumpers must terminate in one of the following methods:

(1) Listed pressure connectors

(2) Terminal bars

(3) Pressure connectors listed for direct burial or concrete encasement [250.70]

(4) Exothermic welding

(5) Machine screws that engage at least two threads or are secured with a nut. **Figure 250–41**

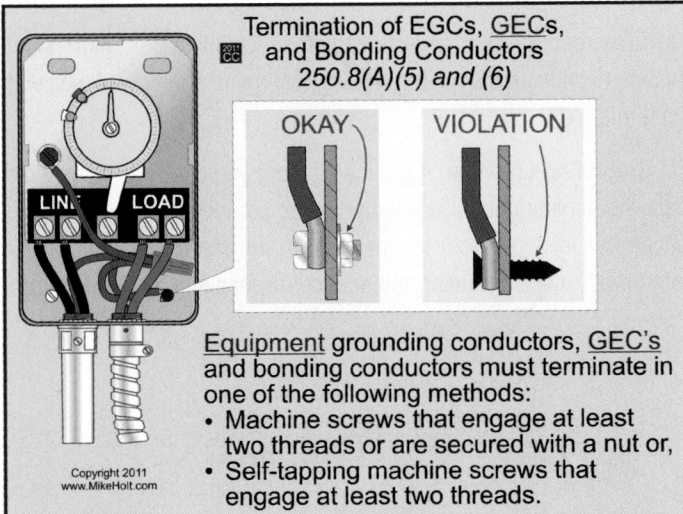

Termination of EGCs, <u>GEC</u>s, and Bonding Conductors
250.8(A)(5) and (6)

OKAY   VIOLATION

<u>Equipment</u> grounding conductors, <u>GEC's</u> and bonding conductors must terminate in one of the following methods:
• Machine screws that engage at least two threads or are secured with a nut or,
• Self-tapping machine screws that engage at least two threads.

Copyright 2011 www.MikeHolt.com

Figure 250–41

(6) Self-tapping machine screws that engage at least two threads

(7) Connections that are part of a listed assembly

(8) Other listed means

(B) Methods Not Permitted. Connection devices or fittings that depend solely on solder aren't allowed.

250.10 Protection of Fittings. Grounding and bonding fittings must be protected from physical damage by:

(1) Locating the fittings so they aren't likely to be damaged.

(2) Enclosing the fittings in metal, wood, or an equivalent protective covering.

Author's Comment: Grounding and bonding fittings can be buried or encased in concrete if they're installed in accordance with 250.53(G), 250.68(A) Ex 1, and 250.70.

250.12 Clean Surfaces. Nonconductive coatings, such as paint, must be removed to ensure good electrical continuity, or the termination fittings must be designed so as to make such removal unnecessary [250.53(A) and 250.96(A)].

Author's Comment: Tarnish on copper water pipe need not be removed before making a termination.

PART II. SYSTEM GROUNDING AND BONDING

250.20 Systems Required to be Grounded.

(A) Systems Below 50V. Systems operating below 50V aren't required to be grounded or bonded in accordance with 250.30 unless the transformer's primary supply is from: **Figure 250–42**

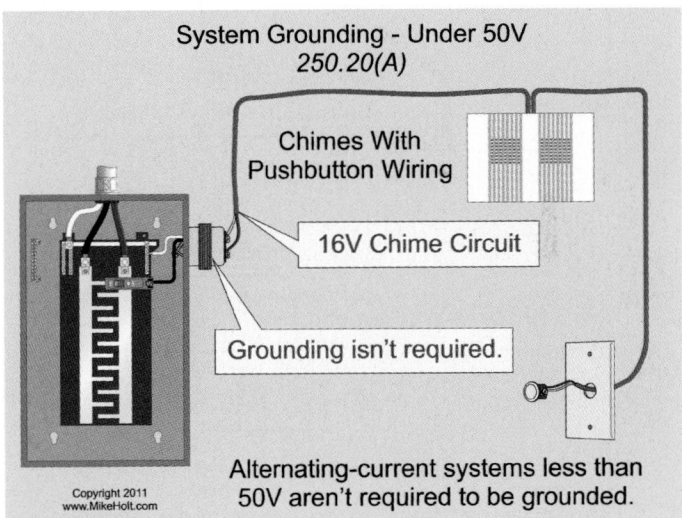

System Grounding - Under 50V
250.20(A)

Chimes With Pushbutton Wiring

16V Chime Circuit

Grounding isn't required.

Copyright 2011 www.MikeHolt.com

Alternating-current systems less than 50V aren't required to be grounded.

Figure 250–42

(1) A 277V or 480V system.

(2) An ungrounded system.

(B) Systems Over 50V. The following systems must be grounded (connected to the earth):

(1) Single-phase systems where the neutral conductor is used as a circuit conductor. **Figure 250–43**

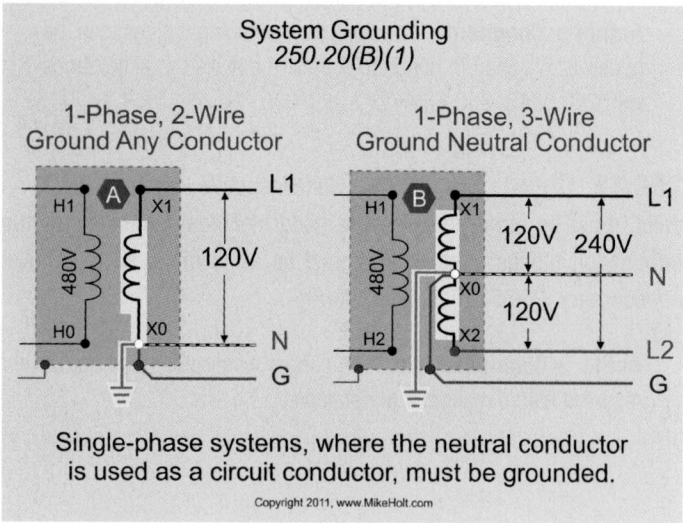

Figure 250–43

(2) Three-phase, wye-connected systems where the neutral conductor is used as a circuit conductor. **Figure 250–44A**

(3) Three-phase, high-leg delta-connected systems where the neutral conductor is used as a circuit conductor. **Figure 250–44B**

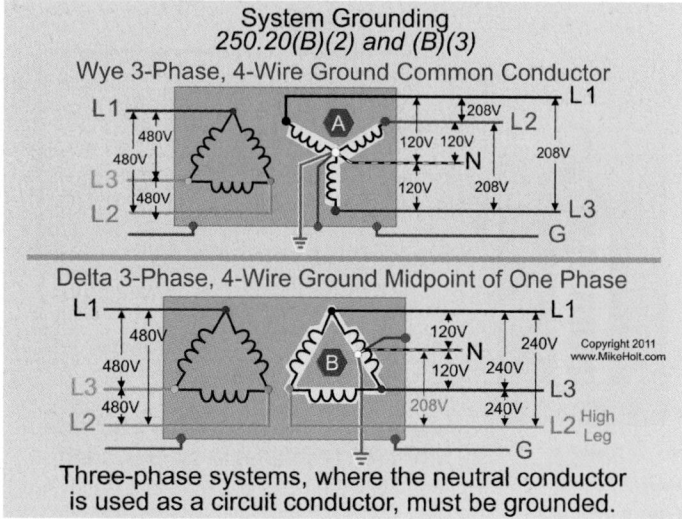

Figure 250–44

250.21 Ungrounded Systems—50V to Less Than 100V.

(B) Ground Detectors.

(1) Systems that aren't required to be grounded in accordance with 250.20(B) [250.21(A)(4)] must have ground detectors installed.

(2) The ground detection sensing equipment must be connected as close as practicable to where the system receives its supply.

(C) Marking. Ungrounded systems must be legibly marked "Ungrounded System" at the source or first disconnecting means of the system, with sufficient durability to withstand the environment involved.

250.24 Service Equipment—Grounding and Bonding.

(A) Grounded System. Service equipment supplied from a grounded system must have the neutral conductor terminate in accordance with (1) through (5).

(1) Grounding Location. A grounding electrode conductor must connect the service neutral conductor to the grounding electrode at any accessible location, from the load end of the service drop or service lateral, up to and including the service disconnecting means. **Figure 250–45**

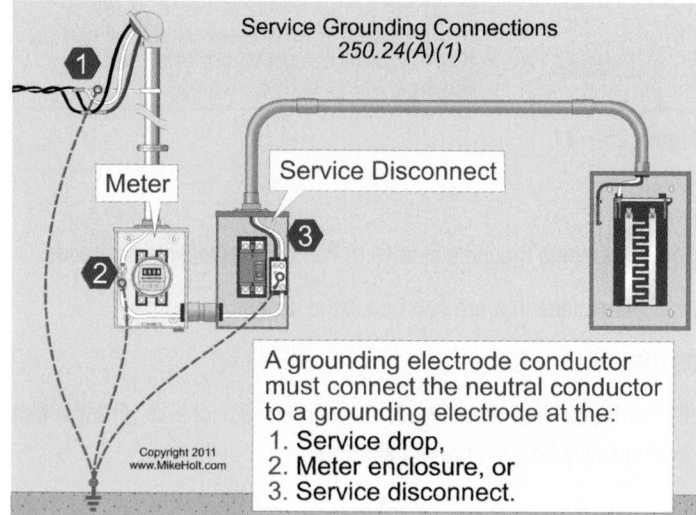

Figure 250–45

Author's Comment: Some inspectors require the service neutral conductor to be grounded (connected to the earth) from the meter socket enclosure, while other inspectors insist that the service neutral conductor be grounded (connected to the earth) only from the service disconnect.

(4) Grounding Termination. When the service neutral conductor is connected to the service disconnecting means [250.24(B)] by a wire or busbar [250.28], the grounding electrode conductor is permitted to terminate to either the neutral terminal or the equipment grounding terminal within the service disconnect.

(5) Neutral-to-Case Connection. A neutral-to-case connection isn't permitted on the load side of service equipment, except as permitted by 250.142(B). **Figure 250–46**

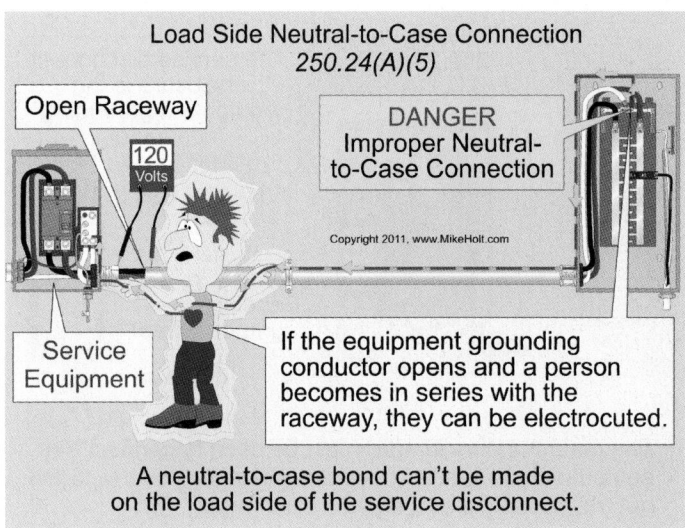

Load Side Neutral-to-Case Connection
250.24(A)(5)

Open Raceway

DANGER
Improper Neutral-to-Case Connection

120 Volts

Copyright 2011, www.MikeHolt.com

Service Equipment

If the equipment grounding conductor opens and a person becomes in series with the raceway, they can be electrocuted.

A neutral-to-case bond can't be made on the load side of the service disconnect.

Figure 250–47

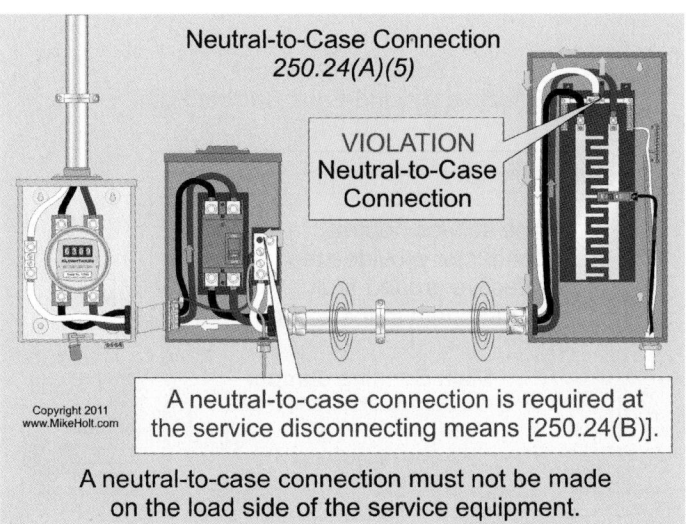

Neutral-to-Case Connection
250.24(A)(5)

VIOLATION
Neutral-to-Case Connection

Copyright 2011
www.MikeHolt.com

A neutral-to-case connection is required at the service disconnecting means [250.24(B)].

A neutral-to-case connection must not be made on the load side of the service equipment.

Figure 250–46

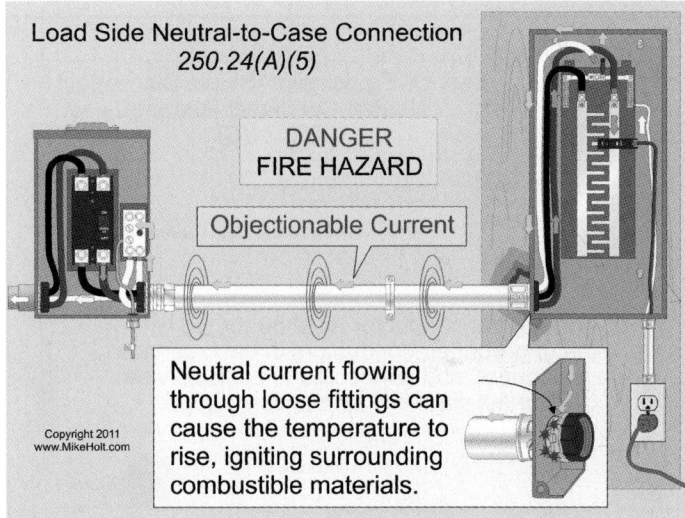

Load Side Neutral-to-Case Connection
250.24(A)(5)

DANGER
FIRE HAZARD

Objectionable Current

Copyright 2011
www.MikeHolt.com

Neutral current flowing through loose fittings can cause the temperature to rise, igniting surrounding combustible materials.

Figure 250–48

Author's Comment: If a neutral-to-case connection is made on the load side of service equipment, dangerous objectionable neutral current will flow on conductive metal parts of electrical equipment [250.6(A)]. Objectionable neutral current on metal parts of electrical equipment can cause electric shock and even death from ventricular fibrillation, as well as a fire. **Figures 250–47 and 250–48**

(B) Bonding. A main bonding jumper [250.28] must be installed for the purpose of connecting the neutral conductor to the metal parts of the service disconnecting means. **Figure 250–49**

(C) Grounded Conductor Brought to Service Equipment. A service neutral conductor from the electric utility must be routed with the ungrounded conductors and terminate to the service disconnecting means via a main bonding jumper [250.24(B)] that's installed between the service neutral conductor and the service disconnecting means enclosure [250.28]. **Figures 250–50 and 250–51**

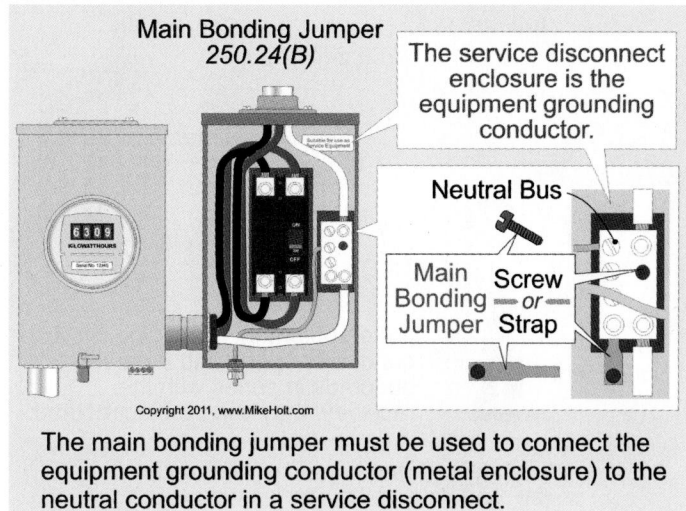

Figure 250–49

The main bonding jumper must be used to connect the equipment grounding conductor (metal enclosure) to the neutral conductor in a service disconnect.

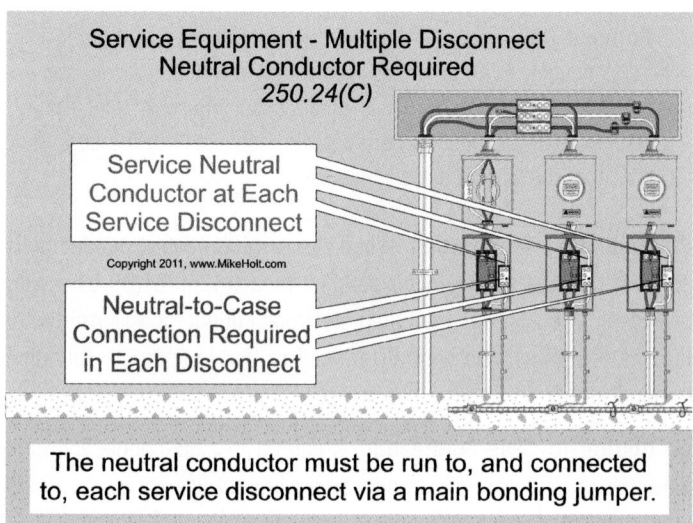

Figure 250–51

The neutral conductor must be run to, and connected to, each service disconnect via a main bonding jumper.

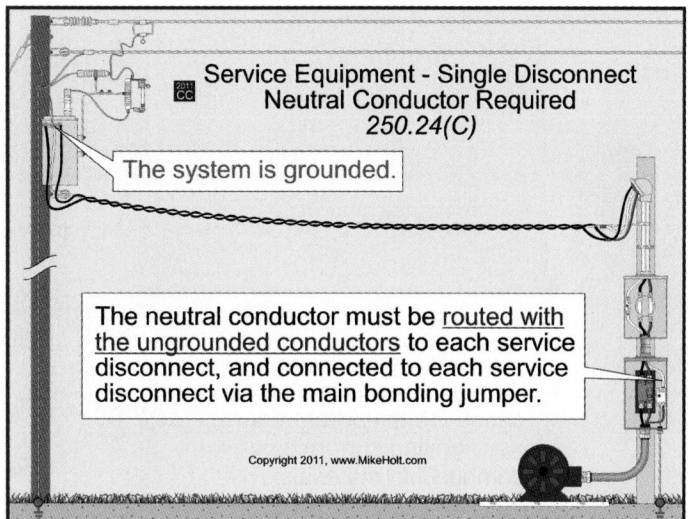

Figure 250–50

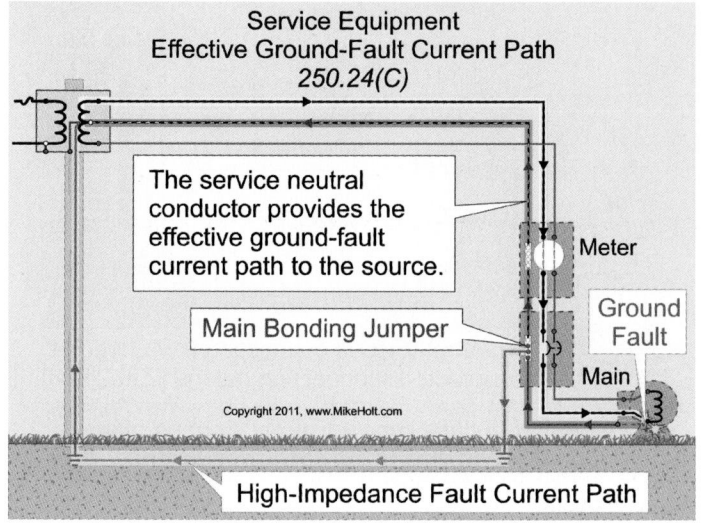

Figure 250–52

Author's Comment: The service neutral conductor provides the effective ground-fault current path to the power supply to ensure that dangerous voltage from a ground fault will be quickly removed by opening the overcurrent device [250.4(A)(3) and 250.4(A)(5)]. **Figure 250–52**

⚠ **DANGER:** *Dangerous voltage from a ground fault won't be removed from metal parts, metal piping, and structural steel if the service disconnecting means enclosure isn't connected to the service neutral conductor. This is because the contact resistance of a grounding electrode to the earth is so great that insufficient fault current returns to the power supply if the earth is the only fault current return path to open the circuit overcurrent device.* **Figure 250–53**

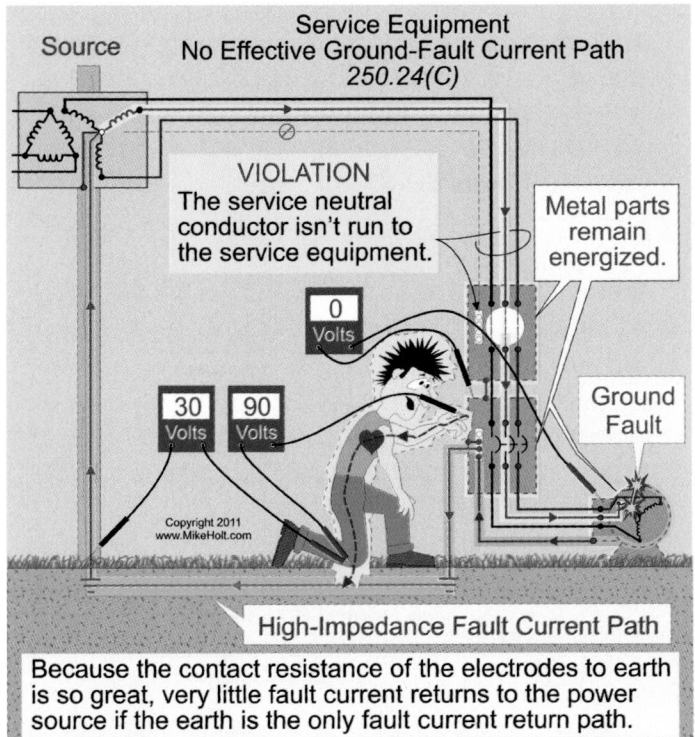

Figure 250–53

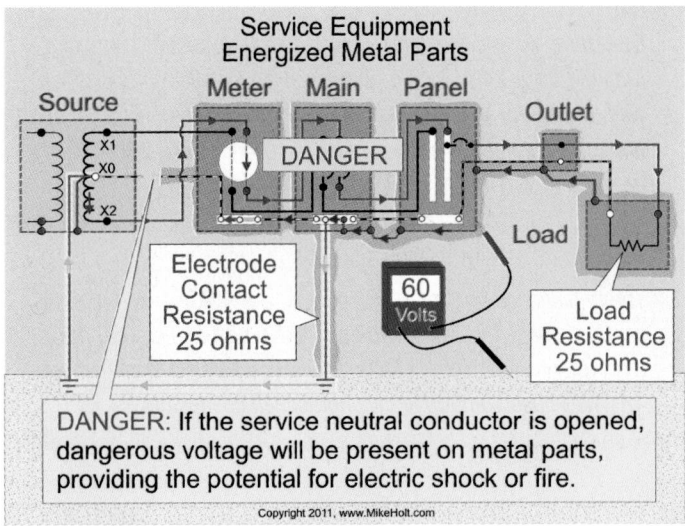

Figure 250–54

Author's Comment: For example, if the neutral conductor is opened, dangerous voltage will be present on metal parts under normal conditions, providing the potential for electric shock. If the earth's ground resistance is 25 ohms and the load's resistance is 25 ohms, the voltage drop across each of these resistors will be half of the voltage source. Since the neutral is connected to the service disconnect, all metal parts will be elevated to 60V above the earth's potential for a 120/240V system. **Figure 250–54**

To determine the actual voltage on the metal parts from an open service neutral conductor, you need to do some complex math calculations. Visit www.MikeHolt.com and go to the "Free Stuff" link to download a spreadsheet for this purpose.

(1) Single Raceway. Because the service neutral conductor serves as the effective ground-fault current path to the source for ground faults, the neutral conductor must be sized so it can safely carry the maximum fault current likely to be imposed on it [110.10 and 250.4(A)(5)]. This is accomplished by sizing the neutral conductor not smaller than specified in Table 250.66, based on the cross-sectional area of the largest ungrounded service conductor. **Figure 250–55**

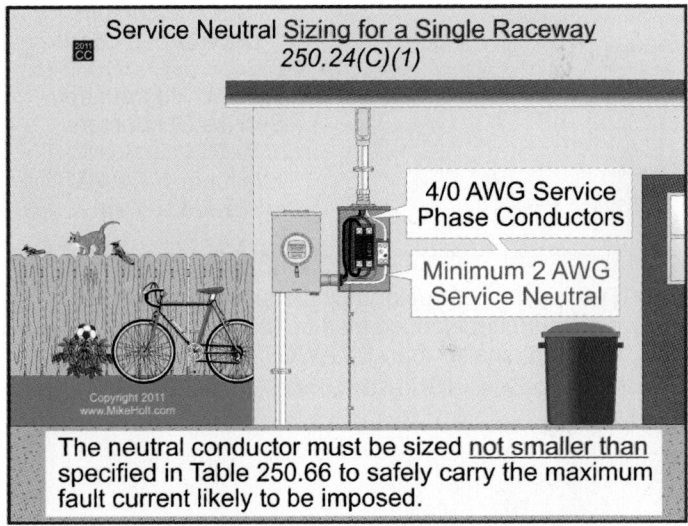

Figure 250–55

Author's Comment: In addition, the neutral conductors must have the capacity to carry the maximum unbalanced neutral current in accordance with 220.61.

Question: *What's the minimum size service neutral conductor required for a 240V, single-phase service installed in one raceway where the ungrounded service conductors are 500 kcmil and the maximum unbalanced load is 100A?* **Figure 250–56**

(a) 3 AWG   (b) 2 AWG   (c) 1 AWG   (d) 1/0 AWG

Answer: *(d) 1/0 AWG [Table 250.66]*

The unbalanced load of 100A requires a 3 AWG service neutral conductor, which is rated 100A at 75°C in accordance with Table 310.15(B)(16) [220.61]. Table 250.66 requires a minimum of 1/0 AWG based on 500 kcmil ungrounded conductors.

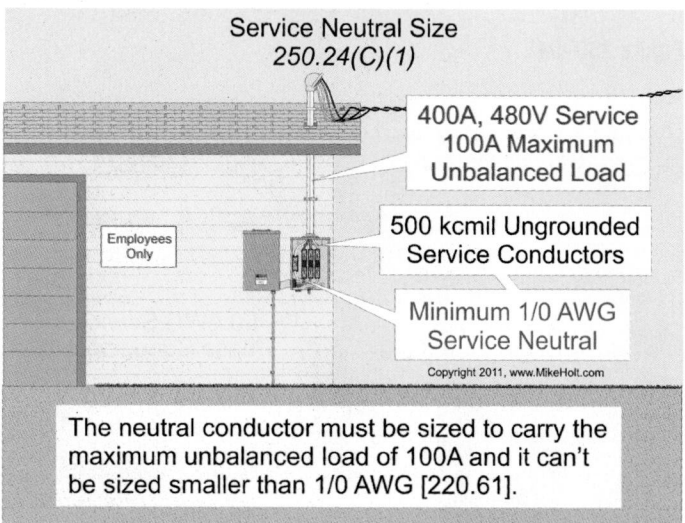

Service Neutral Size
250.24(C)(1)

400A, 480V Service
100A Maximum
Unbalanced Load

500 kcmil Ungrounded
Service Conductors

Minimum 1/0 AWG
Service Neutral

Copyright 2011, www.MikeHolt.com

The neutral conductor must be sized to carry the maximum unbalanced load of 100A and it can't be sized smaller than 1/0 AWG [220.61].

Figure 250–56

(2) Parallel Conductors in Two or More Raceways. If service conductors are paralleled in two or more raceways, a neutral conductor must be installed in each of the parallel raceways. The size of the neutral conductor in each raceway must not be smaller than specified in Table 250.66, based on the cross-sectional area of the largest ungrounded service conductor in each raceway. In no case can the neutral conductor in each parallel set be sized smaller than 1/0 AWG [310.10(H)(1)].

> **Author's Comment:** In addition, the neutral conductors must have the capacity to carry the maximum unbalanced neutral current in accordance with 220.61.

Question: *What's the minimum size service neutral conductor required for a 250V, single-phase service installed in parallel in two raceways where the ungrounded service conductors in each of the raceways are 350 kcmil and the maximum unbalanced load is 100A?* **Figure 250–57**

(a) 3 AWG   (b) 2 AWG   (c) 1 AWG   (d) 1/0 AWG

Answer: *(d) 1/0 AWG per raceway [Table 250.66 and 310.10(H)]*

The unbalanced load of 50A in each raceway requires an 8 AWG service neutral conductor, which is rated 50A at 75°C in accordance with Table 310.15(B)(16) [220.61]. Table 250.66 requires a minimum of 2 AWG, however, the smallest service neutral conductor permitted to be installed in parallel in each raceway must not be smaller than 1/0 AWG [310.10(H) and Table 310.15(B)(16)].

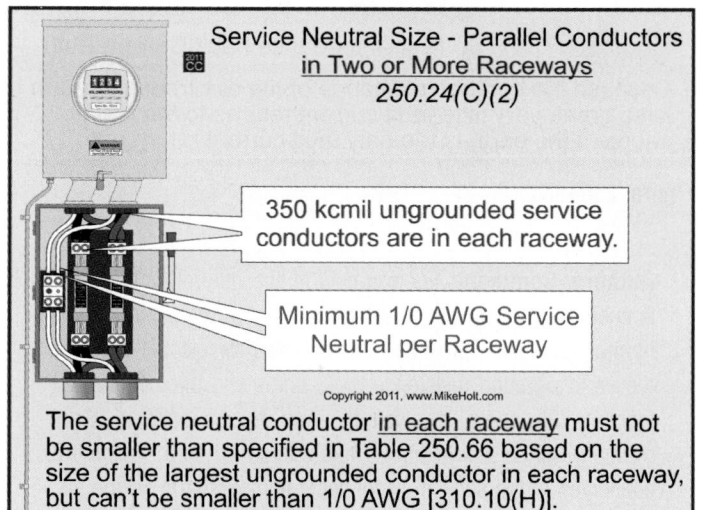

Service Neutral Size - Parallel Conductors
in Two or More Raceways
250.24(C)(2)

350 kcmil ungrounded service
conductors are in each raceway.

Minimum 1/0 AWG Service
Neutral per Raceway

Copyright 2011, www.MikeHolt.com

The service neutral conductor in each raceway must not be smaller than specified in Table 250.66 based on the size of the largest ungrounded conductor in each raceway, but can't be smaller than 1/0 AWG [310.10(H)].

Figure 250–57

(D) Grounding Electrode Conductor. A grounding electrode conductor, sized in accordance with 250.66 based on the area of the ungrounded service conductor, must connect the metal parts of service equipment enclosures to a grounding electrode in accordance with Part III of Article 250.

Question: *What's the minimum size grounding electrode conductor for a 400A service where the ungrounded service conductors are sized at 500 kcmil?* **Figure 250–58**

(a) 3 AWG (b) 2 AWG (c) 1 AWG (d) 1/0 AWG

Answer: *(d) 1/0 AWG [Table 250.66]*

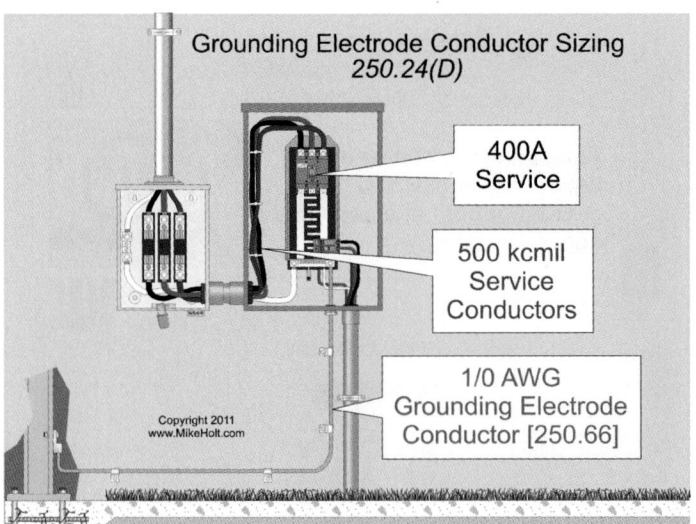

Grounding Electrode Conductor Sizing
250.24(D)

400A Service

500 kcmil Service Conductors

1/0 AWG Grounding Electrode Conductor [250.66]

Copyright 2011 www.MikeHolt.com

Figure 250–58

Author's Comment: If the grounding electrode conductor is connected to a ground rod, the portion of the conductor that's the sole connection to the ground rod isn't required to be larger than 6 AWG copper [250.66(A)]. **Figure 250–59**. If the grounding electrode conductor is connected to a concrete-encased electrode, the portion of the conductor that's the sole connection to the concrete-encased electrode isn't required to be larger than 4 AWG copper [250.66(B)]. **Figure 250–60**

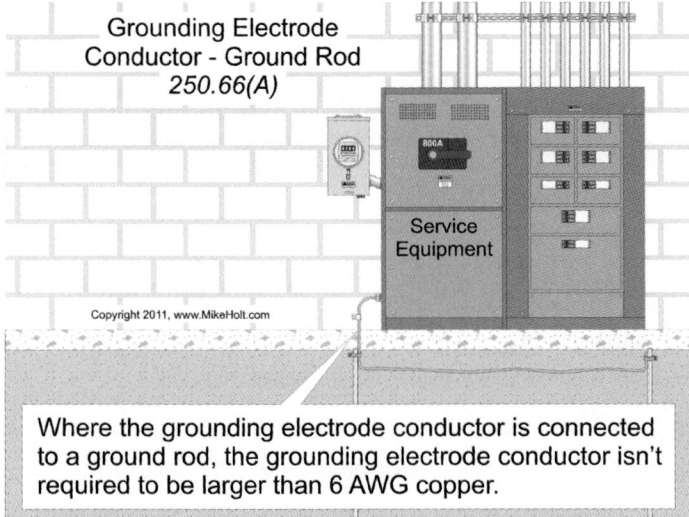

Grounding Electrode Conductor - Ground Rod
250.66(A)

Service Equipment

Copyright 2011, www.MikeHolt.com

Where the grounding electrode conductor is connected to a ground rod, the grounding electrode conductor isn't required to be larger than 6 AWG copper.

Figure 250–59

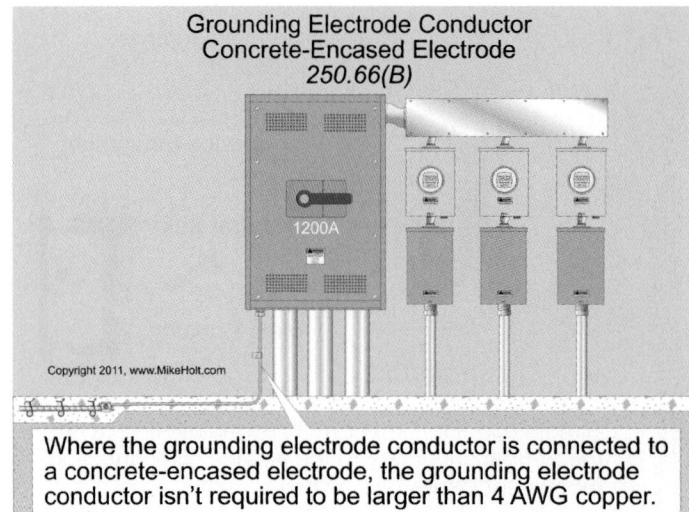

Grounding Electrode Conductor
Concrete-Encased Electrode
250.66(B)

1200A

Copyright 2011, www.MikeHolt.com

Where the grounding electrode conductor is connected to a concrete-encased electrode, the grounding electrode conductor isn't required to be larger than 4 AWG copper.

Figure 250–60

250.28 Main Bonding Jumper and System Bonding Jumper.
Main and system bonding jumpers must be installed as follows:

Author's Comments:

- Main Bonding Jumper. At service equipment, a main bonding jumper must be installed to electrically connect the neutral conductor to the service disconnect enclosure [250.24(B)]. **Figure 250–61**

  The main bonding jumper provides the low-impedance path necessary for fault current to travel back to the power supply to open the circuit overcurrent device to clear a ground fault [250.24(C)]. **Figure 250–62**

 DANGER: *Metal parts of the electrical installation, as well as metal piping and structural steel, will become and remain energized with dangerous voltage from a ground fault if a main bonding jumper isn't installed at service equipment.* Figure 250–63

- System Bonding Jumper. A system bonding jumper must be installed between the neutral terminal of a separately derived system and the circuit equipment grounding conductor [Article 100 Bonding Jumper, System and 250.30(A)(1)]. **Figure 250–64**

 DANGER: *Metal parts of the electrical installation, as well as metal piping and structural steel, will become and remain energized with dangerous voltage from a ground fault if a system bonding jumper isn't installed at a separately derived system.* Figure 250–65

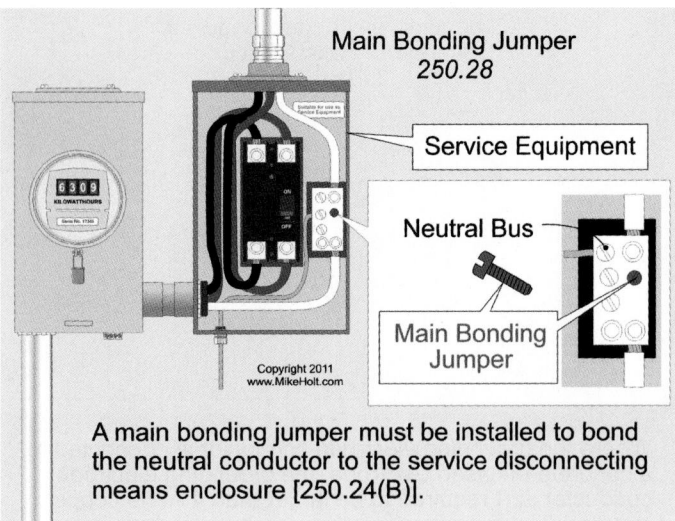

Main Bonding Jumper
250.28

Service Equipment

Neutral Bus

Main Bonding Jumper

A main bonding jumper must be installed to bond the neutral conductor to the service disconnecting means enclosure [250.24(B)].

Figure 250–61

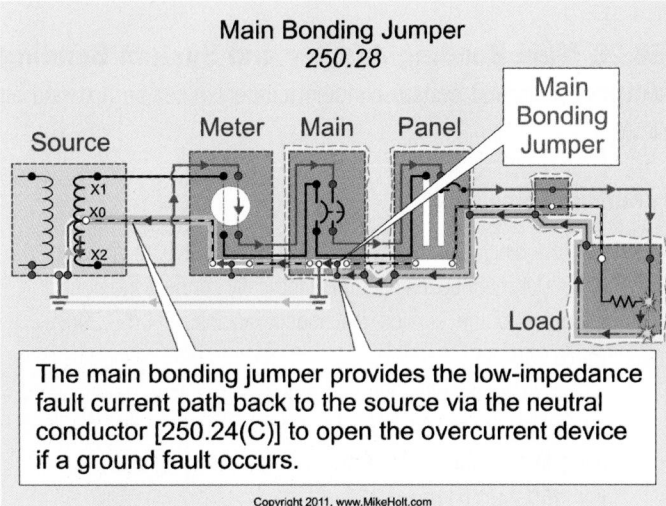

Main Bonding Jumper
250.28

Main Bonding Jumper

Source   Meter   Main   Panel

Load

The main bonding jumper provides the low-impedance fault current path back to the source via the neutral conductor [250.24(C)] to open the overcurrent device if a ground fault occurs.

Figure 250–62

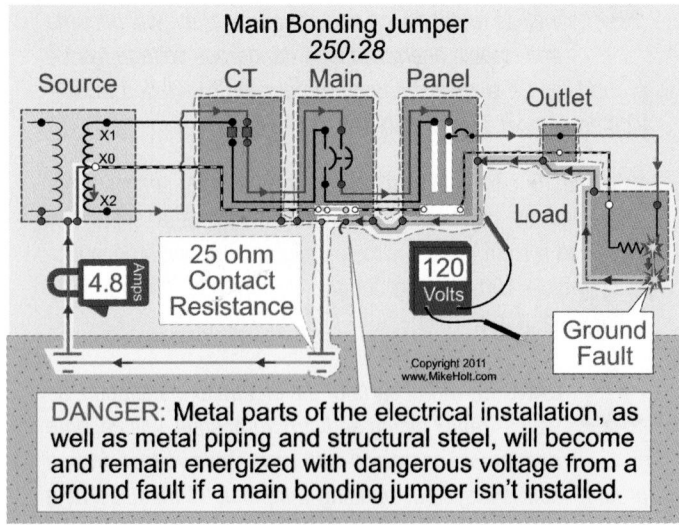

Main Bonding Jumper
250.28

Source   CT   Main   Panel

Outlet

Load

25 ohm Contact Resistance

4.8 Amps

120 Volts

Ground Fault

DANGER: Metal parts of the electrical installation, as well as metal piping and structural steel, will become and remain energized with dangerous voltage from a ground fault if a main bonding jumper isn't installed.

Figure 250–63

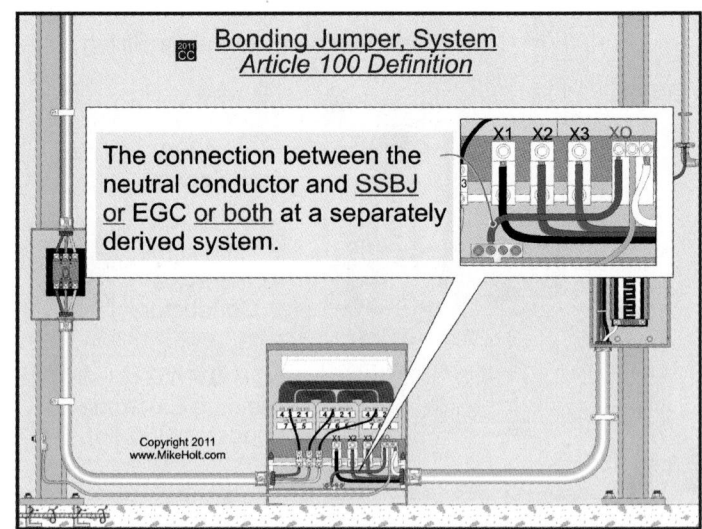

Bonding Jumper, System
Article 100 Definition

The connection between the neutral conductor and SSBJ or EGC or both at a separately derived system.

X1 X2 X3 XO

Figure 250–64

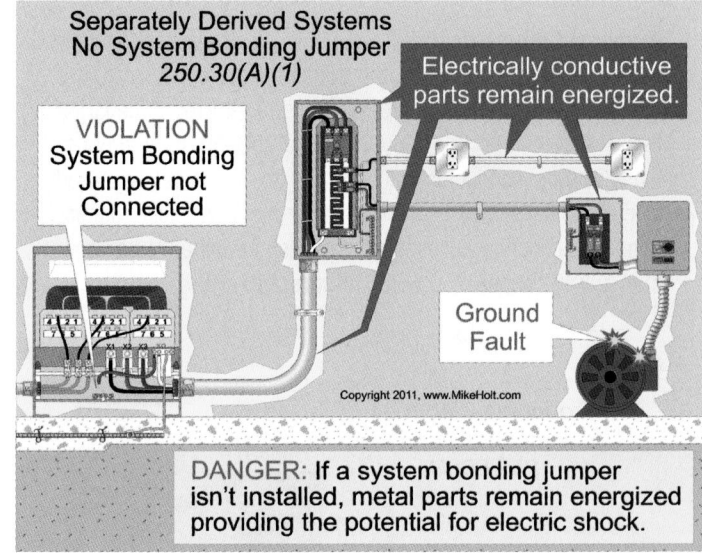

Separately Derived Systems
No System Bonding Jumper
250.30(A)(1)

Electrically conductive parts remain energized.

VIOLATION
System Bonding Jumper not Connected

Ground Fault

DANGER: If a system bonding jumper isn't installed, metal parts remain energized providing the potential for electric shock.

Figure 250–65

(A) Material. The bonding jumper can be a wire, bus, or screw.

(B) Construction. If the bonding jumper is a screw, it must be identified with a green finish visible with the screw installed.

(C) Attachment. Main and system bonding jumpers must terminate by one of the following means in accordance with 250.8(A):

- Listed pressure connectors
- Terminal bars
- Pressure connectors listed as grounding and bonding equipment
- Exothermic welding
- Machine screw-type fasteners that engage not less than two threads or are secured with a nut

- Thread-forming machine screws that engage not less than two threads in the enclosure
- Connections that are part of a listed assembly
- Other listed means

(D) Size.

(1) Main and system bonding jumpers must be sized not smaller than the sizes shown in Table 250.66. If the service or ungrounded conductors of a separately derived system have a total area larger than 1,100 kcmil copper or 1,750 kcmil aluminum, the bonding jumper must have an area not less than 12½ percent of the total conductor area of the largest ungrounded conductor. **Figures 250–66, 250–67, and 250–68**

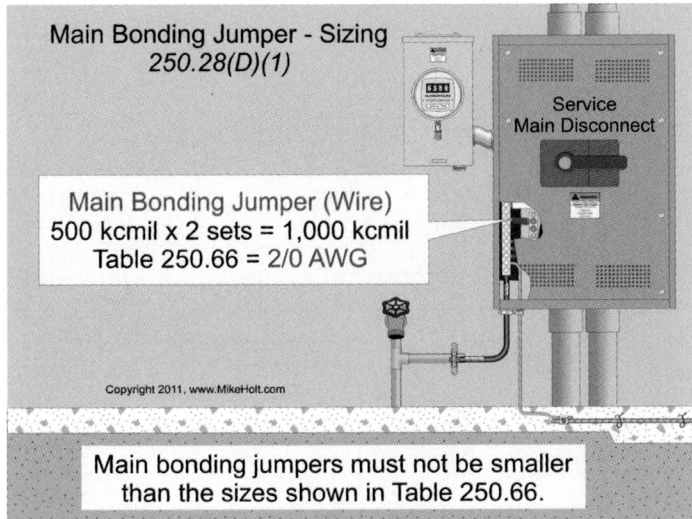

Main Bonding Jumper - Sizing
250.28(D)(1)

Service Main Disconnect

Main Bonding Jumper (Wire)
500 kcmil x 2 sets = 1,000 kcmil
Table 250.66 = 2/0 AWG

Main bonding jumpers must not be smaller than the sizes shown in Table 250.66.

Figure 250–66

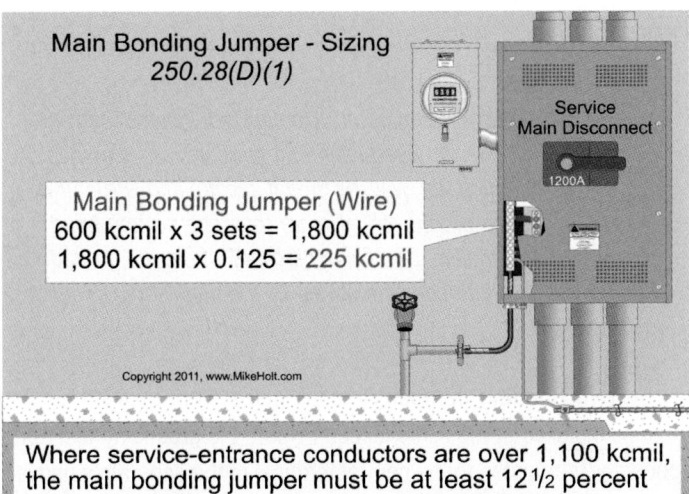

Main Bonding Jumper - Sizing
250.28(D)(1)

Service Main Disconnect

1200A

Main Bonding Jumper (Wire)
600 kcmil x 3 sets = 1,800 kcmil
1,800 kcmil x 0.125 = 225 kcmil

Where service-entrance conductors are over 1,100 kcmil, the main bonding jumper must be at least 12½ percent of the area of the largest ungrounded conductor.

Figure 250–67

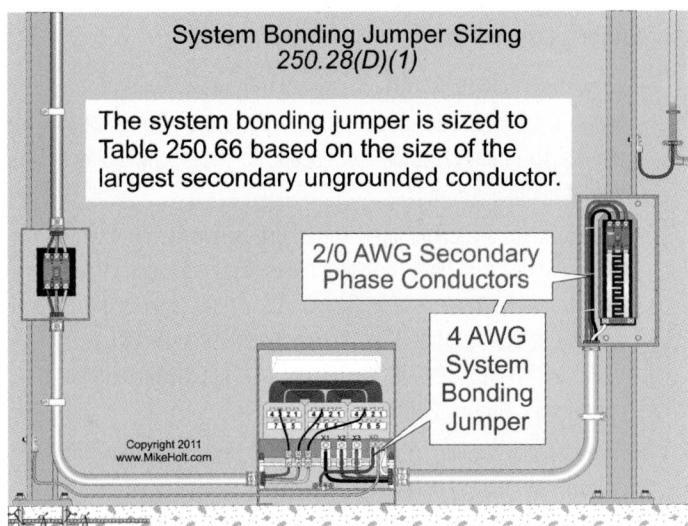

System Bonding Jumper Sizing
250.28(D)(1)

The system bonding jumper is sized to Table 250.66 based on the size of the largest secondary ungrounded conductor.

2/0 AWG Secondary Phase Conductors

4 AWG System Bonding Jumper

Copyright 2011
www.MikeHolt.com

Figure 250–68

250.30 Separately Derived Systems—Grounding and Bonding.

Note 1: An alternate alternating-current power source such as an on-site generator isn't a separately derived system if the neutral conductor is solidly interconnected to a service-supplied system neutral conductor. An example is a generator provided with a transfer switch that includes a neutral conductor that's not switched. **Figure 250–69**

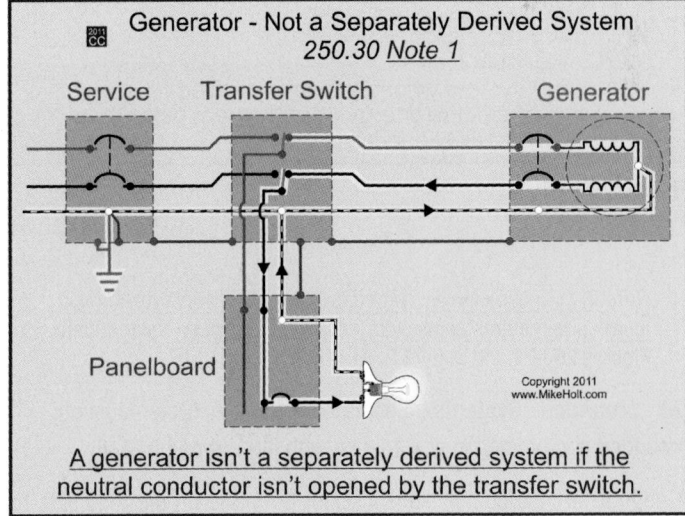

Generator - Not a Separately Derived System
250.30 Note 1

Service   Transfer Switch   Generator

Panelboard

Copyright 2011
www.MikeHolt.com

A generator isn't a separately derived system if the neutral conductor isn't opened by the transfer switch.

Figure 250–69

Author's Comments:

- According to Article 100, a separately derived system is a wiring system whose power is derived from a source where there's no direct electrical connection to the supply conductors of another system.

- Transformers are considered separately derived when the primary conductors have no direct electrical connection from circuit conductors of one system to circuit conductors of another system, other than connections through the earth, metal enclosures, metallic raceways, or equipment grounding conductors. **Figure 250-70**

- A generator having transfer equipment that switches the neutral conductor, or one that has no neutral conductor at all, is a separately derived system and must be grounded and bonded in accordance with 250.30(A). **Figure 250–71**

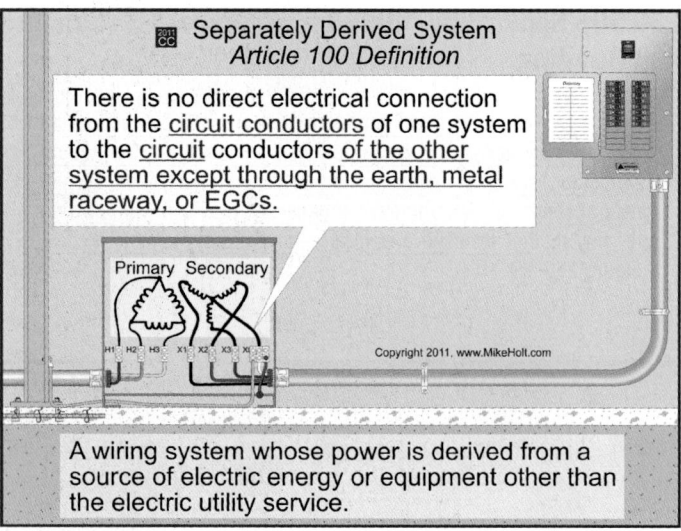

Figure 250–70

Note 2: For nonseparately derived systems, see 445.13 for the minimum size neutral conductors necessary to carry fault current. Figures 250-72 and 250-73

(A) Grounded Systems. Separately derived systems must be grounded and bonded in accordance with (A)(1) through (A)(8).

A neutral-to-case connection must not be made on the load side of the system bonding jumper, except as permitted by 250.142(B).

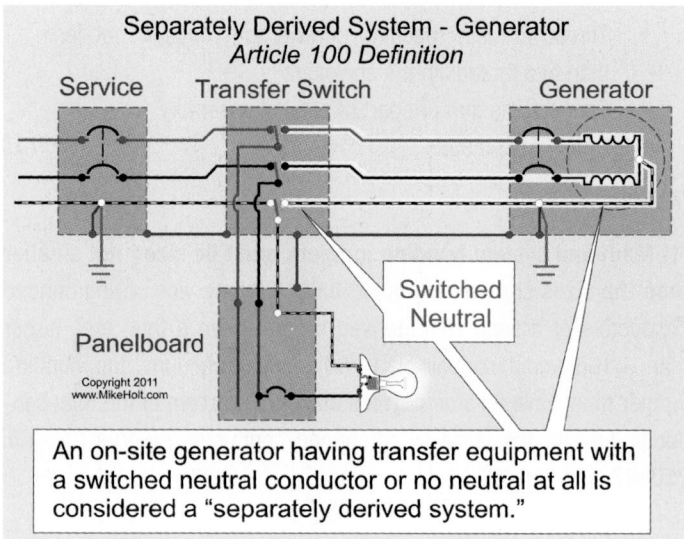

Figure 250–71

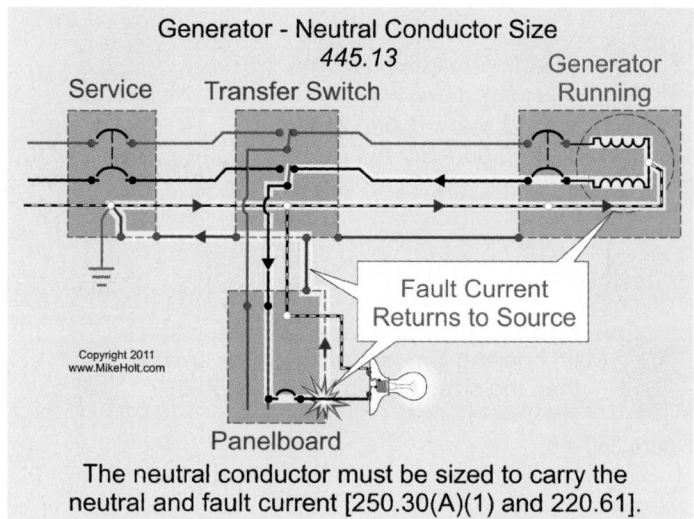

Figure 250–72

CAUTION: *Dangerous objectionable neutral current will flow on conductive metal parts of electrical equipment as well as metal piping and structural steel, in violation of 250.6(A), if more than one system bonding jumper is installed, or if it's not located where the grounding electrode conductor terminates to the neutral conductor.* Figure 250–74

(1) System Bonding Jumper. An unspliced system bonding jumper must be installed at the same location where the grounding electrode conductor terminates to the neutral terminal of the separately derived system; either at the separately derived system or the system disconnecting means, but not at both locations [250.30(A)(5)].

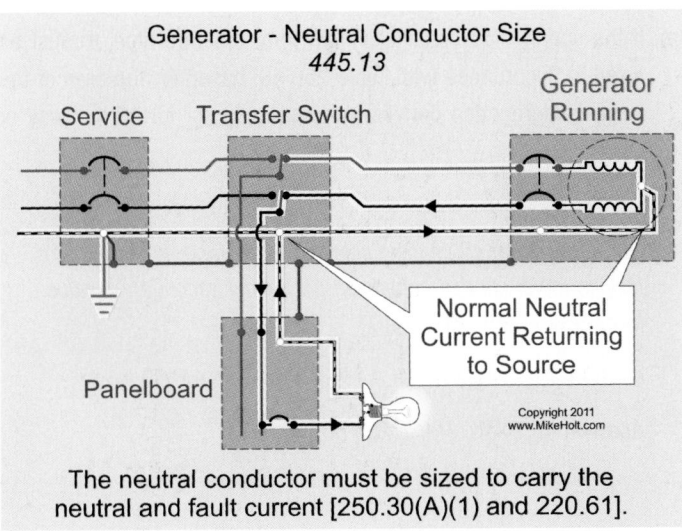

Figure 250–73

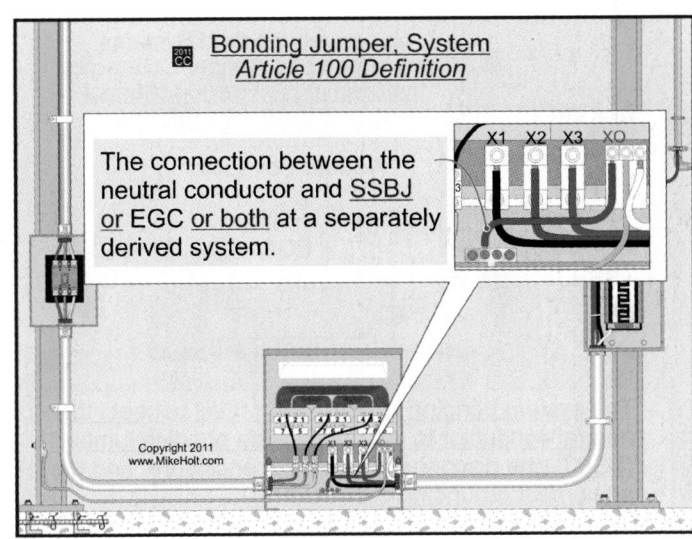

Figure 250–75

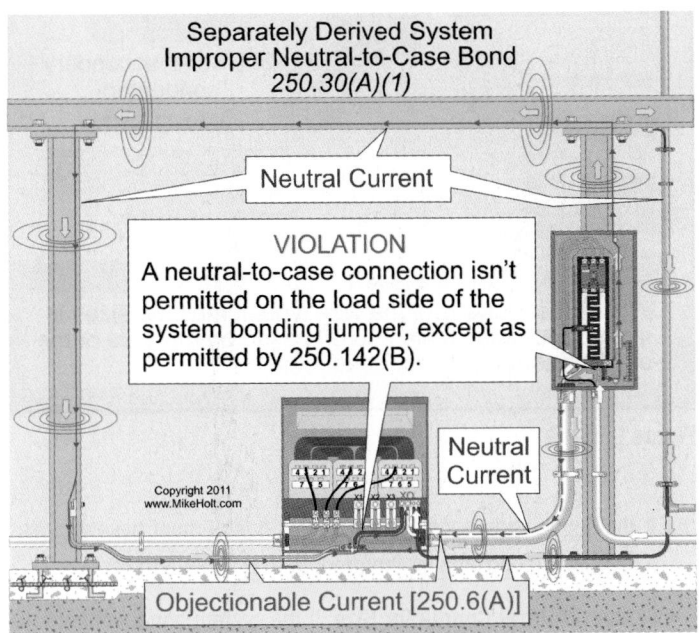

Figure 250–74

Author's Comment: A system bonding jumper is the connection between the neutral conductor and supply side bonding jumper or equipment grounding conductor or both at a separately derived system [Article 100]. **Figure 250-75**

(a) Installed at Source. Where the system bonding jumper is installed at the source of the separately derived system, the jumper must connect the neutral conductor of the derived system to the supply-side bonding jumper and the metal enclosure of the source (transformer case). **Figure 250–76**

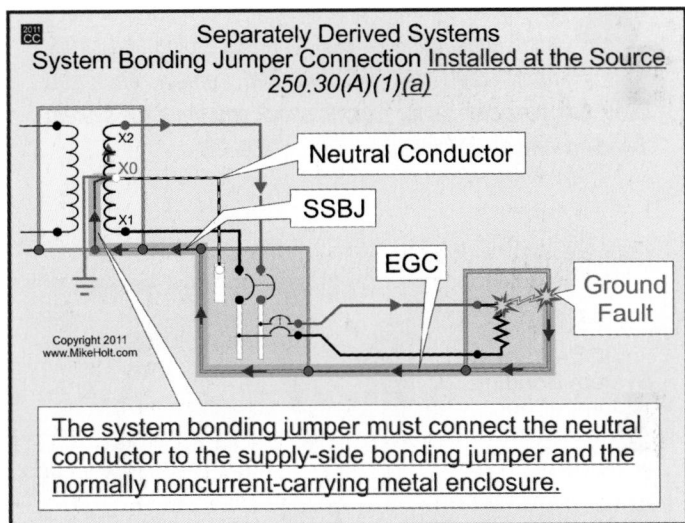

Figure 250–76

(b) Installed at First Disconnecting Means. Where the system bonding jumper is installed at the first disconnecting means of a separately derived system, the jumper must connect the neutral conductor of the derived system to the supply-side bonding jumper and the metal disconnecting means enclosure. **Figure 250–77**

Author's Comment: A system bonding jumper is a conductor, screw, or strap that bonds the metal parts of a separately derived system to the system neutral point [Article 100 Bonding Jumper, System], and it's sized to Table 250.66 in accordance with 250.28(D).

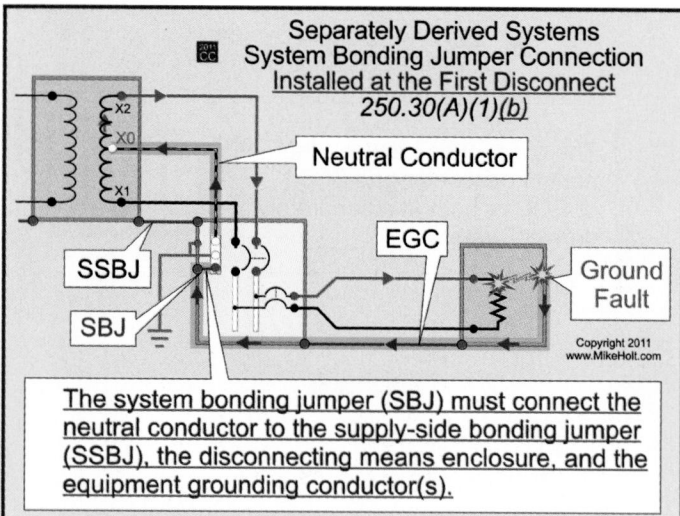

Figure 250–77

⚠ **DANGER:** *During a ground fault, metal parts of electrical equipment, as well as metal piping and structural steel, will become and remain energized providing the potential for electric shock and fire if the system bonding jumper isn't installed.* **Figure 250–78**

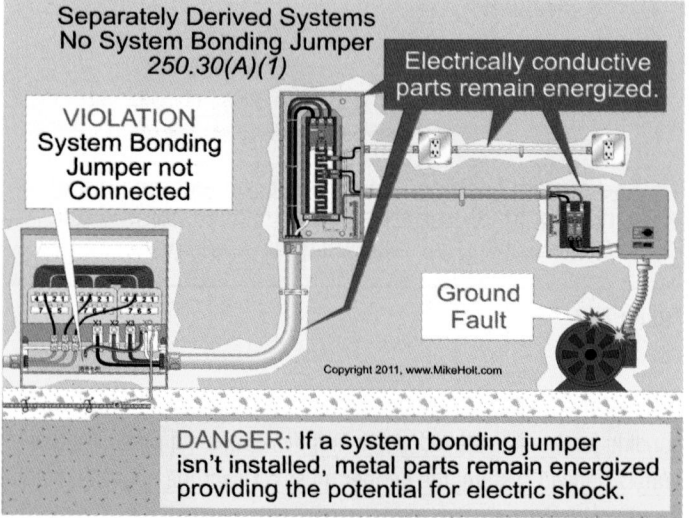

Figure 250–78

(2) Supply-Side Bonding Jumper. If the separately derived system and the first disconnecting means are located in separate enclosures, a supply-side bonding jumper must be run to the derived system disconnecting means. The supply-side bonding jumper can be a nonflexible metal raceway, a wire, or a bus.

(a) If the supply-side bonding jumper is of the wire type, it must be sized in accordance with Table 250.66, based on the area of the largest ungrounded derived system conductor in the raceway or cable.

> **Question:** *What size supply-side bonding jumper is required for flexible metal conduit containing 300 kcmil secondary conductors?* **Figure 250–79**
>
> *(a) 3 AWG　　(b) 2 AWG　　(c) 1 AWG　　(d) 1/0 AWG*
>
> **Answer:** *(b) 2 AWG [Table 250.66]*

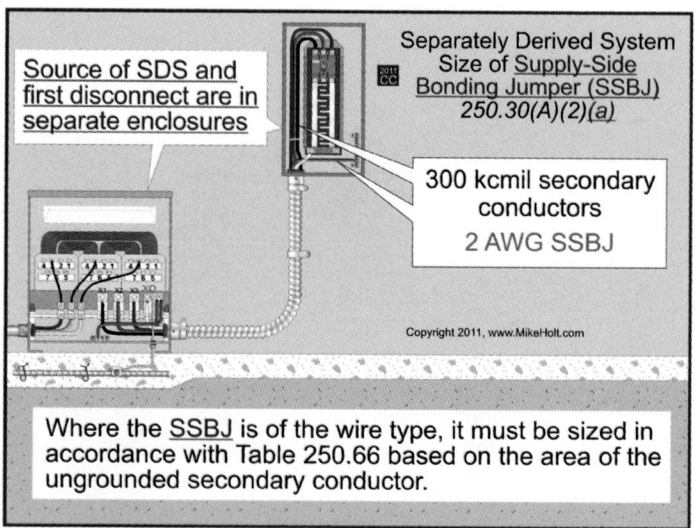

Figure 250–79

(b) If the supply-side bonding jumper is a bus, it must have a cross-sectional area no smaller than required by Table 250.66.

(3) System Neutral Conductor Size. If the system bonding jumper is installed at the disconnecting means instead of at the source, the following requirements apply:

(a) Sizing for Single Raceway. Because the neutral conductor of a derived system serves as the effective ground-fault current path for ground-fault current, it must be routed with the ungrounded conductors of the derived system and be sized not smaller than specified in Table 250.66, based on the area of the ungrounded conductor of the derived system. **Figure 250–80**

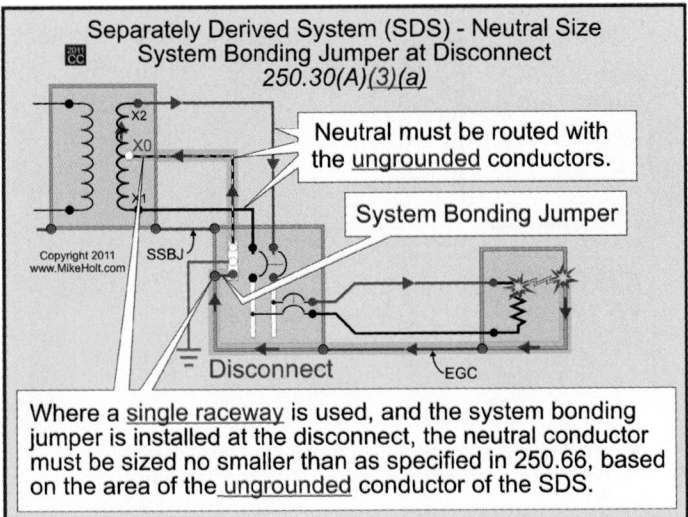

Figure 250–80

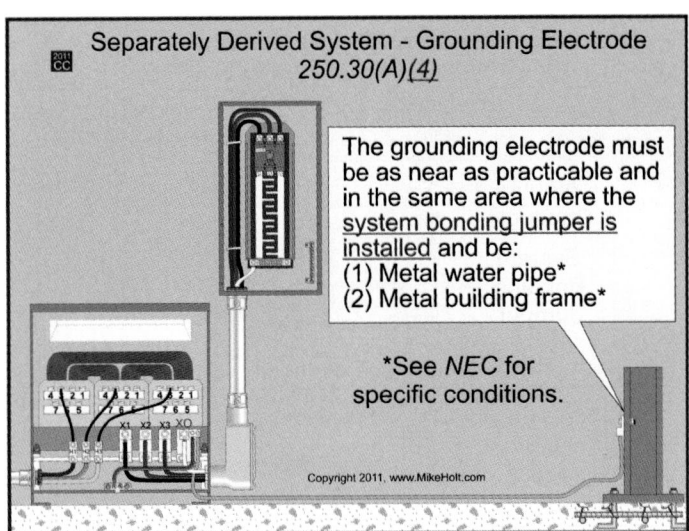

Figure 250–81

(b) Parallel Conductors in Two or More Raceways. If the conductors from the derived system are installed in parallel in two or more raceways, the neutral conductor of the derived system in each raceway or cable must be sized not smaller than specified in Table 250.66, based on the area of the largest ungrounded conductor of the derived system in the raceway or cable. In no case is the neutral conductor of the derived system permitted to be smaller than 1/0 AWG [310.10(H)].

> **Author's Comment:** If the system bonding jumper is installed at the disconnecting means instead of at the source, an equipment bonding conductor must connect the metal parts of the separately derived system to the neutral conductor at the disconnecting means in accordance with 250.30(A)(2).

(4) Grounding Electrode. The grounding electrode must be as near as practicable, and preferably in the same area where the system bonding jumper is installed and be one of the following: **Figure 250–81**

(1) Metal water pipe electrode, within 5 ft of the entry to the building [250.52(A)(1)].

(2) Metal building frame electrode [250.52(A)(2)].

Ex 1: If the electrodes specified in 250.30(A)(4) aren't available, one of the following electrodes can be used:

- *A concrete-encased electrode encased by not less than 2 in. of concrete, located horizontally near the bottom or vertically, and within that portion of concrete foundation or footing that's in direct contact with the earth [250.52(A)(3)].*

- *A ground ring electrode encircling the building/structure, buried not less than 30 in. below grade, consisting of at least 20 ft of bare copper conductor not smaller than 2 AWG [250.52(A)(4) and 250.53(F)].*

- *A ground rod electrode having not less than 8 ft of contact with the soil meeting the requirements of 250.52(A)(5) and 250.53(G)].*

- *Other metal underground systems, piping systems, or underground tanks [250.52(A)(8)].*

Note 1: Interior metal water piping in the area served by separately derived systems must be bonded to the separately derived system in accordance with 250.104(D).

(5) Grounding Electrode Conductor, Single Separately Derived System. The grounding electrode conductor must be sized in accordance with 250.66, based on the area of the largest ungrounded conductor of the derived system. A grounding electrode conductor must connect the neutral terminal of a separately derived system to a grounding electrode of a type identified in 250.30(A)(4) at the same point on the separately derived system where the system bonding jumper is connected. **Figure 250–82**

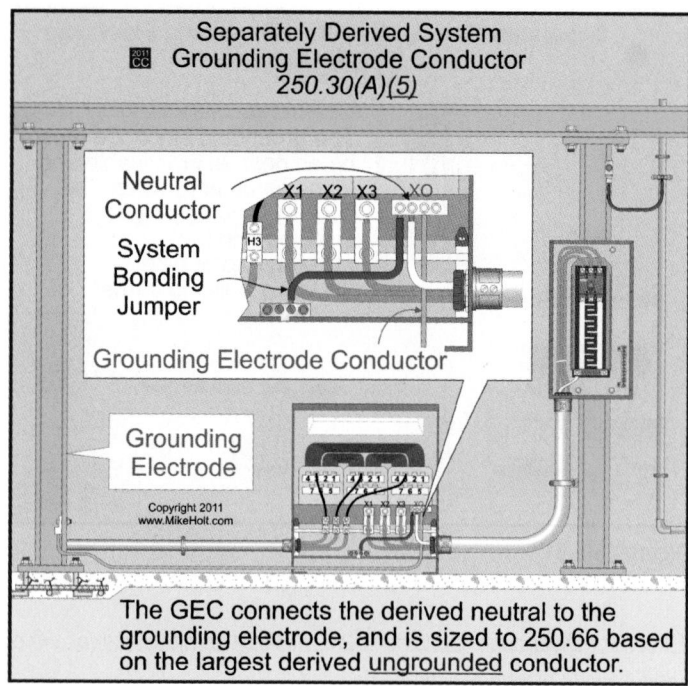

Figure 250–82

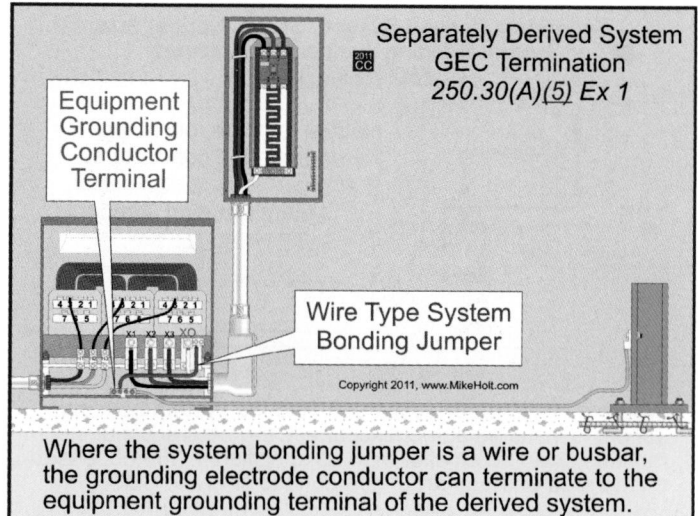

Figure 250–83

Author's Comments:

- System grounding also helps reduce fires in buildings as well as voltage stress on electrical insulation, thereby ensuring longer insulation life for motors, transformers, and other system components.

- To prevent objectionable neutral current from flowing [250.6] onto metal parts, the grounding electrode conductor must originate at the same point on the separately derived system where the system bonding jumper is connected [250.30(A)(1)].

Ex 1: If the system bonding jumper is a wire or busbar, the grounding electrode conductor is permitted to terminate to either the neutral terminal or the equipment grounding terminal, bar, or bus in accordance with 250.30(A)(1). **Figure 250–83**

Ex 3: Separately derived systems rated 1 kVA or less aren't required to be grounded (connected to the earth).

(6) Grounding Electrode Conductor, Multiple Separately Derived Systems. Where there are multiple separately derived systems, a grounding electrode conductor tap from each separately derived system to a common grounding electrode conductor is permitted. This connection is to be made at the same point on the separately derived system where the system bonding jumper is connected [250.30(A)(1)]. **Figure 250–84**

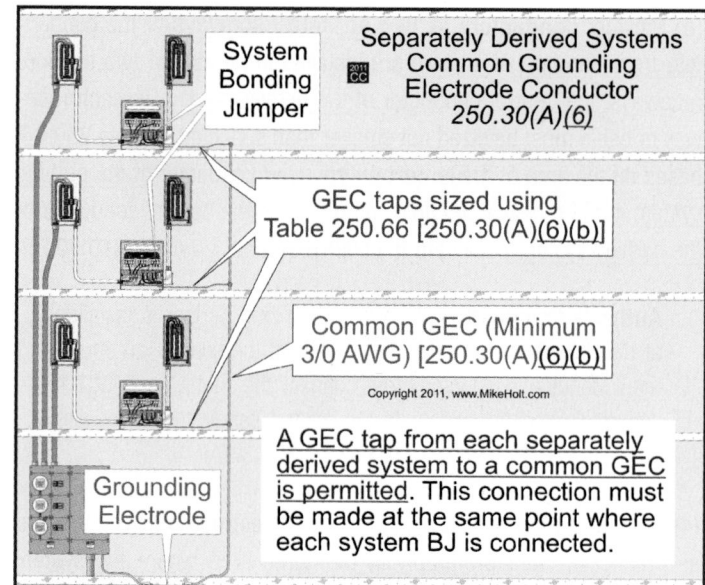

Figure 250–84

Ex 1: If the system bonding jumper is a wire or busbar, the grounding electrode conductor tap can terminate to either the neutral terminal or the equipment grounding terminal, bar, or bus in accordance with 250.30(A)(1).

Ex 2: Separately derived systems rated 1 kVA or less aren't required to be grounded (connected to the earth).

(a) Common Grounding Electrode Conductor. The common grounding electrode conductor can be one of the following:

(1) A conductor not smaller than 3/0 AWG copper or 250 kcmil aluminum.

(2) The metal frame of the building/structure that complies with 250.52(A)(2) or is connected to the grounding electrode system by a conductor not smaller than 3/0 AWG copper or 250 kcmil aluminum.

(b) Tap Conductor Size. Grounding electrode conductor taps must be sized in accordance with Table 250.66, based on the area of the largest ungrounded conductor of the given derived system.

(c) Connections. All tap connections to the common grounding electrode conductor must be made at an accessible location by one of the following methods:

(1) A connector listed as grounding and bonding equipment.

(2) Listed connections to aluminum or copper busbars not less than ¼ in. x 2 in.

(3) Exothermic welding.

Grounding electrode conductor taps must be connected to the common grounding electrode conductor so the common grounding electrode conductor isn't spliced.

(7) Installation. The grounding electrode conductor must comply with the following:

- Be of copper where within 18 in. of the earth [250.64(A)].

- Securely fastened to the surface on which it's carried [250.64(B)].

- Adequately protected if exposed to physical damage [250.64(B)].

- Metal enclosures enclosing a grounding electrode conductor must be made electrically continuous from the point of attachment to cabinets or equipment to the grounding electrode [250.64(E)].

(8) Structural Steel and Metal Piping. To ensure dangerous voltage from a ground fault is removed quickly, structural steel and metal piping in the area served by a separately derived system must be connected to the neutral conductor at the separately derived system in accordance with 250.104(D).

(C) Outdoor Source. If the separately derived system is located outside the building/structure, a connection to the grounding electrode must be made at the separately derived system location. **Figure 250–85**

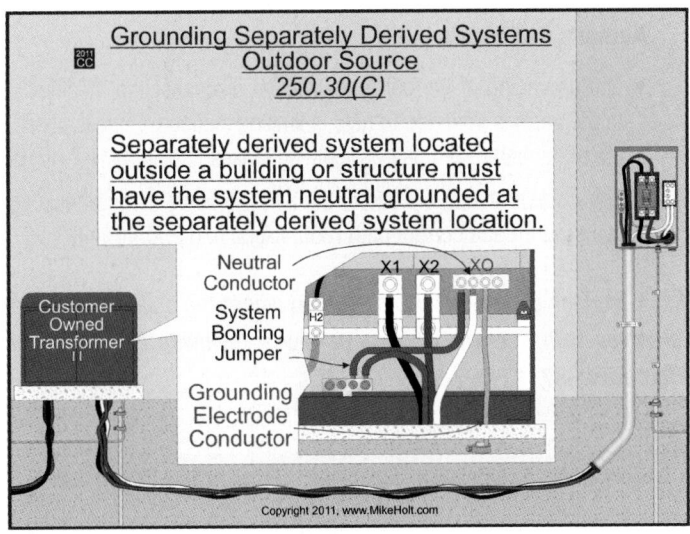

Figure 250–85

250.32 Buildings or Structures Supplied by a Feeder or Branch Circuit.

(A) Grounding Electrode. Each building/structure's disconnect must be connected to an electrode of a type identified in 250.52. **Figure 250–86**

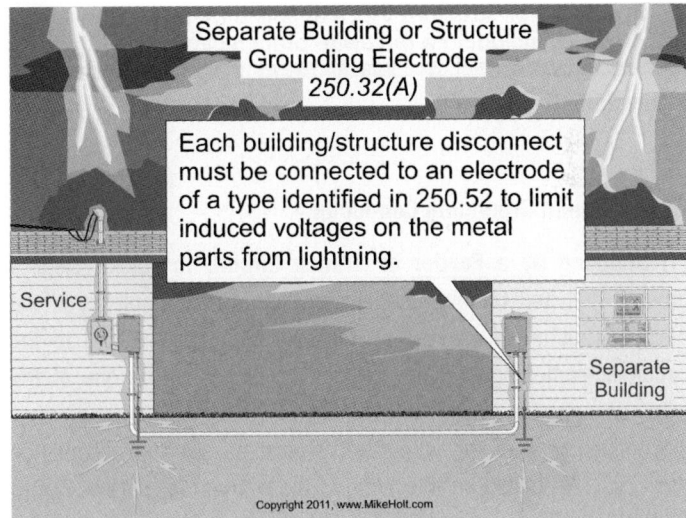

Figure 250–86

Author's Comments:

- The grounding of the building/structure disconnecting means to the earth is intended to help in limiting induced voltages on the metal parts from nearby lightning strikes [250.4(A)(1)].

- The *Code* prohibits the use of the earth to serve as an effective ground-fault current path [250.4(A)(5) and 250.4(B)(4)].

Ex: A grounding electrode isn't required where the building/structure is served with a 2-wire, 3-wire, or 4-wire multiwire branch circuit. **Figure 250–87**

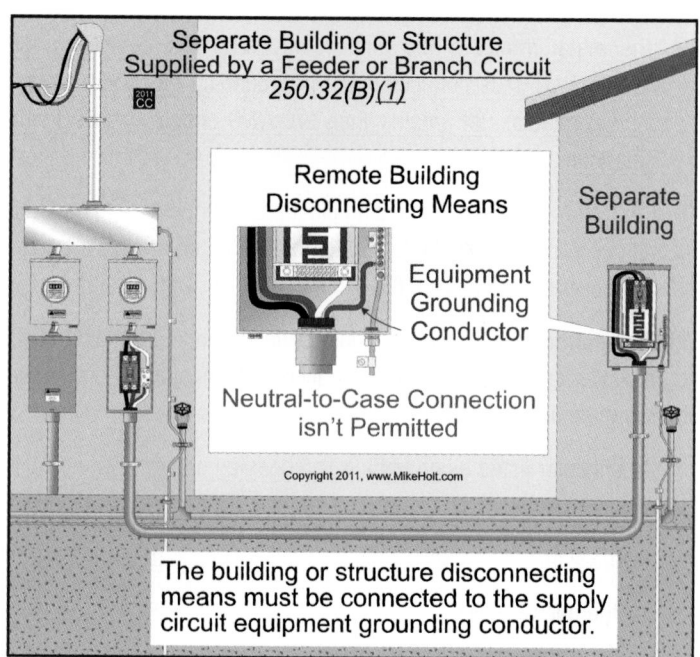

Figure 250–88

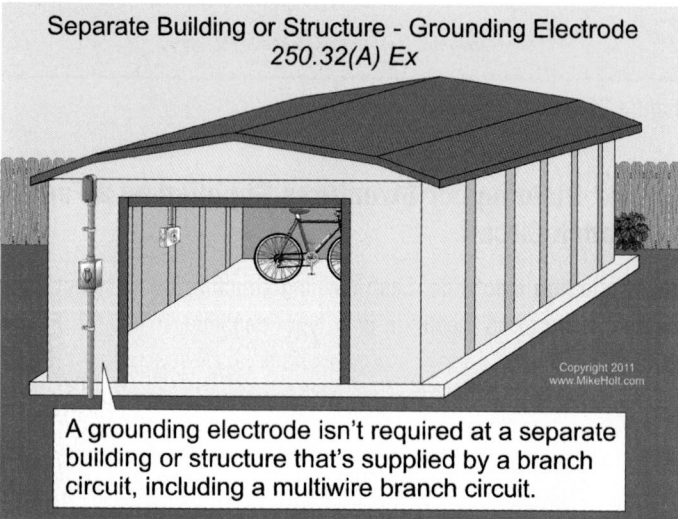

Figure 250–87

(B) Equipment Grounding Conductor.

(1) Supplied by a Feeder or Branch Circuit. To quickly clear a ground fault and remove dangerous voltage from metal parts, the building/structure disconnecting means must be connected to the circuit equipment grounding conductor, which must be one of the types described in 250.118. If the supply circuit equipment grounding conductor is of the wire type, it must be sized in accordance with 250.122, based on the rating of the overcurrent device. **Figure 250–88**

⚠ **CAUTION:** *To prevent dangerous objectionable neutral current from flowing onto metal parts [250.6(A)], the supply circuit neutral conductor isn't permitted to be connected to the remote building/structure disconnecting means [250.142(B)].* **Figure 250–89**

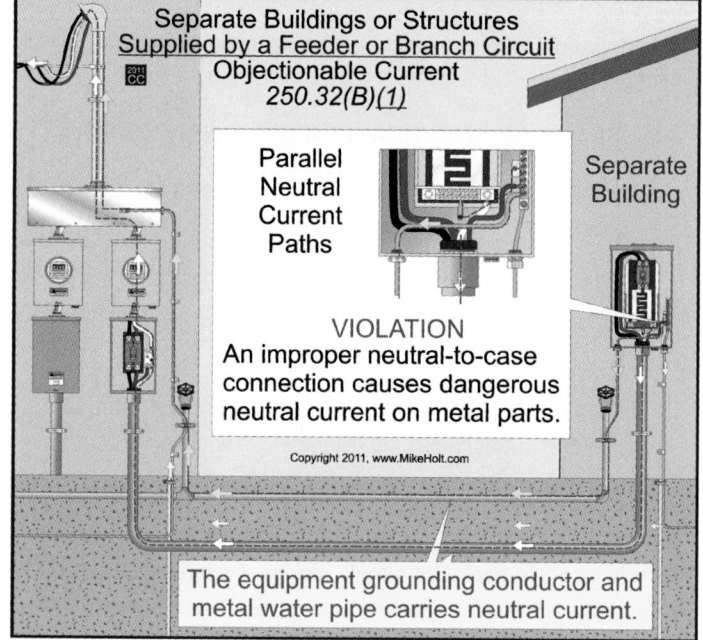

Figure 250–89

Ex: The neutral conductor *can serve as the ground-fault return path* for the building/structure disconnecting means for *existing installations in compliance with previous editions of the Code* where there are no continuous metallic paths between buildings and structures, ground-fault protection of equipment isn't installed on the supply side of the circuit, and the neutral conductor is sized no smaller than the larger of:

(1) The maximum unbalanced neutral load in accordance with 220.61.

(2) The minimum equipment grounding conductor size in accordance with 250.122.

(2) Supplied by Separately Derived System.

(a) With Overcurrent Protection. If overcurrent protection is provided where the conductors originate, the supply conductors must contain an equipment grounding conductor in accordance with 250.32(B)(1).

(b) Without Overcurrent Protection. If overcurrent protection isn't provided for the supply conductors to the building/structure as permitted by 240.21(C)(4), the installation must be grounded and bonded in accordance with 250.30(A).

(E) Grounding Electrode Conductor. The grounding electrode conductor must terminate to the grounding terminal of the disconnecting means, and it must be sized in accordance with 250.66, based on the conductor area of the ungrounded feeder conductor.

> **Question:** What size grounding electrode conductor is required for a building disconnect supplied with a 3/0 AWG feeder? **Figure 250–90**
>
> (a) 4 AWG   (b) 3 AWG   (c) 2 AWG   (d) 1 AWG
>
> **Answer:** (a) 4 AWG [Table 250.66]

Author's Comment: If the grounding electrode conductor is connected to a ground rod, the portion of the conductor that's the sole connection to the ground rod isn't required to be larger than 6 AWG copper [250.66(A)]. If the grounding electrode conductor is connected to a concrete-encased electrode, the portion of the conductor that's the sole connection to the concrete-encased electrode isn't required to be larger than 4 AWG copper [250.66(B)].

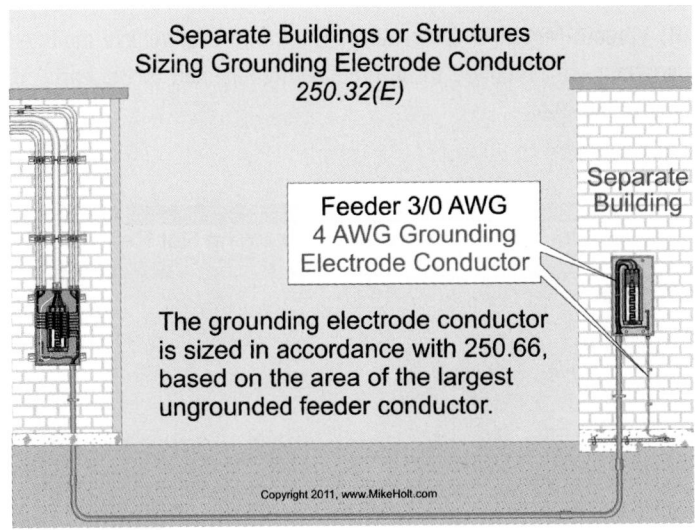

Figure 250–90

250.34 Generators—Portable and Vehicle-Mounted.

(A) Portable Generators. The frame of a portable generator isn't required to be grounded (connected to the earth) if: **Figure 250–91**

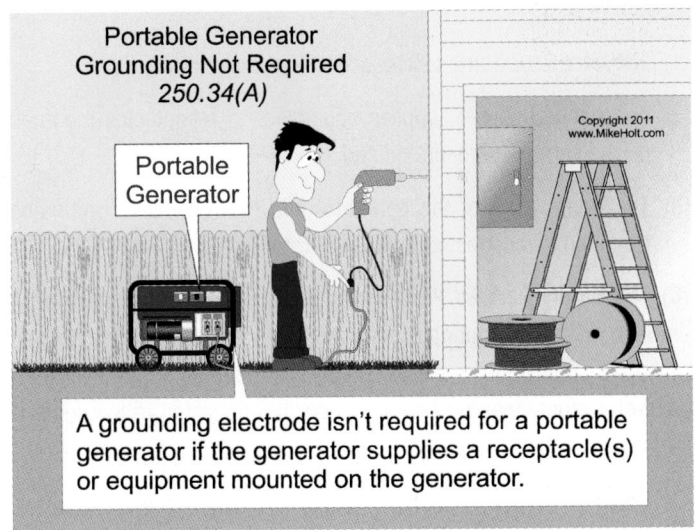

Figure 250–91

(1) The generator only supplies equipment or receptacles mounted on the generator, and

(2) The metal parts of the generator and the receptacle grounding terminal are connected to the generator frame.

(B) Vehicle-Mounted Generators. The frame of a vehicle-mounted generator isn't required to be grounded (connected to the earth) if: Figure 250–92

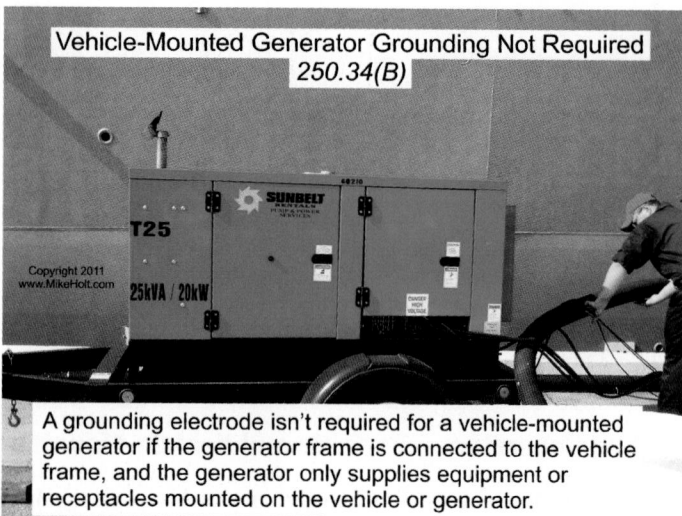

A grounding electrode isn't required for a vehicle-mounted generator if the generator frame is connected to the vehicle frame, and the generator only supplies equipment or receptacles mounted on the vehicle or generator.

Figure 250–92

(1) The generator frame is bonded to the vehicle frame,

(2) The generator only supplies equipment or receptacles mounted on the vehicle or generator, and

(3) The metal parts of the generator and the receptacle grounding terminal are connected to the generator frame.

(C) Separately Derived Portable or Vehicle-Mounted Generator. A portable or vehicle-mounted generator used as a separately derived system to supply equipment or receptacles mounted on the vehicle or generator must have the neutral conductor connected to the generator frame.

Note: A portable or vehicle-mounted generator supplying fixed wiring for a premises must be grounded (connected to the earth) and bonded in accordance with 250.30 for separately derived systems and 250.35 for nonseparately derived systems.

250.35 Permanently Installed Generators.

(A) Separately Derived System. If the generator is installed as a separately derived system, the system must be grounded (connected to the earth) and bonded in accordance with 250.30.

(B) Nonseparately Derived System. A generator without integral overcurrent protection that's not a separately derived system must have a supply-side bonding jumper installed between the generator equipment grounding terminal and the equipment grounding terminal, bar, or bus of the disconnecting mean(s). The supply-side bonding jumper is sized in accordance with 250.102(C), based on the size of the ungrounded circuit conductors of the generator. Figure 250–93

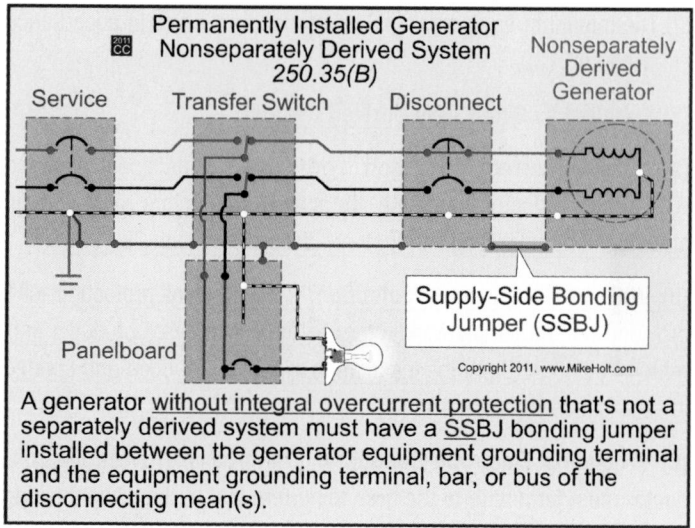

A generator without integral overcurrent protection that's not a separately derived system must have a SSBJ bonding jumper installed between the generator equipment grounding terminal and the equipment grounding terminal, bar, or bus of the disconnecting mean(s).

Figure 250–93

Author's Comment: The frame of a nonseparately derived system generator isn't required to be connected to a grounding electrode.

250.36 High-Impedance Grounded Systems.
High-impedance grounded systems are only permitted for three-phase systems where all of the following conditions are met:

(1) Conditions of maintenance and supervision ensure that only qualified persons service the installation.

(2) Ground detectors are installed on the system [250.21(B)].

(3) Line-to-neutral loads aren't served.

Author's Comment: High-impedance grounded systems are generally referred to as "high-resistance grounded systems" in the industry.

(A) Grounding Impedance Location. To limit fault current to a very low value, high-impedance grounded systems must have a resistor installed between the neutral point of the derived system and the grounding electrode conductor. **Figure 250–94**

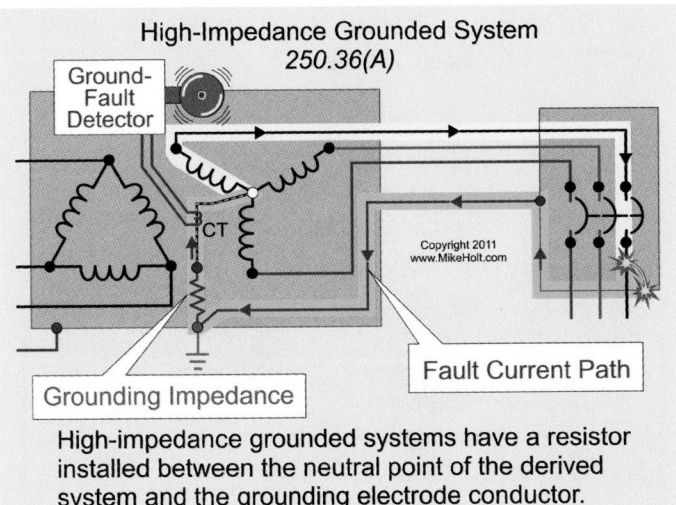

Figure 250–94

Note: For more information on this topic see IEEE 142— *Recommended Practice for Grounding of Industrial and Commercial Power Systems* (Green Book).

PART III. GROUNDING ELECTRODE SYSTEM AND GROUNDING ELECTRODE CONDUCTOR

250.50 Grounding Electrode System. Any grounding electrode described in 250.52(A)(1) through (A)(8) that's present at a building/structure must be bonded together to form the grounding electrode system. **Figure 250–95**

- Underground metal water pipe [250.52(A)(1)]
- Metal frame of the building/structure [250.52(A)(2)]
- Concrete-encased electrode [250.52(A)(3)]
- Ground ring [250.52(A)(4)]
- Ground rod [250.52(A)(5)]
- Other listed electrodes [250.52(A)(6)]
- Grounding plate [250.52(A)(7)]
- Metal underground systems, piping systems, or underground tanks [250.52(A)(8)].

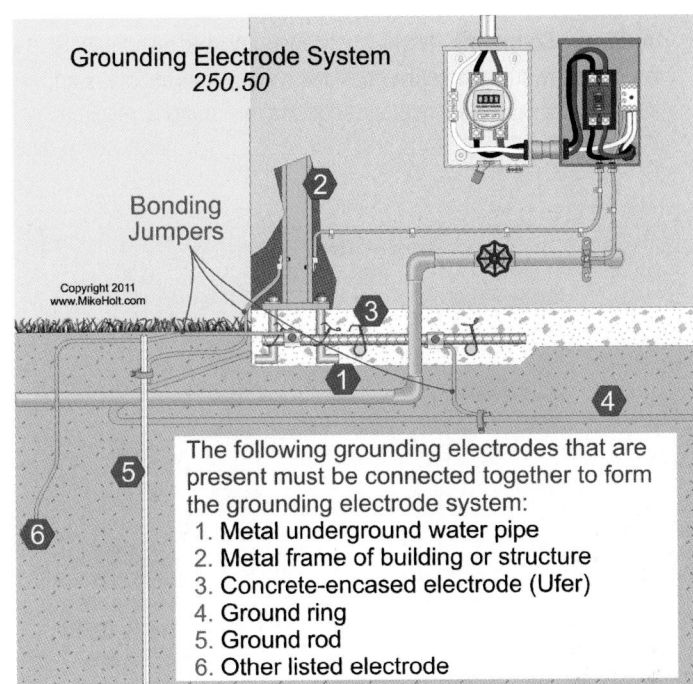

Figure 250–95

Ex: Concrete-encased electrodes aren't required for existing buildings or structures where the conductive steel reinforcing bars aren't accessible without chipping up the concrete. **Figure 250–96**

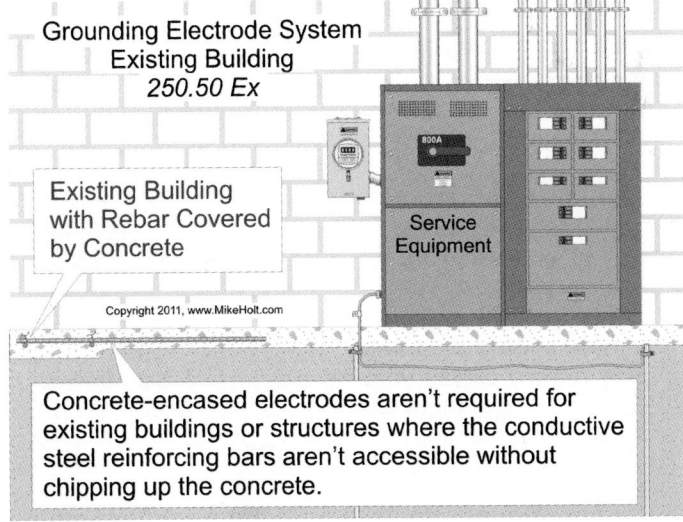

Figure 250–96

Author's Comment: When a concrete-encased electrode is used at a building/structure that doesn't have an underground metal water pipe electrode, no additional electrode is required. **Figure 250–97**

Author's Comment: Controversy about using metal underground water supply piping as a grounding electrode has existed since the early 1900s. The water industry believes that neutral current flowing on water piping corrodes the metal. For more information, contact the American Water Works Association about their report—*Effects of Electrical Grounding on Pipe Integrity and Shock Hazard*, Catalog No. 90702, 1.800.926.7337. **Figure 250–99**

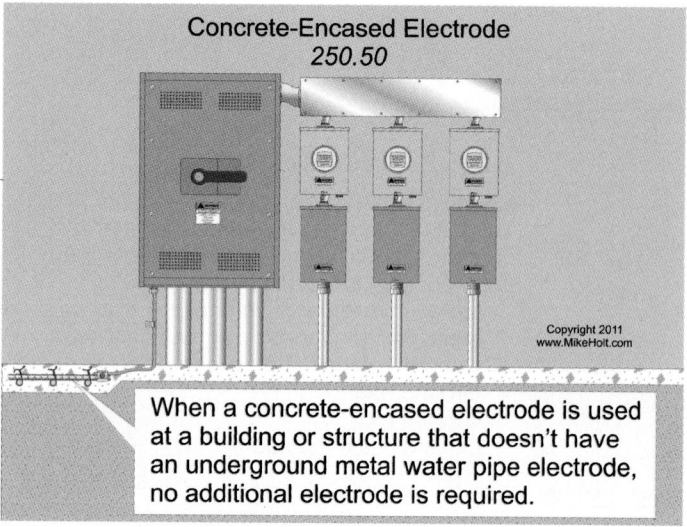

Figure 250–97

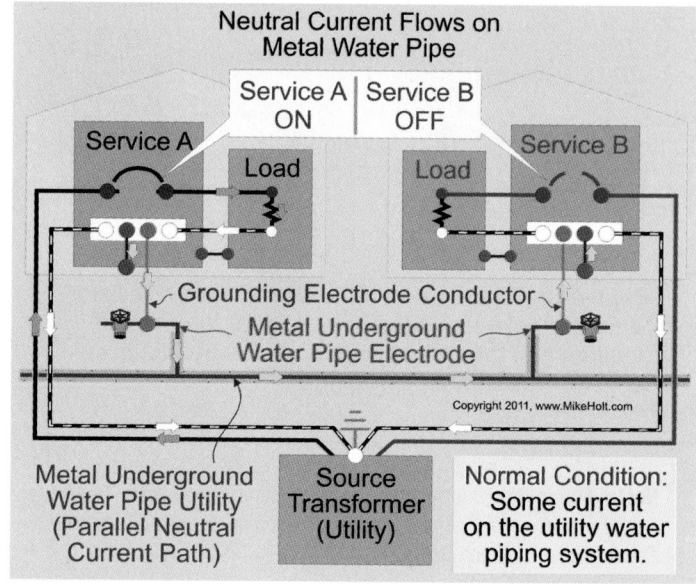

Figure 250–99

250.52 Grounding Electrode Types.

(A) Electrodes Permitted for Grounding.

(1) Underground Metal Water Pipe Electrode. Underground metal water pipe in direct contact with the earth for 10 ft or more can serve as a grounding electrode. **Figure 250–98**

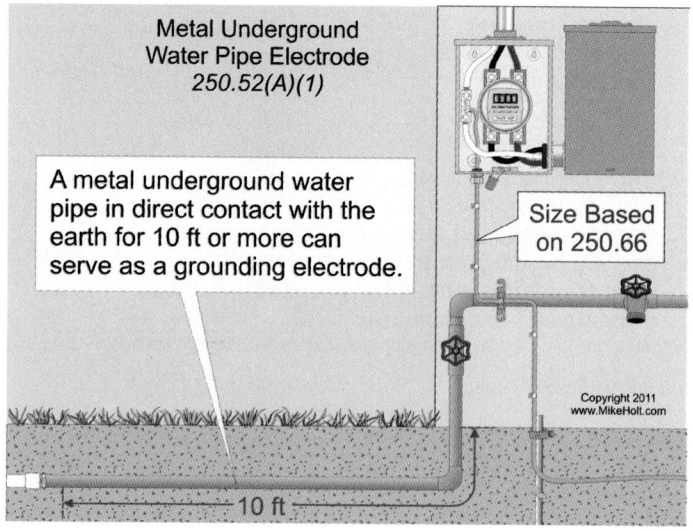

Figure 250–98

(2) Metal Frame Electrode. The metal frame of a building/structure can serve as a grounding electrode when it meets at least one of the following conditions:

(1) At least one structural metal member is in direct contact with the earth for 10 ft or more, with or without concrete encasement.

(2) The bolts securing the structural steel column are connected to a concrete-encased electrode [250.52(A)(3)] by welding, exothermic welding, steel tie wires, or other approved means. **Figure 250–100**

(3) Concrete-Encased Electrode. At least 20 ft of either (1) or (2): **Figure 250–101**

(1) One or more of bare, zinc-galvanized, or otherwise electrically conductive steel reinforcing bars of not less than ½ in. diameter, mechanically connected together by steel tie wires, welding, or other effective means, to create a 20 ft or greater length.

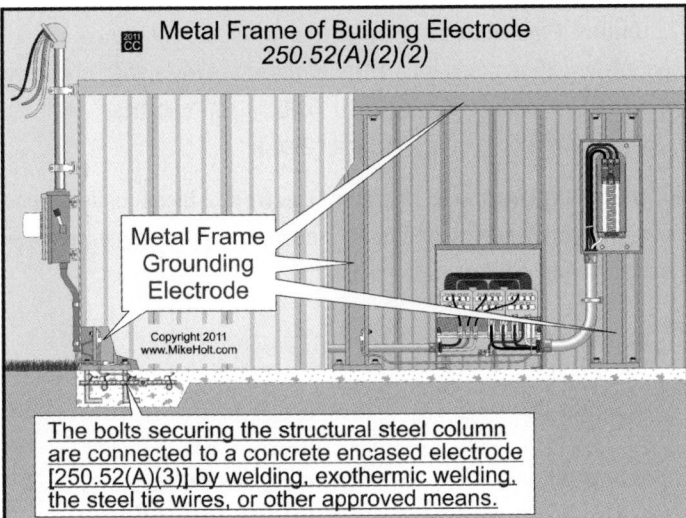

Figure 250–100

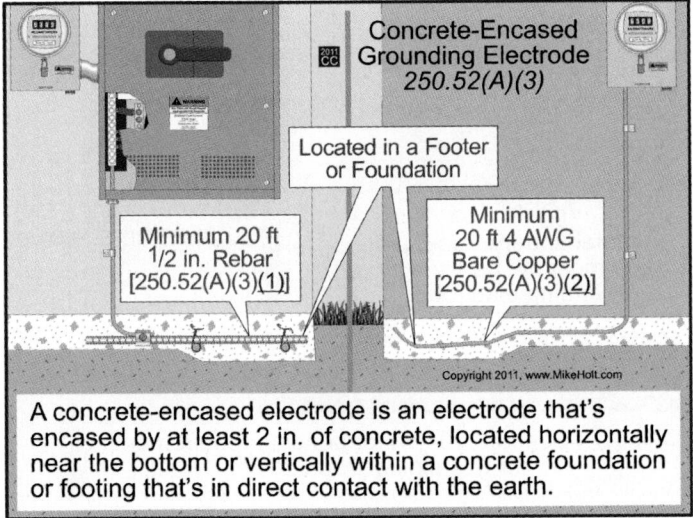

A concrete-encased electrode is an electrode that's encased by at least 2 in. of concrete, located horizontally near the bottom or vertically within a concrete foundation or footing that's in direct contact with the earth.

Figure 250–101

(2) Bare copper conductor not smaller than 4 AWG.

The reinforcing bars or bare copper conductor must be encased by at least 2 in. of concrete located horizontally near the bottom of a concrete footing or vertically within a concrete foundation that's in direct contact with the earth.

If multiple concrete-encased electrodes are present at a building/structure, only one is required to serve as a grounding electrode. **Figure 250–102**

> **Note:** Concrete containing insulation, vapor barriers, films or similar items separating it from the earth isn't considered to be in "direct contact" with the earth.

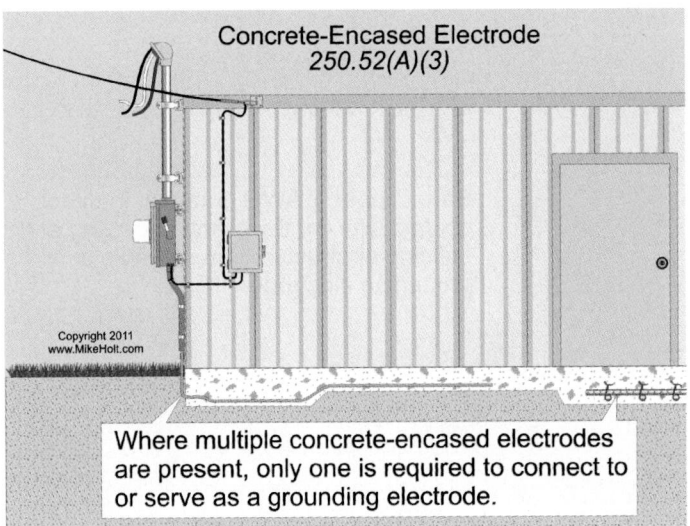

Figure 250–102

Author's Comments:

- The grounding electrode conductor to a concrete-encased grounding electrode isn't required to be larger than 4 AWG copper [250.66(B)].

- The concrete-encased grounding electrode is also called a "Ufer Ground," named after a consultant working for the U.S. Army during World War II. The technique Mr. Ufer came up with was necessary because the site needing grounding had no underground water table and little rainfall. The desert site was a series of bomb storage vaults in the area of Flagstaff, Arizona. This type of grounding electrode generally offers the lowest ground resistance for the cost.

(4) Ground Ring Electrode. A ground ring consisting of at least 20 ft of bare copper conductor not smaller than 2 AWG buried in the earth encircling a building/structure, can serve as a grounding electrode. **Figure 250–103**

> **Author's Comment:** The ground ring must be buried not less than 30 in. [250.53(F)], and the grounding electrode conductor to a ground ring isn't required to be larger than the ground ring conductor size [250.66(C)].

(5) Ground Rod and Pipe Electrode. Ground rod electrodes must not be less than 8 ft in length in contact with the earth [250.53(G)].

(b) Rod-type electrodes must have a diameter of at least ⅝ in., unless listed. **Figure 250–104**

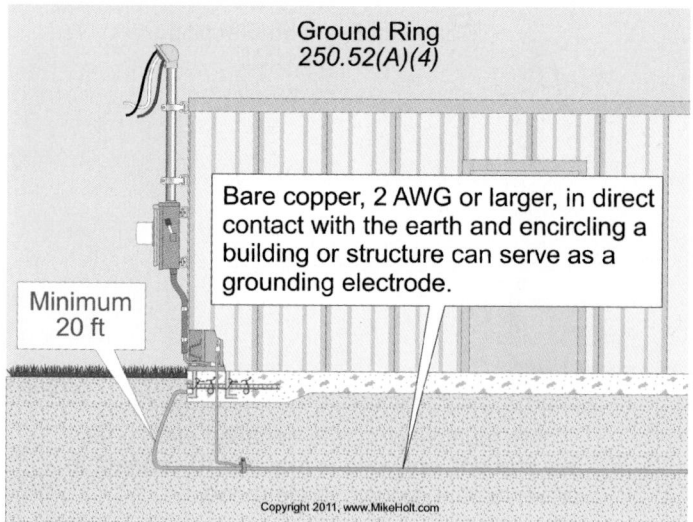

Figure 250–103

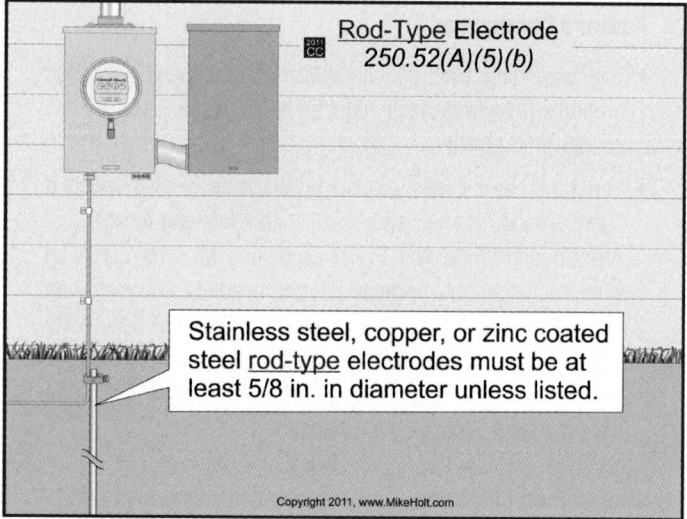

Figure 250–104

Author's Comments:

- The grounding electrode conductor, if it's the sole connection to the ground rod, isn't required to be larger than 6 AWG copper [250.66(A)].

- The diameter of a ground rod has an insignificant effect on the contact resistance of a ground rod to the earth. However, larger diameter ground rods (¾ in. and 1 in.) are sometimes installed where mechanical strength is desired, or to compensate for the loss of the electrode's metal due to corrosion.

(6) Listed Electrode. Other listed grounding electrodes.

(7) Ground Plate Electrode. A bare or conductively coated iron or steel plate with not less than ¼ in. of thickness, or a solid uncoated copper metal plate not less than 0.06 in. of thickness, with an exposed surface area of not less than 2 sq ft.

(8) Metal Underground Systems Electrode. Metal underground piping systems, underground tanks, and underground metal well casings can serve as a grounding electrode.

> **Author's Comment:** The grounding electrode conductor to the metal underground system must be sized in accordance with Table 250.66.

(B) Not Permitted for Use as a Grounding Electrode.

(1) Underground metal gas-piping systems. Figure 250–105

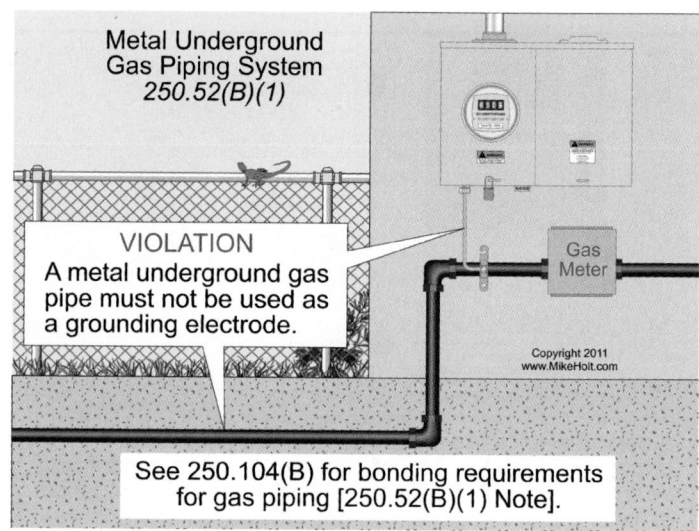

Figure 250–105

(2) Aluminum

250.53 Grounding Electrode Installation Requirements.

(A) Rod, Pipe, or Plate Electrodes.

(1) Below Permanent Moisture Level. If practicable, rod, pipe, and plate electrodes must be embedded below the permanent moisture level and be free from nonconductive coatings such as paint or enamel.

(2) Supplemental Electrode. A single rod, pipe or plate electrode must be supplemented by an additional electrode that's bonded to one of the following: **Figure 250–106**

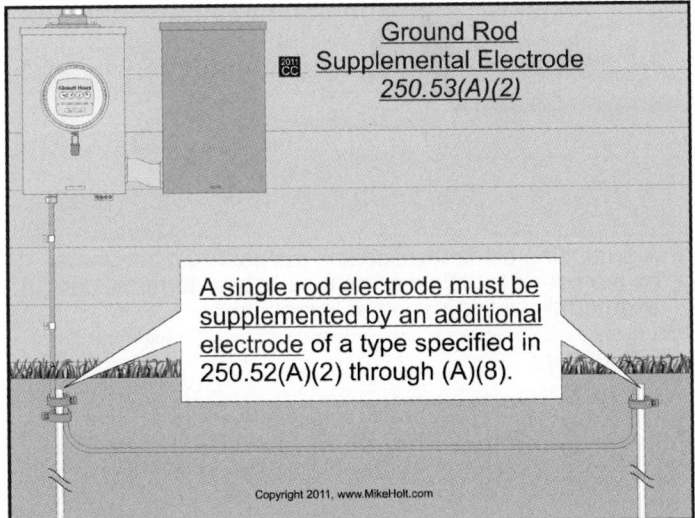

Figure 250–106

(1) The single rod, pipe, or plate electrode

(2) The grounding electrode conductor of the single electrode

(3) The neutral service-entrance conductor

(4) The nonflexible grounded service raceway

(5) The service enclosure

Ex: If a single rod, pipe, or plate grounding electrode has an earth contact resistance of 25 ohms or less, the supplemental electrode isn't required. **Figure 250–107**

(3) Spacing. The supplemental electrode for a single rod, pipe, or plate electrode must be installed not less than 6 ft from the single electrode. **Figure 250–108**

> Note: The efficiency of paralleling electrodes is improved by spacing them at least twice the length of the longest rod.

(B) Electrode Spacing. Ground rods used as the required electrode for power systems must be located no closer than 6 ft from lighting protection or photovoltaic system grounding electrodes. Two or more grounding electrodes that are bonded together are considered a single grounding electrode system. **Figure 250–109**

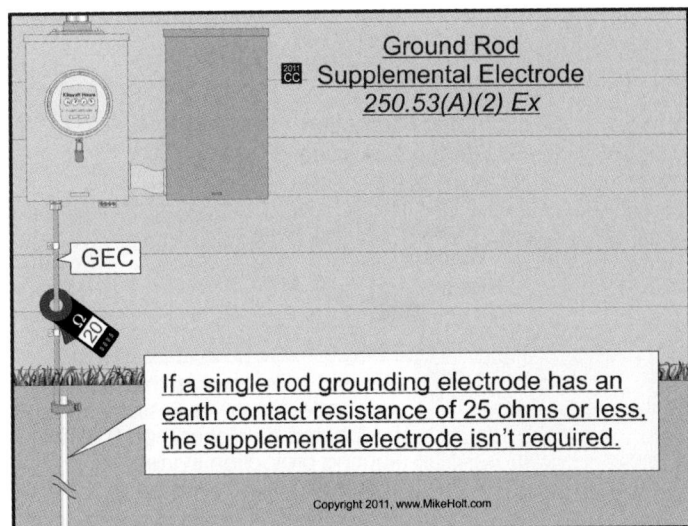

Figure 250–107

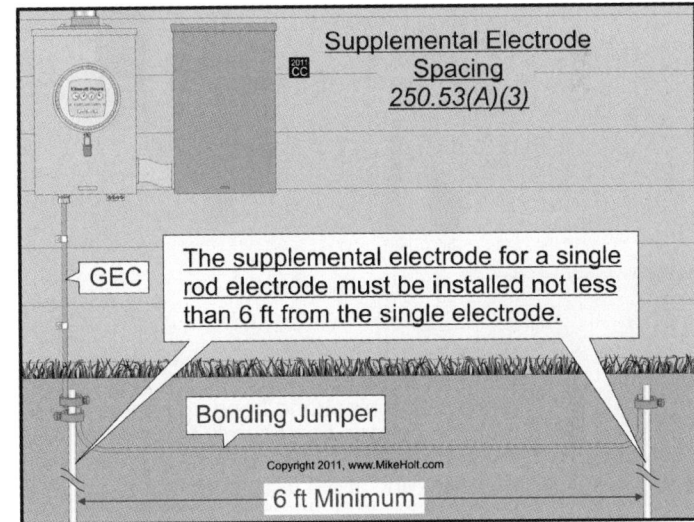

Figure 250–108

(C) Grounding Electrode Bonding Jumper. Grounding electrode bonding jumpers must be copper when within 18 in. of the earth [250.64(A)], be securely fastened to the surface, and be protected if exposed to physical damage [250.64(B)]. The bonding jumper to each electrode must be sized in accordance with 250.66. **Figure 250–110**

The grounding electrode bonding jumpers must terminate by the use of listed pressure connectors, terminal bars, exothermic welding, or other listed means [250.8(A)]. When the termination is encased in concrete or buried, the termination fittings must be listed for this purpose [250.70]. **Figure 250–111**

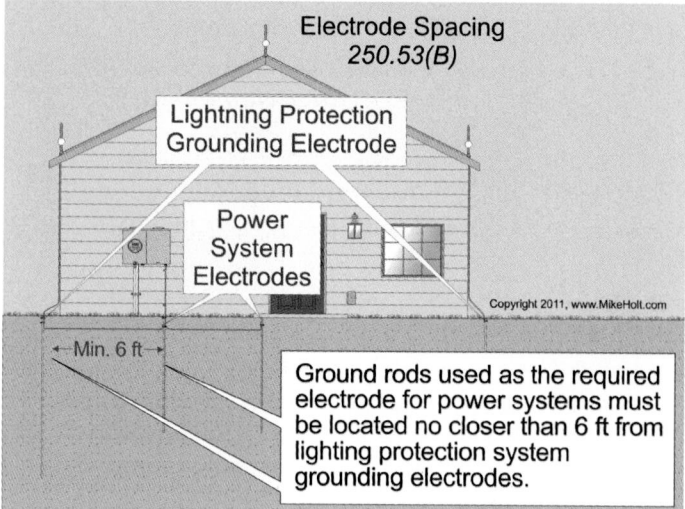

Figure 250–109

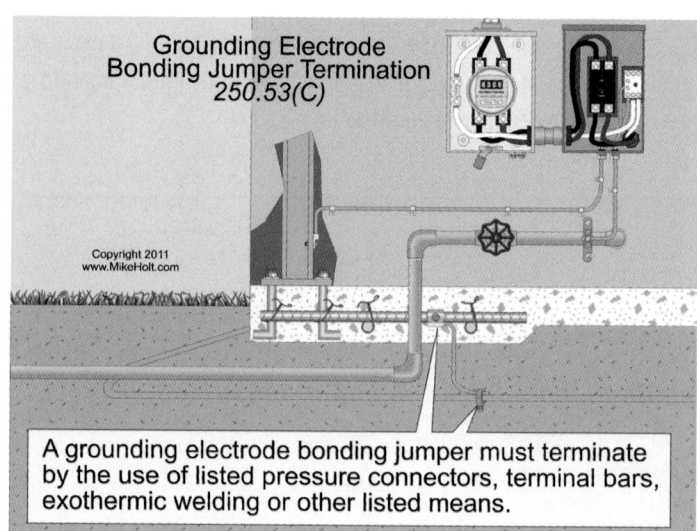

Figure 250–111

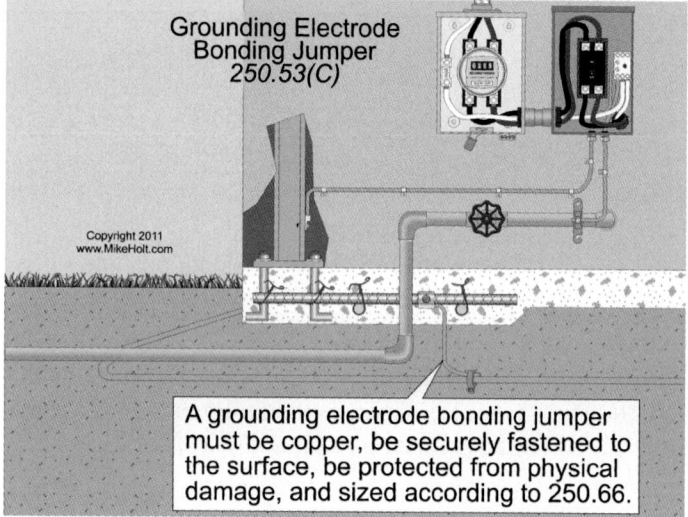

Figure 250–110

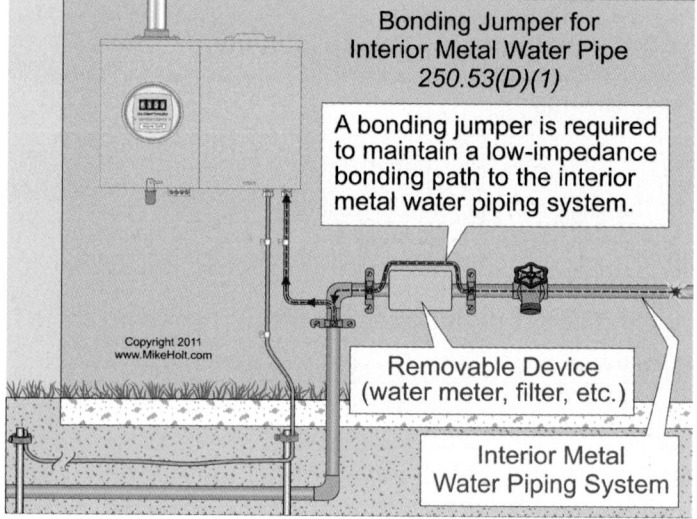

Figure 250–112

(D) Underground Metal Water Pipe Electrode.

(1) Continuity. The bonding connection to the interior metal water piping system, as required by 250.104(A), must not be dependent on water meters, filtering devices, or similar equipment likely to be disconnected for repairs or replacement. When necessary, a bonding jumper must be installed around insulated joints and equipment likely to be disconnected for repairs or replacement to assist in clearing and removing dangerous voltage on metal parts due to a ground fault [250.68(B)]. **Figure 250–112**

(2) Underground Metal Water Pipe Supplemental Electrode Required. When an underground metal water pipe grounding electrode is present [250.52(A)(1)], it must be supplemented by one of the following electrodes:

- Metal frame of the building/structure electrode [250.52(A)(2)]
- Concrete-encased electrode [250.52(A)(3)] **Figure 250–113**
- Ground ring electrode [250.52(A)(4)]
- Ground rod electrode meeting the requirements of 250.52(A)(5)
- Other listed electrodes [250.52(A)(6)]
- Metal underground systems, piping systems, or underground tanks [250.52(A)(8)]

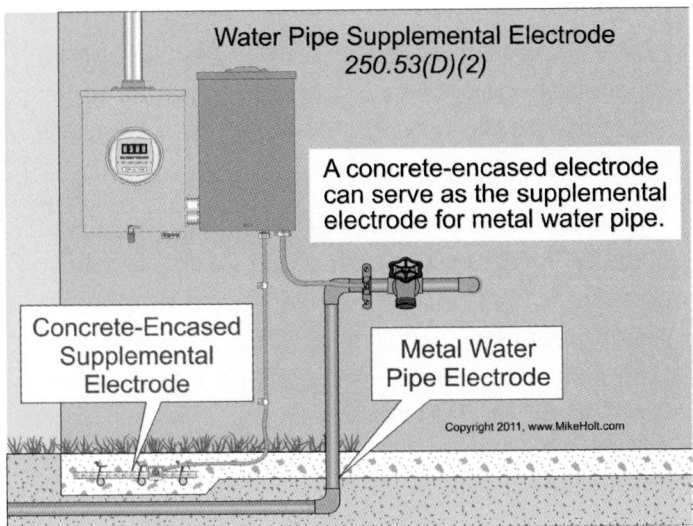

Figure 250–113

The termination of the supplemental grounding electrode conductor must be to one of the following locations: **Figure 250–114**

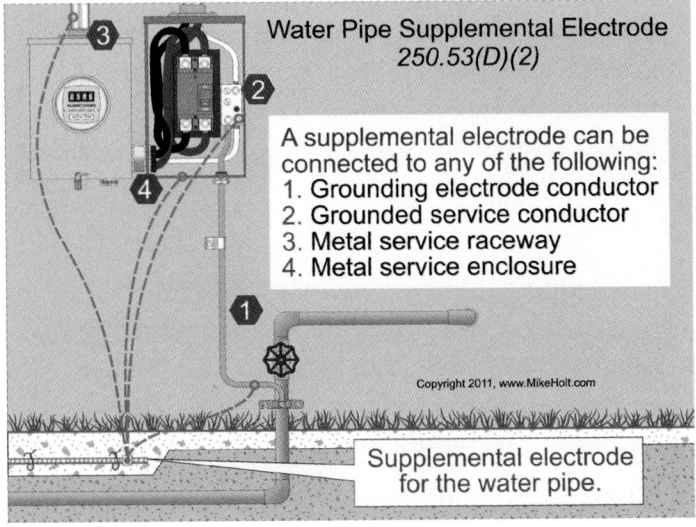

Figure 250–114

(1) Grounding electrode conductor

(2) Service neutral conductor

(3) Metal service raceway

(4) Service equipment enclosure

Ex: The supplemental electrode is permitted to be bonded to interior metal water piping located not more than 5 ft from the point of entrance to the building/structure [250.68(C)(1)].

(E) Supplemental Ground Rod Electrode. The grounding electrode conductor to a ground rod that serves as a supplemental electrode isn't required to be larger than 6 AWG copper.

(F) Ground Ring. A ground ring encircling the building/structure, consisting of at least 20 ft of bare copper conductor not smaller than 2 AWG, must be buried not less than 30 in. [250.52(A)(4)]. **Figure 250–115**

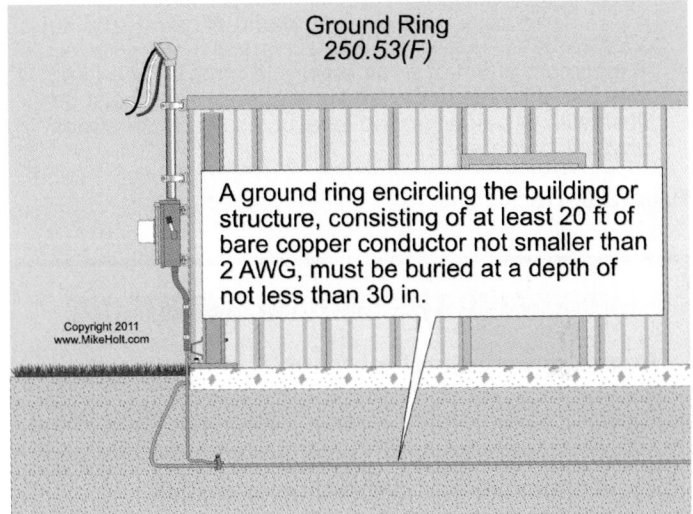

Figure 250–115

(G) Ground Rod Electrodes. Ground rod electrodes must be installed so that not less than 8 ft of length is in contact with the soil. If rock bottom is encountered, the ground rod must be driven at an angle not to exceed 45 degrees from vertical. If rock bottom is encountered at an angle up to 45 degrees from vertical, the ground rod can be buried in a minimum 30 in. deep trench. **Figure 250–116**

The upper end of the ground rod must be flush with or underground unless the grounding electrode conductor attachment is protected against physical damage as specified in 250.10.

> **Author's Comment:** When the grounding electrode attachment fitting is located underground, it must be listed for direct soil burial [250.68(A) Ex 1 and 250.70].

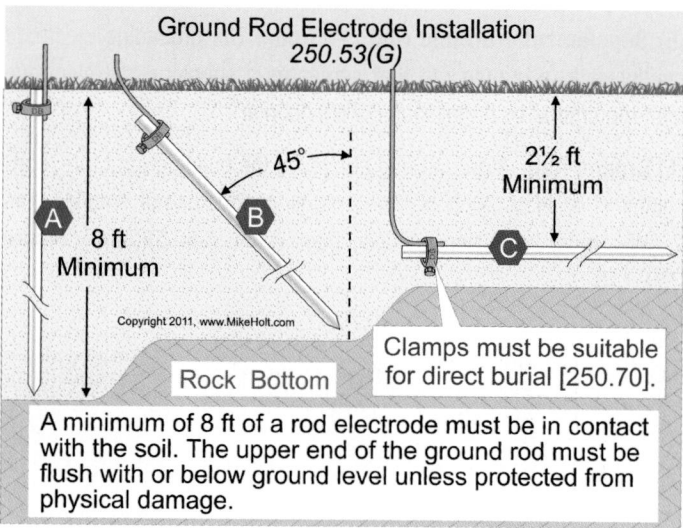

Ground Rod Electrode Installation
250.53(G)

45°

2½ ft
Minimum

8 ft
Minimum

Copyright 2011, www.MikeHolt.com

Rock Bottom

Clamps must be suitable
for direct burial [250.70].

A minimum of 8 ft of a rod electrode must be in contact
with the soil. The upper end of the ground rod must be
flush with or below ground level unless protected from
physical damage.

Figure 250–116

MEASURING THE GROUND RESISTANCE

Measuring the Ground Resistance

A ground resistance clamp meter, or a three-point fall of potential ground resistance meter, can be used to measure the contact resistance of a grounding electrode to the earth.

Ground Clamp Meter. The ground resistance clamp meter
measures the contact resistance of the grounding system to
the earth by injecting a high-frequency signal via the service
neutral conductor to the utility ground, and then measuring the
strength of the return signal through the earth to the grounding
electrode being measured. **Figure 250–117**

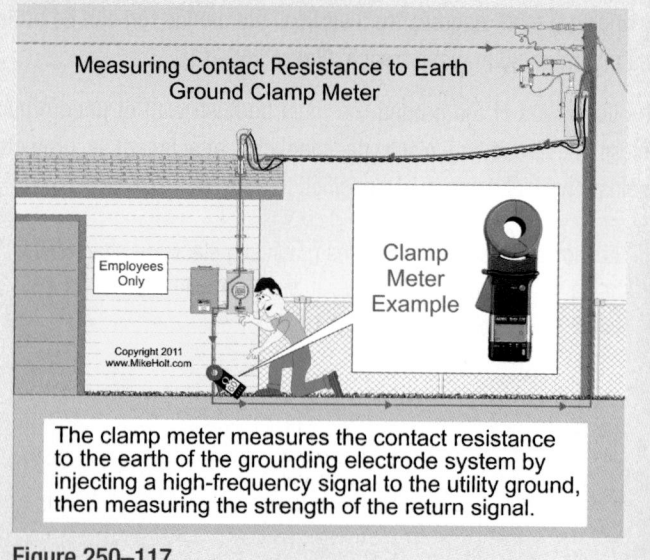

Measuring Contact Resistance to Earth
Ground Clamp Meter

Employees
Only

Clamp
Meter
Example

Copyright 2011
www.MikeHolt.com

The clamp meter measures the contact resistance
to the earth of the grounding electrode system by
injecting a high-frequency signal to the utility ground,
then measuring the strength of the return signal.

Figure 250–117

Fall of Potential Ground Resistance Meter. The three-point fall
of potential ground resistance meter determines the contact
resistance of a single grounding electrode to the earth by using
Ohm's Law: R=E/I.

This meter divides the voltage difference between the electrode to be measured and a driven potential test stake (P) by
the current flowing between the electrode to be measured
and a driven current test stake (C). The test stakes are typically made of ¼ in. diameter steel rods, 24 in. long, driven two-
thirds of their length into the earth.

The distance and alignment between the potential and current
test stakes, and the electrode, is extremely important to the
validity of the earth contact resistance measurements. For an 8
ft ground rod, the accepted practice is to space the current test
stake (C) 80 ft from the electrode to be measured.

The potential test stake (P) is positioned in a straight line
between the electrode to be measured and the current test
stake (C). The potential test stake should be located at approximately 62 percent of the distance the current test stake is
located from the electrode. Since the current test stake (C) for
an 8 ft ground rod is located 80 ft from the grounding electrode, the potential test stake (P) will be about 50 ft from the
electrode to be measured.

> *Question:* If the voltage between the ground rod and the
> potential test stake (P) is 3V and the current between the
> ground rod and the current test stake (C) is 0.20A, then
> the earth contact resistance of the electrode to the earth
> will be _____. **Figure 250–118**
>
> (a) 5 ohms   (b) 10 ohms   (c) 15 ohms   (d) 25 ohms
>
> *Answer:* (c) 15 ohms
>
> Resistance = Voltage/Current
> E (Voltage) = 3V
> I (Current) = 0.20A
> R = E/I
> Resistance = 3V/0.20A
> Resistance = 15 ohms

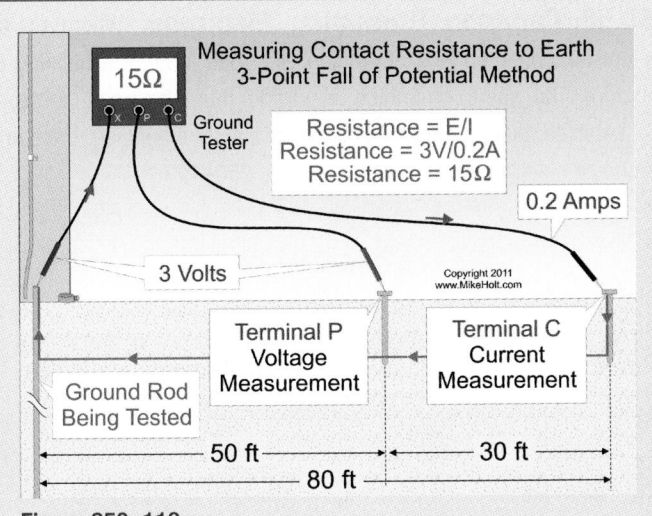

Figure 250–118

Author's Comment: The three-point fall of potential meter can only be used to measure the contact resistance of one electrode to the earth at a time, and this electrode must be independent and not connected to any part of the electrical system. The contact resistance of two electrodes bonded together must not be measured until they've been separated. The contact resistance of two separate electrodes to the earth is calculated as if they're two resistors connected in parallel.

Soil Resistivity

The earth's ground resistance is directly impacted by soil resistivity, which varies throughout the world. Soil resistivity is influenced by electrolytes, which consist of moisture, minerals, and dissolved salts. Because soil resistivity changes with moisture content, the resistance of any grounding system varies with the seasons of the year. Since moisture is stable at greater distances below the surface of the earth, grounding systems are generally more effective if the grounding electrode can reach the water table. In addition, placing the grounding electrode below the frost line helps to ensure less deviation in the system's contact resistance to the earth year round.

The contact resistance to the earth can be lowered by chemically treating the earth around the grounding electrodes with electrolytes designed for this purpose.

250.54 Auxiliary Grounding Electrodes. Auxiliary electrodes can be connected to the circuit equipment grounding conductor. They're not required to be bonded to the building/structure grounding electrode system, the grounding conductor to the electrode isn't required to be sized to 250.66, and their contact resistance to the earth isn't required to comply with the 25 ohm requirement of 250.53(A)(2) Ex. **Figures 250–119 and 250–120**

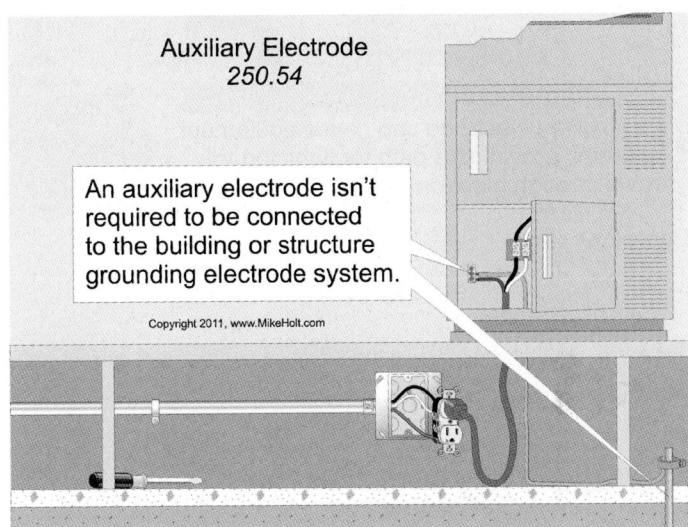

Figure 250–119

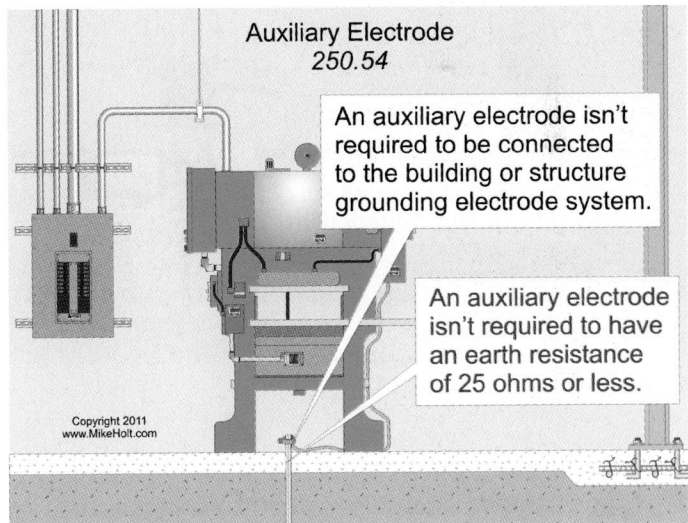

Figure 250–120

⚠️ **CAUTION:** *An auxiliary electrode typically serves no useful purpose, and in some cases it may actually cause equipment failures by providing a path for lightning to travel through electronic equipment.* **Figure 250–121**

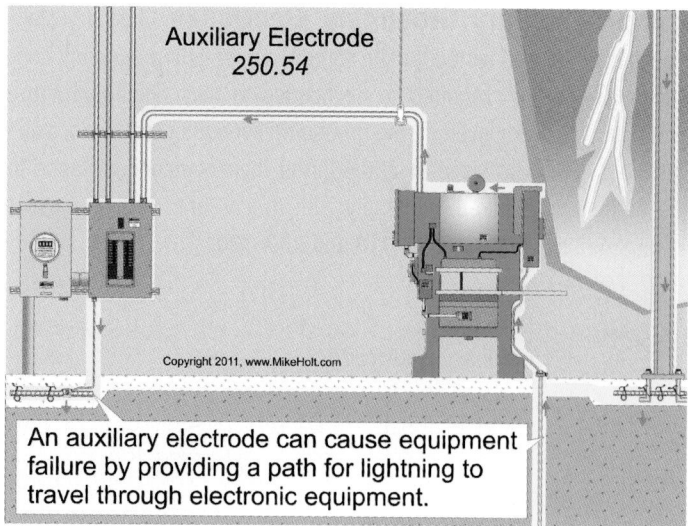

An auxiliary electrode can cause equipment failure by providing a path for lightning to travel through electronic equipment.

Figure 250–121

The earth must not be used as the effective ground-fault current path required by 250.4(A)(5). **Figure 250–122**

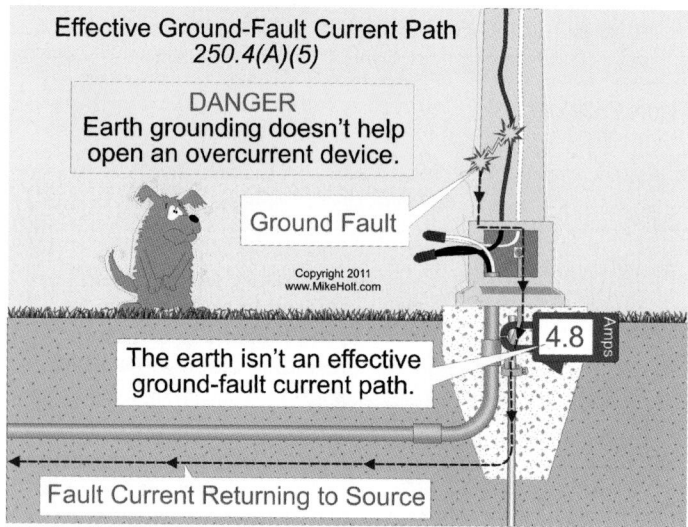

Figure 250–122

DANGER: *Because the contact resistance of an electrode to the earth is so great, very little fault current returns to the power supply if the earth is the only fault current return path. Result—the circuit overcurrent device won't open and clear the ground fault, and all metal parts associated with the electrical installation, metal piping, and structural building steel will become and remain energized.*

250.58 Common Grounding Electrode. Where an ac system is connected to a grounding electrode in or at a building or structure, the same grounding electrode must be used. If separate services, feeders, or branch circuits supply a building, the same grounding electrode must be used. **Figure 250–123**

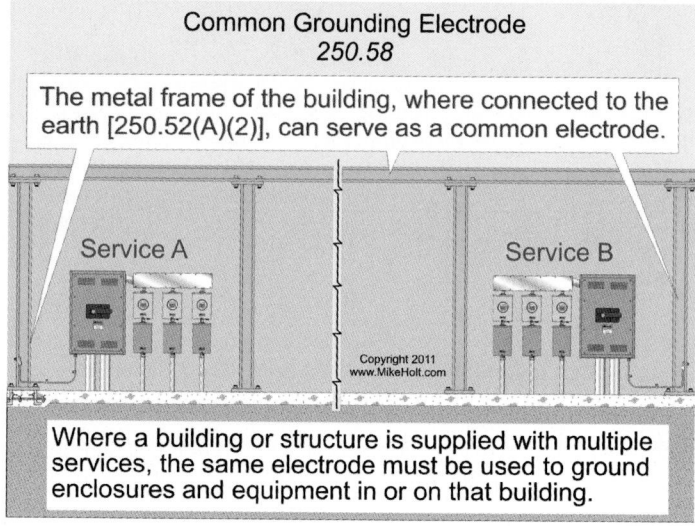

Figure 250–123

Two or more grounding electrodes that are bonded together will be considered as a single grounding electrode system in this sense.

Author's Comment: Metal parts of the electrical installation are grounded (connected to the earth) to reduce induced voltage on the metal parts from lightning so as to prevent fires from a surface arc within the building/structure. Grounding electrical equipment doesn't serve the purpose of providing a low-impedance fault current path to open the circuit overcurrent device in the event of a ground fault.

CAUTION: *Potentially dangerous objectionable neutral current flows on the metal parts when multiple service disconnecting means are connected to the same electrode. This is because neutral current from each service can return to the utility via the common grounding electrode and its conductors. This is especially a problem if a service neutral conductor is opened.* **Figure 250–124**

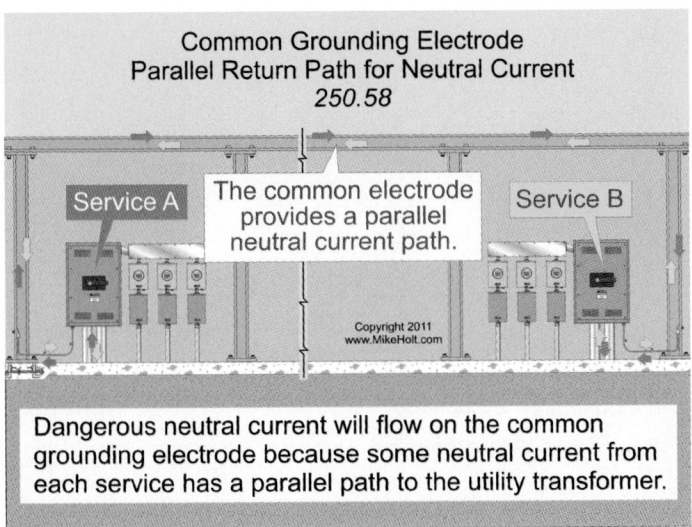

Figure 250–124

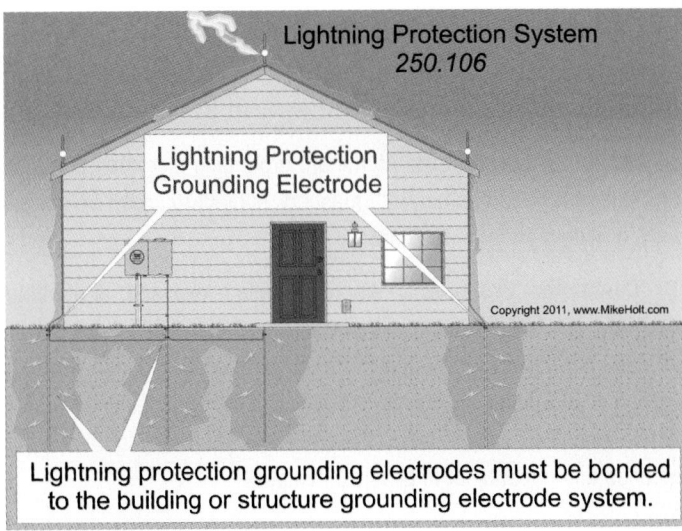

Figure 250–126

250.60 Lightning Protection Electrode. Conductors and electrodes used for <u>strike termination devices of</u> a lightning protection system aren't permitted to be used in lieu of the premises wiring grounding electrode system. **Figure 250–125**

250.62 Grounding Electrode Conductor. The grounding electrode conductor must be solid or stranded, insulated or bare, and it must be copper if within 18 in. of the earth [250.64(A)]. **Figure 250–127**

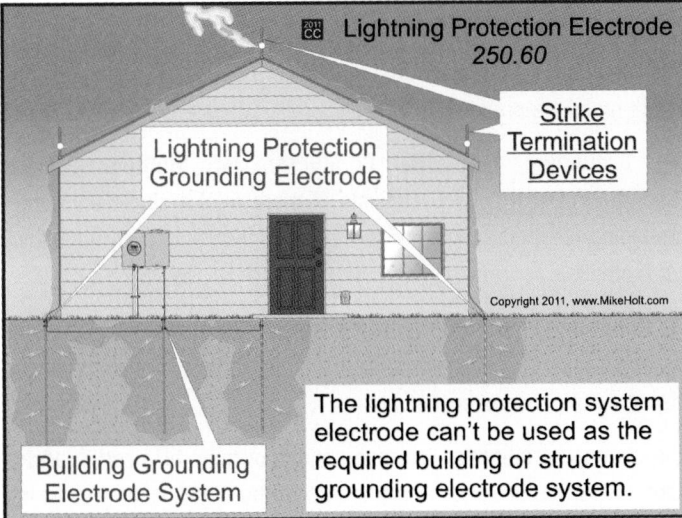

Figure 250–125

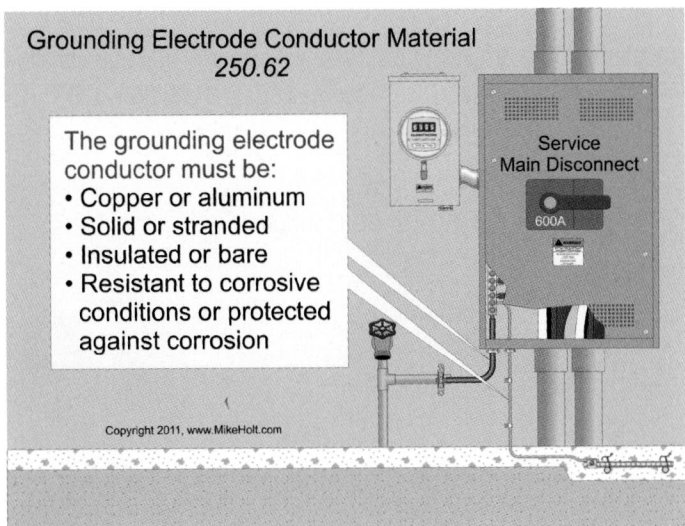

Figure 250–127

Note 2: If a lightning protection system is installed, the lightning protection system must be bonded to the building/structure grounding electrode system so as to limit potential difference between it and the electrical system wiring in accordance with 250.106. **Figure 250–126**

250.64 Grounding Electrode Conductor Installation.

Grounding electrode conductors must be installed as specified in (A) through (F).

(A) Aluminum Conductors. Aluminum grounding <u>electrode</u> conductors must not be in contact with masonry, subject to corrosive conditions, or within 18 in. of the earth.

(B) Conductor Protection. Where installed exposed, grounding electrode conductors must be protected where subject to physical damage and are <u>permitted to be installed on or through framing members.</u> Grounding electrode conductors 6 AWG copper and larger can be installed exposed along the surface of the building if securely fastened and not subject to physical damage.

Grounding electrode conductors sized 8 AWG must be <u>protected by</u> installing them in rigid metal conduit, intermediate metal conduit, PVC conduit, electrical metallic tubing, or <u>reinforced thermosetting resin conduit.</u>

> **Author's Comment:** A ferrous metal raceway containing a grounding electrode conductor must be made electrically continuous by bonding each end of that type of raceway to the grounding electrode conductor [250.64(E)], so it's best to use PVC conduit.

(C) Continuous. Grounding electrode conductor(s) must be installed without a splice or joint except: **Figures 250–128 and 250–129**

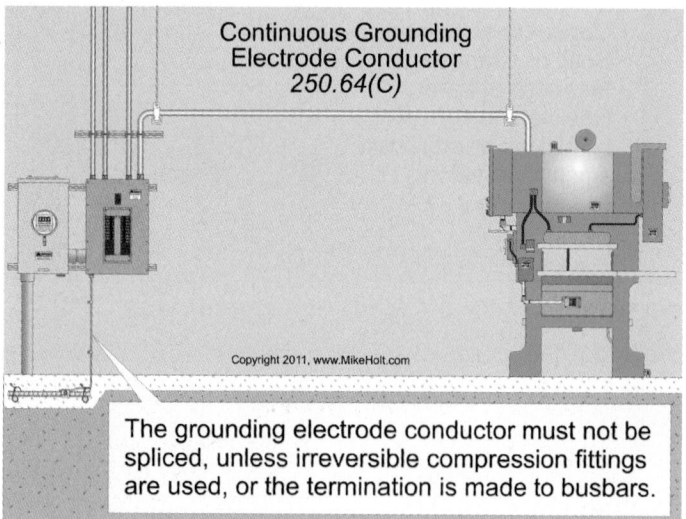

The grounding electrode conductor must not be spliced, unless irreversible compression fittings are used, or the termination is made to busbars.

Figure 250–128

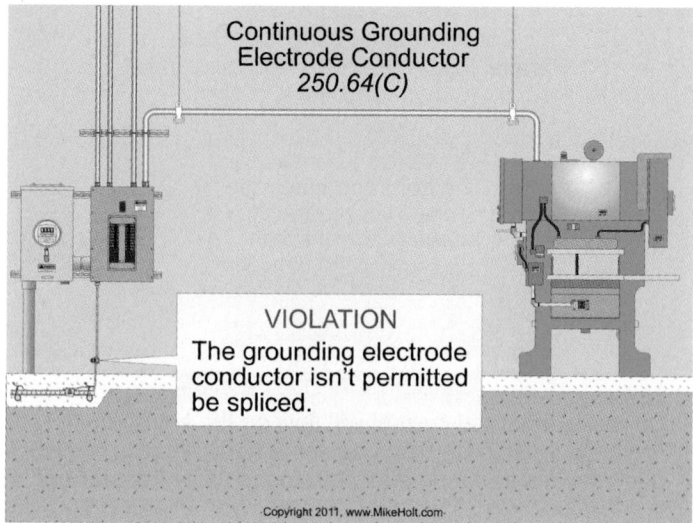

VIOLATION
The grounding electrode conductor isn't permitted be spliced.

Figure 250–129

(1) By irreversible compression-type connectors or exothermic welding.

(2) Sections of busbars connected together to form a grounding electrode conductor.

(3) <u>Bolted, riveted, or welded connections of structural metal frames of buildings or structures.</u>

(4) <u>Threaded, welded, brazed, soldered or bolted-flange connections of metal water piping.</u>

(D) Grounding Electrode Conductor for Multiple Service Disconnects. <u>If</u> a service consists of more than a single enclosure, grounding electrode connections must be made in one of the following methods:

(1) <u>Common</u> Grounding Electrode Conductor and Taps. A grounding electrode conductor tap must extend to the inside of each service disconnecting means enclosure.

The common grounding electrode conductor must be sized in accordance with 250.66, based on the sum of the circular mil area of the largest ungrounded service-entrance conductors. **Figure 250–130**

A grounding electrode conductor must extend from each service disconnecting means, sized not smaller than specified in Table 250.66, based on the area of the largest ungrounded conductor for each service disconnecting means.

The <u>grounding electrode</u> tap conductors must be connected to the common grounding electrode conductor, without splicing the common grounding electrode conductor, by one of the following methods:

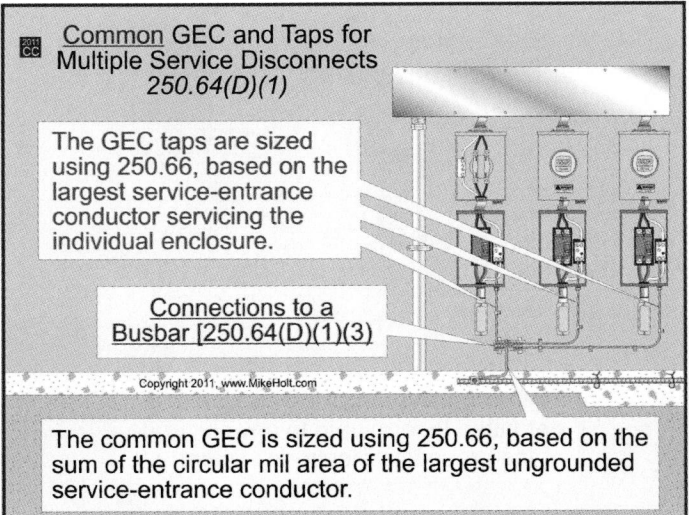

Figure 250–130

(1) Exothermic welding.

(2) Connectors listed as grounding and bonding equipment.

(3) Connections to a busbar not less than ¼ in. × 2 in. that's securely fastened and installed in an accessible location.

(2) Individual Grounding Electrode Conductors. A grounding electrode conductor must be connected between the grounded conductor in each service equipment disconnecting means enclosure and the grounding electrode system, each sized in accordance with 250.66 based on the ungrounded service-entrance conductor(s) supplying the individual service disconnecting means. **Figure 250–131**

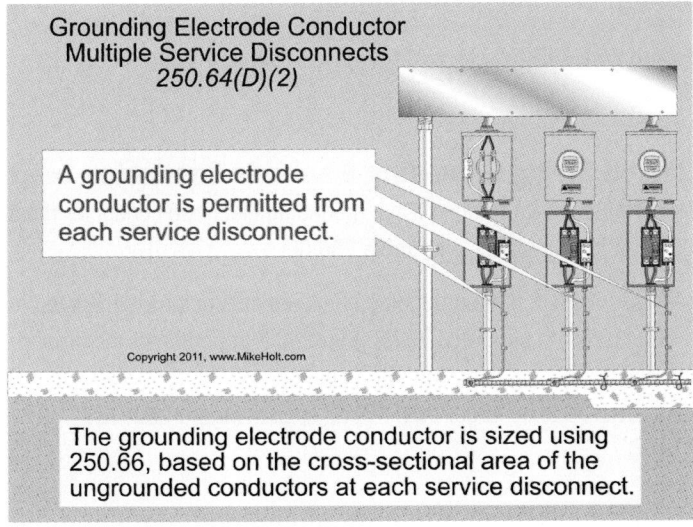

Figure 250–131

(3) Common Location. A single grounding electrode conductor is permitted from a common location, sized not smaller than specified in Table 250.66, based on the area of the ungrounded conductor at the location where the connection is made. **Figure 250–132**

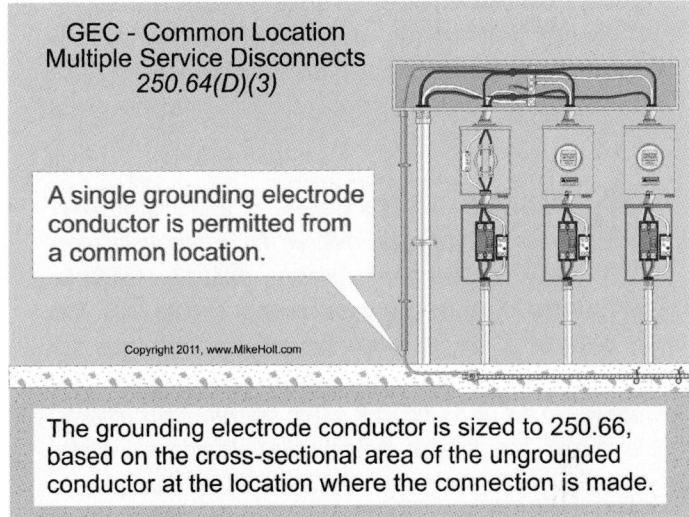

Figure 250–132

(E) Ferrous Metal Enclosures Containing Grounding Electrode Conductors. To prevent inductive choking of grounding electrode conductors, ferrous raceways and enclosures containing grounding electrode conductors must have each end of the raceway or enclosure bonded to the grounding electrode conductor in accordance with 250.92(B) for installations at service equipment. **Figure 250–133**

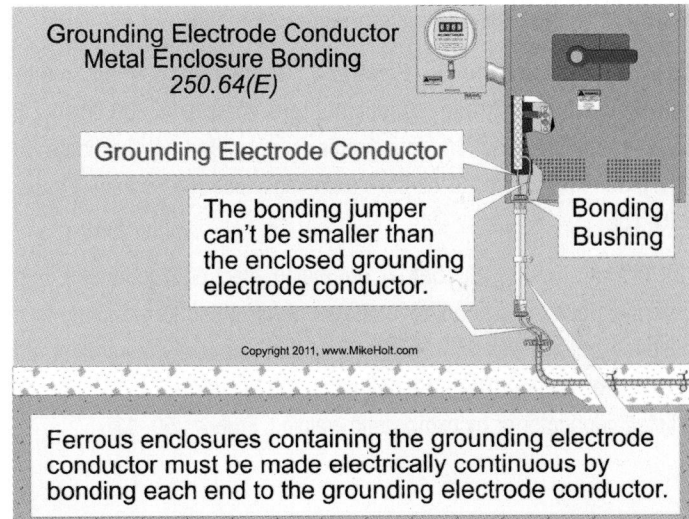

Figure 250–133

For other than service equipment locations, ferrous raceways and enclosures containing grounding electrode conductors must have each end of the raceway or enclosure bonded to the grounding electrode conductor in accordance with 250.92(B)(2) through (B)(4).

Author's Comment: Nonferrous metal raceways, such as aluminum rigid metal conduit, enclosing the grounding electrode conductor aren't required to meet the "bonding each end of the raceway to the grounding electrode conductor" provisions of this section.

⚠ **CAUTION:** *The effectiveness of a grounding electrode is significantly reduced if a ferrous metal raceway containing a grounding electrode conductor isn't bonded to the ferrous metal raceway at both ends. This is because a single conductor carrying high-frequency induced lightning current in a ferrous raceway causes the raceway to act as an inductor, which severely limits (chokes) the current flow through the grounding electrode conductor. ANSI/IEEE 142—Recommended Practice for Grounding of Industrial and Commercial Power Systems (Green Book) states: "An inductive choke can reduce the current flow by 97 percent."*

Author's Comment: To save a lot of time and effort, install the grounding electrode conductor exposed if it's not subject to physical damage [250.64(B)], or enclose it in PVC conduit suitable for the application [352.10(F)].

(F) Termination to Grounding Electrode.

(1) Single Grounding Electrode Conductor. A single grounding electrode conductor is permitted to terminate to any grounding electrode of the grounding electrode system. **Figure 250–134**

(2) Multiple Grounding Electrode Conductors. When multiple grounding electrode conductors are installed [250.64(D)(2)], each grounding electrode conductor is permitted to terminate to any grounding electrode of the grounding electrode system. **Figure 250–135**

(3) Termination to Busbar. A grounding electrode conductor and grounding electrode bonding jumpers are permitted to terminate to a busbar sized not less than ¼ in. × 2 in. that's securely fastened at an accessible location. The terminations to the busbar must be made by a listed connector or by exothermic welding. **Figure 250–136**

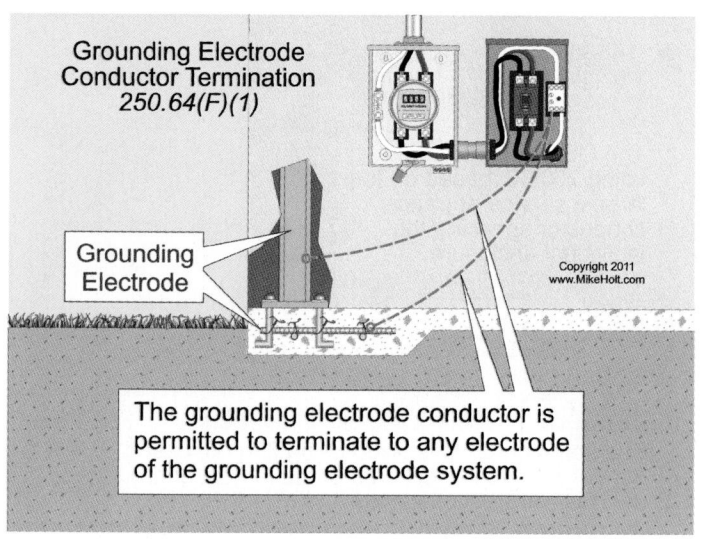

Grounding Electrode Conductor Termination *250.64(F)(1)*

Grounding Electrode

The grounding electrode conductor is permitted to terminate to any electrode of the grounding electrode system.

Figure 250–134

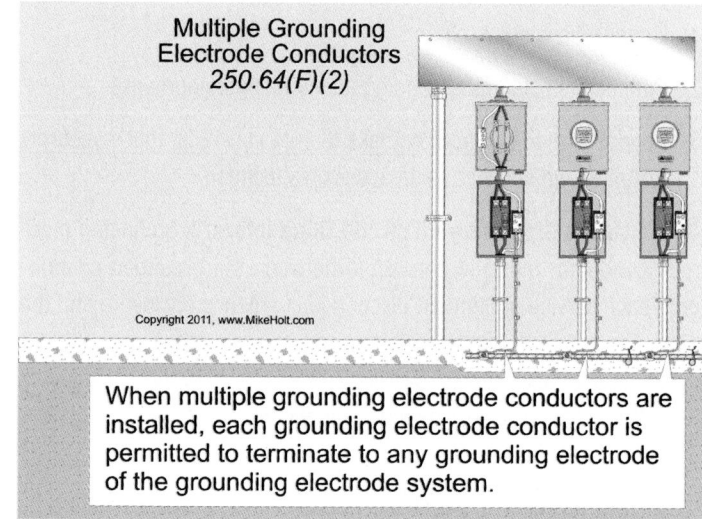

Multiple Grounding Electrode Conductors *250.64(F)(2)*

When multiple grounding electrode conductors are installed, each grounding electrode conductor is permitted to terminate to any grounding electrode of the grounding electrode system.

Figure 250–135

250.66 Sizing Grounding Electrode Conductor. Except as permitted in (A) through (C), a grounding electrode conductor must be sized in accordance with Table 250.66.

(A) Ground Rod. If the grounding electrode conductor is connected to a ground rod as permitted in 250.52(A)(5), that portion of the grounding electrode conductor that's the sole connection to the ground rod isn't required to be larger than 6 AWG copper. **Figure 250–137**

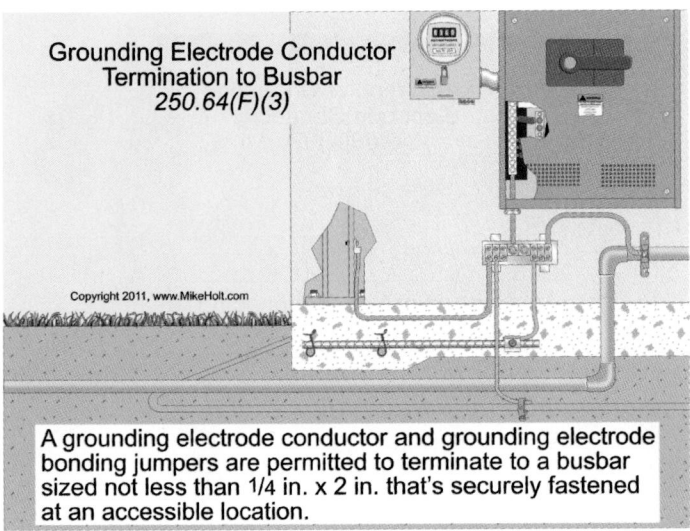

A grounding electrode conductor and grounding electrode bonding jumpers are permitted to terminate to a busbar sized not less than 1/4 in. x 2 in. that's securely fastened at an accessible location.

Figure 250–136

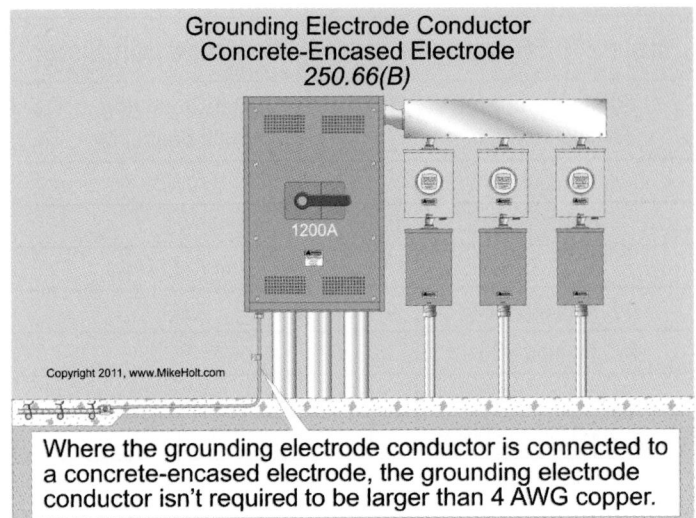

Where the grounding electrode conductor is connected to a concrete-encased electrode, the grounding electrode conductor isn't required to be larger than 4 AWG copper.

Figure 250–138

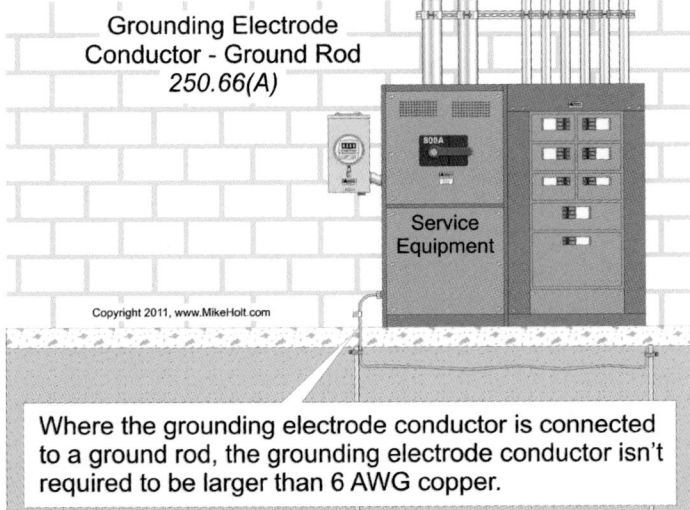

Where the grounding electrode conductor is connected to a ground rod, the grounding electrode conductor isn't required to be larger than 6 AWG copper.

Figure 250–137

Author's Comments:

- A ground ring encircling the building/structure in direct contact with the earth must consist of at least 20 ft of bare copper conductor not smaller than 2 AWG [250.52(A)(4)]. See 250.53(F) for the installation requirements for a ground ring.

- Table 250.66 is used to size the grounding electrode conductor when the conditions of 250.66(A), (B), or (C) don't apply. **Figure 250–139**

(B) Concrete-Encased Grounding Electrode. If the grounding electrode conductor is connected to a concrete-encased electrode, the portion of the grounding electrode conductor that's the sole connection to the concrete-encased electrode isn't required to be larger than 4 AWG copper. **Figure 250–138**

(C) Ground Ring. If the grounding electrode conductor is connected to a ground ring, the portion of the conductor that's the sole connection to the ground ring isn't required to be larger than the conductor used for the ground ring.

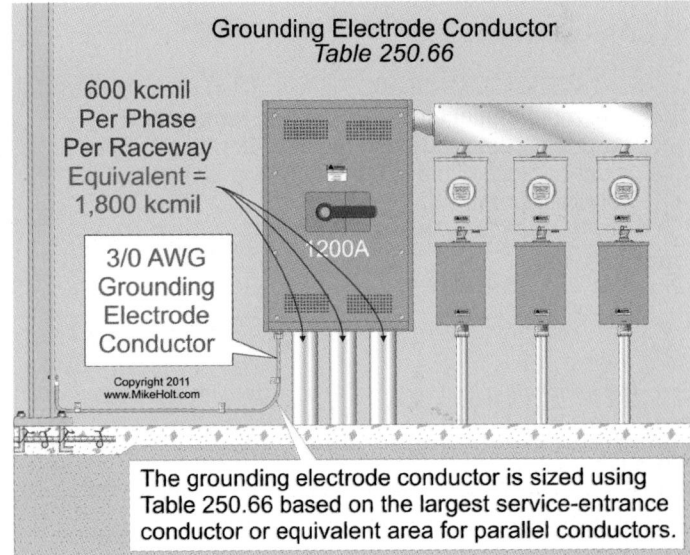

The grounding electrode conductor is sized using Table 250.66 based on the largest service-entrance conductor or equivalent area for parallel conductors.

Figure 250–139

Table 250.66 Sizing Grounding Electrode Conductor	
Conductor or Area of Parallel Conductors	Copper Grounding Electrode Conductor
12 through 2 AWG	8 AWG
1 or 1/0 AWG	6 AWG
2/0 or 3/0 AWG	4 AWG
4/0 through 350 kcmil	2 AWG
400 through 600 kcmil	1/0 AWG
700 through 1,100 kcmil	2/0 AWG
1,200 kcmil and larger	3/0 AWG

250.68 Termination to the Grounding Electrode.

(A) Accessibility. The mechanical elements used to terminate a grounding electrode conductor or bonding jumper to a grounding electrode must be accessible. **Figure 250–140**

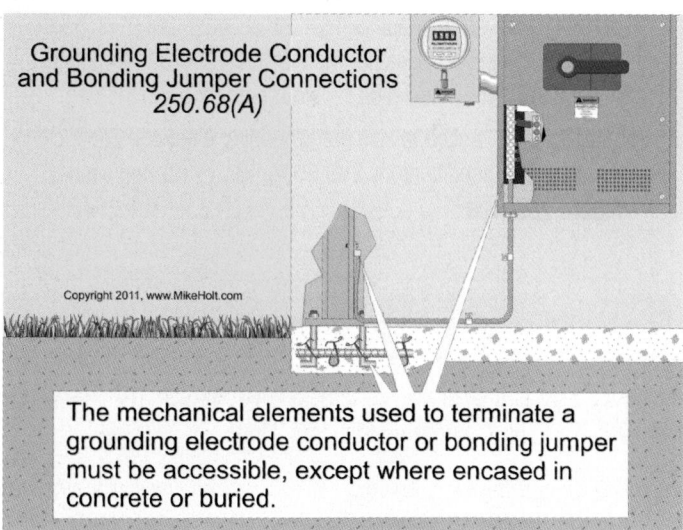

Figure 250–140

Ex 1: The termination isn't required to be accessible if the termination to the electrode is encased in concrete or buried in the earth. **Figure 250–141**

Author's Comment: If the grounding electrode attachment fitting is encased in concrete or buried in the earth, it must be listed for direct soil burial or concrete encasement [250.70].

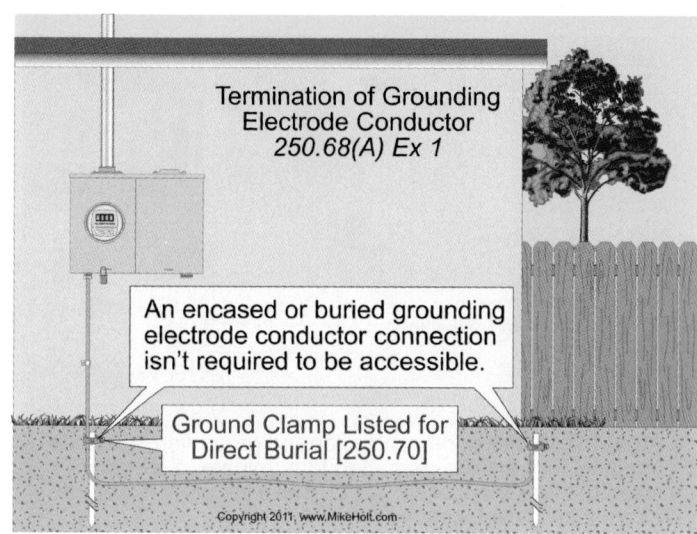

Figure 250–141

Ex 2: Exothermic or irreversible compression connections, together with the mechanical means used to attach to fireproofed structural metal, aren't required to be accessible.

(B) Integrity of Underground Metal Water Pipe Electrode. A bonding jumper must be installed around insulated joints and equipment likely to be disconnected for repairs or replacement for an underground metal water piping system used as a grounding electrode. The bonding jumper must be of sufficient length to allow the removal of such equipment while retaining the integrity of the grounding path. **Figure 250–142**

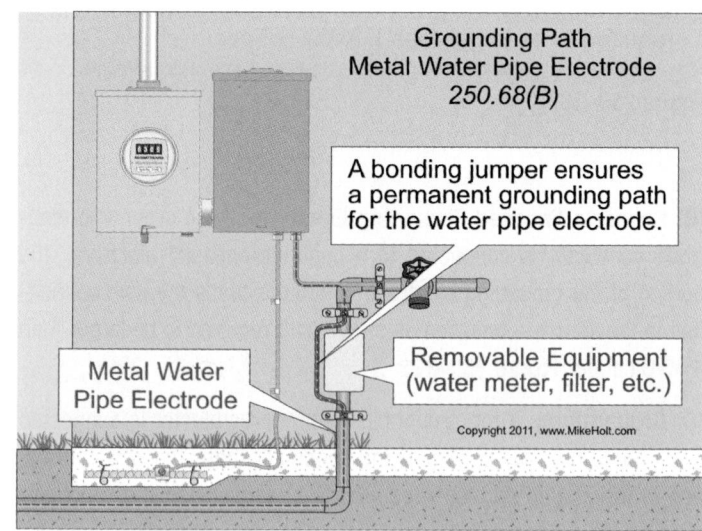

Figure 250–142

(C) Metal Water Pipe and Structural Metal. Grounding electrode conductors and grounding electrode bonding jumpers are permitted to terminate to:

(1) Interior metal water piping located not more than 5 ft from the point of entrance to the building/structure. **Figure 250–143**

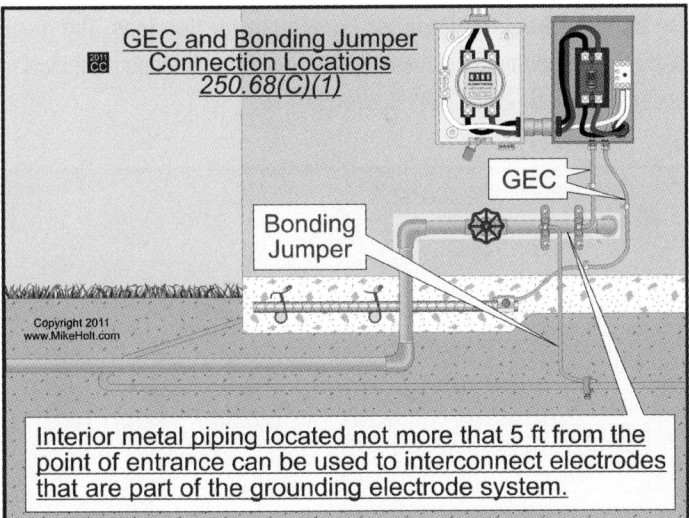

Figure 250–143

Ex: In industrial, institutional, and commercial buildings where conditions of maintenance and supervision ensure only qualified persons service the installation, the entire length of the metal water piping system can be used for grounding purposes, provided the entire length, other than short sections passing through walls, floors, or ceilings, is exposed.

(2) The metal frame of a building/structure that's in direct contact with the earth for 10 ft or more [250.52(A)(2)] or connected to one or more of the following:

(a) Concrete-encased electrode [250.52(A)(3)] or ground ring [250.52(A)(4)],

(b) Ground rod [250.52(A)(5)],

(c) Other approved earth connection.

250.70 Grounding Electrode Conductor Termination Fittings. The grounding electrode conductor must terminate to the grounding electrode by exothermic welding, listed lugs, listed pressure connectors, listed clamps, or other listed means. In addition, fittings terminating to a grounding electrode must be listed for the materials of the grounding electrode.

When the termination to a grounding electrode is encased in concrete or buried in the earth, the termination fitting must be listed for direct soil burial or concrete encasement. No more than one conductor can terminate on a single clamp or fitting unless the clamp or fitting is listed for multiple connections. **Figure 250–144**

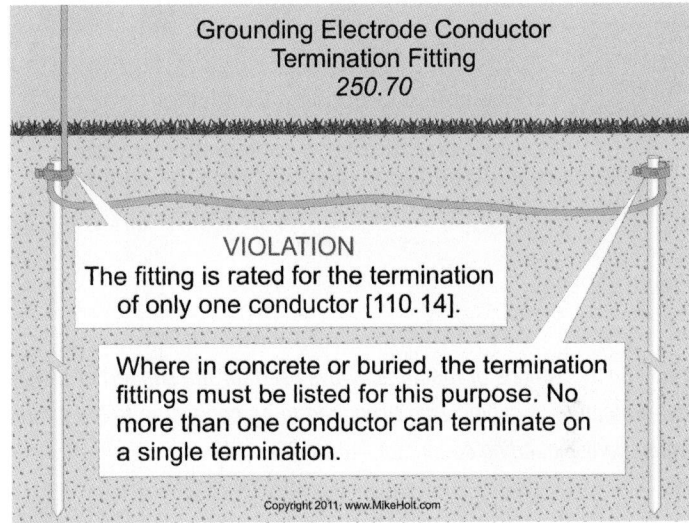

Figure 250–144

PART IV. GROUNDING ENCLOSURE, RACEWAY, AND SERVICE CABLE CONNECTIONS

250.80 Service Raceways and Enclosures. Metal enclosures and raceways containing service conductors must be connected to the neutral conductor at service equipment if the electrical system is grounded or to the grounding electrode conductor for electrical systems that aren't grounded.

Ex: Metal elbows having a minimum of 18 in. of cover installed in an underground nonmetallic raceway system aren't required to be connected to the service neutral or grounding electrode conductor.

250.86 Other Enclosures. Metal raceways and enclosures containing electrical conductors operating at 50V or more [250.20(A)] must be connected to the circuit equipment grounding conductor. **Figure 250–145**

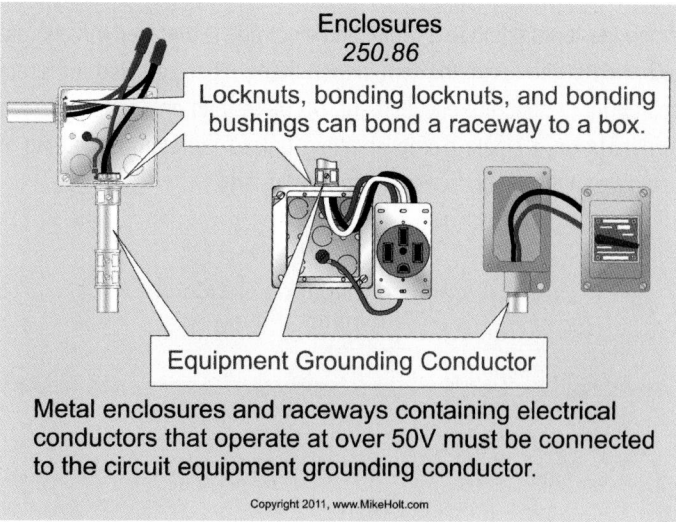

Figure 250–145

Ex 2: Short sections of metal raceways used for the support or physical protection of cables aren't required to be connected to the circuit equipment grounding conductor. **Figure 250–146**

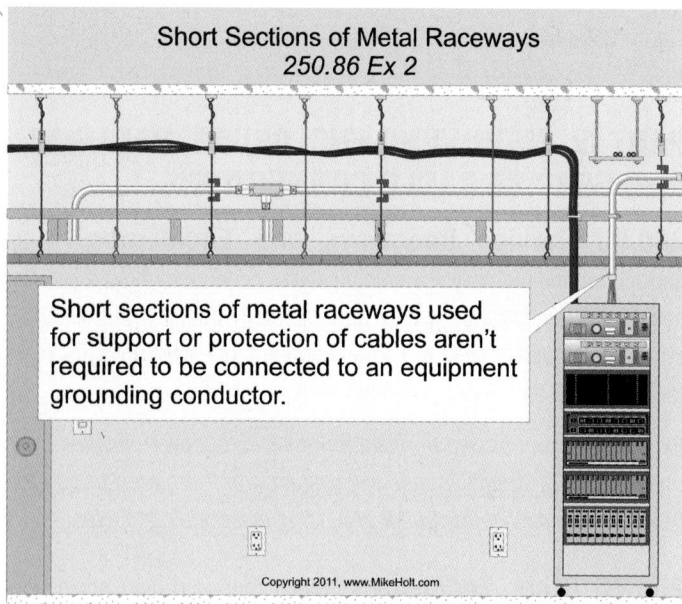

Figure 250–146

Ex 3: A metal elbow installed in a run of underground nonmetallic raceway having a minimum of 18 in. of cover or encased in not less than 2 in. of concrete.

PART V. BONDING

250.90 General. Bonding must be provided to ensure electrical continuity and the capacity to conduct safely any fault current likely to be imposed.

250.92 Bonding Equipment for Services.

(A) Bonding Requirements for Equipment for Services. The metal parts of equipment indicated below must be bonded together in accordance with 250.92(B). **Figure 250–147**

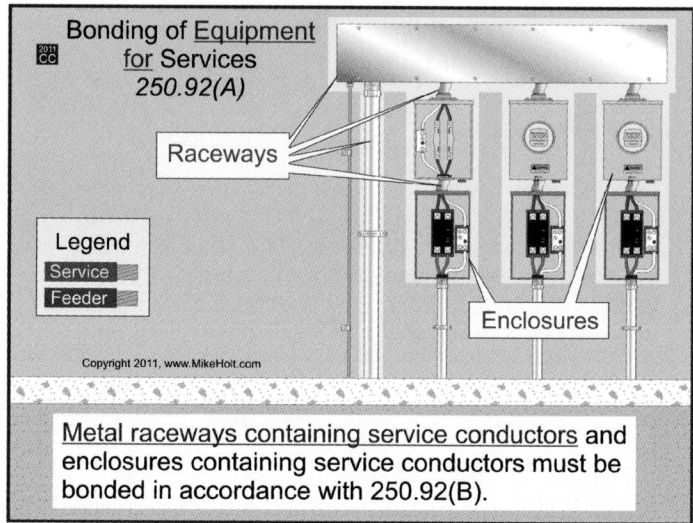

Figure 250–147

(1) Metal raceways containing, enclosing, or supporting service conductors.

(2) Metal enclosures containing service conductors.

> **Author's Comment:** Metal raceways or metal enclosures containing feeder and branch-circuit conductors are required to be connected to the circuit equipment grounding conductor in accordance with 250.86. **Figure 250–148**

(B) Methods of Bonding. Bonding jumpers around reducing washers or oversized, concentric, or eccentric knockouts are required. Standard locknuts are permitted to make a mechanical connection of the raceway(s), but they can't serve as the bonding means required by this section. **Figures 250–149 and 250–150**

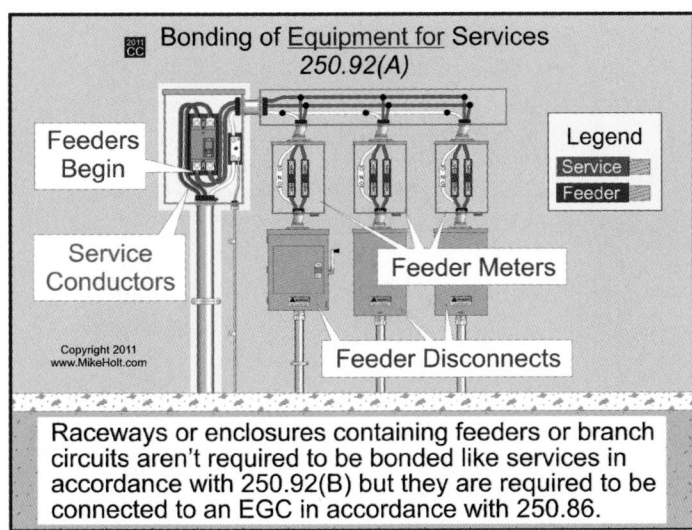

Figure 250–148

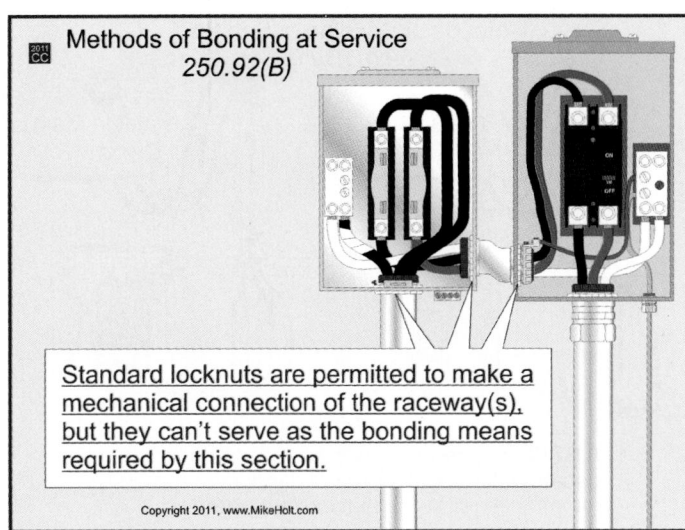

Figure 250–150

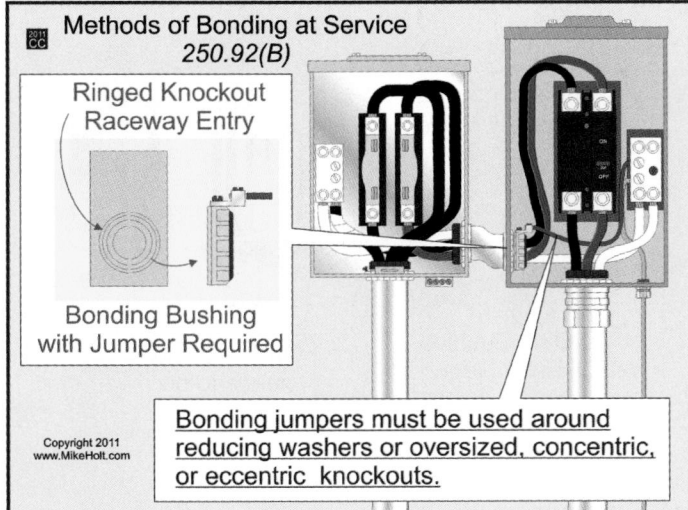

Figure 250–149

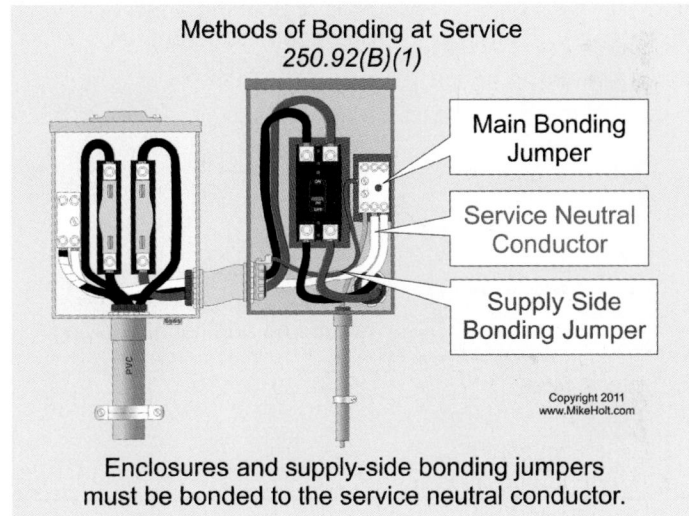

Figure 250–151

Electrical continuity at service equipment, service raceways, and service conductor enclosures must be ensured by one of the following methods:

(1) Neutral Conductor. By bonding the metal parts to the service neutral conductor. **Figure 250–151**

Author's Comments:

- A main bonding jumper is required to bond the service disconnect to the service neutral conductor [250.24(B) and 250.28].

- At service equipment, the service neutral conductor provides the effective ground-fault current path to the power supply [250.24(C)]; therefore, an equipment grounding conductor isn't required to be installed within PVC conduit containing service-entrance conductors [250.142(A)(1) and 352.60 Ex 2]. **Figure 250–152**

(2) Threaded Fittings. By terminating metal raceways to metal enclosures by threaded hubs on enclosures if made up wrenchtight. **Figure 250–153**

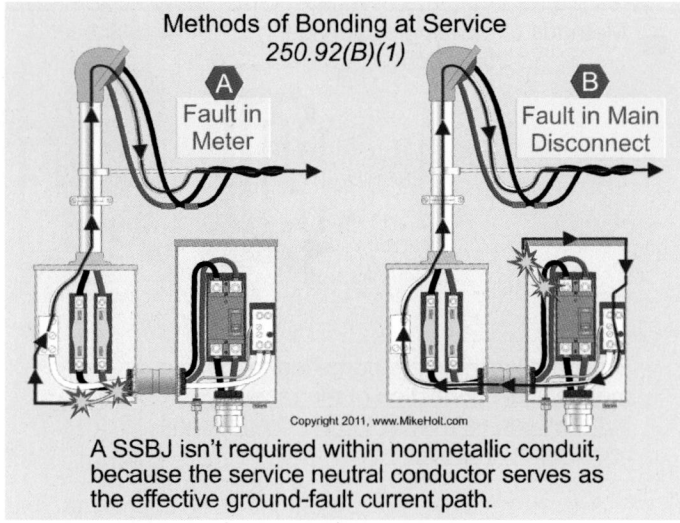

Figure 250–152

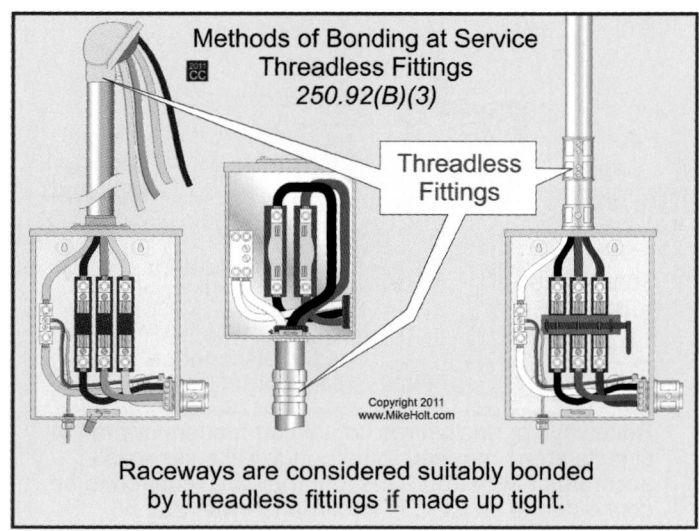

Figure 250–154

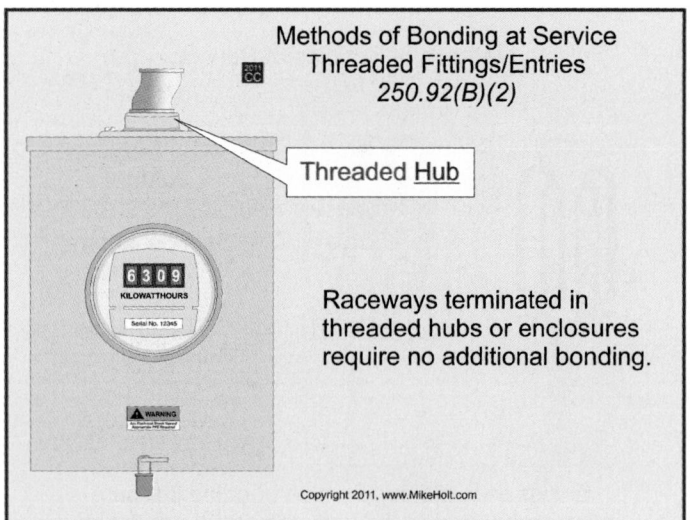

Figure 250–153

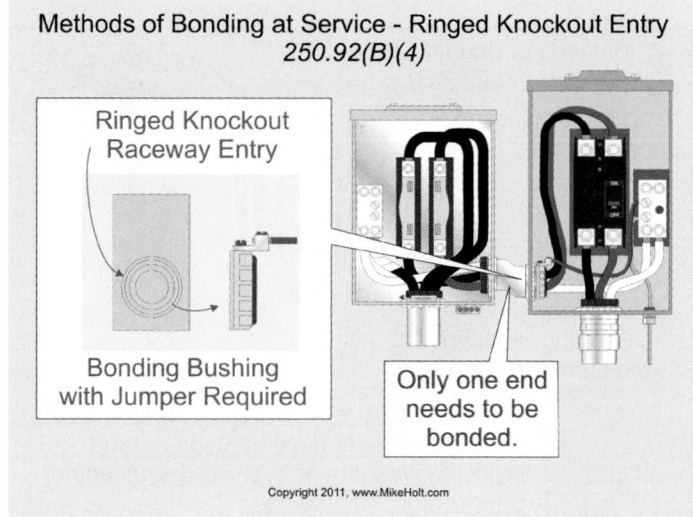

Figure 250–155

(3) Threadless Fittings. By terminating metal raceways to metal enclosures by threadless fittings if made up tight. **Figure 250–154**

(4) Other listed devices, such as bonding-type locknuts, bushings, wedges, or bushings with bonding jumpers.

Author's Comments:

- A listed bonding wedge or bushing with a bonding jumper must be used to bond one end of the service raceway to the service neutral conductor. The bonding jumper used for this purpose must be sized in accordance with Table 250.66, based on the area of the largest ungrounded service conductors within the raceway [250.102(C)]. **Figure 250–155**

- When a metal raceway containing service conductors terminates to an enclosure without a ringed knockout, a bonding-type locknut can be used. **Figure 250–156**

- A bonding locknut differs from a standard locknut in that it's a bonding screw with a sharp point that drives into the metal enclosure to ensure a solid connection.

- Bonding one end of a service raceway to the service neutral provides the low-impedance fault current path to the source. **Figure 250–157**

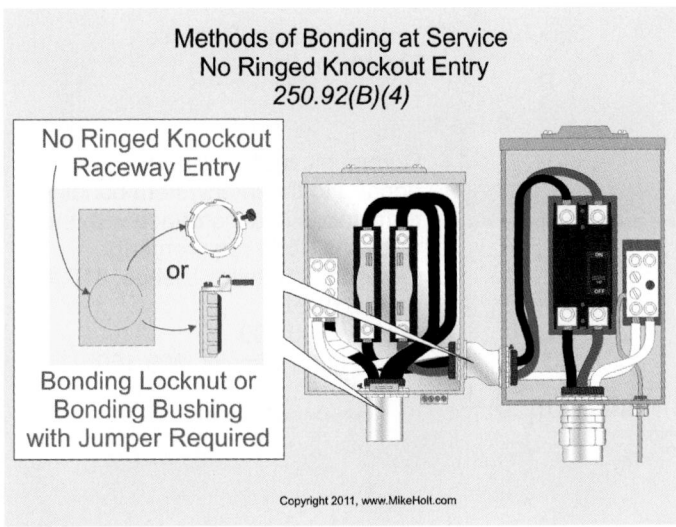

Methods of Bonding at Service
No Ringed Knockout Entry
250.92(B)(4)

No Ringed Knockout
Raceway Entry

or

Bonding Locknut or
Bonding Bushing
with Jumper Required

Copyright 2011, www.MikeHolt.com

Figure 250–156

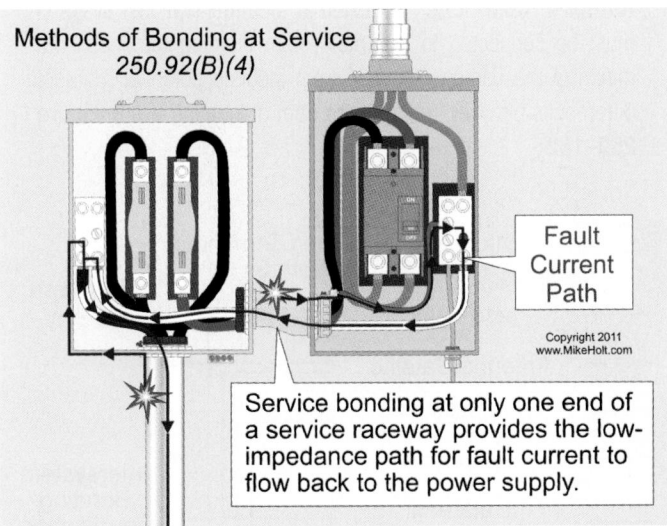

Methods of Bonding at Service
250.92(B)(4)

Fault
Current
Path

Copyright 2011
www.MikeHolt.com

Service bonding at only one end of
a service raceway provides the low-
impedance path for fault current to
flow back to the power supply.

Figure 250–157

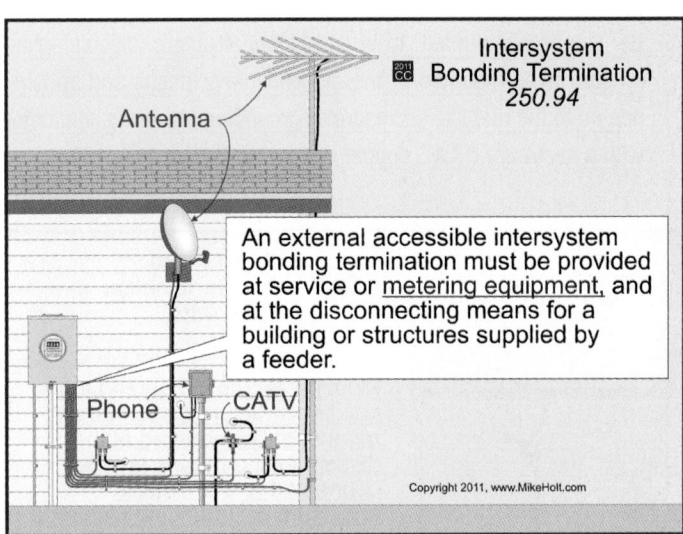

Antenna

Intersystem
Bonding Termination
250.94

An external accessible intersystem
bonding termination must be provided
at service or metering equipment, and
at the disconnecting means for a
building or structures supplied by
a feeder.

Phone   CATV

Copyright 2011, www.MikeHolt.com

Figure 250–158

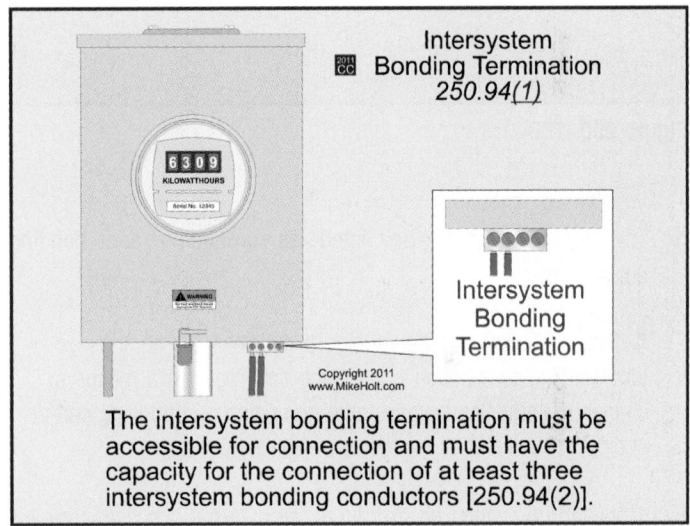

Intersystem
Bonding Termination
250.94(1)

Intersystem
Bonding
Termination

Copyright 2011
www.MikeHolt.com

The intersystem bonding termination must be
accessible for connection and must have the
capacity for the connection of at least three
intersystem bonding conductors [250.94(2)].

Figure 250–159

250.94 Intersystem Bonding Termination. An external accessible intersystem bonding termination for the connection of communications systems bonding conductors must be provided at service equipment or metering equipment enclosure and disconnecting means for buildings or structures supplied by a feeder. **Figure 250–158**. The intersystem bonding termination must:

(1) Be accessible for connection and inspection. **Figure 250–159**

(2) Consist of a set of terminals with the capacity for connection of not less than three intersystem bonding conductors.

(3) Not interfere with opening the enclosure for a service, building/structure disconnecting means, or metering equipment.

(4) Be securely mounted and electrically connected to service equipment, the meter enclosure, or exposed nonflexible metallic service raceway, or be mounted at one of these enclosures and be connected to the enclosure or grounding electrode conductor with a minimum 6 AWG copper conductor.

(5) Be securely mounted to the building/structure disconnecting means, or be mounted at the disconnecting means and be connected to the metallic enclosure or grounding electrode conductor with a minimum 6 AWG copper conductor. **Figure 250–160**

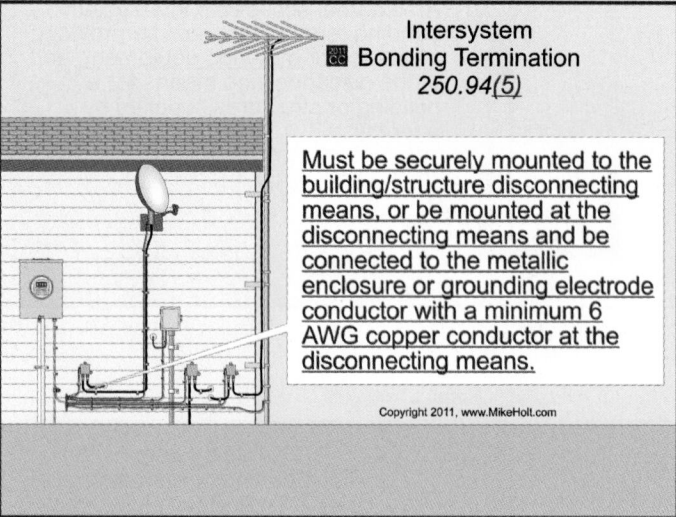

Figure 250–160

(6) The terminals must be listed as grounding and bonding equipment.

Author's Comment: According to Article 100, an intersystem bonding termination is a device that provides a means to connect communications systems grounding and bonding conductors to the building grounding electrode system.

Ex: At existing buildings or structures, an external accessible means for bonding communications systems together can be by the use of a:

(1) Nonflexible metallic raceway,

(2) Grounding electrode conductor, or

(3) Connection approved by the authority having jurisdiction.

Note 2: Communications systems must be bonded to the intersystem bonding termination in accordance with the following *Code* requirements: **Figure 250–161**

- Antennas/Satellite Dishes, 810.15 and 810.21
- CATV, 820.100
- Telephone Circuits, 800.100

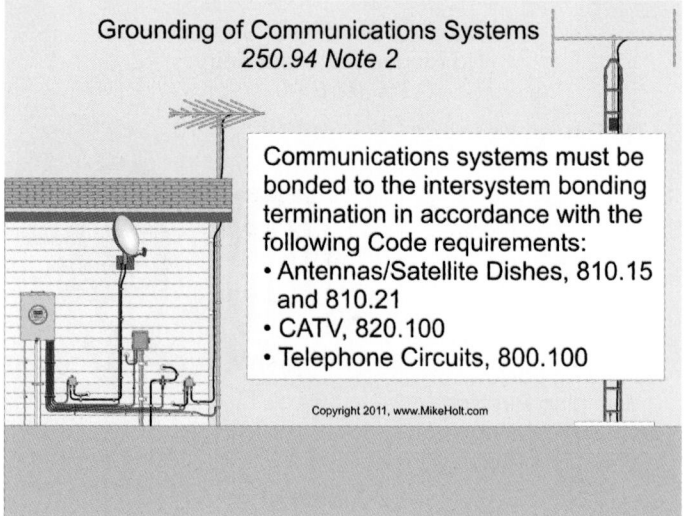

Figure 250–161

Author's Comment: All external communications systems must be connected to the intersystem bonding termination to minimize the damage to them from induced potential (voltage) differences between the systems from a lightning event. **Figure 250–162**

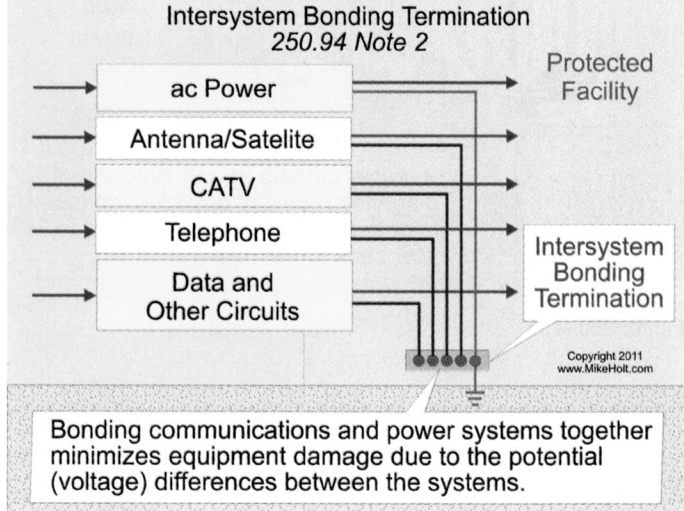

Figure 250–162

250.96 Bonding Other Enclosures.

(A) Maintaining Effective Ground-Fault Current Path. Metal parts intended to serve as equipment grounding conductors including raceways, cables, equipment, and enclosures must be bonded together to ensure they have the capacity to conduct safely any fault current likely to be imposed on them [110.10, 250.4(A)(5), and Note to Table 250.122]. **Figure 250–163**

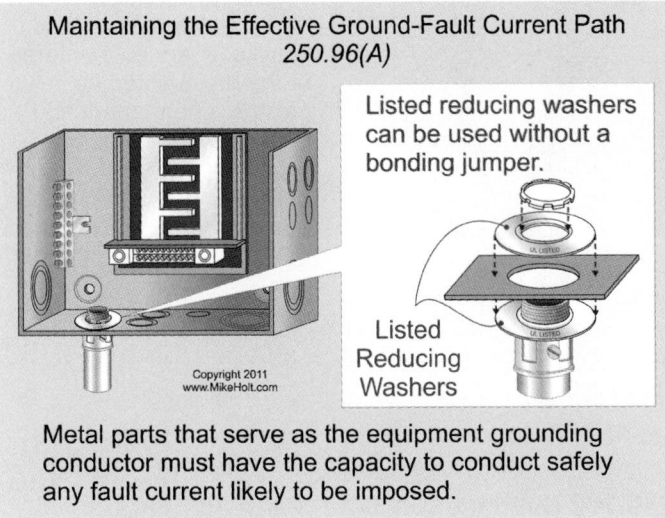

Maintaining the Effective Ground-Fault Current Path
250.96(A)

Listed reducing washers can be used without a bonding jumper.

Listed Reducing Washers

Copyright 2011 www.MikeHolt.com

Metal parts that serve as the equipment grounding conductor must have the capacity to conduct safely any fault current likely to be imposed.

Figure 250–163

Nonconductive coatings such as paint, lacquer, and enamel on equipment must be removed to ensure an effective ground-fault current path, or the termination fittings must be designed so as to make such removal unnecessary [250.12].

Author's Comment: The practice of driving a locknut tight with a screwdriver and pliers is considered sufficient in removing paint and other nonconductive finishes to ensure an effective ground-fault current path.

(B) Isolated Grounding Circuits. An equipment enclosure can be isolated from a metal raceway by a nonmetallic raceway fitting located at the point of attachment of the raceway to the equipment enclosure. The metal raceway must contain an insulated equipment grounding conductor in accordance with 250.146(D). **Figures 250–164 and 250–165**

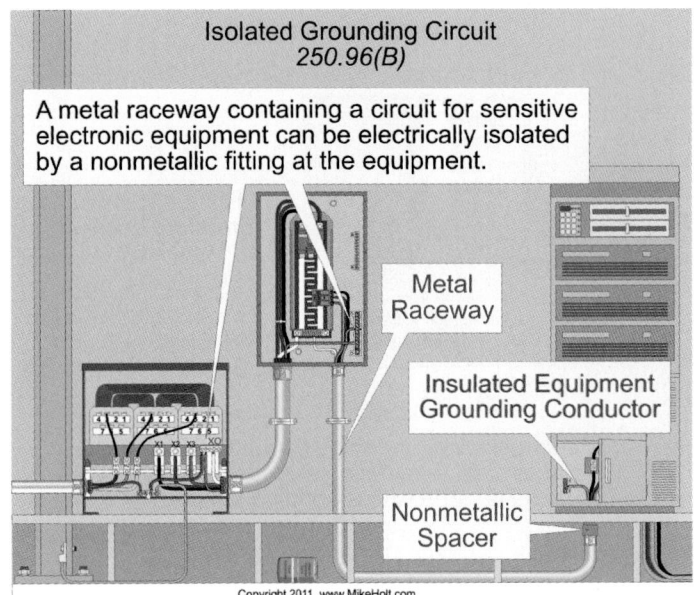

Isolated Grounding Circuit
250.96(B)

A metal raceway containing a circuit for sensitive electronic equipment can be electrically isolated by a nonmetallic fitting at the equipment.

Metal Raceway

Insulated Equipment Grounding Conductor

Nonmetallic Spacer

Copyright 2011, www.MikeHolt.com

Figure 250–164

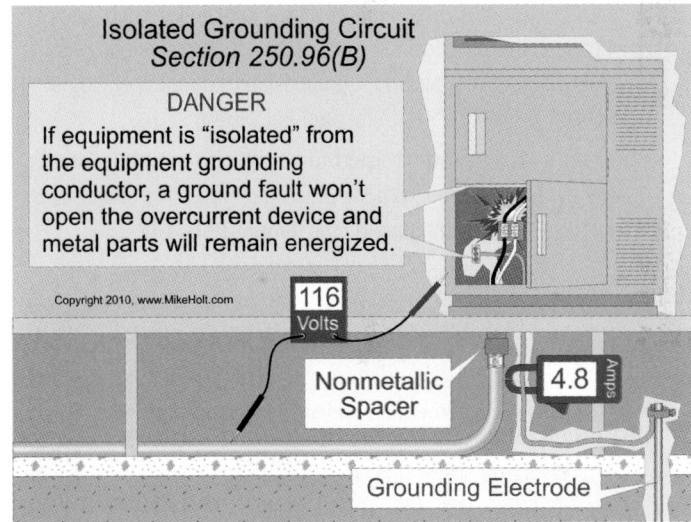

Isolated Grounding Circuit
Section 250.96(B)

DANGER
If equipment is "isolated" from the equipment grounding conductor, a ground fault won't open the overcurrent device and metal parts will remain energized.

Copyright 2010, www.MikeHolt.com

116 Volts

4.8 Amps

Nonmetallic Spacer

Grounding Electrode

Figure 250–165

250.97 Bonding Metal Parts Containing 277V and 480V Circuits.
Metal raceways or cables containing 277V and/or 480V feeder or branch circuits terminating at ringed knockouts must be bonded to the metal enclosure with a bonding jumper sized in accordance with 250.122, based on the rating of the circuit overcurrent device [250.102(D)]. **Figure 250–166**

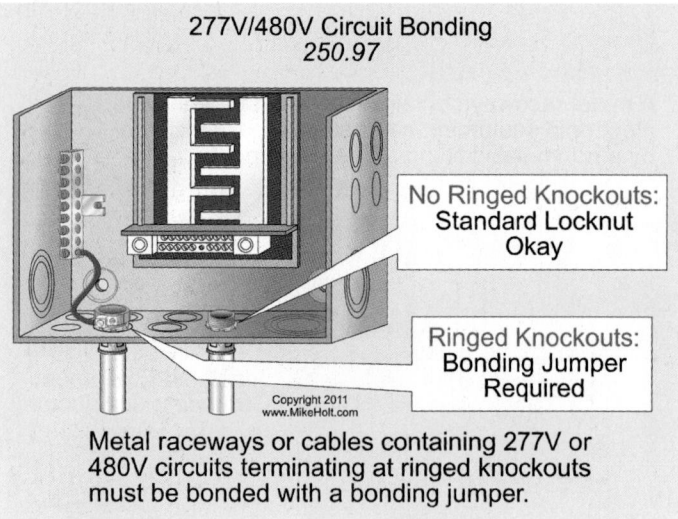

277V/480V Circuit Bonding
250.97

No Ringed Knockouts:
Standard Locknut
Okay

Ringed Knockouts:
Bonding Jumper
Required

Copyright 2011
www.MikeHolt.com

Metal raceways or cables containing 277V or
480V circuits terminating at ringed knockouts
must be bonded with a bonding jumper.

Figure 250–166

Author's Comments:

- Bonding jumpers for raceways and cables containing 277V or 480V circuits are required at ringed knockout terminations to ensure the ground-fault current path has the capacity to safely conduct the maximum ground-fault current likely to be imposed [110.10, 250.4(A)(5), and 250.96(A)].

- Ringed knockouts aren't listed to withstand the heat generated by a 277V ground fault, which generates five times as much heat as a 120V ground fault. **Figure 250–167**

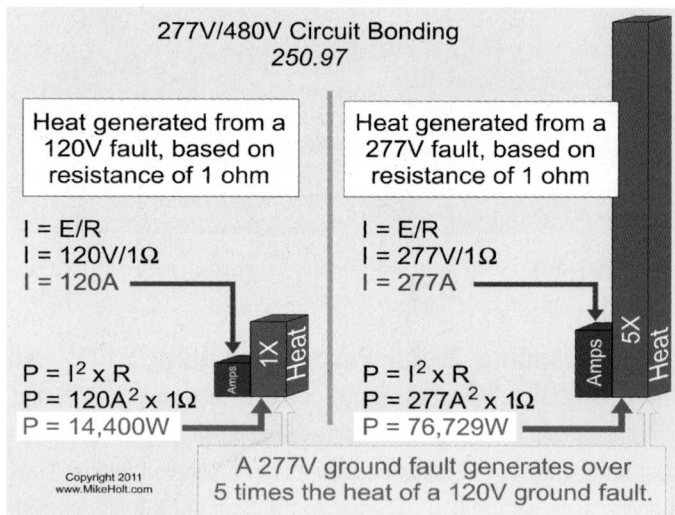

277V/480V Circuit Bonding
250.97

Heat generated from a
120V fault, based on
resistance of 1 ohm

$I = E/R$
$I = 120V/1\Omega$
$I = 120A$

$P = I^2 \times R$
$P = 120A^2 \times 1\Omega$
$P = 14,400W$

Heat generated from a
277V fault, based on
resistance of 1 ohm

$I = E/R$
$I = 277V/1\Omega$
$I = 277A$

$P = I^2 \times R$
$P = 277A^2 \times 1\Omega$
$P = 76,729W$

Copyright 2011
www.MikeHolt.com

A 277V ground fault generates over
5 times the heat of a 120V ground fault.

Figure 250–167

Ex: A bonding jumper isn't required where ringed knockouts aren't encountered, knockouts are totally punched out, or where the box is listed to provide a reliable bonding connection. **Figure 250–168**

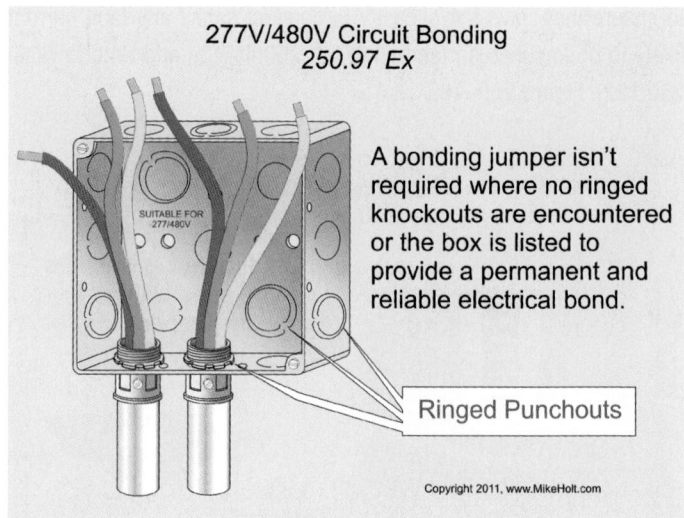

277V/480V Circuit Bonding
250.97 Ex

SUITABLE FOR
277/480V

A bonding jumper isn't
required where no ringed
knockouts are encountered
or the box is listed to
provide a permanent and
reliable electrical bond.

Ringed Punchouts

Copyright 2011, www.MikeHolt.com

Figure 250–168

250.102 Bonding <u>Conductors and</u> Jumpers.

(A) Material. Equipment bonding jumpers must be copper.

(B) Termination. Equipment bonding jumpers must terminate by listed pressure connectors, terminal bars, exothermic welding, or other listed means [250.8(A)].

(C) Size for Supply-Side Bonding Jumper.

(1) Single Raceway Installations. The <u>supply-side</u> bonding jumper is sized to Table 250.66, based on the largest <u>ungrounded</u> conductor within the raceway. If the <u>ungrounded supply</u> conductors are larger than 1,100 kcmil copper or 1,750 kcmil aluminum, the <u>supply-side bonding jumper</u> must be sized not less than 12½ percent of the area of the largest set of <u>ungrounded</u> supply conductors.

(2) Parallel <u>Conductor</u> Installations. If the ungrounded supply conductors are paralleled in two or more raceways or cables, the size of the <u>supply-side bonding jumper for each raceway or cable</u> is sized in accordance with Table 250.66, based on the size of the <u>largest ungrounded</u> conductors in each raceway or cable. <u>A single supply-side bonding jumper for bonding two or more raceways or cables must be sized in accordance with (C)(1).</u>

Question 1: What size supply-side bonding jumper is required for a metal raceway containing 700 kcmil service conductors? **Figure 250–169**

(a) 1 AWG (b) 1/0 AWG (c) 2/0 AWG (d) 3/0 AWG

Answer: (c) 2/0 AWG [Table 250.66]

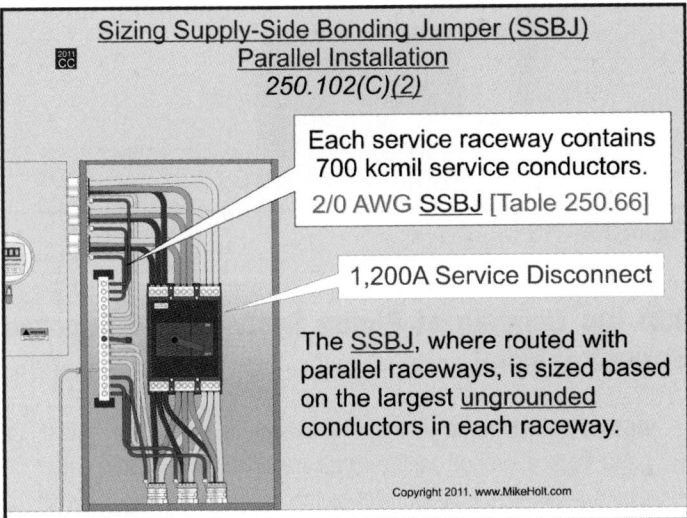

Figure 250–169

Question 2: What size single supply-side bonding jumper is required for three metal raceways containing 700 kcmil service conductors? **Figure 250–170**

(a) 1 AWG (b) 1/0 AWG (c) 2/0 AWG (d) 300 AWG

Answer: (d) 300 kcmil [250.102(C)(1)]

700 kcmil x 3 = 2,100 kcmil
2,100 kcmil x 0.125 = 263 kcmil
Chapter 9, Table 8, use 300 kcmil

(3) Different Materials. If the ungrounded supply conductors and the supply-side bonding jumper are of different materials (copper or aluminum), the supply-side bonding jumper is sized on the assumed use of the same material.

(D) Load Side Equipment Bonding Jumper Sizing. Bonding jumpers on the load side of feeder and branch-circuit overcurrent devices are sized in accordance with 250.122, based on the rating of the circuit overcurrent device.

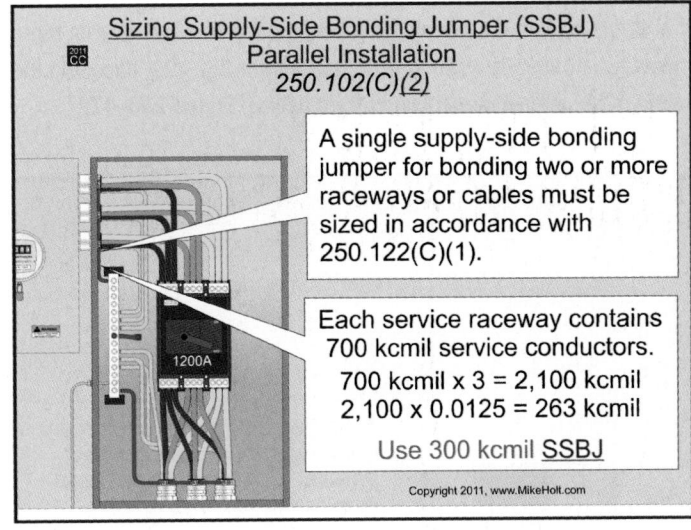

Figure 250–170

Author's Comment: The equipment bonding jumper isn't required to be larger than the largest ungrounded circuit conductors [250.122(A)].

Question: What size equipment bonding jumper is required for a metal raceway where the circuit conductors are protected by a 1,200A overcurrent device? **Figure 250–171**

(a) 1 AWG (b) 1/0 AWG (c) 2/0 AWG (d) 3/0 AWG

Answer: (d) 3/0 AWG [Table 250.122]

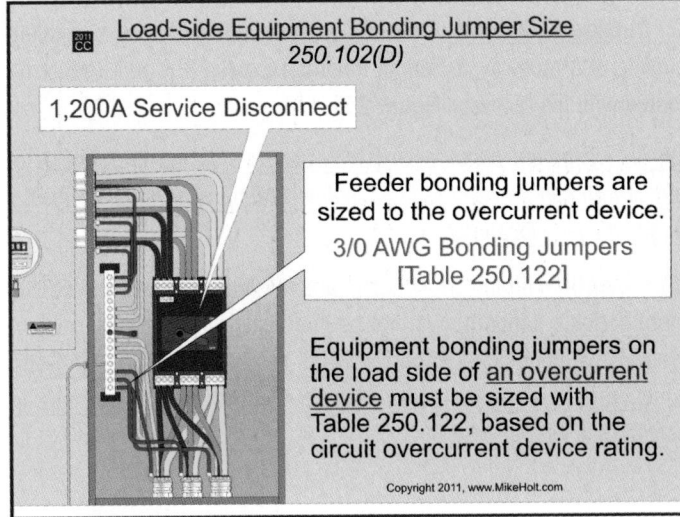

Figure 250–171

If a single equipment bonding jumper is used to bond two or more raceways, it must be sized in accordance with 250.122, based on the rating of the largest circuit overcurrent device. **Figure 250–172**

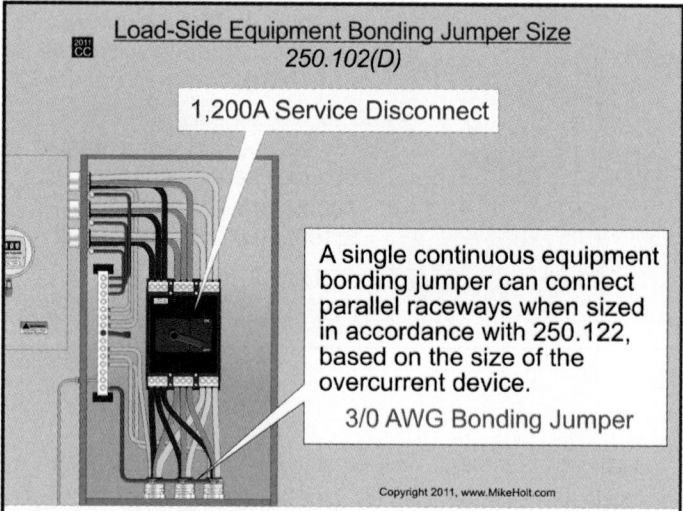

Figure 250–172

(E) Installation. Equipment bonding jumpers, as well as bonding jumpers or conductors can be installed inside or outside of a raceway.

(1) Inside a Raceway or Enclosure. If installed inside a raceway, the conductors must be identified in accordance with 250.119 and if circuit conductors are spliced or terminated on equipment within a metal box, the equipment grounding conductor associated with those circuits must be connected to the box in accordance with 250.148.

(2) Outside a Raceway. If the equipment bonding jumper is installed outside of a raceway, its length must not exceed 6 ft and it must be routed with the raceway. **Figure 250–173**

Ex: An equipment bonding jumper or supply-side bonding jumper of any length can be used to bond isolated sections of metal raceways at outside pole locations.

(3) Protection. Aluminum bonding jumpers or conductors and equipment bonding jumpers must not be in contact with masonry, subject to corrosive conditions, or within 18 in. of the earth [250.64(A)] and conductors must be protected where subject to physical damage in accordance with 250.64(B).

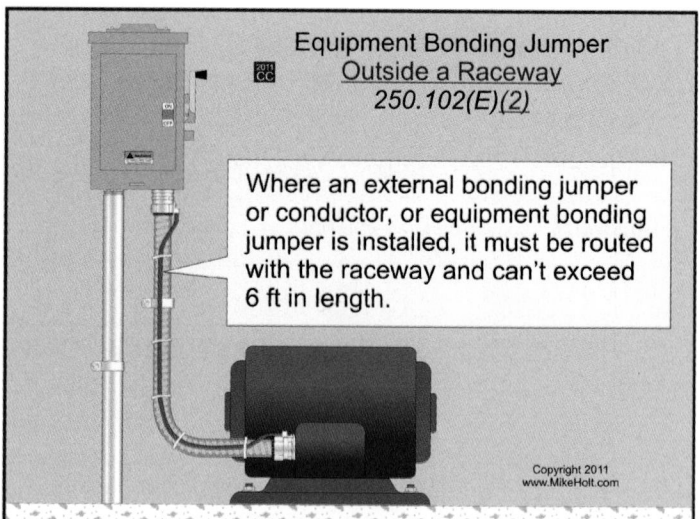

Figure 250–173

250.104 Bonding of Piping Systems and Exposed Structural Metal.

Author's Comment: To remove dangerous voltage on metal parts from a ground fault, electrically conductive metal water piping systems, metal sprinkler piping, metal gas piping, as well as exposed structural steel members likely to become energized, must be connected to an effective ground-fault current path [250.4(A)(4)].

(A) Metal Water Piping System. The metal water piping system must be bonded as required in (A)(1), (A)(2), or (A)(3). The bonding jumper must be copper where within 18 in. of the earth [250.64(A)], securely fastened to the surface on which it's mounted [250.64(B)], and adequately protected if exposed to physical damage [250.64(B)]. In addition, all points of attachment must be accessible.

Author's Comment: Bonding isn't required for isolated sections of metal water piping connected to a nonmetallic water piping system. **Figure 250–174**

(1) Building/Structure Supplied by a Service. The metal water piping system, including the metal sprinkler water piping system of a building/structure supplied with service conductors must be bonded to the: **Figure 250–175**

- Service equipment enclosure,
- Service neutral conductor,
- Grounding electrode conductor of sufficient size, or
- Grounding electrode system.

Figure 250–174

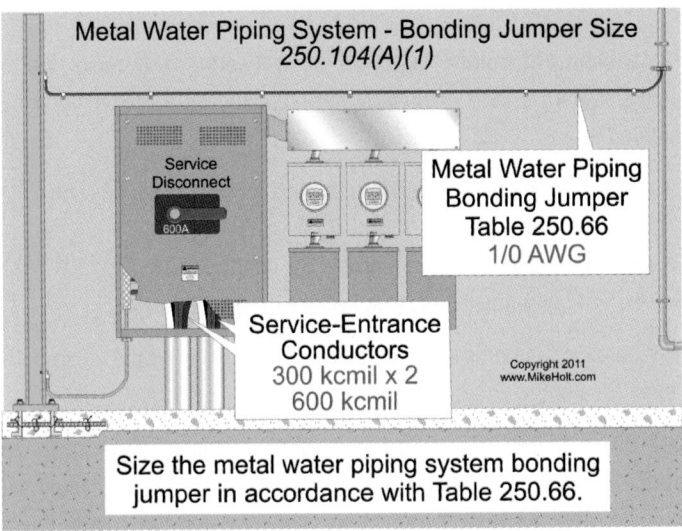

Figure 250–176

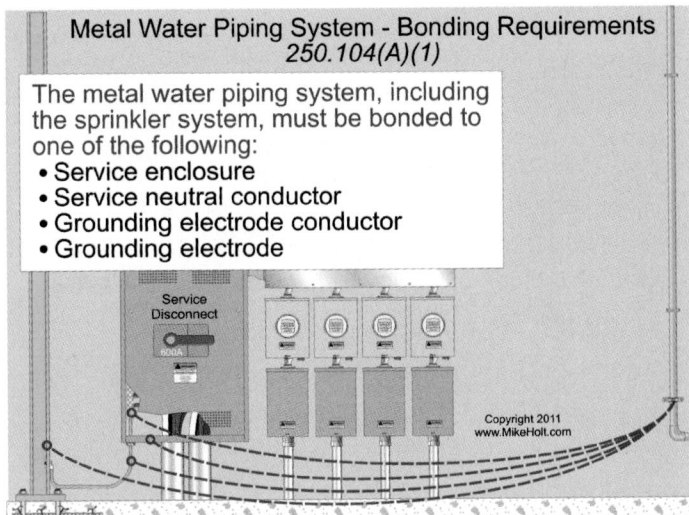

Figure 250–175

The metal water piping system bonding jumper must be sized in accordance with Table 250.66, based on the cross-sectional area of the ungrounded service conductors.

Question: *What size bonding jumper is required for the metal water piping system if the 300 kcmil service conductors are paralleled in two raceways?* **Figure 250–176**

(a) 6 AWG   (b) 4 AWG   (c) 2 AWG   (d) 1/0 AWG

Answer: *(d) 1/0 AWG, based on 600 kcmil conductors, in accordance with Table 250.66*

Author's Comment: If hot and cold metal water pipes are electrically connected, only one bonding jumper is required, either to the cold or hot water pipe.

(2) Multiple Occupancy Building. When the metal water piping system in an individual occupancy is metallically isolated from other occupancies, the metal water piping system for that occupancy can be bonded to the equipment grounding terminal of the occupancy's panelboard. The bonding jumper must be sized in accordance with Table 250.122, based on the ampere rating of the occupancy's feeder overcurrent device. **Figure 250–177**

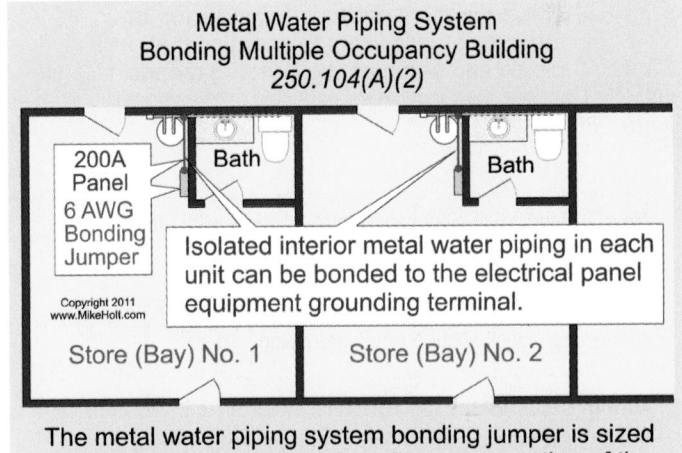

The metal water piping system bonding jumper is sized using Table 250.122 based on the ampere rating of the occupancy's feeder overcurrent device.

Figure 250–177

(3) Building/Structure Supplied by a Feeder. The metal water piping system of a building/structure supplied by a feeder must be bonded to:

- The equipment grounding terminal of the building disconnect enclosure,
- The feeder equipment grounding conductor, or
- The grounding electrode system.

The bonding jumper is sized to Table 250.66, based on the cross-sectional area of the ungrounded feeder conductor.

(B) Other Metal-Piping Systems. Metal-piping systems such as sprinkler, gas, or air that are likely to become energized must be bonded. The equipment grounding conductor for the circuit that's likely to energize the piping can serve as the bonding means. **Figure 250–178**

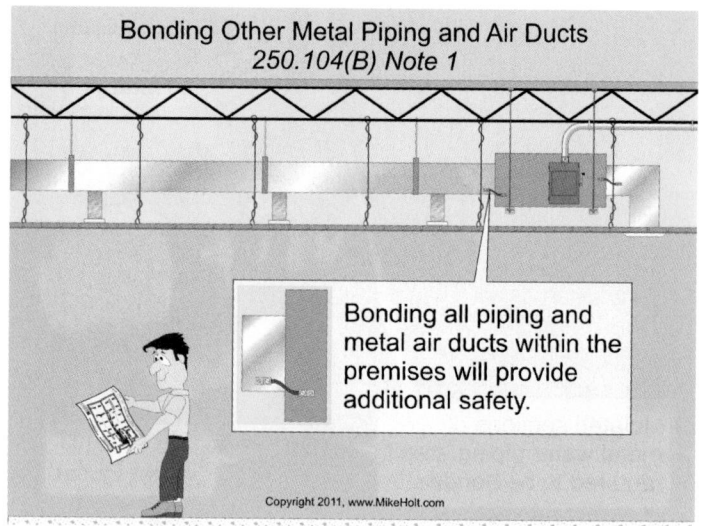

Figure 250–179

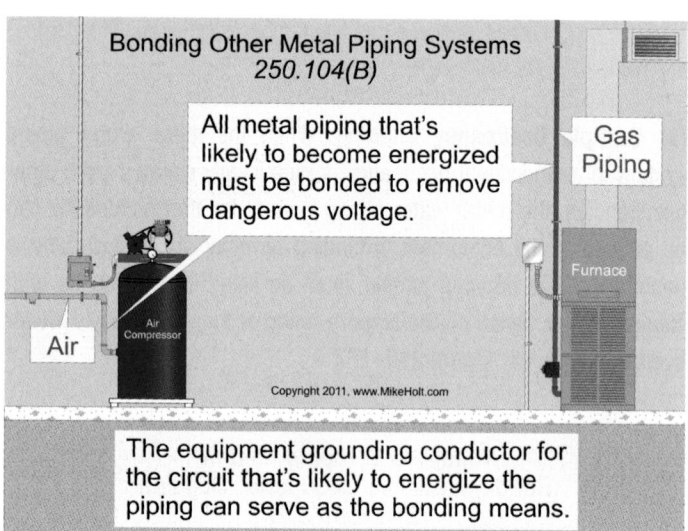

Figure 250–178

Note 1: Bonding all piping and metal air ducts within the premises will provide additional safety. **Figure 250–179**

Note 2: *The National Fuel Gas Code, NFPA 54, Section 7.13 contains further information about bonding gas piping.*

Author's Comment: Informational Notes in the *NEC* are for information purposes only and aren't enforceable as a requirement of the *Code* [90.5(C)].

(C) Structural Metal. Exposed structural metal that forms a metal building frame that's likely to become energized must be bonded to the: **Figure 250–180**

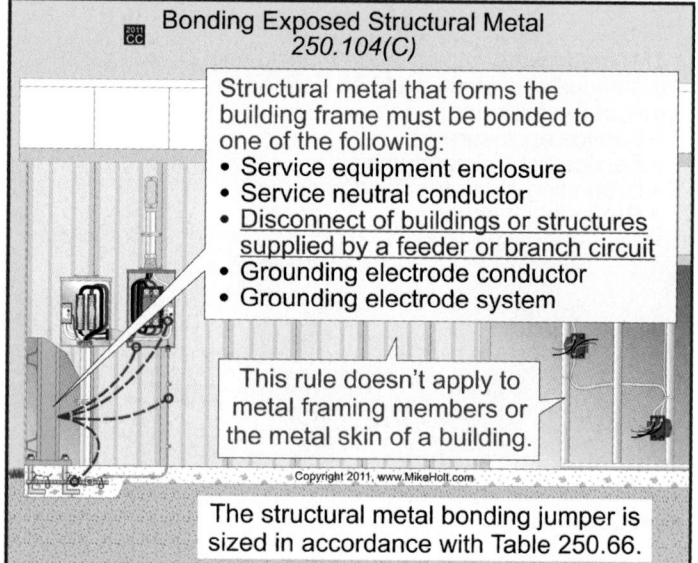

Figure 250–180

- Service equipment enclosure,
- Service neutral conductor,
- Building/structure disconnecting means for buildings or structures supplied by a feeder or branch circuit,
- Grounding electrode conductor if of sufficient size, or
- Grounding electrode system.

Author's Comment: This rule doesn't require the bonding of sheet metal framing members (studs) or the metal skin of a wood frame building.

The bonding jumper must be sized in accordance with Table 250.66, based on the area of the ungrounded supply conductors. The bonding jumper must be copper where within 18 in. of the earth [250.64(A)], securely fastened to the surface on which it's carried [250.64(B)], and adequately protected if exposed to physical damage [250.64(B)]. In addition, all points of attachment must be accessible, except as permitted in 250.68(A).

(D) Separately Derived Systems. Metal water piping systems and structural metal that forms a building frame must be bonded as required in (D)(1) through (D)(3).

(1) Metal Water Pipe. The nearest available point of the metal water piping system in the area served by a separately derived system must be bonded to the neutral point of the separately derived system where the grounding electrode conductor is connected. **Figure 250–181**

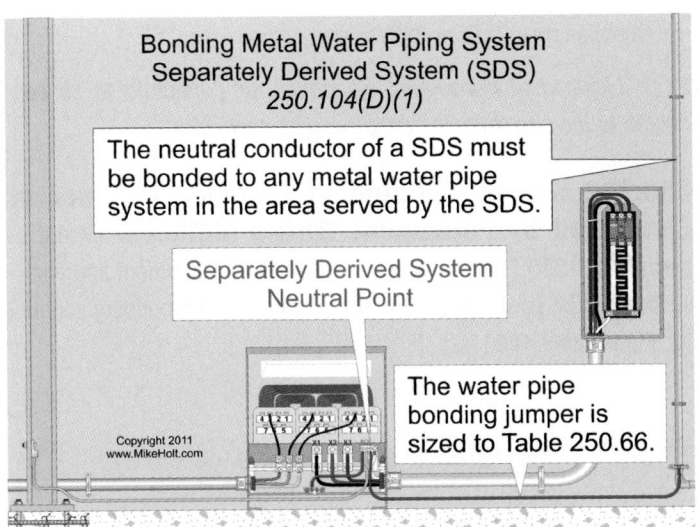

Figure 250–181

The bonding jumper must be sized in accordance with Table 250.66, based on the area of the ungrounded conductor of the derived system.

Ex 2: The metal water piping system is permitted to be bonded to the structural metal building frame if it serves as the grounding electrode [250.52(A)(1)] for the separately derived system. **Figure 250–182**

(2) Structural Metal. Exposed structural metal interconnected to form the building frame must be bonded to the neutral point of each separately derived system where the grounding electrode conductor is connected.

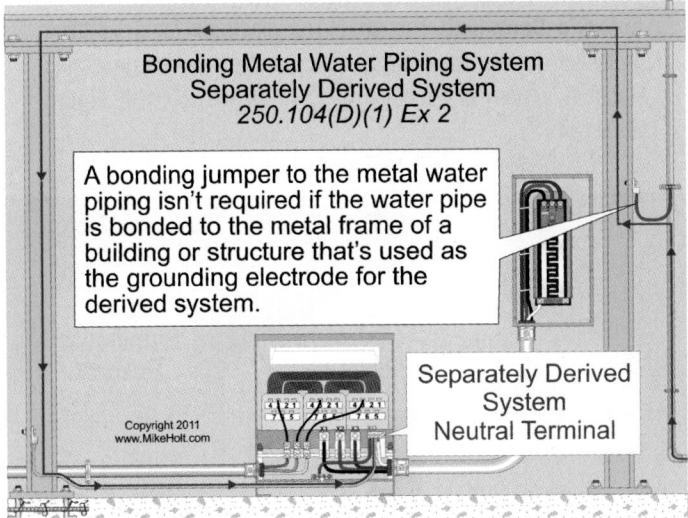

Figure 250–182

The bonding jumper must be sized in accordance with Table 250.66, based on the area of the ungrounded conductors of the derived system.

Ex 1: Bonding to the separately derived system isn't required if the metal structural frame serves as the grounding electrode [250.52(A)(2)] for the separately derived system.

250.106 Lightning Protection System. If a lightning protection system is installed on a building/structure, it must be bonded to the building/structure grounding electrode system. **Figure 250–183**

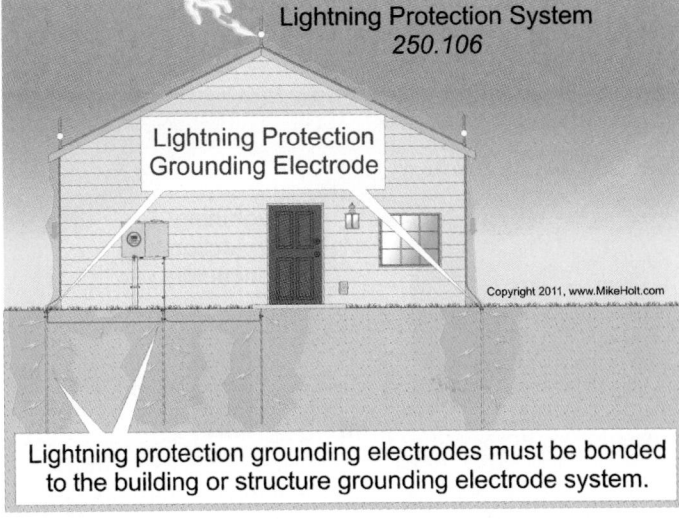

Figure 250–183

Author's Comment: The grounding electrode for a lightning protection system must not be used as the required grounding electrode system for the buildings or structures [250.60]. **Figure 250–184**

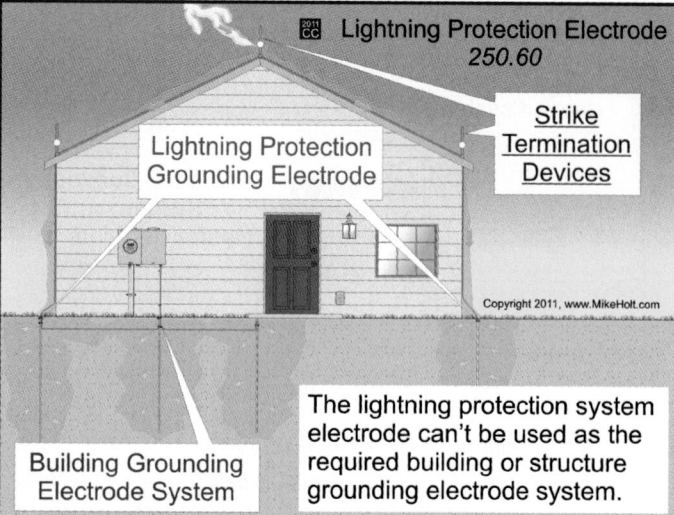

Figure 250–184

Note 1: See NFPA 780—*Standard for the Installation of Lightning Protection Systems,* which contains detailed information on grounding, bonding, and side-flash distance from lightning protection systems.

Note 2: To minimize the likelihood of arcing between metal parts because of induced voltage, metal raceways, enclosures, and other metal parts of electrical equipment may require bonding or spacing from the lightning protection conductors in accordance with NFPA 780—*Standard for the Installation of Lightning Protection Systems.* **Figure 250–185**

Figure 250–185

PART VI. EQUIPMENT GROUNDING AND EQUIPMENT GROUNDING CONDUCTORS

250.110 Fixed Equipment Connected by Permanent Wiring Methods—General.
Exposed metal parts of fixed equipment likely to become energized must be connected to the circuit equipment grounding conductor where the equipment is:

(1) Within 8 ft vertically or 5 ft horizontally of the earth or a grounded metal object

(2) Located in a wet or damp location

(3) In electrical contact with metal

(4) In a hazardous (classified) location [Articles 500 through 517]

(5) Supplied by a wiring method that provides an equipment grounding conductor

(6) Supplied by a 277V or 480V circuit

Ex 3: Listed double-insulated equipment isn't required to be connected to the circuit equipment grounding conductor.

250.112 Specific Equipment Fastened in Place or Connected by Permanent Wiring Methods.
Except as permitted in 250.112(I), exposed metal parts of equipment and enclosures must be connected to the circuit equipment grounding conductor. **Figure 250–186**

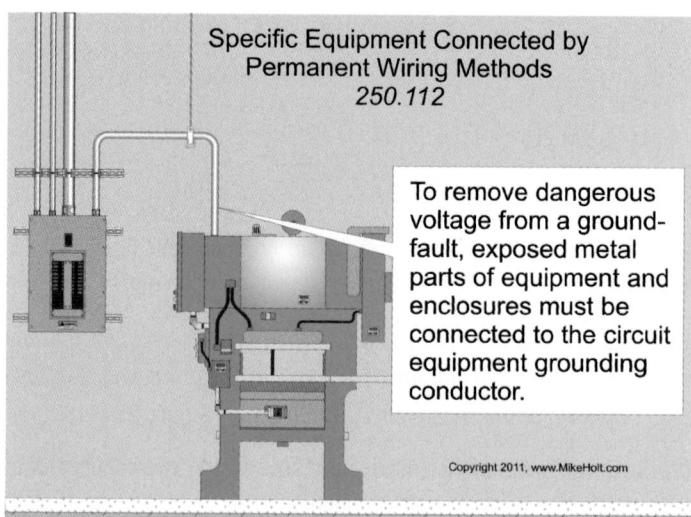

Figure 250–186

(I) Remote-Control, Signaling, and Fire Alarm Circuits. Equipment supplied by circuits operating at 50V or less isn't required to be connected to the circuit equipment grounding conductor. **Figure 250–187**

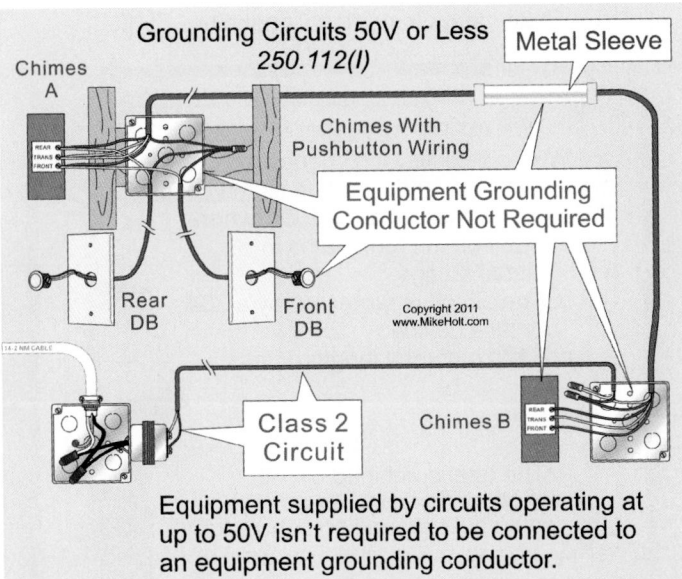

Figure 250–187

Author's Comment: Class 1 power-limited circuits, Class 2, and Class 3 remote-control and signaling circuits, and fire alarm circuits operating at 50V or less don't need to have any metal parts connected to an equipment grounding conductor.

(K) Skid-Mounted Equipment. Electrical equipment permanently mounted on skids, and the skids themselves, must be connected to the equipment grounding conductor sized as required by 250.122.

250.114 Cord-and-Plug-Connected Equipment. Metal

parts of cord-and-plug-connected equipment must be connected to the circuit equipment grounding conductor.

Ex: Listed double-insulated equipment isn't required to be connected to the circuit equipment grounding conductor.

250.118 Types of Equipment Grounding Conductors.

An equipment grounding conductor can be any one or a combination of the following: **Figure 250–188**

Note: The equipment grounding conductor is intended to serve as the effective ground-fault current path. See 250.2. **Figure 250–189**

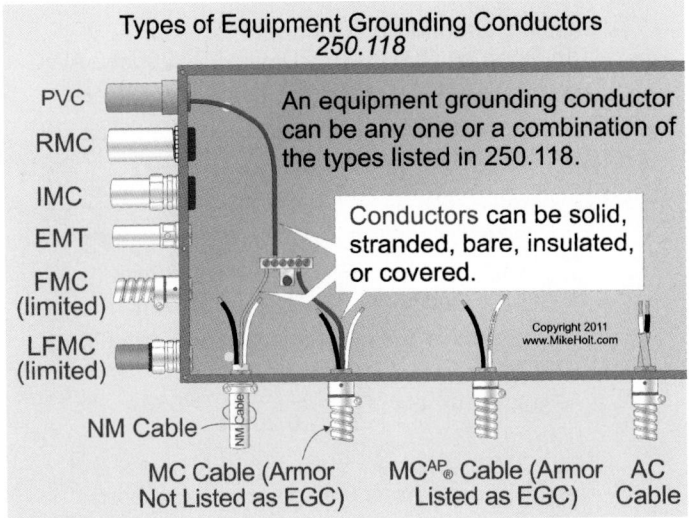

Figure 250–188

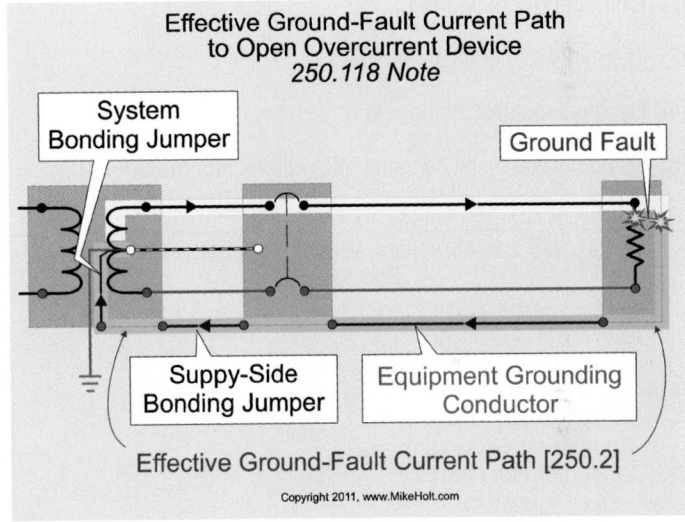

Figure 250–189

Author's Comment: The effective ground-fault path is an intentionally constructed low-impedance conductive path designed to carry fault current from the point of a ground fault on a wiring system to the electrical supply source. Its purpose is to quickly remove dangerous voltage from a ground fault by opening the circuit overcurrent device [250.2]. **Figure 250–190**

(1) A bare or insulated copper or aluminum conductor sized in accordance with 250.122.

Author's Comment: Examples include PVC conduit, Type NM cable, and Type MC cable with an equipment grounding conductor of the wire type.

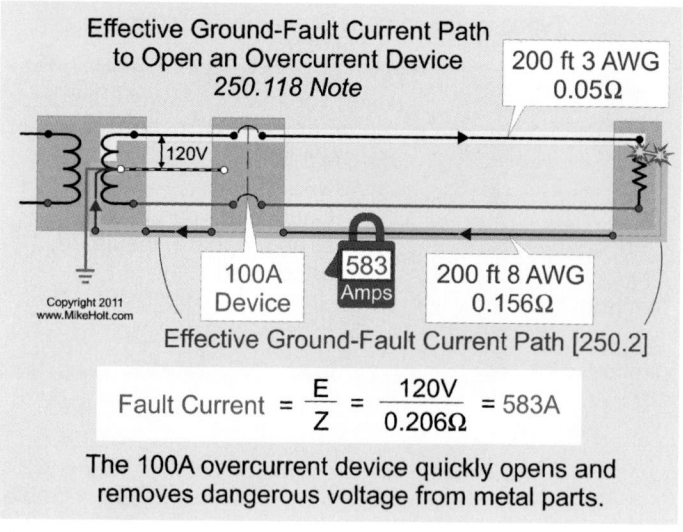

Figure 250–190

(2) Rigid metal conduit (RMC).

(3) Intermediate metal conduit (IMC).

(4) Electrical metallic tubing (EMT).

(5) Listed flexible metal conduit (FMC) where: **Figure 250–191**

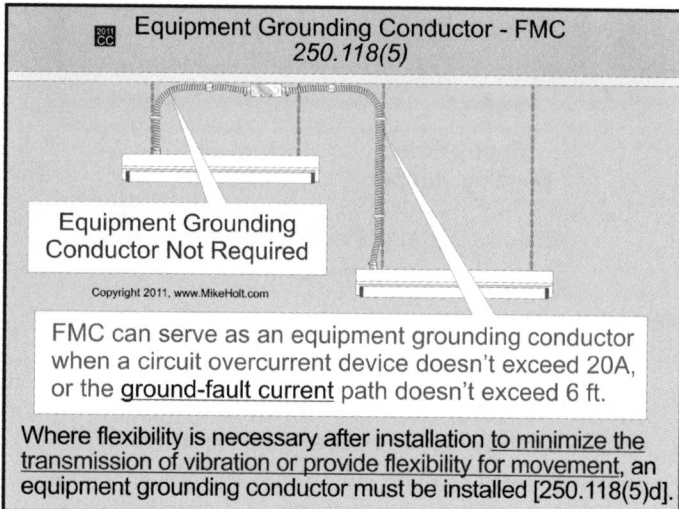

Figure 250–191

a. The raceway terminates in listed fittings.

b. The circuit conductors are protected by an overcurrent device rated 20A or less.

c. The combined length of the flexible conduit in the same ground-fault current path doesn't exceed 6 ft. **Figure 250–192**

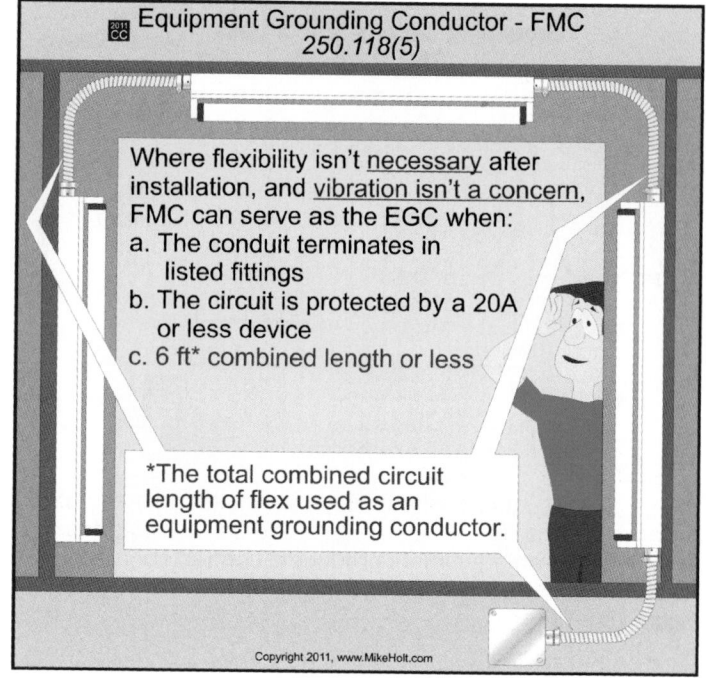

Figure 250–192

d. If flexibility is required to minimize the transmission of vibration from equipment or to provide flexibility for equipment that requires movement after installation, an equipment grounding conductor of the wire type must be installed with the circuit conductors in accordance with 250.102(E), and it must be sized in accordance with 250.122, based on the rating of the circuit overcurrent device.

(6) Listed liquidtight flexible metal conduit (LFMC) where: **Figure 250–193**

a. The raceway terminates in listed fittings.

b. For ⅜ in. through ½ in., the circuit conductors are protected by an overcurrent device rated 20A or less.

c. For ¾ in. through 1¼ in., the circuit conductors are protected by an overcurrent device rated 60A or less.

d. The combined length of the flexible conduit in the same ground-fault current path doesn't exceed 6 ft.

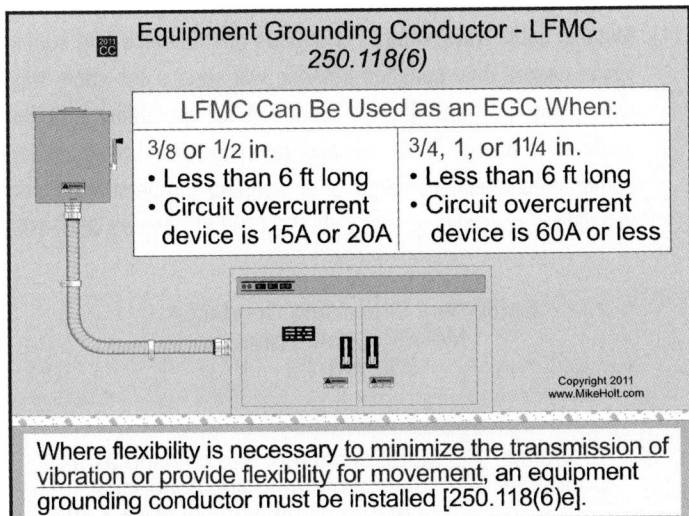

Figure 250–193

e. If flexibility is required to minimize the transmission of vibration from equipment or to provide flexibility for equipment that requires movement after installation, an equipment grounding conductor of the wire type must be installed with the circuit conductors in accordance with 250.102(E), and it must be sized in accordance with 250.122, based on the rating of the circuit overcurrent device.

(8) The sheath of Type AC cable containing an aluminum bonding strip. **Figure 250–194**

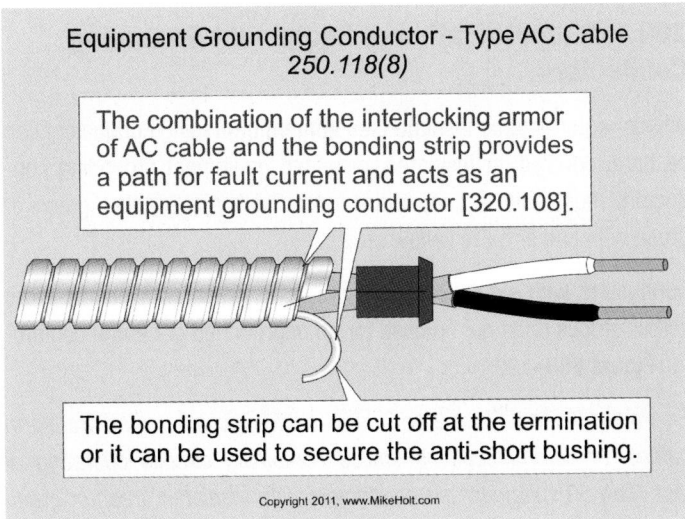

Figure 250–194

Author's Comments:

- The internal aluminum bonding strip isn't an equipment grounding conductor, but it allows the interlocked armor to serve as an equipment grounding conductor because it reduces the impedance of the armored spirals to ensure that a ground fault will be cleared. It's the aluminum bonding strip in combination with the cable armor that creates the circuit equipment grounding conductor. Once the bonding strip exits the cable, it can be cut off because it no longer serves any purpose.

- The effective ground-fault current path must be maintained by the use of fittings specifically listed for Type AC cable [320.40]. See 300.12, 300.15, and 320.100.

(9) The copper sheath of Type MI cable.

(10) Type MC cable that provides an effective ground-fault current path in accordance with one or more of the following:

(a) It contains an insulated or uninsulated equipment grounding conductor in compliance with 250.118(1). **Figure 250–195**

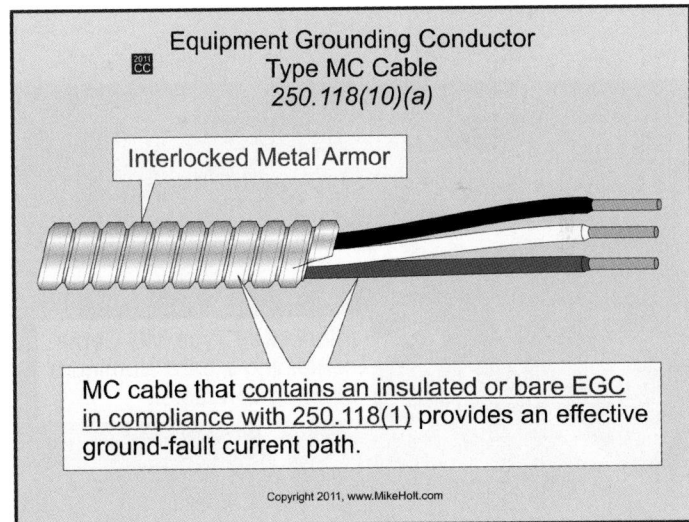

Figure 250–195

(b) The combined metallic sheath and uninsulated equipment grounding/bonding conductor of interlocked metal tape-type MC cable that's listed and identified as an equipment grounding conductor. **Figure 250–196**

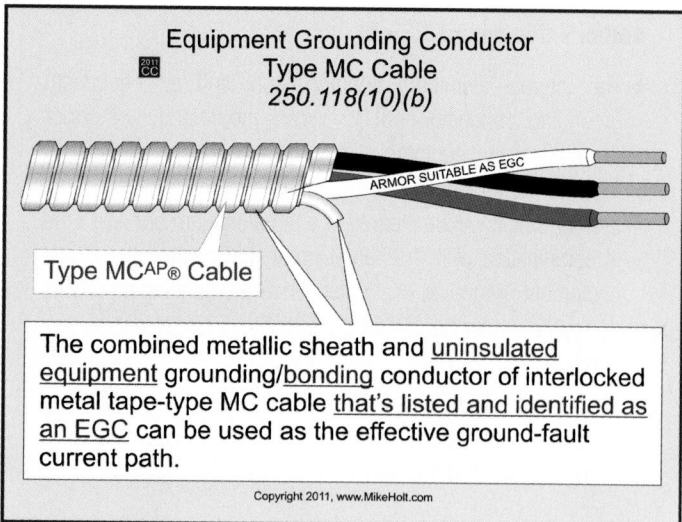

Figure 250–196

Author's Comment: Once the bare aluminum grounding/bonding conductor exits the cable, it can be cut off because it no longer serves any purpose. The effective ground-fault current path must be maintained by the use of fittings specifically listed for Type MCAP® cable [330.40]. See 300.12, 300.15, and 330.100. **Figure 250–197**

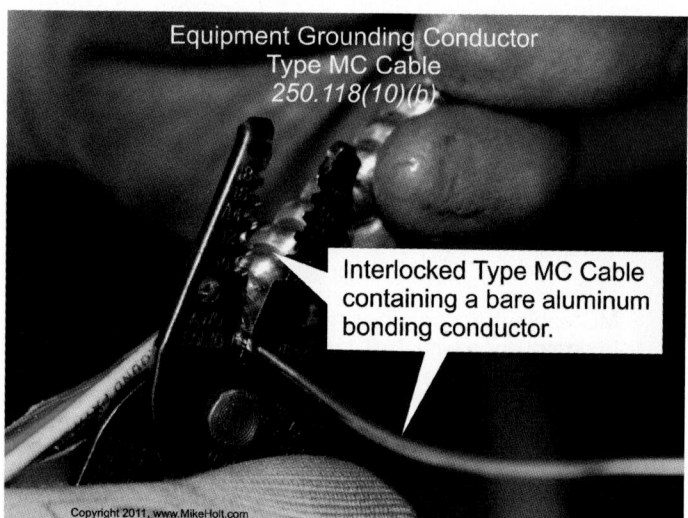

Figure 250–197

(c) The metallic sheath or the combined metallic sheath and equipment grounding conductors of the smooth or corrugated tube-type MC cable that's listed and identified as an equipment grounding conductor.

(11) Metallic cable trays where continuous maintenance and supervision ensure only qualified persons will service the cable tray, with cable tray and fittings identified for grounding and the cable tray, fittings [392.10], and raceways are bonded using bolted mechanical connectors or bonding jumpers sized and installed in accordance with 250.102 [392.60]. **Figure 250–198**

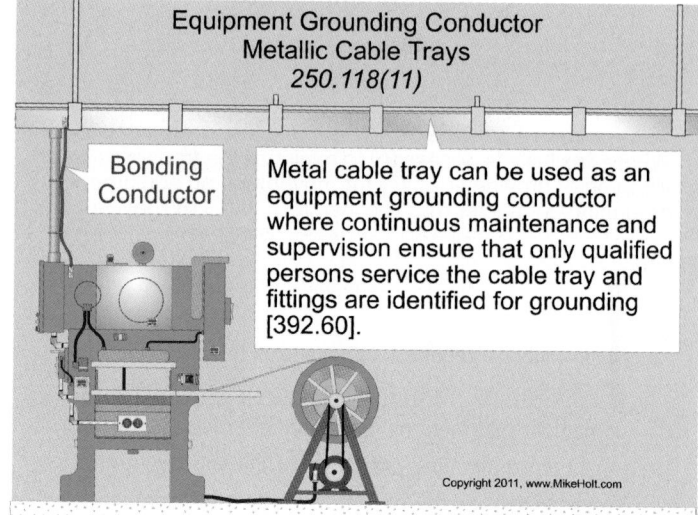

Figure 250–198

(13) Listed electrically continuous metal raceways, such as metal wireways [Article 376] or strut-type channel raceways [384.60].

(14) Surface metal raceways listed for grounding [Article 386].

250.119 Identification of Equipment Grounding Conductors.

Unless required to be insulated, equipment grounding conductors can be bare, covered, or insulated. Insulated equipment grounding conductors must have a continuous outer finish that's either green or green with one or more yellow stripes.

Conductors with insulation that's green, or green with one or more yellow stripes must not be used for an ungrounded or neutral conductor. **Figure 250–199**

Ex: Power-limited, Class 2 or Class 3 cables, power-limited fire alarm cables, or communications cables containing circuits operating at less than 50 volts can use conductors with insulated green or green with one or more yellow stripes for other than equipment grounding conductors [250.20(A) and 250.112(I)]. **Figure 250–200**

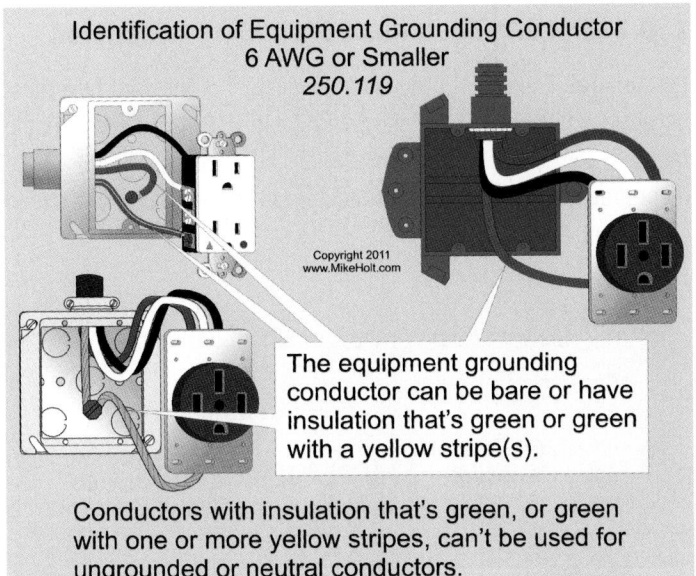

Identification of Equipment Grounding Conductor
6 AWG or Smaller
250.119

Copyright 2011
www.MikeHolt.com

The equipment grounding conductor can be bare or have insulation that's green or green with a yellow stripe(s).

Conductors with insulation that's green, or green with one or more yellow stripes, can't be used for ungrounded or neutral conductors.

Figure 250–199

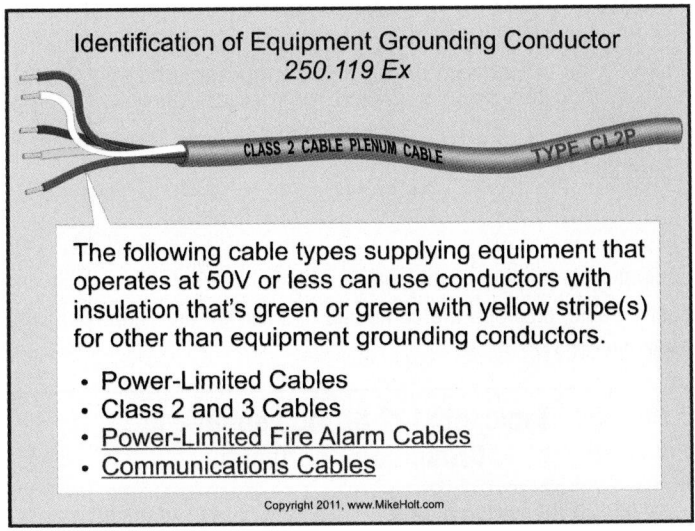

Identification of Equipment Grounding Conductor
250.119 Ex

CLASS 2 CABLE PLENUM CABLE   TYPE CL2P

The following cable types supplying equipment that operates at 50V or less can use conductors with insulation that's green or green with yellow stripe(s) for other than equipment grounding conductors.

- Power-Limited Cables
- Class 2 and 3 Cables
- Power-Limited Fire Alarm Cables
- Communications Cables

Copyright 2011, www.MikeHolt.com

Figure 250–200

Author's Comment: The *NEC* neither requires nor prohibits the use of the color green for the identification of grounding electrode conductors. **Figure 250–201**

(A) Conductors Larger Than 6 AWG.

(1) Identified if Accessible. Insulated equipment grounding conductors larger than 6 AWG can be permanently reidentified at the time of installation at every point where the conductor is accessible.

Ex: Identification of equipment grounding conductors larger than 6 AWG in conduit bodies isn't required.

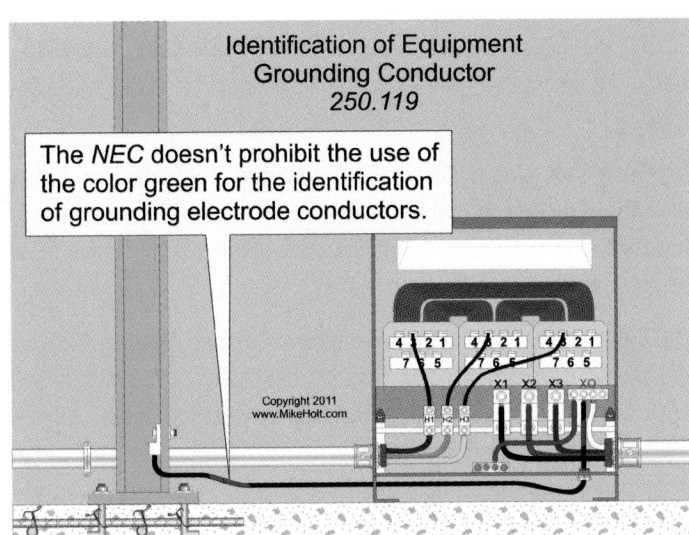

Identification of Equipment
Grounding Conductor
250.119

The *NEC* doesn't prohibit the use of the color green for the identification of grounding electrode conductors.

Copyright 2011
www.MikeHolt.com

Figure 250–201

(2) Identification Method. Equipment grounding conductor identification must encircle the conductor by: **Figure 250–202**

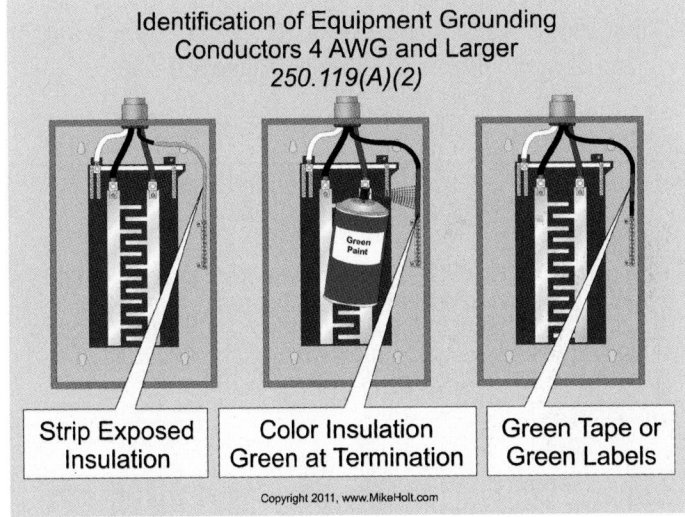

Identification of Equipment Grounding
Conductors 4 AWG and Larger
250.119(A)(2)

Green Paint

| Strip Exposed Insulation | Color Insulation Green at Termination | Green Tape or Green Labels |

Copyright 2011, www.MikeHolt.com

Figure 250–202

a. Removing the insulation at termination

b. Coloring the insulation green at termination

c. Marking the insulation at termination with green tape or green adhesive labels

250.120 Equipment Grounding Conductor Installation.
An equipment grounding conductor must be installed as follows:

(A) Raceway, Cable Trays, Cable Armor, Cablebus, or Cable Sheaths. If it consists of a raceway, cable tray, cable armor, cablebus framework, or cable sheath, fittings for joints and terminations must be made tight using suitable tools.

(C) Equipment Grounding Conductors Smaller Than 6 AWG. If not routed with circuit conductors as permitted in 250.130(C) and 250.134(B) Ex 2, equipment grounding conductors smaller than 6 AWG must be installed in a raceway or cable unless installed within hollow spaces of the framing members of buildings or structures and if not subject to physical damage.

250.121 Use of Equipment Grounding Conductors.
An equipment grounding conductor isn't permitted to be used as a grounding electrode conductor.

Author's Comment: For photovoltaic systems, 690.47(C) permits a combined equipment grounding/grounding electrode conductor if sized to the larger of 250.122 or 250.166 and installed in accordance with 250.64(E). **Figure 250–203**

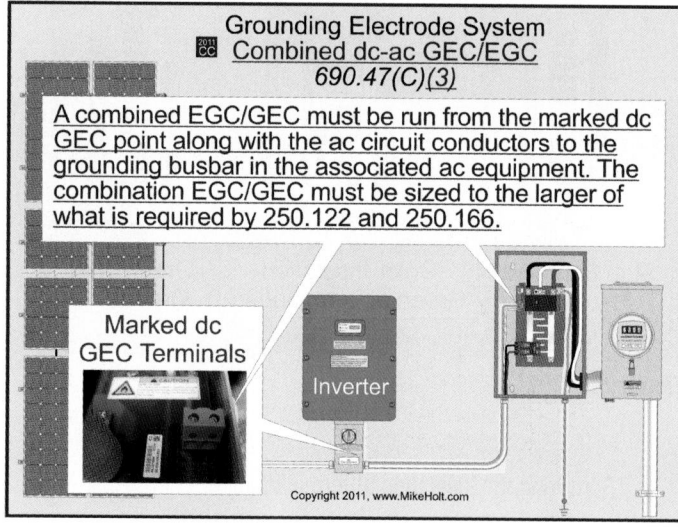

Figure 250-203

250.122 Sizing Equipment Grounding Conductor.

(A) General. Equipment grounding conductors of the wire type must be sized not smaller than shown in Table 250.122, based on the rating of the circuit overcurrent device; however, the circuit equipment grounding conductor isn't required to be larger than the circuit conductors. **Figure 250–204**

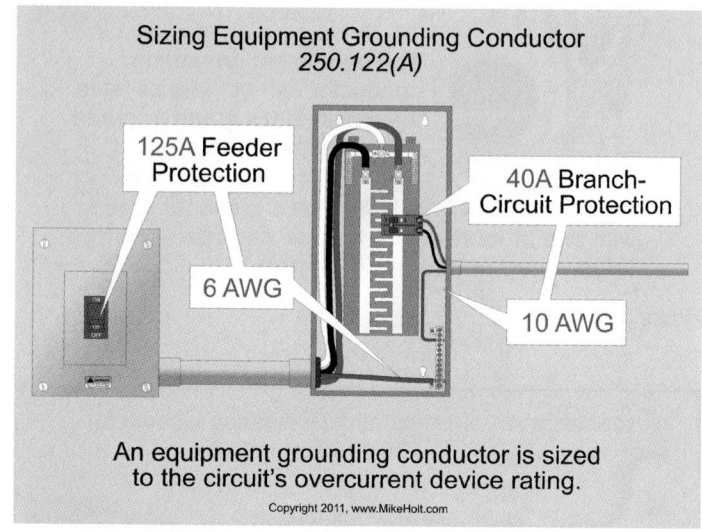

Figure 250–204

Equipment grounding conductors can be sectioned within a multiconductor cable, provided the combined circular mil area complies with Table 250.122.

Table 250.122 Sizing Equipment Grounding Conductor	
Overcurrent Device Rating	Copper Conductor
15A	14 AWG
20A	12 AWG
30A—60A	10 AWG
70A—100A	8 AWG
110A—200A	6 AWG
225A—300A	4 AWG
350A—400A	3 AWG
450A—500A	2 AWG
600A	1 AWG
700A—800A	1/0 AWG
1,000A	2/0 AWG
1,200A	3/0 AWG

(B) Increased in Size. If ungrounded conductors are increased in size from the minimum size, equipment grounding conductors must be proportionately increased in size according to the circular mil area of the ungrounded conductors.

Author's Comment: Ungrounded conductors are sometimes increased in size to accommodate conductor voltage drop, harmonic current heating, short-circuit rating, or simply for future capacity.

Question: If the ungrounded conductors for a 40A circuit are increased in size from 8 AWG to 6 AWG, the circuit equipment grounding conductor must be increased in size from 10 AWG to _____. Figure 250–205

(a) 10 AWG   (b) 8 AWG   (c) 6 AWG   (d) 4 AWG

Answer: (b) 8 AWG

The circular mil area of 6 AWG is 59 percent more than 8 AWG (26,240 Cmil/16,510 Cmil) [Chapter 9, Table 8].

According to Table 250.122, the circuit equipment grounding conductor for a 40A overcurrent device will be 10 AWG (10,380 Cmil), but the circuit equipment grounding conductor for this circuit must be increased in size by a multiplier of 1.59.

Conductor Size = 10,380 Cmil x 1.59
Conductor Size = 16,504 Cmil
Conductor Size = 8 AWG, Chapter 9, Table 8

Size of Equipment Grounding Conductor
250.122(B)

| 8 AWG Conductors Increased to 6 AWG. 59% size increase. 26,240 Cmil/16,510 Cmil | 250.122, 40A = 10 AWG 10,380 Cmil x 1.59 16,504 Cmil = 8 AWG |

When ungrounded conductors are increased in size, the equipment grounding conductor must be proportionately increased in size.

Figure 250–205

(C) Multiple Circuits. When multiple circuits are installed in the same raceway, cable, or cable tray, only one equipment grounding conductor is required for the multiple circuits, sized in accordance with 250.122, based on the rating of the largest circuit overcurrent device. Figures 250–206 and 250–207

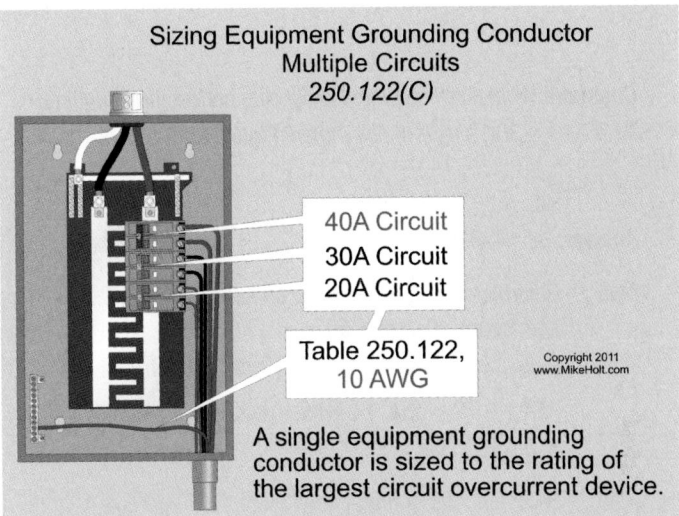

Sizing Equipment Grounding Conductor Multiple Circuits 250.122(C)

40A Circuit
30A Circuit
20A Circuit

Table 250.122, 10 AWG

Copyright 2011 www.MikeHolt.com

A single equipment grounding conductor is sized to the rating of the largest circuit overcurrent device.

Figure 250–206

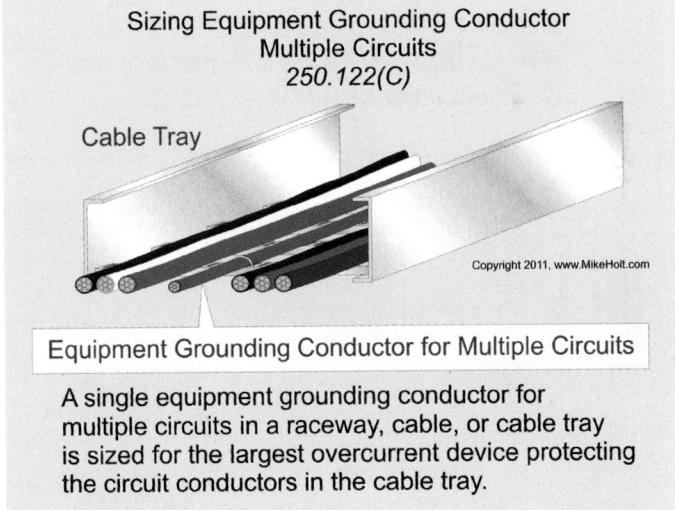

Sizing Equipment Grounding Conductor Multiple Circuits 250.122(C)

Cable Tray

Copyright 2011, www.MikeHolt.com

Equipment Grounding Conductor for Multiple Circuits

A single equipment grounding conductor for multiple circuits in a raceway, cable, or cable tray is sized for the largest overcurrent device protecting the circuit conductors in the cable tray.

Figure 250–207

Author's Comment: Single conductors used as equipment grounding conductors in cable trays must be sized 4 AWG and larger [392.10(B)(1)(c)].

(D) Motor Branch Circuits.

(1) General. The equipment grounding conductor of the wire type must be sized in accordance with Table 250.122, based on the rating of the motor circuit branch-circuit short-circuit and ground-fault overcurrent device, but this conductor isn't required to be larger than the circuit conductors [250.122(A)].

> *Question:* What size equipment grounding conductor is required for a 2 hp, 230V, single-phase motor? **Figure 250–208**
>
> *(a) 14 AWG*   *(b) 12 AWG*   *(c) 10 AWG*   *(d) 8 AWG*
>
> *Answer:* (a) 14 AWG
>
> *Step 1:* Determine the branch-circuit conductor size [430.22(A) and Table 310.15(B)(16)]
>
>   2 hp, 230V Motor FLC = 12A [Table 430.248]
>
>   12A x 1.25 = 15A, 14 AWG, rated 20A at 75°C [Table 310.15(B)(16)]
>
> *Step 2:* Determine the branch-circuit protection [240.6(A), 430.52(C)(1), and Table 430.248]
>
>   12A x 2.50 = 30A
>
> *Step 3:* The circuit equipment grounding conductor must be sized to the 30A overcurrent device—10 AWG [Table 250.122], but it's not required to be sized larger than the circuit conductors—14 AWG.

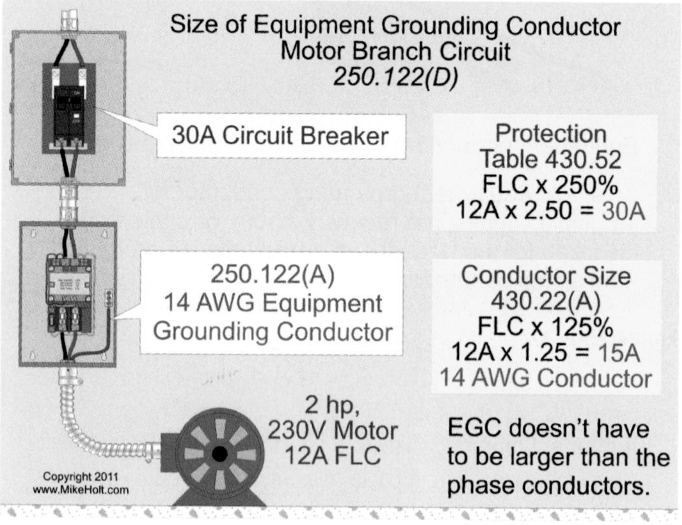

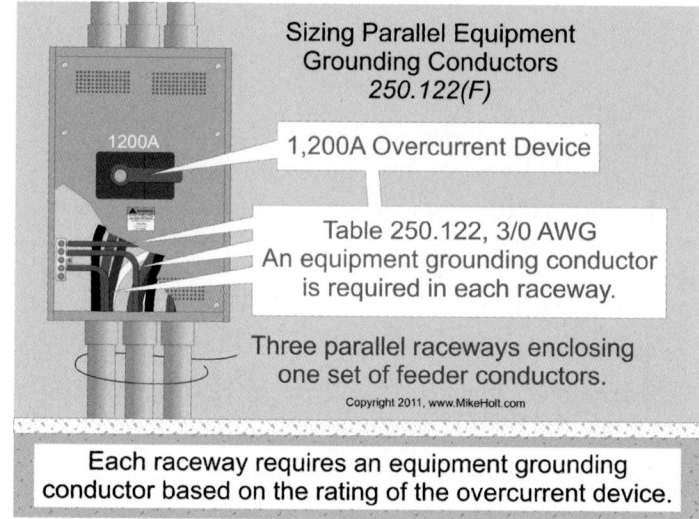

Sizing Parallel Equipment Grounding Conductors 250.122(F)

1,200A Overcurrent Device

Table 250.122, 3/0 AWG An equipment grounding conductor is required in each raceway.

Three parallel raceways enclosing one set of feeder conductors.

Copyright 2011, www.MikeHolt.com

Each raceway requires an equipment grounding conductor based on the rating of the overcurrent device.

Figure 250–209

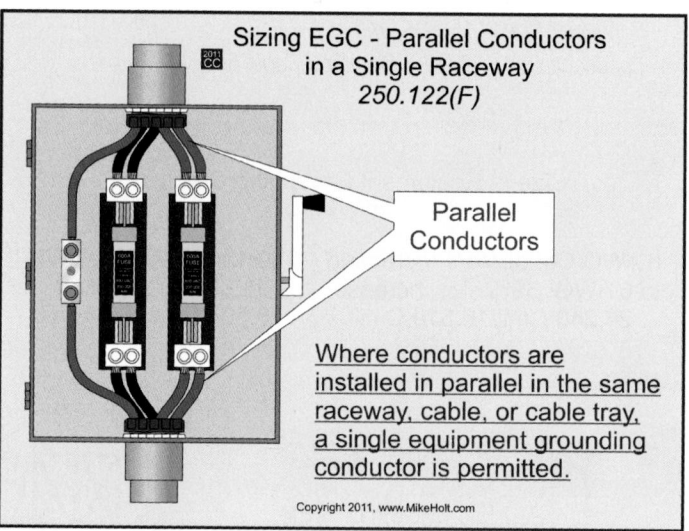

Sizing EGC - Parallel Conductors in a Single Raceway 250.122(F)

Parallel Conductors

Where conductors are installed in parallel in the same raceway, cable, or cable tray, a single equipment grounding conductor is permitted.

Copyright 2011, www.MikeHolt.com

Figure 250–210

Size of Equipment Grounding Conductor Motor Branch Circuit 250.122(D)

30A Circuit Breaker

Protection Table 430.52 FLC x 250% 12A x 2.50 = 30A

250.122(A) 14 AWG Equipment Grounding Conductor

Conductor Size 430.22(A) FLC x 125% 12A x 1.25 = 15A 14 AWG Conductor

2 hp, 230V Motor 12A FLC

EGC doesn't have to be larger than the phase conductors.

Copyright 2011 www.MikeHolt.com

Figure 250–208

(F) Parallel Runs. If circuit conductors are installed in parallel in separate raceways as permitted by 310.10(H), an equipment grounding conductor must be installed for each parallel conductor set. **Figure 250–209.** Where conductors are installed in parallel in the same raceway or cable tray, a single equipment grounding conductor is permitted. **Figure 250–210**

Each equipment grounding conductor must be sized in accordance with Table 250.122, based on the rating of the circuit overcurrent device, but it's not required to be larger than the circuit conductors [250.122(A)].

Author's Comment: In cable trays, single-conductor equipment grounding conductors can be insulated, covered, or bare, but must be sized 4 AWG and larger [392.10(B)(1)(c)].

(G) Feeder Tap Conductors. Equipment grounding conductors for feeder taps must be sized in accordance with Table 250.122, based on the ampere rating of the overcurrent device ahead of the feeder, but in no case is it required to be larger than the feeder tap conductors. **Figure 250–211**

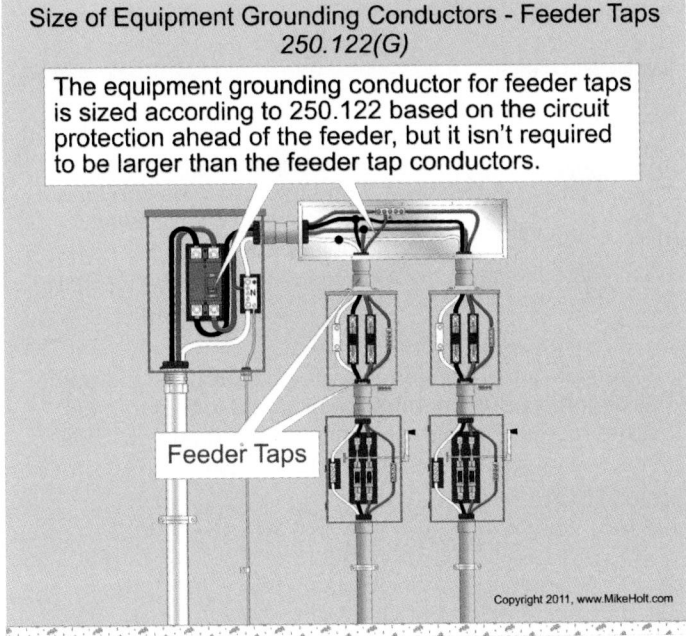

Figure 250–211

250.126 Identification of Wiring Device Terminals.
The terminal of a wiring device for the connection of the equipment grounding conductor must be identified by a green:

(1) Not readily removable terminal screw with a hexagonal head.

(2) Hexagonal, not readily removable terminal nut.

(3) Pressure wire connector. If the terminal for the grounding conductor isn't visible, the conductor entrance hole must be marked with the word "green" or "ground," the letters "G" or "GR," a grounding symbol, or otherwise identified by a distinctive green color.

PART VII. METHODS OF EQUIPMENT GROUNDING

250.130 Replacing Nongrounding Receptacles.

(C) Nongrounding Receptacle Replacement. If a nongrounding receptacle is replaced with a grounding-type receptacle from an outlet box that doesn't contain an equipment grounding conductor, the grounding contacts of the receptacle must be connected to one of the following: **Figure 250–212**

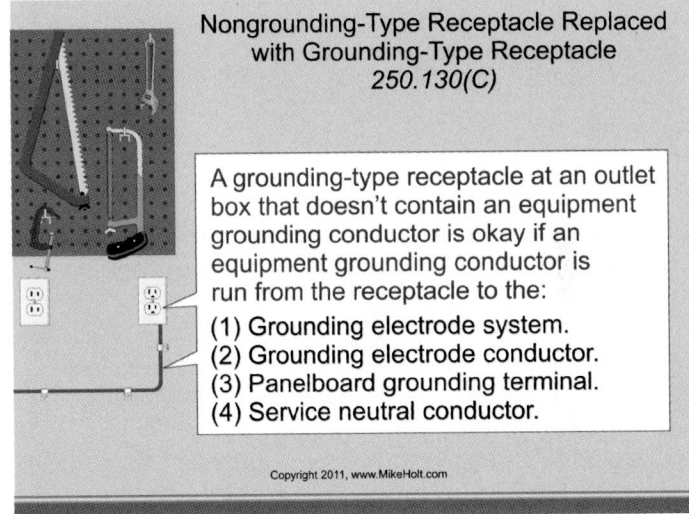

Figure 250–212

(1) Grounding electrode system [250.50]

(2) Grounding electrode conductor

(3) Panelboard equipment grounding terminal

(4) Service neutral conductor

Author's Comment: Branch circuit extensions are only permitted from an outlet box that doesn't contain an equipment grounding conductor if the receptacles on the extension have the grounding contacts connected to the grounding electrode system, grounding electrode conductor, panelboard equipment grounding terminal, or service neutral conductor in accordance with 250.130(C). **Figure 250–213**

Note: A grounding-type receptacle can replace a nongrounding type receptacle, without having the grounding terminal connected to an equipment grounding conductor, if the receptacle is GFCI protected and marked in accordance with 406.4(D)(2). **Figure 250–214**

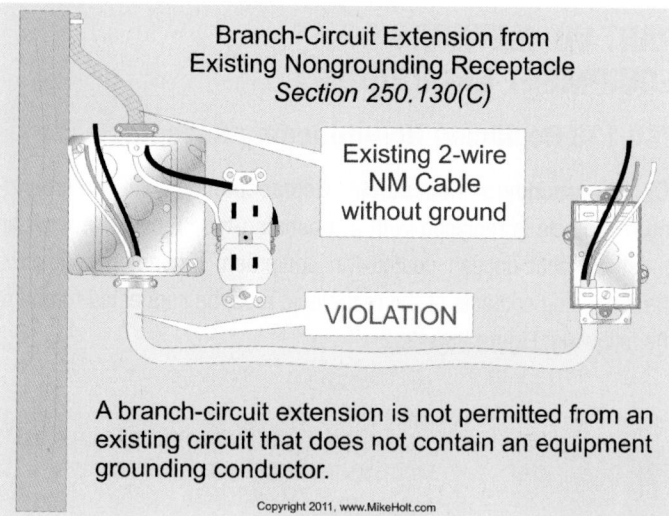

Branch-Circuit Extension from
Existing Nongrounding Receptacle
Section 250.130(C)

Existing 2-wire
NM Cable
without ground

VIOLATION

A branch-circuit extension is not permitted from an
existing circuit that does not contain an equipment
grounding conductor.

Copyright 2011, www.MikeHolt.com

Figure 250–213

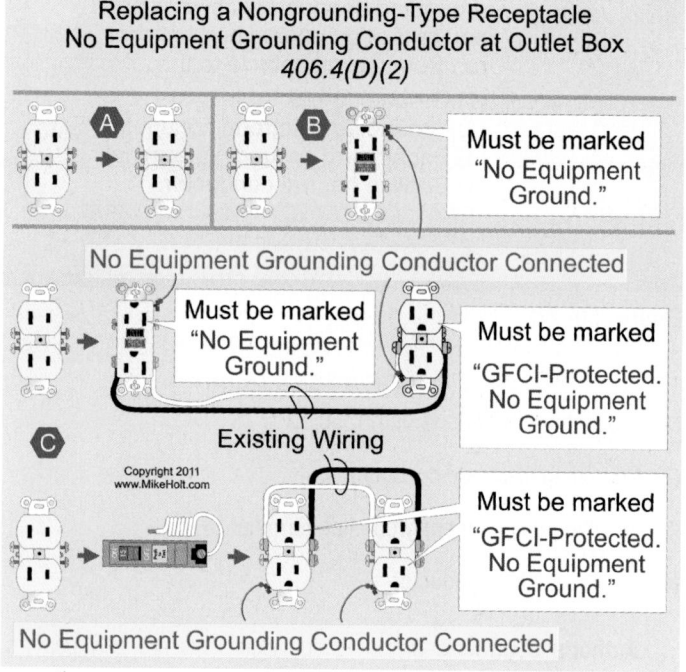

Replacing a Nongrounding-Type Receptacle
No Equipment Grounding Conductor at Outlet Box
406.4(D)(2)

Ⓐ   Ⓑ   Must be marked
            "No Equipment
            Ground."

No Equipment Grounding Conductor Connected

Must be marked
"No Equipment
Ground."

Must be marked
"GFCI-Protected.
No Equipment
Ground."

Existing Wiring

Copyright 2011
www.MikeHolt.com

Ⓒ

Must be marked
"GFCI-Protected.
No Equipment
Ground."

No Equipment Grounding Conductor Connected

Figure 250–214

250.134 Equipment Fastened in Place or Connected by Wiring Methods.
Unless connected to the neutral conductor at services or separately derived systems as permitted or required by 250.142, metal parts of equipment, raceways, and enclosures must be connected to an equipment grounding conductor by one of the following methods:

(A) Equipment Grounding Conductor Types. By connecting to equipment grounding conductors identified in 250.118.

(B) With Circuit Conductors. If an equipment grounding conductor of the wire type is installed, it must be installed in the same raceway, cable tray, trench, cable, or cord with the circuit conductors in accordance with 300.3(B), except as permitted by 250.102(E). **Figures 250–215 and 250–216**

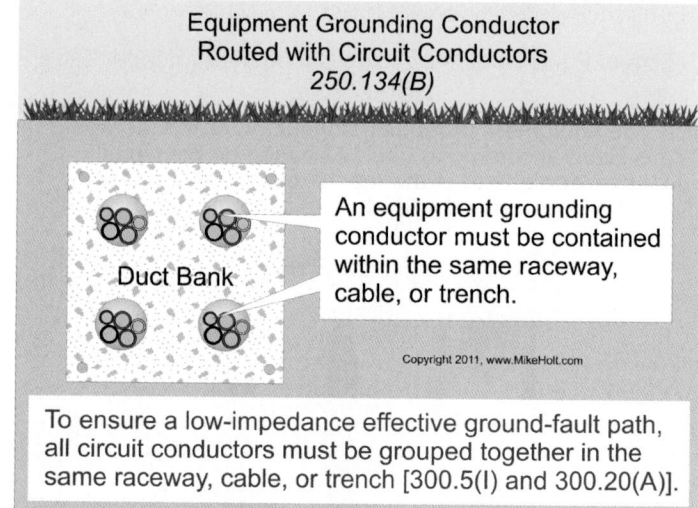

Equipment Grounding Conductor
Routed with Circuit Conductors
250.134(B)

Duct Bank

An equipment grounding
conductor must be contained
within the same raceway,
cable, or trench.

Copyright 2011, www.MikeHolt.com

To ensure a low-impedance effective ground-fault path,
all circuit conductors must be grouped together in the
same raceway, cable, or trench [300.5(I) and 300.20(A)].

Figure 250–215

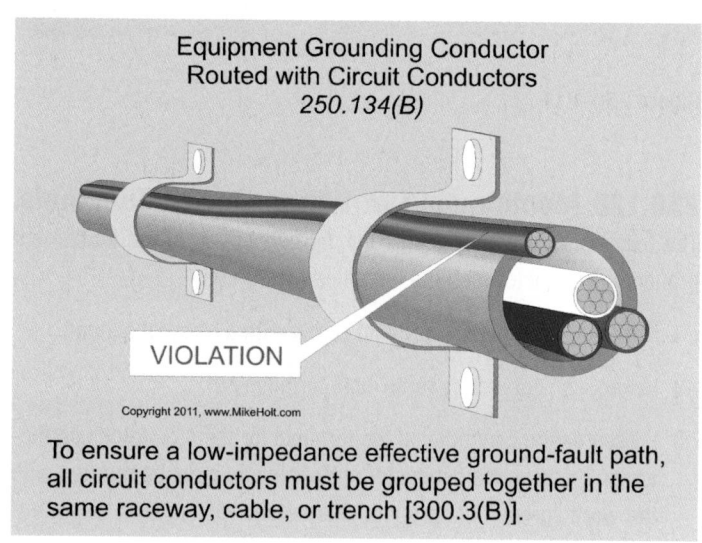

Equipment Grounding Conductor
Routed with Circuit Conductors
250.134(B)

VIOLATION

Copyright 2011, www.MikeHolt.com

To ensure a low-impedance effective ground-fault path,
all circuit conductors must be grouped together in the
same raceway, cable, or trench [300.3(B)].

Figure 250–216

250.136 Equipment Considered Grounded.

(A) Equipment Secured to Grounded Metal Supports. The structural metal frame of a building must not be used as the required equipment grounding conductor.

250.138 Cord-and-Plug-Connected Equipment.

(A) Equipment Grounding Conductor. Metal parts of cord-and-plug-connected equipment must be connected to an equipment grounding conductor that terminates to a grounding-type attachment plug.

250.140 Ranges, Ovens, and Clothes Dryers. The frames of electric ranges, wall-mounted ovens, counter-mounted cooking units, clothes dryers, and outlet boxes that are part of the circuit for these appliances must be connected to the equipment grounding conductor [250.134(A)]. **Figure 250–217**

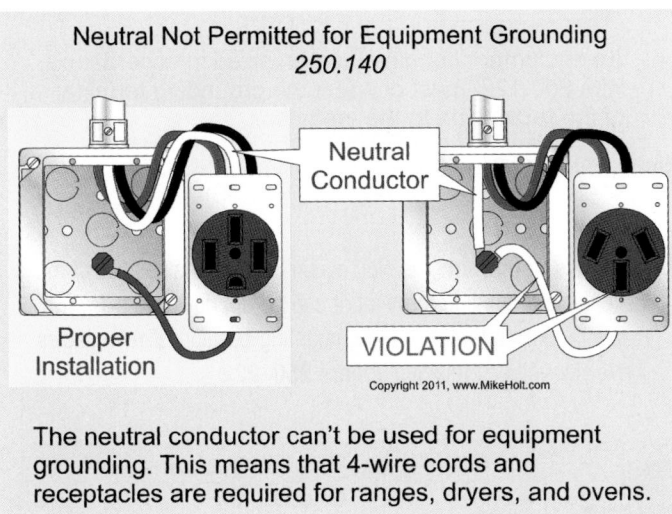

Neutral Not Permitted for Equipment Grounding
250.140

Neutral Conductor

Proper Installation

VIOLATION

Copyright 2011, www.MikeHolt.com

The neutral conductor can't be used for equipment grounding. This means that 4-wire cords and receptacles are required for ranges, dryers, and ovens.

Figure 250–217

⚠ **CAUTION:** *Ranges, dryers, and ovens have their metal cases connected to the neutral conductor at the factory. This neutral-to-case connection must be removed when these appliances are installed in new construction, and a 4-wire cord and receptacle must be used [250.142(B)].*

Ex: For existing installations if an equipment grounding conductor isn't present in the outlet box, the frames of electric ranges, wall-mounted ovens, counter-mounted cooking units, clothes dryers, and outlet boxes that are part of the circuit for these appliances may be connected to the neutral conductor. **Figure 250–218**

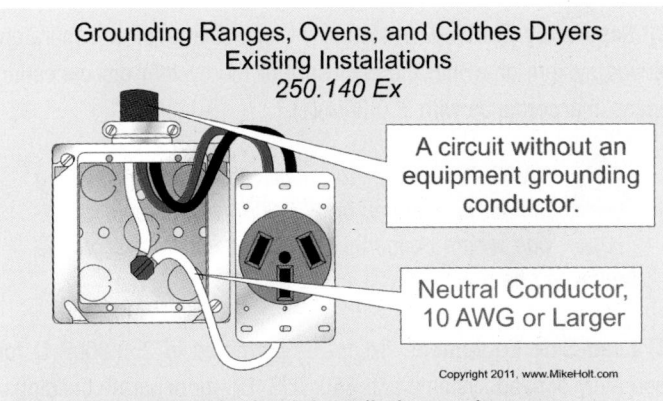

Grounding Ranges, Ovens, and Clothes Dryers
Existing Installations
250.140 Ex

A circuit without an equipment grounding conductor.

Neutral Conductor, 10 AWG or Larger

Copyright 2011, www.MikeHolt.com

For existing branch circuit installations, where an equipment grounding conductor isn't present in the outlet box, the frames and outlet boxes that are part of the circuit can be connected to the circuit neutral conductor.

Figure 250–218

250.142 Use of Neutral Conductor for Equipment Grounding.

Author's Comment: To remove dangerous voltage on metal parts from a ground fault, the metal parts of electrical raceways, cables, enclosures, and equipment must be connected to an equipment grounding conductor of a type recognized in 250.118 in accordance with 250.4(A)(3).

(A) Supply-Side Equipment. The neutral conductor can be used as the circuit equipment grounding conductor for metal parts of equipment, raceways, and enclosures at the following locations:

(1) Service Equipment. On the supply side or within the enclosure of the service disconnect in accordance with 250.24(B). **Figure 250–219**

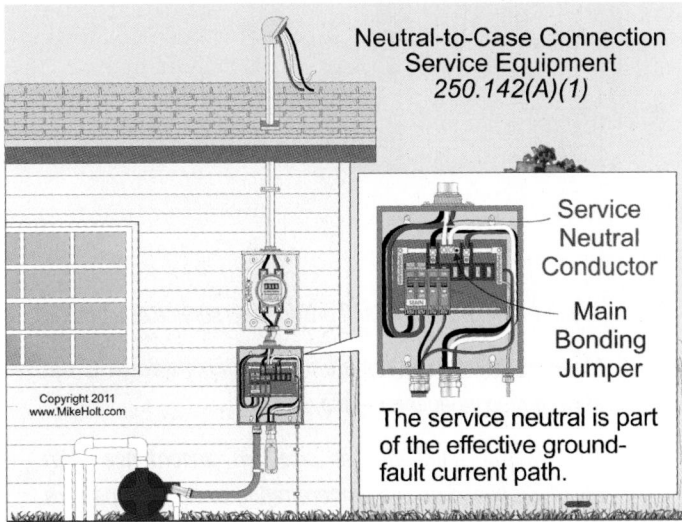

Neutral-to-Case Connection
Service Equipment
250.142(A)(1)

Service Neutral Conductor

Main Bonding Jumper

Copyright 2011 www.MikeHolt.com

The service neutral is part of the effective ground-fault current path.

Figure 250–219

(3) Separately Derived Systems. At the source of a separately derived system or within the enclosure of the system disconnecting means in accordance with 250.30(A)(1).

> ⚠️ **DANGER:** *Failure to install the system bonding jumper as required by 250.30(A)(1) creates a condition where dangerous touch voltage from a ground fault won't be removed.*

(B) Load-Side Equipment. Except as permitted in 250.30(A)(1) for separately derived systems and 250.32(B) Ex, for separate buildings/structures, the neutral conductor isn't permitted to serve as an equipment grounding conductor on the load side of service equipment.

Ex 1: In existing installations, the frames of ranges, wall-mounted ovens, counter-mounted cooking units, and clothes dryers can be connected to the neutral conductor in accordance with 250.140 Ex.

Ex 2: The neutral conductor can be connected to meter socket enclosures on the load side of the service disconnecting means if: **Figure 250–220**

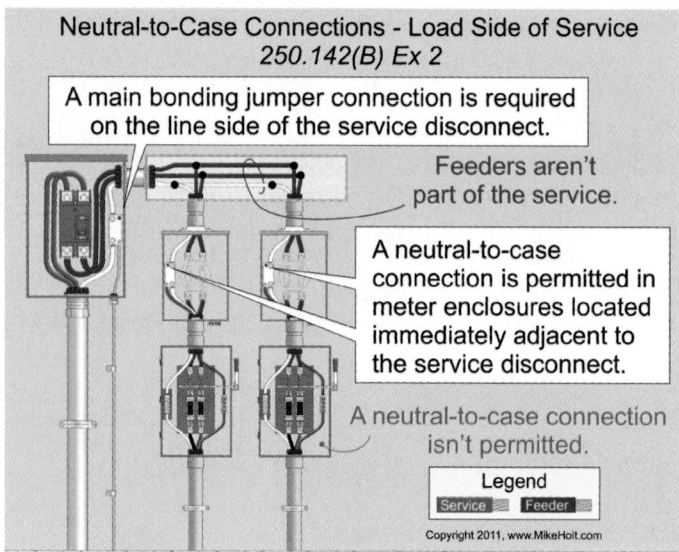

Figure 250–220

(1) Ground-fault protection isn't provided on service equipment,

(2) Meter socket enclosures are immediately adjacent to the service disconnecting means, and

(3) The neutral conductor is sized in accordance with 250.122, based on the ampere rating of the occupancy's feeder overcurrent device.

250.146 Connecting Receptacle Grounding Terminal to Metal Enclosure.

An equipment bonding jumper sized in accordance with 250.122, based on the rating of the circuit overcurrent device, must connect the grounding terminal of a receptacle to a metal box, except as permitted for (A) through (D). **Figure 250–221**

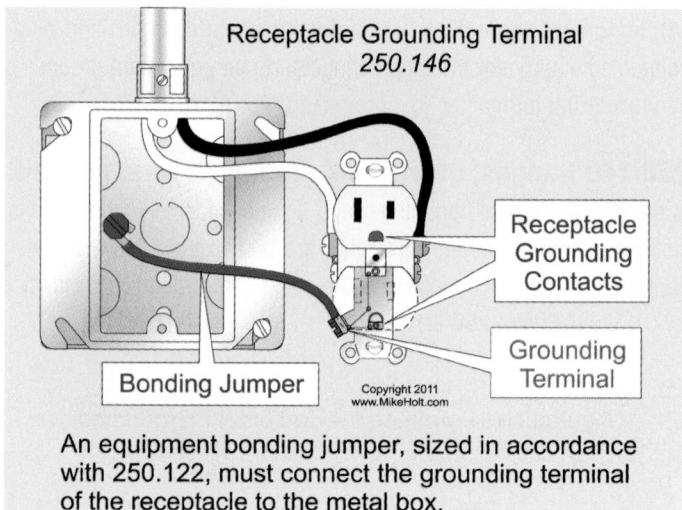

Figure 250–221

Author's Comment: The *NEC* doesn't restrict the position of the receptacle grounding terminal; it can be up, down, or sideways. *Code* proposals to specify the mounting position of receptacles have always been rejected. **Figure 250–222**

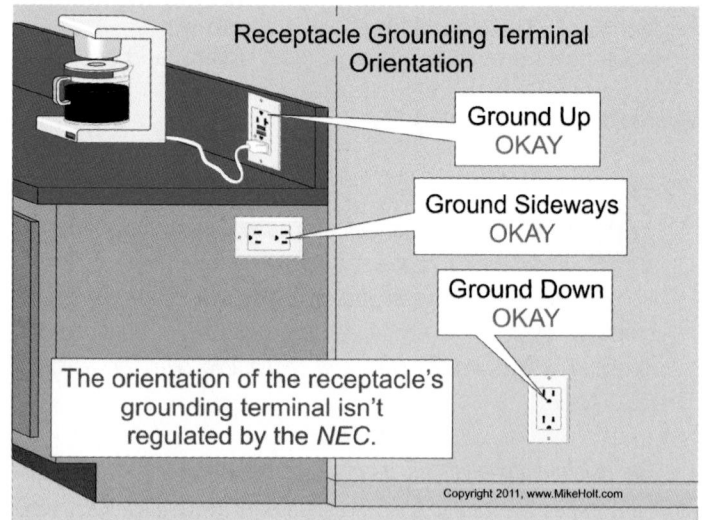

Figure 250–222

(A) Surface-Mounted Box. An equipment bonding jumper from a receptacle to a metal box that's surface mounted isn't required if there's direct metal-to-metal contact between the device yoke and the metal box. To ensure a suitable bonding path between the device yoke and a metal box, at least one of the insulating retaining washers on the yoke screw must be removed. **Figure 250–223**

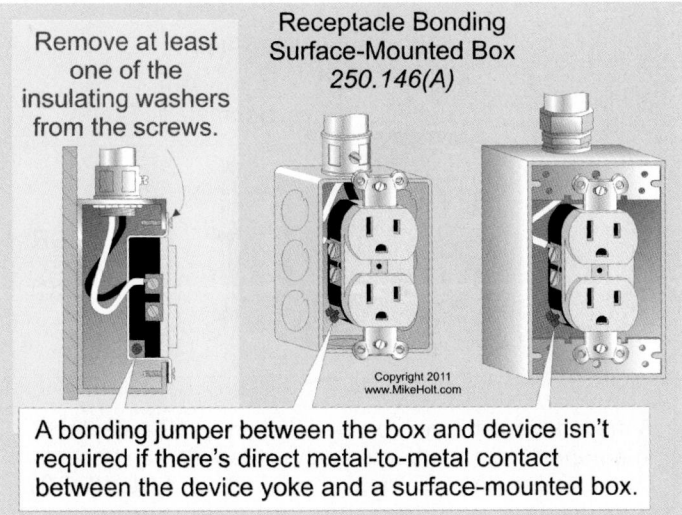

Remove at least one of the insulating washers from the screws.

Receptacle Bonding
Surface-Mounted Box
250.146(A)

Copyright 2011
www.MikeHolt.com

A bonding jumper between the box and device isn't required if there's direct metal-to-metal contact between the device yoke and a surface-mounted box.

Figure 250–223

An equipment bonding jumper isn't required for receptacles attached to listed exposed work covers when the receptacle is attached to the cover with at least two fasteners that have a thread locking or screw or nut locking means, and the cover mounting holes are located on a flat non-raised portion of the cover. **Figure 250–224**

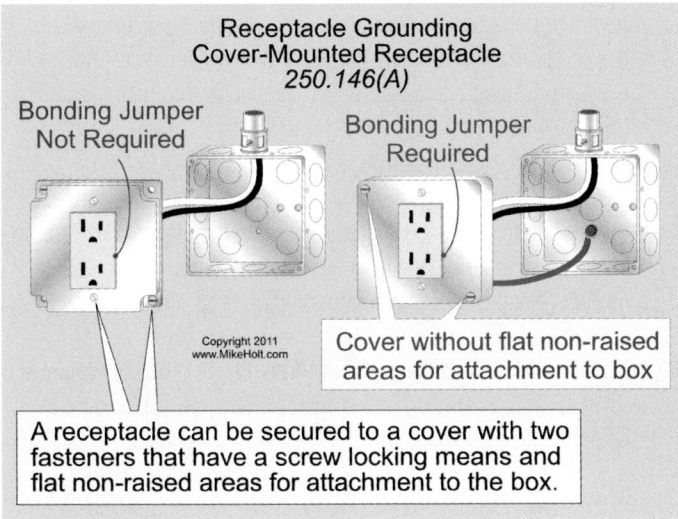

Receptacle Grounding
Cover-Mounted Receptacle
250.146(A)

Bonding Jumper
Not Required

Bonding Jumper
Required

Copyright 2011
www.MikeHolt.com

Cover without flat non-raised areas for attachment to box

A receptacle can be secured to a cover with two fasteners that have a screw locking means and flat non-raised areas for attachment to the box.

Figure 250–224

(B) Self-Grounding Receptacles. Receptacle yokes listed as self-grounding are designed to establish the bonding path between the device yoke and a metal box via the two metal mounting screws. **Figure 250–225**

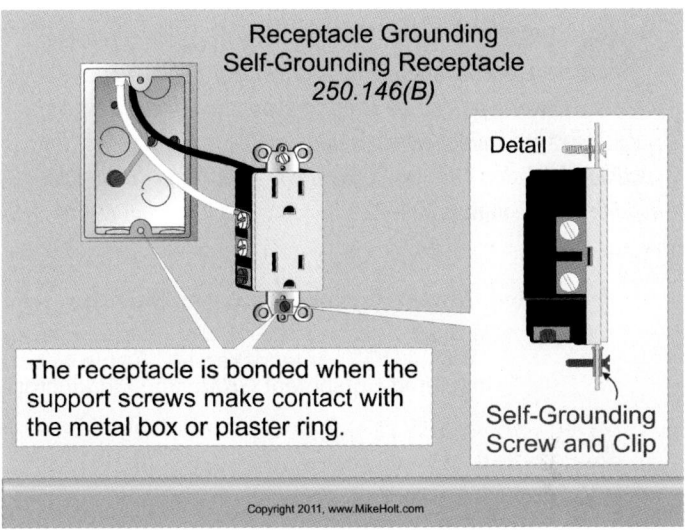

Receptacle Grounding
Self-Grounding Receptacle
250.146(B)

Detail

The receptacle is bonded when the support screws make contact with the metal box or plaster ring.

Self-Grounding
Screw and Clip

Copyright 2011, www.MikeHolt.com

Figure 250–225

(C) Floor Boxes. Listed floor boxes are designed to establish the bonding path between the device yoke and a metal box.

(D) Isolated Ground Receptacles. If installed for the reduction of electrical noise, the grounding terminal of an isolated ground receptacle must be connected to an insulated equipment grounding conductor run with the circuit conductors. **Figure 250–226**

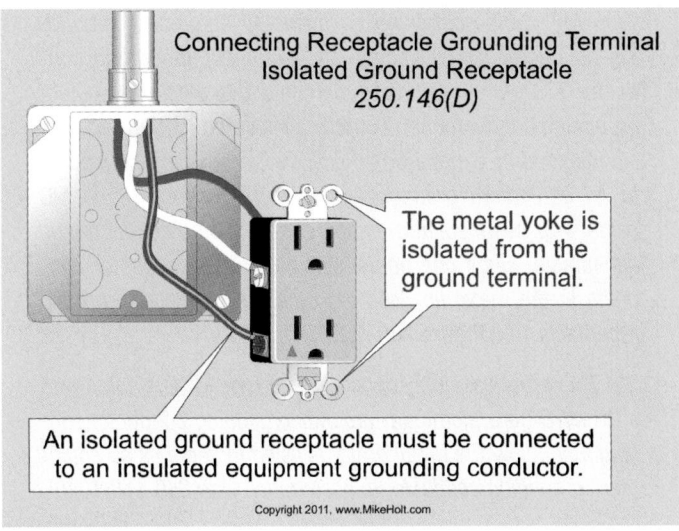

Connecting Receptacle Grounding Terminal
Isolated Ground Receptacle
250.146(D)

The metal yoke is isolated from the ground terminal.

An isolated ground receptacle must be connected to an insulated equipment grounding conductor.

Copyright 2011, www.MikeHolt.com

Figure 250–226

The circuit equipment grounding conductor is permitted to pass through panelboards [408.40 Ex], boxes, wireways, or other enclosures [250.148 Ex] without a connection to the enclosure as long as it terminates at an equipment grounding conductor terminal of the derived system or service.

⚠ **CAUTION:** *Type AC Cable—Type AC cable containing an insulated equipment grounding conductor of the wire type can be used to supply receptacles having insulated grounding terminals because the metal armor of the cable is listed as an equipment grounding conductor [250.118(8)].* **Figure 250–227**

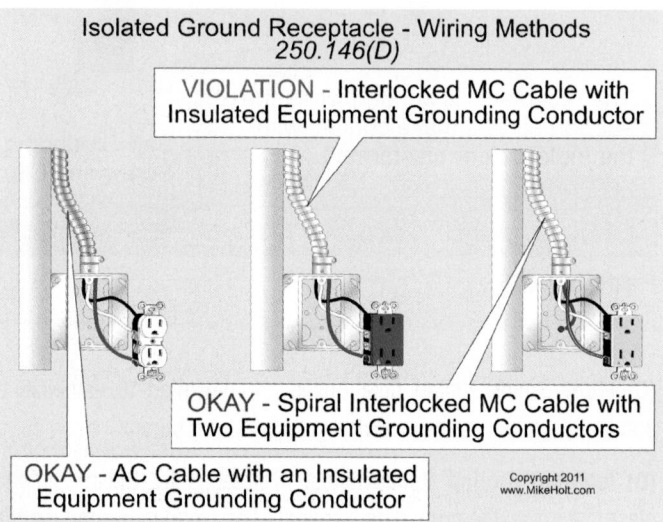

Figure 250–227

Type MC Cable—The metal armor sheath of interlocked Type MC cable containing an insulated equipment grounding conductor isn't listed as an equipment grounding conductor. Therefore, this wiring method with a single equipment grounding conductor can't supply an isolated ground receptacle installed in a metal box (because the box isn't connected to an equipment grounding conductor). However, Type MC cable with two insulated equipment grounding conductors is acceptable, since one equipment grounding conductor connects to the metal box and the other to the isolated ground receptacle. See **Figure 250–227**

The armor assembly of interlocked Type MCAP® cable with a 10 AWG bare aluminum grounding/bonding conductor running just below the metal armor is listed to serve as an equipment grounding conductor in accordance with 250.118(10)(b).

Nonmetallic Boxes—Because the grounding terminal of an isolated ground receptacle is insulated from the metal mounting yoke, a metal faceplate must not be used when an isolated ground receptacle is installed in a nonmetallic box. The reason is that the metal faceplate isn't connected to an equipment grounding conductor [406.3(D)(2)]. **Figure 250–228**

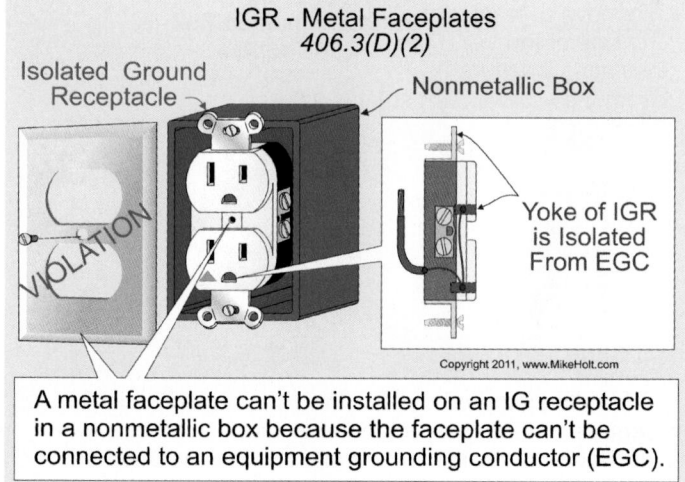

Figure 250–228

Author's Comment: When should an isolated ground receptacle be installed and how should the isolated ground system be designed? These questions are design issues and must not be answered based on the *NEC* alone [90.1(C)]. In most cases, using isolated ground receptacles is a waste of money. For example, IEEE 1100—*Powering and Grounding Electronic Equipment* (Emerald Book) states: "The results from the use of the isolated ground method range from no observable effects, the desired effects, or worse noise conditions than when standard equipment bonding configurations are used to serve electronic load equipment [8.5.3.2]."

In reality, few electrical installations truly require an isolated ground system. For those systems that can benefit from an isolated ground system, engineering opinions differ as to what's a proper design. Making matters worse—of those properly designed, few are correctly installed and even fewer are properly maintained. For more information on how to properly ground electronic equipment, go to: www.MikeHolt.com, click on the "Technical" link, and then visit the "Power Quality" page.

250.148 Continuity and Attachment of Equipment Grounding Conductors in Boxes.

If circuit conductors are spliced or terminated on equipment within a metal box, the equipment grounding conductor associated with those circuits must be connected to the box in accordance with the following: **Figure 250–229**

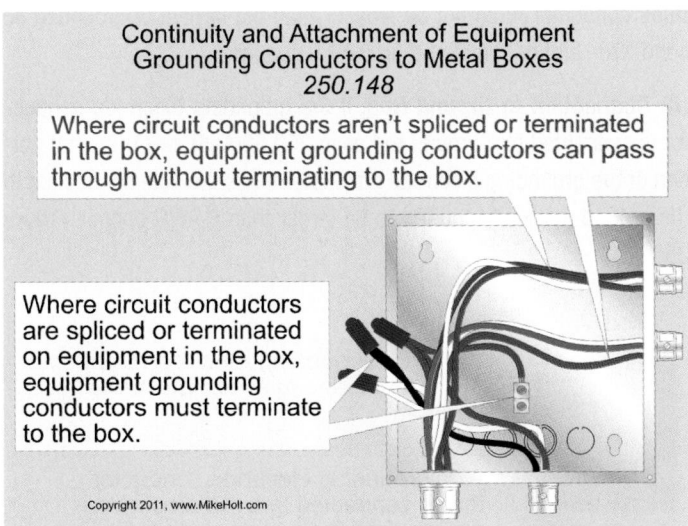

Continuity and Attachment of Equipment
Grounding Conductors to Metal Boxes
250.148

Where circuit conductors aren't spliced or terminated in the box, equipment grounding conductors can pass through without terminating to the box.

Where circuit conductors are spliced or terminated on equipment in the box, equipment grounding conductors must terminate to the box.

Copyright 2011, www.MikeHolt.com

Figure 250–229

Ex: The circuit equipment grounding conductor for an isolated ground receptacle installed in accordance with 250.146(D) isn't required to terminate to a metal box. **Figure 250–230**

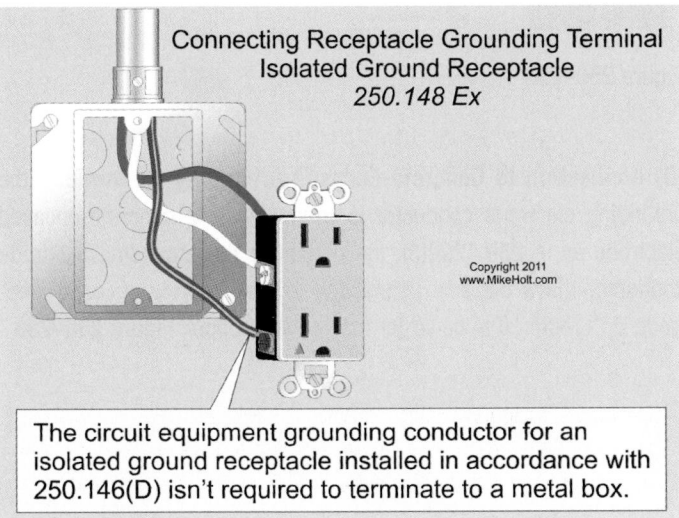

Connecting Receptacle Grounding Terminal
Isolated Ground Receptacle
250.148 Ex

Copyright 2011
www.MikeHolt.com

The circuit equipment grounding conductor for an isolated ground receptacle installed in accordance with 250.146(D) isn't required to terminate to a metal box.

Figure 250–230

(A) Splicing. Equipment grounding conductors must be spliced together with a device listed for the purpose [110.14(B)]. **Figure 250–231**

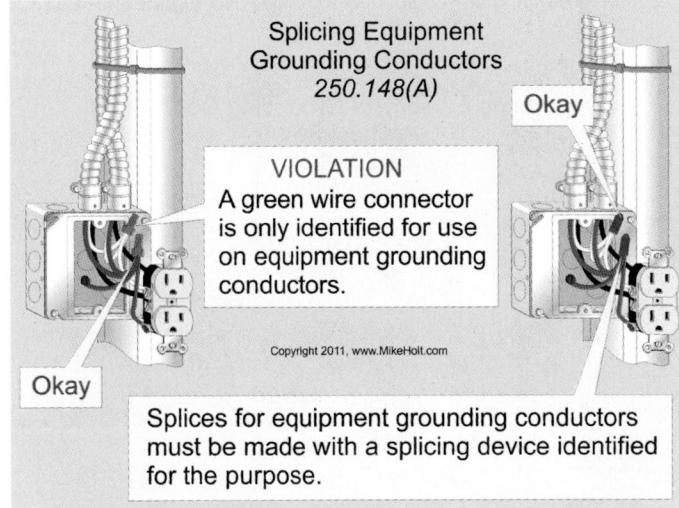

Splicing Equipment
Grounding Conductors
250.148(A)

Okay

VIOLATION
A green wire connector is only identified for use on equipment grounding conductors.

Copyright 2011, www.MikeHolt.com

Okay

Splices for equipment grounding conductors must be made with a splicing device identified for the purpose.

Figure 250–231

Author's Comment: Wire connectors of any color can be used with equipment grounding conductor splices, but green wire connectors can only be used with equipment grounding conductors.

(B) Equipment Grounding Continuity. Equipment grounding conductors must terminate in a manner such that the disconnection or the removal of a receptacle, luminaire, or other device won't interrupt the grounding continuity. **Figure 250–232**

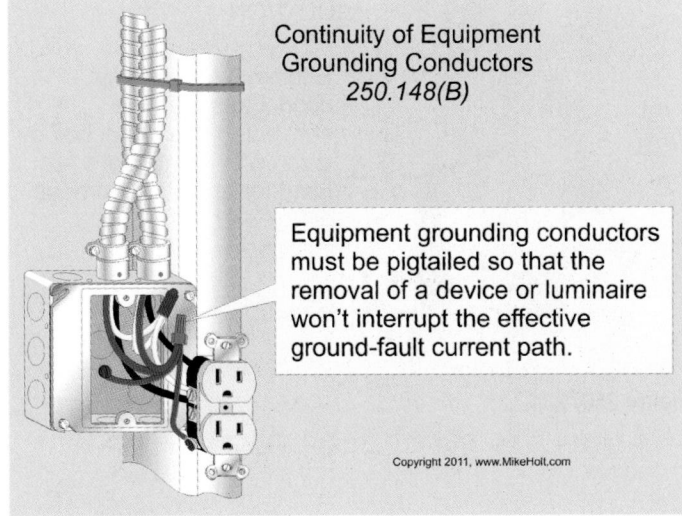

Continuity of Equipment
Grounding Conductors
250.148(B)

Equipment grounding conductors must be pigtailed so that the removal of a device or luminaire won't interrupt the effective ground-fault current path.

Copyright 2011, www.MikeHolt.com

Figure 250–232

(C) Metal Boxes. Equipment grounding conductors within metal boxes must be connected to the metal box with a grounding screw that's not used for any other purpose, an equipment fitting listed for grounding, or a listed grounding device such as a ground clip. **Figure 250–233**

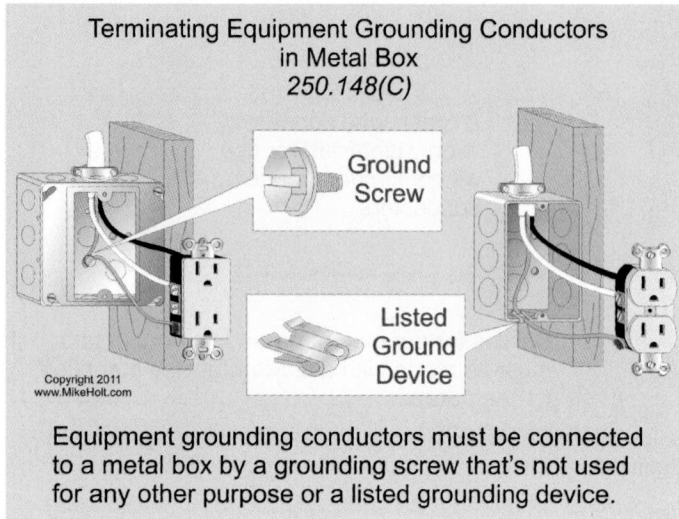

Terminating Equipment Grounding Conductors
in Metal Box
250.148(C)

Ground Screw

Listed Ground Device

Equipment grounding conductors must be connected to a metal box by a grounding screw that's not used for any other purpose or a listed grounding device.

Figure 250–233

Author's Comment: Equipment grounding conductors aren't permitted to terminate to a screw that secures a plaster ring. **Figure 250–234**

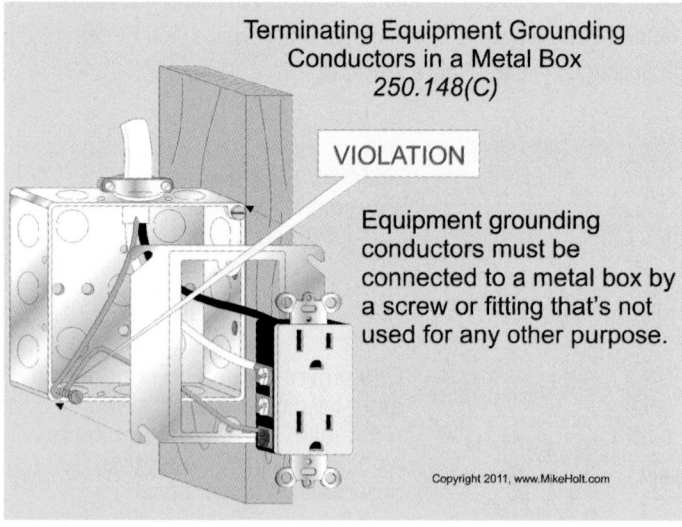

Terminating Equipment Grounding
Conductors in a Metal Box
250.148(C)

VIOLATION

Equipment grounding conductors must be connected to a metal box by a screw or fitting that's not used for any other purpose.

Figure 250–234

PART VIII. DIRECT-CURRENT SYSTEMS

250.166 Sizing Grounding Electrode Conductor.

Except as permitted in (C) through (E), the grounding electrode conductor must be sized in accordance with 250.166(A).

(B) Not Smaller Than the Largest Conductor. The grounding electrode conductor must not be smaller than the largest ungrounded dc conductor, and not smaller than 8 AWG copper.

(C) Connection to Ground Rod. If the grounding electrode conductor is connected to a ground rod as in 250.52(A)(5), or (A)(7), that portion of the grounding electrode conductor that's the sole connection to the ground rod isn't required to be larger than 6 AWG copper. **Figure 250–235**

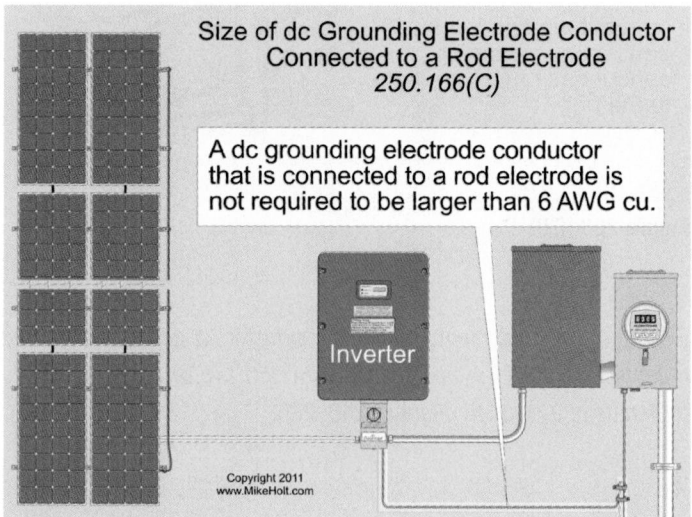

Size of dc Grounding Electrode Conductor
Connected to a Rod Electrode
250.166(C)

A dc grounding electrode conductor that is connected to a rod electrode is not required to be larger than 6 AWG cu.

Inverter

Figure 250–235

(D) Connection to Concrete-Encased Grounding Electrode. If the grounding electrode conductor is connected to a concrete-encased electrode as in 250.52(A)(3), the portion of the grounding electrode conductor that's the sole connection to the concrete-encased electrode isn't required to be larger than 4 AWG copper. **Figure 250–236**

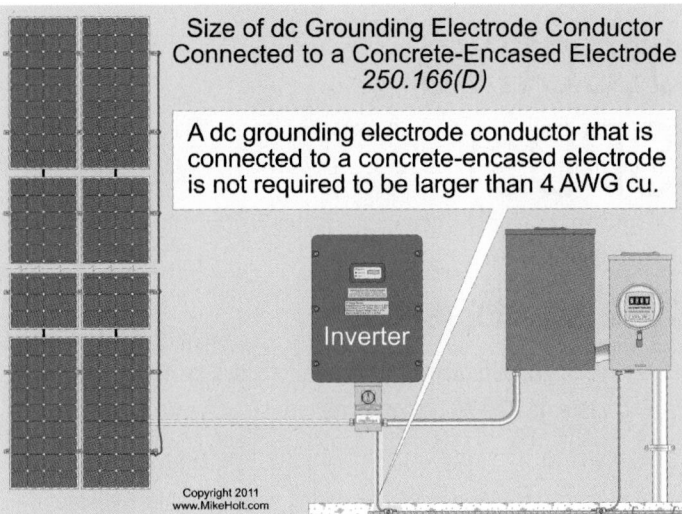

Size of dc Grounding Electrode Conductor
Connected to a Concrete-Encased Electrode
250.166(D)

A dc grounding electrode conductor that is
connected to a concrete-encased electrode
is not required to be larger than 4 AWG cu.

Inverter

Copyright 2011
www.MikeHolt.com

Figure 250–236

ARTICLE
285

Surge Protective Devices (SPDs)

INTRODUCTION TO ARTICLE 285—SURGE PROTECTIVE DEVICES (SPDS)

This article covers the general requirements, installation requirements, and connection requirements for surge protective devices (arresters and TVSSs) rated 1kV or less that are permanently installed on premises wiring systems. The *NEC* doesn't require surge protective devices to be installed, but if they' are, they must comply with this article.

Surge protective devices are designed to reduce transient voltages present on premises power distribution wiring and load-side equipment, particularly electronic equipment such as computers, telecommunications equipment, security systems, and electronic appliances.

These transient voltages can originate from a number of sources, including anything from lightning to a laser printers. The best line of defense for all types of electronic equipment may be the installation of surge protective devices at the electrical service, source of power, as well as at the location of the utilization equipment. **Figures 285–1 and 285–2**

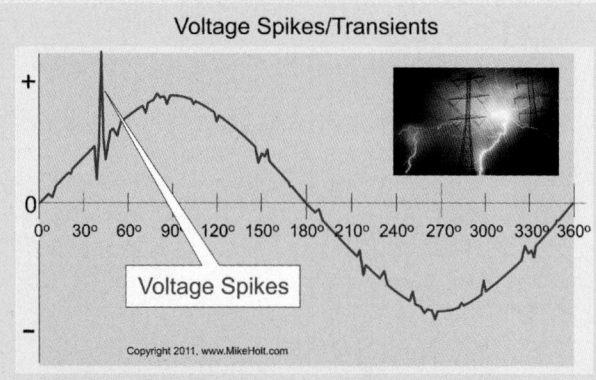

Voltage spikes/transients caused by the switching of utility power lines or power factor correction capacitors, or lightning can reach thousands of volts and amperes.

Figure 285–1

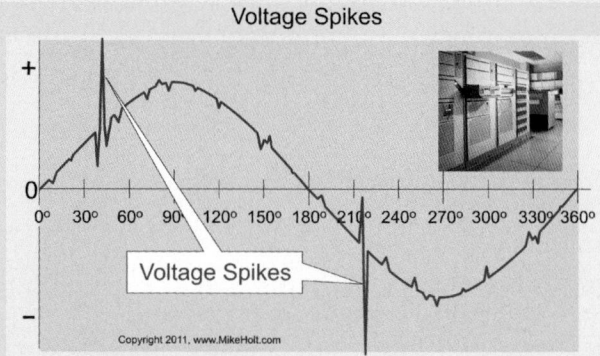

Voltage spikes (transients) produced by premises equipment such as photocopiers, laser printers, and other high reactive loads cycling off, can be in the hundreds of volts.

Figure 285–2

The intent of a surge protection device is to limit transient voltages by diverting or limiting surge current and preventing continued flow of current while remaining capable of repeating these functions [Article 100]. **Figures 285–3 and 285–4**

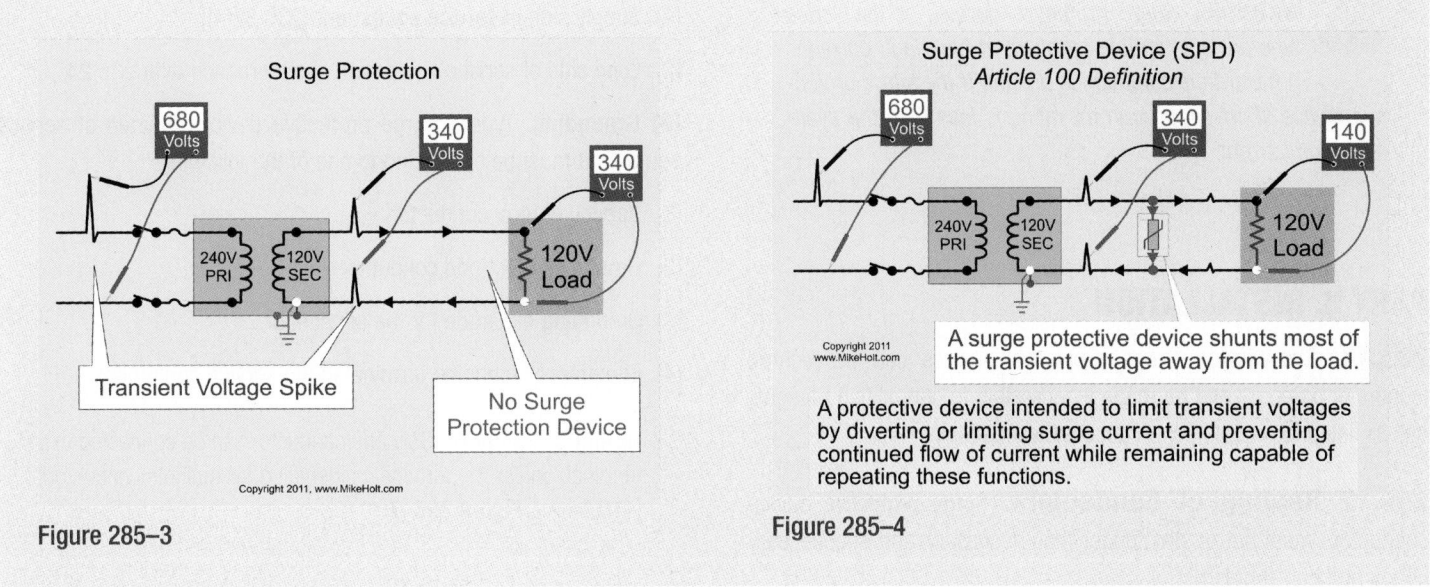

Surge Protection

680 Volts

340 Volts

340 Volts

240V PRI

120V SEC

120V Load

Transient Voltage Spike

No Surge Protection Device

Copyright 2011, www.MikeHolt.com

Figure 285–3

Surge Protective Device (SPD)
Article 100 Definition

680 Volts

340 Volts

140 Volts

240V PRI

120V SEC

120V Load

Copyright 2011
www.MikeHolt.com

A surge protective device shunts most of the transient voltage away from the load.

A protective device intended to limit transient voltages by diverting or limiting surge current and preventing continued flow of current while remaining capable of repeating these functions.

Figure 285–4

PART I. GENERAL

285.1 Scope. This article covers the installation and connection requirements for permanently installed surge protective devices (surge arresters and transient voltage surge suppressors). **Figure 285–5**

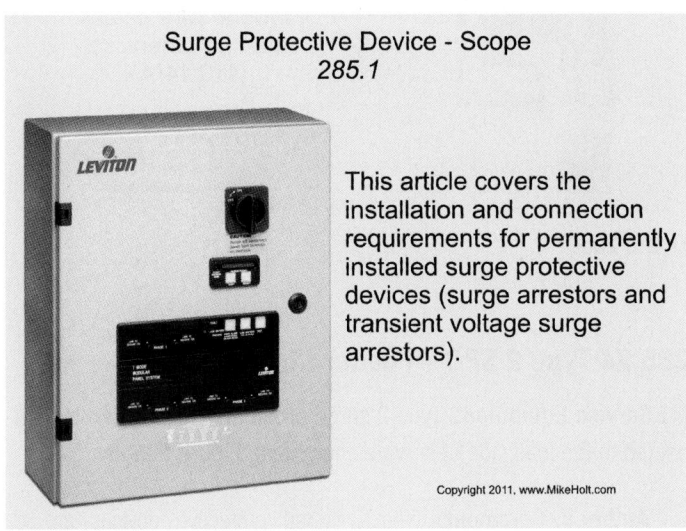

Surge Protective Device - Scope
285.1

LEVITON

This article covers the installation and connection requirements for permanently installed surge protective devices (surge arrestors and transient voltage surge arrestors).

Copyright 2011, www.MikeHolt.com

Figure 285–5

Note 1: Surge arresters rated less than 1,000V are known as Type 1 surge protective devices.

Note 2: Transient voltage surge suppressors (TVSSs) are also known as Type 2 and Type 3 surge protective devices (SPDs).

285.3 Uses Not Permitted. A surge protective device must not be used in:

(1) Circuits that exceed 1,000V.

(2) Ungrounded systems, impedance grounded systems, or corner-grounded delta systems, unless listed specifically for use on these systems.

(3) If the voltage rating of the surge protective device is less than the maximum continuous phase-to-ground voltage available at the point of connection.

285.4 Number Required. If used, the surge protective device must be connected to each ungrounded conductor of the circuit.

285.5 Listing. Surge protective devices must be listed.

Author's Comment: According to UL 1449, *Standard for Surge Protective Devices*, these units are intended to limit the maximum amplitude of transient voltage surges on power lines to specified values. They aren't intended to function as lightning arresters. The adequacy of the voltage suppression level to protect connected equipment from voltage surges hasn't been evaluated.

285.6 Short-Circuit Current Rating. Surge protective devices must be marked with their short-circuit current rating, and they must not be installed if the available fault current exceeds that rating. This short-circuit current marking requirement doesn't apply to receptacles containing surge protective device protection.

⚠️ **WARNING:** *Surge protective devices of the series type are susceptible to failure at high fault currents. A hazardous condition is present if the surge protective device short-circuit current rating is less than the available fault current.*

PART II. INSTALLATION

285.11 Location. Surge protective devices can be located indoors or outdoors and be made inaccessible to unqualified persons, unless listed for installation in accessible locations.

285.12 Routing of Conductors. Surge protective device conductors must not be any longer than necessary, and unnecessary bends must be avoided.

PART III. CONNECTING SURGE PROTECTIVE DEVICES

285.23 Type 1 SPD—Line Side of Service Equipment.

(A) Installation. Type 1 surge protective devices can be connected as follows: Figure 285–6

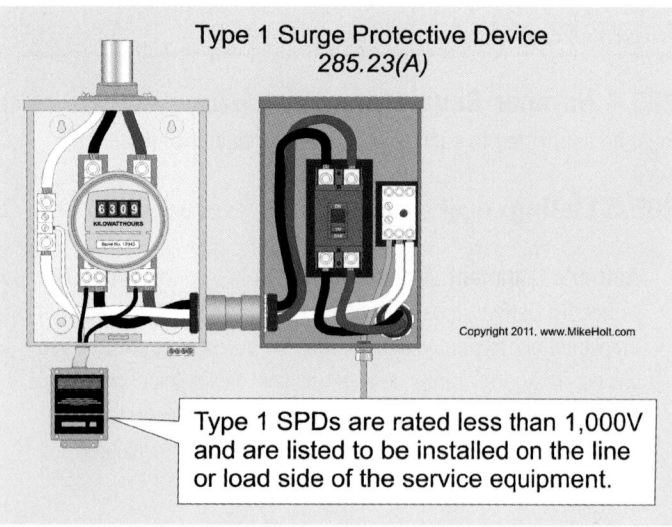

Type 1 Surge Protective Device
285.23(A)

Type 1 SPDs are rated less than 1,000V and are listed to be installed on the line or load side of the service equipment.

Copyright 2011, www.MikeHolt.com

Figure 285–6

(1) Supply side of service equipment [230.82(4)].

(2) Load side of service equipment in accordance with 285.24.

(B) Grounding. Type 1 surge protective devices located at service equipment must be connected to one of the following:

(1) Service neutral conductor,

(2) Grounding electrode conductor,

(3) Grounding electrode for the service, or

(4) Equipment grounding terminal in the service equipment.

> **Author's Comment:** Only one conductor can be connected to a terminal, unless the terminal is identified for multiple conductors [110.14(A)]. **Figure 285–7**

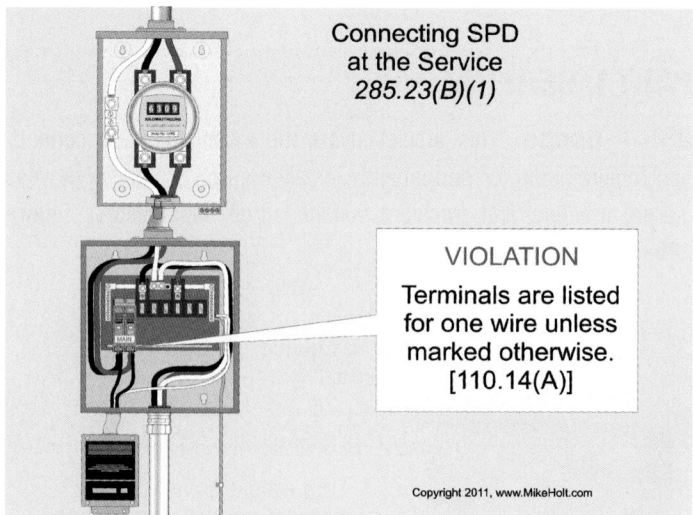

Connecting SPD
at the Service
285.23(B)(1)

VIOLATION
Terminals are listed
for one wire unless
marked otherwise.
[110.14(A)]

Copyright 2011, www.MikeHolt.com

Figure 285–7

285.24 Type 2 SPD—Feeder Circuits.

(A) Service Equipment. Type 2 surge protective devices can be connected to the load side of service equipment. **Figure 285–8**

> **Author's Comment:** Type 2 surge protective devices are listed for installation only on the load side of service equipment because they're not listed to accommodate lightning-induced surges beyond their capacity.

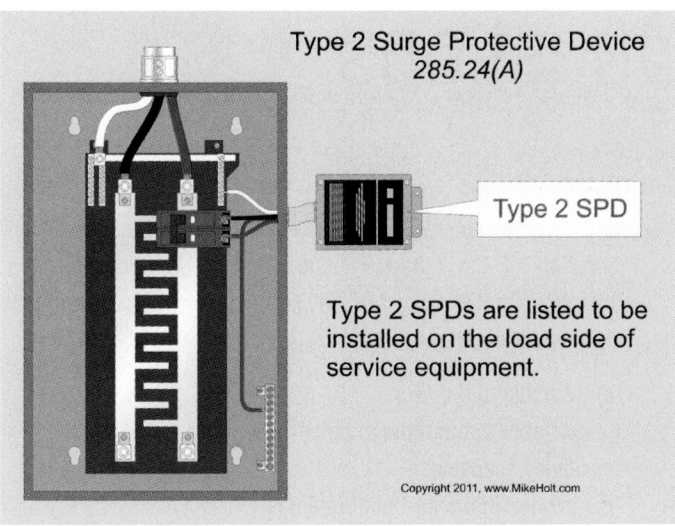

Type 2 Surge Protective Device
285.24(A)

Type 2 SPD

Type 2 SPDs are listed to be installed on the load side of service equipment.

Copyright 2011, www.MikeHolt.com

Figure 285–8

(B) Feeder-Supplied Buildings or Structures. Type 2 surge protective devices can be connected anywhere on the load side of the building/structure overcurrent device.

(C) Separately Derived Systems. Type 2 surge protective devices can be connected anywhere on the premises wiring of the separately derived system.

285.25 Type 3 SPDs—Branch Circuits. Type 3 surge protective devices can be installed on the load side of a branch-circuit overcurrent device. If included in the manufacturer's instructions, the Type 3 SPD connection must be a minimum 30 ft of conductor distance from the service or separately derived system disconnect.

These questions are based on the 2011 *National Electrical Code*. Please use the 2011 *NEC Code* book to answer the following questions.

CHAPTER 2. WIRING AND PROTECTION

Article 200. Use and Identification of Grounded Conductors

1. Article 200 contains the requirements for _____.

   (a) identification of terminals
   (b) grounded conductors in premises wiring systems
   (c) identification of grounded conductors
   (d) all of these

2. An insulated grounded conductor of _____ or smaller shall be identified by a continuous white or gray outer finish, or by three continuous white stripes on other than green insulation along its entire length.

   (a) 8 AWG
   (b) 6 AWG
   (c) 4 AWG
   (d) 3 AWG

3. Grounded conductors _____ and larger can be identified by distinctive white or gray markings at their terminations.

   (a) 10 AWG
   (b) 8 AWG
   (c) 6 AWG
   (d) 4 AWG

4. If neutral conductors of different voltage systems are installed in the same raceway, cable, or enclosure, the means of identification of the different neutrals shall be documented in a manner that's _____ or be permanently posted where the conductors of different systems originate.

   (a) available to the AHJ
   (b) available through the engineer
   (c) readily available
   (d) included in the as-built drawings

5. If used for single-pole, 3-way or 4-way switch loops, the reidentified conductor with white or gray insulation or three continuous white stripes can be used for the supply to the switch but not as a return conductor from the switch to the outlet.

   (a) True
   (b) False

6. Receptacles shall have the terminal intended for connection to the grounded conductor identified by a metal or metal coating that is substantially _____ in color.

   (a) green
   (b) white
   (c) gray
   (d) b or c

7. No _____ shall be attached to any terminal or lead so as to reverse designated polarity.

   (a) grounded conductor
   (b) grounding conductor
   (c) ungrounded conductor
   (d) grounding connector

Article 210. Branch Circuits

1. The rating of a branch circuit shall be determined by the rating of the _____.

    (a) ampacity of the largest device connected to the circuit
    (b) average of the ampacity of all devices
    (c) branch-circuit overcurrent device
    (d) ampacity of the branch-circuit conductors according to Table 310.15(B)(16)

2. Multiwire branch circuits shall _____.

    (a) supply only line-to-neutral loads
    (b) not be permitted in dwelling units
    (c) have their conductors originate from different panelboards
    (d) none of these

3. In dwelling units, the voltage between conductors that supply the terminals of _____ shall not exceed 120V, nominal.

    (a) luminaires
    (b) cord-and-plug-connected loads of 1,440 VA or less
    (c) cord-and-plug-connected loads of more than ¼ hp
    (d) a and b

4. All 15A and 20A, 125V receptacles installed in bathrooms of _____ shall have ground-fault circuit-interrupter (GFCI) protection for personnel.

    (a) guest rooms in hotels/motels
    (b) dwelling units
    (c) office buildings
    (d) all of these

5. All 15A and 20A, 125V receptacles located outdoors of dwelling units, including receptacles installed under the eaves of roofs, must be GFCI protected except for a receptacle that's supplied by a branch circuit dedicated to _____ if the receptacle isn't readily accessible and the equipment or receptacle has ground-fault protection of equipment (GFPE) [426.28 or 427.22].

    (a) fixed electric snow-melting or deicing equipment
    (b) pipeline and vessel heating equipment
    (c) holiday decorative lighting
    (d) a or b

6. GFCI protection shall be provided for all 15A and 20A, 125V receptacles _____ in dwelling unit kitchens.

    (a) installed to serve the countertop surfaces
    (b) within 6 ft of the sink
    (c) for all receptacles
    (d) that are readily accessible

7. All 15A and 20A, 125V receptacles _____ of commercial occupancies shall have GFCI protection.

    (a) in bathrooms
    (b) on rooftops
    (c) in kitchens
    (d) all of these

8. In other than dwelling locations, GFCI protection is required in _____.

    (a) indoor wet locations
    (b) locker rooms adjacent to showering facilities
    (c) garages, service bays, and similar areas
    (d) all of these

9. 15A and 20A, 125V receptacles located in patient bed locations of general care or critical care areas of health care facilities aren't required to be GFCI protected.

    (a) True
    (b) False

10. All 15A and 20A, 125V receptacles installed in garages, service bays, and similar areas where _____ are to be used must be GFCI protected.

    (a) electrical diagnostic equipment
    (b) electrical hand tools
    (c) portable lighting equipment
    (d) all of these

11. There shall be a minimum of one _____ branch circuit for the laundry outlet(s) required by 210.52(F).

    (a) 15A
    (b) 20A
    (c) 30A
    (d) b and c

12. An arc-fault circuit interrupter can be located at the first outlet to provide protection for the remaining portion of the branch circuit if _____.

    (a) the arc-fault circuit interrupter is installed within 8 ft of the branch-circuit overcurrent device
    (b) the circuit conductors up to the arc-fault circuit interrupter are in a metal raceway or steel armored Type AC or Type MC cable with metal outlet and junction boxes
    (c) a and b
    (d) the branch circuit serves only lighting loads

13. Where branch circuit wiring in a dwelling unit is modified, replaced or extended in any of the areas specified in 210.12(A), the branch circuit must be protected by _____.

    (a) a listed combination AFCI located at the origin of the branch circuit
    (b) a listed outlet branch circuit AFCI located at the first receptacle outlet of the existing branch circuit
    (c) a GFCI circuit breaker or receptacle
    (d) a or b

14. Receptacle outlets installed for a specific appliance in a dwelling unit, such as laundry equipment, shall be located within _____ of the intended location of the appliance.

    (a) sight
    (b) 3 ft
    (c) 6 ft
    (d) none of these

15. In a dwelling unit, each wall space _____ or wider requires a receptacle.

    (a) 2 ft
    (b) 3 ft
    (c) 4 ft
    (d) 5 ft

16. Receptacles installed for countertop surfaces as required by 210.52(c) shall not be used to meet the receptacle requirements for wall space as required by 210.52(A).

    (a) True
    (b) False

17. A receptacle connected to a dwelling unit small-appliance circuit can supply gas-fired ranges, ovens, or counter-mounted cooking units.

    (a) True
    (b) False

18. A receptacle outlet shall be installed in dwelling units for every kitchen and dining area countertop space _____, and no point along the wall line shall be more than 2 ft, measured horizontally, from a receptacle outlet in that space.

    (a) wider than 10 in.
    (b) wider than 3 ft
    (c) 18 in. or wider
    (d) 12 in. or wider

19. When breaks occur in dwelling unit kitchen countertop spaces for rangetops, refrigerators or sinks, each countertop surface shall be considered a separate counter space for determining receptacle placement.

    (a) True
    (b) False

20. In dwelling unit bathrooms, not less than one 15A or 20A, 125V receptacle outlet must be installed within _____ from the outside edge of each bathroom basin.

    (a) 20 in.
    (b) 3 ft
    (c) 4 ft
    (d) 6 ft

21. In dwelling units, the required bathroom receptacle outlet can be installed on the side or face of the basin cabinet if no lower than _____ below the countertop.

    (a) 12 in.
    (b) 18 in.
    (c) 24 in.
    (d) 36 in.

22. A laundry receptacle outlet shall not be required in each dwelling unit of a multifamily building, if laundry facilities are provided on the premises for all building occupants.

    (a) True
    (b) False

23. Hallways in dwelling units that are _____ long or longer require a receptacle outlet.

    (a) 6 ft
    (b) 8 ft
    (c) 10 ft
    (d) 12 ft

24. Receptacles installed behind a bed in the guest rooms in hotels and motels shall be located to prevent the bed from contacting an attachment plug, or the receptacle shall be provided with a suitable guard.

    (a) True
    (b) False

25. A 15A or 20A, 125V receptacle outlet shall be located within 25 ft of heating, air-conditioning, and refrigeration equipment for _____ occupancies.

    (a) dwelling
    (b) commercial
    (c) industrial
    (d) all of these

26. In dwelling units, lighting outlets can be controlled by occupancy sensors where equipped with a _____ that will allow the sensor to function as a wall switch.

    (a) manual override
    (b) photo cell
    (c) sensor
    (d) none of these

27. Where a lighting outlet(s) is installed for interior stairways, there shall be a wall switch at each floor level and each landing level that includes an entryway where the stairway between floor levels has six risers or more unless remote, central, or automatic control is used.

    (a) True
    (b) False

28. At least one wall switch-controlled lighting outlet shall be installed in every habitable room and bathroom of a guest room or guest suite of hotels, motels, and similar occupancies. A receptacle outlet controlled by a wall switch may be used to meet this requirement in other than _____.

    (a) bathrooms
    (b) kitchens
    (c) sleeping areas
    (d) a and b

Article 215. Feeders

1. The minimum feeder conductor ampacity, before the application of any adjustment or correction factors, must be no less than the noncontinuous load plus _____ percent of the continuous load.

   (a) 80
   (b) 100
   (c) 125
   (d) 150

2. Dwelling unit or mobile home feeder conductors need not be larger than the service conductors and can be sized according to 310.15(B)(7).

   (a) True
   (b) False

3. Ground-fault protection of equipment shall not be required at a feeder disconnect if ground-fault protection of equipment is provided on the _____ side of the feeder and on the load side of any transformer supplying the feeder.

   (a) load
   (b) supply
   (c) service
   (d) none of these

Article 220. Branch-Circuit, Feeder, and Service Calculations

1. The 3 VA per-square-foot general lighting load for dwelling units does not include _____.

   (a) open porches
   (b) garages
   (c) unused or unfinished spaces not adaptable for future use
   (d) all of these

2. A device comprised of _____ or more receptacles shall be calculated at not less than 90 VA per receptacle.

   (a) one
   (b) two
   (c) three
   (d) four

3. The minimum feeder load for show-window lighting is _____ per-linear-foot.

   (a) 180 VA
   (b) 200 VA
   (c) 300 VA
   (d) 400 VA

4. A dwelling unit containing three 120V small-appliance branch circuits has a calculated load of _____VA for the small appliance circuits.

   (a) 1,500
   (b) 3,000
   (c) 4,500
   (d) 6,000

5. The load for electric clothes dryers in a dwelling unit shall be _____ watts or the nameplate rating, whichever is larger, per dryer.

   (a) 1,500
   (b) 4,500
   (c) 5,000
   (d) 8,000

6. The feeder/service calculated load for a multifamily dwelling containing nine 12 kW ranges is _____.

   (a) 13,000W
   (b) 14,700W
   (c) 16,000W
   (d) 24,000W

7. When applying the demand factors of Table 220.56, the feeder or service demand load shall not be less than the sum of _____.

   (a) the total number of receptacles at 180 VA per receptacle outlet
   (b) the VA rating of all of the small-appliance branch circuits combined
   (c) the largest two kitchen equipment loads
   (d) the kitchen heating and air-conditioning loads

8. There shall be no reduction in the size of the neutral or grounded conductor on _____ loads supplied from a 4-wire, wye-connected, three-phase system.

   (a) dwelling unit
   (b) hospital
   (c) nonlinear
   (d) motel

Article 225. Outside Branch Circuits and Feeders

1. Where mast is used for overhead conductor support, it shall be of adequate strength or be supported by braces or guy wire to withstand safely the strain imposed by the overhead drop.

   (a) True
   (b) False

2. The minimum clearance for overhead feeder conductors that pass over track rails of railroads is _____.

   (a) 10 ft
   (b) 12 ft
   (c) 24.50 ft
   (d) 30 ft

3. The requirement for maintaining a 3 ft vertical clearance from the edge of the roof shall not apply to the final feeder conductor span where the conductors are attached to _____.

   (a) a building pole
   (b) the side of a building
   (c) an antenna
   (d) the base of a building

4. Raceways on exterior surfaces of buildings or other structures shall be arranged to drain, and be suitable for use in _____ locations.

   (a) damp
   (b) wet
   (c) dry
   (d) all of these

5. A building or structure shall be supplied by a maximum of _____ feeder(s) or branch circuit(s), unless specifically permitted otherwise.

   (a) one
   (b) two
   (c) three
   (d) four

6. There shall be no more than _____ switches or circuit breakers to serve as the disconnecting means for a building supplied by a feeder.

   (a) two
   (b) four
   (c) six
   (d) eight

7. When the disconnecting means for a building supplied by a feeder is a power-operated switch or circuit breaker, it shall be able to be opened by hand in the event of a _____.

   (a) ground fault
   (b) short circuit
   (c) power surge
   (d) power failure

8. For installations consisting of not more than two 2-wire branch circuits, the building disconnecting means shall have a rating of not less than _____.

   (a) 15A
   (b) 20A
   (c) 25A
   (d) 30A

Article 230. Services

1. A building or structure shall be supplied by a maximum of _____ service(s), unless specifically permitted otherwise.

   (a) one
   (b) two
   (c) three
   (d) as many as desired

2. Where a building or structure is supplied by more than one service, a permanent plaque or directory shall be installed at each service disconnect location denoting all other services supplying that building or structure and the area served by each.

   (a) True
   (b) False

3. Conductors installed in overhead service masts on the outside surface of the building traveling through the eave of that building are considered to be outside of the building.

   (a) True
   (b) False

4. Service conductors installed as unjacketed multiconductor cable shall have a minimum clearance of _____ from windows that are designed to be opened, doors, porches, stairs, fire escapes, or similar locations.

   (a) 3 ft
   (b) 4 ft
   (c) 6 ft
   (d) 10 ft

5. Overhead service conductors can be supported to hardwood trees.

   (a) True
   (b) False

6. Overhead service conductors installed over roofs shall have a vertical clearance of _____ above the roof surface, unless a lesser distance is permitted by an exception.

   (a) 3 ft
   (b) 8 ft
   (c) 12 ft
   (d) 15 ft

7. If the voltage between overhead service conductors does not exceed 300V and the roof area is guarded or isolated, a reduction in clearance to 3 ft is permitted.

   (a) True
   (b) False

8. Overhead service conductors shall have a horizontal clearance of _____ from a pool.

   (a) 8 ft
   (b) 10 ft
   (c) 12 ft
   (d) 14 ft

9. Where raceway-type service masts are used, all raceway fittings shall be _____ for use with service masts.

   (a) identified
   (b) approved
   (c) of a heavy-duty type
   (d) listed

10. Underground service conductors that supply power to limited loads of a single branch circuit shall not be smaller than _____.

   (a) 14 AWG copper
   (b) 14 AWG aluminum
   (c) 12 AWG copper
   (d) 12 AWG aluminum

11. Service conductors can supply _____ service disconnecting means as permitted in 230.71(A).

    (a) only one
    (b) only two
    (c) up to six
    (d) an unlimited number of

12. One set of service-entrance conductors connected to the supply side of the normal service disconnecting means shall be permitted to supply standby power systems, fire pump equipment, and fire and sprinkler alarms covered by 230.82(5).

    (a) True
    (b) False

13. Cable trays used to support service-entrance conductors shall contain only service-entrance conductors _____.

    (a) unless a solid fixed barrier separates the service-entrance conductors from other conductors
    (b) under 300V
    (c) in industrial locations
    (d) over 600V

14. Service-entrance cables which are not installed underground, where subject to physical damage, shall be protected by _____.

    (a) rigid metal conduit
    (b) IMC
    (c) Schedule 80 PVC conduit
    (d) any of these

15. Service raceways for overhead service drops or overhead service conductors shall have a weatherhead listed for _____.

    (a) wet locations
    (b) damp locations
    (c) Class 2 locations
    (d) NEMA 3R

16. Service heads shall be located _____, unless impracticable.

    (a) above the point of attachment
    (b) below the point of attachment
    (c) even with the point of attachment
    (d) none of these

17. On a three-phase, 4-wire, delta-connected service where the midpoint of one phase winding is grounded, the service conductor having the higher phase voltage-to-ground shall be durably and permanently marked by an outer finish that is _____ in color, or by other effective means, at each termination or junction point.

    (a) orange
    (b) red
    (c) blue
    (d) any of these

18. Service disconnecting means shall not be installed in bathrooms.

    (a) True
    (b) False

19. Each service disconnecting means shall be suitable for _____.

    (a) hazardous (classified) locations
    (b) wet locations
    (c) dry locations
    (d) the prevailing conditions

20. The additional service disconnecting means for fire pumps, emergency systems, legally required standby, or optional standby services, shall be installed remote from the one to six service disconnecting means for normal service to minimize the possibility of _____ interruption of supply.

    (a) intentional
    (b) accidental
    (c) simultaneous
    (d) prolonged

21. When the service disconnecting means is a power-operated switch or circuit breaker, it shall be able to be opened by hand in the event of a _____.

    (a) ground fault
    (b) short circuit
    (c) power surge
    (d) power supply failure

22. For installations consisting of not more than two 2-wire branch circuits, the service disconnecting means shall have a rating of not less than _____.

    (a) 15A
    (b) 20A
    (c) 25A
    (d) 30A

23. Electrical equipment shall not be connected to the supply side of the service disconnecting means, except for a few specific exceptions such as _____.

    (a) Type 1 surge protective devices
    (b) taps used to supply legally required optional standby power systems, fire pump equipment, fire and sprinkler alarms, and load (energy) management devices
    (c) Solar photovoltaic systems
    (d) all of these

Article 240. Overcurrent Protection

1. Overcurrent protection for conductors and equipment is designed to _____ the circuit if the current reaches a value that will cause an excessive or dangerous temperature in conductors or conductor insulation.

    (a) open
    (b) close
    (c) monitor
    (d) record

2. The next higher standard rating overcurrent device above the ampacity of the ungrounded conductors being protected shall be permitted to be used, provided all of the following conditions are met:

    (a) The conductors are not part of a branch circuit supplying more than one receptacle for cord-and-plug-connected portable loads.
    (b) The ampacity of the conductors doesn't correspond with the standard ampere rating of a fuse or circuit breaker.
    (c) The next higher standard rating selected doesn't exceed 800A.
    (d) all of these

3. Flexible cords approved for and used with a specific listed appliance or luminaire shall be considered to be protected by the branch-circuit overcurrent device when _____.

    (a) not more than 6 ft in length
    (b) 20 AWG and larger
    (c) applied within the listing requirements
    (d) 16 AWG and larger

4. The standard ampere ratings for fuses includes _____.

    (a) 1A
    (b) 6A
    (c) 601A
    (d) all of these

5. Ground-fault protection of equipment shall be provided for solidly grounded wye electrical systems of more than 150 volts-to-ground, but not exceeding 600V phase-to-phase for each individual device used as a building or structure main disconnecting means rated _____ or more, unless specifically exempted.

    (a) 1,000A
    (b) 1,500A
    (c) 2,000A
    (d) 2,500A

6. Single-pole breakers with identified handle ties can be used to protect each ungrounded conductor for line-to-line connected loads.

   (a) True
   (b) False

7. The maximum length of a feeder tap conductor in a high-bay manufacturing building over 35 ft high shall be _____.

   (a) 15 ft
   (b) 20 ft
   (c) 50 ft
   (d) 100 ft

8. Overcurrent devices shall be _____.

   (a) accessible (as applied to wiring methods)
   (b) accessible (as applied to equipment)
   (c) readily accessible
   (d) inaccessible to unauthorized personnel

9. Overcurrent devices aren't permitted to be located in the bathrooms of _____.

   (a) dwelling units
   (b) dormitories
   (c) guest rooms or guest suites of hotels or motels
   (d) all of these

10. Handles or levers of circuit breakers, and similar parts that may move suddenly in such a way that persons in the vicinity are likely to be injured by being struck by them, shall be _____.

    (a) guarded
    (b) isolated
    (c) a and b
    (d) a or b

11. Plug fuses of the Edison-base type shall be used _____.

    (a) where overfusing is necessary
    (b) as a replacement in existing installations
    (c) as a replacement for Type S fuses
    (d) 50A and above

12. Type _____ fuse adapters shall be designed so that once inserted in a fuseholder they cannot be removed.

    (a) A
    (b) E
    (c) S
    (d) P

13. Fuseholders for cartridge fuses shall be so designed that it is difficult to put a fuse of any given class into a fuseholder that is designed for a _____ lower or a _____ higher than that of the class to which the fuse belongs.

    (a) voltage, wattage
    (b) wattage, voltage
    (c) voltage, current
    (d) current, voltage

14. Cartridge fuses and fuseholders shall be classified according to their _____ ranges.

    (a) voltage
    (b) amperage
    (c) a or b
    (d) a and b

15. A(n) _____ shall be of such design that any alteration of its trip point (calibration) or the time required for its operation requires dismantling of the device or breaking of a seal for other than intended adjustments.

    (a) Type S fuse
    (b) Edison-base fuse
    (c) circuit breaker
    (d) fuseholder

16. A circuit breaker having an interrupting current rating of other than _____ shall have its interrupting rating marked on the circuit breaker.

    (a) 5,000A
    (b) 10,000A
    (c) 22,000A
    (d) 50,000A

17. A circuit breaker with a _____ voltage rating, such as 240V or 480V, can be used where the nominal voltage between any two conductors does not exceed the circuit breaker's voltage rating.

    (a) straight
    (b) slash
    (c) high
    (d) low

Article 250. Grounding and Bonding

1. A ground-fault current path is an electrically conductive path from the point of a ground fault through normally noncurrent-carrying conductors, equipment, or the earth to the _____.

    (a) ground
    (b) earth
    (c) electrical supply source
    (d) none of these

2. For grounded systems, normally noncurrent-carrying conductive materials enclosing electrical conductors or equipment shall be connected to earth so as to limit the voltage-to-ground on these materials.

    (a) True
    (b) False

3. For grounded systems, electrical equipment and electrically conductive material likely to become energized, shall be installed in a manner that creates a low-impedance circuit capable of safely carrying the maximum ground-fault current likely to be imposed on it from where a ground fault may occur to the _____.

    (a) ground
    (b) earth
    (c) electrical supply source
    (d) none of these

4. Electrically conductive materials that are likely to _____ in ungrounded systems shall be connected together and to the supply system grounded equipment in a manner that creates a low-impedance path for ground-fault current that is capable of carrying the maximum fault current likely to be imposed on it.

    (a) become energized
    (b) require service
    (c) be removed
    (d) be coated with paint or nonconductive materials

5. Currents that introduce noise or data errors in electronic equipment are considered objectionable currents in the context of 250.6(d) of the *NEC*.

    (a) True
    (b) False

6. _____ on equipment to be grounded shall be removed from contact surfaces to ensure good electrical continuity.

    (a) Paint
    (b) Lacquer
    (c) Enamel
    (d) any of these

7. Alternating-current systems of 50V to 1,000V that supply premises wiring systems shall be grounded where supplied by a three-phase, 4-wire, delta-connected system in which the midpoint of one phase winding is used as a circuit conductor.

    (a) True
    (b) False

8. The grounding electrode conductor shall be connected to the grounded service conductor at the _____.

    (a) load end of the service drop
    (b) load end of the service lateral
    (c) service disconnecting means
    (d) any of these

9. The grounded conductor of an alternating-current system operating at less than 1,000V shall be routed with the ungrounded conductors and connected to each disconnecting means grounded conductor terminal or bus, which is then connected to the service disconnecting means enclosure via a(n) _____ that's installed between the service neutral conductor and the service disconnecting means enclosure.

(a) equipment bonding conductor
(b) main bonding jumper
(c) grounding electrode
(d) intersystem bonding terminal

10. A main bonding jumper shall be a _____ or similar suitable conductor.

(a) wire
(b) bus
(c) screw
(d) any of these

11. An unspliced _____ that is sized based on the derived phase conductors shall be used to connect the grounded conductor and the supply-side bonding jumper, or the equipment grounding conductor, or both, at a separately derived system.

(a) system bonding jumper
(b) equipment grounding conductor
(c) grounded conductor
(d) grounding electrode conductor

12. The grounding electrode conductor for a single separately derived system is used to connect the grounded conductor of the derived system to the grounding electrode.

(a) True
(b) False

13. Tap connections to a common grounding electrode conductor for multiple separately derived systems may be made to a copper or aluminum busbar that is _____.

(a) not over ½ in. x 4 in.
(b) not over ¼ in. x 2 in.
(c) at least ¼ in. x 2 in.
(d) a and c

14. When supplying a grounded system at a separate building or structure, an equipment grounding conductor shall be run with the supply conductors and connected to the building or structure disconnecting means.

(a) True
(b) False

15. The size of the grounding electrode conductor for a building or structure supplied by a feeder shall not be smaller than that identified in _____, based on the largest ungrounded supply conductor.

(a) 250.66
(b) 250.122
(c) Table 310.15(B)(16)
(d) none of these

16. High-impedance grounded neutral systems shall be permitted for three-phase ac systems of 480 volts to 1,000 volts where _____.

(a) the conditions of maintenance ensure that only qualified persons service the installation
(b) ground detectors are installed on the system
(c) line-to-neutral loads are not served
(d) all of these

17. A bare 4 AWG copper conductor installed horizontally near the bottom or vertically, and within that portion of a concrete foundation or footing that is in direct contact with the earth can be used as a grounding electrode when the conductor is at least _____ in length.

(a) 10 ft
(b) 15 ft
(c) 20 ft
(d) 25 ft

18. Grounding electrodes that are driven rods require a minimum of _____ in contact with the soil.

(a) 6 ft
(b) 8 ft
(c) 10 ft
(d) 12 ft

19. Where practicable, rod, pipe, and plate electrodes shall be installed _____.

    (a) directly below the electrical meter
    (b) on the north side of the building
    (c) below permanent moisture level
    (d) all of these

20. When a ground ring is used as a grounding electrode, it shall be buried at a depth below the earth's surface of not less than _____.

    (a) 18 in.
    (b) 24 in.
    (c) 30 in.
    (d) 8 ft

21. Buildings or structures supplied by multiple services or feeders must use the same _____ to ground enclosures and equipment in or on that building.

    (a) service
    (b) disconnect
    (c) grounding electrode system
    (d) any of these

22. Grounding electrode conductors smaller than _____ shall be in rigid metal conduit, IMC, PVC conduit, electrical metallic tubing, or cable armor.

    (a) 10 AWG
    (b) 8 AWG
    (c) 6 AWG
    (d) 4 AWG

23. The largest size grounding electrode conductor required is _____ copper.

    (a) 6 AWG
    (b) 1/0 AWG
    (c) 3/0 AWG
    (d) 250 kcmil

24. Exothermic or irreversible compression connections, together with the mechanical means used to attach to fireproofed structural metal, shall not be required to be accessible.

    (a) True
    (b) False

25. Bonding shall be provided where necessary to ensure _____ and the capacity to conduct safely any fault current likely to be imposed.

    (a) electrical continuity
    (b) fiduciary responsibility
    (c) listing requirements
    (d) electrical demand

26. A means external to enclosures for connecting intersystem _____ conductors shall be provided at service equipment or metering equipment enclosure and disconnecting means of buildings or structures supplied by a feeder.

    (a) bonding
    (b) ungrounded
    (c) secondary
    (d) a and b

27. Where installed to reduce electrical noise for electronic equipment, a metal raceway can terminate to a(n) _____ nonmetallic fitting(s) or spacer on the electronic equipment. The metal raceway shall be supplemented by an internal insulated equipment grounding conductor.

    (a) listed
    (b) labeled
    (c) identified
    (d) marked

28. The supply side bonding jumper on the supply side of services shall be sized according to the _____.

    (a) overcurrent device rating
    (b) ungrounded supply conductor size
    (c) service-drop size
    (d) load to be served

29. An equipment bonding jumper can be installed on the outside of a raceway, providing the length of the equipment bonding jumper is not more than _____ and the equipment bonding jumper is routed with the raceway.

    (a) 12 in.
    (b) 24 in.
    (c) 36 in.
    (d) 72 in.

30. Metal gas piping shall be considered bonded by the equipment grounding conductor of the circuit that is likely to energize the piping.

    (a) True
    (b) False

31. Which of the following appliances installed in residential occupancies need not be connected to an equipment grounding conductor?

    (a) toaster
    (b) aquarium
    (c) dishwasher
    (d) refrigerator

32. Listed liquidtight flexible metal conduit (LFMC) is acceptable as an equipment grounding conductor when it terminates in listed fittings and is protected by an overcurrent device rated 60A or less for sizes 3/8 in. through ½ in.

    (a) True
    (b) False

33. An equipment grounding conductor is permitted to be used as a grounding electrode conductor.

    (a) True
    (b) False

34. Equipment grounding conductors for feeder taps are not required to be larger than the tap conductors.

    (a) True
    (b) False

35. A grounded circuit conductor is permitted to ground noncurrent-carrying metal parts of equipment, raceways, and other enclosures on the supply side or within the enclosure of the ac service-disconnecting means.

    (a) True
    (b) False

36. Receptacle yokes designed and _____ as self-grounding can establish the grounding circuit between the device yoke and a grounded outlet box.

    (a) approved
    (b) advertised
    (c) listed
    (d) installed

Article 285. Surge Protection Devices

1. Article 285 covers surge protective devices rated over 1 kV.

    (a) True
    (b) False

2. Surge protective devices shall be listed.

    (a) True
    (b) False

3. The conductors used to connect the surge protective device to ground shall not be any longer than _____ and shall avoid unnecessary bends.

    (a) 6 in.
    (b) 12 in.
    (c) 18 in.
    (d) necessary

Notes

CHAPTER 3

WIRING METHODS AND MATERIALS

INTRODUCTION TO CHAPTER 3—WIRING METHODS AND MATERIALS

Chapter 3 covers wiring methods and materials, and provides some very specific installation requirements for conductors, cables, boxes, raceways, and fittings. This chapter includes detailed information about the installation and restrictions involved with wiring methods.

It may be because of that detail that many people incorrectly apply the rules from this chapter. Be sure to pay careful attention to the details, and be sure that you make your installation in compliance with the rules in the *Code*, not just in the manner that you may have been taught or because "it's always been done that way." This is especially true when it comes to applying the Tables.

Violations of the rules for wiring methods found in Chapter 3 can result in problems with power quality and can lead to fire, shock, and other hazards.

The type of wiring method you'll use depends on several factors: Job specifications, *Code* requirements, the environment, need, and cost are among them.

Chapter 3 begins with rules that are common to most wiring methods [Article 300], it then covers conductors [Article 310], and enclosures [Articles 312 and 314]. The articles that follow become more specific and deal more in-depth with individual wiring methods such as specific types of cables [Articles 320 through 340] and various raceways [Articles 342 through 390]. The chapter winds up with Article 392, a support system, and the final articles [Articles 394 through 398] for open wiring.

Notice as you read through the various wiring methods that the *Code* attempts to use similar subsection numbering for similar topics from one article to the next, using the same digits after the decimal point in the section number for the same topic. This makes it easier to locate specific requirements in a particular article. For example, the rules for securing and supporting can be found in the section that ends with .30 of each article. In addition to this, you'll find a "uses permitted" and "uses not permitted" section in nearly every article.

Wiring Method Articles

- **Article 300—Wiring Methods.** Article 300 contains the general requirements for all wiring methods included in the *NEC*, except for signaling and communications systems, which are covered in Chapters 7 and 8.

- **Article 310—Conductors for General Wiring.** This article contains the general requirements for conductors, such as insulation markings, ampacity ratings, and conductor use. Article 310 doesn't apply to conductors that are part of flexible cords, fixture wires, or conductors that are an integral part of equipment [90.6 and 300.1(B)].

- **Article 312—Cabinets, Cutout Boxes, and Meter Socket Enclosures.** Article 312 covers the installation and construction specifications for cabinets, cutout boxes, and meter socket enclosures.

- **Article 314—Outlet, Device, Pull and Junction Boxes, Conduit Bodies, Fittings, and Handhole Enclosures.** Installation requirements for outlet boxes, pull and junction boxes, as well as conduit bodies, and handhole enclosures are contained in this article.

Cable Articles

Articles 320 through 340 address specific types of cables. If you take the time to become familiar with the various types of cables, you'll:

- Understand what's available for doing the work.
- Recognize cable types that have special *NEC* requirements.
- Avoid buying cable that you can't install due to *Code* requirements you can't meet with that particular wiring method.

Here's a brief overview of each one:

- **Article 320—Armored Cable (Type AC).** Armored cable is an assembly of insulated conductors, 14 AWG through 1 AWG, individually wrapped with waxed paper. The conductors are contained within a flexible spiral metal (steel or aluminum) sheath that interlocks at the edges. Armored cable looks like flexible metal conduit. Many electricians call this metal cable "BX®."

- **Article 330—Metal-Clad Cable (Type MC).** Metal-clad cable encloses insulated conductors in a metal sheath of either corrugated or smooth copper or aluminum tubing, or spiral interlocked steel or aluminum. The physical characteristics of Type MC cable make it a versatile wiring method permitted in almost any location and for almost any application. The most commonly used Type MC cable is the interlocking kind, which looks similar to armored cable or flexible metal conduit.

- **Article 334—Nonmetallic-Sheathed Cable (Type NM).** Nonmetallic-sheathed cable encloses two, three, or four insulated conductors, 14 AWG through 2 AWG, within a nonmetallic outer jacket. Because this cable is nonmetallic, it contains a separate equipment grounding conductor. Nonmetallic-sheathed cable is a common wiring method used for residential and commercial branch circuits. Many electricians call this plastic-sheathed cable "Romex®."

- **Article 336—Power and Control Tray Cable (Type TC).** Power and control tray cable is a factory assembly of two or more insulated conductors under a nonmetallic sheath for installation in cable trays, in raceways, or supported by a messenger wire.

- **Article 338—Service-Entrance Cable (Types SE and USE).** Service-entrance cable can be a single-conductor or a multiconductor assembly within an overall nonmetallic covering. This cable is used primarily for services not over 600V, but is also permitted for feeders and branch circuits.

- **Article 340—Underground Feeder and Branch-Circuit Cable (Type UF).** Underground feeder cable is a moisture-, fungus-, and corrosion-resistant cable suitable for direct burial in the earth, and it comes in sizes 14 AWG through 4/0 AWG [340.104]. Multiconductor UF cable is covered in molded plastic that surrounds the insulated conductors.

Raceway Articles

Articles 342 through 390 address specific types of raceways. Refer to Article 100 for the definition of a raceway. If you take the time to become familiar with the various types of raceways, you'll:

- Understand what's available for doing the work.
- Recognize raceway types that have special *Code* requirements.
- Avoid buying a raceway that you can't install due to *NEC* requirements you can't meet with that particular wiring method.

Here's a brief overview of each one:

- **Article 342—Intermediate Metal Conduit (Type IMC).** Intermediate metal conduit is a circular metal raceway with the same outside diameter as rigid metal conduit. The wall thickness of intermediate metal conduit is less than that of rigid metal conduit, so it's a greater interior cross-sectional area for holding conductors. Intermediate metal conduit is lighter and less expensive than rigid metal conduit, but it's permitted in all the same locations as rigid metal conduit. Intermediate metal conduit also uses a different steel alloy, which makes it stronger than rigid metal conduit, even though the walls are thinner.

- **Article 344—Rigid Metal Conduit (Type RMC).** Rigid metal conduit is similar to intermediate metal conduit, except the wall thickness is greater, so it's a smaller interior cross-sectional area. Rigid metal conduit is heavier than intermediate metal conduit and it's permitted to be installed in any location, just like intermediate metal conduit.

- **Article 348—Flexible Metal Conduit (Type FMC).** Flexible metal conduit is a raceway of circular cross section made of a helically wound, interlocked metal strip of either steel or aluminum. It's commonly called "Greenfield" or "Flex."

- **Article 350—Liquidtight Flexible Metal Conduit (Type LFMC).** Liquidtight flexible metal conduit is a raceway of circular cross section with an outer liquidtight, non-metallic, sunlight-resistant jacket over an inner flexible metal core, with associated couplings, connectors, and fittings. It's listed for the installation of electric conductors. Liquidtight flexible metal conduit is commonly called "Sealtite®" or simply "liquidtight." Liquidtight flexible metal conduit is of similar construction to flexible metal conduit, but it has an outer thermoplastic covering.

- **Article 352—Rigid Polyvinyl Chloride Conduit (Type PVC).** Rigid polyvinyl chloride conduit is a nonmetallic raceway of circular cross section with integral or associated couplings, connectors, and fittings. It's listed for the installation of electrical conductors.

- **Article 356—Liquidtight Flexible Nonmetallic Conduit (Type LFNC).** Liquidtight flexible nonmetallic conduit is a raceway of circular cross section with an outer liquidtight, nonmetallic, sunlight-resistant jacket over an inner flexible core, with associated couplings, connectors, and fittings. It's listed for the installation of electrical conductors. LFNC is available in three types:
  - Type LFNC-A (orange). A smooth seamless inner core and cover bonded together with reinforcement layers inserted between the core and covers.
  - Type LFNC-B (gray). A smooth inner surface with integral reinforcement within the conduit wall.
  - Type LFNC-C (black). A corrugated internal and external surface without integral reinforcement within the conduit wall.

- **Article 358—Electrical Metallic Tubing (EMT).** Electrical metallic tubing is a nonthreaded thinwall raceway of circular cross section designed for the physical protection and routing of conductors and cables. Compared to rigid metal conduit and intermediate metal conduit, electrical metallic tubing is relatively easy to bend, cut, and ream. EMT isn't threaded, so all connectors and couplings are of the threadless type. Today, It's available in a range of colors, such as red and blue.

- **Article 362—Electrical Nonmetallic Tubing (ENT).** Electrical nonmetallic tubing is a pliable, corrugated, circular raceway made of PVC. It's often called "Smurf Pipe" or "Smurf Tube," because it was available only in blue when it came out and at the time the children's cartoon characters "The Smurfs," were popular. It's now available in multiple colors such as red and yellow as well as blue.

- **Article 376—Metal Wireways.** A metal wireway is a sheet metal trough with hinged or removable covers for housing and protecting electrical conductors and cable, in which conductors are placed after the wireway has been installed as a complete system.

- **Article 380—Multioutlet Assemblies.** A multioutlet assembly is a surface, flush, or freestanding raceway designed to hold conductors and receptacles. It's assembled in the field or at the factory.

- **Article 386—Surface Metal Raceways.** A surface metal raceway is a metallic raceway intended to be mounted to the surface with associated accessories, in which conductors are placed after the raceway has been installed as a complete system.

- **Article 388—Surface Nonmetallic Raceways.** A surface nonmetallic raceway is intended to be surface mounted with associated accessories. Conductors are placed inside after the raceway has been installed as a complete system.

Cable Tray

- **Article 392—Cable Trays.** A cable tray system is a unit or assembly of units or sections with associated fittings that form a structural system used to securely fasten or support cables and raceways. A cable tray isn't a raceway; it's a support system for raceways, cables, and enclosures.

Notes

ARTICLE 300
Wiring Methods

INTRODUCTION TO ARTICLE 300—WIRING METHODS

Article 300 contains the general requirements for all wiring methods included in the *NEC*. However, the article doesn't apply to communications systems, which are covered in Chapter 8, except when Article 300 is specifically referenced in Chapter 8.

This article is primarily concerned with how to install, route, splice, protect, and secure conductors and raceways. How well you conform to the requirements of Article 300 will generally be evident in the finished work, because many of the requirements tend to determine the appearance of the installation.

Because of this, it's often easy to spot Article 300 problems if you're looking for *Code* violations. For example, you can easily see when someone runs an equipment grounding conductor outside a raceway instead of grouping all conductors of a circuit together, as required by 300.3(B).

A good understanding of Article 300 will start you on the path to correctly installing the wiring methods included in Chapter 3. Be sure to carefully consider the accompanying illustrations, and refer to the definitions in Article 100 as needed.

PART I. GENERAL

300.1 Scope.

(A) Wiring Installations. Article 300 contains the general requirements for power and lighting wiring methods.

> **Author's Comment:** The requirements contained in Article 300 don't apply to the wiring methods for signaling and communications systems, except where there is a specific reference in Chapter 7 or 8 to a rule in Article 300.
>
> - CATV, 820.3
> - Class 2 and 3 Circuits, 725.3
> - Communications Cables and Raceways, 800.133(A)(2)
> - Fire Alarm Circuits, 760.3

(B) Integral Parts of Equipment. The requirements contained in Article 300 don't apply to the internal parts of electrical equipment. Figure 300–1

(C) Trade Sizes. Designators for raceway trade sizes are given in Table 300.1(C).

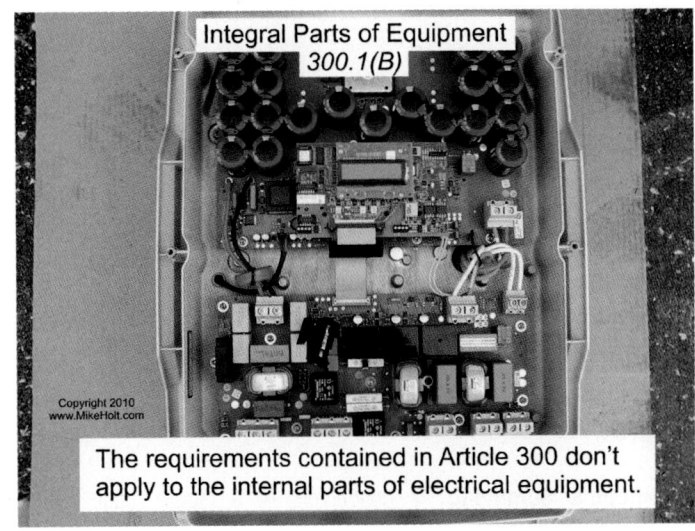

Integral Parts of Equipment
300.1(B)

Copyright 2010
www.MikeHolt.com

The requirements contained in Article 300 don't apply to the internal parts of electrical equipment.

Figure 300–1

> **Author's Comment:** Industry practice is to describe raceways using inch sizes, such as ½ in., 2 in., and so on; however, the proper reference (2005 *NEC* change) is to use "Trade Size ½," or "Trade Size 2." In this textbook we use the term "Trade Size."

300.3 Conductors.

(A) Conductors. Single conductors must be installed within a Chapter 3 wiring method, such as a raceway, cable, or enclosure.

Ex: Overhead conductors can be installed in accordance with 225.6.

(B) Circuit Conductors Grouped Together. All conductors of a circuit must be installed in the same raceway, cable, trench, cord, or cable tray, except as permitted by (1) through (4). **Figure 300–2**

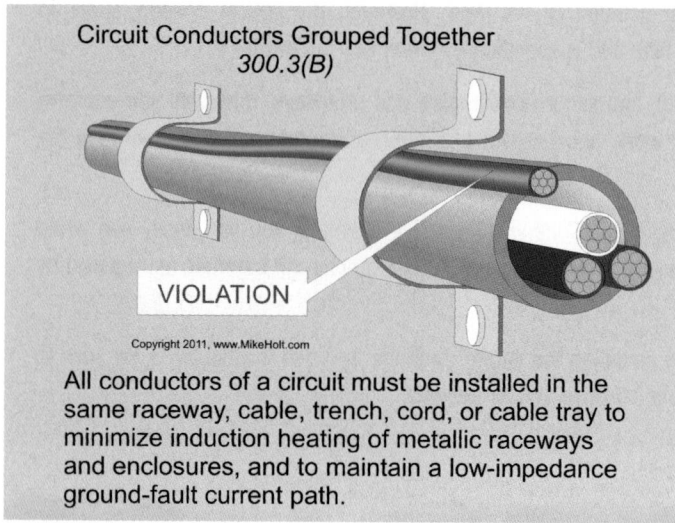

All conductors of a circuit must be installed in the same raceway, cable, trench, cord, or cable tray to minimize induction heating of metallic raceways and enclosures, and to maintain a low-impedance ground-fault current path.

Figure 300–2

(1) Paralleled Installations. Conductors installed in parallel in accordance with 310.10(H) must have all circuit conductors within the same raceway, cable tray, trench, or cable. **Figure 300–3**

Ex: Parallel conductors run underground can be installed in different raceways (Phase A in raceway 1, Phase B in raceway 2, and so forth) if, in order to reduce or eliminate inductive heating, if the raceway is nonmetallic or nonmagnetic and the installation complies with 300.20(B). See 300.5(I) Ex 2.

> **Author's Comment:** All conductors of a circuit must be installed in the same raceway, cable, trench, cord, or cable tray to minimize induction of the heating of ferrous metal raceways and enclosures, and to maintain a low-impedance ground-fault current path [250.4(A)(3)]. **Figure 300–4**

(2) Grounding and Bonding Conductors. Equipment grounding jumpers can be located outside of a flexible raceway if the bonding jumper is installed in accordance with 250.102(E)(2). **Figure 300–5**

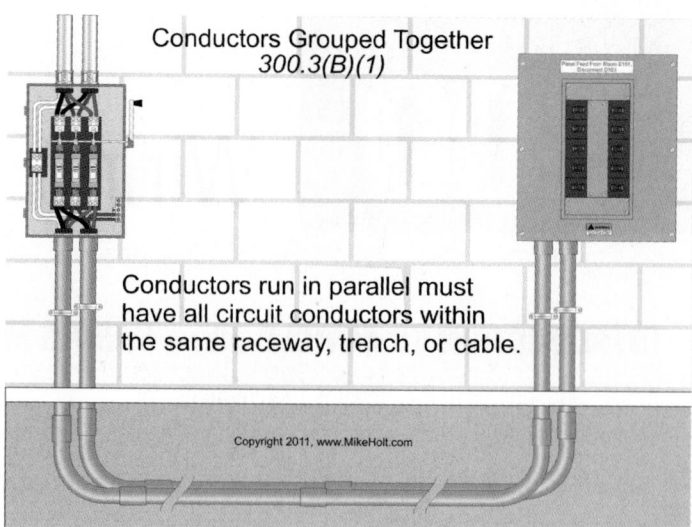

Conductors run in parallel must have all circuit conductors within the same raceway, trench, or cable.

Figure 300–3

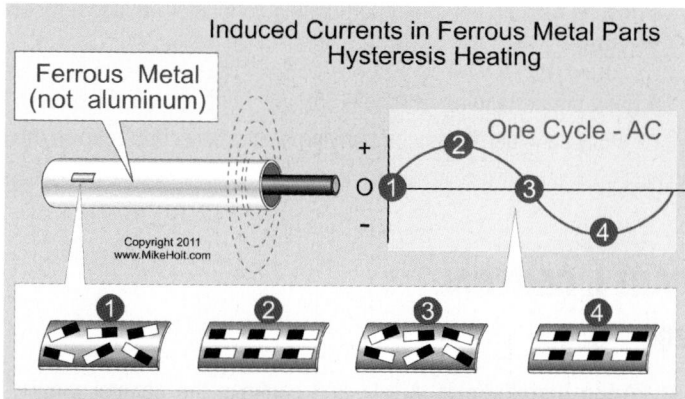

Ferrous metal (steel and iron) molecules align to the polarity of the magnetic field, and when the field reverses, the molecules reverse their polarity. This back-and-forth alignment of the molecules heats up ferrous metal parts.

Figure 300–4

(3) Nonferrous Wiring Methods. Circuit conductors can be installed in different raceways (Phase A in raceway 1, Phase B in raceway 2, and so on) if, in order to reduce or eliminate inductive heating, the raceway is nonmetallic or nonmagnetic and the installation complies with 300.20(B). See 300.3(B)(1) and 300.5(I) Ex 2.

(C) Conductors of Different Systems.

(1) Mixing. Power conductors of alternating-current and direct-current systems rated 600V or less can occupy the same raceway, cable, or enclosure if all conductors have an insulation voltage rating not less than the maximum circuit voltage. **Figure 300–6**

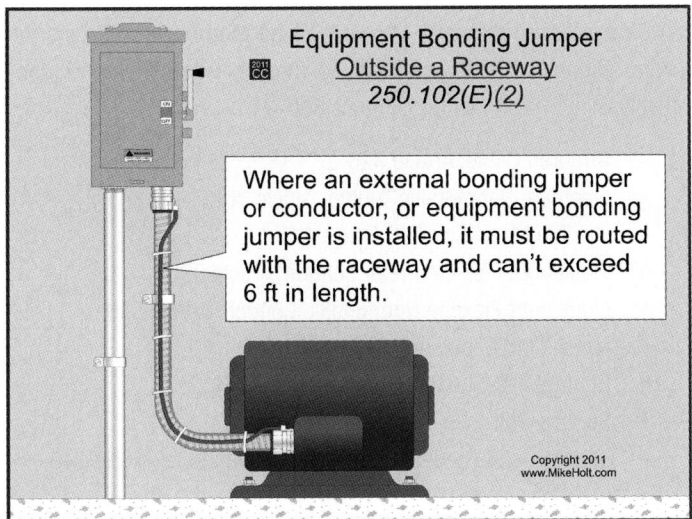

Equipment Bonding Jumper
Outside a Raceway
250.102(E)(2)

Where an external bonding jumper or conductor, or equipment bonding jumper is installed, it must be routed with the raceway and can't exceed 6 ft in length.

Copyright 2011
www.MikeHolt.com

Figure 300–5

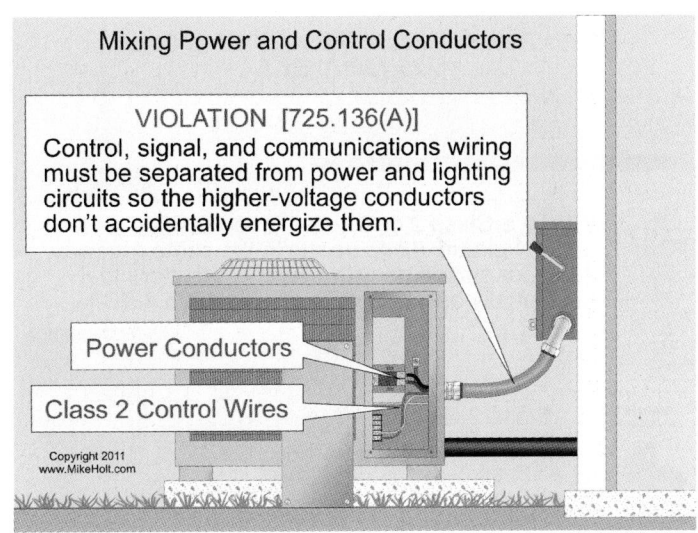

Mixing Power and Control Conductors

VIOLATION [725.136(A)]
Control, signal, and communications wiring must be separated from power and lighting circuits so the higher-voltage conductors don't accidentally energize them.

Power Conductors

Class 2 Control Wires

Copyright 2011
www.MikeHolt.com

Figure 300–7

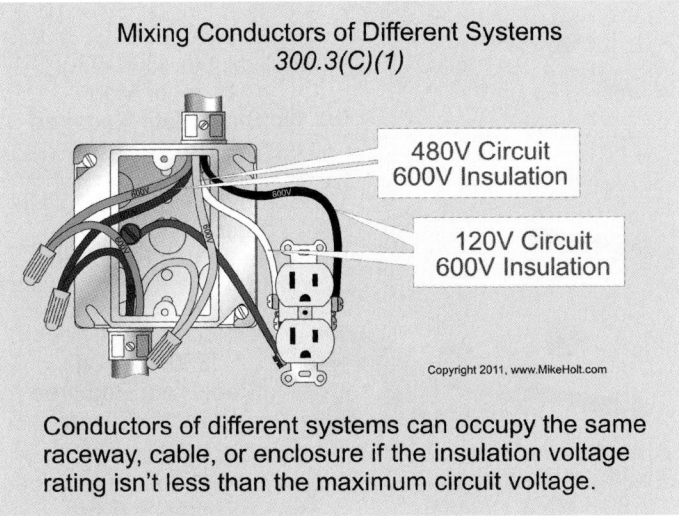

Mixing Conductors of Different Systems
300.3(C)(1)

480V Circuit
600V Insulation

120V Circuit
600V Insulation

Conductors of different systems can occupy the same raceway, cable, or enclosure if the insulation voltage rating isn't less than the maximum circuit voltage.

Copyright 2011, www.MikeHolt.com

Figure 300–6

Author's Comments:

- Control, signal, and communications wiring must be separated from power and lighting circuits so the higher-voltage conductors don't accidentally energize the control, signal, or communications wiring: **Figure 300–7**

  - CATV Coaxial Cable, 820.133(A)
  - Class 1, Class 2, and Class 3 Control Circuits, 725.48 and 725.136(A)
  - Communications Circuits, 800.133(A)(1)(c)
  - Fire Alarm Circuits, 760.136(A)
  - Instrumentation Tray Cable, 727.5
  - Sound Circuits, 640.9(C)

- Class circuit conductors can be installed with associated power conductors [725.48(B)(1)] if all conductors have an insulation voltage rating not less than the maximum circuit voltage [300.3(C)(1)]. **Figure 300–8**

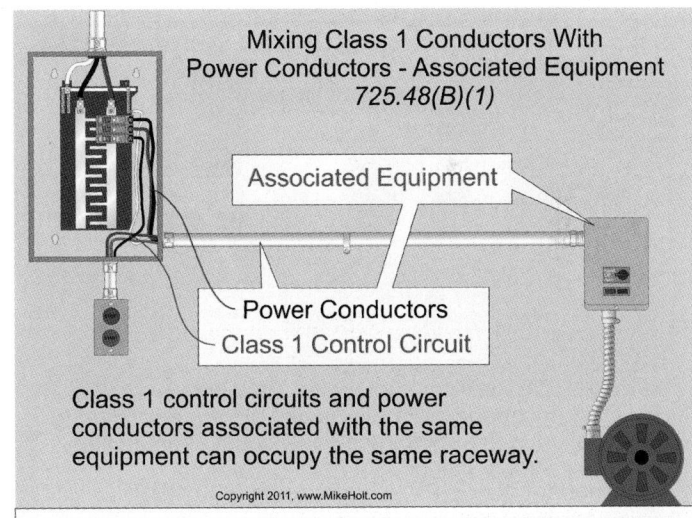

Mixing Class 1 Conductors With
Power Conductors - Associated Equipment
725.48(B)(1)

Associated Equipment

Power Conductors

Class 1 Control Circuit

Class 1 control circuits and power conductors associated with the same equipment can occupy the same raceway.

Copyright 2011, www.MikeHolt.com

Figure 300–8

- A Class 2 circuit that's been reclassified as a Class 1 circuit [725.130(A) Ex 2] can be installed with associated power conductors [725.48(B)(1)] if all conductors have an insulation voltage rating not less than the maximum circuit voltage [300.3(C)(1)]. **Figure 300–9**

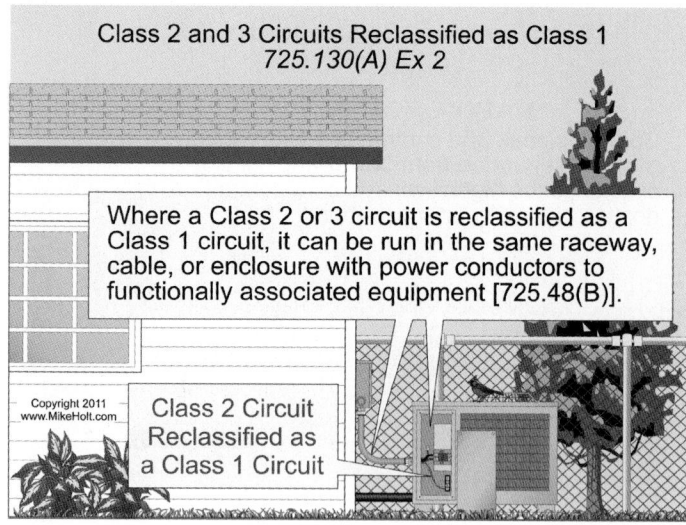

Figure 300–9

Note 2: PV system conductors, both direct current and alternating current, are permitted to be installed in the same raceways, outlet and junction boxes, or similar fittings with each other, but they must be kept entirely independent of all other non-PV system wiring [690.4(B)]. **Figure 300–10**

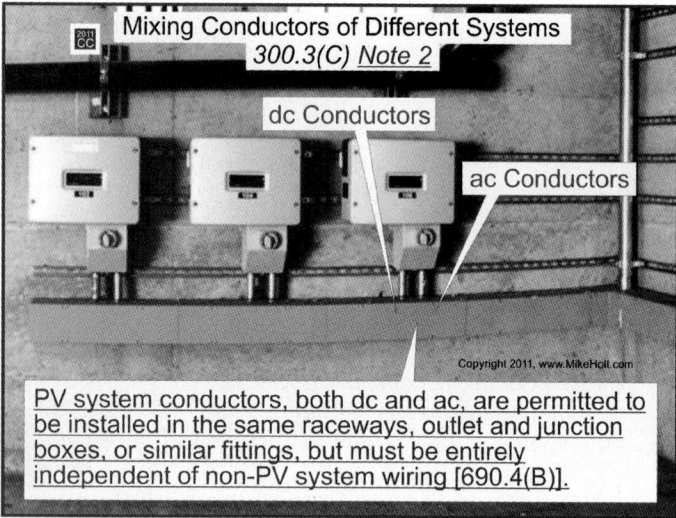

Figure 300–10

300.4 Protection Against Physical Damage. Conductors, raceways, and cables must be protected against physical damage [110.27(B)].

(A) Cables and Raceways Through Wood Members. When the following wiring methods are installed through wood members, they must comply with (1) and (2). **Figure 300–11**

- Armored Cable, Article 320
- Electrical Nonmetallic Tubing, Article 362
- Flexible Metal Conduit, Article 348
- Liquidtight Flexible Metal Conduit, Article 350
- Liquidtight Flexible Nonmetallic Conduit, Article 356
- Metal-Clad Cable, Article 330
- Nonmetallic-Sheathed Cable, Article 334
- Service-Entrance Cable, Article 338
- Underground Feeder and Branch-Circuit Cable, Article 340

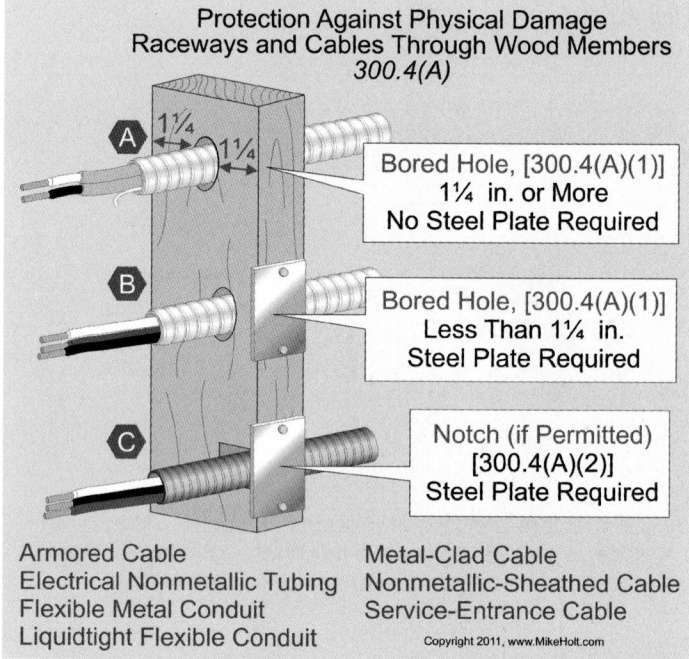

Figure 300–11

(1) Holes in Wood Members. Holes through wood framing members for the above cables or raceways must be not less than 1¼ in. from the edge of the wood member. If the edge of the hole is less than 1¼ in. from the edge, a ¹⁄₁₆ in. thick steel plate of sufficient length and width must be installed to protect the wiring method from screws and nails.

Ex 1: A steel plate isn't required to protect rigid metal conduit, intermediate metal conduit, PVC conduit, or electrical metallic tubing.

Ex 2: A listed and marked steel plate less than ¹⁄₁₆ in. thick that provides equal or better protection against nail or screw penetration is permitted. **Figure 300–12**

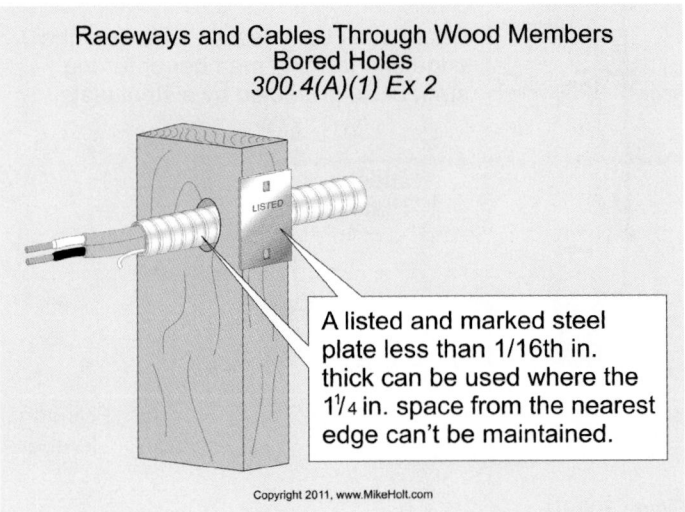

Figure 300–12

> **Author's Comment:** Hardened steel plates thinner than ¹⁄₁₆ in. have been tested and found to provide better protection from screw and nail penetration than the thicker plates.

(2) Notches in Wood Members. If notching of wood framing members for cables and raceways are permitted by the building code, a ¹⁄₁₆ in. thick steel plate of sufficient length and width must be installed to protect the wiring method laid in these wood notches from screws and nails.

> 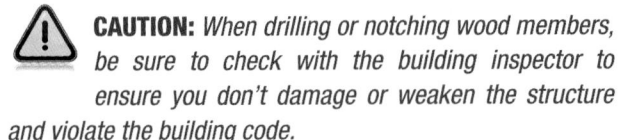 **CAUTION:** *When drilling or notching wood members, be sure to check with the building inspector to ensure you don't damage or weaken the structure and violate the building code.*

Ex 1: A steel plate isn't required to protect rigid metal conduit, intermediate metal conduit, PVC conduit, or electrical metallic tubing.

Ex 2: A listed and marked steel plate less than ¹⁄₁₆ in. thick that provides equal or better protection against nail or screw penetration is permitted. **Figure 300–13**

(B) Nonmetallic-Sheathed Cable and Electrical Nonmetallic Tubing Through Metal Framing Members.

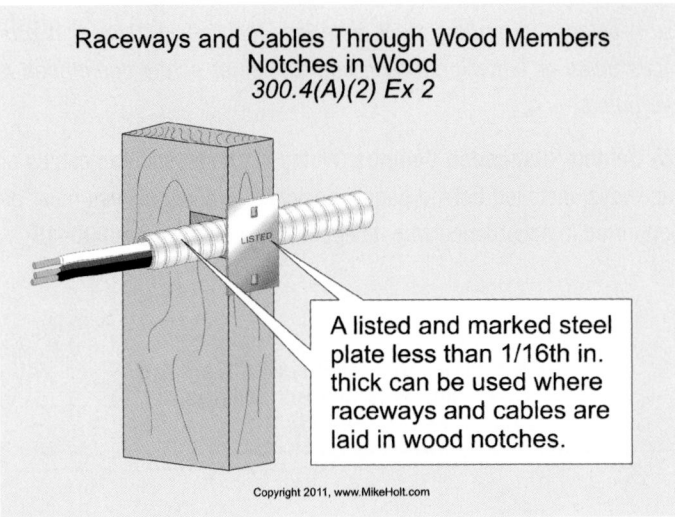

Figure 300–13

(1) Nonmetallic-Sheathed Cable (NM). If Type NM cables pass through factory or field openings in metal framing members, the cable must be protected by listed bushings or listed grommets that cover all metal edges. The protection fitting must be securely fastened in the opening before the installation of the cable. **Figure 300–14**

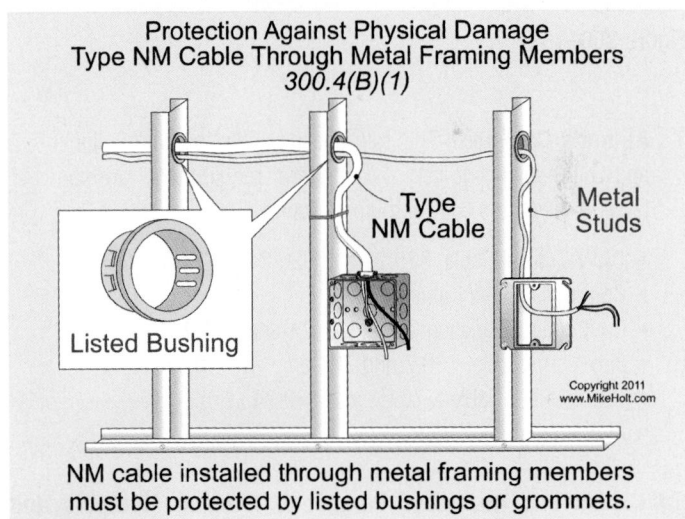

Figure 300–14

(2) Type NM Cable and Electrical Nonmetallic Tubing. If nails or screws are likely to penetrate Type NM cable or electrical nonmetallic tubing, a steel sleeve, steel plate, or steel clip not less than ¹⁄₁₆ in. in thickness must be installed to protect the cable or tubing.

Ex: A listed and marked steel plate less than √₁₆ in. thick that provides equal or better protection against nail or screw penetration is permitted.

(C) Behind Suspended Ceilings. Wiring methods, such as cables or raceways, installed behind panels designed to allow access must be supported in accordance with its applicable article. **Figure 300–15**

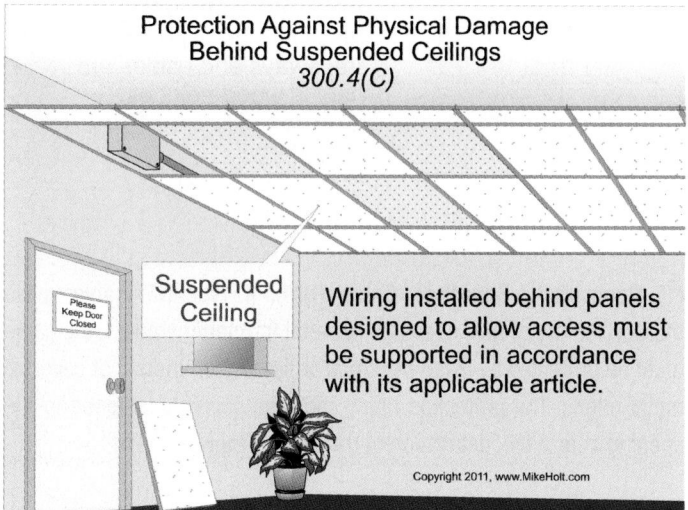

Figure 300–15

Author's Comment: This rule doesn't apply to control, signal, and communications cables, but similar requirements are contained in Chapters 6, 7, and 8 as follows:

- CATV Coaxial Cable, 820.21 and 820.24
- Communications Cable, 800.21
- Control and Signaling Cable, 725.21 and 725.24
- Fire Alarm Cable, 760.7 and 760.8
- Optical Fiber Cable, 770.21 and 770.24
- Audio Cable, 640.6(B)

(D) Cables and Raceways Parallel to Framing Members and Furring Strips. Cables or raceways run parallel to framing members or furring strips must be protected if they're likely to be penetrated by nails or screws, by installing the wiring method so it isn't less than 1¼ in. from the nearest edge of the framing member or furring strip. If the edge of the framing member or furring strip is less than 1¼ in. away, a ¹⁄₁₆ in. thick steel plate of sufficient length and width must be installed to protect the wiring method from screws and nails. **Figure 300–16**

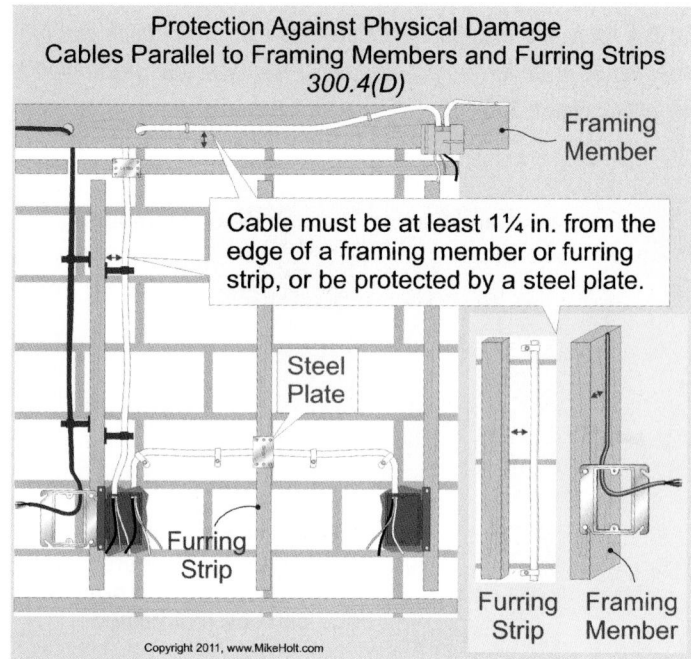

Figure 300–16

Author's Comment: This rule doesn't apply to control, signaling, and communications cables, but similar requirements are contained in Chapters 6, 7, and 8 as follows:

- CATV Coaxial Cable, 820.24
- Communications Cable, 800.24
- Control and Signaling Cable, 725.24
- Optical Fiber Cable, 770.24
- Fire Alarm Cable, 760.8
- Audio Cable, 640.6(B)

Ex 1: Protection isn't required for rigid metal conduit, intermediate metal conduit, PVC conduit, or electrical metallic tubing.

Ex 2: For concealed work in finished buildings, or finished panels for prefabricated buildings if such supporting is impracticable, the cables can be fished between access points.

Ex 3: A listed and marked steel plate less than ¹⁄₁₆ in. thick that provides equal or better protection against nail or screw penetration is permitted.

(E) Wiring Under Roof Decking. Cables, raceways, <u>and enclosures</u> under metal-corrugated sheet roof decking must not be located within 1½ in. of the roof decking, measured from the <u>lowest surface of the roof decking to the top</u> of the cable, raceway, <u>or box. In addition, cables, raceways, and enclosures aren't permitted in concealed locations of metal-corrugated sheet decking type roofing.</u>

Note: Roof decking material will be installed or replaced after the initial raceway or cabling which may be penetrated by the screws or other mechanical devices designed to provide "hold down" strength of the waterproof membrane or roof insulating material.

Ex: Spacing from roof decking doesn't apply to rigid metal conduit and intermediate metal conduit.

(F) Cables and Raceways Installed in Grooves. Cables and raceways installed in a groove must be protected by a ¹⁄₁₆ in. thick steel plate or sleeve, or by 1¼ in. of free space.

Author's Comment: An example is Type NM cable installed in a groove cut into the Styrofoam-type insulation building block structure and then covered with wallboard.

Ex 1: Protection isn't required if the cable is installed in rigid metal conduit, intermediate metal conduit, PVC conduit, or electrical metallic tubing.

Ex 2: A listed and marked steel plate less than √₁₆ in. thick that provides equal or better protection against nail or screw penetration is permitted.

(G) Insulating Fittings. If raceways contain insulated circuit conductors 4 AWG and larger that enter an enclosure, the conductors must be protected from abrasion during and after installation by a fitting identified to provide a smooth, rounded insulating surface, such as an insulating bushing. **Figure 300–17**

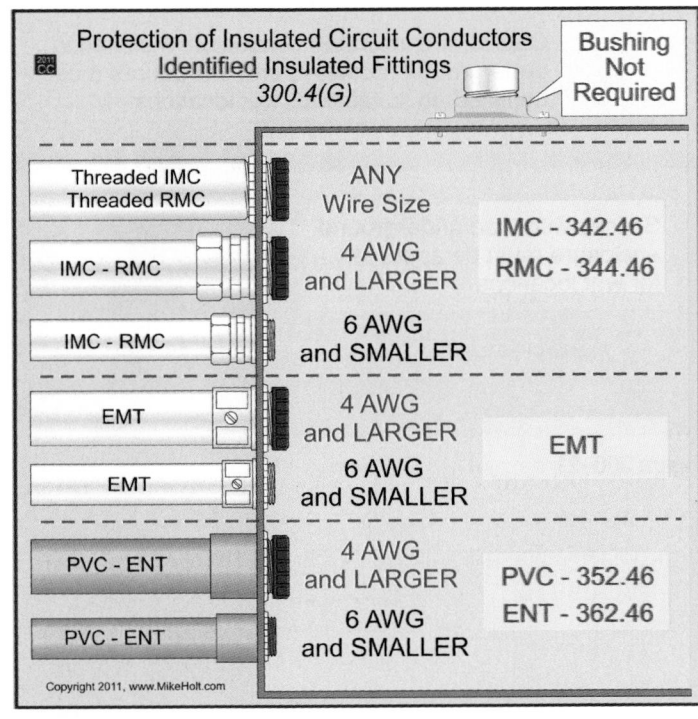

Figure 300–17

Author's Comments:

- If IMC or RMC conduit enters an enclosure without a connector, a bushing must be provided, regardless of the conductor size [342.46 and 344.46].
- An insulated fitting isn't required for a grounding electrode. **Figure 300–18**

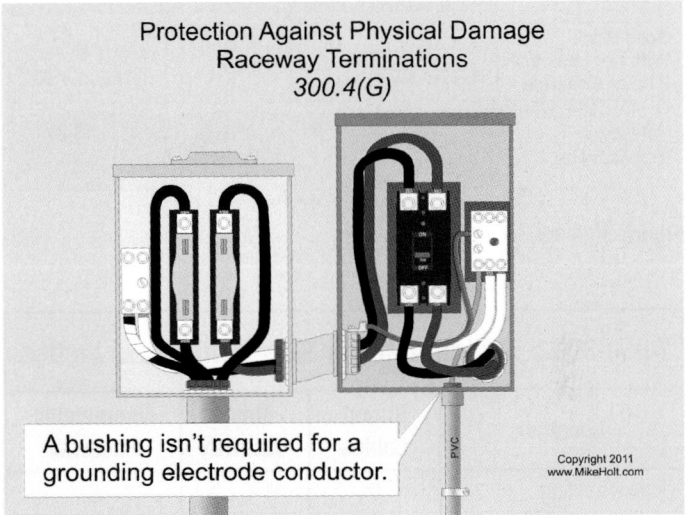

Figure 300–18

Ex: Insulating bushings aren't required if a raceway terminates in a threaded raceway entry that provides a smooth, rounded, or flared surface for the conductors. An example would be a meter hub fitting or a Meyer's hub-type fitting.

(H) Structural Joints. A listed expansion/deflection fitting or other means approved by the authority having jurisdiction must be used where a raceway crosses a structural joint intended for expansion, contraction or deflection.

300.5 Underground Installations.

(A) Minimum Burial Depths. When cables or raceways are installed underground, they must have a minimum "cover" in accordance with Table 300.5. **Figure 300–19**

Underground Installations - Minimum Cover Depths
Table 300.5

	UF or USE Cables or Conductors	RMC or IMC	PVC not Encased in Concrete	Residential 15A & 20A GFCI 120V Branch Ckts
Street Driveway Parking Lot	24 in.	24 in.	24 in.	24 in.
Driveways One - Two Family	18 in.	18 in.	18 in.	12 in.
Solid Rock With not Less than 2 in. of Concrete	Raceway Only			Raceway Only
All Other Applications	24 in.	6 in.	18 in.	12 in.

Copyright 2011, www.MikeHolt.com

Figure 300–19

Table 300.5 Minimum Cover Requirements in Inches

Location	Buried Cables	Metal Raceway	Nonmetallic Raceway
Under Building	0	0	0
Dwelling Unit	24/12*	6	18
Dwelling Unit Driveway	18/12*	6	18/12*
Under Roadway	24	24	24
Other Locations	24	6	18

Residential branch circuits rated 120V or less with GFCI protection and maximum overcurrent protection of 20A. Note: This is a summary of the NEC's Table 300.5. See the table in the NEC for full details.

Note 1 to Table 300.5 defines "Cover" as the distance from the top of the underground cable or raceway to the top surface of finished grade. Figure 300–05 02 N1

Author's Comment: The cover requirements contained in 300.5 don't apply to the following signaling, communications, and other power-limited wiring systems: **Figure 300–20**

- CATV, 90.3
- Class 2 and 3 Circuits, 725.3
- Communications Cables and Raceways, 90.3
- Fire Alarm Circuits, 760.3
- Optical Fiber Cables and Raceways, 770.3

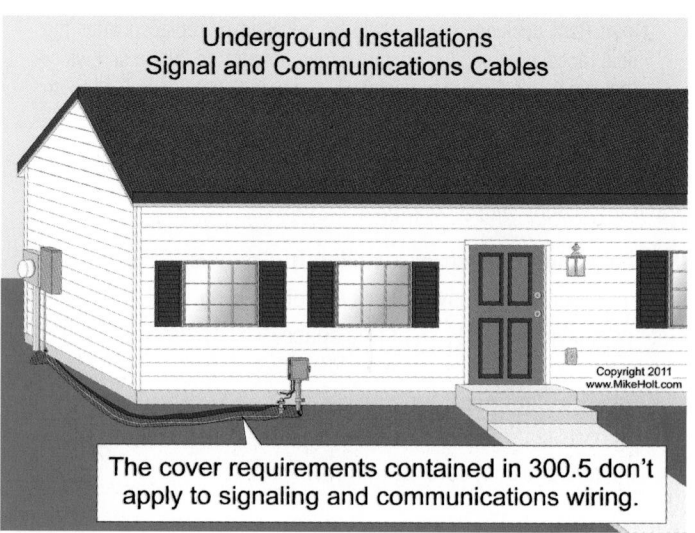

Underground Installations
Signal and Communications Cables

Copyright 2011 www.MikeHolt.com

The cover requirements contained in 300.5 don't apply to signaling and communications wiring.

Figure 300–20

(B) Wet Locations. The interior of enclosures or raceways installed in an underground installation are considered to be a wet location. Cables and insulated conductors installed in underground enclosures or raceways must be listed for use in wet locations according to 310.10(C). Splices within an underground enclosure must be listed as suitable for wet locations [110.14(B)]. **Figure 300–21**

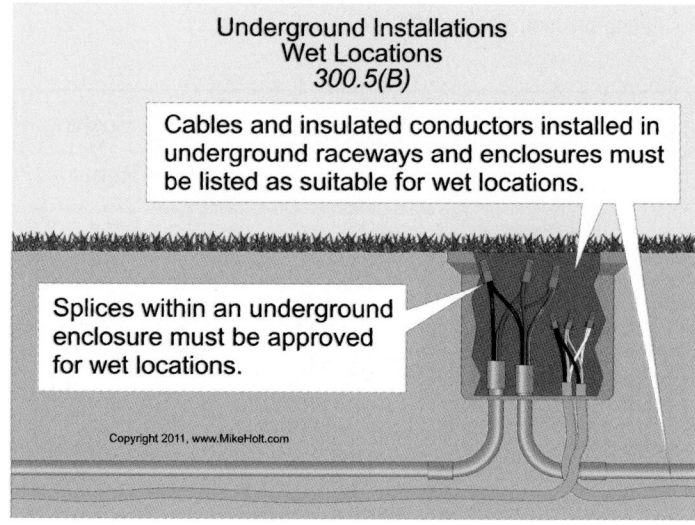

Underground Installations
Wet Locations
300.5(B)

Cables and insulated conductors installed in underground raceways and enclosures must be listed as suitable for wet locations.

Splices within an underground enclosure must be approved for wet locations.

Copyright 2011, www.MikeHolt.com

Figure 300–21

Author's Comment: The definition of a "Wet Location" as contained in Article 100, includes installations underground, in concrete slabs in direct contact with the earth, locations subject to saturation with water, and unprotected locations exposed to weather. If raceways are installed in wet locations above grade, the interior of these raceways is also considered to be a wet location [300.9].

(C) Cables Under Buildings. Cables installed under a building must be installed in a raceway that extends past the outside walls of the building.

Ex 2: Type MC Cable listed for direct burial is permitted under a building without installation in a raceway [330.10(A)(5)]. **Figure 300–22**

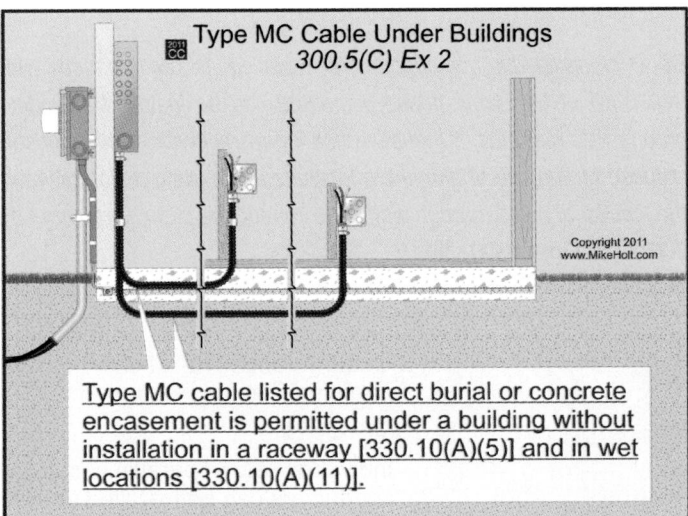

Figure 300–22

(D) Protecting Underground Cables and Conductors. Direct-buried conductors and cables such as Types MC, UF, and USE must be protected from damage in accordance with (1) through (4).

(1) Emerging from Grade. Direct-buried cables or conductors that emerge from grade must be installed in an enclosure or raceway to protect against physical damage. Protection isn't required to extend more than 18 in. below grade, and protection above ground must extend to a height of not less than 8 ft. **Figure 300–23**

(2) Conductors Entering Buildings. Conductors that enter a building must be protected to the point of entrance.

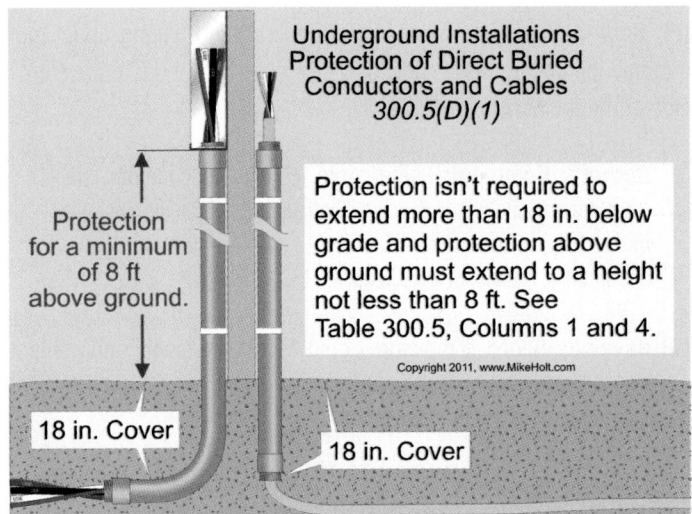

Figure 300–23

(4) Enclosure or Raceway Damage. If direct-buried cables, enclosures, or raceways are subject to physical damage, the conductors must be installed in rigid metal conduit, intermediate metal conduit, or Schedule 80 PVC conduit.

(E) Underground Splices and Taps. Direct-buried conductors or cables can be spliced or tapped underground without a splice box [300.15(G)], if the splice or tap is made in accordance with 110.14(B). **Figure 300–24**

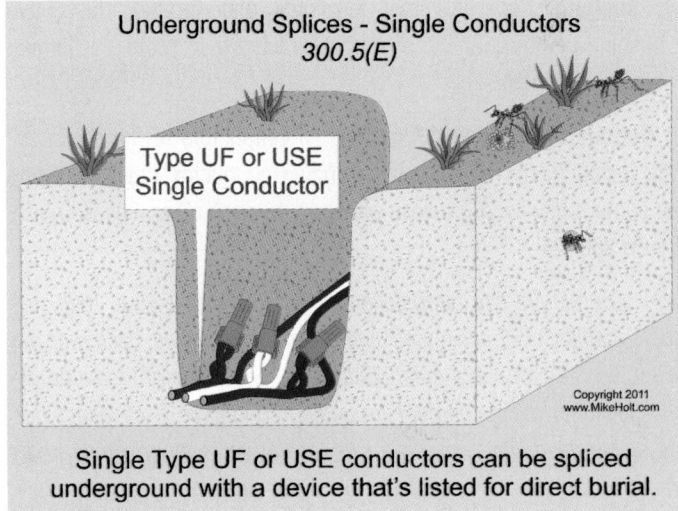

Figure 300–24

(F) Backfill. Backfill material for underground wiring must not damage the underground cable or raceway, or contribute to the corrosion of the metal raceway.

> **Author's Comment:** Large rocks, chunks of concrete, steel rods, mesh, and other sharp-edged objects must not be used for backfill material, because they can damage the underground conductors, cables, or raceways.

(G) Raceway Seals. If moisture could enter a raceway and contact energized live parts, a seal must be installed at one or both ends of the raceway.

> **Author's Comment:** This is a common problem for equipment located downhill from the supply, or in underground equipment rooms. See 230.8 for service raceway seals and 300.7(A) for different temperature area seals.

> **Note:** Hazardous explosive gases or vapors make it necessary to seal underground raceways that enter the building in accordance with 501.15.

> **Author's Comment:** It isn't the intent of this Note to imply that sealing fittings of the types required in hazardous locations be installed in unclassified locations, except as required in Chapter 5. This also doesn't imply that the sealing material provides a watertight seal, but only that it prevents moisture from entering the raceways.

(H) Bushing. Raceways that terminate underground must have a bushing or fitting at the end of the raceway to protect emerging cables or conductors.

(I) Conductors Grouped Together. All conductors of the same circuit, including the equipment grounding conductor, must be inside the same raceway, or in close proximity to each other. See 300.3(B). Figure 300–25

Ex 1: Conductors can be installed in parallel in raceways, multiconductor cables, or direct-buried single-conductor cables. Each raceway or multiconductor cable must contain all conductors of the same circuit including the equipment grounding conductor. Each direct-buried single-conductor cable must be located in close proximity in the trench to the other single conductor cables in the same parallel set of conductors, including equipment grounding conductors.

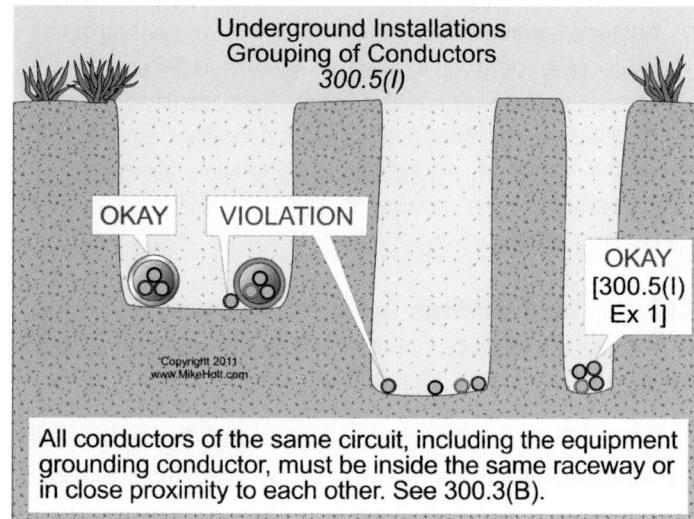

Figure 300–25

Ex 2: Parallel circuit conductors installed in accordance with 310.10(H) of the same phase or neutral can be installed in underground PVC conduits, if inductive heating at raceway terminations is reduced by the use of aluminum locknuts and cutting a slot between the individual holes through which the conductors pass as required by 300.20(B). **Figure 300–26**

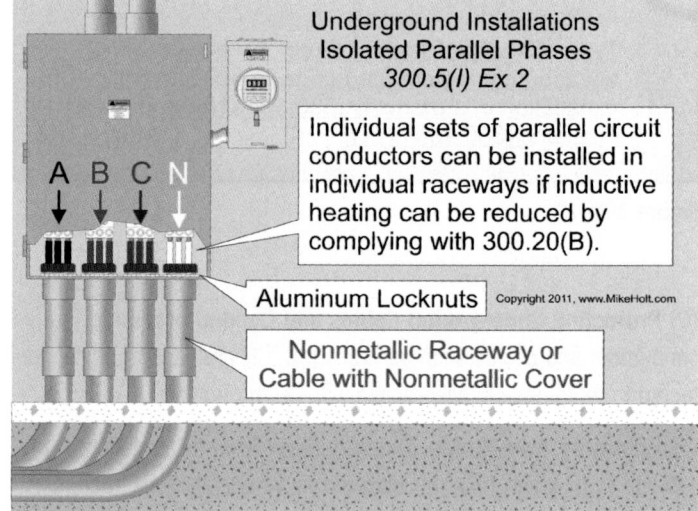

Figure 300–26

> **Author's Comment:** Installing ungrounded and neutral conductors in different PVC conduits makes it easier to terminate larger parallel sets of conductors, but it will result in higher levels of electromagnetic fields (EMF).

(J) Earth Movement. Direct-buried conductors, cables, or raceways that are subject to movement by settlement or frost must be arranged to prevent damage to conductors or equipment connected to the wiring.

(K) Directional Boring. Cables or raceways installed using directional boring equipment must be approved by the authority having jurisdiction for this purpose.

> **Author's Comment:** Directional boring technology uses a directional drill, which is steered continuously from point "A" to point "B." When the drill head comes out of the earth at point "B," it's replaced with a back-reamer and the duct or raceway being installed is attached to it. The size of the boring rig (hp, torque, and pull-back power) comes into play, along with the types of soil, in determining the type of raceways required. For telecommunications work, multiple poly innerducts are pulled in at one time. At major crossings, such as expressways, railroads, or rivers, outerduct may be installed to create a permanent sleeve for the innerducts.
>
> "Innerduct" and "outerduct" are terms usually associated with optical fiber cable installations, while "unitduct" comes with factory installed conductors. All of these come in various sizes. Galvanized rigid metal conduit, Schedule 40 and Schedule 80 PVC, HDPE conduit and nonmetallic underground conduit with conductors (NUCC) are common wiring methods used with directional boring installations.

300.6 Protection Against Corrosion and Deterioration.

Raceways, cable trays, cablebus, cable armor, boxes, cable sheathing, cabinets, elbows, couplings, fittings, supports, and support hardware must be suitable for the environment. **Figure 300–27**

(A) Ferrous Metal Equipment. Ferrous metal raceways, enclosures, cables, cable trays, fittings, and support hardware must be protected against corrosion by a coating of listed corrosion-resistant material. Where conduit is threaded in the field, the threads must be coated with an approved electrically conductive, corrosion-resistant compound, such as cold zinc.

> **Author's Comment:** Nonferrous metal raceways, such as aluminum rigid metal conduit, don't have to meet the provisions of this section.

(1) Protected from Corrosion Solely by Enamel. If ferrous metal parts are protected from corrosion solely by enamel, they must not be used outdoors or in wet locations as described in 300.6(D).

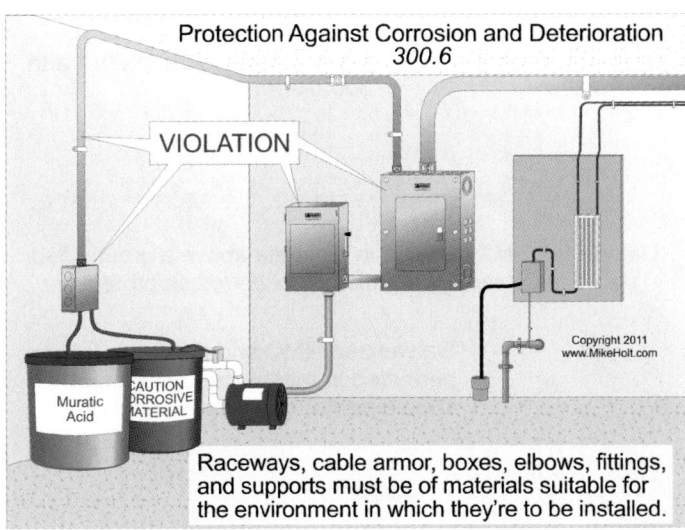

Figure 300–27

(2) Organic Coatings on Boxes or Cabinets. Boxes or cabinets having a system of organic coatings marked "Raintight," "Rainproof," or "Outdoor Type," can be installed outdoors.

(3) In Concrete or in Direct Contact with the Earth. Ferrous metal raceways, cable armor, boxes, cable sheathing, cabinets, elbows, couplings, nipples, fittings, supports, and support hardware can be installed in concrete or in direct contact with the earth, or in areas subject to severe corrosive influences if made of material approved for the condition, or if provided with corrosion protection approved for the condition.

> **Author's Comment:** Galvanized steel electrical metallic tubing can be installed in concrete at grade level and in direct contact with the earth, but supplementary corrosion protection is usually required (UL White Book, *Guide Information for Electrical Equipment*, www.ul.com/regulators/2008_WhiteBook.pdf). Electrical metallic tubing can be installed in concrete above the ground floor slab generally without supplementary corrosion protection. **Figure 300–28**

(B) Aluminum Equipment. Aluminum raceways, cable trays, cablebus, cable armor, boxes, cable sheathing, cabinets, elbows, couplings, nipples, fittings, supports, and support hardware embedded or encased in concrete or in direct contact with the earth must be provided with supplementary corrosion protection.

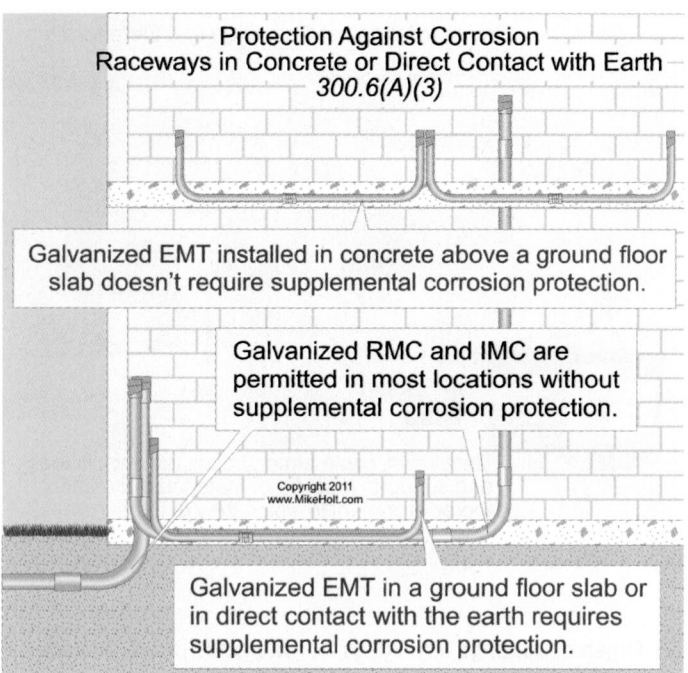

Figure 300–28

(C) Nonmetallic Equipment. Nonmetallic raceways, cable trays, cablebus, boxes, cables with a nonmetallic outer jacket and internal metal armor or jacket, cable sheathing, cabinets, elbows, couplings, nipples, fittings, supports, and support hardware must be made of material identified for the condition, and must comply with (1) and (2). **Figure 300–29**

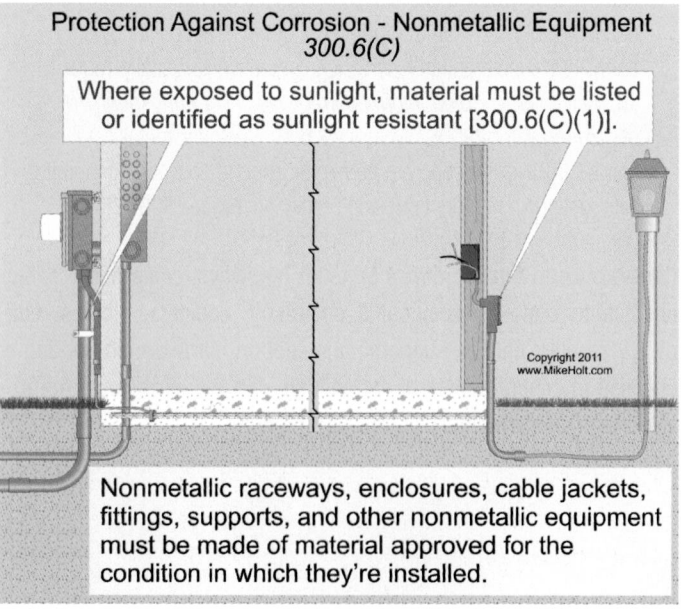

Figure 300–29

(1) Exposed to Sunlight. If exposed to sunlight, the materials must be listed or identified as sunlight resistant.

(2) Chemical Exposure. If subject to exposure to chemical solvents, vapors, splashing, or immersion, materials or coatings must either be inherently resistant to chemicals based upon their listing, or be identified for the specific chemical.

(D) Indoor Wet Locations. In portions of dairy processing facilities, laundries, canneries, and other indoor wet locations, and in locations where walls are frequently washed or where there are surfaces of absorbent materials, such as damp paper or wood, the entire wiring system, where installed exposed, including all boxes, fittings, raceways, and cables, must be mounted so there's at least ¼ in. of airspace between it and the wall or supporting surface.

> **Author's Comment:** See the definitions of "Exposed" and "Location, Wet" in Article 100.

Ex: Nonmetallic raceways, boxes, and fittings are permitted without the airspace on a concrete, masonry, tile, or similar surface.

Note: Areas where acids and alkali chemicals are handled and stored may present corrosive conditions, particularly when wet or damp. Severe corrosive conditions may also be present in portions of meatpacking plants, tanneries, glue houses, and some stables; in installations immediately adjacent to a seashore or swimming pool, spa, hot tub, and fountain areas; in areas where chemical deicers are used; and in storage cellars or rooms for hides, casings, fertilizer, salt, and bulk chemicals.

300.7 Raceways Exposed to Different Temperatures.

(A) Sealing. If a raceway is subjected to different temperatures, and where condensation is known to be a problem, the raceway must be filled with a material approved by the authority having jurisdiction that will prevent the circulation of warm air to a colder section of the raceway. An explosionproof seal isn't required for this purpose. **Figure 300–30**

(B) Expansion Fittings. Raceways must be provided with expansion fittings where necessary to compensate for thermal expansion and contraction. **Figure 300–31**

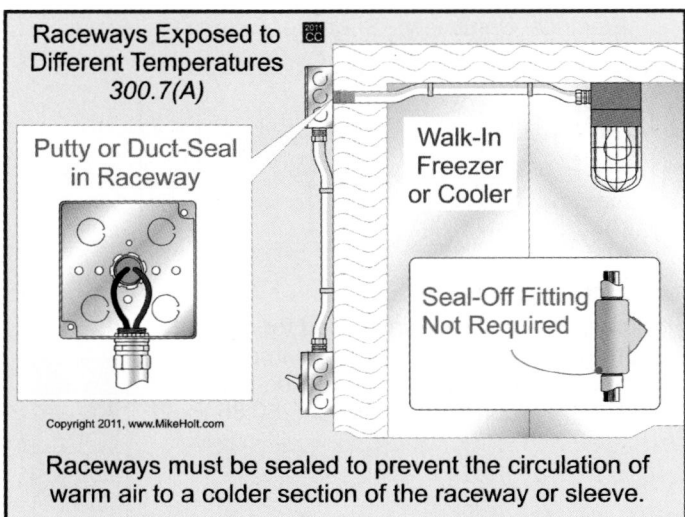

Figure 300–30

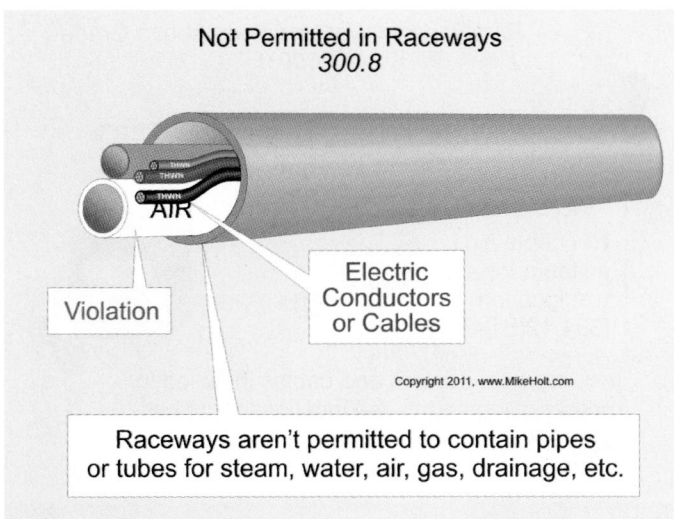

Figure 300–32

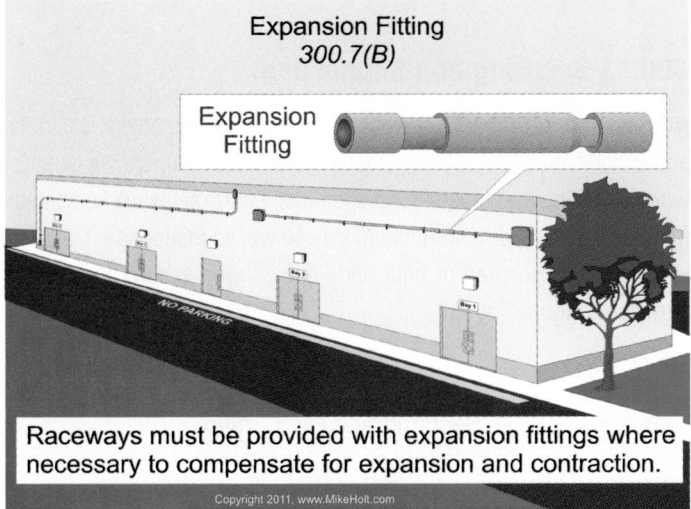

Figure 300–31

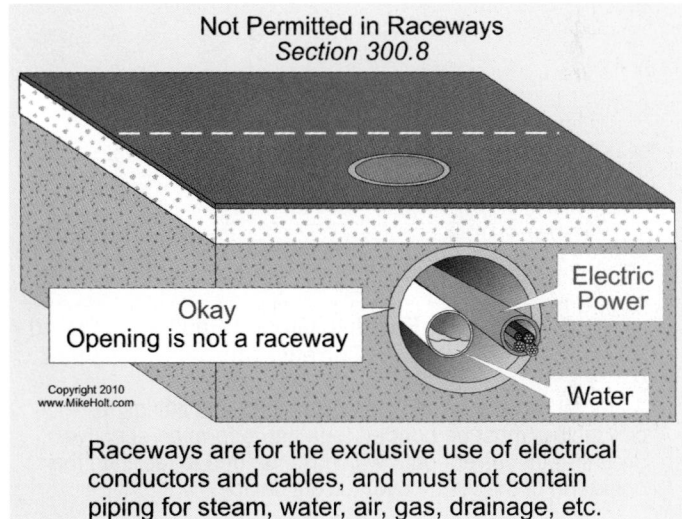

Figure 300–33

Note: Table 352.44 provides the expansion characteristics for PVC conduit. The expansion characteristics for metal raceways are determined by multiplying the values from Table 352.44 by 0.20, and the expansion characteristics for aluminum raceways are determined by multiplying the values from Table 352.44 by 0.40. Table 354.44 provides the expansion characteristics for reinforced thermosetting resin conduit (RTRC).

300.8 Not Permitted in Raceways. Raceways are designed for the exclusive use of electrical conductors and cables, and aren't permitted to contain nonelectrical components, such as pipes or tubes for steam, water, air, gas, drainage, and so forth. **Figures 300–32 and 300–33**

300.9 Raceways in Wet Locations Above Grade. Insulated conductors and cables installed in raceways in aboveground wet locations must be listed for use in wet locations according to 310.10(C). **Figure 300–34**

300.10 Electrical Continuity. Metal raceways, cables, boxes, fittings, cabinets, and enclosures for conductors must be metallically joined together to form a continuous, low-impedance fault current path capable of carrying any fault current likely to be imposed on it [110.10, 250.4(A)(3), and 250.122]. **Figure 300–35**

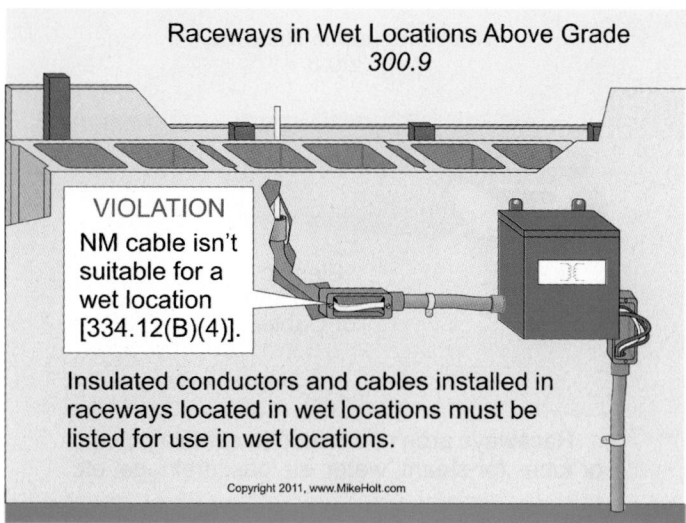

Raceways in Wet Locations Above Grade
300.9

VIOLATION

NM cable isn't suitable for a wet location [334.12(B)(4)].

Insulated conductors and cables installed in raceways located in wet locations must be listed for use in wet locations.

Copyright 2011, www.MikeHolt.com

Figure 300–34

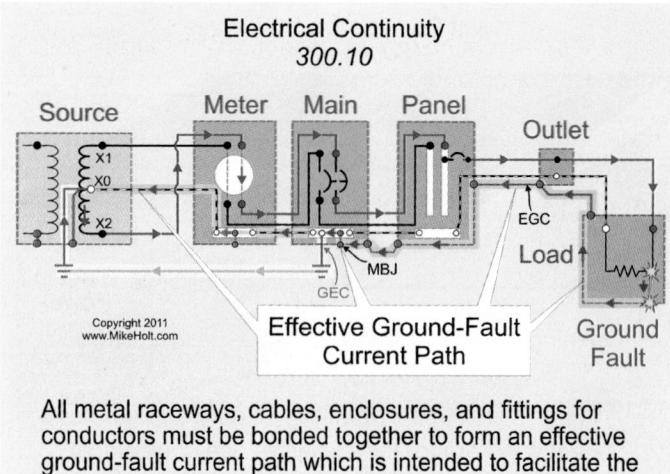

Electrical Continuity
300.10

Copyright 2011 www.MikeHolt.com

Effective Ground-Fault Current Path

All metal raceways, cables, enclosures, and fittings for conductors must be bonded together to form an effective ground-fault current path which is intended to facilitate the operation of the circuit overcurrent device.

Figure 300–35

Metal raceways and cable assemblies must be mechanically secured to boxes, fittings, cabinets, and other enclosures.

Ex 1: Short lengths of metal raceways used for the support or protection of cables aren't required to be electrically continuous, nor are they required to be connected to an equipment grounding conductor of a type recognized in 250.118 [250.86 Ex 2 and 300.12 Ex]. **Figure 300–36**

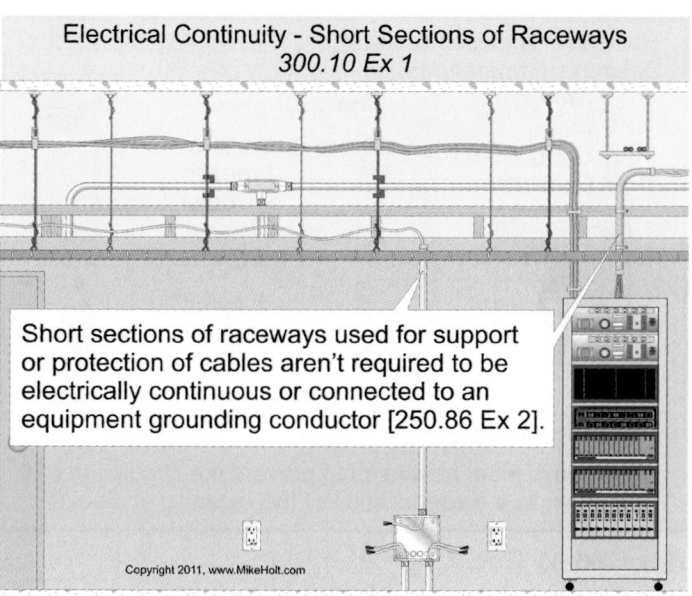

Electrical Continuity - Short Sections of Raceways
300.10 Ex 1

Short sections of raceways used for support or protection of cables aren't required to be electrically continuous or connected to an equipment grounding conductor [250.86 Ex 2].

Copyright 2011, www.MikeHolt.com

Figure 300–36

300.11 Securing and Supporting.

(A) Secured in Place. Raceways, cable assemblies, boxes, cabinets, and fittings must be securely fastened in place. The ceiling-support wires or ceiling grid must not be used to support raceways and cables (power, signaling, or communications). However, independent support wires that are secured at both ends and provide secure support are permitted. **Figure 300–37**

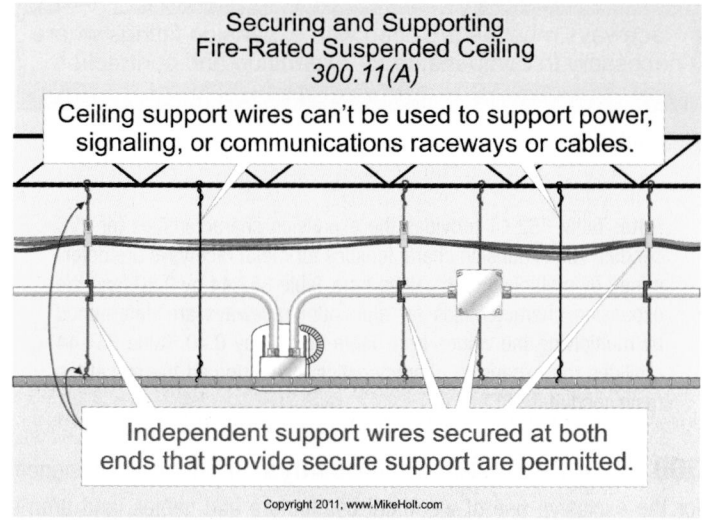

Securing and Supporting
Fire-Rated Suspended Ceiling
300.11(A)

Ceiling support wires can't be used to support power, signaling, or communications raceways or cables.

Independent support wires secured at both ends that provide secure support are permitted.

Copyright 2011, www.MikeHolt.com

Figure 300–37

Author's Comment: Outlet boxes [314.23(D)] and luminaires can be secured to the suspended-ceiling grid if securely fastened to the ceiling-framing members by mechanical means such as bolts, screws, or rivets, or by the use of clips or other securing means identified for use with the type of ceiling-framing member(s) used [410.36(B)].

(1) Fire-Rated Ceiling Assembly. Electrical wiring within the cavity of a fire-rated floor-ceiling or roof-ceiling assembly can be supported by independent support wires attached to the ceiling assembly. The independent support wires must be distinguishable from the suspended-ceiling support wires by color, tagging, or other effective means.

(2) Nonfire-Rated Ceiling Assembly. Wiring in a nonfire-rated floor-ceiling or roof-ceiling assembly can be supported by independent support wires attached to the ceiling assembly. The independent support wires must be distinguishable from the suspended-ceiling support wires by color, tagging, or other effective means. **Figure 300–38**

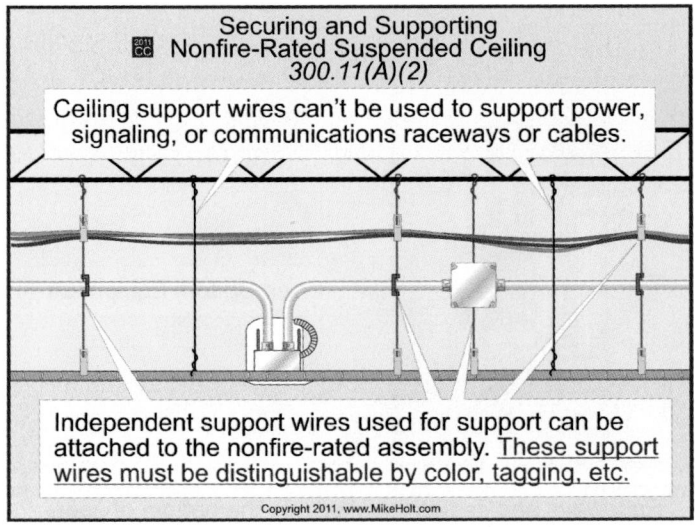

Figure 300–38

(B) Raceways Used for Support. Raceways must not be used as a means of support for other raceways, cables, or nonelectrical equipment, except as permitted in (1) through (3). **Figure 300–39**

(1) Identified. If the raceway or means of support is identified for the purpose.

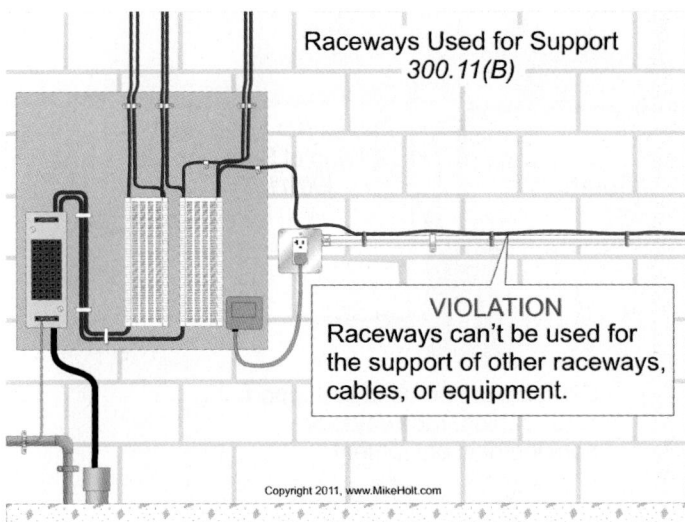

Figure 300–39

(2) Class 2 and 3 Circuits. Class 2 and 3 cable can be supported by the raceway that supplies power to the equipment controlled by the Class 2 or 3 circuit. **Figure 300–40**

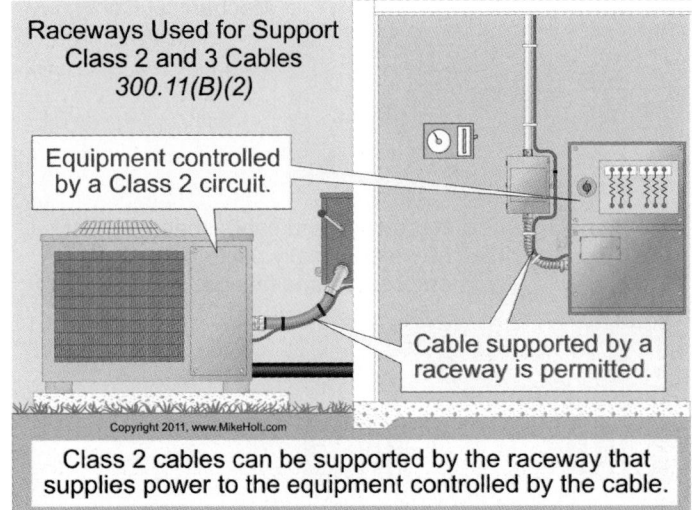

Figure 300–40

(3) Boxes Supported by Raceways. Raceways are permitted as a means of support for threaded boxes and conduit bodies in accordance with 314.23(E) and (F), or to support luminaires in accordance with 410.36(E).

(C) Cables Not Used as Means of Support. Cables must not be used to support other cables, raceways, or nonelectrical equipment. **Figure 300–41**

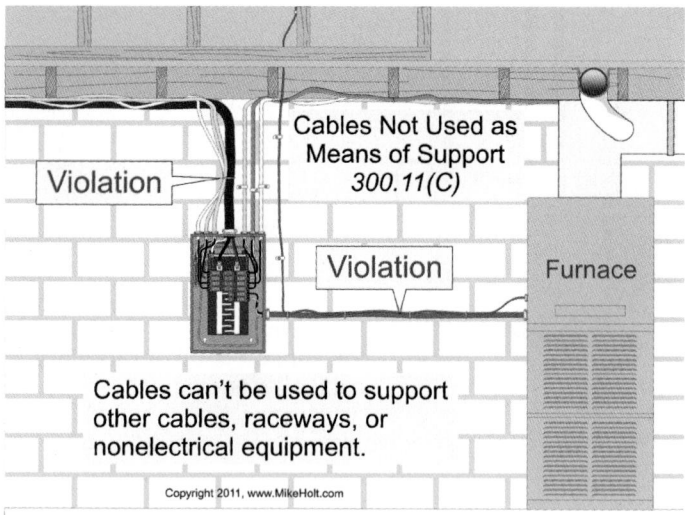

Figure 300–41

300.12 Mechanical Continuity. Raceways and cable sheaths must be mechanically continuous between boxes, cabinets, and fittings. **Figure 300–42**

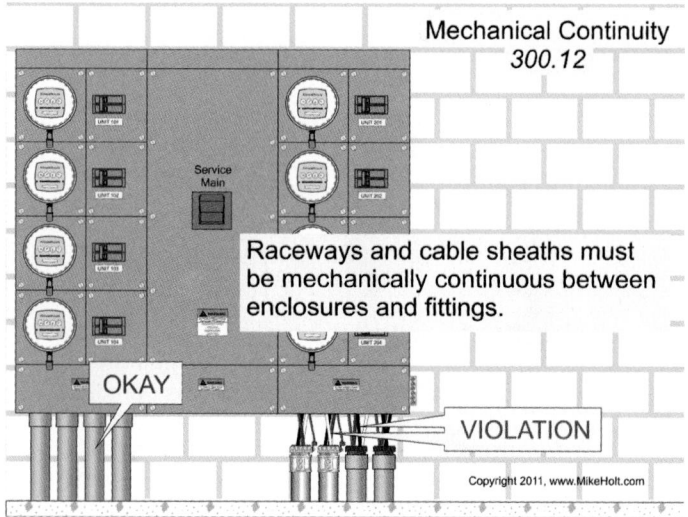

Figure 300–42

Ex 1: Short sections of raceways used to provide support or protection of cable from physical damage aren't required to be mechanically continuous [250.86 Ex 2 and 300.10 Ex 1]. **Figure 300–43**

Ex 2: Raceways at the bottom of open-bottom equipment, such as switchboards, motor control centers, and transformers, aren't required to be mechanically secured to the equipment. **Figure 300–44**

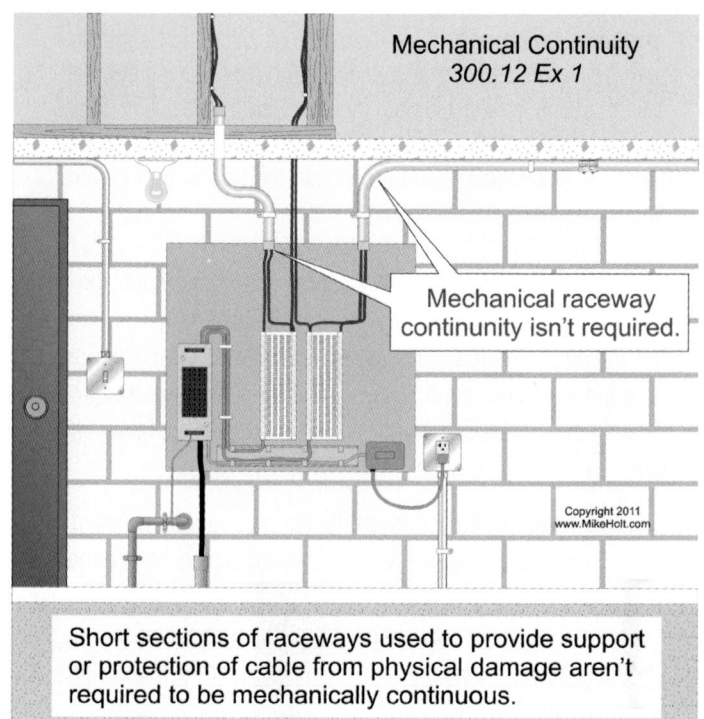

Short sections of raceways used to provide support or protection of cable from physical damage aren't required to be mechanically continuous.

Figure 300–43

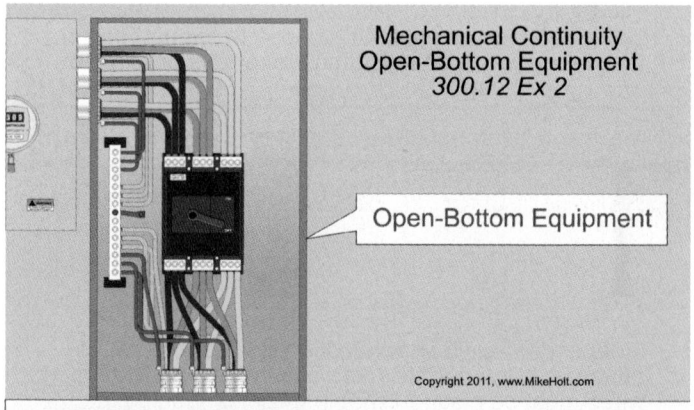

Raceways and cables installed into the bottom of open-bottom equipment aren't required to be mechanically secured to the equipment.

Figure 300–44

Author's Comment: When raceways are stubbed into an open-bottom switchboard, the raceway, including the end fitting, can't rise more than 3 in. above the bottom of the switchboard enclosure [408.5].

300.13 Splices and Pigtails.

A) Conductor Splices. Splices must be in enclosures as per 300.15 and aren't permitted in raceways, except as permitted by 376.56, 386.56, or 388.56. **Figure 300–45**

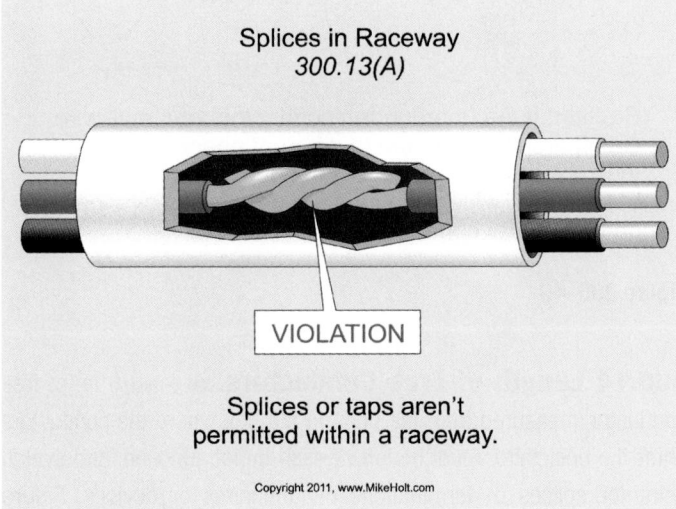

Splices in Raceway
300.13(A)

VIOLATION

Splices or taps aren't
permitted within a raceway.

Copyright 2011, www.MikeHolt.com

Figure 300–45

(B) Conductor Continuity. Continuity of the neutral conductor of a multiwire branch circuit must not be interrupted by the removal of a wiring device. In these applications the neutral conductors must be spliced together, and a pigtail must be provided for the wiring device. **Figure 300–46**

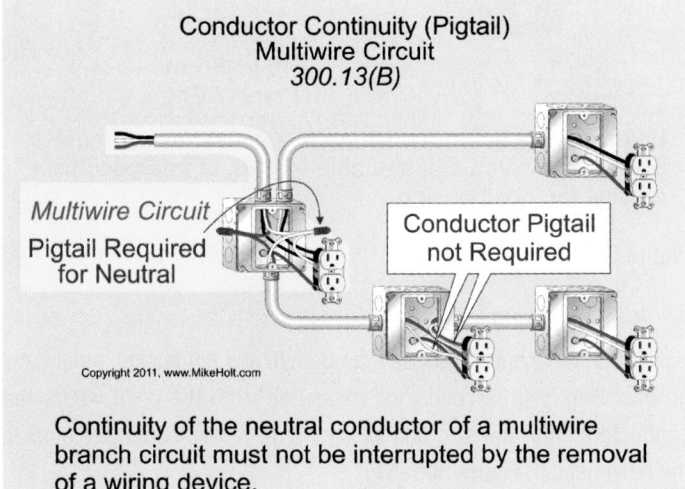

**Conductor Continuity (Pigtail)
Multiwire Circuit**
300.13(B)

Multiwire Circuit
Pigtail Required
for Neutral

Conductor Pigtail
not Required

Copyright 2011, www.MikeHolt.com

Continuity of the neutral conductor of a multiwire
branch circuit must not be interrupted by the removal
of a wiring device.

Figure 300–46

Author's Comment: The opening of the ungrounded conductors, or the neutral conductor of a 2-wire circuit during the replacement of a device, doesn't cause a safety hazard, so pigtailing these conductors isn't required [110.14(B)].

 CAUTION: *If the continuity of the neutral conductor of a multiwire circuit is interrupted (opened), the resultant over- or undervoltage can cause a fire and/or destruction of electrical equipment.*

Example: *A 3-wire, single-phase, 120/240V multiwire circuit supplies a 1,200W, 120V hair dryer and a 600W, 120V television.* **Figure 300–47**

If the neutral conductor of the multiwire circuit is interrupted, it will cause the 120V television to operate at 160V and consume 1,067W of power (instead of 600W) for only a few seconds before it burns up. **Figure 300–48**

Step 1: Determine the resistance of each appliance, $R = E^2/P$.

R of the hair dryer = 120V2/1,200W
R of the hair dryer = 12 ohms

R of the television = 120V2/600W
R of the television = 24 ohms

Step 2: Determine the current of the circuit, I = E/R.

E = 240V
R = 36 ohms (12 ohms + 24 ohms)
I = 240V/36 ohms
I = 6.70A

Step 3: Determine the operating voltage for each appliance, E = I x R.

I = 6.70A
R = 12 ohms for hair dryer and 24 ohms for TV

Voltage of hair dryer = 6.70A x 12 ohms
Voltage of hair dryer = 80V

Voltage of television = 6.70A x 24 ohms
Voltage of television = 160V

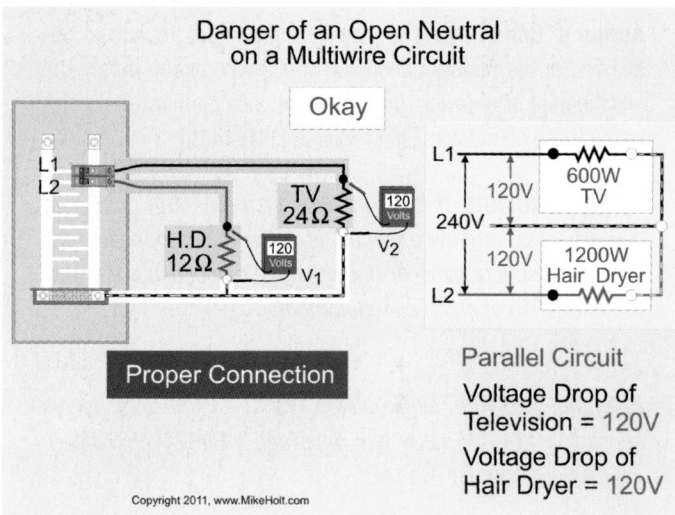

Figure 300–47

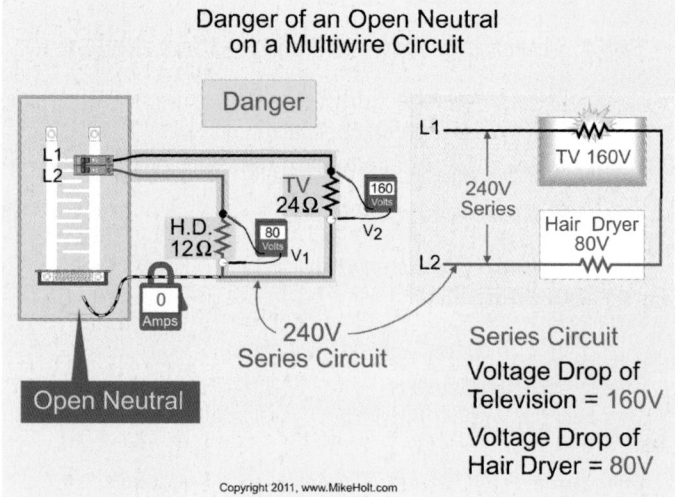

Figure 300–48

WARNING: *Failure to terminate the ungrounded conductors to separate phases can cause the neutral conductor to become overloaded, and the insulation can be damaged or destroyed by excessive heat. Conductor overheating is known to decrease the service life of insulating materials, which creates the potential for arcing faults in hidden locations, and can ultimately lead to fires. It isn't known just how long conductor insulation lasts, but heat does decrease its life span.* **Figure 300–49**

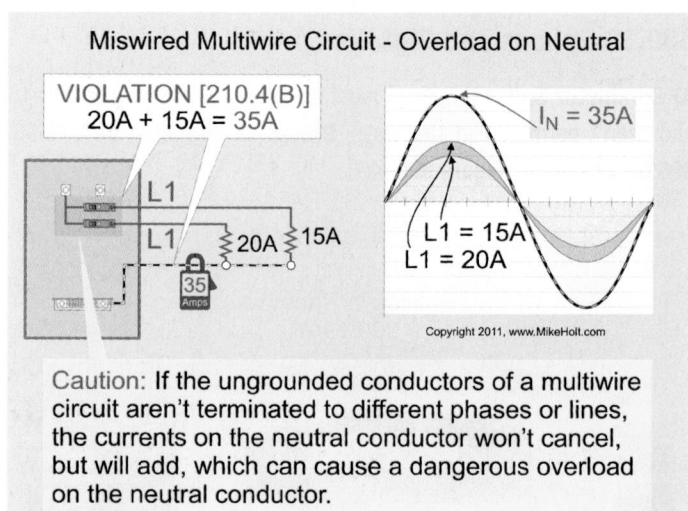

Figure 300–49

300.14 Length of Free Conductors. At least 6 in. of free conductor, measured from the point in the box where the conductors enter the enclosure, must be left at each outlet, junction, and switch point for splices or terminations of luminaires or devices. **Figure 300–50**

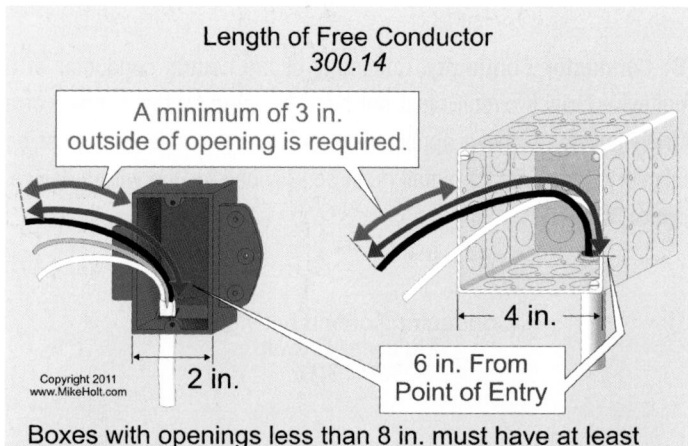

Figure 300–50

Boxes that have openings less than 8 in. in any dimension, must have at least 6 in. of free conductor, measured from the point where the conductors enter the box, and at least 3 in. of free conductor outside the box opening. **Figure 300–51**

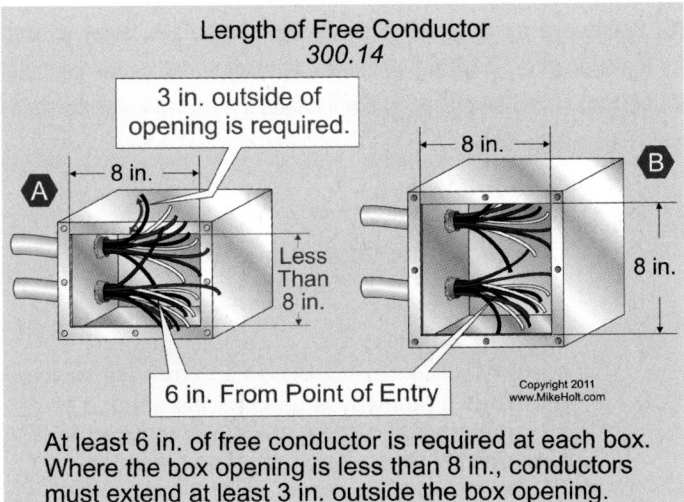

Length of Free Conductor
300.14

3 in. outside of opening is required.

8 in.

Ⓐ

Less Than 8 in.

8 in.

Ⓑ

8 in.

6 in. From Point of Entry

Copyright 2011 www.MikeHolt.com

At least 6 in. of free conductor is required at each box. Where the box opening is less than 8 in., conductors must extend at least 3 in. outside the box opening.

Figure 300–51

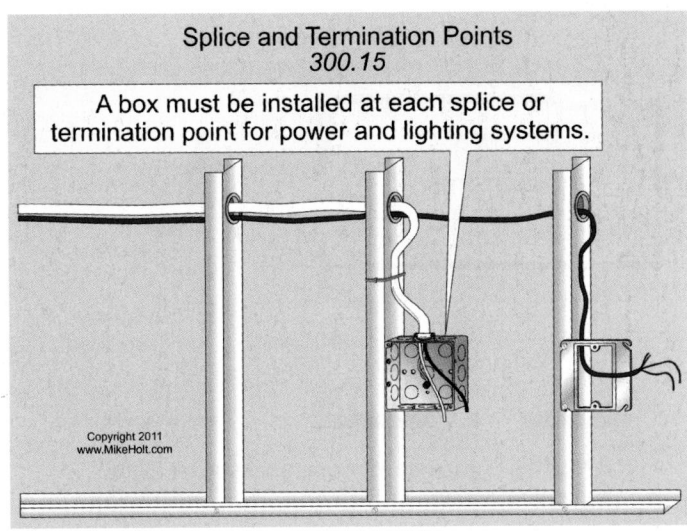

Splice and Termination Points
300.15

A box must be installed at each splice or termination point for power and lighting systems.

Copyright 2011 www.MikeHolt.com

Figure 300–52

Author's Comment: The following text was the Panels' Statement when it rejected my proposal to require the free conductor length to be unspliced in the 2008 *NEC*. "The purpose of Section 300.14 is to permit access to the end of the conductor. Whether this conductor is spliced or unspliced does not affect the length of this free end of the conductor. Many conductors originate inside the box and are spliced to other conductors within the box but extend out of the box for connection to a device of some kind. Making this change would not permit this very common application. Even the exception to this section states that unspliced or unterminated conductors do not have to comply with 300.14."

Ex: Six inches of free conductor isn't required for conductors that pass through a box without a splice or termination.

300.15 Boxes or Conduit Bodies. A box must be installed at each splice or termination point, except as permitted for: **Figure 300–52**

- Cabinet or Cutout Boxes, 312.8
- Conduit Bodies, 314.16(C) **Figure 300–53**
- Luminaires, 410.64
- Surface Raceways, 386.56 and 388.56
- Wireways, 376.56

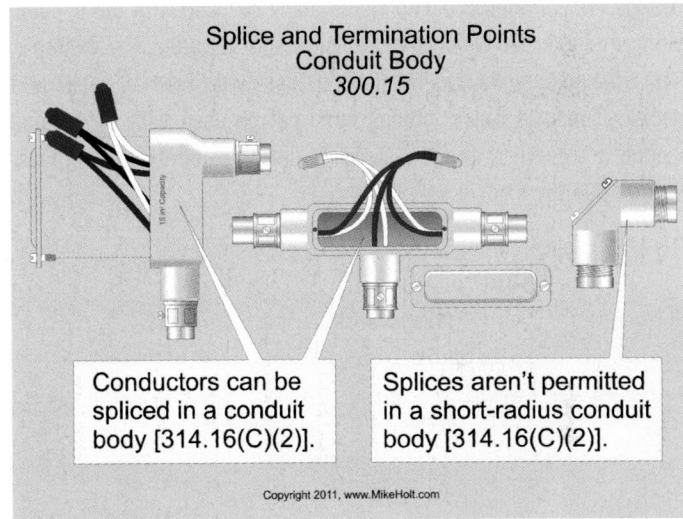

Splice and Termination Points
Conduit Body
300.15

Conductors can be spliced in a conduit body [314.16(C)(2)].

Splices aren't permitted in a short-radius conduit body [314.16(C)(2)].

Copyright 2011, www.MikeHolt.com

Figure 300–53

Author's Comment: Boxes aren't required for the following signaling and communications cables or raceways: **Figure 300–54**

- CATV, 90.3
- Class 2 and 3 Control and Signaling, 725.3
- Communications, 90.3
- Optical Fiber, 770.3

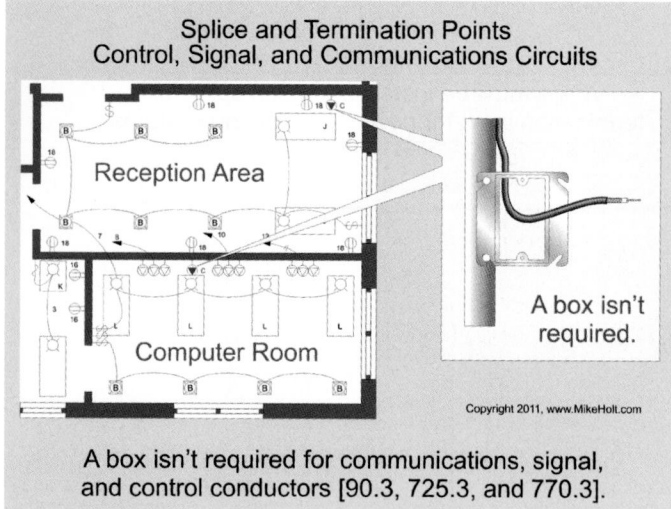

A box isn't required for communications, signal, and control conductors [90.3, 725.3, and 770.3].

Figure 300–54

Fittings and Connectors. Fittings can only be used with the specific wiring methods for which they're listed and designed. For example, Type NM cable connectors must not be used with Type AC cable, and electrical metallic tubing fittings must not be used with rigid metal conduit or intermediate metal conduit, unless listed for the purpose. **Figure 300–55**

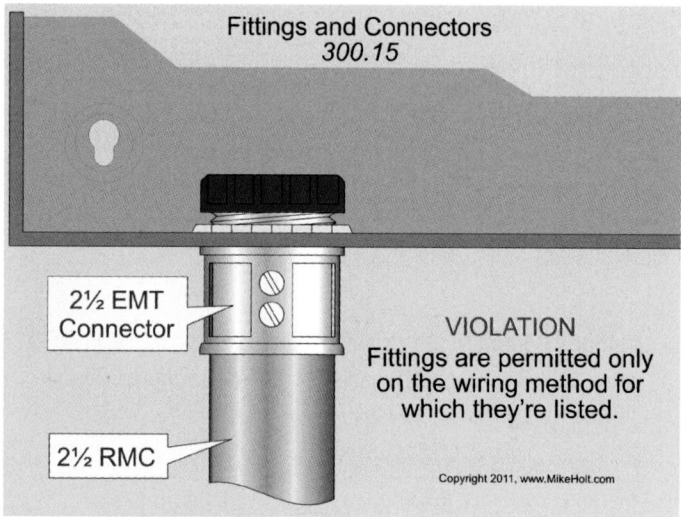

Figure 300–55

Author's Comment: PVC conduit couplings and connectors are permitted with electrical nonmetallic tubing if the proper glue is used in accordance with manufacturer's instructions [110.3(B)]. See 362.48.

(C) Raceways for Support or Protection. When a raceway is used for the support or protection of cables, a fitting to reduce the potential for abrasion must be placed at the location the cables enter the raceway. **Figure 300–56**

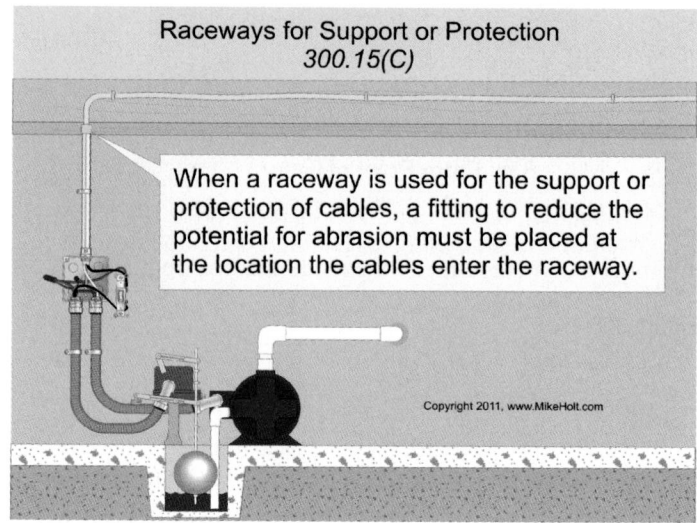

Figure 300–56

(F) Fitting. A fitting is permitted in lieu of a box or conduit body where conductors aren't spliced or terminated within the fitting if it's accessible after installation. **Figure 300–57**

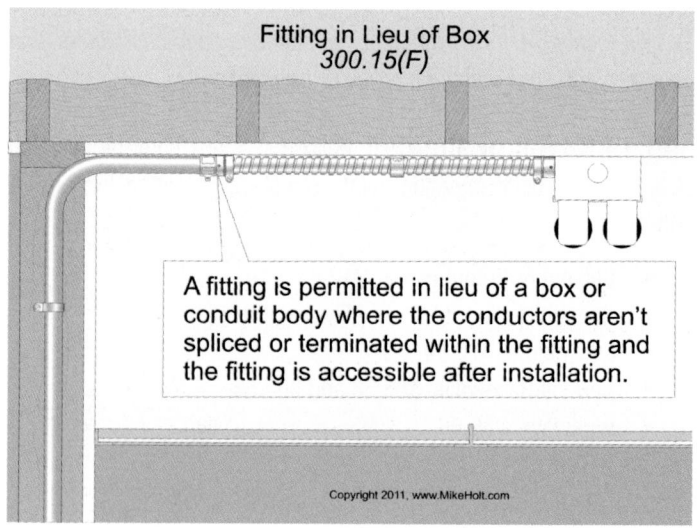

Figure 300–57

(G) Underground Splices. A box or conduit body isn't required where a splice is made underground if the conductors are spliced with a splicing device listed for direct burial. See 110.14(B) and 300.5(E).

> **Author's Comment:** See the definition of "Conduit Body" in Article 100.

(I) Enclosures. A box or conduit body isn't required where a splice is made in a cabinet or in cutout boxes containing switches or over-current devices if the splices or taps don't fill the wiring space at any cross section to more than 75 percent, and the wiring at any cross section doesn't exceed 40 percent. See 312.8 and 404.3(B). **Figure 300–58**

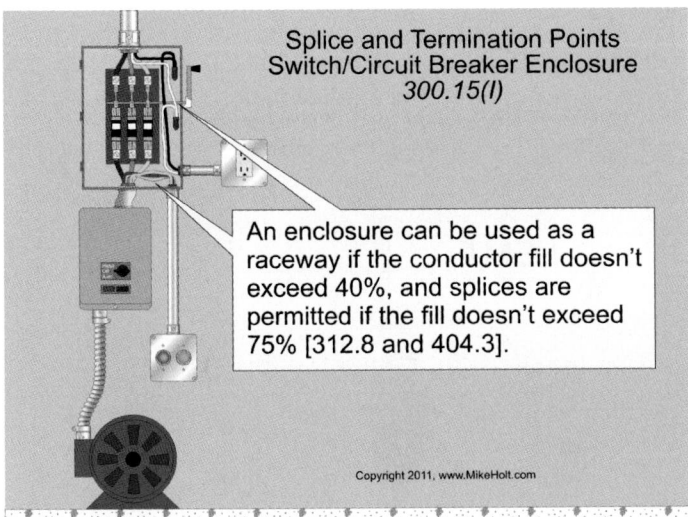

Splice and Termination Points
Switch/Circuit Breaker Enclosure
300.15(I)

An enclosure can be used as a raceway if the conductor fill doesn't exceed 40%, and splices are permitted if the fill doesn't exceed 75% [312.8 and 404.3].

Copyright 2011, www.MikeHolt.com

Figure 300–58

> **Author's Comment:** See the definitions of "Cabinet" and "Cutout Box" in Article 100.

(L) Handhole Enclosures. A box or conduit body isn't required for conductors installed in a handhole enclosure. Splices must be made in accordance with 314.30. **Figure 300–59**

> **Author's Comment:** Splices or terminations within a handhole must be accomplished by the use of fittings listed as suitable for wet locations [110.14(B) and 314.30(C)].

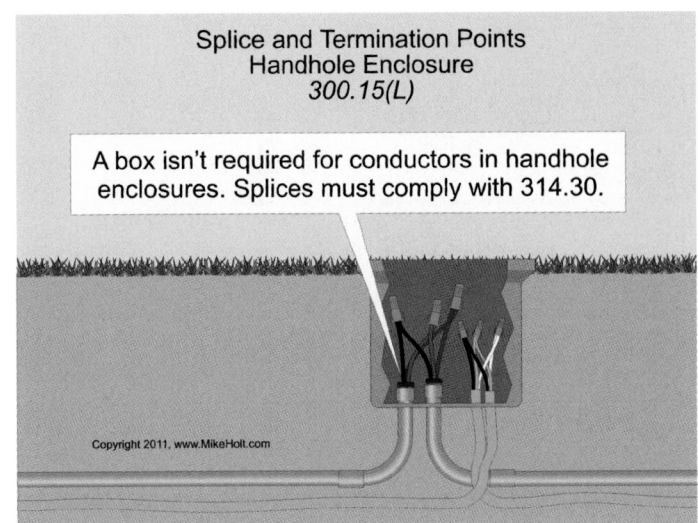

Splice and Termination Points
Handhole Enclosure
300.15(L)

A box isn't required for conductors in handhole enclosures. Splices must comply with 314.30.

Copyright 2011, www.MikeHolt.com

Figure 300–59

300.16 Raceway or Cable to Open or Concealed Wiring.

(B) Bushing. A bushing is permitted in lieu of a box or terminal where the conductors emerge from a raceway and enter or terminate at equipment such as open switchboards, unenclosed control equipment, or similar equipment.

300.17 Raceway Sizing. Raceways must be large enough to permit the installation and removal of conductors without damaging the conductor's insulation.

> **Author's Comments:**
> - When all conductors in a raceway are the same size and of the same insulation type, the number of conductors permitted can be determined by Annex C.
> - When different size conductors are installed in a raceway, conductor fill is limited to the percentages in Table 1 of Chapter 9. **Figure 300–60**

Table 1, Chapter 9	
Number	**Percent Fill**
1 Conductor	53%
2 Conductors	31%
3 or more	40%

The above percentages are based on conditions where the length of the conductor and number of raceway bends are within reasonable limits [Chapter 9, Table 1, Note 1].

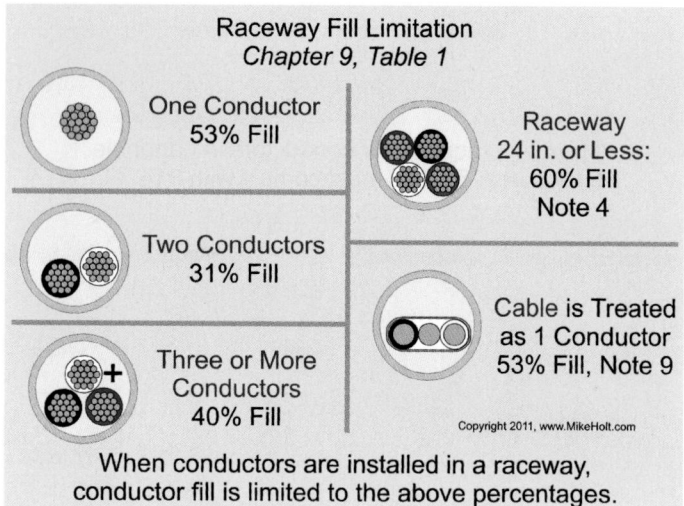

Figure 300–60

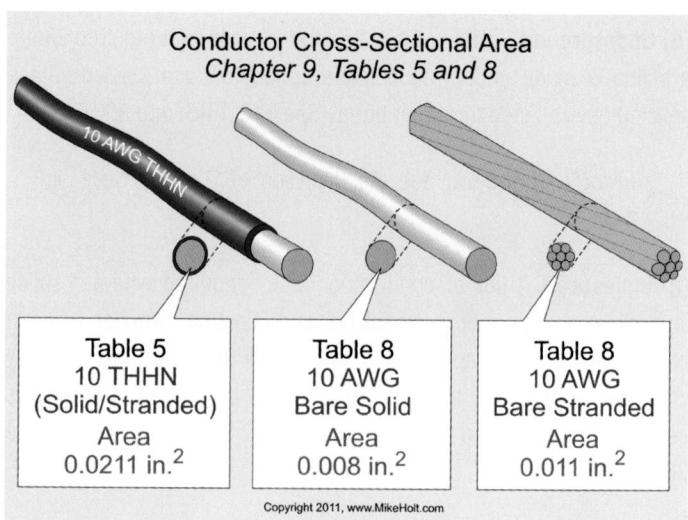

Figure 300–62

Question: *How many 12 THHN conductors can be installed in trade size ¾ electrical metallic tubing?* **Figure 300–61**

(a) 12   *(b) 13*   *(c) 14*   *(d) 16*

Answer: *(d) 16 conductors [Annex C, Table C1]*

Step 1: *When sizing a raceway, first determine the total area of conductors (Chapter 9, Table 5 for insulated conductors and Chapter 9, Table 8 for bare conductors).* **Figure 300–62**

Step 2: *Select the raceway from Chapter 9, Table 4, in accordance with the percent fill listed in Chapter 9, Table 1.* **Figure 300–63**

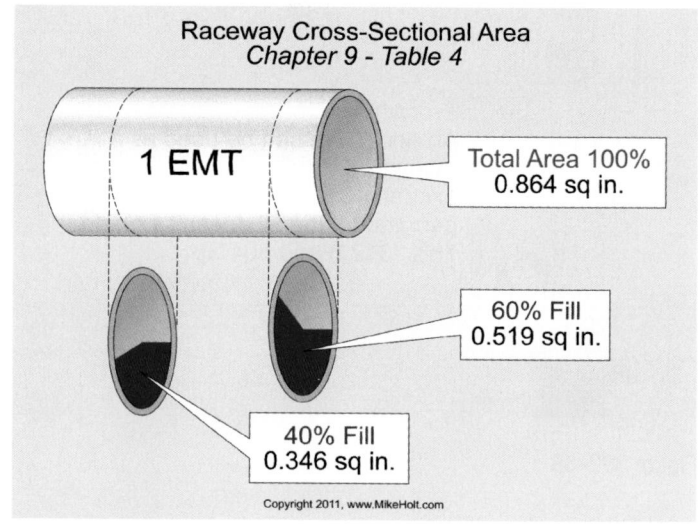

Figure 300–63

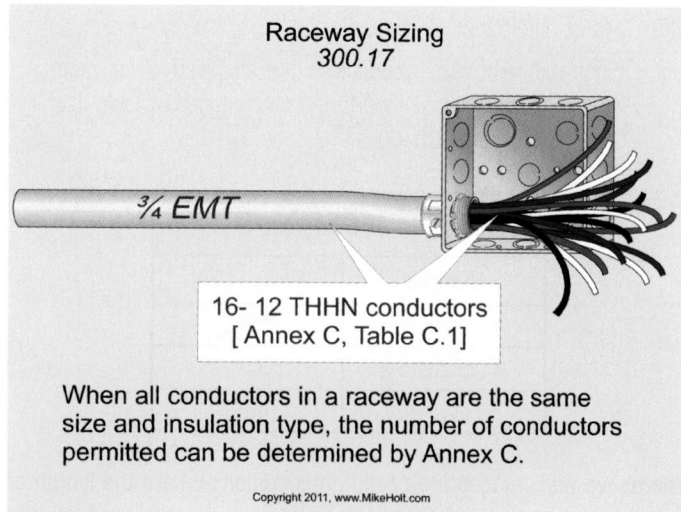

Figure 300–61

Question: *What trade size Schedule 40 PVC conduit is required for the following conductors?* **Figure 300–64**
3—500 THHN
1—250 THHN
1—3 THHN

(a) 2   *(b) 3*   *(c) 4*   *(d) 6*

Answer: *(b) 3*

continued on next page

Step 1: Determine the total area of conductors
[Chapter 9, Table 5]:

500 THHN	0.7073 x 3 =	2.1219 in.²
250 THHN	0.3970 x 1 =	0.3970 in.²
3 THHN	0.0973 x 1 =	+ 0.0973 in.²
Total Area =		2.6162 in.²

Step 2: Select the raceway at 40 percent fill
[Chapter 9, Table 4]:

Trade size 3 Schedule 40 PVC = 2.907 sq in. of conductor fill at 40%.

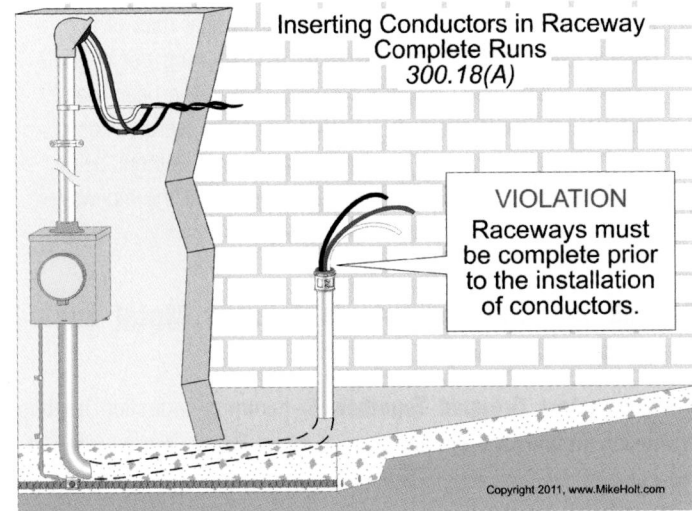

Figure 300–65

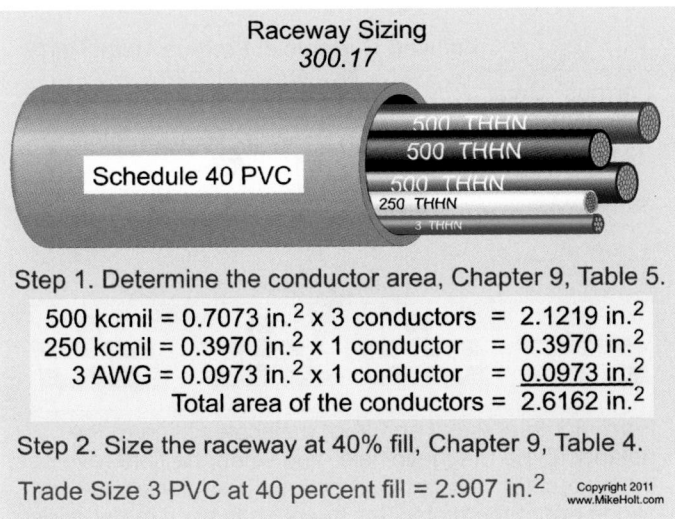

Raceway Sizing
300.17

Step 1. Determine the conductor area, Chapter 9, Table 5.

500 kcmil = 0.7073 in.² x 3 conductors = 2.1219 in.²
250 kcmil = 0.3970 in.² x 1 conductor = 0.3970 in.²
3 AWG = 0.0973 in.² x 1 conductor = 0.0973 in.²
Total area of the conductors = 2.6162 in.²

Step 2. Size the raceway at 40% fill, Chapter 9, Table 4.

Trade Size 3 PVC at 40 percent fill = 2.907 in.²   Copyright 2011 www.MikeHolt.com

Figure 300–64

300.18 Inserting Conductors in Raceways.

(A) Complete Runs. To protect conductor insulation from abrasion during installation, raceways must be mechanically completed between the pulling points before conductors are installed. See 300.10 and 300.12. **Figure 300–65**

Ex: Short sections of raceways used for the protection of cables from physical damage aren't required to be installed complete between outlet, junction, or splicing points.

(B) Welding. Metal raceways must not be supported, terminated, or connected by welding to the raceway.

300.19 Supporting Conductors in Vertical Raceways.

(A) Spacing Intervals. If the vertical rise of a raceway exceeds the values of Table 300.19(A), the conductors must be supported at the top, or as close to the top as practical. Intermediate support must also be provided in increments that don't exceed the values of Table 300.19(A). **Figure 300–66**

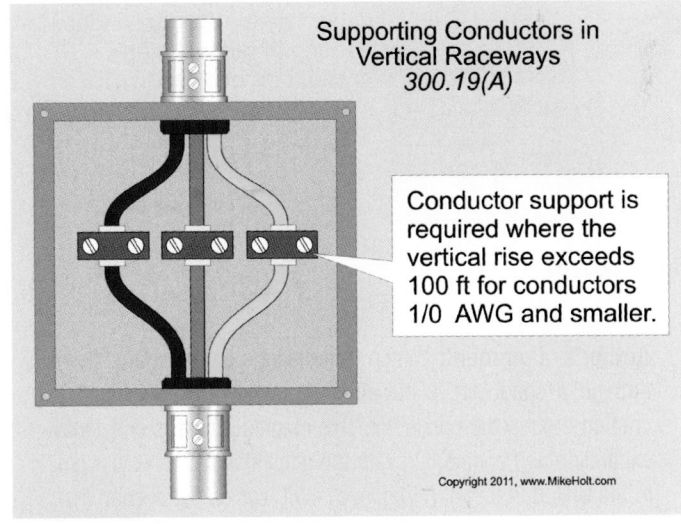

Figure 300–66

Author's Comment: The weight of long vertical runs of conductors can cause the conductors to actually drop out of the raceway if they aren't properly secured. There have been many cases where conductors in a vertical raceway were released from the pulling "basket" or "grip" (at the top) without being secured, and the conductors fell down and out of the raceway, injuring those at the bottom of the installation.

300.20 Induced Currents in Ferrous Metal Enclosures and Raceways.

(A) Conductors Grouped Together. To minimize induction heating of ferrous metal raceways and ferrous metal enclosures for alternating-current circuits, and to maintain an effective ground-fault current path, all conductors of a circuit must be installed in the same raceway, cable, trench, cord, or cable tray. See 250.102(E), 300.3(B), 300.5(I), and 392.8(D). **Figure 300–67**

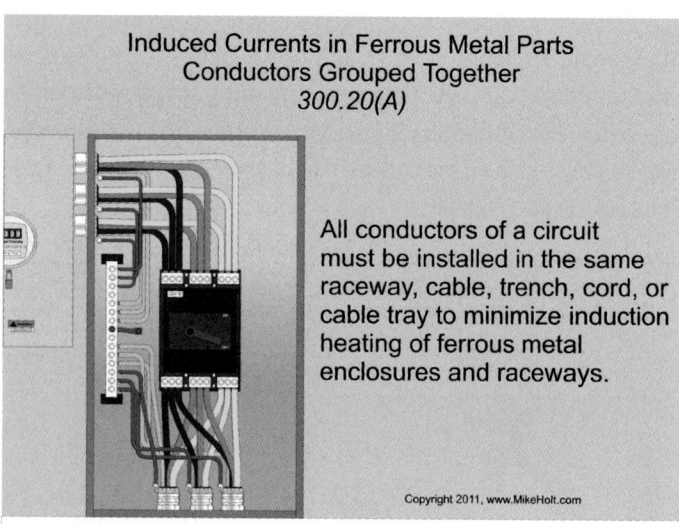

Figure 300–67

Author's Comment: When alternating current (ac) flows through a conductor, a pulsating or varying magnetic field is created around the conductor. This magnetic field is constantly expanding and contracting with the amplitude of the ac current. In the United States, the frequency is 60 cycles per second (Hz). Since ac reverses polarity 120 times per second, the magnetic field that surrounds the conductor also reverses its direction 120 times per second. This expanding and collapsing magnetic field induces eddy currents in the ferrous metal parts that surround the conductors, causing the metal parts to heat up from hysteresis heating.

Magnetic materials naturally resist the rapidly changing magnetic fields. The resulting friction produces its own additional heat—hysteresis heating—in addition to eddy current heating. A metal which offers high resistance is said to have high magnetic "permeability." Permeability can vary on a scale of 100 to 500 for magnetic materials; nonmagnetic materials have a permeability of one.

Simply put, the molecules of steel and iron align to the polarity of the magnetic field and when the magnetic field reverses, the molecules reverse their polarity as well. This back-and-forth alignment of the molecules heats up the metal, and the more the current flows, the greater the heat rises in the ferrous metal parts. **Figure 300–68**

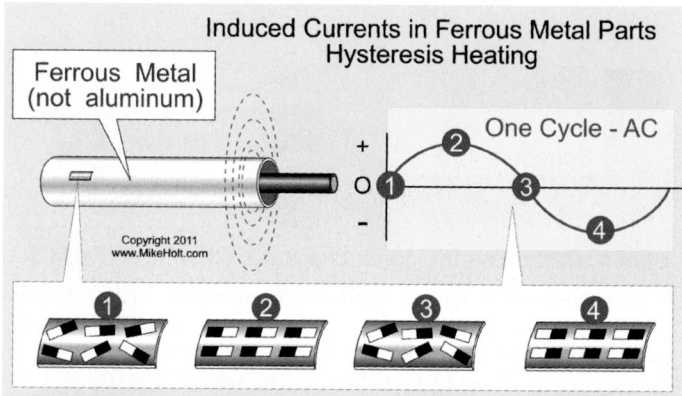

Figure 300–68

When conductors of the same circuit are grouped together, the magnetic fields of the different conductors tend to cancel each other out, resulting in a reduced magnetic field around the conductors. The lower magnetic field reduces induced currents in the ferrous metal raceways or enclosures, which reduces the hysteresis heating of the surrounding metal enclosure.

⚠ **WARNING:** There's been much discussion in the press on the effects of electromagnetic fields on humans. According to the Institute of Electrical and Electronics Engineers (IEEE), there's insufficient information at this time to define an unsafe electromagnetic field level.

(B) Single Conductors. When single conductors are installed in nonmetallic raceways as permitted in 300.5(I) Ex 2, the inductive heating of the metal enclosure must be minimized by the use of aluminum locknuts and by cutting a slot between the individual holes through which the conductors pass. **Figure 300–69**

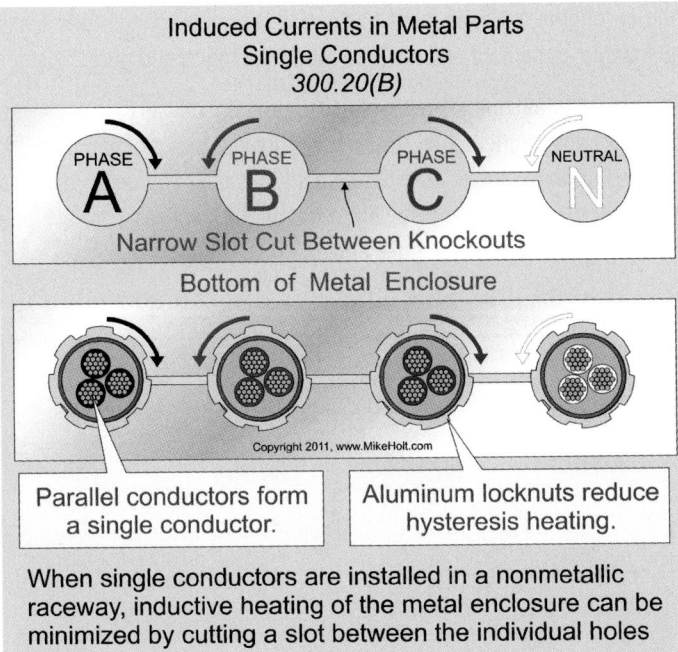

Figure 300–69

Note: Because aluminum is a nonmagnetic metal, aluminum parts don't heat up due to hysteresis heating.

Author's Comment: Aluminum conduit, locknuts, and enclosures carry eddy currents, but because aluminum is nonferrous, it doesn't heat up [300.20(B) Note].

300.21 Spread of Fire or Products of Combustion.

Electrical circuits and equipment must be installed in such a way that the spread of fire or products of combustion won't be substantially increased. Openings into or through fire-rated walls, floors, and ceilings for electrical equipment must be fire-stopped using methods approved by the authority having jurisdiction to maintain the fire-resistance rating of the fire-rated assembly. **Figure 300–70**

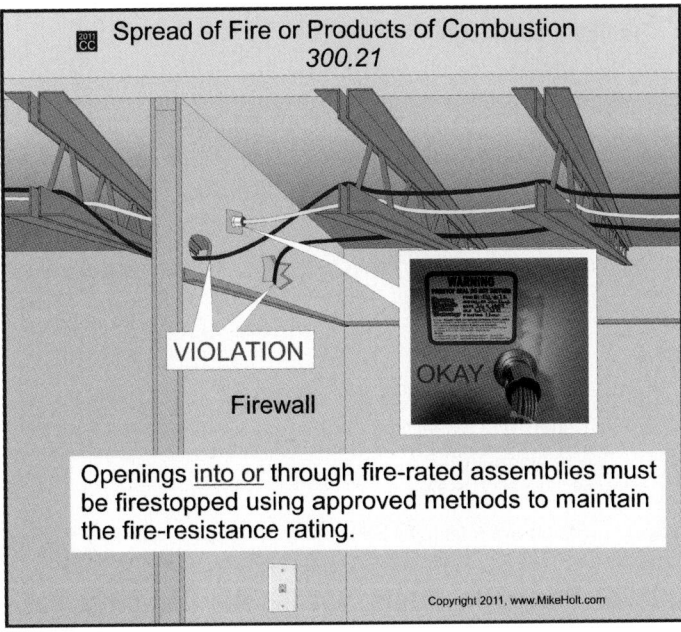

Figure 300–70

Author's Comment: Fire-stopping materials are listed for the specific types of wiring methods and the construction of the assembly that they penetrate.

Note: Directories of electrical construction materials published by qualified testing laboratories contain listing and installation restrictions necessary to maintain the fire-resistive rating of assemblies. Outlet boxes must have a horizontal separation not less than 24 in. when installed in a fire-rated assembly, unless an outlet box is listed for closer spacing or protected by fire-resistant "putty pads" in accordance with manufacturer's instructions. **Figure 300–71**

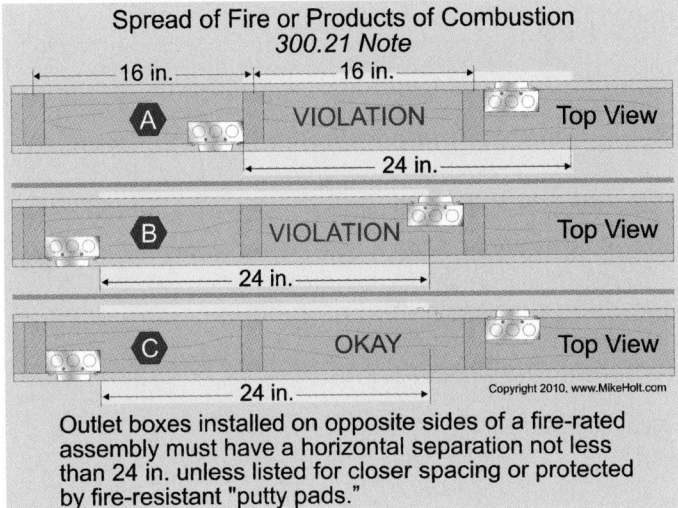

Figure 300–71

Author's Comments:

- Boxes installed in fire-resistance-rated assemblies must be listed for the purpose. If steel boxes are used, they must be secured to the framing member, so cut-in type boxes aren't permitted (UL White Book, *Guide Information for Electrical Equipment,* www.ul.com/regulators/2008_WhiteBook.pdf).

- This rule also applies to control, signaling, and communications cables or raceways.

  - CATV, 820.26
  - Communications, 800.26
  - Control and Signaling, 725.25
  - Fire Alarm, 760.3(A)
  - Optical Fiber, 770.26
  - Sound Systems, 640.3(A)

300.22 Wiring in Ducts Not for Air Handling, Fabricated Ducts for Environmental Air, and Other Spaces For Environmental Air (Plenums).

The provisions of this section apply to the installation and uses of electrical wiring and equipment in ducts used for dust, loose stock, or vapor removal; ducts specifically fabricated for environmental air, and spaces used for environmental air (plenums).

(A) Ducts Used for Dust, Loose Stock, or Vapor. Ducts that transport dust, loose stock, or vapors must not have any wiring method installed within them. **Figure 300–72**

Ducts Used for Dust, Loose Stock, or Vapor
300.22(A)

Ducts that transport dust, loose stock, or vapors must not have any wiring method installed within them.

SAFETY FIRST — EYE PROTECTION REQUIRED

DANGER — NO SMOKING, MATCHES OR OPEN LIGHTS

Copyright 2011, www.MikeHolt.com

Figure 300–72

(B) Ducts Specifically Fabricated for Environmental Air. If necessary for direct action upon, or sensing of, the contained air, Type MC cable that has a smooth or corrugated impervious metal sheath without an overall nonmetallic covering, electrical metallic tubing, flexible metallic tubing, intermediate metal conduit, or rigid metal conduit without an overall nonmetallic covering can be installed in ducts specifically fabricated to transport environmental air. Flexible metal conduit in lengths not exceeding 4 ft can be used to connect physically adjustable equipment and devices within the fabricated duct.

Equipment is only permitted within the duct specifically fabricated to transport environmental air if necessary for the direct action upon, or sensing of, the contained air. Equipment, devices, and/or illumination are only permitted to be installed in the duct if necessary to facilitate maintenance and repair. **Figure 300–73**

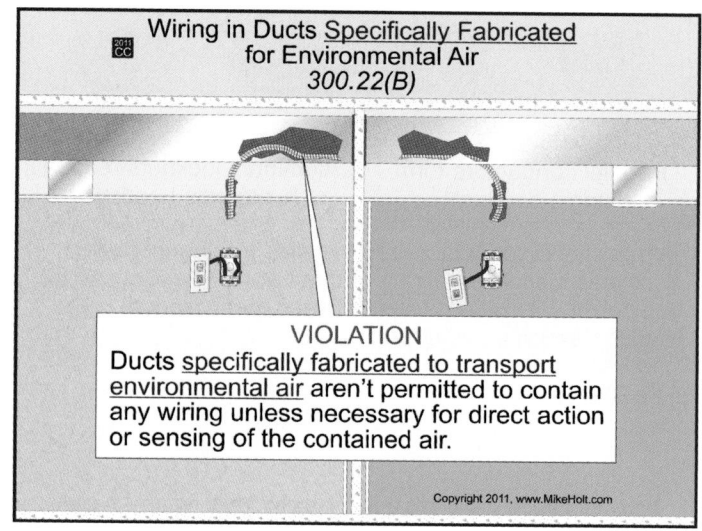

Wiring in Ducts Specifically Fabricated for Environmental Air
300.22(B)

VIOLATION
Ducts specifically fabricated to transport environmental air aren't permitted to contain any wiring unless necessary for direct action or sensing of the contained air.

Copyright 2011, www.MikeHolt.com

Figure 300–73

(C) Other Spaces Used for Environmental Air (Plenums). This section applies to spaces used for air-handling purposes, but not fabricated for environmental air-handling purposes. This requirement doesn't apply to habitable rooms or areas of buildings, the prime purpose of which isn't air handling.

> **Note 1:** The spaces above a suspended ceiling or below a raised floor used for environmental air are examples of the type of space to which this section applies. **Figure 300–74**

> **Note 2:** The phrase "other space used for environmental air (plenum)" correlates with the term "plenum" in NFPA 90A, *Standard for the Installation of Air-Conditioning and Ventilating Systems*, and other mechanical codes where the ceiling cavity plenum is used for return air purposes, as well as some other air-handling spaces.

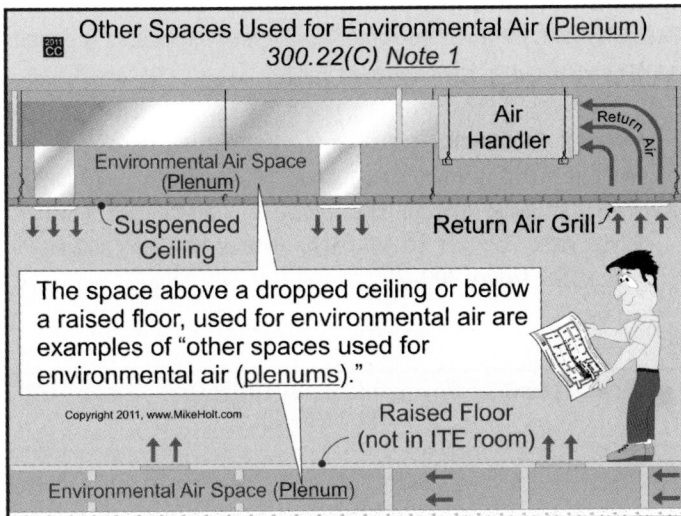

Figure 300–74

Author's Comment: For the purpose of this book, when the *NEC* references "other space used for environmental air (plenum)," the term cavity plenum space' will be used.

(1) Wiring Methods. Electrical metallic tubing, rigid metal conduit, intermediate metal conduit, armored cable, metal-clad cable without a nonmetallic cover, and flexible metal conduit can be installed in cavity plenum space. If accessible, surface metal raceways or metal wireways with metal <u>covers</u> can be installed in cavity plenum space. **Figure 300–75**

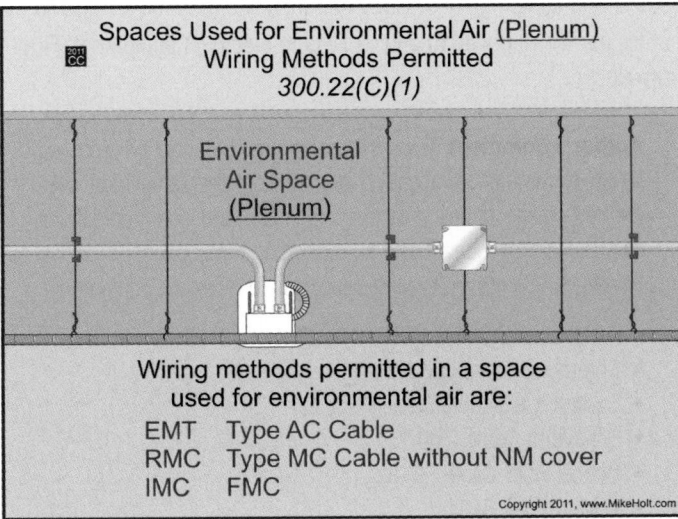

Figure 300–75

Author's Comments:

- PVC conduit [Article 352], electrical nonmetallic tubing [Article 362], liquidtight flexible conduit, and nonmetallic cables aren't permitted to be installed in spaces used for environmental air because they give off deadly toxic fumes when burned or superheated.

- Plenum-rated control, signaling, and communications cables and raceways are permitted in cavity plenum space: **Figure 300–76**

  - CATV, 820.179(A)
  - Communications, 800.21
  - Control and Signaling, 725.154(A)
  - Fire Alarm, 760.7
  - Optical Fiber Cables and Raceways, 770.113(C)
  - Sound Systems, 640.9(C) and 725.154(A)

- Any wiring method suitable for the condition can be used in a space not used for environmental air-handling purposes. **Figure 300–77**

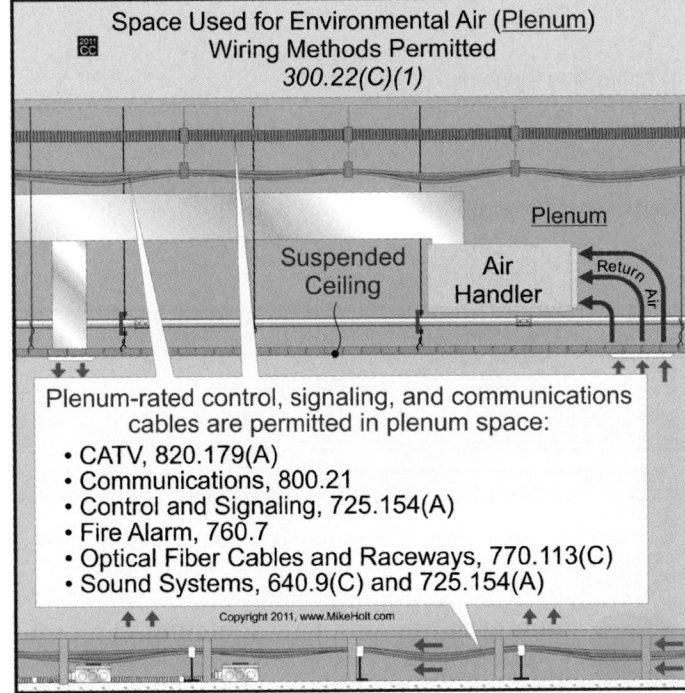

Figure 300–76

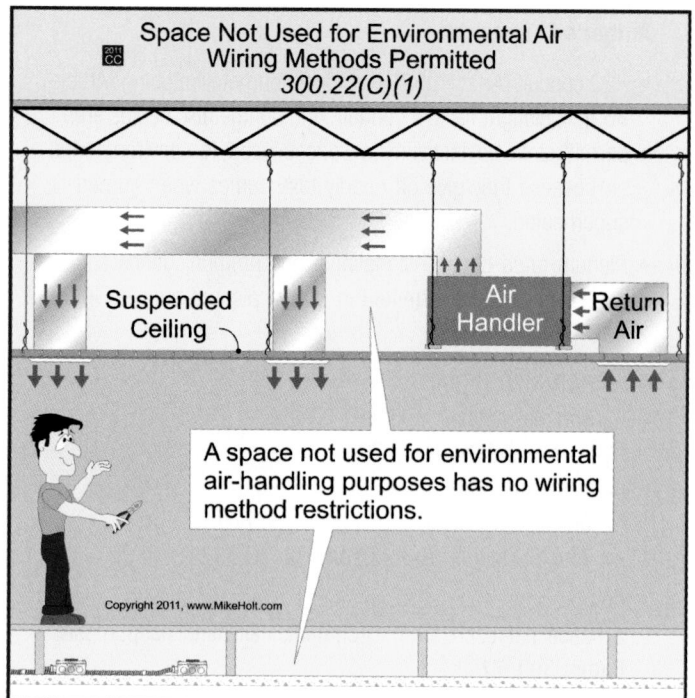

Figure 300–77

(2) Cable Tray Systems.

(a) Metal Cable Tray Systems. Metal cable tray systems can be installed to support the wiring methods and equipment permitted by this section. **Figure 300–78**

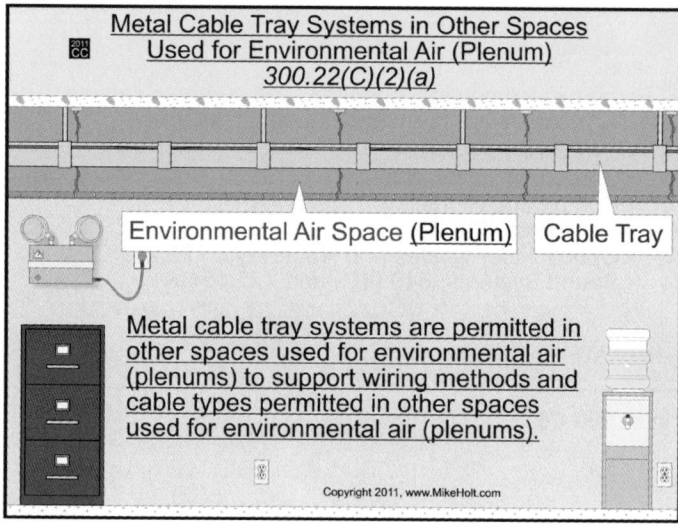

Figure 300–78

(3) Equipment. Electrical equipment with metal enclosures is permitted to be installed in cavity plenum space.

Author's Comment: Examples of electrical equipment permitted in cavity plenum space would be air-handlers, junction boxes, dry-type transformers; however transformers must not be rated not over 50 kVA when located in hollow spaces [450.13(B)]. **Figure 300–79**

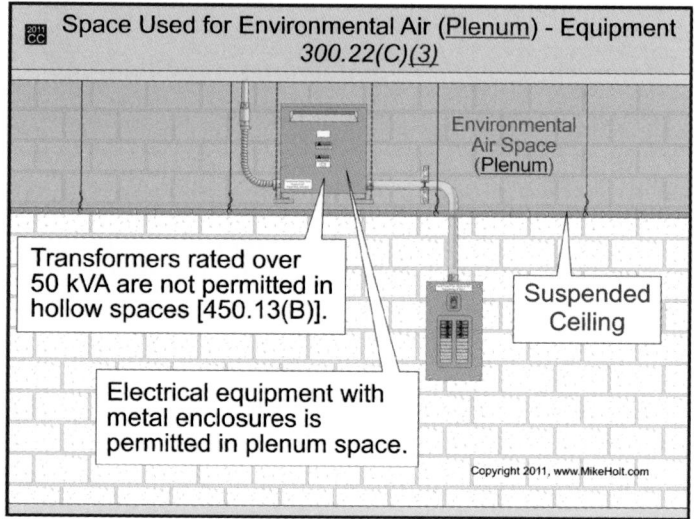

Figure 300–79

300.23 Panels Designed to Allow Access. Wiring, cables, and equipment installed behind panels must be located so the panels can be removed to give access to electrical equipment. **Figure 300–80**

Author's Comment: Access to equipment must not be hindered by an accumulation of cables that prevent the removal of suspended-ceiling panels. Control, signaling, and communications cables must be located and supported so the suspended-ceiling panels can be moved to provide access to electrical equipment.

- CATV Coaxial Cable, 820.21
- Communications Cable, 800.21
- Control & Signaling Cable, 725.21
- Fire Alarm Cable, 760.7
- Optical Fiber Cable, 770.21
- Audio Cable, 640.5

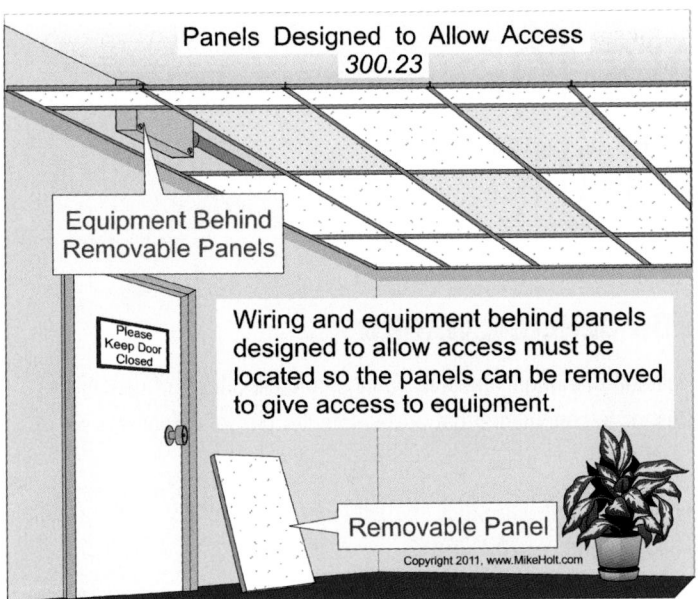

Figure 300–80

INTRODUCTION TO ARTICLE 310—CONDUCTORS FOR GENERAL WIRING

This article contains the general requirements for conductors, such as insulation markings, ampacity ratings, and conditions of use. Article 310 doesn't apply to conductors that are part of flexible cords, fixture wires, or to conductors that are an integral part of equipment [90.7 and 300.1(B)].

People often make errors in applying the ampacity tables contained in Article 310. If you study the explanations carefully, you'll avoid common errors such as applying Table 310.15(B)(17) when you should be applying Table 310.15(B)(16).

Why so many tables? Why does Table 310.15(B)(17) list the ampacity of 6 THHN as 105 amperes, yet Table 310.15(B)(16) lists the same conductor as having an ampacity of only 75 amperes? To answer that, go back to Article 100 and review the definition of ampacity. Notice the phrase "conditions of use." These tables set a maximum current value at which premature failure of the conductor insulation shouldn't occur during normal use, under the conditions described in the tables.

The designations THHN, THHW, RHH, and so on, are insulation types. Every type of insulation has a limit to how much heat it can withstand. When current flows through a conductor, it creates heat. How well the insulation around a conductor can dissipate that heat depends on factors such as whether that conductor is in free air or not. Think about what happens when you put on a sweater, a jacket, and then a coat—all at the same time. You heat up. Your skin can't dissipate heat with all that clothing on nearly as well as it dissipates heat in free air. The same principal applies to conductors.

Conductor insulation also fails with age. That's why we conduct cable testing and take other measures to predict failure and replace certain conductors (for example, feeders or critical equipment conductors) while they're still within design specifications. But conductor insulation failure takes decades under normal use—and it's a maintenance issue. However, if a conductor is forced to exceed the ampacity listed in the appropriate table, and as a result its design temperature is exceeded, insulation failure happens much more rapidly—often catastrophically. Consequently, exceeding the allowable ampacity of a conductor is a serious safety issue.

PART I. GENERAL

310.1 Scope. Article 310 contains the general requirements for conductors, such as insulation markings, ampacity ratings, and their use. This article doesn't apply to conductors that are an integral part of equipment [90.7 and 300.1(B)].

PART II. INSTALLATION

310.10 Uses Permitted. Conductors described in 310.104 can be used in any of the wiring methods recognized in Chapter 3 as permitted in this Code [110.8].

(B) Dry and Damp Locations. Insulated conductors typically used in dry and damp locations include THHN, THHW, THWN, or THWN-2.

> **Author's Comment:** Refer to Table 310.104 for a complete list of conductors that may be installed in dry or damp locations.

(C) Wet Locations. Insulated conductors typically used in wet locations include:

(2) Types THHW, THWN, THWN-2, XHHW, or XHHW-2

> **Author's Comment:** Refer to Table 310.104 for a complete list of conductors that may be installed in wet locations.

(D) Locations Exposed to Direct Sunlight. Insulated conductors and cables exposed to the direct rays of the sun must be:

(1) Listed as sunlight resistant or marked as being sunlight resistant. Figure 310–1

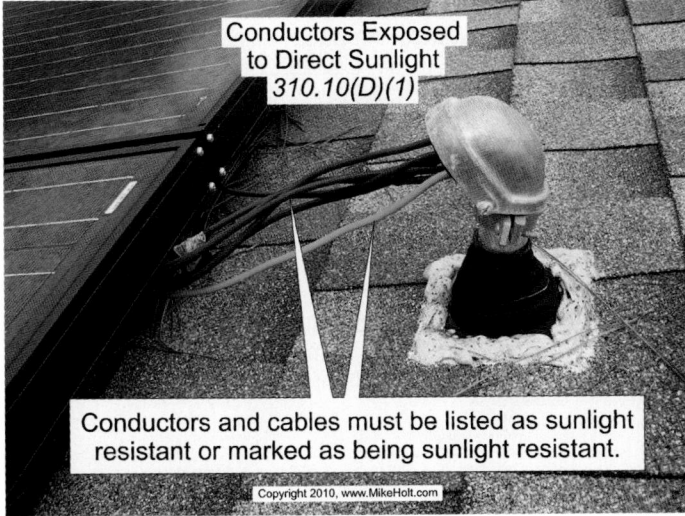

Figure 310–1

> **Author's Comment:** SE cable and the conductors contained in the cable are listed as sunlight resistant. However, according to the UL listing standard, the conductors contained in SE cable aren't required to be marked as sunlight resistant.

(2) Covered with insulating material, such as tape or sleeving materials that are listed as being sunlight resistant or marked as being sunlight resistant.

(G) Corrosive Conditions. Conductor insulation must be suitable for any substance to which it may be exposed that may have a detrimental effect on the conductor's insulation, such as oil, grease, vapor, gases, fumes, liquids, or other substances. See 110.11.

(H) Conductors in Parallel.

(1) General. Ungrounded and neutral conductors can be connected in parallel, only in sizes 1/0 AWG and larger.

(2) Conductor Characteristics. When circuit conductors are installed in parallel, the conductors must be connected so that the current will be evenly distributed between the individual parallel conductors by requiring all circuit conductors within each parallel set to: Figure 310–2

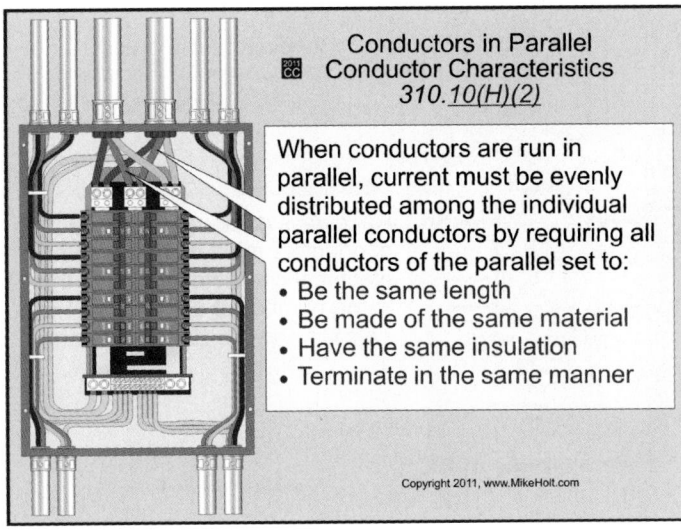

Figure 310–2

(1) Be the same length.

(2) Consist of the same conductor material (copper/aluminum).

(3) Be the same size in circular mil area (minimum 1/0 AWG).

(4) Have the same type of insulation (like THHN).

(5) Terminate in the same method (set screw versus compression).

> **Author's Comment:** Conductors aren't required to have the same physical characteristics as those of another ungrounded or neutral conductor to achieve balance.

(3) Separate Raceways or Cables. Raceways or cables containing parallel conductors must have the same electrical characteristics and the same number of conductors. Figure 310–3

> **Author's Comment:** If one set of parallel conductors is installed in a metallic raceway and the other conductors are installed in PVC conduit, the conductors in the metallic raceway will have an increased opposition to current flow (impedance) as compared to the conductors in the nonmetallic raceway. This results in an unbalanced distribution of current between the parallel conductors.

Parallel sets of conductors aren't required to have the same physical characteristics as those of another set to achieve balance.

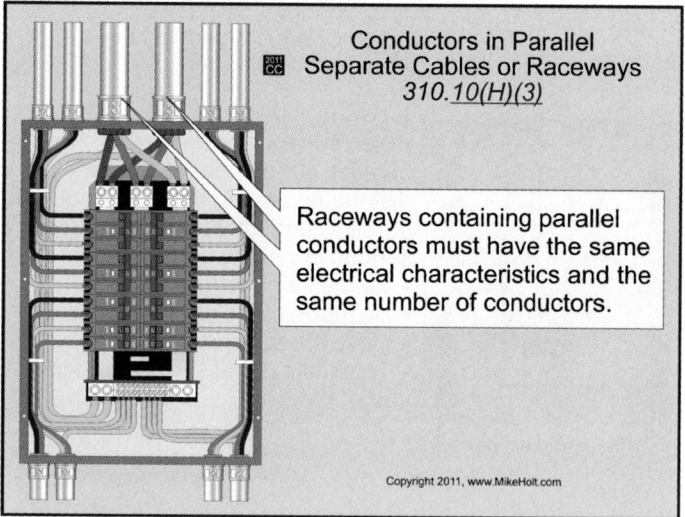

Figure 310–3

Author's Comment: For example, a 400A feeder with a neutral load of 240A can be paralleled as follows: **Figure 310–4**

- Phase A, Two—250 kcmil THHN aluminum, 100 ft
- Phase B, Two—3/0 THHN copper, 104 ft
- Phase C, Two—3/0 THHN copper, 102 ft
- Neutral, Two—1/0 THHN aluminum, 103 ft
- Equipment Grounding Conductor, Two—3 AWG copper, 101 ft*

The minimum 1/0 AWG requirement doesn't apply to equipment grounding conductors [310.10(H)(5)].

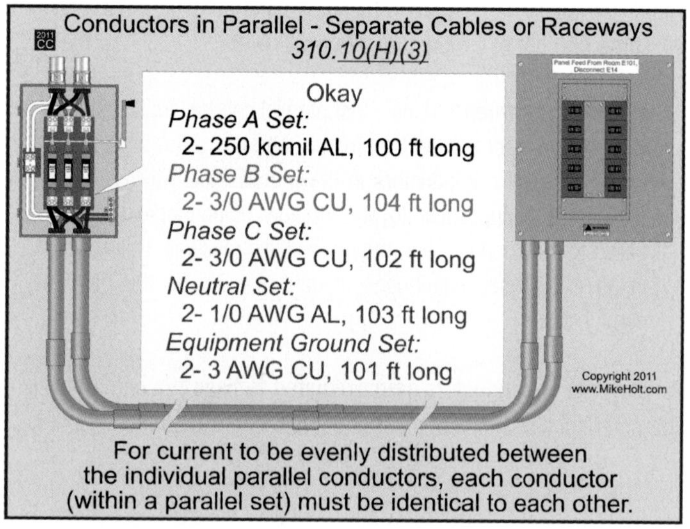

(4) Conductor Ampacity Adjustment. Each current-carrying conductor of a paralleled set of conductors must be counted as a current-carrying conductor for the purpose of conductor ampacity adjustment, in accordance with Table 310.15(B)(3)(a). **Figure 310–5**

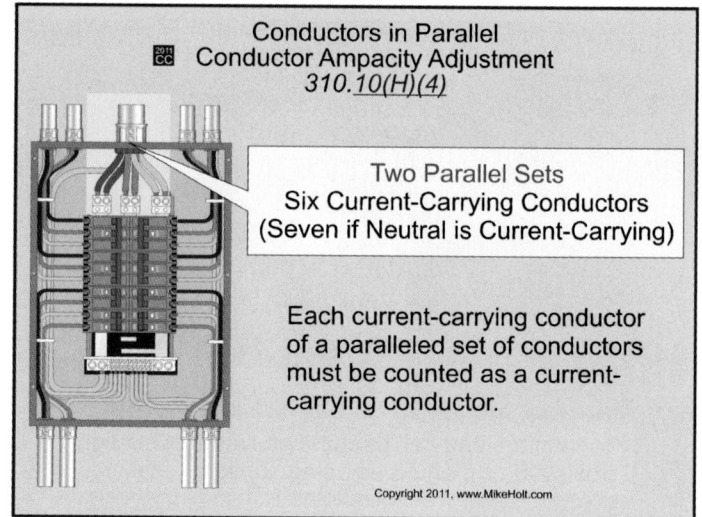

Figure 310–5

(5) Equipment Grounding Conductors. The equipment grounding conductors for circuits in parallel must be sized in accordance with 250.122(F). **Figure 310–6**

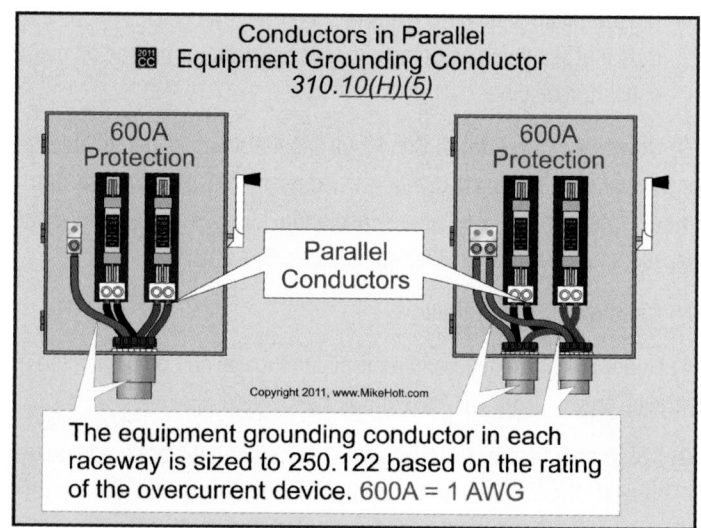

Figure 310–6

Figure 310–4

Author's Comment: The minimum 1/0 AWG parallel conductor size rule of 310.10(H) doesn't apply to equipment grounding conductors.

(6) Equipment Bonding Jumpers. Equipment bonding jumpers are sized in accordance with 250.102.

Author's Comment: The equipment bonding jumper isn't required to be larger than the largest ungrounded circuit conductors supplying the equipment.

310.15 Conductor Ampacity.

Author's Comment: According to Article 100, ampacity means the <u>maximum</u> current, in amperes, a conductor can carry continuously, where the temperature of the conductor won't be raised in excess of its insulation temperature rating. **Figure 310–7**

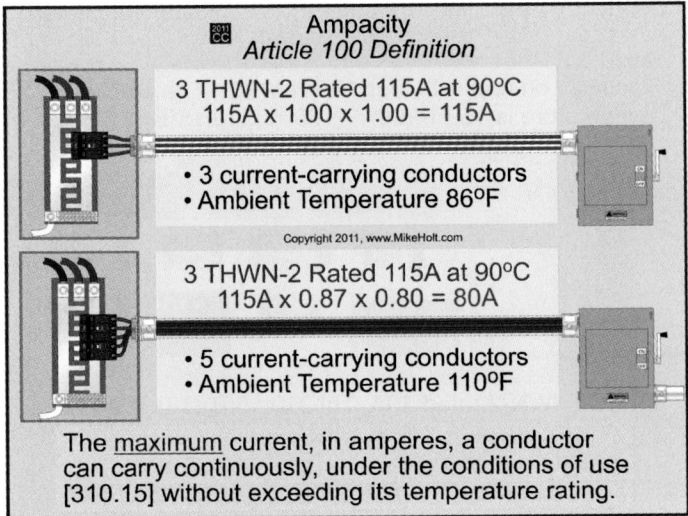

Figure 310–7

(A) General Requirements.

(1) Tables for Engineering Supervision. The ampacity of a conductor can be determined either by using the tables in accordance with 310.15(B), or under engineering supervision as provided in 310.15(C).

Note 1: Ampacities provided by this section don't take voltage drop into consideration. See 210.19(A) Note 4, for branch circuits and 215.2(D) Note 2, for feeders.

(2) Conductor Ampacity—Lower Rating. Where more than <u>one ampacity applies</u> for a given circuit length, the lowest value must be used. **Figure 310–8**

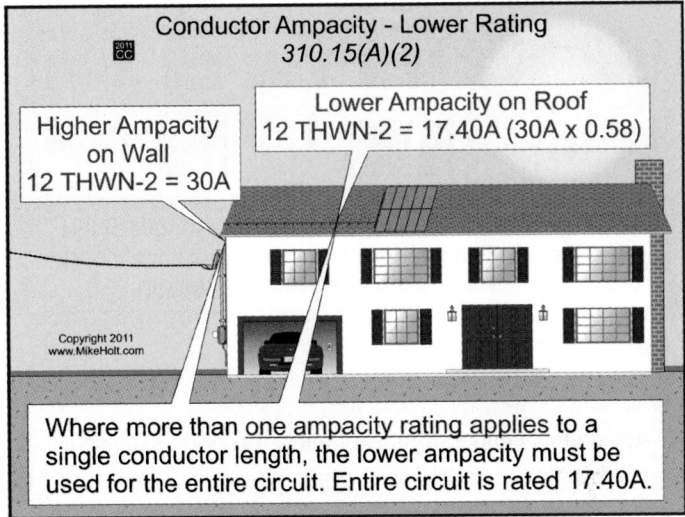

Figure 310–8

Ex: When different ampacities apply to a length of conductor, the higher ampacity is permitted for the entire circuit if the reduced ampacity length doesn't exceed 10 ft and its length doesn't exceed 10 percent of the length of the higher ampacity. **Figures 310–9 and 310–10**

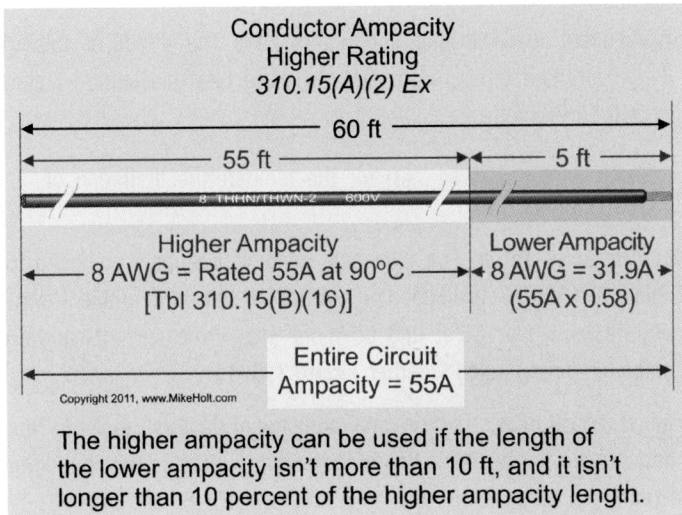

Figure 310–9

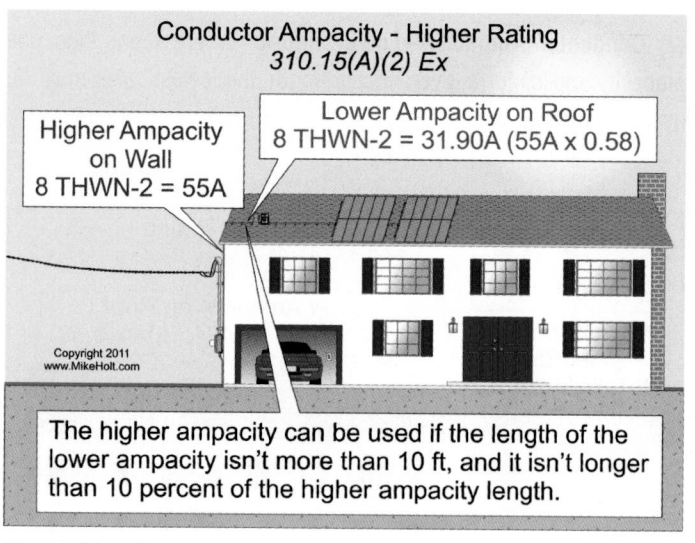

Figure 310–10

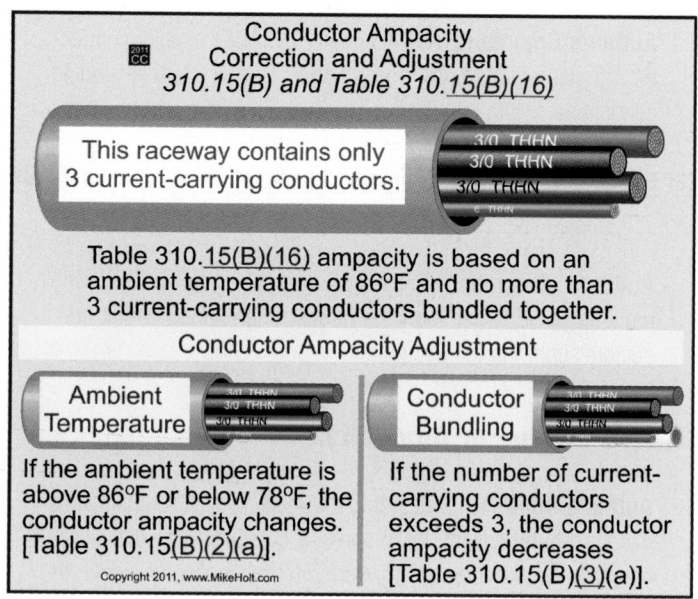

Figure 310–11

(3) Insulation Temperature Limitation. Conductors must not be used where the operating temperature exceeds that designated for the type of insulated conductor involved.

Note 1: The insulation temperature rating of a conductor [Table 310.104(A)] is the maximum temperature a conductor can withstand over a prolonged time period without serious degradation. The main factors to consider for conductor operating temperature include:

(1) Ambient temperature may vary along the conductor length as well as from time to time [Table 310.15(B)(2)(a)].

(2) Heat generated internally in the conductor—load current flow.

(3) The rate at which generated heat dissipates into the ambient medium.

(4) Adjacent load-carrying conductors have the effect of raising the ambient temperature and impeding heat dissipation [Table 310.15(B)(3)(a)].

Note 2: See 110.14(C)(1) for the temperature limitation of terminations.

(B) Ampacity Table. The allowable conductor ampacities listed in Table 310.15(B)(16) are based on conditions where the ambient temperature isn't over 86°F, and no more than three current-carrying conductors are bundled together. **Figure 310–11**

The temperature correction and adjustment factors apply to the conductor ampacity, based on the temperature rating of the conductor insulation in accordance with Table 310.15(B)(16). **Figure 310–12**

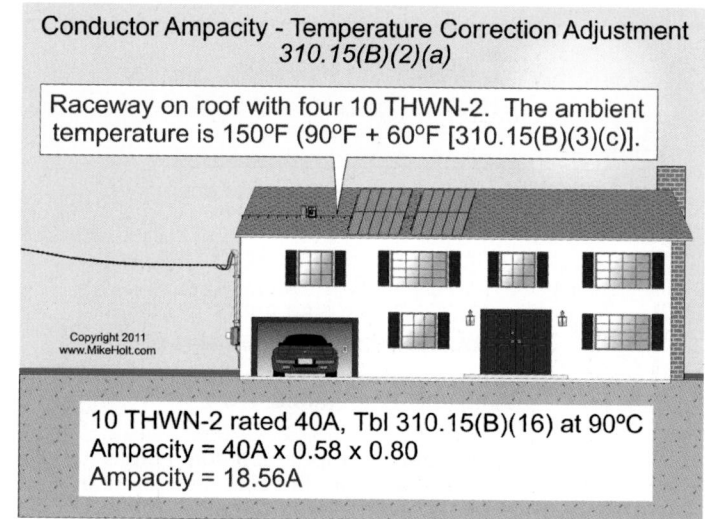

Figure 310–12

(2) Conductor Ampacity Ambient Temperature Correction. When conductors are installed in an ambient temperature other than 78°F to 86°F, the ampacities listed in Table 310.15(B)(16) must be corrected in accordance with the multipliers listed in Table 310.15(B)(2) (a). **Figure 310–13**

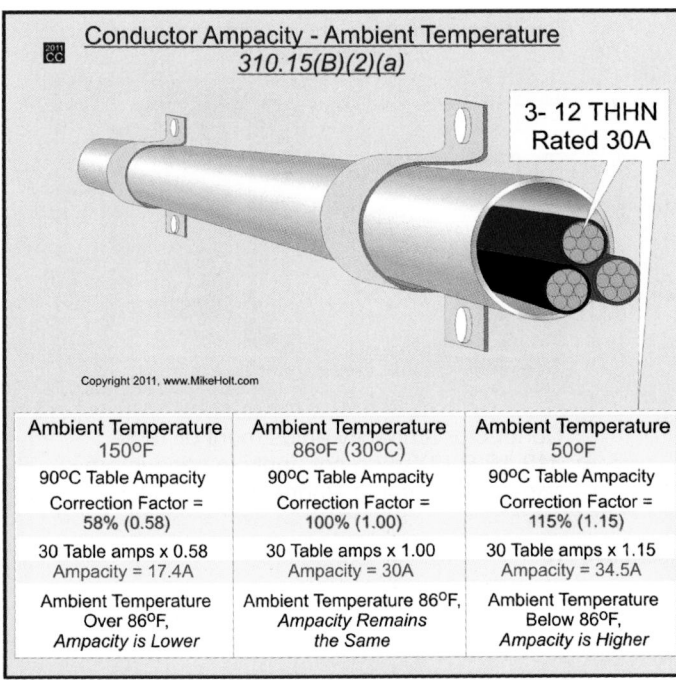

Conductor Ampacity - Ambient Temperature
310.15(B)(2)(a)

3- 12 THHN
Rated 30A

Copyright 2011, www.MikeHolt.com

Ambient Temperature 150ºF	Ambient Temperature 86ºF (30ºC)	Ambient Temperature 50ºF
90ºC Table Ampacity Correction Factor = 58% (0.58)	90ºC Table Ampacity Correction Factor = 100% (1.00)	90ºC Table Ampacity Correction Factor = 115% (1.15)
30 Table amps x 0.58 Ampacity = 17.4A	30 Table amps x 1.00 Ampacity = 30A	30 Table amps x 1.15 Ampacity = 34.5A
Ambient Temperature Over 86ºF, Ampacity is Lower	Ambient Temperature 86ºF, Ampacity Remains the Same	Ambient Temperature Below 86ºF, Ampacity is Higher

Figure 310–13

Table 310.15(B)(2)(a) Ambient Temperature Correction

Ambient Temperature °F	Ambient Temperature °C	Correction Factor 75°C Conductors	Correction Factor 90°C Conductors
50 or less	10 or less	1.20	1.15
51–59°F	11–15°C	1.15	1.12
60–68°F	16–20°C	1.11	1.08
69–77°F	21–25°C	1.05	1.04
78–86°F	26–30°C	1.00	1.00
87–95°F	31–35°C	0.94	0.96
96–104°F	36–40°C	0.88	0.91
105–113°F	41–45°C	0.82	0.87
114–122°F	46–50°C	0.75	0.82
123–131°F	51–55°C	0.67	0.76
132–140°F	56–60°C	0.58	0.71
141–149°F	61–65°C	0.47	0.65
150–158°F	66–70°C	0.33	0.58
159–167°F	71–75°C	0.00	0.50
168–176°F	76–80°C	0.00	0.41
177–185°F	81–85°C	0.00	0.29

Question: *What's the corrected ampacity of 3/0 THHN/THWN conductors in a dry location if the ambient temperature is 108°F?*

(a) 173A   (b) 196A   (c) 213A   (d) 241A

Answer: *(b) 196A*

Conductor Ampacity [90°C] = 225A
Correction Factor [Table 310.(B)(2)(a)] = 0.87
Corrected Ampacity = 225A x 0.87
Corrected Ampacity = 196A

Question: *What's the corrected ampacity of 3/0 THHN/THWN conductors in a wet location if the ambient temperature is 108°F?*

(a) 164A   (b) 196A   (c) 213A   (d) 241A

Answer: *(a) 164A*

Conductor Ampacity [75°C] = 200A
Correction Factor [Table 310.(B)(2)(a)] = 0.82
Corrected Ampacity = 200A x 0.82
Corrected Ampacity = 164A

(3) Conductor Ampacity Adjustment.

(a) Four or More Current-Carrying Conductors in a Raceway or Cable. Where four or more current-carrying power conductors are in a raceway longer than 24 in. [310.15(B)(3)(a)(3)], or where cables are bundled for a length longer than 24 in., the ampacity of each conductor must be reduced in accordance with Table 310.15(B)(3)(a).

Table 310.15(B)(3)(a) Conductor Ampacity Adjustment for More Than Three Current-Carrying Conductors in a Raceway or Cable

Number of Conductors[1]	Adjustment
4–6	0.80 or 80%
7–9	0.70 or 70%
10–20	0.50 or 50%
21–30	0.45 or 50%
31–40	0.40 or 40%
41 and above	0.35 or 35%

[1]Number of conductors is the total number of conductors in the raceway or cable adjusted in accordance with 310.15(B)(5) and (6).

Author's Comment: Conductor ampacity reduction is required when four or more current-carrying conductors are bundled because heat generated by current flow is not able to dissipate as quickly as three or fewer current-carry conductors. **Figures 310–14 and 310–15**

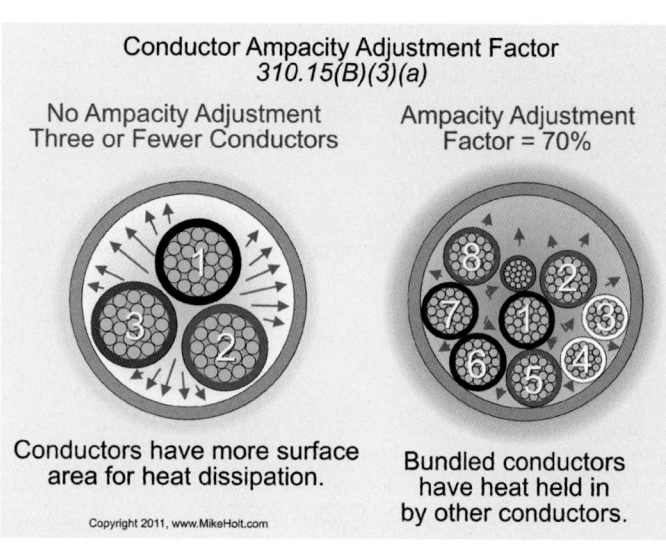

Figure 310–14

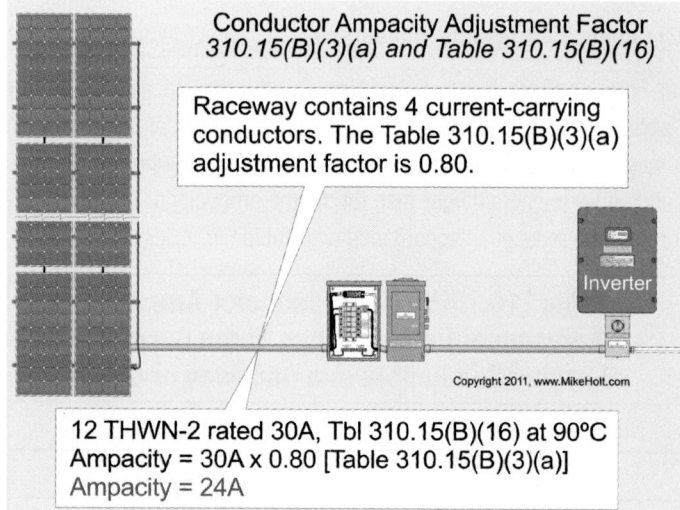

Figure 310–15

(1) Conductor ampacity adjustment of Table 310.15(B)(3)(a) does not apply to conductors installed in cable trays, 392.80 apply.

(2) Conductor ampacity adjustment of Table 310.15(B)(3)(a) does not apply to conductors in raceways having a length not exceeding 24 in. **Figure 310–16**

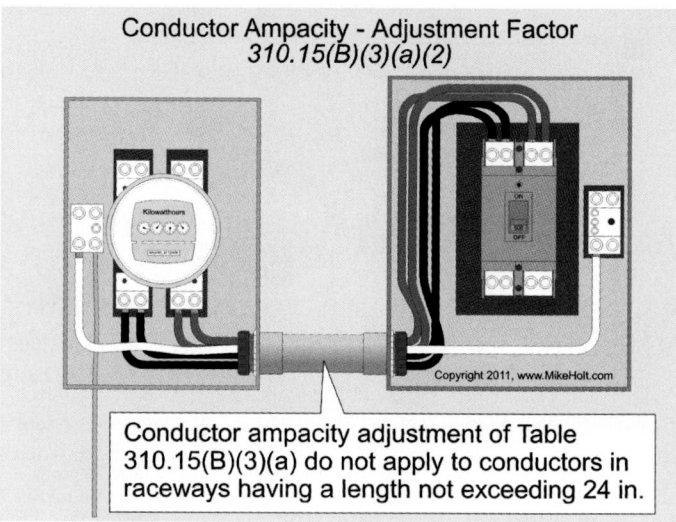

Figure 310–16

(4) Conductor ampacity adjustment of Table 310.15(B)(3)(a) does not apply to conductors within Type AC or Type MC cable under the following conditions: **Figure 310–17**

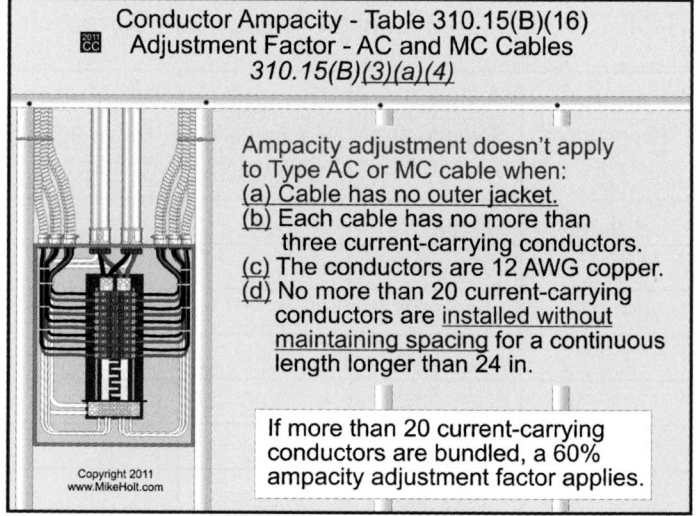

Figure 310–17

(a) The cables don't have an outer jacket,

(b) Each cable has no more than three current-carrying conductors,

(c) The conductors are 12 AWG copper, and

(d) No more than 20 current-carrying conductors (ten 2-wire cables or six 3-wire cables) are installed without maintaining spacing for a continuous length longer than 24 in.

(5) Ampacity adjustment of 60 percent applies to conductors within Type AC or Type MC cable without an overall outer jacket under the following conditions:

(b) The number of current-carrying conductors exceeds 20.

(c) The cables are stacked or bundled longer than 24 in. without spacing being maintained.

(c) Circular Raceways Exposed to Sunlight on Rooftops. When applying ampacity adjustment correction factors, the ambient temperature adjustment contained in Table 310.15(B)(3)(c) is added to the outdoor ambient temperature for conductors installed in circular raceways exposed to direct sunlight on or above rooftops to determine the applicable ambient temperature for ampacity correction factors in Table 310.15(B)(2)(a) or Table 310.15(B)(2)(b). **Figures 310–18 and 310–19**

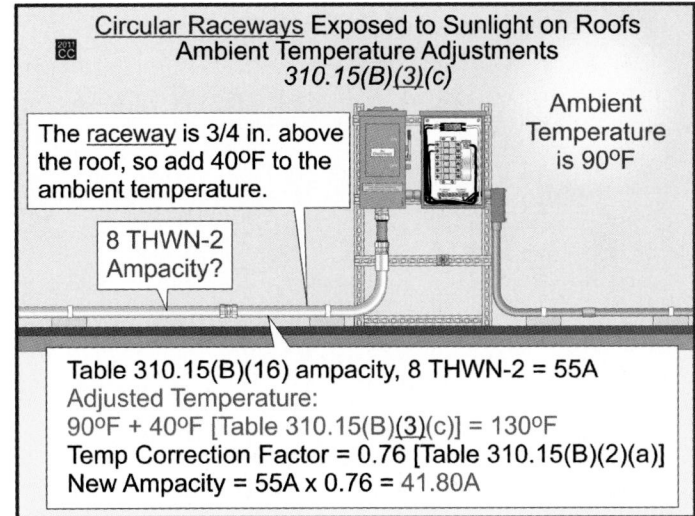

Figure 310–19

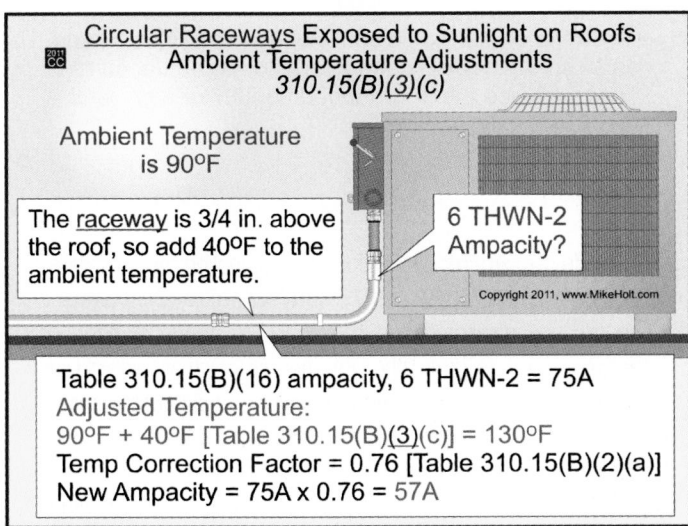

Figure 310–18

Note 1: See the ASHRAE *Handbook—Fundamentals* (www.ashrae. org) as a source for the average ambient temperatures in various locations.

Note 2: The temperature adders in Table 310.15(B)(3)(c) are based on the results of averaging the ambient temperatures.

Table 310.15(B)(3)(c) Ambient Temperature Adder for Raceways On or Above Rooftops		
Distance of Raceway Above Roof	C°	F°
0 to ½ in.	33	60
Above ½ in. to 3½ in.	22	40
Above 3½ in. to 12 in.	17	30
Above 12 in. to 36 in.	14	25

Author's Comment: This rule requires the ambient temperature used for ampacity correction to be adjusted where conductors or cables are installed in a circular raceway on or above a rooftop and the raceway is exposed to direct sunlight. The reasoning is that the air inside circular raceways in direct sunlight is significantly hotter than the surrounding air, and appropriate ampacity corrections must be made in order to comply with 310.10.

(5) Neutral Conductors.

(a) The neutral conductor of a 3-wire, single-phase, 120/240V system, or 4-wire, three-phase, 120/208V or 277/480V wye-connected system, isn't considered a current-carrying conductor for conductor ampacity adjustment of 310.15(B)(3)(a). **Figure 310–20**

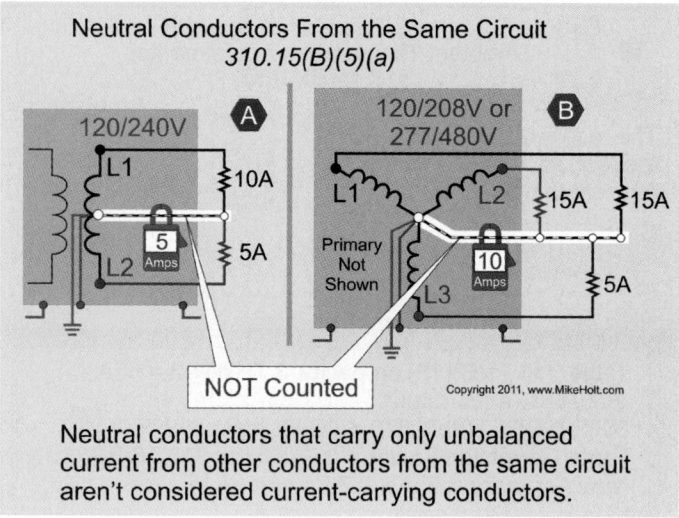

Figure 310–20

(b) The neutral conductor of a 3-wire circuit from a 4-wire, three-phase, 120/208V or 277/480V wye-connected system is considered a current-carrying conductor for conductor ampacity adjustment of 310.15(B)(3)(a).

Author's Comment: When a 3-wire circuit is supplied from a 4-wire, three-phase, 120/208V or 277/480V wye-connected system, the neutral conductor carries approximately the same current as the ungrounded conductors. **Figure 310–21**

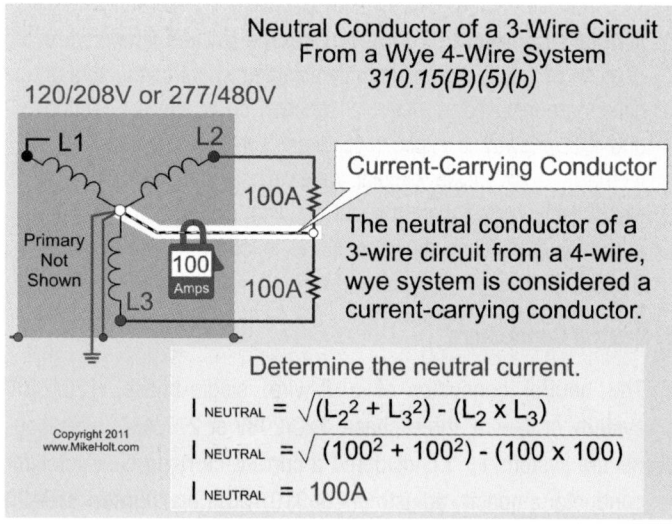

Figure 310–21

(c) The neutral conductor of a 4-wire, three-phase, 120/208V or 277/480V wye-connected system is considered a current-carrying conductor for conductor ampacity adjustment of 310.15(B)(3)(a) if more than 50 percent of the neutral load consists of nonlinear loads. **Figure 310–22**

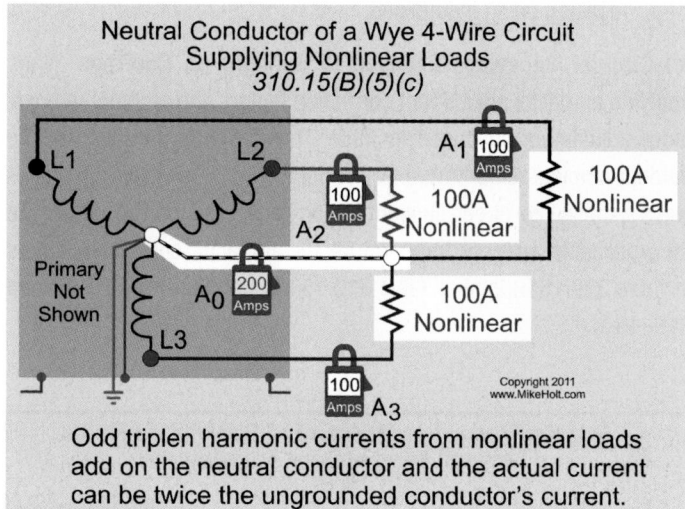

Figure 310–22

Author's Comment: Nonlinear loads supplied by a 4-wire, three-phase, 120/208V or 277/480V wye-connected system can produce unwanted and potentially hazardous odd triplen harmonic currents (3rd, 9th, 15th, and so on) that can add on the neutral conductor. To prevent fire or equipment damage from excessive harmonic neutral current, the designer should consider increasing the size of the neutral conductor or installing a separate neutral for each phase. For more information, visit www.MikeHolt.com, click on the "Technical" link, then the "Power Quality" link. Also see 210.4(A) Note, 220.61 Note 2, and 450.3 Note 2.

(6) Grounding Conductors. Grounding and bonding conductors aren't considered current carrying. **Figure 310–23**

(7) Dwelling Unit Feeder/Service Conductors. For individual dwelling units of one-family, two-family, and multifamily dwellings, Table 310.15(B)(7) can be used to size 3-wire, single-phase, 120/240V service conductors. **Figure 310–24**

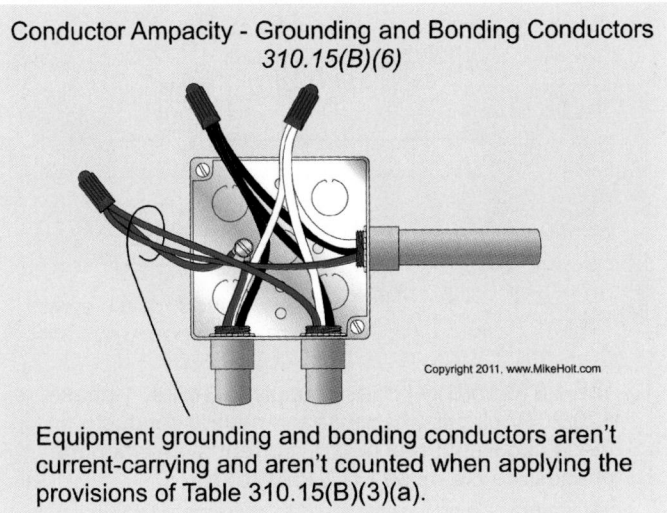

Conductor Ampacity - Grounding and Bonding Conductors
310.15(B)(6)

Equipment grounding and bonding conductors aren't current-carrying and aren't counted when applying the provisions of Table 310.15(B)(3)(a).

Figure 310–23

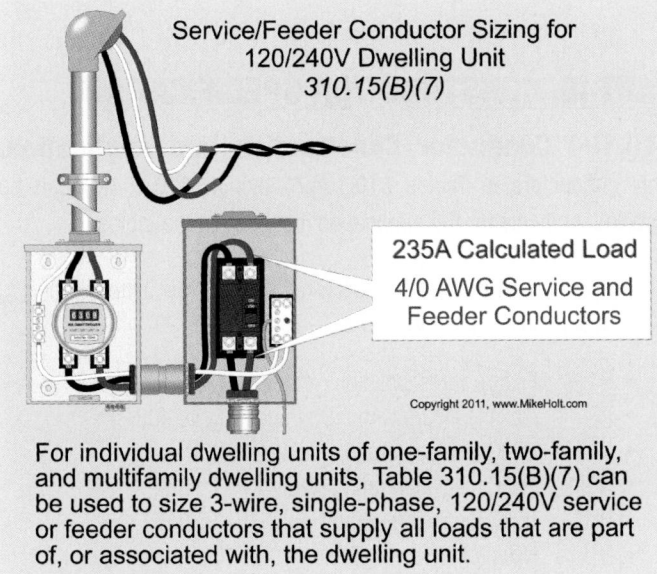

Service/Feeder Conductor Sizing for 120/240V Dwelling Unit
310.15(B)(7)

235A Calculated Load

4/0 AWG Service and Feeder Conductors

For individual dwelling units of one-family, two-family, and multifamily dwelling units, Table 310.15(B)(7) can be used to size 3-wire, single-phase, 120/240V service or feeder conductors that supply all loads that are part of, or associated with, the dwelling unit.

Figure 310–24

Author's Comment: Table 310.15(B)(7) can't be used for service conductors for two-family or multifamily dwelling buildings. Figure 310–25

Feeder conductors for individual dwelling units aren't required to be sized larger than service conductors sized to 310.15(B)(7) [215.2(A)(4)].

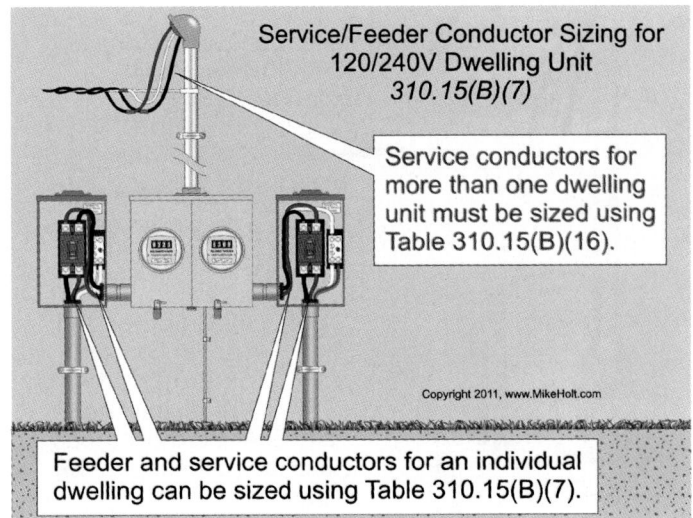

Service/Feeder Conductor Sizing for 120/240V Dwelling Unit
310.15(B)(7)

Service conductors for more than one dwelling unit must be sized using Table 310.15(B)(16).

Feeder and service conductors for an individual dwelling can be sized using Table 310.15(B)(7).

Figure 310–25

Neutral Conductor Sizing. For individual dwelling units of one-family, two-family, and multifamily dwellings, Table 310.15(B)(7) can be used to size the neutral conductor of a 3-wire, single-phase, 120/240V service or feeder that carries all loads associated with the dwelling unit, based on the calculated load in accordance with 220.61.

⚠ **CAUTION:** *Because the service neutral conductor is required to serve as the effective ground-fault current path, it must be sized so it can safely carry the maximum fault current likely to be imposed on it [110.10 and 250.4(A)(5)]. This is accomplished by sizing the neutral conductor in accordance with Table 250.66, based on the area of the largest ungrounded service conductor [250.24(C)(1)].*

Question: What size service conductors are required if the calculated load for a dwelling unit equals 195A, and the maximum unbalanced neutral load is 100A? **Figure 310–26**

(a) 1/0 AWG and 6 AWG   (b) 2/0 AWG and 4 AWG
(c) 3/0 AWG and 2 AWG   (d) 4/0 AWG and 1 AWG

Answer: (b) 2/0 AWG and 4 AWG

Service Conductor: 2/0 AWG rated 200A [Table 310.15(B)(7)]

Neutral Conductor: 4 AWG is rated 100A in accordance with Table 310.15(B)(7). In addition, 250.24(C) requires the neutral conductor to be sized no smaller than 4 AWG based on 2/0 AWG service conductors in accordance with Table 250.66.

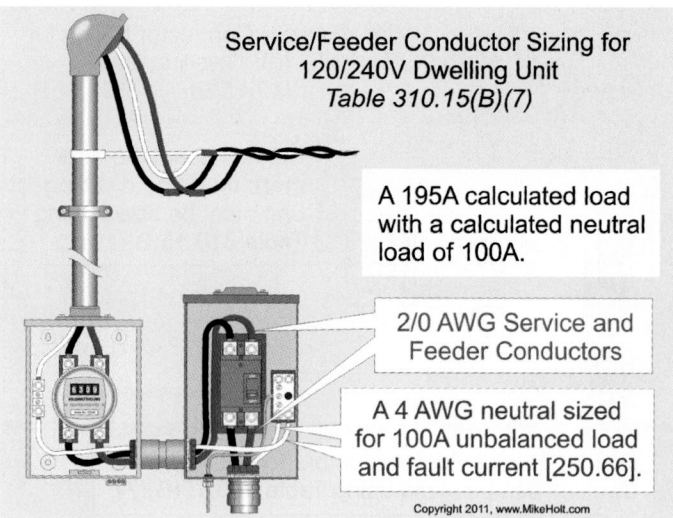

Service/Feeder Conductor Sizing for
120/240V Dwelling Unit
Table 310.15(B)(7)

A 195A calculated load
with a calculated neutral
load of 100A.

2/0 AWG Service and
Feeder Conductors

A 4 AWG neutral sized
for 100A unbalanced load
and fault current [250.66].

Copyright 2011, www.MikeHolt.com

Figure 310–26

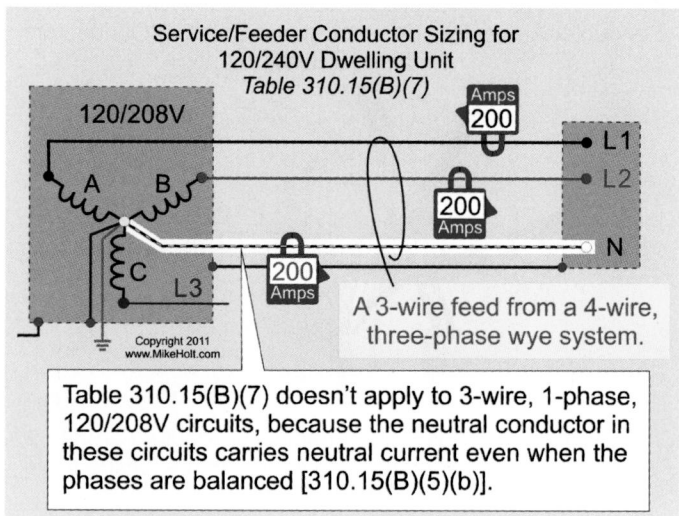

Service/Feeder Conductor Sizing for
120/240V Dwelling Unit
Table 310.15(B)(7)

120/208V

A 3-wire feed from a 4-wire,
three-phase wye system.

Copyright 2011
www.MikeHolt.com

Table 310.15(B)(7) doesn't apply to 3-wire, 1-phase,
120/208V circuits, because the neutral conductor in
these circuits carries neutral current even when the
phases are balanced [310.15(B)(5)(b)].

Figure 310–27

Table 310.15(B)(7) Conductor Sizes for 120/240V, 3-Wire, Single-Phase Dwelling Services and Feeders		
Amperes	Copper	Aluminum
100	4 AWG	2 AWG
110	3 AWG	1 AWG
125	2 AWG	1/0 AWG
150	1 AWG	2/0 AWG
175	1/0 AWG	3/0 AWG
200	2/0 AWG	4/0 AWG
225	3/0 AWG	250 kcmil
250	4/0 AWG	300 kcmil
300	250 kcmil	350 kcmil
350	350 kcmil	500 kcmil
400	400 kcmil	600 kcmil

⚠️ **WARNING:** *Table 310.15(B)(7) doesn't apply to 3-wire feeder/service conductors connected to a three-phase, 120/208V system, because the neutral conductor in these systems always carries neutral current, even when the load on the phases are balanced [310.15(B)(5)(b)]. For more information on this topic, see 220.61(C)(1).* **Figure 310–27**

PART III. CONSTRUCTION SPECIFICATION

310.104 Conductor Construction and Application.

Only conductors in Tables 310.104(A) though 310.104(G) can be installed, and only for the application identified in the tables.

Author's Comment: The following explains the lettering on conductor insulation: **Figures 310–28 and 310–29**

- F   Fixture wires (solid or 7 strands) [Table 402.3]
- FF   Flexible fixture wire (19 strands) [Table 402.3]
- No H   60°C insulation rating [Table 310.104(A)]
- H   75°C insulation rating [Table 310.104(A)]
- HH   90°C insulation rating [Table 310.104(A)]
- N   Nylon outer cover [Table 310.104(A)]
- R   Thermoset insulation [Table 310.104(A)]
- T   Thermoplastic insulation [Table 310.104(A)]
- U   Underground [Table 310.104(A)]
- W   Wet or damp locations [Table 310.104(A)]
- X   Cross-linked polyethylene insulation [Table 310.104(A)]

Table 310.15(B)(16) Allowable Ampacities of Insulated Conductors
Based on Not More Than Three Current-Carrying Conductors and Ambient Temperature of 30°C (86°F)*

Size	Temperature Rating of Conductor, See Table 310.13						Size
	60°C (140°F)	75°C (167°F)	90°C (194°F)	60°C (140°F)	75°C (167°F)	90°C (194°F)	
AWG kcmil	TW UF	THHW THW THWN XHHW	THHN THW-2 THWN-2 THHW XHHW XHHW-2 Dry Location	TW UF	THHN THW THWN XHHW	THHN THW-2 THWN-2 THHW XHHW XHHW-2	AWG kcmil
	Copper			Aluminum/Copper-Clad Aluminum			
14*	15	20	25				14*
12*	20	25	30	15	20	25	12*
10*	30	35	40	25	30	35	10*
8	40	50	55	35	40	45	8
6	55	65	75	40	50	55	6
4	70	85	95	55	65	75	4
3	85	100	115	65	75	85	3
2	95	115	130	75	90	100	2
1	110	130	145	85	100	115	1
1/0	125	150	170	100	120	135	1/0
2/0	145	175	195	115	135	150	2/0
3/0	165	200	225	130	155	175	3/0
4/0	195	230	260	150	180	205	4/0
250	215	255	290	170	205	230	250
300	240	285	320	195	230	260	300
350	260	310	350	210	250	280	350
400	280	335	380	225	270	305	400
500	320	380	430	260	310	350	500

*See 240.4(D)

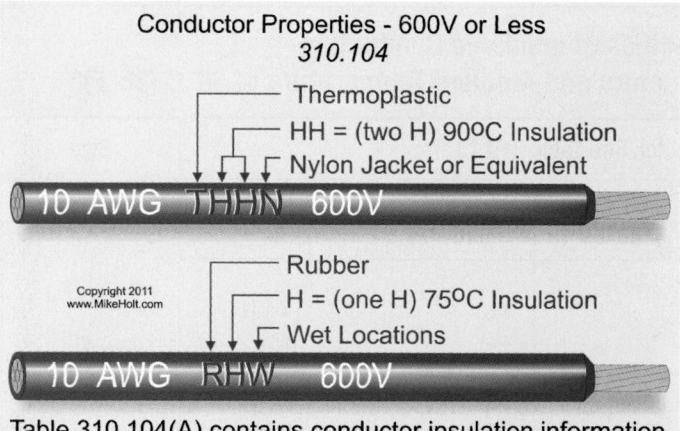

Conductor Properties - 600V or Less
310.104

Thermoplastic
HH = (two H) 90°C Insulation
Nylon Jacket or Equivalent

10 AWG THHN 600V

Rubber
H = (one H) 75°C Insulation
Wet Locations

10 AWG RHW 600V

Copyright 2011
www.MikeHolt.com

Table 310.104(A) contains conductor insulation information, such as operating temperature and applications. These conductors can be used in any Chapter 3 wiring method.

Figure 310–28

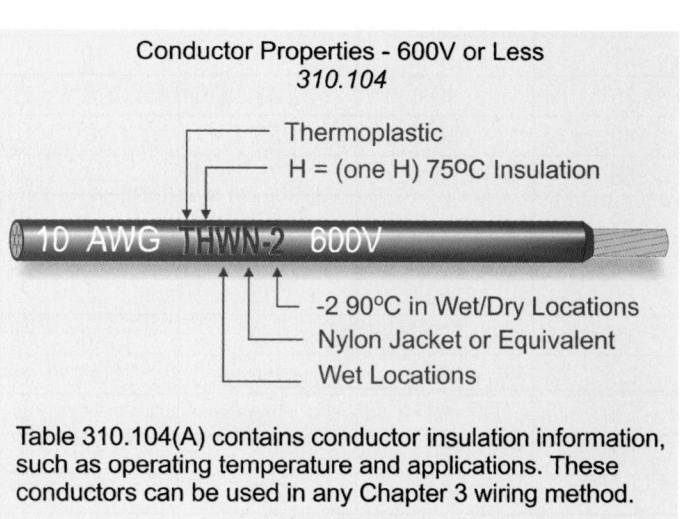

Conductor Properties - 600V or Less
310.104

Thermoplastic
H = (one H) 75°C Insulation

10 AWG THWN-2 600V

-2 90°C in Wet/Dry Locations
Nylon Jacket or Equivalent
Wet Locations

Table 310.104(A) contains conductor insulation information, such as operating temperature and applications. These conductors can be used in any Chapter 3 wiring method.

Copyright 2011, www.MikeHolt.com

Figure 310–29

310.106 Conductors

(A) Minimum Size Conductors. The smallest conductor permitted for branch circuits for residential, commercial, and industrial locations is 14 AWG copper, except as permitted elsewhere in this *Code*.

Author's Comment: There's a misconception that 12 AWG copper is the smallest conductor permitted for commercial or industrial facilities. Although this isn't true based on *NEC* rules, it may be a local code requirement.

(C) Stranded Conductors. Conductors 8 AWG and larger must be stranded when installed in a raceway. **Figure 310–30**

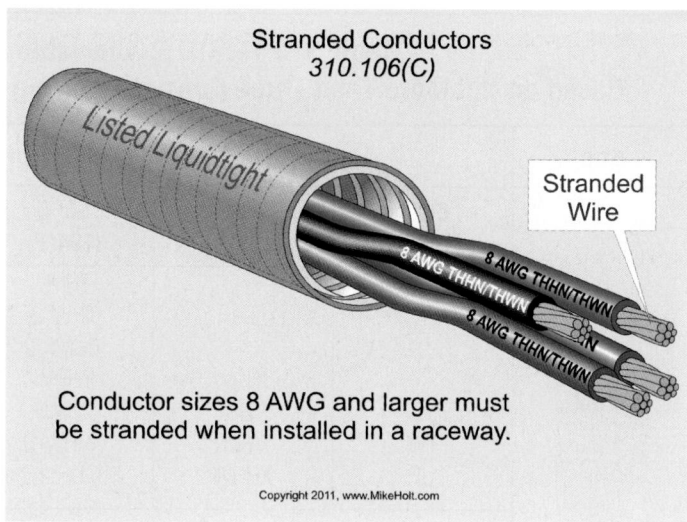

Stranded Conductors
310.106(C)

Listed Liquidtight

Stranded Wire

8 AWG THHN/THWN
8 AWG THHN/THWN
8 AWG THHN/THWN

Conductor sizes 8 AWG and larger must be stranded when installed in a raceway.

Copyright 2011, www.MikeHolt.com

Figure 310–30

Author's Comment: Solid conductors are often used for the grounding electrode conductor [250.62] and for the bonding of pools, spas, and outdoor hot tubs [680.26(C)]. Technically, the practice of installing 8 AWG and larger solid conductors in a raceway for the protection of grounding and bonding conductors is a violation of this rule.

(D) Insulated. Conductors must be insulated <u>except where specific permission allows them to be covered or bare</u>. **Figure 310–31**

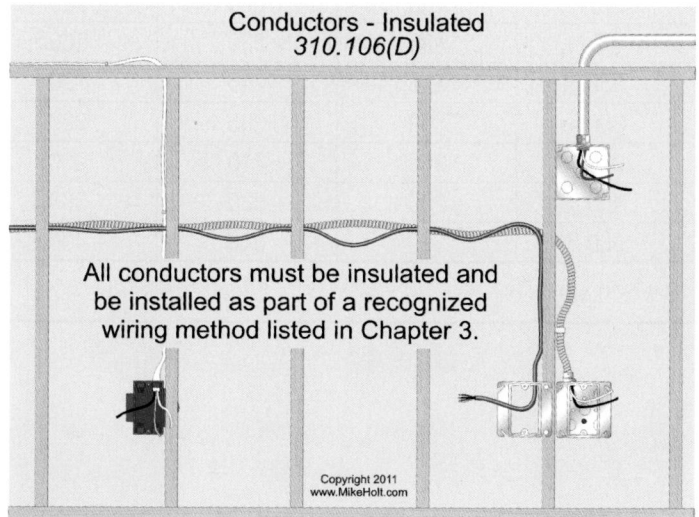

Conductors - Insulated
310.106(D)

All conductors must be insulated and be installed as part of a recognized wiring method listed in Chapter 3.

Copyright 2011
www.MikeHolt.com

Figure 310–31

Author's Comment: Equipment grounding conductors are permitted to be bare, see 250.118(1). **Figure 310–32**

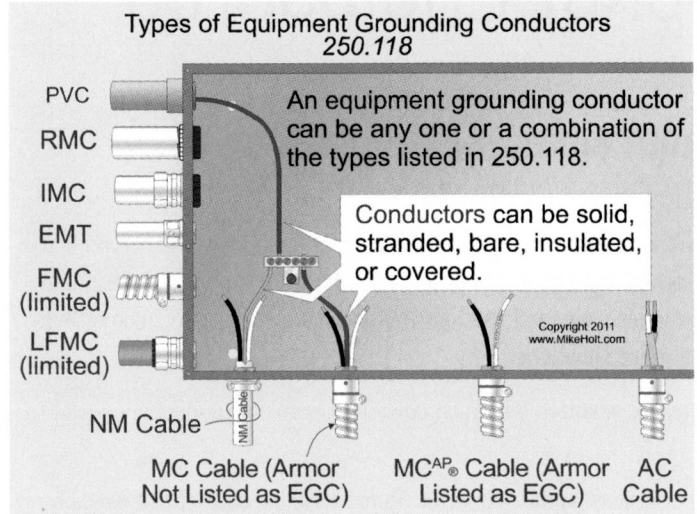

Figure 310–32

310.110 Conductor Identification.

(A) Grounded Conductor. Grounded conductors must be identified in accordance with 200.6.

(B) Equipment Grounding Conductor. Equipment grounding conductors must be identified in accordance with 250.119.

(C) Ungrounded Conductors. Ungrounded conductors must be clearly distinguishable from neutral and equipment grounding conductors. **Figure 310–33**

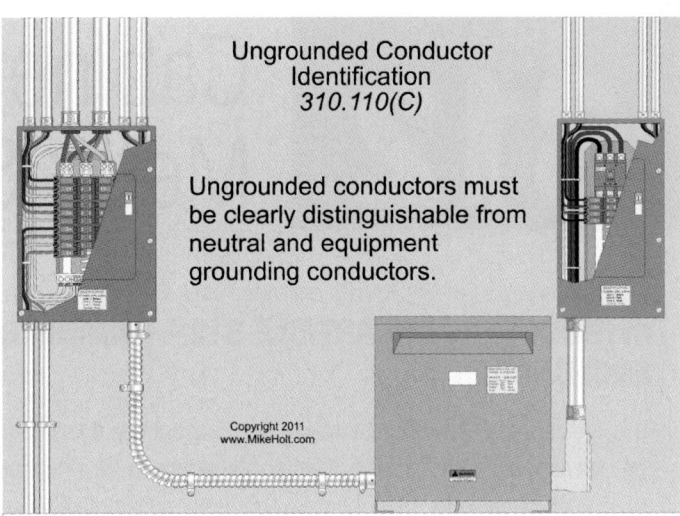

Figure 310–33

Author's Comments:

- If the premises wiring system has branch circuits or feeders supplied from more than one nominal voltage system, each ungrounded conductor of the branch circuit or feeder, if accessible, must be identified by system. The means of identification can be by separate color coding, marking tape, tagging, or other means approved by the authority having jurisdiction. Such identification must be permanently posted at each panelboard [210.5(C) and 215.12].

- The *NEC* doesn't require color coding of ungrounded conductors, except for the high-leg conductor when a neutral conductor is present [110.15 and 230.56]. Although not required, electricians often use the following color system for power and lighting conductor identification:

  - 120/240V, single-phase—black, red, and white

  - 120/208V, three-phase—black, red, blue, and white

  - 120/240V, three-phase, delta-connected system—black, orange, blue, and white

  - 277/480V, three-phase, wye-connected system—brown, orange, yellow, and gray; or, brown, purple, yellow, and gray

ARTICLE
312

Cabinets, Cutout Boxes, and Meter Socket Enclosures

INTRODUCTION TO ARTICLE 312—CABINETS, CUTOUT BOXES, AND METER SOCKET ENCLOSURES

This article addresses the installation and construction specifications for the items mentioned in its title. In Article 310, we observed that the conditions of use have an effect on the ampacity of a conductor. Likewise, the conditions of use have an effect on the selection and application of cabinets, cutout boxes, and meter socket enclosures. For example, you can't use just any enclosure in a wet location or in a hazardous location. The conditions of use impose special requirements for these situations.

For all such enclosures, certain requirements apply—regardless of the use. For example, you must cover any openings, protect conductors from abrasion, and allow sufficient bending room for conductors.

Notice that Article 408 covers switchboards and panelboards, with primary emphasis on the interior, or "guts" while the cabinet that would be used to enclose a panelboard is covered here in Article 312. Therefore you'll find that some important considerations such as wire-bending space at terminals of panelboards are included in this article.

Article 312 covers the installation and construction specifications for cabinets, cutout boxes, and meter socket enclosures. [312.1].

Author's Comment: A cabinet is an enclosure for either surface mounting or flush mounting and provided with a frame in which a door may be hung. A cutout box is designed for surface mounting with a swinging door [Article 100]. The industry name for a meter socket enclosure is "meter can."

312.1 Scope. Article 312 covers the installation and construction specifications for cabinets, cutout boxes, and meter socket enclosures. **Figure 312–1**

Author's Comment: A cabinet is an enclosure for either surface mounting or flush mounting and provided with a frame in which a door may be hung. A cutout box is designed for surface mounting with a swinging door [Article 100]. The industry name for a meter socket enclosure is "meter can."

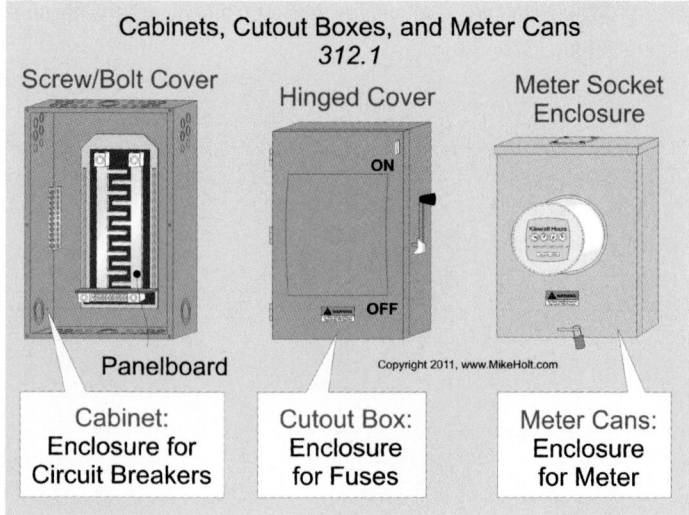

Figure 312–1

PART I. INSTALLATION

312.2 Damp or Wet Locations.

Enclosures in damp or wet locations must prevent moisture or water from entering or accumulating within the enclosure, and must be weatherproof. When the enclosure is surface mounted in a wet location, the enclosure must be mounted with not less than a ¼ in. air space between it and the mounting surface. See 300.6(D).

If raceways or cables enter above the level of uninsulated live parts of an enclosure in a wet location, a fitting listed for wet locations must be used for termination.

> **Author's Comment:** A fitting listed for use in a wet location with a sealing locknut is suitable for this application.

Ex: The ¼ in. air space isn't required for nonmetallic equipment, raceways, or cables.

312.3 Installed in Walls.

Cabinets or cutout boxes installed in walls of concrete, tile, or other noncombustible material must be installed so that the front edge of the enclosure is set back no more than ¼ in. from the finished surface. In walls constructed of wood or other combustible material, cabinets or cutout boxes must be flush with the finished surface or project outward.

312.4 Repairing Gaps.

Gaps around cabinets and cutout boxes that are recessed in noncombustible surfaces (plaster, drywall, or plasterboard) having a flush-type cover, must be repaired so that there will be no gap more than ⅛ in. at the edge of the cabinet or cutout box. **Figure 312–2**

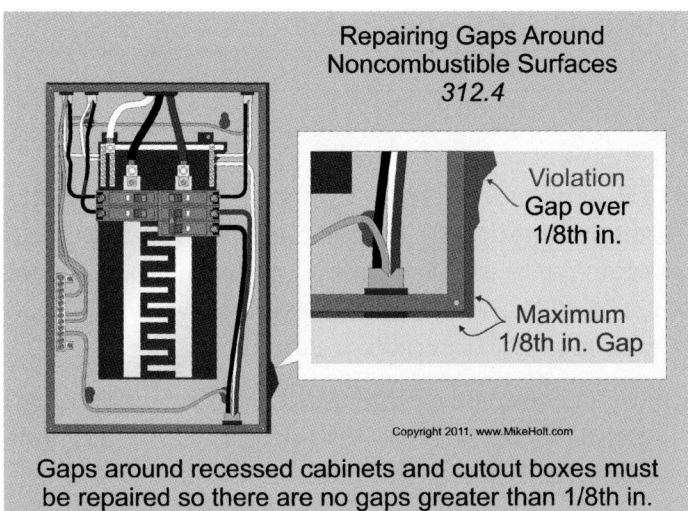

Repairing Gaps Around
Noncombustible Surfaces
312.4

Violation
Gap over
1/8th in.

Maximum
1/8th in. Gap

Copyright 2011, www.MikeHolt.com

Gaps around recessed cabinets and cutout boxes must be repaired so there are no gaps greater than 1/8th in.

Figure 312–2

312.5 Enclosures.

(A) Unused Openings. Openings intended to provide entry for conductors must be adequately closed. **Figure 312–3**

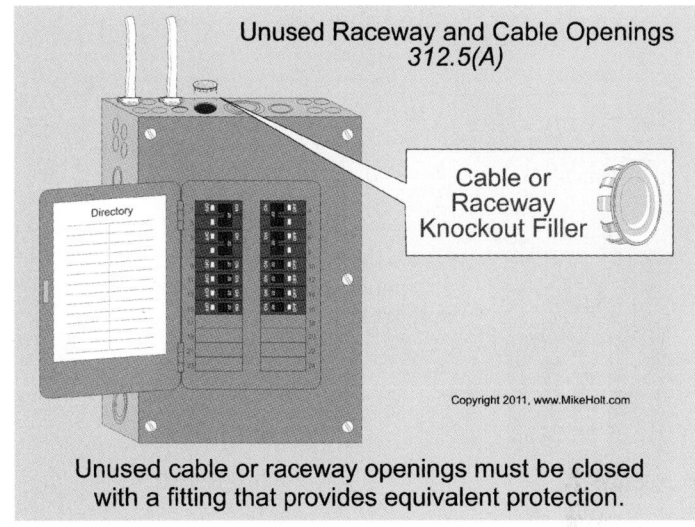

Unused Raceway and Cable Openings
312.5(A)

Cable or
Raceway
Knockout Filler

Directory

Copyright 2011, www.MikeHolt.com

Unused cable or raceway openings must be closed with a fitting that provides equivalent protection.

Figure 312–3

> **Author's Comment:** Unused openings for circuit breakers must be closed by means that provide protection substantially equivalent to the wall of the enclosure [408.7]. **Figure 312–4**

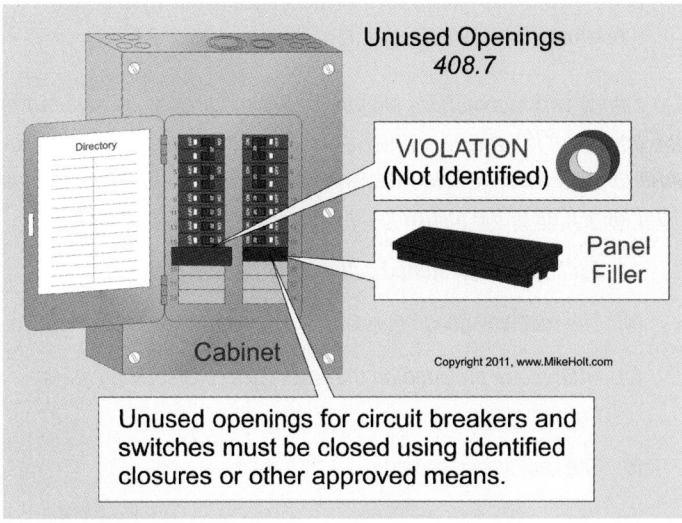

Unused Openings
408.7

Directory

VIOLATION
(Not Identified)

Panel
Filler

Cabinet

Copyright 2011, www.MikeHolt.com

Unused openings for circuit breakers and switches must be closed using identified closures or other approved means.

Figure 312–4

(C) Cable Termination. Cables must be secured to the enclosure with fittings designed and listed for the cable. See 300.12 and 300.15. Figure 312–5

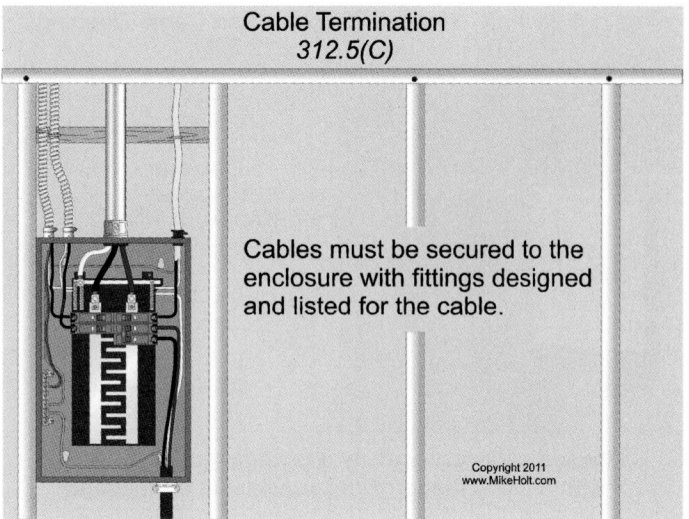

Figure 312–5

Author's Comment: Cable clamps or cable connectors must be used with only one cable, unless that clamp or fitting is identified for more than one cable. Some Type NM cable clamps are listed for two Type NM cables within a single fitting (UL White Book, *Guide Information for Electrical Equipment,* www.ul.com/regulators/2008_WhiteBook.pdf).

Ex: Cables with nonmetallic sheaths aren't required to be secured to the enclosure if the cables enter the top of a surface-mounted enclosure through a nonflexible raceway not less than 18 in. or more than 10 ft long, if all of the following conditions are met: Figure 312–6

(a) *Each cable is fastened within 1 ft from the raceway.*

(b) *The raceway doesn't penetrate a structural ceiling.*

(c) *Fittings are provided on the raceway to protect the cables from abrasion.*

(d) *The raceway is sealed.*

(e) *Each cable sheath extends not less than ¼ in. into the panelboard.*

(f) *The raceway is properly secured.*

(g) *Conductor fill is limited to Chapter 9, Table 1 percentages.*

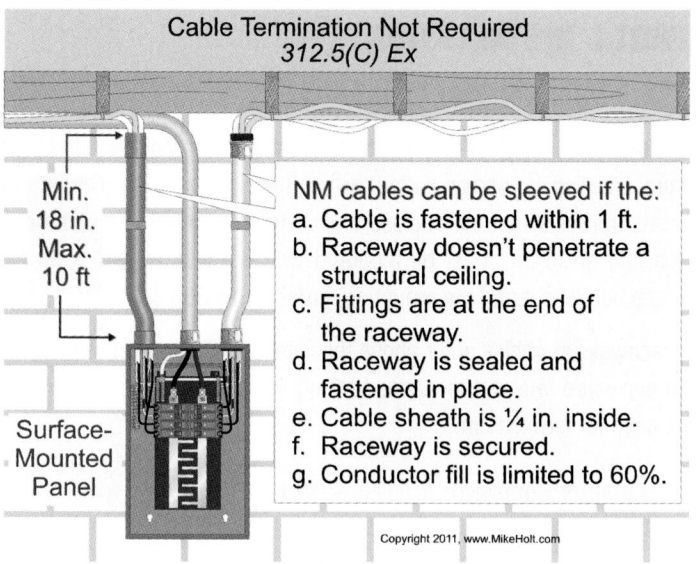

Figure 312–6

312.6 Deflection of Conductors. Enclosures for conductors must be sized to allow conductors to be deflected in accordance with Table 312.6(A).

Table 312.6(A) Minimum Wire-Bending Space	
Wire Size (AWG or kcmil)	Inches
8–6	1½
4–3	2
2	2½
1	3
1/0–2/0	3½
3/0–4/0	4
250	4½
300–350	5
400–500	6
600–700	8

312.8 Enclosures With Splices, Taps, and Feed-Through Conductors. Cabinets, cutout boxes, and meter socket enclosures can be used for conductors as feeding through, spliced, or tapping off to other enclosures, switches, or overcurrent devices where all of the following conditions are met:

(1) The total area of the conductors at any cross section doesn't exceed 40 percent of the cross-sectional area of the space. Figure 312–7

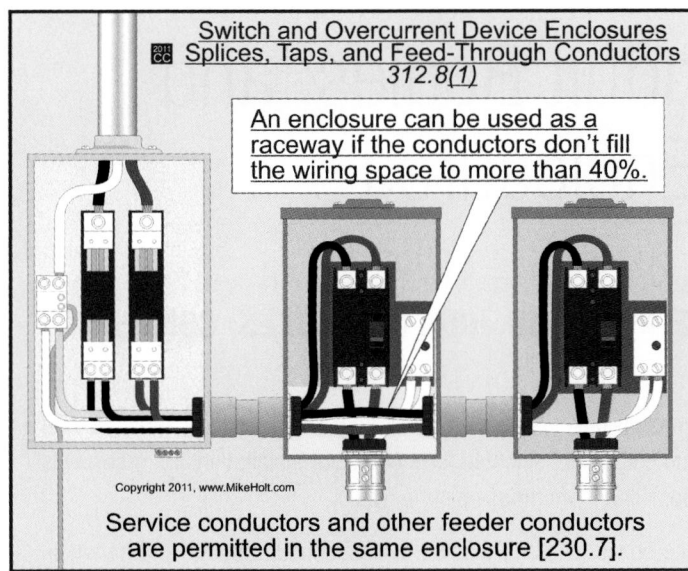

Figure 312–7

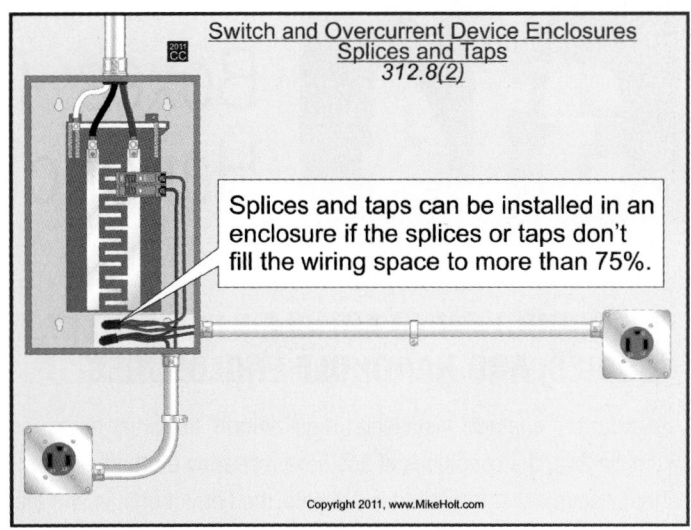

Figure 312–8

(2) The total area of conductors, splices, and taps installed at any cross section doesn't exceed 75 percent of the cross-sectional area of that space. **Figure 312–8**

(3) A warning label on the enclosure identifies the disconnecting means for feed-through conductors. **Figure 312–9**

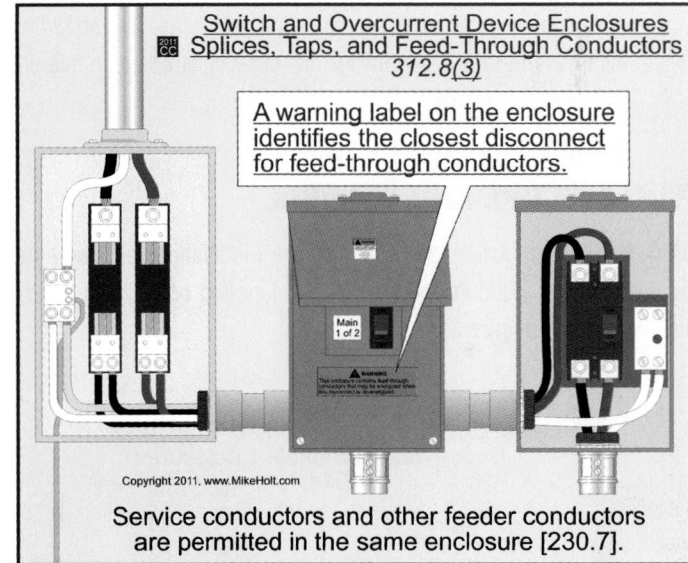

Figure 312–9

ARTICLE 314

Outlet, Device, Pull and Junction Boxes; Conduit Bodies; and Handhole Enclosures

INTRODUCTION TO ARTICLE 314—OUTLET, DEVICE, PULL AND JUNCTION BOXES; CONDUIT BODIES; AND HANDHOLE ENCLOSURES

Article 314 contains installation requirements for outlet boxes, pull and junction boxes, conduit bodies, and handhole enclosures. As with Article 312, the conditions of use have a bearing on the type of material and equipment selected for a particular installation. If a raceway is installed in a wet location, for example, the correct fittings and the proper installation methods must be used.

Article 314 provides guidance for selecting and installing outlet and device boxes, pull and junction boxes, conduit bodies, and handhole enclosures. Information in this article will help you size an outlet box using the proper cubic-inch capacity as well as calculating the minimum dimensions for larger pull boxes. There are limits on the amount of weight that can be supported by an outlet box and rules on how to support a device or outlet box to various surfaces. This article will help you understand these type of rules so that your installation will be compliant with the *NEC*. As always, the clear illustrations in this unit will help you visualize the finished installation.

PART I. SCOPE AND GENERAL

314.1 Scope. Article 314 contains the installation requirements for outlet boxes, conduit bodies, pull and junction boxes, and handhole enclosures. **Figure 314–1**

Outlet Boxes, Conduit Bodies, Pull/Junction Boxes, and Handhole Enclosures
314.1

Outlet Boxes

Junction Box

Conduit Body

Handhole Enclosure

Copyright 2011
www.MikeHolt.com

Article 314 contains the installation requirements for outlet boxes, conduit bodies, pull and junction boxes, and handhole enclosures.

Figure 314–1

314.3 Nonmetallic Boxes. Nonmetallic boxes can only be used with nonmetallic cables and raceways.

Ex 1: Metal raceways and metal cables can be used with nonmetallic boxes if all raceways are bonded together in the nonmetallic box.

314.4 Metal Boxes. Metal boxes containing circuits that operate at 50V or more must be connected to an equipment grounding conductor of a type listed in 250.118 [250.112(I) and 250.148]. **Figure 314–2**

PART II. INSTALLATION

314.15 Damp or Wet Locations. Boxes and conduit bodies in damp or wet locations must prevent moisture or water from entering or accumulating within the enclosure. Boxes, conduit bodies, and fittings installed in wet locations must be listed for use in wet locations. **Figure 314–3**

> **Author's Comment:** If handhole enclosures without bottoms are installed, all enclosed conductors and any splices or terminations must be listed as suitable for wet locations [314.30(C)].

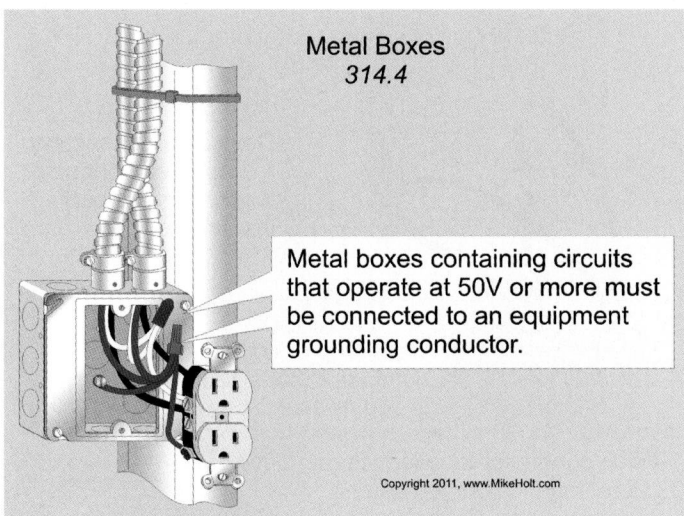

Metal Boxes
314.4

Metal boxes containing circuits that operate at 50V or more must be connected to an equipment grounding conductor.

Copyright 2011, www.MikeHolt.com

Figure 314–2

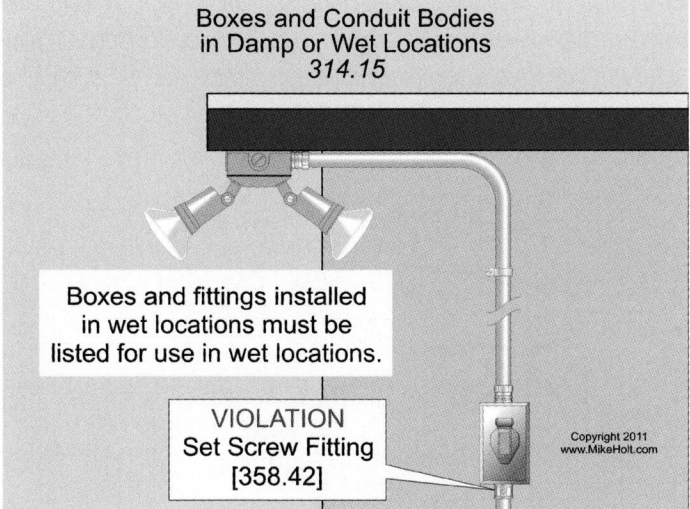

Boxes and Conduit Bodies in Damp or Wet Locations
314.15

Boxes and fittings installed in wet locations must be listed for use in wet locations.

VIOLATION
Set Screw Fitting
[358.42]

Copyright 2011 www.MikeHolt.com

Figure 314–3

314.16 Number of 6 AWG and Smaller Conductors in Boxes and Conduit Bodies.

Boxes containing 6 AWG and smaller conductors must be sized to provide sufficient free space for all conductors, devices, and fittings. In no case can the volume of the box, as calculated in 314.16(A), be less than the volume requirement as calculated in 314.16(B).

Conduit bodies must be sized in accordance with 314.16(C).

Author's Comment: The requirements for sizing boxes and conduit bodies containing conductors 4 AWG and larger are contained in 314.28. The requirements for sizing handhole enclosures are contained in 314.30(A).

(A) Box Volume Calculations. The volume of a box includes the total volume of its assembled parts, including plaster rings, extension rings, and domed covers that are either marked with their volume in cubic inches (cu in.), or are made from boxes listed in Table 314.16(A). **Figure 314–4**

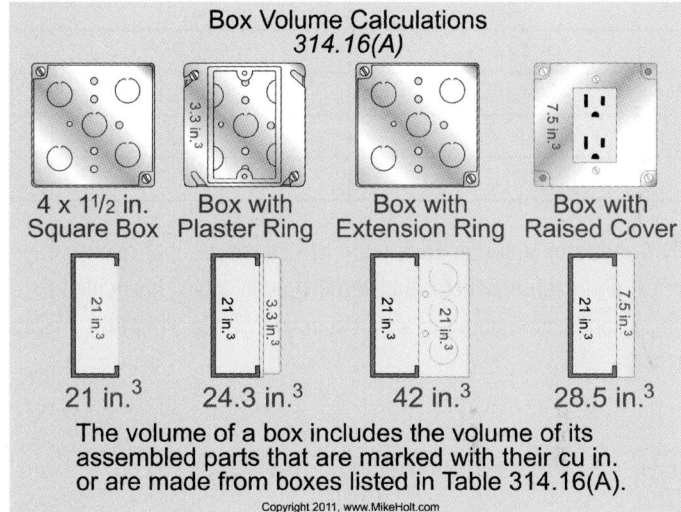

Box Volume Calculations
314.16(A)

4 x 1½ in. Square Box — 21 in.³
Box with Plaster Ring — 24.3 in.³
Box with Extension Ring — 42 in.³
Box with Raised Cover — 28.5 in.³

The volume of a box includes the volume of its assembled parts that are marked with their cu in. or are made from boxes listed in Table 314.16(A).

Copyright 2011, www.MikeHolt.com

Figure 314–4

(B) Box Fill Calculations. The calculated conductor volume determined by (1) through (5) and Table 314.16(B) are added together to determine the total volume of the conductors, devices, and fittings. Raceway and cable fittings, including locknuts and bushings, aren't counted for box fill calculations. **Figure 314–5**

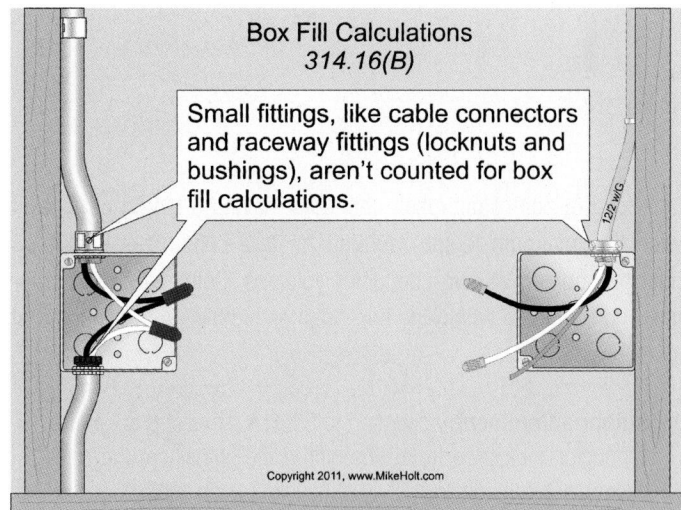

Box Fill Calculations
314.16(B)

Small fittings, like cable connectors and raceway fittings (locknuts and bushings), aren't counted for box fill calculations.

Copyright 2011, www.MikeHolt.com

Figure 314–5

Table 314.16(B) Volume Allowance Required per Conductor	
Conductor AWG	Volume cu in.
18	1.50
16	1.75
14	2.00
12	2.25
10	2.50
8	3.00
6	5.00

(1) Conductor Volume. Each unbroken conductor that runs through a box, and each conductor that terminates in a box, is counted as a single conductor volume in accordance with Table 314.16(B). **Figure 314–6**

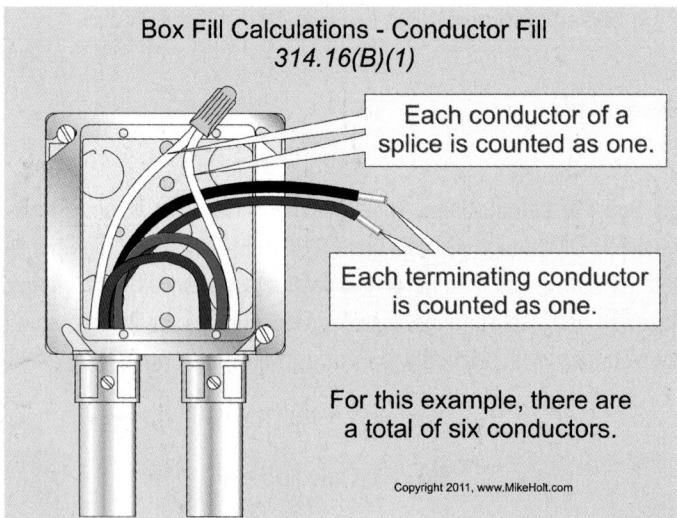

Figure 314–6

Each loop or coil of unbroken conductor having a length of at least twice the minimum length required for free conductors in 300.14 must be counted as two conductor volumes. Conductors that originate and terminate within the box, such as pigtails, aren't counted at all. **Figure 314–7**

Author's Comment: According to 300.14, at least 6 in. of free conductor, measured from the point in the box where the conductors enter the enclosure, must be left at each outlet, junction, and switch point for splices or terminations of luminaires or devices.

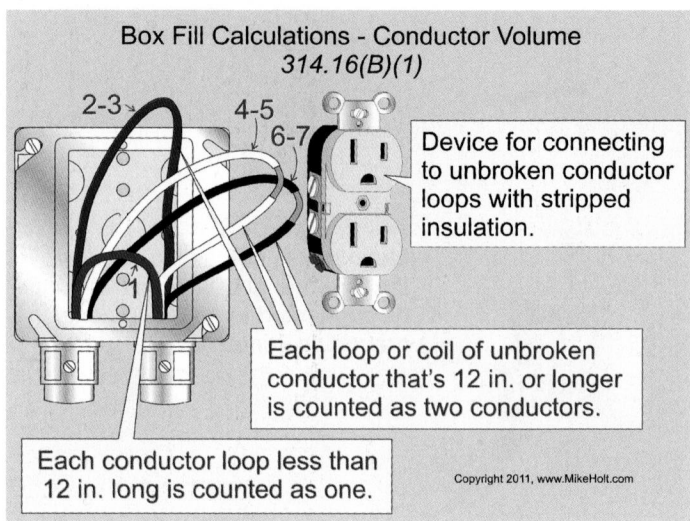

Figure 314–7

Ex: Equipment grounding conductors, and up to four 16 AWG and smaller fixture wires, can be omitted from box fill calculations if they enter the box from a domed luminaire or similar canopy, such as a ceiling paddle fan canopy. **Figure 314–8**

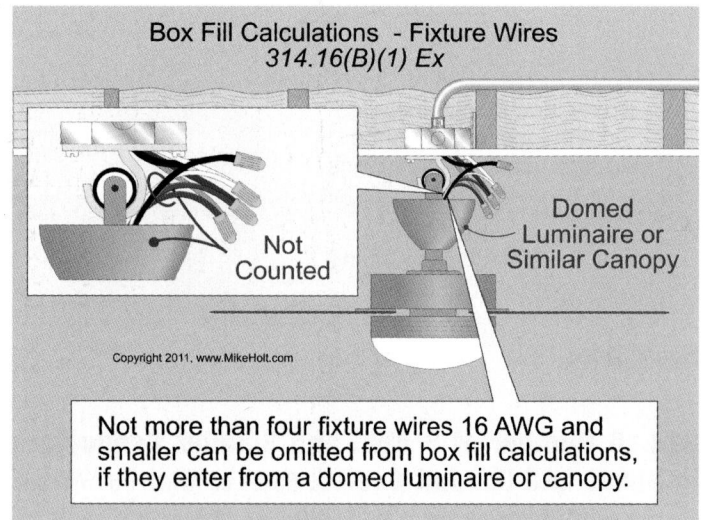

Figure 314–8

(2) Cable Clamp Volume. One or more internal cable clamps count as a single conductor volume in accordance with Table 314.16(B), based on the largest conductor that enters the box. Cable connectors that have their clamping mechanism outside of the box aren't counted. **Figure 314–9**

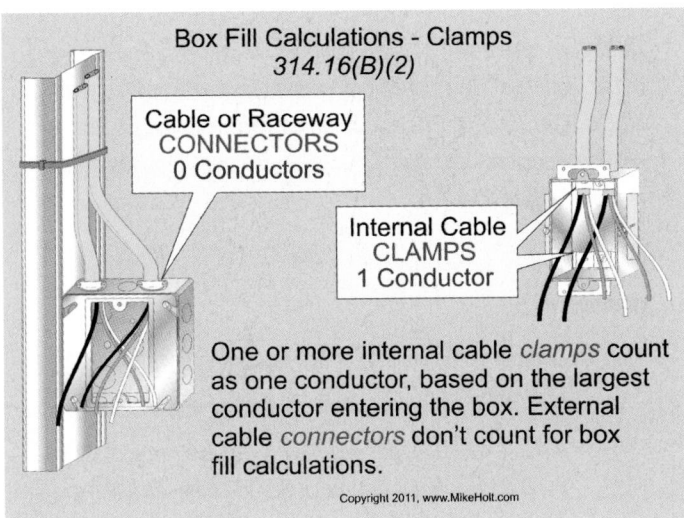

Figure 314–9

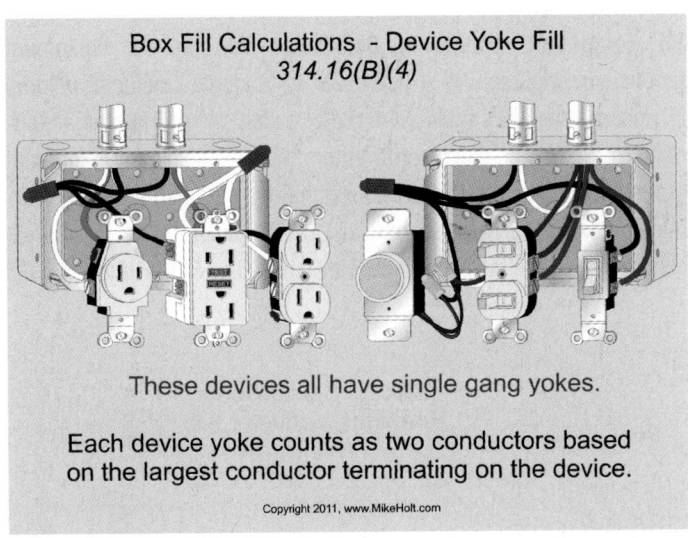

Figure 314–11

(3) Support Fitting Volume. Each luminaire stud or luminaire hickey counts as a single conductor volume in accordance with Table 314.16(B), based on the largest conductor that enters the box. **Figure 314–10**

Each multigang-device yoke counts as two conductor volumes for each gang, based on the largest conductor that terminates on the device in accordance with Table 314.16(B). **Figure 314–12**

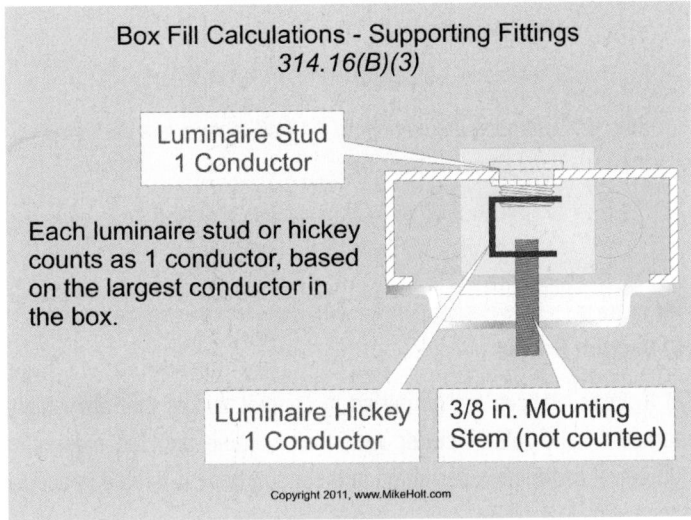

Figure 314–10

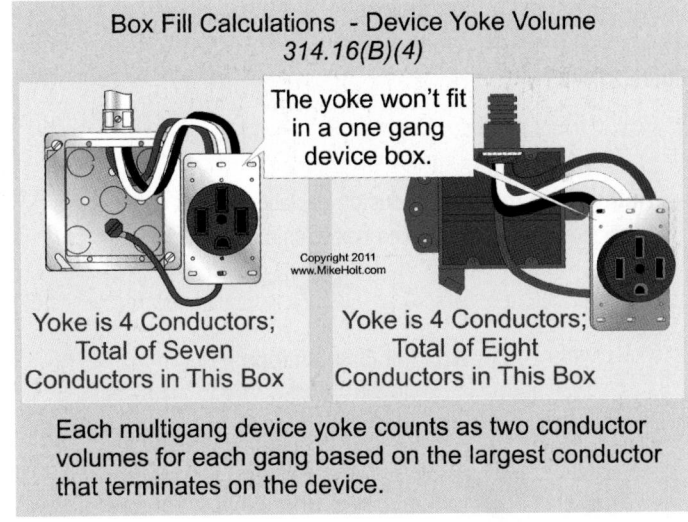

Figure 314–12

Author's Comment: Luminaire stems don't need to be counted as a conductor volume.

Author's Comment: A device that's too wide for mounting in a single-gang box, as described in Table 314.16(A), is counted based on the number of gangs required for the device.

(4) Device Yoke Volume. Each single-gang device yoke (regardless of the ampere rating of the device) counts as two conductor volumes, based on the largest conductor that terminates on the device in accordance with Table 314.16(B). **Figure 314–11**

(5) Equipment Grounding Conductor Volume. All equipment grounding conductors in a box count as a single conductor volume in accordance with Table 314.16(B), based on the largest equipment grounding conductor that enters the box. Insulated equipment grounding conductors for receptacles having insulated grounding terminals (isolated ground receptacles) [250.146(D)], count as a single conductor volume in accordance with Table 314.16(B). **Figure 314–13**

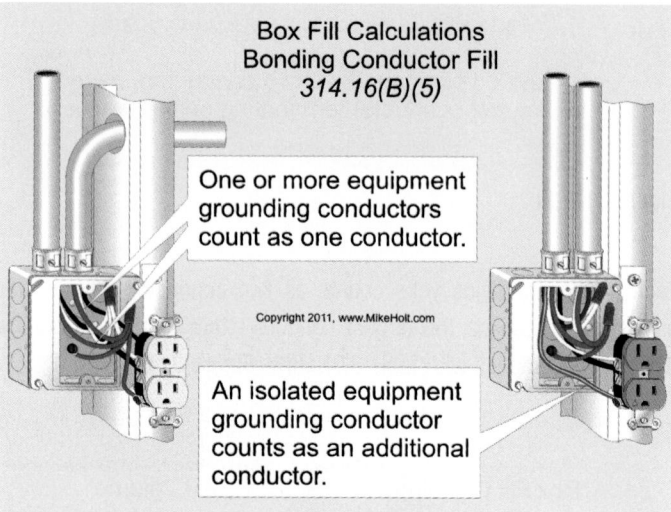

Box Fill Calculations
Bonding Conductor Fill
314.16(B)(5)

One or more equipment grounding conductors count as one conductor.

Copyright 2011, www.MikeHolt.com

An isolated equipment grounding conductor counts as an additional conductor.

Figure 314–13

Author's Comment: Conductor insulation isn't a factor that's considered when determining box volume calculations.

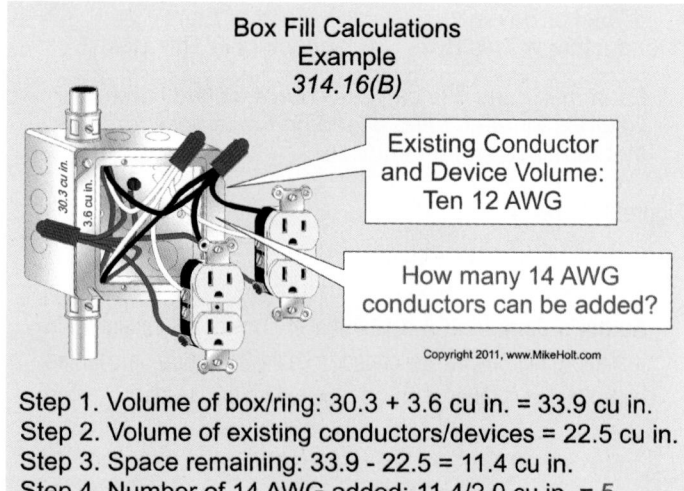

Box Fill Calculations
Example
314.16(B)

Existing Conductor and Device Volume: Ten 12 AWG

How many 14 AWG conductors can be added?

Copyright 2011, www.MikeHolt.com

Step 1. Volume of box/ring: 30.3 + 3.6 cu in. = 33.9 cu in.
Step 2. Volume of existing conductors/devices = 22.5 cu in.
Step 3. Space remaining: 33.9 - 22.5 = 11.4 cu in.
Step 4. Number of 14 AWG added: 11.4/2.0 cu in. = 5

Figure 314–14

Question: *How many 14 AWG conductors can be pulled through a 4 in. square x 2½ in. deep box with a plaster ring with a marking of 3.60 cu in.? The box contains two receptacles, five 12 AWG conductors, and two 12 AWG equipment grounding conductors.* **Figure 314–14**

(a) 3   (b) 5   (c) 7   (d) 9

Answer: *(b) 5*

Step 1: Determine the volume of the box assembly [314.16(A)]:

Box 30.30 cu in. + 3.60 cu in. plaster ring = 33.90 cu in.

A 4 x 4 x 2⅛ in. box will have a gross volume of 34 cu in., but the interior volume is 30.30 cu in., as listed in Table 314.16(A).

Step 2: Determine the volume of the devices and conductors in the box:

Two—receptacles	4—12 AWG
Five—12 AWG	5—12 AWG
Two—12 AWG Grounds	1—12 AWG

Total 10—12 AWG x 2.25 cu in. = 22.50 cu in.

Step 3: Determine the remaining volume permitted for the 14 AWG conductors:

33.90 cu in. - 22.50 cu in. = 11.40 cu in.

Step 4: Determine the number of 14 AWG conductors permitted in the remaining volume:

14 AWG = 2.00 cu in. each [Table 314.16(B)]
11.40 cu in./2.00 cu in. = 5 conductors

(C) Conduit Bodies.

(2) Splices. Splices are permitted in conduit bodies that are legibly marked by the manufacturer with their volume and the maximum number of conductors permitted in a conduit body is limited in accordance with 314.16(B).

Question: *How many 12 AWG conductors can be spliced in a 15 cu in. conduit body?* **Figure 314–15**

(a) 4   (b) 6   (c) 8   (d) 10

Answer: *(b) 6 conductors (15 cu in./2.25 cu in.)*

12 AWG = 2.25 cu in. [Table 314.16(B)]
15 cu in./2.25 cu in. = 6

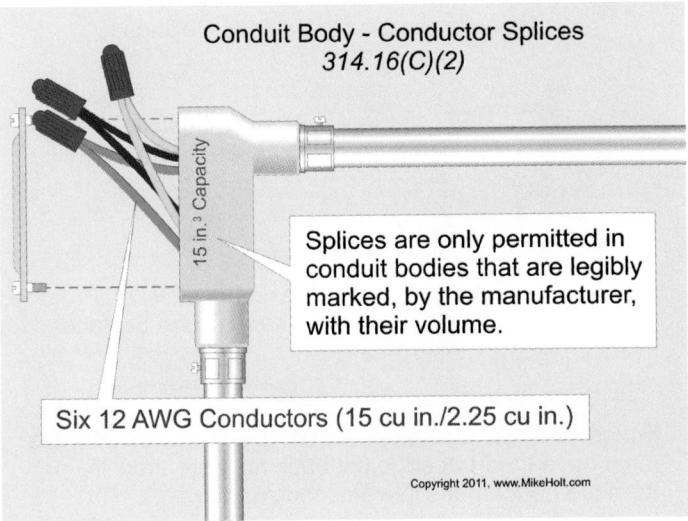

Figure 314–15

(3) Short-Radius Conduit Bodies. Capped elbows, handy ells, and service-entrance elbows aren't permitted to contain any splices. Figure 314–16

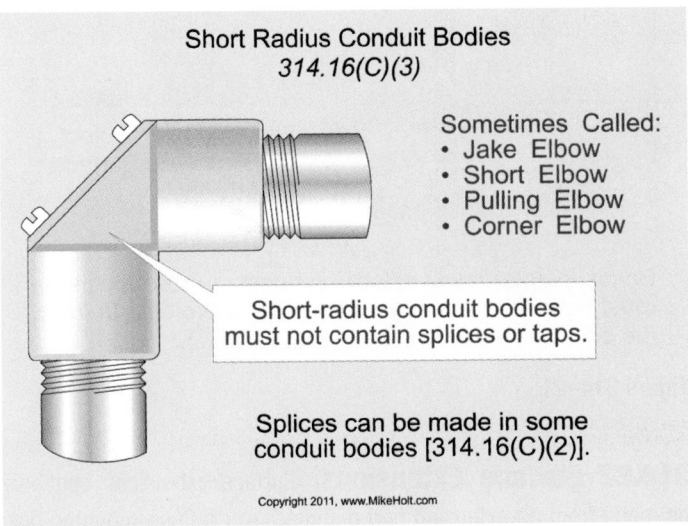

Figure 314–16

314.17 Conductors That Enter Boxes or Conduit Bodies.

(A) Openings to Be Closed. Openings through which cables or raceways enter must be adequately closed.

Author's Comment: Unused cable or raceway openings in electrical equipment must be effectively closed by fittings that provide protection substantially equivalent to the wall of the equipment [110.12(A)]. **Figure 314–17**

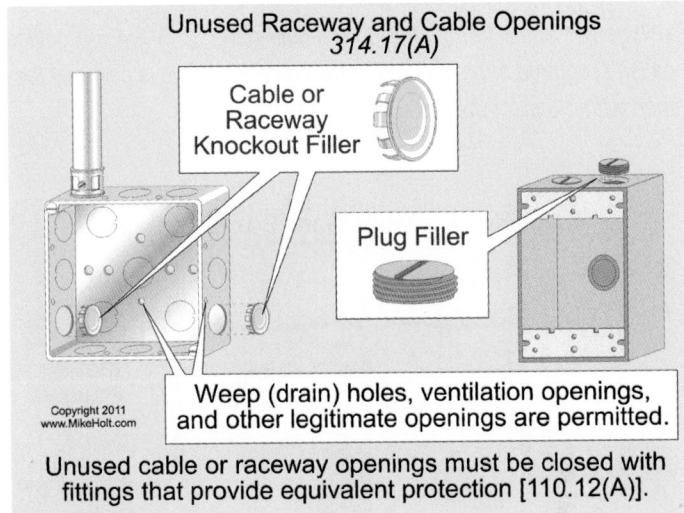

Figure 314–17

(B) Metal Boxes and Conduit Bodies. Raceways and cables must be mechanically fastened to metal boxes or conduit bodies by fittings designed for the wiring method. See 300.12 and 300.15.

(C) Nonmetallic Boxes and Conduit Bodies. Raceways and cables must be securely fastened to nonmetallic boxes or conduit bodies by fittings designed for the wiring method [300.12 and 300.15]. **Figure 314–18**

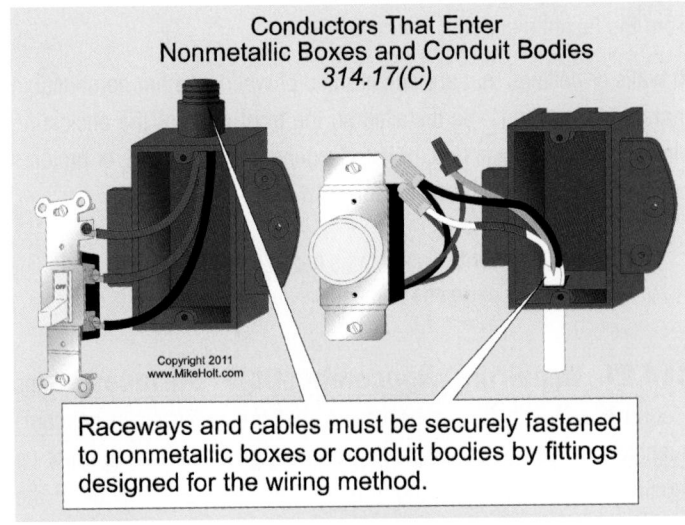

Figure 314–18

The sheath of type NM cable must extend not less than ¼ in. into the nonmetallic box.

Author's Comment: Two Type NM cables can terminate in a single cable clamp, if the clamp is listed for this purpose.

Ex: Type NM cable terminating to a single-gang (2 ¼ x 4 in.) device box isn't required to be secured to the box if the cable is securely fastened within 8 in. of the box. **Figure 314–19**

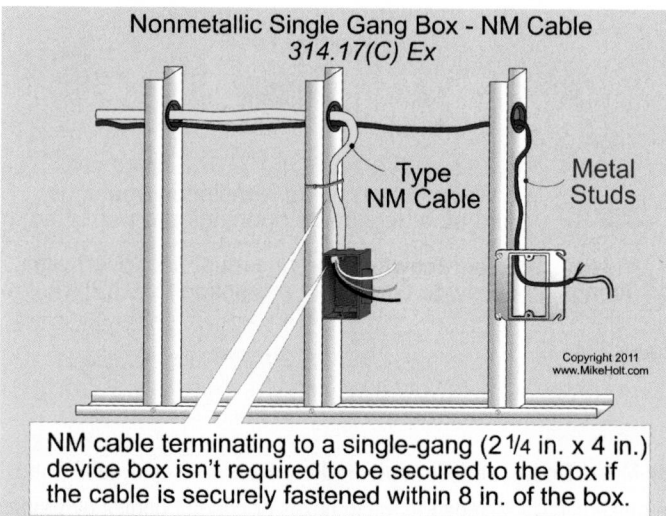

NM cable terminating to a single-gang (2 ¼ in. x 4 in.) device box isn't required to be secured to the box if the cable is securely fastened within 8 in. of the box.

Figure 314–19

314.20 Boxes Recessed in Walls or Ceilings.
Boxes having flush-type covers that are recessed in walls or ceilings of non-combustible material must have the front edge of the box, plaster ring, extension ring, or listed extender set back no more than ¼ in. from the finished surface. **Figure 314–20**

In walls or ceilings that are constructed of wood or other combustible material, boxes must be installed so the front edge of the enclosure, plaster ring, extension ring, or listed extender is flush with, or projects out from, the finished surface. **Figure 314–21**

Author's Comment: Plaster rings and extension rings are available in a variety of depths to meet the above requirements.

314.21 Repairing Noncombustible Surfaces.
Gaps around boxes with flush-type covers that are recessed in noncombustible surfaces (such as plaster, drywall, or plasterboard) must be repaired so there will be no gap more than ⅛ in. at the edge of the box. **Figure 314–22**

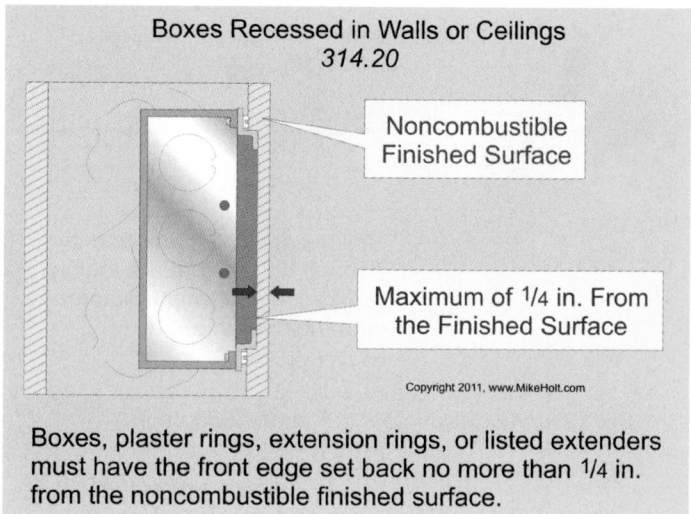

Boxes, plaster rings, extension rings, or listed extenders must have the front edge set back no more than ¼ in. from the noncombustible finished surface.

Figure 314–20

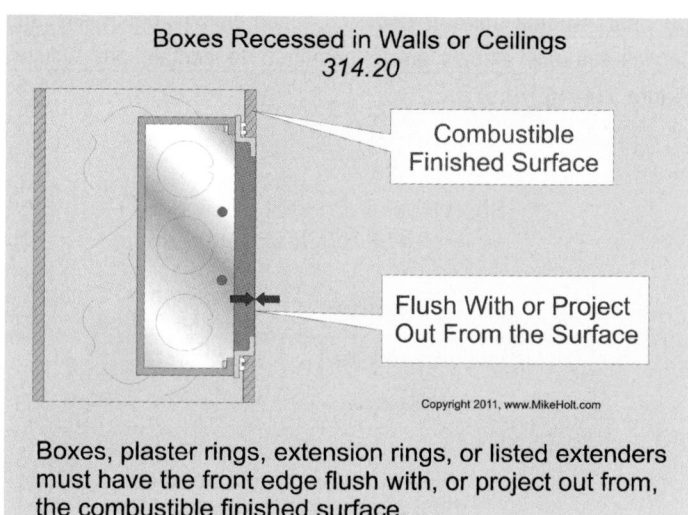

Boxes, plaster rings, extension rings, or listed extenders must have the front edge flush with, or project out from, the combustible finished surface.

Figure 314–21

314.22 Surface Extensions.
Surface extensions can only be made from an extension ring mounted over a flush-mounted box. **Figure 314–23**

Ex: A surface extension can be made from the cover of a flush-mounted box if the cover is designed so it's unlikely to fall off if the mounting screws become loose. The surface extension wiring method must be flexible to permit the removal of the cover and provide access to the box interior, and equipment grounding continuity must be independent of the connection between the box and the cover. **Figure 314–24**

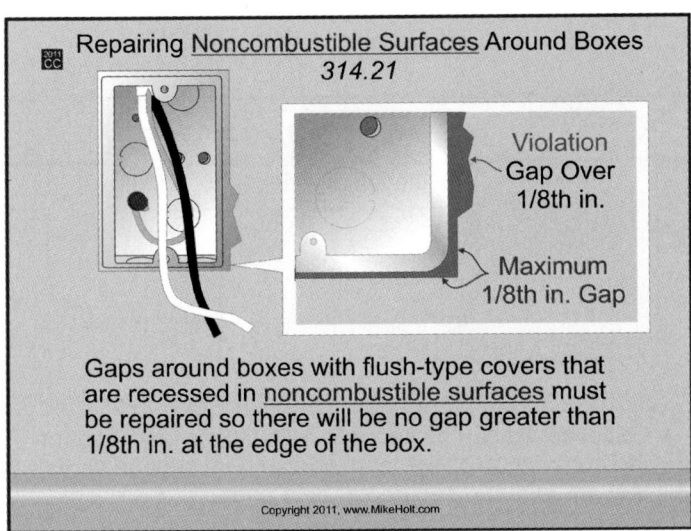

Figure 314–22

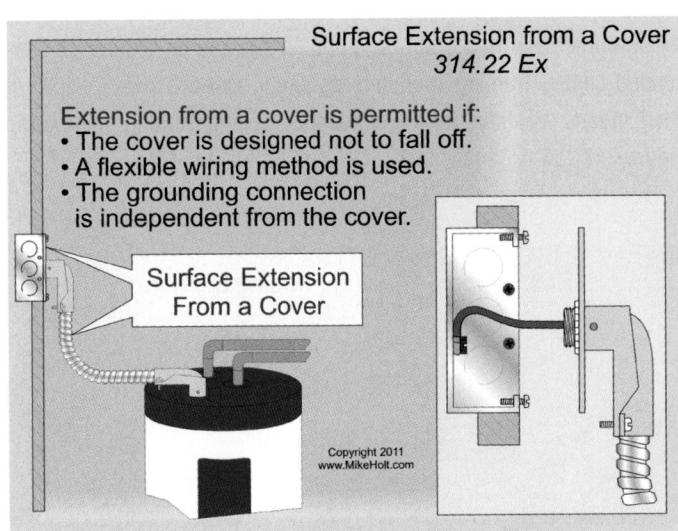

Figure 314–24

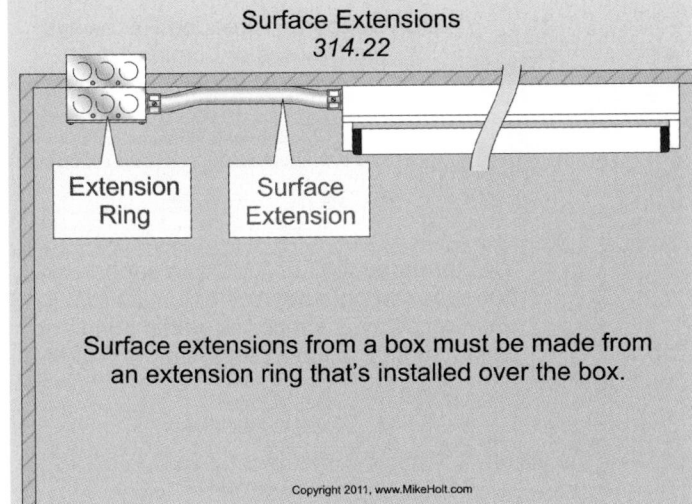

Figure 314–23

314.23 Support of Boxes and Conduit Bodies. Boxes
must be securely supported by one of the following methods:

(A) Surface. Boxes can be fastened to any surface that provides adequate support.

(B) Structural Mounting. Boxes can be supported from a structural member of a building or supported from grade by a metal, plastic, or wood brace.

(1) Nails and Screws. Nails or screws can be used to fasten boxes, provided the exposed threads of screws are protected to prevent abrasion of conductor insulation.

(2) Braces. Metal braces no less than 0.02 in. thick and wood braces not less than a nominal 1 in. x 2 in. can support a box.

(C) Finished Surface Support. Boxes can be secured to a finished surface (drywall or plaster walls or ceilings) by clamps, anchors, or fittings identified for the purpose. **Figure 314–25**

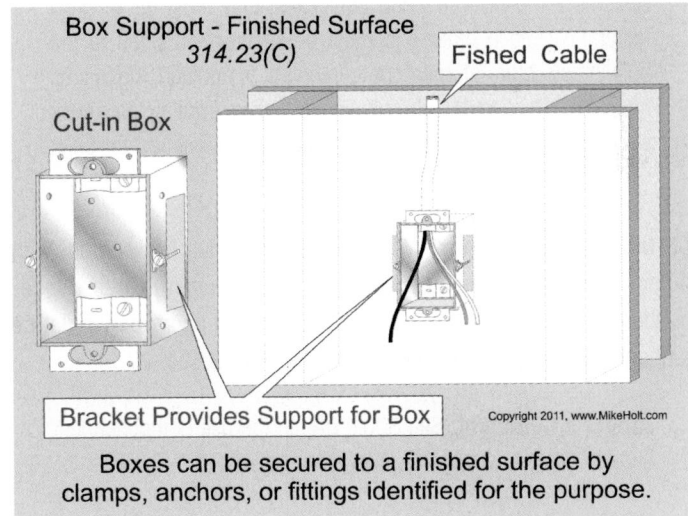

Figure 314–25

(D) Suspended-Ceiling Support. Outlet boxes can be supported to the structural or supporting elements of a suspended ceiling, if securely fastened by one of the following methods:

(1) Ceiling-Framing Members. An outlet box can be secured to suspended-ceiling framing members by bolts, screws, rivets, clips, or other means identified for the suspended-ceiling framing member(s). **Figure 314–26**

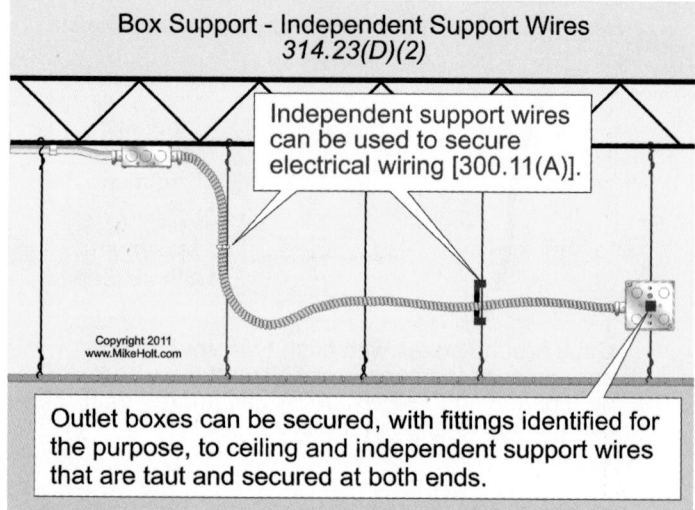

Figure 314–27

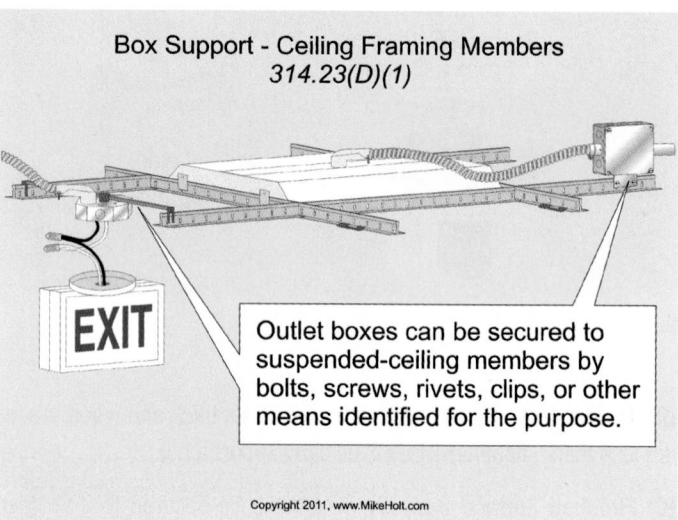

Figure 314–26

Author's Comment: If framing members of suspended-ceiling systems are used to support luminaires, they must be securely fastened to each other and must be securely attached to the building structure at appropriate intervals. In addition, luminaires must be attached to the suspended-ceiling framing members with screws, bolts, rivets, or clips listed and identified for such use [410.36(B)].

(2) Independent Support Wires. Outlet boxes can be secured, with fittings identified for the purpose, to the ceiling-support wires. If independent support wires are used for outlet box support, they must be taut and secured at both ends [300.11(A)]. **Figure 314–27**

Author's Comment: See 300.11(A) on the use of independent support wires to support raceways and cables.

(E) Raceway—Boxes and Conduit Bodies Without Devices or Luminaires. Two intermediate metal or rigid metal conduits, threaded wrenchtight into the enclosure, can be used to support an outlet box that doesn't contain a device or luminaire, if each raceway is supported within 36 in. of the box or within 18 in. of the box if all conduit entries are on the same side. **Figure 314–28**

Ex: Conduit bodies are permitted to be supported by any of the following wiring methods:

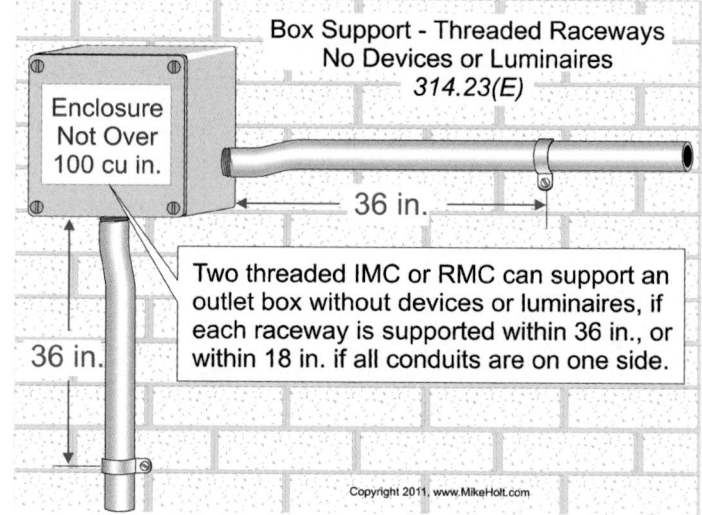

Figure 314–28

(1) Intermediate metal conduit, Type IMC

(2) Rigid metal conduit, Type RMC

(3) Rigid polyvinyl chloride conduit, Type PVC

(4) Reinforced thermosetting resin conduit, Type RTRC

(5) Electrical metallic tubing, Type EMT

(F) Raceway—Boxes and Conduit Bodies with Devices or Luminaires. Two intermediate metal or rigid metal conduits, threaded wrenchtight into the enclosure, can be used to support an outlet box containing devices or luminaires, if each raceway is supported within 18 in. of the box. **Figure 314–29**

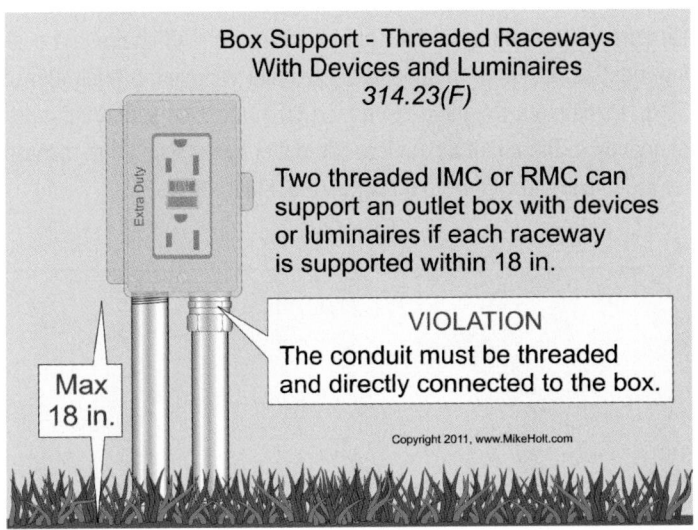

Figure 314–29

(H) Pendant Boxes.

(1) Flexible Cord. Boxes containing a hub can be supported from a cord connected to fittings that prevent tension from being transmitted to joints or terminals [400.10]. **Figure 314–30**

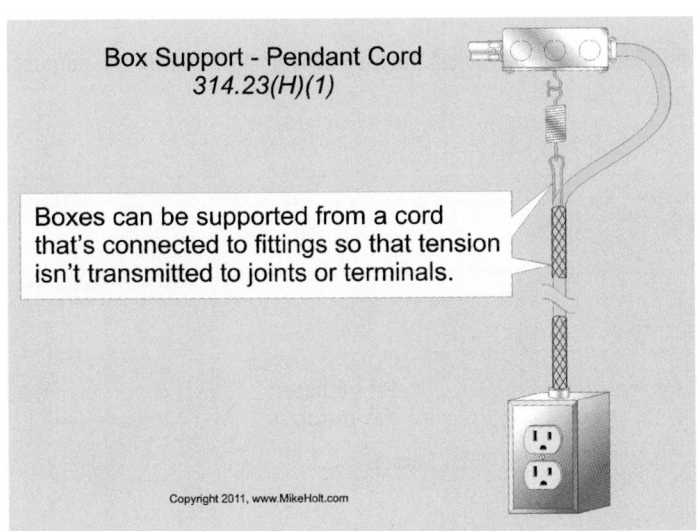

Figure 314–30

Author's Comment: Only cords identified for use as pendants in Table 400.4 may be used for pendants.314.25 Covers and Canopies. When the installation is complete, each outlet box must be provided with a cover or faceplate, unless covered by a fixture canopy, lampholder, or similar device. **Figure 314–31**

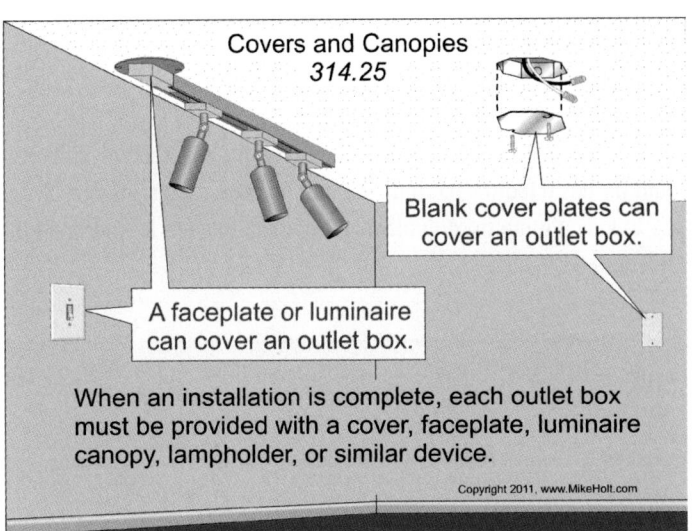

Figure 314–31

(A) Nonmetallic or Metallic. Nonmetallic covers are permitted on any box, but metal covers are only permitted if they can be connected to an equipment grounding conductor of a type recognized in 250.118, in accordance with 250.110 [250.4(A)(3)]. **Figure 314–32**

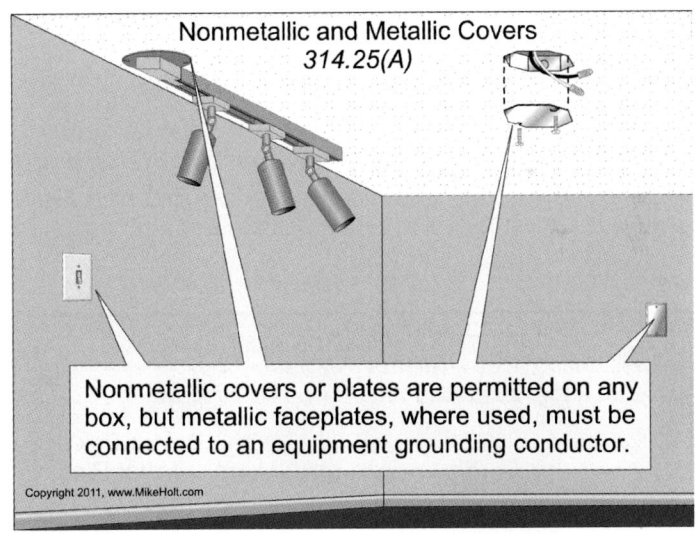

Figure 314–32

Author's Comment: Metal switch faceplates [404.9(B)] and metal receptacle faceplates [406.6(A)] must be connected to an equipment grounding conductor.

314.27 Outlet Box.

(A) Boxes at Luminaire Outlets.

(1) Luminaire Outlets in the Wall. Boxes for a luminaire in a wall must be designed for the purpose and marked on the interior of the box to indicate the maximum weight of the luminaire if other than 50 lb. **Figure 314–33**

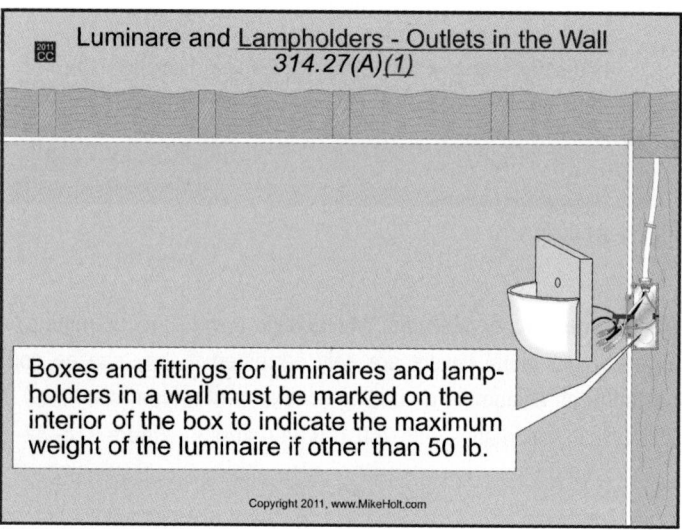

Figure 314–33

Ex: A wall-mounted luminaire weighing no more than 6 lb can be supported to a device box or plaster ring secured to a device box. **Figure 314–34**

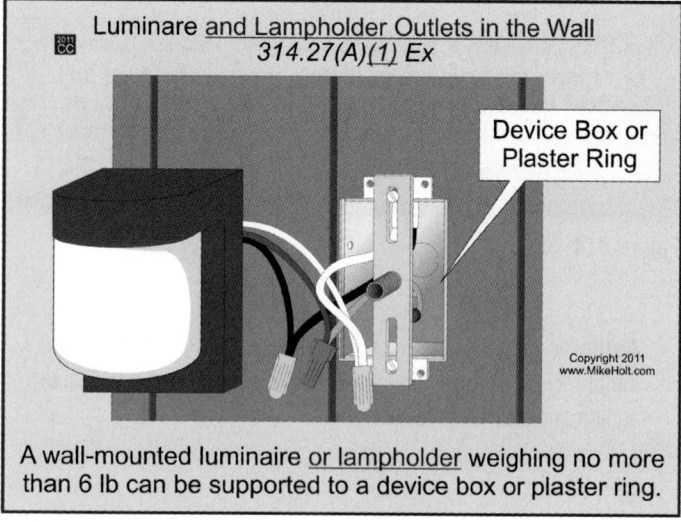

Figure 314–34

(2) Luminaire Outlets in the Ceiling. Boxes for a luminaire in a ceiling must be designed to support a luminaire weighing a minimum of 50 lb. Luminaires weighing more than 50 lb must be supported independently of the outlet box unless the outlet box is listed and marked for the maximum weight to be supported. **Figure 314–35**

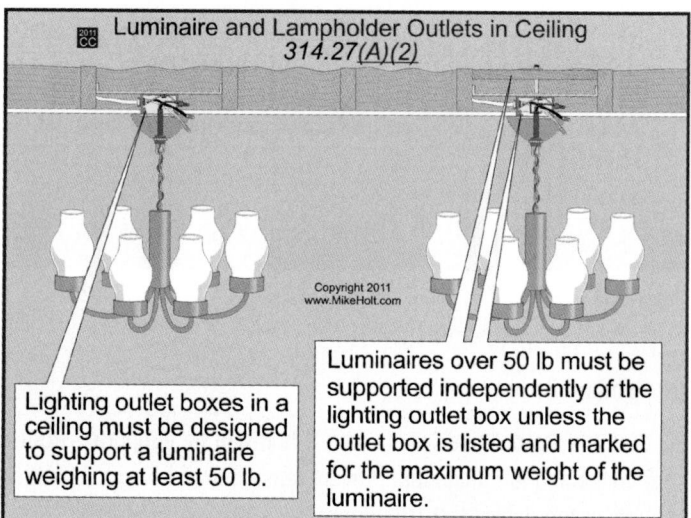

Figure 314–35

(B) Floor Box. Floor boxes must be specifically listed for the purpose. **Figure 314–36**

Figure 314–36

(C) Ceiling Paddle Fan Box. Outlet boxes for a ceiling paddle fan must be listed and marked as suitable for the purpose, and must not support a fan weighing more than 70 lb. Outlet boxes for a ceiling paddle fan that weighs more than 35 lb must include the maximum weight to be supported in the required marking. **Figure 314-37**

Figure 314-37

Author's Comment: If the maximum weight isn't marked on the box, and the fan weighs over 35 lb, the fan must be supported independently of the outlet box. Ceiling paddle fans over 70 lb must be supported independently of the outlet box.

Where spare, separately switched, ungrounded conductors are provided to a ceiling-mounted outlet box, in a location acceptable for a ceiling-suspended (paddle) fan in single or multifamily dwellings, the outlet box or outlet box system must be listed for the support of a ceiling-suspended (paddle) fan.

(D) Utilization Equipment. Boxes used for the support of utilization equipment must be designed to support equipment that weighs a minimum of 50 lb [314.27(A)].

Ex: Utilization equipment weighing 6 lb or less is permitted to be supported by any box or plaster ring secured to a box, provided the equipment is secured with no fewer than two No. 6 or larger screws. Figure 314-38

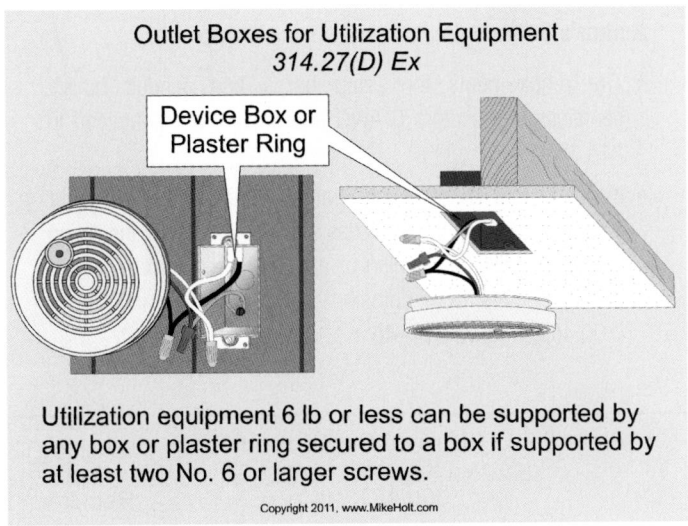

Figure 314-38

314.28 Boxes and Conduit Bodies for Conductors 4 AWG and Larger.
Boxes and conduit bodies containing conductors 4 AWG and larger that are required to be insulated must be sized so the conductor insulation won't be damaged. **Figure 314-39**

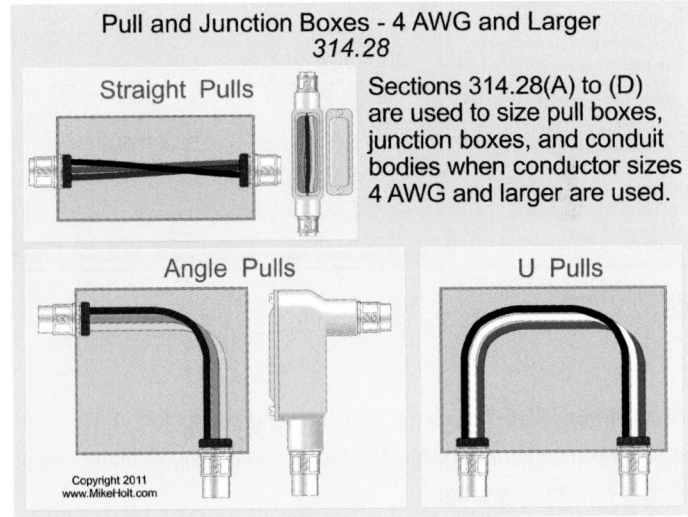

Figure 314-39

Author's Comments:

- The requirements for sizing boxes and conduit bodies containing conductors 6 AWG and smaller are contained in 314.16.

- If conductors 4 AWG and larger enter a box or other enclosure, a fitting that provides a smooth, rounded, insulating surface, such as a bushing or adapter, is required to protect the conductors from abrasion during and after installation [300.4(G)]. **Figure 314–40**

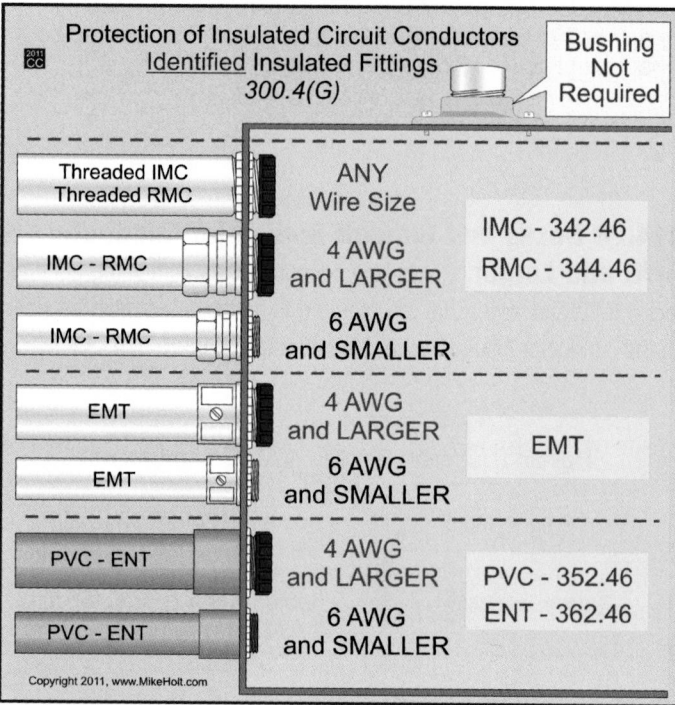

Figure 314–40

(A) Minimum Size. For raceways containing conductors 4 AWG and larger, the minimum dimensions of boxes and conduit bodies must comply with the following:

(1) Straight Pulls. The minimum distance from where the conductors enter the box or conduit body to the opposite wall must not be less than eight times the trade size of the largest raceway. **Figure 314–41**

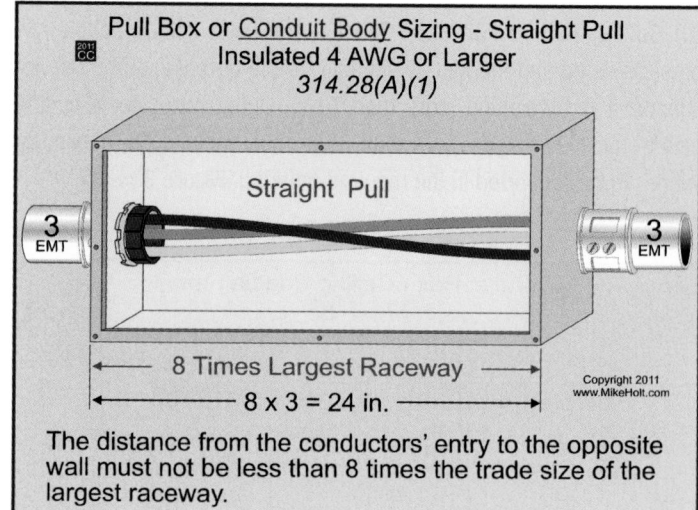

The distance from the conductors' entry to the opposite wall must not be less than 8 times the trade size of the largest raceway.

Figure 314–41

(2) Angle Pulls, U Pulls, or Splices.

- **Angle Pulls.** The distance from the raceway entry of the box or conduit body to the opposite wall must not be less than six times the trade size of the largest raceway, plus the sum of the trade sizes of the remaining raceways on the same wall and row. **Figure 314–42**

- **U Pulls.** When a conductor enters and leaves from the same wall of the box, the distance from where the raceways enter to the opposite wall must not be less than six times the trade size of the largest raceway, plus the sum of the trade sizes of the remaining raceways on the same wall and row. **Figure 314–43**

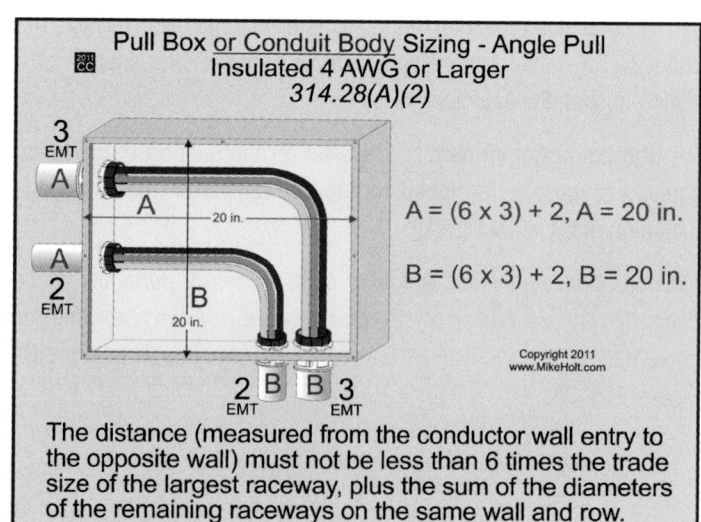

The distance (measured from the conductor wall entry to the opposite wall) must not be less than 6 times the trade size of the largest raceway, plus the sum of the diameters of the remaining raceways on the same wall and row.

Figure 314–42

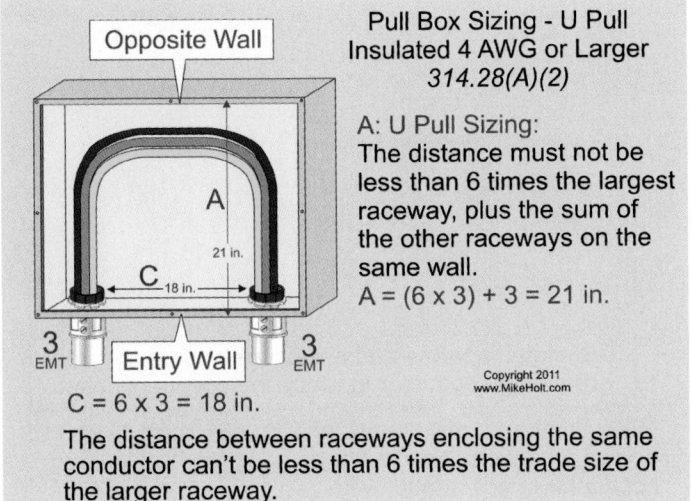

Pull Box Sizing - U Pull
Insulated 4 AWG or Larger
314.28(A)(2)

A: U Pull Sizing:
The distance must not be less than 6 times the largest raceway, plus the sum of the other raceways on the same wall.

A = (6 x 3) + 3 = 21 in.

C = 6 x 3 = 18 in.

The distance between raceways enclosing the same conductor can't be less than 6 times the trade size of the larger raceway.

Figure 314–43

- **Splices.** When conductors are spliced, the distance from where the raceways enter to the opposite wall must not be less than six times the trade size of the largest raceway, plus the sum of the trade sizes of the remaining raceways on the same wall and row. **Figure 314–44**

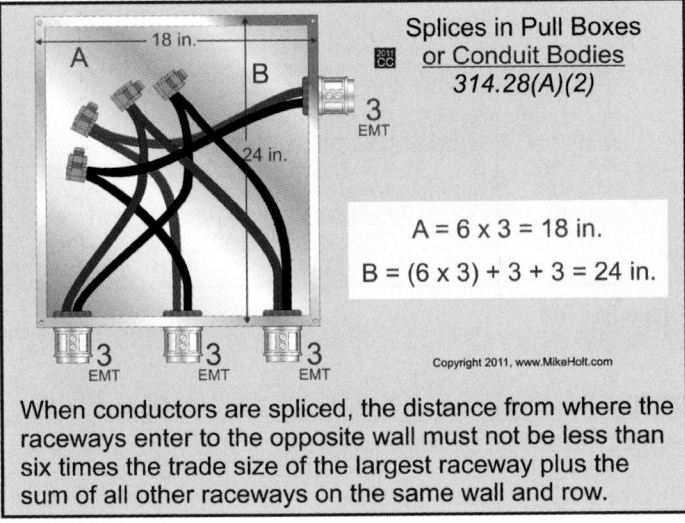

Splices in Pull Boxes
or Conduit Bodies
314.28(A)(2)

A = 6 x 3 = 18 in.

B = (6 x 3) + 3 + 3 = 24 in.

When conductors are spliced, the distance from where the raceways enter to the opposite wall must not be less than six times the trade size of the largest raceway plus the sum of all other raceways on the same wall and row.

Figure 314–44

- **Rows.** If there are multiple rows of raceway entries, each row is calculated individually and the row with the largest distance must be used. **Figure 314–45**

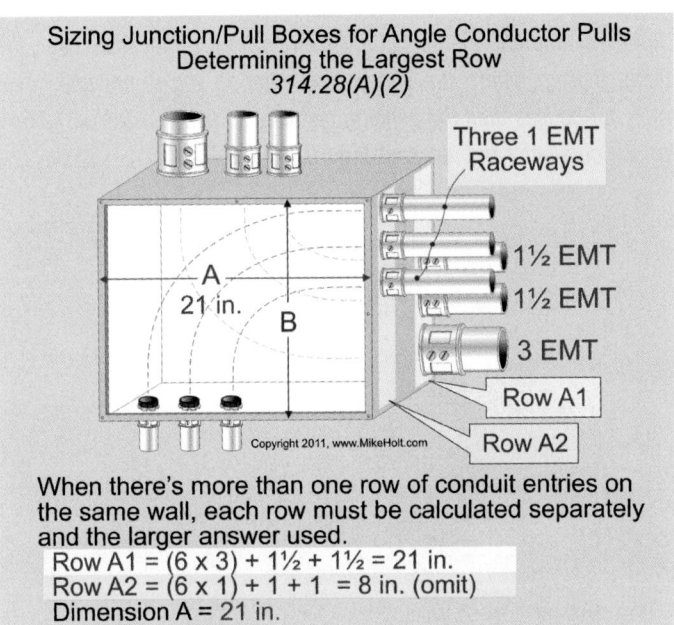

Sizing Junction/Pull Boxes for Angle Conductor Pulls
Determining the Largest Row
314.28(A)(2)

Three 1 EMT Raceways

1½ EMT

1½ EMT

3 EMT

Row A1

Row A2

When there's more than one row of conduit entries on the same wall, each row must be calculated separately and the larger answer used.
Row A1 = (6 x 3) + 1½ + 1½ = 21 in.
Row A2 = (6 x 1) + 1 + 1 = 8 in. (omit)
Dimension A = 21 in.

Figure 314–45

- **Distance Between Raceways.** The distance between raceways enclosing the same conductor must not be less than six times the trade size of the largest raceway, measured from the raceways' nearest edge-to-nearest edge. **Figure 314–46**

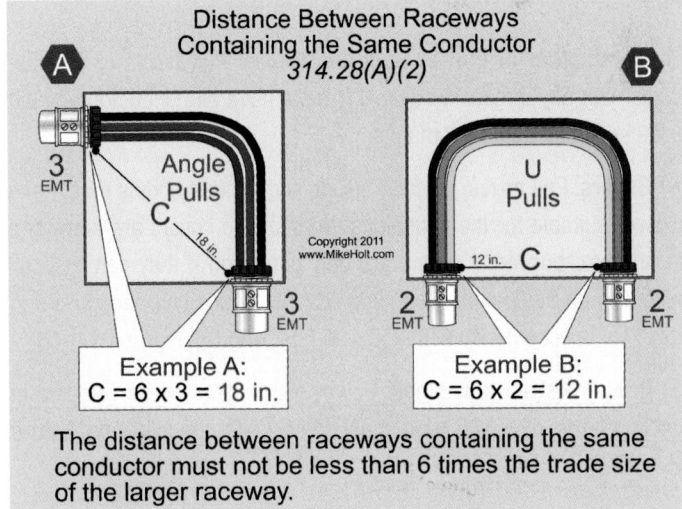

Distance Between Raceways
Containing the Same Conductor
314.28(A)(2)

Angle Pulls

U Pulls

Example A:
C = 6 x 3 = 18 in.

Example B:
C = 6 x 2 = 12 in.

The distance between raceways containing the same conductor must not be less than 6 times the trade size of the larger raceway.

Figure 314–46

Ex: When conductors enter an enclosure with a removable cover, the distance from where the conductors enter to the removable cover must not be less than the bending distance as listed in Table 312.6(A) for one conductor per terminal. **Figure 314–47**

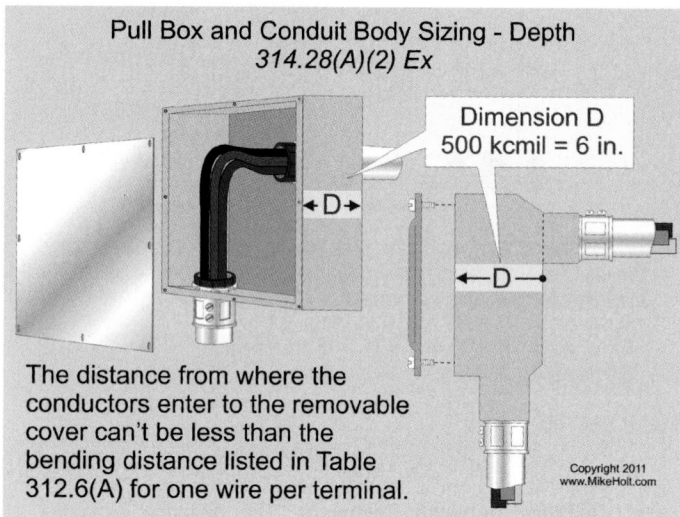

Figure 314–47

(3) Smaller Dimensions. Boxes or conduit bodies smaller than those required in 314.28(A)(1) and 314.28(A)(2) are permitted, if the enclosure is permanently marked with the maximum number and maximum size of conductors.

(B) Conductors in Pull or Junction Boxes. Pull boxes or junction boxes with any dimension over 6 ft must have all conductors cabled or racked in an approved manner.

(C) Covers. Pull boxes, junction boxes, and conduit bodies must have a cover suitable for the conditions. Nonmetallic covers are permitted on any box, but metal covers are only permitted if they can be connected to an equipment grounding conductor of a type recognized in 250.118, in accordance with 250.110 [250.4(A)(3)]. **Figure 314–48**

(E) Power Distribution Block. Power distribution blocks installed in junction boxes over 100 cu in. must comply with the following: **Figure 314–49**

(1) Installation. Be listed as a power distribution block.

(2) Size. Be installed in a box not smaller than required by the installation instructions of the power distribution block.

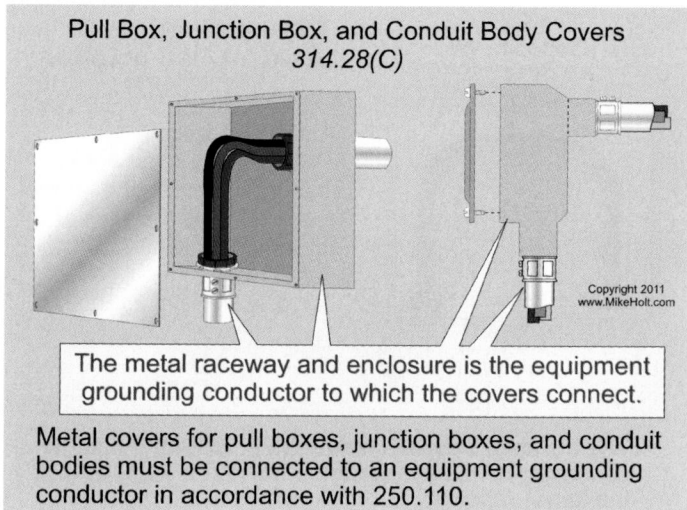

Figure 314–48

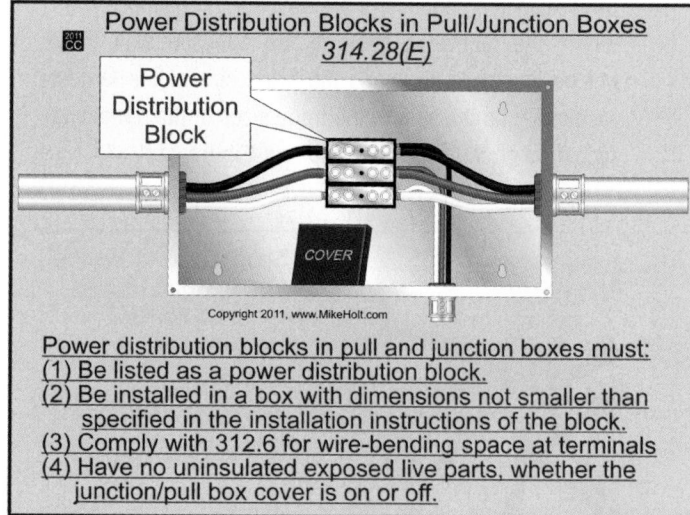

Figure 314–49

(3) Wire-Bending Space. The junction box is sized so that the wire-bending space requirements of 312.6 can be met.

(4) Live Parts. Exposed live parts on the power distribution block aren't present when the junction box cover is removed.

(5) Through Conductors. Where the junction box has conductors that don't terminate on the power distribution block(s), the through conductors must be arranged so the power distribution block terminals are unobstructed following installation.

314.29 Wiring to be Accessible. Boxes, conduit bodies, and handhole enclosures must be installed so that the wiring is accessible without removing any part of the building, sidewalks, paving, or earth. Figure 314–50

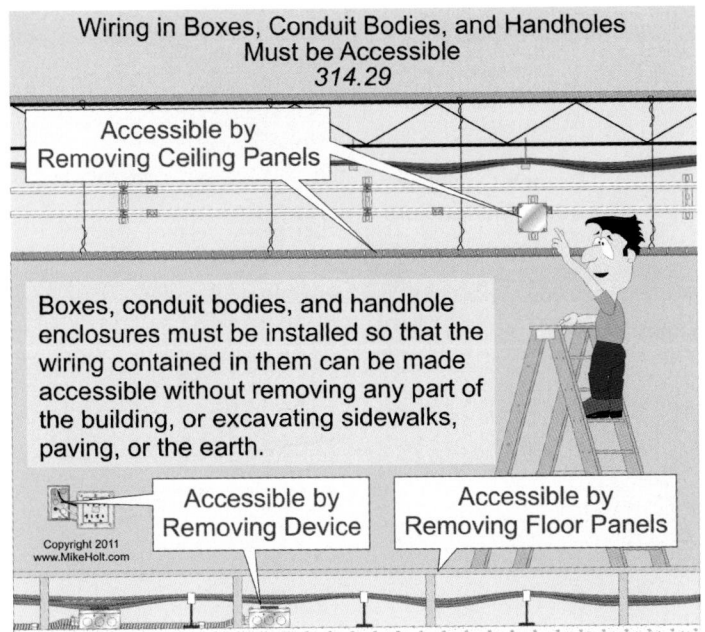

Figure 314–50

Ex: Listed boxes and handhole enclosures can be buried if covered by gravel, light aggregate, or noncohesive granulated soil, and their location is effectively identified and accessible for excavation.

314.30 Handhole Enclosures. Handhole enclosures must be identified for underground use, and be designed and installed to withstand all loads likely to be imposed on them. **Figure 314–51**

(A) Size. Handhole enclosures must be sized in accordance with 314.28(A). For handhole enclosures without bottoms, the measurement to the removable cover is taken from the end of the raceway or cable assembly. When the measurement is taken from the end of the raceway or cable assembly, the values in Table 312.6(A) for one wire to terminal can be used [314.28(A)(2) Ex].

(B) Mechanical Raceway and Cable Connection. Underground raceways and cables entering a handhole enclosure aren't required to be mechanically connected to the handhole enclosure. **Figure 314–52**

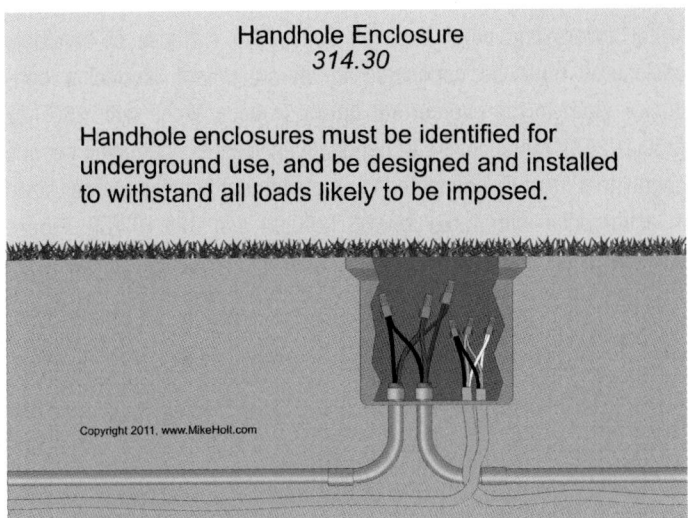

Figure 314–51

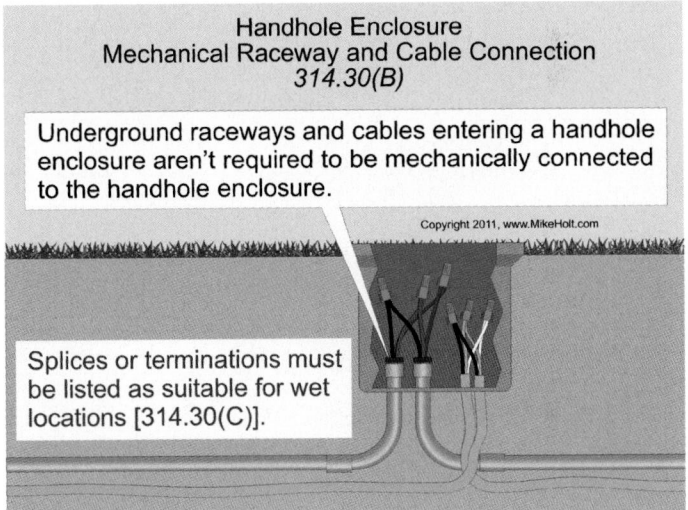

Figure 314–52

(C) Enclosure Wiring. Splices or terminations within a handhole must be listed as suitable for wet locations [110.14(B)].

(D) Covers. Handhole enclosure covers must have an identifying mark or logo that prominently identifies the function of the enclosure, such as "electric." Handhole enclosure covers must require the use of tools to open, or they must weigh over 100 lb.

Metal covers and other exposed conductive surfaces of handhole enclosures must be connected to an equipment grounding conductor sized to the overcurrent device in accordance with 250.122 [250.102(D)]. Metal covers of handhole enclosures containing service conductors must be connected to an equipment bonding jumper sized in accordance with Table 250.66 [250.92 and 250.102(C)]. **Figure 314–53**

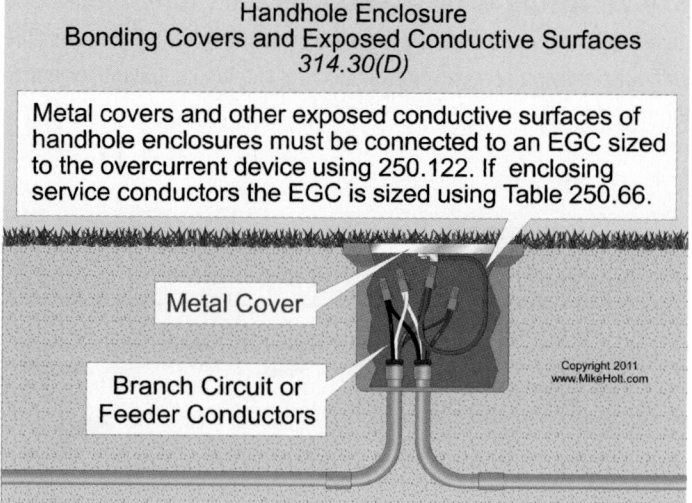

Handhole Enclosure
Bonding Covers and Exposed Conductive Surfaces
314.30(D)

Metal covers and other exposed conductive surfaces of handhole enclosures must be connected to an EGC sized to the overcurrent device using 250.122. If enclosing service conductors the EGC is sized using Table 250.66.

Metal Cover

Branch Circuit or
Feeder Conductors

Copyright 2011
www.MikeHolt.com

Figure 314–53

320

Armored Cable (Type AC)

INTRODUCTION TO ARTICLE 320—ARMORED CABLE (TYPE AC)

Armored cable is an assembly of insulated conductors, 14 AWG through 1 AWG, individually wrapped within waxed paper and contained within a flexible spiral metal sheath. The outside appearance of armored cable looks like flexible metal conduit as well as metal-clad cable to the casual observer. This cable has been referred to as "BX®" cable over the years and used in residential wiring in some areas of the country.

PART I. GENERAL

320.1 Scope. This article covers the use, installation, and construction specifications of armored cable, Type AC.

320.2 Definition.

Armored Cable (Type AC). A fabricated assembly of conductors in a flexible underlined interlocked metal armor with an internal bonding strip in intimate contact with the armor for its entire length. See 320.100. **Figure 320–1**

Armored Cable - Type AC
320.2 Definition

Waxed Paper Jute

Interlocked Spiral Metal Sheath

Bonding Strip

A fabricated assembly of conductors in a flexible interlocked metal armor with an internal bonding strip in intimate contact with the armor for its entire length.

Copyright 2011, www.MikeHolt.com

Figure 320–1

Author's Comment: The conductors are contained within a flexible metal sheath that interlocks at the edges, with an internal aluminum bonding strip, giving the cable an outside appearance similar to that of flexible metal conduit. Many electricians call this metal cable "BX®" The advantages of any flexible cables, as compared to raceway wiring methods, are that there's no limit to the number of bends between terminations and the cable can be quickly installed.

PART II. INSTALLATION

320.10 Uses Permitted. Type AC cable is permitted as follows:

(1) Feeders and branch circuits in both exposed and concealed installations.

(2) Cable trays.

(3) Dry locations.

(4) Embedded in plaster or brick, except in damp or wet locations.

(5) Air voids where not exposed to excessive moisture or dampness.

Note: The "Uses Permitted" isn't an all-inclusive list, which indicates that other suitable uses are permitted if approved by the authority having jurisdiction.

Author's Comment: Type AC cable is also permitted to be installed in a cavity plenum space [300.22(C)(1)].

320.12 Uses Not Permitted. Type AC cable must not be installed in any of the following locations:

(1) If subject to physical damage.

(2) In damp or wet locations.

(3) In air voids of masonry block or tile walls where such walls are exposed or subject to excessive moisture or dampness.

(4) Where exposed to corrosive <u>conditions.</u>

320.15 Exposed Work. Exposed Type AC cable must closely follow the surface of the building finish or running boards. Type AC cable installed on the bottom of floor or ceiling joists must be secured at every joist, and must not be subject to physical damage. **Figure 320–2**

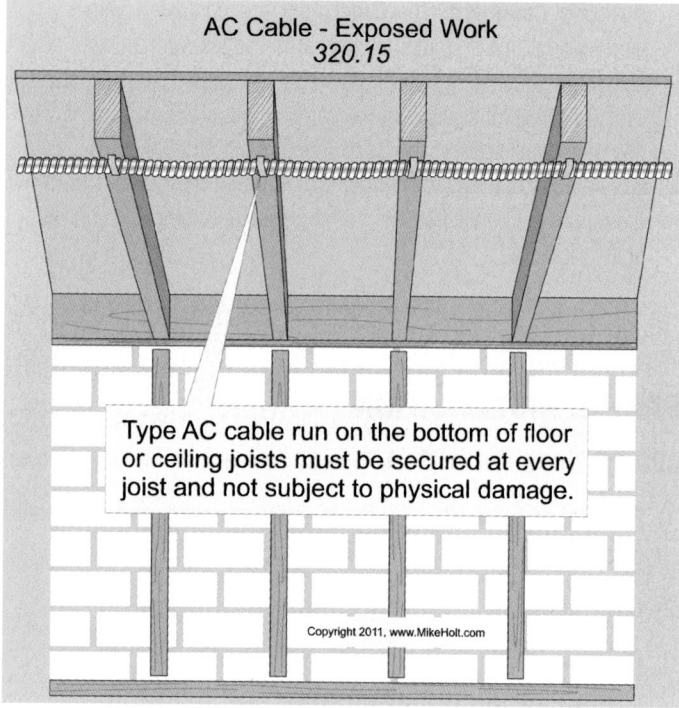

Type AC cable run on the bottom of floor or ceiling joists must be secured at every joist and not subject to physical damage.

Copyright 2011, www.MikeHolt.com

Figure 320–2

320.17 Through or Parallel to Framing Members.

Type AC cable installed through, or parallel to, framing members or furring strips must be protected against physical damage from penetration by screws or nails by maintaining 1¼ in. of separation, or by installing a suitable metal plate in accordance with 300.4(A), (C), and (D).

Author's Comments:

- 300.4(A)(1) Drilling Holes in Wood Members. When drilling holes through wood framing members for cables, the edge of the holes must be not less than 1¼ in. from the edge of the wood member. **Figure 320–3A**

  If the edge of the hole is less than 1¼ in. from the edge, a ¹⁄₁₆ in. thick steel plate of sufficient length and width must be installed to protect the wiring method from screws and nails. **Figure 320–3B**

- 300.4(A)(2) Notching Wood Members. If notching of wood framing members for cables is permitted by the building code, a ¹⁄₁₆ in. thick steel plate of sufficient length and width must be installed to protect the cables and raceways from screws and nails. **Figure 320–3C**

- 300.4(D) Cables Parallel to Framing Members and Furring Strips. Cables installed parallel to framing members or furring strips must be protected where likely to be penetrated by nails or screws. The wiring method must be installed so it's at least 1¼ in. from the nearest edge of the framing members or furring strips, or a ¹⁄₁₆ in. thick steel plate must protect the wiring method. **Figure 320–4**

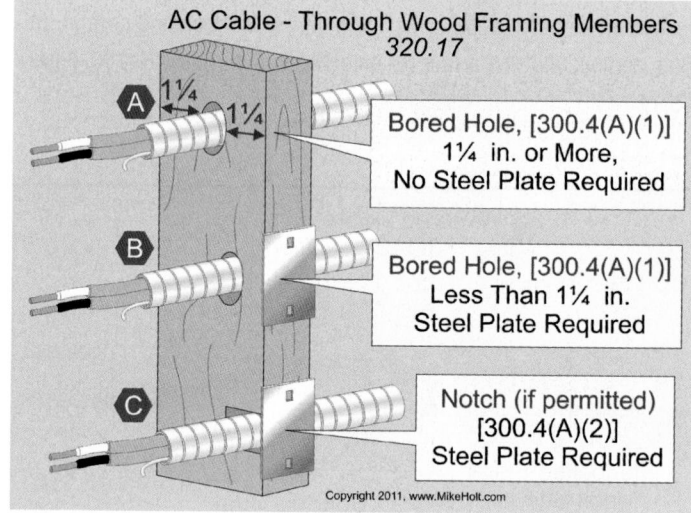

AC Cable - Through Wood Framing Members
320.17

Ⓐ Bored Hole, [300.4(A)(1)] 1¼ in. or More, No Steel Plate Required

Ⓑ Bored Hole, [300.4(A)(1)] Less Than 1¼ in. Steel Plate Required

Ⓒ Notch (if permitted) [300.4(A)(2)] Steel Plate Required

Copyright 2011, www.MikeHolt.com

Figure 320–3

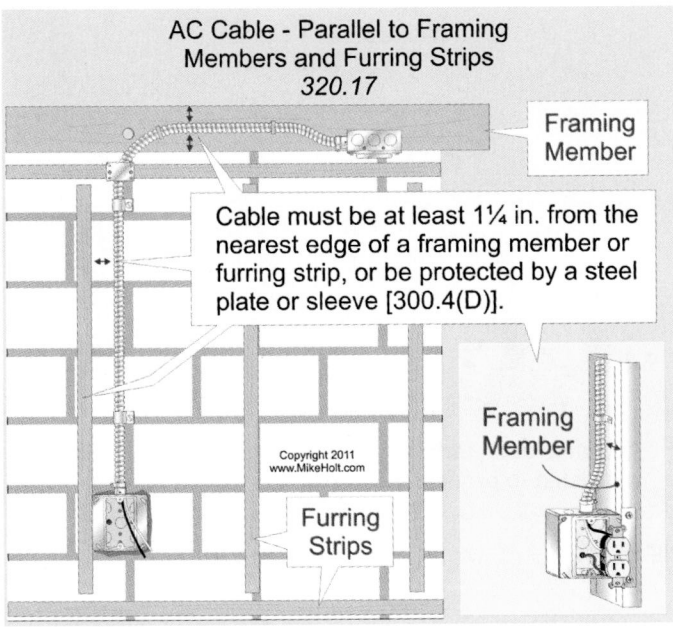

AC Cable - Parallel to Framing Members and Furring Strips
320.17

Framing Member

Cable must be at least 1¼ in. from the nearest edge of a framing member or furring strip, or be protected by a steel plate or sleeve [300.4(D)].

Framing Member

Furring Strips

Copyright 2011
www.MikeHolt.com

Figure 320–4

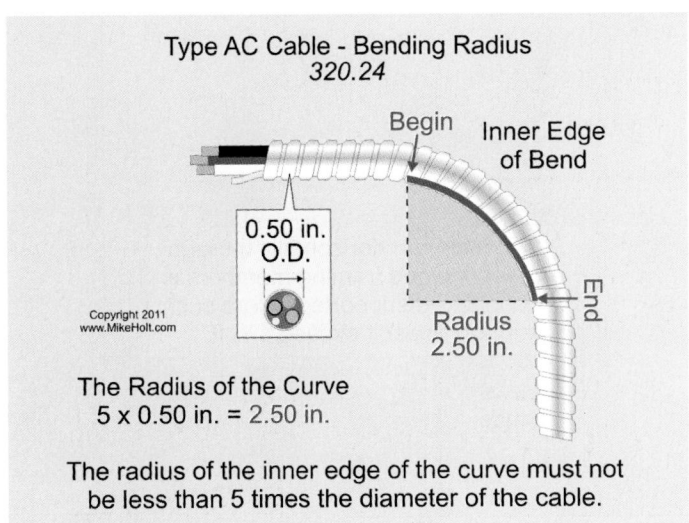

Type AC Cable - Bending Radius
320.24

Begin   Inner Edge of Bend

0.50 in. O.D.

Radius 2.50 in.

End

Copyright 2011
www.MikeHolt.com

The Radius of the Curve
5 x 0.50 in. = 2.50 in.

The radius of the inner edge of the curve must not be less than 5 times the diameter of the cable.

Figure 320–5

320.23 In Accessible Attics or Roof Spaces.

(A) Cables Run Across the Top of Floor Joists. Where run across the top of floor joists, or across the face of rafters or studding within 7 ft of floor or floor joists, the cable must be protected by substantial guard strips that are at least as high as the cable. If this space isn't accessible by permanent stairs or ladders, protection is required only within 6 ft of the nearest edge of the scuttle hole or attic entrance.

(B) Cable Installed Parallel to Framing Members. Where Type AC cable is installed on the side of rafters, studs, ceiling joists, or floor joists, no protection is required if the cable is installed and supported so the nearest outside surface of the cable or raceway is at least 1¼ in. from the nearest edge of the framing member [300.4(D)].

320.24 Bends.
Type AC cable must not be bent in a manner that will damage the cable. This is accomplished by limiting bending of the inner edge of the cable to a radius of not less than five times the diameter of the cable. **Figure 320–5**

320.30 Securing and Supporting.

(A) General. Type AC cable must be supported and secured by staples, cable ties, straps, hangers, or similar fittings, designed and installed so as not to damage the cable.

(B) Securing. Type AC cable must be secured within 12 in. of every outlet box, junction box, cabinet, or fitting, and at intervals not exceeding 4½ ft. **Figure 320–6**

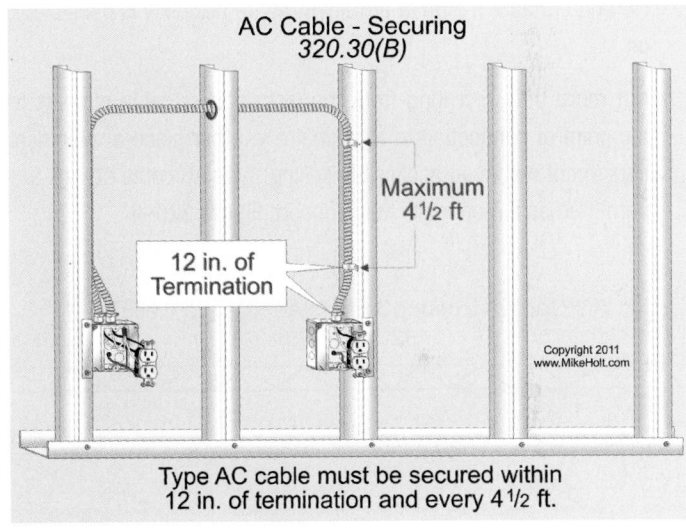

AC Cable - Securing
320.30(B)

Maximum 4½ ft

12 in. of Termination

Copyright 2011
www.MikeHolt.com

Type AC cable must be secured within 12 in. of termination and every 4½ ft.

Figure 320–6

Author's Comment: Type AC cable is considered secured when installed horizontally through openings in wooden or metal framing members [320.30(C)].

(C) Supporting. Type AC cable must be supported at intervals not exceeding 4½ ft. Cables installed horizontally through wooden or metal framing members are considered supported if support doesn't exceed 4½ ft. **Figure 320–7**

(D) Unsupported Cables. Type AC cable can be unsupported where the cable is:

(1) Fished through concealed spaces in finished buildings or structures, if support is impracticable; or

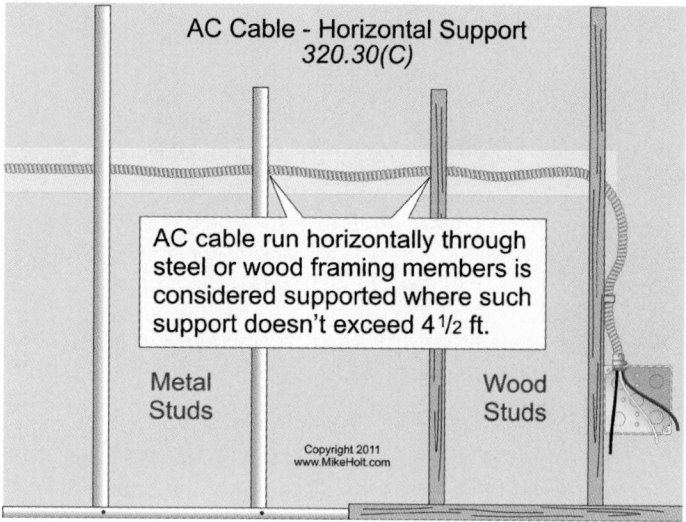

Figure 320–7

(2) Not more than 2 ft long at terminals where flexibility is necessary; or

(3) Not more than 6 ft long from the last point of cable support to the point of connection to a luminaire or other piece of electrical equipment within an accessible ceiling. Type AC cable fittings are permitted as a means of cable support. **Figure 320–8**

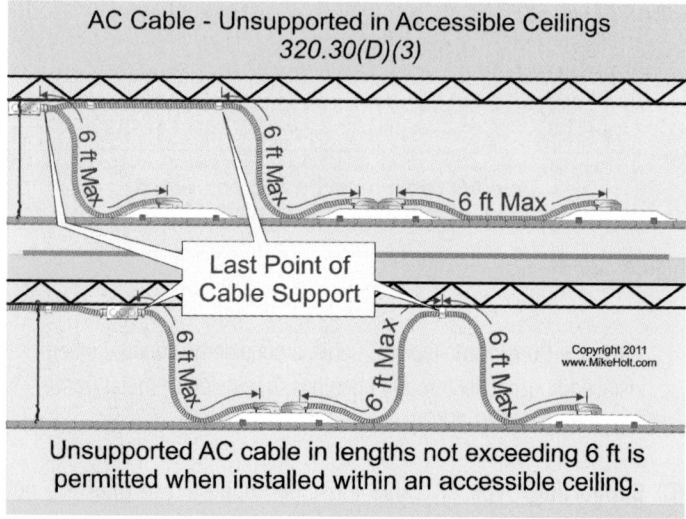

Figure 320–8

320.40 Boxes and Fittings. Type AC cable must terminate in boxes or fittings specifically listed for Type AC cable to protect the conductors from abrasion [300.15]. **Figure 320–9**

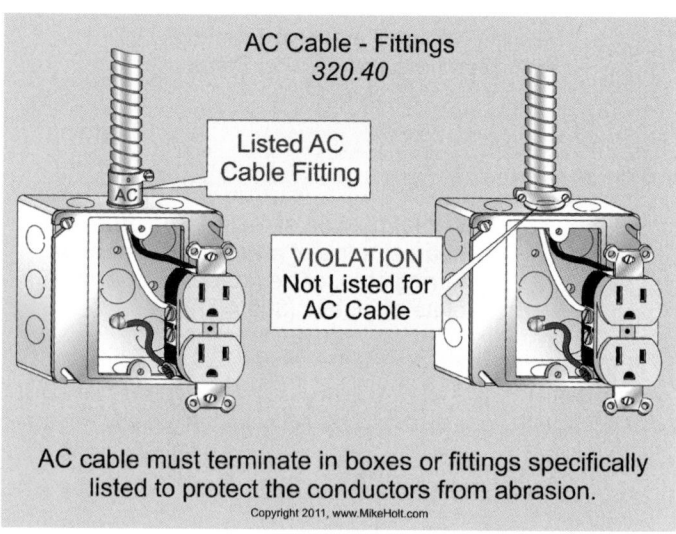

Figure 320–9

An insulating anti-short bushing, sometimes called a "redhead," must be installed at all Type AC cable terminations. The termination fitting must permit the visual inspection of the anti-short bushing once the cable has been installed. **Figure 320–10**

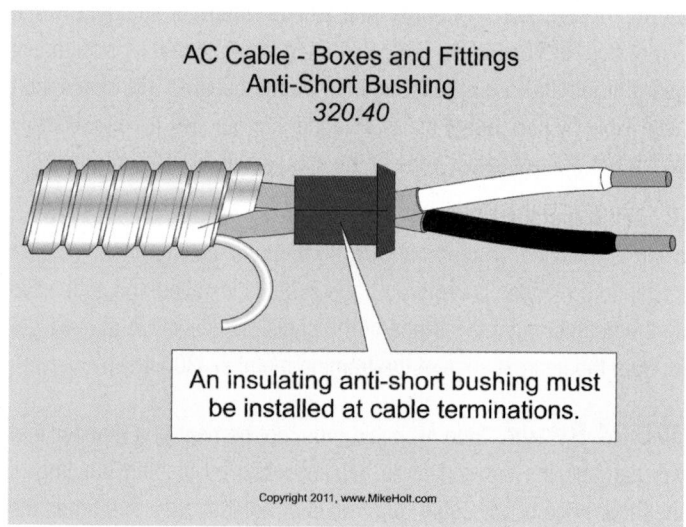

Figure 320–10

Author's Comments:

- The internal aluminum bonding strip within the cable serves no electrical purpose once outside the cable, and can be cut off, but many electricians use it to secure the anti-short bushing to the cable. See 320.108.

• Conductors 4 AWG and larger that enter an enclosure must be protected from abrasion during and after installation by a fitting that provides a smooth, rounded, insulating surface, such as an insulating bushing unless the design of the box, fitting, or enclosure provides equivalent protection in accordance with 300.4(G).

320.80 Conductor Ampacity.

(A) Thermal Insulation. Conductor ampacity is calculated on the 90°C insulation rating of the conductors, however the conductors must be sized to the termination temperature rating in accordance with 110.14(C)(1). **Figure 320–11**

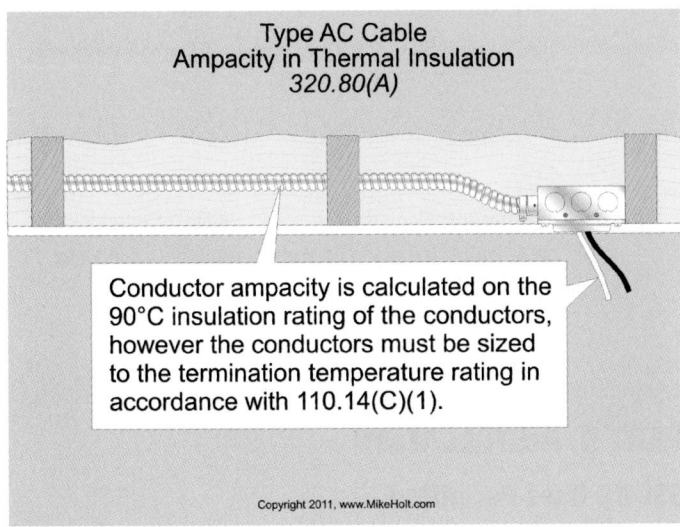

Figure 320–11

Question: What's the ampacity of four 12 THHN current-carrying conductors installed in Type AC cable?

(a) 18A   (b) 24A   (c) 27A   (d) 30A

Answer: (b) 24A

Table 310.15(B)(16) ampacity if 12 THHN is 30A
Conductor Adjusted Ampacity = 30A x 0.80 [Table 310.15(B)(3)(a)]
Conductor Adjusted Ampacity = 24A

PART III. CONSTRUCTION SPECIFICATIONS

320.100 Construction. Type AC cable has an armor of flexible metal tape with an internal aluminum bonding strip in intimate contact with the armor for its entire length.

Author's Comments:

• The best method of cutting Type AC cable is to use a tool specially designed for the purpose, such as a rotary armor cutter.

• When cutting Type AC cable with a hacksaw, be sure to cut only one spiral of the cable and be careful not to nick the conductors; this is done by cutting the cable at an angle. Breaking the cable spiral (bending the cable very sharply), then cutting the cable with a pair of dikes isn't a good practice.

320.108 Equipment Grounding Conductor. Type AC cable must provide an adequate path for fault current as required by 250.4(A)(5) or 250.4(B)(4) to act as an equipment grounding conductor. **Figure 320–12**

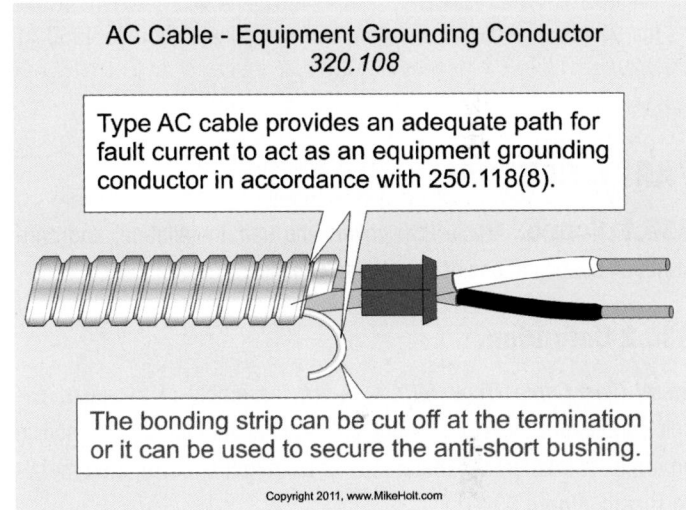

Figure 320–12

Author's Comment: The internal aluminum bonding strip isn't an equipment grounding conductor, but it allows the interlocked armor to serve as an equipment grounding conductor because it reduces the impedance of the armored spirals to ensure that a ground fault will be cleared. It's the combination of the aluminum bonding strip and the cable armor that creates the equipment grounding conductor. Once the bonding strip exits the cable, it can be cut off because it no longer serves any purpose. The effective ground-fault current path must be maintained by the use of fittings specifically listed for Type AC cable [320.40]. See 300.12, 300.15, and 300.100.

Metal-Clad Cable (Type MC)

INTRODUCTION TO ARTICLE 330—METAL-CLAD CABLE (TYPE MC)

Metal-clad cable encloses insulated conductors in a metal sheath of either corrugated or smooth copper or aluminum tubing, or spiral inter-locked steel or aluminum. The physical characteristics of Type MC cable make it a versatile wiring method that you can use in almost any location, and for almost any application. The most commonly used Type MC cable is the interlocking kind, which looks similar to armored cable or flexible metal conduit. Traditional interlocked Type MC cable isn't permitted to serve as an equipment grounding conductor, there-fore this cable must contain an insulated equipment grounding conductor in accordance with 250.118(1). There is a fairly new product called interlocked Type MCᴬᴾ cable containing an aluminum grounding/bonding conductor running just below the metal armor, which allows the sheath to serve as an equipment grounding conductor [250.118(10)(b)].

PART I. GENERAL

330.1 Scope. Article 330 covers the use, installation, and construction specifications of metal-clad cable.

330.2 Definition.

Metal-Clad Cable (Type MC). A factory assembly of insulated circuit conductors, with or without optical fiber members, enclosed in an armor of interlocking metal tape or a smooth or corrugated metallic sheath. **Figure 330–1**

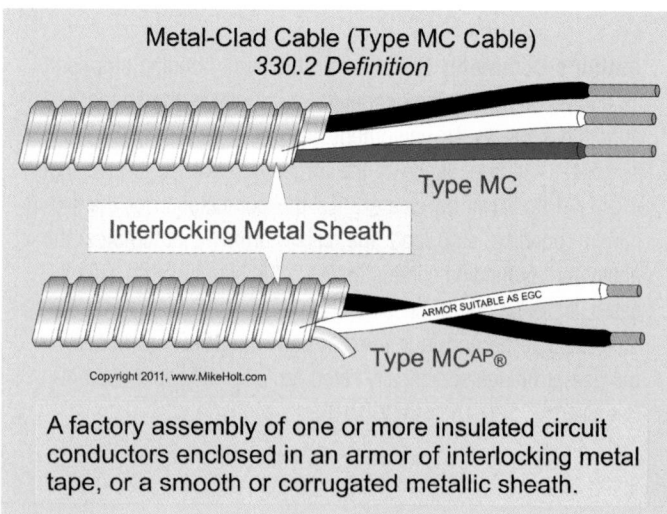

Figure 330–1

Author's Comment: Because the outer sheath of interlocked Type MC cable isn't listed as an equipment grounding conductor, it contains an equipment grounding conductor [330.108].

PART II. INSTALLATION

330.10 Uses Permitted.

(A) General Uses.

(1) In branch circuits, feeders, and services

(2) In power, lighting, control, and signal circuits

(3) Indoors or outdoors

(4) Exposed or concealed

(5) Directly buried (if identified for the purpose)

(6) In a cable tray

(7) In a raceway

(8) As aerial cable on a messenger

(9) In hazardous locations as permitted in 501.10(B), 502.10(B), and 503.10

(10) Embedded in plaster or brick

(11) In wet locations, if any of the following are met:

a. The metallic covering is impervious to moisture.

b. A moisture-impervious jacket is provided under the metal covering.

c. The insulated conductors under the metallic covering are listed for use in wet locations and a corrosion-resistant jacket is provided over the metallic sheath.

(12) If single-conductor cables are used, all circuit conductors must be grouped together to minimize induced voltage on the sheath [300.3(B)].

(B) Specific Uses.

(1) Cable Tray. Type MC cable installed in a cable tray must comply with 392.10, 392.12, 392.10(E), 392.10(L), 392.10(N), 392.30(A), 392.46, and 392.56.

(2) Direct Buried. Direct-buried cables must be protected in accordance with 300.5.

(3) Installed as Service-Entrance Cable. Type MC cable is permitted for service entrances, when installed in accordance with 230.43.

(4) Installed Outside of Buildings or Structures. Type MC cable installed outside of buildings or structures must comply with 225.10, 396.10, and 396.12.

> **Note:** The "Uses Permitted" isn't an all-inclusive list, which indicates that other suitable uses are permitted if approved by the authority having jurisdiction.

330.12 Uses Not Permitted. Type MC cable must not be used where:

(1) Subject to physical damage.

(2) Exposed to the destructive corrosive conditions in (a) or (b), unless the metallic sheath or armor is resistant or protected by material resistant to the conditions:

(a) Direct burial in the earth or embedded in concrete unless identified for the application.

(b) Exposed to cinder fills, strong chlorides, caustic alkalis, or vapors of chlorine or of hydrochloric acids.

330.17 Through or Parallel to Framing Members.

Type MC cable installed through or parallel to framing members or furring strips must be protected against physical damage from penetration of screws or nails by maintaining a 1¼ in. separation, or by installing a suitable metal plate in accordance with 300.4(A) and (D).

Author's Comments:

- 300.4(A)(1) Drilling Holes in Wood Members. When drilling holes through wood framing members for cables, the edge of the holes must be not less than 1¼ in. from the edge of the wood member. **Figure 330–2A**

  If the edge of the hole is less than 1¼ in. from the edge, a ¹⁄₁₆ in. thick steel plate of sufficient length and width must be installed to protect the wiring method from screws and nails. **Figure 330–2B**

- 300.4(A)(2) Notching Wood Members. If notching of wood framing members for cables is permitted by the building code, a ¹⁄₁₆ in. thick steel plate of sufficient length and width must be installed to protect the cables and raceways from screws and nails. **Figure 330–2C**

- 300.4(D) Cables Parallel to Framing Members and Furring Strips. Cables installed parallel to framing members or furring strips must be protected where likely to be penetrated by nails or screws. The wiring method must be installed so it's at least 1¼ in. from the nearest edge of the framing member or furring strips, or a ¹⁄₁₆ in. thick steel plate must protect it. **Figure 330–3**

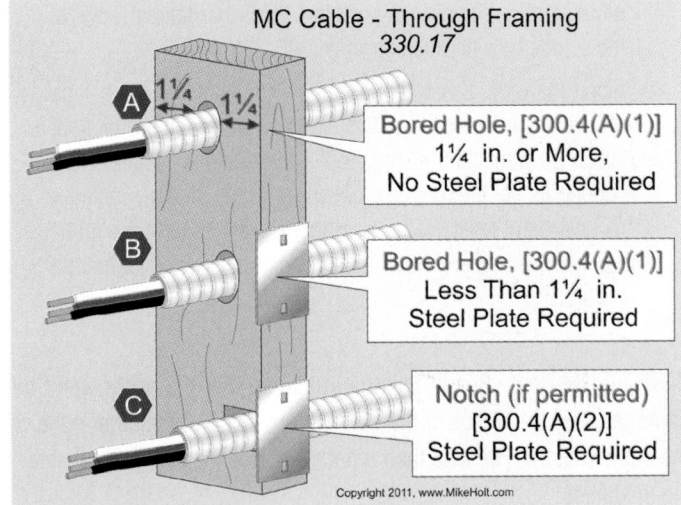

Figure 330–2

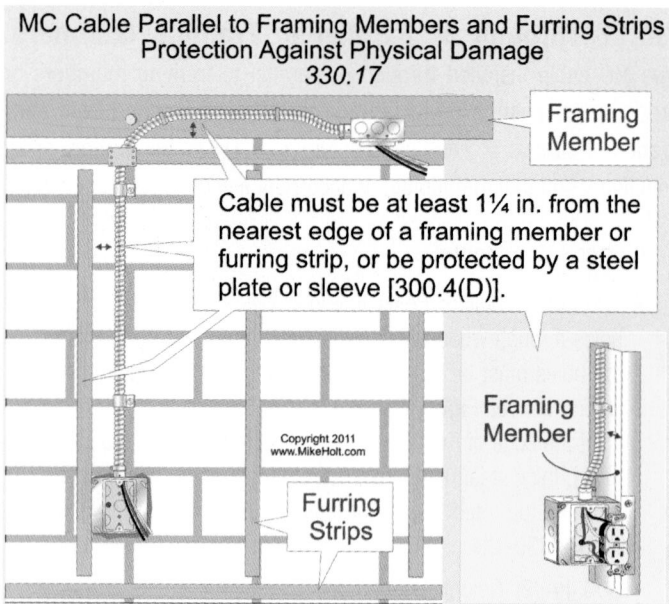

Figure 330–3

330.23 In Accessible Attics or Roof Spaces. Type MC
cable installed in accessible attics or roof spaces must comply with 320.23.

Author's Comments:

- On the Surface of Floor Joists, Rafters, or Studs. In attics and roof spaces that are accessible, substantial guards must protect cables installed across the top of floor joists, or across the face of rafters or studding within 7 ft of floor or floor joists. If this space isn't accessible by permanent stairs or ladders, protection is required only within 6 ft of the nearest edge of the scuttle hole or attic entrance [320.23(A)].

- Along the Side of Framing Members [320.23(B)]. When Type MC cable is installed on the side of rafters, studs, or floor joists, no protection is required if the cable is installed and supported so the nearest outside surface of the cable or raceway is at least 1¼ in. from the nearest edge of the framing member where nails or screws are likely to penetrate [300.4(D)].

330.24 Bends. Bends must be made so that the cable won't be damaged, and the radius of the curve of any bend at the inner edge of the cable must not be less than what's dictated in each of the following instances:

(A) Smooth-Sheath Cables.

(1) Smooth-sheath Type MC cables must not be bent so the bending radius of the inner edge of the cable is less than 10 times the external diameter of the metallic sheath for cable up to ¾ in. in external diameter.

(B) Interlocked or Corrugated Sheath. Interlocked- or corrugated-sheath Type MC cable must not be bent so the bending radius of the inner edge of the cable is less than seven times the external diameter of the cable. **Figure 330–4**

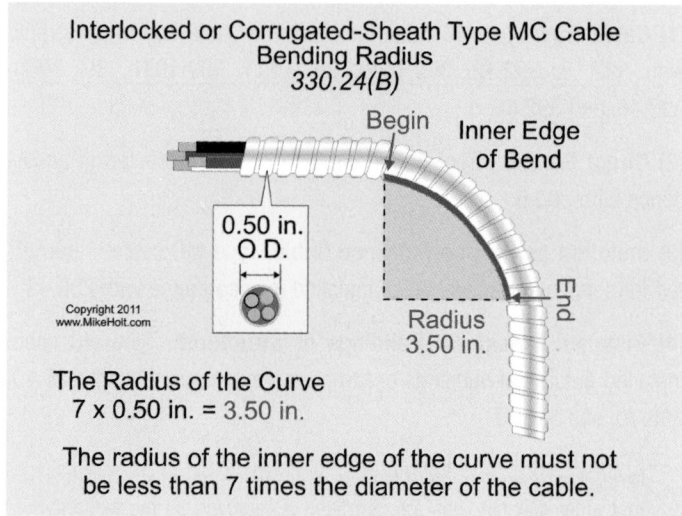

Figure 330–4

330.30 Securing and Supporting.

(A) General. Type MC cable must be supported and secured by staples, cable ties, straps, hangers, or similar fittings designed and installed so as not to damage the cable.

(B) Securing. Type MC cable with four or less conductors sized no larger than 10 AWG, must be secured within 12 in. of every outlet box, junction box, cabinet, or fitting and at intervals not exceeding 6 ft. **Figure 330–5**

(C) Supporting. Type MC cable must be supported at intervals not exceeding 6 ft. Cables installed horizontally through wooden or metal framing members are considered secured and supported if such support doesn't exceed 6 ft intervals. **Figure 330–6**

(D) Unsupported Cables. Type MC cable can be unsupported if the cable is:

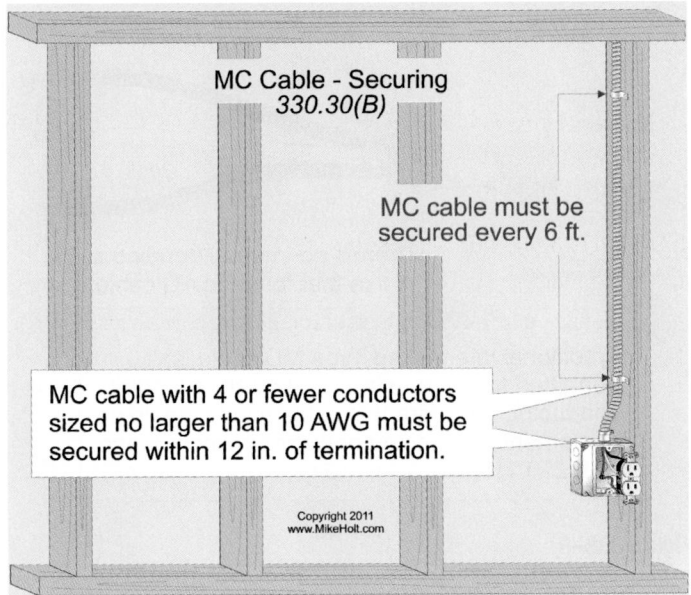

MC Cable - Securing
330.30(B)

MC cable must be secured every 6 ft.

MC cable with 4 or fewer conductors sized no larger than 10 AWG must be secured within 12 in. of termination.

Copyright 2011
www.MikeHolt.com

Figure 330–5

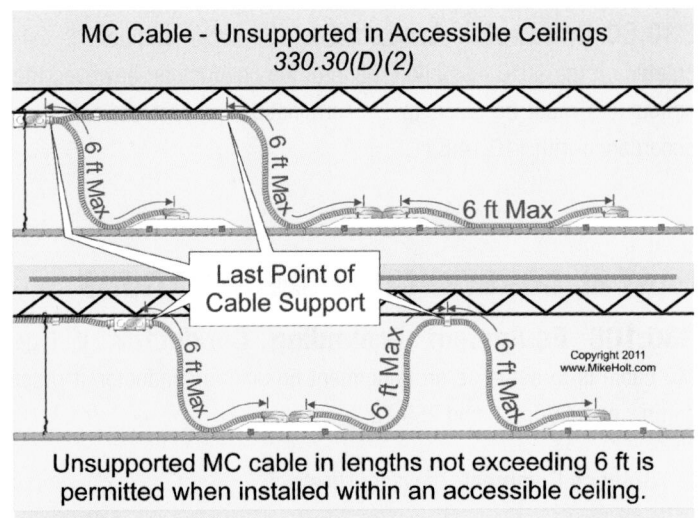

MC Cable - Unsupported in Accessible Ceilings
330.30(D)(2)

6 ft Max

6 ft Max

6 ft Max

Last Point of Cable Support

6 ft Max

6 ft Max

6 ft Max

Copyright 2011
www.MikeHolt.com

Unsupported MC cable in lengths not exceeding 6 ft is permitted when installed within an accessible ceiling.

Figure 330–7

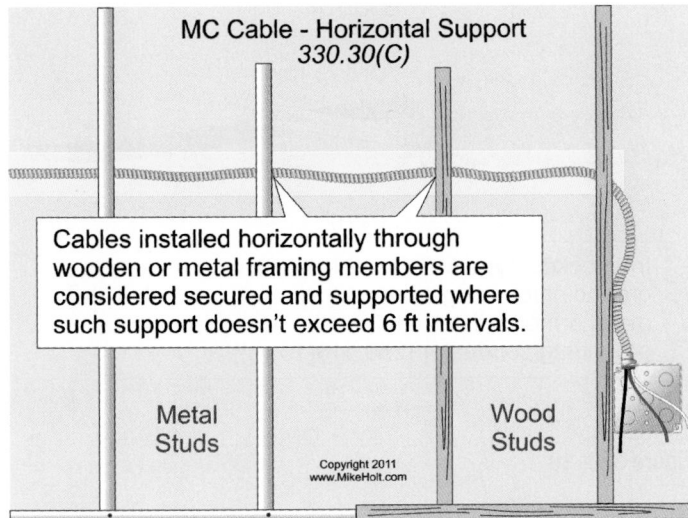

MC Cable - Horizontal Support
330.30(C)

Cables installed horizontally through wooden or metal framing members are considered secured and supported where such support doesn't exceed 6 ft intervals.

Metal Studs

Wood Studs

Copyright 2011
www.MikeHolt.com

Figure 330–6

(1) Fished through concealed spaces in finished buildings or structures, if support is impracticable, or

(2) Not more than 6 ft long from the last point of cable support to the point of connection to luminaires or other electrical equipment within an accessible ceiling. Type MC cable fittings are permitted as a means of cable support. **Figure 330–7**

330.40 Fittings. Fittings used to secure Type MC cable to boxes or other enclosures must be listed and identified for such use [300.15]. **Figure 330–8**

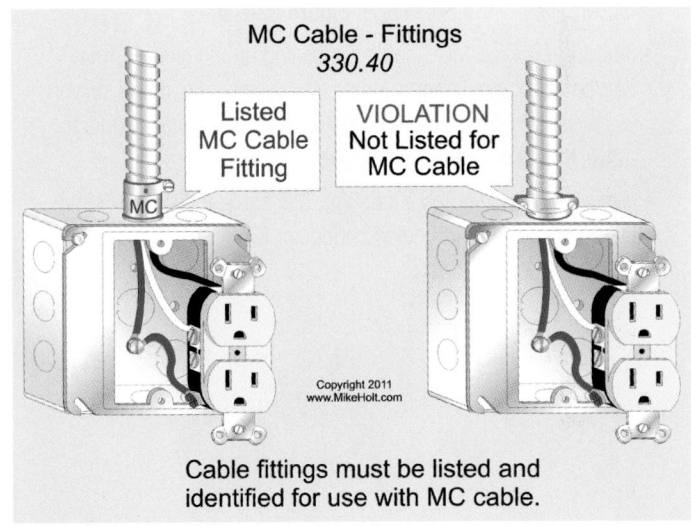

MC Cable - Fittings
330.40

Listed MC Cable Fitting

VIOLATION
Not Listed for MC Cable

Copyright 2011
www.MikeHolt.com

Cable fittings must be listed and identified for use with MC cable.

Figure 330–8

Author's Comments:

• The *NEC* doesn't require anti-short bushings (red heads) at the termination of Type MC cable, but if they're supplied it's considered by many to be a good practice to use them.

• Conductors 4 AWG and larger that enter an enclosure must be protected from abrasion during and after installation by a fitting that provides a smooth, rounded, insulating surface, such as an insulating bushing unless the design of the box, fitting, or enclosure provides equivalent protection in accordance with 300.4(G).

330.80 Conductor Ampacities. Conductor ampacity is calculated on the 90°C insulation rating of the conductors; however, the conductors must be sized to the termination temperature rating in accordance with 110.14(C)(1).

PART III. CONSTRUCTION SPECIFICATIONS

330.108 Equipment Grounding Conductor. If Type MC cable is to serve as an equipment grounding conductor, it must comply with 250.118 and 250.122.

Author's Comment: The outer sheath of:

- Traditional interlocked Type MC cable isn't permitted to serve as an equipment grounding conductor, therefore this cable must contain an insulated equipment grounding conductor in accordance with 250.118(1). **Figure 330–9**

- Interlocked Type MC^AP cable containing an aluminum grounding/bonding conductor running just below the metal armor is listed to serve as an equipment grounding conductor [250.118(10)(b)]. **Figure 330–10**

- Smooth or corrugated-tube Type MC cable is listed to serve as an equipment grounding conductor [250.118(10)(c)].

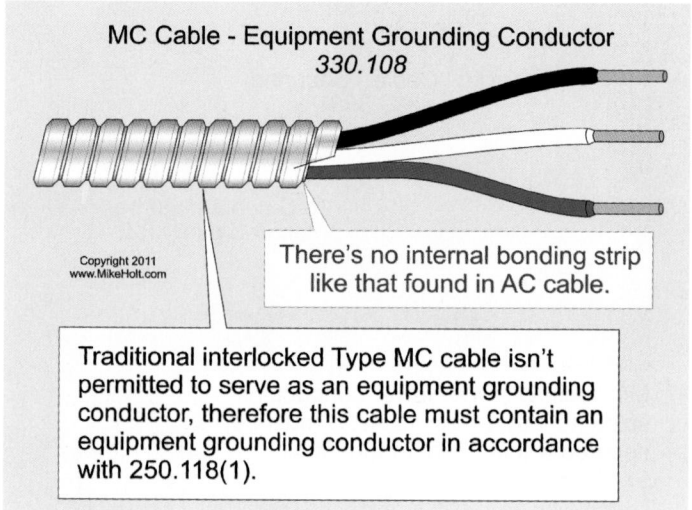

Figure 330–9

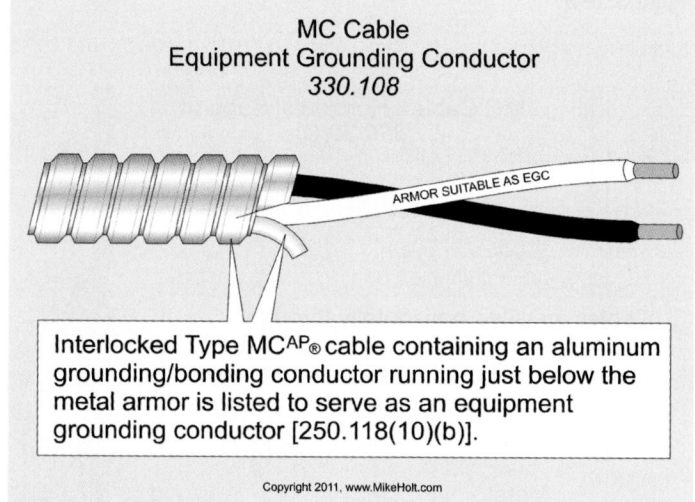

Figure 330–10

ARTICLE 334

Nonmetallic-Sheathed Cable (Types NM and NMC)

INTRODUCTION TO ARTICLE 334—NONMETALLIC-SHEATHED CABLE (TYPES NM AND NMC)

Nonmetallic-sheathed cable is flexible, inexpensive, and easily installed. It provides very limited physical protection for the conductors, so the installation restrictions are strict. Its low cost and relative ease of installation make it a common wiring method for residential and commercial branch circuits. In the field, Type NM cable is typically referred to as "Romex®."

PART I. GENERAL

334.1 Scope. Article 334 covers the use, installation, and construction specifications of nonmetallic-sheathed cable.

334.2 Definition.

Nonmetallic-Sheathed Cable (Types NM and NMC). A wiring method that encloses two or more insulated conductors, 14 AWG through 2 AWG, within a nonmetallic jacket.

- NM cable has insulated conductors enclosed within an overall nonmetallic jacket.
- NMC cable has insulated conductors enclosed within an overall, corrosion resistant, nonmetallic jacket. **Figure 334–1**

Author's Comment: It's the generally accepted practice in the electrical industry to call Type NM cable "Romex®," a registered trademark of the Southwire Company.

334.6 Listed. Types NM and NMC cables must be listed.

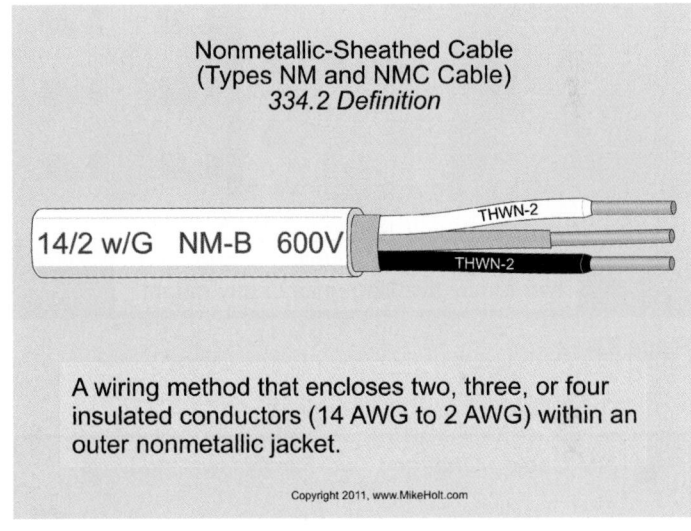

Nonmetallic-Sheathed Cable
(Types NM and NMC Cable)
334.2 Definition

14/2 w/G   NM-B   600V   THWN-2 / THWN-2

A wiring method that encloses two, three, or four insulated conductors (14 AWG to 2 AWG) within an outer nonmetallic jacket.

Copyright 2011, www.MikeHolt.com

Figure 334–1

PART II. INSTALLATION

334.10 Uses Permitted. Type NM and Type NMC cables can be used in the following:

(1) One- and two-family dwellings of any height, <u>and their attached/ detached garages or storage buildings.</u> **Figures 334–2 and 334–3**

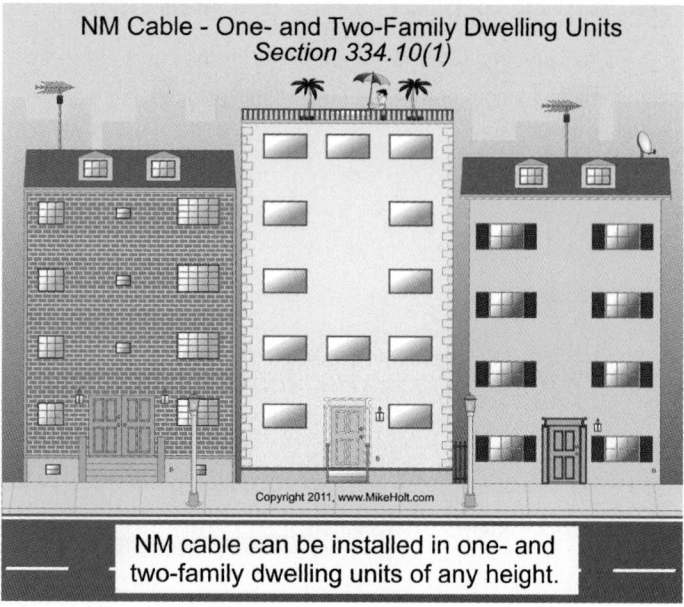

NM cable can be installed in one- and two-family dwelling units of any height.

Figure 334–2

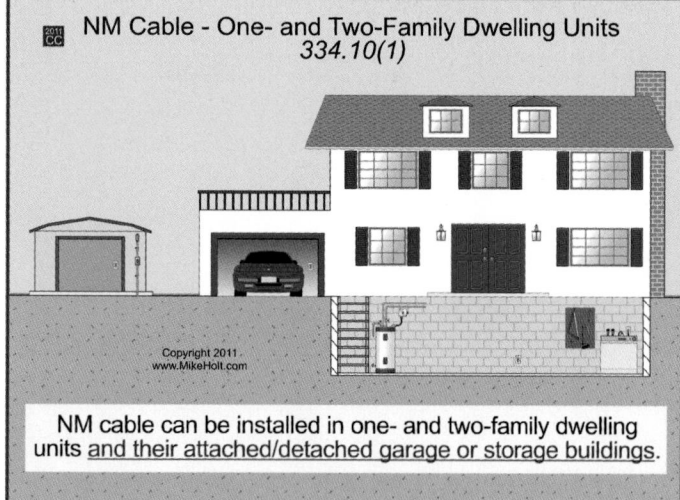

NM cable can be installed in one- and two-family dwelling units <u>and their attached/detached garage or storage buildings</u>.

Figure 334–3

(2) Multifamily dwellings permitted to be of Types III, IV, and V construction. **Figure 334–4**

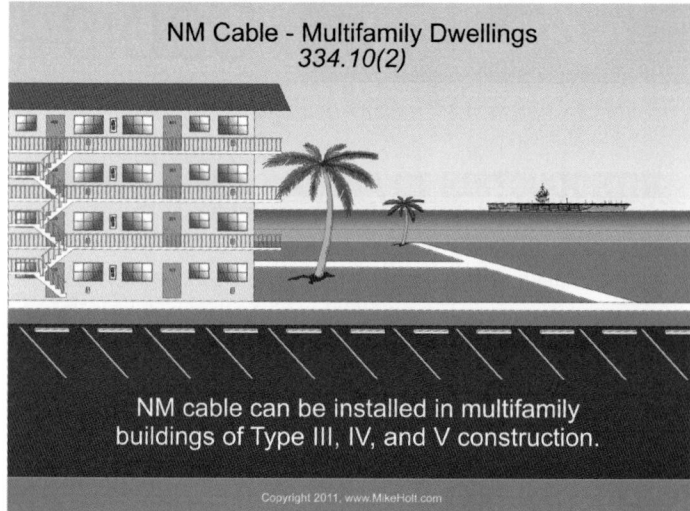

NM cable can be installed in multifamily buildings of Type III, IV, and V construction.

Figure 334–4

(3) Other structures permitted to be of Types III, IV, and V construction, except as prohibited in 334.12. Cables must be concealed within walls, floors, or ceilings that provide a thermal barrier of material with at least a 15-minute finish rating, as identified in listings of fire-rated assemblies. **Figure 334–5**

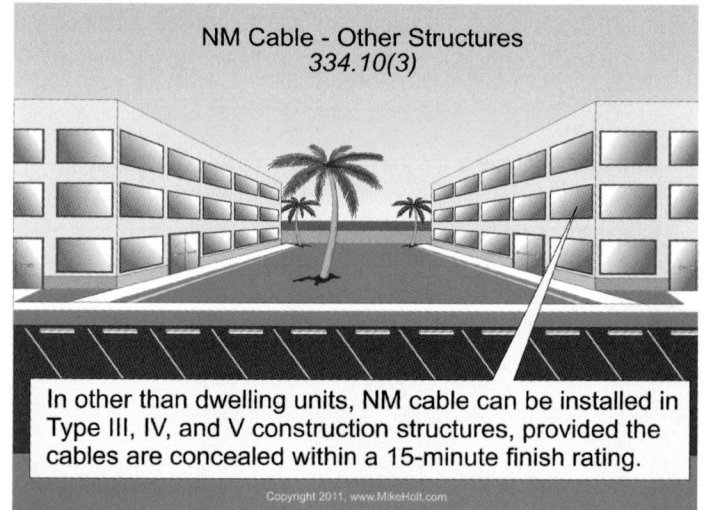

In other than dwelling units, NM cable can be installed in Type III, IV, and V construction structures, provided the cables are concealed within a 15-minute finish rating.

Figure 334–5

Author's Comment: See the definition of "Concealed" in Article 100.

Note 1: Building constructions are defined in NFPA 220-2006, *Standard on Types of Building Construction*, the applicable building code, or both.

Note 2: See Annex E for the determination of building types [NFPA 220, Table 3-1].

334.12 Uses Not Permitted.

(A) Types NM and NMC.

(1) In any dwelling or structure not specifically permitted in 334.10(1), (2), and (3).

(2) Exposed in dropped or suspended ceilings in other than one- and two-family and multifamily dwellings. **Figure 334–6**

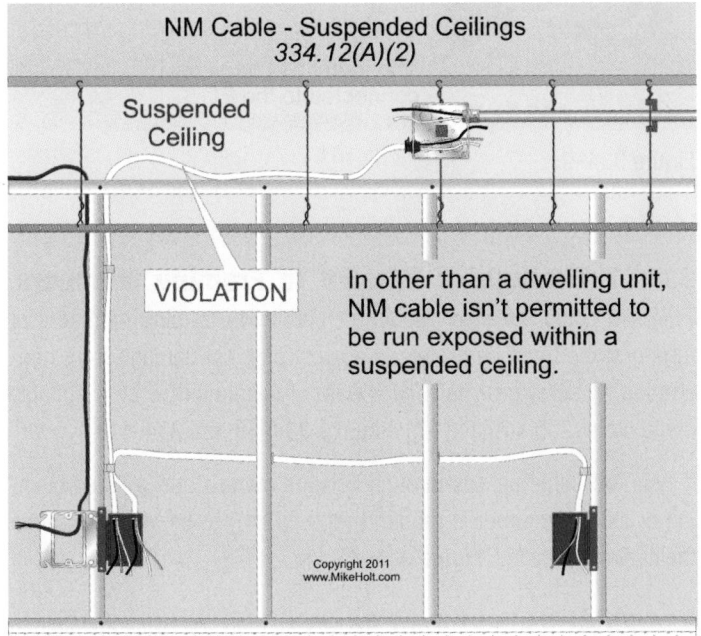

Figure 334–6

(3) As service-entrance cable.

(4) In commercial garages having hazardous locations, as defined in 511.3.

(5) In theaters and similar locations, except where permitted in 518.4(B).

(6) In motion picture studios.

(7) In storage battery rooms.

(8) In hoistways, or on elevators or escalators.

(9) Embedded in poured cement, concrete, or aggregate.

(10) In any hazardous location, except where permitted by 501.10(B)(3), 502.10(B)(3), and 504.20.

(B) Type NM. Type NM cables must not be used under the following conditions, or in the following locations:

(1) If exposed to corrosive fumes or vapors.

(2) If embedded in masonry, concrete, adobe, fill, or plaster.

(3) In a shallow chase in masonry, concrete, or adobe and covered with plaster, adobe, or similar finish.

(4) In wet or damp locations. **Figure 334–7**

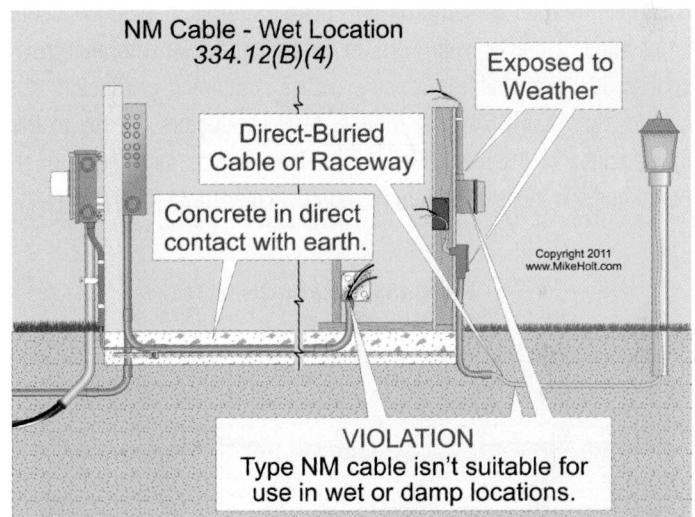

Figure 334–7

Author's Comment: Type NM cable isn't permitted in ducts or cavity plenum spaces [300.22], or for wiring in patient care areas [517.13].

334.15 Exposed.

(A) Surface of the Building. Exposed Type NM cable must closely follow the surface of the building.

(B) Protected from Physical Damage. Nonmetallic-sheathed cable must be protected from physical damage by rigid metal conduit, intermediate metal conduit, Schedule 80 PVC conduit, Type RTRC-XW conduit, electrical metallic tubing, guard strips, or other means approved by the authority having jurisdiction.

> **Author's Comment:** When installed in a raceway, the cable must be protected from abrasion by a fitting installed on the end of the raceway [300.15(C)].

Type NMC cable installed in shallow chases in masonry, concrete, or adobe, must be protected against nails or screws by a steel plate not less than 1/16 in. thick [300.4(F)] and covered with plaster, adobe, or similar finish.

> **Author's Comment:** If Type NM cable is installed in a metal raceway, the raceway isn't required to be connected to an equipment grounding conductor [250.86 Ex 2 and 300.12 Ex].

(C) In Unfinished Basements and Crawl Spaces. If Type NM cable is installed at angles with joists in unfinished basements and crawl spaces, it's permissible to secure cables containing conductors not smaller than two 6 AWG or three 8 AWG conductors directly to the lower edges of the joists. Smaller cables must be installed through bored holes in joists or on running boards. **Figure 334–8**

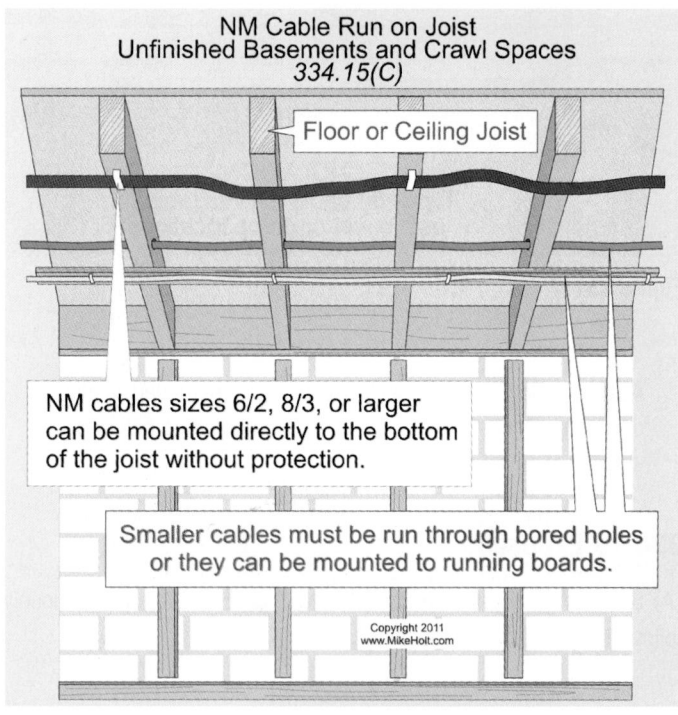

Figure 334–8

Type NM cable installed on a wall of an unfinished basement or crawl space subject to physical damage must be protected in accordance with 300.4, or be installed in a raceway with a nonmetallic bushing or adapter at the point where the cable enters the raceway, and the NM cable must be secured within 12 in. of the point where the cable enters the raceway. **Figure 334–9**

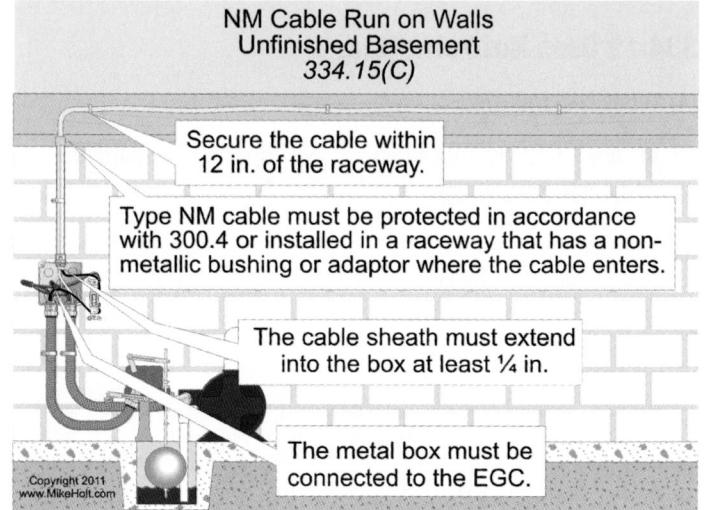

Figure 334–9

334.17 Through or Parallel to Framing Members.
Type NM cable installed through or parallel to framing members or furring strips must be protected against physical damage from penetration by screws or nails by 1¼ in. of separation or by a suitable metal plate [300.4(A) and (D)]. **Figures 334–10 and 334–11**

If Type NM cable passes through holes in metal studs, a listed bushing or listed grommet is required [300.4(B)(1)] to be in place before the cable is installed. **Figure 334–12**

334.23 Attics and Roof Spaces.
Type NM cable installed in accessible attics or roof spaces must comply with 320.23.

> **Author's Comments:**
>
> • On the Surface of Floor Joists, Rafters, or Studs. In attics and roof spaces that are accessible, substantial guards must protect cables installed across the top of floor joists, or across the face of rafters or studding within 7 ft of the floor or floor joists. If this space isn't accessible by permanent stairs or ladders, protection is required only within 6 ft of the nearest edge of the scuttle hole or attic entrance [320.23(A)].

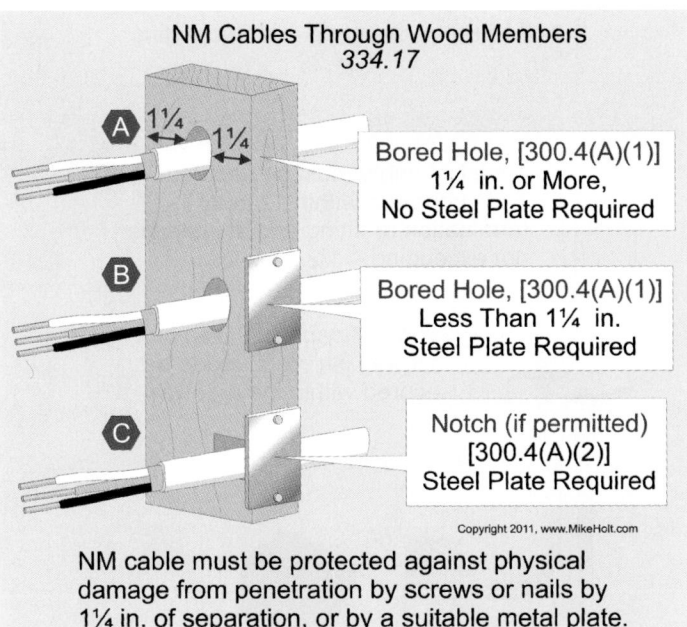

NM Cables Through Wood Members
334.17

Ⓐ 1¼ ↔ 1¼

Bored Hole, [300.4(A)(1)]
1¼ in. or More,
No Steel Plate Required

Ⓑ

Bored Hole, [300.4(A)(1)]
Less Than 1¼ in.
Steel Plate Required

Ⓒ

Notch (if permitted)
[300.4(A)(2)]
Steel Plate Required

Copyright 2011, www.MikeHolt.com

NM cable must be protected against physical damage from penetration by screws or nails by 1¼ in. of separation, or by a suitable metal plate.

Figure 334–10

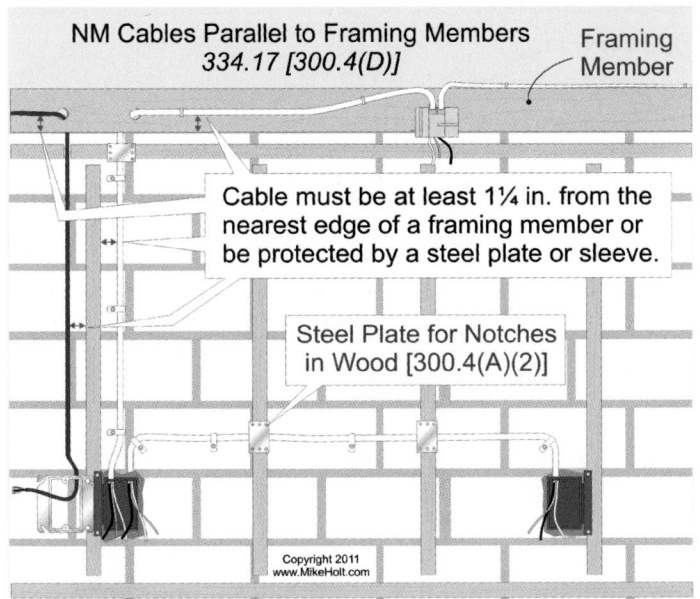

NM Cables Parallel to Framing Members
334.17 [300.4(D)]   Framing Member

Cable must be at least 1¼ in. from the nearest edge of a framing member or be protected by a steel plate or sleeve.

Steel Plate for Notches in Wood [300.4(A)(2)]

Copyright 2011
www.MikeHolt.com

Figure 334–11

- Along the Side of Framing Members [320.23(B)]. When Type NM cable is installed on the side of rafters, studs, or floor joists, no protection is required if the cable is installed and supported so the nearest outside surface of the cable or raceway is at least 1¼ in. from the nearest edge of the framing member if nails or screws are likely to penetrate [300.4(D)].

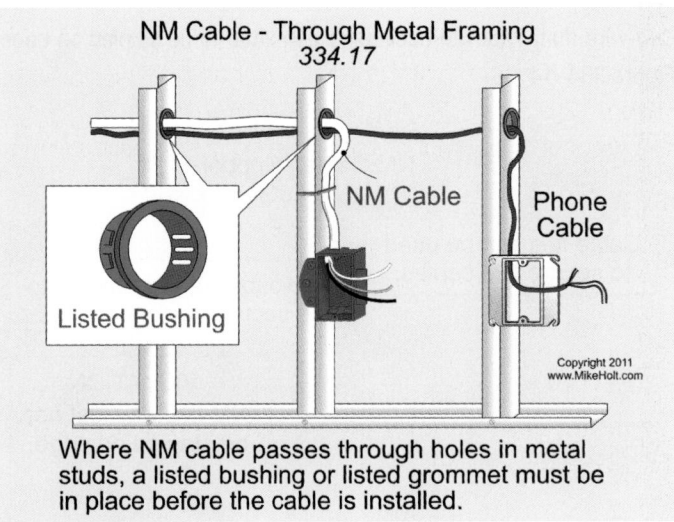

NM Cable - Through Metal Framing
334.17

Listed Bushing

NM Cable   Phone Cable

Copyright 2011
www.MikeHolt.com

Where NM cable passes through holes in metal studs, a listed bushing or listed grommet must be in place before the cable is installed.

Figure 334–12

334.24 Bends. When the cable is bent, it must not be damaged and the radius of the curve of the inner edge of any bend must not be less than five times the diameter of the cable. **Figure 334–13**

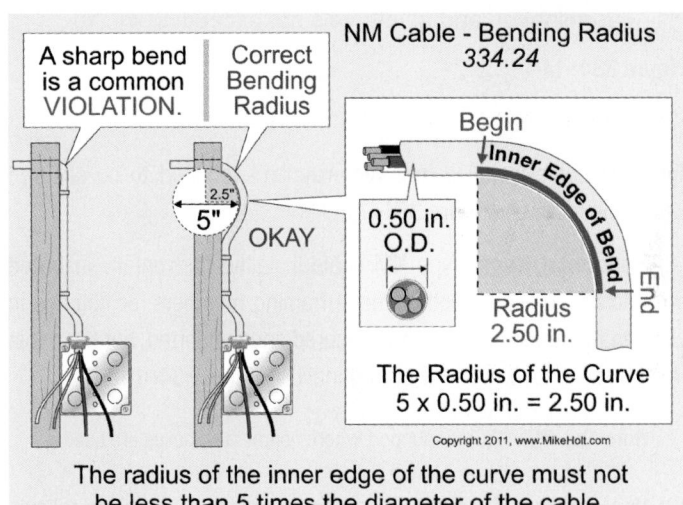

NM Cable - Bending Radius
334.24

A sharp bend is a common VIOLATION.   Correct Bending Radius

2.5"
5" OKAY

0.50 in. O.D.

Begin
Inner Edge of Bend
Radius 2.50 in.
End

The Radius of the Curve
5 x 0.50 in. = 2.50 in.

Copyright 2011, www.MikeHolt.com

The radius of the inner edge of the curve must not be less than 5 times the diameter of the cable.

Figure 334–13

334.30 Securing and Supporting. Staples, straps, cable ties, hangers, or similar fittings must secure Type NM cable in a manner that won't damage the cable. Type NM cable must be secured within 12 in. of every box, cabinet, enclosure, or termination fitting, except as permitted by 314.17(C) Ex or 312.5(C) Ex, and at intervals not exceeding 4¼ ft.

Two-wire (flat) Type NM cable isn't permitted to be stapled on edge. **Figure 334–14**

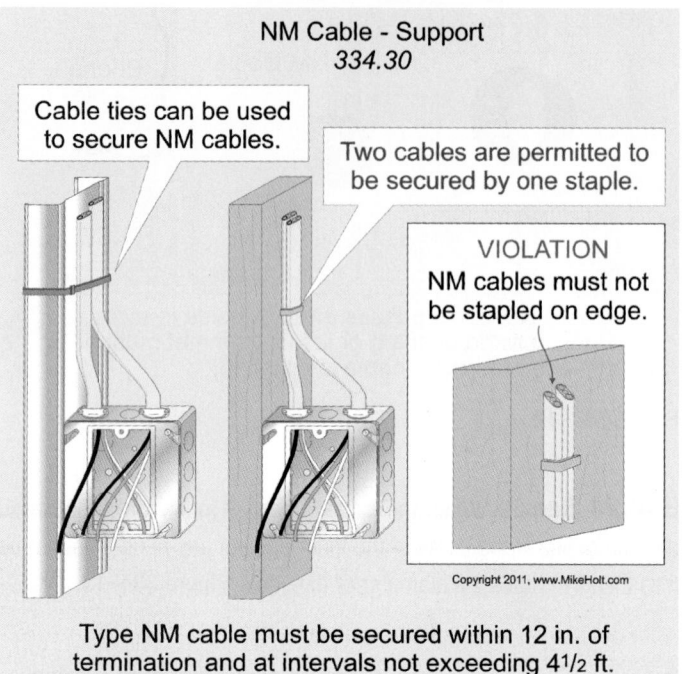

Figure 334–14

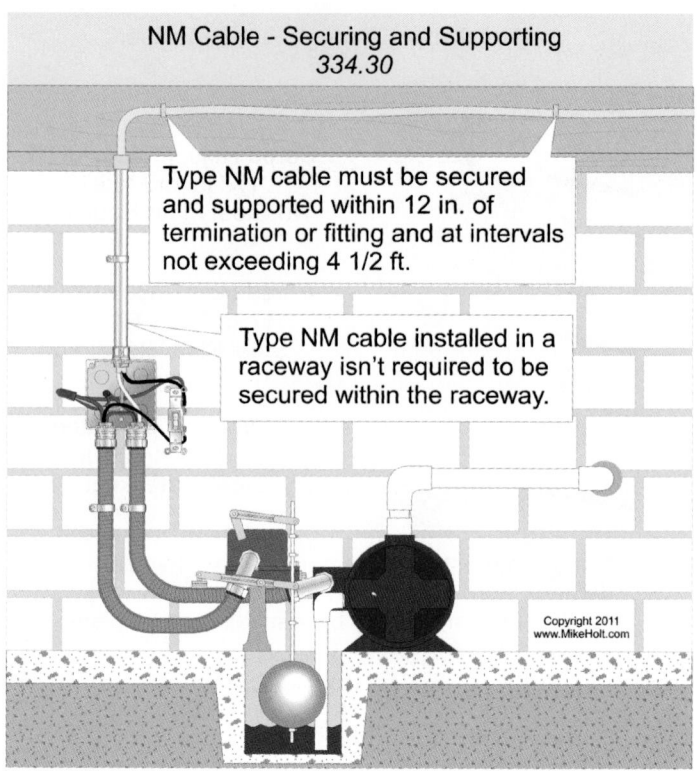

Figure 334–15

Type NM cable installed in a raceway isn't required to be secured within the raceway. **Figure 334–15**

(A) Horizontal Runs. Type NM cable installed horizontally in bored or punched holes in wood or metal framing members, or notches in wooden members is considered secured and supported, but the cable must be secured within 1 ft of termination. **Figure 334–16**

Note: See 314.17(C) for support where nonmetallic boxes are used.

(B) Unsupported. Type NM cable can be unsupported in the following situations:

(1) If Type NM cable is fished between concealed access points in finished buildings or structures, and support is impracticable.

(2) Not more than 4½ ft of unsupported cable is permitted from the last point of support within an accessible ceiling for the connection of luminaires or equipment.

Author's Comment: Type NM cable isn't permitted as a wiring method above accessible ceilings, except in dwellings [334.12(A)(2)].

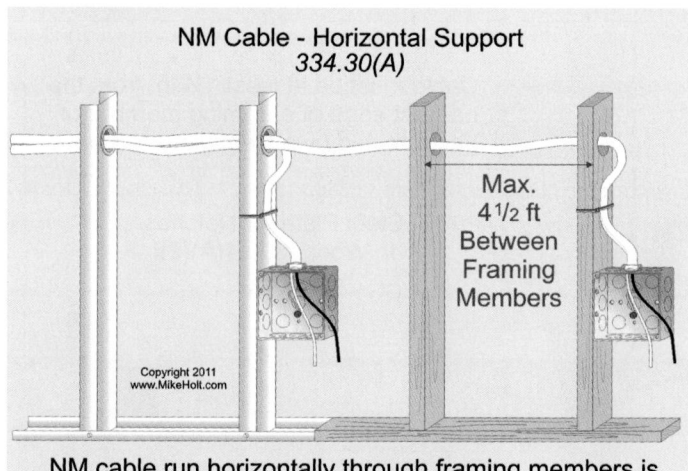

Figure 334–16

334.80 Conductor Ampacity. Conductor ampacity is calculated on the 90°C insulation rating of the conductor in accordance with Table 310.15(B)(16), however the conductors must be sized to the termination temperature rating of 60°C.

Question: What size Type NM cable is required to supply a 9.60 kW, 240V, single-phase fixed space heater with a 3A blower motor? The terminals are rated 75°C. **Figure 334–17**

(a) 2 AWG   (b) 4 AWG   (c) 6 AWG   (d) 8 AWG

Answer: (b) 4 AWG

Step 1: Determine the total load in amperes:

$I = VA/E$

$I = 9,600W/240V + 3A$

$I = 40A + 3A$

$I = 43A$

Step 2: Conductor and Protection Size [424.3(B)]. Size the ungrounded conductors and overcurrent device at no less than 125 percent of the total heating load.

Conductor/Protection Size = Load x 1.25

Conductor/Protection Size = 43A x 1.25

Conductor/Protection Size = 53.75A

According to Table 310.15(B)(16), a 6 AWG conductor rated 55A at 60°C, protected with a 60A overcurrent device [240.6(A)].

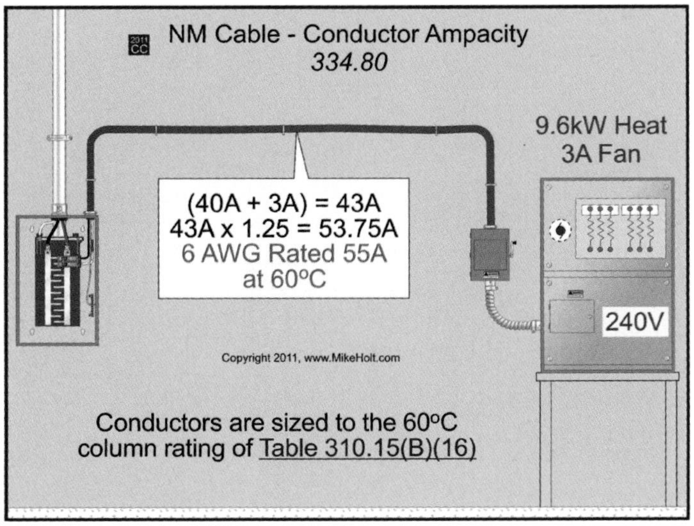

If multiple Type NM cables pass through the same wood framing opening that's to be sealed with thermal insulation, caulking, or sealing foam, the allowable ampacity of each conductor must be adjusted in accordance with Table 310.15(B)(3)(a). **Figure 334–18**

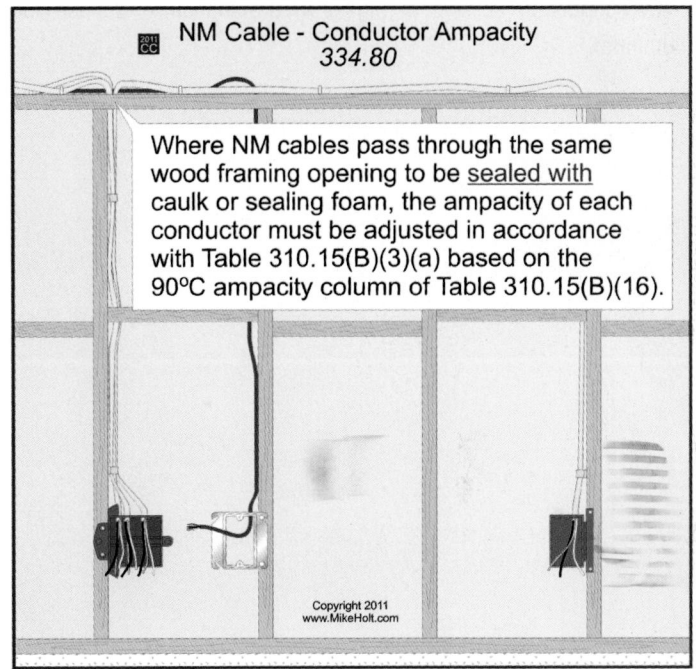

Figure 334–18

Author's Comment: This requirement has no effect on conductor sizing if you bundle no more than nine current-carrying 14 or 12 AWG conductors together. For example, three 14/2 cables and one 14/3 cable (nine current-carrying 14 THHN conductors) are bundled together in a dry location, the ampacity for each conductor (25A at 90°C, Table 310.15(B)(16)) is adjusted by a 70 percent adjustment factor [Table 310.15(B)(3)(a)].

Adjusted Conductor Ampacity = 25A x 0.70

Adjusted Conductor Ampacity = 17.50A

NM Cable - Conductor Ampacity
334.80

9.6kW Heat
3A Fan

(40A + 3A) = 43A
43A x 1.25 = 53.75A
6 AWG Rated 55A
at 60°C

240V

Copyright 2011, www.MikeHolt.com

Conductors are sized to the 60°C
column rating of Table 310.15(B)(16)

Figure 334–17

PART III. CONSTRUCTION SPECIFICATIONS

334.100 Construction. The outer cable sheath of Type NM cable must be constructed with nonmetallic material.

334.104 Conductors. The conductors must be 14 AWG through 2 AWG copper, or 12 AWG through 2 AWG aluminum or copper-clad aluminum.

334.108 Equipment Grounding Conductor. Type NM cable must have an insulated, covered, or bare equipment grounding conductor.

334.112 Insulation. NM conductor insulation must be rated 90°C (194°F).

> **Note:** Types NM cable identified by the markings NM-B meet this requirement.

Service-Entrance Cable (Types SE and USE)

INTRODUCTION TO ARTICLE 338—SERVICE-ENTRANCE CABLE (TYPES SE AND USE)

Service-entrance cable is a single conductor or multiconductor assembly with or without an overall moisture-resistant covering. This cable is used primarily for services not over 600V, but can also be used for feeders and branch circuits when the limitations of this article are observed.

PART I. GENERAL

338.1 Scope. Article 338 covers the use, installation, and construction specifications of service-entrance cable, Types SE and USE.

338.2 Definitions.

Service-Entrance Cable. Service-entrance cable is a single or multiconductor assembly, with or without an overall covering, used primarily for services not over 600V. **Figure 338–1**

Service-Entrance Cable
338.2 Definition

A single or multiconductor assembly with or without an overall covering used primarily for services not over 600V.

Aboveground

SE | SER

SE cable is permitted only in aboveground installations and is permitted for branch circuits or feeders when installed according to 338.10(B).

Copyright 2011, www.MikeHolt.com

Underground Only

USE | USE-2

USE cable is identified for underground use. Its covering is moisture resistant but not flame retardant, and it isn't suitable for use within a premises.

Figure 338–1

Type SE. SE and SER cables have a flame-retardant, moisture-resistant covering and are permitted only in aboveground installations. These cables are permitted for branch circuits or feeders when installed in accordance with 338.10(B).

> **Author's Comment:** SER cable is SE cable with an insulated neutral, resulting in three insulated conductors with an uninsulated equipment grounding conductor. SER cable is round, while 2-wire SE cable is flat.

Type USE. USE cable is identified as a wiring method permitted for underground use; its covering is moisture resistant, but not flame retardant.

> **Author's Comment:** USE cable isn't permitted to be installed indoors [338.10(B)], except single-conductor USE dual rated as RHH/RHW.

PART II. INSTALLATION

338.10 Uses Permitted.

(A) Service-Entrance Conductors. Service-entrance cable used as service-entrance conductors must be installed in accordance with Article 230.

(B) Branch Circuits or Feeders.

(1) Insulated Conductor. Type SE service-entrance cable is permitted for branch circuits and feeders where the circuit conductors are insulated.

(2) Uninsulated Conductor. SE cable is permitted for branch circuits and feeders if the insulated conductors are used for circuit wiring, and the uninsulated conductor is only used for equipment grounding purposes. **Figure 338–2**

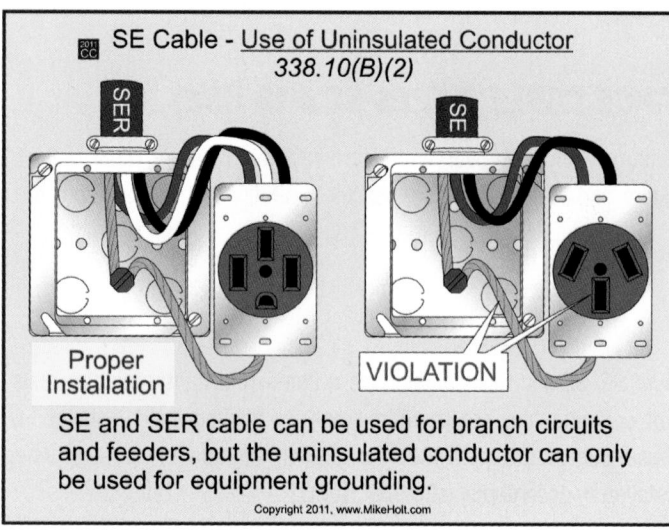

SE Cable - Use of Uninsulated Conductor
338.10(B)(2)

Proper Installation

VIOLATION

SE and SER cable can be used for branch circuits and feeders, but the uninsulated conductor can only be used for equipment grounding.

Copyright 2011, www.MikeHolt.com

Figure 338–2

Ex: In existing installations, uninsulated conductors may be used for the neutral conductor if the uninsulated neutral conductor of the cable originates in service equipment.

(3) Temperature Limitations. SE cable must not be subjected to conductor temperatures exceeding its insulation rating.

(4) Installation Methods for Branch Circuits and Feeders. SE cable used for branch circuits or feeders must comply with (a) and (b).

(a) Interior Installations. SE cable used for interior branch circuit or feeder wiring must be installed in accordance with the same requirements as Type NM Cable—Article 334, excluding 334.80.

The maximum conductor temperature rating can be used [310.15(B) (2)] for ampacity adjustment and correction purposes, but when installed in thermal insulation the conductors must be sized in accordance with Table 310.15(B)(16) 60°C rated conductor column.

 CAUTION: *Underground service-entrance cable (USE) is not permitted for interior wiring because it does not have a flame-retardant insulation. It would only be permitted in interior wiring when dual listed as wire type in accordance with Table 310.104, such as RHW.*

(b) Exterior Installations. The cable must be supported in accordance with 334.30 and where run underground the cable must comply with Part II of Article 340.

338.12 Uses Not Permitted.

(A) Service-Entrance Cable. SE cable isn't permitted under the following conditions or locations:

(1) If subject to physical damage unless protected in accordance with 230.50(A).

(2) Underground with or without a raceway.

(B) Underground Service-Entrance Cable. USE cable isn't permitted:

(1) For interior wiring.

(2) Above ground, except where protected against physical damage in accordance with 300.5(D).

338.24 Bends. Bends in cable must be made so the protective coverings of the cable aren't damaged, and the radius of the curve of the inner edge is at least five times the diameter of the cable.

ARTICLE 340

Underground Feeder and Branch-Circuit Cable (Type UF)

INTRODUCTION TO ARTICLE 340—UNDERGROUND FEEDER AND BRANCH-CIRCUIT CABLE (TYPE UF)

UF cable is a moisture-, fungus-, and corrosion-resistant cable suitable for direct burial in the earth.

PART I. GENERAL

340.1 Scope. Article 340 covers the use, installation, and construction specifications of underground feeder and branch-circuit cable, Type UF.

340.2 Definition.

Underground Feeder and Branch-Circuit Cable (Type UF). A factory assembly of insulated conductors with an integral or an overall covering of nonmetallic material suitable for direct burial in the earth. Notice that Type UF is not allowed as a service cable. **Figure 340–1**

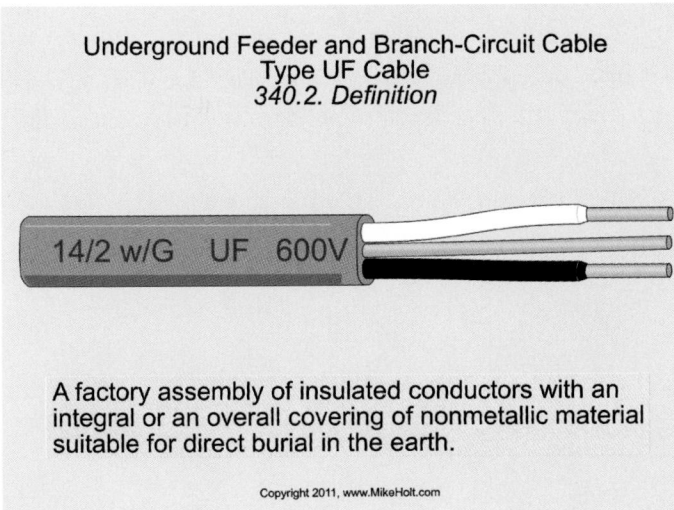

Underground Feeder and Branch-Circuit Cable
Type UF Cable
340.2. Definition

14/2 w/G   UF   600V

A factory assembly of insulated conductors with an integral or an overall covering of nonmetallic material suitable for direct burial in the earth.

Copyright 2011, www.MikeHolt.com

Figure 340–1

Author's Comments:

- UF cable is a moisture-, fungus-, and corrosion-resistant cable suitable for direct burial in the earth. It comes in sizes 14 AWG through 4/0 AWG [340.104]. The covering of multiconductor Type UF cable is molded plastic that encases the insulated conductors.

- Because the covering of Type UF cable encapsulates the insulated conductors, it's difficult to strip off the outer jacket to gain access to the conductors, but this covering provides excellent corrosion protection. Be careful not to damage the conductor insulation or cut yourself when you remove the outer cover.

340.6 Listing Requirements. Type UF cable must be listed.

PART II. INSTALLATION

340.10 Uses Permitted.

(1) Underground, in accordance with 300.5.

(2) As a single conductor in the same trench or raceway with circuit conductors.

(3) As interior or exterior wiring in wet, dry, or corrosive locations.

(4) As Type NM cable, when installed in accordance with Article 334.

(5) For solar photovoltaic systems, in accordance with 690.31.

(6) As single-conductor cables for nonheating leads for heating cables, as provided in 424.43.

(7) Supported by cable trays.

340.12 Uses Not Permitted.

(1) As services [230.43].

(2) In commercial garages [511.3].

(3) In theaters [520.5].

(4) In motion picture studios [530.11].

(5) In storage battery rooms [Article 480].

(6) In hoistways [Article 620].

(7) In hazardous locations, except as <u>specifically</u> permitted <u>by other</u> <u>articles</u> in the *Code*.

(8) Embedded in concrete.

(9) Exposed to direct sunlight unless identified.

(10) If subject to physical damage. **Figure 340–2**

(11) As overhead messenger-supported wiring.

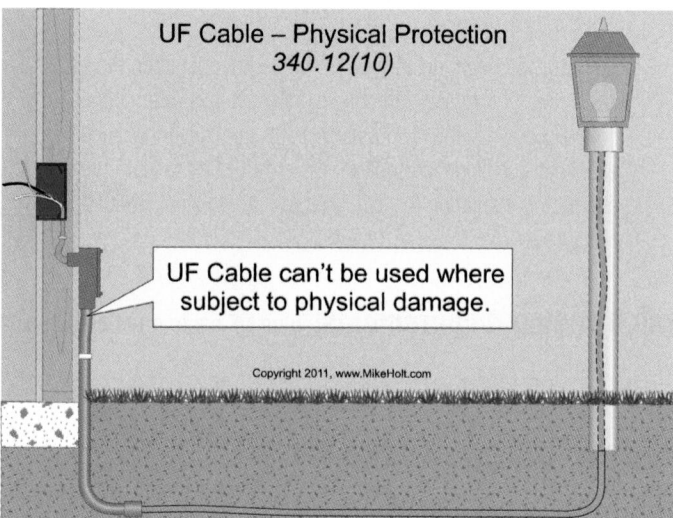

Figure 340–2

Author's Comment: UF cable isn't permitted in ducts or cavity plenum spaces [300.22], or in patient care areas [517.13].

340.24 Bends. Bends in cables must be made so that the protective coverings of the cable aren't damaged, and the radius of the curve of the inner edge must not be less than five times the diameter of the cable.

340.80 Ampacity. The ampacity of conductors contained in UF cable is based on the 60°C insulation rating listed in Table 310.15(B)(16).

340.112 Insulation. The conductors of UF cable must be one of the moisture-resistant types listed in Table 310.104(A) suitable for branch-circuit wiring. If installed as a substitute wiring method for Type NM cable, the conductor insulation must be rated 90°C (194°F).

Intermediate Metal Conduit (Type IMC)

PART I. GENERAL

342.1 Scope. Article 342 covers the use, installation, and construction specifications of intermediate metal conduit and associated fittings.

342.2 Definition.

Intermediate Metal Conduit (Type IMC). A listed steel raceway of circular cross section that can be threaded with integral or associated couplings. It's listed for the installation of electrical conductors, and is used with listed fittings to provide electrical continuity. **Figure 342–1**

Intermediate Metal Conduit (Type IMC)
342.2 Definition

A listed steel circular raceway that can be threaded with integral or associated couplings.

Compression   Set Screw

Threadless IMC Fittings

Copyright 2011, www.MikeHolt.com

Figure 342–1

Author's Comment: The type of steel from which intermediate metal conduit is manufactured, the process by which it's made, and the corrosion protection applied are all equal, or superior, to that of rigid metal conduit.

342.6 Listing Requirements. Intermediate metal conduit and its associated fittings, such as elbows and couplings, must be listed.

PART II. INSTALLATION

342.10 Uses Permitted.

(A) All Atmospheric Conditions and Occupancies. Intermediate metal conduit is permitted in all atmospheric conditions and occupancies.

(B) Corrosion Environments. Intermediate metal conduit, elbows, couplings, and fittings can be installed in concrete, in direct contact with the earth, or in areas subject to severe corrosive influences if provided with corrosion protection and judged suitable for the condition in accordance with 300.6.

(C) Cinder Fill. IMC can be installed in or under cinder fill subject to permanent moisture when protected on all sides by 2 in. of non-cinder concrete; where the conduit isn't less than 18 in. under the fill; or where protected by corrosion protection judged suitable for the condition.

(D) Wet Locations. Support fittings, such as screws, straps, and so forth, installed in a wet location must be made of corrosion-resistant material, or be protected by corrosion-resistant coatings in accordance with 300.6.

⚠️ **CAUTION:** *Supplementary coatings for corrosion protection haven't been investigated by a product testing and listing agency, and these coatings are known to cause cancer in laboratory animals. There's a documented case where an electrician was taken to the hospital for lead poisoning after using a supplemental coating product (asphalted paint) in a poorly ventilated area. As with all products, be sure to read and follow all product instructions, including material data safety sheets, particularly when petroleum-based chemicals (volatile organic compounds) may be in the material.*

342.14 Dissimilar Metals.
If practical, contact with dissimilar metals should be avoided to prevent the deterioration of the metal because of galvanic action. Aluminum fittings and enclosures, however, are permitted with steel intermediate metal conduit.

342.20 Trade Size.

(A) Minimum. Intermediate metal conduit smaller than trade size ½ must not be used.

(B) Maximum. Intermediate metal conduit larger than trade size 4 must not be used.

342.22 Number of Conductors.
The number of conductors in IMC isn't permitted to exceed the percentage fill specified in Table 1, Chapter 9. Raceways must be large enough to permit the installation and removal of conductors without damaging the conductor insulation. When all conductors in a raceway are the same size and insulation, the number of conductors permitted can be found in Annex C for the raceway type.

> *Question:* How many 10 THHN conductors can be installed in trade size 1 IMC?
>
> (a) 12   (b) 14   (c) 16   (d) 18
>
> *Answer:* (d) 18 conductors [Annex C, Table C4]

Author's Comment: See 300.17 for additional examples on how to size raceways when conductors aren't all the same size.

Cables can be installed in intermediate metal conduit, as long as the number of cables doesn't exceed the allowable percentage fill specified in Table 1, Chapter 9.

342.24 Bends.
Raceway bends must not be made in any manner that would damage the raceway, or significantly change its internal diameter (no kinks). The radius of the curve of the inner edge of any field bend must not be less than shown in Table 2, Chapter 9.

Author's Comment: This is usually not a problem, because benders are made to comply with this table. However, when using a hickey bender (short-radius bender), be careful not to over-bend the raceway.

342.26 Number of Bends (360°).
To reduce the stress and friction on conductor insulation, the maximum number of bends (including offsets) between pull points must not exceed 360°. **Figure 342–2**

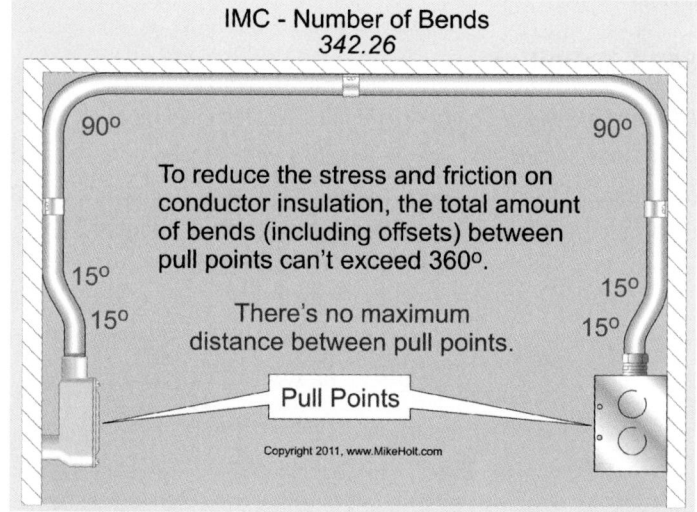

IMC - Number of Bends
342.26

To reduce the stress and friction on conductor insulation, the total amount of bends (including offsets) between pull points can't exceed 360°.

There's no maximum distance between pull points.

Pull Points

Copyright 2011, www.MikeHolt.com

Figure 342–2

Author's Comment: There's no maximum distance between pull boxes because this is a design issue, not a safety issue.

342.28 Reaming.
When the raceway is cut in the field, reaming is required to remove the burrs and rough edges.

Author's Comment: It's a commonly accepted practice to ream small raceways with a screwdriver or the backside of pliers. However, when the raceway is cut with a three-wheel pipe cutter, a reaming tool is required to remove the sharp edge of the indented raceway. When conduits are threaded in the field, the threads must be coated with an electrically conductive, corrosion-resistant compound approved by the authority having jurisdiction, in accordance with 300.6(A).

342.30 Securing and Supporting.
Intermediate metal conduit must be installed as a complete system in accordance with 300.18 [300.10 and 300.12], and it must be securely fastened in place and supported in accordance with (A) and (B).

(A) Securely Fastened. IMC must be secured in accordance with one of the following:

(1) Fastened within 3 ft of each outlet box, junction box, device box, cabinet, conduit body, or other conduit termination. **Figure 342–3**

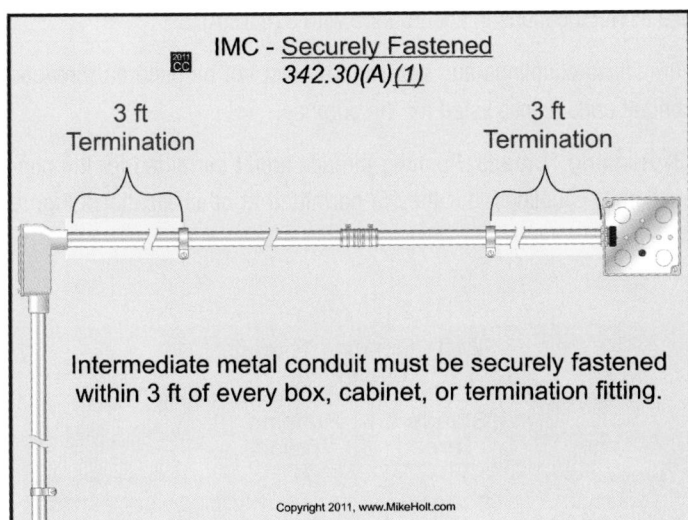

Figure 342–3

Author's Comment: Fastening is required within 3 ft of terminations, not within 3 ft of each coupling.

(2) When structural members don't permit the raceway to be secured within 3 ft of a box or termination fitting, the raceway must be secured within 5 ft of the termination. **Figure 342–4**

(3) Conduits aren't required to be securely fastened within 3 ft of the service head for an above-the-roof termination of a mast.

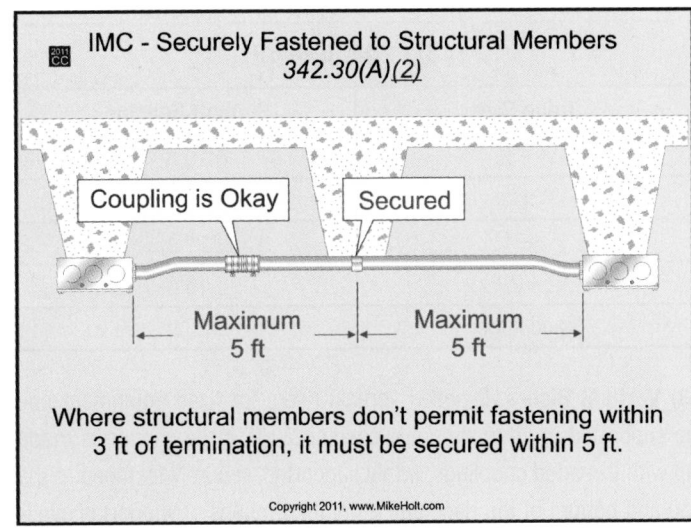

Figure 342–4

(B) Supports.

(1) General. Intermediate metal conduit must generally be supported at intervals not exceeding 10 ft.

(2) Straight Horizontal Runs. Straight horizontal runs made with threaded couplings can be supported in accordance with the distances listed in Table 344.30(B)(2). **Figure 342–5**

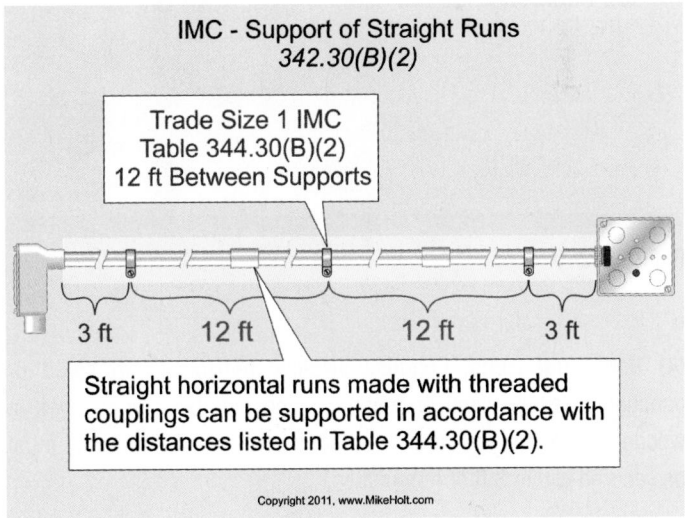

Figure 342–5

Table 344.30(B)(2)	
Trade Size	Support Spacing
½–¾	10 ft
1	12 ft*
1¼–1½	14 ft
2–2½	16 ft
3 and larger	20 ft

(3) Vertical Risers. Exposed vertical risers for fixed equipment can be supported at intervals not exceeding 20 ft, if the conduit is made up with threaded couplings, firmly supported, securely fastened at the top and bottom of the riser, and if no other means of support is available. **Figure 342–6**

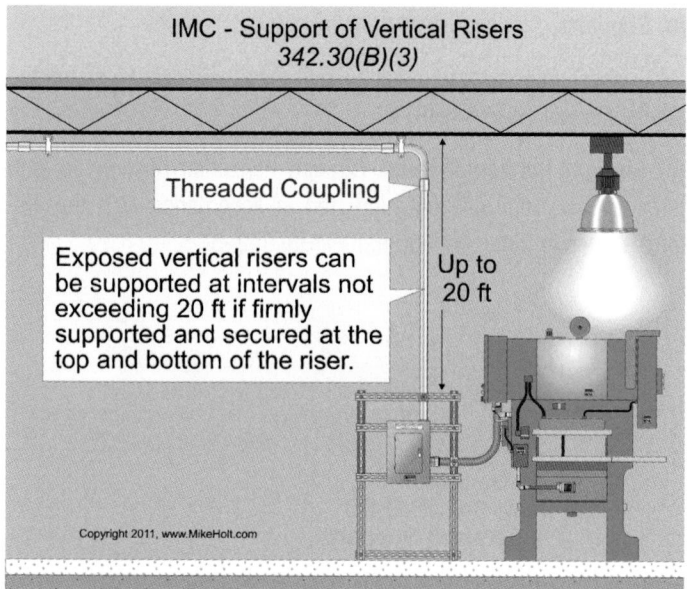

Figure 342–6

(4) Horizontal Runs. Conduits installed horizontally in bored or punched holes in wood or metal framing members, or notches in wooden members are considered supported, but the raceway must be secured within 3 ft of termination.

Author's Comment: IMC must be provided with expansion fittings if necessary to compensate for thermal expansion and contraction [300.7(B)]. The expansion characteristics for metal raceways are determined by multiplying the values from Table 352.44 by 0.20, and the expansion characteristics for aluminum raceways is determined by multiplying the values from Table 352.44 by 0.40 [300.7 Note].

342.42 Couplings and Connectors.

(A) Installation. Threadless couplings and connectors must be made up tight to maintain an effective ground-fault current path to safely conduct fault current in accordance with 250.4(A)(5), 250.96(A), and 300.10.

Author's Comment: Loose locknuts have been found to burn clear before a fault was cleared because loose termination fittings increase the impedance of the fault current path.

If buried in masonry or concrete, threadless fittings must be the concrete-tight type. If installed in wet locations, fittings must be listed for use in wet locations in accordance with 314.15(A).

Threadless couplings and connectors must not be used on threaded conduit ends unless listed for the purpose.

(B) Running Threads. Running threads aren't permitted for the connection of couplings, but they're permitted at other locations. **Figure 342–7**

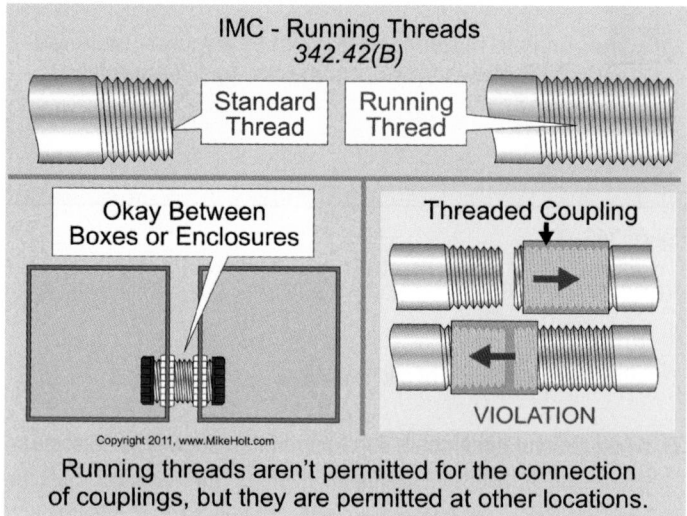

Figure 342–7

342.46 Bushings. To protect conductors from abrasion, a metal or plastic bushing must be installed on conduit termination threads, regardless of conductor size, unless the box, fitting, or enclosure is <u>designed to provide this</u> protection.

Note: Conductors 4 AWG and larger that enter an enclosure must be protected from abrasion, during and after installation, by a fitting that provides a smooth, rounded, insulating surface, such as an insulating bushing, unless the design of the box, fitting, or enclosure provides equivalent protection, in accordance with 300.4(G). **Figure 342–8**

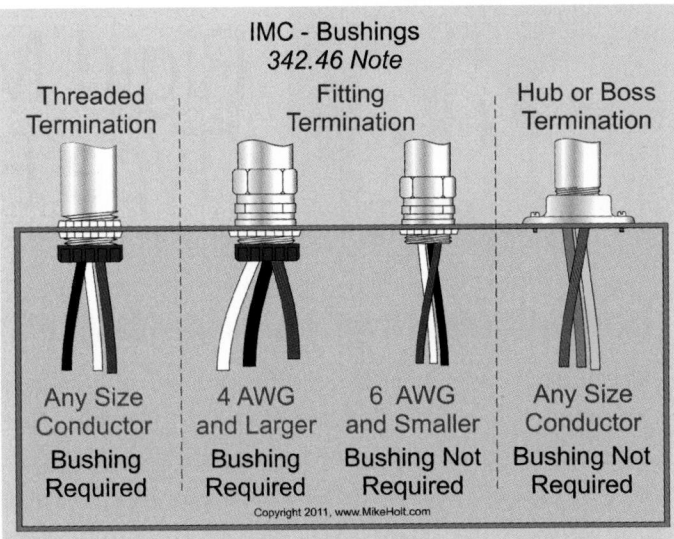

Conductors 4 AWG and larger must be protected by a fitting that provides a smooth, rounded, insulating surface, such as an insulating bushing [300.4(G)].

Figure 342–8

ARTICLE 344

Rigid Metal Conduit (Type RMC)

INTRODUCTION TO ARTICLE 344—RIGID METAL CONDUIT (TYPE RMC)

Rigid metal conduit, commonly called "rigid," has long been the standard raceway for providing protection from physical impact and from difficult environments. The outside diameter of rigid metal conduit is the same as intermediate metal conduit. However, the wall thickness of rigid metal conduit is greater than intermediate metal conduit; therefore it's a smaller interior cross-sectional area. Rigid metal conduit is heavier and more expensive than intermediate metal conduit, and it can be used in any location. Rigid metal conduit is manufactured in both galvanized steel and aluminum; the steel type is much more common.

PART I. GENERAL

344.1 Scope.
Article 344 covers the use, installation, and construction specifications of rigid metal conduit and associated fittings.

344.2 Definition.

Rigid Metal Conduit (Type RMC). A listed metal raceway of circular cross section with integral or associated couplings, listed for the installation of electrical conductors, and used with listed fittings to provide electrical continuity. **Figure 344–1**

Rigid Metal Conduit (Type RMC)
344.2 Definition

A listed metal circular raceway that can be threaded with integral or associated couplings.

Compression   Set Screw

Threadless RMC Fittings

Copyright 2011, www.MikeHolt.com

Figure 344–1

Author's Comment: When the mechanical and physical characteristics of rigid metal conduit are desired and a corrosive environment is anticipated, a PVC-coated raceway system is commonly used. This type of raceway is frequently used in the petrochemical industry. The common trade name of this coated raceway is "Plasti-bond®," and it's commonly referred to as "Rob Roy conduit." The benefits of the improved corrosion protection can be achieved only when the system is properly installed. Joints must be sealed in accordance with the manufacturer's instructions, and the coating must not be damaged with tools such as benders, pliers, and pipe wrenches. Couplings are available with an extended skirt that can be properly sealed after installation.

344.6 Listing Requirements.
Rigid metal conduit, elbows, couplings, and associated fittings must be listed.

PART II. INSTALLATION

344.10 Uses Permitted.

(A) Atmospheric Conditions and Occupancies.

(1) Galvanized Steel and Stainless Steel. Galvanized steel and stainless steel rigid metal conduit is permitted in all atmospheric conditions and occupancies.

(2) Red Brass. Red brass rigid metal conduit is permitted for direct burial and swimming pool applications.

(3) Aluminum. Rigid aluminum conduit is permitted if judged suitable for the environment.

(B) Corrosion Environments.

(1) Galvanized Steel and Stainless Steel. Rigid metal conduit fittings, elbows, and couplings can be installed in concrete, in direct contact with the earth, or in areas subject to severe corrosive influences judged suitable for the condition.

(2) Aluminum. Rigid aluminum conduit must be provided with supplementary corrosion protection approved by the authority having jurisdiction if encased in concrete or in direct contact with the earth.

(C) Cinder Fill. Galvanized steel, stainless steel, and red brass RMC is permitted in or under cinder fill subject to permanent moisture, when protected on all sides by a layer of noncinder concrete not less than 2 in. thick; where the conduit isn't less than 18 in. under the fill; or where protected by corrosion protection judged suitable for the condition.

(D) Wet Locations. Support fittings, such as screws, straps, and so forth, installed in a wet location must be made of corrosion-resistant material or protected by corrosion-resistant coatings in accordance with 300.6.

> ⚠️ **CAUTION:** *Supplementary coatings (asphalted paint) for corrosion protection haven't been investigated by a product testing and listing agency, and these coatings are known to cause cancer in laboratory animals.*

344.14 Dissimilar Metals. If practical, contact with dissimilar metals should be avoided to prevent the deterioration of the metal because of galvanic action. Aluminum fittings and enclosures are permitted, however, with rigid metal conduit.

344.20 Trade Size.

(A) Minimum. Rigid metal conduit smaller than trade size ½ must not be used.

(B) Maximum. Rigid metal conduit larger than trade size 6 must not be used.

344.22 Number of Conductors. Raceways must be large enough to permit the installation and removal of conductors without damaging the conductors' insulation. When all conductors in a raceway are the same size and insulation, the number of conductors permitted can be found in Annex C for the raceway type.

> *Question: How many 8 THHN conductors can be installed in trade size 1½ RMC?*
>
> *(a) 16   (b) 18   (c) 20   (d) 22*
>
> *Answer: 22 conductors [Annex C, Table C8]*

Author's Comment: See 300.17 for additional examples on how to size raceways when conductors aren't all the same size.

Cables can be installed in rigid metal conduit, as long as the number of cables doesn't exceed the allowable percentage fill specified in Table 1, Chapter 9.

344.24 Bends. Raceway bends must not be made in any manner that would damage the raceway, or significantly change its internal diameter (no kinks). The radius of the curve of the inner edge of any field bend must not be less than shown in Table 2, Chapter 9.

Author's Comment: This is usually not a problem because benders are made to comply with this table. However, when using a hickey bender (short-radius bender), be careful not to over-bend the raceway.

344.26 Number of Bends (360°). To reduce the stress and friction on conductor insulation, the maximum number of bends (including offsets) between pull points must not exceed 360°. **Figure 344–2**

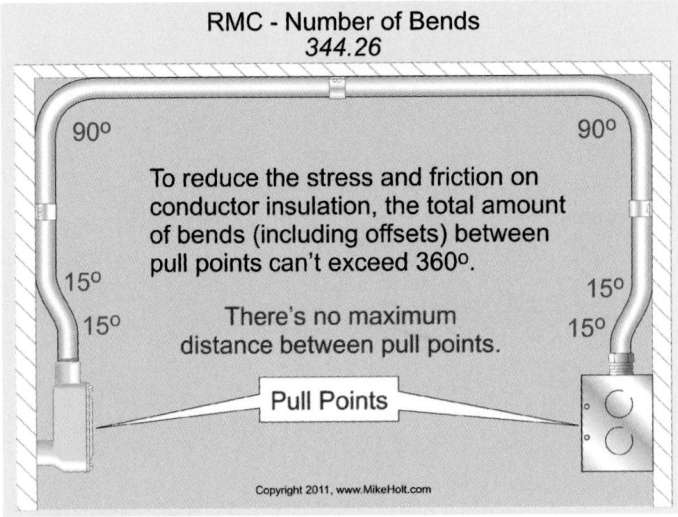

RMC - Number of Bends
344.26

90°   90°

To reduce the stress and friction on conductor insulation, the total amount of bends (including offsets) between pull points can't exceed 360°.

15°   15°

15°   15°

There's no maximum distance between pull points.

Pull Points

Copyright 2011, www.MikeHolt.com

Figure 344–2

Author's Comment: There's no maximum distance between pull boxes because this is a design issue, not a safety issue.

344.28 Reaming. When the raceway is cut in the field, reaming is required to remove the burrs and rough edges.

Author's Comment: It's a commonly accepted practice to ream small raceways with a screwdriver or the backside of pliers. However, when the raceway is cut with a three-wheel pipe cutter, a reaming tool is required to remove the sharp edge of the indented raceway. When conduit is threaded in the field, the threads must be coated with an electrically conductive, corrosion-resistant compound approved by the authority having jurisdiction, in accordance with 300.6(A).

344.30 Securing and Supporting. Rigid metal conduit must be installed as a complete system in accordance with 300.18 [300.10 and 300.12], and it must be securely fastened in place and supported in accordance with (A) and (B).

(A) Securely Fastened. RMC must be secured in accordance with one of the following: **Figure 344–3**

- Fastened within 3 ft of each outlet box, junction box, device box, cabinet, conduit body, or other conduit termination.

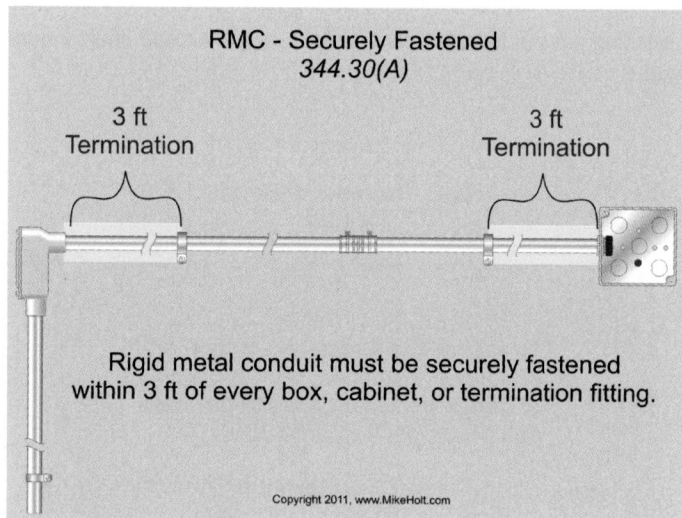

Figure 344–3

Author's Comment: Fastening is required within 3 ft of terminations, not within 3 ft of each coupling.

- When structural members don't permit the raceway to be secured within 3 ft of a box or termination fitting, the raceway must be secured within 5 ft of the termination. **Figure 344–4**

- Conduits aren't required to be securely fastened within 3 ft of the service head for an above-the-roof termination of a mast.

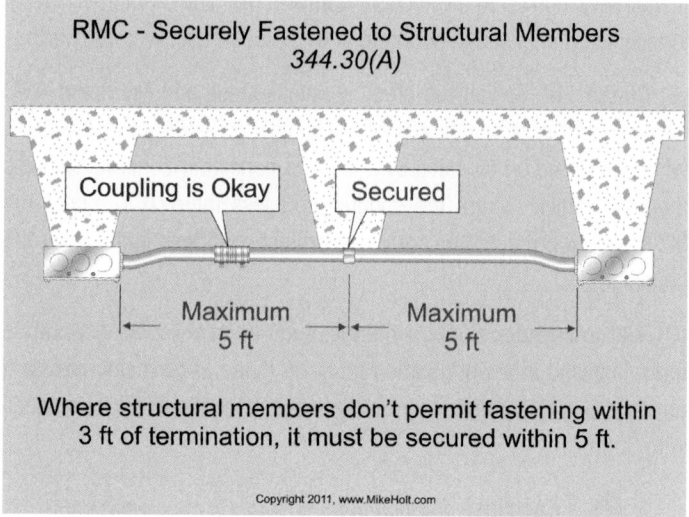

Figure 344–4

(B) Supports.

(1) General. Rigid metal conduit must be supported at intervals not exceeding 10 ft.

(2) Straight Horizontal Runs. Straight horizontal runs made with threaded couplings can be supported in accordance with the distances listed in Table 344.30(B)(2). **Figure 344–5**

Table 344.30(B)(2)	
Trade Size	Support Spacing
½–¾	10 ft
1	12 ft*
1¼–1½	14 ft
2–2½	16 ft
3 and larger	20 ft

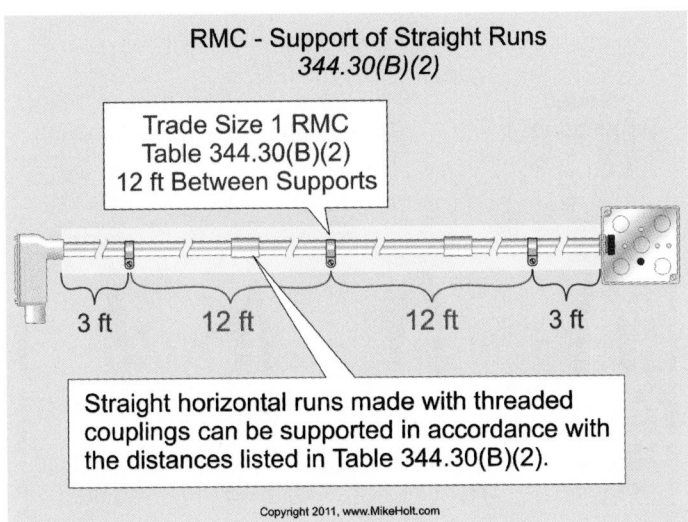

Figure 344–5

(3) Vertical Risers. Exposed vertical risers for fixed equipment can be supported at intervals not exceeding 20 ft, if the conduit is made up with threaded couplings, firmly supported, securely fastened at the top and bottom of the riser, and if no other means of support is available. **Figure 344–6**

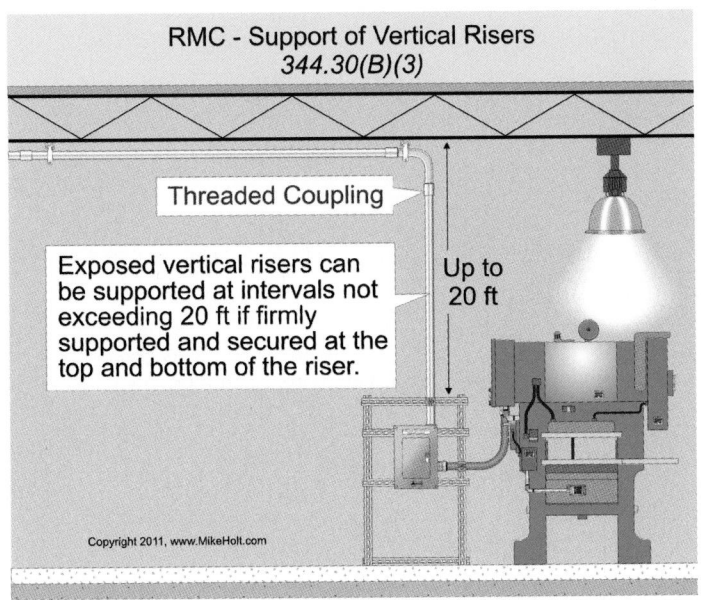

Figure 344–6

(4) Horizontal Runs. Conduits installed horizontally in bored or punched holes in wood or metal framing members, or notches in wooden members, are considered supported, but the raceway must be secured within 3 ft of termination.

Author's Comment: Rigid metal conduit must be provided with expansion fittings if necessary to compensate for thermal expansion and contraction [300.7(B)]. The expansion characteristics for metal raceways are determined by multiplying the values from Table 352.44 by 0.20, and the expansion characteristics for aluminum raceways is determined by multiplying the values from Table 352.44 by 0.40 [300.7 Note].

344.42 Couplings and Connectors.

(A) Installation. Threadless couplings and connectors must be made up tight to maintain an effective ground-fault current path to safely conduct fault current in accordance with 250.4(A)(5), 250.96(A), and 300.10.

Author's Comment: Loose locknuts have been found to burn clear before a fault was cleared because loose connections increase the impedance of the fault current path.

If buried in masonry or concrete, threadless fittings must be the concrete-tight type. If installed in wet locations, fittings must be listed for use in wet locations, in accordance with 314.15(A).

Threadless couplings and connectors must not be used on threaded conduit ends, unless listed for the purpose.

(B) Running Threads. Running threads aren't permitted for the connection of couplings, but they're permitted at other locations. **Figure 344–7**

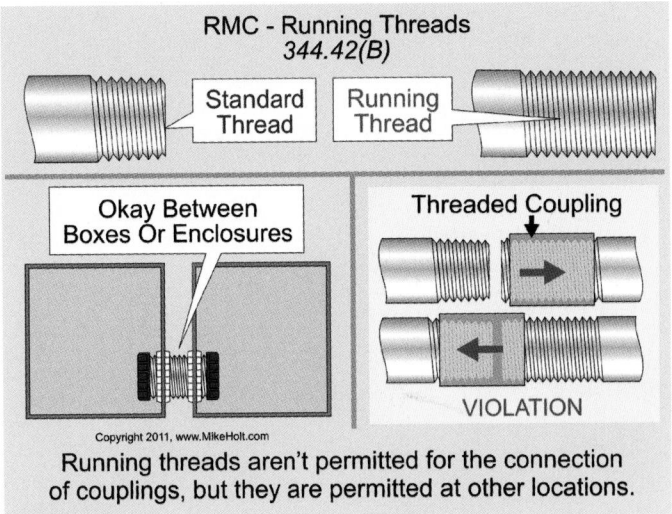

Figure 344–7

344.46 Bushings. To protect conductors from abrasion, a metal or plastic bushing must be installed on conduit threads at terminations, regardless of conductor size, unless the box, fitting, or enclosure is <u>designed to provide this</u> protection.

Note: Conductors 4 AWG and larger that enter an enclosure must be protected from abrasion, during and after installation, by a fitting that provides a smooth, rounded, insulating surface, such as an insulating bushing, unless the design of the box, fitting, or enclosure provides equivalent protection, in accordance with 300.4(G). **Figure 344–8**

PART III. CONSTRUCTION SPECIFICATIONS

344.130 Standard Lengths. The standard length of RMC is 10 ft including an attached coupling, and each end must be threaded. Longer or shorter lengths with or without a coupling and threaded or unthreaded are permitted.

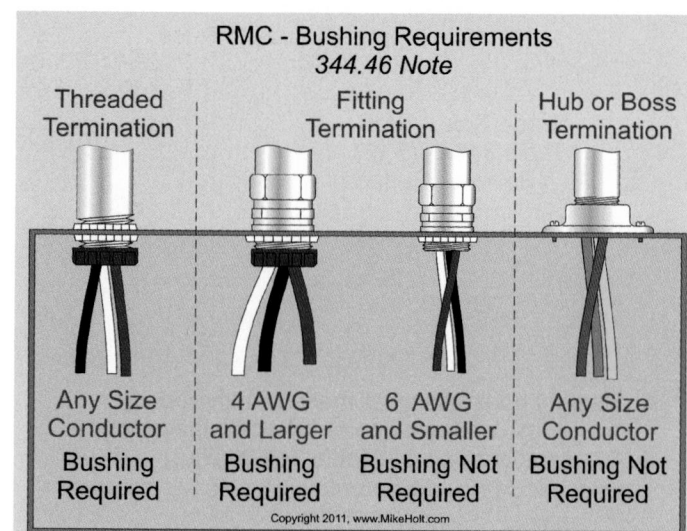

Conductors 4 AWG and larger must be protected by a fitting that provides a smooth, rounded, insulating surface, such as an insulating bushing [300.4(G)].

Figure 344–8

Flexible Metal Conduit (Type FMC)

INTRODUCTION TO ARTICLE 348—FLEXIBLE METAL CONDUIT (TYPE FMC)

Flexible metal conduit (FMC), commonly called "Greenfield" or "flex," is a raceway of an interlocked metal strip of either steel or aluminum. It's primarily used for the final 6 ft or less of raceways between a more rigid raceway system and equipment that moves, shakes, or vibrates. Examples of such equipment include pump motors and industrial machinery.

PART I. GENERAL

348.1 Scope. Article 348 covers the use, installation, and construction specifications for flexible metal conduit and associated fittings.

348.2 Definition.

Flexible Metal Conduit (Type FMC). A raceway of circular cross section made of a helically wound, formed, interlocked metal strip.

348.6 Listing Requirements. Flexible metal conduit and associated fittings must be listed.

PART II. INSTALLATION

348.10 Uses Permitted. Flexible metal conduit is permitted exposed or concealed.

348.12 Uses Not Permitted.

(1) In wet locations.

(2) In hoistways, other than as permitted in 620.21(A)(1).

(3) In storage battery rooms.

(4) In any hazardous location, except as permitted by 501.10(B).

(5) Exposed to material having a deteriorating effect on the installed conductors.

(6) Underground or embedded in poured concrete.

(7) If subject to physical damage.

348.20 Trade Size.

(A) Minimum. Flexible metal conduit smaller than trade size ½ must not be used, except trade size ⅜ can be used for the following applications:

(1) For enclosing the leads of motors.

(2) Not exceeding 6 ft in length: **Figure 348–1**

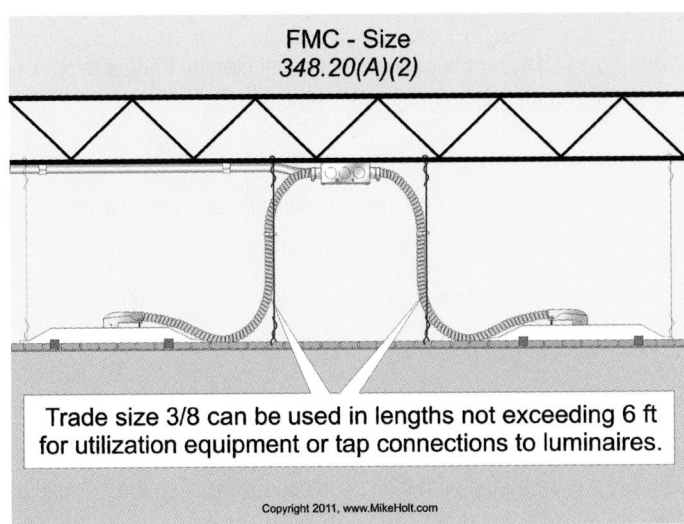

FMC - Size
348.20(A)(2)

Trade size 3/8 can be used in lengths not exceeding 6 ft for utilization equipment or tap connections to luminaires.

Copyright 2011, www.MikeHolt.com

Figure 348–1

a. For utilization equipment,

b. As part of a listed assembly, or

c. For luminaire tap connections, in accordance with 410.117(C).

(3) In manufactured wiring systems, 604.6(A).

(4) In hoistways, 620.21(A)(1).

(5) As part of a listed luminaire assembly in accordance with 410.137(C).

(B) Maximum. Flexible metal conduit larger than trade size 4 must not be used.

348.22 Number of Conductors.

Trade Size ½ and Larger. Flexible metal conduit must be large enough to permit the installation and removal of conductors without damaging the conductors' insulation. When all conductors in a raceway are the same size and insulation, the number of conductors permitted can be found in Annex C for the raceway type.

> **Question:** *How many 6 THHN conductors can be installed in trade size 1 flexible metal conduit?*
>
> (a) 2   (b) 4   (c) 6   (d) 8
>
> **Answer:** *(c) 6 conductors [Annex C, Table C3]*

Author's Comment: See 300.17 for additional examples on how to size raceways when conductors aren't all the same size.

Trade Size ⅜. The number and size of conductors in trade size ⅜ flexible metal conduit must comply with Table 348.22.

> **Question:** *How many 12 THHN conductors can be installed in trade size 3/8 flexible metal conduit that uses outside fittings?*
>
> (a) 1   (b) 3   (c) 5   (d) 7
>
> **Answer:** *(b) 3 conductors [Table 348.22]*

One insulated, covered, or bare equipment grounding conductor of the same size is permitted with the circuit conductors. See the "*" note at the bottom of Table 348.22.

Cables can be installed in flexible metal conduit as long as the number of cables doesn't exceed the allowable percentage fill specified in Table 1, Chapter 9.

348.24 Bends. Bends must be made so that the conduit won't be damaged, and its internal diameter won't be effectively reduced. The radius of the curve of the inner edge of any field bend must not be less than shown in Table 2, Chapter 9 using the column "Other Bends."

348.26 Number of Bends (360°). To reduce the stress and friction on conductor insulation, the maximum number of bends (including offsets) between pull points must not exceed 360°.

> **Author's Comment:** There's no maximum distance between pull boxes because this is a design issue, not a safety issue.

348.28 Trimming. The cut ends of flexible metal conduit must be trimmed to remove the rough edges, but this isn't necessary if fittings are threaded into the convolutions.

348.30 Securing and Supporting.

(A) Securely Fastened. Flexible metal conduit must be securely fastened by a means approved by the authority having jurisdiction within 1 ft of termination, and it must be secured and supported at intervals not exceeding 4½ ft. **Figure 348–2**

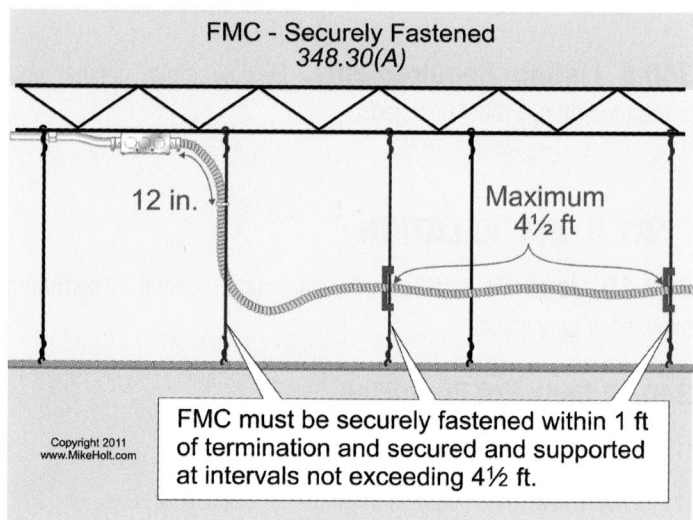

Figure 348–2

Ex 1: Flexible metal conduit isn't required to be securely fastened or supported where fished between access points through concealed spaces and supporting is impracticable.

Ex 2: If flexibility is necessary after installation, unsecured lengths from the last point the raceway is securely fastened must not exceed: Figure 348–3

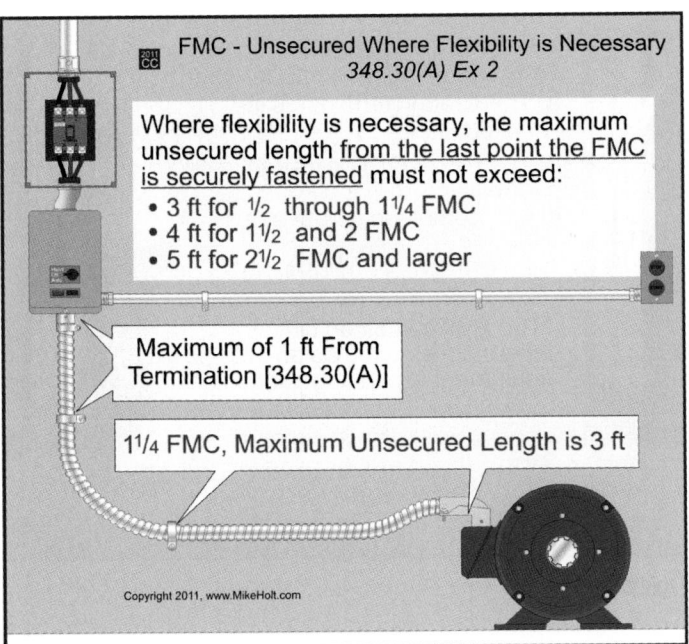

FMC - Unsecured Where Flexibility is Necessary
348.30(A) Ex 2

Where flexibility is necessary, the maximum unsecured length <u>from the last point the FMC is securely fastened</u> must not exceed:
- 3 ft for ½ through 1¼ FMC
- 4 ft for 1½ and 2 FMC
- 5 ft for 2½ FMC and larger

Maximum of 1 ft From Termination [348.30(A)]

1¼ FMC, Maximum Unsecured Length is 3 ft

Copyright 2011, www.MikeHolt.com

Figure 348–3

(1) 3 ft for trade sizes ½ through 1¼

(2) 4 ft for trade sizes 1½ through 2

(3) 5 ft for trade sizes 2½ and larger

Ex 4: FMC to a luminaire or electrical equipment within an accessible ceiling is permitted to be unsupported for not more than 6 ft from the last point where the raceway is securely fastened. **Figure 348–4**

(B) Horizontal Runs. Flexible metal conduit installed horizontally in bored or punched holes in wood or metal framing members, or notches in wooden members, is considered supported, but the raceway must be secured within 1 ft of terminations. **Figure 348–5**

348.42 Fittings. Angle connectors must not be <u>concealed.</u>

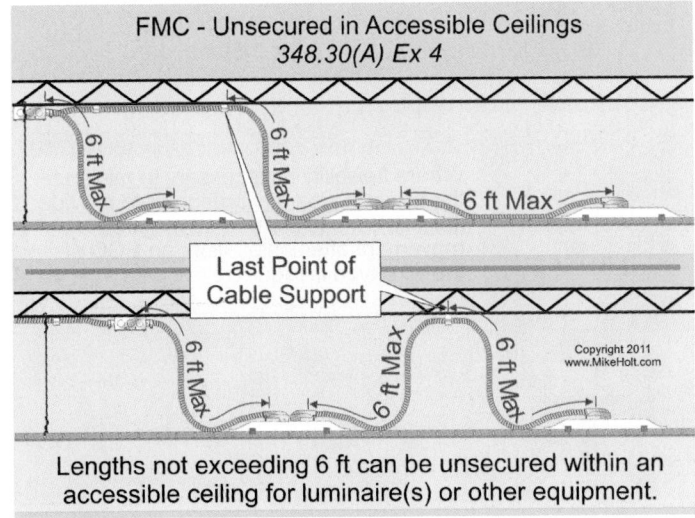

FMC - Unsecured in Accessible Ceilings
348.30(A) Ex 4

6 ft Max

6 ft Max

6 ft Max

Last Point of Cable Support

6 ft Max

6 ft Max

6 ft Max

6 ft Max

Copyright 2011
www.MikeHolt.com

Lengths not exceeding 6 ft can be unsecured within an accessible ceiling for luminaire(s) or other equipment.

Figure 348–4

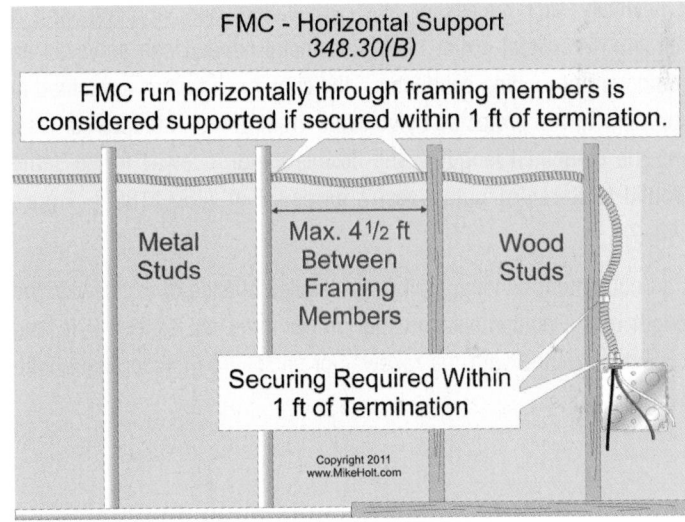

FMC - Horizontal Support
348.30(B)

FMC run horizontally through framing members is considered supported if secured within 1 ft of termination.

Metal Studs

Max. 4½ ft Between Framing Members

Wood Studs

Securing Required Within 1 ft of Termination

Copyright 2011
www.MikeHolt.com

Figure 348–5

348.60 Grounding and Bonding. If flexibility is <u>necessary to minimize the transmission of vibration from equipment or to provide flexibility for equipment that requires movement</u> after installation, an equipment grounding conductor of the wire type must be installed with the circuit conductors in accordance with 250.118(5), based on the rating of the circuit overcurrent device in accordance with 250.122. **Figure 348–6**

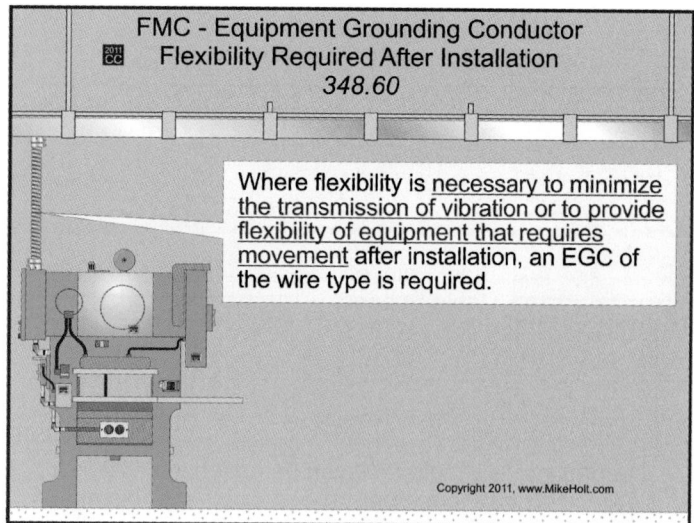

Figure 348-6

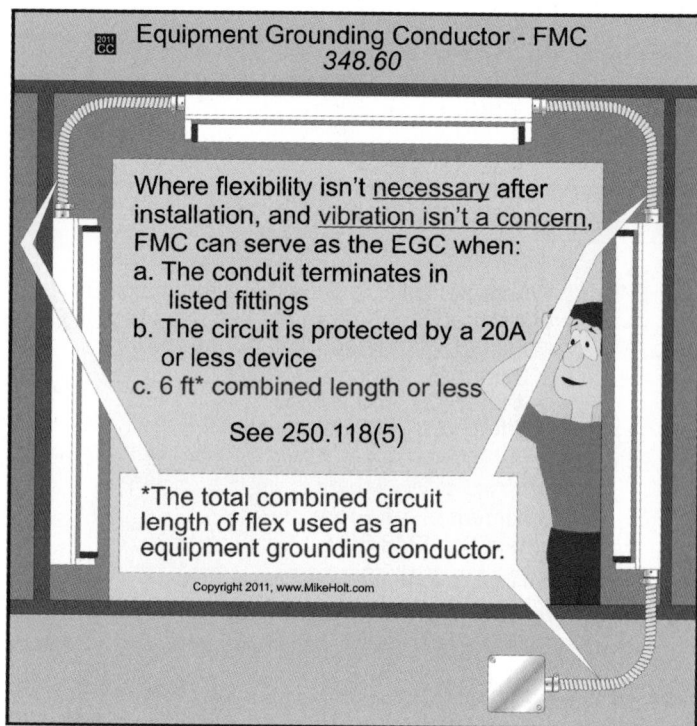

Figure 348-7

If flexibility isn't <u>necessary</u> after installation, <u>and vibration isn't a concern,</u> the metal armor of flexible metal conduit can serve as an equipment grounding conductor if the circuit conductors contained in the raceway are protected by an overcurrent device rated 20A or less, and the combined length of the flexible metal raceway in the same ground-fault return path doesn't exceed 6 ft [250.118(5)]. **Figure 348-7**

If an equipment bonding jumper is installed outside of a raceway, the length of the equipment bonding jumper must not exceed 6 ft, and it must be routed with the raceway or enclosure in accordance with 250.102(E)(2).

ARTICLE 350

Liquidtight Flexible Metal Conduit (Type LFMC)

INTRODUCTION TO ARTICLE 350—LIQUIDTIGHT FLEXIBLE METAL CONDUIT (TYPE LFMC)

Liquidtight flexible metal conduit (LFMC), with its associated connectors and fittings, is a flexible raceway commonly used for connections to equipment that vibrate or are required to move occasionally. Liquidtight flexible metal conduit is commonly called "Sealtight®" or "liquidtight." Liquidtight flexible metal conduit is of similar construction to flexible metal conduit, but it also has an outer liquidtight thermoplastic covering. It has the same primary purpose as flexible metal conduit, but it also provides protection from moisture and some corrosive effects.

PART I. GENERAL

350.1 Scope. Article 350 covers the use, installation, and construction specifications of liquidtight flexible metal conduit and associated fittings.

350.2 Definition.

Liquidtight Flexible Metal Conduit (Type LFMC). A raceway of circular cross section, having an outer liquidtight, nonmetallic, sunlight-resistant jacket over an inner flexible metal core, with associated connectors and fittings for the installation of electric conductors. Figure 350–1

350.6 Listing Requirements. Liquidtight flexible metal conduit and its associated fittings must be listed.

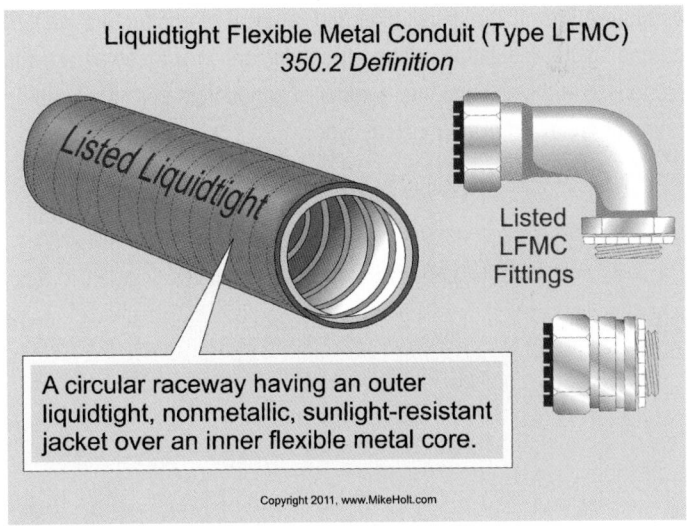

Liquidtight Flexible Metal Conduit (Type LFMC)
350.2 Definition

A circular raceway having an outer liquidtight, nonmetallic, sunlight-resistant jacket over an inner flexible metal core.

Listed LFMC Fittings

Copyright 2011, www.MikeHolt.com

Figure 350–1

PART II. INSTALLATION

350.10 Uses Permitted.

(A) Permitted Use. Listed liquidtight flexible metal conduit is permitted, either exposed or concealed, at any of the following locations:

(1) If flexibility or protection from liquids, vapors, or solids is required.

(2) In hazardous locations, as permitted in 501.10(B), 502.10(A)(2), 502.10(B)(2), or 503.10(A)(2).

(3) For direct burial, if listed and marked for this purpose.

350.12 Uses Not Permitted.

(1) If subject to physical damage.

(2) If the combination of the ambient and conductor operating temperatures exceeds the rating of the raceway.

350.20 Trade Size.

(A) Minimum. Liquidtight flexible metal conduit smaller than trade size ½ must not be used.

Ex: Liquidtight flexible metal conduit can be smaller than trade size ½ if installed in accordance with 348.20(A).

Author's Comment: According to 348.20(A), LFMC smaller than trade size ½ is permitted for the following:

(1) For enclosing the leads of motors.
(2) Not exceeding 6 ft in length:
    a. For utilization equipment,
    b. As part of a listed assembly, or
    c. For tap connections to luminaires as permitted by 410.117(C).
(3) In manufactured wiring systems, 604.6(A).
(4) In hoistways, 620.21(A)(1).
(5) As part of a listed assembly to connect wired luminaire sections, 410.137(C).

(B) Maximum. Liquidtight flexible metal conduit larger than trade size 4 must not be used.

350.22 Number of Conductors.

(A) Raceway Trade Size ½ and Larger. Raceways must be large enough to permit the installation and removal of conductors without damaging the insulation. When all conductors in a raceway are the same size and insulation, the number of conductors permitted can be found in Annex C for the raceway type.

> *Question:* How many 6 THHN conductors can be installed in trade size 1 LFMC? **Figure 350–2**
>
> (a) 3   (b) 5   (c) 7   (d) 9
>
> *Answer:* (c) 7 conductors [Annex C, Table C.7]

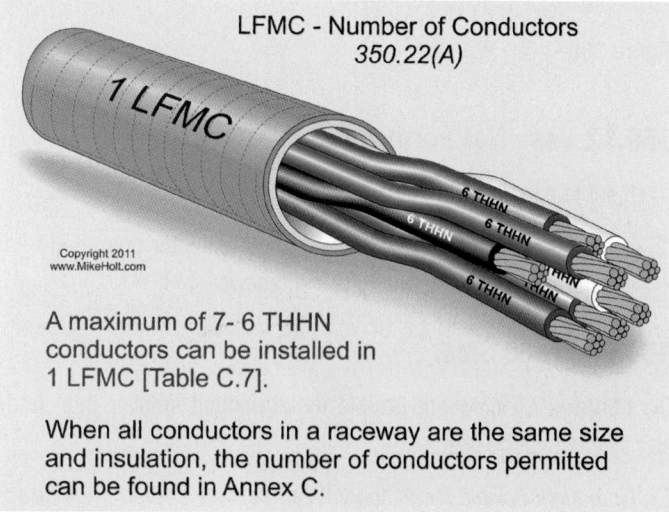

LFMC - Number of Conductors
350.22(A)

1 LFMC

6 THHN

Copyright 2011
www.MikeHolt.com

A maximum of 7- 6 THHN conductors can be installed in 1 LFMC [Table C.7].

When all conductors in a raceway are the same size and insulation, the number of conductors permitted can be found in Annex C.

Figure 350–2

Author's Comment: See 300.17 for additional examples on how to size raceways when conductors aren't all the same size.

Cables can be installed in liquidtight flexible metal conduit as long as the number of cables doesn't exceed the allowable percentage fill specified in Table 1, Chapter 9.

(B) Raceway Trade Size ⅜. The number and size of conductors in a trade size ⅜ liquidtight flexible metal conduit must comply with Table 348.22.

> *Question:* How many 12 THHN conductors can be installed in trade size 3⁄8 LFMC that uses outside fittings?
>
> (a) 1   (b) 3   (c) 5   (d) 7
>
> *Answer:* (b) 3 conductors [Table 348.22]

One insulated, covered, or bare equipment grounding conductor of the same size is permitted with the circuit conductors. See the "*" note at the bottom of Table 348.22.

350.24 Bends. Bends must be made so that the conduit won't be damaged and the internal diameter of the conduit won't be effectively reduced. The radius of the curve of the inner edge of any field bend must not be less than shown in Table 2, Chapter 9 using the column "Other Bends."

350.26 Number of Bends (360°). To reduce the stress and friction on conductor insulation, the maximum number of bends (including offsets) between pull points must not exceed 360°.

> **Author's Comment:** There's no maximum distance between pull boxes because this is a design issue, not a safety issue.

350.30 Securing and Supporting. Liquidtight flexible metal conduit must be securely fastened in place and supported in accordance with (A) and (B).

(A) Securely Fastened. Liquidtight flexible metal conduit must be securely fastened by a means approved by the authority having jurisdiction within 1 ft of termination, and must be secured and supported at intervals not exceeding 4½ ft. **Figure 350–3**

Ex 1: Liquidtight flexible metal conduit isn't required to be securely fastened or supported where fished between access points through concealed spaces and supporting is impracticable.

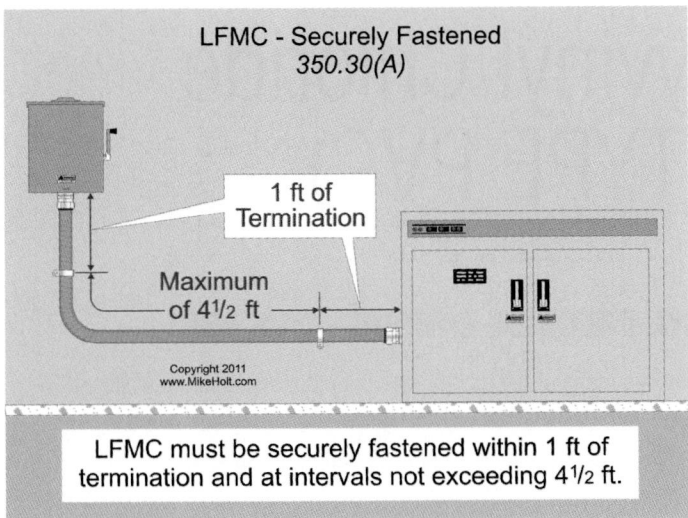

LFMC - Securely Fastened
350.30(A)

1 ft of Termination

Maximum of 4½ ft

Copyright 2011
www.MikeHolt.com

LFMC must be securely fastened within 1 ft of termination and at intervals not exceeding 4½ ft.

Figure 350–3

Ex 2: If flexibility is necessary after installation, unsecured lengths from the last point where the raceway is securely fastened must not exceed: **Figure 350–4**

(1) 3 ft for trade sizes ½ through 1¼
(2) 4 ft for trade sizes 1½ through 2
(3) 5 ft for trade sizes 2½ and larger

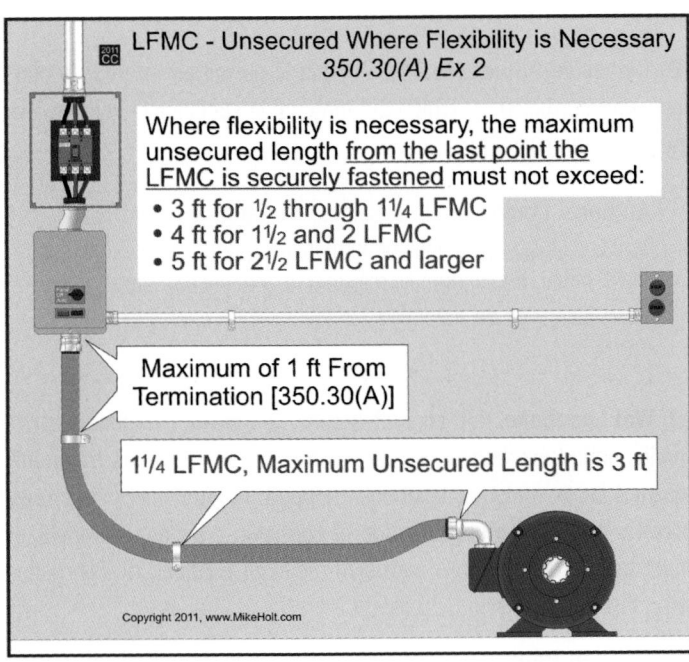

LFMC - Unsecured Where Flexibility is Necessary
350.30(A) Ex 2

Where flexibility is necessary, the maximum unsecured length from the last point the LFMC is securely fastened must not exceed:
• 3 ft for ½ through 1¼ LFMC
• 4 ft for 1½ and 2 LFMC
• 5 ft for 2½ LFMC and larger

Maximum of 1 ft From Termination [350.30(A)]

1¼ LFMC, Maximum Unsecured Length is 3 ft

Copyright 2011, www.MikeHolt.com

Figure 350–4

Ex 4: Lengths not exceeding 6 ft from the last point where the raceway is securely fastened can be unsecured within an accessible ceiling for luminaire(s) or other equipment.

(B) Horizontal Runs. Liquidtight flexible metal conduit installed horizontally in bored or punched holes in wood or metal framing members, or notches in wooden members, is considered supported, but the raceway must be secured within 1 ft of termination.

350.42 Fittings. Angle connectors must not be concealed.

350.60 Grounding and Bonding. If flexibility is necessary to minimize the transmission of vibration from equipment or to provide flexibility for equipment that requires movement after installation, an equipment grounding conductor of the wire type must be installed with the circuit conductors in accordance with 250.118(6), based on the rating of the circuit overcurrent device in accordance with 250.122. **Figure 350–5**

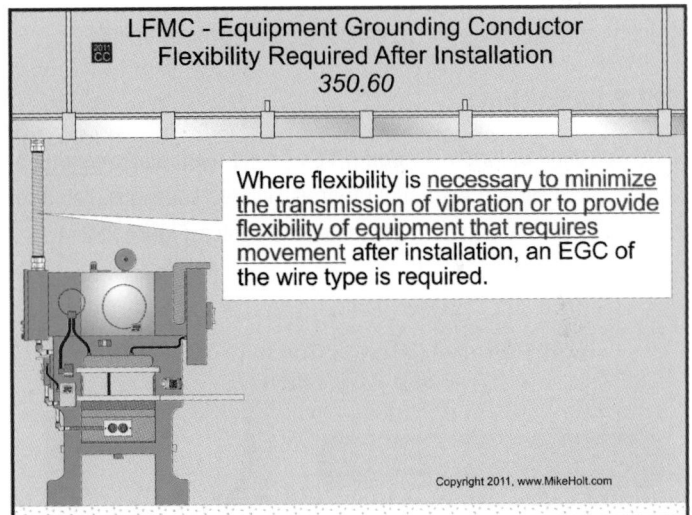

LFMC - Equipment Grounding Conductor
Flexibility Required After Installation
350.60

Where flexibility is necessary to minimize the transmission of vibration or to provide flexibility of equipment that requires movement after installation, an EGC of the wire type is required.

Copyright 2011, www.MikeHolt.com

Figure 350–5

If flexibility isn't necessary after installation, and vibration isn't a concern, the metal armor of flexible metal conduit can serve as an equipment grounding conductor if the circuit conductors contained in the raceway are protected by an overcurrent device rated 20A or less, and the combined length of the flexible metal raceway in the same ground-fault return path doesn't exceed 6 ft [250.118(6)].

If an equipment bonding jumper is installed outside of a raceway, the length of the equipment bonding jumper must not exceed 6 ft, and it must be routed with the raceway or enclosure in accordance with 250.102(E)(2).

ARTICLE 352

Rigid Polyvinyl Chloride Conduit (TYPE PVC)

INTRODUCTION TO ARTICLE 352—RIGID POLYVINYL CHLORIDE CONDUIT (TYPE PVC)

Rigid polyvinyl chloride conduit (PVC) is a rigid nonmetallic conduit that provides many of the advantages of rigid metal conduit, while allowing installation in areas that are wet or corrosive. It's an inexpensive raceway, and easily installed. It's lightweight, easily cut, glued together, and relatively strong. However, conduits manufactured from polyvinyl chloride (PVC) are brittle when cold, and they sag when hot. This type of conduit is commonly used as an underground raceway because of its low cost, ease of installation, and resistance to corrosion and decay.

PART I. GENERAL

352.1 Scope.
Article 352 covers the use, installation, and construction specifications of PVC conduit and associated fittings.

352.2 Definition.

Rigid Polyvinyl Chloride Conduit (PVC). A rigid nonmetallic underline conduit of circular cross section with integral or associated couplings, listed for the installation of electrical conductors and cables. **Figure 352–1**

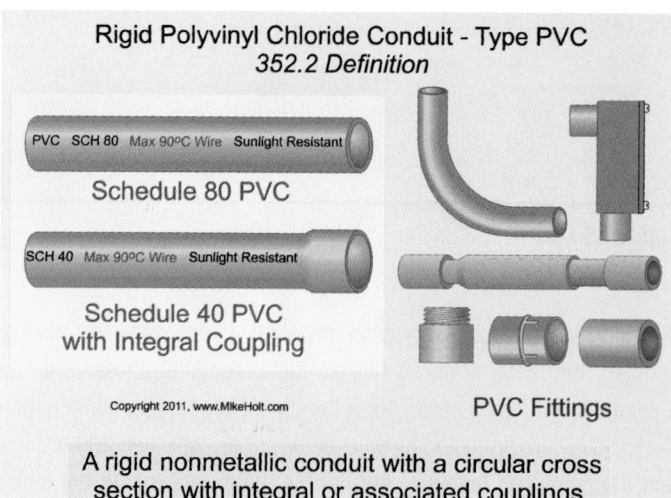

A rigid nonmetallic conduit with a circular cross section with integral or associated couplings.

Figure 352–1

PART II. INSTALLATION

352.10 Uses Permitted.

> **Note:** In extreme cold, PVC conduit can become brittle, and is more susceptible to physical damage.

(A) Concealed. PVC conduit can be concealed within walls, floors, or ceilings, directly buried or embedded in concrete in buildings of any height.

(B) Corrosive Influences. PVC conduit is permitted in areas subject to severe corrosion for which the material is specifically approved by the authority having jurisdiction.

> **Author's Comment:** If subject to exposure to chemical solvents, vapors, splashing, or immersion, materials or coatings must either be inherently resistant to chemicals based upon their listing, or be identified for the specific chemical reagent [300.6(C)(2)].

(D) Wet Locations. PVC conduit is permitted in wet locations such as dairies, laundries, canneries, car washes, and other areas frequently washed or in outdoor locations. Support fittings such as straps, screws, and bolts must be made of corrosion-resistant materials, or must be protected with a corrosion-resistant coating, in accordance with 300.6(A).

(E) Dry and Damp Locations. PVC conduit is permitted in dry and damp locations, except where limited in 352.12.

(F) Exposed. Schedule 40 PVC conduit is permitted for exposed locations where not subject to physical damage. **Figure 352–2**

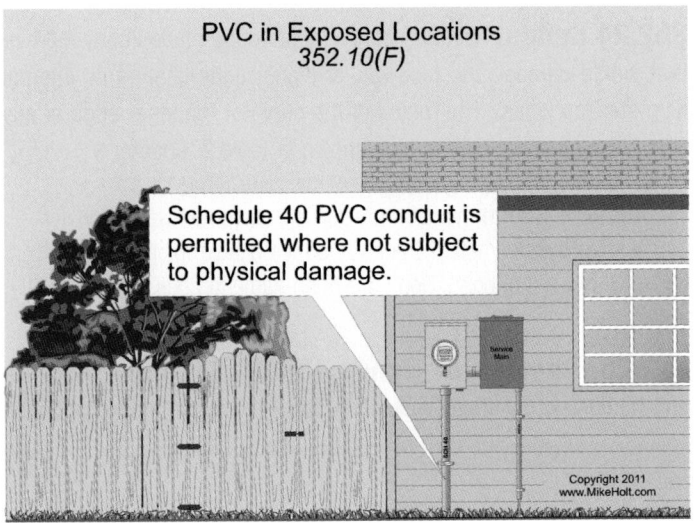

PVC in Exposed Locations
352.10(F)

Schedule 40 PVC conduit is permitted where not subject to physical damage.

Copyright 2011
www.MikeHolt.com

Figure 352–2

If PVC conduit is exposed to physical damage, the raceway must be identified for the application.

Note: PVC Schedule 80 conduit is identified for use in areas subject to physical damage. **Figure 352–3**

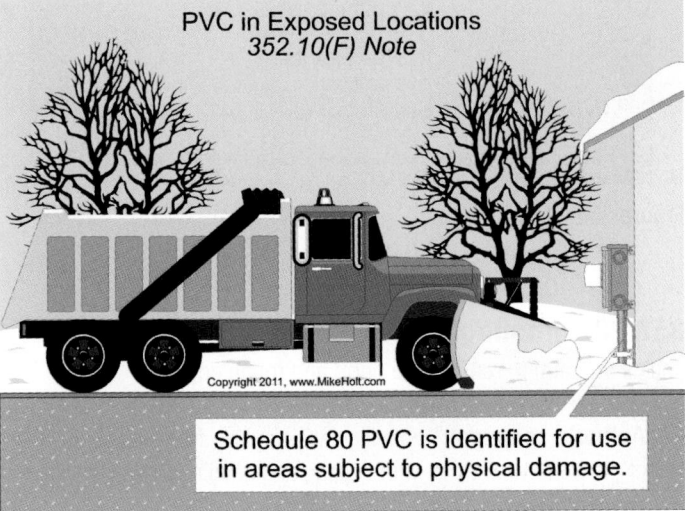

PVC in Exposed Locations
352.10(F) Note

Copyright 2011, www.MikeHolt.com

Schedule 80 PVC is identified for use in areas subject to physical damage.

Figure 352–3

(G) Underground. PVC conduit installed underground must comply with the burial requirements of 300.5.

(H) Support of Conduit Bodies. PVC conduit is permitted to support nonmetallic conduit bodies that aren't larger than the largest trade size of an entering raceway. These conduit bodies can't support luminaires or other equipment, and aren't permitted to contain devices, other than splicing devices permitted by 110.14(B) and 314.16(C)(2).

(I) Insulation Temperature Limitations. Conductors rated at a temperature higher than the listed temperature rating of PVC conduit must not be operated at a temperature above the raceway's listed temperature rating. **Figure 352–4**

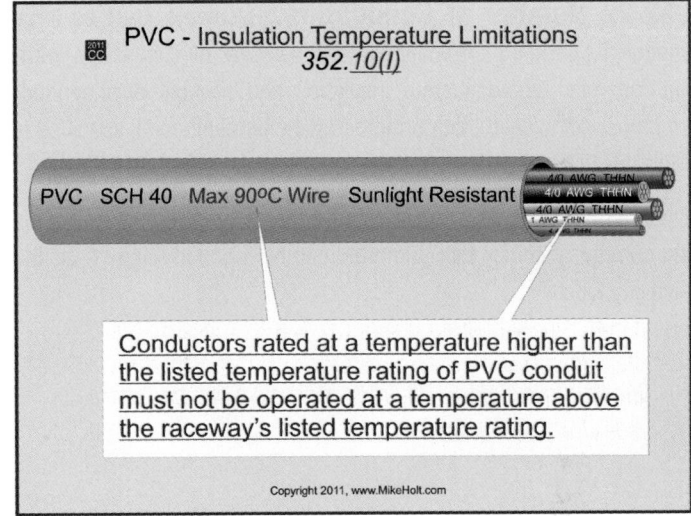

PVC - Insulation Temperature Limitations
352.10(I)

PVC SCH 40   Max 90ºC Wire   Sunlight Resistant

4/0 AWG THHN

Conductors rated at a temperature higher than the listed temperature rating of PVC conduit must not be operated at a temperature above the raceway's listed temperature rating.

Copyright 2011, www.MikeHolt.com

Figure 352–4

352.12 Uses Not Permitted.

(A) Hazardous Locations. PVC conduit isn't permitted to be used in hazardous locations except as permitted by 501.10(A)(1)(a) Ex, 503.10(A), 504.20, 514.8 Ex 2, and 515.8.

(2) In Class I, Division 2 locations, except as permitted in 501.10(B)(7).

(B) Support of Luminaires. PVC conduit must not be used for the support of luminaires or other equipment not described in 352.10(H).

Author's Comment: PVC conduit is permitted to support conduit bodies in accordance with 314.23(E) Ex.

(C) Physical Damage. Schedule 40 PVC conduit must not be installed if subject to physical damage, unless identified for the application.

> **Author's Comment:** PVC Schedule 80 conduit is identified for use in areas subject to physical damage [352.10(F) Note].

(D) Ambient Temperature. PVC conduit must not be installed if the ambient temperature exceeds 50°C (122°F).

352.20 Trade Size.

(A) Minimum. PVC conduit smaller than trade size ½ must not be used.

(B) Maximum. PVC conduit larger than trade size 6 must not be used.

352.22 Number of Conductors. Raceways must be large enough to permit the installation and removal of conductors without damaging the conductors' insulation, and the number of conductors must not exceed that permitted by the percentage fill specified in Table 1, Chapter 9.

When all conductors in a raceway are the same size and insulation, the number of conductors permitted can be found in Annex C for the raceway type.

> *Question: How many 4/0 THHN conductors can be installed in trade size 2 Schedule 40 PVC?*
>
> *(a) 2   (b) 4   (c) 6   (d) 8*
>
> ***Answer:*** *(b) 4 conductors [Annex C, Table C10]*

> **Author's Comment:** Schedule 80 PVC conduit has the same outside diameter as Schedule 40 PVC conduit, but the wall thickness of Schedule 80 PVC conduit is greater, which results in a reduced interior area for conductor fill.

> *Question: How many 4/0 THHN conductors can be installed in trade size 2 Schedule 80 PVC conduit?*
>
> *(a) 3   (b) 5   (c) 7   (d) 9*
>
> ***Answer:*** *(a) 3 conductors [Annex C, Table C9]*

> **Author's Comment:** See 300.17 for additional examples on how to size raceways when conductors aren't all the same size.

Cables can be installed in PVC conduit, as long as the number of cables doesn't exceed the allowable percentage fill specified in Table 1, Chapter 9.

352.24 Bends. Raceway bends must not be made in any manner that would damage the raceway, or significantly change its internal diameter (no kinks). The radius of the curve of the inner edge of any field bend must not be less than shown in Table 2, Chapter 9.

> **Author's Comment:** Be sure to use equipment designed for heating the nonmetallic raceway so it's pliable for bending (for example, a "hot box"). Don't use open-flame torches.

352.26 Number of Bends (360°). To reduce the stress and friction on conductor insulation, the maximum number of bends (including offsets) between pull points must not exceed 360°. **Figure 352–5**

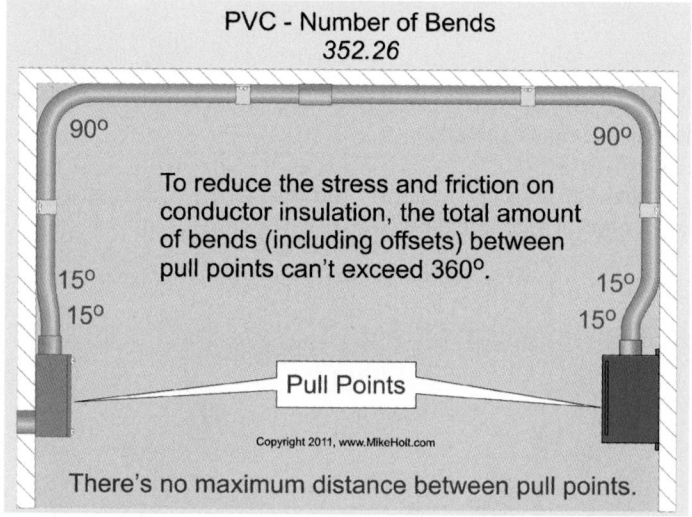

Figure 352–5

352.28 Trimming. The cut ends of PVC conduit must be trimmed (inside and out) to remove the burrs and rough edges.

> **Author's comment:** Trimming PVC conduit is very easy; most of the burrs will rub off with fingers, and a knife will smooth the rough edges.

352.30 Securing and Supporting. PVC conduit must be securely fastened and supported in accordance with (A) and (B).

(A) Secured. PVC conduit must be secured within 3 ft of every box, cabinet, or termination fitting, such as a conduit body. **Figure 352–6**

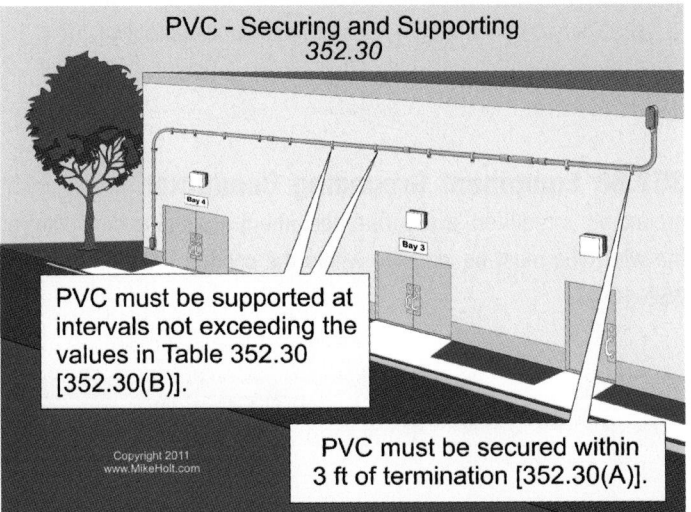

Figure 352–6

(B) Supports. PVC conduit must be supported at intervals not exceeding the values in Table 352.30, and the raceway must be fastened in a manner that permits movement from thermal expansion or contraction. See **Figure 352–6.**

Table 352.30

Trade Size	Support Spacing
½–1	3 ft
1¼–2	5 ft
2½–3	6 ft
3½–5	7 ft
6	8 ft

PVC conduit installed horizontally in bored or punched holes in wood or metal framing members, or notches in wooden members, is considered supported, but the raceway must be secured within 3 ft of termination.

352.44 Expansion Fittings. If PVC conduit is installed in a straight run between securely mounted items, such as boxes, cabinets, elbows, or other conduit terminations, expansion fittings must be provided to compensate for thermal expansion and contraction of the raceway in accordance with Table 352.44, if the length change is determined to be ¼ in. or greater. **Figure 352–7**

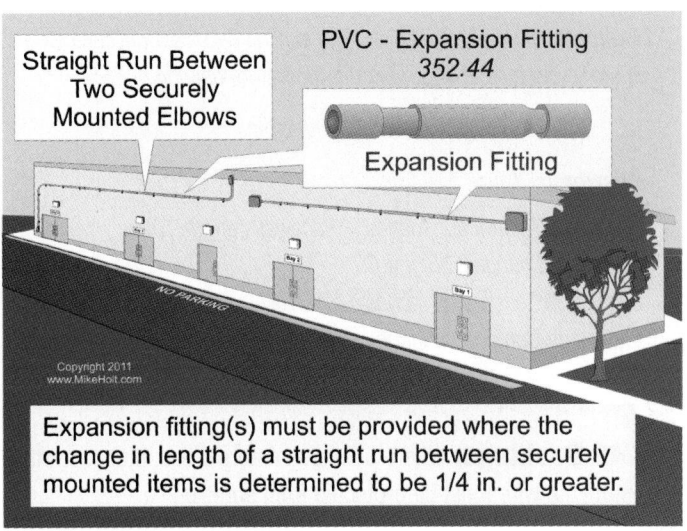

Figure 352–7

Author's Comment: Table 352.44 in the *NEC* was created based on the following formula: **Figure 352–8**

Expansion/Contraction Inches =
Raceway Length/100 x [(Temp Change/100) x 4.00]

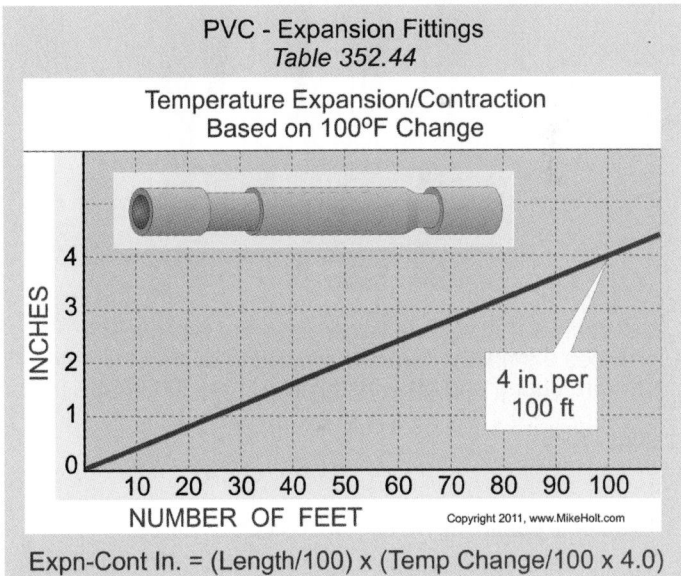

Figure 352–8

Example: How much will a 25 ft run of PVC conduit contract when it's located in an ambient temperature change of 25°F?

(a) 1 in.　　　(b) 2 in.　　　(c) 3 in.　　　(d) 4 in.

Answer: (a) 1 in.

Expansion/Contraction Inches = Raceway Length/100 x ((Temp °F Change/100) x 4.00)

Expansion/Contraction Inches = (25/100) x ((25/100) x 4.00)

Expansion/Contraction Inches = 0.25 in.

352.46 Bushings.
Where a conduit enters a box, fitting, or other enclosure, the wire must be protected from abrasion.

Note: Conductors 4 AWG and larger that enter an enclosure must be protected from abrasion, during and after installation, by a fitting that provides a smooth, rounded insulating surface, such as an insulating bushing, unless the design of the box, fitting, or enclosure provides equivalent protection, in accordance with 300.4(G). **Figure 352–9**

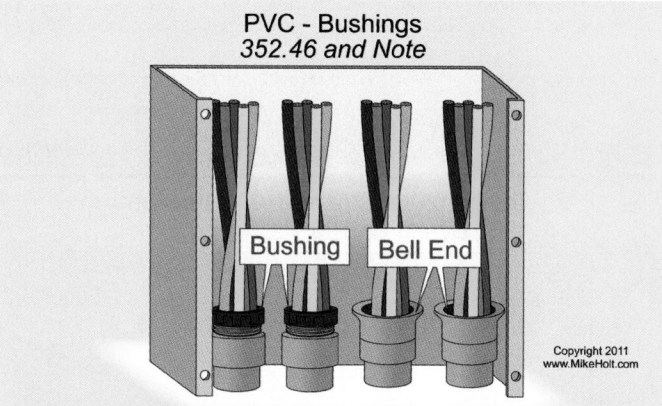

PVC - Bushings
352.46 and Note

Bushing　Bell End

Copyright 2011
www.MikeHolt.com

Conductors 4 AWG and larger require a fitting that provides a smooth, rounded, insulating surface to protect the wire during and after installation. See 300.4(G).

Figure 352–9

Author's Comment: When PVC conduit is stubbed into an open-bottom switchboard, the raceway, including the end fitting (bell-end), must not rise more than 3 in. above the bottom of the switchboard enclosure [300.16(B) and 408.5].

352.48 Joints.
Joints, such as couplings and connectors, must be made in a manner approved by the authority having jurisdiction.

Author's Comment: Follow the manufacturer's instructions for the raceway, fittings, and glue. Some glue requires the raceway surface to be cleaned with a solvent before the application of the glue. After applying glue to both surfaces, a quarter turn of the fitting is required.

352.60 Equipment Grounding Conductor.
If equipment grounding is required, a separate equipment grounding conductor of the wire type must be installed within the conduit [300.2(B)]. **Figure 352–10**

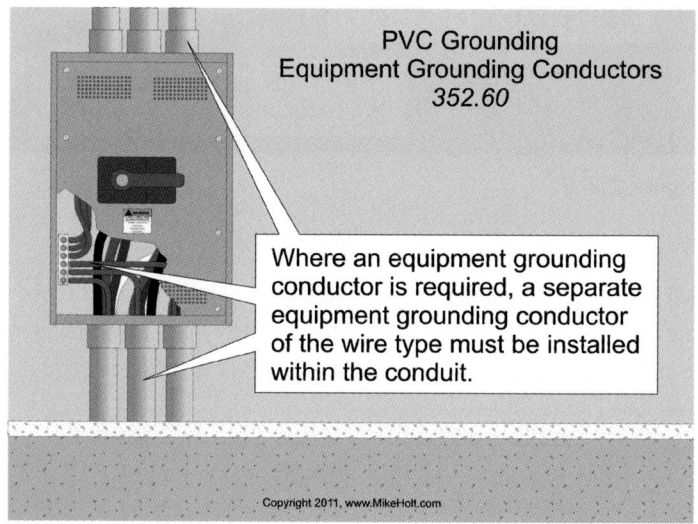

PVC Grounding
Equipment Grounding Conductors
352.60

Where an equipment grounding conductor is required, a separate equipment grounding conductor of the wire type must be installed within the conduit.

Copyright 2011, www.MikeHolt.com

Figure 352–10

Ex 2: An equipment grounding conductor isn't required in PVC conduit if the neutral conductor is used to ground service equipment, as permitted in 250.142(A) [250.24(C)]. **Figure 352–11**

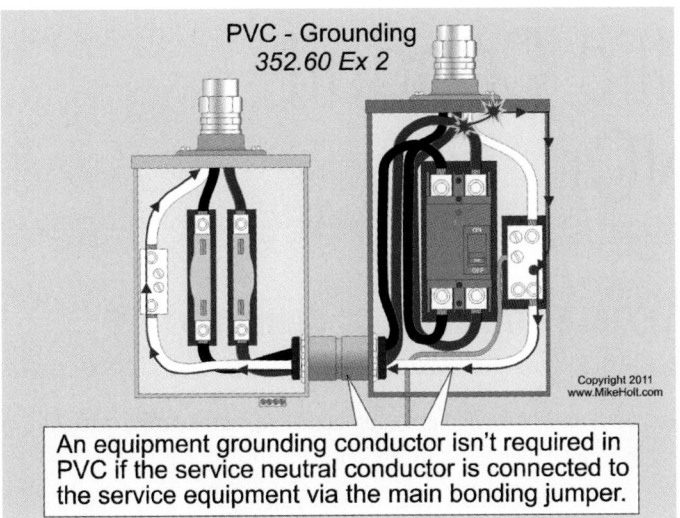

PVC - Grounding
352.60 Ex 2

Copyright 2011
www.MikeHolt.com

An equipment grounding conductor isn't required in PVC if the service neutral conductor is connected to the service equipment via the main bonding jumper.

Figure 352–11

Liquidtight Flexible Nonmetallic Conduit (Type LFNC)

INTRODUCTION TO ARTICLE 356—LIQUIDTIGHT FLEXIBLE NONMETALLIC CONDUIT (TYPE LFNC)

Liquidtight flexible nonmetallic conduit (LFNC) is a listed raceway of circular cross section having an outer liquidtight, nonmetallic, sunlight-resistant jacket over an inner flexible core with associated couplings, connectors, and fittings.

PART I. GENERAL

356.1 Scope. Article 356 covers the use, installation, and construction specifications of liquidtight flexible nonmetallic conduit and associated fittings.

356.2 Definition.

Liquidtight Flexible Nonmetallic Conduit (Type LFNC). A listed raceway of circular cross section, having an outer liquidtight, nonmetallic, sunlight-resistant jacket over a flexible inner core, with associated couplings, connectors, and fittings, listed for the installation of electrical conductors. **Figure 356–1**

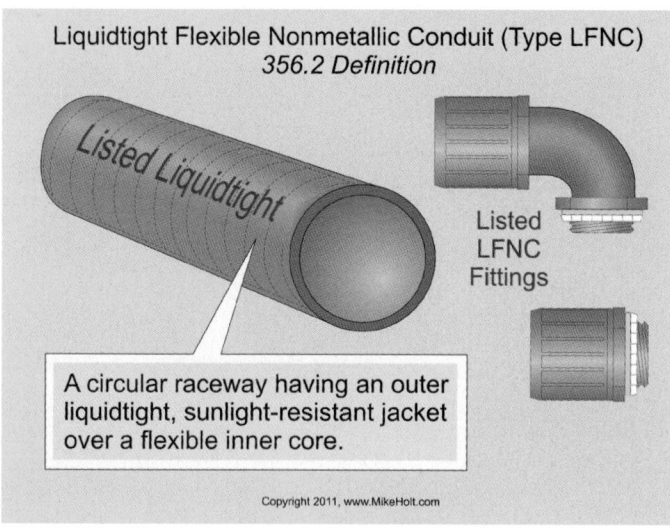

Figure 356–1

(1) Type LFNC-A (orange color). A smooth seamless inner core and cover having reinforcement layers between the core and cover.

(2) Type LFNC-B (gray color). A smooth inner surface with integral reinforcement within the conduit wall.

(3) Type LFNC-C (black color). A corrugated internal and external surface without integral reinforcement.

356.6 Listing Requirement. Liquidtight flexible nonmetallic conduit, and its associated fittings, must be listed.

PART II. INSTALLATION

356.10 Uses Permitted. Listed liquidtight flexible nonmetallic conduit is permitted, either exposed or concealed, at any of the following locations:

(1) If flexibility is required.

(2) If protection from liquids, vapors, or solids is required.

(3) Outdoors, if listed and marked for this purpose.

(4) Directly buried in the earth, if listed and marked for this purpose.

(5) LFNC-B (gray color) is permitted in lengths over 6 ft if secured according to 356.30.

(6) LFNC-B (black color) as a listed manufactured prewired assembly.

(7) Encasement in concrete if listed for direct burial.

356.12 Uses Not Permitted.

(1) If subject to physical damage.

(2) If the combination of ambient and conductor temperature will produce an operating temperature above the rating of the raceway.

(3) Longer than 6 ft, except if approved by the authority having jurisdiction as essential for a required degree of flexibility.

(4) If the operating voltage of the contained conductors exceeds 600 volts, nominal.

(5) In any hazardous location, except as permitted by 501.10(B), 502.10(A) and (B), and 504.20.

356.20 Trade Size.

(A) Minimum. Liquidtight flexible nonmetallic conduit smaller than trade size ½ isn't permitted, except as permitted in the following:

(1) Enclosing the leads of motors, 430.245(B).

(2) For tap connections to lighting fixtures as permitted by 410.117(C).

(B) Maximum. Liquidtight flexible nonmetallic conduit larger than trade size 4 isn't permitted.

356.22 Number of Conductors. Raceways must be large enough to permit the installation and removal of conductors without damaging the insulation. When all conductors in a raceway are the same size and insulation, the number of conductors permitted can be found in Annex C for the raceway type. **Figure 356–2**

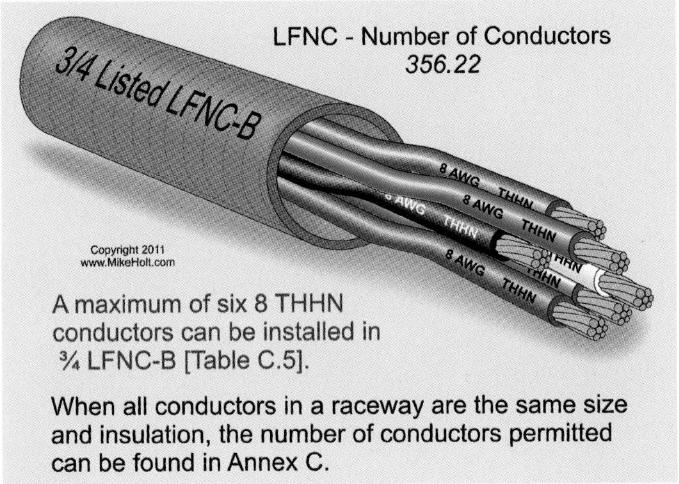

> **Question:** How many 8 THHN conductors can be installed in trade size ¾ LFNC-B?
>
> **Answer:** Six conductors [Annex C, Table C5]

Author's Comment: See 300.17 for additional examples on how to size raceways when conductors aren't all the same size.

Cables can be installed in liquidtight flexible nonmetallic conduit, as long as the number of cables doesn't exceed the allowable percentage fill specified in Table 1, Chapter 9.

356.24 Bends. Raceway bends must not be made in any manner that would damage the raceway or significantly change its internal diameter (no kinks). The radius of the curve of the inner edge of any field bend must not be less than shown in Table 2, Chapter 9 using the column "Other Bends."

356.26 Number of Bends (360°). To reduce the stress and friction on conductor insulation, the maximum number of bends (including offsets) between pull points must not exceed 360°.

Author's Comment: There's no maximum distance between pull boxes because this is a design issue, not a safety issue.

356.30 Securing and Supporting. LFNC-B (gray color) must be securely fastened and supported in accordance with one of the following: **Figure 356–3**

LFNC - Number of Conductors
356.22

A maximum of six 8 THHN conductors can be installed in ¾ LFNC-B [Table C.5].

When all conductors in a raceway are the same size and insulation, the number of conductors permitted can be found in Annex C.

Figure 356–2

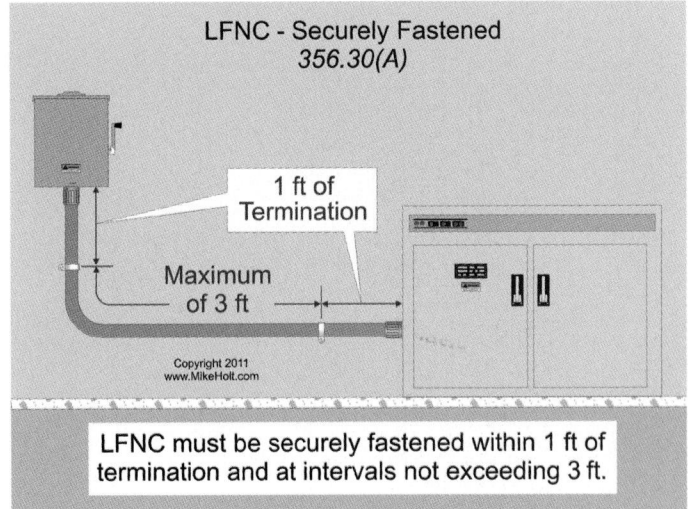

LFNC - Securely Fastened
356.30(A)

1 ft of Termination

Maximum of 3 ft

LFNC must be securely fastened within 1 ft of termination and at intervals not exceeding 3 ft.

Figure 356–3

(1) The conduit must be securely fastened at intervals not exceeding 3 ft, and within 1 ft of termination when installed longer than 6 ft.

(2) Securing or supporting isn't required if it's fished, installed in lengths not exceeding 3 ft at terminals if flexibility is required, or installed in lengths not exceeding 6 ft for tap conductors to luminaires, as permitted in 410.117(C).

(3) Horizontal runs of liquidtight flexible nonmetallic conduit installed horizontally in bored or punched holes in wood or metal framing members, or notches in wooden members, are considered supported, but the raceway must be secured within 1 ft of termination.

(4) Securing or supporting of LFNC-B (gray color) isn't required if installed in lengths not exceeding 6 ft from the last point where the raceway is securely fastened for connections within an accessible ceiling to luminaire(s) or other equipment.

356.42 Fittings. Only fittings listed for use with liquidtight flexible nonmetallic conduit can be used [300.15]. Angle connector fittings must not be used in concealed raceway installations. Straight liquidtight flexible nonmetallic conduit fittings are permitted for direct burial or encasement in concrete.

> **Author's Comment:** Conductors 4 AWG and larger that enter an enclosure must be protected from abrasion, during and after installation, by a fitting that provides a smooth, rounded, insulating surface, such as an insulating bushing, unless the design of the box, fitting, or enclosure provides equivalent protection, in accordance with 300.4(G).

356.60 Equipment Grounding Conductor. If equipment grounding is required, a separate equipment grounding conductor of the wire type must be installed within the conduit [300.2(B)]. **Figure 356–4**

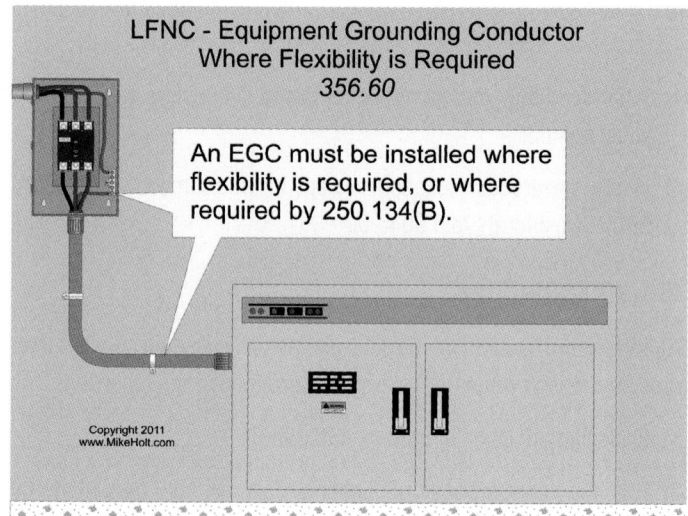

Figure 356–4

If an equipment bonding jumper is installed outside of a raceway, the length of the equipment bonding jumper must not exceed 6 ft, and it must be routed with the raceway or enclosure in accordance with 250.102(E)(2).

Electrical Metallic Tubing (Type EMT)

INTRODUCTION TO ARTICLE 358—ELECTRICAL METALLIC TUBING (TYPE EMT)

Electrical metallic tubing (EMT) is a lightweight raceway that's relatively easy to bend, cut, and ream. Because it isn't threaded, all connectors and couplings are of the threadless type and provide quick, easy, and inexpensive installation when compared to other metallic conduit systems, which makes it very popular. Electrical metallic tubing is manufactured in both galvanized steel and aluminum; the steel type is the most common type used.

PART I. GENERAL

358.1 Scope. Article 358 covers the use, installation, and construction specifications of electrical metallic tubing.

358.2 Definition.

Electrical Metallic Tubing (Type EMT). A metallic tubing of circular cross section used for the installation and physical protection of electrical conductors when joined together with fittings. **Figure 358–1**

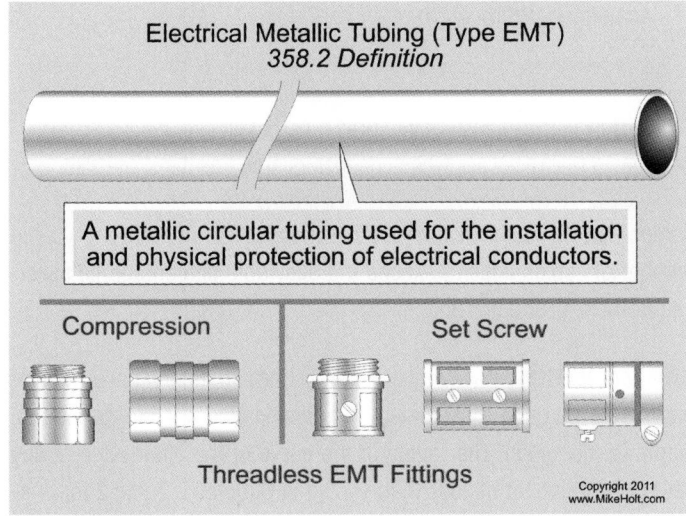

Figure 358–1

358.6 Listing Requirement. Electrical metallic tubing, elbows, and associated fittings must be listed.

PART II. INSTALLATION

358.10 Uses Permitted.

(A) Exposed and Concealed. Electrical metallic tubing is permitted exposed or concealed.

(B) Corrosion Protection. Electrical metallic tubing, elbows, couplings, and fittings can be installed in concrete, in direct contact with the earth, or in areas subject to severe corrosive influences if protected by corrosion protection and <u>approved as</u> suitable for the condition. **Figure 358–2**

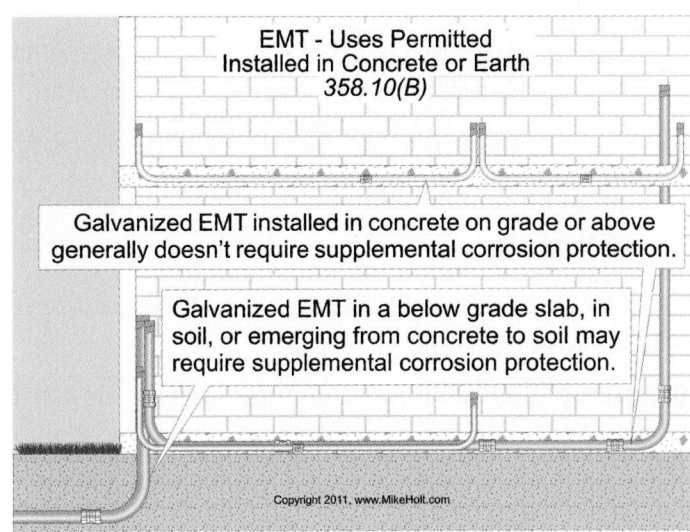

Figure 358–2

CAUTION: *Supplementary coatings for corrosion protection (asphalted paint) haven't been investigated by a product testing and listing agency, and these coatings are known to cause cancer in laboratory animals.*

(C) Wet Locations. Support fittings, such as screws, straps, and so on, installed in a wet location must be made of corrosion-resistant material, or a corrosion-resistant coating must protect them in accordance with 300.6.

> **Author's Comment:** Fittings used in wet locations must be listed for the application (wet location) [314.15]. For more information, visit http://www.etpfittings.com/.

358.12 Uses Not Permitted. EMT must not be used under the following conditions:

(1) Where, during installation or afterward, it will be subject to severe physical damage.

(2) If protected from corrosion solely by enamel.

(3) In cinder concrete or cinder fill where subject to permanent moisture, unless encased in not less than 2 in. of concrete.

(4) In any hazardous location, except as permitted by 502.10, 503.10, and 504.20.

(5) For the support of luminaires or other equipment (like boxes), except conduit bodies no larger than the largest trade size of the tubing that can be supported by the raceway. **Figure 358–3**

(6) If practical, contact with dissimilar metals must be avoided to prevent the deterioration of the metal because of galvanic action.

Ex: Aluminum fittings are permitted on steel electrical metallic tubing, and steel fittings are permitted on aluminum EMT.

358.20 Trade Size.

(A) Minimum. Electrical metallic tubing smaller than trade size ½ isn't permitted.

(B) Maximum. Electrical metallic tubing larger than trade size 4 isn't permitted.

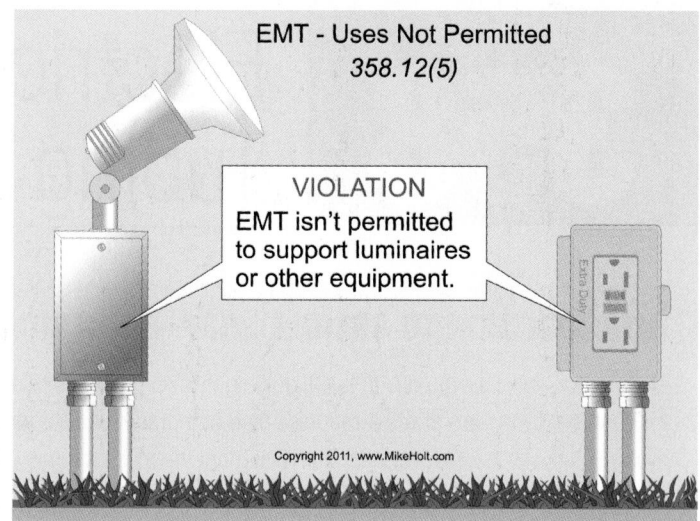

EMT - Uses Not Permitted
358.12(5)

VIOLATION
EMT isn't permitted to support luminaires or other equipment.

Copyright 2011, www.MikeHolt.com

Figure 358–3

358.22 Number of Conductors. Raceways must be large enough to permit the installation and removal of conductors without damaging the conductor insulation. When all conductors in a raceway are the same size and insulation, the number of conductors permitted can be found in Annex C for the raceway type.

> *Question: How many 12 THHN conductors can be installed in trade size 1 EMT?* **Figure 358–4**
>
> *(a) 26   (b) 28   (c) 30   (d) 32*
>
> **Answer:** *(a) 26 conductors [Annex C, Table C.1]*

> **Author's Comment:** See 300.17 for additional examples on how to size raceways when conductors aren't all the same size.

Cables can be installed in electrical metallic tubing, as long as the number of cables doesn't exceed the allowable percentage fill specified in Table 1, Chapter 9.

358.24 Bends. Raceway bends must not be made in any manner that would damage the raceway, or significantly change its internal diameter (no kinks). The radius of the curve of the inner edge of any field bend must not be less than shown in Chapter 9, Table 2 for one-shot and full shoe benders.

> **Author's Comment:** This typically isn't a problem, because most benders are made to comply with this table.

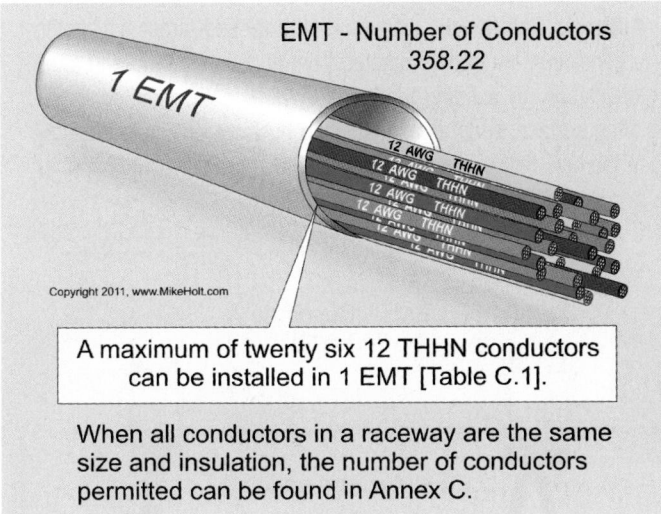

A maximum of twenty six 12 THHN conductors can be installed in 1 EMT [Table C.1].

When all conductors in a raceway are the same size and insulation, the number of conductors permitted can be found in Annex C.

Figure 358–4

358.26 Number of Bends (360°). To reduce the stress and friction on conductor insulation, the maximum number of bends (including offsets) between pull points can't exceed 360°. **Figure 358–5**

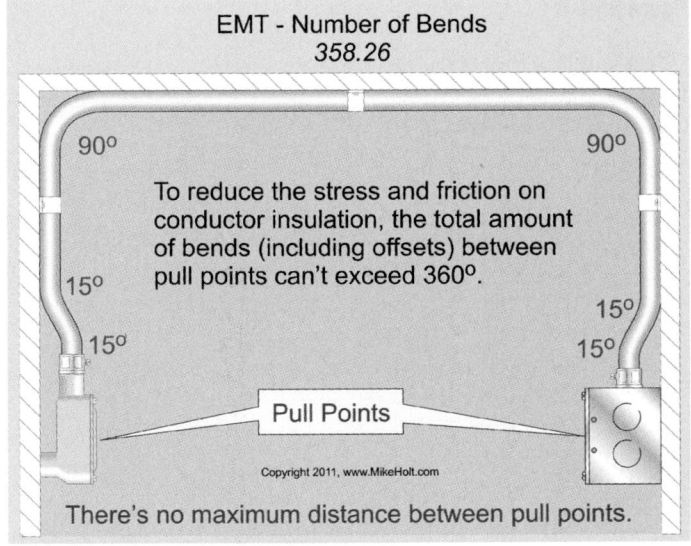

Figure 358–5

Author's Comment: There's no maximum distance between pull boxes because this is a design issue, not a safety issue.

358.28 Reaming and Threading.

(A) Reaming. Reaming to remove the burrs and rough edges is required when the raceway is cut.

> **Author's Comment:** It's considered an accepted practice to ream small raceways with a screwdriver or the backside of pliers.

(B) Threading. Electrical metallic tubing must not be threaded.

358.30 Securing and Supporting. Electrical metallic tubing must be installed as a complete system in accordance with 300.18 [300.10 and 300.12], and it must be securely fastened in place and supported in accordance with (A) and (B).

(A) Securely Fastened. Electrical metallic tubing must generally be securely fastened within 3 ft of every box, cabinet, or termination fitting, and at intervals not exceeding 10 ft. **Figure 358–6**

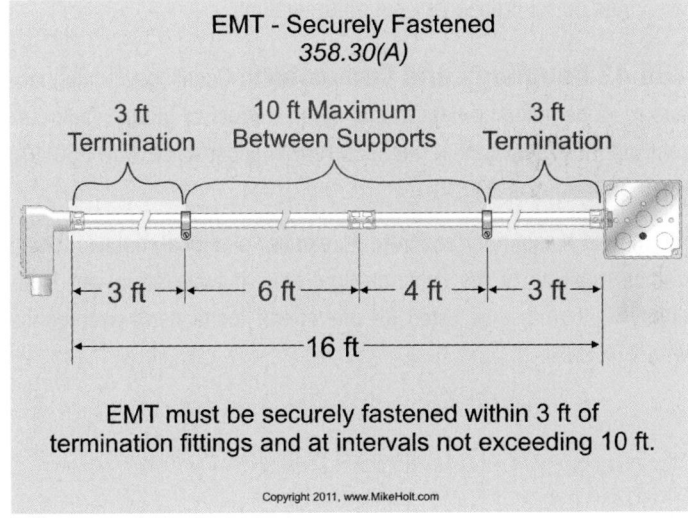

Figure 358–6

> **Author's Comment:** Fastening is required within 3 ft of termination, not within 3 ft of a coupling.

Ex 1: When structural members don't permit the raceway to be secured within 3 ft of a box or termination fitting, an unbroken raceway can be secured within 5 ft of a box or termination fitting. **Figure 358–7**

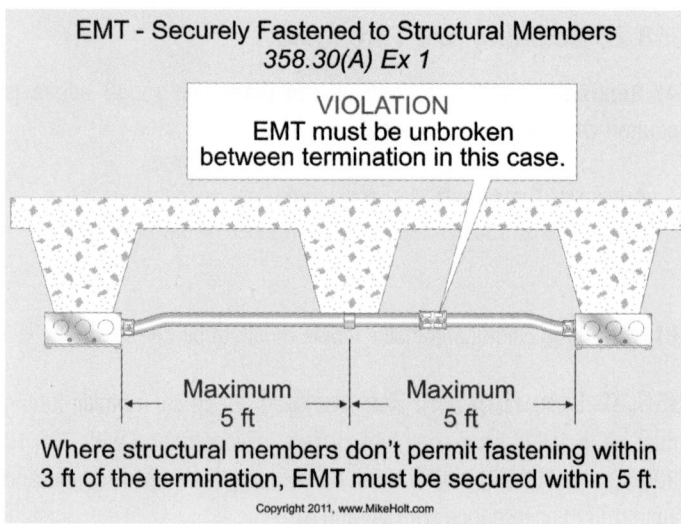

Figure 358–7

(B) Horizontal Runs. Electrical metallic tubing installed horizontally in bored or punched holes in wood or metal framing members, or notches in wooden members, is considered supported, but the raceway must be secured within 3 ft of termination.

358.42 Couplings and Connectors. Couplings and connectors must be made up tight to maintain an effective ground-fault current path to safely conduct fault current in accordance with 250.4(A)(5), 250.96(A), and 300.10.

If buried in masonry or concrete, threadless electrical metallic tubing fittings must be of the concrete-tight type. If installed in wet locations, fittings must be listed for use in wet locations in accordance with 314.15(A).

Author's Comment: Conductors 4 AWG and larger that enter an enclosure must be protected from abrasion, during and after installation, by a fitting that provides a smooth, rounded, insulating surface, such as an insulating bushing, unless the design of the box, fitting, or enclosure provides equivalent protection, in accordance with 300.4(G). **Figure 358–8**

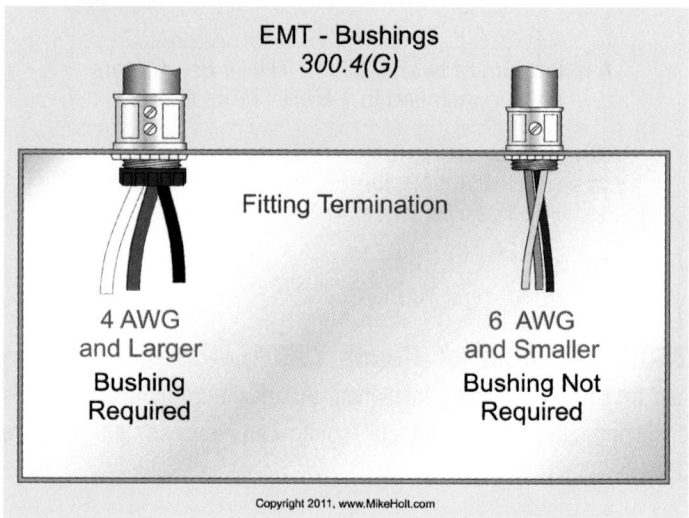

Figure 358–8

ARTICLE 362

Electrical Nonmetallic Tubing (Type ENT)

INTRODUCTION TO ARTICLE 362—ELECTRICAL NONMETALLIC TUBING (TYPE ENT)

Electrical nonmetallic tubing (ENT) is a pliable, corrugated, circular raceway made of polyvinyl chloride. In some parts of the country, the field name for electrical nonmetallic tubing is "Smurf Pipe" or "Smurf Tube," because it was only available in blue when it originally came out at the time the children's cartoon characters "The Smurfs" were most popular. Today, the raceway is available in a rainbow of colors such as white, yellow, red, green, and orange, and is sold in both fixed lengths and on reels.

PART I. GENERAL

362.1 Scope. Article 362 covers the use, installation, and construction specifications of electrical nonmetallic tubing and associated fittings.

362.2 Definition.

Electrical Nonmetallic Tubing (Type ENT). A pliable corrugated raceway of circular cross section, with integral or associated couplings, connectors, and fittings listed for the installation of electrical conductors. **Figure 362–1**

Electrical nonmetallic tubing can be bent by hand with a reasonable force, but without other assistance.

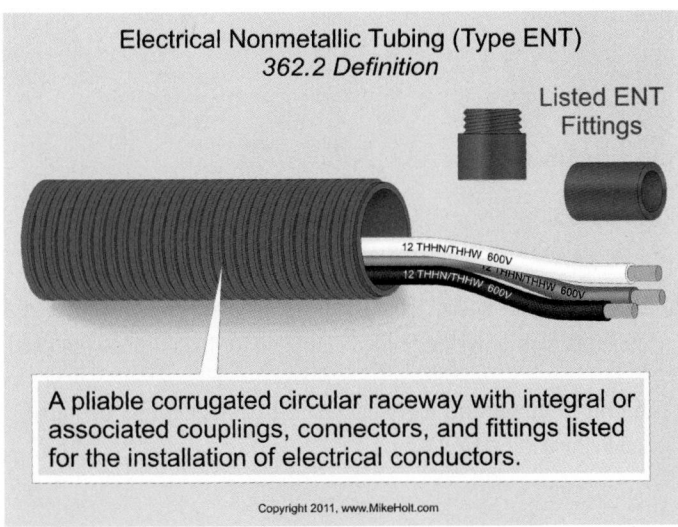

Figure 362–1

PART II. INSTALLATION

362.10 Uses Permitted.

Definition of First Floor. The first floor of a building is the floor with 50 percent or more of the exterior wall surface area level with or above finished grade. If one additional level not designed for human habitation and used only for vehicle parking, storage, or similar use is at ground level, then the first of the three permissible floors can be the next higher floor.

(1) In buildings not exceeding three floors. **Figure 362–2**

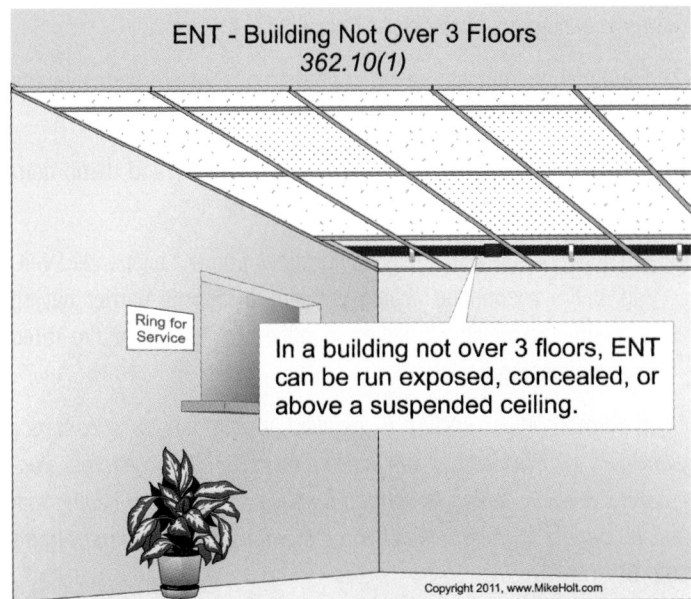

Figure 362–2

a. Exposed, where not prohibited by 362.12.

b. Concealed within walls, floors, and ceilings.

(2) In buildings exceeding three floors, electrical nonmetallic tubing can be installed concealed in walls, floors, or ceilings that provide a thermal barrier having a 15-minute finish rating, as identified in listings of fire-rated assemblies. **Figure 362–3**

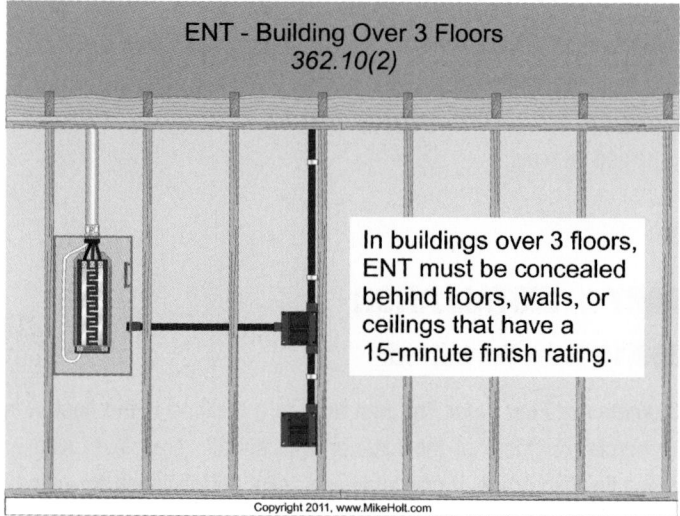

Figure 362–3

Ex to (2): If a fire sprinkler system is installed on all floors, in accordance with NFPA 13, Standard for the Installation of Sprinkler Systems, electrical nonmetallic tubing is permitted exposed or concealed in buildings of any height. **Figure 362–4**

(3) Electrical nonmetallic tubing is permitted in severe corrosive and chemical locations, when identified for this use.

(4) Electrical nonmetallic tubing is permitted in dry and damp concealed locations, if not prohibited by 362.12.

(5) Electrical nonmetallic tubing is permitted above a suspended ceiling, if the suspended ceiling provides a thermal barrier having a 15-minute finish rating, as identified in listings of fire-rated assemblies. **Figure 362–5**

Ex: If a fire sprinkler system is installed on all floors, in accordance with NFPA 13, Standard for the Installation of Sprinkler Systems, electrical nonmetallic tubing is permitted above a suspended ceiling that doesn't have a 15-minute finish rated thermal barrier material. **Figure 362–6**

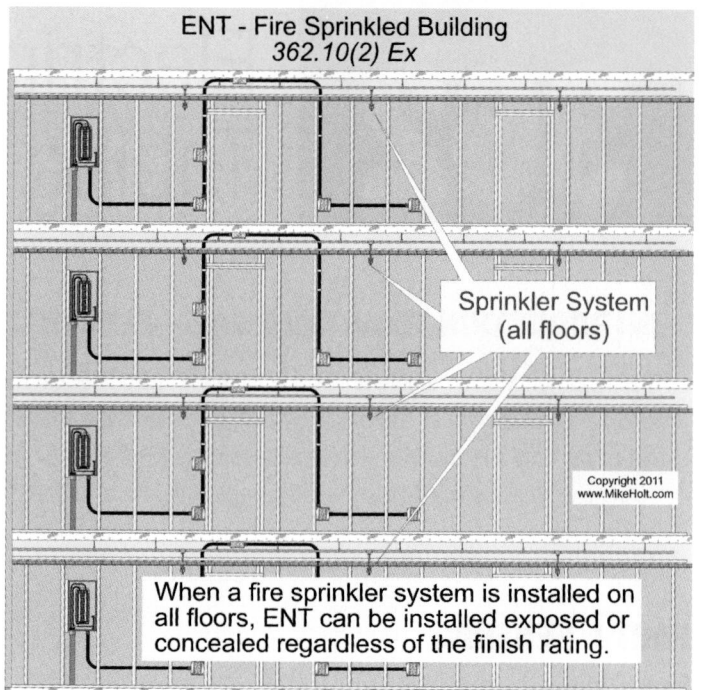

Figure 362–4

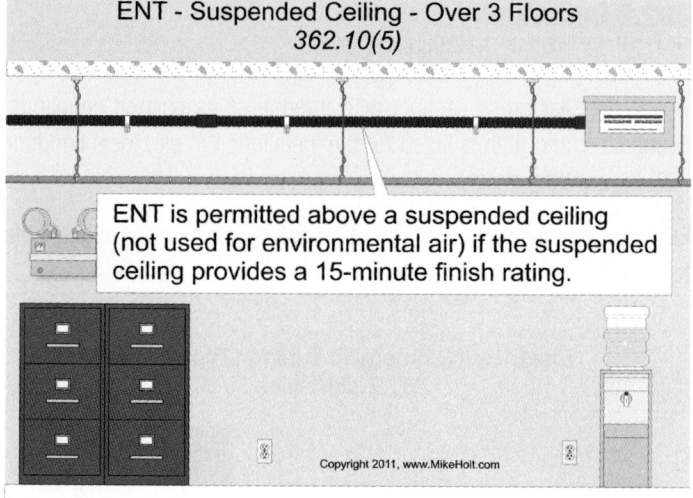

Figure 362–5

(6) Electrical nonmetallic tubing can be encased or embedded in a concrete slab provided fittings identified for the purpose are used.

Author's Comment: Electrical nonmetallic tubing isn't permitted in the earth [362.12(5)].

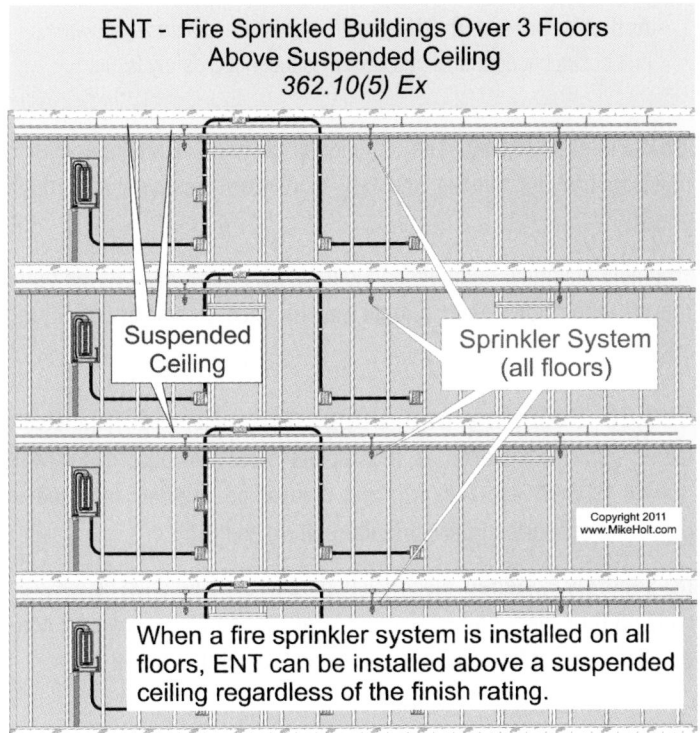

ENT - Fire Sprinkled Buildings Over 3 Floors Above Suspended Ceiling
362.10(5) Ex

Suspended Ceiling

Sprinkler System (all floors)

When a fire sprinkler system is installed on all floors, ENT can be installed above a suspended ceiling regardless of the finish rating.

Figure 362–6

(7) Electrical nonmetallic tubing is permitted in wet locations indoors, or in a concrete slab on or below grade, with fittings listed for the purpose.

(8) Listed prewired electrical nonmetallic tubing with conductors is permitted in trade sizes ½, ¾, and 1.

(9) Conductors rated at a temperature higher than the listed temperature rating of ENT must not be operated at a temperature above the raceways listed temperature rating. **Figure 362–7**

362.12 Uses Not Permitted.

(1) In any hazardous location, except as permitted by 504.20 and 505.15(A)(1).

(2) For the support of luminaires or equipment. See 314.2.

(3) If the ambient temperature exceeds 50°C (122°F).

(4) For direct earth burial.

Author's Comment: Electrical nonmetallic tubing can be encased in concrete [362.10(6)].

(5) As a wiring method for systems over 600V.

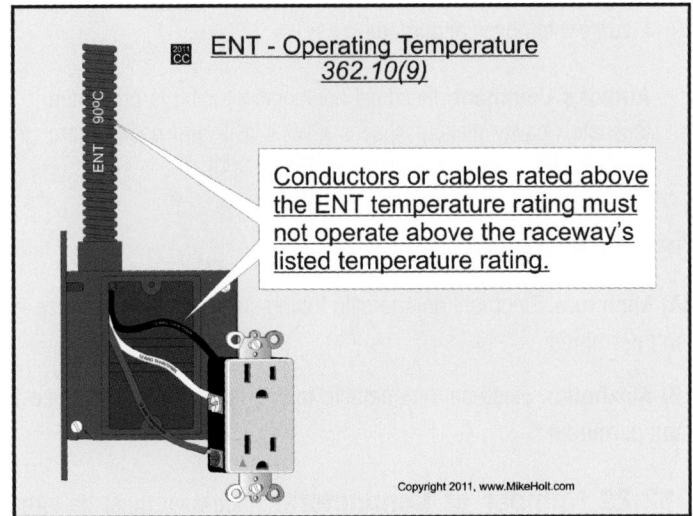

ENT - Operating Temperature
362.10(9)

Conductors or cables rated above the ENT temperature rating must not operate above the raceway's listed temperature rating.

Figure 362–7

(6) Exposed in buildings over three floors, except as permitted by 362.10(2) and (5) Ex.

(7) In assembly occupancies or theaters, except as permitted by 518.4 and 520.5.

(8) Exposed to the direct rays of the sun for an extended period, unless listed as sunlight resistant.

Author's Comment: Exposing electrical nonmetallic tubing to the direct rays of the sun for an extended time may result in the product becoming brittle, unless it's listed to resist the effects of ultraviolet (UV) radiation. **Figure 362–8**

ENT - Exposed to Direct Sun
362.12(8)

ENT isn't permitted to be exposed to the direct rays of the sun for extended periods unless listed as sunlight resistant.

Figure 362–8

(9) If subject to physical damage.

Author's Comment: Electrical nonmetallic tubing is prohibited in ducts, cavity plenum spaces [300.22(C)], and patient care area circuits in health care facilities [517.13(A)].

362.20 Trade Sizes.

(A) Minimum. Electrical nonmetallic tubing smaller than trade size ½ isn't permitted.

(B) Maximum. Electrical nonmetallic tubing larger than trade size 2 isn't permitted.

362.22 Number of Conductors.
Raceways must be large enough to permit the installation and removal of conductors without damaging the conductors' insulation, and the number of conductors must not exceed that permitted by the percentage fill specified in Table 1, Chapter 9.

When all conductors in a raceway are the same size and insulation, the number of conductors permitted can be found in Annex C for the raceway type.

> *Question: How many 12 THHN conductors can be installed in trade size ½ ENT?*
>
> *(a) 5   (b) 7   (c) 9   (d) 11*
>
> *Answer: (b) 7 conductors [Annex C, Table C2]*

Author's Comment: See 300.17 for additional examples on how to size raceways when conductors aren't all the same size.

Cables can be installed in electrical nonmetallic tubing, as long as the cables don't exceed the allowable percentage fill specified in Table 1, Chapter 9.

362.24 Bends.
Raceway bends must not be made in any manner that would damage the raceway, or significantly change its internal diameter (no kinks). The radius of the curve to the centerline of any field bend must not be less than shown in Chapter 9, Table 2, using the column "Other Bends."

362.26 Number of Bends (360°).
To reduce the stress and friction on conductor insulation, the maximum number of bends (including offsets) between pull points can't exceed 360°.

Author's Comment: There's no maximum distance between pull boxes because this is a design issue, not a safety issue.

362.28 Trimming.
The cut ends of electrical nonmetallic tubing must be trimmed (inside and out) to remove the burrs and rough edges.

Trimming electrical nonmetallic tubing is very easy; most of the burrs rub off with fingers, and a knife can be used to smooth the rough edges.

362.30 Securing and Supporting.
Electrical nonmetallic tubing must be installed as a complete system in accordance with 300.18 [300.10 and 300.12], and it must be securely fastened in place and supported in accordance with (A) and (B).

(A) Securely Fastened. Electrical nonmetallic tubing must be secured within 3 ft of every box, cabinet, or termination fitting, such as a conduit body, and at intervals not exceeding 3 ft. **Figure 362–9**

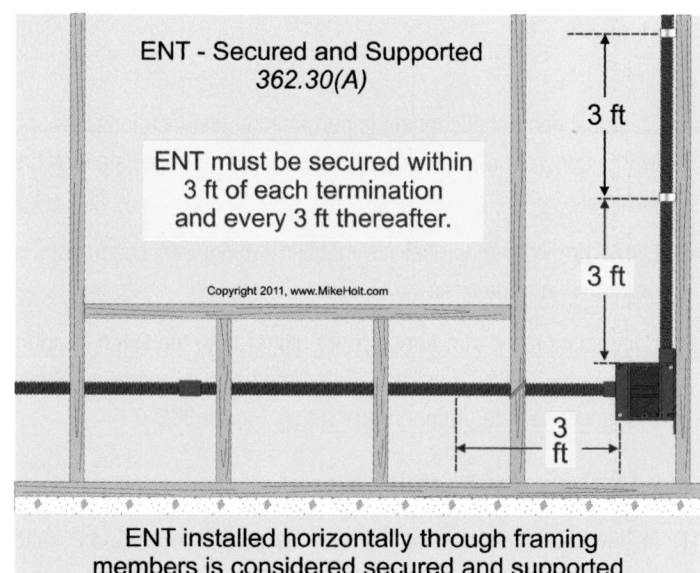

ENT - Secured and Supported
362.30(A)

ENT must be secured within 3 ft of each termination and every 3 ft thereafter.

3 ft

3 ft

3 ft

Copyright 2011, www.MikeHolt.com

ENT installed horizontally through framing members is considered secured and supported.

Figure 362–9

Ex 2: Lengths not exceeding 6 ft from the last point if the raceway is securely fastened within an accessible ceiling to luminaire(s) or other equipment.

Ex 3: If fished between access points through concealed spaces and supporting is impractical.

(B) Horizontal Runs. Electrical nonmetallic tubing installed horizontally in bored or punched holes in wood or metal framing members, or notches in wooden members, is considered supported, but the raceway must be secured within 3 ft of terminations.

362.46 Bushings. Conductors 4 AWG and larger that enter an enclosure from a fitting must be protected from abrasion, during and after installation, by a fitting that provides a smooth, rounded, insulating surface, such as an insulating bushing, unless the design of the box, fitting, or enclosure provides equivalent protection, in accordance with 300.4(G).

362.48 Joints. Joints, such as couplings and connectors, must be made in a manner approved by the authority having jurisdiction.

> **Author's Comment:** Follow the manufacturer's instructions for the raceway, fittings, and glue. According to product listings, PVC conduit fittings are permitted with electrical nonmetallic tubing.

> ⚠️ **CAUTION:** *Glue used with electrical nonmetallic tubing must be listed for ENT. Glue for PVC conduit must not be used with electrical nonmetallic tubing because it damages the plastic from which ENT is manufactured.*

362.60 Equipment Grounding Conductor. If equipment grounding is required, a separate equipment grounding conductor of the wire type must be installed within the raceway. **Figure 362–10**

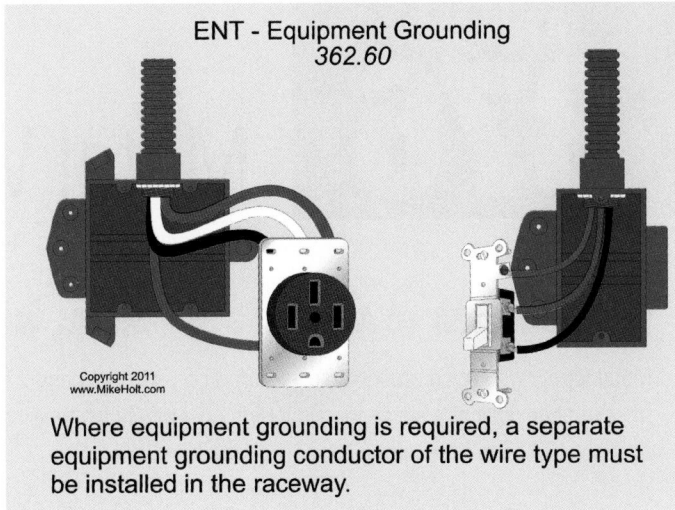

ENT - Equipment Grounding
362.60

Where equipment grounding is required, a separate equipment grounding conductor of the wire type must be installed in the raceway.

Copyright 2011
www.MikeHolt.com

Figure 362–10

ARTICLE 376

Metal Wireways

INTRODUCTION TO ARTICLE 376—METAL WIREWAYS

Metal wireways are commonly used where access to the conductors within the raceway is required to make terminations, splices, or taps to several devices at a single location. High cost precludes their use for other than short distances, except in some commercial or industrial occupancies where the wiring is frequently revised.

Author's Comment: Both metal wireways and nonmetallic wireways are often called "troughs" or "gutters" in the field.

PART I. GENERAL

376.1 Scope. Article 376 covers the use, installation, and construction specifications of metal wireways and associated fittings.

376.2 Definition.

Metal Wireway. A sheet metal trough with hinged or removable covers for housing and protecting electric conductors and cable, and in which conductors are placed after the wireway has been installed. **Figure 376–1**

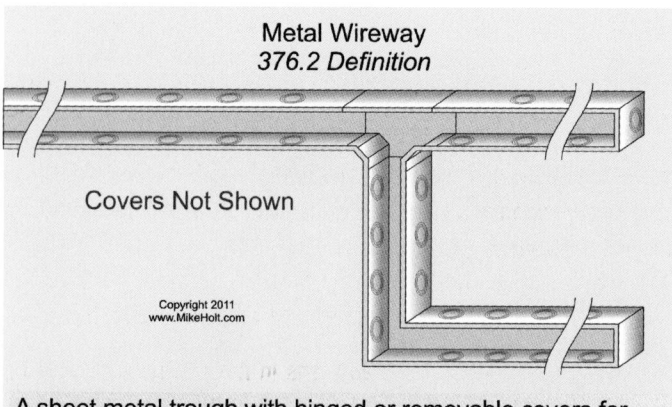

Metal Wireway
376.2 Definition

Covers Not Shown

Copyright 2011
www.MikeHolt.com

A sheet metal trough with hinged or removable covers for housing and protecting electric wires and cable, and in which conductors are placed after the wireway has been installed.

Figure 376–1

PART II. INSTALLATION

376.10 Uses Permitted.

(1) Exposed.

(2) In any hazardous locations, as permitted by other articles in the Code.

(3) Wet locations where listed for the purpose.

(4) Unbroken through walls, partitions, and floors.

> **Author's Comment:** See 501.10(B), 502.10(B), and 504.20 for metal wireways used in hazardous locations.

376.12 Uses Not Permitted.

(1) Where subject to severe physical damage.

(2) Where subject to corrosive environments.

376.21 Conductors—Maximum Size. The maximum size conductor permitted in a wireway must not be larger than that for which the wireway is designed.

376.22 Number of Conductors and Ampacity. The number of conductors and their ampacity must comply with 376.22(A) and (B).

(A) Number of Conductors. The maximum number of conductors permitted in a wireway is limited to 20 percent of the cross-sectional area of the wireway. **Figure 376–2**

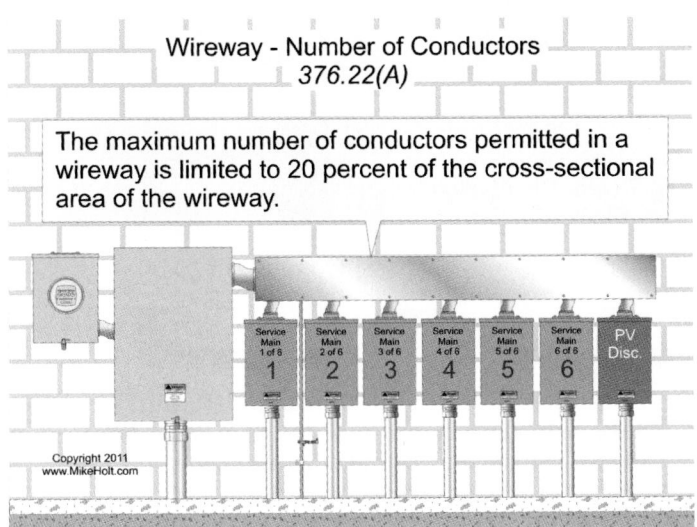

Figure 376–2

Author's Comment: Splices and taps must not fill more than 75 percent of the wiring space at any cross section [376.56].

(B) Conductor Ampacity Adjustment Factors. When more than 30 current-carrying conductors are installed in any cross-sectional area of the wireway, the conductor ampacity, as listed in Table 310.15(B)(16), must be adjusted in accordance with Table 310.15(B)(3)(a). **Figure 376–3**

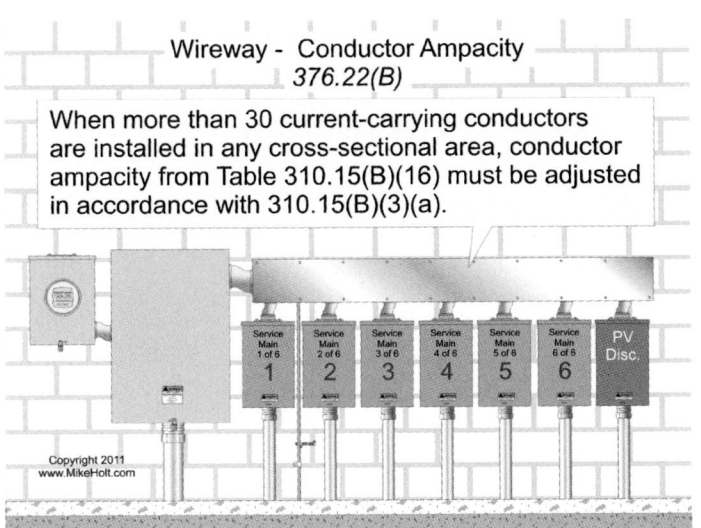

Figure 376–3

Signaling and motor control conductors between a motor and its starter used only for starting duty aren't considered current carrying for conductor ampacity adjustment.

376.23 Wireway Sizing.

(A) Sizing for Conductor Bending Radius. If conductors are bent within a metal wireway, the wireway must be sized to meet the bending radius requirements contained in Table 312.6(A), based on one wire per terminal. **Figure 376–4**

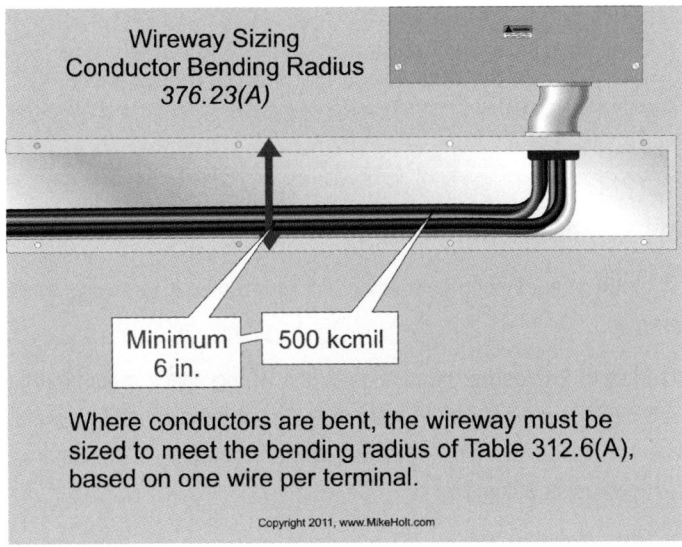

Figure 376–4

376.30 Supports. Wireways must be supported in accordance with (A) and (B).

(A) Horizontal Support. If installed horizontally, metal wireways must be supported at each end and at intervals not exceeding 5 ft.

(B) Vertical Support. If installed vertically, metal wireways must be securely supported at intervals not exceeding 15 ft, with no more than one joint between supports.

376.56 Splices, Taps, and Power Distribution Blocks.

(A) Splices and Taps. Splices and taps in metal wireways must be accessible, and they must not fill the wireway to more than 75 percent of its cross-sectional area. **Figure 376–5**

Author's Comment: The maximum number of conductors permitted in a metal wireway is limited to 20 percent of its cross-sectional area at any point [376.22(A)].

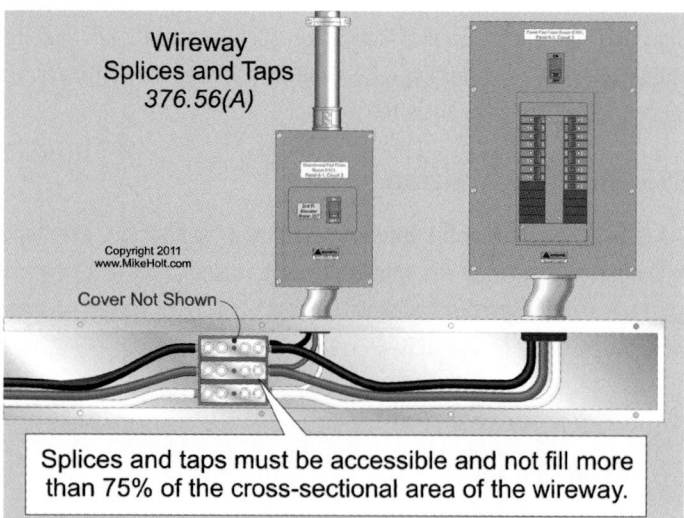

Wireway
Splices and Taps
376.56(A)

Copyright 2011
www.MikeHolt.com

Cover Not Shown

Splices and taps must be accessible and not fill more than 75% of the cross-sectional area of the wireway.

Figure 376–5

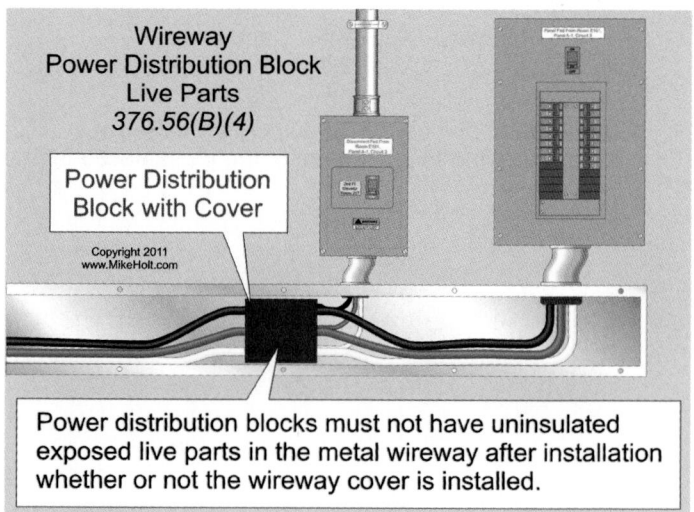

Wireway
Power Distribution Block
Live Parts
376.56(B)(4)

Power Distribution
Block with Cover

Copyright 2011
www.MikeHolt.com

Power distribution blocks must not have uninsulated exposed live parts in the metal wireway after installation whether or not the wireway cover is installed.

Figure 376–6

(B) Power Distribution Blocks.

(1) Installation. Power distribution blocks installed in wireways must be listed.

(2) Size of Enclosure. In addition to the wiring space requirements [376.56(A)], the power distribution block must be installed in a metal wireway not smaller than specified in the installation instructions of the power distribution block.

(3) Wire-Bending Space. Wire-bending space at the terminals of power distribution blocks must comply with 312.6(B).

(4) Live Parts. Power distribution blocks must not have uninsulated exposed live parts in the metal wireway after installation, whether or not the wireway cover is installed. **Figure 376–6**

Multioutlet Assemblies

INTRODUCTION TO ARTICLE 380—MULTIOUTLET ASSEMBLIES

A multioutlet assembly is a surface, flush, or freestanding raceway designed to hold conductors and receptacles, and is assembled in the field or at the factory [Article 100]. It's not limited to systems commonly referred to by the trade names "Plugtrak®" or "Plugmold®."

PART I. GENERAL

380.1 Scope. Article 380 covers the use, installation, and construction specifications of multioutlet assemblies.

> **Author's Comment:** A multioutlet assembly is a surface, flush or freestanding raceway designed to hold conductors and receptacles assembled in the field or at the factory [Article 100]. **Figure 380–1**

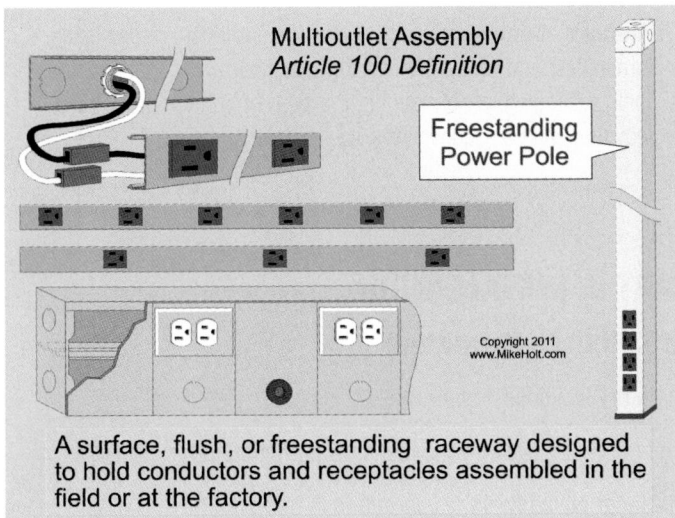

Multioutlet Assembly
Article 100 Definition

Freestanding Power Pole

Copyright 2011
www.MikeHolt.com

A surface, flush, or freestanding raceway designed to hold conductors and receptacles assembled in the field or at the factory.

Figure 380–1

PART II. INSTALLATION

380.10 Uses Permitted. Multioutlet assemblies are only permitted in dry locations.

380.12 Uses Not Permitted.

(1) Concealed.

(2) If subject to severe physical damage.

(3) If the voltage is 300V or more between conductors, unless the metal has a thickness not less than 0.04 in.

(4) If subject to corrosive vapors.

(5) In hoistways.

(6) In any hazardous location, except as permitted by 501.10(B).

380.76 Through Partitions. Metal multioutlet assemblies can pass through a dry partition provided no receptacle is concealed in the wall, and the cover of the exposed portion of the system can be removed.

ARTICLE
386

Surface Metal Raceways

PART I. GENERAL

386.1 Scope. This article covers the use, installation, and construction specifications of surface metal raceways and associated fittings.

386.2 Definition.

Surface Metal Raceway. A metallic raceway intended to be mounted to the surface, with associated accessories, in which conductors are placed after the raceway has been installed as a complete system [300.18(A)]. **Figure 386–1**

Surface Metal Raceways
386.2 Definition

A raceway intended to be mounted to the surface, in which conductors are placed after the raceway has been installed as a complete system.

Copyright 2011, www.MikeHolt.com

Figure 386–1

Author's Comment: Surface metal raceways are available in different shapes and sizes and can be mounted on walls, ceilings, or floors. Some surface metal raceways have two or more separate compartments, which permit the separation of power and lighting conductors from low-voltage or limited-energy conductors or cables (control, signal, and communications cables and conductors) [386.70].

386.6 Listing Requirements. Surface metal raceways and associated fittings must be listed.

Author's Comment: Enclosures for switches, receptacles, luminaires, and other devices are identified by the markings on their packaging, which identify the type of surface metal raceway that can be used with the enclosure.

PART II. INSTALLATION

386.10 Uses Permitted.

(1) In dry locations. **Figure 386–2**

(2) In Class I, Division 2 locations, as permitted in 501.10(B)(3).

(3) Under raised floors, as permitted in 645.5(E)(2).

(4) Run through walls and floors, if access to the conductors is maintained on both sides of the wall, partition, or floor.

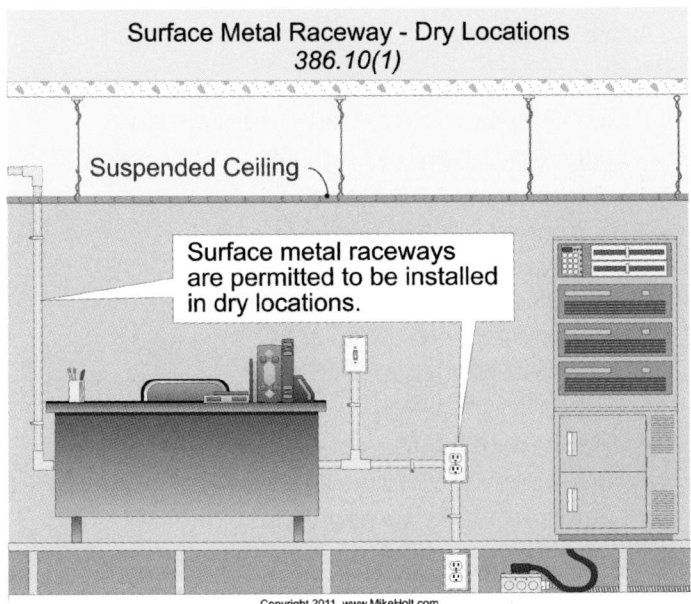

Figure 386–2

The ampacity <u>adjustment</u> factors of 310.15(B)(3)(a) don't apply to conductors installed in surface metal raceways if all of the following conditions are met: **Figure 386–3**

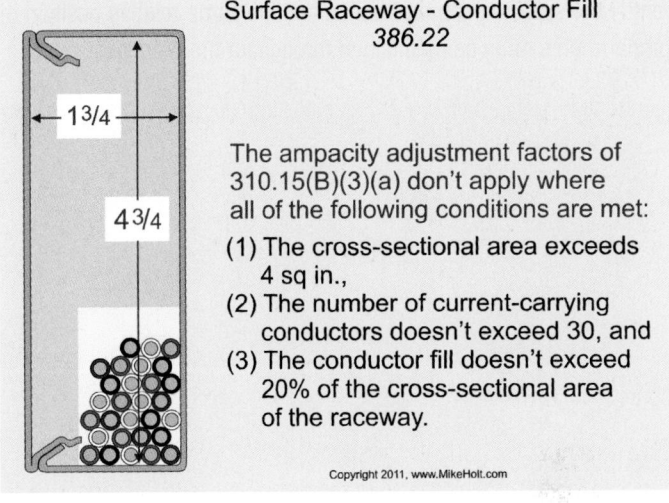

Figure 386–3

386.12 Uses Not Permitted.

(1) If subject to severe physical damage, unless otherwise approved by the authority having jurisdiction.

(2) If the voltage is 300V or more between conductors, unless the metal has a thickness not less than 0.04 in.

(3) If subject to corrosive vapors.

(4) In hoistways.

(5) If concealed, except as permitted in 386.10.

386.21 Size of Conductors.
The maximum size conductor permitted in a surface metal wireway must not be larger than that for which the wireway is designed.

> **Author's Comment:** Because partial packages are often purchased, you may not always receive this information.

386.22 Number of Conductors.
The number of conductors or cables installed in a surface metal raceway must not be more than the number for which the raceway is designed. Cables can be installed in surface metal raceways as long as the number of cables doesn't exceed the allowable percentage fill specified in Table 1, Chapter 9.

(1) The cross-sectional area of the raceway exceeds 4 sq in.

(2) The number of current-carrying conductors doesn't exceed 30, and

(3) The sum of the cross-sectional areas of all contained conductors doesn't exceed 20 percent of the interior cross-sectional area of the raceway.

386.30 Securing and Supporting.
Surface metal raceways must be secured and supported at intervals in accordance with the manufacturer's installation instructions.

386.56 Splices and Taps.
Splices and taps must be accessible, and must not fill the raceway to more than 75 percent of its cross-sectional area.

386.60 Equipment Grounding Conductor.
Surface metal raceway fittings must be mechanically and electrically joined together in a manner that doesn't subject the conductors to abrasion. Surface metal raceways that allow a transition to another wiring method, such as knockouts for connecting raceways, must have a means for the termination of an equipment grounding conductor. A surface metal raceway is considered suitable as an equipment grounding conductor, in accordance with 250.118(14).

386.70 Separate Compartments. If surface metal raceways have separate compartments within a single raceway, power and lighting conductors can occupy one compartment, and the other compartment may contain control, signaling, or communications wiring. Stamping, imprinting, or color coding of the interior finish must identify the separate compartments, and the same relative position of compartments must be maintained throughout the premises.

Author's Comments:

- Separation from power conductors is required by the *NEC* for the following low-voltage and limited-energy systems:
  - CATV, 820.44(F)(1)
  - Communications, 800.133(A)(1)
  - Control and Signaling, 725.136(B)
  - Fire Alarms, 760.136(B)
  - Intrinsically Safe Systems, 504.30(A)(2)
  - Instrumentation Tray Cable, 727.5
  - Radio and Television, 810.18(C)
  - Sound Systems, 640.9(C)

- Nonconductive optical fiber cables can occupy the same cable tray or raceway as conductors for electric light, power, Class 1, or nonpower-limited fire alarm circuits [770.133(A)].

Cable Trays

INTRODUCTION TO ARTICLE 392—CABLE TRAYS

A cable tray system is a unit or an assembly of units or sections with associated fittings that forms a structural system used to securely fasten or support cables and raceways. Cable tray systems include ladder, ventilated trough, ventilated channel, solid bottom, and other similar structures. Cable trays are manufactured in many forms, from a simple hanger or wire mesh to a substantial, rigid, steel support system. Cable trays are designed and manufactured to support specific wiring methods, as identified in 392.10(A).

PART I. GENERAL

392.1 Scope. Article 392 covers cable tray systems, including ladder, ventilated trough, ventilated channel, solid bottom, and other similar structures.

392.2 Definition.

Cable Tray System. A unit or assembly of units or sections with associated fittings forming a rigid structural system used to securely fasten or support cables, raceways, and boxes. **Figure 392–1**

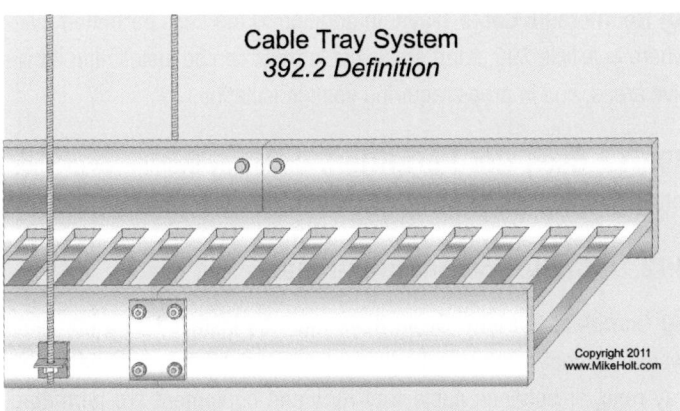

Cable Tray System
392.2 Definition

A unit or assembly of units or sections with associated fittings forming a rigid structural system used to securely fasten or support cables, raceways, and boxes.

Figure 392–1

Author's Comment: Cable tray isn't a type of raceway. It's a support system for cables and raceways.

PART II. INSTALLATION

392.10 Uses Permitted. Cable trays can be used as a support system for service, feeder, or branch-circuit conductors, as well as communications circuits, control circuits, and signaling circuits. **Figure 392–2**

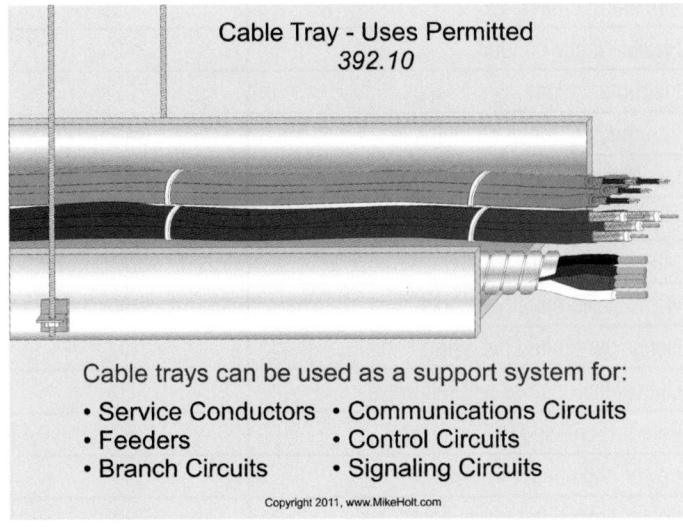

Cable Tray - Uses Permitted
392.10

Cable trays can be used as a support system for:
- Service Conductors
- Communications Circuits
- Feeders
- Control Circuits
- Branch Circuits
- Signaling Circuits

Copyright 2011, www.MikeHolt.com

Figure 392–2

Author's Comment: Cable trays used to support service-entrance conductors must contain only service-entrance conductors unless a solid fixed barrier separates the service-entrance conductors from other conductors [230.44].

Author's Comments:

- Cable tray installations aren't limited to industrial establishments.

- If exposed to the direct rays of the sun, insulated conductors and jacketed cables must be identified as being sunlight resistant. The manufacturer must identify cable trays and associated fittings for their intended use.

(A) Wiring Methods. Any wiring methods listed in Table 392.10(A) can be installed in a cable tray.

Table 392.10(A) Wiring Methods	
Wiring Method	**Article/Section**
Armored Cable	320
CATV cables	820
CATV raceways	820
Class 2 & 3 cables	725
Communications cables	800
Communications raceways	800
Electrical metallic tubing	358
Electrical nonmetallic tubing	362
Fire alarm cables	760
Flexible metal conduit	348
Instrumentation tray cable	727
Intermediate metal conduit	342
Liquidtight flexible metal conduit	350
Liquidtight flexible nonmetallic conduit	356
Metal-clad cable	330
Nonmetallic-sheathed cable	334
Nonpower-limited fire alarm cable	760
Optical fiber cables and raceways	770
Polyvinyl chloride PVC conduit	352
Power and control tray cable	336
Power-limited fire alarm cable	760
Power-limited tray cable	725.154(C) and 725.179(E) and 725.71(F)
Rigid metal conduit	344
Service-entrance cable	338
Signaling raceway	725
Underground feeder and branch-circuit cable	340

Author's Comment: Control, signal, and communications cables must be separated from the power conductors by a barrier or maintain a 2 in. separation.

- Coaxial Cables, 820.133(A)(1)(b) Ex 1
- Class 2 and 3 Cables, 725.136(B) and 725.136(I)
- Communications Cables, 800.133(A)(2) Ex 1
- Fire Alarm Cables, 760.136(G)
- Optical Fiber Cables, 770.133(B)
- Intrinsically Safe Systems Cables, 504.30(A)(2) Ex 1
- Radio and Television Cables, 810.18(B) Ex 1

(B) In Industrial Establishments.

(1) Where conditions of maintenance and supervision ensure that only qualified persons service the installed cable tray system, single conductor cables can be installed in accordance with the following:

(a) 1/0 AWG and larger listed and marked for use in cable trays.

(c) Equipment grounding conductors must be 4 AWG and larger.

(C) Hazardous Locations. Cable trays in hazardous locations must contain only the cable types and raceways permitted by the *Code* for the application

Author's Comment: For permitted cable types, see 501.10, 502.10, 503.10, 504.20, and 505.15.

(D) Nonmetallic Cable Trays. In addition to the uses permitted elsewhere in Article 392, nonmetallic cable trays can be installed in corrosive areas, and in areas requiring voltage isolation.

392.12 Uses Not Permitted.
Cable tray systems aren't permitted in hoistways, or where subject to severe physical damage.

392.18 Cable Tray Installations

(A) Complete System. Cable trays must be installed as a complete system, except mechanically discontinuous segments between cable tray runs, or between cable tray runs and equipment are permitted. The system must provide for the support of the cables and raceways in accordance with their corresponding articles.

A bonding jumper, sized in accordance with 250.102 and installed in accordance with 250.96, must bond the sections of cable tray, or the cable tray and the raceway or equipment.

(B) Completed Before Installation. Each run of cable tray must be completed before the installation of cables or conductors.

(D) Through Partitions and Walls. Cable trays can extend through partitions and walls, or vertically through platforms and floors if the installation is made in accordance with the firestopping requirements of 300.21.

(E) Exposed and Accessible. Cable trays must be exposed and accessible, except as permitted by 392.10(H).

(F) Adequate Access. Sufficient space must be provided and maintained about cable trays to permit adequate access for installing and maintaining the cables.

(G) Raceways, Cables, and Boxes Supported from Cable Trays. In industrial facilities where conditions of maintenance and supervision ensure only qualified persons will service the installation, and if the cable tray system is designed and installed to support the load, cable tray systems can support raceways, cables, boxes, and conduit bodies. **Figure 392–3**

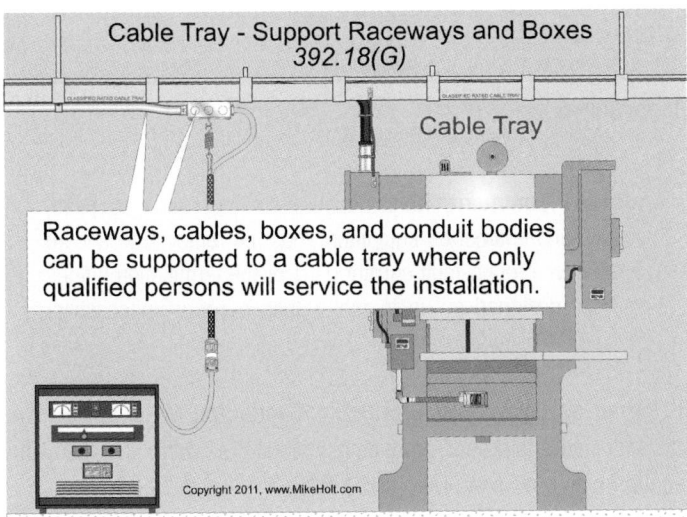

Figure 392–3

For raceways terminating at the tray, a listed cable tray clamp or adapter must be used to securely fasten the raceway to the cable tray system. The raceway must be supported in accordance with the appropriate raceway article.

Raceways or cables running parallel to the cable tray system can be attached to the bottom or side of a cable tray system. The raceway or cable must be fastened and supported in accordance with the appropriate raceway or cable's *Code* article.

Boxes and conduit bodies attached to the bottom or side of a cable tray system must be fastened and supported in accordance with 314.23.

392.20 Cable and Conductor Installation

(C) Connected in Parallel. To prevent unbalanced current in the parallel conductors due to inductive reactance, all circuit conductors of a parallel set [310.10(H)] must be bundled together and secured to prevent excessive movement due to fault current magnetic forces.

(D) Single Conductors. Single conductors of a circuit not connected in parallel must be installed in a single layer, unless the conductors are bound together.

392.22 Number of Conductors or Cables.

(A) Number of Multiconductor Cables in Cable Trays. The number of multiconductor cables, rated 2,000 volts or less, permitted in a single cable tray must not exceed the requirements of this section. The conductor sizes herein apply to both aluminum and copper conductors.

(1) Any Mixture of Cables. If ladder or ventilated trough cable trays contain multiconductor power or lighting cables, the maximum number of cables must conform to the following:

(a) If all of the cables are 4/0 AWG and larger, the sum of the diameters of all cables must not exceed the cable tray width, and the cables must be installed in a single layer.

392.30 Securing and Supporting.

(A) Fastened Securely. Cables installed vertically must be securely fastened to transverse members of the cable tray.

(B) Support. Supports for cable trays must be provided to prevent stress on cables where they enter raceways or other enclosures from cable tray systems. Cable trays must be supported in accordance with the manufacturer's installation instructions.

392.46 Bushed Raceway. A box isn't required where cables or conductors exit a bushed raceway used for the support or protection of the conductors.

392.56 Cable Splices. Splices are permitted in a cable tray if the splice is accessible and insulated by a method approved by the authority having jurisdiction. Splices can project above the side rails of the cable tray if not subject to physical damage. **Figure 392–4**

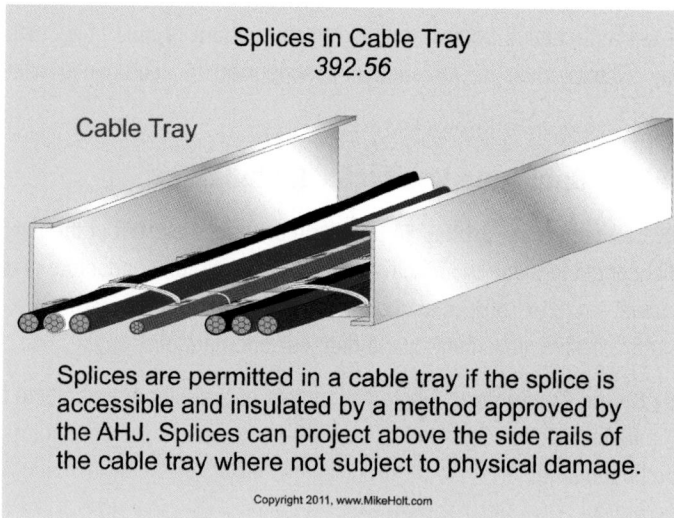

Figure 392–4

392.60 Equipment Grounding Conductor.

(A) Metallic Cable Trays. Metallic cable trays can be used as equipment grounding conductors where continuous maintenance and supervision ensure that qualified persons service the installed cable tray system. **Figure 392–5**

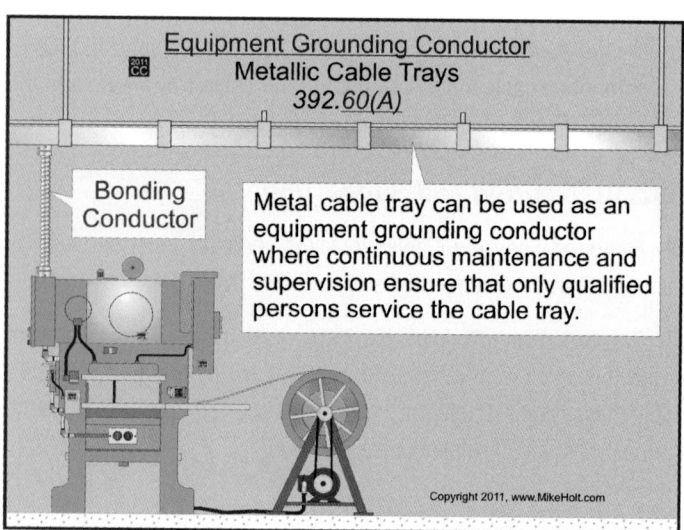

Figure 392–5

The metallic cable trays that support conductors must be bonded together to ensure that they have the capacity to conduct safely any fault current likely to be imposed in accordance with 250.96(A).

Metal cable trays containing communications, data, and signaling conductors and cables must be electrically continuous through listed connections or the use of a bonding jumper not smaller than 10 AWG. **Figure 392–6**

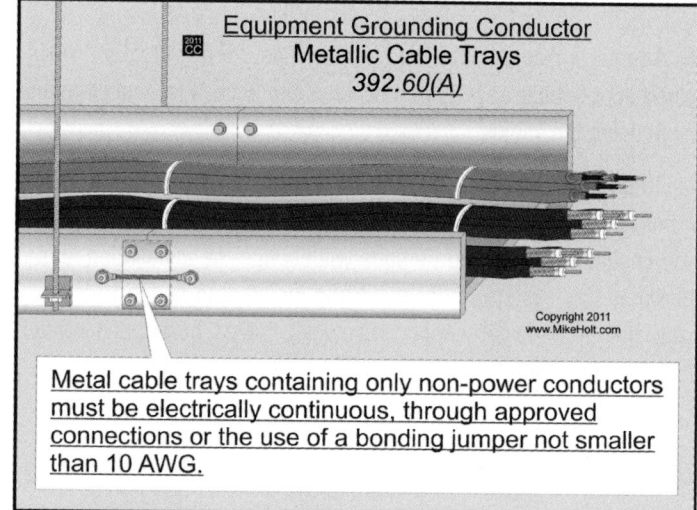

Figure 392–6

Author's Comment: Nonconductive coatings such as paint, lacquer, and enamel on equipment must be removed to ensure an effective ground-fault current path, or the termination fittings must be designed so as to make such removal unnecessary [250.12].

(B) Serve as Equipment Grounding Conductor. Metal cable trays can serve as equipment grounding conductors where the following requirements have been met [392.10(C)]:

(1) Cable tray sections and fittings are identified for grounding. **Figure 392–7**

Author's Comment: Identification will be marked on each cable tray section.

(4) Cable tray sections, fittings, and connected raceways are effectively bonded to each other to ensure electrical continuity and the capacity to conduct safely any fault current likely to be imposed on them [250.96(A)]. This is accomplished by using bolted mechanical connectors or bonding jumpers sized in accordance with 250.102.

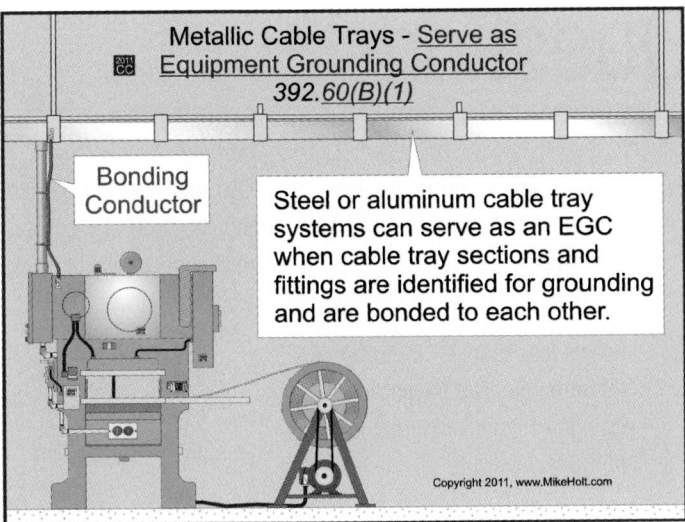

Metallic Cable Trays - <u>Serve as</u>
<u>Equipment Grounding Conductor</u>
392.60(B)(1)

Bonding Conductor

Steel or aluminum cable tray systems can serve as an EGC when cable tray sections and fittings are identified for grounding and are bonded to each other.

Copyright 2011, www.MikeHolt.com

Figure 392–7

392.80 Ampacity of Conductors.

(A) Ampacity in Cable Trays.

(1) The allowable ampacity of multiconductor cables installed according to the requirements of 392.22(A) must be as given in Table 310.15(B)(16) and Table 310.15(B)(18).

(a) The conductor ampacity adjustment factors of 310.15(B)(3)(a) apply to a given cable if it contains more than three current-carrying conductors. The conductor adjustment factors only apply to the number of current-carrying conductors in the cable and not to the number of conductors in the cable tray.

These questions are based on the 2011 *National Electrical Code*. Please use the 2011 *NEC Code* book to answer the following questions.

CHAPTER 3. WIRING METHODS AND MATERIALS

Article 300. Wiring Methods

1. Conductors shall be installed within a raceway, cable, or enclosure.

   (a) True
   (b) False

2. Where cables or nonmetallic raceways are installed through bored holes in joists, rafters, or wood members, holes shall be bored so that the edge of the hole is _____ the nearest edge of the wood member.

   (a) not less than 1¼ in. from
   (b) immediately adjacent to
   (c) not less than 1/16 in. from
   (d) 90° away from

3. Where Type NM cables pass through cut or drilled slots or holes in metal members, the cable shall be protected by _____ which are installed in the opening prior to the installation of the cable and which securely cover all metal edges.

   (a) listed bushings
   (b) listed grommets
   (c) plates
   (d) a or b

4. Where cables and nonmetallic raceways are installed parallel to framing members, the nearest outside surface of the cable or raceway shall be _____ the nearest edge of the framing member where nails or screws are likely to penetrate.

   (a) not less than 1¼ in. from
   (b) immediately adjacent to
   (c) not less than 1/16 in. from
   (d) 90°away from

5. When installed under metal-corrugated sheet roof decking, the rules for spacing from roof decking apply equally to rigid metal conduit and intermediate metal conduit.

   (a) True
   (b) False

6. What is the minimum cover requirement for direct burial Type UF cable installed outdoors that supplies a 120V, 30A circuit?

   (a) 6 in.
   (b) 12 in.
   (c) 18 in.
   (d) 24 in.

7. What is the minimum cover requirement for Type UF cable supplying power to a 120V, 15A GFCI-protected circuit outdoors under a driveway of a one-family dwelling?

   (a) 6 in.
   (b) 12 in.
   (c) 16 in.
   (d) 24 in.

8. The interior of underground raceways shall be considered a _____ location.

   (a) wet
   (b) dry
   (c) damp
   (d) corrosive

9. Direct-buried service conductors that are not encased in concrete and that are buried 18 in. or more below grade shall have their location identified by a warning ribbon placed in the trench at least _____ above the underground installation.

   (a) 6 in.
   (b) 10 in.
   (c) 12 in.
   (d) 18 in.

10. Conduits or raceways through which moisture may contact live parts shall be _____ at either or both ends.

    (a) sealed
    (b) plugged
    (c) bushed
    (d) a or b

11. Each direct-buried single conductor cable must be located _____ in the trench to the other single conductor cables in the same parallel set of conductors, including equipment grounding conductors.

    (a) perpendicular
    (b) bundled together
    (c) in close proximity
    (d) spaced apart

12. Raceways, cable trays, cablebus, auxiliary gutters, cable armor, boxes, cable sheathing, cabinets, elbows, couplings, fittings, supports, and support hardware shall be of materials suitable for _____.

    (a) corrosive locations
    (b) wet locations
    (c) the environment in which they are to be installed
    (d) none of these

13. Ferrous metal raceways, boxes, fittings, supports, and support hardware can be installed in concrete or in direct contact with the earth or other areas subject to severe corrosive influences, where _____ approved for the conditions.

    (a) the soil is
    (b) made of material
    (c) the qualified installer is
    (d) none of these

14. Where nonmetallic wiring methods are subject to exposure to chemical solvents or vapors, they shall be inherently resistant to chemicals based upon their being _____.

    (a) listed for the chemical
    (b) identified for the chemical
    (c) a and b
    (d) a or b

15. Where portions of a cable raceway or sleeve are subjected to different temperatures and condensation is known to be a problem, the _____ shall be filled with an approved material to prevent the circulation of warm air to a colder section of the raceway or sleeve.

    (a) raceway
    (b) sleeve
    (c) a or b
    (d) none of these

16. Where raceways are installed in wet locations above grade, the interior of these raceways shall be considered a _____ location.

    (a) wet
    (b) dry
    (c) damp
    (d) corrosive

17. Where independent support wires of a ceiling assembly are used to support raceways, cable assemblies, or boxes above a ceiling, they shall be secured at _____ ends.

    (a) one
    (b) both
    (c) a or b
    (d) none of these

18. Ceiling-support wires used for the support of electrical raceways and cables within nonfire-rated assemblies shall be distinguishable from the suspended-ceiling framing support wires.

    (a) True
    (b) False

19. Metal or nonmetallic raceways, cable armors, and cable sheaths _____ between cabinets, boxes, fittings or other enclosures or outlets.

    (a) can be attached with electrical tape
    (b) are allowed gaps for expansion
    (c) shall be continuous
    (d) none of these

20. In multiwire branch circuits, the continuity of the _____ conductor shall not be dependent upon the device connections.

    (a) ungrounded
    (b) grounded
    (c) grounding electrode
    (d) a and b

21. A box or conduit body shall not be required where cables enter or exit from conduit or tubing that is used to provide cable support or protection against physical damage.

    (a) True
    (b) False

22. A bushing shall be permitted in lieu of a box or terminal where the conductors emerge from a raceway and enter or terminate at equipment such as open switchboards, unenclosed control equipment, or similar equipment.

    (a) True
    (b) False

23. Prewired raceway assemblies shall be used only where specifically permitted in the *NEC* for the applicable wiring method.

    (a) True
    (b) False

24. A vertical run of 4/0 AWG copper shall be supported at intervals not exceeding _____.

    (a) 40 ft
    (b) 80 ft
    (c) 100 ft
    (d) 120 ft

25. Electrical installations in hollow spaces, vertical shafts, and ventilation or air-handling ducts shall be made so that the possible spread of fire or products of combustion is not _____.

    (a) substantially increased
    (b) allowed
    (c) inherent
    (d) possible

26. Equipment and devices shall only be permitted within ducts or plenum chambers specifically fabricated to transport environmental air if necessary for their direct action upon, or sensing of, the _____.

    (a) contained air
    (b) air quality
    (c) air temperature
    (d) none of these

27. _____ shall be permitted to support the wiring methods and equipment permitted to be used in other spaces used for environmental air (plenum).

    (a) Metal cable tray system
    (b) Nonmetallic wireways
    (c) PVC conduit
    (d) Surface nonmetallic raceways

Article 310. Conductors for General Wiring

1. In general, the minimum size conductor permitted for use in parallel installations is _____ AWG.

    (a) 10
    (b) 4
    (c) 1
    (d) 1/0

2. Where conductors in parallel are run in separate raceways, the raceways shall have the same electrical characteristics.

    (a) True
    (b) False

3. There are four principal determinants of conductor operating temperature, one of which is _____ generated internally in the conductor as the result of load current flow, including fundamental and harmonic currents.

   (a) friction
   (b) magnetism
   (c) heat
   (d) none of these

4. Each current-carrying conductor of a paralleled set of conductors shall be counted as a current-carrying conductor for the purpose of applying the adjustment factors of 310.15(B)(3)(a).

   (a) True
   (b) False

5. When bare conductors are installed with insulated conductors, their ampacities shall be limited to _____.

   (a) 60°C
   (b) 75°C
   (c) 90°C
   (d) the lowest temperature rating for any of the insulated conductors

6. On a three-phase, 4-wire, wye circuit, where the major portion of the load consists of nonlinear loads, the neutral conductor shall be counted when applying 310.15(B)(3)(a) adjustment factors.

   (a) True
   (b) False

7. When determining the number of current-carrying conductors, a grounding or bonding conductor shall not be counted when applying the provisions of 310.15(B)(3)(a) _____.

   (a) True
   (b) False

8. THWN insulated conductors are rated _____.

   (a) 75°C
   (b) for wet locations
   (c) a and b
   (d) not enough information

9. The minimum size conductor permitted for branch circuits under 600V is _____ AWG.

   (a) 14
   (b) 12
   (c) 10
   (d) 8

Article 312. Cabinets, Cutout Boxes, and Meter Socket Enclosures

1. Where raceways or cables enter above the level of uninsulated live parts of cabinets, cutout boxes, and meter socket enclosures in a wet location, a(n) _____ shall be used.

   (a) fitting listed for wet locations
   (b) explosionproof seal
   (c) fitting listed for damp locations
   (d) insulated fitting

2. Each cable entering a cutout box _____.

   (a) shall be secured to the cutout box
   (b) can be sleeved through a chase
   (c) shall have a maximum of two cables per connector
   (d) all of these

Article 314. Outlet, Device, Pull and Junction Boxes; Conduit Bodies; Fittings; and Handhole Enclosures

1. According to the *NEC*, the volume of a 3 x 2 x 2 in. device box is _____.

   (a) 8 cu in.
   (b) 10 cu in.
   (c) 12 cu in.
   (d) 14 cu in.

2. When counting the number of conductors in a box, a conductor running through the box with an unbroken loop or coil not less than twice the minimum length required for free conductors shall be counted as _____ conductor(s).

(a) one
(b) two
(c) three
(d) four

3. For the purposes of determining box fill, each device or utilization equipment in the box which is wider than a single device box counts as two conductors for each _____ required for the mounting.

(a) inch
(b) kilometer
(c) gang
(d) box

4. Conduit bodies that are durably and legibly marked by the manufacturer with their volume can contain splices, taps, or devices.

(a) True
(b) False

5. Noncombustible surfaces that are broken or incomplete around boxes employing a flush-type cover or faceplate shall be repaired so there will be no gaps or open spaces larger than _____ at the edge of the box.

(a) 1/16 in.
(b) 1/8 in.
(c) ¼ in.
(d) ½ in.

6. A wood brace used for supporting a box for structural mounting shall have a cross-section not less than nominal _____.

(a) 1 in. x 2 in.
(b) 2 in. x 2 in.
(c) 2 in. x 3 in.
(d) 2 in. x 4 in.

7. In completed installations, each outlet box shall have a _____.

(a) cover
(b) faceplate
(c) canopy
(d) any of these

8. Listed outlet boxes to support ceiling-suspended fans that weigh more than _____ lb shall have the maximum allowable weight marked on the box.

(a) 35 lb
(b) 50 lb
(c) 60 lb
(d) 70 lb

9. Power distribution blocks shall be permitted in pull and junction boxes over 100 cubic inches when they comply with the provisions of 314.28(E).

(a) True
(b) False

10. _____ shall be installed so that the wiring contained can be rendered accessible without removing any part of the building or, in underground circuits, without excavating sidewalks, paving, or earth.

(a) Boxes
(b) Conduit bodies
(c) Handhole enclosures
(d) all of these

11. Conductors, splices or terminations in a handhole enclosure shall be listed as _____.

(a) suitable for wet locations
(b) suitable for damp locations
(c) suitable for direct burial in the earth
(d) none of these

Article 320. Armored Cable (Type AC)

1. Type _____ cable is a fabricated assembly of insulated conductors in a flexible interlocked metallic armor.

   (a) AC
   (b) MC
   (c) NM
   (d) b and c

2. Armored cable shall not be installed _____.

   (a) in damp or wet locations
   (b) where subject to physical damage
   (c) where exposed to corrosive conditions
   (d) all of these

3. When Type AC cable is run across the top of a floor joist in an attic without permanent ladders or stairs, substantial guard strips within _____ of the scuttle hole, or attic entrance, shall protect the cable.

   (a) 3 ft
   (b) 4 ft
   (c) 5 ft
   (d) 6 ft

4. Type AC cable can be supported and secured by _____.

   (a) staples
   (b) cable ties
   (c) straps
   (d) all of these

5. Armored cable used to connect recessed luminaires or equipment within an accessible ceiling can be unsecured for lengths up to _____.

   (a) 2 ft
   (b) 3 ft
   (c) 4½ ft
   (d) 6 ft

Article 330. Metal-Clad Cable (Type MC)

1. Type _____ is a factory assembly of insulated circuit conductors within an armor of interlocking metal tape, or a smooth or corrugated metallic sheath.

   (a) AC
   (b) MC
   (c) NM
   (d) b and c

2. Smooth-sheath Type MC cable with an external diameter not greater than ¾ in. shall have a bending radius not more than _____ times the cable external diameter.

   (a) five
   (b) 10
   (c) 12
   (d) 13

3. Type MC cable shall be secured at intervals not exceeding _____.

   (a) 3 ft
   (b) 4 ft
   (c) 6 ft
   (d) 8 ft

4. Fittings used for connecting Type MC cable to boxes, cabinets, or other equipment shall _____.

   (a) be nonmetallic only
   (b) be listed and identified for such use
   (c) be listed and identified as weatherproof
   (d) include anti-shorting bushings

Article 334. Nonmetallic-Sheathed Cable (Types NM and NMC)

1. Type _____ cable is a wiring method that encloses two or more insulated conductors within a nonmetallic jacket.

   (a) AC
   (b) MC
   (c) NM
   (d) b and c

2. Type NM and Type NMC cables shall be permitted in _____.

   (a) in one- and two-family dwellings and their attached/ detached garages or storage buildings
   (b) multifamily dwellings permitted to be of Types III, IV, and V construction
   (c) other structures permitted to be of Types III, IV, and V construction, except as prohibited in 334.12.
   (d) any of these

3. Type NM cable shall closely follow the surface of the building finish or running boards when run exposed.

   (a) True
   (b) False

4. Where Type NM cable is run at angles with joists in unfinished basements and crawl spaces, it is permissible to secure cables not smaller than _____ conductors directly to the lower edges of the joist.

   (a) two, 6 AWG
   (b) three, 8 AWG
   (c) three, 10 AWG
   (d) a or b

5. Type NM cable protected from physical damage by a raceway shall not be required to be _____ within the raceway.

   (a) covered
   (b) insulated
   (c) secured
   (d) unspliced

6. For Type NM and NMC cable, the conductor ampacity used for ambient temperature correction [310.15(B)(2)(a)], conductor bundling adjustment [310.15(B)(3)(a)], or both, is based on the 90°C conductor insulation rating [310.15(B)(2)], provided the adjusted or corrected ampacity doesn't exceed that for a _____ rated conductor.

   (a) 60°C
   (b) 75°C
   (c) 90°C
   (d) 120°C

Article 338. Service-Entrance Cable (Types SE and USE)

1. Type SE cable shall be permitted to be used as _____ in wiring systems where all of the circuit conductors of the cable are of the thermoset or thermoplastic type.

   (a) branch circuits
   (b) feeders
   (c) a or b
   (d) neither a or b

2. Type USE cable is not permitted for _____ wiring.

   (a) underground
   (b) interior
   (c) a or b
   (d) a and b

Article 340. Underground Feeder and Branch-Circuit Cable (Type UF)

1. Type _____ cable is a factory assembly of conductors with an overall covering of nonmetallic material suitable for direct burial in the earth.

   (a) NM
   (b) UF
   (c) SE
   (d) TC

2. Type UF cable can be used in commercial garages.

    (a) True
    (b) False

3. Type UF cable shall not be used where subject to physical damage.

    (a) True
    (b) False

4. The overall covering of Type UF cable is _____.

    (a) flame retardant
    (b) moisture, fungus, and corrosion resistant
    (c) suitable for direct burial in the earth
    (d) all of these

Article 342. Intermediate Metal Conduit (Type IMC)

1. IMC can be installed in or under cinder fill subject to permanent moisture _____.

    (a) where the conduit is not less than 18 in. under the fill
    (b) when protected on all sides by 2 in. of noncinder concrete
    (c) where protected by corrosion protection judged suitable for the condition
    (d) any of these

2. A run of IMC shall not contain more than the equivalent of _____ quarter bends between pull points such as conduit bodies and boxes.

    (a) one
    (b) two
    (c) three
    (d) four

3. Trade size 1 IMC shall be supported at intervals not exceeding _____.

    (a) 8 ft
    (b) 10 ft
    (c) 12 ft
    (d) 14 ft

4. Threadless couplings approved for use with IMC in wet locations shall be _____.

    (a) rainproof
    (b) listed for wet locations
    (c) moistureproof
    (d) concrete-tight

Article 344. Rigid Metal Conduit (Type RMC)

1. Galvanized steel, stainless steel and red brass RMC can be installed in concrete, in direct contact with the earth, or in areas subject to severe corrosive influences when protected by _____ and judged suitable for the condition.

    (a) ceramic
    (b) corrosion protection
    (c) backfill
    (d) a natural barrier

2. Aluminum fittings and enclosures can be used with _____ conduit where not subject to severe corrosive influences.

    (a) steel rigid metal
    (b) aluminum rigid metal
    (c) PVC-coated rigid conduit only
    (d) a and b

3. Cut ends of RMC shall be _____ or otherwise finished to remove rough edges.

    (a) threaded
    (b) reamed
    (c) painted
    (d) galvanized

4. Threadless couplings and connectors used with RMC buried in masonry or concrete shall be the _____ type.

    (a) raintight
    (b) wet and damp location
    (c) nonabsorbent
    (d) concrete-tight

5. Each length of RMC shall be clearly and durably identified in every _____.

(a) 3 ft
(b) 5 ft
(c) 10 ft
(d) 20 ft

Article 348. Flexible Metal Conduit (Type FMC)

1. FMC can be installed exposed or concealed where not subject to physical damage.

(a) True
(b) False

2. Cut ends of FMC shall be trimmed or otherwise finished to remove rough edges, except where fittings _____.

(a) are the crimp-on type
(b) thread into the convolutions
(c) contain insulated throats
(d) are listed for grounding

3. Flexible metal conduit shall not be required to be _____ where fished between access points through concealed spaces in finished buildings or structures and supporting is impracticable.

(a) secured
(b) supported
(c) complete
(d) (a) and (b)

4. In an FMC installation, _____ connectors shall not be concealed.

(a) straight
(b) angle
(c) grounding-type
(d) none of these

Article 350. Liquidtight Flexible Metal Conduit (Type LFMC)

1. Liquidtight flexible metal conduit must be securely fastened by a means approved by the authority having jurisdiction within _____ of termination.

(a) 6 in.
(b) 10 in.
(c) 1 ft
(d) 10 ft

2. For liquidtight flexible metal conduit, if flexibility is necessary after installation, unsecured lengths from the last point the raceway is securely fastened must not exceed _____.

(a) 3 ft for trade sizes ½ through 1 ¼
(b) 4 ft for trade sizes 1 ½ through 2
(c) 5 ft for trade sizes 2 ½ and larger
(d) all of these

3. Where flexibility _____, liquidtight flexible metal conduit shall be permitted to be used as an equipment grounding conductor when installed in accordance with 250.118(6).

(a) is required after installation
(b) is not required after installation
(c) either a or d
(d) is optional

Article 352. Rigid Polyvinyl Chloride Conduit (Type PVC)

1. PVC conduit shall be permitted for exposed work where subject to physical damage if identified for such use.

(a) True
(b) False

2. PVC conduit shall not be used _____, unless specifically permitted.

(a) in hazardous (classified) locations
(b) for the support of luminaires or other equipment
(c) where subject to physical damage unless identified for such use
(d) all of these

3. Bends in PVC conduit shall _____ between pull points.

(a) not be made
(b) not be limited in degrees
(c) be limited to 360 degrees
(d) be limited to 180 degrees

4. Where PVC conduit enters a box, fitting, or other enclosure, a bushing or adapter shall be provided to protect the conductor from abrasion unless the design of the box, fitting, or enclosure affords equivalent protection.

(a) True
(b) False

5. PVC conduit and fittings for use above ground shall have the following characteristics _____.

(a) flame retardant
(b) resistance to low temperatures and sunlight
(c) resistance to distortion from heat
(d) all of these

Article 356. Liquidtight Flexible Nonmetallic Conduit (Type LFNC)

1. LFNC shall be permitted for _____.

(a) direct burial where listed and marked for the purpose
(b) exposed work
(c) outdoors where listed and marked for this purpose
(d) all of these

2. Bends in LFNC shall _____ between pull points.

(a) not be made
(b) not be limited in degrees
(c) be limited to 360 degrees
(d) be limited to 180 degrees

Article 358. Electrical Metallic Tubing (Type EMT)

1. _____ is a listed thin-wall, metallic tubing of circular cross section used for the installation and physical protection of electrical conductors when joined together with listed fittings.

(a) LFNC
(b) EMT
(c) NUCC
(d) RTRC

2. When EMT is installed in wet locations, all supports, bolts, straps, and screws shall be _____.

(a) of corrosion-resistant materials
(b) protected against corrosion
(c) a or b
(d) of nonmetallic materials only

3. EMT shall not be threaded.

(a) True
(b) False

Article 362. Electrical Nonmetallic Tubing (Type ENT)

1. ENT is composed of a material resistant to moisture and chemical atmospheres, and is _____.

(a) flexible
(b) flame retardant
(c) fireproof
(d) flammable

2. When a building is supplied with a fire sprinkler system, ENT can be installed above any suspended ceiling.

(a) True
(b) False

3. ENT is not permitted in hazardous (classified) locations, unless permitted in other articles of the *Code*.

(a) True
(b) False

4. ENT shall not be used where exposed to the direct rays of the sun, unless identified as _____.

(a) high-temperature rated
(b) sunlight resistant
(c) Schedule 80
(d) never can be

5. Cut ends of ENT shall be trimmed inside and _____ to remove rough edges.

(a) outside
(b) tapered
(c) filed
(d) beveled

6. Bushings or adapters shall be provided at ENT terminations to protect the conductors from abrasion, unless the box, fitting, or enclosure design provides equivalent protection.

(a) True
(b) False

7. The _____ of conductors used in prewired ENT manufactured assemblies shall be identified by means of a printed tag or label attached to each end of the manufactured assembly.

(a) type
(b) size
(c) quantity
(d) all of these

Article 376. Metal Wireways

1. Metal wireways are sheet metal troughs with _____ for housing and protecting electric conductors and cable.

(a) removable covers
(b) hinged covers
(c) a or b
(d) none of these

2. Wireways can pass transversely through a wall _____.

(a) if the length passing through the wall is unbroken
(b) if the wall is of fire-rated construction
(c) in hazardous (classified) locations
(d) if the wall is not of fire-rated construction

3. The sum of the cross-sectional areas of all contained conductors at any cross-section of a metal wireway shall not exceed _____.

(a) 50 percent
(b) 20 percent
(c) 25 percent
(d) 80 percent

4. Where insulated conductors are deflected within a metal wireway, the wireway shall be sized to meet the bending requirements corresponding to _____ wire per terminal in Table 312.6(A).

(a) one
(b) two
(c) three
(d) four

5. Power distribution blocks installed in metal wireways shall _____.

(a) allow for sufficient wire-bending space at terminals
(b) not have uninsulated exposed live parts
(c) a or b
(d) a and b

Article 380. Multioutlet Assembly

1. A multioutlet assembly shall not be installed _____.

    (a) in hoistways
    (b) where subject to severe physical damage
    (c) where subject to corrosive vapors
    (d) all of these

Article 386. Surface Metal Raceways

1. Unbroken lengths of surface metal raceways can be run through dry _____.

    (a) walls
    (b) partitions
    (c) floors
    (d) all of these

2. The voltage between conductors in a surface metal raceway shall not exceed _____ unless the metal has a thickness of not less than 0.040 in. nominal.

    (a) 150V
    (b) 300V
    (c) 600V
    (d) 1,000V

3. The maximum number of conductors permitted in any surface raceway shall be _____.

    (a) no more than 30 percent of the inside diameter
    (b) no greater than the number for which it was designed
    (c) no more than 75 percent of the cross-sectional area
    (d) that which is permitted in Table 312.6(A)

4. Surface metal raceways shall be secured and supported at intervals _____.

    (a) in accordance with the manufacturer's installation instructions
    (b) appropriate for the building design
    (c) not exceeding 4 ft
    (d) not exceeding 8 ft

5. Surface metal raceway enclosures providing a transition from other wiring methods shall have a means for connecting a(n) _____.

    (a) grounded conductor
    (b) ungrounded conductor
    (c) equipment grounding conductor
    (d) all of these

Article 392. Cable Trays

1. A cable tray is a unit or assembly of units or sections and associated fittings forming a _____ system used to securely fasten or support cables and raceways.

    (a) structural
    (b) flexible
    (c) movable
    (d) secure

2. Where exposed to the direct rays of the sun, insulated conductors and jacketed cables installed in cable trays shall be _____ as being sunlight resistant.

    (a) listed
    (b) approved
    (c) identified
    (d) none of these

3. Any of the following wiring methods can be installed in a cable tray:

    (a) metal raceways
    (b) nonmetallic raceways
    (c) cables
    (d) all of these

4. Each run of cable tray shall be _____ before the installation of cables.

    (a) tested for 25 ohms resistance
    (b) insulated
    (c) completed
    (d) all of these

5. In industrial facilities where conditions of maintenance and supervision ensure that only qualified persons will service the installation, cable tray systems can be used to support _____.

   (a) raceways
   (b) cables
   (c) boxes and conduit bodies
   (d) all of these

6. Where single conductor cables comprising each phase, neutral, or grounded conductor of a circuit are connected in parallel in a cable tray, the conductors shall be installed _____, to prevent current unbalance in the paralleled conductors due to inductive reactance.

   (a) in groups consisting of not more than three conductors per phase or neutral
   (b) in groups consisting of not more than one conductor per phase or neutral
   (c) as individual conductors securely bound to the cable tray
   (d) in separate groups

7. A box shall not be required where cables or conductors from cable trays are installed in bushed conduit and tubing used as support or for protection against _____.

   (a) abuse
   (b) unauthorized access
   (c) physical damage
   (d) tampering

8. Metal cable trays containing only non-power conductors such as communication, data, signal, conductors and cables must be electrically continuous, through listed connections or the use of an insulated stranded bonding jumper not smaller than _____.

   (a) 12 AWG
   (b) 10 AWG
   (c) 6 AWG
   (d) 4 AWG

9. Steel or aluminum cable tray systems shall be permitted to be used as an equipment grounding conductor, provided the cable tray sections and fittings are identified as _____, among other requirements.

   (a) an equipment grounding conductor
   (b) special
   (c) industrial
   (d) all of these

10. Cable trays shall _____.

    (a) include fittings or other suitable means for changes in direction and elevation
    (b) have side rails or equivalent structural members
    (c) be made of corrosion-resistant material or protected from corrosion as required by 300.6
    (d) all of these

CHAPTER 4

EQUIPMENT FOR GENERAL USE

INTRODUCTION TO CHAPTER 4—EQUIPMENT FOR GENERAL USE

With the first three chapters behind you, the final chapter in the NEC for building a solid foundation in general work is Chapter 4. This chapter helps you apply the first three chapters to installations involving general equipment. These first four chapters follow a natural sequential progression. Each of the next four NEC Chapters—5, 6, 7, and 8—build upon the first four, but in no particular order. You need to understand all of the first four chapters to properly apply any of the next four.

As in the preceding chapters, Chapter 4 is also arranged logically. Here are the groupings:

- Flexible cords and cables, fixture wires, switches, and receptacles.
- Switchboards and panelboards.
- Lamps, luminaires, appliances, and space heaters.
- Motors, refrigeration equipment, generators, and transformers.
- Capacitors and other components.

These groupings make sense. For example, motors, refrigeration equipment, generators, and transformers are all inductive equipment.

This logical arrangement of the *NEC* is something to keep in mind when you're searching for a particular item. You know, for example, that transformers are general equipment. So you'll find the *Code* requirements for them in Chapter 4. You know they're wound devices, so you'll find transformer requirements located somewhere near motor requirements.

- **Article 400—Flexible Cords and Flexible Cables.** Article 400 covers the general requirements, applications, and construction specifications for flexible cords and flexible cables.

- **Article 402—Fixture Wires.** This article covers the general requirements and construction specifications for fixture wires.

- **Article 404—Switches.** The requirements of Article 404 apply to switches of all types. These include snap (toggle) switches, dimmer switches, fan switches, knife switches, circuit breakers used as switches, and automatic switches such as time clocks, timers, and switches and circuit breakers used for disconnecting means.

- **Article 406—Receptacles, Cord Connectors, and Attachment Plugs (Caps).** This article covers the rating, type, and installation of receptacles, cord connectors, and attachment plugs (cord caps). It also covers flanged surface inlets.

- **Article 408—Switchboards and Panelboards.** Article 408 covers specific requirements for switchboards, panelboards, and distribution boards that supply lighting and power circuits.

- **Article 410—Luminaires, Lampholders, and Lamps.** This article contains the requirements for luminaires, lampholders, and lamps. Because of the many types and applications of luminaires, manufacturer's instructions are very important and helpful for proper installation. Underwriters Laboratories produces a pamphlet called the *Luminaire Marking Guide*, which provides information for properly installing common types of incandescent, fluorescent, and high-intensity discharge (HID) luminaires.

- **Article 411—Lighting Systems Operating at 30V or Less.** Article 411 covers lighting systems, and their associated components, that operate at 30V or less.

- **Article 422—Appliances.** This article covers electric appliances used in any occupancy.

- **Article 424—Fixed Electric Space-Heating Equipment.** Article 424 covers fixed electric equipment used for space heating. For the purpose of this article, heating equipment includes heating cable, unit heaters, boilers, central systems, and other fixed electric space-heating equipment. Article 424 doesn't apply to process heating and room air-conditioning.

- **Article 430—Motors, Motor Circuits, and Controllers.** This article contains the specific requirements for conductor sizing, overcurrent protection, control circuit conductors, motor controllers, and disconnecting means. The installation requirements for motor control centers are covered in Article 430, Part VIII.

- **Article 440—Air-Conditioning and Refrigeration Equipment.** Article 440 applies to electrically driven air-conditioning and refrigeration equipment with a motorized hermetic refrigerant compressor. The requirements in this article are in addition to, or amend, the requirements in Article 430 and other articles.

- **Article 445—Generators.** Article 445 contains the electrical installation requirements for generators and other requirements, such as where they can be installed, nameplate markings, conductor ampacity, and disconnecting means.

- **Article 450—Transformers.** This article covers the installation of transformers.

- **Article 480—Batteries.** Article 480 covers stationary installations of storage batteries.

Flexible Cords and Flexible Cables

INTRODUCTION TO ARTICLE 400—FLEXIBLE CORDS AND FLEXIBLE CABLES

This article covers the general requirements, applications, and construction specifications for flexible cords and flexible cables. The *NEC* doesn't consider flexible cords to be wiring methods like those defined in Chapter 3.

Always use a cord (and fittings) identified for the application. Table 400.4 will help you in that regard. For example, use cords listed for a wet location if you're using them outdoors. The jacket material of any cord is tested to maintain its insulation properties and other characteristics in the environments for which its been listed. Tables 400.5(A)(1) and 400.5(A)(2) are also important tables to turn to when looking for the ampacity of flexible cords and cables.

400.1 Scope. Article 400 covers the general requirements, applications, and construction specifications for flexible cords and flexible cables as contained in Table 400.4.

> **Author's Comment:** Extension cords must not be used as a substitute for fixed wiring [400.8(1)], but they can be used for temporary wiring if approved by the authority having jurisdiction in accordance with 590.2(B).

400.3 Suitability. Flexible cords and flexible cables, as well as their fittings must be suitable for the use and location. **Figure 400–1**

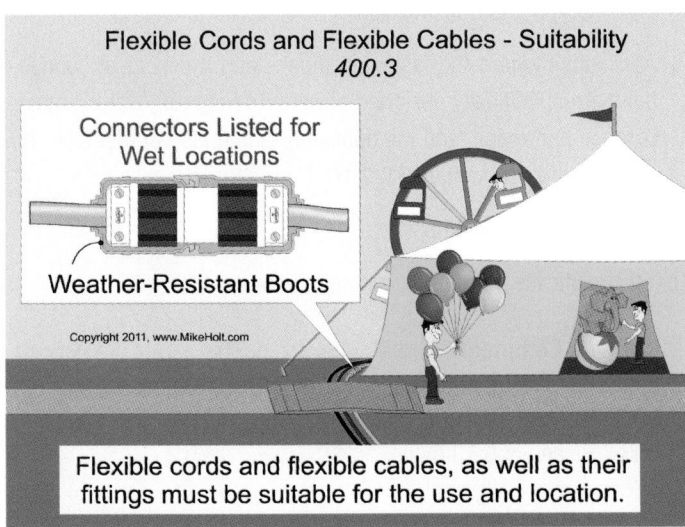

Flexible Cords and Flexible Cables - Suitability
400.3

Connectors Listed for Wet Locations

Weather-Resistant Boots

Copyright 2011, www.MikeHolt.com

Flexible cords and flexible cables, as well as their fittings must be suitable for the use and location.

Figure 400–1

400.4 Types of Flexible Cords and Flexible Cables. The use of flexible cords and flexible cables must conform to the descriptions contained in Table 400.4.

> **Author's Comment:** The suffix "W" at the end of a cord type designates that the cord is water and sunlight resistant [Table 400.4, Note 15].

400.5 Ampacity of Flexible Cords and Flexible Cables.

(A) Ampacity Tables. Table 400.5(A)(1) lists the allowable ampacity for copper conductors in flexible cords and flexible cables and 400.5(A)(2) lists the allowable ampacity for copper conductors in flexible cords and flexible cables with not more than three current-carrying conductors at an ambient temperature of 86°F.

Where the number of current-carrying conductors in a cable or raceway exceeds three, the allowable ampacity of each conductor must be adjusted in accordance with the following multipliers: **Figure 400–2**

Table 400.5 Adjustment Factor	
Current Carrying	**Ampacity Multiplier**
4–6 Conductors	0.80
7–9 Conductors	0.70
10–20 Conductors	0.50

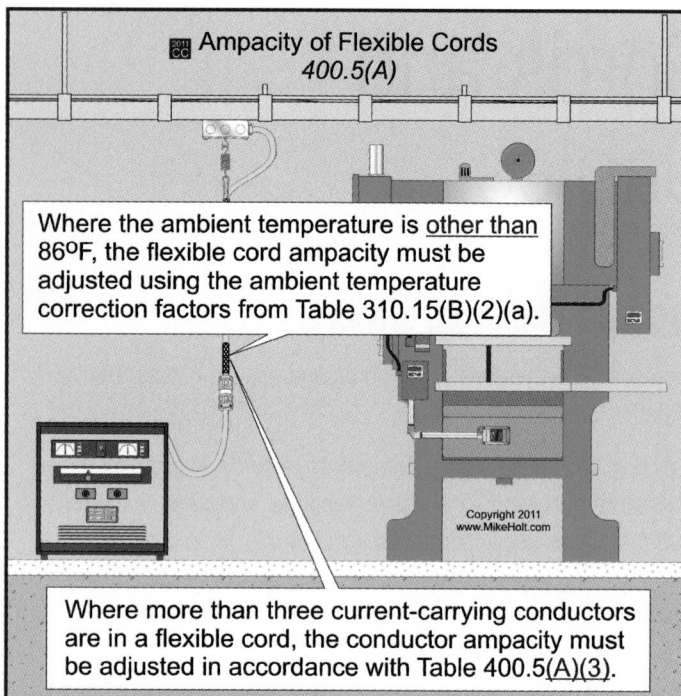

Ampacity of Flexible Cords
400.5(A)

Where the ambient temperature is <u>other than</u> 86°F, the flexible cord ampacity must be adjusted using the ambient temperature correction factors from Table 310.15(B)(2)(a).

Where more than three current-carrying conductors are in a flexible cord, the conductor ampacity must be adjusted in accordance with Table 400.5<u>(A)(3)</u>.

Copyright 2011
www.MikeHolt.com

Figure 400–2

If the ambient temperature is other than 86°F, the flexible cord or flexible cable ampacity, as listed in Table 400.5(A)(1) or 400.5(A)(2), must be adjusted by using the ambient temperature correction factors listed in Table 310.15(B)(2)(a).

Author's Comments:

- Temperature ratings for flexible cords and flexible cables aren't contained in the *NEC*, but UL listing standards state that flexible cords and flexible cables are rated for 60°C unless marked otherwise.

- See 400.13 for overcurrent protection requirements for flexible cords and flexible cables.

400.7 Uses Permitted.

(A) Uses Permitted. Flexible cords and flexible cables within the scope of this article can be used for the following applications:

(1) Pendants [210.50(A) and 314.23(H)].

Author's Comment: Only cords identified for use as pendants in Table 400.4 may be used for pendants.

(2) Wiring of luminaires [410.24(A) and 410.62(B)].

(3) Connection of portable luminaires, portable and mobile signs, or appliances [422.16].

(4) Elevator cables.

(5) Wiring of cranes and hoists.

(6) Connection of utilization equipment to facilitate frequent interchange [422.16]. **Figure 400–3**

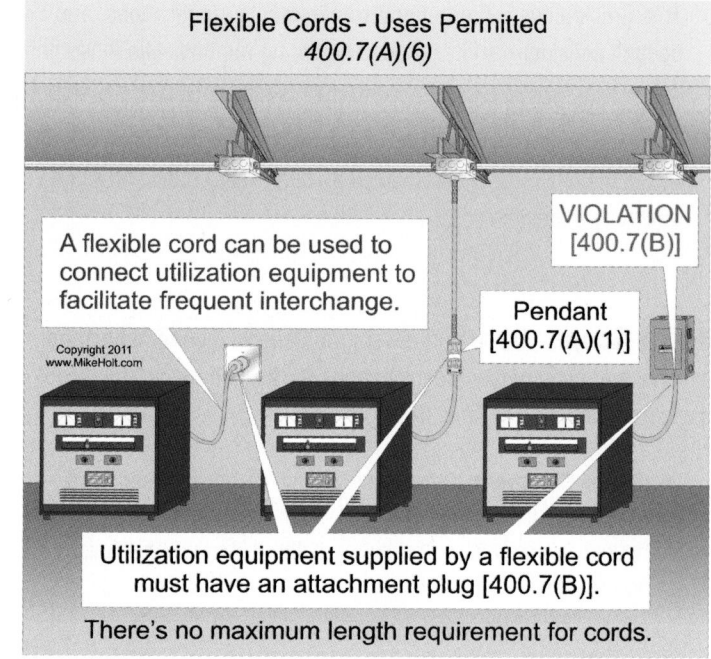

Flexible Cords - Uses Permitted
400.7(A)(6)

A flexible cord can be used to connect utilization equipment to facilitate frequent interchange.

Copyright 2011
www.MikeHolt.com

VIOLATION
[400.7(B)]

Pendant
[400.7(A)(1)]

Utilization equipment supplied by a flexible cord must have an attachment plug [400.7(B)].

There's no maximum length requirement for cords.

Figure 400–3

(7) Prevention of the transmission of noise or vibration [422.16].

(8) Appliances where the fastening means and mechanical connections are specifically designed to permit ready removal for maintenance and repair, and the appliance is intended or identified for flexible cord connections [422.16].

(9) Connection of moving parts.

(10) If specifically permitted elsewhere in this *Code*.

Author's Comment: Flexible cords and flexible cables are permitted for fixed permanent wiring by 501.10(A)(2) and (B)(2), 501.140, 502.4(A)(1)(e), 502.4(B)(2), 503.3(A)(2), 550.10(B), 553.7(B), and 555.13(A)(2).

(B) Attachment Plugs. Attachment plugs are required for flexible cords used in any of the following applications: **Figure 400–4**

- Portable luminaires, portable and mobile signs, or appliances [400.7(A)(3)].
- Stationary equipment to facilitate its frequent interchange [400.7(A)(6) and 422.16].
- Appliances specifically designed to permit ready removal for maintenance and repair, and identified for flexible cord connection [400.7(A)(8)].

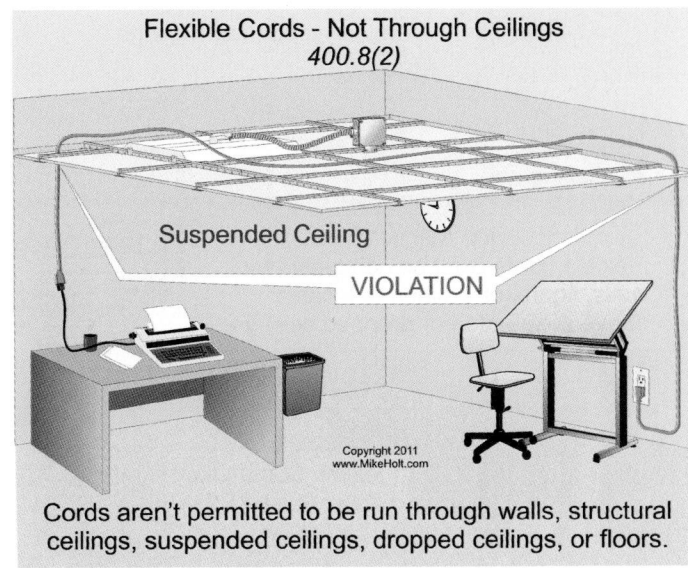

Flexible Cords - Not Through Ceilings
400.8(2)

Suspended Ceiling

VIOLATION

Cords aren't permitted to be run through walls, structural ceilings, suspended ceilings, dropped ceilings, or floors.

Figure 400–5

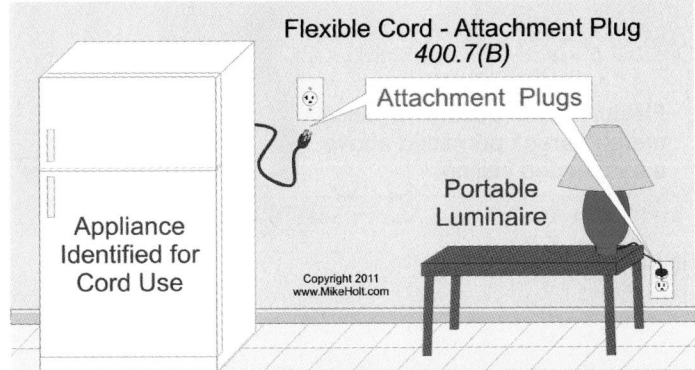

Flexible Cord - Attachment Plug
400.7(B)

Attachment Plugs

Portable Luminaire

Appliance Identified for Cord Use

Flexible cords must have an attachment plug for:
• Portable luminaires or appliances [400.7(A)(3)]
• Equipment to facilitate frequent interchange [400.7(A)(6)]
• Appliances identified for flexible cord usage [400.7(A)(8)]

Figure 400–4

Author's Comment: An attachment plug can serve as the disconnecting means for stationary appliances [422.33] and room air conditioners [440.63].

400.8 Uses Not Permitted. Unless specifically permitted in 400.7, flexible cords must not be:

(1) Used as a substitute for the fixed wiring of a structure.

(2) Run through holes in walls, structural ceilings, suspended or dropped ceilings, or floors. **Figure 400–5**

Author's Comment: According to an article in the *International Association of Electrical Inspectors* magazine (*IAEI News*), a flexible cord installed through a cabinet for an appliance isn't considered as being installed through a wall. **Figure 400–6**

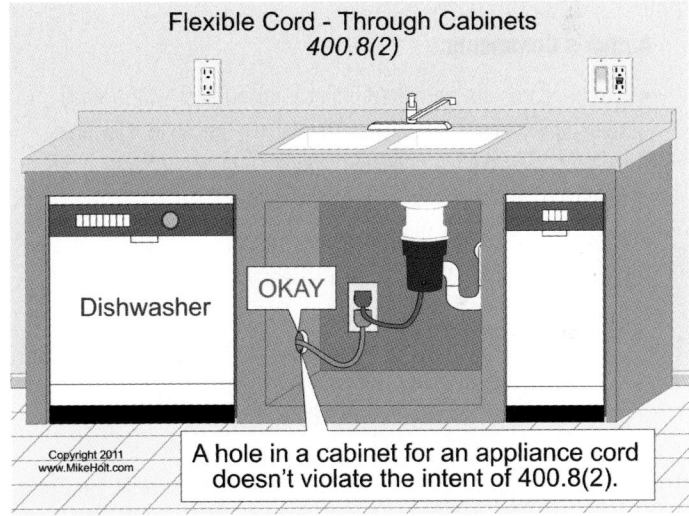

Flexible Cord - Through Cabinets
400.8(2)

Dishwasher   OKAY

A hole in a cabinet for an appliance cord doesn't violate the intent of 400.8(2).

Figure 400–6

(3) Run through doorways, windows, or similar openings.

(4) Attached to building surfaces.

(5) Concealed by walls, floors, or ceilings, or located above suspended or dropped ceilings. **Figure 400–7**

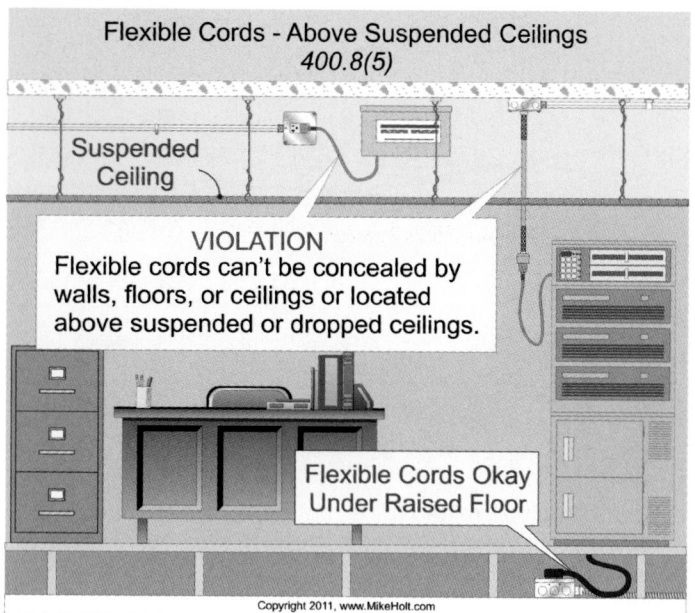

Figure 400–7

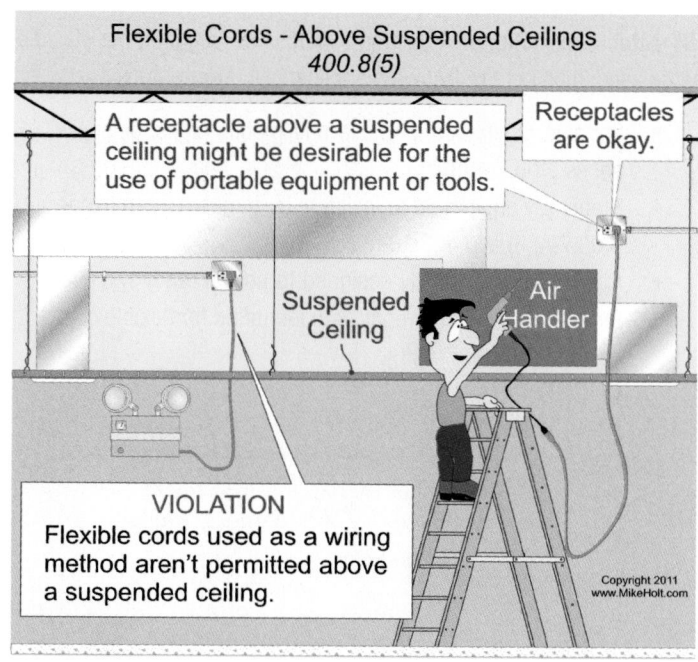

Figure 400–8

Author's Comments:

- Flexible cords are permitted under a raised floor (with removable panels) used for environmental air, because this area isn't considered a concealed space. See the definition of "Exposed" in Article 100.

- Receptacles are permitted above a suspended ceiling, but a flexible cord isn't. Why install a receptacle above a ceiling if the flexible cord isn't permitted in this space? Because the receptacle can be used for portable tools; it just can't be used for cord-and-plug-connected equipment fastened in place, such as a projector. **Figure 400–8**

(6) Installed in raceways, except as permitted elsewhere in the *Code*.

(7) If subject to physical damage.

Author's Comment: Even cords listed as "extra-hard usage" must not be used where subject to physical damage.

400.10 Pull at Joints and Terminals. Flexible cords must be installed so tension won't be transmitted to the conductor terminals.

Note: This can be accomplished by knotting the cord, winding the cord with tape, or by using fittings designed for the purpose, such as strain-relief fittings. **Figure 400–9**

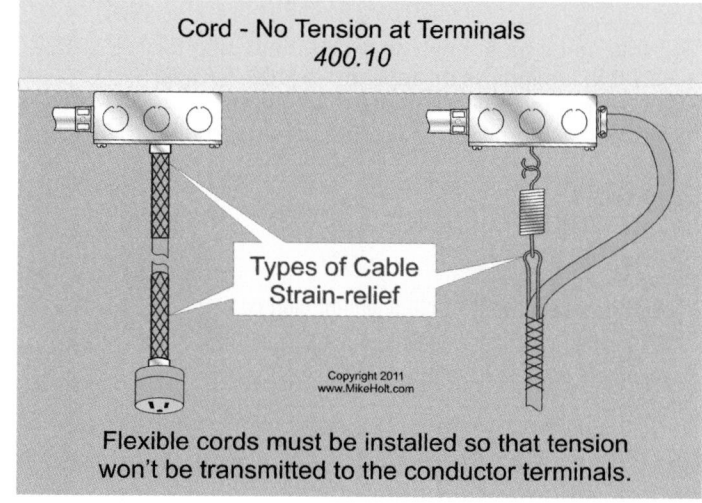

Figure 400–9

Author's Comment: When critical health and economic activities are dependent on flexible cord-supplied equipment, the best method is a factory-made, stress-relieving, listed device, not an old-timer's knot.

400.14 Protection from Damage. Flexible cords must be protected by bushings or fittings where passing through holes in covers, outlet boxes, or similar enclosures.

In industrial establishments where the conditions of maintenance and supervision ensure that only qualified persons will service the installation, flexible cords or flexible cables not exceeding 50 ft can be installed in aboveground raceways.

400.23 Equipment Grounding Conductor Identification. A conductor intended to be used as an equipment grounding conductor must have a continuous green color or a continuous identifying marker distinguishing it from the other conductor(s). Conductors with green insulation, or green with one or more yellow stripes must not be used for an ungrounded or neutral conductor [250.119].

ARTICLE
402

Fixture Wires

INTRODUCTION TO ARTICLE 402—FIXTURE WIRES

This article covers the general requirements and construction specifications for fixture wires. One such requirement is that no fixture wire can be smaller than 18 AWG. Another requirement is that fixture wires must be of a type listed in Table 402.3. That table makes up the bulk of Article 402. Table 402.5 lists the allowable ampacity for fixture wires.

402.1 Scope. Article 402 covers the general requirements and construction specifications for fixture wires.

402.3 Types. Fixture wires must be of a type contained in Table 402.3.

402.5 Allowable Ampacity of Fixture Wires. The allowable ampacity of fixture wires is as follows:

Table 402.5 Allowable Ampacity for Fixture Wires

Wire AWG	Wire Ampacity
18	6A
16	8A
14	17A
12	23A
10	28A

402.6 Minimum Size. Fixture wires must not be smaller than 18 AWG.

402.7 Raceway Size. Raceways must be large enough to permit the installation and removal of conductors without damaging conductor insulation. The number of fixture wires permitted in a single raceway must not exceed the percentage fill specified in Table 1, Chapter 9.

> **Author's Comment:** When all conductors in a raceway are the same size and insulation, the number of conductors permitted can be found in Annex C for the raceway type.

> **Question:** How many 18 TFFN conductors can be installed in trade size ½ electrical metallic tubing? **Figure 402–1**
>
> (a) 12   (b) 14   (c) 19   (d) 22
>
> **Answer:** (d) 22 conductors [Annex C, Table C.1]

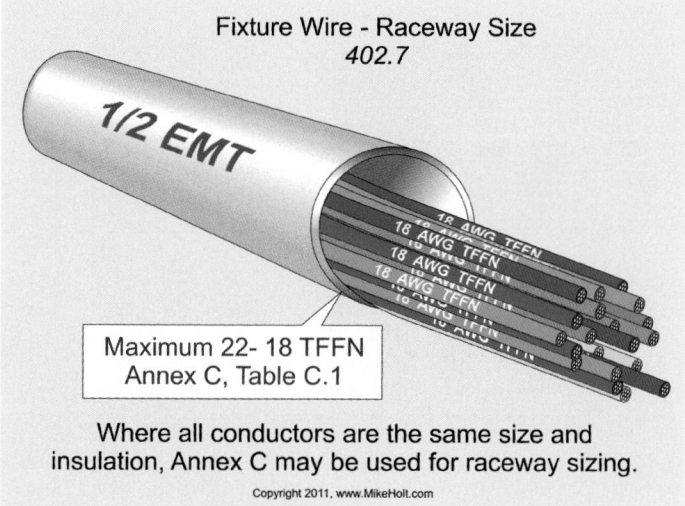

Fixture Wire - Raceway Size
402.7

1/2 EMT

Maximum 22- 18 TFFN
Annex C, Table C.1

Where all conductors are the same size and insulation, Annex C may be used for raceway sizing.

Copyright 2011, www.MikeHolt.com

Figure 402–1

> **Author's Comment:** See 300.17 for additional examples on how to size raceways when conductors aren't all the same size.

402.8 Neutral Conductor. Fixture wire used as a neutral conductor must be identified by continuous white stripes.

> **Author's Comment:** To prevent electric shock, the screw shell of a luminaire or lampholder must be connected to the neutral conductor [200.10(C) and 410.50]. **Figure 402–2**

Figure 402–2

402.10 Uses Permitted.

(2) Fixture wires are permitted for the connection of luminaires. **Figure 402–3**

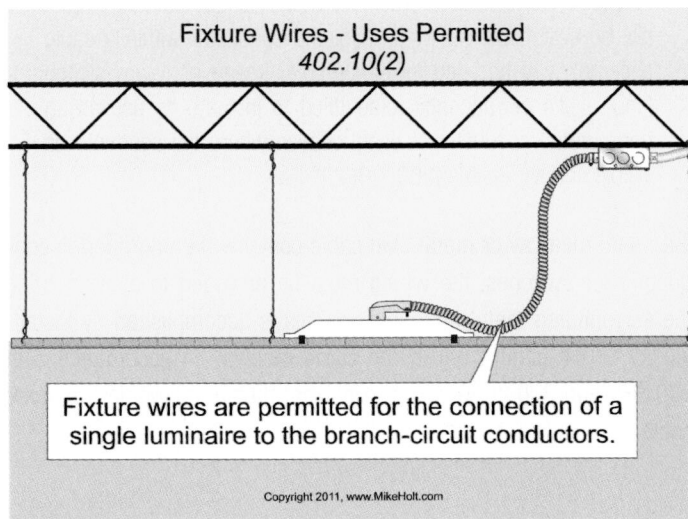

Figure 402–3

> **Author's Comment:** Fixture wires can also be used for elevators and escalators [620.11(C)], Class 1 control and power-limited circuits [725.49(B)], and nonpower-limited fire alarm circuits [760.49(B)].

402.11 Uses Not Permitted. Fixture wires must not be used for branch-circuit wiring, except as permitted elsewhere in the *Code*. **Figure 402–4**

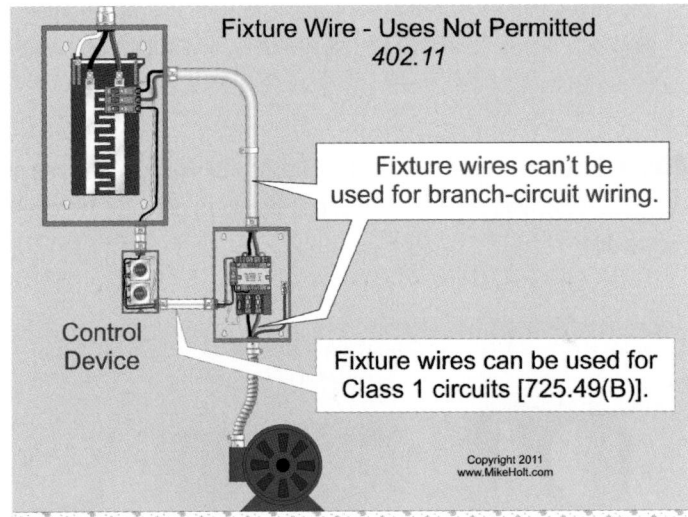

Figure 402–4

402.12 Overcurrent Protection. Fixture wires must be protected against overcurrent according to the requirements contained in 240.5.

> **Author's Comment:** Fixture wires used for motor control circuit taps must have overcurrent protection in accordance with 430.72(A), and Class 1 remote-control circuits must have overcurrent protection in accordance with 725.43.

ARTICLE
404

Switches

INTRODUCTION TO ARTICLE 404—SWITCHES

The requirements of Article 404 apply to switches of all types, including snap (toggle) switches, dimmer switches, fan switches, knife switches, circuit breakers used as switches, and automatic switches, such as time clocks and timers.

404.1 Scope. The requirements of Article 404 apply to all types of switches, switching devices, and circuit breakers used as switches. Figure 404–1

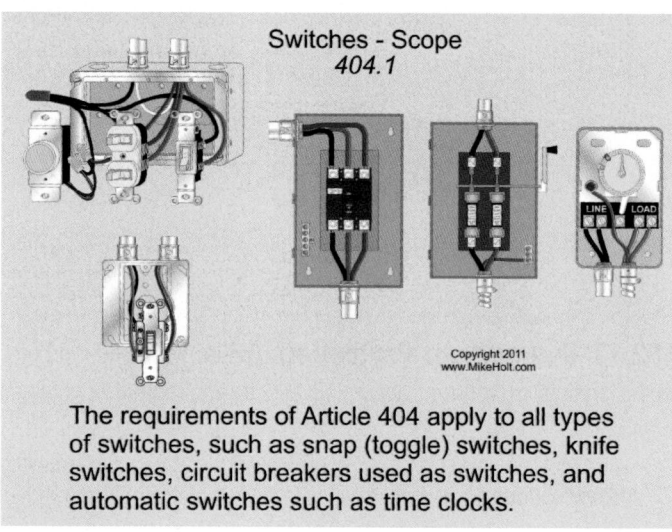

Switches - Scope
404.1

The requirements of Article 404 apply to all types of switches, such as snap (toggle) switches, knife switches, circuit breakers used as switches, and automatic switches such as time clocks.

Figure 404–1

404.2 Switch Connections.

(A) Three-Way and Four-Way Switches. Wiring for 3-way and 4-way switching must be done so that only the ungrounded conductors are switched. Figure 404–2

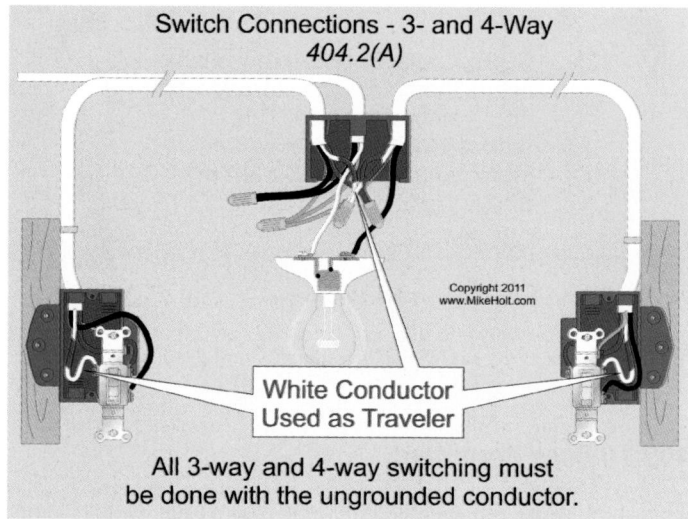

Switch Connections - 3- and 4-Way
404.2(A)

Copyright 2011
www.MikeHolt.com

White Conductor
Used as Traveler

All 3-way and 4-way switching must
be done with the ungrounded conductor.

Figure 404–2

Author's Comment: In other words, the neutral conductor must not be switched. The white insulated conductor within a cable assembly can be used for single-pole, 3-way, or 4-way switch loops if it's permanently reidentified to indicate its use as an ungrounded conductor at each location where the conductor is visible and accessible [200.7(C)(2)].

If a metal raceway or metal-clad cable contains the ungrounded conductors for switches, the wiring must be arranged to avoid heating the surrounding metal by induction. This is accomplished by installing all circuit conductors in the same raceway in accordance with 300.3(B) and 300.20(A), or ensuring that they're all within the same cable.

Ex: A neutral conductor isn't required in the same raceway or cable with travelers and switch leg (switch loop) conductors. **Figure 404–3**

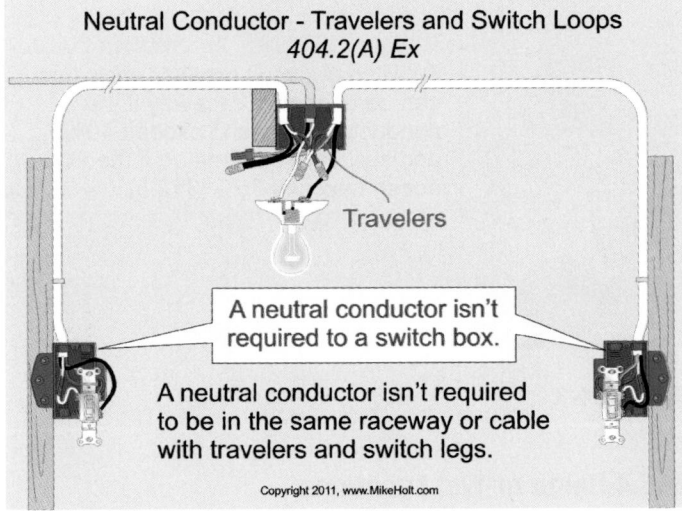

Neutral Conductor - Travelers and Switch Loops
404.2(A) Ex

Travelers

A neutral conductor isn't required to a switch box.

A neutral conductor isn't required to be in the same raceway or cable with travelers and switch legs.

Copyright 2011, www.MikeHolt.com

Figure 404–3

(B) Switching Neutral Conductors. Only the ungrounded conductor is permitted to be used for switching, and the grounded conductor must not be disconnected by switches or circuit breakers. **Figure 404–4**

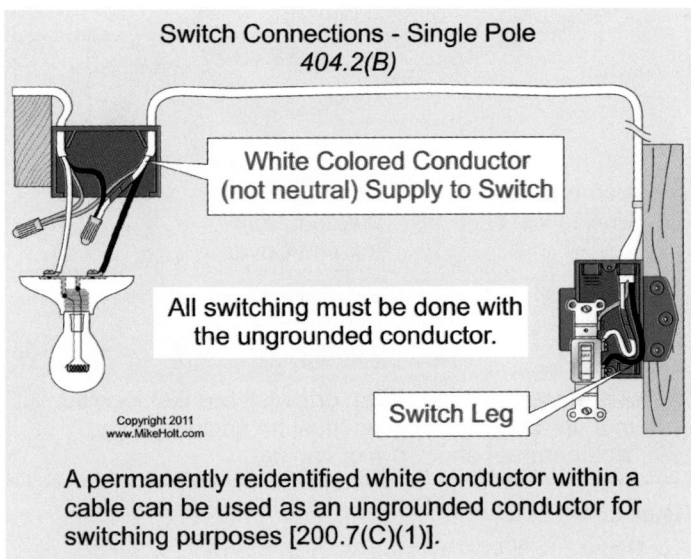

Switch Connections - Single Pole
404.2(B)

White Colored Conductor
(not neutral) Supply to Switch

All switching must be done with the ungrounded conductor.

Copyright 2011
www.MikeHolt.com

Switch Leg

A permanently reidentified white conductor within a cable can be used as an ungrounded conductor for switching purposes [200.7(C)(1)].

Figure 404–4

Ex: A switch or circuit breaker is permitted to disconnect a grounded circuit conductor where it disconnects all circuit conductors simultaneously.

(C) Switches Controlling Lighting Loads. Switches controlling line-to-neutral lighting loads must have a neutral provided at the switch location.

Ex: The neutral conductor isn't required at the switch location if:

(1) The conductors for switches enter the device box through a raceway that has sufficient cross-sectional area to accommodate a neutral conductor. **Figure 404–5**

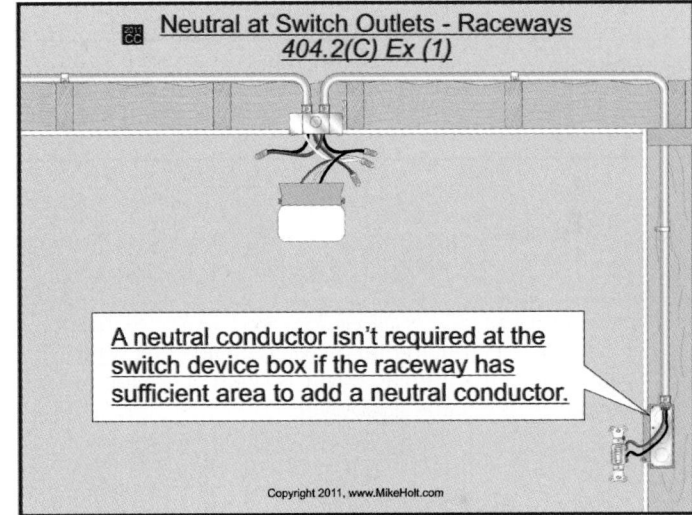

Neutral at Switch Outlets - Raceways
404.2(C) Ex (1)

A neutral conductor isn't required at the switch device box if the raceway has sufficient area to add a neutral conductor.

Copyright 2011, www.MikeHolt.com

Figure 404–5

(2) Cable assemblies for switches enter the box through a framing cavity that's open at the top or bottom on the same floor level, or switches enter the box through a wall, floor, or ceiling that's unfinished on one side. **Figures 404–6 and 404–7**

Note: The purpose of the neutral conductor is to complete a circuit path for electronic lighting control devices.

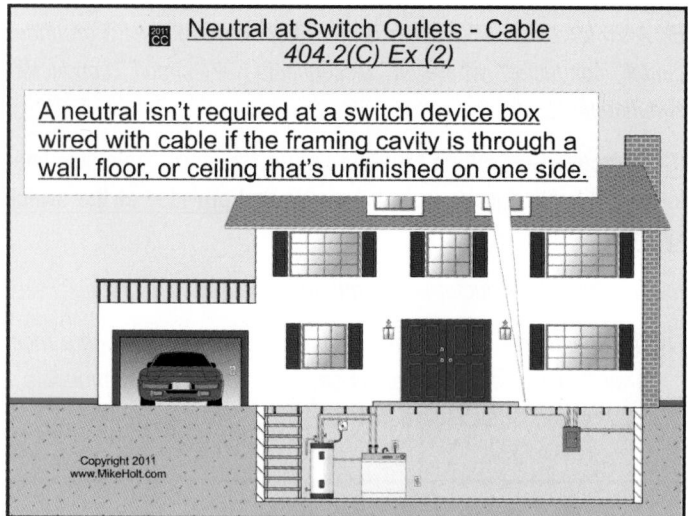

Figure 404–6

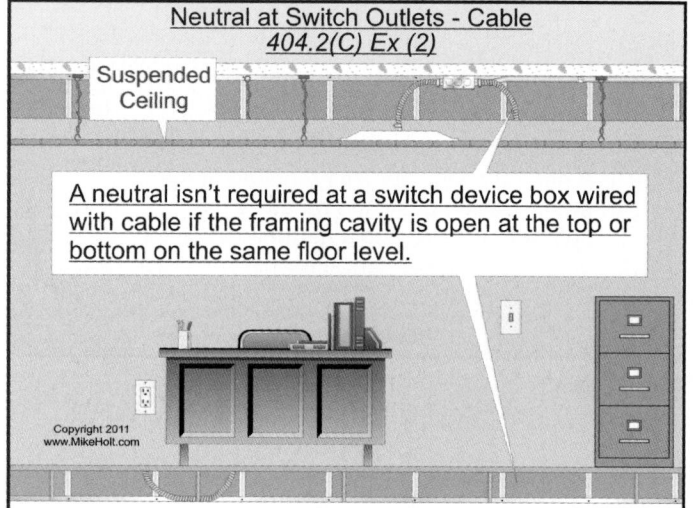

Figure 404–7

404.3 Switch Enclosures.

(A) General. Switches and circuit breakers used as switches must be of the externally operable type mounted in an enclosure listed for the intended use.

(B) Used for Raceways or Splices. Switch or circuit-breaker enclosures can contain splices and taps if the splices and/or taps don't fill the wiring space at any cross section to more than 75 percent. Switch or circuit-breaker enclosures can have conductors feed through them if the wiring doesn't fill the wiring space at any cross section to more than 40 percent in accordance with 312.8. **Figure 404–8**

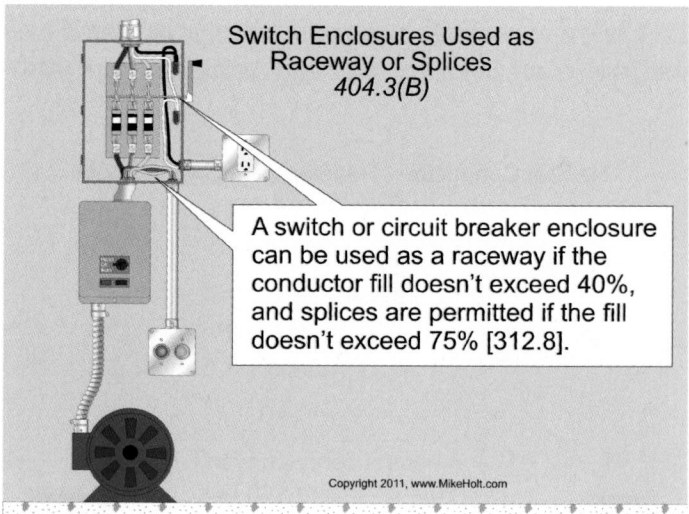

Figure 404–8

404.4 Damp or Wet Locations.

(A) Surface-Mounted Switches or Circuit Breakers. Surface-mounted switches and circuit breakers in a damp or wet location must be installed in a weatherproof enclosure. The enclosure must be installed so not less than ¼ in. of airspace is provided between the enclosure and the wall or other supporting surface [312.2]. **Figure 404–9**

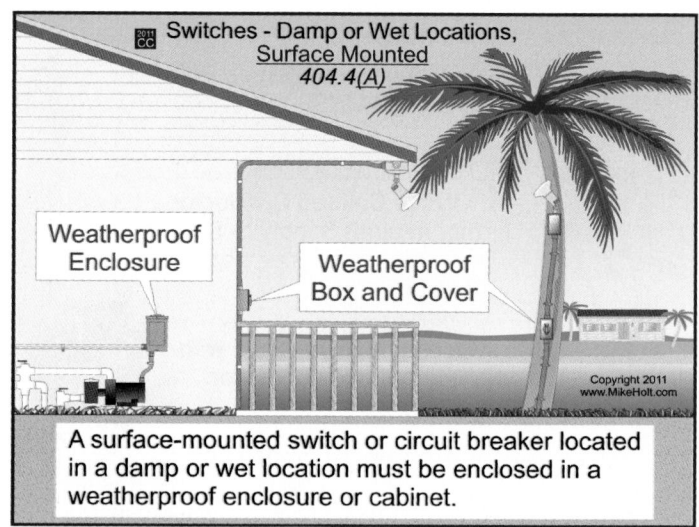

Figure 404–9

(B) Flush-Mounted Switches or Circuit Breakers. A flush-mounted switch or circuit breaker in a damp or wet location must have a weatherproof cover. **Figure 404–10**

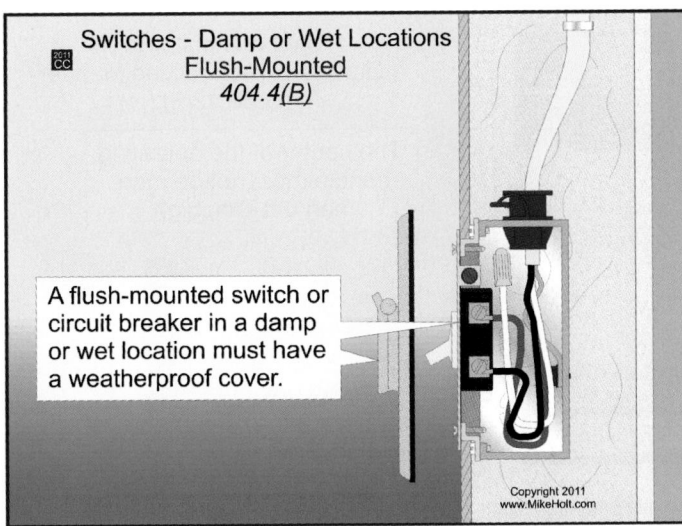

Figure 404–10

(C) Switches in Bathtub or Shower Spaces. Switches can be located next to but not within a bathtub, hydromassage bathtub, or shower space unless installed as part of a listed tub or shower assembly. **Figure 404–11**

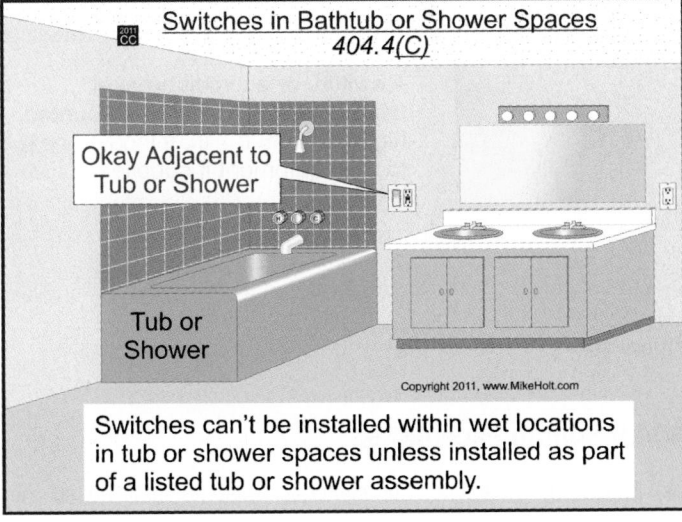

Figure 404–11

404.6 Position of Knife Switches.

(A) Single-Throw Knife Switch. Single-throw knife switches must be installed so gravity won't tend to close them.

(C) Connection of Switches. Single-throw knife switches, molded case switches, and circuit breakers used as switches must have the terminals supplying the load deenergize when the switch is in the open position.

Exception: The blades and terminals supplying the load can be energized when the switch is in the open position. For such installations, a permanent sign must on the switch enclosure or immediately adjacent to open switch is required to read:

⚠️ **WARNING — LOAD SIDE TERMINALS MAY BE ENERGIZED BY BACKFEED.**

404.7 Indicating. Switches, motor circuit switches, and circuit breakers used as switches must be marked to indicate whether they're in the "on" or "off" position. When the switch is operated vertically, it must be installed so the "up" position is the "on" position [240.81]. **Figure 404–12**

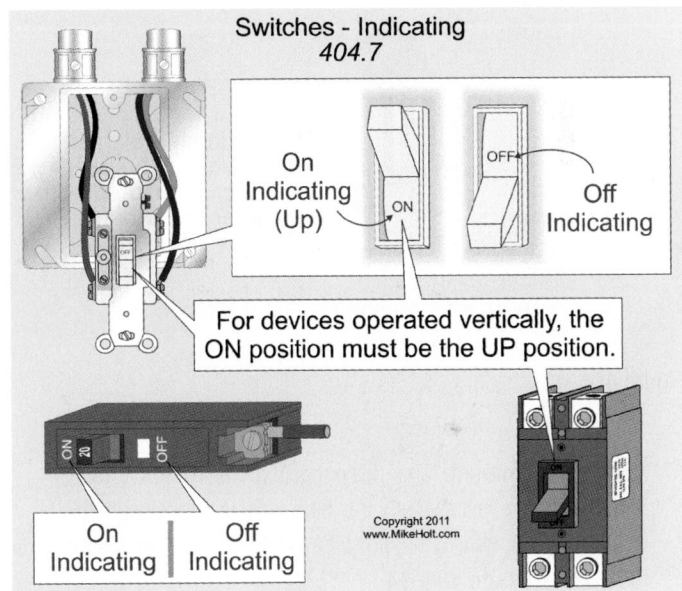

Figure 404–12

Ex 1: Double-throw switches, such as 3-way and 4-way switches, aren't required to be marked "on" or "off."

Ex 2: On busway installations, tap switches employing a center-pivoting handle can be open or closed with either end of the handle in the up or down position. The switch position must be clearly indicated and must be visible from the floor or from the usual point of operation.

404.8 Accessibility and Grouping.

(A) Location. Switches and circuit breakers used as switches must be capable of being operated from a readily accessible location. They must also be installed so the center of the grip of the operating handle of the switch or circuit breaker, when in its highest position, isn't more than 6 ft 7 in. above the floor or working platform [240.24(A)]. **Figure 404–13**

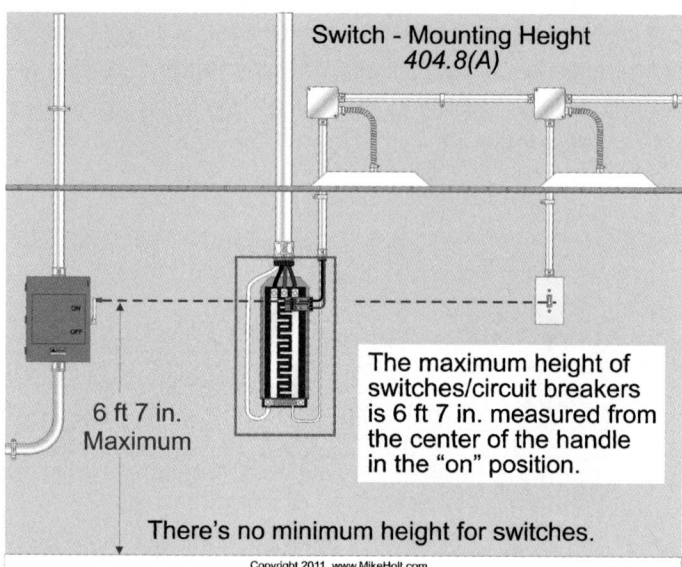

Figure 404–13

Author's Comment: The disconnecting means for a mobile home must be installed so the bottom of the enclosure isn't less than 2 ft above the finished grade or working platform [550.32(F)]. **Figure 404–14**

Ex 1: On busways, fusible switches and circuit breakers can be located at the same level as the busway where suitable means is provided to operate the handle of the device from the floor.

Ex 2: Switches and circuit breakers used as switches can be mounted above 6 ft 7 in. if they're next to the equipment they supply, and are accessible by portable means [240.24(A)(4)]. **Figure 404–15**

(B) Voltage Between Devices. Snap switches must not be grouped or ganged in enclosures with other snap switches, receptacles, or similar devices if the voltage between devices exceeds 300V, unless the devices are separated by barriers. **Figures 404–16 and 404–17**

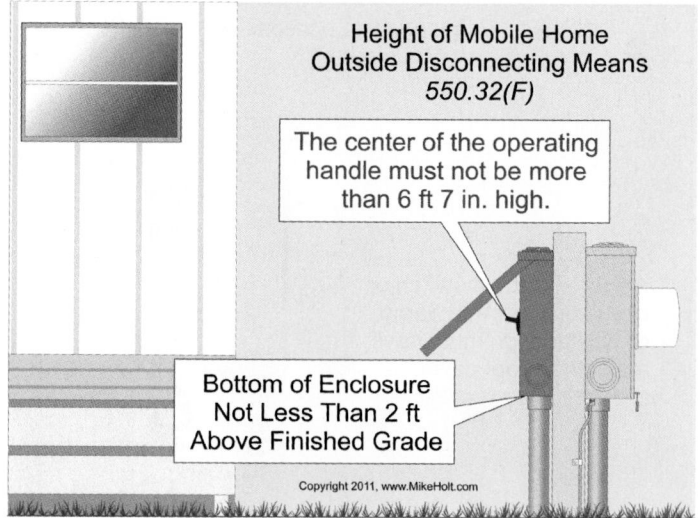

Figure 404–14

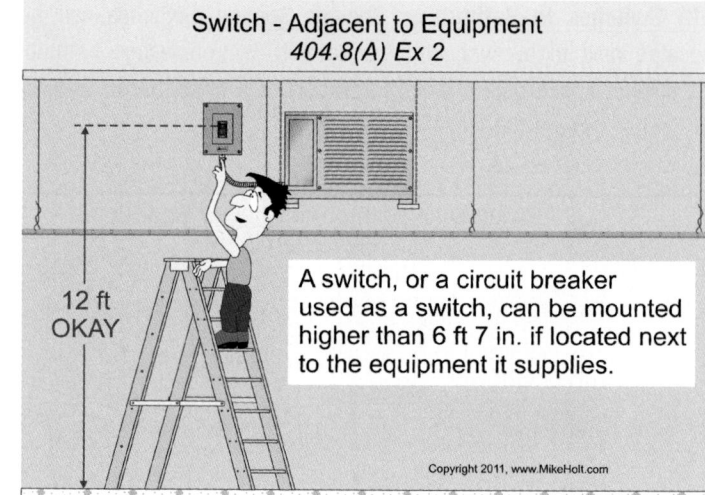

Figure 404–15

404.9 Switch Faceplates.

(A) Mounting. Faceplates for switches must be installed so they completely cover the outlet box opening and, where flush mounted, the faceplate must seat against the wall surface.

(B) Grounding. The metal mounting yokes for switches, dimmers, and similar control switches must be connected to an equipment grounding conductor of a type recognized in 250.118, whether or not a metal faceplate is installed. The metal mounting yoke is considered part of the effective ground-fault current path [250.2] by the use of one of the following means:

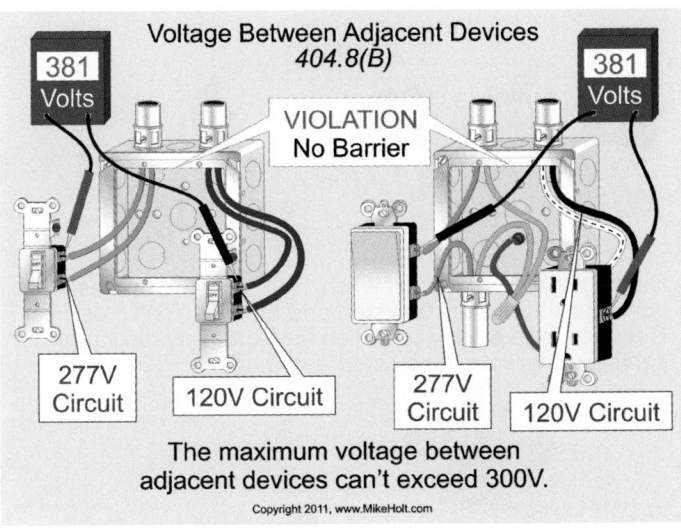

Figure 404–16

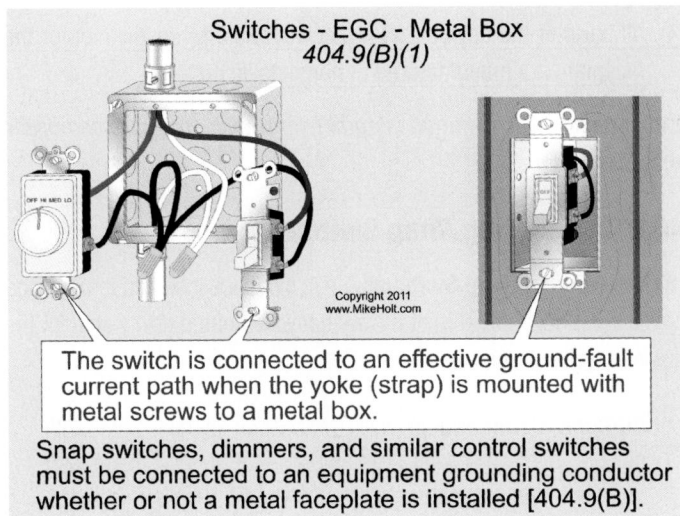

The switch is connected to an effective ground-fault current path when the yoke (strap) is mounted with metal screws to a metal box.

Snap switches, dimmers, and similar control switches must be connected to an equipment grounding conductor whether or not a metal faceplate is installed [404.9(B)].

Figure 404–18

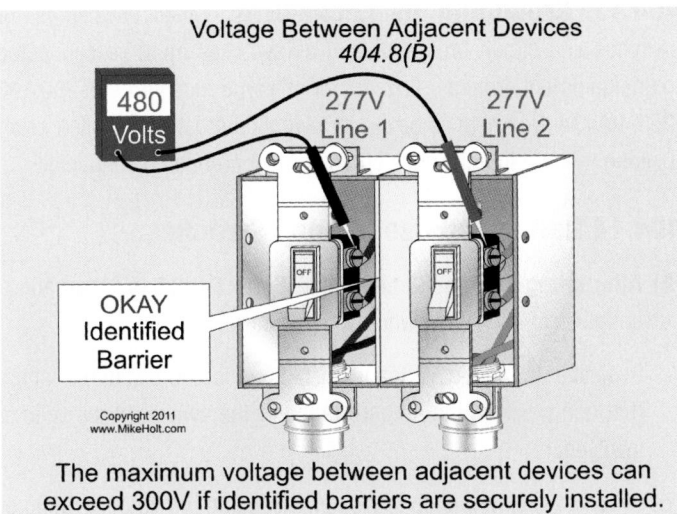

Figure 404–17

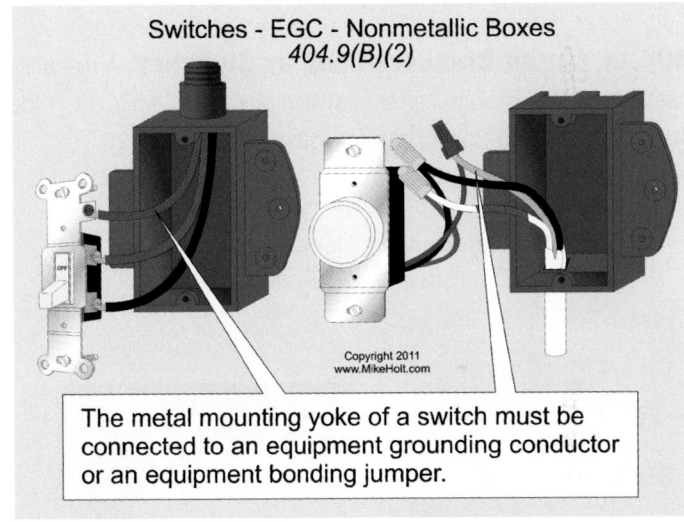

The metal mounting yoke of a switch must be connected to an equipment grounding conductor or an equipment bonding jumper.

Figure 404–19

(1) Mounting Screw. The switch is mounted with metal screws to a metal box or a metal cover that's connected to an equipment grounding conductor of a type recognized in 250.118. **Figure 404–18**

> **Author's Comment:** Direct metal-to-metal contact between the device yoke of a switch and the box isn't required.

(2) Equipment Grounding Conductor. An equipment grounding conductor or equipment bonding jumper is connected to the grounding terminal of the metal mounting yoke. **Figure 404–19**

Ex 1: The metal mounting yoke of a replacement switch isn't required to be connected to an equipment grounding conductor if the wiring at the existing switch doesn't contain an equipment grounding conductor, and the switch faceplate is nonmetallic with nonmetallic screws, or the replacement switch is GFCI protected.

Ex 2: Listed assemblies aren't required to be connected to an equipment grounding conductor if all of the following conditions are met:

(1) The device is provided with a nonmetallic faceplate that can't be installed on any other type of device,

(2) The device doesn't have mounting means to accept other configurations of faceplates,

(3) The device is equipped with a nonmetallic yoke, and

(4) All parts of the device that are accessible after installation of the faceplate are manufactured of nonmetallic material.

Ex 3: A snap switch with an integral nonmetallic enclosure complying with 300.15(E).

404.10 Mounting Snap Switches.

(B) Mounting of Snap Switches. Snap switches installed in recessed boxes must have the ears of the switch yoke seated firmly against the finished wall surface.

> **Author's Comment:** In walls or ceilings of noncombustible material, such as drywall, boxes must not be set back more than ¼ in. from the finished surface. In combustible walls or ceilings, boxes must be flush with, or project slightly from, the finished surface [314.20]. There must not be any gaps more than ⅛ in. at the edge of the box [314.21].

404.11 Circuit Breakers Used as Switches. A manually operable circuit breaker used as a switch must show when it's in the "on" (closed) or "off" (open) position [404.7]. **Figure 404–20**

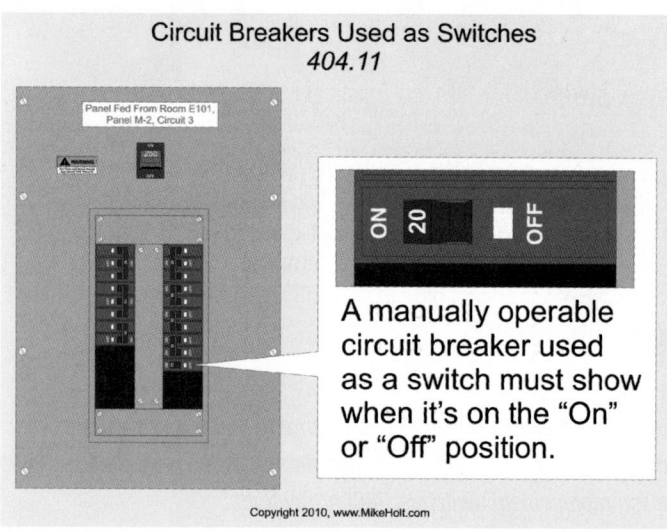

Figure 404–20

> **Author's Comment:** Circuit breakers used to switch fluorescent lighting must be listed and marked "SWD" or "HID." Circuit breakers used to switch high-intensity discharge lighting must be listed and must be marked "HID" [240.83(D)]. **Figure 404–21**

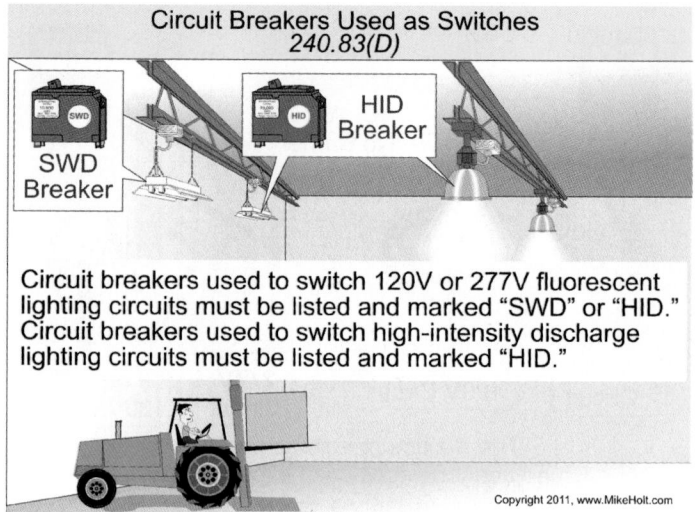

Figure 404–21

404.12 Grounding of Enclosures. Metal enclosures for switches and circuit breakers used as switches must be connected to an equipment grounding conductor of a type recognized in 250.118 [250.4(A)(3)]. Nonmetallic boxes for switches must be installed using a wiring method that includes an equipment grounding conductor.

404.14 Rating and Use of Snap Switches.

(A) Alternating-Current General-Use Snap Switches. Alternating-current general-use snap switches can control:

(1) Resistive and inductive loads, including electric-discharge lamps that don't exceed the ampere rating of the switch, at the voltage involved.

(2) Tungsten-filament lamp loads not exceeding the ampere rating of the switch at 120V.

(3) Motor loads rated 2 hp or less that don't exceed 80 percent of the ampere rating of the switch. See 430.109(C).

(B) Alternating-Current or Direct-Current General-Use Snap Switch. A form of general-use snap switch suitable for use on either alternating-current or direct-current circuits for controlling:

(1) Resistive loads not exceeding the ampere rating of the switch at the voltage applied.

(2) Inductive loads not exceeding 50 percent of the ampere rating of the switch at the applied voltage or rated in horsepower for motor loads.

(3) Tungsten-filament lamp loads not exceeding the ampere rating of the switch at the applied voltage if T-rated.

(C) CO/ALR Snap Switches. Snap switches rated 20A or less connected to aluminum wire must be marked CO/ALR. See 406.3(C).

> **Author's Comment:** According to UL listing requirements, aluminum conductors must not terminate in screwless (push-in) terminals of a snap switch (UL White Book, *Guide Information for Electrical Equipment*, www.ul.com/regulators/2008_WhiteBook. pdf).

(E) Dimmers. General-use dimmer switches are only permitted to control permanently installed incandescent luminaires. **Figure 404–22**

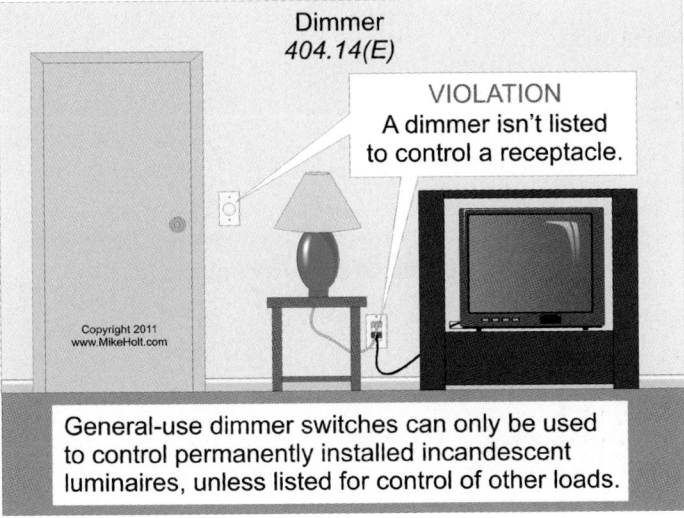

Figure 404–22

404.15 Switch Marking.

(A) Markings. Switches must be marked with the current, voltage, and if horsepower rated, the maximum rating for which they're designed.

(B) Off Indication. If in the off position, a switching device with a marked "off" position must completely disconnect all ungrounded conductors of the load it controls.

> **Author's Comment:** If an electronic occupancy sensor is used for switching, voltage will be present and a small current of 0.05 mA can flow through the circuit when the switch is in the "off" position. This small amount of current can startle a person, perhaps causing a fall. To solve this problem, manufacturers have simply removed the word "off" from the switch. **Figure 404–23**

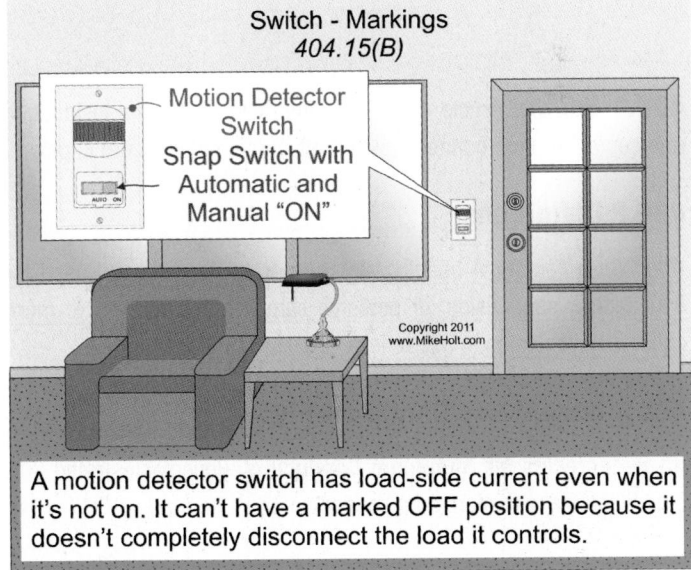

Figure 404–23

Receptacles, Cord Connectors, and Attachment Plugs (Caps)

INTRODUCTION TO ARTICLE 406—RECEPTACLES, CORD CONNECTORS, AND ATTACHMENT PLUGS (CAPS)

This article covers the rating, type, and installation of receptacles, cord connectors, and attachment plugs (cord caps). It also addresses their grounding requirements. Some key points to remember include:

- Follow the grounding requirements of the specific type of device you're using.
- Provide GFCI protection where specified by 406.4(D)(3).
- Mount receptacles according to the requirements of 406.5, which are highly detailed.

406.1 Scope. Article 406 covers the rating, type, and installation of receptacles, cord connectors, and attachment plugs (cord caps).

406.2 Definitions.

Child Care Facility. A building/structure or portions thereof used for educational, supervision, or personal care services for five or more children seven years in age or less.

406.3 Receptacle Rating and Type.

(C) Receptacles for Aluminum Conductors. Receptacles rated 20A or less for use with aluminum conductors must be marked CO/ALR.

> **Author's Comment:** According to UL listing requirements, aluminum conductors must not terminate in screwless (push-in) terminals of a receptacle (UL White Book, *Guide Information for Electrical Equipment,* www.ul.com/regulators/2008_WhiteBook.pdf).

(D) Isolated Ground Receptacles. Receptacles of the isolated grounding conductor type must be identified by an orange triangle marking on the face of the receptacle. **Figure 406–1**

(1) Receptacles having insulated grounding terminals (isolated ground receptacles) must have the grounding contact connected to an insulated equipment grounding conductor installed with the circuit conductors, in accordance with 250.146(D). **Figure 406–2**

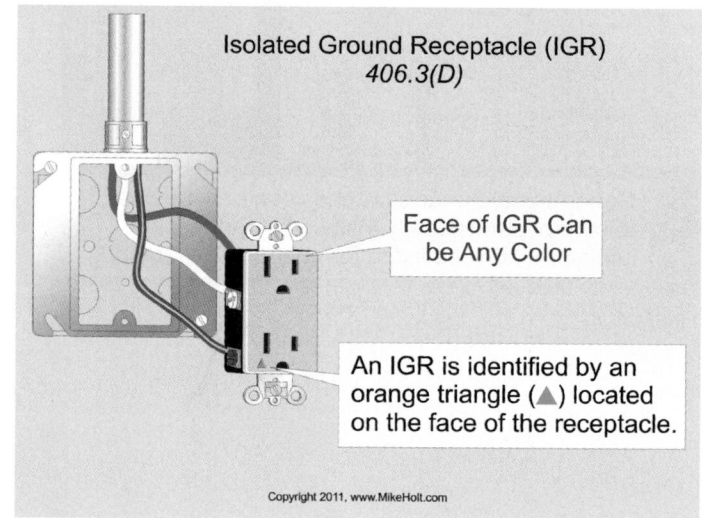

Isolated Ground Receptacle (IGR)
406.3(D)

Face of IGR Can be Any Color

An IGR is identified by an orange triangle (▲) located on the face of the receptacle.

Copyright 2011, www.MikeHolt.com

Figure 406–1

(2) Receptacles having insulated grounding terminals (isolated ground receptacles) installed in nonmetallic boxes must be covered with a nonmetallic faceplate, because a metal faceplate secured to an isolated ground receptacle isn't connected to an equipment grounding conductor. This connection is usually made through the yoke of the receptacle, but with isolated ground receptacles the yoke isn't connected to the isolated equipment grounding conductor [250.4(A)(3)]. **Figure 406–3**

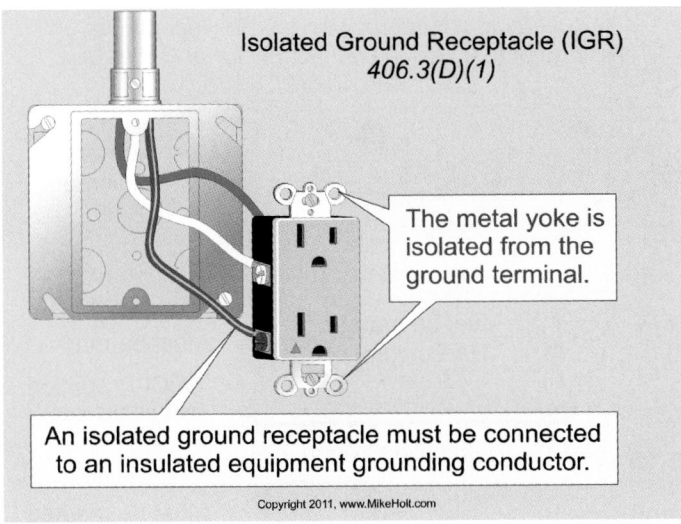

Isolated Ground Receptacle (IGR)
406.3(D)(1)

The metal yoke is isolated from the ground terminal.

An isolated ground receptacle must be connected to an insulated equipment grounding conductor.

Copyright 2011, www.MikeHolt.com

Figure 406–2

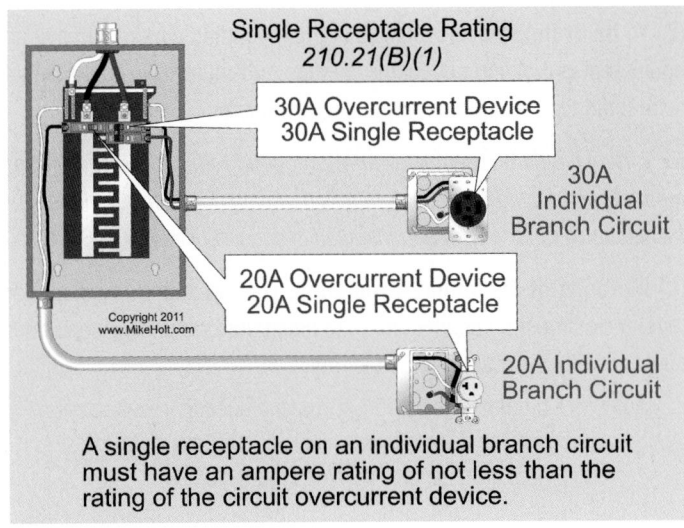

Single Receptacle Rating
210.21(B)(1)

30A Overcurrent Device
30A Single Receptacle

30A Individual Branch Circuit

20A Overcurrent Device
20A Single Receptacle

Copyright 2011
www.MikeHolt.com

20A Individual Branch Circuit

A single receptacle on an individual branch circuit must have an ampere rating of not less than the rating of the circuit overcurrent device.

Figure 406–4

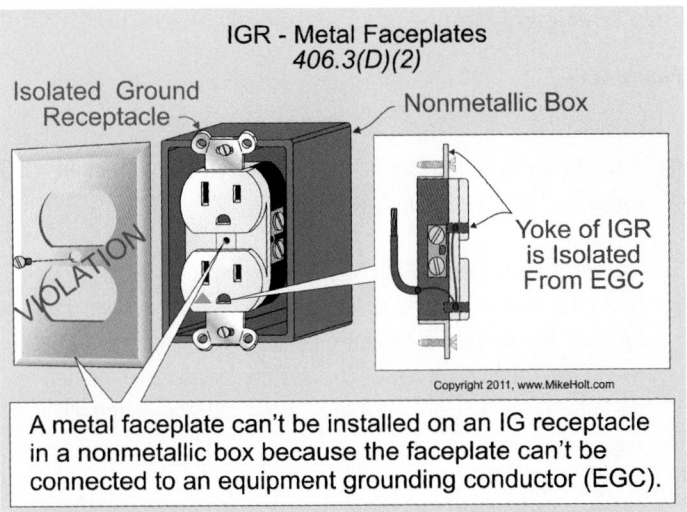

IGR - Metal Faceplates
406.3(D)(2)

Isolated Ground Receptacle

Nonmetallic Box

VIOLATION

Yoke of IGR is Isolated From EGC

Copyright 2011, www.MikeHolt.com

A metal faceplate can't be installed on an IG receptacle in a nonmetallic box because the faceplate can't be connected to an equipment grounding conductor (EGC).

Figure 406–3

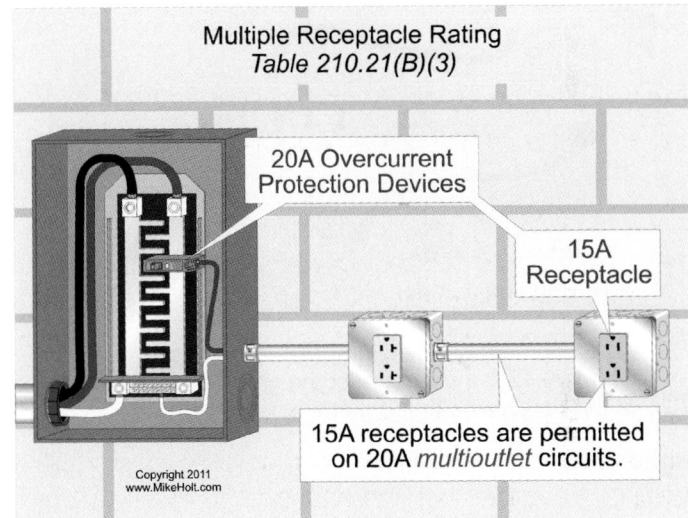

Multiple Receptacle Rating
Table 210.21(B)(3)

20A Overcurrent Protection Devices

15A Receptacle

15A receptacles are permitted on 20A *multioutlet* circuits.

Copyright 2011
www.MikeHolt.com

Figure 406–5

406.4 General Installation Requirements.

(A) Grounding Type. Receptacles installed on 15A and 20A branch circuits must be of the grounding type. Single receptacles must have an ampere rating not less than the rating of the branch circuit [210.21(B)(1)], and multioutlet receptacles (duplex receptacles) must have a rating in accordance with Table 210.21(B)(3). **Figures 406–4 and 406–5**

Table 210.21(B)(3) Receptacle Ratings	
Circuit Rating	Receptacle Rating
15A	15A
20A	15A or 20A
30A	30A
40A	40A or 50A
50A	50A

Ex: Nongrounding-type receptacles are permitted for replacement in an existing outlet box if no equipment grounding conductor exists in the outlet box, in accordance with 406.5(D).

(B) To be Grounded. Receptacles of the grounding type must have an equipment grounding conductor contact, and must have that contact connected to an equipment grounding conductor.

Ex 2: Replacement receptacles aren't required to have their grounding contacts connected to an equipment grounding conductor if the receptacles are GFCI protected and installed in accordance with 406.4(D).

(C) Methods of Equipment Grounding. The grounding terminals for receptacles must be connected to an equipment grounding conductor supplied with the branch-circuit wiring.

Author's Comment: See 250.146 for the specific requirements on connecting the grounding terminals of receptacles to the circuit equipment grounding conductor. **Figure 406–6**

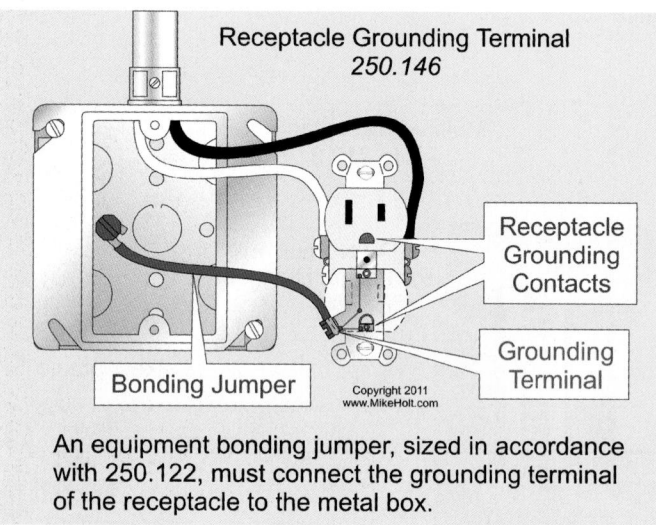

Receptacle Grounding Terminal
250.146

Receptacle Grounding Contacts

Bonding Jumper

Grounding Terminal

Copyright 2011
www.MikeHolt.com

An equipment bonding jumper, sized in accordance with 250.122, must connect the grounding terminal of the receptacle to the metal box.

Figure 406–6

(D) Receptacle Replacement.

(1) Grounding-Type Receptacles. If an equipment grounding conductor exists, grounding-type receptacles must replace nongrounding-type receptacles, and the receptacle's grounding terminal must be connected to an equipment grounding conductor in accordance with 406.4(C).

(2) Nongrounding-Type Receptacles. If no equipment grounding conductor exists in the outlet box for the receptacle, such as old 2-wire Type NM cable without an equipment grounding conductor, existing nongrounding-type receptacles can be replaced in accordance with (a), (b), or (c): **Figure 406–7**

(a) Another nongrounding-type receptacle.

(b) A GFCI-type receptacle marked "No Equipment Ground."

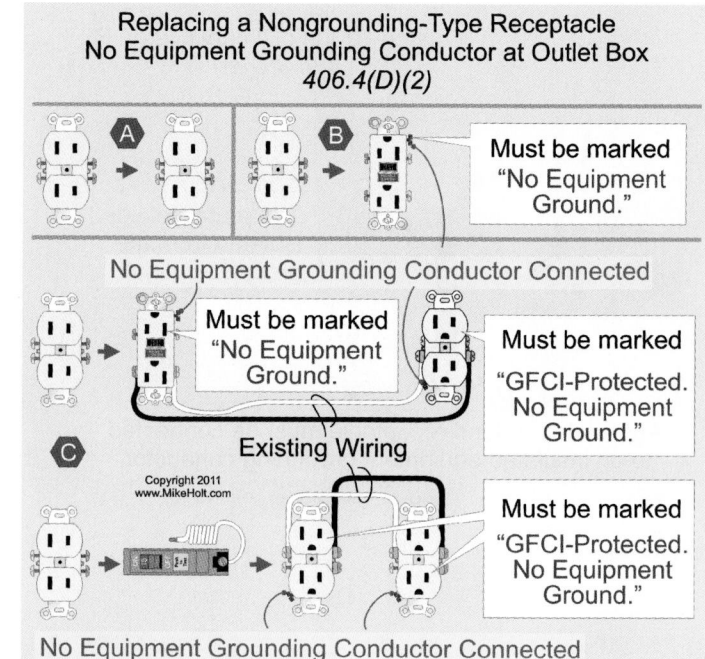

Replacing a Nongrounding-Type Receptacle
No Equipment Grounding Conductor at Outlet Box
406.4(D)(2)

Must be marked "No Equipment Ground."

No Equipment Grounding Conductor Connected

Must be marked "No Equipment Ground."

Must be marked "GFCI-Protected. No Equipment Ground."

Existing Wiring

Copyright 2011
www.MikeHolt.com

Must be marked "GFCI-Protected. No Equipment Ground."

No Equipment Grounding Conductor Connected

Figure 406–7

(c) A grounding-type receptacle, if GFCI protected and marked "GFCI Protected" and "No Equipment Ground."

Author's Comment: GFCI protection functions properly on a 2-wire circuit without an equipment grounding conductor because the circuit equipment grounding conductor serves no role in the operation of the GFCI-protection device. See the definition of "Ground-Fault Circuit Interrupter" for more information. **Figure 406–8**

⚠ **CAUTION:** *The permission to replace nongrounding-type receptacles with GFCI-protected grounding-type receptacles doesn't apply to new receptacle outlets that extend from an existing outlet box that's not connected to an equipment grounding conductor. Once you add a receptacle outlet (branch-circuit extension), the receptacle must be of the grounding type and it must have its grounding terminal connected to an equipment grounding conductor of a type recognized in 250.118, in accordance with 250.130(C).* **Figure 406–9**

(3) GFCI Protection Required. When existing receptacles are replaced in locations where GFCI protection is currently required, the replacement receptacles must be GFCI protected. This includes the replacement of receptacles in dwelling unit bathrooms, garages, outdoors, crawl spaces, unfinished basements, kitchen countertops, rooftops, or within 6 ft of laundry, utility, and wet bar sinks.

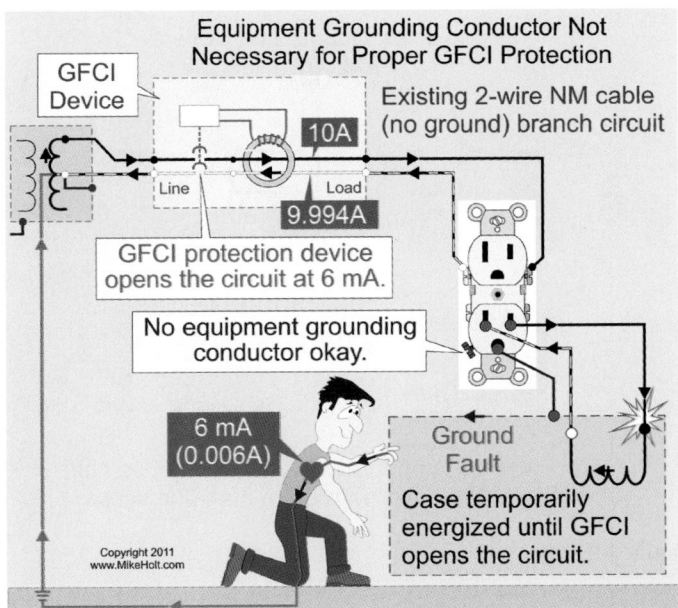

Figure 406–8

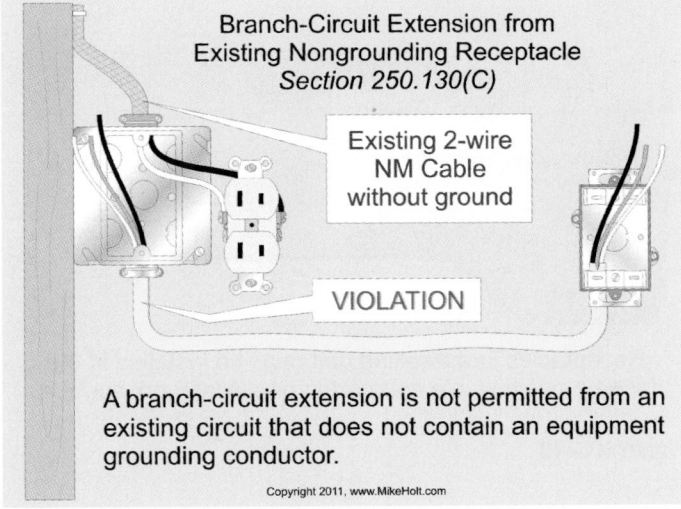

Figure 406–9

Author's Comment: See 210.8 in this textbook for specific GFCI-protection requirements.

(4) Arc-Fault Circuit Interrupters. Effective January 1, 2014, where a receptacle outlet is supplied by a branch circuit that requires arc-fault circuit-interrupter protection [210.12(A)], a replacement receptacle at this outlet must be one of the following:

(1) A listed (receptacle) outlet branch-circuit type arc-fault circuit-interrupter receptacle.

(2) A receptacle protected by a listed (receptacle) outlet branch-circuit type arc-fault circuit-interrupter type receptacle.

(3) A receptacle protected by a listed combination type arc-fault circuit interrupter type circuit breaker.

(5) Tamper-Resistant Receptacles. Listed tamper-resistant receptacles must be provided where replacements are made at receptacle outlets that are required to be tamper resistant in accordance with 406.12 for dwelling units, 406.13 for guest rooms and guest suites, and 406.14 for child care facilities.

(6) Weather-Resistant Receptacles. Weather-resistant receptacles must be provided where replacements are made at receptacle outlets that are required to be so protected in accordance with 406.9(A) and (B).

406.5 Receptacle Mounting. Receptacles must be installed in outlet boxes designed for the purpose.

Author's Comment: The position of the ground terminal of a receptacle isn't specified in the *NEC*. The ground terminal can be up, down, or to the side. Proposals to specify the mounting position of the ground terminal have been rejected through many Code cycles. For more information on this subject, visit www.MikeHolt.com. **Figure 406–10**

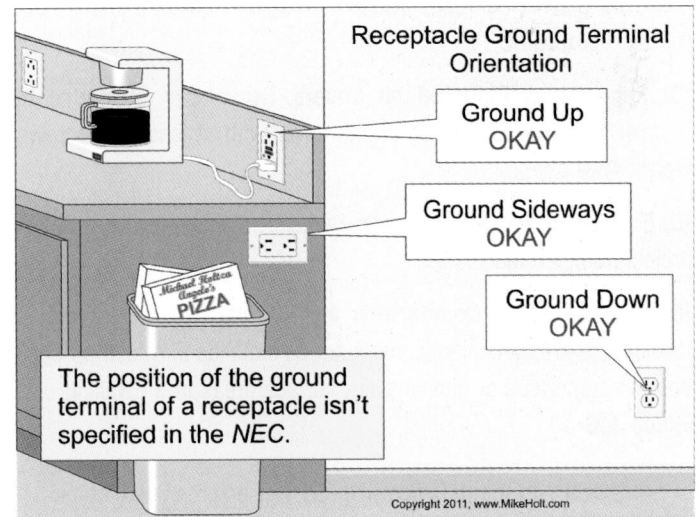

Figure 406–10

(A) Boxes Set Back. Receptacles in outlet boxes that are set back from the finished surface, as permitted by 314.20, must be installed so the mounting yoke of the receptacle is held rigidly to the finished surface or outlet box. **Figure 406–11**

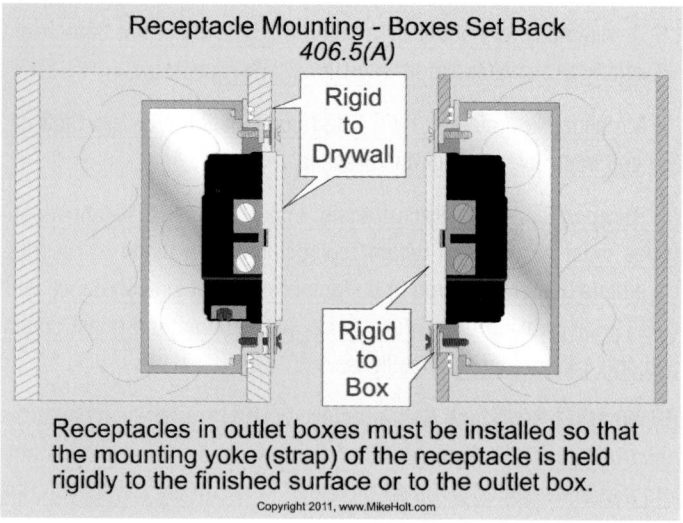

Receptacles in outlet boxes must be installed so that the mounting yoke (strap) of the receptacle is held rigidly to the finished surface or to the outlet box.

Figure 406–11

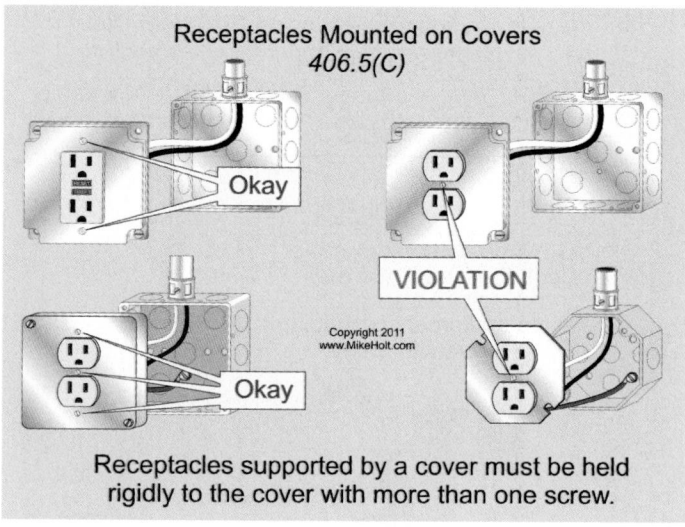

Receptacles supported by a cover must be held rigidly to the cover with more than one screw.

Figure 406–12

Author's Comment: In walls or ceilings of noncombustible material, such as drywall, outlet boxes must not be set back more than ¼ in. from the finished surface. In walls or ceilings of combustible material, outlet boxes must be flush with the finished surface [314.20]. There must not be any gaps more than ⅛ in. at the edge of the outlet box [314.21].

(B) Boxes Flush with the Surface. Receptacles mounted in outlet boxes that are flush with the finished surface must be installed so the mounting yoke of the receptacle is held rigidly against the outlet box or raised box cover.

(C) Receptacles Mounted on Covers. Receptacles supported by a cover must be held rigidly to the cover with at least two screws. Figure 406–12

(D) Position of Receptacle Faces. Receptacles must be flush with, or project from, the faceplates.

(E) Receptacles in Countertops and Similar Work Surfaces in Dwelling Units. Receptacles must not be installed in a face-up position in countertops or similar work surface areas in a dwelling unit. Figure 406–13

Author's Comment: Receptacle outlet assemblies listed for the application can be installed in dwelling unit kitchen and bathroom countertops [210.52(C)(5) and 210.52(D)].

(G) Voltage Between Devices. Receptacles must not be in enclosures with other switches or receptacles if the voltage between the devices exceeds 300V, unless the devices are installed in enclosures

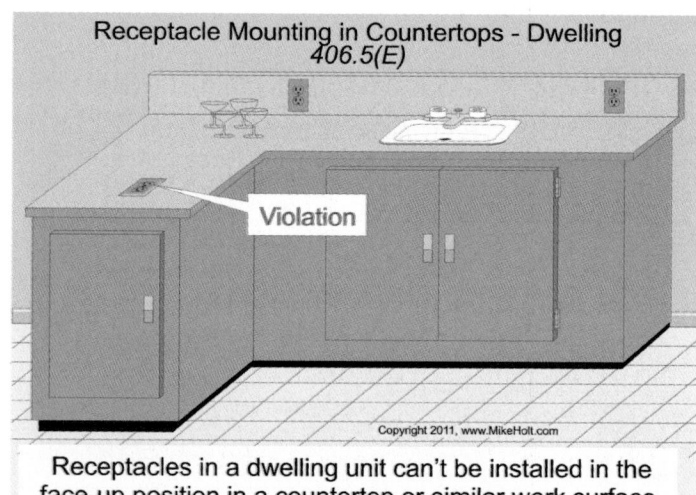

Receptacles in a dwelling unit can't be installed in the face-up position in a countertop or similar work surface.

Figure 406–13

equipped with barriers identified for the purpose, that are securely installed between adjacent devices. Figure 406–14

406.6 Receptacle Faceplates. Faceplates for receptacles must completely cover the outlet openings.

(B) Grounding. Metal faceplates for receptacles must be connected to the circuit equipment grounding conductor.

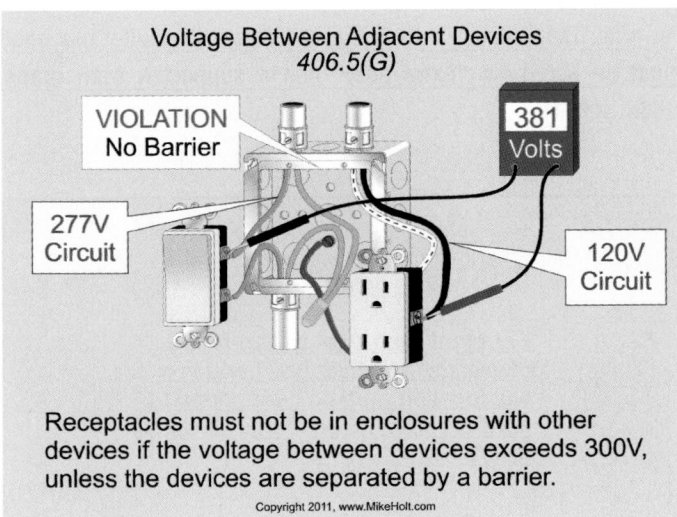

Figure 406–14

Author's Comment: The *NEC* doesn't specify how this is accomplished, but 517.13(B) Ex 1 for health care facilities permits the metal mounting screw(s) securing the faceplate to a metal outlet box or wiring device to be suitable for this purpose. **Figure 406–15**

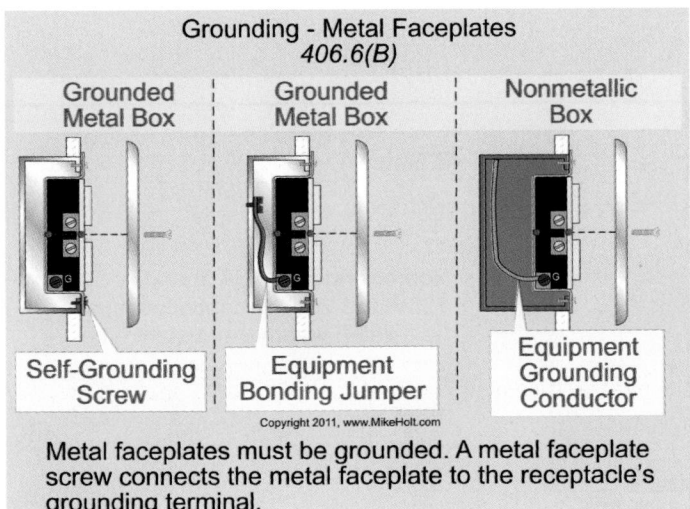

Figure 406–15

406.7 Attachment Plugs, Cord Connectors, and Flanged Surface Devices.
Attachment plugs and cord connectors must be listed for the purpose and marked with the manufacturer's name or identification and voltage and ampere ratings.

(A) Exposed Live Parts. Attachment plugs, cord connectors, and flanged surface devices must have no exposed current-carrying parts, except the prongs, blades, or pins.

(B) No Energized Parts. Attachment plugs must be installed so their prongs, blades, or pins aren't energized unless inserted into an energized receptacle or cord connector. **Figure 406–16**

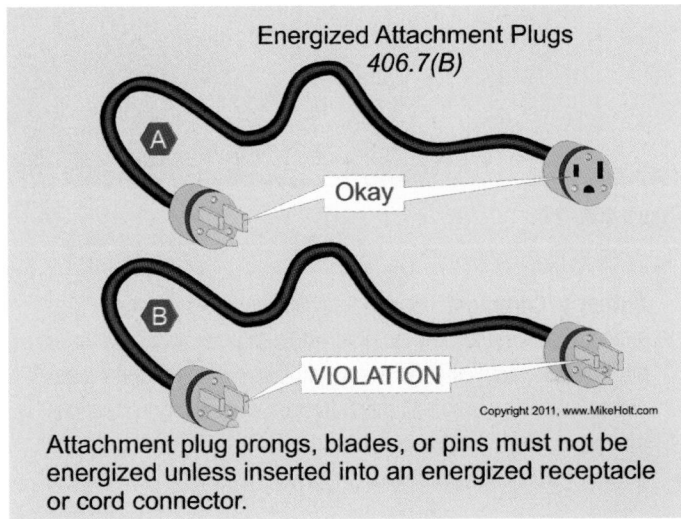

Figure 406–16

(D) Flanged Surface Inlet. A flanged surface inlet must be installed so the prongs, blades, or pins aren't energized unless an energized cord connector is inserted into it.

> **Author's Comment:** The use of flanged "inlets," such as those on computers, transfer switches, and so forth, for detachable power cords is increasing.

406.9 Receptacles in Damp or Wet Locations.

(A) Damp Locations. Receptacles installed in a damp location must be installed in an enclosure that's weatherproof when an attachment plug cap isn't inserted, and the receptacle cover is closed, or an enclosure that's weatherproof when an attachment plug is inserted. All nonlocking 15A and 20A, 125V and 250V receptacles in a damp location must be listed as weather resistant. **Figure 406–17**

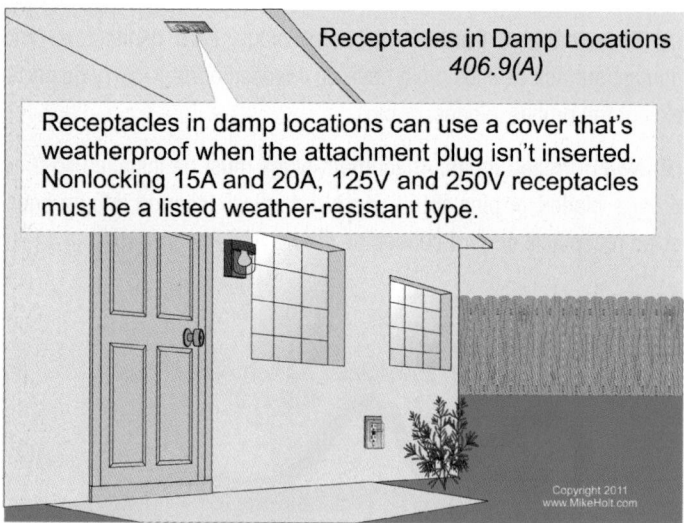

Figure 406–17

Author's Comment: Damp locations include locations protected from weather and not subject to saturation with water or other liquids, as well as locations partially protected under canopies, marquees, roofed open porches, and interior locations that are subject to moderate degrees of moisture, such as some basements, barns, and cold-storage warehouses [Article 100].

(B) Wet Locations.

(1) 15A and 20A Receptacles. All 15A and 20A receptacles installed in a wet location must be within an enclosure that's weatherproof when an attachment plug is inserted. **Figure 406–18**

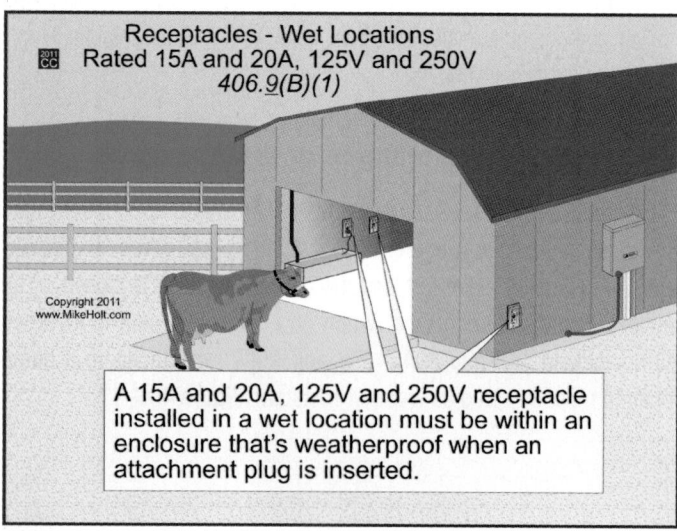

Figure 406–18

For other than one- or two-family dwellings, the outlet box hood must be listed for "extra-duty" use if supported from grade. **Figure 406–19**

Figure 406–19

All nonlocking type 15A and 20A, 125V and 250V receptacles in a wet location must be listed as weather resistant. **Figure 406–20**

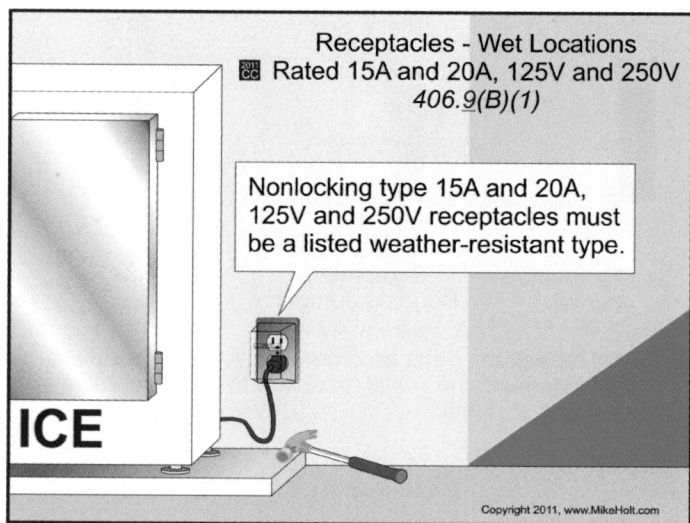

Figure 406–20

Author's Comment: Exposed plastic surface material of weather-resistant receptacles must have UV resistance to ensure that deterioration from sunlight doesn't take place, or that it's minimal. In testing, receptacles are subjected to temperature cycling from very cold to very warm conditions, and then subjected to additional dielectric testing. The rapid transition from the cold to warm temperatures will change the relative humidity and moisture content on the device, and the dielectric test ensures that this won't create a breakdown of the insulation properties.

Ex: Receptacles rated 15A and 20A that are subjected to routine high-pressure washing spray may have an enclosure that's weatherproof when the attachment plug is removed.

Author's Comment: A wet location is an area subject to saturation with water, as well as unprotected locations that are exposed to weather [Article 100].

(2) Other Receptacles. Receptacles rated 30A or more installed in a wet location must comply with (a) or (b).

(a) Wet Location Covers. A receptacle that's in a wet location, where the load isn't attended while in use, must be installed in an enclosure that's weatherproof when an attachment plug is inserted.

(b) Damp Location Covers. A receptacle installed in a wet location that will only be used while someone is in close proximity to it, such as one used with portable tools, can have an enclosure that's weatherproof when the attachment plug is removed and the cover is closed.

(C) Bathtub and Shower Space. Receptacles must not be installed within or directly over a bathtub or shower stall. **Figure 406–21**

(E) Flush Mounting with Faceplate. The enclosure for a receptacle installed in an outlet box that's flush-mounted on a finished surface must be made weatherproof by a weatherproof faceplate that provides a watertight connection between the plate and the finished surface.

406.11 Connecting Receptacle Grounding Terminal to Equipment Grounding Conductor.
The grounding terminal of receptacles must be connected to an equipment grounding conductor in accordance with 250.146.

406.12 Tamper-Resistant Receptacles in Dwelling Units.
All nonlocking type 15A and 20A, 125V receptacles in the following areas of a dwelling unit [210.52] must be listed as tamper resistant.

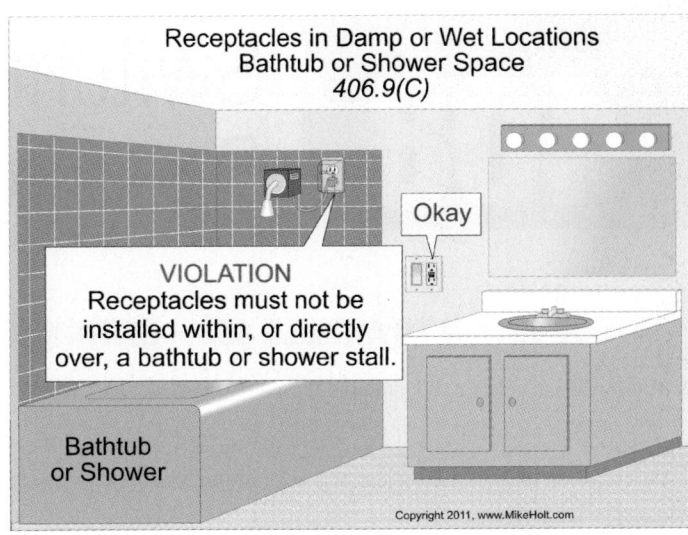

Figure 406–21

- Wall Space—210.52(A)
- Small-Appliance Circuit—210.52(B)
- Countertop Space—210.52(C)
- Bathroom Area—210.52(D)
- Outdoors—210.52(E)
- Laundry Area—210.52(F)
- Garage and Outbuildings—210.52(G)
- Hallways—210.52(H)

Ex: Receptacles in the following locations aren't required to be tamper-resistant:

(1) Receptacles located more than 5½ ft above the floor.

(2) Receptacles that are part of a luminaire or appliance.

(3) A receptacle located within dedicated space for an appliance that in normal use isn't easily moved from one place to another.

(4) Nongrounding receptacles used for replacements as permitted in 406.4(D)(2)(a).

406.13 Tamper-Resistant Receptacles in Guest Rooms and Guest Suites.
Nonlocking type 15A and 20A, 125V receptacles in guest rooms and guest suites must be listed as tamper resistant.

406.14 Tamper-Resistant Receptacles in Child Care Facilities.
Nonlocking type 15A and 20A, 125V receptacles in child care facilities must be listed as tamper resistant.

ARTICLE 408

Switchboards and Panelboards

INTRODUCTION TO ARTICLE 408—SWITCHBOARDS AND PANELBOARDS

Article 408 covers the specific requirements for switchboards and panelboards that control power and lighting circuits. Some key points to remember:

- One objective of Article 408 is that the installation prevents contact between current-carrying conductors and people or equipment.
- The circuit directory of a panelboard must clearly identify the purpose or use of each circuit that originates in the panelboard.
- You must understand the detailed grounding and overcurrent protection requirements for panelboards.

PART I. GENERAL

408.1 Scope. Article 408 covers the specific requirements for switchboards, and panelboards that control power and lighting circuits. **Figure 408–1**

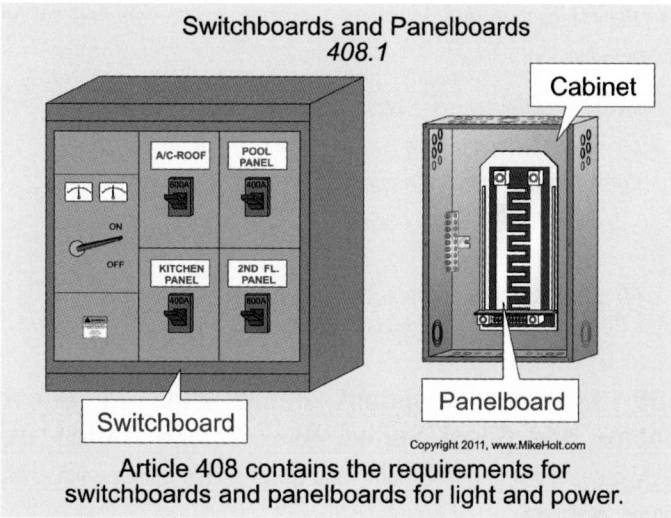

Figure 408–1

Author's Comment: For the purposes of this textbook, we'll only cover the requirements for panelboards.

408.3 Arrangement of Busbars and Conductors.

(D) Terminals. In switchboards and panelboards, terminals for neutral and equipment grounding conductors must be located so it's not necessary to reach beyond uninsulated live parts in order to make connections.

(E) Panelboard Phase Arrangement. Panelboards supplied by a 4-wire, delta-connected, three-phase (high-leg) system must have the high-leg conductor (which operates at 208V to ground) terminate to the "B" phase of the panelboard. **Figure 408–2**

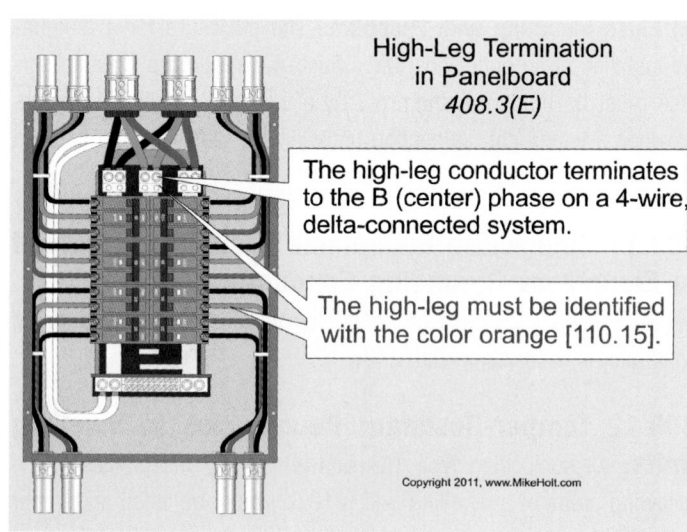

Figure 408–2

Ex: The high-leg conductor can terminate to the "C" phase when the meter is located in the same section of a switchboard or panelboard.

Note: Orange identification, or some other effective means, is required for the high-leg conductor [110.15 and 230.56]. **Figure 408–3**

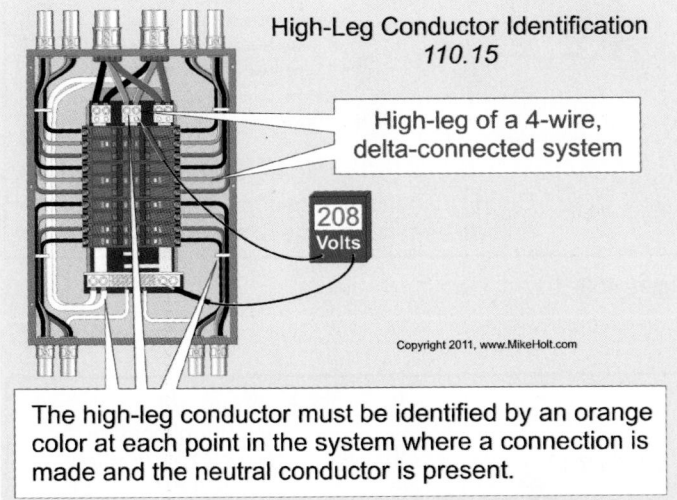

Figure 408–3

WARNING: *The ANSI standard for meter equipment requires the high-leg conductor (208V to neutral) to terminate on the "C" (right) phase of the meter socket enclosure. This is because the demand meter needs 120V and it gets it from the "B" phase.* **Figure 408–4**

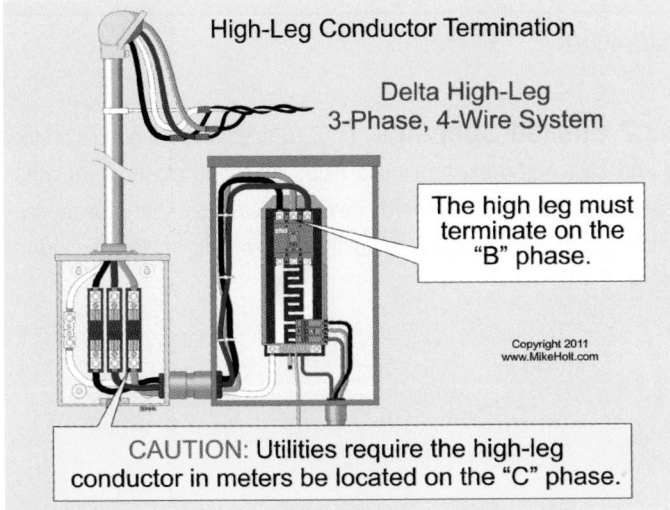

Figure 408–4

WARNING: *When replacing equipment in existing facilities that contain a high-leg conductor, use care to ensure that the high-leg conductor is replaced in the original location. Prior to 1975, the high-leg conductor was required to terminate on the "C" phase of panelboards and switchboards. Failure to re-terminate the high leg in accordance with the existing installation can result in 120V circuits being inadvertently connected to the 208V high leg, with disastrous results.*

(F) Switchboard or Panelboard Identification.

(1) High-Leg Identification. A switchboard or panelboard containing a 4-wire, delta-connected system where the midpoint of one phase winding is grounded shall be legibly and permanently field-marked as follows: **Figure 408–5**

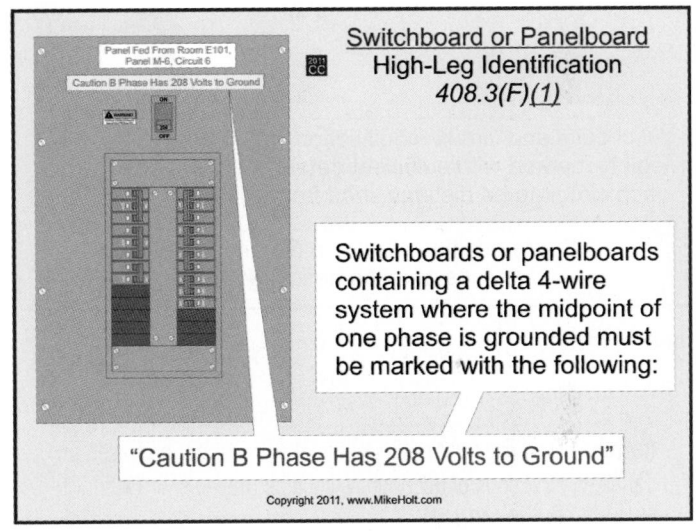

Figure 408–5

"CAUTION _____ PHASE HAS _____ VOLTS TO GROUND"

(2) Ungrounded Systems. A switchboard or panelboard containing an ungrounded electrical system as permitted in 250.21 shall be legibly and permanently field-marked as follows:

"CAUTION UNGROUNDED SYSTEM OPERATING AT _____ VOLTS BETWEEN CONDUCTORS"

408.4 Field Identification.

(A) Circuit Directory or Circuit Identification. All circuits, and circuit modifications, must be legibly identified as to their clear, evident, and specific purpose. Spare positions that contain unused overcurrent devices must also be identified. Identification must include sufficient detail to allow each circuit to be distinguished from all others, and the identification must be on a circuit directory located on the face or inside of the door of the panelboard. See 110.22. **Figure 408–6**

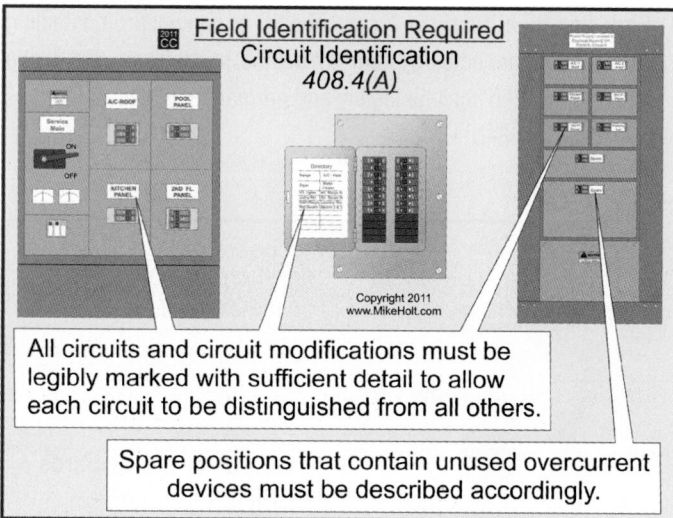

Figure 408–6

Author's Comment: Circuit identification must not be based on transient conditions of occupancy, such as Steven's, or Brittney's bedroom. **Figure 408–7**

(B) Source of Supply. All switchboards and panelboards supplied by a feeder in other than one- or two-family dwellings must be marked as to the device or equipment where the power supply originates. **Figure 408–8**

408.5 Clearance for Conductors Entering Bus Enclosures.

If raceways enter a switchboard, floor-standing panelboard, or similar enclosure, the raceways, including end fittings, must not rise more than 3 in. above the bottom of the enclosure.

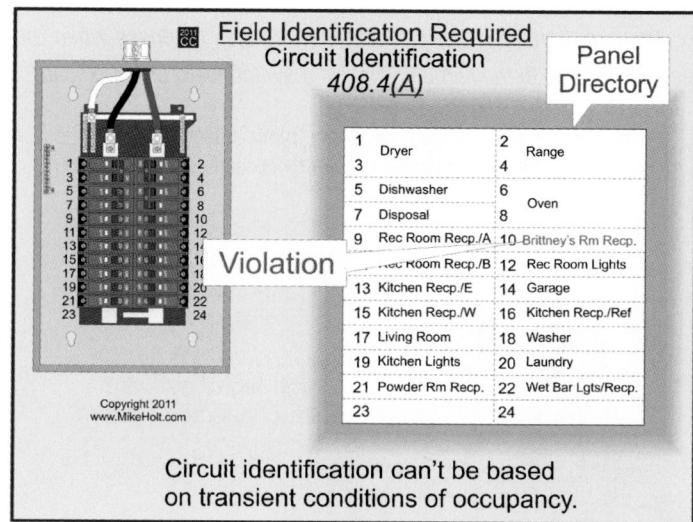

Figure 408–7

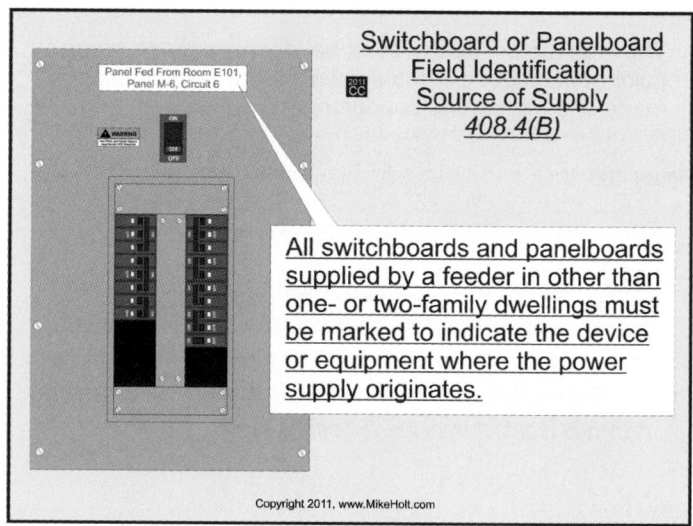

Figure 408–8

408.7 Unused Openings.

Unused openings for circuit breakers and switches must be closed using identified closures, or other means approved by the authority having jurisdiction, that provide protection substantially equivalent to the wall of the enclosure. **Figure 408–9**

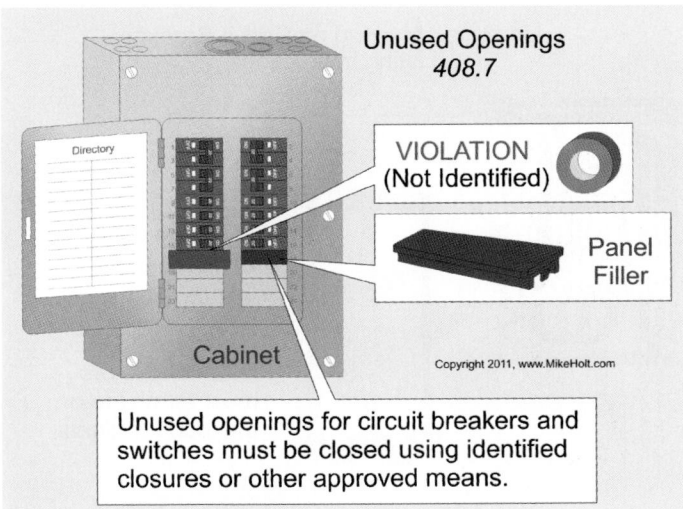

Unused Openings
408.7

VIOLATION
(Not Identified)

Panel Filler

Directory

Cabinet

Copyright 2011, www.MikeHolt.com

Unused openings for circuit breakers and switches must be closed using identified closures or other approved means.

Figure 408–9

PART III. PANELBOARDS

408.36 Overcurrent Protection of Panelboards.

Each panelboard must be provided with overcurrent protection located within, or at any point on the supply side of, the panelboard. The overcurrent device must have a rating not greater than that of the panelboard, and it can be located within or on the supply side of the panelboard. **Figure 408–10**

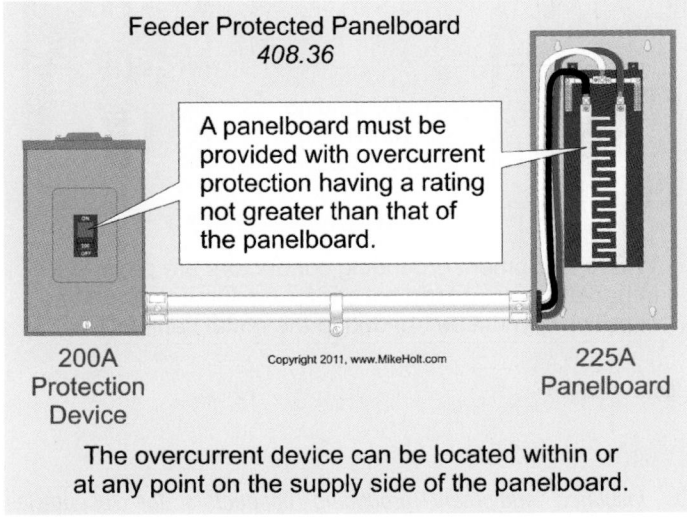

Feeder Protected Panelboard
408.36

A panelboard must be provided with overcurrent protection having a rating not greater than that of the panelboard.

200A Protection Device

Copyright 2011, www.MikeHolt.com

225A Panelboard

The overcurrent device can be located within or at any point on the supply side of the panelboard.

Figure 408–10

Ex 1: Individual overcurrent protection isn't required for panelboards used as service equipment in accordance with 230.71.

(B) Panelboards Supplied Through a Transformer. When a panelboard is supplied from a transformer, as permitted in 240.21(C), the overcurrent protection for the panelboard must be on the secondary side of the transformer. The required overcurrent protection can be in a separate enclosure ahead of the panelboard, or it can be in the panelboard. **Figure 408–11**

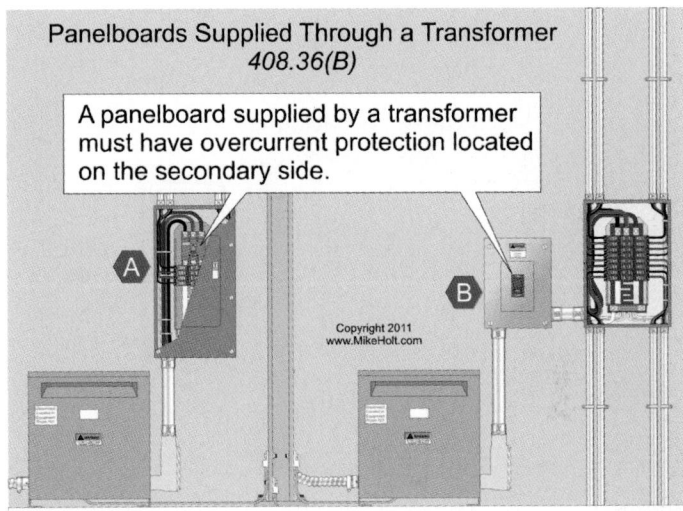

Panelboards Supplied Through a Transformer
408.36(B)

A panelboard supplied by a transformer must have overcurrent protection located on the secondary side.

A

B

Copyright 2011
www.MikeHolt.com

Figure 408–11

(D) Back-Fed Devices. Plug-in circuit breakers that are back-fed from field-installed conductors must be secured in place by an additional fastener that requires other than a pull to release the breaker from the panelboard. **Figure 408–12**

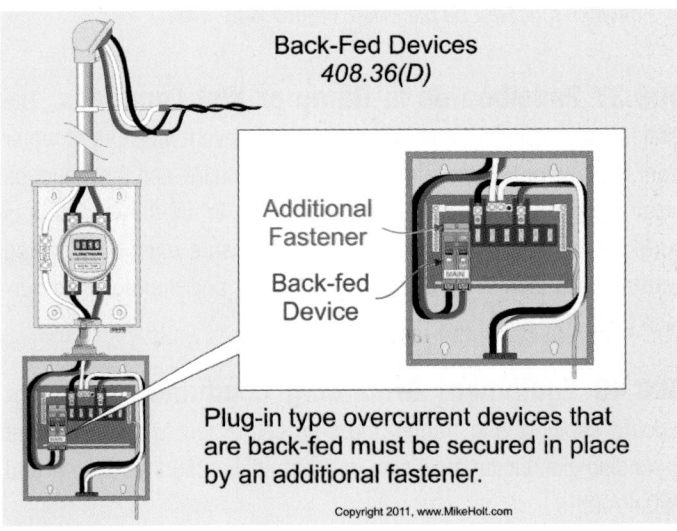

Back-Fed Devices
408.36(D)

Additional Fastener

Back-fed Device

Plug-in type overcurrent devices that are back-fed must be secured in place by an additional fastener.

Copyright 2011, www.MikeHolt.com

Figure 408–12

Author's Comments:

- The purpose of the breaker fastener is to prevent the circuit breaker from being accidentally removed from the panelboard while energized, thereby exposing someone to dangerous voltage.

- For photovoltaic systems, conductors from the PV ac inverter is permitted to backfed dedicated circuit breakers that aren't marked "Line" and "Load" [705.12(D)(5)]. **Figure 408–13**

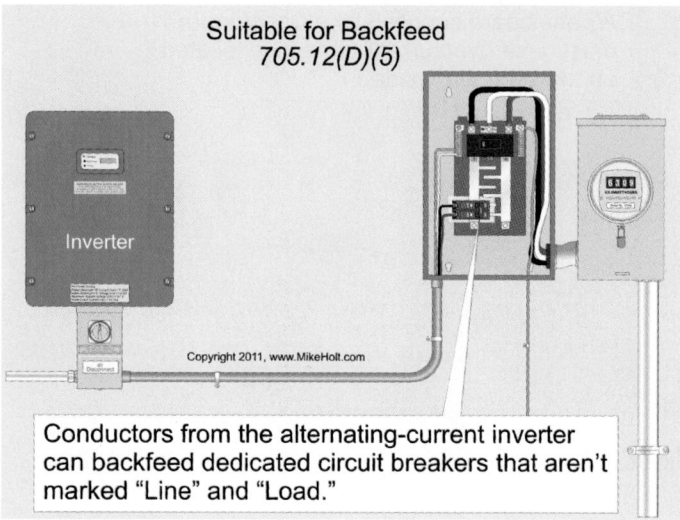

Figure 408–13

> ⚠ **CAUTION:** *Circuit breakers marked "Line" and "Load" must be installed in accordance with listing or labeling instructions [110.3(B)]; therefore, these types of devices must not be back-fed.* Figure 408–14

408.37 Panelboards in Damp or Wet Locations. The
enclosures (cabinets) for panelboards must prevent moisture or water from entering or accumulating within the enclosure, and they must be weatherproof when located in a wet location. When the enclosure is surface mounted in a wet location, the enclosure must be mounted with not less than ¼ in. air space between it and the mounting surface [312.2].

408.40 Equipment Grounding Conductor. Metal pan-
elboard cabinets and frames must be connected to an equipment grounding conductor of a type recognized in 250.118 [215.6 and 250.4(A)(3)].

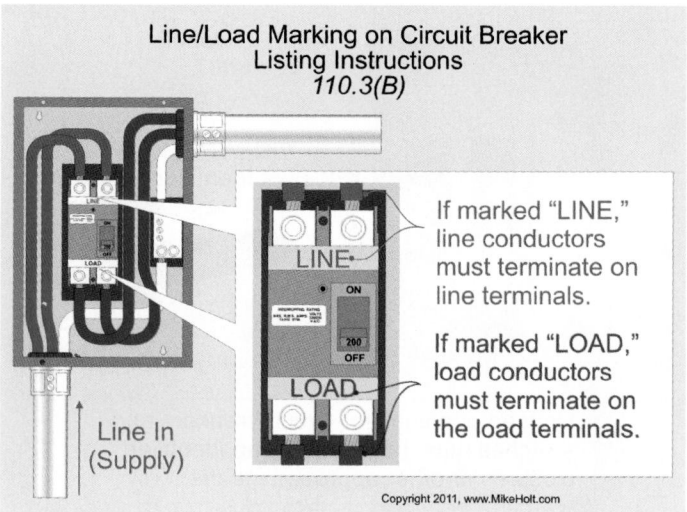

Figure 408–14

If the panelboard cabinet is used with nonmetallic raceways or cables, or where separate equipment grounding conductors are provided, a terminal bar for the circuit equipment grounding conductors must be bonded to the metal cabinet. Figure 408–15

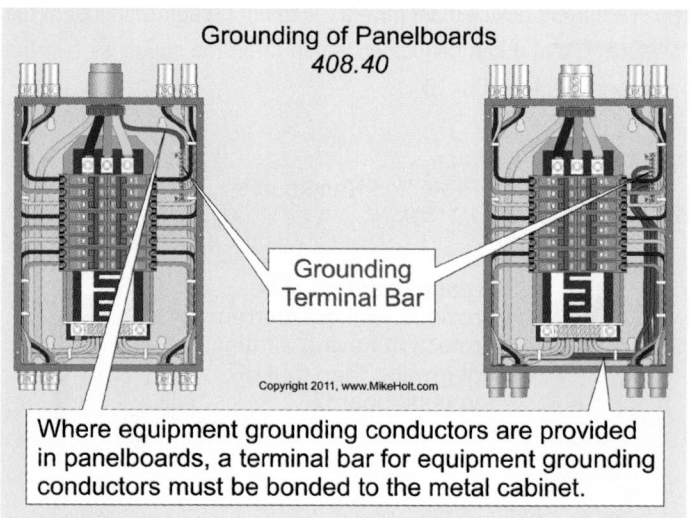

Figure 408–15

Ex: Insulated equipment grounding conductors for receptacles having insulated grounding terminals (isolated ground receptacles) [250.146(D)] can pass through the panelboard without terminating onto the equipment grounding terminal of the panelboard cabinet. Figure 408–16

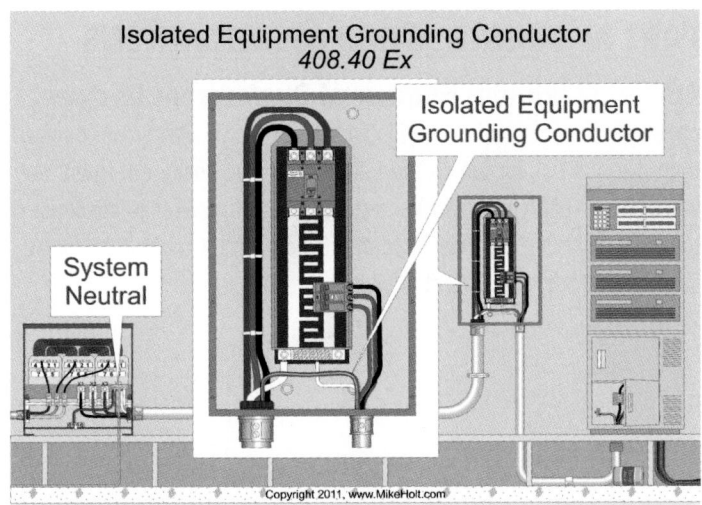

Isolated Equipment Grounding Conductor
408.40 Ex

An isolated equipment grounding conductor can pass through a metal enclosure, but it must terminate to the system neutral.

Figure 408–16

Equipment grounding conductors must not terminate on the neutral terminal bar, and neutral conductors must not terminate on the equipment grounding terminal bar, except as permitted by 250.142 for services and separately derived systems. **Figure 408–17**

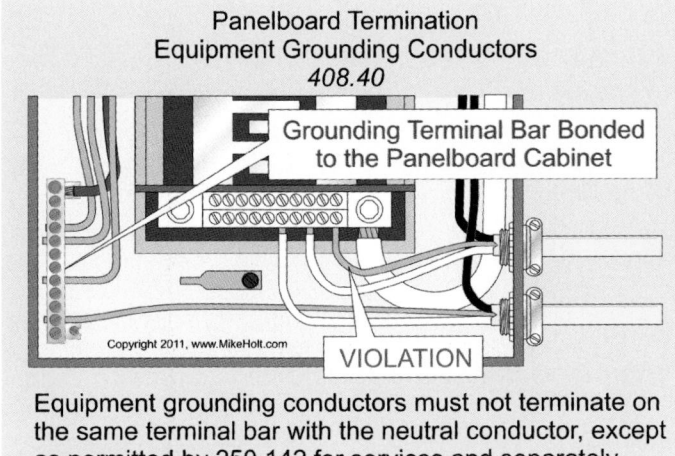

Panelboard Termination
Equipment Grounding Conductors
408.40

Equipment grounding conductors must not terminate on the same terminal bar with the neutral conductor, except as permitted by 250.142 for services and separately derived systems.

Figure 408–17

Author's Comment: See the definition of "Separately Derived System" in Article 100.

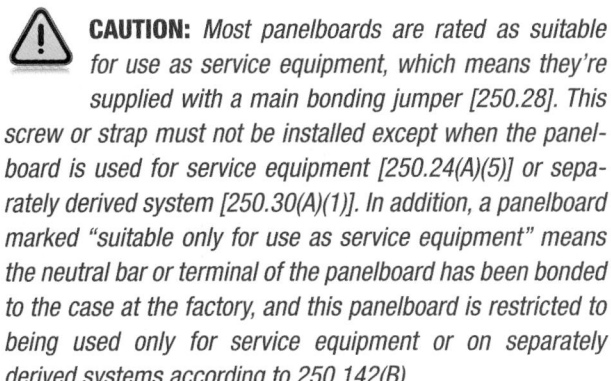

CAUTION: *Most panelboards are rated as suitable for use as service equipment, which means they're supplied with a main bonding jumper [250.28]. This screw or strap must not be installed except when the panelboard is used for service equipment [250.24(A)(5)] or separately derived system [250.30(A)(1)]. In addition, a panelboard marked "suitable only for use as service equipment" means the neutral bar or terminal of the panelboard has been bonded to the case at the factory, and this panelboard is restricted to being used only for service equipment or on separately derived systems according to 250.142(B).*

408.41 Neutral Conductor Terminations. Each neutral conductor within a panelboard must terminate to an individual terminal. **Figure 408–18**

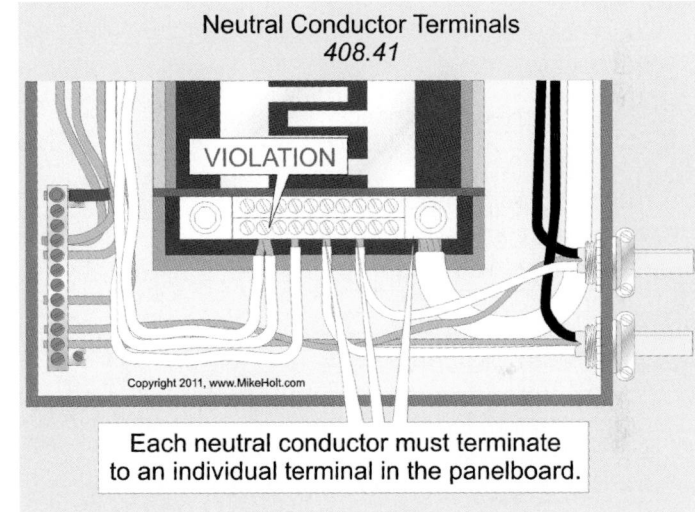

Neutral Conductor Terminals
408.41

Each neutral conductor must terminate to an individual terminal in the panelboard.

Figure 408–18

Author's Comment: If two neutral conductors are connected to the same terminal, and someone removes one of them, the other neutral conductor might unintentionally be removed as well. If that happens to the neutral conductor of a multiwire circuit, it can result in excessive line-to-neutral voltage for one of the circuits, as well as undervoltage for the other circuit. See 300.13(B) of this textbook for details. **Figure 408–19**

This requirement doesn't apply to equipment grounding conductors, because the voltage of a circuit isn't affected if an equipment grounding conductor is accidentally removed. **Figure 408–20**

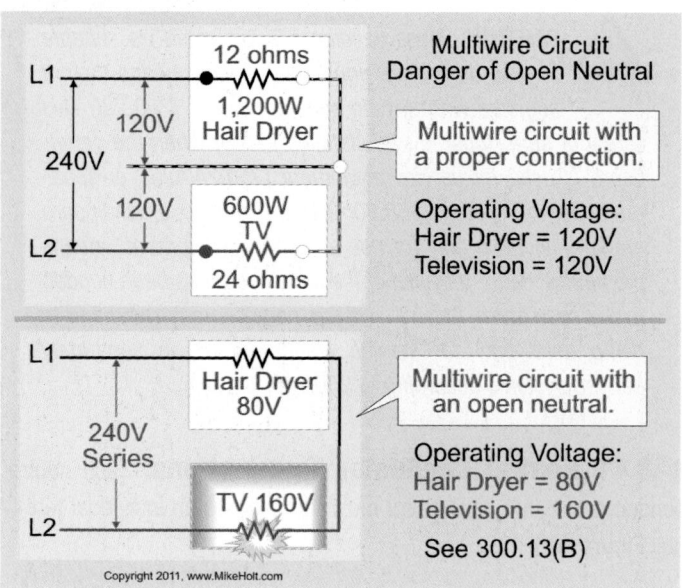

Figure 408–19

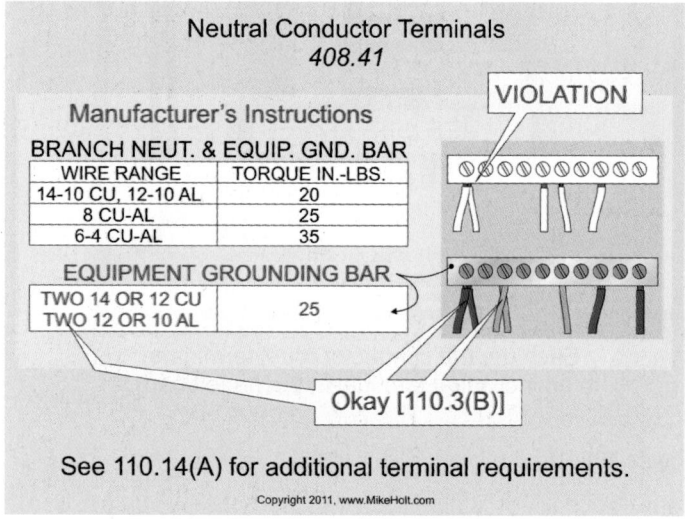

Figure 408–20

PART IV. CONSTRUCTION SPECIFICATIONS

408.54 Maximum Number of Overcurrent Devices. A panelboard must prevent the installation of more overcurrent devices than the number for which the panelboard was designed, rated, and listed. When applying this rule, a 2-pole circuit breaker is considered to be two overcurrent devices, and a 3-pole circuit breaker is considered to be three overcurrent devices.

Luminaires, Lampholders, and Lamps

INTRODUCTION TO ARTICLE 410—LUMINAIRES, LAMPHOLDERS, AND LAMPS

This article covers luminaires, lampholders, lamps, decorative lighting products, lighting accessories for temporary seasonal and holiday use, including portable flexible lighting products, and the wiring and equipment of such products and lighting installations. Even though Article 410 is highly detailed, it's broken down into 16 parts. The first five are sequential, and apply to all luminaires, lampholders, and lamps:

- General, Part I
- Location, Part II
- Boxes and Covers, Part III
- Supports, Part IV
- Equipment Grounding Conductors, Part V

This is mostly mechanical information, and it's not hard to follow or absorb. Part VI, Wiring, ends the sequence. The seventh, ninth, and tenth parts provide requirements for manufacturers to follow—use only equipment that conforms to these requirements. Part VIII provides requirements for installing lampholders. The rest of Article 410 addresses specific types of lighting.

Author's Comment: Article 411 addresses "Lighting Systems Operating at 30 Volts or Less."

PART I. GENERAL

410.1 Scope. This article covers luminaires, lampholders, lamps, decorative lighting products, lighting accessories for temporary seasonal and holiday use, portable flexible lighting products, and the wiring and equipment of such products and lighting installations. **Figure 410–1**

> **Author's Comment:** Because of the many types and applications of luminaires, manufacturers' instructions are very important and helpful for proper installation. UL produces a pamphlet called the Luminaire Marking Guide, which provides information for properly installing common types of incandescent, fluorescent, and high-intensity discharge (HID) luminaires.

410.2 Definitions.

Closet Storage Space. Storage space is defined as a volume bounded by the sides and back closet walls, extending from the closet floor vertically to a height of 6 ft or the highest clothes-hanging rod at a horizontal distance of 2 ft from the sides and back of the closet walls.

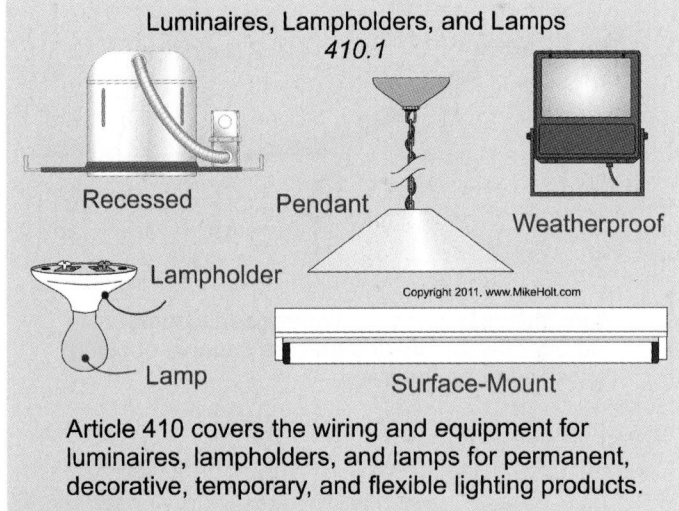

Article 410 covers the wiring and equipment for luminaires, lampholders, and lamps for permanent, decorative, temporary, and flexible lighting products.

Figure 410–1

Storage space continues vertically to the closet ceiling for a distance of 1 ft or the width of the shelf, whichever is greater. **Figure 410–2**

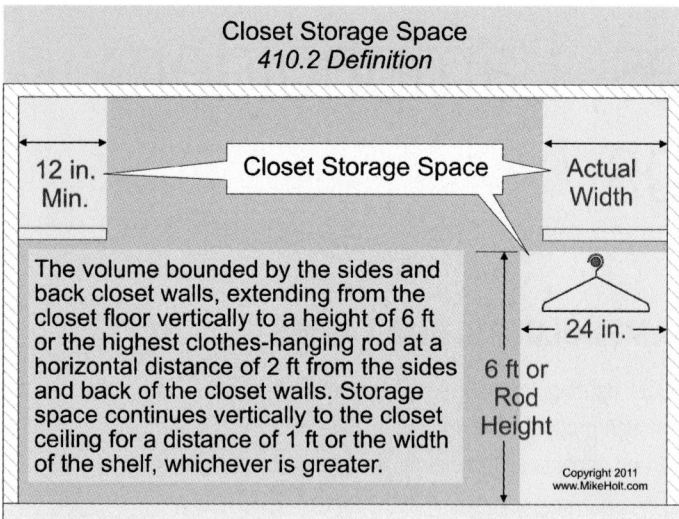

Figure 410–2

Author's Comment: This definition consists of approximately 125 words in one sentence, perhaps the longest sentence in the *Code*. Take a breath and don't get lost when reading it!

Lighting Track. This is a manufactured assembly, designed to support and energize luminaires that can be readily repositioned on the track, and whose length may be altered by the addition or subtraction of sections of track. **Figure 410–3**

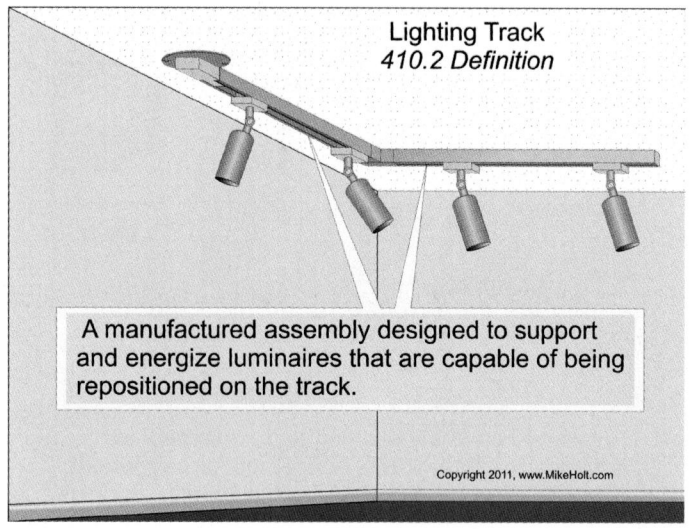

Figure 410–3

410.6 Listing Required. Luminaires and lampholders must be listed.

PART II. LUMINAIRE LOCATIONS

410.10 Luminaires in Specific Locations.

(A) Wet or Damp Locations. Luminaires in wet or damp locations must be installed in a manner that prevents water from accumulating in any part of the luminaire. Luminaires marked "Suitable for Dry Locations Only" must be installed only in a dry location; luminaires marked "Suitable for Damp Locations" can be installed in either a damp or dry location; and luminaires marked "Suitable for Wet Locations" can be installed in a dry, damp, or wet location. **Figure 410–4**

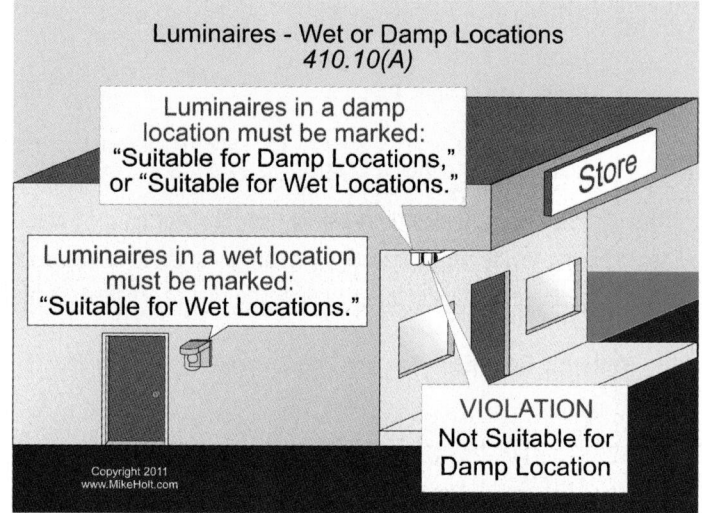

Figure 410–4

Author's Comment: A dry location can be subjected to occasional dampness or wetness. See the definition of "Location, Dry" in Article 100.

(B) Corrosive Locations. Luminaires installed in corrosive locations must be suitable for the location.

(C) In Ducts or Hoods. Luminaires can be installed in commercial cooking hoods if all of the following conditions are met: **Figure 410–5**

(1) The luminaire is identified for use within commercial cooking hoods.

(2) The luminaire is constructed so that all exhaust vapors, grease, oil, or cooking vapors are excluded from the lamp and wiring compartment.

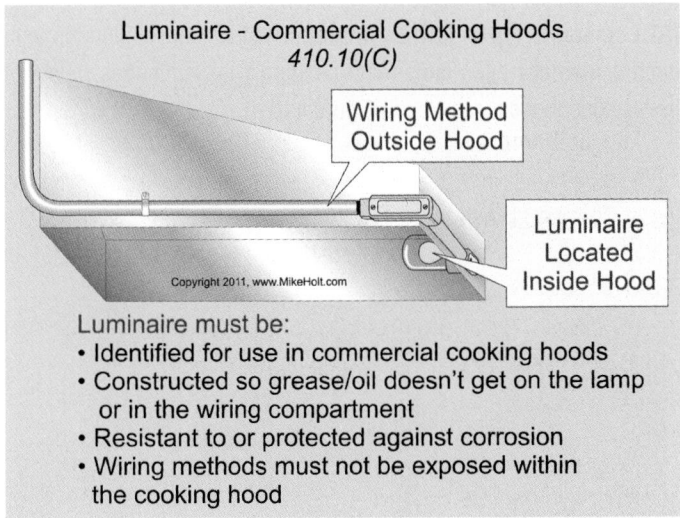

Figure 410–5

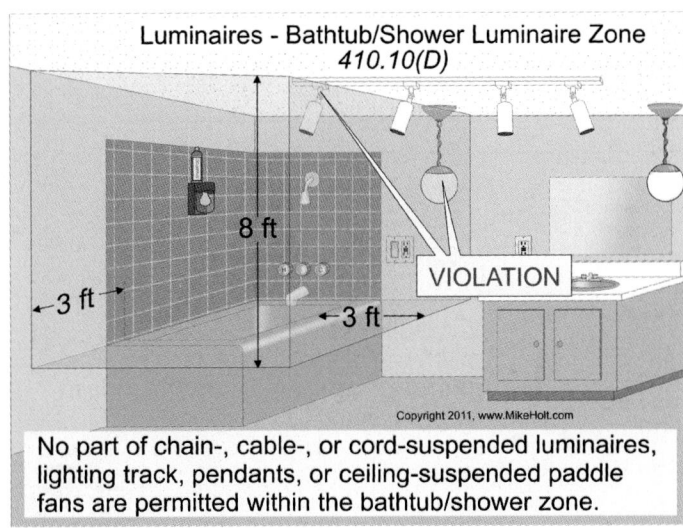

Figure 410–6

(3) The luminaire is corrosion resistant, or protected against corrosion, and the surface must be smooth so as not to collect deposits and to facilitate cleaning.

(4) Wiring methods and materials supplying the luminaire must not be exposed within the cooking hood.

Author's Comment: Standard gasketed luminaires must not be installed in a commercial cooking hood because accumulations of grease and oil can result in a fire caused by high temperatures on the glass globe.

(D) Bathtub and Shower Areas. No part of chain-, cable-, or cord-suspended luminaires, track luminaires, or ceiling paddle fans can be located within 3 ft horizontally and 8 ft vertically from the top of the bathtub rim or shower stall threshold. **Figure 410–6**

Author's Comment: See 404.4 for switch requirements and 406.9(C) for receptacle requirements within or near bathtubs or shower stalls.

Luminaires located within the actual outside dimensions of a bathtub or shower to a height of 8 ft from the top of the bathtub rim or shower threshold must be marked for damp locations. If subject to shower spray, the luminaires must be marked for wet locations. **Figure 410–7**

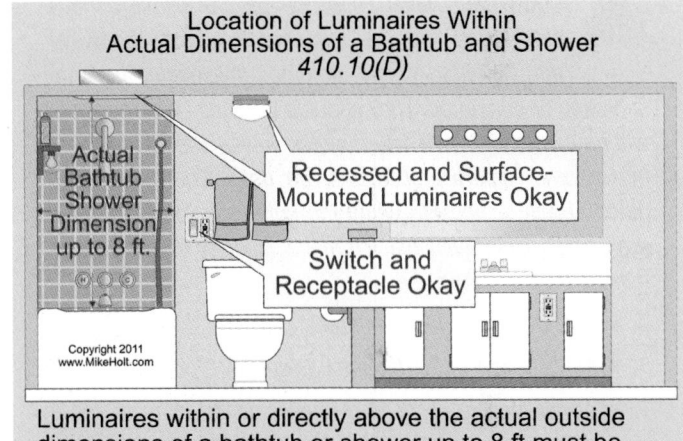

Figure 410–7

(E) Luminaires in Indoor Sports, Mixed-Use, and All-Purpose Facilities. Luminaires using a mercury vapor or metal halide lamp that are subject to physical damage and are installed in playing and spectator seating areas of indoor sports, mixed-use, or all-purpose facilities must be of the type that has a glass or plastic lamp shield. Such luminaires can have an additional guard. **Figure 410–8**

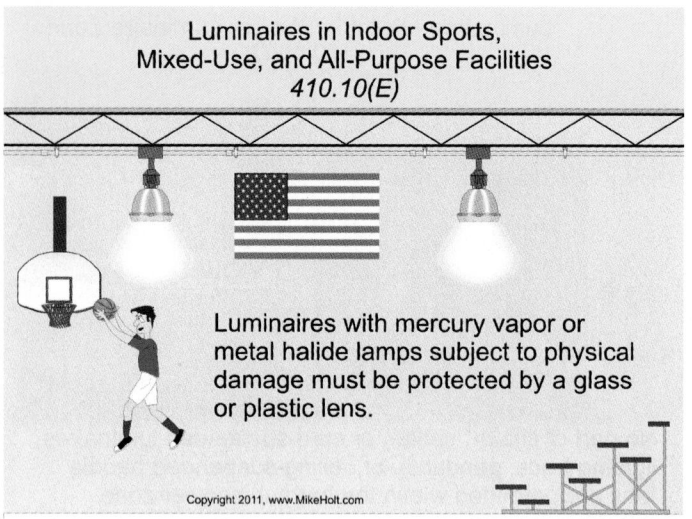

Figure 410–8

⚠ **WARNING:** *Metal halide lamps can cause serious skin burns and eye inflammation from shortwave ultraviolet radiation if the outer envelope of the lamp is broken or punctured. They shouldn't be used where people will remain more than a few minutes unless adequate shielding or other safety precautions are used. Lamps that will automatically extinguish when the outer envelope is broken are commercially available. If a metal halide or mercury vapor lamp is broken during use:*

- *Turn off the light immediately,*
- *Move people out of the area as quickly a possible, and*
- *Advise people exposed to the damaged lamp to see a doctor if symptoms of skin burns or eye irritation occur.*

410.11 Luminaires Near Combustible Material.
Luminaires must be installed or be equipped with shades or guards so that combustible material isn't subjected to temperatures in excess of 90°C (194°F).

410.16 Luminaires in Clothes Closets.

(A) Luminaire Types Permitted. Only the following types of luminaires are permitted to be installed in a clothes closet:

(1) Surface or recessed incandescent or LED luminaires with an enclosed light source.

(2) Surface or recessed fluorescent luminaires.

(3) Surface-mounted or recessed LED luminaires identified for use within the closet storage space.

(B) Luminaire Types Not Permitted. Incandescent luminaires with open or partially open lamps and pendant-type luminaires must not be installed in a clothes closet. **Figure 410–9**

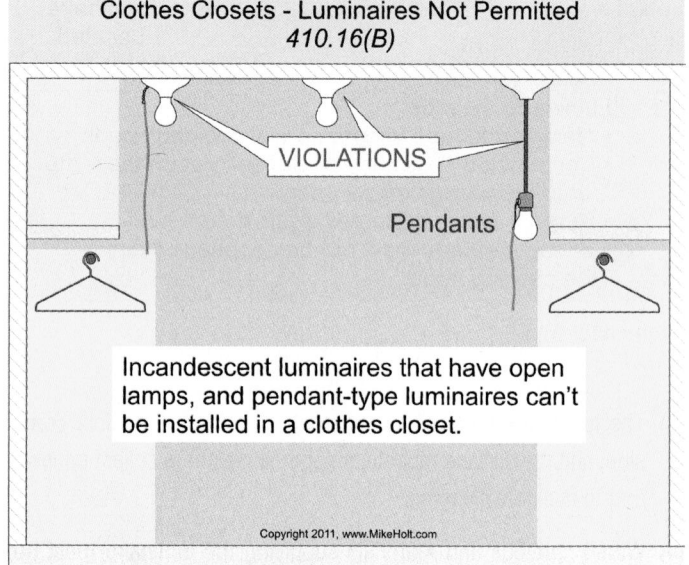

Figure 410–9

(C) Installation of Luminaires. Luminaires must maintain a minimum clearance from the closet storage space as follows:

(1) 12 in. for surface-mounted incandescent or LED luminaires with an enclosed light source. **Figure 410–10**

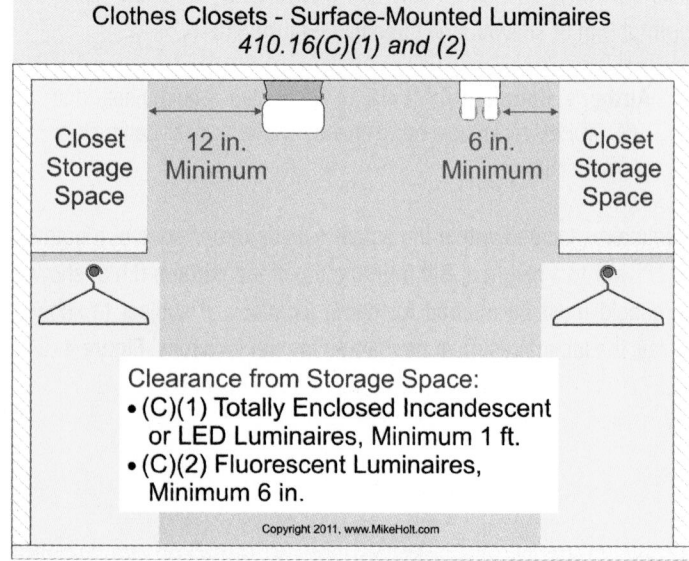

Figure 410–10

(2) 6 in. for surface-mounted fluorescent luminaires.

(3) 6 in. for recessed incandescent or LED luminaires with an enclosed light source. **Figure 410–11**

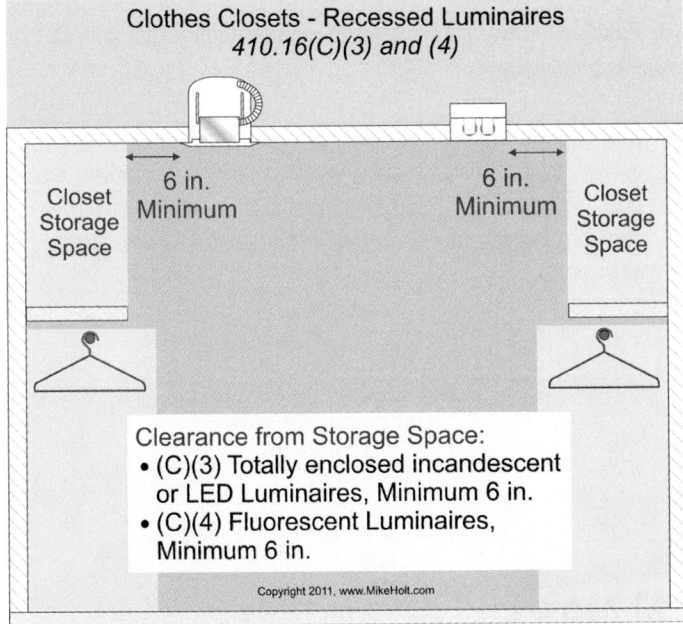

Figure 410–11

(4) 6 in. for recessed fluorescent luminaires.

(5) Surface-mounted fluorescent or LED luminaires are permitted within the <u>closet</u> storage space if identified for this use. **Figure 410–12**

410.18 Space for Cove Lighting. Coves must have adequate space so that lamps and equipment can be properly installed and maintained.

PART III. LUMINAIRE OUTLET BOXES AND COVERS

410.22 Outlet Boxes to be Covered. Outlet boxes for luminaires must be covered with a luminaire, lampholder, or blank faceplate. See 314.25. **Figure 410–13**

410.24 Connection of Electric-Discharge <u>and LED</u> Luminaires.

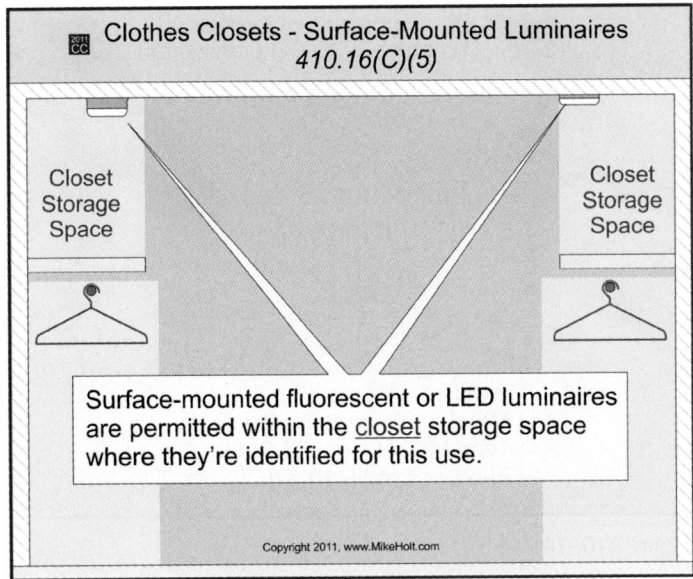

Figure 410–12

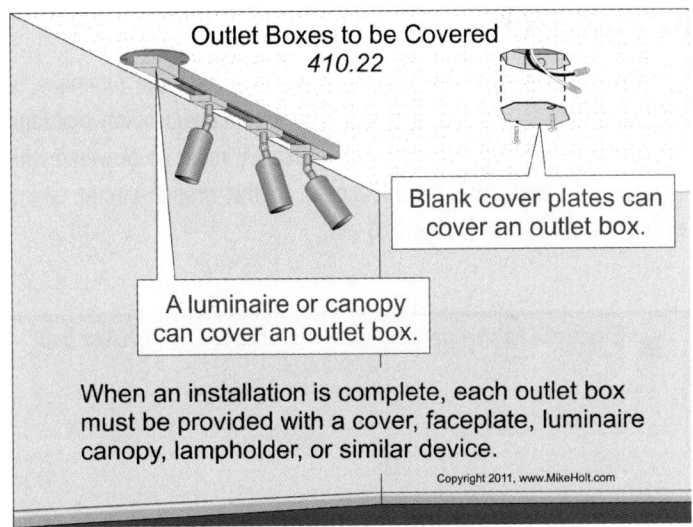

Figure 410–13

(A) Luminaires Supported Independently of the Outlet Box. Electric-discharge <u>and LED</u> luminaires supported independently of the outlet box must be connected to the branch circuit with a raceway, or with Types MC, AC, or NM cable. **Figure 410–14**

Electric-discharge luminaires can be cord-connected if the luminaires are provided with internal adjustments to position the lamp [410.62(B)].

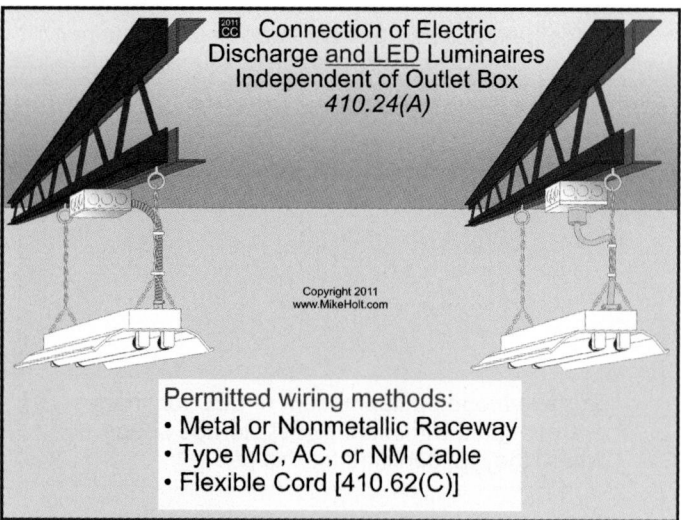

Figure 410–14

Electric-discharge luminaires can be cord-connected if the cord is visible for its entire length and is plugged into a receptacle, and the installation complies with 410.62(C).

(B) Access to Outlet Box. When an electric-discharge luminaire or LED luminaire is surface mounted over a concealed outlet box, and not supported by the outlet box, the luminaire must be provided with suitable openings that permit access to the branch-circuit wiring within the outlet box. **Figure 410–15**

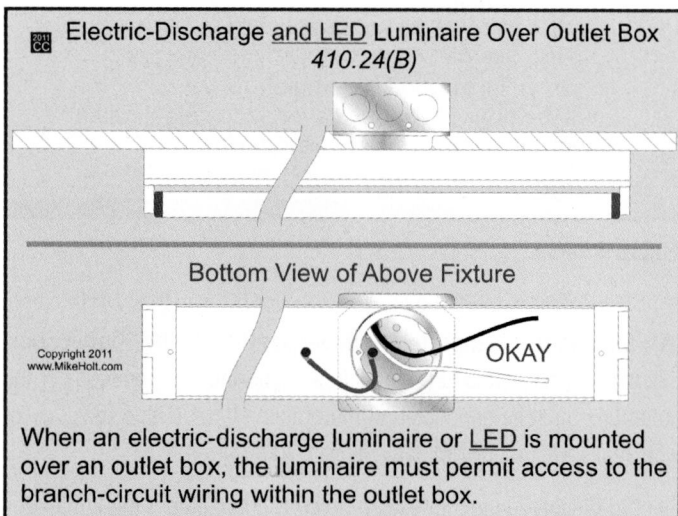

Figure 410–15

PART IV. LUMINAIRE SUPPORTS

410.30 Supports.

(A) General Support Requirements. Luminaires and lampholders must be securely supported.

(B) Poles. A poles can be used to support luminaires, and can be used as a raceway.

> **Author's Comment:** With security being a high priority, many owners want to install security cameras on existing parking lot poles. However, 820.133(A)(1)(b) prohibits the mixing of power and communications conductors in the same raceway. **Figure 410–16**

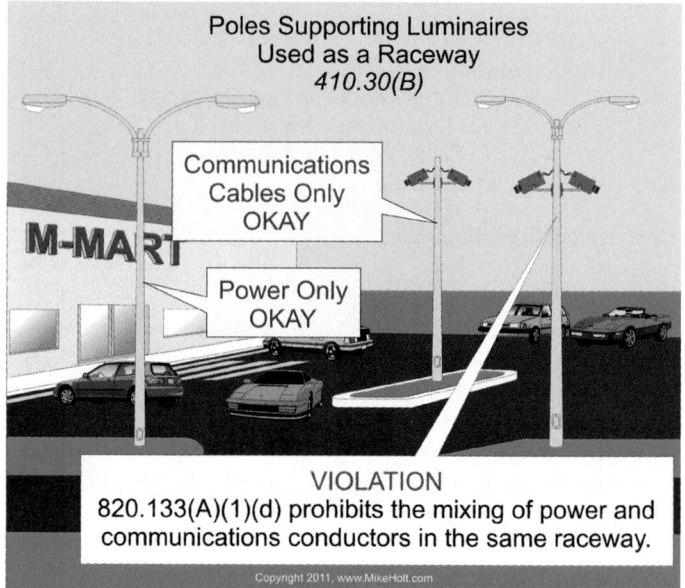

Figure 410–16

In addition, they must comply with the requirements of (1) through (6).

(1) The pole must have an accessible 2 in. x 4 in. handhole with a cover suitable for use in wet locations that provides access to the supply conductors within the pole.

Ex 1: The handhole isn't required for a pole that's 8 ft or less in height, if the supply conductors for the luminaire are accessible by removing the luminaire. **Figure 410–17**

Ex 2: The handhole can be omitted on poles that are 20 ft or less in height, if the pole is provided with a hinged base.

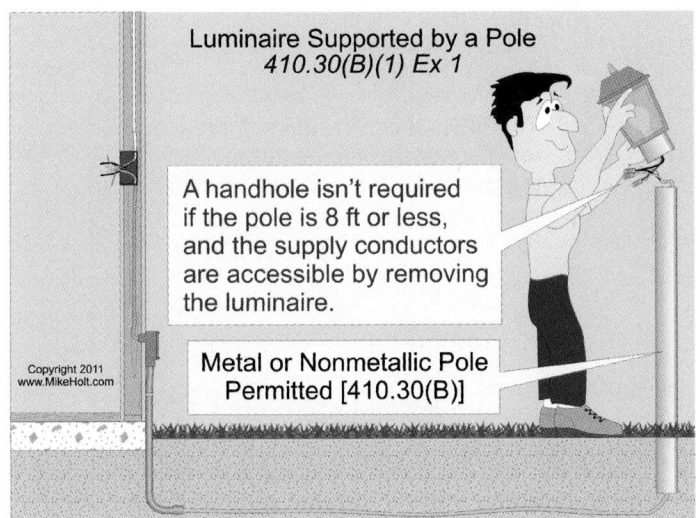

Luminaire Supported by a Pole
410.30(B)(1) Ex 1

A handhole isn't required if the pole is 8 ft or less, and the supply conductors are accessible by removing the luminaire.

Metal or Nonmetallic Pole Permitted [410.30(B)]

Copyright 2011
www.MikeHolt.com

Figure 410–17

(2) When the supply raceway or cable doesn't enter the pole, a threaded fitting or nipple must be welded, brazed, or attached to the pole opposite the handhole opening for the supply conductors.

(3) A metal pole must have an equipment grounding terminal accessible from the handhole.

Ex: A grounding terminal isn't required in a pole that's 8 ft or less in height above grade if the splices are accessible by removing the luminaire.

(5) Metal poles used for the support of luminaires must be connected to an equipment grounding conductor of a type recognized in 250.118 [250.4(A)(5)]. **Figure 410–18**

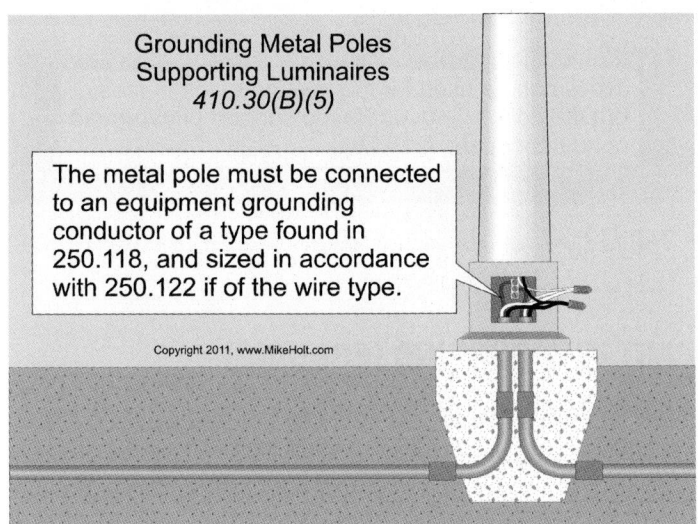

Grounding Metal Poles
Supporting Luminaires
410.30(B)(5)

The metal pole must be connected to an equipment grounding conductor of a type found in 250.118, and sized in accordance with 250.122 if of the wire type.

Copyright 2011, www.MikeHolt.com

Figure 410–18

DANGER: *Because the contact resistance of an electrode to the earth is so high, very little fault current returns to the power supply if the earth is the only fault current return path. Result—the circuit overcurrent device won't open and clear the ground fault, and the metal pole will become and remain energized by the circuit voltage.* **Figure 410–19**

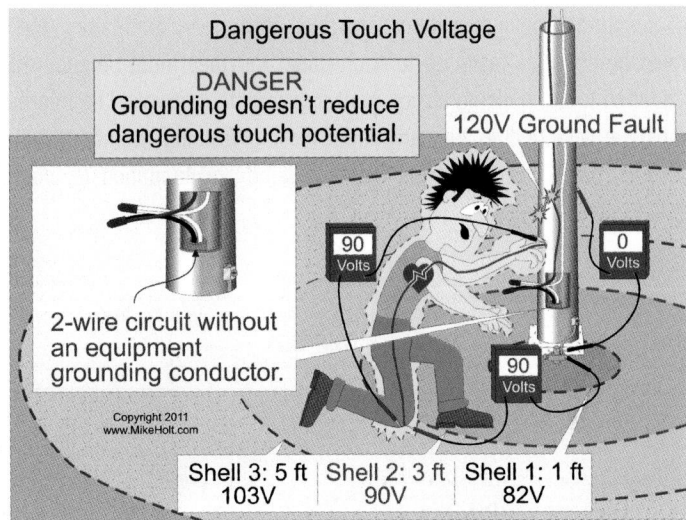

Dangerous Touch Voltage

DANGER
Grounding doesn't reduce dangerous touch potential.

120V Ground Fault

90 Volts

0 Volts

90 Volts

2-wire circuit without an equipment grounding conductor.

Copyright 2011
www.MikeHolt.com

Shell 3: 5 ft	Shell 2: 3 ft	Shell 1: 1 ft
103V	90V	82V

Figure 410–19

(6) Conductors in vertical metal poles must be supported when the vertical rise exceeds 100 ft [Table 300.19(A)].

Author's Comment: When provided by the manufacturer of roadway lighting poles, so-called J-hooks must be used to support conductors, as they're part of the listing instructions [110.3(B)].

410.36 Means of Support.

(A) Outlet Boxes. Outlet boxes designed for the support of luminaires must be supported by one of the following methods:

- Fastened to any surface that provides adequate support [314.23(A)].
- Supported from a structural member of a building or from grade by a metal, plastic, or wood brace [314.23(B)].
- Secured to a finished surface (drywall or plaster walls or ceilings) by clamps, anchors, or fittings identified for the application [314.23(C)].
- Secured to the structural or supporting elements of a suspended ceiling [314.23(D)].

- Supported by two intermediate metal conduits or rigid metal conduits threaded wrenchtight [314.23(E) and (F)].
- Embedded in concrete or masonry [314.23(G)].
- Outlet boxes for luminaires can support a luminaire that weighs up to 50 lb, unless the box is listed for the luminaries' actual weight [314.27(A)(2)].

(B) Suspended-Ceiling Framing Members. If framing members of suspended-ceiling systems are used to support luminaires, they must be securely fastened to each other and they must be securely attached to the building structure at appropriate intervals. Luminaires must be attached to the suspended-ceiling framing members with screws, bolts, rivets, or clips that are listed and identified for such use. **Figure 410–20**

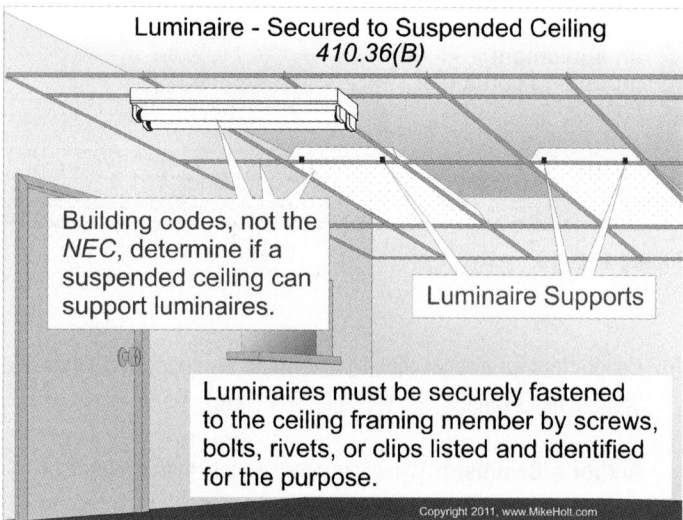

Figure 410–20

Author's Comment:

- The *NEC* doesn't require independent support wires for suspended-ceiling luminaires that aren't installed in a fire-rated ceiling; however, building codes often do. **Figure 410–21**
- Raceways and cables within a suspended ceiling must be supported in accordance with 300.11(A). Outlet boxes can be secured to the ceiling-framing members by bolts, screws, rivets, clips, or independent support wires that are taut and secured at both ends [314.23(D)].

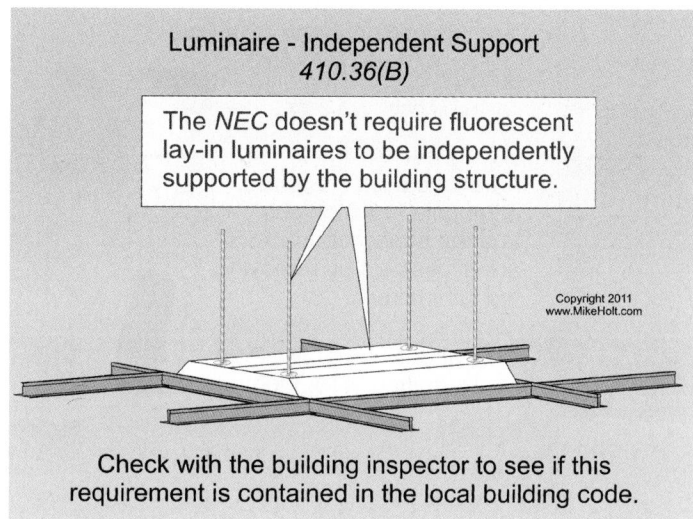

Figure 410–21

(G) Luminaires Supported by Trees. Trees can be used to support luminaires, but they must not be used to support overhead conductor spans [225.26]. **Figure 410–22**

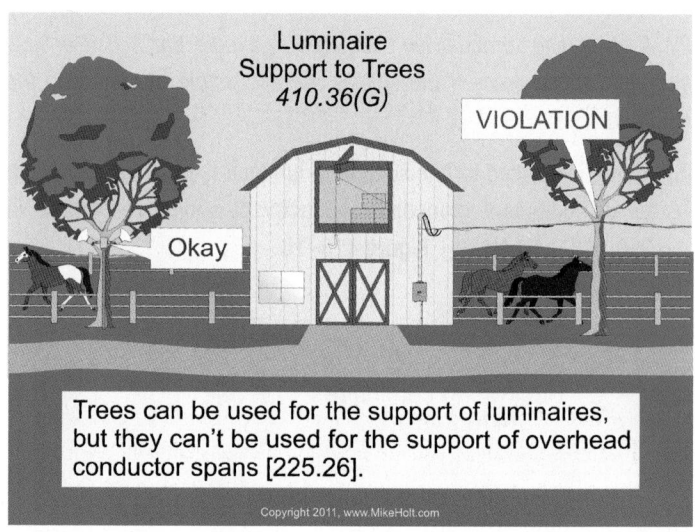

Figure 410–22

PART V. GROUNDING (BONDING)

410.44 Methods of Grounding. Luminaires must be connected to an equipment grounding conductor of a type recognized in 250.118. If of the wire type, the circuit equipment grounding conductor must be sized in accordance with 250.122, based on the rating of the overcurrent device.

Ex 1: If an equipment grounding conductor isn't present in the outlet box for a luminaire, the luminaire must be made of insulating material and must not have any exposed conductive parts.

Ex 2: Replacement luminaires can be installed in an outlet box that doesn't contain an equipment grounding conductor if the luminaire is connected to one of the following:

(1) Grounding electrode system [250.50].

(2) Grounding electrode conductor.

(3) Panelboard equipment grounding terminal.

(4) Service neutral conductor within the service equipment enclosure.

Ex 3: GFCI-protected replacement luminaires aren't required to be connected to an equipment grounding conductor of a type recognized in 250.118 if no equipment grounding conductor exists at the outlet box.

> **Author's Comment:** This is similar to the rule for receptacle replacements in locations where an equipment grounding conductor isn't present in the outlet box [406.4(D)(3)].

PART VI. WIRING OF LUMINAIRES

410.50 Polarization of Luminaires. Luminaires must have the neutral conductor connected to the screw shell of the lampholder [200.10(C)], and the neutral conductor must be properly identified in accordance with 200.6.

410.62 Cord-Connected Luminaires.

(B) Adjustable Luminaires. Luminaires that require adjusting or aiming after installation can be cord connected, with or without an attachment plug, provided the exposed cord is of the hard usage or extra-hard usage type. The cord must not be longer than necessary for luminaire adjustment, and it must not be subject to strain or physical damage [400.10]. **Figure 410–23**

(C) Electric-Discharge and LED Luminaires. A luminaire can be cord connected if: **Figure 410–24**

(1) The luminaire is mounted directly below the outlet box, and

(2) The flexible cord:

   a. Is visible for its entire length,

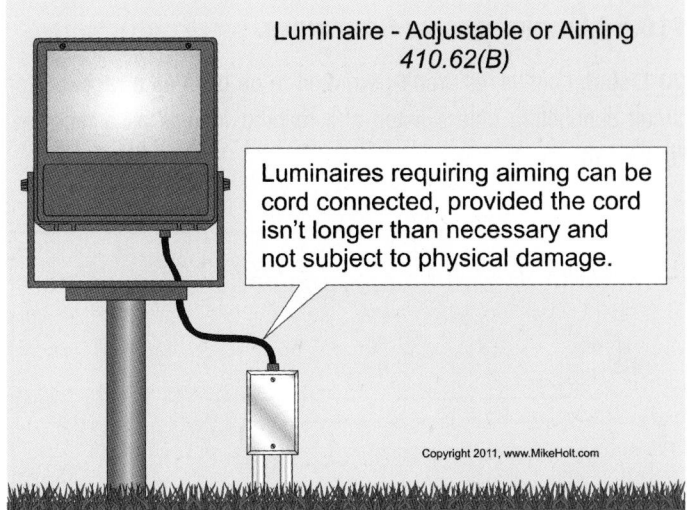

Luminaire - Adjustable or Aiming
410.62(B)

Luminaires requiring aiming can be cord connected, provided the cord isn't longer than necessary and not subject to physical damage.

Copyright 2011, www.MikeHolt.com

Figure 410–23

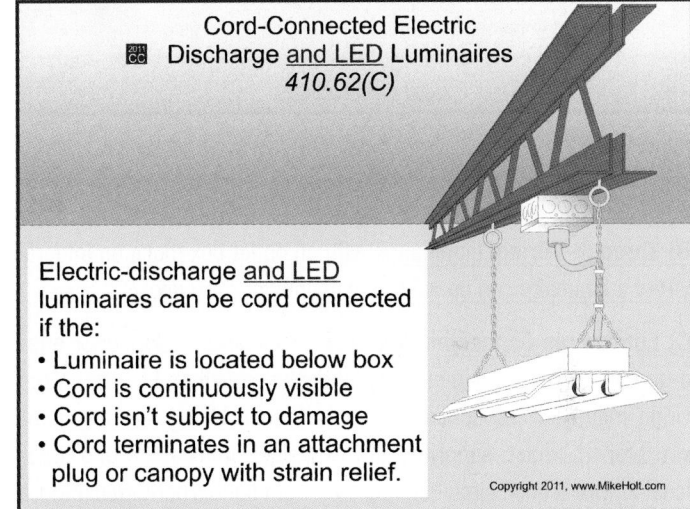

Cord-Connected Electric
Discharge and LED Luminaires
410.62(C)

Electric-discharge and LED luminaires can be cord connected if the:
• Luminaire is located below box
• Cord is continuously visible
• Cord isn't subject to damage
• Cord terminates in an attachment plug or canopy with strain relief.

Copyright 2011, www.MikeHolt.com

Figure 410–24

   b. Isn't subject to strain or physical damage [400.10], and

   c. Terminates in an attachment plug, canopy with strain relief, or manufactured wiring system connector in accordance with 604.6(C).

> **Author's Comment:** The *Code* doesn't require twist-lock receptacles for this application.

410.64 Luminaires as Raceways.

(A) Listed. Luminaires aren't permitted to be used as a raceway for circuit conductors unless listed and marked for use as a raceway. **Figure 410–25**

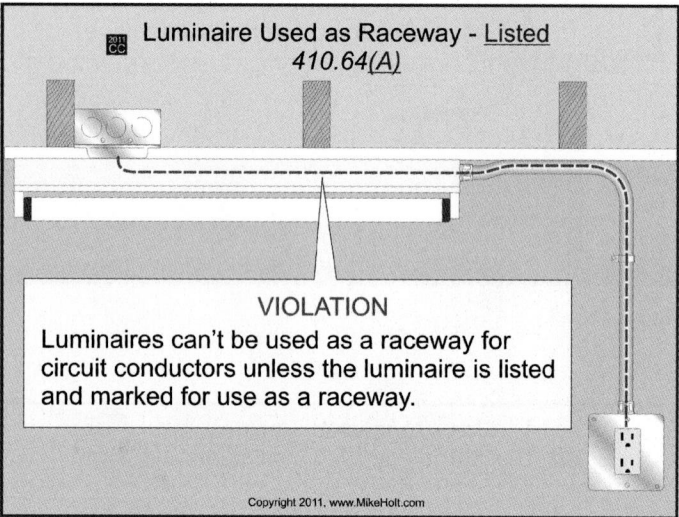

Figure 410–25

(B) Through-Wiring. Luminaires with an outlet box that's an integral part of a luminaire can be used as a conductor raceway.

(C) Luminaires Connected Together. Luminaires designed for end-to-end assembly, or luminaires connected together by recognized wiring methods, can contain a 2-wire branch circuit, or one multiwire branch circuit, supplying the connected luminaires. One additional 2-wire branch circuit supplying a night light is permitted. **Figure 410–26**

410.68 Conductors and Ballasts. Conductors within 3 in. of ballast, LED driver, power supply, or transformer must have an insulation temperature rating not lower than 90°C.

PART VIII. INSTALLATION OF LAMPHOLDERS

410.90 Screw-Shell Lampholders. Lampholders of the screw-shell type must be installed for use as lampholders only.

Author's Comment: A receptacle adapter that screws into a lampholder is a violation of this section. **Figure 410–27**

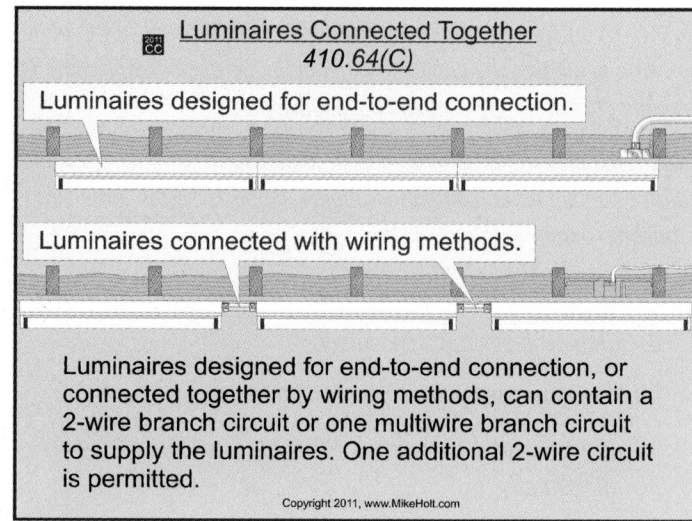

Figure 410–26

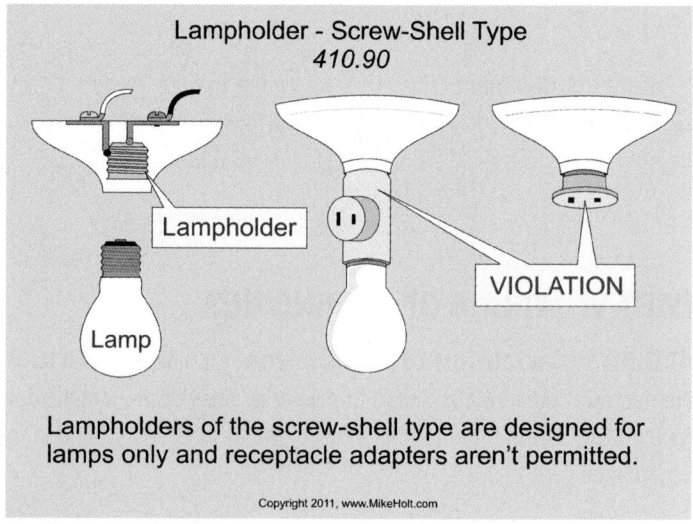

Figure 410–27

410.96 Lampholders in Wet or Damp Locations. Lampholders installed in wet locations must be listed for use in wet locations and lampholders installed in damp locations must be listed for damp or wet locations.

410.97 Lampholders Near Combustible Material.

Lampholders must be constructed, installed, or equipped with shades or guards so that combustible material isn't subjected to temperatures in excess of 90°C (194°F).

PART X. RECESSED LUMINAIRES

410.110 General. Luminaires installed in recessed cavities in walls or ceilings, <u>including suspended ceilings,</u> must comply with this Part (X. Recessed Luminaires).

410.115 Thermally Protected.

(C) Recessed Incandescent Luminaires. Recessed incandescent luminaires must be identified as thermally protected.

> **Author's Comment:** When higher-wattage lamps or improper trims are installed, the lampholder contained in a recessed luminaire can overheat, activating the thermal overcurrent device and causing the luminaire to cycle on and off.

Ex 2: Thermal protection isn't required for recessed Type IC luminaires whose design, construction, and thermal performance characteristics are equivalent to a thermally protected luminaire.

410.116 Recessed Luminaire Clearances.

(A) Clearances From Combustible Materials.

(1) Non-Type IC Luminaires. A recessed luminaire that isn't identified for contact with insulation must have all recessed parts, except the points of supports, spaced not less than ¼ in. from combustible materials. **Figure 410–28**

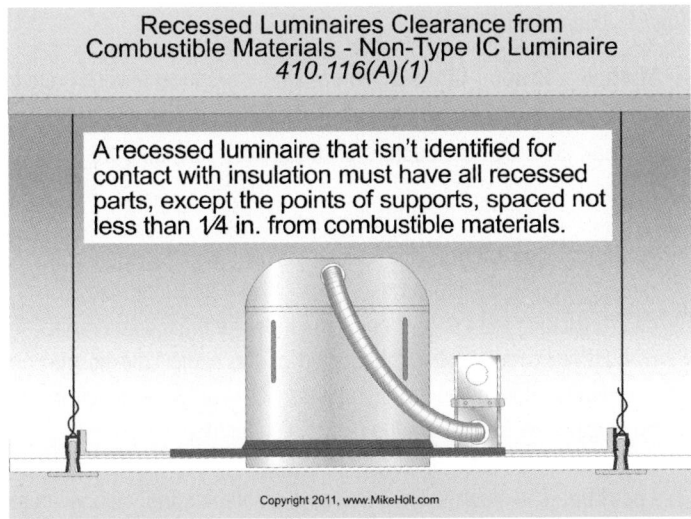

Recessed Luminaires Clearance from
Combustible Materials - Non-Type IC Luminaire
410.116(A)(1)

A recessed luminaire that isn't identified for contact with insulation must have all recessed parts, except the points of supports, spaced not less than 1⁄4 in. from combustible materials.

Copyright 2011, www.MikeHolt.com

Figure 410–28

(2) Type IC Luminaires. A Type IC luminaire (identified for contact with insulation) can be in contact with combustible materials. **Figure 410–29**

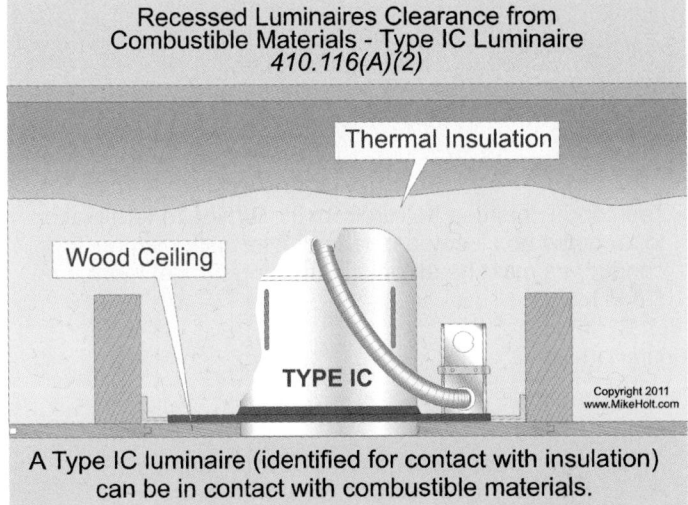

Recessed Luminaires Clearance from
Combustible Materials - Type IC Luminaire
410.116(A)(2)

Thermal Insulation

Wood Ceiling

TYPE IC

Copyright 2011
www.MikeHolt.com

A Type IC luminaire (identified for contact with insulation)
can be in contact with combustible materials.

410–29

(B) Installation. Thermal insulation must not be installed above a recessed luminaire or within 3 in. of the luminaries' enclosure, wiring compartment, or ballast, <u>transformer, LED driver, or power supply</u> unless identified for contact with insulation, Type IC.

410.117 Wiring.

(C) Tap Conductors. Fixture wires installed in accordance with Article 402 and protected against overcurrent in accordance with 240.5(B)(2), are permitted to run from the luminaire to an outlet box located at least 1 ft away from the luminaire, as long as the conductors aren't over 6 ft long. **Figure 410–30**

PART XII. ELECTRIC-DISCHARGE LIGHTING

410.130 General.

(F) High-Intensity Discharge Luminaires.

(5) Metal Halide Lamp Containment. Luminaires containing a metal halide lamp, other than a thick-glass parabolic reflector lamp (PAR), must be provided with a containment barrier that encloses the lamp, or the luminaire must only allow the use of a Type "O" lamp that has an internal arc-tube shield. **Figure 410–31**

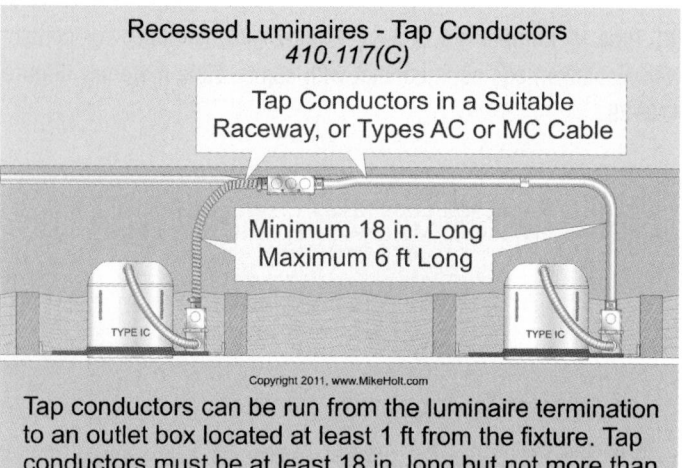

Recessed Luminaires - Tap Conductors
410.117(C)

Tap Conductors in a Suitable Raceway, or Types AC or MC Cable

Minimum 18 in. Long
Maximum 6 ft Long

Tap conductors can be run from the luminaire termination to an outlet box located at least 1 ft from the fixture. Tap conductors must be at least 18 in. long but not more than 6 ft in length.

Figure 410–30

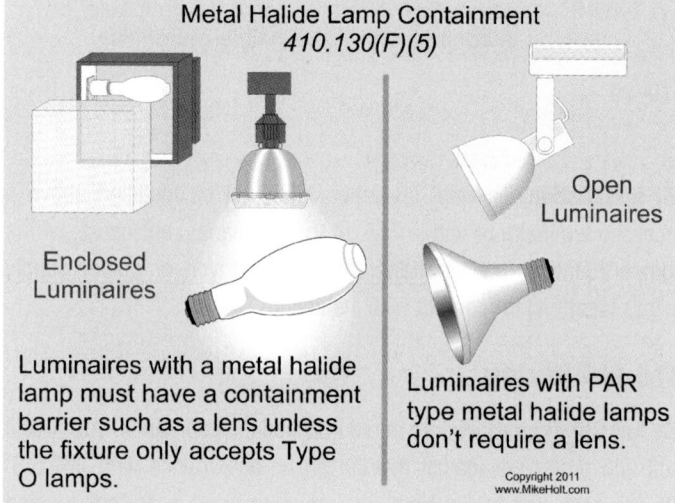

Metal Halide Lamp Containment
410.130(F)(5)

Open Luminaires

Enclosed Luminaires

Luminaires with a metal halide lamp must have a containment barrier such as a lens unless the fixture only accepts Type O lamps.

Luminaires with PAR type metal halide lamps don't require a lens.

Figure 410–31

Author's Comments:

- Fires have resulted from arc lamps exploding on start-up, shattering the lamp globe and showering glass and hot quartz fragments from metal halide lamp failures. The possibility of failure increases significantly as the lamp approaches and exceeds its rated life. It's projected that one violent rupture occurs in every 100,000 failures.

- "O-rated" lamps, which have an internal arc-tube shield, have been designed to meet ANSI containment standards for the installation of a metal halide lamp in an open fixture.

(G) Disconnecting Means.

(1) General. In indoor locations, other than dwellings and associated accessory structures, fluorescent luminaires that utilize double-ended lamps (typical fluorescent lamps) and contain ballasts that can be serviced in place must have a disconnecting means.

For existing installed luminaires, a disconnecting means must be added at the time a ballast is replaced.

> **Author's Comment:** Changing the ballast while the circuit feeding the luminaire is energized has become a regular practice because a local disconnect isn't available.

Ex 2: A disconnecting means isn't required for the emergency illumination required in 700.16.

Ex 3: For cord-and-plug-connected luminaires, an accessible separable connector, or an accessible plug and receptacle, is permitted to serve as the disconnecting means.

Ex 4: A disconnecting means isn't required in industrial establishments with restricted public access where written procedures and conditions of maintenance and supervision ensure that only qualified persons will service the installation.

Ex 5: If more than one luminaire is installed and is supplied by a branch circuit that isn't of the multiwire type, a disconnecting means isn't required for every luminaire; but, only when the light switch for the space ensures that some of the luminaires in the space will still provide illumination.

(2) Multiwire Branch Circuits. When connected to multiwire branch circuits, the fluorescent luminaire disconnect must simultaneously break all circuit conductors of the ballast, including the neutral conductor.

> **Author's Comment:** This rule requires the disconnecting means to open "all circuit conductors of a multiwire branch circuit," including the neutral conductor. If the neutral conductor in a multiwire circuit isn't disconnected at the same time as the ungrounded conductors, a false sense of security can result in an unexpected shock from the neutral conductor.

(3) Location. The fluorescent luminaire disconnecting means must be accessible to qualified persons, and if the disconnecting means is external to the luminaire, it must be a single device and must be located in sight from the luminaire.

PART XIV. TRACK LIGHTING

410.151 Installation.

(A) Track Lighting. Track lighting must be permanently installed and permanently connected to the branch-circuit wiring. Lampholders for track lighting are designed for lamps only, so a receptacle adapter isn't permitted [410.90].

(B) Circuit Rating. The connected load on a lighting track must not exceed the rating of the track, and an overcurrent device whose rating exceeds the rating of the track must not supply the track. Figure 410–32

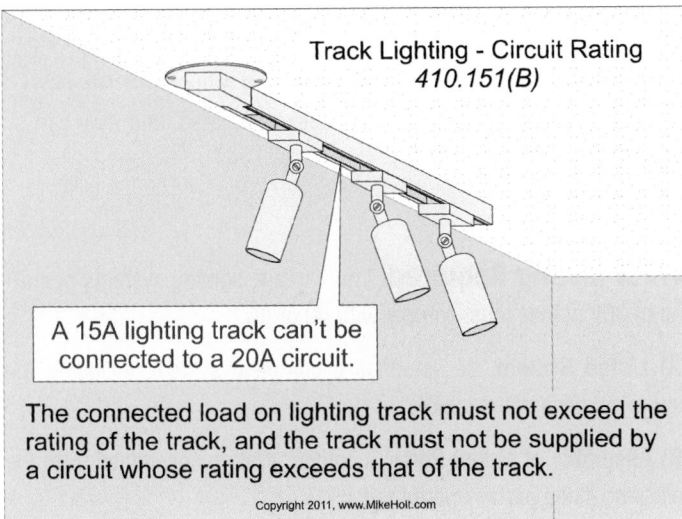

A 15A lighting track can't be connected to a 20A circuit.

The connected load on lighting track must not exceed the rating of the track, and the track must not be supplied by a circuit whose rating exceeds that of the track.

Copyright 2011, www.MikeHolt.com

Figure 410–32

Note: The feeder or service load calculations of 220.43(B) don't limit the number of feet of track on a circuit, nor do they limit the number of luminaires mounted on an individual track. **Figure 410–33**

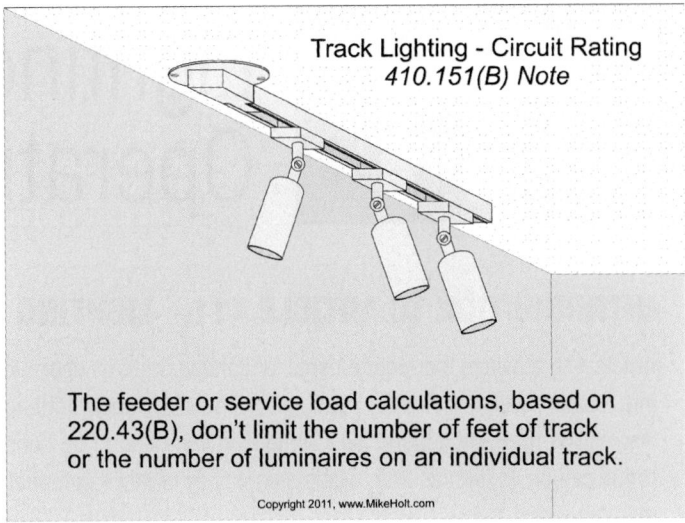

The feeder or service load calculations, based on 220.43(B), don't limit the number of feet of track or the number of luminaires on an individual track.

Copyright 2011, www.MikeHolt.com

Figure 410–33

(C) Locations Not Permitted. Track lighting must not be installed:

(1) If it's likely to be subjected to physical damage.

(2) In wet or damp locations.

(3) If subject to corrosive vapors.

(4) In storage battery rooms.

(5) In any hazardous location.

(6) If concealed.

(7) If extended through walls, partitions, or floors.

(8) Less than 5 ft above the finished floor, except where protected from physical damage or where the track operates below 30V open-circuit voltage.

(9) Within 3 ft horizontally and 8 ft vertically from the top of a bathtub rim or shower space [410.4(D)].

410.154 Fastening. Track lighting must be securely mounted to support the weight of the luminaires. A single track section 4 ft or shorter in length must have two supports, and, where installed in a continuous row, each individual track section of not more than 4 ft in length must have one additional support.

Lighting Systems Operating at 30V or Less

INTRODUCTION TO ARTICLE 411—LIGHTING SYSTEMS OPERATING AT 30V OR LESS

Article 411 provides the requirements for lighting systems operating at 30V or less, which are often found in such applications as landscaping, kitchen over-the-counter lighting, commercial display lighting, and museums. Don't let the half-page size of Article 411 give you the impression that 30V lighting isn't something you need to be concerned about. These systems are limited in their voltage, but the current rating can be as high as 25A, which means they're still a potential source of fire. Installation of these systems is widespread and becoming more so.

Many of these systems now use LEDs, and 30V halogen lamps are also fairly common. All 30V lighting systems have an ungrounded secondary circuit supplied by an isolating transformer. These systems have restrictions that effect where they can be located, and they can have a maximum supply breaker size of 25A.

411.1 Scope. Article 411 covers the installation of lighting systems that operate at 30V or less, as well as their associated components.

411.2 Definition.

Lighting Systems Operating at 30V or Less. A lighting system consisting of an isolating power supply, luminaires, and associated equipment identified for the use. The lighting system power supply must be rated not more than 25A and not more than 30V. **Figure 411–1**

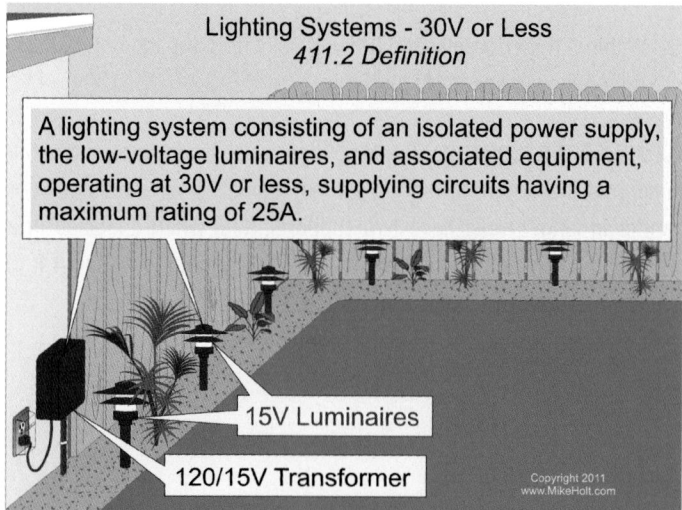

Figure 411–1

411.3 Listing Required. Low-voltage lighting systems operating at 30V or less must comply with (A) or (B).

(A) Listed System. Be listed as a complete system, including the power supply and luminaires.

(B) Assembly of Listed Parts. A lighting system assembled from the following listed parts is permitted:

(1) Low-voltage luminaires.

(2) Low-voltage luminaire power supply.

(3) Class 2 power supply.

(4) Low-voltage luminaire fitting.

(5) Cords that the luminaires and power supply are listed for use with.

(6) Cable, conductors in a raceway, or other fixed wiring method for the secondary circuit.

The luminaires, power supply, and luminaire fittings of an exposed bare conductor lighting system must be listed for use as part of the same identified lighting system.

411.4 Specific Location Requirements.

(A) Walls, Floors, and Ceilings. Conductors concealed or installed through a wall, floor, or ceiling must comply with (1) or (2):

(1) Lighting system conductors must be installed within a Chapter 3 wiring method.

(2) Lighting system conductors supplied by a listed Class 2 power supply can use Class 2 cables, installed in accordance with 725.130.

(B) Pools, Spas, Fountains, and Similar Locations. Low-voltage lighting systems must not be installed less than 10 ft from the edge of the water. **Figure 411–2**

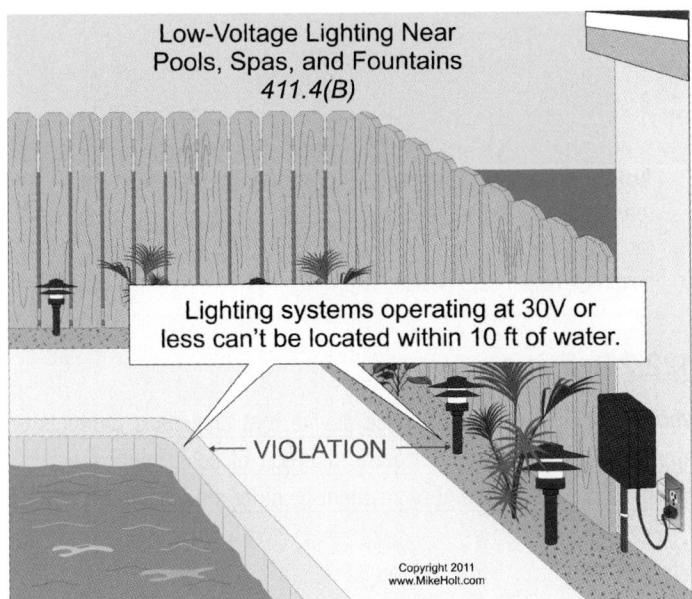

Figure 411–2

411.5 Secondary Circuits.

(A) Grounding. Secondary circuits aren't permitted to be grounded.

(B) Isolation. The secondary circuit must be insulated from the branch circuit by an isolating transformer.

(C) Bare Conductors. Exposed bare conductors and current-carrying parts must not be installed less than 7 ft above the finished floor, unless listed for a lower height.

(D) Insulated Conductors. Exposed insulated secondary circuit conductors must be:

(1) Supplied by a Class 2 power source with Class 2 cable in accordance with Article 725.

(2) Installed at least 7 ft above the finished floor unless listed for a lower installation height.

(3) Installed in a Chapter 3 wiring method.

ARTICLE 422

Appliances

INTRODUCTION TO ARTICLE 422—APPLIANCES

Article 422 covers electric appliances used in any occupancy. The meat of this article is contained in Parts II and III. Parts IV and V are primarily for manufacturers, but you should examine appliances for compliance before installing them. If the appliance has a label from a recognized labeling authority (for example, UL), it complies [90.7].

PART I. GENERAL

422.1 Scope. The scope of Article 422 includes appliances in any occupancy that are fastened in place, permanently connected, or cord-and-plug-connected. **Figure 422–1**

Appliances
422.1

Paddle Fans
Ranges
Ovens
Water Heaters
Refrigerators and Freezers
Waste Disposer
Cooktops
Dishwashers
Dryers
Trash Compactors
Washers
Drinking Fountains and Coolers
Room Air Conditioners

Copyright 2011
www.MikeHolt.com

Article 422 covers appliances in any occupancy.

Figure 422–1

Author's Comment: Appliances are electrical equipment, other than industrial equipment, built in standardized sizes, such as ranges, ovens, cooktops, refrigerators, drinking water coolers, or beverage dispensers [Article 100].

422.2 Definitions.

Vending Machine. A self-service device that dispenses products or merchandise, designed to require insertion of coin, paper currency, token, card, key, or receipt of payment by other means. **Figure 422–2**

Vending Machine
422.2 Definition

Copyright 2011, www.MikeHolt.com

Vending Machine: A self-serve device that dispenses products or merchandise without replenishing the device between each vending operation and is designed to require insertion of money, tokens, or other means of payment.

Figure 422–2

422.3 Other Articles. Motor-operated appliances must comply with Article 430, and appliances containing hermetic refrigerant motor compressors must comply with Article 440.

Author's Comment: Room air-conditioning equipment must be installed in accordance with Part VII of Article 440.

PART II. BRANCH-CIRCUIT REQUIREMENTS

422.10 Branch-Circuit Rating.

(A) Individual Circuits. The branch-circuit ampere rating for an individual appliance must not be less than the branch-circuit rating marked on the appliance [110.3(B)].

The branch-circuit rating for motor-operated appliances must be in accordance with 430.6(A) and 430.22.

A branch-circuit for an appliance that's a continuous load must be rated not less than 125 percent of the marked ampere rating of the appliance [210.19(A)(1)].

Branch circuits for household ranges and cooking appliances can be sized in accordance with Table 220.55, and 210.19(A)(3).

(B) Circuits Supplying Two or More Loads. Branch circuits supplying appliances and other loads must be sized in accordance with the following:

- Cord-and-plug-connected equipment must not be rated more than 80 percent of the branch-circuit ampere rating [210.23(A)(1)]. **Figure 422–3**

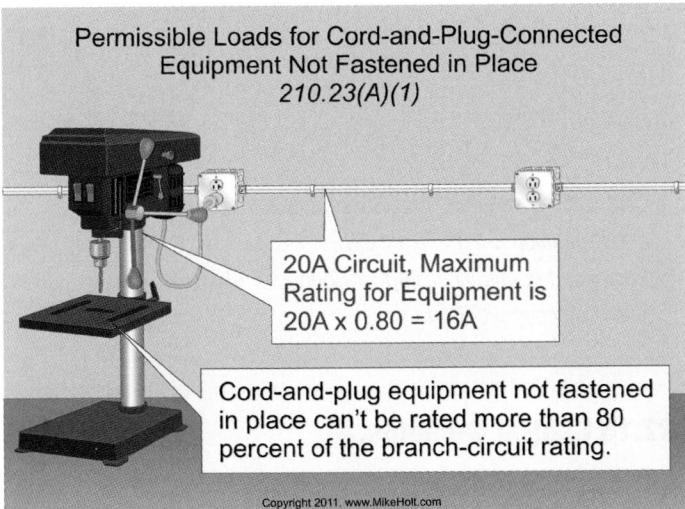

Figure 422–3

- Equipment fastened in place must not be rated more than 50 percent of the branch-circuit ampere rating, if the circuit supplies both luminaires and receptacles [210.23(A)(2)]. **Figure 422–4**

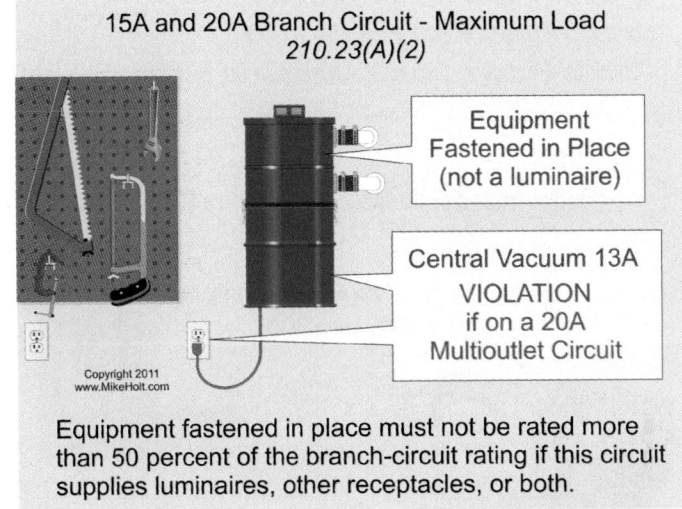

Figure 422–4

422.11 Overcurrent Protection.

(A) Branch-Circuits. Branch-circuit conductors must have overcurrent protection in accordance with 240.4, and the overcurrent device rating must not exceed the rating marked on the appliance.

(E) Nonmotor Appliances. The appliance overcurrent device must:

(1) Not exceed the rating marked on the appliance.

(2) Not exceed 20A if the overcurrent device rating isn't marked, and the appliance is rated 13.30A or less, or

(3) Not exceed 150 percent of the appliance rated current if the overcurrent device rating isn't marked, and the appliance is rated over 13.30A. Where 150 percent of the appliance rating doesn't correspond to a standard overcurrent device ampere rating listed in 240.6(A), the next higher standard rating is permitted.

Question: *What is the maximum size overcurrent protection for a 4,500W, 240V water heater?* **Figure 422–5**

(a) 20A   *(b) 30A*   *(c) 40A*   *(d) 50A*

Answer: (b) 30A

Conductor/Protection Size = 4,500W/240V

Conductor/Protection Size = 18.75A x 1.50

Conductor/Protection Size = 28A, next size up, 30A [240.6(A)]

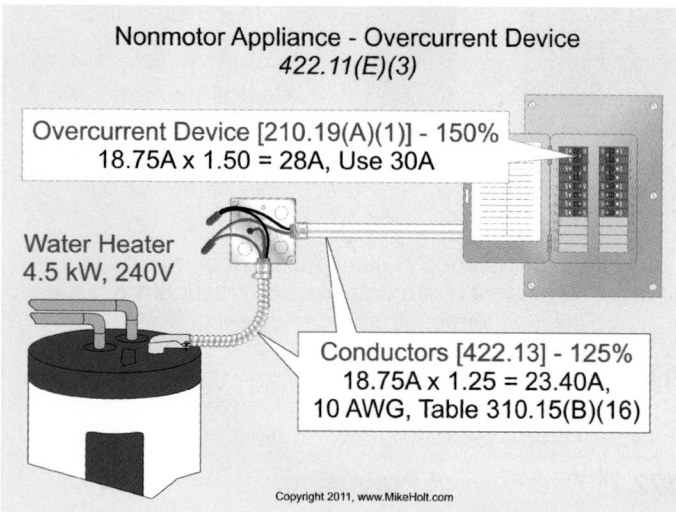

Figure 422–5

422.12 Central Heating Equipment (Furnaces). An
individual branch circuit must supply central heating equipment, such as gas, oil, or coal furnaces.

Author's Comment: This rule isn't intended to apply to a listed wood-burning fireplace with a fan, since the fireplace isn't central heating equipment.

Ex 1: Auxiliary equipment to the central heating equipment, such as pumps, valves, humidifiers, and electrostatic air cleaners, can be connected to the central heater circuit.

Author's Comment: Electric space-heating equipment must be installed in accordance with Article 424—Electric Space-Heating Equipment.

Ex 2: Permanently connected air-conditioning equipment can be connected to the individual branch circuit that supplies central heating equipment.

422.13 Storage Water Heaters. An electric water heater
having a capacity of 120 gallons or less is considered a continuous load, for the purpose of sizing branch circuits.Author's Comment: Branch-circuit conductors and overcurrent devices must have a rating of at least 125 percent of the ampere rating of a continuous load [210.19(A)(1) and 210.20(A)]. **Figure 422–6**

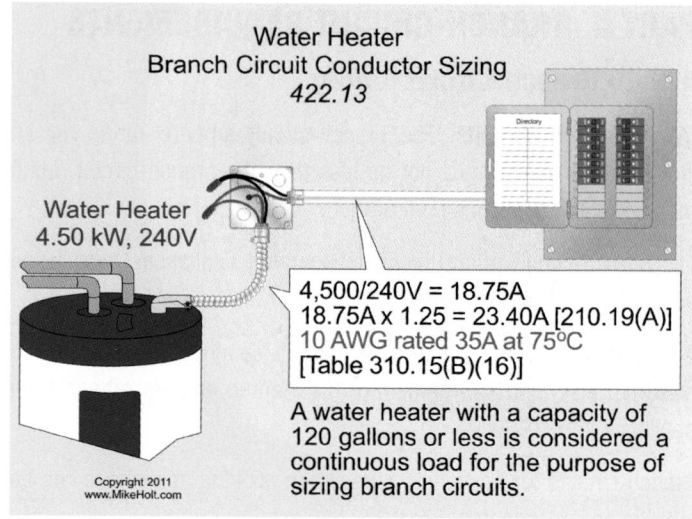

Figure 422–6

Question: *What's the calculated load for conductor sizing and overcurrent protection for a 4,500W, 240V water heater?*

(a) 15A   *(b) 20A*   *(c) 25A*   *(d) 30A*

Answer: (c) 25A

$I = P/E$

$P = 4,500W$

$E = 240V$

$I = 4,500W/240V$

$I = 18.75A$

Calculated Continuous Load for Conductor Sizing and Protection = 18.75A x 1.25

Calculated Continuous Load for Conductor Sizing and Protection = 23.44A

422.15 Central Vacuums.

(A) Circuit Loading. Central vacuum systems must be on a separate circuit if the rating of the equipment exceeds 50 percent of the ampere rating of the circuit [210.23(A)(2)].

Author's Comment: 210.23(A)(2) specifies that equipment fastened in place, other than luminaires, must not be rated more than 50 percent of the branch-circuit ampere rating if this circuit supplies both luminaires and receptacles. Due to this requirement, a separate 15A circuit is required for a central vacuum receptacle outlet if the rating of the central vacuum exceeds 7.50A. A separate 20A circuit is required for a central vacuum receptacle outlet if the rating of the central vacuum exceeds 10A, but not 16A [210.23(A)(2)]. **Figure 422-7**

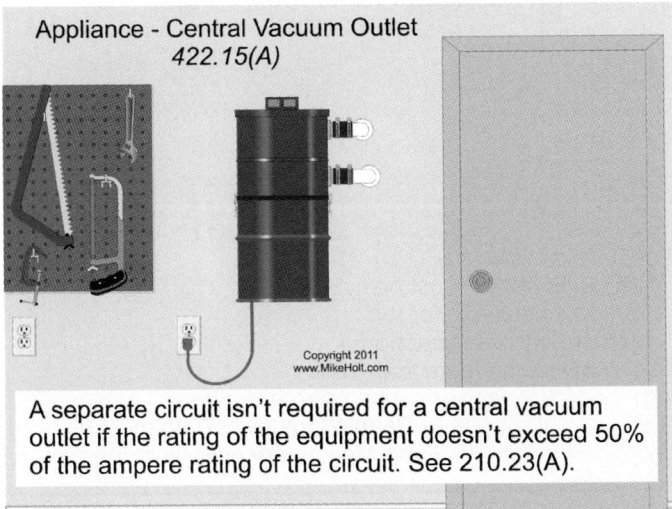

Appliance - Central Vacuum Outlet
422.15(A)

A separate circuit isn't required for a central vacuum outlet if the rating of the equipment doesn't exceed 50% of the ampere rating of the circuit. See 210.23(A).

Figure 422-7

422.16 Flexible Cords.

(A) General. Flexible cords are permitted to:

(1) Facilitate frequent interchange, or to prevent the transmission of noise and vibration [400.7(A)(6) and 400.7(A)(7)].

(2) Facilitate the removal of appliances fastened in place, where the fastening means and mechanical connections are specifically designed to permit ready removal [400.8(A)(8)].

Author's Comment: Flexible cords must not be used for the connection of water heaters, furnaces, and other appliances fastened in place, unless the appliances are specifically identified to be used with a flexible cord. **Figure 422-8**

(B) Specific Appliances.

(1) Waste (Garbage) Disposals. A flexible cord is permitted for a waste disposal if:

(1) The cord has a grounding-type attachment plug.

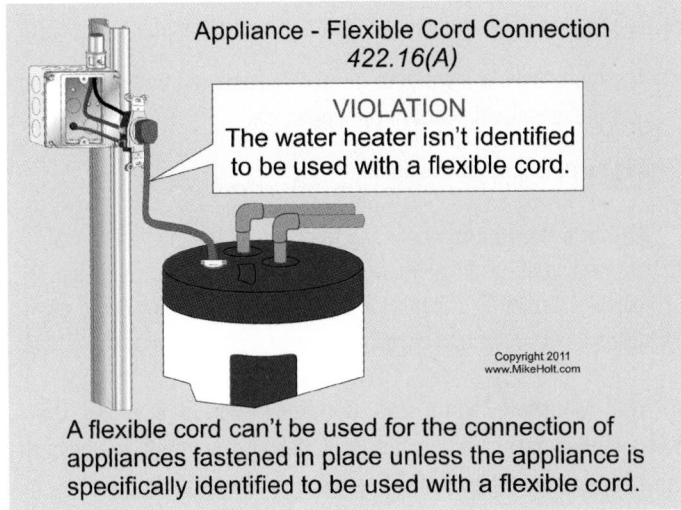

Appliance - Flexible Cord Connection
422.16(A)

VIOLATION
The water heater isn't identified to be used with a flexible cord.

A flexible cord can't be used for the connection of appliances fastened in place unless the appliance is specifically identified to be used with a flexible cord.

Figure 422-8

(2) The cord length is at least 18 in. and not longer than 3 ft.

(3) The waste disposal receptacle is located to avoid damage to the cord.

(4) The waste disposal receptacle is accessible.

(2) Dishwashers and Trash Compactors. A cord is permitted for a dishwasher or trash compactor if:

(1) The cord has a grounding-type attachment plug.

(2) The cord length is at least 3 ft and not longer than 4 ft, measured from the rear plane of the appliance. **Figure 422-9**

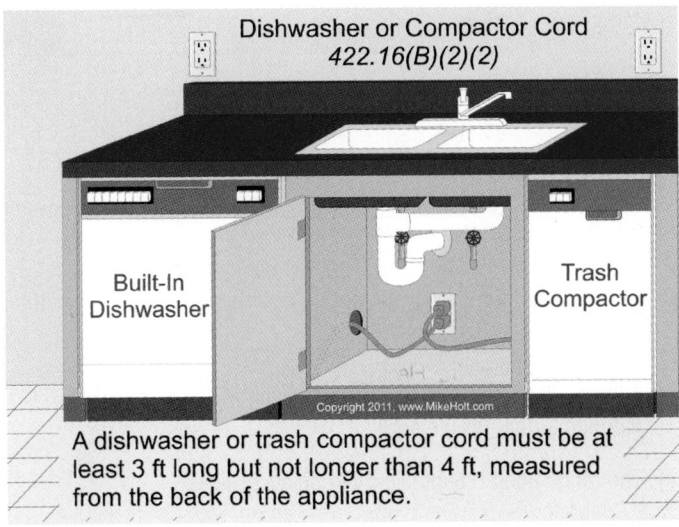

Dishwasher or Compactor Cord
422.16(B)(2)(2)

Built-In Dishwasher

Trash Compactor

A dishwasher or trash compactor cord must be at least 3 ft long but not longer than 4 ft, measured from the back of the appliance.

Figure 422-9

(3) The appliance receptacle is located to avoid damage to the cord.

(4) The receptacle is located in the space occupied by the appliance or in the space adjacent to the appliance.

(5) The receptacle is accessible.

Author's Comment: According to an article in the International Association of Electrical Inspectors magazine (IAEI News), a cord installed through a cabinet for an appliance isn't considered as being installed through a wall.

(3) Wall-Mounted Ovens and Counter-Mounted Cooking Units. Wall-mounted ovens and counter-mounted cooking units can be cord-and-plug-connected for ease in servicing for installation.

(4) Range Hoods. Range hoods can be cord-and-plug-connected if all of the following conditions are met: **Figure 422–10**

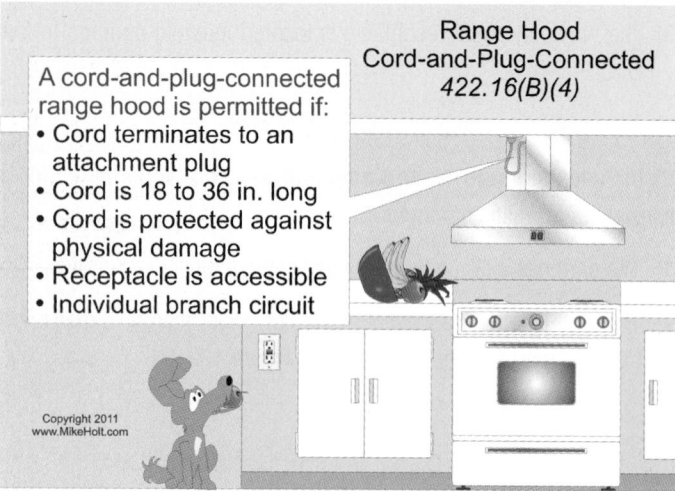

Figure 422–10

(1) The flexible cord terminates with a grounding-type attachment plug.

(2) The length of the cord must not be less than 18 in. or longer than 36 in.

(3) The range hood receptacle must be located to avoid physical damage to the flexible cord.

(4) The range hood receptacle must be accessible.

(5) The range hood receptacle must be supplied by an individual branch circuit.

Author's Comment: An above the range microwave that contains a fan listed as a range hood must comply with this section, if it's cord-and-plug-connected.

422.18 Support of Ceiling Paddle Fans. Ceiling paddle fans must be supported by a listed fan outlet box, or outlet box system, in accordance with 314.27(C). **Figure 422–11**

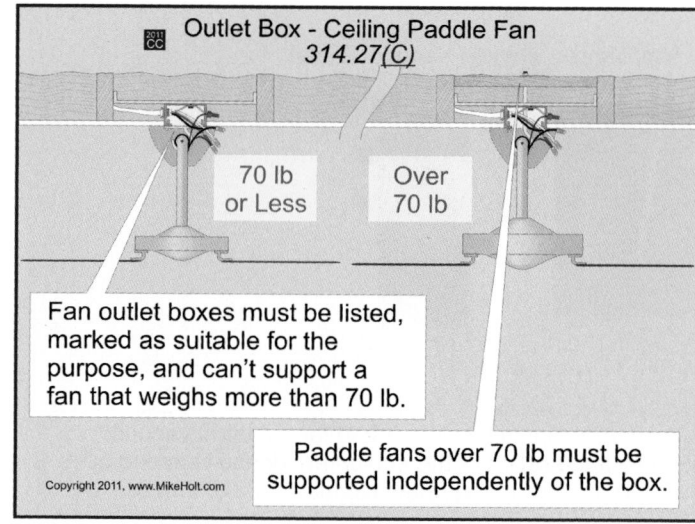

Figure 422–11

PART III. DISCONNECT

422.30 General. Each appliance must have a means that disconnects <u>simultaneously</u> all ungrounded circuit conductors.

422.31 Permanently Connected Appliance Disconnects.

(A) Appliances Rated at Not Over 300 VA or ⅛ Horsepower. The branch-circuit overcurrent device, such as a plug fuse or circuit breaker, can serve as the appliance disconnect.

(B) <u>Appliances Rated Over 300 VA.</u> A switch or circuit breaker can serve as the disconnect means if it's located within sight of the appliance, or the switch or circuit breaker is capable of being locked in the open position. The provision for locking or adding a lock to the disconnecting means must be on the switch or circuit breaker and remain in place with or without the lock installed. **Figure 422–12**

Author's Comment: According to Article 100, within sight means that it's visible and not more than 50 ft from one to the other.

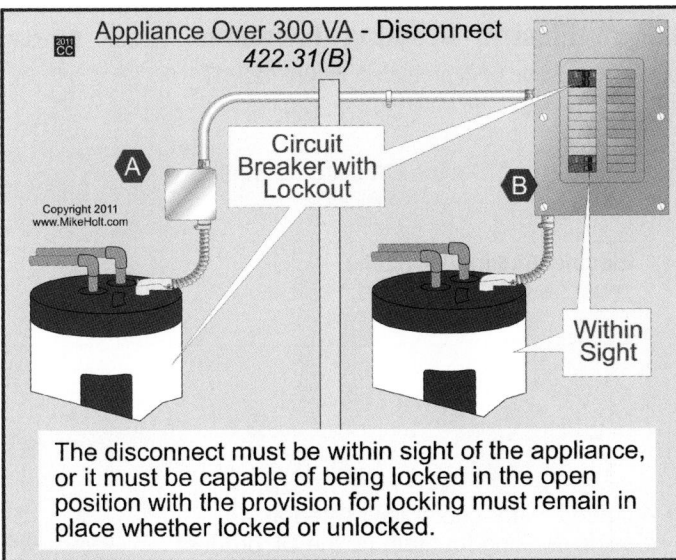

Figure 422–12

(C) Motor-Operated Appliances Rated Over $\frac{1}{8}$ Horsepower. A switch or circuit breaker located within sight from the motor-operated appliance can serve as the appliance disconnect.

Ex: An appliance containing a unit switch that complies with 422.34.

422.33 Cord-and-Plug-Connected Appliance Disconnects.

(A) Attachment Plugs and Receptacles. An accessible plug and receptacle can serve as the disconnecting means for a cord-and-plug-connected appliance. **Figure 422–13**

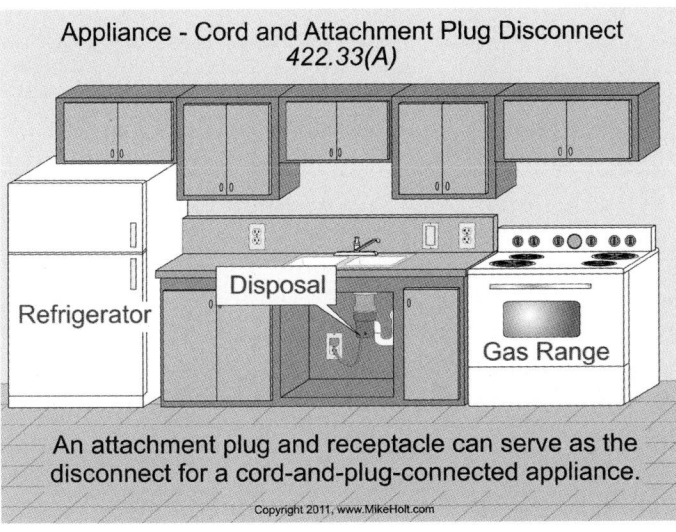

Figure 422–13

(B) Cord-and-Plug-Connected Ranges. The plug and receptacle of a cord-and-plug-connected household electric range can serve as the range disconnecting means, if the plug is accessible from the front of the range by the removal of a drawer. **Figure 422–14**

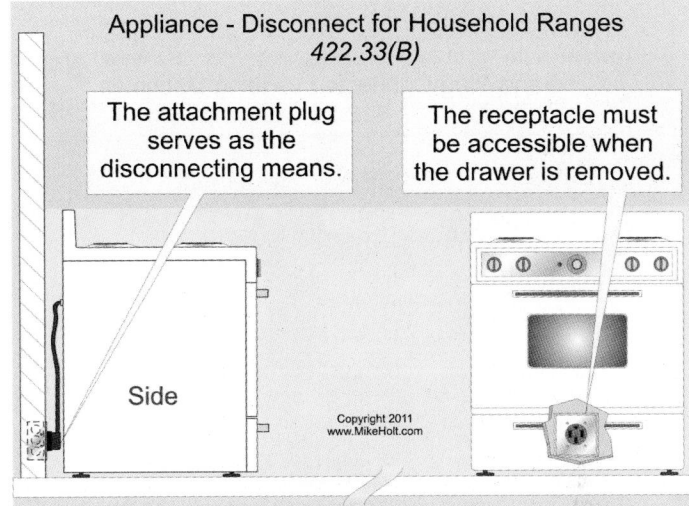

Figure 422–14

422.34 Unit Switches as Disconnects. A unit switch with a marked "off" position that's a part of the appliance can serve as the appliance disconnect, if it disconnects all ungrounded conductors. **Figure 422–15**

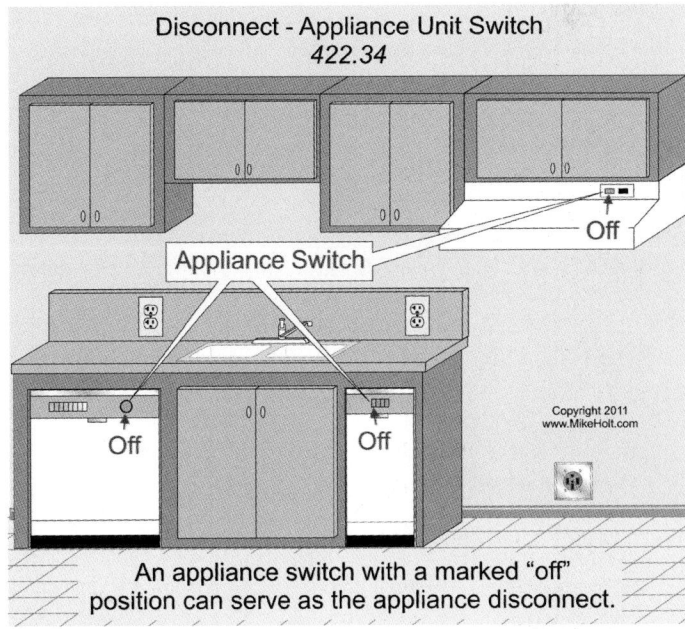

Figure 422–15

422.51 Cord-and-Plug-Connected Vending Machines.

Cord-and-plug-connected vending machines must include a GFCI as an integral part of the attachment plug, or within 12 in. of the attachment plug. Older machines that aren't so equipped must be connected to a GFCI-protected outlet. **Figure 422–16**

Cord-and-Plug-Connected Vending Machines
422.51

Cord-and-plug-connected vending machines must
have an attachment cord with integral GFCI protection.

Copyright 2011
www.MikeHolt.com

Figure 422–16

Author's Comment: Because electric vending machines are often located in damp or wet locations in public places, and are used by people standing on the ground, reliance on an equipment grounding conductor for protection against electrocution is insufficient.

422.52 Electric Drinking Fountains. Electric drinking fountains must be GFCI protected. **Figure 422–17**

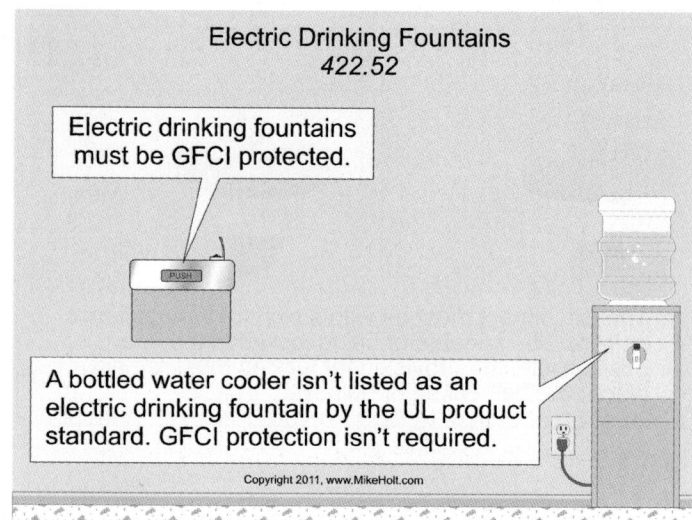

Electric Drinking Fountains
422.52

Electric drinking fountains
must be GFCI protected.

A bottled water cooler isn't listed as an
electric drinking fountain by the UL product
standard. GFCI protection isn't required.

Copyright 2011, www.MikeHolt.com

Figure 422–17

ARTICLE 424

Fixed Electric Space-Heating Equipment

INTRODUCTION TO ARTICLE 424—FIXED ELECTRIC SPACE-HEATING EQUIPMENT

Many people are surprised to see how many pages Article 424 has. This is a nine-part article on fixed electric space heaters. Why so much text for what seems to be a simple application? The answer is that Article 424 covers a variety of applications—heaters come in various configurations for various uses. Not all of these parts are for the electrician in the field—the requirements in Part IV are for manufacturers.

Fixed space heaters (wall-mounted, ceiling-mounted, or free-standing) are common in many utility buildings and other small structures, as well as in some larger structures. When used to heat floors, space-heating cables address the thermal layering problem typical of forced-air systems—so it's likely you'll encounter them. Duct heaters are very common in large office and educational buildings. These provide a distributed heating scheme. Locating the heater in the ductwork, but close to the occupied space, eliminates the waste of transporting heated air through sheet metal routed in unheated spaces, so it's likely you'll encounter those as well.

PART I. GENERAL

424.1 Scope.
Article 424 contains the installation requirements for fixed electrical equipment used for space heating, such as heating cables, unit heaters, boilers, or central systems.

> **Author's Comment:** Wiring for fossil-fuel heating equipment, such as gas, oil, or coal central furnaces, must be installed in accordance with Article 422, specifically 422.12.

424.3 Branch Circuits.

(B) Branch-Circuit Sizing. For the purpose of sizing branch-circuit conductors, fixed electric space-heating equipment <u>and motor(s)</u> are to be considered a continuous load.

> **Author's Comment:** The branch-circuit conductors and overcurrent devices for fixed electric space-heating equipment must have an ampacity not less than 125 percent of the total heating load [210.19(A)(1) and 210.20(A)].

Question: What size conductor and overcurrent device are required for a 9.60 kW, 240V fixed electric space heater that has a 3A blower motor with 75°C terminals? **Figure 424–1**

(a) 10 AWG, 30A   (b) 8 AWG, 40A
(c) 6 AWG, 60A   (d) 4 AWG, 80A

Answer: (c) 6 AWG, 60A

Step 1: Determine the total load:

$I = VA/E$
$I = 9,6000\ VA/240V$
$I = 40A + 3A = 43A$

Step 2: Size the conductors at 125 percent of the total current load [110.14(C)(1), 210.19(A)(1), and Table 310.15(B)(16)]:

Conductor = 43A x 1.25
Conductor = 53.75A, 6 AWG, rated 65A at 75°C

Step 3: Size the overcurrent device at 125 percent of the total current load [210.20(A), 240.4(B), and 240.6(A)]:

Overcurrent Protection = 43A x 1.25
Overcurrent Protection = 53.75A, next size up is 60A

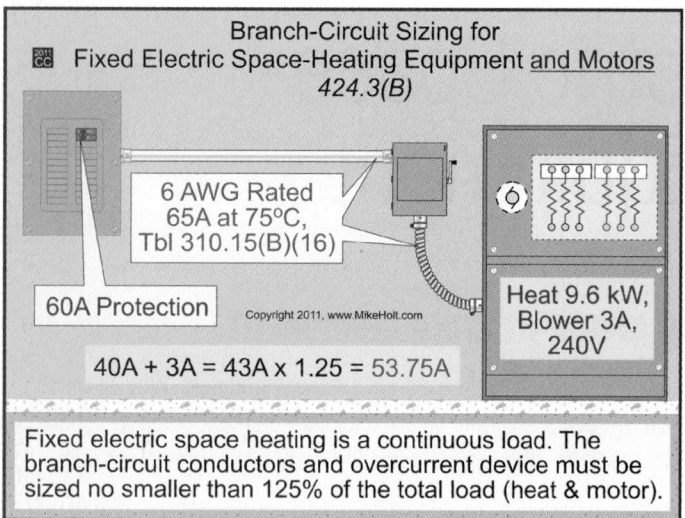

Figure 424–1

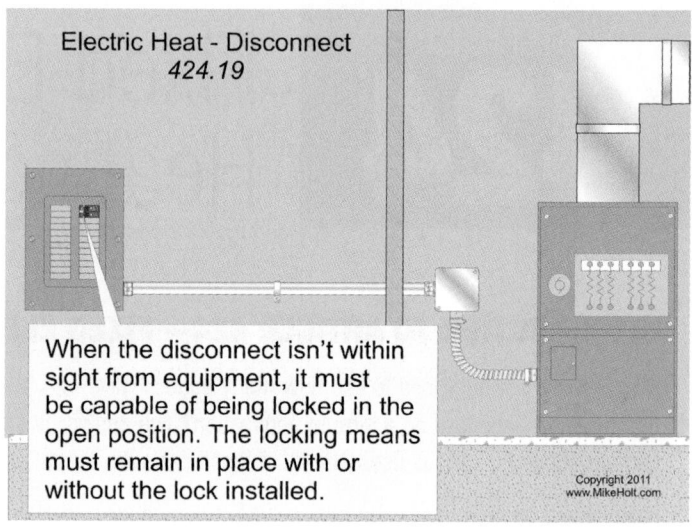

Figure 424–2

424.9 Permanently Installed Electric Baseboard Heaters with Receptacles.
If a permanently installed electric baseboard heater has factory-installed receptacle outlets, the receptacles must not be connected to the heater circuits.

Note: Listed baseboard heaters include instructions that prohibit their installation below receptacle outlets.

PART III. ELECTRIC SPACE-HEATING EQUIPMENT

424.19 Disconnecting Means. Means must be provided to simultaneously disconnect the heater, motor controller, and supplementary overcurrent devices of all fixed electric space-heating equipment from all ungrounded conductors.

The disconnecting means must be capable of being locked in the open position. The provision for locking or adding a lock to the disconnecting means must be on the switch or circuit breaker, and it must remain in place with or without the lock installed. **Figure 424–2**

(A) Heating Equipment with Supplementary Overcurrent Protection. The disconnecting means for fixed electric space-heating equipment with supplementary overcurrent protection must be within sight from the supplementary overcurrent devices.

Author's Comment: According to Article 100, within sight means that it's visible and not more than 50 ft from one to the other.

(B) Heating Equipment Without Supplementary Overcurrent Protection. For fixed electric space-heating equipment, the branch-circuit circuit breaker is permitted to serve as the disconnecting means if the circuit breaker is within sight from the heater or it's capable of being locked in the open position.

(C) Unit Switch as Disconnect. A unit switch with a marked "off" position that's an integral part of the equipment can serve as the heater disconnecting means, if it disconnects all ungrounded conductors of the circuit. **Figure 424–3**

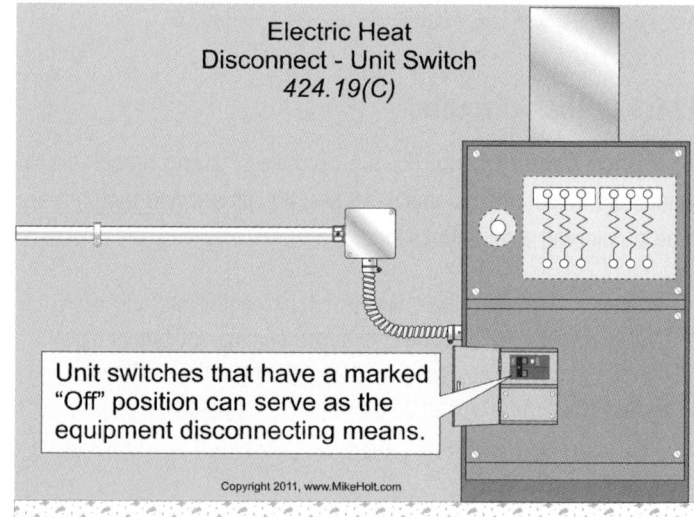

Figure 424–3

PART V. ELECTRIC SPACE-HEATING CABLES

424.36 Clearances of Wiring in Ceilings.
Wiring located above heated ceilings must be spaced not less than 2 in. above the heated ceiling and is considered as operating at an ambient temperature of 50°C.

424.38 Area Restrictions.

(A) Must Not Extend Beyond the Room or Area. Heating cables must not extend beyond the room or area in which they originate.

(B) Uses Prohibited. Heating cables must not be installed:

(1) In closets.

(2) Over walls.

(3) Over partitions that extend to the ceiling.

424.39 Clearance from Other Objects and Openings.
Heating elements of cables must be separated at least 8 in. from the edge of outlet boxes and junction boxes used for mounting surface luminaires and 2 in. from recessed luminaires and their trims.

424.44 Installation of Cables in Concrete or Poured Masonry Floors.

(G) GFCI Protection. GFCI protection is required for electric space-heating cables that are embedded in concrete or poured masonry floors of bathrooms, kitchens, and hydromassage bathtub locations. Figure 424–4

> **Author's Comment:** See 680.28(C)(3) for restrictions on the installation of radiant-heating cables for spas and hot tubs installed outdoors.

PART VI. DUCT HEATERS

424.65 Disconnect for Electric Duct Heater Controllers.
Means must be provided to disconnect the heater, motor controller, and supplementary overcurrent devices from all ungrounded conductors of the circuit. The disconnecting means must be within sight from the equipment, or it must be capable of being locked in the open position [424.19(A)]. The provision for locking or adding a lock to the disconnecting means must be on the switch or circuit breaker, and must remain in place with or without the lock installed. A portable locking means doesn't meet the "locked in the open position" requirement. **Figure 424–5**

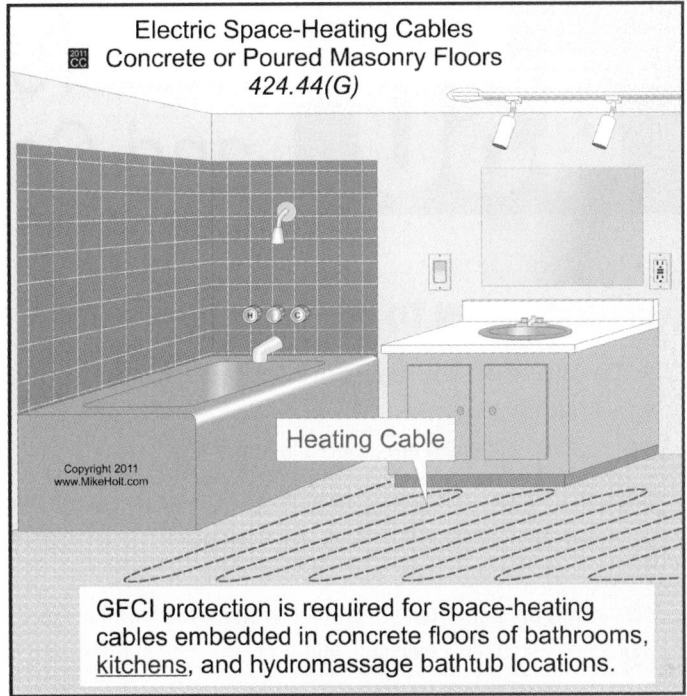

Electric Space-Heating Cables
Concrete or Poured Masonry Floors
424.44(G)

Heating Cable

GFCI protection is required for space-heating cables embedded in concrete floors of bathrooms, kitchens, and hydromassage bathtub locations.

Figure 424–4

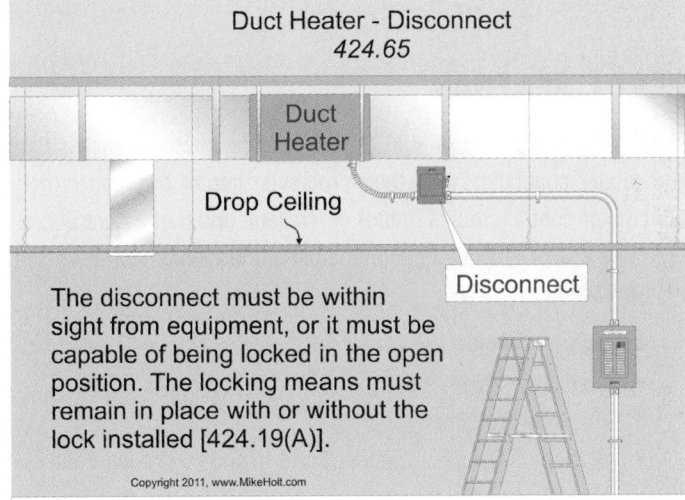

Duct Heater - Disconnect
424.65

Duct Heater

Drop Ceiling

Disconnect

The disconnect must be within sight from equipment, or it must be capable of being locked in the open position. The locking means must remain in place with or without the lock installed [424.19(A)].

Copyright 2011, www.MikeHolt.com

Figure 424–5

> **Author's Comment:** The disconnecting means for a duct heater isn't required to be readily accessible. Therefore, it can be located within a suspended ceiling area adjacent to the duct heater as long as it's accessible by portable means [240.24(A)(4) and 404.8(A) Ex 2].

ARTICLE 430

Motors, Motor Circuits, and Controllers

INTRODUCTION TO ARTICLE 430—MOTORS, MOTOR CIRCUITS, AND CONTROLLERS

Article 430 contains the specific rules for conductor sizing, overcurrent protection, control circuit conductors, controllers, and disconnecting means for electric motors. The installation requirements for motor control centers are covered in Part VIII, and air-conditioning and refrigeration equipment are covered in Article 440.

Article 430 is one of the longest articles in the *NEC*. It's also one of the most complex, but motors are also complex equipment. They're electrical and mechanical devices, but what makes motor applications complex is the fact that they're inductive loads with a high-current demand at start-up that's typically six, or more, times the running current. This makes overcurrent protection for motor applications necessarily different from the protection employed for other types of equipment. So don't confuse general overcurrent protection with motor protection—you must calculate and apply them differently using the rules in Article 430.

You might be uncomfortable with the allowances for overcurrent protection found in this article, such as protecting a 10 AWG conductor with a 60A overcurrent protection device, but as you learn to understand how motor protection works, you'll understand why these allowances aren't only safe, but necessary.

PART I. GENERAL

430.1 Scope. Article 430 covers motors, motor branch-circuit and feeder conductors and their protection, motor overload protection, motor control circuits, motor controllers, and motor control centers. This article is divided into many parts, the most important being: Figure 430–1

- General—Part I
- Conductor Size—Part II
- Overload Protection—Part III
- Branch Circuit Short-Circuit and Ground-Fault Protection—Part IV
- Feeder Short-Circuit and Ground-Fault Protection—Part V
- Motor Control Circuits—Part VI
- Motor Controllers—Part VII
- Motor Control Centers—Part VIII
- Disconnecting Means—Part IX

Note 1: Article 440 contains the installation requirements for electrically driven air-conditioning and refrigeration equipment [440.1]. Also see 110.26(E) for dedicated space requirements for motor control centers.

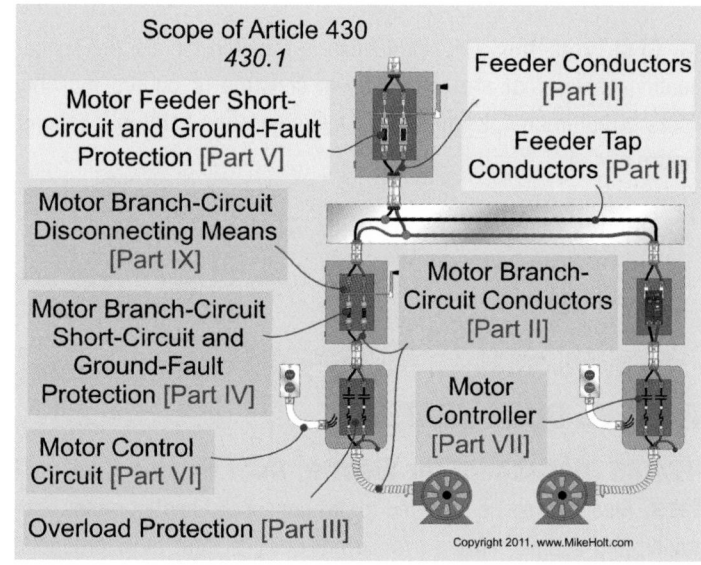

Figure 430–1

430.2 Definitions.

Adjustable-Speed Drive. A combination of the power converter, motor, and motor mounted auxiliary devices such as encoders, tachometers, thermal switches and detectors, air blowers, heaters, and vibration sensors.

Author's Comment: Adjustable-speed drives are often referred to as "variable-speed drives" or "variable-frequency drives."

Controller. A switch or device used to start and stop a motor by making and breaking the motor circuit current. **Figure 430–2**

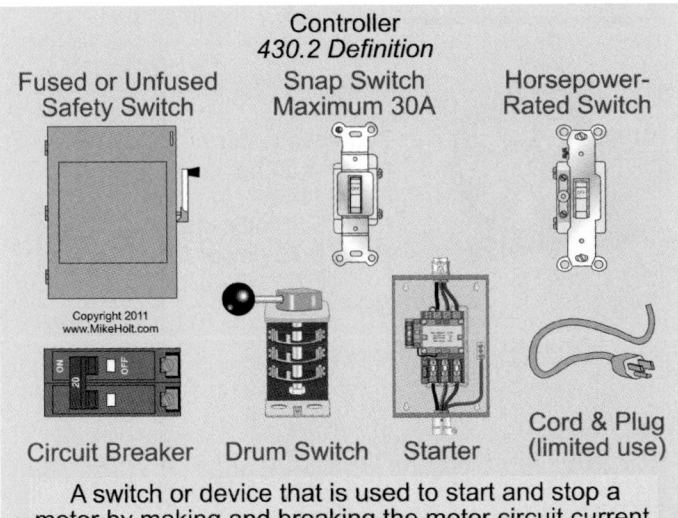

Figure 430–2

Author's Comments:

- A controller can be a horsepower-rated switch, snap switch, or circuit breaker. A pushbutton that operates an electromechanical relay isn't a controller because it doesn't meet the controller rating requirements of 430.83. Devices such as start-stop stations and pressure switches are control devices, not motor controllers. **Figure 430–3**

- Controllers discussed in Article 430 are those that meet this definition, not the definition of "Controller" in Article 100.

Motor Control Circuit. The circuit that carries the electric signals that direct the performance of the controller. **Figure 430–4**

430.6 Table FLC versus Motor Nameplate Current Rating.

(A) General Requirements. Figure 430–5

(1) Table Full-Load Current (FLC). The motor full-load current ratings listed in Tables 430.247, 430.248, and 430.250 are used to determine the conductor ampacity [430.22], the branch-circuit short-circuit and ground-fault overcurrent device size [430.52 and 430.62], and the ampere rating of disconnecting switches [430.110].

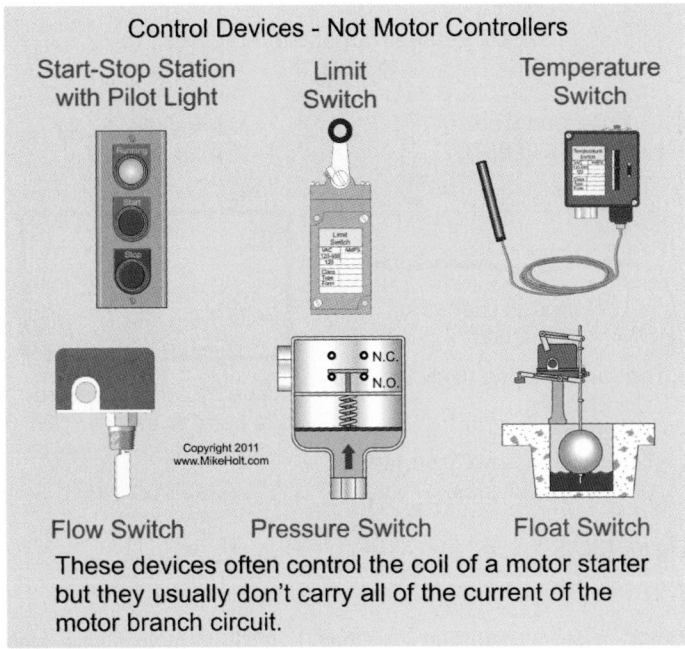

Figure 430–3

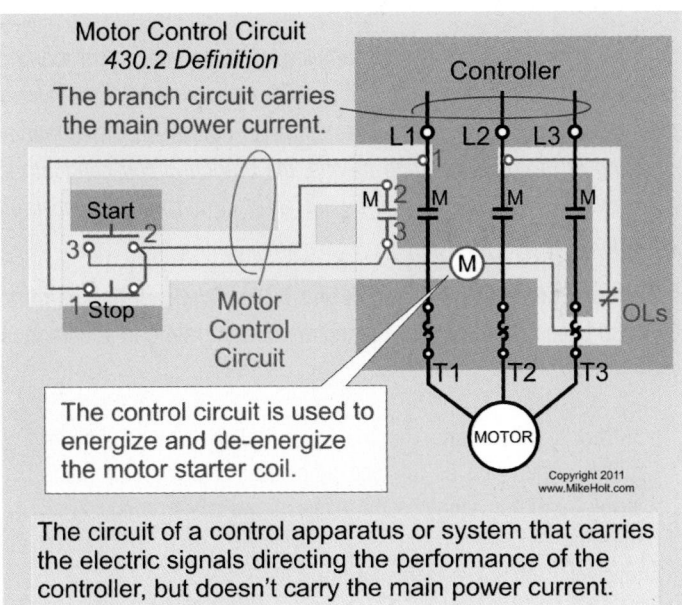

Figure 430–4

Author's Comment: The actual current rating on the motor nameplate full-load amperes (FLA) [430.6(A)(2)] isn't permitted to be used to determine the conductor ampacity, the branch-circuit short-circuit and ground-fault overcurrent device size, nor the ampere rating of disconnecting switches.

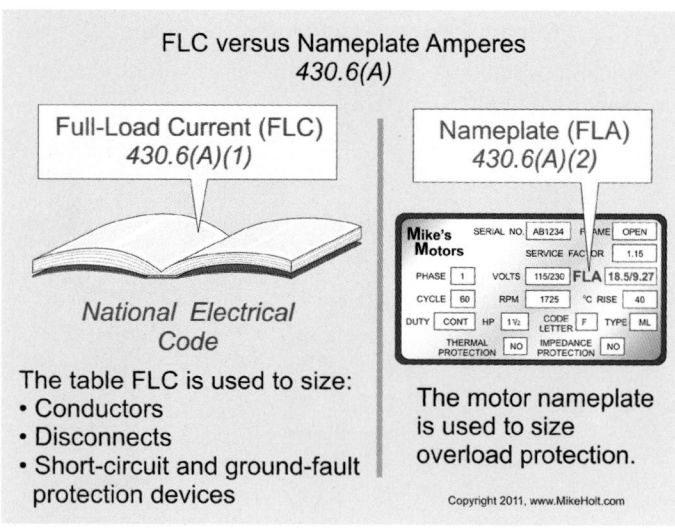

Figure 430–5

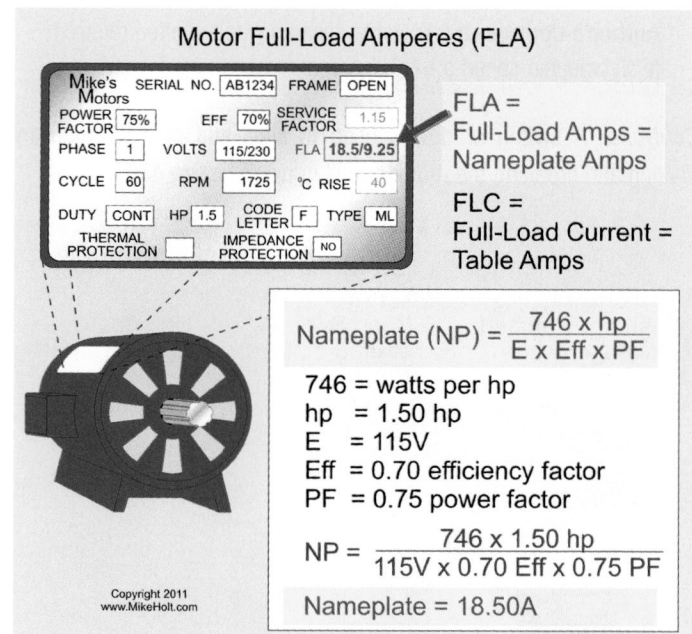

Figure 430–6

Motors built to operate at less than 1,200 RPM or that have high torques may have higher full-load currents, and multispeed motors have full-load current varying with speed, in which case the nameplate current ratings must be used.

Ex 3: For a listed motor-operated appliance, the actual current marked on the nameplate of the appliance must be used instead of the horsepower rating on the appliance nameplate to determine the ampacity or rating of the disconnecting means, the branch-circuit conductors, the controller, and the branch-circuit short-circuit and ground-fault protection.

(2) Motor Nameplate Current Rating (FLA). Overload devices must be sized based on the motor nameplate current rating in accordance with 430.31.

> **Author's Comment:** The motor nameplate full-load ampere rating is identified as full-load amperes (FLA). The FLA rating is the current in amperes the motor draws while producing its rated horsepower load at its rated voltage, based on its rated efficiency and power factor. **Figure 430–6**

The actual current drawn by the motor depends upon the load on the motor and on the actual operating voltage at the motor terminals. That is, if the load increases, the current also increases, or if the motor operates at a voltage below its nameplate rating, the operating current will increase.

> ⚠️ **CAUTION:** *To prevent damage to motor windings from excessive heat (caused by excessive current), never load a motor above its horsepower rating, and be sure the voltage source matches the motor's voltage rating.*

430.8 Marking on Controllers. A controller must be marked with the manufacturer's name or identification, the voltage, the current or horsepower rating, the short-circuit current rating, and other necessary data to properly indicate the applications for which it's suitable.

Ex 1: The short-circuit current rating isn't required for controllers applied in accordance with 430.81(A), 430.81(B), or 430.83(C).

Ex 2: The short-circuit rating isn't required on the controller when the short-circuit current rating of the controller is marked elsewhere on the assembly.

Ex 3: The short-circuit rating isn't required on the controller when the assembly into which it's installed has a marked short-circuit current rating.

Ex 4: A short-circuit rating isn't required on controllers rated less than 2 hp at 300V or less, if they're listed for use on general-purpose branch circuits.

430.9 Motor Controller Terminal Requirements.

(B) Copper Conductors. Motor controllers and terminals of control circuit devices must be connected with copper conductors.

(C) Torque Requirements. Motor control conductors 14 AWG and smaller must be torqued at a minimum of 7 lb-in. for screw-type pressure terminals, unless identified otherwise. See 110.3(B) and 110.14 Note.

430.14 Location of Motors.

(A) Ventilation and Maintenance. Motors must be located so adequate ventilation is provided and maintenance can be readily accomplished.

430.17 The Highest Rated Motor. When sizing motor circuit conductors, the highest rated motor is the motor with the highest rated full-load current rating (FLC).

> **Question:** Which of the following motors has the highest FLC rating? **Figure 430–7**
>
> (a) 10 hp, three-phase, 208V   (b) 5 hp, single-phase, 208V
> (c) 3 hp, single-phase, 120V   (d) none of these
>
> **Answer:** (c) 3 hp, single-phase, 120V
>
> 10 hp = 30.80A [Table 430.250]
> 5 hp = 30.80A [Table 430.248]
> 3 hp = 34.00A [Table 430.248]

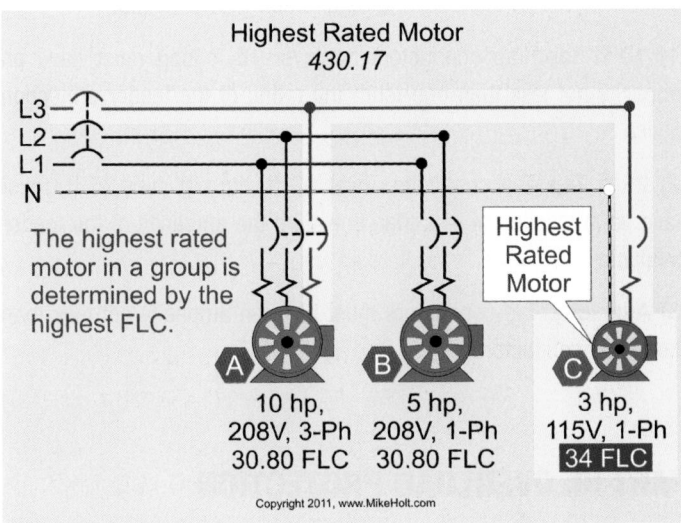

Figure 430–7

PART II. CONDUCTOR SIZE

430.22 Single Motor Conductor Size. Conductors to a single motor must be sized not less than 125 percent of the motor FLC rating as listed in Table 430.247 Direct-Current Motors, Table 430.248 Single-Phase Motors, or Table 430.250 Three-Phase Motors. Figure 430–8

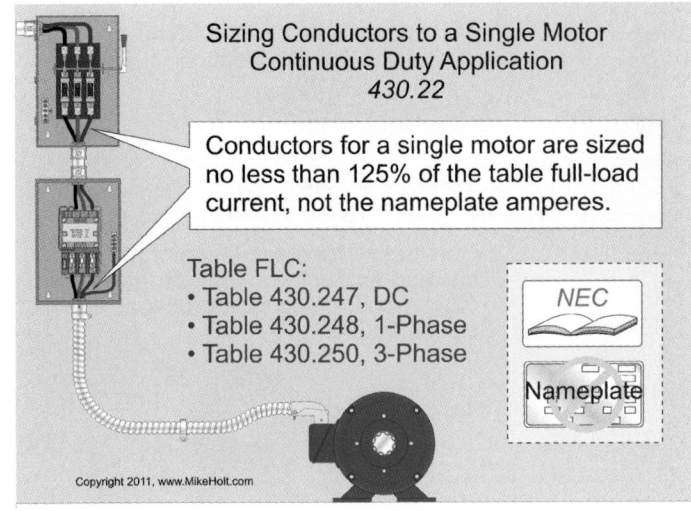

Figure 430–8

> **Question:** What size branch-circuit conductor is required for a 7½ hp, 230V, three-phase motor? **Figure 430–9**
>
> (a) 14 AWG   (b) 12 AWG   (c) 10 AWG   (d) 8 AWG
>
> **Answer:** (c) 10 AWG
>
> Motor FLC = 22A [Table 430.250]
>
> Conductor's Size = 22A x 1.25
> Conductor's Size = 27.50A, 10 AWG, rated 30A at 75°C [Table 310.15(B)(16)]
>
> Note: The branch-circuit short-circuit and ground-fault protection device using an inverse time breaker is sized at 60A according to 430.52(C)(1) Ex 1:
>
> Circuit Protection = 22A x 2.50
> Circuit Protection = 55A, next size up 60A [240.6(A)]

430.24 Several Motors—Conductor Size. Circuit conductors that supply several motors must not be sized smaller than the sum of the following:

(1) 125 percent of the full-load current of the highest rated motor

(2) The full-load current ratings of other motors

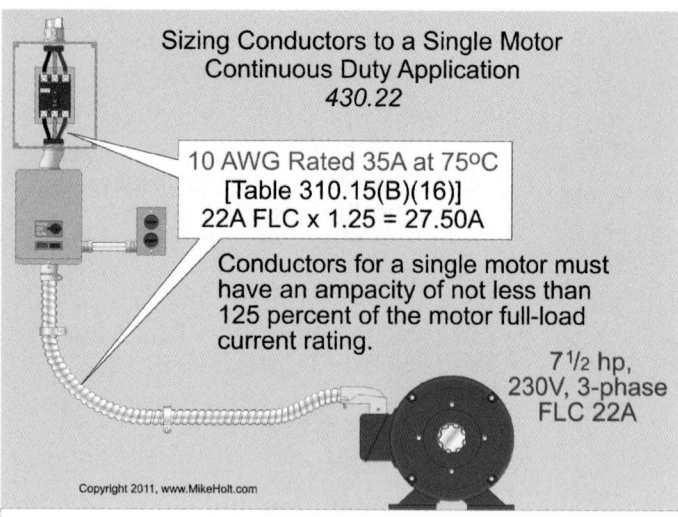

Figure 430–9

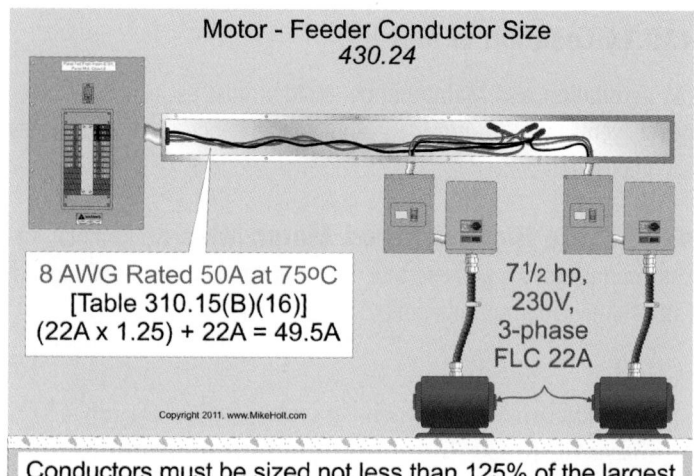

Figure 430–10

Question: What size feeder conductor is required for two 7½ hp, 230V, three-phase motors, if the terminals are rated for 75°C?
Figure 430–10

(a) 14 AWG   *(b) 12 AWG*   *(c) 10 AWG*   *(d) 8 AWG*

Answer: (d) 8 AWG

Motor FLC = 22A [Table 430.250]

Motor Feeder Conductor = (22A x 1.25) + 22A

Motor Feeder Conductor = 49.50A, 8 AWG rated 50A at 75°C [Table 310.15(B)(16)]

Author's Comment: The feeder overcurrent device (inverse time circuit breaker) must comply with 430.62 as follows:

Step 1: Determine the largest branch-circuit overcurrent device rating [240.6(A) and 430.52(C)(1) Ex 1]:

            22A x 2.50 = 55A, next size up 60A

Step 2: Size the feeder overcurrent device in accordance with 240.6(A) and 430.62:

            Feeder Inverse Time Breaker: 60A + 22A = 82A, next size down, 80A

Author's Comment: The "next size up protection" rule for branch circuits [430.52(C)(1) Ex 1] doesn't apply to motor feeder short-circuit and ground-fault protection device sizing.

430.28 Motor Feeder Taps. Motor circuit conductors tapped from a feeder must have an ampacity in accordance with 430.22, and the tap conductors must terminate in a branch-circuit short-circuit and ground-fault protection device sized in accordance with 430.52. In addition, one of the following requirements must be met:

(1) 10 ft Tap. Tap conductors not over 10 ft long must have an ampacity not less than one-tenth the rating of the feeder protection device.

(2) 25 ft Tap. Tap conductors over 10 ft, but not over 25 ft, must have an ampacity not less than one-third the ampacity of the feeder conductor.

(3) Ampacity. Tap conductors must have an ampacity not less than the feeder conductors.

PART III. OVERLOAD PROTECTION

Part III contains the requirements for overload devices. Overload devices are intended to protect motors, motor control equipment, and motor branch-circuit conductors against excessive heating due to motor overloads and failure to start.

Overload is the operation of equipment in excess of the normal, full-load current rating, which, if it persists for a sufficient amount of time, will cause damage or dangerous overheating of the equipment.

Author's Comment: Article 100 defines overcurrent as "current in excess of the rated current of equipment or the ampacity of a conductor from an overload, a short circuit, or a ground fault." Because of the difference between starting and running current, the overcurrent protection for motors is generally accomplished by having the overload device separate from the motor's short-circuit and ground-fault protection device (Article 430 Part IV). **Figure 430–11**

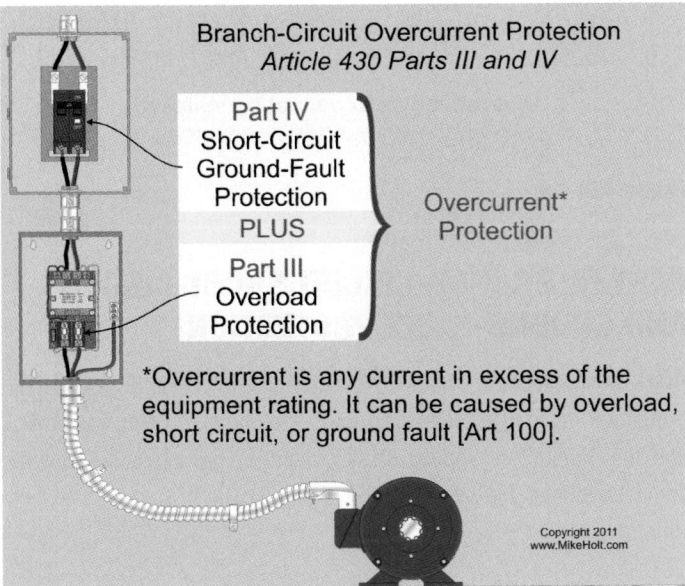

Figure 430–11

430.31 Overload. Overload devices (sometimes called "heaters") are intended to provide overload protection, and come in a variety of configurations; they can be conventional or electronic. In addition, a fuse sized in accordance with 430.32 can be used for circuit overload protection [430.55]. **Figure 430–12**

Note: An overload is a condition where equipment is operated above its current rating, or where current is in excess of the conductor ampacity. When an overload condition persists for a sufficient length of time, it could result in equipment failure or a fire from damaging or dangerous overheating. A fault, such as a short circuit or ground fault, isn't an overload [Article 100].

Author's Comments:

- Motor overload protection sizing is usually accomplished by installing the correct "heater" or setting the overload device in accordance with the controller's instructions, based on the motor nameplate current rating.

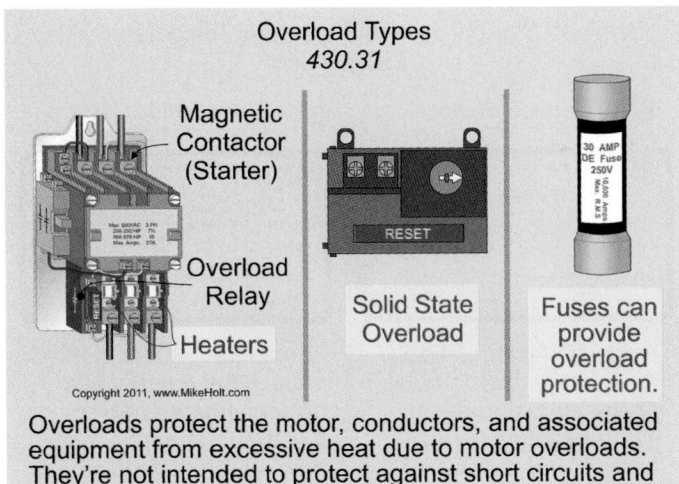

Overloads protect the motor, conductors, and associated equipment from excessive heat due to motor overloads. They're not intended to protect against short circuits and ground faults.

Figure 430–12

- The intended level of protection required in Article 430 Part III is for overload and failure-to-start protection only, in order to protect against the motor becoming a fire hazard.

Overload protection isn't required if it might introduce additional or increased hazards, as in the case of fire pumps.

Note: See 695.7 for the protection requirements for fire pump supply conductors.

430.32 Overload Sizing for Continuous-Duty Motors.

(A) Motors Rated More Than One Horsepower. Motors rated more than 1 hp, used in a continuous-duty application without integral thermal protection, must have an overload device sized as follows:

(1) Separate Overload Device. A separate overload device must be selected to open at no more than the following percent of the motor nameplate full-load current rating: **Figure 430–13**

Service Factor. Motors with a marked service factor (SF) of 1.15 or more on the nameplate must have the overload device sized no more than 125 percent of the motor nameplate current rating.

Author's Comment: A service factor of 1.15 means the motor is designed to operate periodically at 115 percent of its rated horsepower.

Temperature Rise. Motors with a nameplate temperature rise of 40°C or less must have the overload device sized no more than 125 percent of the motor nameplate current rating.

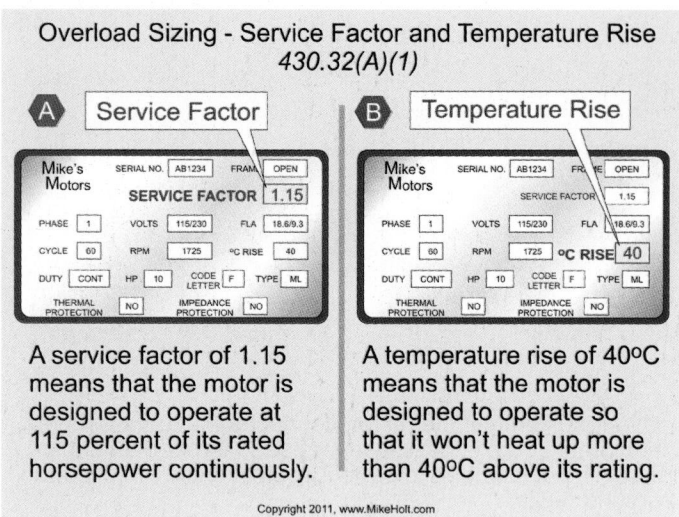

Figure 430–13

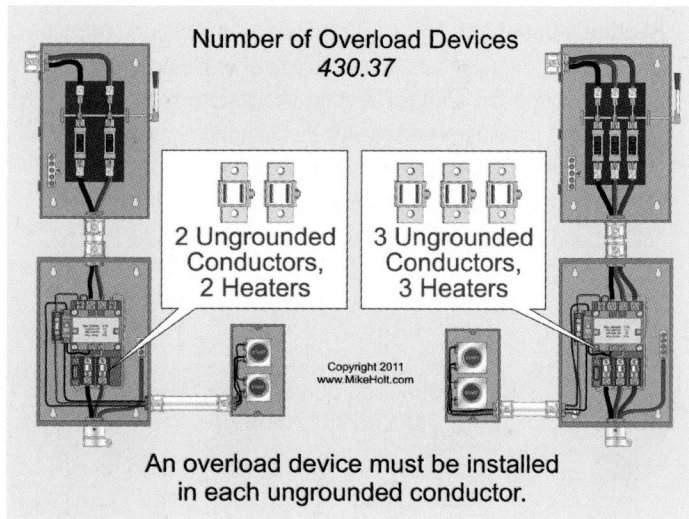

Figure 430–14

Author's Comment: A motor with a nameplate temperature rise of 40°C means the motor is designed to operate so that it won't heat up more than 40°C above its rated ambient temperature when operated at its rated load and voltage. Studies have shown that when the operating temperature of a motor is increased 10°C, the motor winding insulating material's anticipated life is reduced by 50 percent.

All Other Motors. No more than 115 percent of the motor "nameplate current rating."

430.36 Use of Fuses for Overload Protection. If fuses are used for overload protection, one must be provided for each ungrounded conductor of the circuit.

Author's Comment: If remote control isn't required for a motor, considerable savings can be achieved by using dual-element fuses (eliminate a motor controller) sized in accordance with 430.32 to protect the motor and the circuit conductors against overcurrent, which includes overload, short circuit, and ground faults. See 430.55 for more information.

430.37 Number of Overload Devices. An overload device must be installed in each ungrounded conductor. **Figure 430–14**

PART IV. BRANCH-CIRCUIT SHORT-CIRCUIT AND GROUND-FAULT PROTECTION

430.51 General. A branch-circuit short-circuit and ground-fault protective device protects the motor, the motor control equipment, and the conductors against short circuits or ground faults, but not against overload. **Figure 430–15**

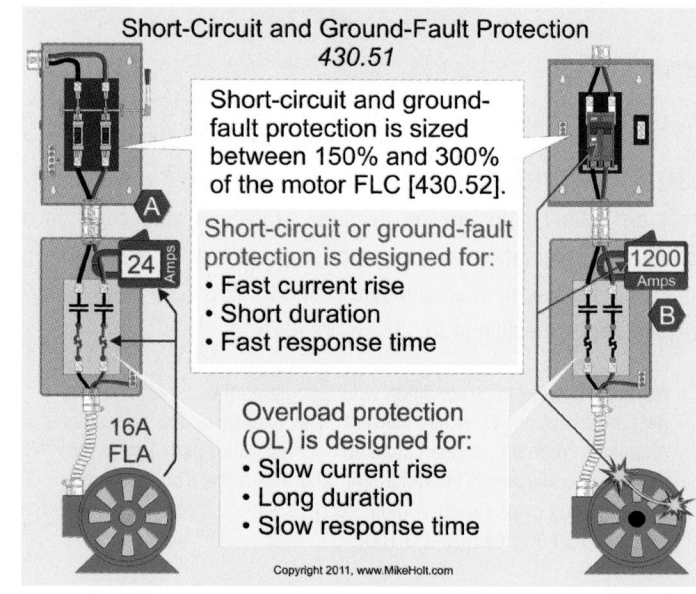

Figure 430–15

Author's Comment: Overload protection must comply with the requirements contained in 430.32.

Motor-Starting Current. When voltage is first applied to the field winding of an induction motor, only the conductor resistance opposes the flow of current through the motor winding. Because the conductor resistance is so low, the motor will have a very large inrush current. Figure 430–16

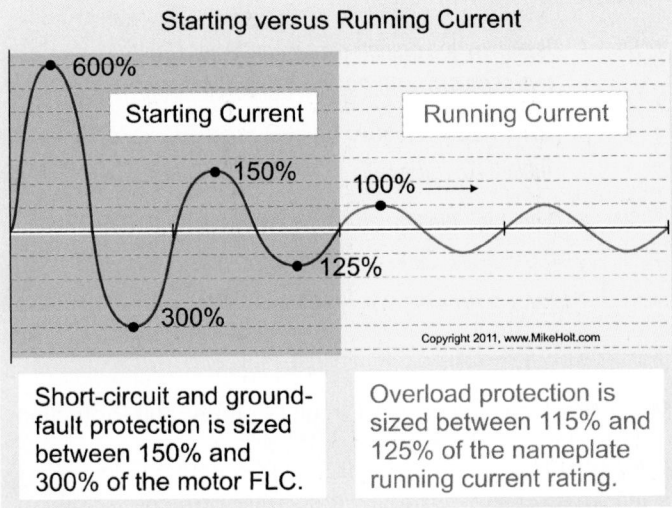

Starting versus Running Current

600%

Starting Current | Running Current

150%

100% →

125%

300%

Copyright 2011, www.MikeHolt.com

Short-circuit and ground-fault protection is sized between 150% and 300% of the motor FLC.

Overload protection is sized between 115% and 125% of the nameplate running current rating.

Figure 430–16

Motor-Running Current. Once the rotor begins turning, there's an increase in counter-electromotive force which reduces the starting current to running current. See Figure 430–16.

Motor Locked-Rotor Current (LRC). If the rotating part of the motor winding (armature) becomes jammed so it can't rotate, no counter-electromotive force (CEMF) will be produced in the motor winding. This results in a decrease in conductor impedance to the point that it's effectively a short circuit. Result—the motor operates at locked-rotor current (LRC), often six times the full-load ampere rating, depending on the motor code letter rating [430.7(B)], and this will cause the motor winding to overheat and be destroyed if the current isn't quickly reduced or removed.

Author's Comment: The *National Electrical Code* requires that most motors be provided with overcurrent protection to prevent damage to the motor winding because of locked-rotor current.

430.52 Branch-Circuit Short-Circuit and Ground-Fault Protection.

(A) General. The motor branch-circuit short-circuit and ground-fault protective device must comply with 430.52(B) and 430.52(C).

(B) All Motors. A motor branch-circuit short-circuit and ground-fault protective device must be capable of carrying the motor's starting current.

(C) Rating or Setting.

(1) Table 430.52. Each motor branch circuit must be protected against short circuit and ground faults by a protective device sized no greater than the following percentages listed in Table 430.52.

Table 430.52			
Motor Type	Nontime Delay	Dual-Element Fuse	Inverse Time Breaker
Wound Rotor	150%	150%	150%
Direct Current	150%	150%	150%
All Other Motors	300%	175%	250%

Question: What size conductor and inverse time circuit breaker are required for a 2 hp, 230V, single-phase motor? **Figure 430–17**

(a) 14 AWG, 30A breaker   (b) 14 AWG, 35A breaker
(c) 14 AWG, 40A breaker   (d) 14 AWG, 45A breaker

Answer: (a) 14 AWG, 30A breaker

Step 1: Determine the branch-circuit conductor [Table 310.15(B)(16), 430.22, and Table 430.248]:

    12A x 1.25 = 15A, 14 AWG, rated 20A at 75°C [Table 310.15(B)(16)]

Step 2: Determine the branch-circuit protection [240.6(A), 430.52(C)(1), and Table 430.248]:

    12A x 2.50 = 30A

Author's Comment: I know it bothers many in the electrical industry to see a 14 AWG conductor protected by a 30A circuit breaker, but branch-circuit conductors are protected against overloads by the overload device, which is sized between 115 and 125 percent of the motor nameplate current rating [430.32]. The small conductor rule contained in 240.4(D) which limits 15A protection for 14 AWG doesn't apply to motor circuit protection. See 240.4(D) and 240.4(G).

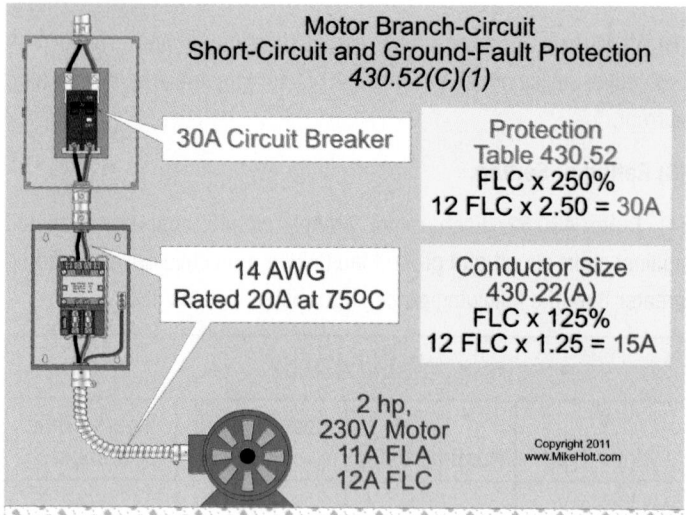

Figure 430–17

Ex 1: If the motor short-circuit and ground-fault protective device values derived from Table 430.52 don't correspond with the standard overcurrent device ratings listed in 240.6(A), the next higher overcurrent device rating can be used. Figure 430–18

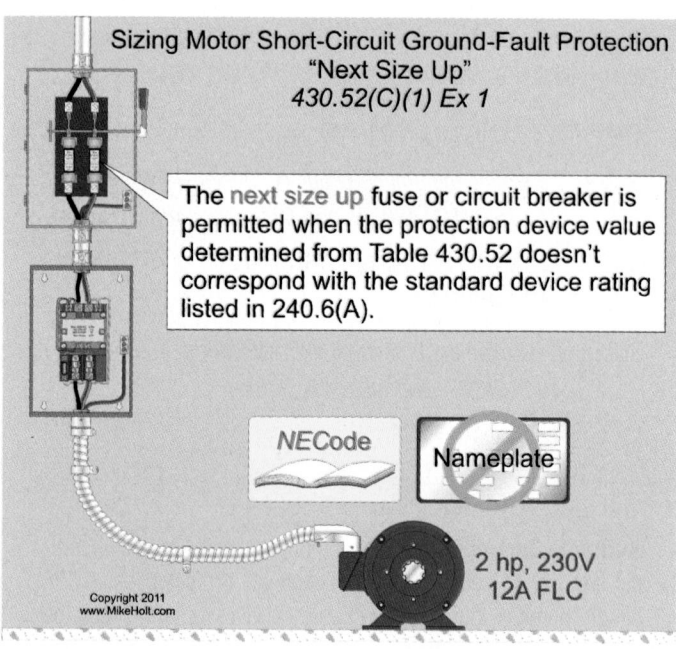

Figure 430–18

Question: What size conductor and inverse time circuit breaker are required for a 7½ hp, 230V, three-phase motor? Figure 430–19

(a) 10 AWG, 50A breaker   (b) 10 AWG, 60A breaker

(c) a or b   (d) none of these

Answer: (b) 10 AWG, 60A breaker

Step 1: Determine the branch-circuit conductor [Table 310.15(B)(16), 430.22, and Table 430.250]:

   22A x 1.25 = 27.50A, 10 AWG, rated 30A at 75°C [Table 310.15(B)(16)]

Step 2: Determine the branch-circuit protection [240.6(A), 430.52(C)(1) Ex 1, and Table 430.250]:

   22A x 2.50 = 55A, next size up = 60A

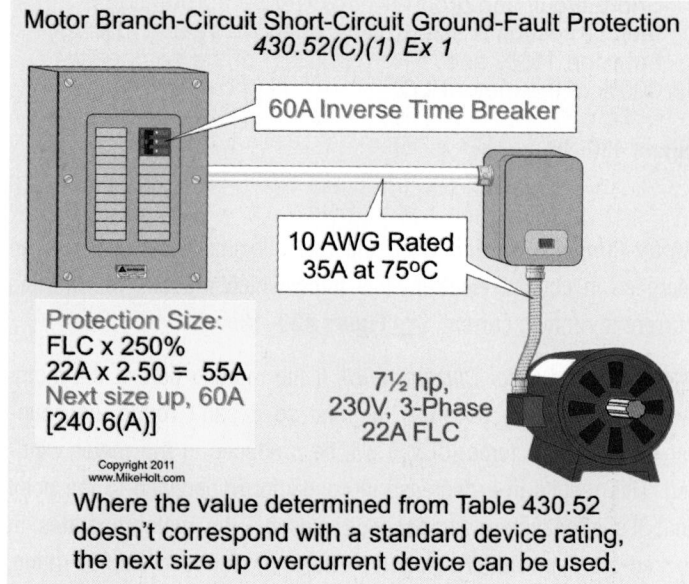

Figure 430–19

430.55 Single Overcurrent Device.

A motor can be protected against overload, short circuit, and ground fault by a single overcurrent device sized to the overload requirements contained in 430.32.

Question: What size dual-element fuse is permitted to protect a 5 hp, 230V, single-phase motor with a service factor of 1.15 and a nameplate current rating of 28A? **Figure 430–20**

(a) 20A   (b) 25A   (c) 30A   (d) 35A

Answer: (d) 35A

Overload Protection [430.32(A)(1)]

28A x 1.25 = 35A

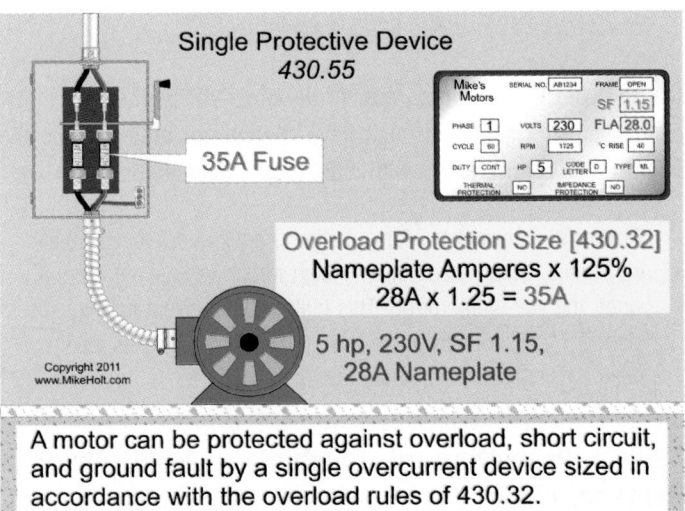

A motor can be protected against overload, short circuit, and ground fault by a single overcurrent device sized in accordance with the overload rules of 430.32.

Figure 430–20

PART V. FEEDER SHORT-CIRCUIT AND GROUND-FAULT PROTECTION

430.62 Feeder Protection.

(A) Motors Only. Feeder conductors must be protected against short circuits and ground faults by a protective device sized not more than the largest rating of the branch-circuit short-circuit and ground-fault protective device for any motor, plus the sum of the full-load currents of the other motors in the group.

Question: What size feeder protection (inverse time breakers with 75°C terminals) and conductors are required for the following two motors? **Figure 430–21**

Motor 1—20 hp, 460V, three-phase = 27A FLC [Table 430.250]
Motor 2—10 hp, 460V, three-phase = 14A FLC

(a) 8 AWG, 70A breaker   (b) 8 AWG, 80A breaker
(c) 8 AWG, 90A breaker   (d) 10 AWG, 90A breaker

Answer: (b) 8 AWG, 80A breaker

Step 1: Determine the feeder conductor size [430.24]:
(27A x 1.25) + 14A = 48A
8 AWG rated 50A at 75°C [110.14(C)(1) and Table 310.15(B)(16)]

Step 2: Feeder protection [430.62(A)] isn't greater than the largest branch-circuit ground-fault and short-circuit protective device plus the other motor FLC.

Step 3: Determine the largest branch-circuit ground-fault and short-circuit protective device [430.52(C)(1) Ex]:
20 hp Motor = 27A x 2.50 = 68, next size up = 70A
10 hp Motor = 14A x 2.50 = 35A

Step 4: Determine the size feeder protection:
Not more than 70A + 14A, = 84A, next size down = 80A [240.6(A)]

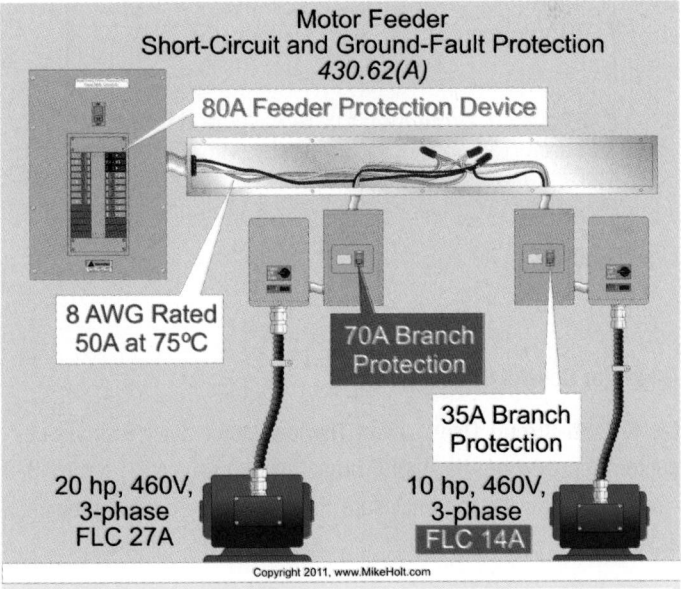

Feeder Protection Device Not to be Larger Than 70A + 14A

Figure 430–21

Author's Comment: The "next size up protection" rule for branch circuits [430.52(C)(1) Ex 1] doesn't apply to a motor feeder protection device rating.

Conductor Size	Overcurrent Protection
18 AWG	7A
16 AWG	10A
14 AWG	45A
12 AWG	60A
10 AWG	90A

PART VI. MOTOR CONTROL CIRCUITS

430.72 Overcurrent Protection for Control Circuits.

(A) Class 1 Control Conductors. Motor control conductors that aren't tapped from the branch-circuit protective device are classified as a Class 1 remote-control circuit, and they must have overcurrent protection in accordance with 725.43.

Author's Comment: Section 725.43 states that overcurrent protection for conductors 14 AWG and larger must comply with the conductor ampacity from Table 310.15(B)(16). Overcurrent protection for 18 AWG must not exceed 7A, and a 10A device must protect 16 AWG conductors. **Figure 430–22**

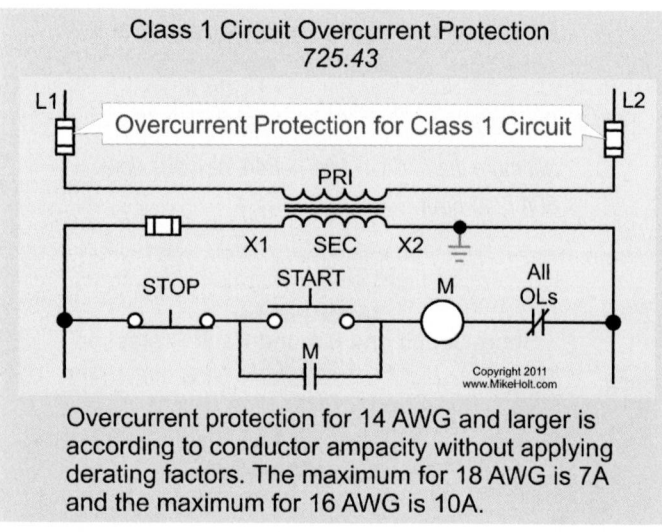

Class 1 Circuit Overcurrent Protection
725.43

Overcurrent Protection for Class 1 Circuit

Overcurrent protection for 14 AWG and larger is according to conductor ampacity without applying derating factors. The maximum for 18 AWG is 7A and the maximum for 16 AWG is 10A.

Figure 430–22

(B) Motor Control Conductors.

(2) Branch-Circuit Overcurrent Device. Motor control circuit conductors tapped from the motor branch-circuit protection device that extends beyond the tap enclosure must have overcurrent protection as follows:

Author's Comment: The above limitations don't apply to the internal wiring of industrial control panels listed in UL *508 Standard for Practical Application Guidelines.*

(C) Control Circuit Transformer Protection. Transformers for motor control circuit conductors must have overcurrent protection on the primary side in accordance with 430.72(C)(1) through (6).

Author's Comment: Many control transformers have small iron cores, which result in very high inrush (excitation) current when the coil is energized. This high inrush current can cause standard fuses to blow, so you should only use the fuses recommended by the control transformer manufacturer.

430.73 Protection of Conductors from Physical Damage. If physical damage would result in a hazard, the conductors of a remote motor control circuit installed outside the control device must be protected by installing the conductors in a raceway or be protected from physical damage.

430.75 Disconnect for Control Circuits.

(A) Control Circuit Disconnect. Motor control circuit conductors must have a disconnecting means that simultaneously opens all sources of supply when the disconnecting means is in the open position. If the control circuit conductors are tapped from the controller disconnect, the controller disconnecting means can serve as the disconnecting means for the control circuit conductors [430.102(A)].

If the control circuit conductors aren't tapped from the controller disconnect, a separate disconnecting means is required for the control circuit conductors, and it must be located adjacent to the controller disconnect. **Figure 430–23**

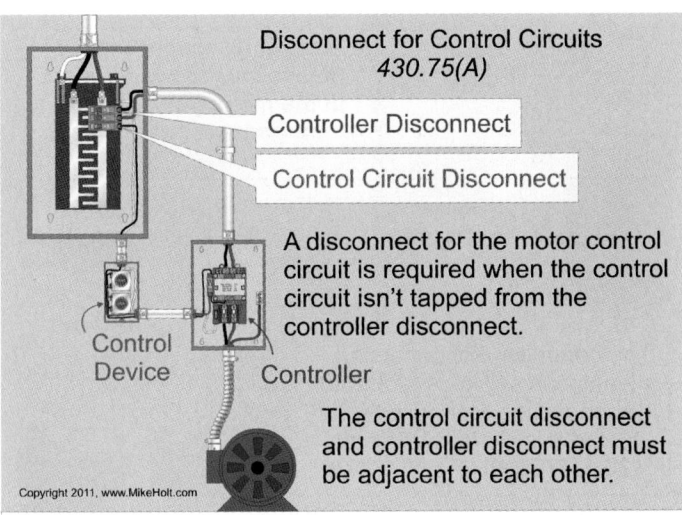

Figure 430–23

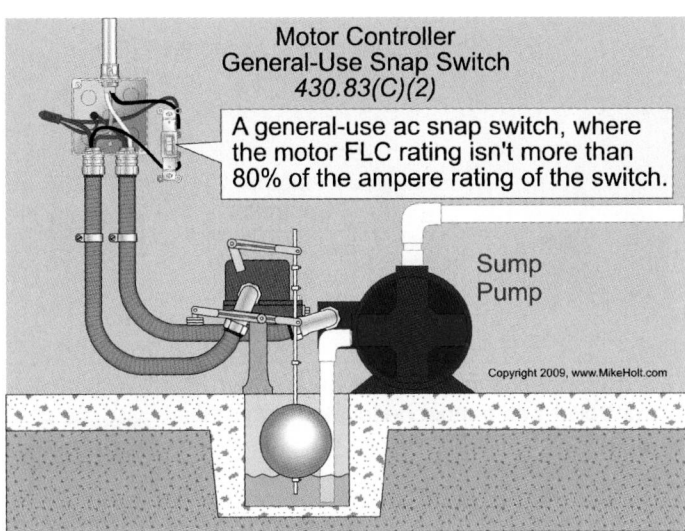

Figure 430–24

PART VII. MOTOR CONTROLLERS

430.83 Controller Rating.

(A) General. The controller must have one of the following ratings:

(1) Horsepower Rating. Controllers, other than circuit breakers and molded case switches, must have a horsepower rating not less than that of the motor.

(2) Circuit Breakers. A circuit breaker can serve as a motor controller [430.111].

> **Author's Comment:** Circuit breakers aren't required to be horsepower rated.

(3) Molded Case Switch. A molded case switch, rated in amperes, can serve as a motor controller.

> **Author's Comment:** A molded case switch isn't required to be horsepower rated.

(C) Stationary Motors of Two Horsepower or Less. For stationary motors rated at 2 hp or less, the controller can be:

(2) General-Use Snap Switch. A general-use alternating-current snap switch, where the motor full-load current rating isn't more than 80 percent of the ampere rating of the switch. **Figure 430–24**

> **Author's Comment:** A general-use snap switch is a general-use switch constructed for installation in device boxes or on box covers, or otherwise used in conjunction with wiring systems recognized by this *Code*.

430.84 Need Not Open All Conductors of the Circuit.

The motor controller can open only as many conductors of the circuit as necessary to start and stop the motor.

> **Author's Comment:** The controller is only required to start and stop the motor; it isn't a disconnecting means. See the disconnecting means requirement in 430.103 for more information.

430.87 Controller for Each Motor.
Each motor must have its own individual controller.

PART IX. DISCONNECTING MEANS

430.102 Disconnect Requirement.

(A) Controller Disconnect. A disconnecting means is required for each motor controller, and it must be located within sight from the controller. **Figures 430–25 and 430–26**

> **Author's Comment:** According to Article 100, within sight means that it's visible and not more than 50 ft from one to the other.

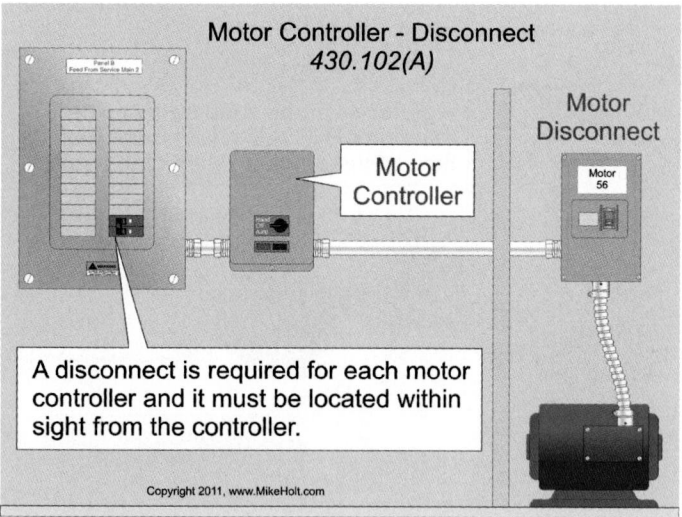

Figure 430–25

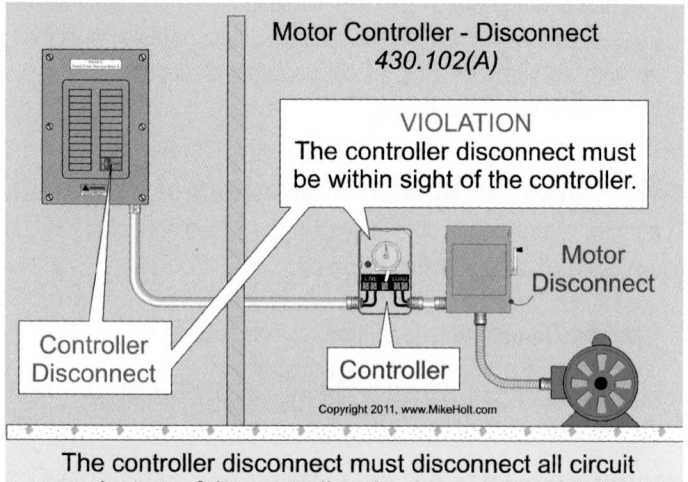

Figure 430–26

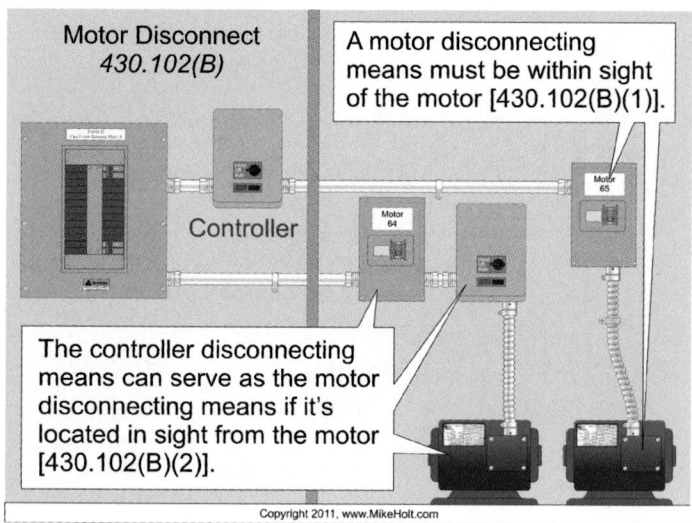

Figure 430–27

Ex to (1) and (2): A motor disconnecting means isn't required under either condition (a) or (b), if the controller disconnecting means [430.102(A)] is capable of being locked in the open position. The provision for locking or adding a lock to the disconnecting means must be installed on or at the switch or circuit breaker, and it must remain in place with or without the lock installed. **Figure 430–28**

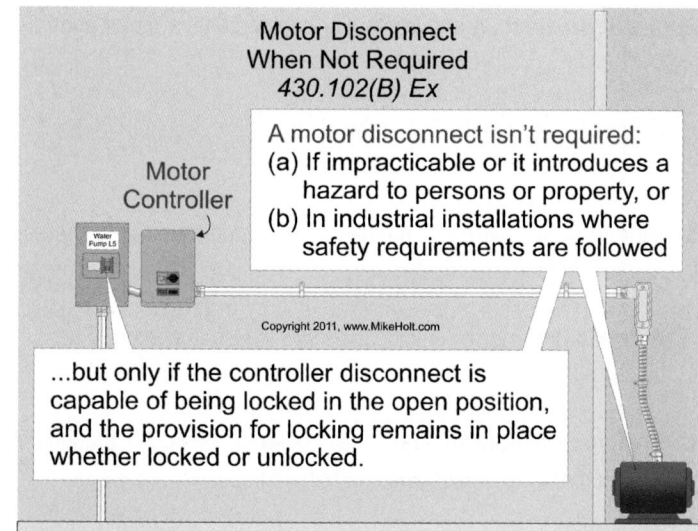

Figure 430–28

(B) Motor Disconnect. A motor disconnect must be provided in accordance with (B)(1) or (B)(2). **Figure 430–27**

(1) Separate Motor Disconnect. A disconnecting means is required for each motor, and it must be located in sight from the motor location and the driven machinery location.

(2) Controller Disconnect. The controller disconnecting means [430.102(A)] can serve as the disconnecting means for the motor, if the disconnect is located in sight from the motor location.

(a) *If locating the disconnecting means is impracticable or introduces additional or increased hazards to persons or property.*

(b) In industrial installations, with written safety procedures, where conditions of maintenance and supervision ensure only qualified persons will service the equipment.

Note 2: For information on lockout/tagout procedures, see NFPA 70E, *Standard for Electrical Safety in the Workplace.*

430.103 Operation of Disconnect.
The disconnecting means for the motor controller and the motor must open all ungrounded supply conductors simultaneously, and it must be designed so that it won't close automatically. **Figure 430–29**

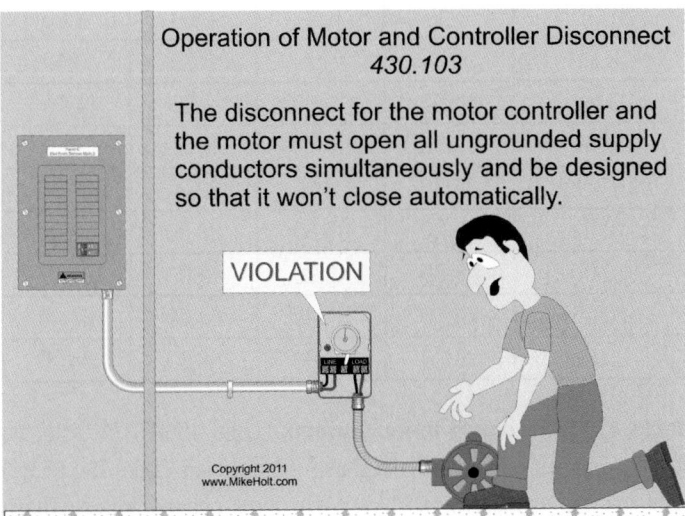

Operation of Motor and Controller Disconnect
430.103

The disconnect for the motor controller and the motor must open all ungrounded supply conductors simultaneously and be designed so that it won't close automatically.

VIOLATION

Copyright 2011
www.MikeHolt.com

Figure 430–29

430.104 Marking and Mounting.
The controller and motor disconnecting means must indicate whether they're in the "on" or "off" position.

> **Author's Comment:** The disconnecting means must be legibly marked to identify its intended purpose [110.22 and 408.4], and when operated vertically, the "up" position must be the "on" position [240.81 and 404.6(C)].

430.107 Readily Accessible.
Either the controller disconnecting means or the motor disconnecting means required by 430.102 must be readily accessible. **Figure 430–30**

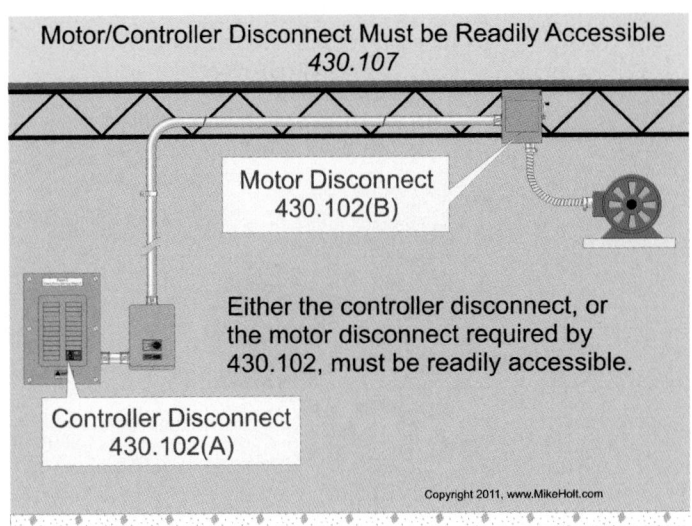

Motor/Controller Disconnect Must be Readily Accessible
430.107

Motor Disconnect
430.102(B)

Either the controller disconnect, or the motor disconnect required by 430.102, must be readily accessible.

Controller Disconnect
430.102(A)

Copyright 2011, www.MikeHolt.com

Figure 430–30

430.109 Disconnecting Means Rating.

(A) General. The disconnecting means for the motor controller and/or the motor must be a:

(1) Motor-Circuit Switch. A listed horsepower-rated motor-circuit switch.

(2) Molded Case Circuit Breaker. A listed molded case circuit breaker.

(3) Molded Case Switch. A listed molded case switch.

(6) Manual Motor Controller. A listed manual motor controller marked "Suitable as Motor Disconnect."

(B) Stationary Motors of ⅛ Horsepower or Less. For stationary motors of ⅛ hp or less, the branch-circuit overcurrent device is permitted to serve as the disconnecting means.

(C) Stationary Motors of Two Horsepower or Less.

(2) General-Use Snap Switch. A general-use alternating-current snap switch, where the motor full-load current rating isn't more than 80 percent of the ampere rating of the switch. **Figure 430–31**

(F) Cord-and-Plug-Connected Motors. A horsepower-rated attachment plug and receptacle, flanged surface inlet and cord connector, or attachment plug cord connector having a horsepower rating not less than the motor rating can be used as the motor disconnecting means.

430.111 Combination Controller and Disconnect.
A horsepower-rated switch or circuit breaker can serve as both a controller and disconnecting means if it opens all ungrounded conductors to the motor as required by 430.103.

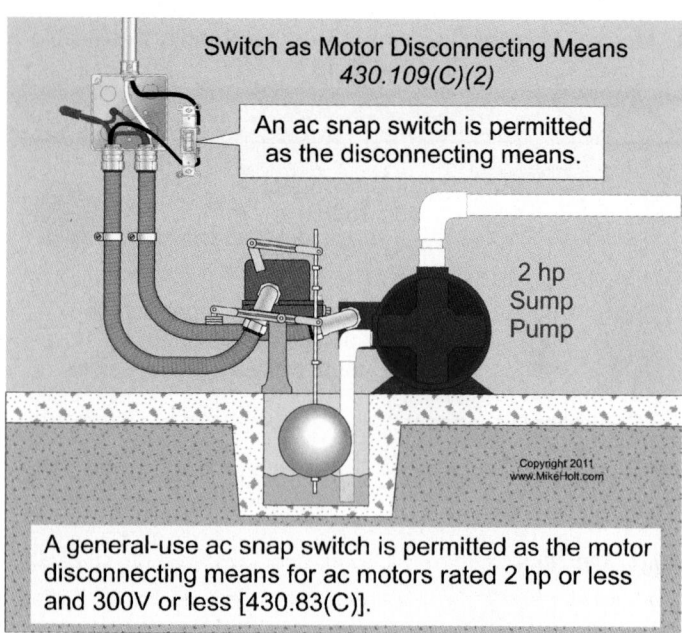

Switch as Motor Disconnecting Means
430.109(C)(2)

An ac snap switch is permitted as the disconnecting means.

2 hp Sump Pump

Copyright 2011
www.MikeHolt.com

A general-use ac snap switch is permitted as the motor disconnecting means for ac motors rated 2 hp or less and 300V or less [430.83(C)].

Figure 430–31

PART XIV. TABLES

Table 430.248 Full-Load Current, Single-Phase Motors. Table 430.248 lists the full-load current for single-phase alternating-current motors. These values are used to determine motor conductor sizing, ampere ratings of disconnects, controller rating, and branch-circuit and feeder protection, but not overload protection [430.6(A)(1) and 430.6(A)(2)].

Table 430.248 FLC Single-Phase AC Motors				
	115V	200V	208V	230V
1/2 hp	9.80	5.60	5.40	4.90
3/4 hp	13.80	7.90	7.60	6.90
1 hp	16.00	9.20	8.80	8.00
1 1/2 hp	20.00	11.50	11.00	11.00
2 hp	24.00	13.90	13.20	12.00
3 hp	34.00	19.60	18.70	17.00
5 hp	56.00	32.20	30.80	28.00
7 1/2 hp	80.00	46.00	44.00	40.00
10 hp	100.00	57.50	55.00	50.00

Table 430.250 Full-Load Current, Three-Phase Motors. Table 430.250 lists the full-load current for three-phase alternating-current motors. The values are used to determine motor conductor sizing, ampere ratings of disconnects, controller rating, and branch-circuit and feeder protection, but not overload protection [430.6(A)(1) and 430.6(A)(2)].

Table 430.250 FLC Three-Phase AC Motors				
	200V	208V	230V	460V
1/2 hp	2.50	2.40	2.20	1.10
3/4 hp	3.70	3.50	3.20	1.60
1 hp	4.80	4.60	4.20	2.10
1 1/2 hp	6.90	6.60	6.00	3.00
2 hp	7.80	7.50	6.80	3.40
3 hp	11.00	10.60	9.60	4.00
5 hp	17.50	16.70	15.20	7.60
7 1/2 hp	25.30	24.20	22.00	11.00
10.00	32.20	30.80	28.00	14.00
15.00	48.30	46.20	42.00	21.00
20.00	62.10	59.40	54.00	27.00
25.00	78.20	74.80	68.00	34.00

Table 430.251 Locked-Rotor Currents. Table 430.251(A) lists the locked-rotor current for single-phase motors, and Table 430.251(B) contains the locked-rotor current for three-phase motors. These values are used in the selection of controllers and disconnecting means when the horsepower rating isn't marked on the motor nameplate.

ARTICLE 440

Air-Conditioning and Refrigeration Equipment

INTRODUCTION TO ARTICLE 440—AIR-CONDITIONING AND REFRIGERATION EQUIPMENT

This article applies to electrically driven air-conditioning and refrigeration equipment. The rules in this article add to, or amend, the rules in Article 430 and other articles.

Each equipment manufacturer has the motor for a given air-conditioning unit built to its own specifications. Cooling and other characteristics are different from those of nonhermetic motors. For each motor, the manufacturer has worked out all of the details and supplied the correct protection, conductor sizing, and other information on the nameplate. So when wiring an air conditioner, trust the information on the nameplate and don't try to over-complicate the situation. The math for sizing the overcurrent protection and conductor minimum ampacity has already been done for you.

PART I. GENERAL

440.1 Scope. Article 440 applies to electrically driven air-conditioning and refrigeration equipment.

440.2 Definitions.

Hermetic Refrigerant Motor-Compressor. A compressor and motor enclosed in the same housing, operating in the refrigerant.

Rated-Load Current. The current resulting when the motor-compressor operates at rated load and rated voltage.

440.3 Other Articles.

(B) Equipment with No Hermetic Motor-Compressors. Air-conditioning and refrigeration equipment that don't have hermetic refrigerant motor-compressors, such as furnaces with evaporator coils, must comply with Article 422 for appliances, Article 424 for electric space heating, and Article 430 for motors.

(C) Household Refrigerant Motor-Compressor Appliances. Household refrigerators and freezers, drinking water coolers, and beverage dispensing machines are listed as appliances, and their installation must also comply with Article 422 for appliances. **Figure 440–1**

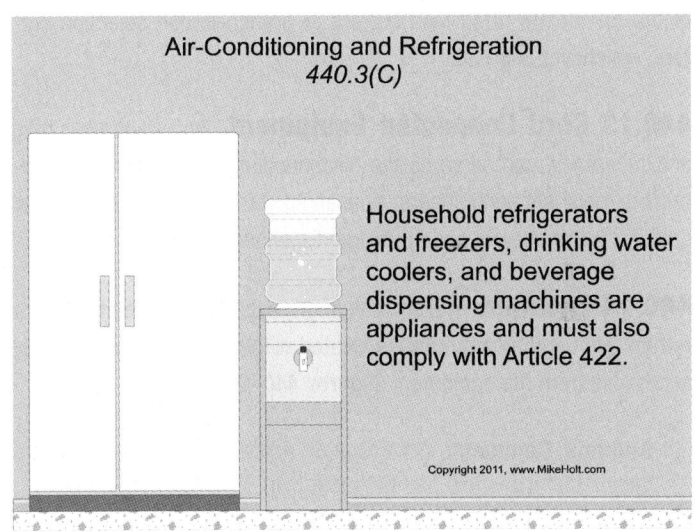

Air-Conditioning and Refrigeration
440.3(C)

Household refrigerators and freezers, drinking water coolers, and beverage dispensing machines are appliances and must also comply with Article 422.

Copyright 2011, www.MikeHolt.com

Figure 440–1

440.4 Marking on Hermetic Refrigerant Motor-Compressors and Equipment.

(B) Multimotor and Combination-Load Equipment. Multimotor and combination-load equipment must have a visible nameplate marked with the maker's name, rating in volts, number of phases, minimum conductor ampacity, and the maximum rating of the branch-circuit short-circuit and ground-fault protective device.

Author's Comment: The minimum conductor ampacity is calculated in accordance with 440.33 and the branch circuit short-circuit and ground-fault protective device rating is sized with 440.22(B)(1).

440.6 Ampacity and Rating.

(A) Hermetic Refrigerant Motor-Compressor. For a hermetic refrigerant motor-compressor, the rated-load current marked on the nameplate of the equipment is to be used in determining the rating of the disconnecting means, the branch-circuit conductors, the controller, and the branch-circuit short-circuit and ground-fault protection.

PART II. DISCONNECTING MEANS

440.12 Rating and Interrupting Capacity.

(A) Hermetic Refrigerant Motor-Compressor.

(1) Ampere Rating. The ampere rating must be at least 115 percent of the nameplate rated-load current or branch-circuit selection current, whichever is greater.

440.13 Cord-Connected Equipment. An attachment plug and receptacle can serve as the disconnecting means for cord-connected room air conditioners, household refrigerators and freezers, drinking water coolers and beverage dispensers.

440.14 Location. A disconnecting means for air-conditioning or refrigeration equipment must be located within sight from and readily accessible from the equipment. **Figures 440–2 and 440–3**

> **Author's Comment:** According to Article 100, within sight means that it's visible and not more than 50 ft from one to the other.

The disconnecting means can be mounted on or within the air-conditioning equipment, but it must not be located on panels designed to allow access to the equipment, or where it will obscure the equipment nameplate. **Figure 440–4**

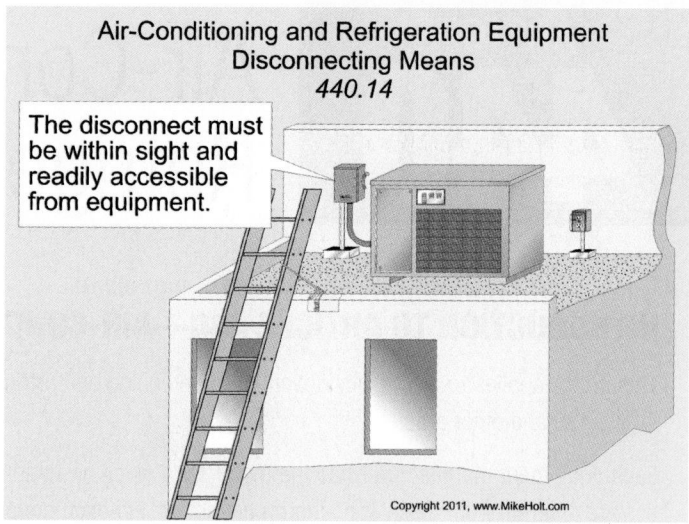

Figure 440–2

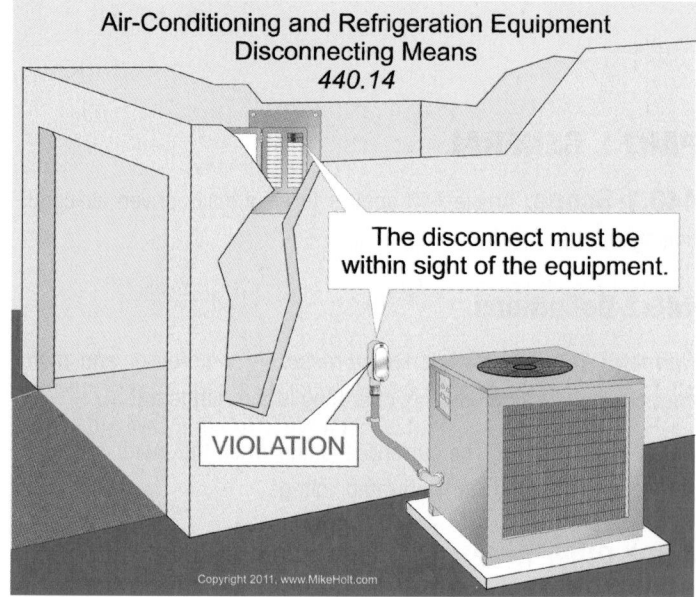

Figure 440–3

Ex 1: A disconnecting means isn't required to be within sight from the equipment, if the disconnecting means is capable of being individually locked in the open position, and if the equipment is essential to an industrial process in a facility that has written safety procedures, and where the conditions of maintenance and supervision ensure only qualified persons service the equipment. The provision for locking or adding a lock to the disconnecting means must be on the switch or circuit breaker, and it must remain in place with or without the lock installed.

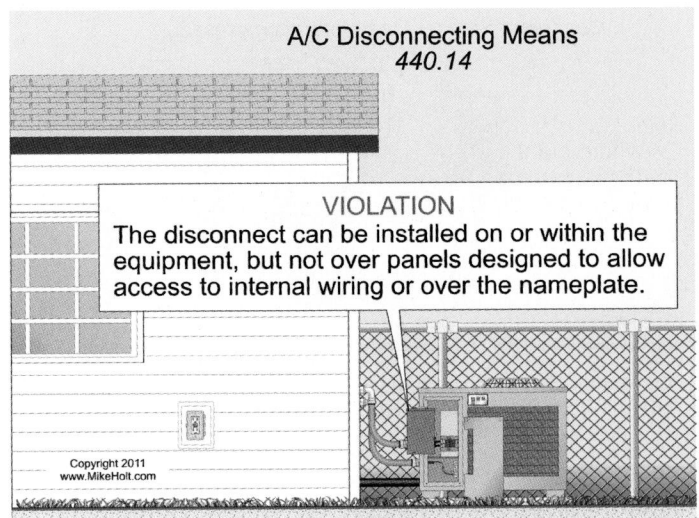

Figure 440–4

Ex 2: An accessible attachment plug and receptacle can serve as the disconnecting means.

Author's Comment: The receptacle for the attachment plug isn't required to be readily accessible.

PART III. OVERCURRENT PROTECTION

440.21 General. The branch-circuit conductors, control equipment, and circuits supplying hermetic refrigerant motor-compressors must be protected against short circuits and ground faults in accordance with 440.22.

Author's Comment: If the equipment nameplate specifies "Maximum Fuse Size," then a one-time or dual-element fuse must be used.

440.22 Short-Circuit and Ground-Fault Overcurrent Device Size.

(A) Single Motor-Compressors. The short-circuit and ground-fault protective device must not be more than 175 percent of the motor-compressor current rating. If the protective device sized at 175 percent isn't capable of carrying the starting current of the motor-compressor, the next size larger protective device can be used, but in no case can it exceed 225 percent of the motor-compressor current rating.

Question: What size conductor and protection are required for a 24A motor-compressor connected to a 240V circuit? **Figure 440–5**

(a) 10 AWG, 40A	*(b) 10 AWG, 60A*
(c) a or b	*(d) 10 AWG, 90A*

Answer: *(a) 10 AWG, 40A*

Step 1: Determine the branch-circuit conductor [Table 310.15(B)(16) and 440.32]:

24A x 1.25 = 30A, 10 AWG, rated 30A at 75°C [Table 310.15(B)(16)]

Step 2: Determine the branch-circuit protection [240.6(A) and 440.22(A)]:

24A x 1.75 = 42A, next size down = 40A

If the 40A short-circuit and ground-fault protective device isn't capable of carrying the starting current, then the protective device can be sized up to 225 percent of the equipment load current rating. 24A x 2.25 = 54A, next size down 50A

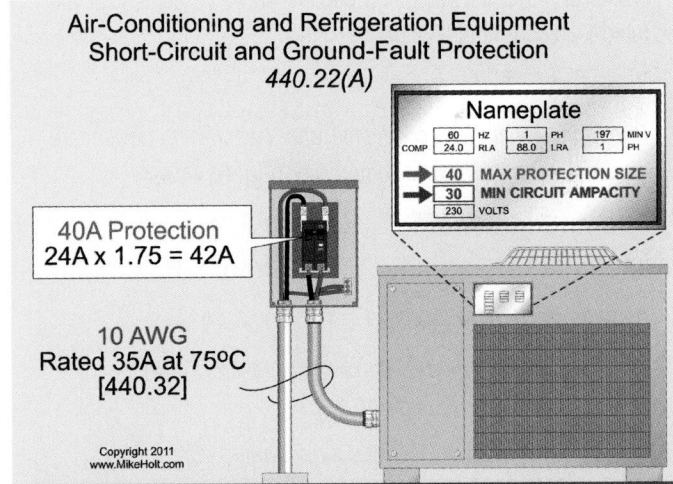

A short-circuit and ground-fault protection device must not be greater than 175% of the equipment load current rating.

Figure 440–5

(B) Multimotor and Combination-Load Equipment. If the equipment incorporates more than one hermetic refrigerant motor-compressor, or a hermetic refrigerant motor-compressor and other motors or other loads, the equipment must have a visible nameplate containing the maximum rating of the branch-circuit short-circuit and ground-fault protective device.

> **Author's Comment:** The branch-circuit conductors are sized at 125 percent of the largest motor-compressor current, plus the sum of the rated-load currents of the other compressors [440.33].

PART IV. CONDUCTOR SIZING

440.32 Conductor Size for Single Motor-Compressors.
Branch-circuit conductors to a single motor-compressor must have an ampacity not less than 125 percent of the motor-compressor rated-load current or the branch-circuit selection current, whichever is greater.

> **Author's Comment:** Branch-circuit conductors for a single motor-compressor must have short-circuit and ground-fault protection sized between 175 percent and 225 percent of the rated-load current [440.22(A)].

> **Question:** What size conductor and overcurrent device are required for an 18A motor compressor? **Figure 440–6**
>
> (a) 12 AWG, 30A   (b) 10 AWG, 50A
> (c) a or b   (d) 10 AWG, 60A
>
> **Answer:** (a) 12 AWG, 30A
>
> Step 1: Determine the branch-circuit conductor [Table 310.15(B)(16) and 440.32]:
>
> 18A x 1.25 = 22.50A, 12 AWG, rated 25A at 75°C [Table 310.15(B)(16)]
>
> Step 2: Determine the branch-circuit protection [240.6(A) and 440.22(A)]:
>
> 18A x 1.75 = 31.50A, next size down = 30A
>
> If the 30A short-circuit and ground-fault protection device isn't capable of carrying the starting current, then the protective device can be sized up to 225 percent of the equipment load current rating. 18A x 2.25 = 40.50A, next size down 40A

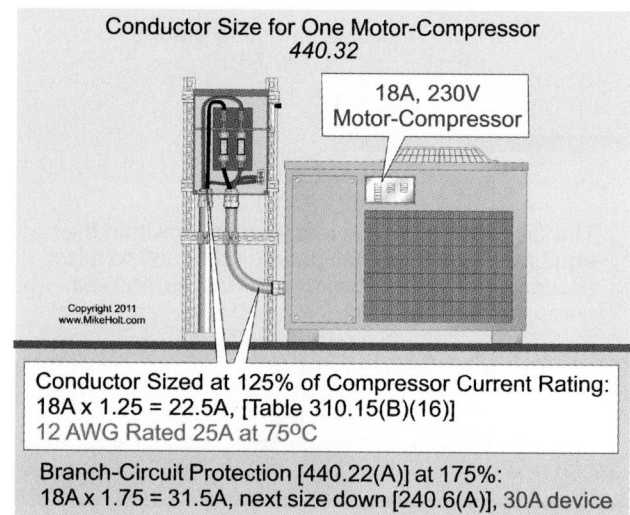

Conductor Size for One Motor-Compressor
440.32

18A, 230V Motor-Compressor

Conductor Sized at 125% of Compressor Current Rating:
18A x 1.25 = 22.5A, [Table 310.15(B)(16)]
12 AWG Rated 25A at 75°C

Branch-Circuit Protection [440.22(A)] at 175%:
18A x 1.75 = 31.5A, next size down [240.6(A)], 30A device

Figure 440–6

> **Author's Comment:** A 30A or 40A overcurrent device is permitted to protect a 12 AWG conductor for an air-conditioning circuit. See 240.4(G) for details.

PART VII. ROOM AIR CONDITIONERS

The requirements in this Part apply to a cord-and-plug-connected room air conditioner of the window or in-wall type that incorporates a hermetic refrigerant motor-compressor rated not over 40A, 250V, single-phase [440.60].

440.62 Branch-Circuit Requirements.

(A) Sizing Conductors and Protection. Branch-circuit conductors for a cord-and-plug-connected room air conditioner must have an ampacity not less than 125 percent of the rated-load current [440.32].

(B) Separate Circuit. If the room air conditioner is the only load on a circuit, the marked rating of the air conditioner must not exceed 80 percent of the rating of the circuit overcurrent device.

(C) Other Loads on Circuit. The total rating of a cord-and-plug-connected room air conditioner must not exceed 50 percent of the rating of a branch circuit where lighting outlets, other appliances, or general-use receptacles are also supplied. **Figure 440–7**

440.63 Disconnecting Means.
An attachment plug and receptacle or cord connector can serve as the disconnecting means for a room air conditioner, provided: **Figure 440–8**

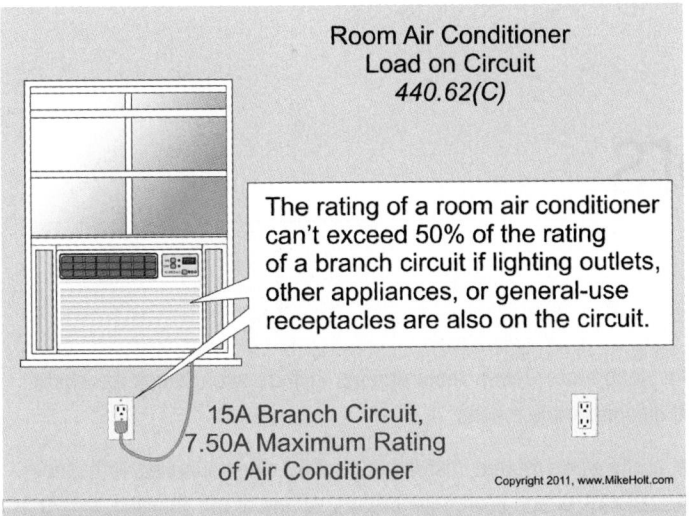

Figure 440–7

(1) The manual controls on the room air conditioner are readily accessible and within 6 ft of the floor, or

(2) A readily accessible disconnecting means is within sight from the room air conditioner.

440.64 Supply Cords. If a flexible cord is used to supply a room air conditioner, the cord must not exceed 10 ft for 120V units, or 6 ft for 208V or 240V units.

440.65 Leakage Current Detector-Interrupter and Arc-Fault Circuit Interrupter. Single-phase cord-and-plug-connected room air conditioners must be provided with a factory-installed leakage current detector, or with an arc-fault circuit-interrupter (AFCI).

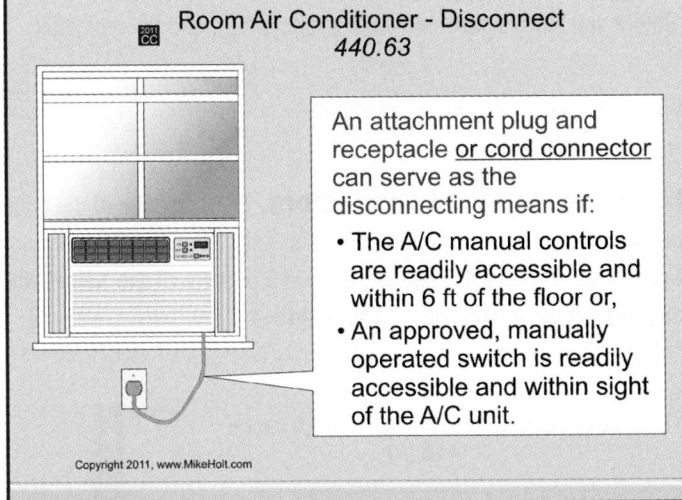

Figure 440–8

ARTICLE 445

Generators

INTRODUCTION TO ARTICLE 445—GENERATORS

This article contains the electrical installation, and other requirements, for generators. These requirements include such things as where generators can be installed, nameplate markings, conductor ampacity, and disconnecting means.

Generators are basically motors that operate in reverse—they produce electricity when rotated, instead of rotating when supplied with electricity. Article 430, which covers motors, is the longest article in the *NEC*. Article 445, which covers generators, is one of the shortest. At first, this might not seem to make sense. But you don't need to size and protect conductors to a generator. You do need to size and protect them to a motor.

Generators need overload protection, and it's necessary to size the conductors that come from the generator. But these considerations are much more straightforward than the equivalent considerations for motors. Before you study Article 445, take a moment to read the definition of "Separately Derived System" in Article 100.

445.1 Scope. Article 445 contains the installation <u>and other requirements</u> for generators.

> **Author's Comment:** Generators, associated wiring, and equipment must be installed in accordance with the following requirements depending on their use:
>
> - Article 695, Fire Pumps
> - Article 700, Emergency Systems
> - Article 701, Legally Required Standby Systems
> - Article 702, Optional Standby Systems

445.11 Marking. Each generator must be provided with a nameplate indicating the manufacturer's name, rated frequency, power factor, number of phases, rating in kilowatts or kilovolt amperes, volts and amperes corresponding to the rating, RPM, insulation class and rated ambient temperature or rated temperature rise, and time rating.

445.12 Overcurrent Protection.

(A) Generators. Generators must be protected from <u>overload</u> by inherent design, circuit breakers, fuses, or other identified overcurrent protective means.

445.13 Ampacity of Conductors. The ampacity of the conductors from the generator to distribution devices containing overcurrent protection must not be less than 115 percent of the nameplate current rating of the generator. **Figure 445–1**

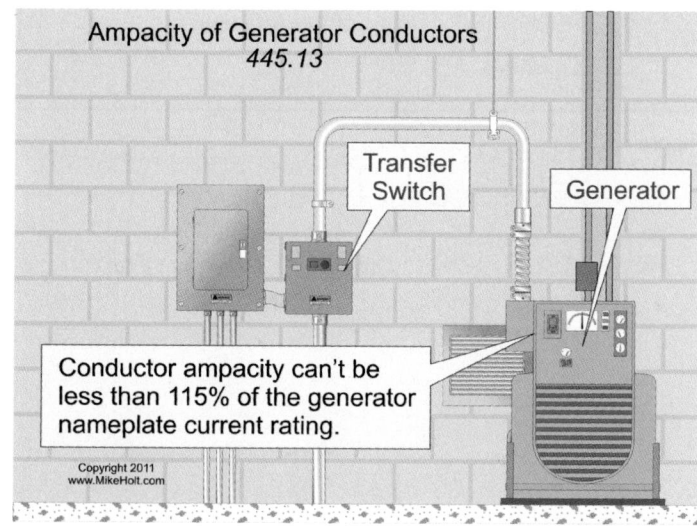

Figure 445–1

Generators that aren't a separately derived system must have the neutral conductor sized to: **Figure 445–2**

- Carry the maximum unbalanced current as determined by 220.61.
- Serve as the low-impedance fault current path.

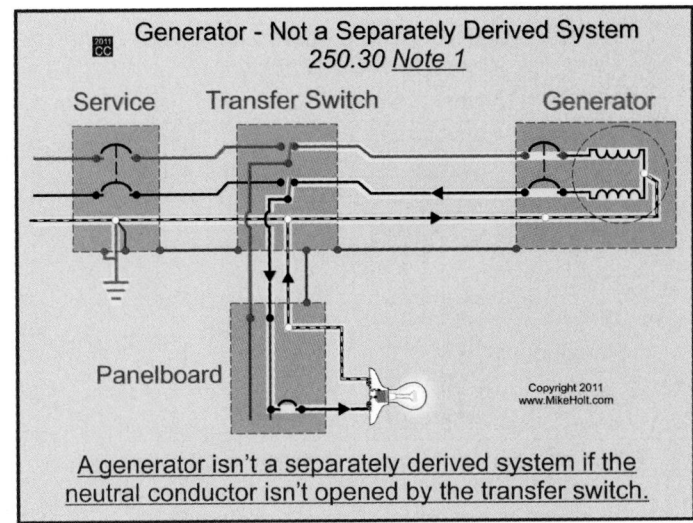

Figure 445–3

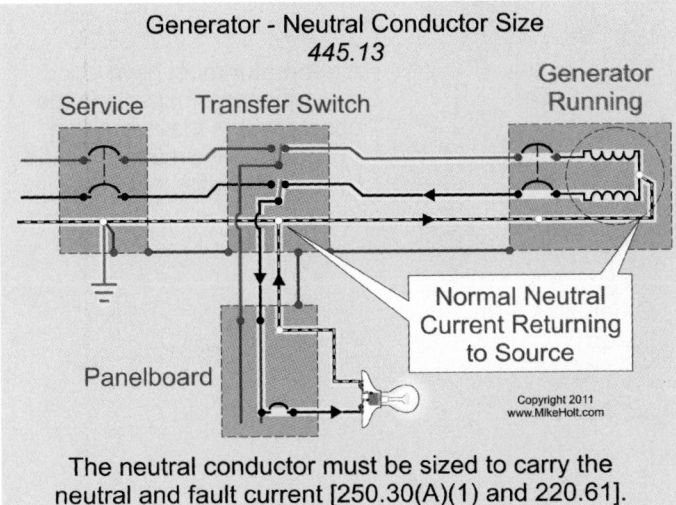

Figure 445–2

Author's Comment: If the feeder conductors from the generator terminate in a transfer switch that doesn't open the neutral conductor, the generator isn't considered a separately derived system [250.30 Note 1]. **Figure 445–3.** A neutral-to-case bond isn't permitted at the generator. Under this condition, the neutral conductor from the normal power to the transfer switch, and the neutral conductor from the generator to the transfer switch, are required to provide the low-impedance fault current path back to the power source. **Figure 445–4**

Separately derived system generators must have the neutral conductor sized not less than required to carry the maximum unbalanced current as determined by 220.61.

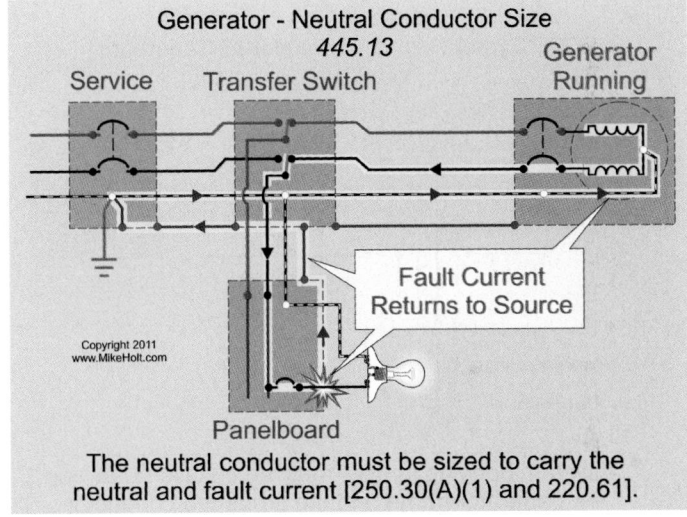

Figure 445–4

Author's Comment: If the feeder conductors from the generator terminate in a transfer switch that opens the neutral conductor, the generator is considered a separately derived system [Article100]. **Figure 445–5.** A neutral-to-case connection (system bonding jumper) is required at the generator [250.30(A)(1)] to provide a low-impedance fault current path back to the power source. **Figure 445–6**

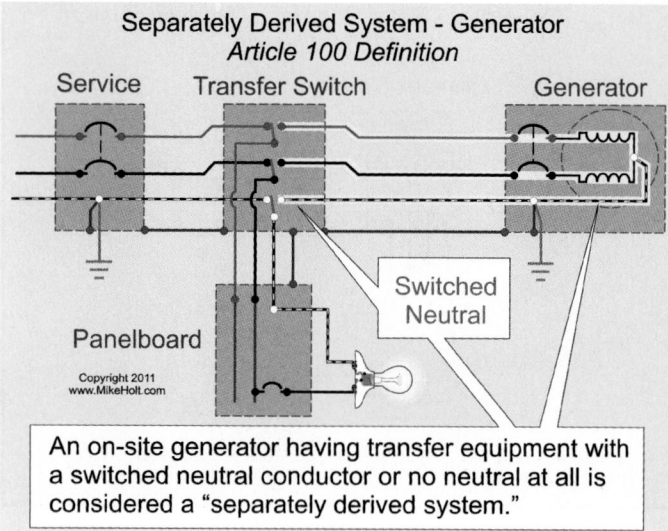

An on-site generator having transfer equipment with a switched neutral conductor or no neutral at all is considered a "separately derived system."

Figure 445–5

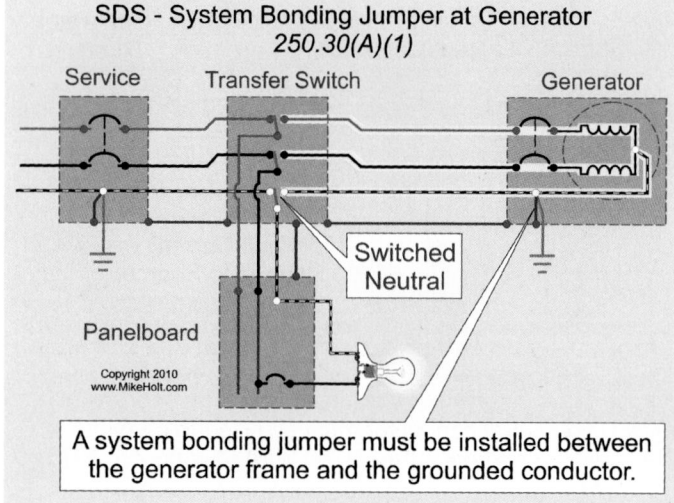

A system bonding jumper must be installed between the generator frame and the grounded conductor.

Figure 445–6

445.18 Disconnecting Means.
Generators must have one or more disconnecting means that disconnects all power, except where: Figure 445–7

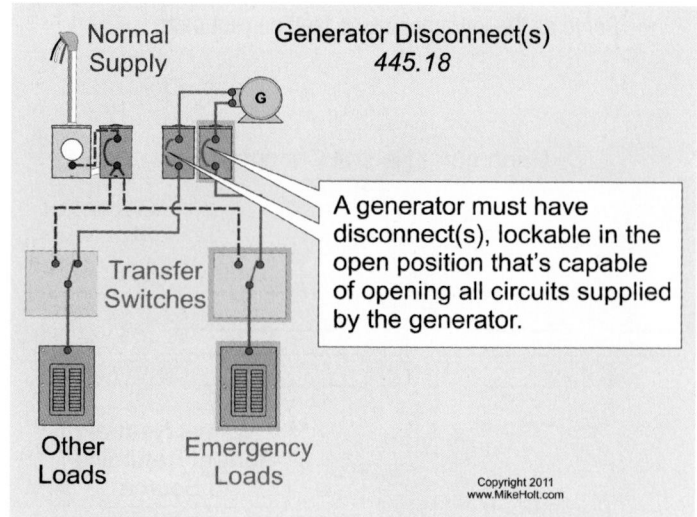

A generator must have disconnect(s), lockable in the open position that's capable of opening all circuits supplied by the generator.

Figure 445–7

(1) The driving means for the generator can be readily shut down, and

(2) The generator isn't arranged to operate in parallel with another generator or other source of voltage.

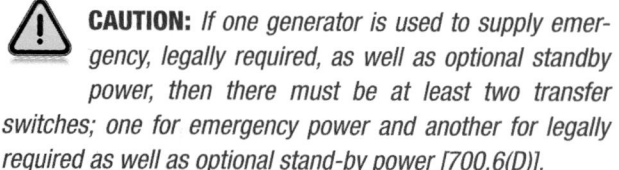 **CAUTION:** *If one generator is used to supply emergency, legally required, as well as optional standby power, then there must be at least two transfer switches; one for emergency power and another for legally required as well as optional stand-by power [700.6(D)].*

445.19 Generators Supplying Multiple Loads.
A single generator is permitted to supply more than one load.

ARTICLE 450 Transformers

INTRODUCTION TO ARTICLE 450—TRANSFORMERS

Article 450 opens by saying, "This article covers the installation of all transformers." Then it lists eight exceptions. So what does Article 450 really cover? Essentially, it covers power transformers and most kinds of lighting transformers.

A major concern with transformers is preventing overheating. The *Code* doesn't completely address this issue. Article 90 explains that the *NEC* isn't a design manual, and it assumes that the person using the *Code* has a certain level of expertise. Proper transformer selection is an important part of preventing transformer overheating.

The *NEC* assumes you've already selected a transformer suitable to the load characteristics. For the *Code* to tell you how to do that would push it into the realm of a design manual. Article 450 then takes you to the next logical step—providing overcurrent protection and the proper connections. But this article doesn't stop there; 450.9 provides ventilation requirements, and 450.13 contains accessibility requirements.

Part I of Article 450 contains the general requirements such as guarding, marking, and accessibility, Part II contains the requirements for different types of transformers, and Part III covers transformer vaults.

PART I. GENERAL

450.1 Scope. Article 450 covers the installation requirements of transformers and transformer vaults. **Figure 450–1**

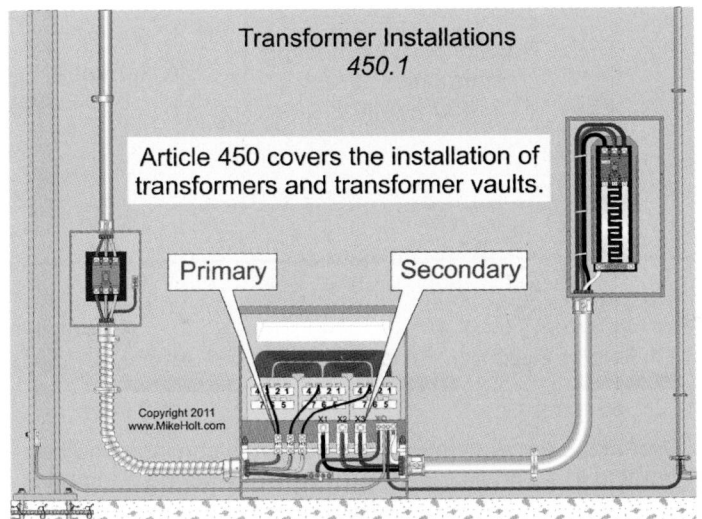

Figure 450–1

450.3 Overcurrent Protection.

Note 2: Nonlinear loads on 4-wire, wye-connected secondary wiring can increase heat in a transformer without operating the primary overcurrent device. **Figure 450–2**

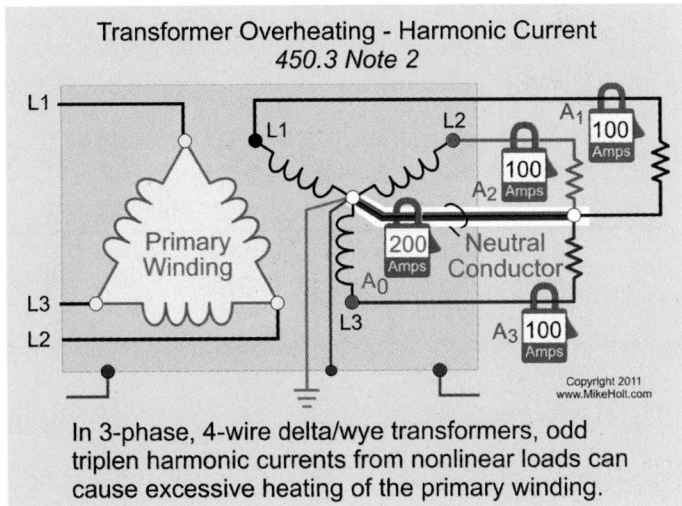

Figure 450–2

(B) Overcurrent Protection for Transformers Not Over 600V. The primary winding of a transformer must be protected against overcurrent in accordance with the percentages listed in Table 450.3(B) and all applicable notes.

Table 450.3(B) Primary Protection Only	
Primary Current Rating	**Maximum Protection**
9A or More	125%, see Note 1
Less Than 9A	167%
Less Than 2A	300%

Note 1. If 125 percent of the primary current doesn't correspond to a standard rating of a fuse or nonadjustable circuit breaker, the next higher rating is permitted [240.6(A)].

Question: What's the primary overcurrent device rating and conductor size required for a 45 kVA, three-phase, 480V transformer that's fully loaded? The terminals are rated 75°C. **Figure 450–3**

(a) 8 AWG, 40A
(b) 6 AWG, 50A
(c) 6 AWG, 60A
(d) 4 AWG, 70A

Answer: (d) 4 AWG, 70A

Step 1: Determine the primary current:

$$I = VA/(E \times 1.732)$$
$$I = 45,000 \, VA/(480V \times 1.732)$$
$$I = 54A$$

Step 2: Determine the primary overcurrent device rating [240.6(A)]:

54A x 1.25 = 68A, next size up 70A, Table 450.3(B), Note 1

Step 3: The primary conductor must be sized to carry 54A continuously (54A x 1.25 = 68A) [215.2(A)(1)] and be protected by a 70A overcurrent device [240.4(B)]. A 4 AWG conductor rated 85A at 75°C meets all of the requirements [110.14(C)(1) and 310.15(B)(16)].

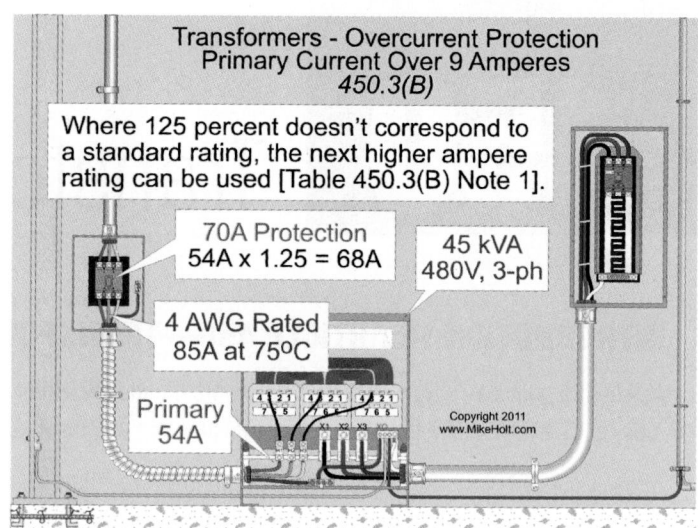

Figure 450–3

450.9 Ventilation. Transformers must be installed in accordance with the manufacturer's instructions, and their ventilating openings must not be blocked [110.3(B)].

Note 2: Transformers can become excessively heated above their rating because nonlinear loads can increase heat in a transformer without operating its overcurrent protective device [450.3 Note].

Author's Comment: The heating from harmonic currents is proportional to the square of the harmonic frequency. This means the 3rd order harmonic currents (180 Hz) will heat at nine times the rate of 60 Hz current. **Figure 450–4**

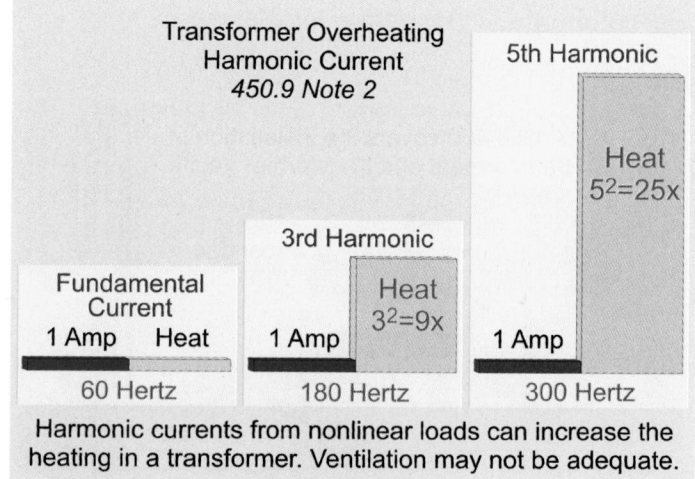

Figure 450–4

450.11 Marking. Transformers must be provided with a nameplate identifying the manufacturer of the transformer and indicating the transformer's rated kVA, primary and secondary voltage, impedance if 25 kVA or larger, and required clearances for transformers with ventilating openings.

450.13 Transformer Accessibility. Transformers must be readily accessible to qualified personnel for inspection and maintenance, except as permitted by (A) or (B).

(A) Open Installations. Dry-type transformers can be located in the open on walls, columns, or structures. **Figure 450–5**

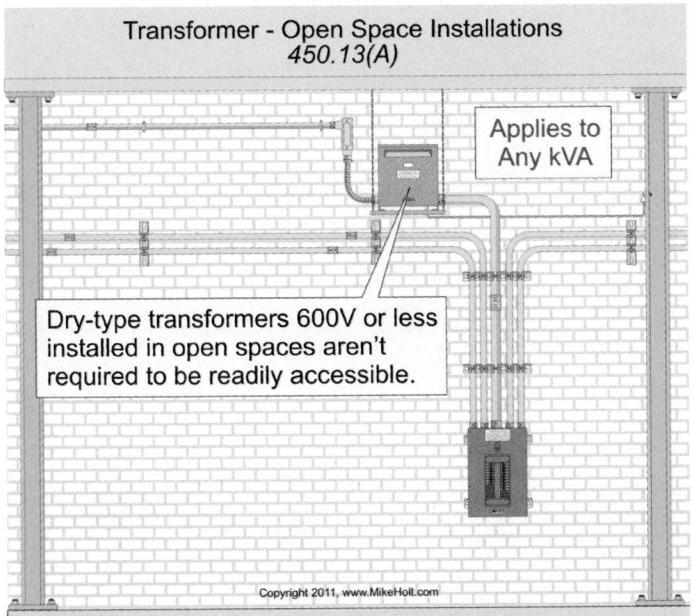

Figure 450–5

(B) Suspended Ceilings. Dry-type transformers, rated not more than 50 kVA, are permitted above suspended ceilings or in hollow spaces of buildings, if not permanently closed in by the structure. **Figure 450–6**

Author's Comment: Dry-type transformers not exceeding 50 kVA with a metal enclosure can be installed above a suspended-ceiling space used for environmental air-handling purposes (plenum) [300.22(C)(3)].

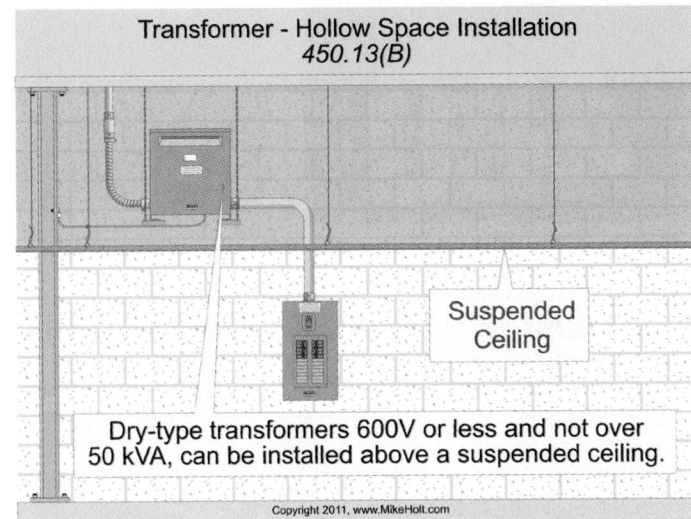

Figure 450–6

450.14 Disconnecting Means. A disconnect is required to disconnect all transformer ungrounded primary conductors. The disconnect must be located within sight of the transformer, unless the location of the disconnect is field-marked on the transformer and the disconnect is lockable. **Figure 450–7**

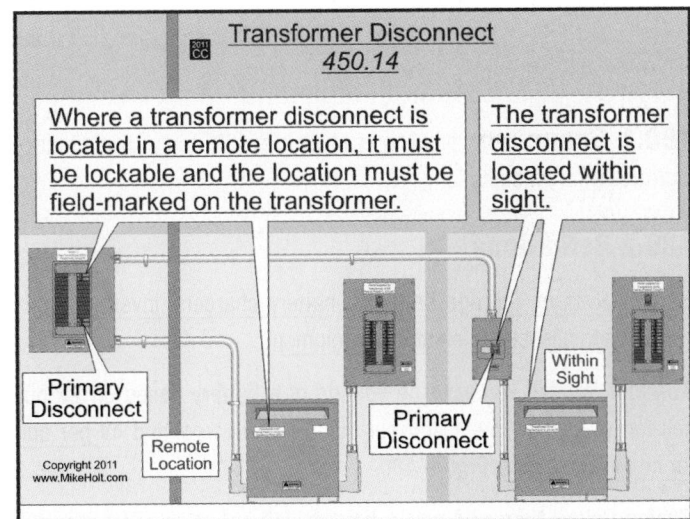

Figure 450–7

Author's Comment: Within sight means that it's visible and not more than 50 ft from one to the other [Article 100].

ARTICLE
480

Storage Batteries

INTRODUCTION TO ARTICLE 480—STORAGE BATTERIES

The stationary battery is the heart of any uninterruptible power supply. Article 480 addresses stationary batteries for commercial and industrial grade power supplies, not the small, "point of use" UPS boxes.

Stationary batteries are also used in other applications, such as emergency power systems. Regardless of the application, if it uses stationary batteries then Article 480 applies.

Lead-acid stationary batteries fall into two general categories: flooded, and valve regulated (VRLA). These differ markedly in such ways as maintainability, total cost of ownership, and scalability. The *NEC* doesn't address these differences, as they're engineering issues and not fire safety or electrical safety issues [90.1].

The *Code* doesn't address such design issues as optimum tier height, distance between tiers, determination of charging voltage, or string configuration. Nor does it address battery testing, monitoring, or maintenance. All of these involve highly specialized areas of knowledge, and are required for optimizing operational efficiency. Standards other than the *NEC* address these issues.

What the *Code* does address, in Article 480, are issues related to preventing electrocution and the ignition of the gases that all stationary batteries (even "sealed" ones) emit.

480.1 Scope. The provisions of Article 480 apply to stationary storage battery installations.

480.2 Definitions.

Battery System. Storage batteries, battery chargers, inverters, converters, and associated electrical equipment.

Nominal Battery Voltage. The voltage of a battery based on 2V per cell for lead-acid type, 1.50V per cell for alkali type, and 4V per cell for lithium-ion types. **Figure 480–1**

Sealed Cell or Battery. A cell or battery with no provision for the routine addition of water or electrolyte.

Storage Battery. Battery consisting of one or more rechargeable cells.

480.3 Wiring and Equipment Supplied from Batteries. Wiring and equipment supplied from storage batteries must be in accordance with Chapters 1 through 4.

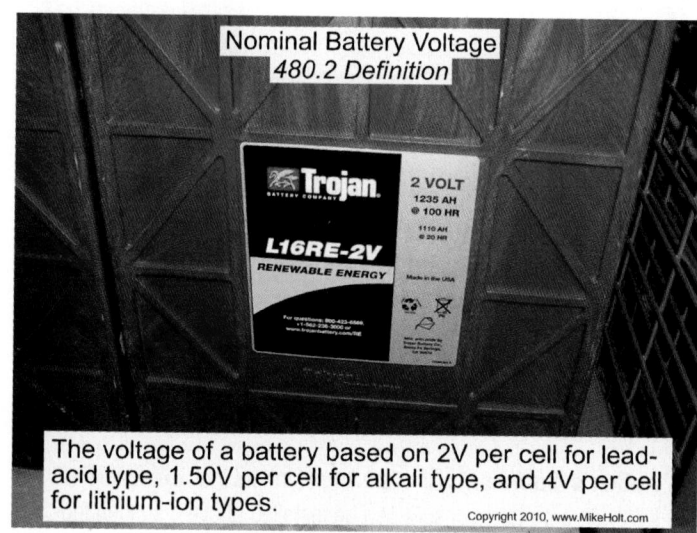

Nominal Battery Voltage
480.2 Definition

The voltage of a battery based on 2V per cell for lead-acid type, 1.50V per cell for alkali type, and 4V per cell for lithium-ion types.
Copyright 2010, www.MikeHolt.com

Figure 480–1

480.4 Overcurrent Protection for Prime Movers.

Overcurrent protection for ungrounded battery conductors is required and the overcurrent protection device must be located as close as practical to the storage battery terminals [240.21(H)].

The requirement contained in 300.3 that single conductors be installed where part of a recognized wiring method of Chapter 3 and all conductors of the circuit be contained within the same raceway or cable doesn't apply.

480.5 Disconnecting Means.

A readily accessible disconnecting means is required within sight of the storage battery for all ungrounded battery system conductors operating at over 50V nominal.

> **Author's Comment:** According to Article 100, within sight means that it's visible and not more than 50 ft from one to the other.

> **Note:** Overcurrent protection for ungrounded battery conductors must be located as close as practical to the storage battery terminals [240.21(H)].

480.8 Racks and Trays.

Racks and trays must be:

(A) Racks. Racks (rigid frames designed to support battery cells or trays) must be made of one of the following: **Figure 480–2**

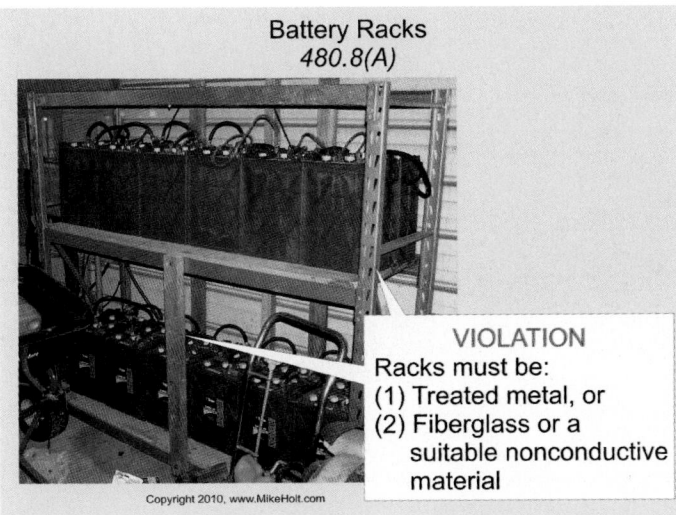

Battery Racks
480.8(A)

VIOLATION
Racks must be:
(1) Treated metal, or
(2) Fiberglass or a
    suitable nonconductive
    material

Copyright 2010, www.MikeHolt.com

Figure 480–2

(1) Metal, treated to be resistant to deteriorating action by the electrolyte and provided with nonconducting or continuous insulating material members directly supporting the cells.

(2) Fiberglass or other suitable nonconductive materials.

(B) Trays. Trays (boxes of nonconductive material) must be constructed or treated so as to be resistant to deteriorating action by the electrolyte. **Figure 480–3**

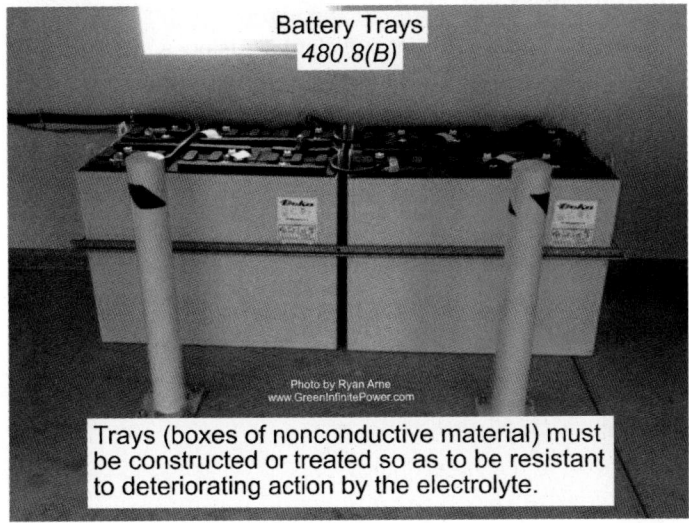

Battery Trays
480.8(B)

Photo by Ryan Arne
www.GreenInfinitePower.com

Trays (boxes of nonconductive material) must be constructed or treated so as to be resistant to deteriorating action by the electrolyte.

Figure 480–3

480.9 Battery Locations.

(A) Ventilation. Provisions must permit sufficient diffusion and ventilation of battery gases to prevent the accumulation of an explosive mixture. **Figure 480–4**

(B) Live Parts. Live parts of battery systems must be protected in accordance with 110.27.

> **Author's Comment:** According to 110.27, electrical equipment must not be installed where subject to physical damage, unless en closures or guards are arranged and of such strength as to prevent damage [110.27(B)]. In addition, entrances to rooms and other guarded locations containing exposed live parts must be marked with conspicuous signs forbidding unqualified persons to enter [110.27(C)].

(C) Working Space. The required working space requirements of 110.26 are measured from the edge of the battery rack.

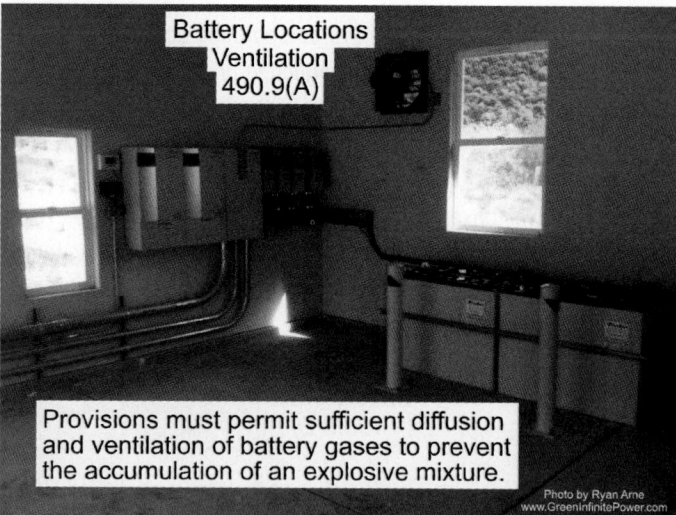

Battery Locations
Ventilation
490.9(A)

Provisions must permit sufficient diffusion
and ventilation of battery gases to prevent
the accumulation of an explosive mixture.

Photo by Ryan Arne
www.GreenInfinitePower.com

Figure 480–4

These questions are based on the 2011 *National Electrical Code*. Please use the 2011 *NEC Code* book to answer the following questions.

CHAPTER 4. EQUIPMENT FOR GENERAL USE

Article 400. Flexible Cords and Flexible Cables

1. The allowable ampacity of flexible cords and cables is found in _____.

   (a) Table 310.15(B)(16)
   (b) Tables 400.5(A)(1) and (2)
   (c) Chapter 9, Table 1
   (d) Table 430.52

2. Conductors within flexible cords and cables shall not be associated together in such a way that the _____ temperature of the conductors is exceeded.

   (a) operating
   (b) governing
   (c) ambient
   (d) limiting

3. Flexible cords and cables can be used for _____.

   (a) wiring of luminaires
   (b) connection of portable luminaires or appliances
   (c) connection of utilization equipment to facilitate frequent interchange
   (d) all of these

4. Flexible cords and cables shall not be concealed behind building _____, or run through doorways, windows, or similar openings.

   (a) structural ceilings
   (b) suspended or dropped ceilings
   (c) floors or walls
   (d) all of these

5. In industrial establishments where conditions of maintenance and supervision ensure that only qualified persons service the installation, flexible cords and cables can be installed in aboveground raceways that are no longer than _____, to protect the flexible cord or cable from physical damage.

   (a) 25 ft
   (b) 50 ft
   (c) 100 ft
   (d) no limit

Article 402. Fixture Wire

1. The number of fixture wires in a single conduit or tubing shall not exceed the percentage fill specified in _____.

   (a) Chapter 9, Table 1
   (b) Table 250.66
   (c) Table 310.15(B)(16)
   (d) 240.6

Article 404. Switches

1. Three-way and four-way switches shall be wired so that all switching is done only in the _____ circuit conductor.

   (a) ungrounded
   (b) grounded
   (c) equipment ground
   (d) neutral

2. As a general rule, switches controlling line-to-neutral lighting loads must have a neutral provided at the switch location.

   (a) True
   (b) False

3. Switches shall not be installed within wet locations in tub or shower spaces unless installed as part of a listed tub or shower assembly.

   (a) True
   (b) False

4. Switches and circuit breakers used as switches shall be installed so that they may be operated from a readily accessible place.

   (a) True
   (b) False

5. A multipole, general-use snap switch shall not be fed from more than a single circuit unless it is listed and marked as a 2-circuit or 3-circuit switch, or unless its voltage rating is not less than the nominal _____ voltage of the system supplying the circuits.

   (a) line-to-ground
   (b) line-to-neutral
   (c) line-to-line
   (d) phase-to-phase

6. A snap switch that does not have means for connection to an equipment grounding conductor shall be permitted for replacement purposes only where the wiring method does not include an equipment grounding conductor and the switch is _____.

   (a) provided with a faceplate of nonconducting, noncombustible material with nonmetallic screws
   (b) GFCI protected
   (c) a or b
   (d) none of these

7. A snap switch with integral nonmetallic enclosure complying with 300.15(E) is required to be connected to an equipment grounding conductor.

   (a) True
   (b) False

8. Metal enclosures for switches or circuit breakers shall be connected to the circuit _____.

   (a) grounded conductor
   (b) grounding conductor
   (c) equipment grounding conductor
   (d) any of these

9. AC or DC general-use snap switches may be used for control of inductive loads not exceeding _____ percent of the ampere rating of the switch at the applied voltage.

   (a) 50
   (b) 75
   (c) 90
   (d) 100

10. Switches shall be marked with _____.

    (a) current
    (b) voltage
    (c) maximum horsepower, if horsepower rated
    (d) all of these

Article 406. Receptacles, Cord Connectors, and Attachment Plugs (Caps)

1. Receptacles rated _____ or less directly connected to aluminum conductors shall be listed and marked CO/ALR.

   (a) 15A
   (b) 20A
   (c) 25A
   (d) 30A

2. Receptacles and cord connectors having equipment grounding conductor contacts shall have those contacts connected to a(n) _____ conductor.

   (a) grounded
   (b) ungrounded
   (c) equipment grounding
   (d) neutral

3. When replacing receptacles in locations that would require GFCI protection under the current *NEC*, _____ receptacles shall be installed.

   (a) dedicated
   (b) isolated ground
   (c) GFCI-protected
   (d) grounding

4. Weather-resistant receptacles _____ where replacements are made at receptacle outlets that are required to be so protected elsewhere in the *Code*.

   (a) shall be provided
   (b) are not required
   (c) are optional
   (d) are not allowed

5. Receptacles mounted to and supported by a cover shall be secured by more than one screw unless listed and identified for securing by a single screw.

   (a) True
   (b) False

6. Metal faceplates for receptacles shall be grounded.

   (a) True
   (b) False

7. An outdoor receptacle in a location protected from the weather, or in another damp location, shall be installed in an enclosure that is weatherproof when the receptacle is _____.

   (a) covered
   (b) enclosed
   (c) protected
   (d) none of these

8. Nonlocking 15A and 20A, 125V and 250V receptacles installed in damp locations shall be listed as _____.

   (a) raintight
   (b) watertight
   (c) weatherproof
   (d) weather resistant

9. Where installed in a wet location, all _____ receptacle(s) shall be listed as weather-resistant.

   (a) 125V, 30A nonlocking
   (b) 250V, 15A nonlocking
   (c) 125V, 30A locking
   (d) 250V, 15A locking

10. A receptacle shall not be installed within, or directly over, a bathtub or shower space.

   (a) True
   (b) False

11. A receptacle installed in an outlet box flush-mounted in a finished surface in a damp or wet location shall be made weatherproof by means of a weatherproof faceplate assembly that provides a _____ connection between the plate and the finished surface.

   (a) sealed
   (b) weathertight
   (c) sealed and protected
   (d) watertight

12. Nonlocking type 15A and 20A, 125V receptacles in a dwelling unit shall be listed as tamper resistant except _____.

   (a) Receptacles located more than 5½ ft above the floor.
   (b) Receptacles that are part of a luminaire or appliance.
   (c) A receptacle located within dedicated space for an appliance that in normal use is not easily moved from one place to another.
   (d) all of these

13. Nonlocking type 15A and 20A, 125V receptacles in a dwelling unit shall be listed as tamper resistant except nongrounding receptacles used for replacements for existing nongrounding receptacles as permitted in 406.4(D)(2)(a).

(a) True
(b) False

14. Nonlocking type 15A and 20A, 125V receptacles in _____ must be listed as tamper resistant.

(a) restaurants
(b) guest rooms and guest suites
(c) office buildings
(d) b and c

15. Nonlocking type 15A and 20A, 125V receptacles in _____ must be listed as tamper resistant.

(a) theatres
(b) arcades
(c) child care facilities
(d) major repair garages

Article 408. Switchboards and Panelboards

1. Each switchboard or panelboard used as service equipment shall be provided with a main bonding jumper within the panelboard, or within one of the sections of the switchboard, for connecting the grounded service-entrance conductor on its _____ side to the switchboard or panelboard frame.

(a) load
(b) supply
(c) phase
(d) high-leg

2. A switchboard or panelboard containing a 4-wire, _____ system where the midpoint of one phase winding is grounded, shall be legibly and permanently field-marked to caution that one phase has a higher voltage-to-ground.

(a) wye-connected
(b) delta-connected
(c) solidly grounded
(d) ungrounded

3. The purpose or use of panelboard circuits and circuit _____, including spare positions, shall be legibly identified on a circuit directory located on the face or inside of the door of a panelboard, and at each switch or circuit breaker on a switchboard.

(a) manufacturers
(b) conductors
(c) feeders
(d) modifications

4. Conduits and raceways, including end fittings, shall not rise more than _____ above the bottom of a switchboard enclosure.

(a) 3 in.
(b) 4 in.
(c) 5 in.
(d) 6 in.

5. For switchboards that are not totally enclosed, a space of _____ or more shall be provided between the top of the switchboard and any combustible ceiling.

(a) 12 in.
(b) 18 in.
(c) 2 ft
(d) 3 ft

6. A panelboard shall be protected by an overcurrent device within the panelboard, or at any point on the _____ side of the panelboard.

(a) load
(b) supply
(c) a or b
(d) none of these

7. When equipment grounding conductors are installed in panel-boards, a _____ shall be secured inside the cabinet.

   (a) grounded conductor
   (b) terminal lug
   (c) terminal bar
   (d) none of these

8. A panelboard shall be provided with physical means to prevent the installation of more _____ devices than that number for which the panelboard was designed, rated, and listed.

   (a) overcurrent
   (b) equipment
   (c) circuit breaker
   (d) all of these

Article 410 Luminaires, Lampholders, and Lamps

1. Lighting track is a manufactured assembly and its length may not be altered by the addition or subtraction of sections of track.

   (a) True
   (b) False

2. A luminaire marked Suitable for Wet Locations _____ be permitted to be used in a damp location.

   (a) shall
   (b) shall not
   (c) a or b
   (d) none of these

3. Luminaires located within the actual outside dimension of a bathtub and shower shall be marked for damp locations, or marked for wet locations where they are _____.

   (a) below 7 ft in. height
   (b) below 6 ft 7 in. in height
   (c) subject to shower spray
   (d) not GFCI-protected

4. Unless an individual switch is provided for each luminaire located over combustible material, lampholders shall be located at least _____ above the floor, or shall be located or guarded so that the lamps cannot be readily removed or damaged.

   (a) 3 ft
   (b) 6 ft
   (c) 8 ft
   (d) 10 ft

5. Surface-mounted fluorescent luminaires in clothes closets shall be permitted on the wall above the door, or on the ceiling, provided there is a minimum clearance of _____ between the luminaire and the nearest point of a storage space.

   (a) 3 in.
   (b) 6 in.
   (c) 9 in.
   (d) 12 in.

6. The *NEC* allows a lighting outlet on the wall in a clothes closet when it is at least 6 in. away from storage space.

   (a) True
   (b) False

7. Electric-discharge and LED luminaires supported independently of the outlet box shall be connected to the branch circuit through _____.

   (a) raceways
   (b) Type MC, AC, MI, or NM cable
   (c) flexible cords
   (d) any of these

8. Handholds in poles supporting luminaires shall not be required for poles _____ or less in height above finished grade, if the pole is provided with a hinged base.

   (a) 5 ft
   (b) 10 ft
   (c) 15 ft
   (d) 20 ft

9. Luminaires attached to the framing of a suspended ceiling shall be secured to the framing member(s) by mechanical means such as _____.

(a) bolts
(b) screws
(c) rivets
(d) any of these

10. Exposed metal conductive parts of luminaires shall be _____.

(a) connected to an equipment grounding conductor
(b) painted
(c) removed
(d) a and b

11. Replacement luminaires can be installed in an outlet box that doesn't contain an equipment grounding conductor if an equipment grounding conductor is added from the luminaire and is connected to _____.

(a) the grounding electrode system or grounding electrode conductor
(b) the panelboard equipment grounding terminal
(c) the service neutral conductor within the service equipment enclosure
(d) any of these

12. Luminaires shall be wired with conductors having insulation suitable for the environmental conditions and _____ to which the conductors will be subjected.

(a) temperature
(b) voltage
(c) current
(d) all of these

13. No _____ splices or taps shall be made within or on a luminaire.

(a) unapproved
(b) untested
(c) uninspected
(d) unnecessary

14. An electric-discharge or LED luminaire or listed assembly can be cord-connected if located _____ the outlet, the cord is visible for its entire length outside the luminaire, and the cord is not subject to strain or physical damage.

(a) within
(b) directly below
(c) directly above
(d) adjacent to

15. Luminaires designed for end-to-end assembly, or luminaires connected together by _____, can contain a 2-wire branch circuit, or one multiwire branch circuit, supplying the connected luminaires. One additional 2-wire branch circuit supplying one or more of the connected luminaires is permitted.

(a) rigid metal conduit
(b) recognized wiring methods
(c) flexible wiring methods
(d) EMT

16. Portable luminaires shall be wired with _____ recognized by 400.4, and have an attachment plug of the polarized or grounding type.

(a) flexible cable
(b) flexible cord
(c) nonmetallic flexible cable
(d) nonmetallic flexible cord

17. Lampholders installed in damp locations shall be listed for use in _____ locations.

(a) damp
(b) wet
(c) dry
(d) a or b

18. A recessed luminaire shall be installed so that adjacent combustible material will not be subjected to temperatures in excess of _____ °C.

(a) 75
(b) 90
(c) 125
(d) 150

19. Type IC recessed luminaires are permitted to make contact with combustible material at _____.

    (a) recessed parts
    (b) points of support
    (c) portions passing through or finishing off the opening in the building structure
    (d) all of these

20. The raceway or cable for tap conductors to recessed luminaires shall have a minimum length of _____.

    (a) 6 in.
    (b) 12 in.
    (c) 18 in.
    (d) 24 in.

21. Luminaires containing a metal halide lamp (other than a thick glass PAR lamp) shall be provided with a containment barrier that encloses the lamp, or shall be provided with a physical means that only allows the use of a(n) _____.

    (a) Type O lamp
    (b) Type CB lamp
    (c) a or b
    (d) inert gas

22. In indoor locations other than dwellings and associated accessory buildings, fluorescent luminaires that utilize double-ended lamps and contain ballast(s) and can be serviced in place shall have a disconnecting means either internal or external to each luminaire.

    (a) True
    (b) False

23. If more than one luminaire is installed on a branch circuit that isn't of the multiwire type, a disconnecting means isn't required for every luminaire when the light switch for the space ensures that some of the luminaires in the space will still provide illumination.

    (a) True
    (b) False

24. Surface-mounted luminaires with a ballast shall have a minimum clearance of _____ from combustible low-density cellulose fiberboard, unless the luminaire is marked for surface mounting on combustible low-density cellulose fiberboard.

    (a) ½ in.
    (b) 1 in.
    (c) 1½ in.
    (d) 2 in.

25. The connected load on lighting track is permitted to exceed the rating of the track under some conditions.

    (a) True
    (b) False

26. Lighting track shall not be installed less than _____ above the finished floor except where protected from physical damage or where the track operates at less than 30V rms, open-circuit voltage.

    (a) 4 ft
    (b) 5 ft
    (c) 5½ ft
    (d) 6 ft

27. Lighting track shall have two supports for a single section of _____ or shorter in length and each individual section of not more than 4 ft attached to it shall have one additional support, unless the track is identified for supports at greater intervals.

    (a) 2 ft
    (b) 4 ft
    (c) 6 ft
    (d) 8 ft

Article 411. Lighting Systems Operating at 30 Volts or Less

1. Lighting systems operating at 30V or less shall be listed or assembled with listed components.

    (a) True
    (b) False

2. Lighting systems operating at 30V or less shall not be installed within _____ ft of pools, spas, fountains, or similar locations.

(a) 5 ft
(b) 6 ft
(c) 10 ft
(d) 20 ft

Article 422. Appliances

1. Branch-circuit conductors to individual appliances shall not be sized _____ than required by the appliance markings.

(a) larger
(b) smaller

2. If a protective device rating is marked on an appliance, the branch-circuit overcurrent device rating shall not exceed _____ percent of the protective device rating marked on the appliance.

(a) 50
(b) 80
(c) 100
(d) 115

3. If a branch circuit supplies a single nonmotor-operated appliance, the rating of overcurrent protection shall not exceed _____ if the overcurrent protection rating is not marked and the appliance is rated 13.30A or less.

(a) 15A
(b) 20A
(c) 25A
(d) 30A

4. Central heating equipment, other than fixed electric space-heating equipment, shall be supplied by a(n) _____ branch circuit.

(a) multiwire
(b) individual
(c) multipurpose
(d) small-appliance

5. A waste disposal can be cord-and-plug-connected, but the cord shall not be less than 18 in. or more than _____ in length.

(a) 30 in.
(b) 36 in.
(c) 42 in.
(d) 48 in.

6. Wall-mounted ovens and counter-mounted cooking units shall be permitted to be _____.

(a) permanently connected
(b) cord-and-plug-connected
(c) a or b
(d) none of these

7. For permanently connected appliances rated over _____ the branch-circuit circuit breaker can serve as the disconnecting means where the circuit breaker is within sight from the appliance, or is capable of being locked in the open position with a permanently installed locking provision that remains in place with or without the lock installed.

(a) 200 VA
(b) 300 VA
(c) 400 VA
(d) 500 VA

8. If an appliance of more than 1/8 hp is provided with a unit switch that complies with 422.34(A), (B), (C), or (D), the switch or circuit breaker serving as the other disconnecting means shall be permitted to be out of sight from the appliance.

(a) True
(b) False

9. For cord-and-plug-connected household electric ranges, an attachment plug and receptacle connection at the rear base of the range can serve as the disconnecting means, if it is _____.

(a) less than 40A
(b) a flush-mounted receptacle
(c) GFCI-protected
(d) accessible by the removal of a drawer

10. Cord-and-plug connected vending machines manufactured or remanufactured on or after January 1, 2005 shall include a ground-fault circuit interrupter as an integral part of the attachment plug or in the power-supply cord within 12 in. of the attachment plug. Older vending machines not incorporating integral GFCI protection shall _____.

(a) be remanufactured
(b) be disabled
(c) be connected to a GFCI-protected outlet
(d) be connected to an AFCI-protected circuit

11. Each electric appliance shall be provided with a(n) _____ giving the identifying name and the rating in volts and amperes, or in volts and watts.

(a) pamphlet
(b) nameplate
(c) auxiliary statement
(d) owner's manual

Article 424. Fixed Electric Space-Heating Equipment

1. If a permanently installed electric baseboard heater has factory-installed receptacle outlets, the receptacle is permitted to be connected to the heater circuits.

(a) True
(b) False

2. Fixed electric space-heating equipment shall be installed to provide the _____ spacing between the equipment and adjacent combustible material, unless it is listed for direct contact with combustible material.

(a) required
(b) minimum
(c) maximum
(d) safest

3. A unit switch with a marked _____ position that is part of a fixed space heater, and disconnects all ungrounded conductors, shall be permitted to serve as the required disconnecting means.

(a) on
(b) closed
(c) off
(d) none of these

4. Resistance-type heating elements in electric space-heating equipment shall be protected at not more than _____.

(a) 24A
(b) 36A
(c) 48A
(d) 60A

5. On electric space-heating cables, blue leads indicate a cable rated for use on a nominal circuit voltage of _____.

(a) 120V
(b) 208V
(c) 240V
(d) 277V

6. Electric space-heating cables shall not extend beyond the room or area in which they _____.

(a) provide heat
(b) originate
(c) terminate
(d) are connected

7. The minimum clearance between an electric space-heating cable and an outlet box used for surface luminaires shall not be less than _____.

(a) 6 in.
(b) 8 in.
(c) 14 in.
(d) 18 in.

8. Duct heater controller equipment shall have a disconnecting means installed within _____ the controller except as allowed by 424.19(A).

   (a) 25 ft of
   (b) sight from
   (c) the side of
   (d) none of these

9. A heating panel is a complete assembly provided with a junction box or length of flexible conduit for connection to a(n) _____.

   (a) wiring system
   (b) service
   (c) branch circuit
   (d) approved conductor

Article 430. Motors, Motor Circuits and Controllers

1. The motor _____ currents listed in Tables 430.247 through 430.250 shall be used to determine the ampacity of motor circuit conductors and short-circuit and ground-fault protection devices.

   (a) nameplate
   (b) full-load
   (c) power factor
   (d) service factor

2. Torque requirements for motor control circuit device terminals shall be a minimum of _____ lb-in. (unless otherwise identified) for screw-type pressure terminals used for 14 AWG and smaller copper conductors.

   (a) 7
   (b) 9
   (c) 10
   (d) 15

3. Motors shall be located so that adequate _____ is provided and so that maintenance, such as lubrication of bearings and replacing of brushes, can be readily accomplished.

   (a) space
   (b) ventilation
   (c) protection
   (d) all of these

4. Branch-circuit conductors supplying a single continuous-duty motor shall have an ampacity not less than _____ rating.

   (a) 125 percent of the motor's nameplate current
   (b) 125 percent of the motor's full-load current as determined by 430.6(A)(1)
   (c) 125 percent of the motor's full locked-rotor
   (d) 80 percent of the motor's full-load current

5. Overload devices are intended to protect motors, motor control apparatus, and motor branch-circuit conductors against _____.

   (a) excessive heating due to motor overloads
   (b) excessive heating due to failure to start
   (c) short circuits and ground faults
   (d) a and b

6. Motor overload protection shall not be shunted or cut out during the starting period if the motor is _____.

   (a) not automatically started
   (b) automatically started
   (c) manually started
   (d) none of these

7. A motor _____ device that can restart a motor automatically after overload tripping shall not be installed if automatic restarting of the motor can result in injury to persons.

   (a) short-circuit
   (b) ground-fault
   (c) overcurrent
   (d) overload

8. The motor branch-circuit short-circuit and ground-fault protective device shall be capable of carrying the _____ current of the motor.

    (a) varying
    (b) starting
    (c) running
    (d) continuous

9. A feeder supplying fixed motor load(s) shall have a protective device with a rating or setting _____ branch-circuit short-circuit and ground-fault protective device for any motor in the group, plus the sum of the full-load currents of the other motors of the group.

    (a) not greater than the largest rating or setting of the
    (b) 125 percent of the largest rating of any
    (c) equal to the largest rating of any
    (d) none of these

10. Motor control circuit transformers, with a primary current rating of less than 2A, can have the primary protection device set at no more than _____ percent of the rated primary current rating.

    (a) 150
    (b) 200
    (c) 400
    (d) 500

11. The branch-circuit protective device can serve as the controller for a stationary motor rated at _____ or less that is normally left running and cannot be damaged by overload or failure to start.

    (a) 1/8 hp
    (b) ¼ hp
    (c) 3/8 hp
    (d) ½ hp

12. For stationary motors of 2 hp or less and 300V or less on ac circuits, the controller can be an ac-rated only general-use snap switch where the motor full-load current rating is not more than _____ percent of the rating of the switch.

    (a) 50
    (b) 60
    (c) 70
    (d) 80

13. A _____ shall be located in sight from the motor location and the driven machinery location.

    (a) controller
    (b) protection device
    (c) disconnecting means
    (d) all of these

14. The disconnecting means for a motor controller shall be designed so that it does not _____ automatically.

    (a) open
    (b) close
    (c) restart
    (d) shut down

15. A motor disconnecting means can be a _____.

    (a) listed molded case circuit breaker
    (b) listed motor-circuit switch rated in horsepower
    (c) listed molded case switch
    (d) any of these

16. A horsepower-rated _____ having a horsepower rating not less than the motor rating shall be permitted to serve as the disconnecting means.

    (a) attachment plug and receptacle
    (b) flanged surface inlet and cord connector
    (c) automatic controller
    (d) a or b

17. A switch or circuit breaker can be used as both the controller and disconnecting means if it _____.

(a) opens all ungrounded conductors

(b) is protected by an overcurrent device in each ungrounded conductor

(c) is manually operable, or both power and manually operable

(d) all of these

Article 440. Air-Conditioning and Refrigerating Equipment

1. Article 440 applies to electric motor-driven air-conditioning and refrigerating equipment that has a hermetic refrigerant motor-compressor.

(a) True

(b) False

2. The rules of _____ shall apply to air-conditioning and refrigerating equipment that does not incorporate a hermetic refrigerant motor-compressor.

(a) Article 422

(b) Article 424

(c) Article 430

(d) all of these

3. A disconnecting means that serves a hermetic refrigerant motor-compressor shall have an ampere rating of at least _____ percent of the nameplate rated-load current or branch-circuit selection current, whichever is greater.

(a) 80

(b) 100

(c) 115

(d) 125

4. The disconnecting means for air-conditioning and refrigerating equipment shall be _____ from the air-conditioning or refrigerating equipment.

(a) readily accessible

(b) within sight

(c) a or b

(d) a and b

5. Where the air conditioner disconnecting means is not within sight from the equipment, the provision for locking or adding a lock to the disconnecting means shall be on the switch or circuit breaker and remain in place _____ the lock installed.

(a) with

(b) without

(c) with or without

(d) none of these

6. Branch-circuit conductors supplying a single air-conditioner motor-compressor shall have an ampacity not less than _____ percent of either the motor-compressor rated-load current or the branch-circuit selection current, whichever is greater.

(a) 100

(b) 125

(c) 150

(d) 200

7. A hermetic motor-compressor controller shall have a _____ current rating not less than the respective nameplate rating(s) on the compressor.

(a) continuous-duty full-load

(b) locked-rotor

(c) a or b

(d) a and b

8. The total rating of a cord-and-plug-connected room air conditioner, connected to the same branch circuit which supplies lighting units, other appliances, or general-use receptacles, shall not exceed _____ percent of the branch-circuit rating.

(a) 40
(b) 50
(c) 70
(d) 80

9. When supplying a room air conditioner rated 120V, the length of a flexible supply cord shall not exceed _____.

(a) 4 ft
(b) 6 ft
(c) 8 ft
(d) 10 ft

Article 445. Generators

1. Article 445 contains installation and other requirements for generators.

(a) True
(b) False

2. Constant-voltage generators, except ac generator exciters, shall be protected from overcurrent by _____ or other acceptable overcurrent protective means suitable for the conditions of use.

(a) inherent design
(b) circuit breakers
(c) fuses
(d) any of these

3. Separately derived system generators must have the _____ conductor sized not smaller than required to carry the maximum unbalanced current as determined by 220.61.

(a) neutral
(b) grounding
(c) a and b
(d) none of these

Article 450. Transformers and Transformer Vaults

1. The primary overcurrent protection for a transformer rated 600V, nominal, or less, with no secondary protection and having a primary current rating of over 9A must be set at not more than _____ percent.

(a) 125
(b) 167
(c) 200
(d) 300

2. Transformers with ventilating openings shall be installed so that the ventilating openings _____.

(a) are a minimum 18 in. above the floor
(b) are not blocked by walls or obstructions
(c) are aesthetically located
(d) are vented to the exterior of the building

3. For transformers, other than Class 2 and Class 3, a means is required to disconnect all transformer ungrounded primary conductors. The disconnecting means must be located within sight of the transformer unless the _____.

(a) disconnect location is field-marked on the transformer
(b) disconnect is lockable
(c) disconnect is non-fusible
(d) a and b

4. Dry-type transformers installed indoors rated over _____ shall be installed in a vault.

(a) 1,000V
(b) 20,000V
(c) 35,000V
(d) 50,000V

5. Transformer vaults shall be located where they can be ventilated to the outside air without using flues or ducts, where _____.

(a) permitted
(b) practicable
(c) required
(d) all of these

6. Each doorway leading into a transformer vault from the building interior shall be provided with a tight-fitting door having a minimum fire rating of _____ hours.

(a) 2
(b) 3
(c) 4
(d) 6

7. Ventilation openings for transformer vaults must be as far as possible from _____.

(a) doors
(b) windows
(c) combustible material
(d) any of these

Article 480. Storage Batteries

1. The provisions of Article _____ apply to stationary storage battery installations.

(a) 450
(b) 460
(c) 470
(d) 480

2. Nominal battery voltage, as it relates to storage batteries, is defined as the voltage of a battery based on the _____ of cells in the battery.

(a) number
(b) type
(c) a and b
(d) a or b

3. Wiring and equipment supplied from storage batteries must be in accordance with Chapters 1 through 4 of the *NEC* unless otherwise permitted by 480.4.

(a) True
(b) False

4. A _____ disconnecting means is required within sight of the storage battery for all ungrounded battery system conductors operating at over 50V nominal.

(a) accessible
(b) readily accessible
(c) safety
(d) all of these

5. Racks (rigid frames designed to support battery cells or trays) must be made of one of the following:

(a) Metal, treated to be resistant to deteriorating action by the electrolyte and provided with nonconducting or continuous insulating material members directly supporting the cells
(b) Fiberglass
(c) Other suitable nonconductive materials
(d) Any of these

6. The required working space requirements of 110.26 are measured from the edge of the battery _____.

(a) terminals
(b) enclosure
(c) rack
(d) any of these

Final Exam A Questions

These questions are based on the 2011 *National Electrical Code*. Please use the 2011 *NEC Code* book to answer the following questions.

Final Exam A

1. "_____" means acceptable to the authority having jurisdiction.
   - (a) Identified
   - (b) Listed
   - (c) Approved
   - (d) Labeled

2. A bare 4 AWG copper conductor installed horizontally near the bottom or vertically, and within that portion of a concrete foundation or footing that is in direct contact with the earth can be used as a grounding electrode when the conductor is at least _____ in length.
   - (a) 10 ft
   - (b) 15 ft
   - (c) 20 ft
   - (d) 25 ft

3. A building or structure shall be supplied by a maximum of _____ service(s), unless specifically permitted otherwise.
   - (a) one
   - (b) two
   - (c) three
   - (d) as many as desired

4. A Class A GFCI protection device is designed to trip when the ground-fault current to ground is _____ or higher.
   - (a) 4 mA
   - (b) 5 mA
   - (c) 6 mA
   - (d) none of these

5. A dwelling unit containing three 120V small-appliance branch circuits has a calculated load of _____VA for the small appliance circuits.
   - (a) 1,500
   - (b) 3,000
   - (c) 4,500
   - (d) 6,000

6. A hermetic motor-compressor controller shall have a _____ current rating not less than the respective nameplate rating(s) on the compressor.
   - (a) continuous-duty full-load
   - (b) locked-rotor
   - (c) a or b
   - (d) a and b

7. A main bonding jumper shall be a _____ or similar suitable conductor.
   - (a) wire
   - (b) bus
   - (c) screw
   - (d) any of these

8. A multipole, general-use snap switch shall not be fed from more than a single circuit unless it is listed and marked as a 2-circuit or 3-circuit switch, or unless its voltage rating is not less than the nominal _____ voltage of the system supplying the circuits.
   - (a) line-to-ground
   - (b) line-to-neutral
   - (c) line-to-line
   - (d) phase-to-phase

9. A receptacle outlet shall be installed in dwelling units for every kitchen and dining area countertop space _____, and no point along the wall line shall be more than 2 ft, measured horizontally, from a receptacle outlet in that space.
   - (a) wider than 10 in.
   - (b) wider than 3 ft
   - (c) 18 in. or wider
   - (d) 12 in. or wider

10. A switch or circuit breaker can be used as both the controller and disconnecting means if it _____.

    (a) opens all ungrounded conductors
    (b) is protected by an overcurrent device in each ungrounded conductor
    (c) is manually operable, or both power and manually operable
    (d) all of these

11. A wood brace used for supporting a box for structural mounting shall have a cross-section not less than nominal _____.

    (a) 1 in. x 2 in.
    (b) 2 in. x 2 in.
    (c) 2 in. x 3 in.
    (d) 2 in. x 4 in.

12. All 15A and 20A, 125V receptacles installed in garages, service bays, and similar areas where _____ are to be used must be GFCI protected.

    (a) electrical diagnostic equipment
    (b) electrical hand tools
    (c) portable lighting equipment
    (d) all of these

13. Aluminum fittings and enclosures can be used with _____ conduit where not subject to severe corrosive influences.

    (a) steel rigid metal
    (b) aluminum rigid metal
    (c) PVC-coated rigid conduit only
    (d) a and b

14. An unspliced _____ that is sized based on the derived phase conductors shall be used to connect the grounded conductor and the supply-side bonding jumper, or the equipment grounding conductor, or both, at a separately derived system.

    (a) system bonding jumper
    (b) equipment grounding conductor
    (c) grounded conductor
    (d) grounding electrode conductor

15. Bends in LFNC shall _____ between pull points.

    (a) not be made
    (b) not be limited in degrees
    (c) be limited to 360 degrees
    (d) be limited to 180 degrees

16. Branch-circuit conductors supplying a single air-conditioner motor-compressor shall have an ampacity not less than _____ percent of either the motor-compressor rated-load current or the branch-circuit selection current, whichever is greater.

    (a) 100
    (b) 125
    (c) 150
    (d) 200

17. Buildings or structures supplied by multiple services or feeders must use the same _____ to ground enclosures and equipment in or on that building.

    (a) service
    (b) disconnect
    (c) grounding electrode system
    (d) any of these

18. Cable trays used to support service-entrance conductors shall contain only service-entrance conductors _____.

    (a) unless a solid fixed barrier separates the service-entrance conductors from other conductors
    (b) under 300V
    (c) in industrial locations
    (d) over 600V

19. Ceiling-support wires used for the support of electrical raceways and cables within nonfire-rated assemblies shall be distinguishable from the suspended-ceiling framing support wires.

    (a) True
    (b) False

20. Concrete, brick, or tile walls are considered _____, as applied to working space requirements.

    (a) inconsequential
    (b) in the way
    (c) grounded
    (d) none of these

21. Conductors, splices or terminations in a handhole enclosure shall be listed as _____.

    (a) suitable for wet locations
    (b) suitable for damp locations
    (c) suitable for direct burial in the earth
    (d) none of these

22. Conduits or raceways through which moisture may contact live parts shall be _____ at either or both ends.

    (a) sealed
    (b) plugged
    (c) bushed
    (d) a or b

23. Cut ends of ENT shall be trimmed inside and _____ to remove rough edges.

    (a) outside
    (b) tapered
    (c) filed
    (d) beveled

24. Dry-type transformers installed indoors rated over _____ shall be installed in a vault.

    (a) 1,000V
    (b) 20,000V
    (c) 35,000V
    (d) 50,000V

25. Each direct-buried single conductor cable must be located _____ in the trench to the other single conductor cables in the same parallel set of conductors, including equipment grounding conductors.

    (a) perpendicular
    (b) bundled together
    (c) in close proximity
    (d) spaced apart

26. Each length of RMC shall be clearly and durably identified in every _____.

    (a) 3 ft
    (b) 5 ft
    (c) 10 ft
    (d) 20 ft

27. Each switchboard or panelboard used as service equipment shall be provided with a main bonding jumper within the panelboard, or within one of the sections of the switchboard, for connecting the grounded service-entrance conductor on its _____ side to the switchboard or panelboard frame.

    (a) load
    (b) supply
    (c) phase
    (d) high-leg

28. Electrical installations in hollow spaces, vertical shafts, and ventilation or air-handling ducts shall be made so that the possible spread of fire or products of combustion is not _____.

    (a) substantially increased
    (b) allowed
    (c) inherent
    (d) possible

29. EMT shall not be threaded.

    (a) True
    (b) False

30. ENT shall not be used where exposed to the direct rays of the sun, unless identified as _____.

    (a) high-temperature rated
    (b) sunlight resistant
    (c) Schedule 80
    (d) never can be

31. Equipment or materials included in a list published by a testing laboratory acceptable to the authority having jurisdiction is said to be "_____."

    (a) book
    (b) digest
    (c) manifest
    (d) listed

32. Explanatory material, such as references to other standards, references to related sections of the *NEC*, or information related to a *Code* rule, are included in the form of Informational Notes.

    (a) True
    (b) False

33. Fittings used for connecting Type MC cable to boxes, cabinets, or other equipment shall _____.

    (a) be nonmetallic only
    (b) be listed and identified for such use
    (c) be listed and identified as weatherproof
    (d) include anti-shorting bushings

34. Flexible cords and cables shall not be concealed behind building _____, or run through doorways, windows, or similar openings.

    (a) structural ceilings
    (b) suspended or dropped ceilings
    (c) floors or walls
    (d) all of these

35. For grounded systems, electrical equipment and electrically conductive material likely to become energized, shall be installed in a manner that creates a low-impedance circuit capable of safely carrying the maximum ground-fault current likely to be imposed on it from where a ground fault may occur to the _____.

    (a) ground
    (b) earth
    (c) electrical supply source
    (d) none of these

36. For installations consisting of not more than two 2-wire branch circuits, the service disconnecting means shall have a rating of not less than _____.

    (a) 15A
    (b) 20A
    (c) 25A
    (d) 30A

37. For stationary motors of 2 hp or less and 300V or less on ac circuits, the controller can be an ac-rated only general-use snap switch where the motor full-load current rating is not more than _____ percent of the rating of the switch.

    (a) 50
    (b) 60
    (c) 70
    (d) 80

38. For transformers, other than Class 2 and Class 3, a means is required to disconnect all transformer ungrounded primary conductors. The disconnecting means must be located within sight of the transformer unless the _____.

    (a) disconnect location is field-marked on the transformer
    (b) disconnect is lockable
    (c) disconnect is non-fusible
    (d) a and b

39. Galvanized steel, stainless steel and red brass RMC can be installed in concrete, in direct contact with the earth, or in areas subject to severe corrosive influences when protected by _____ and judged suitable for the condition.

    (a) ceramic
    (b) corrosion protection
    (c) backfill
    (d) a natural barrier

40. Ground-fault protection of equipment shall be provided for solidly grounded wye electrical systems of more than 150 volts-to-ground, but not exceeding 600V phase-to-phase for each individual device used as a building or structure main disconnecting means rated _____ or more, unless specifically exempted.

    (a) 1,000A
    (b) 1,500A
    (c) 2,000A
    (d) 2,500A

41. Grounding electrodes that are driven rods require a minimum of _____ in contact with the soil.

    (a) 6 ft
    (b) 8 ft
    (c) 10 ft
    (d) 12 ft

42. Handles or levers of circuit breakers, and similar parts that may move suddenly in such a way that persons in the vicinity are likely to be injured by being struck by them, shall be _____.

    (a) guarded
    (b) isolated
    (c) a and b
    (d) a or b

43. If a branch circuit supplies a single nonmotor-operated appliance, the rating of overcurrent protection shall not exceed _____ if the overcurrent protection rating is not marked and the appliance is rated 13.30A or less.

    (a) 15A
    (b) 20A
    (c) 25A
    (d) 30A

44. If an appliance of more than 1/8 hp is provided with a unit switch that complies with 422.34(A), (B), (C), or (D), the switch or circuit breaker serving as the other disconnecting means shall be permitted to be out of sight from the appliance.

    (a) True
    (b) False

45. If the voltage between overhead service conductors does not exceed 300V and the roof area is guarded or isolated, a reduction in clearance to 3 ft is permitted.

    (a) True
    (b) False

46. In a dwelling unit, each wall space _____ or wider requires a receptacle.

    (a) 2 ft
    (b) 3 ft
    (c) 4 ft
    (d) 5 ft

47. In dwelling unit bathrooms, not less than one 15A or 20A, 125V receptacle outlet must be installed within _____ from the outside edge of each bathroom basin.

    (a) 20 in.
    (b) 3 ft
    (c) 4 ft
    (d) 6 ft

48. In dwelling units, the voltage between conductors that supply the terminals of _____ shall not exceed 120V, nominal.

    (a) luminaires
    (b) cord-and-plug-connected loads of 1,440 VA or less
    (c) cord-and-plug-connected loads of more than ¼ hp
    (d) a and b

49. In industrial establishments where conditions of maintenance and supervision ensure that only qualified persons service the installation, flexible cords and cables can be installed in aboveground raceways that are no longer than _____, to protect the flexible cord or cable from physical damage.

    (a) 25 ft
    (b) 50 ft
    (c) 100 ft
    (d) no limit

50. In locations where electrical equipment is likely to be exposed to _____, enclosures or guards shall be so arranged and of such strength as to prevent such damage.

    (a) corrosion
    (b) physical damage
    (c) magnetic fields
    (d) weather

51. Installations of communications equipment that are under the exclusive control of communications utilities, and located outdoors or in building spaces used exclusively for such installations _____ covered by the *NEC*.

    (a) are
    (b) are sometimes
    (c) are not
    (d) may be

52. Lighting systems operating at 30V or less shall be listed or assembled with listed components.

    (a) True
    (b) False

53. Lighting track shall have two supports for a single section of _____ or shorter in length and each individual section of not more than 4 ft attached to it shall have one additional support, unless the track is identified for supports at greater intervals.

    (a) 2 ft
    (b) 4 ft
    (c) 6 ft
    (d) 8 ft

54. Listed liquidtight flexible metal conduit (LFMC) is acceptable as an equipment grounding conductor when it terminates in listed fittings and is protected by an overcurrent device rated 60A or less for sizes 3/8 in. through ½ in.

    (a) True
    (b) False

55. Luminaires containing a metal halide lamp (other than a thick glass PAR lamp) shall be provided with a containment barrier that encloses the lamp, or shall be provided with a physical means that only allows the use of a(n) _____.

    (a) Type O lamp
    (b) Type CB lamp
    (c) a or b
    (d) inert gas

56. Luminaires shall be wired with conductors having insulation suitable for the environmental conditions and _____ to which the conductors will be subjected.

    (a) temperature
    (b) voltage
    (c) current
    (d) all of these

57. Metal faceplates for receptacles shall be grounded.

    (a) True
    (b) False

58. Metal wireways are sheet metal troughs with _____ for housing and protecting electric conductors and cable.

    (a) removable covers
    (b) hinged covers
    (c) a or b
    (d) none of these

59. Motors shall be located so that adequate _____ is provided and so that maintenance, such as lubrication of bearings and replacing of brushes, can be readily accomplished.

    (a) space
    (b) ventilation
    (c) protection
    (d) all of these

60. No _____ splices or taps shall be made within or on a luminaire.

    (a) unapproved
    (b) untested
    (c) uninspected
    (d) unnecessary

61. Nonlocking 15A and 20A, 125V and 250V receptacles installed in damp locations shall be listed as _____.

    (a) raintight
    (b) watertight
    (c) weatherproof
    (d) weather resistant

62. Nonlocking type 15A and 20A, 125V receptacles in a dwelling unit shall be listed as tamper resistant except _____.

    (a) Receptacles located more than 5½ ft above the floor.
    (b) Receptacles that are part of a luminaire or appliance.
    (c) A receptacle located within dedicated space for an appliance that in normal use is not easily moved from one place to another.
    (d) all of these

63. One set of service-entrance conductors connected to the supply side of the normal service disconnecting means shall be permitted to supply standby power systems, fire pump equipment, and fire and sprinkler alarms covered by 230.82(5).

    (a) True
    (b) False

64. Overcurrent protection for conductors and equipment is designed to _____ the circuit if the current reaches a value that will cause an excessive or dangerous temperature in conductors or conductor insulation.

    (a) open
    (b) close
    (c) monitor
    (d) record

65. Overload devices are intended to protect motors, motor control apparatus, and motor branch-circuit conductors against _____.

    (a) excessive heating due to motor overloads
    (b) excessive heating due to failure to start
    (c) short circuits and ground faults
    (d) a and b

66. Power distribution blocks installed in metal wireways shall _____.

    (a) allow for sufficient wire-bending space at terminals
    (b) not have uninsulated exposed live parts
    (c) a or b
    (d) a and b

67. PVC conduit shall not be used _____, unless specifically permitted.

    (a) in hazardous (classified) locations
    (b) for the support of luminaires or other equipment
    (c) where subject to physical damage unless identified for such use
    (d) all of these

68. Racks (rigid frames designed to support battery cells or trays) must be made of one of the following:

    (a) Metal, treated to be resistant to deteriorating action by the electrolyte and provided with nonconducting or continuous insulating material members directly supporting the cells.
    (b) Fiberglass.
    (c) Other suitable nonconductive materials.
    (d) Any of these

69. Receptacles installed behind a bed in the guest rooms in hotels and motels shall be located to prevent the bed from contacting an attachment plug, or the receptacle shall be provided with a suitable guard.

    (a) True
    (b) False

70. Recognized as suitable for the specific purpose, function, use, environment, and application is the definition of "_____."

    (a) labeled
    (b) identified (as applied to equipment)
    (c) listed
    (d) approved

71. Separately derived system generators must have the _____ conductor sized not smaller than required to carry the maximum unbalanced current as determined by 220.61.

    (a) neutral
    (b) grounding
    (c) a and b
    (d) none of these

72. Service disconnecting means shall not be installed in bathrooms.

    (a) True
    (b) False

73. Smooth-sheath Type MC cable with an external diameter not greater than ¾ in. shall have a bending radius not more than _____ times the cable external diameter.

    (a) five
    (b) 10
    (c) 12
    (d) 13

74. Surface metal raceways shall be secured and supported at intervals _____.

    (a) in accordance with the manufacturer's installation instructions
    (b) appropriate for the building design
    (c) not exceeding 4 ft
    (d) not exceeding 8 ft

75. Switches shall be marked with _____.

    (a) current
    (b) voltage
    (c) maximum horsepower, if horsepower rated
    (d) all of these

76. The _____ is the necessary equipment, usually consisting of a circuit breaker(s) or switch(es) and fuse(s) and their accessories, connected to the load end of service conductors, and intended to constitute the main control and cutoff of the supply.

    (a) service equipment
    (b) service
    (c) service disconnect
    (d) service overcurrent device

77. The authority having jurisdiction has the responsibility for _____.

    (a) making interpretations of rules
    (b) deciding upon the approval of equipment and materials
    (c) waiving specific requirements in the *Code* and permitting alternate methods and material if safety is maintained
    (d) all of these

78. The connected load on lighting track is permitted to exceed the rating of the track under some conditions.

    (a) True
    (b) False

79. The grounding electrode conductor for a single separately derived system is used to connect the grounded conductor of the derived system to the grounding electrode.

    (a) True
    (b) False

80. The load for electric clothes dryers in a dwelling unit shall be _____ watts or the nameplate rating, whichever is larger, per dryer.

    (a) 1,500
    (b) 4,500
    (c) 5,000
    (d) 8,000

81. The minimum feeder conductor ampacity, before the application of any adjustment or correction factors, must be no less than the noncontinuous load plus _____ percent of the continuous load.

    (a) 80
    (b) 100
    (c) 125
    (d) 150

82. The motor _____ currents listed in Tables 430.247 through 430.250 shall be used to determine the ampacity of motor circuit conductors and short-circuit and ground-fault protection devices.

    (a) nameplate
    (b) full-load
    (c) power factor
    (d) service factor

83. The next higher standard rating overcurrent device above the ampacity of the ungrounded conductors being protected shall be permitted to be used, provided all of the following conditions are met:

    (a) The conductors are not part of a branch circuit supplying more than one receptacle for cord-and-plug-connected portable loads.
    (b) The ampacity of the conductors doesn't correspond with the standard ampere rating of a fuse or circuit breaker.
    (c) The next higher standard rating selected doesn't exceed 800A.
    (d) all of these

84. The provisions of Article _____ apply to stationary storage battery installations.

    (a) 450
    (b) 460
    (c) 470
    (d) 480

85. The requirement for maintaining a 3 ft vertical clearance from the edge of the roof shall not apply to the final feeder conductor span where the conductors are attached to _____.

    (a) a building pole
    (b) the side of a building
    (c) an antenna
    (d) the base of a building

86. The sum of the cross-sectional areas of all contained conductors at any cross-section of a metal wireway shall not exceed _____.

    (a) 50 percent
    (b) 20 percent
    (c) 25 percent
    (d) 80 percent

87. There shall be a minimum of one _____ branch circuit for the laundry outlet(s) required by 210.52(F).

    (a) 15A
    (b) 20A
    (c) 30A
    (d) b and c

88. Threadless couplings and connectors used with RMC buried in masonry or concrete shall be the _____ type.

    (a) raintight
    (b) wet and damp location
    (c) nonabsorbent
    (d) concrete-tight

89. Trade size 1 IMC shall be supported at intervals not exceeding _____.

    (a) 8 ft
    (b) 10 ft
    (c) 12 ft
    (d) 14 ft

90. Type _____ cable is a factory assembly of conductors with an overall covering of nonmetallic material suitable for direct burial in the earth.

    (a) NM
    (b) UF
    (c) SE
    (d) TC

91. Type IC recessed luminaires are permitted to make contact with combustible material at _____.

    (a) recessed parts
    (b) points of support
    (c) portions passing through or finishing off the opening in the building structure
    (d) all of these

92. Type NM cable shall closely follow the surface of the building finish or running boards when run exposed.

    (a) True
    (b) False

93. Unbroken lengths of surface metal raceways can be run through dry _____.

    (a) walls
    (b) partitions
    (c) floors
    (d) all of these

94. Unused openings other than those intended for the operation of equipment, intended for mounting purposes, or permitted as part of the design for listed equipment shall be _____.

    (a) filled with cable clamps or connectors only
    (b) taped over with electrical tape
    (c) repaired only by welding or brazing in a metal slug
    (d) effectively closed to afford protection substantially equivalent to the wall of the equipment

95. What is the minimum cover requirement for direct burial Type UF cable installed outdoors that supplies a 120V, 30A circuit?

    (a) 6 in.
    (b) 12 in.
    (c) 18 in.
    (d) 24 in.

96. When applying the demand factors of Table 220.56, the feeder or service demand load shall not be less than the sum of _____.

    (a) the total number of receptacles at 180 VA per receptacle outlet
    (b) the VA rating of all of the small-appliance branch circuits combined
    (c) the largest two kitchen equipment loads
    (d) the kitchen heating and air-conditioning loads

97. When EMT is installed in wet locations, all supports, bolts, straps, and screws shall be _____.

    (a) of corrosion-resistant materials
    (b) protected against corrosion
    (c) a or b
    (d) of nonmetallic materials only

98. When supplying a grounded system at a separate building or structure, an equipment grounding conductor shall be run with the supply conductors and connected to the building or structure disconnecting means.

    (a) True
    (b) False

99. When Type AC cable is run across the top of a floor joist in an attic without permanent ladders or stairs, substantial guard strips within _____ of the scuttle hole, or attic entrance, shall protect the cable.

    (a) 3 ft
    (b) 4 ft
    (c) 5 ft
    (d) 6 ft

100. Where conductors in parallel are run in separate raceways, the raceways shall have the same electrical characteristics.

    (a) True
    (b) False

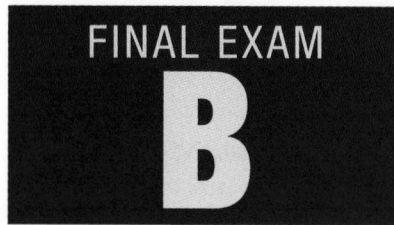
Final Exam B Questions

These questions are based on the 2011 *National Electrical Code*. Please use the 2011 *NEC Code* book to answer the following questions.

Final Exam B

1. _____ is a listed thin-wall, metallic tubing of circular cross section used for the installation and physical protection of electrical conductors when joined together with listed fittings.
   (a) LFNC
   (b) EMT
   (c) NUCC
   (d) RTRC

2. 15A and 20A, 125V receptacles located in patient bed locations of general care or critical care areas of health care facilities aren't required to be GFCI protected.
   (a) True
   (b) False

3. A building or structure shall be supplied by a maximum of _____ feeder(s) or branch circuit(s), unless specifically permitted otherwise.
   (a) one
   (b) two
   (c) three
   (d) four

4. A circuit breaker having an interrupting current rating of other than _____ shall have its interrupting rating marked on the circuit breaker.
   (a) 5,000A
   (b) 10,000A
   (c) 22,000A
   (d) 50,000A

5. A disconnecting means that serves a hermetic refrigerant motor-compressor shall have an ampere rating of at least _____ percent of the nameplate rated-load current or branch-circuit selection current, whichever is greater.
   (a) 80
   (b) 100
   (c) 115
   (d) 125

6. A ground-fault current path is an electrically conductive path from the point of a ground fault through normally noncurrent-carrying conductors, equipment, or the earth to the _____.
   (a) ground
   (b) earth
   (c) electrical supply source
   (d) none of these

7. A load is considered to be continuous if the maximum current is expected to continue for _____ or more.
   (a) one-half hour
   (b) 1 hour
   (c) 2 hours
   (d) 3 hours

8. A multioutlet assembly shall not be installed _____.
   (a) in hoistways
   (b) where subject to severe physical damage
   (c) where subject to corrosive vapors
   (d) all of these

9. A receptacle connected to a dwelling unit small-appliance circuit can supply gas-fired ranges, ovens, or counter-mounted cooking units.
   (a) True
   (b) False

10. A single receptacle is a single contact device with no other contact device on the same _____.

    (a) circuit
    (b) yoke
    (c) run
    (d) equipment

11. A unit switch with a marked _____ position that is part of a fixed space heater, and disconnects all ungrounded conductors, shall be permitted to serve as the required disconnecting means.

    (a) on
    (b) closed
    (c) off
    (d) none of these

12. All 15A and 20A, 125V receptacles _____ of commercial occupancies shall have GFCI protection.

    (a) in bathrooms
    (b) on rooftops
    (c) in kitchens
    (d) all of these

13. Alternating-current systems of 50V to 1,000V that supply premises wiring systems shall be grounded where supplied by a three-phase, 4-wire, delta-connected system in which the midpoint of one phase winding is used as a circuit conductor.

    (a) True
    (b) False

14. An insulated grounded conductor of _____ or smaller shall be identified by a continuous white or gray outer finish, or by three continuous white stripes on other than green insulation along its entire length.

    (a) 8 AWG
    (b) 6 AWG
    (c) 4 AWG
    (d) 3 AWG

15. Any of the following wiring methods can be installed in a cable tray:

    (a) Metal raceways.
    (b) Nonmetallic raceways.
    (c) Cables.
    (d) all of these

16. At least one wall switch-controlled lighting outlet shall be installed in every habitable room and bathroom of a guest room or guest suite of hotels, motels, and similar occupancies. A receptacle outlet controlled by a wall switch may be used to meet this requirement in other than _____.

    (a) bathrooms
    (b) kitchens
    (c) sleeping areas
    (d) a and b

17. Bonding shall be provided where necessary to ensure _____ and the capacity to conduct safely any fault current likely to be imposed.

    (a) electrical continuity
    (b) fiduciary responsibility
    (c) listing requirements
    (d) electrical demand

18. Branch-circuit conductors to individual appliances shall not be sized _____ than required by the appliance markings.

    (a) larger
    (b) smaller

19. Cable trays shall _____.

    (a) include fittings or other suitable means for changes in direction and elevation
    (b) have side rails or equivalent structural members
    (c) be made of corrosion-resistant material or protected from corrosion as required by 300.6
    (d) all of these

20. Cartridge fuses and fuseholders shall be classified according to their _____ ranges.

    (a) voltage
    (b) amperage
    (c) a or b
    (d) a and b

21. Communications wiring such as telephone, antenna, and CATV wiring within a building shall not be required to comply with the installation requirements of Chapters 1 through 7, except where specifically referenced in Chapter 8.

    (a) True
    (b) False

22. Conductors shall be installed within a raceway, cable, or enclosure.

    (a) True
    (b) False

23. Conduits and raceways, including end fittings, shall not rise more than _____ above the bottom of a switchboard enclosure.

    (a) 3 in.
    (b) 4 in.
    (c) 5 in.
    (d) 6 in.

24. Cord-and-plug connected vending machines manufactured or remanufactured on or after January 1, 2005 shall include a ground-fault circuit interrupter as an integral part of the attachment plug or in the power-supply cord within 12 in. of the attachment plug. Older vending machines not incorporating integral GFCI protection shall _____.

    (a) be remanufactured
    (b) be disabled
    (c) be connected to a GFCI-protected outlet
    (d) be connected to an AFCI-protected circuit

25. Direct-buried service conductors that are not encased in concrete and that are buried 18 in. or more below grade shall have their location identified by a warning ribbon placed in the trench at least _____ above the underground installation.

    (a) 6 in.
    (b) 10 in.
    (c) 12 in.
    (d) 18 in.

26. Each cable entering a cutout box _____.

    (a) shall be secured to the cutout box
    (b) can be sleeved through a chase
    (c) shall have a maximum of two cables per connector
    (d) all of these

27. Each doorway leading into a transformer vault from the building interior shall be provided with a tight-fitting door having a minimum fire rating of _____ hours.

    (a) 2
    (b) 3
    (c) 4
    (d) 6

28. Each run of cable tray shall be _____ before the installation of cables.

    (a) tested for 25 ohms resistance
    (b) insulated
    (c) completed
    (d) all of these

29. Electric space-heating cables shall not extend beyond the room or area in which they _____.

    (a) provide heat
    (b) originate
    (c) terminate
    (d) are connected

30. Electrically conductive materials that are likely to _____ in ungrounded systems shall be connected together and to the supply system grounded equipment in a manner that creates a low-impedance path for ground-fault current that is capable of carrying the maximum fault current likely to be imposed on it.

    (a) become energized
    (b) require service
    (c) be removed
    (d) be coated with paint or nonconductive materials

31. ENT is composed of a material resistant to moisture and chemical atmospheres, and is _____.

    (a) flexible
    (b) flame retardant
    (c) fireproof
    (d) flammable

32. Equipment and devices shall only be permitted within ducts or plenum chambers specifically fabricated to transport environmental air if necessary for their direct action upon, or sensing of, the _____.

    (a) contained air
    (b) air quality
    (c) air temperature
    (d) none of these

33. Equipment or materials to which a symbol or other identifying mark of a product evaluation organization that is acceptable to the authority having jurisdiction has been attached is known as "_____."

    (a) listed
    (b) labeled
    (c) approved
    (d) identified

34. Exposed metal conductive parts of luminaires shall be _____.

    (a) connected to an equipment grounding conductor
    (b) painted
    (c) removed
    (d) a and b

35. Fixed electric space-heating equipment shall be installed to provide the _____ spacing between the equipment and adjacent combustible material, unless it is listed for direct contact with combustible material.

    (a) required
    (b) minimum
    (c) maximum
    (d) safest

36. FMC can be installed exposed or concealed where not subject to physical damage.

    (a) True
    (b) False

37. For grounded systems, normally noncurrent-carrying conductive materials enclosing electrical conductors or equipment shall be connected to earth so as to limit the voltage-to-ground on these materials.

    (a) True
    (b) False

38. For liquidtight flexible metal conduit, if flexibility is necessary after installation, unsecured lengths from the last point the raceway is securely fastened must not exceed _____.

    (a) 3 ft for trade sizes ½ through 1 ¼
    (b) 4 ft for trade sizes 1 ½ through 2
    (c) 5 ft for trade sizes 2 ½ and larger
    (d) all of these

39. For switchboards that are not totally enclosed, a space of _____ or more shall be provided between the top of the switchboard and any combustible ceiling.

    (a) 12 in.
    (b) 18 in.
    (c) 2 ft
    (d) 3 ft

40. For Type NM and NMC cable, the conductor ampacity used for ambient temperature correction [310.15(B)(2)(a)], conductor bundling adjustment [310.15(B)(3)(a)], or both, is based on the 90ºC conductor insulation rating [310.15(B)(2)], provided the adjusted or corrected ampacity doesn't exceed that for a _____ rated conductor.

    (a) 60°C
    (b) 75°C
    (c) 90°C
    (d) 120°C

41. Grounded conductors _____ and larger can be identified by distinctive white or gray markings at their terminations.

    (a) 10 AWG
    (b) 8 AWG
    (c) 6 AWG
    (d) 4 AWG

42. Grounding electrode conductors smaller than _____ shall be in rigid metal conduit, IMC, PVC conduit, electrical metallic tubing, or cable armor.

    (a) 10 AWG
    (b) 8 AWG
    (c) 6 AWG
    (d) 4 AWG

43. Handholds in poles supporting luminaires shall not be required for poles _____ or less in height above finished grade, if the pole is provided with a hinged base.

    (a) 5 ft
    (b) 10 ft
    (c) 15 ft
    (d) 20 ft

44. High-impedance grounded neutral systems shall be permitted for three-phase ac systems of 480 volts to 1,000 volts where _____.

(a) the conditions of maintenance ensure that only qualified persons service the installation
(b) ground detectors are installed on the system
(c) line-to-neutral loads are not served
(d) all of these

45. If a protective device rating is marked on an appliance, the branch-circuit overcurrent device rating shall not exceed _____ percent of the protective device rating marked on the appliance.

(a) 50
(b) 80
(c) 100
(d) 115

46. If neutral conductors of different voltage systems are installed in the same raceway, cable, or enclosure, the means of identification of the different neutrals shall be documented in a manner that's _____ or be permanently posted where the conductors of different systems originate.

(a) available to the AHJ
(b) available through the engineer
(c) readily available
(d) included in the as-built drawings

47. IMC can be installed in or under cinder fill subject to permanent moisture _____.

(a) where the conduit is not less than 18 in. under the fill
(b) when protected on all sides by 2 in. of noncinder concrete
(c) where protected by corrosion protection judged suitable for the condition
(d) any of these

48. In completed installations, each outlet box shall have a _____.

(a) cover
(b) faceplate
(c) canopy
(d) any of these

49. In dwelling units, the required bathroom receptacle outlet can be installed on the side or face of the basin cabinet if no lower than _____ below the countertop.

(a) 12 in.
(b) 18 in.
(c) 24 in.
(d) 36 in.

50. In indoor locations other than dwellings and associated accessory buildings, fluorescent luminaires that utilize double-ended lamps and contain ballast(s) and can be serviced in place shall have a disconnecting means either internal or external to each luminaire.

(a) True
(b) False

51. In judging equipment for approval, considerations such as the following shall be evaluated:

(a) Mechanical strength.
(b) Wire-bending space.
(c) Arcing effects.
(d) all of these

52. In other than dwelling locations, GFCI protection is required in _____.

(a) indoor wet locations
(b) locker rooms adjacent to showering facilities
(c) garages, service bays, and similar areas
(d) all of these

53. LFNC shall be permitted for _____.

(a) direct burial where listed and marked for the purpose
(b) exposed work
(c) outdoors where listed and marked for this purpose
(d) all of these

54. Lighting track is a manufactured assembly and its length may not be altered by the addition or subtraction of sections of track.

(a) True
(b) False

55. Liquidtight flexible metal conduit must be securely fastened by a means approved by the authority having jurisdiction within _____ of termination.

    (a) 6 in.
    (b) 10 in.
    (c) 1 ft
    (d) 10 ft

56. Luminaires attached to the framing of a suspended ceiling shall be secured to the framing member(s) by mechanical means such as _____.

    (a) bolts
    (b) screws
    (c) rivets
    (d) any of these

57. Luminaires located within the actual outside dimension of a bathtub and shower shall be marked for damp locations, or marked for wet locations where they are _____.

    (a) below 7 ft in. height
    (b) below 6 ft 7 in. in height
    (c) subject to shower spray
    (d) not GFCI-protected

58. Metal enclosures for switches or circuit breakers shall be connected to the circuit _____.

    (a) grounded conductor
    (b) grounding conductor
    (c) equipment grounding conductor
    (d) any of these

59. Metal or nonmetallic raceways, cable armors, and cable sheaths _____ between cabinets, boxes, fittings or other enclosures or outlets.

    (a) can be attached with electrical tape
    (b) are allowed gaps for expansion
    (c) shall be continuous
    (d) none of these

60. Motor overload protection shall not be shunted or cut out during the starting period if the motor is _____.

    (a) not automatically started
    (b) automatically started
    (c) manually started
    (d) none of these

61. No _____ shall be attached to any terminal or lead so as to reverse designated polarity.

    (a) grounded conductor
    (b) grounding conductor
    (c) ungrounded conductor
    (d) grounding connector

62. Noncombustible surfaces that are broken or incomplete around boxes employing a flush-type cover or faceplate shall be repaired so there will be no gaps or open spaces larger than _____ at the edge of the box.

    (a) 1/16 in.
    (b) 1/8 in.
    (c) ¼ in.
    (d) ½ in.

63. Nonlocking type 15A and 20A, 125V receptacles in _____ must be listed as tamper resistant.

    (a) theatres
    (b) arcades
    (c) child care facilities
    (d) major repair garages

64. On a three-phase, 4-wire, wye circuit, where the major portion of the load consists of nonlinear loads, the neutral conductor shall be counted when applying 310.15(B)(3)(a) adjustment factors.

    (a) True
    (b) False

65. Overcurrent devices aren't permitted to be located in the bathrooms of _____.

    (a) dwelling units
    (b) dormitories
    (c) guest rooms or guest suites of hotels or motels
    (d) all of these

66. Overhead service conductors shall have a horizontal clearance of _____ from a pool.

    (a) 8 ft
    (b) 10 ft
    (c) 12 ft
    (d) 14 ft

67. Portable luminaires shall be wired with _____ recognized by 400.4, and have an attachment plug of the polarized or grounding type.

    (a) flexible cable
    (b) flexible cord
    (c) nonmetallic flexible cable
    (d) nonmetallic flexible cord

68. PVC conduit and fittings for use above ground shall have the following characteristics _____.

    (a) flame retardant
    (b) resistance to low temperatures and sunlight
    (c) resistance to distortion from heat
    (d) all of these

69. Raceways on exterior surfaces of buildings or other structures shall be arranged to drain, and be suitable for use in _____ locations.

    (a) damp
    (b) wet
    (c) dry
    (d) all of these

70. Receptacles and cord connectors having equipment grounding conductor contacts shall have those contacts connected to a(n) _____ conductor.

    (a) grounded
    (b) ungrounded
    (c) equipment grounding
    (d) neutral

71. Receptacles mounted to and supported by a cover shall be secured by more than one screw unless listed and identified for securing by a single screw.

    (a) True
    (b) False

72. Replacement luminaires can be installed in an outlet box that doesn't contain an equipment grounding conductor if an equipment grounding conductor is added from the luminaire and is connected to _____.

    (a) the grounding electrode system or grounding electrode conductor
    (b) the panelboard equipment grounding terminal
    (c) the service neutral conductor within the service equipment enclosure
    (d) any of these

73. Separately installed pressure connectors shall be used with conductors at the _____ not exceeding the ampacity at the listed and identified temperature rating of the connector.

    (a) voltages
    (b) temperatures
    (c) listings
    (d) ampacities

74. Service raceways for overhead service drops or overhead service conductors shall have a weatherhead listed for _____.

    (a) wet locations
    (b) damp locations
    (c) Class 2 locations
    (d) NEMA 3R

75. Special permission is the written consent from the _____.

    (a) testing laboratory
    (b) manufacturer
    (c) owner
    (d) authority having jurisdiction

76. Surface-mounted luminaires with a ballast shall have a minimum clearance of _____ from combustible low-density cellulose fiberboard, unless the luminaire is marked for surface mounting on combustible low-density cellulose fiberboard.

    (a) ½ in.
    (b) 1 in.
    (c) 1½ in.
    (d) 2 in.

77. Switches shall not be installed within wet locations in tub or shower spaces unless installed as part of a listed tub or shower assembly.

    (a) True
    (b) False

78. The 3 VA per-square-foot general lighting load for dwelling units does not include _____.

    (a) open porches
    (b) garages
    (c) unused or unfinished spaces not adaptable for future use
    (d) all of these

79. The branch-circuit protective device can serve as the controller for a stationary motor rated at _____ or less that is normally left running and cannot be damaged by overload or failure to start.

    (a) ⅛ hp
    (b) ¼ hp
    (c) ⅜ hp
    (d) ½ hp

80. The feeder/service calculated load for a multifamily dwelling containing nine 12 kW ranges is _____.

    (a) 13,000W
    (b) 14,700W
    (c) 16,000W
    (d) 24,000W

81. The largest size grounding electrode conductor required is _____ copper.

    (a) 6 AWG
    (b) 1/0 AWG
    (c) 3/0 AWG
    (d) 250 kcmil

82. The minimum clearance between an electric space-heating cable and an outlet box used for surface luminaires shall not be less than _____.

    (a) 6 in.
    (b) 8 in.
    (c) 14 in.
    (d) 18 in.

83. The minimum size conductor permitted for branch circuits under 600V is _____ AWG.

    (a) 14
    (b) 12
    (c) 10
    (d) 8

84. The *NEC* defines a "_____" as all circuit conductors between the service equipment, the source of a separately derived system, or other power-supply source and the final branch-circuit overcurrent device.

    (a) service
    (b) feeder
    (c) branch circuit
    (d) all of these

85. The primary overcurrent protection for a transformer rated 600V, nominal, or less, with no secondary protection and having a primary current rating of over 9A must be set at not more than _____ percent.

    (a) 125
    (b) 167
    (c) 200
    (d) 300

86. The rating of a branch circuit shall be determined by the rating of the _____.

    (a) ampacity of the largest device connected to the circuit
    (b) average of the ampacity of all devices
    (c) branch-circuit overcurrent device
    (d) ampacity of the branch-circuit conductors according to Table 310.15(B)(16)

87. The standard ampere ratings for fuses includes _____.

    (a) 1A
    (b) 6A
    (c) 601A
    (d) all of these

88. The voltage between conductors in a surface metal raceway shall not exceed _____ unless the metal has a thickness of not less than 0.040 in. nominal.

    (a) 150V
    (b) 300V
    (c) 600V
    (d) 1,000V

89. This *Code* covers the installation of _____ for public and private premises, including buildings, structures, mobile homes, recreational vehicles, and floating buildings.

    (a) optical fiber cables
    (b) electrical equipment
    (c) raceways
    (d) all of these

90. THWN insulated conductors are rated _____.

    (a) 75°C
    (b) for wet locations
    (c) a and b
    (d) not enough information

91. Type _____ cable is a fabricated assembly of insulated conductors in a flexible interlocked metallic armor.

    (a) AC
    (b) MC
    (c) NM
    (d) b and c

92. Type _____ is a factory assembly of insulated circuit conductors within an armor of interlocking metal tape, or a smooth or corrugated metallic sheath.

    (a) AC
    (b) MC
    (c) NM
    (d) b and c

93. Type NM cable protected from physical damage by a raceway shall not be required to be _____ within the raceway.

    (a) covered
    (b) insulated
    (c) secured
    (d) unspliced

94. Type UF cable shall not be used where subject to physical damage.

    (a) True
    (b) False

95. Underground service conductors that supply power to limited loads of a single branch circuit shall not be smaller than _____.

    (a) 14 AWG copper
    (b) 14 AWG aluminum
    (c) 12 AWG copper
    (d) 12 AWG aluminum

96. Ventilation openings for transformer vaults must be as far as possible from _____.

    (a) doors
    (b) windows
    (c) combustible material
    (d) any of these

97. What is the minimum cover requirement for Type UF cable supplying power to a 120V, 15A GFCI-protected circuit outdoors under a driveway of a one-family dwelling?

    (a) 6 in.
    (b) 12 in.
    (c) 16 in.
    (d) 24 in.

98. When breaks occur in dwelling unit kitchen countertop spaces for rangetops, refrigerators or sinks, each countertop surface shall be considered a separate counter space for determining receptacle placement.

    (a) True
    (b) False

99. When equipment grounding conductors are installed in panelboards, a _____ shall be secured inside the cabinet.

    (a) grounded conductor
    (b) terminal lug
    (c) terminal bar
    (d) none of these

100. When the *Code* uses "_____," it means the identified actions are allowed but not required, and they may be options or alternative methods.

    (a) shall
    (b) shall not
    (c) shall be permitted
    (d) a or b

Index